ANNALS AND ANTIQUITIES OF RAJAST'HAN

ANNALS AND ANTIQUITIES
OF
RAJAST'HAN

OR, THE CENTRAL AND WESTERN RAJPOOT STATES OF INDIA

JAMES TOD
LATE POLITICAL AGENT TO THE WESTERN RAJPOOT STATES

IN TWO VOLUMES

I

Rupa & Co

First published 1829 by
Routledge & Kegan Paul Ltd., London

First in Rupa Paperback 1997
Fourth Impression 2005

Published by
Rupa & Co
7/16, Ansari Road, Daryaganj,
New Delhi 110 002

Sales Centres:

Allahabad Bangalore Chandigarh Chennai
Hyderabad Jaipur Kathmandu
Kolkata Mumbai Pune

ISBN 81-7167-366-X (Set)

Printed in India by
Gopsons Papers Ltd.
A-14 Sector 60
Noida 201 301

PUBLISHER'S NOTE TO PRESENT EDITION

In presenting this edition at a popular price of the *Annals and Antiquities of Rajast'han,* by the late Lieut.-Colonel James Tod (1782–1835), in a complete and an unabridged form, the Publishers have been at pains to minimise as far as possible the discrepancies of spelling in the original. Certain obvious mistakes have been rectified ; the Index has been revised and amplified ; and the proofs of both volumes have been carefully read and collated, with a view to providing students of the work with an accurate text in readable type. The Map is reproduced from the original map prepared by the Author, with the omission of the less significant names.

The Publishers are indebted to Mr. Douglas Sladen, who contributes a Preface to the work, for enlisting the interest of H.H. The Maharaj Rana of Jhalawar, to whom this edition is inscribed.

1914 G. R. & S. Ltd.

DEDICATED TO

HIS HIGHNESS THE MAHARAJ RANA OF JHALAWAR,

TO WHOM

THE REPUBLICATION OF THIS

CLASSIC OF INDIA

IS DUE

PREFACE

TOD'S *Rajast'han* has for three quarters of a century been recognised as one of the chief English Classics upon India. It has for many years been out of print, and the price of a copy has been prohibitive. It stands at this moment at twenty pounds. But the enormous length of the book—it is as long as eight ordinary novels—precluded any publisher from taking the risk of reprinting it as a whole, though Messrs. George Routledge & Sons Ltd. had reprinted a portion of it.

Last year, when H.H. The Maharaj Rana of Jhalawar, the heir of Zalim Sing the Great, the hero who figures most largely in its pages, was in England, I suggested to him that something ought to be done to prevent a book of such value remaining inaccessible to students, and he at once said that he was willing to share the burden of any firm of publishers who undertook the republication.

I approached Messrs. George Routledge & Sons Ltd., who had made the former reprint, and who make a specialty of resuscitating out-of-print Classics, and they were equally prompt in accepting their share of the responsibility.

The result is that the libraries of Great Britain and India and the Empire will be able to place on their shelves at a popular price this indispensable and immensely valuable Classic, which not one in a hundred of them has previously been able to include in its catalogue.

On the life of Zalim Sing the Great, the Indian Machiavelli, the Rajpoot Prince who practically saved the British Power in India, nearly a hundred years ago, I am at present engaged. It was the difficulty of procuring a copy of Tod's *Rajast'han* for my work on this subject, which led to my approaching the Maharaj Rana and Messrs. George Routledge & Sons Ltd. for its republication, now happily accomplished.

DOUGLAS SLADEN.

THE AVENUE HOUSE, RICHMOND, SURREY.
1914

[Original Dedication of the First Volume]

TO

HIS MOST GRACIOUS MAJESTY

GEORGE THE FOURTH

SIRE,

The gracious permission accorded me, to lay at the foot of the Throne the fruit of my labours, allows me to propitiate Your Majesty's consideration towards the object of this work, the prosecution of which I have made a paramount duty.

The Rajpoot princes, happily rescued, by the triumph of the British arms, from the yoke of lawless oppression, are now the most remote tributaries to Your Majesty's extensive empire; and their admirer and annalist may, perhaps, be permitted to hope, that the sighs of this ancient and interesting race for the restoration of their former independence, which it would suit our wisest policy to grant, may be deemed not undeserving Your Majesty's regard.

With entire loyalty and devotion, I subscribe myself.

YOUR MAJESTY'S

Most faithful subject and servant,

JAMES TOD.

BIRD HURST, CROYDON,

20th June 1829.

AUTHOR'S INTRODUCTION

Much disappointment has been felt in Europe at the sterility of the historic muse of Hindust'han. When Sir William Jones first began to explore the vast mines of Sanscrit literature, great hopes were entertained that the history of the world would acquire considerable accessions from this source. The sanguine expectations that were then formed have not been realised ; and, as it usually happens, excitement has been succeeded by apathy and indifference. It is now generally regarded as an axiom, that India possesses no national history ; to which we may oppose the remark of a French Orientalist, who ingeniously asks, whence Abulfuzil obtained the materials for his outlines of ancient Hindu history ?[1] Mr. Wilson has, indeed, done much to obviate this prejudice, by his translation of the *Raj Tarringini*, or History of Cashmer,[2] which clearly demonstrates that regular historical composition was an art not unknown in Hindust'han, and affords satisfactory ground for concluding that these productions were once less rare than at present, and that further exertion may bring more relics to light. Although the labours of Colebrooke, Wilkins, Wilson, and others of our own countrymen, emulated by many learned men in France and Germany,[3] have revealed to Europe some of the hidden lore of India ; still it is not pretended that we have done much more than pass the threshold of Indian science ; and we are consequently not competent to speak decisively of its extent or its character. Immense libraries, in various parts of India, are still intact, which have survived the devastations of the Islamite. The collections of Jessulmér and Puttun, for example, escaped the scrutiny of even the lynx-eyed Alla, who conquered both these kingdoms, and who would have shown as little mercy to those literary treasures, as Omar displayed towards the Alexandrine library. Many other minor collections, consisting of thousands of volumes each, exist in Central and Western India, some of which are the private property of princes, and others belong to the Jain communities.[4]

[1] M. Abel Rémusat, in his *Mélanges Asiatiques*, makes many apposite and forcible remarks on this subject, which, without intention, convey a just reproof to the lukewarmness of our countrymen. The institution of the Royal Asiatic Society, especially that branch of it devoted to Oriental translations, may yet redeem this reproach.

[2] *Asiatic Researches*, vol. xv.

[3] When the genius and erudition of such men as Schlegel are added to the zeal which characterises that celebrated writer, what revelations may we not yet expect from the cultivation of oriental literature ?

[4] Some copies of these Jain MSS. from Jessulmér, which were written from five to eight centuries back, I presented to the Royal Asiatic Society. Of the vast numbers of these MS. books in the libraries of Puttun and Jessulmér, many are of the most remote antiquity, and in a character no longer understood by

If we consider the political changes and convulsions which have happened in Hindust'han since Mahmood's invasion, and the intolerant bigotry of many of his successors, we shall be able to account for the paucity of its national works on history, without being driven to the improbable conclusion, that the Hindus were ignorant of an art which has been cultivated in other countries from almost the earliest ages. Is it to be imagined that a nation so highly civilised as the Hindus, amongst whom the exact sciences flourished in perfection, by whom the fine arts, architecture, sculpture, poetry, music, were not only cultivated, but taught and defined by the nicest and most elaborate rules, were totally unacquainted with the simple art of recording the events of their history, the characters of their princes, and the acts of their reigns ? Where such traces of *mind* exist, we can hardly believe that there was a want of competent recorders of events, which synchronical authorities tell us were worthy of commemoration. The cities of Hastinapoor and Indraprest'ha, of Anhulwara and Somanat'ha, the triumphal columns of Dehli and Cheetore, the shrines of Aboo and Girnar, the cave-temples of Elephanta and Ellora, are so many attestations of the same fact ; nor can we imagine that the age in which these works were erected was without an historian. Yet from the Mahabharat, or Great War, to Alexander's invasion, and from that grand event to the era of Mahmood of Ghizni, scarcely a paragraph of pure native Hindu history (except as before stated) has hitherto been revealed to the curiosity of western scholars. In the heroic history of Pirthi-raj, the last of the Hindu sovereigns of Dehli, written by his bard Chund, we find notices which authorise the inference that works similar to his own were then extant, relating to the period between Mahmood and Shabudin (A.D. 1000–1193) ; but these have disappeared.

After eight centuries of galling subjection to conquerors totally ignorant of the classical language of the Hindus ; after almost every capital city had been repeatedly stormed and sacked by barbarous, bigoted, and exasperated foes ; it is too much to expect that the literature of the country should not have sustained, in common with other important interests, irretrievable losses. My own animadversions upon the defective condition of the annals of Rajwarra have more than once been checked by a very just remark : "when our princes were in exile, driven from hold to hold, and compelled to dwell in the clefts of the mountains, often doubtful whether they would not be forced to abandon the very meal preparing for them, was that a time to think of historical records ?"

Those who expect from a people like the Hindus a species of composi-

their possessors, or only by the supreme pontiff and his initiated librarians. There is one volume held so sacred for its magical contents, that it is suspended by a chain in the temple of Chintamun, at the last-named capital in the desert, and is only taken down to have its covering renewed, or at the inauguration of a pontiff. Tradition assigns its authorship to Somaditya Sooru Acharya, a pontiff of past days, before the Islamite had crossed the waters of the Indus, and whose diocese extended far beyond that stream. His magic mantle is also here preserved, and used on every new installation. The character is, doubtless, the nail-headed Pali ; and could we introduce the ingenious, indefatigable, and modest Mons. E. Burnouf, with his able coadjutor Dr. Lassen, into the temple, we might learn something of this Sybilline volume, without their incurring the risk of loss of sight, which befel the last individual, a female Yati of the Jains, who sacrilegiously endeavoured to acquire its contents.

tion of precisely the same character as the historical works of Greece and Rome, commit the very egregious error of overlooking the peculiarities which distinguish the natives of India from all other races, and which strongly discriminate their intellectual productions of every kind from those of the West. Their philosophy, their poetry, their architecture, are marked with traits of originality; and the same may be expected to pervade their history, which, like the arts enumerated, took a character from its intimate association with the religion of the people. It must be recollected, moreover, that until a more correct taste was imparted to the literature of England and of France, by the study of classical models, the chronicles of both these countries, and indeed of all the polished nations of Europe, were, at a much more recent date, as crude, as wild, and as barren, as those of the early Rajpoots.

In the absence of regular and legitimate historical records, there are, however, other native works (they may, indeed, be said to abound), which, in the hands of a skilful and patient investigator, would afford no despicable materials for the history of India. The first of these are the *Purans* and genealogical legends of the princes, which, obscured as they are by mythological details, allegory, and improbable circumstances, contain many facts that serve as beacons to direct the research of the historian. What Hume remarks of the annals and annalists of the Saxon Heptarchy, may be applied with equal truth to those of the Rajpoot *Seven States*:[1] "they abound in names, but are extremely barren of events; or they are related so much without circumstances and causes, that the most profound and eloquent writer must despair of rendering them either instructive or entertaining to the reader. The monks" (for which we may read "Brahmins"), "who lived remote from public affairs, considered the civil transactions as subservient to the ecclesiastical, and were strongly affected with credulity, with the love of wonder, and with a propensity to imposture."

The heroic poems of India constitute another resource for history. Bards may be regarded as the primitive historians of mankind. Before fiction began to engross the attention of poets, or rather, before the province of history was dignified by a class of writers who made it a distinct department of literature, the functions of the bard were doubtless employed in recording real events and in commemorating real personages. In India, Calliope has been worshipped by the bards from the days of Vyasu, the contemporary of Job, to the time of Beni-dása, the present chronicler of Méwar. The poets are the chief, though not the sole, historians of Western India; neither is there any deficiency of them, though they speak in a peculiar tongue, which requires to be translated into the sober language of probability. To compensate for their magniloquence and obscurity, their pen is free: the despotism of the Rajpoot princes does not extend to the poet's lay, which flows unconfined except by the shackles of the *chund bhojoonga*, or 'serpentine stanza'; no slight restraint, it must be confessed, upon the freedom of the historic muse. On the other hand, there is a sort of compact or understanding between the bard and the prince, a barter of "solid pudding against empty praise," whereby the fidelity of the poetic chronicle is somewhat impaired. This sale of "fame," as the bards term it, by the court-laureates and historio-

[1] Méwar, Marwar, Ambér, Bikanér, Jessulmér, Kotah, and Boondí.

graphers of Rajast'han, will continue until there shall arise in the community a class sufficiently enlightened and independent, to look for no other recompense for literary labour than public distinction.

Still, however, these chroniclers dare utter truths, sometimes most unpalatable to their masters. When offended, or actuated by a virtuous indignation against immorality, they are fearless of consequences ; and woe to the individual who provokes them ! Many a resolution has sunk under the lash of their satire, which has condemned to eternal ridicule names that might otherwise have escaped notoriety. The *vis*, or poison of the bard, is more dreaded by the Rajpoot than the steel of the foe

The absence of all mystery or reserve with regard to public affairs in the Rajpoot principalities, in which every individual takes an interest, from the noble to the porter at the city-gates, is of great advantage to the chronicler of events. When matters of moment in the disorganised state of the country rendered it imperative to observe secrecy, the Rana of Méwar, being applied to on the necessity of concealing them, rejoined as follows : " this is *Chaomookhi-raj* ; [1] Eklinga the sovereign, I his vicegerent ; in him I trust, and I have no secrets from my children." To this publicity may be partly ascribed the inefficiency of every general alliance against common foes ; but it gives a kind of patriarchal character to the government, and inspires, if not loyalty and patriotism in their most exalted sense, feelings at least much akin to them.

A material drawback upon the value of these bardic histories is, that they are confined almost exclusively to the martial exploits of their heroes, and to the *rung-rin-bhom*, or 'field of slaughter.' Writing for the amusement of a warlike race, the authors disregard civil matters and the arts and pursuits of peaceful life ; love and war are their favourite themes. Chund, the last of the great bards of India, tells us, indeed, in his preface, " that he will give rules for governing empires ; the laws of grammar and composition ; lessons in diplomacy, home and foreign, etc." : and he fulfils his promise, by interspersing precepts on these points in various episodes throughout his work.

Again : the bard, although he is admitted to the knowledge of all the secret springs which direct each measure of the government, enters too deeply into the intrigues, as well as the levities, of the court, to be qualified to pronounce a sober judgment upon its acts.

Nevertheless, although open to all these objections, the works of the native bards afford many valuable data, in facts, incidents, religious opinions, and traits of manners ; many of which, being carelessly introduced, are thence to be regarded as the least suspicious kind of historical evidence. In the heroic history of Pirthi-raj, by Chund, there occur many geographical as well as historical details, in the description of his sovereign's wars, of which the bard was an eye-witness, having been his friend, his herald, his ambassador, and finally discharging the melancholy office of accessory to his death, that he might save him from dishonour. The poetical histories of Chund were collected by the great Umra Sing of Méwar, a patron of literature, as well as a warrior and a legislator.

Another species of historical records is found in the accounts given by the Brahmins of the endowments of the temples, their dilapidation

[1] 'Government of *four mouths*,' alluding to the quadriform image of the tutelary divinity.

and repairs, which furnish occasions for the introduction of historical and chronological details. In the legends, respecting places of pilgrimage and religious resort, profane events are blended with superstitious rites and ordinances, local ceremonies and customs. The controversies of the Jains furnish, also, much historical information, especially with reference to Guzzerat and Nehrwala, during the Chaulac dynasty. From a close and attentive examination of the Jain records, which embody all that those ancient sectarians knew of science, many chasms in Hindu history might be filled up. The party-spirit of the rival sects of India was, doubtless, adverse to the purity of history; and the very ground upon which the Brahmins built their ascendancy was the ignorance of the people. There appears to have been in India, as well as in Egypt in early times, a coalition between the hierarchy and the state, with the view of keeping the mass of the nation in darkness and subjugation.

These different records, works of a mixed historical and geographical character which I know to exist; *rasahs* or poetical legends of princes, which are common; local *Puranas*, religious comments, and traditionary couplets;[1] with authorities of a less dubious character, namely, inscriptions "cut on the rock," coins, copper-plate grants, containing charters of immunities, and expressing many singular features of civil government, constitute, as I have already observed, no despicable materials for the historian, who would, moreover, be assisted by the synchronisms which are capable of being established with ancient Pagan and later Mahomedan writers.

From the earliest period of my official connection with this interesting country, I applied myself to collect and explore its early historical records, with a view of throwing some light upon a people scarcely yet known in Europe and whose political connection with England appeared to me to be capable of undergoing a material change, with benefit to both parties. It would be wearisome to the reader to be minutely informed of the process I adopted, to collect the scattered relics of Rajpoot history into the form and substance in which he now sees them. I began with the sacred genealogy from the *Puranas*; examined the *Mahabharat*, and the poems of Chund (a complete chronicle of his times); the voluminous historical poems of Jessulmér, Marwar, and Méwar;[2] the histories of the Kheetchies, and those of the Hara princes of Kotah and Boondí, etc., by their respective bards. A portion of the materials compiled by Jey Sing of Ambér or Jeipoor (one of the greatest patrons of science amongst the modern Hindu princes), to illustrate the history of his race, fell into my hands. I have reason to believe that there existed more copious materials, which his profligate descendant, the late prince, in his division of the

[1] Some of these preserve the names of princes who invaded India between the time of Mahmood of Ghizni and Shabudin, who are not mentioned by Ferishta, the Mahomedan historian. The invasion of Ajmér and the capture of Biana, the seat of the Yadu princes, were made known to us by this means.

[2] Of Marwar, there were the *Vijya Vulas*, the *Surya Prukas*, and *Kheat*, or legends, besides detached fragments of reigns. Of Méwar, there was the *Khoman Rassah*, a modern work formed from old materials which are lost, and commencing with the attack of Cheetore by Mahmood, supposed to be the son of Kasim of Sinde, in the very earliest ages of Mahomedanism: also the *Juggut Vulas*, the *Raj-prukas*, and the *Jeya Vulas*, all poems composed in the reigns of the princes whose names they bear, but generally introducing succinctly the early parts of history. Besides these, there were fragments of the Jeipoor family, from their archives; and the *Mán Cheritra*, or history of Raja Maun.

empire with a prostitute, may have disposed of on the partition of the library of the state, which was the finest collection in Rajast'han. Like some of the renowned princes of Timur's dynasty, Jey Sing kept a diary, termed *Calpadruma*, in which he noted every event : a work written by such a man and at such an interesting juncture, would be a valuable acquisition to history. From the Duttea prince I obtained a transcript of the journal of his ancestor, who served with such *éclat* amongst the great feudatories of Arungzéb's army, and from which Scott made many extracts in his history of the Dekhan.

For a period of ten years, I was employed, with the aid of a learned Jain, in ransacking every work which could contribute any facts or incidents to the history of the Rajpoots, or diffuse any light upon their manners and character. Extracts and versions of all such passages were made by my Jain assistant into the more familiar dialects (which are formed from the Sanscrit) of these tribes, in whose language my long residence amongst them enabled me to converse with facility. At much expense, and during many wearisome hours, to support which required no ordinary degree of enthusiasm, I endeavoured to possess myself not merely of their history, but of their religious notions, their familiar opinions, and their characteristic manners, by associating with their chiefs and bardic chroniclers, and by listening to their traditionary tales and allegorical poems. I might ultimately, as the circle of my inquiries enlarged, have materially augmented my knowledge of these subjects ; but ill-health compelled me to relinquish this pleasing though toilsome pursuit, and forced me to revisit my native land just as I had obtained permission to look across the threshold of the Hindu Minerva ; whence, however, I brought some relics, the examination of which I now consign to other hands. The large collection of ancient Sanscrit and Bakha MSS., which I conveyed to England, have been presented to the Royal Asiatic Society, in whose library they are deposited. The contents of many, still unexamined, may throw additional light on the history of ancient India. I claim only the merit of having brought them to the knowledge of European scholars ; but I may hope that this will furnish a stimulus to others to make similar exertions.

The little exact knowledge that Europe has hitherto acquired of the Rajpoot states, has probably originated a false idea of the comparative importance of this portion of Hindust'han. The splendour of the Rajpoot courts, however, at an early period of the history of that country, making every allowance for the exaggeration of the bards, must have been great. Northern India was rich from the earliest times ; that portion of it, situated on either side the Indus, formed the richest satrapy of Darius. It has abounded in the more striking events which constitute the materials for history : there is not a petty state in Rajast'han that has not had its Thermopylæ, and scarcely a city that has not produced its Leonidas. But the mantle of ages has shrouded from view what the magic pen of the historian might have consecrated to endless admiration : Somnat'h might have rivalled Delphos ; the spoils of Hind might have vied with the wealth of the Lybian king ; and compared with the array of the Pandus, the army of Xerxes would have dwindled into insignificance. But the Hindus either never had, or have unfortunately lost, their Herodotus and Xenophon.

If "the moral effect of history depend on the sympathy it excites," the annals of these states possess commanding interest. The struggles of a brave people for independence during a series of ages, sacrificing whatever was dear to them for the maintenance of the religion of their forefathers, and sturdily defending to death, and in spite of every temptation, their rights and national liberty, form a picture which it is difficult to contemplate without emotion. Could I impart to the reader but a small portion of the enthusiastic delight with which I have listened to the tales of times that are past, amid scenes where their events occurred, I should not despair of triumphing over the apathy which dooms to neglect almost every effort to enlighten my native country on the subject of India; nor should I apprehend any ill effect from the sound of names, which, musical and expressive as they are to a Hindu, are dissonant and unmeaning to a European ear: for it should be remembered that almost every Eastern name is significant of some quality, personal or mental. Seated amidst the ruins of ancient cities, I have listened to the traditions respecting their fall; or have heard the exploits of their illustrious defenders related by their descendants near the altars erected to their memory. I have, whilst in the train of the southern Goths (the Mahrattas), as they carried desolation over the land, encamped on or traversed many a field of battle, of civil strife or foreign aggression, to read in the rude memorials on the tumuli of the slain their names and history. Such anecdotes and records afford data of history as well as of manners. Even the couplet recording the erection of a "column of victory," or of a temple or its repairs, contributes something to our stock of knowledge of the past.

As far as regards the antiquity of the dynasties now ruling in Central and Western India, there are but two, the origin of which is not perfectly within the limits of historical probability; the rest having owed their present establishments to the progress of the Moslem arms, their annals are confirmed by those of their conquerors. All the existing families, indeed, have attained their present settlements subsequently to the Mahomedan invasions, except Méwar, Jessulmér, and some smaller principalities in the desert; whilst others of the first magnitude, such as the Pramara and Solanki, who ruled at Dhar and Anhulwarra, have for centuries ceased to exist.

I have been so hardy as to affirm and endeavour to prove the common origin of the martial tribes of Rajast'han and those of ancient Europe. I have expatiated at some length upon the evidence in favour of the existence of a feudal system in India, similar to that which prevailed in the early ages on the European continent, and of which relics still remain in the laws of our own nation. Hypotheses of this kind are, I am aware, viewed with suspicion, and sometimes assailed with ridicule. With regard to the notions which I have developed on these questions, and the frequent allusions to them in the pages of this volume, I entertain no obstinate prepossessions or prejudices in their favour. The world is too enlightened at the present day to be in danger of being misled by any hypothetical writer, let him be ever so skilful; but the probability is, that we have been induced, by the multitude of false theories which time has exposed, to fall into the opposite error, and that we have become too sceptical with regard to the common origin of the people of the east and west. However, I submit my proofs to the candid judgment of the world: the analogies, if not conclusive on the questions, are still sufficiently curious and remarkable to repay the trouble of perusal and to provoke further investigation ; and they may, it is hoped, vindicate the author for endeavouring to elucidate the subject, " by steering through the dark channels of antiquity by the feeble lights of forgotten chronicles and imperfect records."

I am conscious that there is much in this work which demands the indulgence of the public ; and I trust it will not be necessary for me to assign a more powerful argument in plea than that which I have already adverted to, namely, the state of my health, which has rendered it a matter of considerable difficulty, indeed I may say of risk, to bring my bulky materials even into their present imperfect form. I should observe, that it never was my intention to treat the subject in the severe style of history, which would have excluded many details useful to the politician as well as to the curious student. I offer this work as a copious collection of materials for the future historian ; and am far less concerned at the idea of giving too much, than at the apprehension of suppressing what might possibly be useful.

Some variations occur (notwithstanding great care) in the orthography and accentuation of the numerous proper names. The long *i* is occasionally marked *í*, and sometimes printed as *ee* ; the Italian *u* is, in like manner, sometimes *ú*, and now and then written as *oo*, etc. The only variation which can occasion the smallest difficulty to the reader, is the name of the Hindu sovereign of Dehli, who is called *Pirthwirájá* and *Pirthiraj*.

CONTENTS

GEOGRAPHY OF RAJAST'HAN, OR RAJPOOTANA

HISTORY OF THE RAJPOOT TRIBES

CHAPTER I

CHAPTER II

CHAPTER III

CHAPTER IV

CHAPTER V

CHAPTER VI

CHAPTER VII

CHAPTER VIII

SKETCH OF A FEUDAL SYSTEM IN RAJAST'HAN

PAGE

CHAPTER I

CHAPTER II

CHAPTER III

CHAPTER IV

CHAPTER V

APPENDIX

ANNALS OF MÉWAR

CHAPTER I

CHAPTER II

CHAPTER III

CHAPTER IV

CHAPTER V

CHAPTER VI

CHAPTER VII

CHAPTER VIII

CHAPTER IX

CHAPTER X

CHAPTER XI

CHAPTER XII

CHAPTER XIII

CHAPTER XIV

CHAPTER XV

CHAPTER XVI

CHAPTER XVII

PERSONAL NARRATIVE OF THE AUTHOR

CHAPTER XXV

Journey to Marwar

CHAPTER XXVI

CHAPTER XXVII

CHAPTER XXVIII

APPENDIX

ANNALS AND ANTIQUITIES OF RAJAST'HAN

GEOGRAPHY OF RAJAST'HAN OR RAJPOOTANA

RAJAST'HAN is the collective and classical denomination of that portion of India which is 'the abode [1] of (Rajpoot) princes.' In the familiar dialect of these countries it is termed *Rajwarra*, but by the more refined *Raét'hána*, corrupted to *Rajpootana*, the common designation amongst the British to denote the Rajpoot principalities.

What might have been the nominal extent of Rajast'han prior to the Mahomedan conqueror Shabudin (when it probably reached beyond the Jumna and Ganges, even to the base of the Himalaya) cannot now be known. At present we may adhere to its restrictive definition, still comprehending a wide space and a variety of interesting races.

Previous to the erection of the minor Mahommedan monarchies of Mandoo and Ahmedabad (the capitals of Malwa and Guzzerat), on the ruins of Dhar and Anhulwarra Puttun, the term Rajast'han would have been appropriated to the space comprehended in the map prefixed to this work: the valley of the Indus on the west, and Boondelkhund [2] on the east; to the north, the sandy tracts (south of the Sutledge) termed *Jungul dés*; and the Vindhya mountains to the south.

This space comprehends nearly 8° of latitude and 9° of longitude, being from 22° to 30° north latitude, and 69° to 78° east longitude, embracing a superficial area of 350,000 square miles.

Although it is proposed to touch upon the annals of all the states in this extensive tract, with their past and present condition, those in the centre will claim the most prominent regard; especially Méwar, which, copiously treated of, will afford a specimen, obviating the necessity of like details of the rest.

[1] Or 'regal (*raj*) dwelling (*t'han*).

[2] It is rather singular that the Sinde river will mark this eastern boundary, as does the Indus (or great Sinde) that to the west. East of this minor Sinde the Hindu princes are not of pure blood, and are excluded from Rajast'han or Rajwarra.

The order in which these states will be reviewed is as follows :—

1. Méwar, or Oodipoor.
2. Marwar, or Jodpoor.
3. Bikanér and Kishengurh.
4. Kotah } or Harouti.
5. Boondi }
6. Ambér, or Jeipoor, with its branches, dependent and independent.
7. Jesselmér.
8. The Indian desert to the valley of the Indus.

The basis of this work is the geography of the country, the historical and statistical portion being consequent and subordinate thereto. It was, indeed, originally designed to be essentially geographical ; but circumstances have rendered it impossible to execute the intended details, or even to make the map [1] so perfect as the superabundant material at the command of the author might have enabled him to do ; a matter of regret to himself rather than of loss to the general reader, to whom geographic details, however important, are usually dry and uninteresting.

It was also intended to institute a comparison between the map and such remains of ancient geography as can be extracted from the Poorans and other Hindu authorities ; which, however, must be deferred to a future period, when the deficiency of the present rapid and general sketch may be supplied, should the author be enabled to resume his labours.

The laborious research, in the course of which these data were accumulated, commenced in 1806, when the author was attached to the embassy sent, at the close of the Mahratta wars, to the court of Sindia. This chieftain's army was then in Méwar, at that period almost a *terra incognita*, the position of whose two capitals, Oodipoor and Cheetore, in the best existing maps, was precisely reversed ; that is, Cheetore was inserted S.E. of Oodipoor, instead of E.N.E. ; a proof of the scanty knowledge possessed at that period.

In other respects there was almost a total blank. In the maps prior to 1806 nearly all the western and central states of Rajast'han will be found wanting. It had been imagined, but a little time before, that the rivers had a southerly course into the Nerbudda ; a notion corrected by the father of Indian geography, the distinguished Rennell.

This blank the author filled up ; and in 1815, for the first time, the geography of Rajast'han was put into combined form and presented to the Marquis of Hastings, on the eve of a general war, when the labour of ten years was amply rewarded by its becoming in part the foundation of that illustrious commander's plans of the campaign. It is a duty owing to himself to state that every map, without exception, printed since this period, has its foundation, as regards Central and Western India, in the labours of the author.[2]

[1] Engraved by that meritorious artist Mr. Walker, engraver to the East-India Company, who, I trust, will be able to make a fuller use of my materials hereafter.

[2] When the war of 1817 broke out, copies of my map on a reduced scale were sent to all the divisions of the armies in the field, and came into possession of many of the staff. Transcripts were made which were brought to Europe, and portions introduced into every recent map of India. One map has, indeed,

The route of the embassy was from Agra, through the southern frontier of Jeipoor, to Oodipoor. A portion of this had been surveyed, and points laid down from celestial observation, by Dr. W. Hunter, which I adopted as the basis of my enterprise. The Resident Envoy [1] to the court of Sindia was possessed of the valuable sketch of the route of Colonel Palmer's embassy in 1791, as laid down by Dr. Hunter, the foundation of my subsequent surveys, as it merited from its importance and general accuracy. It embraced all the extreme points of Central India: Agra, Nirwur, Ditteah, Jhansi, Bhopal, Sarangpoor, Oojein, and on return from this, the first meridian of the Hindus, by Kotah, Boondi, Rampoora (Tonk), Biana, to Agra. The position of all these places was more or less accurately fixed, according to the time which could be bestowed, by astronomical observation.

At Rampoora Hunter ceased to be my guide: and from this point commenced the new survey of Oodipoor, where we arrived in June 1806. The position then assigned to it, with most inadequate instruments, has been changed only 1′ of longitude, though the latitude amounted to about 5′.

From Oodipoor the subsequent march of the army with which we moved led past the celebrated Cheetore, and through the centre of Malwa, crossing in detail all the grand streams flowing from the Vindhya, till we halted for a season on the Boondelkhund frontier at Kémlassa. In this journey of seven hundred miles I twice crossed the lines of route of the former embassy, and was gratified to find my first attempts generally coincide with their established points.

In 1807 the army having undertaken the siege of Rahtgurh, I determined to avail myself of the time which Mahrattas waste in such a process, and to pursue my favourite project. With a small guard I determined to push through untrodden fields, by the banks of the Bétwa to Chandéri, and in its latitude proceed in a westerly direction towards Kotah, trace the course once more of all those streams from the south, and the points of junction of the most important (the Cali Sinde, Parbutti, and Bunas) with the Chumbul; and having effected this, continue my journey to Agra. This I accomplished in times very different from the present, being often obliged to strike my tents and march at midnight, and more than once the object of plunder.[2] The chief points in this route were Kémlassa, Rajwarra, Kotra on the Bétwa, Kunniadana,[3] Booradongur,[4]

been given, in a manner to induce a supposition that the furnisher of the materials was the author of them. It has fulfilled a prediction of the Marquis of Hastings, who, foreseeing the impossibility of such materials remaining private property, "and the danger of their being appropriated by others," and desirous that the author should derive the full advantage of his labours, had it signified that the claims for recompense, on the records of successive governments, should not be deferred.

It will not be inferred the author is surprised at what he remarks. While he claims priority for himself, he is the last person to wish to see a halt in science—

"For emulation has a thousand sons."

[1] My esteemed friend, Græme Mercer, Esq. (of Maevisbank), who stimulated my exertions with his approbation.

[2] Many incidents in these journeys would require no aid of imagination to touch on the romantic, but they can have no place here.

[3] Eastern tableland.

[4] Sinde River.

Shahabad, Barah,[1] Polaitah,[2] Baroda, Seopoor, Palli,[3] Rintimbore, Kerowly, Sri Muttra, and Agra.

On my return to the Mahratta camp I resolved further to increase the sphere, and proceeded westward by Bhurtpoor, Kut'hoomur, Saintri, to Jeipoor, Tonk, Indurgurh, Googul, Chupra, Raghoogurh, Arone, Koorwye, Bhorasso, to Saugur: a journey of more than one thousand miles. I found the camp nearly where I left it.

With this ambulatory court I moved everywhere within this region, constantly employed in surveying till 1812 when Sindia's court became stationary. It was then I formed my plans for obtaining a knowledge of those countries into which I could not personally penetrate.

In 1810–11 I had despatched two parties, one to the Indus, the other to the desert south of the Sutledge. The first party, under Shekh Abul Birkat, journeyed westward, by Oodipoor, through Guzzerat, Saurashtra and Cutch, Lukput and Hyderabad (the capital of the Sindie government); crossed the Indus to Tatta, proceeded up the right bank to Seewan; recrossed, and continued on the left bank as far as Khyrpoor, the residence of one of the triumvirate governors of Sinde, and having reached the insulated Bekher[4] (the capital of the Sogdi of Alexander) returned by the desert of Oomrasoomra to Jesselmér, Marwar, and Jeipoor, and joined me in camp at Nirwar. It was a perilous undertaking; but the Shekh was a fearless and enterprising character, and moreover a man with some tincture of learning. His journals contained many hints and directions for future research in the geography, statistics, and manners of the various races amongst whom he travelled.

The other party was conducted by a most valuable man, Madarri Lall, who became a perfect adept in these expeditions of geographical discovery, and other knowledge resulting therefrom. There is not a district of any consequence in the wide space before the reader which was not traversed by this spirited individual, whose qualifications for such complicated and hazardous journeys were never excelled. Ardent, persevering, prepossessing, and generally well-informed, he made his way when others might have perished.[5]

From these remote regions the best informed native inhabitants were, by persuasion and recompense, conducted to me; and I could at all times, in the Mahratta camp at Gwalior, from 1812 to 1817, have provided a native of the valley of the Indus, the deserts of Dhat, Oomrasoomra, or any of the states of Rajast'han.

The precision with which Kasids and other public conveyers of letters, in countries where posts are little used, can detail the peculiarities of a

[1] Parbutti River. [2] Cali Sinde River.

[3] Passage of the Chumbul and junction of the Par.

[4] The Shekh brought me specimens of the rock, which is siliceous; and also a piece of brick of the very ancient fortress of Seewan, and some of the grain from its pits, charred and alleged by tradition to have lain there since the period of Raja Bhirtirri, the brother of Vicramaditya. It is not impossible that it might be owing to Alexander's terrific progress, and to their supplies being destroyed by fire. Seewan is conjectured by Captain Pottinger to be the capital of Musicanus.

[5] His health was worn out at length, and he became the victim of depressed spirits. He died suddenly: I believe poisoned. Futtah, almost as zealous as Madarri, also died in the pursuit. Geography has been destructive to all who have pursued it with ardour in the East.

long line of route, and the accuracy of their distances, would scarcely be credited in Europe. I have no hesitation in asserting that if a correct estimate were obtained of the measured *coss* of a country, a line might be laid down upon a flat surface with great exactitude. I have heard it affirmed that it was the custom of the old Hindoo governments to have measurements made of the roads from town to town, and that the *Aboo Mahatma* [1] contains a notice of an instrument for that purpose. Indeed, the singular coincidence between lines measured by the perambulator and the estimated distances of the natives, is the best proof that the latter are deduced from some more certain method than mere computation.

I never rested satisfied with the result of one set of my parties, with the single exception of Madarri's, always making the information of one a basis for the instruction of another, who went over the same ground; but with additional views and advantages, and with the aid of the natives brought successively by each, till I exhausted every field.

Thus, in a few years, I had filled several volumes with lines of route throughout this space; and having many frontier and intermediate points, the positions of which were fixed, a general outline of the result was constructed, wherein all this information was laid down. I speak more particularly of the western states, as the central portion, or that watered by the Chumbul and its tributary streams, whether from the elevated Aravulli on the west, or from the Vindhya mountains on the south, has been personally surveyed and measured in every direction, with an accuracy sufficient for every political or military purpose, until the grand trigonometrical survey from the peninsula shall be extended throughout India. These countries form an extended plain to the Sutledge north, and west to the Indus, rendering the amalgamation of geographical materials much less difficult than where mountainous regions intervene.

After having laid down these varied lines in the outline described, I determined to check and confirm its accuracy by recommencing the survey on a new plan, viz. trigonometrically.

My parties were again despatched to resume their labours over fields now familiar to them. They commenced from points whose positions were fixed (and my knowledge enabled me to give a series of such), from each of which, as a centre, they collected every radiating route to every town within the distance of twenty miles. The points selected were generally such as to approach equilateral triangles; and although to digest the information became a severe toil, the method will appear, even to the casual observer, one which must throw out its own errors; for these lines crossed in every direction, and consequently corrected each other. By such means did I work my way in those unknown tracts, and the result is in part before the reader. I say, in part; for my health compels me reluctantly to leave out much which could be combined from *ten folios* of journeys extending throughout these regions.

In 1815, as before stated, an outline map containing all the information thus obtained, and which the subsequent crisis rendered of essential importance, was presented by me to the Governor-General of India. Upon the very eve of the war I constructed and presented another, of the greater portion of Malwa, to which it appeared expedient to confine the

[1] A valuable and ancient work, which I presented to the Royal Asiatic Society.

operations against the Pindarries. The material feature in this small map was the general position of the Vindhya mountains, the sources and course of every river originating thence, and the passes in this chain, an object of primary importance. The boundaries of the various countries in this tract were likewise defined, and it became essentially useful in the subsequent dismemberment of the Peishwa's dominions.

In the construction of this map I had many fixed points, both of Dr. Hunter's and my own, to work from ; and it is gratifying to observe that though several measured lines have since been run through this space, not only the general, but often the identical features of mine, have been preserved in the maps since given to the world. As considerable improvement has been made by several measured lines through this tract, and many positions affixed by a scientific and zealous geographer, I have had no hesitation in incorporating a small portion of this improved geography in the map now presented.[1]

Many surveyed lines were made by me, from 1817 to 1822 ; and here I express my obligations to my kinsman,[2] to whom alone I owe any aid for improving this portion of my geographical labours. This officer made a circuitous survey, which comprehended nearly the extreme points of Méwar, from the capital, by Cheetore, Mandelgurh, Jehajpoor, Rajmahl, and in return by Bunai, Bednore, Deogurh, to the point of outset. From these extreme points he was enabled to place many intermediate ones, for which Méwar is so favourable, by reason of its isolated hills.

In 1820 I made an important journey across the Aravulli, by Komulmér, Pali, to Jodpoor, the capital of Marwar, and thence by Mairta, tracing the course of the Looni to its source at Ajmér ; and from this celebrated residence of the Chohan kings and Mogul emperors, returning through the central lands of Méwar, by Bunai and Bunéra, to the capital.

I had the peculiar satisfaction to find that my position of Jodpoor, which has been used as a capital point in fixing the geography west and north, was only 3′ of space out in latitude, and little more in longitude ; which accounted for the coincidence of my position of Bikanér with that assigned by Mr. Elphinstone, in his account of the embassy to Caubul.

Besides Oodipoor, Jodpoor, Ajmér, etc., whose positions I had fixed by observations, and the points laid down by Hunter, I availed myself of a few positions given to me by that enterprising traveller, the author of the journey into Khorassan,[3] who marched from Dehli, by Nagore and Jodpoor. to Oodipoor.

The outline of the countries of Guzzerat,[4] the Saurashtra peninsula, and Cutch, inserted chiefly by way of connection, is entirely taken from the labours of that distinguished geographer, the late General Reynolds. We had both gone over a great portion of the same field, and my testimony

[1] It is, however, limited to Malwa, whose geography was greatly improved and enlarged by the labours of Captain Dangerfield ; and though my materials could fill up the whole of this province, I merely insert the chief points to connect it with Rajast'han.

[2] Captain P. T. Waugh, 10th Regiment Light Cavalry, Bengal.

[3] Mr. J. B. Fraser.

[4] My last journey, in 1822–23, was from Oodipoor, through these countries towards the Delta of the Indus, but more with a view to historical and antiquarian than geographical research. It proved the most fuitful of all my many journeys.

is due to the value of his researches in countries into which he never personally penetrated, evincing what may be done by industry, and the use of such materials as I have described.

I shall conclude with a rapid sketch of the physiognomy of these regions; minute and local descriptions will appear more appropriately in the respective historical portions.

Rajast'han presents a great variety of feature. Let me place the reader on the highest peak of the insulated Aboo, 'the saint's pinnacle,'[1] as it is termed, and guide his eye in a survey over this wide expanse, from the 'blue waters' of the Indus west, to the 'withy-covered'[2] Bétwa on the east. From this, the most elevated spot in Hindust'han, overlooking by fifteen hundred feet the Aravulli mountains, his eye descends to the plains of Medpát[3] (the classic term for Méwar), whose chief streams flowing from the base of the Aravulli, join the Béris and Bunas, and are prevented from uniting with the Chumbul only by the Pat-ár[4] or plateau of Central India.

Ascending this plateau near the celebrated Cheetore, let the eye deviate slightly from the direct eastern line, and pursue the only practicable path by Ruttungurh, and Singolli, to Kotah, and he will observe its three successive steppes, the miniature representation of those of Russian Tartary. Let the observer here glance across the Chumbul and traverse Harouti to its eastern frontier, guarded by the fortress of Shahabad: thence abruptly descend the plateau to the level of the Sinde, still proceeding eastward, until the table-mountain, the western limit of Boondelkhund, affords a resting point.

To render this more distinct, I present a profile of the tract described from Aboo to Kotra on the Bétwa:[5] from Aboo to the Chumbul, the result of barometrical measurement, and from the latter to the Bétwa from my general observations[6] of the irregularities of surface. The result is, that the Bétwa at Kotra is one thousand feet above the sea level, and one thousand lower than the city and valley of Oodipoor, which again is on the same level with *the base* of Aboo, two thousand feet above the sea. This line, the general direction of which is but a short distance from the tropic, is about six geographic degrees in length: yet is this small space highly diversified, both in its inhabitants and the production of the soil, whether hidden or revealed.

Let us now from our elevated station (still turned to the east) carry the eye both south and north of the line described, which nearly bisects

[1] Gūru Sikr.

[2] Its classic name is *Vitraventi*, *Vitra* being the common willow in Sanscrit; said by Wilford to be the same in Welsh.

[3] Literally 'the central (*médya*) flat.'

[4] Meaning 'table (*pát*) mountain (*ár*).'—Although *ár* may not be found in any Sanscrit dictionary with the signification 'mountain,' yet it appears to be a primitive root possessing such meaning—instance, *Ar-boodha*, 'hill of Booddha'; *Aravulli*, 'hill of strength.' *Ar* is Hebrew for 'mountain' (qu. *Ararat*?) Ορος in Greek? The common word for a mountain in Sanscrit, *gir*, is equally so in Hebrew.

[5] The Bétwa river runs under the tableland just alluded to, on the east.

[6] I am familiar with these regions, and confidently predict that when a similar measurement shall be made from the Bétwa to Kotah, these results will little err, and the error will be in having made Kotah somewhat too elevated, and the bed of the Bétwa a little too low.

Media-désa,[1] 'the *central land*' of Rajast'han; best defined by the course of the Chumbul and its tributary streams, to its confluence with the Jumna: while the regions west of the transalpine Aravulli[2] may as justly be defined Western Rajast'han.

Looking to the south, the eye rests on the long extended and strongly defined line of the Vindhya mountains, the proper bounds of Hindust'han and the Dekhan. Though, from our elevated stand on 'the Saint's Pinnacle' of Aboo, we look down on the Vindhya as a range of diminished importance, it is that our position is the least favourable to viewing its grandeur, which would be most apparent from the south; though throughout this skirt of descent, irregular elevations attain a height of many hundred feet above such points of its abrupt descent.

The Aravulli itself may be said to connect with the Vindhya, and the point of junction to be towards Champanér; though it might be as correct to say the Aravulli thence rose upon and stretched from the Vindhya. Whilst it is much less elevated than more to the north, it presents bold features throughout,[3] south by Lunawarra, Dongurpoor, and Edur, to Amba Bhawani and Oodipoor.

Still looking from Aboo over the table-land of Malwa, we observe her plains of black loam furrowed by the numerous streams from the highest points of the Vindhya, pursuing their northerly course; some meandering through valleys or falling over precipices; others bearing down all opposition, and actually forcing an exit through the central plateau to join the Chumbul.

Having thus glanced at the south, let us cast the eye north of this line, and pause on the alpine Aravulli.[4] Let us take a section of it, from the capital, Oodipoor, the line of our station on Aboo, passing through Oguna, Panurwa, and Meerpoor, to the western descent near Sirohi, a space of nearly sixty miles in a direct line, where "hills o'er hills and alps on alps arise," from the ascent at Oodipoor, to the descent to Marwar. All this space to the Sirohi frontier is inhabited by communities of the aboriginal races, living in a state of primeval and almost savage independence, owning no paramount power, paying no tribute, but with all the simplicity of republics; their leaders, with the title of Rawut, being hereditary. Thus the Rawut of the Oguna commune can assemble five thousand bows, and several others can on occasion muster considerable numbers. Their habitations are dispersed through the valleys in small rude hamlets, near their pastures or places of defence.[5]

[1] Central India, a term which I first applied as the title of the map presented to the Marquis of Hastings, in 1815, "of Central and Western India," and since become familiar.

[2] Let it be remembered that the Aravulli, though it loses its tabular form, sends its branches north, terminating at Dehli.

[3] Those who have marched from Baroda towards Malwa and marked the irregularities of surface, will admit this chain of connection of the Vindhya and Aravulli.

[4] 'The refuge of strength,' a title justly merited, from its affording protection to the most ancient sovereign race which holds dominion, whether in the east or west—the ancient stock of the Sooryavans, the Heliadæ of India, our 'children of the sun,' the princes of Méwar.

[5] It was my intention to have penetrated through their singular abodes; and I had negotiated, and obtained of these 'forest lords' a promise of hospitable

Let me now transport the reader to the citadel pinnacle of Komulmér,[1] thence surveying the range running north to Ajmér, where, shortly after, it loses its tabular form, and breaking into lofty ridges, sends numerous branches through the Shekhavati federation, and Alwar, till in low heights it terminates at Dehli.

From Komulmér to Ajmér the whole space is termed Mérwarra, and is inhabited by the mountain race of Mér or Mair, the habits and history of which singular class will be hereafter related. The range averages from six to fifteen miles in breadth, having upwards of one hundred and fifty villages and hamlets scattered over its valleys and rocks, abundantly watered, not deficient in pasture, and with cultivation enough for all internal wants, though it is raised with infinite labour on terraces, as the vine is cultivated in Switzerland and on the Rhine.

In vain does the eye search for any trace of wheel-carriage across this compound range from Edur to Ajmér; and it consequently well merits its appellation *ara*, 'the *barrier*,' for the strongest arm of modern warfare, artillery, would have to turn the chain by the north, to avoid the impracticable descent to the west.[2]

Guiding the eye along the chain, several fortresses are observed on pinnacles guarding the passes on either side, while numerous rills descend, pouring over the declivities, seeking their devious exit between the projecting ribs of the mountain. The Béris, the Bunas, the Kotaseri, the Khari, the Dye, all uniting with the Bunas to the east, while to the west the still more numerous streams which fertilise the rich province of Godwar, unite to 'the Salt River,' *the Looni*, and mark the true line of the desert. Of these the chief are the Sookri and the Bandi; while others which are not perennial, and depend on atmospheric causes for their supply, receive the general denomination of '*rayl*,' indicative of rapid mountain torrents, carrying in their descent a vast volume of alluvial deposit, to enrich the siliceous soil below.

However grand the view of the chaotic mass of rock from this elevated site of Komulmér, it is from the plains of Marwar that its majesty is most apparent; where its 'splintered pinnacles' are seen rising over each

passport, of which I have never allowed myself to doubt, as the virtues of pledged faith and hospitality are ever to be found in stronger keeping in the inverse ratio of civilisation. Many years ago one of my parties was permitted to range through this tract. In one of the passes of their lengthened valleys 'The Lord of the Mountain' was dead: the men were all abroad, and his widow alone in the hut. Madarri told his story, and claimed her surety and passport; which the Bheelni delivered from the quiver of her late lord; and the arrow carried in his hand was as well recognised as the cumbrous roll with all its seals and appendages of a traveller in Europe.

[1] *Mér* signifies 'a hill' in Sanscrit, hence *Komul*, or properly *Koombhomér*, is 'the hill' or 'mountain of Koombho,' a prince whose exploits are narrated. Likewise *Ajmér* is the 'hill of Ajya,' the 'Invincible' hill. *Mér* is with the long é, like *Mère* in French, in classical orthography.

[2] At the point of my descent this was characteristically illustrated by my Rajpoot friend of Sémur, whose domain had been invaded and cow-pens emptied, but a few days before, by the mountain bandit of Sirohi. With their booty they took the shortest and not most practicable road: but though their alpine kine are pretty well accustomed to leaping in such abodes, it would appear they had hesitated here. The difficulty was soon got over by one of the Meenas, who with his dagger transfixed one and rolled him over the height, his carcase serving at once as a precedent and a *stepping-stone* for his horned kindred.

other in varied form, or frowning over the dark indented recesses of its forest-covered and rugged declivities.

On reflection, I am led to pronounce the Aravulli a connection of the 'Appennines of India'; the Ghats on the Malabar coast of the peninsula: nor does the passage of the Nerbudda or the Tapti, through its diminished centre, militate against the hypothesis, which might be better substantiated by the comparison of their intrinsic character and structure.

The general character of the Aravulli is its primitive formation : granite, reposing in variety of angle (the general dip is to the east) on massive, compact, dark blue slate, the latter rarely appearing much above the surface or base of the superincumbent granite. The internal valleys abound in variegated quartz and a variety of schistus slate of every hue, which gives a most singular appearance to the roofs of the houses and temples when the sun shines upon them. Rocks of gneiss and of syenite appear in the intervals ; and in the diverging ridges west of Ajmér, the summits are quite dazzling with the enormous masses of vitreous rose-coloured quartz.

The Aravulli and its subordinate hills are rich both in mineral and metallic products ; and, as stated in the annals of Méwar, to the latter alone can be attributed the resources which enabled this family so long to struggle against superior power, and to raise those magnificent structures which would do honour to the most potent kingdoms of the west.

The mines are royalties ; their produce a monopoly, increasing the personal revenue of their prince. '*Án-Dán-Kán*' is a triple figurative expression, which comprehends the sum of sovereign rights in Rajast'han, being *allegiance*, *commercial duties*, *mines*. The tin-mines of Méwar were once very productive, and yielded, it is asserted, no inconsiderable portion of silver: but the caste of miners is extinct, and political reasons, during the Mogul domination, led to the concealment of such sources of wealth. Copper of a very fine description is likewise abundant, and supplies the currency ; and the chief of Saloombra even coins by sufferance from the mines on his own estate. *Soorma*, or the oxide of antimony, is found on the western frontier. The garnet, amethystine quartz, rock crystal, the chrysolite, and inferior kinds of the emerald family, are all to be found within Méwar ; and though I have seen no specimens decidedly valuable, the Rana has often told me that, according to tradition, his native hills contained every species of mineral wealth.

Let us now quit our alpine station on the Aravulli, and make a tour of the *Pátár*, or plateau of Central India, not the least important feature of this interesting region. It possesses a most decided character, and is distinct from the Vindhya to the south and the Aravulli to the west, being of the secondary formation, or trap, of the most regular horizontal stratification.

The circumference of the plateau is best explained in the map, though its surface is most unequally detailed, and is continually alternating its character between the tabular form and clustering ridges.

Commencing the tour at Mandelgurh, let us proceed south, skirting Cheetore (both on insulated rocks detached from the plateau), thence by Jawud, Dantolli, Rampoora,[1] Bhanpoora, the Mokundurra Pass,[2] to

[1] Near this the Chumbul first breaks into the Pátár.

[2] Here is the celebrated pass through the mountains.

Gagrown (where the Cali Sinde forces an entrance through its table-barrier to Eklaira)[1] and Mergwas (where the Parbutti, taking advantage of the diminished elevation, passes from Malwa to Harouti), and by Raghoogurh, Shahabad, Gazeegurh, Guswanee, to Jadoowati, where the plateau terminates on the Chumbul, east; while from the same point of outset, Mandelgurh, soon losing much of its table form, it stretches away in bold ranges, occasionally tabular, as in the Boondi fortress, by Dublana, Indurgurh,[2] and Lakhéri,[2] to Rint'humbor and Kerowli, terminating at Dholpoor Bari.

The elevation and inequalities of this plateau are best seen by crossing it from west to east, from the plains to the level of the Chumbul, where, with the exception of the short flat between Kotah and Palli ferry, this noble stream is seen rushing through the rocky barrier.

At Rint'humbor the plateau breaks into lofty ranges, their white summits sparkling in the sun; cragged but not peaked, and preserving the characteristic formation, though disunited from the mass. Here there are no less than seven distinct ranges (*Sát-parra*), through all of which the Bunas has to force a passage to unite with the Chumbul. Beyond Rint'humbor, and the whole way from Kerowli to the river, is an irregular table-land, on the edge of whose summit are the fortresses of Ootgeer, Mundrél, and that more celebrated of T'hoon. But east of the eastern side there is still another steppe of descent, which may be said to originate near the fountain of the Sinde at Latoti, and passing by Chanderi, Kuniadhana, Nirwar, and Gwalior, terminates at Deogurh, in the plains of Gohud. The descent from this second steppe is into Boondelkhund and the valley of the Bétwa.

Distinguished as is this elevated region of the surface of Central India, its summit is but little higher than the general elevation of the crest of the Vindhya, and upon a level with the valley of Oodipoor and base of the Aravulli. The slope or descent, therefore, from both these ranges to the skirts of the plateau, is great and abrupt, of which the most intelligible and simple proof appears in the course of these streams. Few portions of the globe attest more powerfully the force exerted by the action of waters to subdue every obstacle, than a view of the rock-bound channels of these streams in this adamantine barrier. Four streams—one of which, the Chumbul, would rank with the Rhine and almost with the Rhone—have here forced their way, laying bare the stratification from the water's level to the summit, from three to six hundred feet in perpendicular height, the rock appearing as if chiselled by the hand of man. Here the geologist may read the book of nature in distinct character: few tracts (from Rampoora to Kotah) will be found more interesting to him, to the antiquarian, or to the lover of nature in her most rugged attire.

The surface of this extensive plateau is greatly diversified. At Kotah, the bare protruding rock in some places presents not a trace of vegetation; but where it bevels off to the banks of the Par, it is one of the richest and most productive soils in India, and better cultivated than any spot even of British India. In its indented sides are glens of the most romantic description (as the fountain of '*the Snake King*' near Hinglaz), and deep

[1] Here the Newaz breaks the chain.

[2] Both celebrated passes, where the ranges are very complicated.

dells, the source of small streams, where many treasures of art,[1] in temples and ancient dwellings, yet remain to reward the traveller.

This central elevation, as before described, is of the secondary formation, called trap. Its prevailing colour, where laid bare by the Chumbul, is milk-white: it is compact and close-grained, and though perhaps the mineral offering the greatest resistance to the chisel, the sculptures at the celebrated Burolli evince its utility to the artist. White is also the prevailing colour to the westward. About Kotah it is often mixed white and porphyritic, and about Shahabad of a mixed red and brown tint. When exposed to the action of the atmosphere in its eastern declivity the decomposed and rough surface would almost cause it to be mistaken for gritstone.

This formation is not favourable to mineral wealth. The only metals are lead and iron; but their ores, especially the latter, are abundant. There are mines, said to be of value, of sulphuret of lead (*galena*) in the Gwalior province, from which I have had specimens, but these also are closed. The natives fear to extract their mineral wealth; and though abounding in lead, tin, and copper, they are indebted almost entirely to Europe even for the materials of their culinary utensils.

Without attempting a delineation of inferior ranges, I will only further direct the reader's attention to an important deduction from this superficial review of the physiognomy of Rajwarra.

There are two distinctly marked declivities or slopes in Central India: the chief is that from west to east, from the great rampart, the Aravulli (interposed to prevent the drifting of the sands into the central plains, bisected by the Chumbul and his hundred arms) to the Bétwa; the other slope is from south to north, from the Vindhya, the southern buttress of Central India, to the Jumna.

Extending our definition, we may pronounce the course of the Jumna to indicate the central fall of that immense vale which has its northern slope from the base of the Himalaya, and the southern from that of the Vindhya mountains.

It is not in contemplation to delineate the varied course of the magnificent Nerbudda, though I have abundant means; for the moment we ascend the summit of the tropical[2] Vindhya, to descend into the valley of the Nerbudda, we abandon Rajast'han and the Rajpoots for the aboriginal races, the first proprietors of the land. These I shall leave to others, and commence and end with the Chumbul, the paramount lord of the floods of Central India.

The Chumbul has *his* fountains in a very elevated point of the Vindhya, amidst a cluster of hills on which is bestowed the local appellation of 'Janapava.' It has three co-equal sources from the same cluster, the Chumbul, Chambela, and Gumbheer; while no less than nine other streams have their origin on the south side, and pour their waters into the Nerbudda.

The Sipra from Peepuldo, the little Sinde[3] from Dewas, and other

[1] I have rescued a few of these from oblivion to present to my countrymen.

[2] Hence its name, *Vind'hya*, 'the barrier,' to the further progress of the sun in his northern declination.

[3] This is the *fourth Sinde* of India. We have, first, the *Sinde* or Indus; this little Sinde; then the Cali Sinde, or 'black river'; and again the Sinde rising at Latoti, on the plateau west and above Seronge.

Sin is a Scythic word for river (now unused), so applied by the Hindus.

minor streams passing Oojein, all unite with the Chumbul in different stages before he breaks through the plateau.

The Cali Sinde, from Baugri, and its petty branch, the Sodwia, from Raghoogurh ; the Newaz (or Jamneeri), from Morsookri and Magurda ; the Parbutti, from the pass of Amlakhéra, with its more eastern arm from Doulutpoor, uniting at Furher, are all points in the crest of the Vindhya range, whence they pursue their course through the plateau, rolling over precipices,[1] till engulphed in the Chumbul at the ferries of Noonérah and Palli. All these unite on the right bank.

On the left bank his flood is increased by the Bunas, fed by the perennial streams from the Aravulli, and the Béris from the lakes of Oodipoor ; and after watering Méwar, the southern frontier of Jeipoor, and the highlands of Kerowli, the river turns south to unite at the holy *Sungum*,[2] Rameswar. Minor streams contribute (unworthy however of separate notice), and after a thousand involutions he reaches the Jumna, at the holy *Triveni*,[3] or 'triple-allied' stream, between Etawa and Kalpi.

The course of the Chumbul, not reckoning the minor sinuosities, is upwards of five hundred miles ; and along its banks specimens of nearly every race now existing in India may be found : Sondies, Chunderawuts, Seesodias, Haras, Gore, Jadoon, Sikerwal, Goojur,[4] Jat,[4] Tuar, Chohan, Bhadoria, Kutchwaha, Sengar, Boondela ; each in associations of various magnitudes, from the substantive state of the little republic communes between the Chumbul and Cohari.[5]

Having thus sketched the central portion of Rajast'han, or that eastward of the Aravulli, I shall give a rapid general[6] view of that to the west, conducting the reader over the '*T'hul ca Teeba*,' or 'sand hills' of the desert, to the valley of the Indus.

Let the reader again take post on Aboo, by which he may be saved a painful journey over the *T'hul*.[7] The most interesting object in this arid 'region of death' is the 'salt river,' the Looni, with its many arms falling from the Aravulli to enrich the best portion of the principality of Jodpoor, and distinctly marking the line of that extensive plain of ever-shifting sand, termed in Hindu geography *Maroost'hulli*, corrupted to *Marwar*.

The Looni, from its sources, the sacred lakes of Poshkur and Ajmér, and the more remote arm from Purbutsir to its embouchure in the great western salt marsh, the Rin, has a course of more than three hundred miles.

In the term 'Erinos' of the historians of Alexander, we have the corruption of the word 'Run' or 'Rin,'[8] still used to describe that extensive fen formed by the deposits of the Looni, and the equally saturated

[1] The falls of the Cali Sinde through the rocks at Gagrown and the Parbutti at Chupra (Googul) are well worthy of a visit. The latter, though I encamped twice at Chupra, from which it was reputed five miles, I did not see.

[2] *Sungum* is the point of confluence of two or more rivers, always sacred to Mahadeva.

[3] The Jumna, Chumbul, and Sinde.

[4] The only tribes not of Rajpoot blood.

[5] The 'virgin' stream.

[6] I do not repeat the names of towns forming the arrondissements of the various states ; they are distinctly laid down in the boundary lines of each.

[7] T'hul is the general term for the sand ridges of the desert.

[8] Most probably a corruption of 'aranya,' or *desert* ; so that the Greek mode of writing it is more correct than the present.

saline streams from the southern desert of Dhat. It is one hundred and fifty miles in length ; and where broadest, from Bhooj to Buliari, about seventy : in which direction the caravans cross, having as a place of halt an insulated oasis in this mediterranean salt marsh. In the dry season, nothing meets the eye but an extensive and glaring sheet of salt, spread over its insidious surface, full of dangerous quicksands : and in the rains it is a dirty saline solution, up to the camels' girths in many places. The little oasis, the *Khari Cába*, furnishes pasture for this useful animal and rest for the traveller pursuing his journey to either bank.

It is on the desiccated borders [1] of this vast salt marsh that the illusory phenomenon, the *mirage*, presents its fantastic appearance, pleasing to all but the wearied traveller, who sees a haven of rest in the embattled towers, the peaceful hamlet,[2] or shady grove, to which he hastens in vain ; receding as he advances, till "the sun in his might," dissipating these "cloud cap'd towers," reveals the vanity of his pursuit.

Such phenomena are common to the desert, more particularly where these extensive saline depositions exist, but varying from certain causes. In most cases, this powerfully magnifying and reflecting medium is a vertical stratum ; at first dense and opaque, it gradually attenuates with increased temperature, till the maximum of heat, which it can no longer resist, drives it off in an etherial vapour. This optical deception, well known to the Rajpoots, is called *see-kote*, or 'winter castles,' because chiefly visible in the cold season : hence, possibly, originated the equally illusory and delightful 'Chateau en Espagne,' so well known in the west.[3]

From the north bank of the Looni to the south, and the Shekhavat frontier to the east, the sandy region commences. Bíkanér, Jodpoor, Jessulmér, are all sandy plains, increasing in volume as you proceed westward. All this portion of territory is incumbent on a sandstone formation : soundings of all the new wells made from Jodpoor to Ajmér, yielded the same result ; sand, concrete siliceous deposits, and chalk.

Jessulmér is everywhere encircled by desert ; and that portion round the capital might not be improperly termed an oasis, in which wheat, barley, and even rice are produced. The fortress is erected on the extremity of a range of some hundred feet in elevation, which can be traced beyond its southern confines to the ruins of the ancient Chotun erected upon them, and which tradition has preserved as the capital of a tribe, or prince, termed Happa, of whom no other trace exists. It is not unlikely

[1] It is here the wild ass (*gorkhur*) roams at large, untamable as in the day of the Arabian Patriarch of Uz, "his house the wilderness, the barren land (or, according to the Hebrew, *salt places*), his dwelling ; who scorneth the multitude of the city, neither regardeth the crying of the driver."—Job xxxix, 6, 7.

[2] Poorwa.

[3] I have beheld it from the top of the ruined fortress of Hissar with unlimited range of vision, no object to diverge its ray, save the miniature forests ; the entire circle of the horizon a chain of more than fancy could form of palaces, towers, and these airy "pillars of heaven" terminating in turn their ephemeral existence. But in the deserts of Dhát and Oomrasoomra, where the shepherds pasture their flocks, and especially where the alkaline plant is produced, the stratification is more horizontal, and produces more of the watery deception.

It is this illusion to which the inspired writer refers, when he says, "the mock pool of the desert shall become real water." The inhabitants of the desert term it *Chitram*, literally 'the picture,' by no means an unhappy designation.

that this ridge may be connected with that which runs through the rich province of Jalore ; consequently an offset from the base of Aboo.

Though all these regions collectively bear the term *Maroost'hulli*, or 'region of death' (the emphatic and figurative phrase for the desert), the restrictive definition applies to a part only, that under the dominion of the Rahtore race.

From Bhalotra on the Looni, throughout the whole of Dhát and Oomrasoomra, the western portion of Jessulmér, and a broad stripe between the southern limits of Daodpotra and Bíkanér, there is real solitude and desolation. But from the Sutledge to the Rin, a space of five hundred miles of longitudinal distance, and varying in breadth from fifty to one hundred miles, numerous oases are found, where the shepherds from the valley of the Indus and the T'hul pasture their flocks. The springs of water in these places have various appellations, *tir*, *par*, *var*, *dur*, all expressive of the element, round which assemble the Rajurs, Sodas, Mangulias, and Sehraies,[1] inhabiting the desert.

I will not touch on the salt lakes or natron beds, or the other products of the desert, vegetable or mineral ; though the latter might soon be described, being confined to the jasper rock near Jessulmér, which has been much used in the beautiful arabesques of that fairy fabric, at Agra, the mausoleum of Shah Jehan's queen.

Neither shall I describe the valley of the Indus, or that portion eastward of the stream, the termination of the sand ridges of the desert. I will merely remark, that the small stream which breaks from the Indus at Dura, seven miles north of the insulated Bekher, and falls into the ocean at Lukput, shows the breadth of this eastern portion of the valley, which forms the western boundary of the desert. A traveller proceeding from the Kheechee or *flats* of Sinde to the east, sees the line of the desert distinctly marked, with its elevated *teebas*, or sand ridges under which flows the Sandkra which is generally dry except at periodical inundations. These sand-hills are of considerable elevation, and may be considered the limit of the inundation of the 'sweet river,' the *Meeta Muran*, a Scythic or Tatar name for river, and by which alone the Indus is known, rom the Punjnud [2] to the ocean.

[1] *Sehraie*, from *sehara*, 'desert.' Hence *Sarrazin*, or *Saracen*, is a corruption from *sehara*, 'desert,' and *zuddun*, 'to strike,' contracted. *Razuni*, 'to strike on the road' (*ra*). *Ra-ber*, '*on* the road,' corrupted by the Pindarries to *labur*, the designation of their forays.

[2] The confluent arms or sources of the Indus.

HISTORY OF THE RAJPOOT TRIBES

CHAPTER I

Genealogies of the Rajpoot princes—The Pooráns—Connection of the Rajpoots with the Scythic tribes.

BEING desirous of epitomising the chronicles of the martial races of Central and Western India, it was essential to ascertain the sources whence they draw, or claim to draw, their lineage. For this purpose I obtained from the library of the Rana of Oodipoor their sacred volumes, the *Pooráns*, and laid them before a body of pundhits, over whom presided the learned Jetty Gyanchandra. From these extracts were made of all the genealogies of the great races of Soorya and Chandra, and of facts historical and geographical.

Most of the *Pooráns* [1] contain portions of historical as well as geographical knowledge; but the *Bhagvat*, the *Scanda*, the *Agni*, and the *Bhavishya*, are the chief guides. It is rather fortunate than to be regretted that their chronologies do not perfectly agree. The number of princes in each line varies, and names are transposed; but we recognise distinctly the principal features in each, affording the conclusion that they are the productions of various writers, borrowing from some common original source.

The *Genesis* [2] of India commences with an event described in the history of almost all nations, the deluge, which, though treated with the fancy peculiar to the orientals, is not the less entitled to attention. The essence of the extract from the *Agni Poorán* is this: "When ocean quitted his bounds and caused universal destruction by Brimha's command, Vaivaswata [3] Menu (Noah), who dwelt near the Himaleh [4] mountains, was giving water to the gods in the Kritmala river, when a small fish fell into his hand. A voice commanded him to preserve it. The fish expanded to an enormous size. Menu, with his sons and their wives,

[1] "Every Purána," says the first authority existing in Sanscrit lore, "treats of five subjects: the creation of the universe; its progress, and the renovation of the world; the genealogy of gods and heroes; chronology, according to a fabulous system; and heroic history, containing the achievements of demi-gods and heroes. Since each purána contains a cosmogony, both mythological and heroic history, the works which bear that title may not unaptly be compared to the Grecian theogonies."—"Essay on the Sanscrit and Pracrit Languages," by H. T. Colebrooke, Esq.; *As. Res.*, vol. vii. p. 202.

[2] Resolvable into Sanscrit, *jenem*, 'birth,' and *es* and *iswar*, 'lords.'

[3] Son of the sun.

[4] The snowy Caucasus. Sir William Jones, in an extract from a work entitled *Essence of the Poorános*, says that this event took place at Dravira in the Dekhan.

and the sages, with the seed of every living thing, entered into a vessel which was fastened to a horn on the head of the fish, and thus they were preserved."

Here, then, the grand northern chain is given to which the abode of the great patriarch of mankind approximated. In the *Bhavishya* it is stated, that " Vaivaswata (sun-born) Menu ruled at the mountain Soomér. Of his seed was Cacoosta Rajah, who obtained sovereignty at Ayodia,[1] and his descendants filled the land and spread over the earth."

I am aware of the meaning given to *Soomér*, that thus the Hindus designated the north pole of the earth. But they had also a mountain with this same appellation of pre-eminence of *Méru*, ' the hill,' with the prefix *Soo*, ' good, sacred ' : *the Sacred Hill.*

In the geography of the *Agni Poorán*, the term is used as a substantial geographical limit ;[2] and some of the rivers flowing from the mountainous ranges, whose relative position with Soomér are there defined, still retain their ancient appellations. Let us not darken the subject, by supposing only allegorical meanings attached to explicit points. In the distribution of their seven dwipas, or continents, though they interpose seas of curds, milk, or wine, we should not reject strong and evident facts, because subsequent ignorant interpolators filled up the page with puerilities.

This sacred mountain (Soomér) is claimed by the Brahmins as the abode of Mahadeva,[3] Adiswar,[4] or Bághés,[5] ; by the Jains, as the abode of Adnat'h,[6] the first Jiniswára, or Jain lord. Here they say he taught mankind the arts of agriculture and civilised life. The Greeks claimed it as the abode of Bacchus ; and hence the Grecian fable of this god being taken from the thigh of Jupiter, confounding *meros* (thigh) with the *méru* (hill) of this Indian deity. In this vicinity the followers of Alexander had their Saturnalia, drank to excess of the wine from its indigenous vines, and bound their brows with ivy (*véla*)[7] sacred to the Bághés of the east and west, whose votaries alike indulge in " strong drink."

These traditions appear to point to one spot, and to one individual, in the early history of mankind, when the Hindu and the Greek approach a common focus ; for there is little doubt that Adnat'h, Adiswára, Osiris, Bághés, Bacchus, Menu, Menes, designate the patriarch of mankind, Noah.

The Hindus can at this time give only a very general idea of the site of Méru ; but they appear to localise it in a space of which Bamian,

[1] The present Oude, capital of one of the twenty-two satrapies constituting the Mogul Empire, and for some generations held by the titular Vizir, who has recently assumed the regal title.

[2] " To the south of Sooméru are the mountains Himawun, Hemcoota, and Nissida ; to the north are the countries Nïl, Suwét, and Sringie. Between Hemachil and the ocean the land is Bharatkhand, called Coocarma Bhoomi (*land of vice*, opposed to Aryaverta, or *land of virtue*), in which the seven grand ranges are Mahendrachil, Mulliachil, Sujrachil, Sactimun, Rikyachil, Vindyachil, and Paryâtra."—*Agni Poorán*.

[3] The Creator, literally ' the Great God.'

[4] The ' first lord.'

[5] Bághés, ' the tiger lord.' He wears a tiger's or panther's hide ; which he places beneath him. So Bacchus did. The phallus is the emblem of each. Bághés has several temples in Méwar.

[6] First lord.

[7] Véla is the general term for a climber, sacred to the Indian Bacchus (Bághés, Adiswára, or Mahadeva), whose priests, following his example, are fond of intoxicating beverages, or drugs. The im-mur, or immortal véla, is a noble climber.

Caubul, and Ghizni, would be the exterior points. The former of these cities is known to possess remains of the religion of Boodha, in its caves and colossal statues.[1] The Paropamisan Alexandria is near Bamian; but the Méru and Nyssa[2] of Alexander are placed more to the eastward by the Greek writers, and according to the cautious Arrian between the Cophas and Indus. Authority localises it between Peshawur and Jillalabad, and calls it *Mér-coh*, or *Mar-coh*,[3] "a bare rock 2000 feet high with caves to the westward, termed Bé-dowlut by the Emperor Hemayoon from its dismal appearance."[4] This designation, however, of Deshté

[1] "In Zohac Bamian, the castle, a monument of great antiquity, is in good condition, while the castle of Bamian is in ruins.

"In the midst of the mountains are twelve thousand caves cut out of the rock, and ornamented with carving and plaster reliefs. These are called summij, and were the winter retreat of the natives. Here are three astonishing idols: one representing a man eighty ells high; another of a woman fifty, and a third of a child fifteen ells in height. In one of these summijes is a tomb, where is *a coffin containing a corpse, concerning which the oldest man can give no account: it is held in high veneration.* The ancients were possessed of some medical preparations, with which they anointed dead bodies, and by which they suffered no injury from time."—*Ayin Akbery*, vol. ii. p. 169.

[2] Nissida is mentioned in the *Poorán* as a mountain. If in the genitive case (which the final syllable marks), it would be a local term given from the city of Nissa.

[3] *Mér*, Sanscrit, and *coh*, Persian, for a 'hill.'

[4] *Asiatic Researches*, vol. vi. p. 497. Wilford appears to have borrowed largely from that ancient store-house (as the Hindu would call it) of learning, Sir Walter Raleigh's *History of the World*. He combines, however, much of what that great man had so singularly acquired and condensed, with what he himself collected, and with the aid of imagination has formed a curious mosaic. But when he took a peep into "the chorographical description of the Terrestrial Paradise," I am surprised he did not separate the nurseries of mankind before and after the flood. There is one passage, also, of Sir Walter Raleigh which would have aided his hypothesis, that Eden was in Higher Asia, between the common sources of the Jihun and other grand rivers; the abundance of the *ficus Indica*, or burtree, sacred to the first lord, Adnat'h or Mahadeva.

"Now for the tree of knowledge of good and evil, some men have presumed further; especially Gorapius Bocanus, who giveth himself the honour to have found out the kind of this tree, which none of the writers of former times could ever guess at, whereat Gorapius much marvelleth."

——"Both together went
Into the thickest wood; there soon they chose
The fig tree; not that kind for fruit renowned,
But such as at this day, to Indians known
In Malabar or Deccan, spreads her arms
Branching so broad and long, that in the ground
The bended twigs take root, and daughters grow
About the mother tree, a pillar'd shade
High overarched, and echoing walks between.
There oft the Indian herdsman, shunning heat,
Shelters in cool and tends his pasturing herds."
——"Those leaves
They gathered, broad as Amazonian targe."

—*Paradise Lost*, Book ix.

Sir Walter strongly supports the Hindu hypothesis regarding the locality of the nursery for rearing mankind, and that "India was the first planted and peopled countrie after the flood" (p. 99). His first argument is, that it was a place where the vine and olive were indigenous, as amongst the Sacæ Scythæ (and as they still are, together with oats, between Caubul and Bamian); and that Ararat could not be in Armenia, because the Gordian mountains on which

Bé-dowlut, or 'unhappy plain,' was given to the tract between the cities beforementioned.

The only scope of these remarks on Soomér is to show that the Hindus themselves do not make India within the Indus the cradle of their race, but west, amidst the hills of Caucasus,[1] whence the sons of Vaivaswata, or the 'sun-born,' migrated eastward to the Indus and Ganges, and founded their first establishment in Kosulya, the capital, Ayodia, or Oude.

Most nations have indulged the desire of fixing the source whence they issued, and few spots possess more interest than this elevated *Media-Bhoomi*, or 'central region' of Asia, where the Amu, Oxus, or Jihoon, and other rivers, have their rise, and in which both the Soorya and Indu[2] races (*Sacæ*) claim *the hill*,[3] sacred to a great patriarchal ancestor, whence they migrated eastward.

the ark rested were in longitude 75°, and the Valley of Shináár 79° to 80°, which would be reversing the tide of migration. "As they journeyed *from the East*, they found a plain, in the land of Shinar, and they dwelt there"—(Genesis, chap. 11, ver. 2). He adds, "Ararat, named by Moses, is not any one hill, but a general term for the great Caucasian range; therefore we must blow up this mountain Ararat, or dig it down and carry it out of Armenia, or find it elsewhere in a warmer country, and east from Shinár." He therefore places it in Indo-Scythia, in 140° of longitude and 35° to 37° of latitude, "where the mountains do build themselves exceeding high": and concludes, "It was in the plentiful warm East where Noah rested, where he planted the vine, where he tilled the ground and lived thereon. Placuit vero Noacho agriculturæ studium in quâ tractanda ipse omnium peritissimus esse dicitur; ob eamque rem, suâ ipsius linguâ, *Ish-Adamath*:[1] hoc est, *Telluris Vir*, appellatur, celebratusque est. The study of husbandry pleased Noah (says the excellent learned man, Arius Montanus) in the order and knowledge of which it is said that Noah excelled all men, and therefore was he called in his own language, *a man exercised in the earth*." The title, character, and abode, exactly suit the description the Jains give of their first Jiniswára, Adnat'h, the first lordly man, who taught them agriculture, even to "muzzling the bull in treading out the corn."

Had Sir Walter been aware that the Hindu sacred books styled their country *Aryaverta*,[2] and of which the great Imaus is the northern boundary, he would doubtless have seized it for his Ararat.

[1] Hindu, or Indu-cush or kho, is the local appellation; 'mountains of the moon.'

[2] Solar and lunar.

[3] *Méru*, 'the hill,' is used distinctively, as in Jessul-mér (the capital of the Bhatti tribe in the Western Desert), 'the hill of Jessul'; Mérwarra, or the 'mountainous region'; and its inhabitants Méras, or 'mountaineers.' Thus, also, in the grand epic the *Ramayuna* (Book i. p. 236), Méra is the mountain-nymph, the daughter of Méru and spouse of Himavut; from whom sprung two daughters, the river goddess Gunga and the mountain nymph Parbutti. She is, in the *Mahabharat*, also termed Syeela, the daughter of Syeel, another designation of the snowy chain; and hence mountain streams are called in Sanscrit *silletee*. Syeela bears the same attributes with the Phrygian Cybele, who was

---

[1] In Sanscrit, *Ish*, 'Lord,' *áda*, 'the first,' *mat'h* or *mut'h*, 'Earth.' Here the Sanscrit and Hebrew have the same meaning, 'first lord of the earth.' In these remote Rajpoot regions, where early manners and language remain, the strongest phrase to denote a man or human being is literally 'earth.' A chief describing a fray between his own followers and borderers whence death ensued, says, '*Mera mat'hi mara*,' 'My earth has been struck': a phrase requiring no comment, and denoting that he must have blood in return.

[2] *Aryaverta*, or the land of promise or virtue, cannot extend to the flat plains of India south of the Himavut; for this is styled in the *Poor*á*ns* the very reverse, '*coocarma des*,' or land of vice.

The Rajpoot tribes could scarcely have acquired some of their still existing Scythic habits and warlike superstitions on the burning plains of Ind. It was too hot to hail with fervent adoration the return of the sun from his southern course to enliven the northern hemisphere. This should be the religion of a colder clime, brought from their first haunts, the sources of the Jihoon and Jaxartes. The grand solstitial festival, the *Aswamedha*, or sacrifice of the horse (the type of the sun), practised by the children of Vaivaswata, the 'sun-born,' was most probably simultaneously introduced from Scythia into the plains of Ind, and west, by the sons of Odin, Woden, or Boodha, into Scandinavia, where it became the *Hi-él* or *Hi-ul*,[1] the festival of the winter solstice; the grand jubilee of northern nations, and in the first ages of Christianity, being so near the epoch of its rise, gladly used by the first fathers of the church to perpetuate that event.[2]

CHAPTER II

Genealogies continued—Fictions in the Pooráns—Union of the regal and the priestly characters—Legends of the Pooráns confirmed by the Greek historians.

THE chronicles of the *Bhagvat* and *Agni*, containing the genealogies of the Soorya (*sun*) and Indu (*moon*) races, shall now be examined. The first of these, by calculation, brings down the chain to a period six centuries subsequent to Vicramaditya (A.D. 650), so that these books may have been remodelled or commented on about this period: their fabrication cannot be supposed.

Although portions of these genealogies by Sir William Jones, Mr. Bentley, and Colonel Wilford, have appeared in the volumes of the *Asiatic Researches*, yet no one should rest satisfied with the inquiries of others, if by any process he can reach the fountain-head himself.

If, after all, these are fabricated genealogies of the ancient families of India, the fabrication is of ancient date, and they are all they know themselves upon the subject. The step next in importance to obtaining a

also the daughter of a mountain of the same name; the one is carried, the other drawn, by lions. Thus the Greeks also metamorphosed *Parbut Pámer*, or 'the mountain Pámer,' into Paropamisan, applied to the Hindu Kho west of Bamian: but the *Parbut put Pámer*, or 'Pámer chief of hills,' is mentioned by the bard *Chund* as being far east of that tract, and under it resided Hamira, one of the great feudatories of Prithwi-raja of Dehli. Had it been Paropanisan (as some authorities write it), it would better accord with the locality where it takes up the name, being near to Nyssa and Méru, of which Parbut or Pahár would be a version, and form Paronisan, 'the Mountain of Nyssa,' the range Nissida of the Pooráns.

[1] *Hya* or *Hi*, in Sanscrit, 'horse'—*El*, 'sun': whence ἵππος and ἥλοσι. Ηλ appears to have been a term of Scythian origin for the sun; and Heri, the Indian Apollo, is addressed as the sun. Hiul, or Jul, of northern nations (qu. *Noel* of France?), is the Hindu Sacranta, of which more will be said hereafter.

[2] Mallet's *Northern Antiquities*.

perfect acquaintance with the genuine early history of nations, is to learn what those nations repute to be such.

Doubtless the original *Pooráns* contained much valuable historical matter ; but, at present, it is difficult to separate a little pure metal from the base alloy of ignorant expounders and interpolators. I have but skimmed the surface : research, to the capable, may yet be rewarded by many isolated facts and important transactions, now hid under the veil of ignorance and allegory.

The Hindus, with the decrease of intellectual power, their possession of which is evinced by their architectural remains, where just proportion and elegant mythological device are still visible, lost the relish for the beauty of truth, and adopted the monstrous in their writings, as well as their edifices. But for detection and shame, matters of history would be hideously distorted even in civilised Europe ; but in the East, in the moral decrepitude of ancient Asia, with no judge to condemn, no public to praise, each priestly expounder may revel in an unfettered imagination, and reckon his admirers in proportion to the mixture of the marvellous.[1] Plain historical truths have long ceased to interest this artificially-fed people.

If at such a comparatively modern period as the third century before Christ, the Babylonian historian Berosus composed his fictions, which assigned to that monarchy such incredible antiquity, it became capable of refutation from the many historians of repute who preceded him. But on the fabulist of India we have no such check. If Vyasu himself penned these legends as *now* existing, then is the stream of knowledge corrupt from the fountain-head. If such the source, the stream, filtering through ages of ignorance, has only been increased by fresh impurities. It is difficult to conceive how the arts and sciences could advance, when it is held impious to doubt the truth of whatever has been handed down, and still more to suppose that the degenerate could improve thereon. The highest ambition of the present learned priesthood, generation after generation, is to be able to comprehend what has thus reached them, and to form commentaries upon past wisdom ; which commentaries are commented on *ad infinitum*. Whoever dare now aspire to improve thereon must keep the secret in his own breast. They are but the expounders of the olden oracles ; were they more they would be infidels. But this could not always have been the case.

With the Hindus, as with other nations, the progress to the heights of science they attained must have been gradual ; unless we take from them the merit of original invention, and set them down as borrowers of a system. These slavish fetters of the mind must have been forged at a later period, and it is fair to infer that the monopoly of science and religion were simultaneous. What must be the effect of such monopoly on the impulses and operations of the understanding ? Where such exists, knowledge could not long remain stationary ; it must perforce retro-

[1] The celebrated Goguet remarks on the madness of most nations pretending to trace their origin to infinity. The Babylonians, the Egyptians, and the Scythians, particularly, piqued themselves on their high antiquity, and the first assimilate with the Hindus in boasting they had observed the course of the stars 473,000 years. Each heaped ages on ages ; but the foundations of this pretended antiquity are not supported by probability, and are even of modern invention.—*Origin of Laws.*

grade. Could we but discover the period when religion [1] ceased to be a *profession* and became hereditary (and that such there was these very genealogies bear evidence), we might approximate the era when science attained its height.

In the early ages of these Solar and Lunar dynasties, the priestly office was not hereditary in families ; it was a profession ; and the genealogies exhibit frequent instances of branches of these races terminating their martial career in the commencement of a religious sect, or *gotra*, and of their descendants reassuming their warlike occupations. Thus, of the ten sons of Icshwáca,[2] three are represented as abandoning worldly affairs and taking to religion ; and one of these, Canin, is said to be the first who made an *agnihotra*, or pyreum, and worshipped fire, while another son embraced commerce. Of the Lunar line and the six sons of Proorwa, the name of the fourth was Reh ; "from him the fifteenth generation was Harita, who with his eight brothers took to the office of religion, and established the Causika Gotra, or *tribe* of Brahmins."

From the twenty-fourth prince in lineal descent from Yáyát, by name Bhardhwaja, originated a celebrated sect, who still bear his name, and are the spiritual teachers of several Rajpoot tribes.

Of the twenty-sixth prince, Munevu, two sons devoted themselves to religion, and established celebrated sects, viz. Mahavira, whose descendants were the Poshkur Brahmins ; and Sanskritti, whose issue were learned in the *védas*. From the line of Ujamida these ministers of religion were continually branching off.

In the very early periods, the princes of the Solar line, like the Egyptians and Romans, combined the offices of the priesthood with kingly power, and this whether Brahminical or Boodhist.[3] Many of the royal line, before and subsequent to Rama passed great part of their lives as ascetics ; and in ancient sculpture and drawings, the head is as often adorned with the braided lock of the ascetic, as with the diadem of royalty.[4]

The greatest monarchs bestowed their daughters on these royal hermits and sages. Ahelya, the daughter of the powerful Panchalica,[5] became the wife of the ascetic Gotama. The sage Jamdagni espoused the daughter

[1] It has been said that the Brahminical religion was foreign to India ; but as to the period of importation we have but loose assertion. We can easily give credit to various creeds and tenets of faith being from time to time incorporated, ere the present books were composed, and that previously the sons of royalty alone possessed the office. Authorities of weight inform us of these grafts ; for instance, Mr. Colebrooke gives a passage in his *Indian Classes*: "A chief of the twice-born tribe was brought by Vishnu's eagle from Saca Dwipa ; hence Saca Dwipa Brahmins were known in Jambu Dwipa." By Saca Dwipa, Scythia is understood, of which more will be said hereafter.

Ferishta also, translating from ancient authorities, says, to the same effect, that "in the reign of Mahraje, King of Canouj, a Brahmin came from Persia, who introduced magic, idolatry, and the worship of the stars" : so that there is no want of authority for the introduction of new tenets of faith.

[2] See Table I.

[3] Some of the earlier of the twenty-four *Tirt'hancaras*, or Jain hierarchs, trace their origin from the solar race of princes.

[4] Even now the Rana of Méwar mingles spiritual duties with those of royalty, and when he attends the temple of the tutelary deity of his race, he performs himself all the offices of the high priest for the day. In this point a strong resemblance exists to many of the races of antiquity.

[5] Prince of the country of Punj-áb, or five streams east of the Indus.

of Sehesra [1] Arjoona, of Muhésvati,[2] king of the Hihya tribe, a great branch of the Yadu race.

Among the Egyptians, according to Herodotus, the priests succeeded to sovereignty, as they and the military class alone could hold lands ; and Sethos, the priest of Vulcan, caused a revolution, by depriving the military of their estates.

We have various instances in India of the Brahmins from Jamdagni to the Mahratta Peishwa, contesting for sovereignty ; power [3] and homage being still their great aim, as in the days of Vishwamitra [4] and Vasishta,

[1] The legend of this monarch stealing his son-in-law's, the hermit's, cow (of which the *Ramayuna* gives another version), the incarnation of Parswa-ram, son of Jamdagni, and his exploits, appear purely allegorical, signifying the violence and oppression of royalty over the earth (*prithu*), personified by the sacred *gao*, or cow ; and that the Brahmins were enabled to wrest royalty from the martial tribe, shows how they had multiplied.

On the derivatives from the word *gao*, I venture an etymology for others to pursue :—

ΓΑΪΑ, *γέα, γῆ* (*Dor. γᾶ*), that which produces all things (from *γάω, genero*) ; the earth.—*Jones's Dictionary*.

ΓΆΛΑ, Milk. *Gao-la*, Herdsman, in Sanscrit. Γαλατικοί, Κέλτοι, Galatians, or Gauls, and Celts (allowed to be the same), would be the shepherd races, the pastoral invaders of Europe.

[2] Mahéswar, on the Nerbudda river.

[3] Hindust'han abounds with Brahmins, who make excellent soldiers, as far as bravery is a virtue ; but our officers are cautious, from experience, of admitting too many into a troop or company, for they still retain their intriguing habits. I have seen nearly as many of the Brahmins as of military in some companies ; a dangerous error.

[4] The Brahmin Vasishta possessed a cow named Shuboola, so fruitful that with her assistance he could accomplish whatever he desired. By her aid he entertained King Vishwamitra and his army. It is evident that this cow denotes some *tract of country which the priest held* (bearing in mind that *gao, prithu*, signify 'the earth,' as well as 'cow') : a grant, beyond doubt, by some of Vishwamitra's unwise ancestors, and which he wished to resume. From her were supplied "the oblations to the gods and the *pitriswars* (father-gods, or ancestors), the perpetual sacrificial fire, the burnt-offerings and sacrifices." This was "the fountain of devotional acts"; this was the Shuboola for which the king offered "a hundred thousand cows"; this was "the jewel of which a king only should be propríetor."—The subjects of the Brahmin appeared not to relish such transfer, and by "the lowing of the cow Shuboola" obtained numerous foreign auxiliaries, which enabled the Brahmin to set his sovereign at defiance. Of these "the Pehlavi (Persian) kings, *the dreadful Sakas* (Sacæ), and *Yavanas* (Greeks), with scymitars and gold armour, the Kambojas," etc., were each in turn created by the all-producing cow. The armies of the Pehlavi kings were cut to pieces by Vishwamitra ; who at last, by continual reinforcements, was overpowered by the Brahmin's levies.

These reinforcements would appear to have been the ancient Persians, the Sacæ, the Greeks, the inhabitants of Assam and southern India, and various races out of the pale of the Hindu religion ; all classed under the term *M'lech'ha*, equivalent to the 'barbarian' of the Greeks and Romans.

The King Vishwamitra, defeated and disgraced by this powerful priest, "like a serpent with his teeth broken, like the sun robbed by the eclipse of its splendour, was filled with perturbation. Deprived of his sons and array, stripped of his pride and confidence, he was left without resource as a bird bereft of his wings." He abandoned his kingdom to his son, and like all Hindu princes in distress, determined, by penitential rites and austerities, "to obtain Brahminhood."

He took up his abode at the sacred Poshkur, living on fruits and roots, and fixing his mind, said, "I will become a Brahmin." By these penances he attained such spiritual power that he was enabled to usurp the Brahmin's office. The theocrats caution Vishwamitra, thus determined to become a

the royal sages whom "Janaka, sovereign of Mit'hila, addressed with folded hands in token of superiority."

But this deference for the Brahmins is certainly, with many Rajpoot classes, very weak. In obedience to prejudice, they show them outward civility; but, unless when their fears or wishes interfere, they are less esteemed than the bards.

The story of the King Vishwamitra of Gadhipoora[1] and the Brahmin Vasishta, which fills so many sections of the first book of the *Ramayuna*,[2] exemplifies, under the veil of allegory, the contests for power between the Brahminical and military classes, and will serve to indicate the probable period when the castes became immutable. Stripped of its allegory, the legend appears to point to a time when the division of the classes was yet imperfect; though we may infer, from the violence of the struggle, that it was the last in which '*Brahminhood*' could be obtained by the military.

Vishwamitra was the son of Gadhi (of the race of Causika), King of Gadhipoora, and contemporary of Umbareesha, King of Ayodia or Oude, the fortieth prince from Icshwáca; consequently about two hundred years anterior to Rama. This event therefore, whence we infer that the system of castes was approaching perfection, was probably about one thousand four hundred years before Christ.

If proof can be given that these genealogies existed in the days of Alexander, the fact would be interesting. The legend in the *Poориáns*, of the origin of the Lunar race, appears to afford this testimony.

Vyasu, the author of the grand epic the *Mahabharat*, was son of Santana (of the race of Heri),[3] sovereign of Dehli, by Yojnaganda, a fisherman's daughter,[4] consequently illegitimate. He became the spiritual father, or preceptor, of his nieces, the daughters of Vichitravira, the son and successor of Santana.

Vichitravira had no male offspring. Of his three daughters, one was

Brahmin by austerity, that "the divine books are to be observed with care only by *those acquainted with their evidence*; nor does it become thee (Vishwamitra) to subvert the order of things established by the ancients."

The history of his wanderings, austerities, and the temptations thrown in his way, is related. The celestial fair were commissioned to break in upon his meditations. The mother of love herself descended; while Indra, joining the cause of the Brahmins, took the shape of the kokila, and added the melody of his notes to the allurements of Rembha, and the perfumed zephyrs which assailed the royal saint in the wilderness. He was proof against all temptation, and condemned the fair to become a pillar of stone. He persevered "till every passion was subdued," till "not a tincture of sin appeared in him," and gave such alarm to the whole priesthood, that they dreaded lest his excessive sanctity should be fatal to them: they feared "mankind would become atheists." "The gods and Brimha at their head were obliged to grant his desire of Brahminhood; and Vashista, conciliated by the gods, acquiesced in their wish, and formed a friendship with Vishwamitra."

[1] Canouj, the ancient capital of the present race of Marwar.

[2] See translation of this epic, by Messrs. Carey and Marshman.

[3] Heri-cúla.

[4] It is a very curious circumstance, that Hindu legend gives to two of their most celebrated authors, whom they have invested with a sacred character, a descent from the aboriginal and impure tribes of India: Vyasu from a fisherman, and Valmika, the author of the other grand epic the *Ramayuna*, from a budhék or robber, an associate of the *Bhil* tribe at Aboo. The conversion of Valmika (said to have been miraculous, when in the act of robbing the shrine of the deity), is worked into a story of considerable effect, in the works of Chund, from olden authority.

named Pandea ;[1] and Vyasu, being the sole remaining male branch of the house of Santana, took his niece, and *spiritual daughter*, Pandea, to wife, and became the father of Pandu, afterwards sovereign of Indraprest'ha.

Arrian gives the story thus : " He (Hercules [2]) had a daughter when he was advanced in years ;[3] and being unable to find a husband worthy of

[1] The reason for this name is thus given. One of these daughters being by a slave, it was necessary to ascertain which : a difficult matter, from the seclusion in which they were kept. It was therefore left to Vyasu to discover the pure of birth ; who determined that nobility of blood would show itself, and commanded that the princesses should walk uncovered before him. The elder, from shame, closed her eyes, and from her was born the blind Dhertarashtra, sovereign of Hastinapoora ; the second, from the same feeling, covered herself with yellow ochre, called *pandu*, and henceforth she bore the name of Pandea, and her son was called Pandu ; while the third stepped forth unabashed. She was adjudged not of gentle blood, and her issue was Vidura.

[2] A generic term for the sovereigns of the race of Heri, used by Arrian as a proper name. A section of the *Mahabharat* is devoted to the history of the Hericúla, of which race was Vyasu.

Arrian notices the similarity of the Theban and the Hindu Hercules, and cites as authority the ambassador of Seleucus, Megasthenes, who says : " He uses the same habit with the Theban ; and is particularly worshipped by the Suraseni, who " have two great cities belonging to them, namely, *Methoras* (Mat'hoora) and *Clisoboras*."

Diodorus has the same legend, with some variety. He says : " Hercules was born amongst the Indians, and like the Greeks they furnish him with a club and lion's hide. In strength (*bala*) he excelled all men, and cleared the sea and land of monsters and wild beasts. He had many sons, but only one daughter. It is said that he built Palibothra, and divided his kingdom amongst his sons (the Balica-pútras, sons of Bali). They never colonised ; but in time most of the cities assumed a democratical form of government (though some were monarchical) till Alexander's time." The combats of Hercules, to which Diodorus alludes, are those in the legendary haunts of the *Hericúlas*, during their twelve years' exile from the seats of their forefathers.

How invaluable such remnants of the ancient race of Heri-cúla ! How refreshing to the mind yet to discover, amidst the ruins on the Yamuna, Hercules (Baldeva, god of strength) retaining his club and lion's hide, standing on his pedestal at Buldeo, and yet worshipped by the *Suraseni* ! This name was given to a large tract of country round Mat'hoora, or rather round Soorpoora, the ancient capital founded by Soorséh, the grandfather of the Indian brother-deities, Crishna and Baldeva, Apollo and Hercules. The title would apply to either ; though Baldeva has the attributes of the ' god of strength.' Both are *es* (lords) of the race (*cúla*) of *Heri* (Heri-cul-és), of which the Greeks might have made the compound Hercules. Might not a colony after the great war have migrated westward ? The period of the return of the Heraclidæ, the descendants of Atreus (Atri is progenitor of the Heri-cúla) would answer : it was about half a century after the great war.

It is unfortunate that Alexander's historians were unable to penetrate into the arcana of the Hindus, as Herodotus appears to have done with those of the Egyptians. The shortness of Alexander's stay, the unknown language in which their science and religion were hid, presented an insuperable difficulty. They could have made very little progress in the study of the language without discovering its analogy to their own.

[3] Arrian generally exercises his judgment in these matters, and is the reverse of credulous. On this point he says, " My opinion of this story is, that if Hercules were capable of having an affair of this kind, and getting children, he was not so near his end as they wish to make us believe."

Sandrocottus is mentioned by Arrian to be of this line ; and we can have no hesitation, therefore, in giving him a place in the dynasty of Pooru, the second son of Yáyát, whence the patronymic used by the race now extinct, as was *Yadu*, the elder brother of Pooru. Hence Sandrocottus, if not a Pooru himself, is connected with the chain of which the links are Jarasand'ha (a hero of the *Bharat*) Ripoonjaya, the twenty-third in descent, when a new race, headed by Sonuka

her, he *married her himself*, that he might supply the throne of India with monarchs. Her name was Pandea, and he caused the whole province in which she was born to receive its name from her."

This is the very legend contained in the *Pooráns*, of Vyasu (who was Heri-cul-és, or chief of the race of Heri) and his *spiritual daughter* Pandea from whom the grand race *the Pandua*; and from whom Dehli and its dependencies were designated the Pandua sovereignty.

Her issue ruled for thirty-one generations in direct descents, or from 1120 to 610 before Christ; when the military minister,[1] connected by blood was chosen by the chiefs who rebelled against the last Pandu king, represented as "neglectful of all the cares of government," and whose deposition and death introduced a new dynasty.

Two other dynasties succeeded in like manner by the usurpation of these military ministers, until Vicramaditya, when the Pandua sovereignty and era of Yoodishtra were both overturned.

Indraprest'ha remained without a sovereign, supreme power being removed from the north to the southern parts of India, till the fourth, or, according to some authorities, the eighth century after Vicrama, when the throne of Yoodishtra was once more occupied by the Tuár tribe of Rajpoots, claiming descents from the *Pandus*. To this ancient capital, thus re-founded, the new appellation of *Dehli* was given; and the dynasty of the founder, Anungpal, lasted to the twelfth century, when he abdicated in favour of his grandson,[2] Pirthwirájá, the last imperial Rajpoot sovereign of India, whose defeat and death introduced the Mahomedans.

This line has also closed with the pageant of a prince, and a colony returned from the extreme west is now the sole arbiter of the thrones of *Pandu* and *Timoor*.

Britain has become heir to the monuments of Indraprest'ha raised by the descendants of Boodha and Ella; to the iron pillar of the Pandus, "whose pedestal[3] is fixed in hell"; to the columns reared to victory, inscribed with characters yet unknown; to the massive ruins of its ancient continuous cities, encompassing a space still larger than the largest city in the world, whose mouldering domes and sites of fortresses,[4] the very

and Séhesnag, about six hundred years before Christ, usurped the seat of the lineal descendants of Pooru; in which line of usurpation is Chandragupta, of the tribe Mori, the Sandrocottus of Alexander, a branch of this Sehesnag, Takshac, or *Snake* race, a race which, stripped of its allegory, will afford room for subsequent dissertation. The Prasii of Arrian would be the stock of Pooru: Prág is claimed in the annals yet existing as the cradle of their race. This is the modern Allahabad; and the Eranaboas must be the Jumna, and the point of junction with the Ganges, where we must place the capital of the *Prasii*.

[1] Analogous to the *maire du palais* of the first races of the Franks.

[2] His daughter's son. This is not the first or only instance of the Salic law of India being set aside. There are two in the history of the sovereigns of Anhulwarra Puttun. In all adoptions of this nature, when the child "binds round his head the turban" of his adopted father, he is finally severed from the stock whence he had his birth.

[3] The kheel, or iron pillar of the Pandus, is mentioned in the poems of Chund. An infidel Tuár prince wished to prove the truth of the tradition of its depth of foundation: "blood gushed up from the earth's centre, the pillar became loose (*dhilli*)," as did the fortune of the house from such impiety. This is the origin of *Dehli*.

[4] I doubt if Shapoor is yet known. I traced its extent from the remains of a tower between Hemayoon's tomb and the grand column, the Cootub. In 1809 I resided four months at the mausoleum of Sufder Jung, the ancestor of the

names of which are lost, present a noble field for speculation on the ephemeral nature of power and glory. What monument would Britain bequeath to distant posterity of her succession to this dominion? Not one: except it be that of a still less perishable nature, the monument of national benefit. Much is in our power: much has been given, and posterity will demand the result.

CHAPTER III

Genealogies continued—Comparisons between the lists of Sir W. Jones, Mr. Bentley, Captain Wilford, and the Author—Synchronisms.

VYASU gives but fifty-seven princes of the Solar line, from Vaivaswata Menu to Rama; and no list which has come under my observation exhibits more than fifty-eight, for the same period, of the Lunar race. How different from the Egyptian priesthood, who, according to Herodotus, gave a list up to that period of three hundred and thirty [1] sovereigns from their first prince, also the '*sun-born* [2] *Menes*!'

Icshwáca was the son of Menu, and the first who moved to the eastward, and founded Ayodia.

Boodha (Mercury) founded the Lunar line; but we are not told who established their first capital, Poorag,[3] though we are authorised to infer that it was founded by Pooru, the sixth in descent from Boodha.

A succession of fifty-seven princes occupied Ayodia from Icshwáca to Rama. From Yayat's sons the Lunar races descend in unequal lengths. The lines from Yadu,[4] concluding with Crishna and his cousin Kansa, exhibit fifty-seven and fifty-nine descents from Yayat; while Yoodishtra,[5] Sul,[6] Jarasandha,[7] and Vahoorita,[8] all contemporaries of Crishna and Kansa, are fifty-one, forty-six, and forty-seven generations, respectively, from the common ancestor, Yayat.

There is a wide difference between the Solar and the Yadu branches

present King of Oude, amidst the ruins of Indraprest'ha, several miles from inhabited Dehli, but with which these ruins forms detached links of connection. I went to that retirement with a friend now no more, Lieutenant Macartney, a name well known and honoured. We had both been employed in surveying the canals which had their sources in common from the head of the Jumna, where this river leaves its rocky barriers, the Sewalik chain, and issues into the plains of Hindust'han. These canals on each side, fed by the parent stream, returned the waters again into it; one through the city of Dehli, the other on the opposite side.

[1] Herodotus, *Melpomene*, chap. xlv. p. 200.

[2] The Egyptians claim the sun, also, as the first founder of the kingdom of Egypt.

[3] The Jessulmér annals give in succession Poorag, Mat'hoora, Koosust'hulli, Dwarica, as capitals of the Indu or Lunar race, in the ages preceding the bharat or great war. Hastinapoor was founded twenty generations after these, by Hasti, from whom ramified the three grand Sacæ, viz. Ujmída, Déomída, and Pooramída, which diversified the Yadu race.

[4] See Table I.

[5] Of Dehli—Indraprest'ha.

[6] *Sul*, the founder of *Arore* on the Indus, a capital I had the good fortune to discover. *Sul* is the *Sehr* of Abul Fuzil.

[7] Jarasandha of Bahar.

[8] Vahoorita, unknown yet.

of the Lunar lines; yet is that now given fuller than any I have met with. Sir William Jones' lists of the Solar line give fifty-six, and of the Lunar (Boodha to Yoodishtra) forty-six, being one less in each than in the tables now presented; nor has he given the important branch terminating with Crishna. So close an affinity between lists, derived from such different authorities as this distinguished character and myself had access to, shows that there was some general source extitled to credit.

Mr. Bentley's [1] lists agree with Sir William Jones', exhibiting fifty-six and forty-six, respectively, for the last-mentioned Solar and Lunar races. But, on a close comparison, he has either copied them or taken from the same original source; afterwards transposing names which, though aiding a likely hypothesis, will not accord with their historical belief.

Colonel Wilford's [2] Solar list is of no use: but his two dynasties of Pooru and Yadu of the Lunar race are excellent, that part of the line of Pooru, from Jarasandha to Chandragoopta, being the only correct one in print.

It is surprising Wilford did not make use of Sir William Jones' Solar chronology; but he appears to have dreaded bringing down Rama to the period of Crishna, as he is known to have preceded by four generations "the great war" of the Yadu races.

It is evident that the Lunar line has reached us defective. It is supposed so by their genealogists; and Wilford would have increased the error by taking it as the standard, and reducing the Solar to conform thereto.

Mr. Bentley's method is therefore preferable; namely, to suppose eleven princes omitted in the Lunar between Janmeyja and Prachinwat. But as there is no authority for this, the Lunar princes are distributed in the tables collaterally with the Solar, preserving contemporaneous affinity where synchronisms will authorise. By this means all hypothesis will be avoided, and the genealogies will speak for themselves.

There is very little difference between Sir William Jones' and Colonel Wilford's lists, in that main branch of the Lunar race, of which Pooru, Hasti, Ujmida, Cooru, Santana, and Yoodishtra, are the most distinguished links. The coincidence is so near as to warrant a supposition of identity of source; but close inspection shows Wilford to have had a fuller supply, for he produces new branches, both of Hasti's and Cooru's progeny. He has also one name (Bhimséna) towards the close, which is in my lists, but not in Sir William Jones'; and immediately following Bhimséna, both these lists exhibit *Dulipa*, wanting in my copy of the *Bhagvat*, though contained in the *Agni Poorán*: proofs of the diversity of the sources of supply, and highly gratifying when the remoteness of those sources is considered. There is also in my lists *Tunsu*, the nineteenth from Boodha, who is not in the lists either of Sir William Jones or Wilford. Again; Wilford has a *Suhotra* preceding Hasti, who is not in Sir William Jones' genealogies.[3]

Again; *Jahnu* is made the successor to Cooru; whereas the *Poorán* (whence my extracts) makes Parikhit the successor, who adopts the son of Jahnu. This son is Porat'ha, who has a place in all three. Other variations are merely orthographical.

[1] *Asiatic Researches*, vol. v. p. 341. [2] *Ibid.* vol. v. p. 241.

[3] I find them, however, in the *Agni Poorán*.

A comparison of Sir William Jones' Solar genealogies with my tables will yield nearly the same satisfactory result as to original authenticity. I say Sir William Jones' list, because there is no other efficient one. We first differ at the fourth from Icshwáca. In my list this is Un-Prit'hu, of which he makes two names, Aneas and Prit'hu. Thence to Pooroocutsa, the eighteenth, the difference is only in orthography. To Irisuaka, the twenty-third in mine, the twenty-sixth in Sir William Jones' list, one name is above accounted for; but here are two wanting in mine, Irasadadya and Hyaswa. There is, also, considerable difference in the orthography of those names which we have in common. Again; we differ as to the successors of Champa, the twenty-seventh, the founder of Champapoor in Bahar. In Sir Williams', Sudeva succeeds, and he is followed by Vijya: but my authorities state these both to be sons of Champa, and that Vijya, the younger, was his successor, as the elder, Sudeva, took to religious austerity. The thirty-third and thirty-sixth, Kesi and Dulipa, are not noticed by Sir William Jones; but there is a much more important person than either of these omitted, who is a grand link of connection, and affording a good synchronism of the earliest history. This is Ambarisha, the fortieth, the contemporary of Gadhi, who was the founder of Gadhipoora or Canouj. Nala, Suroora, and Dulipa (Nos. 44, 45, 54 of my lists), are all omitted by Sir William Jones.

This comparative analysis of the chronologies of both these grand races cannot fail to be satisfactory. Those which I furnish are from the sacred genealogies in the library of a prince who claims common origin with them, and are less liable to interpolation. There is scarcely a chief of character for knowledge who cannot repeat the genealogy of his line. The Prince of Méwar has a peculiarly retentive memory in this way. The professed genealogists, the Bháts, must have them graven on their memory, and the Charunas (the encomiasts) ought to be well versed therein.

The first table exhibits two dynasties of the Solar race of Princes of Ayodia and Mit'hil Dés, or Tirhoot, which latter I have seen nowhere else. It also exhibits four great and three lesser dynasties of the Lunar race; and an eighth line is added, of the race of Yadu, from the annals of the Bhatti tribe at Jessulmér.

Ere quitting this halting-place in the genealogical history of the ancient races, where the celebrated names of Rama, Crishna, and Yoodishtra, close the brazen age of India, and whose issue introduce the present iron age, or kal yuga, I shall shortly refer to the few synchronic points which the various authorities admit.

Of periods so remote, approximations to truth are the utmost to be looked for; and it is from the *Ramayuna* and the *Pooráns* these synchronisms are hazarded.

The first commences with a celebrated name of the Solar line, Harchandra, son of Trisunkha, still proverbial for his humility. He is the twenty-fourth,[1] and declared contemporary of Parswa-rama, who slew the celebrated Sehesra-Arjoona [2] of the Hihya (Lunar) race, Prince of Mahés-

[1] Syadri Khanda of the *Scanda Poorána*.

[2] In the *Bhavishya Poorána* this prince, Sehesra-Arjoona, is termed a chakraverta, or paramount sovereign. That he conquered Kurkotaka of the Takshac, Toorshka, or Snake race, and brought with him the population of Mahesvati,

vati on the Nerbudda. This is confirmed by the *Ramayuna*, which details the destruction of the military class and assumption of political power by the Brahmins, under their chief Parswa-rama, marking the period when the military class "lost the umbrella of royalty," and, as the Brahmins ridiculously assert, their purity of blood. This last, however, their own books sufficiently contradict, as the next synchronism will show.

This synchronism we have in Ságára, the thirty-second prince of the Solar line, the contemporary of Taljanga, of the Lunar line, the sixth in descent from Sehesra Arjoona, who had five sons preserved from the general slaughter of the military class by Parswa-rama, whose names are given in the *Bhavishya*.

Wars were constantly carried on between these great rival races, Soorya and Indu, recorded in the *Poordns* and *Ramayuna*. The *Bhavishya* describes that between Ságára and Taljanga "to resemble that of their ancestors, in which the Hihyas suffered as severely as before." But that they had recovered all their power since Parswa-rama, is evident from their having completely retaliated on the Sooryas, and expelled the father [1] of Ságára from his capital of Ayodia. Ságára and Taljanga appear to have been contemporary with Hasti of Hastinapoora, and with Anga, descended from Boodha, the founder of Angdésa,[2] or Ongdeas, and the Anga race.

The *Ramayuna* affords another synchronism ; namely, that Ambarisha of Ayodia, the fortieth prince of the Solar line, was the contemporary of Gadhi, the founder of Canouj, and of Lompada the Prince of Angdésa.

The last synchronism is that of Crishna and Yoodishtra, which terminates the brazen, and introduces the kal yuga or iron age. But this is

and founded Hemanágára in the north of India, on his expulsion from his dominions on the Nerbudda. Traditionary legends yet remain of this prince on the Nerbudda, where he is styled Sehesra Bahu, or 'with a thousand arms,' figurative of his numerous progeny.

The Takshac, or Snake race, here alluded to, will hereafter engage our attention. The names of animals in early times, planets, and things inanimate, all furnished symbolic appellations for the various races. In Scripture we have the fly, the bee, the ram, to describe the princes of Egypt, Assyria, and Macedonia ; here we have the snake, horse, monkey, etc.

The Snake or Takshac race was one of the most extensive and earliest of Higher Asia, and celebrated in all its extent, and to which I shall have to recur hereafter.

In the *Ramayuna* it is stated that the sacrificial horse was stolen by "a serpent (Takshac) assuming the form of Anunta."

[1] "Usita, the father of Ságára, expelled by hostile kings of the Haihyas, the Talajunghas, and the Susoo-vindhas, fled to the Himvat mountains, where he died leaving his wives pregnant, and from one of these Ságára was born." [1] It was to preserve the Solar race from the destruction which threatened it from the prolific Lunar race, that the Brahmin Parswa-rama armed : evidently proving that the Brahminical faith was held by the Solar race ; while the religion of *Boodha*, the great progenitor of the Lunar, still governed his descendants. This strengthened the opposition of the sages of the Solar line to Vishwamitra's (of Boodha's or the Lunar line) obtaining Brahminhood. That Crishna, of Lunar stock, prior to founding a new sect, worshipped Boodha, is susceptible of proof.

[2] Angdés, Ongdés, or Oondés, adjoins Thibet. The inhabitants call themselves Hoongias, and appear to be the Hong-niu of the Chinese authors, the Hüns (Hoons) of Europe and India, which prove this Tartar race to be Lunar, and of Boodha.

---

[1] Forty-first section, Book i. of the *Ramayuna*, translation by Carey.

in the Lunar line; nor have we any guide by which the difference can be adjusted between the appearance of Rama of the Solar, and Crishna of the Lunar races.

Thus of the race of Crust'ha we have Kansa, Prince of Mat'hoora, the fifty-ninth, and his cousin Crishna, the fifty-eighth from Boodha; while of the line of Pooru, descending through Ujmida and Deomida, we have Sul, Jarasandha, and Yoodishtra, the fifty-first, fifty-third, and fifty-fourth, respectively.

The race of Anga gives Prit'hoo-séna as one of the actors and survivors of the *Mahabharat*, and the fifty-third from Boodha.

Thus, taking an average of the whole, we may consider fifty-five princes to be the number of descents from Boodha to Crishna and Yoodishtra; and, admitting an average of twenty years for each reign, a period of eleven hundred years: which being added to a like period calculated from thence to Vicramaditya, who reigned fifty-six years before Christ, I venture to place the establishment in India Proper of these two grand races, distinctively called those of Soorya and Chandra, at about 2256 years before the Christian era; at which period, though somewhat later, the Egyptian, Chinese, and Assyrian monarchies are generally stated to have been established,[1] and about a century and a half after that great event, the Flood.

Though a passage in the *Agni Poorán* indicates that the line of Soorya, of which Icshwáca was the head, was the first colony which entered India from central Asia, yet we are compelled to place the patriarch Boodha as his contemporary, he being stated to have come from a distant region, and married to Ella, the sister of Icshwáca.

Ere we proceed to make any remarks on the descendants of Crishna and Arjoona, who carry on the Lunar line, or of the Cushites and Lavites, from Cush and Lava, the sons of Rama, who carry on that of the Sun, a few observations on the chief kingdoms established by their progenitors on the continent of India will be hazarded in the ensuing chapter.

CHAPTER IV

Foundations of states and cities by the different tribes.

AYODIA[2] was the first city founded by the race of Soorya. Like other capitals, its importance must have risen by slow degrees; yet, making

[1] Egyptian, under Misraim, B.C. 2188; Assyrian, 2059; Chinese, 2207.

[2] The picture drawn by Valmiki of the capital of the Solar race is so highly coloured, that Ayodia might stand for Utopia, and it would be difficult to find such a catalogue of metropolitan embellishments, in this, the iron age of Oude. "On the banks of the Surayoo is a large country called Koshula, in which is Ayodhia, built by *Menu*, twelve yojuns (forty-eight miles) in extent, with streets regular and well watered. It was filled with merchants, beautified by gardens, ornamented with stately gates and high-arched porticos, furnished with arms, crowded with chariots, elephants, and horses, and with ambassadors from foreign lands; embellished with palaces whose domes resembled the mountain tops, dwellings of equal height, resounding with the delightful music of the tabor, the flute, and the harp. It was surrounded by an impassable moat, and guarded by archers. Desarat'ha was its king, a mighty charioteer. There were no

every allowance for exaggeration, it must have attained great splendour long anterior to Rama. Its site is well known at this day under the contracted name of Oude, which also designates the country appertaining to the titular vizier of the Mogul empire ; which country, twenty-five years ago, nearly marked the limits of Kosula, the pristine kingdom of the Soorya race. Overgrown greatness characterised all the ancient Asiatic capitals, and that of Ayodia was immense. Lucknow, the present capital, is traditionally asserted to have been one of the suburbs of ancient Oude, and so named by Rama, in compliment to his brother Lacshman.

Nearly coeval in point of time with Ayodia was Mit'hila,[1] the capital of a country of the same name, founded by Mit'hila, the grandson of Icshwáca.

The name of Janika,[2] son of Mit'hila, eclipsed that of the founder, and became the patronymic of this branch of the Solar race.

These are the two chief capitals of the kingdoms of the Solar line described in this early age ; though there were others of a minor order, such as Rotas, Champapoora, etc., all founded previously to Rama.

By the numerous dynasties of the Lunar race of Boodha many kingdoms were founded. Much has been said of the antiquity of Poorág ; yet the first capital of the Indu or Lunar race appears to have been founded by Sehesra Arjoona, of the Hihya tribe. This was Mahésvati on the Nerbudda, still existing in Muheswar.[3] The rivalry between the Lunar race and that of the Sooryas of Ayodia, in whose aid the priesthood armed, and expelled Sehesra Arjoona from Mahésvati, has been mentioned. A small branch of these ancient Hihyas[4] yet exist in the line of the Nerbudda, near the very top of the valley at Sohagpoor, in Bhagel-khund, aware of their ancient lineage ; and, though few in number, are still celebrated for their valour.[5]

Koosust'hulli Dwarica, the capital of Crishna, was founded prior to Poorág, to Soorpoor, or Mat'hoora. The *Bhagvat* attributes the foundation of the city to Anirt, the brother of Icshwáca, of the Solar race, but states not how or when the Yadus became possessed thereof.

The ancient annals of the Jessulmér family of the Yadu stock give the priority of foundation to *Poorág*, next to *Mat'hoora*, and last to *Dwarica*.

atheists. The affections of the men were in their consorts. The women were chaste and obedient to their lords, endowed with beauty, wit, sweetness, prudence, and industry, with bright ornaments and fair apparel ; the men devoted to truth and hospitality, regardful of their superiors, their ancestors and their gods.

" There were eight councillors ; two chosen priests profound in the law, besides another inferior council of six. Of subdued appetites, disinterested, forbearing, pleasant, patient ; not avaricious ; well acquainted with their duties and popular customs ; attentive to the army, the treasury ; impartially awarding punishment even on their own sons ; never oppressing even an enemy ; not arrogant ; comely in dress ; never confident about doubtful matters ; devoted to the sovereign."

[1] Mit'hila, the modern Tirhoot in Bengal.

[2] Koosad'hwuja, father of Seeta (spouse of Rama), is also called Janika ; a name common in this line, and borne by the third prince in succession after *Sooverna Roma*, the ' golden-haired ' chief Mit'hila.

[3] Familiarly designated as Sehesra Bahu Ka Bustee, or ' the town of the thousand-armed.'

[4] The Hihya race, of the line of Boodha, may claim affinity with the Chinese race which first gave monarchs to China.

[5] Of this I have heard the most romantic proofs in very recent times.

All these cities are too well known to require description; especially Poorág, at the confluence of the Yamuna and Ganges. The Prasii were the descendants of Poorú[1] of Poorág, visited by Megasthenes, ambassador of Seleucus, and the principal city of the Yadus, ere it sent forth the four branches from Satwati. At Poorág resided the celebrated Bharat, the husband of Sacoontala.

In the *Ramayuna*, the Susoovindhas[2] (another Yadu race) are inscribed as allied with the Hihyas in the wars with the race of Soorya; and of this race was Sisoopal[3] (the founder of Chedya[4]), one of the foes of Crishna.

We are assured by Alexander's historians that the country and people round Mat'hoora, when he invaded India, were termed *Surséni*. There are two princes of the name of Sursén in the immediate ancestry of Crishna; one his grandfather, the other eight generations anterior. Which of these founded the capital Soorpoor,[5] whence the country and inhabitants had their appellation, we cannot say. Mathoora and Clesobaras are mentioned by the historians of Alexander as the chief cities of the Suraseni. Though the Greeks sadly disfigure names, we cannot trace any affinity between Clesobaras and Soorpoor.

The city of Hastinapoora was built by Hasti, a name celebrated in the Lunar dynasties. The name of this city is still preserved on the Ganges, about forty miles south of Hari-dwar,[6] where the Ganges breaks through the Sewaluk mountains and enters the plains of India. This

1 Poorú became the patronymic of this branch of the Lunar race. Of this Alexander's historians made Porus. The *Suraseni* of *Methoras* (descendants of the Soor Sén of Mat'hoora) were all *Poorus*, the Prasii of Megasthenes. Allahabad yet retains its Hindu name of Poorag, pronounced Prag.

2 The Hares. Seesodia is said to have the same derivation.

3 The princes of Rinthum-bowur, expelled by Pirthwiraja of Dehli, were of this race.

4 The modern Chanderi is said to be this capital, and one of the few to which no Englishman has obtained entrance, though I tried hard in 1807. Doubtless it would afford food for curiosity; for, being out of the path of armies in the days of conquest and revolution, it may, and I believe does retain, much worthy of research.

5 I had the pleasure, in 1814, of discovering a remnant of this city, which the Yamuna has overwhelmed. The sarced place of pilgrimage, Bhatéswara, stands on part of it. My discovery of it was doubly gratifying, for while I found out the Suraseni of the Greeks, I obtained a medal of the little known Apollodotus, who carried his arms to the mouths of the Indus, and possibly to the centre of the land of the Yadus. He is not included by Bayer in his lists of the kings of Bactria, but we have only an imperfect knowledge of the extent of that dynasty The *Bhagvat Poorán* asserts thirteen Yavan or Ionian princes to have ruled in Balich-dés, or Bactria, in which they mention Pushpamitra *Doomitra*. We are justified in asserting this to be Demetrius, the son of Euthydemus, but who did not succeed his father, as Menander intervened. Of this last conqueror I also possess a medal, obtained amongst the Suraseni, and struck in commemoration of victory, as the winged messenger of heavenly peace extends the palm branch from her hand. These two will fill up a chasm in the Bactrian annals, for Menander is well known to them. Apollodotus would have perished but for Arrian, who wrote the Periplus of the Erythræan sea in the second century, while commercial agent at Baroach, or classically Brigugatcha, the Barugaza of the Greeks.

Without the notice this writer has afforded us, my Apollodotus would have lost half its value. Since my arrival in Europe I have also been made acquainted with the existence of a medal of Demetrius, discovered in Bokhara, and on which an essay has been written by a *sçavant* at St. Petersburg.

6 The portal of Huri or Hari, whose trisula or trident is there.

mighty stream, rolling its masses of waters from the glaciers of the Himalaya, and joined by many auxiliary streams, frequently carries destruction before it. In one night a column of thirty feet in perpendicular height has been known to bear away all within its sweep, and to such an occurrence the capital of Hasti is said to have owed its ruin.[1]

As it existed, however, long after the Mahabharat, it is surprising it is not mentioned by the historians of Alexander, who invaded India probably about eight centuries after that event. In this abode of the sons of Pooru resided Porus, one of the two princes of that name, opponents of Alexander, and probably Barusar the son of Chandragoopta, surmised to be the Abisares and Sandracoptos of Grecian authorities. Of the two princes named Porus mentioned by Alexander's historians, one resided in the very cradle of the Pooru dynasties; the abode of the other bordered on the Punjâb: warranting an assertion that the Pori of Alexander were of the Lunar race, and destroying all the claims various authors[2] have advanced on behalf of the princes of Méwar.[3]

Hasti sent forth three grand branches, Ujamida, Deomida, and Poormida. Of the two last we lose sight altogether; but Ujamida's progeny spread over all the northern parts of India, in the Punjâb and across the Indus. The period, probably one thousand six hundred years before Christ.

From Ujamida,[4] in the fourth generation, was Bajaswa, who obtained possessions towards the Indus, and whose five sons gave their name, *Panchalica*, to the Punjâb, or space watered by the five rivers. The capital founded by the younger brother, Kampila, was named Kampilnagara.[5]

The descendants of Ujamida by his second wife, Késunee, founded another kingdom and dynasty, celebrated in the heroic history of northern India. This is the *Cúsika* dynasty.

Cush had four sons, two of whom, Cushnabha and Cushamba, are well known to traditional history, and by the still surviving cities founded by them. Cushnabha founded the city of Muhadya on the Ganges, afterwards changed to Canyacubja, or Canouj, which maintained its celebrity until the Mahomedan invasion of Shabudin (A.D. 1193), when this overgrown city was laid prostrate for ever. It was not unfrequently called

[1] Wilford says this event is mentioned in two *Pooráns* as occurring in the sixth or eighth generation of the great war. Those who have travelled in the Doáb must have remarked where both the Ganges and Jumna have shifted their beds.

[2] Sir Thomas Roe; Sir Thomas Herbert; the Holstein ambassador (by Olearius); Della Valle; Churchill, in his collection: and borrowing from these, D'Anville, Bayer, Orme, Rennell, etc.

[3] The ignorance of the family of Méwar of the fact would by no means be a conclusive argument against it, could it be otherwise substantiated; but the race of Soorya was completely eclipsed at that period by the Lunar and new races which soon poured in from the west of the Indus, and in time displaced them all.

[4] Ujamida, by his wife Nila, had five sons, who spread their branches (Sachæ) on both sides the Indus. Regarding three the Pooráns are silent, which implies their migration to distant regions. Is it possible they might be the origin of the Medes? These Medes are descendants of *Ydyát, third son of the patriarch Menu*; and Madai, founder of the Medes, was of Japhet's line. Aja-mede, the patronymic of the branch of *Bajaswa*, is from *Aja* 'a goat.' The Assyrian Mede, in Scripture, is typified by the goat.

[5] Of this house was Droopdevi, the wife, in common, of the five Pandua brothers: manners peculiar to Scythia.

Gadhipoora, or the 'city of Gadhi.' This practice of multiplying names of cities in the east is very destructive to history. Abul Fuzil has taken from Hindu authorities an account of Canouj ; and could we admit the authority of a poet on such subjects, Chund, the bard of Pirthwirájá,[1] would afford materials. Ferishta states it in the early ages to have been twenty-five coss (thirty-five miles) in circumference, and that there were thirty thousand shops for the sale of the areca or beetle-nut only ; and this in the sixth century, at which period the Rahtore dynasty, which terminated with Jeichund, in the twelfth, had been in possession from the end of the fifth century.

Cushamba also founded a city, called after his own name *Causambi.*[2] The name was in existence in the eleventh century ; and ruins might yet exist, if search were made on the shores of the Ganges, from Canouj southward.

The other sons built two capitals, Dharmarunya and Vasumuttee ; but of neither have we any correct knowledge.

Cooru had two sons, Sudina and Parikhita. The descendants of the former terminated with Jarasandha, whose capital was Rajgraha (the modern Rajmahl) on the Ganges, in the province of Bahar. From Parikhita descended the monarchs Santana and Balica : the first producing the rivals of the Great War, Yoodishtra and Duryodhana ; the other the Balicaputras.

Duryodhana, the successor to the throne of Cooru, resided at the ancient capital, Hastinapoora ; while the junior branch, Yoodishtra, founded Indraprest'ha, on the Yamuna of Jumna, which name in the eighth century was changed to Dehli.

The sons of Balica founded two kingdoms ; *Palibot'hra*, on the lower Ganges : and *Arore*,[3] on the eastern bank of the Indus, founded by Sehl.

[1] King of Dehli.

[2] An inscription was discovered at Kurrah on the Ganges, in which Yaspal is mentioned as prince of the realm of Causambi.—*As. Res.* vol. ix. p. 440. Wilford, in his Essay on the Geography of the Purans, says "Causambi, near Alluhabad."—*As. Res.* vol. xiv.

[3] Arore, or Alore, was the capital of Sinde in remote antiquity : a bridge over the stream which branched from the Indus, near Dura, is almost the sole vestige of this capital of the Sogdi of Alexander. On its site the shepherds of the desert have established an extensive hamlet ; it is placed on a ridge of siliceous rock, seven miles east of the insular Bekher, and free from the inundations of the Indus. The Soda tribe, a powerful branch of the Pramara race, has ruled in these countries from remote antiquity, and to a very late period they were lords of Omrakote and Oomrasoomra, in which divisions was Arore.

Sehl and his capital were known to Abul Fuzil, though he was ignorant of its position, which he transferred to Debeil, or Dewul, the modern Tatta. This indefatigable historian thus describes it : "In ancient times there lived a raja named Sehris (Sehl), whose capital was Alore, and his dominions extended north to Cashmere and south to the ocean."

Sehl, or Sehr, became a titular appellation of the country, its princes, and its inhabitants, the Sehraes.

Alore appears to have been the capital of the kingdom of Sigertis, conquered by Menander of Bactria. Ebn Haukul, the Arabian geographer, mentions it ; but a superfluous point in writing has changed Arore into Azore, or Azour, as translated by Sir W. Ouseley.

The illustrious D'Anville mentions it ; but, in ignorance of its position, quoting Abulfeda, says, in grandeur "Azour est presque comparable à Mooltan."

I have to claim the discovery of several ancient capital cities in the north of India ; Soorpoor, on the Jumna, the capital of the Yadus ; Alore. on the Indus,

One great arm of the tree of Yáyát remains unnoticed, that of Ooru or Oorvasu, written by others *Turvasu*.

Ooru was the father of a line of kings who founded several empires.

Viroota, the eighth prince from Ooru, had eight sons, two of whom are particularly mentioned as sending forth two grand shoots, Druhya and Babru.

From Druhya a dynasty was established in the north. Ar, with his son Khandar, is stated to have founded a state: Pritchita is said to have become king of Mile-cha-dés, or the *barbarous regions*.

This line terminated with Dushkhanta, the father of the celebrated Sacoontala, married to Bharat, and who, labouring under the displeasure of some offended deity, is said by the Hindus to have been the cause of all the woes which subsequently befell the race.

The four grandsons of Dushkhanta, Kalinjra, Keril, Pand, and Chowal, gave their names to countries.

Kalinjra is the celebrated fortress in Boondelkhund, so well known for its antiquities, which have claimed considerable notice.

Of the second, Keril, it is only known that in the list of the thirty-six royal races in the twelfth century, the Keril makes one, but the capital is unknown.

The kingdom founded by Pand may be that on the coast of Malabar, the Pandu-Mandel of the Hindus, the *Regia Pandiona* of the geographers of the west, and of which, probably, Tanjore is the modern capital.

Chowal [1] is in the Saurashtra peninsula, and on the coast, towards Jugut Koont, 'the world's end,' and still retains its appellation.

The other shoot from Babru became celebrated. The thirty-fourth prince, *Anga*, founded the kingdom of Anga-désa, of which Champa [2] Malini was the capital, established about the same time with Canouj, probably fifteen hundred years before Christ. With him the patronymic was changed, and the Anga race became famous in ancient Hindu history;

the capital of the Sodas; Mundodri, capital of the Puriharas; Chandravati, at the foot of the Aravulli mountains; and Balabhipoora, in Guzzerat, capital of the Balica-raes, the Balharas of Arab travellers. The Balla Rajpoot of Saurashtra may have given the name to Balabhipoora, as descendants of *Balica*, from Sehl of Arore. The blessing of the bard to them is yet, *Tattá Mooltán ca Ráo* ('lord of Tattá and Mooltán,' the seats of the Balica-putras): nor is it improbable that a branch of these under the Indian Hercules, Bala-ram, who left India after the Great War, may have founded Balich, or Balkh, emphatically called the "mother of cities.' The Jessulmér annals assert that the Yadu and Balica branches of the Indu race ruled Khorassan after the Great War, the Indo-Scythic races of Grecian authors.

Besides the Balicas, and the numerous branches of the Indo-Medes, many of the sons of Cooru dispersed over these regions: amongst whom we may place Ootooru Cooru (*Northern Coorus*) of the *Pooráns*, the Ottorocuræ of the Greek authors. Both the Indu and Soorya races were eternally sending their superfluous population to those distant regions, when probably the same primeval religion governed the races east and west of the Indus.

[1] From Chowal on the coast, in journeying towards Joonagurh, and about seven miles from the former, are the remains of an ancient city.

[2] From the description in the *Ramayuna* of King Desarat'ha proceeding to Champa-malina, the capital of Lompada, king of Anga (sixth in descent from the founder), it is evident that it was a very mountainous region, and the deep forests and large rivers presented serious obstructions to his journey. From this I should imagine it impossible that Anga-désa should apply to a portion of Bengal, in which there is a Champa-malina, described by Colonel Francklin in his Essay on Palibothra.

and to this day *An-dês* still designates the Alpine regions of Thibet bordering on Chinese Tartary.

Pristooséna terminates the line of Anga; and as he survived the disasters of the Great War, his race probably multiplied in those regions, where caste appears never to have been introduced.

Thus have we rapidly reviewed the dynasties of Soorya and Chandra, from Menu and Boodha to Rama, Crishna, Yoodishtra, and Jarasandha; establishing, it is hoped, some new points, and perhaps adding to the credibility of the whole.

The wrecks of almost all the vast cities founded by them are yet to be traced in ruins. The city of Icshwáca and Rama, on the Sarjoo; Indraprest'ha, Mat'hoora, Soorpoora, Poorag on the Yamuna; Hastinapoora, Canyacubja, Raj-graha on the Ganges; Mahéswar on the Nerbudda; Arore on the Indus; and Koosust'hulli Dwarica on the shore of the Indian ocean. Each has left some memorial of former grandeur: research may discover others.

There is yet an unexplored region in Panchalica; Kampilnagara its capital, and those cities established west of the Indus by the sons of Bajaswa.

Traces of the early Indo-Scythic nations may possibly reward the search of some adventurous traveller who may penetrate into Transoxiana, on the sites of Cyropolis, and the most northern Alexandria; in Balkh, and amidst the caves of Bamian.

The plains of India retain yet many ancient cities, from whose ruins somewhat may be gleaned to add a mite to knowledge; and where inscriptions may be found in a character which, though yet unintelligible, will not always remain so in this age of discovery. For such let the search be general, and when once a key is obtained, they will enlighten each other. Wherever the races of Cooru, Ooru, and Yadu have swayed, have been found ancient and yet undeciphered characters.

Much would reward him who would make a better digest of the historical and geographical matter in the *Pooráns*. But we must discard the idea that the history of Rama, the *Mahabharat* of Crishna and the five Pandua [1] brothers, are mere allegory: an idea supported by some, although their races, their cities, and their coins still exist. Let us master the characters on the columns of Indraprest'ha, of Poorag and Méwar, on the rocks of Joonagurh [2] at Bijollí, on the Aravulli, and in the Jain temples scattered over India, and then we shall be able to arrive at just and satisfactory conclusions.

[1] The history and exploits of the Pandus and Hériculas are best known in the most remote parts of India: amidst the forest-covered mountains of Saurashtra, the deep woods and caves of Herimba and Virat (still the shelter of the savage Bhil and Koli), or on the craggy banks of the Charmati (Chumbul). In each, tradition has localised the shelter of these heroes when exiled from the Yamuna; and colossal figures cut from the mountain, ancient temples and caves inscribed with characters yet unknown, attributed to the Pandus, confirm the legendary tale.

[2] The 'ancient city,' *par éminence*, is the only name this old capital, at the foot of, and guarding, the sacred mount Girnar, is known by. Abul Fuzil says it had long remained desolate and unknown, and was discovered by mere accident. Tradition even being silent, they gave it the emphatic appellation of Juna (old) Gur'h (fortress). I have little doubt that it is the Asildurga, or Asilgurh, of the Grahilote annals; where it is said that prince Asil raised a fortress, called after him, near to Girnar, by the consent of the Dabi prince, his uncle.

CHAPTER V

The dynastics which succeeded Rama and Crishna—The Pandu family—Periods of the different dynasties.

Having investigated the line from Icshwáca to Rama, and that from Boodha (the parent and first emigrant of the Indu [1] race, from Saca Dwipa, or Scythia, to Hindust'han) to Crishna and Yoodishtra, a period of twelve hundred years, we proceed to the second division and second table of the genealogies.

From Rama all the tribes termed Sooryavansa, or 'Race of the Sun,' claim descent, as the present princes of Méwar, Jeipoor, Marwar, Bikanér, and their numerous clans; while from the Lunar (Indu) line of Boodha and Crishna, the families of Jessulmér and Cutch (the Bhatti [2] and Jaréja races), extending throughout the Indian desert from the Sutledge to the ocean, deduce their pedigrees.

Rama preceded Crishna: but as their historians, Valmika and Vyasu, who wrote the events they witnessed, were contemporaries, it could not have been by many years.

The present table contains the dynasties which succeeded these great beacons of the Solar and Lunar races, and are three in number.[3]

1. The Sooryavansa, descendants of Rama.
2. The Induvansa, descendants of Pandu through Yoodishtra.
3. The Induvansa, descendants of Jarasandha, monarch of Rajgraha.

The *Bhagvat* and *Agni Pooráns* are the authorities for the lines from Rama and Jarasandha; while that of Pandu is from the *Raj-Tarringini* and *Rajaolie*.

The existing Rajpoot tribes of the Solar race claim descent from Lava and Cush, the two elder sons of Rama; nor do I believe any existing tribes trace their ancestry to his other children, or to his brothers.

From the eldest son, Lava, the Ranas of Méwar claim descent: so do the Birgoogir tribe, formerly powerful within the confines of the present Ambér, whose representative now dwells at Anoopshehr on the Ganges.

From Cush descend the Cushwaha [4] princes of Nirwar and Ambér, and their numerous clans. Ambér, though the first in power, is but a scion of Nirwar, transplanted about one thousand years back, whose chief, the representative of the celebrated Prince Nala, enjoys but a sorry district [5] of all his ancient possessions.

The house of Marwar also claims descent from this stem, which appears to originate in an error of the genealogists, confounding the race of Cush

[1] Indu, Som, Chandra, in Sanscrit 'the moon'; hence the Lunar race is termed the Chandra-vansa, Som-vansa, or Indu-vansa, most probably the root of *Hindu*.

[2] The isolated and now dependent chieftainship of Dhát, of which Omrakote is the capital, separates the Bhattis from the Jaréjas. Dhát is now amalgamated with Sinde. Its prince, of Pramara race and Soda tribe, ancient lords of all Sinde.

[3] A fourth and fifth might have been given, but imperfect. First the descendants of Cush, second son of Rama, from whence the princes of Nirwar and Ambér: secondly, the descendants of Crishna, from whom the princes of Jessulmér.

[4] In modern times always written and pronounced *Cutchwaha*.

[5] It is in the plateau of Central India, near Shahabad.

with the Causika of Canouj and Causambi. Nor do the Solar genealogists admit this assumed pedigree.

The Ambér prince in his genealogies traces the descent of the Méwar [1] family from Rama to Sumitra, through Lava, the eldest brother, and not through Cush,[2] as in some copies of the *Pooráns*, and in that whence Sir William Jones had his lists.

Mr. Bentley, taking this genealogy from the same authority as Sir William Jones, has mutilated it by a transposition, for which his reasons are insufficient, and militate against every opinion of the Hindus. Finding the names Vrihadbalu and Vridasura, declared to be princes contemporary with Yoodishtra, he transposes the whole ten princes of his list intervening between Takshac [3] and Bahuman.[4]

Bahuman,[5] or 'the man with arms' (Derazdusht or Longimanus) is the thirty-fourth prince from Rama; and his reign must be placed nearly intermediate between Rama and Sumitra, or his contemporary Vicrama, and in the sixth century from either.

Sumitra concludes the line of Soorya or Rama from the *Bhagvat Poorán.* Thence it is connected with the present line of Méwar, by Jey Sing's authorities; which list has been compared with various others, chiefly Jain, as will be related in the annals of Méwar.

It will be seen that the line of Soorya exhibits fifty-six princes, from Lava, the son of Rama, to Sumitra, the last prince given in the *Pooráns.* Sir William Jones exhibits fifty-seven.

To these fifty-six reigns I should be willing to allow the average of twenty years, which would give 1120 from Rama to Sumitra, who preceded by a short period Vicramaditya; and as 1100 have been already calculated to have preceded the era of Rama and Yoodishtra, the inference is, that 2200 years elapsed from Icshwáca, the founder of the Solar line, to Sumitra.

[1] Whatever dignity attaches to this pedigree, whether true or false, every prince, and every Hindu of learning, admit the claims of the princes of Méwar as heir to 'the chair of Rama'; and a degree of reverence has consequently attached, not only to his person, but to the seat of his power.

When Madajee Sindia was called by the Rana to reduce a traitorous noble in Cheetore, such was the reverence which actuated that (in other respects) little scrupulous chieftain, that he could not be prevailed on to point his cannon on the walls within which consent established 'the throne of Rama.' The Rana himself, then a youth, had to break the ice, and fired a cannon against his own ancient abode.

[2] Bryant, in his *Analysis*, mentions that the children of the Cushite Ham used his name in salutation as a mark of recognition. 'Ram, Ram,' is the common salutation in these Hindu countries; the respondent often joining Seeta's name with that of her consort Rama, 'Seeta Ram.'

[3] Twenty-eighth prince from Rama in Mr. Bentley's list, and twenty-fifth in mine.

[4] Thirty-seventh in Mr. Bentley's list and thirty-fourth in mine; but the intervening names being made to follow Rama, Bahuman (written by him *Banumat*) follows Takshac.

[5] The period of time, also, would allow of their grafting the son of Artaxerxes and father of Darius, the worshipper of Mithras, on the stem of the adorers of Soorya, while a curious notice of the Raja Jey Sing's on a subsequent name on this list which he calls Noshirwan, strengthens the coincidence. Bahuman (see article 'Bahaman,' D'Herbelot's *Bibl. Orient.*) actually carried his arms into India, and invaded the kingdoms of the Solar race of Mit'hila and Magadha. The time is appropriate to the first Darius and his father; and Herodotus tells us that the richest and best of the satrapies of his empire was the Hindu.

From the *Raj-Tarringini* and *Rajaolie*, the Induvansa family (descendants of Pandu through Yoodishtra) is supplied. These works, celebrated in Rajwarra as collections of genealogies and historical facts, by the Pundhits Vedyadhara and Ragonat'h, were compiled under the eye of the most learned prince of his period, Sowae Jey Sing of Ambér, and give the various dynasties which ruled at Indraprest'ha, or Dehli, from Yoodishtra to Vicramaditya ; and although barren of events, may be considered of value in filling up a period of entire darkness.

The *Tarringini* commences with Adnat'h [1] or Rishubdeva,[2] being the Jain [3] theogony. Rapidly noticing the leading princes of the dynasties discussed, they pass to the birth of the kings Dhertarashtra and Pandu, and their offspring, detailing the causes of their civil strife, to that conflict termed the Mahabharat or Great War.

The origin of every family, whether of east or west, is involved in fable. That of the Pandu [4] is entitled to as much credence as the birth of Romulus, or other founders of a race.

Such traditions [5] were probably invented to cover some great disgrace in the Pandu family, and have relation to the story already related of Vyasu, and the debasement of this branch of the Héri-culas. Accordingly, on the death of Pandu, Duryodhanu, nephew of Pandu (son of Dhertarashtra, who from blindness could not inherit), asserted their illegitimacy before the assembled kin at Hastinapoora.

With the aid, however, of the priesthood, and the blind Dhertarashtra, his nephew, Yoodishtra, elder son of Pandu, was invested by him with the seal of royalty, in the capital, Hastinapoora.

Duryodhanu's plots against the Pandu and his partisans were so numerous that the five brothers determined to leave for a while their ancestral abodes on the Ganges. They sought shelter in foreign countries about the Indus, and were first protected by Droopdeva, king of Panchalica, at whose capital, Kampilnagara, the surrounding princes had arrived as suitors for the hand of his daughter, Droopdevi.[6] But the prize was destined for the exiled Pandu, and the skill of Arjoona in archery obtained him the fair, who "threw round his neck the (burmala) garland of marriage." The disappointed princes indulged their resentment against the exile ; but by Arjoona's bow they suffered the fate of Penelope's suitors, and the Pandu brought home his bride, who became the wife in common of the five brothers : manners [7] decisively Scythic.

[1] First lord. [2] Lord of the Bull. [3] Vedhydar was a Jain.

[4] Pandu not being blessed with progeny, his queen made use of a charm by which she enticed the deities from their spheres. To Dherma Raj (Minos) she bore Yoodishtra ; by Pavan (Eolus) she had Bhima ; by Indra (Jupiter Cœlus) she had Arjoona, who was taught by his sire the use of the bow, so fatal in the Great War ; and Nycula and Sydeva owed their birth to Aswini Kumar (Esculapius) the physician of the gods.

[5] We must not disregard the intellect of the Ambér prince, who allowed these ancient traditions to be incorporated with the genealogy compiled under his eye. The prince who obtained De Silva from Emmanuel III. of Portugal, who combined the astronomical tables of Europe and Asia, and raised these monuments of his scientific genius in his favourite pursuit (astronomy) in all the capital cities of India, while engrossed in war and politics, requires neither eulogy nor defence.

[6] Droopdeva was of the Aswa race, being descended from Bajaswa (or Hyaswa) of the line of Ujamida.

[7] This marriage, so inconsistent with Hindu delicacy, is glossed over. Admitting the polyandrism, but in ignorance of its being a national custom, puerile

The deeds of the brothers abroad were bruited in Hastinapoora, and the blind Dhertarashtra's influence effected their recall. To stop, however, their intestine feuds, he partitioned the Pandu sovereignty; and while his son, Duryodhanu, retained Hastinapoora, Yoodishtra founded the new capital of Indraprest'ha; but shortly after the Mahabharat he abdicated in favour of his grand nephew, Parikhita, introducing a new era, called after himself, which existed for eleven hundred years, when it was overturned, and Indraprest'ha was conquered by Vicramaditya Túar of Oojein, of the same race, who established an era of his own.

On the division of the Pandu sovereignty, the new kingdom of Indraprest'ha eclipsed that of Hastinapoora. The brothers reduced to obedience the surrounding [1] nations, and compelled their princes to sign tributary engagements (*paenamah*).[2]

Yoodishtra, firmly seated on his throne, determined to signalise his reign and paramount sovereignty, by the imposing and solemn rites of '*Aswamedha*' [3] and '*Rajsoo*.'

In these magnificent ceremonies, in which princes alone officiate, every duty, down to that of porter, is performed by royalty.

The 'Steed of Sacrifice' was liberated under Arjoona's care, having wandered whither he listed for twelve months; and none daring to accept this challenge of supremacy, he was reconducted to Indraprest'ha, where, in the meanwhile, the hall of sacrifice was prepared, and all the princes of the land were summoned to attend.

The hearts of the Coorus [4] burned with envy at the assumption of supremacy by the Pandus, for the Prince of Hastinapoora's office was to serve out the sacred food.

The rivalry between the races burst forth afresh; but Duryodhanu, who so often failed in his schemes against the safety of his antagonists, determined to make the virtue of Yoodishtra the instrument of his success. He availed himself of the national propensity for play, in which the Rajpoot continues to preserve his Scythic [5] resemblance. Yoodishtra fell into the snare prepared for him. He lost his kingdom, his wife, and even his personal liberty and that of his brothers, for twelve years, and became an exile from the plains of the Yamuna.

The traditional history of these wanderers during the term of proba-

reasons are interpolated. In the early annals of the same race, predecessors of the Jessulmér family, the younger son is made to succeed: also Scythic or Tatar.

The manners of the Scythæ described by Herodotus are found still to exist among their descendants: "a pair of slippers at the wife's door" is a signal well understood by all Eimauk husbands.—Elphinstone's *Caubul*, vol. ii. p. 251.

[1] *Tarringini.*

[2] *Paenamah* is a word peculiarly expressive of subserviency to paramount authority, whether the engagement be in money or service: from *paé*, 'the foot.'

[3] Sacrifice of the horse to the sun, of which a full description is given hereafter.

[4] Duryodhanu, as the elder branch, retained his title as head of the Coorus; while the junior, Yoodishtra, on the separation of authority, adopted his father's name, Pandu, as the patronymic of his new dynasty. The site of the great conflict (or Mahabharat) between these rival clans, is called Cooru-Khétu, or 'Field of the Coorus.'

[5] Herodotus describes the ruinous passion for play amongst the Scythic hordes, and which may have been carried west by Odin into Scandinavia and Germany. Tacitus tells us that the Germans, like the Pandus, staked even personal liberty, and were sold as slaves by the winner.

tion, their many lurking places now sacred, the return to their ancestral abodes, and the grand battle (Mahabharat) which ensued, form highly interesting episodes in the legends of Hindu antiquity.

To decide this civil strife, every tribe and chief of fame, from the Caucasus to the ocean, assembled on Cooru-Khétu, the field on which the empire of India has since more than once been contested[1] and lost.

This combat was fatal to the dominant influence of the "fifty-six tribes of Yadu." On each of its eighteen days' combat, myriads were slain; for "the father knew not the son, nor the disciple his perceptor."

Victory brought no happiness to Yoodishtra. The slaughter of his friends disgusted him with the world, and he determined to withdraw from it; previously performing, at Hastinapoora, funeral rites for Duryodhanu (slain by the hands of Bhima), whose ambition and bad faith had originated this exterminating war.

"Having regained his kingdom, he proclaimed a new era, and placing on the throne of Indraprest'ha, Parikhita, grandson to Arjoona, retired to Dwarica with Crishna and Buldeva: and since the war to the period of writing, 4636 years have elapsed."[2]

Yoodishtra, Buldeva, and Crishna, having retired with the wreck of this ill-fated struggle to Dwarica, the two former had soon to lament the death of Crishna, slain by one of the aboriginal tribes of Bhils; against whom, from their shattered condition, they were unable to contend. After this event, Yoodishtra, with Buldeva and a few followers, entirely withdrew from India, and emigrating northwards, by Sinde, to the Himalayan mountains, are there abandoned by Hindu traditional history, and are supposed to have perished in the snows.[3]

[1] On it the last Hindu monarch, Pirthwirájá, lost his kingdom, his liberty, and life.

[2] *Raj Tarringini*. The period of writing was A.D. 1740.

[3] Having ventured to surmise analogies between the Hercules of the east and west, I shall carry them a point farther. Amidst the snows of Caucasus, Hindu legend abandons the Hericúlas, under their leaders Yoodishtra and Buldeva: yet if Alexander established his altars in Panchalica, amongst the sons of Pooru and the Hericúlas, what physical impossibility exists that a colony of them, under Yoodishtra and Buldeva, eight centuries anterior, should have penetrated to Greece? Comparatively far advanced in science and arms, the conquest would have been easy. When Alexander attacked the "free cities" of Panchalica, the Poorus and Hericúlas who opposed him evinced the recollections of their ancestor, in carrying the figure of Hercules as their standard. Comparison proves a common origin to Hindu and Grecian mythology; and Plato says the Greeks had theirs from Egypt and the East. May not this colony of the Hericúlas be the Heraclidæ, who penetrated into the Peloponnesus (according to Volney) 1078 years before Christ, sufficiently near our calculated period of the Great War?

The Heraclidæ claimed from Atreus: the Hericúlas claim from Atri.

Euristhenes was the first king of the Heraclidæ: Yoodishtra has sufficient affinity in name to the first Spartan king, not to startle the etymologist, the *d* and *r* being always permutable in Sanscrit.

The Greeks or Ionians are descended from Yavan, or Javan, the seventh from Japhet. The Hericúlas are also Yavans claiming from Javan or Yavan, the thirteenth in descent from Yáyát, the third son of the primeval patriarch.

The ancient Heraclidæ of Greece asserted they were as old as the sun, and older than the moon. May not this boast conceal the fact that the Heliadæ (or *Suryavansa*) of Greece had settled there anterior to the colony of the Indu (Lunar) race of Hericúla?

In all that relates to the mythological history of the Indian demi-gods, Buldeva

From Parikhita, who succeeded Yoodishtra, to Vicramaditya, four [1] dynasties are given in a continuous chain, exhibiting sixty-six princes to Rájpál, who, invading Kemaon, was slain by Sukwanta. The Kemaon conqueror seized upon Dehli, but was soon dispossessed by Vicramaditya, who transferred the seat of imperial power from Indraprest'ha to Avanti, or Oojein, from which time it became the first meridian of the Hindu astronomy.

Indraprest'ha ceased to be a regal abode for eight centuries, when it was re-established by Anungpal,[2] the founder of the Tuár race, claiming descent from the Pandus. Then the name of Dehli superseded that of Indraprest'ha.

"Sukwanta, a prince from the northern mountains of Kemaon, ruled fourteen years, when he was slain by Vicramaditya; [3] and from the Bharat to this period 2915 years have elasped." [4]

Such a period asserted to have elapsed while sixty-six princes occupied the throne, gives an average of forty-four years to each; which is incredible, if not absolutely impossible.

In another passage the compiler says: "I have read many books (shastras), and all agreed to make one hundred princes, all of Khetri [5] race, occupy the throne of Dehli from Yoodishtra to Pirthwirájá, a period of 4100 years,[6] after which the Rawad [7] race succeeded."

It is fortunate for these remnants of historical data that they have only extended the duration of reigns, and not added more heads. Sixty-six links are quite sufficient to connect Yoodishtra and Vicramaditya.

We cannot object to the "one hundred princes" who fill the space assigned from Yoodishtra to Pirthwirájá, though there is no proportion

(Hercules), Crishna or Karnya (Apollo), and Boodha (Mercury), a powerful and almost perfect resemblance can be traced between those of Hindu legend, Greece, and Egypt. Buldeva (the god of strength) Hericúla, is still worshipped as in the days of Alexander; his shrine at Buldeo in Vrij (the Suraseni of the Greeks), his club a ploughshare, and a lion's skin his covering.

An Hindu intaglio of rare value, represents Hercules exactly as described by Arrian, with a monogram consisting of two ancient characters now unknown, but which I have found wherever tradition assigns a spot to the Hericúlas; especially in Saurashtra, where they were long concealed on their exile from Dehli.

This we may at once decide to be the exact figure of Hercules which Arrian describes his descendants to have carried as their standard, when Porus opposed Alexander. The intaglio will appear in the *Trans. R.A.S.*

[1] The twenty-eighth prince, Khemraj, was the last in lineal descent from Parikhita, the grand nephew of Yoodishtra. The first dynasty lasted 1864 years. The second dynasty was of Viserwa, and consisted of fourteen princes; this lasted five hundred years. The third dynasty was headed by Mahraj, and terminated by Untinai, the fifteenth prince. The fourth dynasty was headed by Dhoodsen, and terminated by Rájpál, the ninth and last king.—*Raj Tarringini.*

[2] The *Raj Tarringini* gives the date A.V. 848, or A.D. 792, for this; and adds: "Princes from Sewaluk, or northern hills, held it during this time, and it long continued desolate until the Túars."

[3] Fifty-six years, A.C. [4] Ragoonat'h. [5] Rajpoot, or Chátrya.

[6] This period of 4100 years may have been arrived at by the compiler taking for granted the number of years mentioned by Ragoonat'h as having elapsed from the Mahabharat to Vicramaditya, namely, 2915, and adding thereto the well authenticated period of Pirthwirájá, who was born in Samvat 1215: for if 2915 be subtracted from 4100, it leaves 1185, the period within thirty years of the birth of Pirthwirájá, according to the Chohan chronicles.

[7] Solar.

between the number which precedes and that which follows Vicramaditya, the former being sixty-six, the latter only thirty-four princes, although the period cannot differ half a century.

Let us apply a test to these one hundred kings, from Yoodishtra to Pirthwirájá : the result will be 2250 years.

This test is derived from the average rate of reigns of the chief dynasties of Rajast'han, during a period of 633 [1] to 663 [2] years, or from Pirthwirájá to the present date.

Of Méwar	. .	34 [3] princes, or 19 years to each reign.		
Of Marwar	. .	28 princes, or $23\frac{1}{4}$	,,	,,
Of Ambér	. .	29 princes, or $22\frac{1}{2}$	,,	,,
Of Jessulmér	. .	28 princes, or $23\frac{1}{4}$	,,	,,

giving an average of twenty-two years for each reign.

It would not be proper to ascribe a longer period to each reign, and it were perhaps better to give the minimum, nineteen, to extended dynasties ; and to the sixty-six princes from Yoodishtra and Vicramaditya not even so much, four revolutions [4] and usurpations marking this period.

The remaining line, that of Jarasandha, taken from the *Bhagvat*, is of considerable importance, and will afford scope for further speculation.

Jarasandha was the monarch of Rajgrahi,[5] or Behar, whose son Sydeva, and grandson Marjairi, are declared to have been contemporaries of the Mahabharat, and consequently coeval with Parikhita, the Dehli sovereign.

The direct line of Jarasandha terminates in twenty-three descents with Ripoonjya, who was slain, and his throne assumed by his minister, Sonuka, whose dynasty terminated in the fifth generation with Nundivardan. Sonuka derived no personal advantage from his usurpation, as he immediately placed his son, Pradhyota, on the throne. To these five princes one hundred and thirty-eight years are assigned.

A new race entered Hindust'han, led by a conqueror termed Sehesnag, from Sehesnagdésa,[6] who ascended the Pandu throne, and whose line terminates in ten descents with Mahananda, of spurious birth. This last prince, who was also named Bykyat, carried on an exterminating warfare against the ancient Rajpoot princes of pure blood, the *Poorâns* declaring that since the dynasty of Sehesnag the princes were Soodras. Three hundred and sixty years are allotted to these ten princes.

A fourth dynasty commenced with Chandragoopta Mori, of the same

[1] From S. 1250, or A.D. 1194, captivity and dethronement of Pirthwirájá.

[2] From S. 1212, A.D. 1516, the founding of Jessulmér by Jessul, to the accession of Guj Sing, the present prince, in S. 1876, or A.D. 1820.

[3] Many of its early princes were killed in battle ; and the present prince's father succeeded his own nephew, which was retrograding.

[4] The historians sanction the propriety of these changes, in their remarks, that the deposed were "deficient in [capacity for] the cares and duties of government."

[5] Rajgrahi, or Rajmahl, capital of Magad-dés, or Behar.

[6] Figuratively, the country of the 'head of the Snakes' ; *Nag*, *Tak*, or *Takshac*, being synonymous : and which I conclude to be the abode of the ancient Scythic *Tachari* of Strabo, the *Tak-i-uks* of the Chinese, the *Tajuks* of the present day of Turkistan. This race appears to be the same with that of the Toorshka (of the *Poorâns*), who ruled on the Ârverma (the Araxes), in Saca-Dwipa, or Scythia.

Takshac race. The Mori dynasty consisted of ten princes, who are stated to have passed away in one hundred and thirty-seven years.

The fifth dynasty of eight princes were from Sringi-dés, and are said to have ruled one hundred and twelve years, when a prince of Canva-dés deprived the last of life and kingdom. Of these eight princes, four were of pure blood, when Kistna, by a Soodra woman, succeeded. The dynasty of Canva-dés terminates in twenty-three generations with Salombdhi.

Thus from the Great War six successive dynasties are given, presenting a continuous chain of eighty-two princes, reckoning from Sahadeva, the successor of Jarasandha, to Salombdhi.

To some of the short dynasties periods are assigned of moderate length: but as the first and last are without such data, the test already decided on must be applied; which will yield 1704 years, being six hundred and four after Vicramaditya, whose contemporary will thus be Basdeva, the fifty-fifth prince from Sahadeva of the sixth dynasty, said to be a conqueror from the country of Kuttér. If these calculations possess any value, the genealogies of the *Bhagvat* are brought down to the close of the fifth [1] century following Vicramaditya. As we cannot admit the gift of prophesy to the compilers of these books, we may infer that they remodelled their ancient chronicles during the reign of Salombdhi, about the year of Vicrama 600, or A.D. 546.

With regard to calculations already adduced, as to the average number of years for the reigns of the foregoing dynasties, a comparison with those which history affords of other parts of the world will supply the best criterion of the correctness of the assumed data.

From the revolt of the ten tribes against Rehoboam [2] to the capture of Jerusalem, a period of three hundred and eighty-seven years, twenty kings sat on the throne of Judah, making each reign nineteen and a half years; but if we include the three anterior reigns of Saul, David, and Solomon, prior to the revolt, the result will be twenty-six and a half years each.

From the dismemberment of the Assyrian [3] empire under Sardanapalus, nearly nine hundred years before Christ, the three consequent confluent dynasties of Babylonia, Assyria, and Media, afford very different results for comparison.

The Assyrian preserves the medium, while the Babylonish and Median run into extremes. Of the nine princes who swayed Babylon, from the period of its separation from, till its reunion to Assyria, a space of fifty-two years, Darius, who ruled Media sixty years, outlived the whole. Of the line of Darius there were but six princes, from the separation of

[1] Mr. Bentley [1] states, that the astronomer, Brahmagupta, flourished about A.D. 527, or of Vicrama 583, shortly preceding the reign of Salombdhi; that he was the founder of the system called the Calpa of Brahma, on which the present Hindu chronology is founded, and to which Mr. Bentley says their historical data was transferred. This would strengthen my calculations; but the weight of Mr. Bentley's authority has been much weakened by his unwarrantable attack on Mr. Colebrooke, whose extent of knowledge is of double value from his entire aversion to hypothesis.

[2] 987 years before Christ.

[3] For these and the following dates I am indebted to Goguet's chronological tables in his *Origin of Laws*.

---

[1] "On the Hindu System of Astronomy," *As. Res.* vol. viii. pp. 236–7.

the kingdoms to their reunion under Cyrus, a period of one hundred and seventy-four years, or twenty-nine to each reign.

The Assyrian reigns form a juster medium. From Nebuchadnezzar to Sardanapalus we have twenty-two years to a reign; but from thence to the extinction of this dynasty, eighteen.

The first eleven kings, the Heraclidæ of Lacedæmon, commencing with Euristhenes (1078 before Christ), average thirty-two years; while in republican Athens, nearly contemporary, from the first perpetual archon until the office became decennial in the seventh Olympiad, the reigns of the twelve chief magistrates average twenty-eight years and a half.

Thus we have three periods, Jewish, Spartan, and Athenian, each commencing about eleven hundred years before Christ, not half a century remote from the Mahabharat; with those of Babylonia, Assyria, and Media, commencing where we quit the Grecian, in the eighth century before the Christian era, the Jewish ending in the sixth century.

However short, compared with our Solar and Lunar dynasties, yet these, combined with the average reigns of existing Hindu dynasties, will aid the judgment in estimating the periods to be assigned to the lines thus afforded, instead of following the improbable value attached by the Brahmins.

From such data, longevity appears in unison with climate and simplicity of life: the Spartan yielding the maximum of thirty-two to a reign, while the more luxurious Athens gives twenty-eight and a half. The Jews, from Saul to their exile 'to the waters of Babylon,' twenty-six and a half. The Medes equal the Lacedæmonians, and in all history can only be paralleled by the princes of Anhulwarra, one of whom, Chaond, almost equalled Darius.

Of the separated ten tribes, from the revolt to the captivity, twenty kings of Israel passed away in two centuries, or ten years each.

The Spartan and Assyrian present the extremes of thirty-two and eighteen, giving a medium of twenty-five years to a reign.

The average result of our four Hindu dynasties, in a period of nearly seven hundred years, is twenty-two years.

From all which data, I would presume to assign from twenty to twenty-two years to each reign in lines of fifty princes.

If the value thus obtained be satisfactory, and the lines of dynasties derived from so many authorities correct, we shall arrive at the same conclusion with Mr. Bentley; who, by the more philosophical process of astronomical and genealogical combination, places Yoodishtra's era in the year 2825 of the world; which being taken from 4004 (the world's age at the birth of Christ) will leave 1179 before Christ for Yoodishtra's era, or 1123 before Vicramaditya.

CHAPTER VI

Genealogical history of the Rajpoot tribes subsequent to Vicramaditya—Foreign races which entered India—Analogies between the Scythians, the Rajpoots, and the tribes of Scandinavia.

HAVING thus brought down the genealogical history of the ancient martial races of India, from the earliest period to Yoodishtra and Crishna, and thence to Vicramaditya and the present day, a few observations on the races invading India during that time, and now ranked amongst the thirty-six royal races of Rajast'han, affording scope for some curious analogies, may not be inopportune.

The tribes here alluded to are the Hya or Aswa, the Takshac, and the Jit or Gete; the similitude of whose theogony, names in their early genealogies, and many other points, with the Chinese, Tatar, Mogul, Hindu, and Scythic races, would appear to warrant the assertion of one common origin.

Though the periods of the passage of these tribes into India cannot be stated with exactitude, the regions whence they migrated may more easily be ascertained.

Let us compare the origin of the Tatars and Moguls, as given by their historian, Abulgazi, with the races we have been treating of from the *Pooráns*.

Mogul was the name of the Tatarian patriarch. His son was Ogz,[1] the founder of all the races of those northern regions, called Tatars and Mogul.

Ogz, or Oguz, had six sons.[2] First, Kiun,[3] 'the sun,' the Soorya of the Pooráns; secondly, Ay,[4] 'the moon,' the Indu of the Pooráns.

In the latter, Ayu, we have even the same name as in the Pooráns for the Lunar ancestor.

The Tatars all claim from Ayu, 'the moon,' the Indus of the Pooráns. Hence with them, as with the German tribes, the moon was always a male deity.

The Tatar Ay had a son, Juldus. His son was Hyu, from whom [5] came the first race of the kings of China.

The Pooranic Ayu had a son, Yadu (pronounced Jadoo); from whose third son, Hyu, the Hindu genealogist deduces no line, and from whom the Chinese may claim their Indu [5] origin.

El Khan (ninth fron Ay) had two sons: first, Kaian; and secondly, Nagas; whose descendants peopled all Tatary.

From Kaian, Jungeez Khan claimed descent.

[1] Query, if from Mogul and Ogz, compounded, we have not the Magog, son of Japhet, of Scripture?

[2] The other four sons are the remaining elements, personified: whence the six races of Tatars. The Hindus had long but two races, till the four agni-cula made them also six, and now thirty-six!

[3] In Tatar, according to Abulgazi, the sun and moon.

[4] De Guignes.

[5] Sir W. Jones says the Chinese assert their Hindu origin; but a comparison proves both these Indu races to be of Scythic origin.

Nagas was probably the founder of the Takshac, or *Snake* race [1] of the Pooráns and Tatar genealogists, the Tak-i-uk Moguls of De Guignes.

Such are the comparative genealogical origin of the three races. Let us compare their theogony, the fabulous birth assigned by each for the founder of the Indu race.

1. The Pooranic. "Ella (*the earth*), daughter of the sun-born Icshwáca, while wandering in the forests was encountered by Boodha (*Mercury*), and from the rape of Ella sprung the Indu race."

2. The Chinese account of the birth of Yu (Ayu), their first monarch. "A star [2] (Mercury or Fo), struck his mother while journeying. She conceived, and gave to the world Yu, the founder of the first dynasty which reigned in China. Yu divided China into nine provinces, and began to reign 2207 [3] years before Christ."

Thus the Ay of the Tatars, the Yu of the Chinese, and the Ayu of the Pooráns, evidently indicate the great Indu (Lunar) progenitor of the three races.

Boodha (Mercury), the son of Indu (the moon), became the patriarchal and spiritual leader; as Fo, in China; Woden and Teutates,[4] of the tribes migrating to Europe.

Hence it follows that the religion of Boodha must be coeval with the existence of these nations; that it was brought into India Proper by them, and guided them until the schism of Crishna and the Sooryas, worshippers of Bal, in time depressed them, when the Boodha religion was modified into its present mild form, the Jain.

Let us contrast with these the origin of the Scythic nations, as related by Diodorus; [5] when it will be observed the same legends were known to him which have been handed down by the Pooráns and Abulgazi.

"The Scythians had their first abodes on the Araxes.[6] Their origin was from a virgin born of the earth (Ella),[7] of the shape of a woman from the waist upwards, and below a serpent (symbol of Boodha or Mercury); that Jupiter had a son by her, named Scythes,[8] whose name the nation adopted. Scythes had two sons, Palas and Napas (*qu.* the Nagas, or Snake race, of the Tatar genealogy ?), who were celebrated for their great actions, and who divided the countries; and the nations were called after them, the Palians (*qu.* Pali ?) [9] and Napians. They led their forces as far as the Nile on Egypt, and subdued many nations. They enlarged the

[1] Naga and Takshac are Sanscrit names for a snake or serpent, the emblem of Boodha or Mercury. The Naga race, so well known to India, the Takshacs or Takiuks of Scythia, invaded India about six centuries before Christ.

[2] De Guignes, *Sur les Dynasties des Huns*, vol. i. p. 7.

[3] Nearly the calculated period from the Pooráns.

[4] *Taut'h*, 'father' in Sanscrit. *Qu.* Teuths, and Toth, the Mercury of Egypt ?

[5] Diodorus, *Siculus*, book ii.

[6] The Arverma of the Pooráns; the Jaxartes or Sihoon. The Pooráns thus describe Saca-Dwipa or Scythia. Diodorus (lib. ii.) makes the Hemodus the boundary between Saca-Scythia and India Proper.

[7] Ella, the mother of the Lunar race, is the earth personified. Ertha of the Saxons; ἔρα of the Greeks; *ard* in Hebrew.

[8] Scythes, from *Sacatai*, 'Saca-dwipa,' and *és*, 'Lord': Lord of Sacatai, or Scythia.

[9] *Qu.* Whether the Scythic Pali may not be the shepherd invaders of Egypt. The Pali character yet exists, and appears the same as ancient fragments of the Boodha inscriptions in my possession: many letters assimilate with the Coptic.

empire of the Scythians as far as the Eastern ocean, and to the Caspian and lake Mœotis. The nation had many kings, from whom the Sacans (*Sacæ*), the Massagetæ (*Getes* or *Jits*), the Ari-aspians (*Aswas* of Aria), and many other races. They overran Assyria and Media,[1] overturning the empire, and transplanting the inhabitants to the Araxes under the name of Sauro-Matians."[2]

As the Sacæ, Gete, Aswa, and Takshac are names which have crept in amongst our thirty-six royal races, common with others also to early civilisation in Europe, let us seek further ancient authority on the original abodes.

Strabo[3] says: "All the tribes east of the Caspian are called Scythic. The Dahæ[4] next the sea, the Massagetæ (*great* Gete) and Sacæ more eastward; but every tribe has a particular name. All are nomadic: but of these nomades the best known are the *Asi*,[5] the *Pasiani*, *Tachari*, *Sacaranli*, who took Bactria from the Greeks. The Sacæ[6] ('races') have made in Asia irruptions similar to those of the Cimmerians; thus they have been seen to possess themselves of Bactria, and the best district of Armenia, called after them *Sacasenæ*."[7]

Which of the tribes of Rajast'han are the offspring of the Aswa and Medes, of Indu race, returned under new appellations, we shall not now stop to inquire, limiting our hypothesis to the fact of invasions, and adducing some evidence of such being simultaneous with migrations of the same bands into Europe. Hence the inference of a common origin between the Rajpoot and early races of Europe; to support which, a similar mythology, martial manners and poetry, language, and even music and architectural ornaments, may be adduced.[8]

Of the first migrations of the Indu-Scythic Getes, Takshac, and Asi, into India, that of Sehesnag (Takshac), from Sehesnagdés (Tocharist'han ?) or Sehesnag, six centuries, by calculation, before Christ, is the first noticed

[1] The three great branches of the Indu (Lunar) Aswa bore the epithet of *Mida* (pronounced *Mede*), viz. Poora-mede, Uja-mede, and Deomede. *Qu.* The Aswa invaders of Assyria and Media, the sons of Bajaswa, expressly stated to have multiplied in the countries west of the Indus, emigrating from their paternal seats in Panchalica ?

[2] Sun worshippers, the Sooryavansa.

[3] Strabo, lib. xi. p. 254.

[4] Dahya (one of the thirty-six tribes), now extinct.

[5] The Asi and Tachari, the Aswa and Takshac, or Toorshka races, of the Pooráns, of Saca-Dwipa.

"C'est vraisemblablement d'après le nom de Tachari, que M. D'Anville aura cru devoir placer les tribus ainsi dénommées dans le territoire qui s'appelle aujourdhui Tokarist'han, situé, dit ce grand géographe, entre les montagnes et le Gihon ou Amou."—Note 3, liv. xi. p. 254, Strabon.

[6] Once more I may state *Sacæ* in Sanscrit has the aspirate, *Sac'hæ*: literally, the 'branches' or 'races.'

[7] "La Sacasene étoit une contrée de l'Arménie sur les confins de l'Albanie ou du Shirvan."—Note 4, tome i. p. 191, Strabon. "The Sacasenæ were the ancestors of the Saxons."—Turner's *History of the Anglo-Saxons*.

[8] Herodotus (*Melpomene*, p. 190) says: "The Cimmerians, expelled by the Massagetæ, migrated to the Crimea." Here were the Thyssagetæ, or western Getæ; and thence both the Gete and Cimbri found their way to the Baltic.

Rubruquis the Jesuit, describing the monuments of the Comani in the Deshté Kipchak, whence these tribes, says, "their monuments and circles of stones are like our Celtic or Druidical remains."—Bell's *Collection*.

The Comani are a branch of the Catti tribe of Saurashtra, whose pallias, or funeral monumental pillars, are seen in groups at every town and village. The Catti were one of the early German tribes.

by the Pooráns. About this period a grand irruption of the same races conquered Asia Minor, and eventually Scandinavia; and not long after the Asi and Tachari overturned the Greek kingdom of Bactria, the Romans felt the power of the Asi,[1] the Catti, and Cimbri, from the Baltic shore.

"If we can show the Germans to have been originally Scythæ or Goths (Getes or Jits), a wide field of curiosity and inquiry is open to the origin of government, manners, etc.; all the antiquities of Europe will assume a new appearance, and, instead of being traced to the bands of Germany, as Montesquieu and the greatest writers have hitherto done, may be followed through long descriptions of the manners of the Scythians, etc., as given by Herodotus. Scandinavia was occupied by the Scythæ five hundred years before Christ. These Scythians worshipped Mercury (Budha), Woden or Odin, and believed themselves his progeny. The Gothic mythology, by parallel, might be shown to be Grecian, whose gods were the progeny of Cœlus and Terra (Budha and Ella).[2] Dryads, satyrs, fairies, and all the Greek and Roman superstition, may be found in the Scandinavian creed. The Goths consulted the heart of victims, had oracles, had sybils, had a Venus in Freya, and Parcæ in the Valkyrie." [3]

Ere we proceed to trace these mythological resemblances, let us adduce further opinions in proof of the position assumed of a common origin of the tribes of early Europe and the Scythic Rajpoot.

The translator of Abulgazi, in his preface, observes: "Our contempt for the Tatars would lessen did we consider how nearly we stand related to them, and that our ancestors originally came from the north of Asia, and that our customs, laws, and way of living, were formerly the same as theirs. In short, that we are no other than a colony of Tatars.

"It was from Tatary those people came, who, under the successive names of Cymbrians,[4] Kelts, and Gauls, possessed all the northern part of Europe. What were the Goths, Huns, Alans, Swedes, Vandals, Franks, but swarms of the same hive? The Swedish chronicles bring the Swedes [5] from Cashgar, and the affinity between the Saxon language and Kipchak is great; and the Keltick language still subsisting in Britany and Wales is a demonstration that the inhabitants are descended from Tatar nations."

From between the parallels of 30° and 50° of north latitude, and from 75° to 95° of east longitude, the highlands of Central Asia, alike removed from the fires of the equator and the cold of the arctic circle, migrated the

[1] Asi was the term applied to the Getes, Yeuts, or Juts, when they invaded Scandinavia and founded Yeutland or Jutland.—See '*Edda*,' Mallet's Introduction.

[2] Mercury and earth.

[3] Pinkerton, *On the Goths*, vol. ii. p. 94.

[4] Camari was one of the eight sons of Japhet, says Abulgazi: whence the Camari, Cimmerii, or Cimbri. Camari is one of the tribes of Saurashtra.

[5] The Suiones, Suevi, or Su. Now the Su, Yuchi, or Yuti, are Getes, according to De Guignes. Marco Polo calls Cashgar, where he was in the sixth century, the birthplace of the Swedes; and De la Croix adds, that in 1691 Sparvenfeldt, the Swedish ambassador at Paris, told him he had read in Swedish chronicles that Cashgar was their country. When the Huns were chased from the north of China, the greater part retired into the southern countries adjoining Europe. The rest passed directly to the Oxus and Jaxartes; thence they spread to the Caspian and Persian frontiers. In Mawer-ool-nehr (Transoxiana) they mixed with the Su, the Yuchi, or Getes, who were particularly powerful, and extended into Europe. One would be tempted to regard them as the ancestors of those Getes who were known in Europe. Some bands of Su might equally pass into the north of Europe, known as the Suevi.

races which passed into Europe and within the Indus. We must therefore voyage up the Indus, cross the Paropamisan, to the Oxus or Jihoon, to Sakitai [1] or Saca-Dwipa, and from thence and the Deshté Kipchak conduct the Takshacs, the Getes, the Camari, the Catti, and the Huns, into the plains of Hindust'han.

We have much to learn in these unexplored regions, the abode of ancient civilisation, and which, so late as Jungeez Khan's invasion, abounded with large cities. It is an error to suppose that the nations of Higher Asia were merely pastoral; and De Guignes, from original authorities, informs us that when the Su invaded the Yuchi or Jits, they found upwards of a hundred cities containing the merchandise of India, and with the currency bearing the effigies of the prince.

Such was the state of Central Asia long before the Christian era, though now depopulated and rendered desert by desolating wars, which have raged in these countries, and to which Europe can exhibit no parallel. Timoor's wars, in more modern times, against the Getic nation, will illustrate the paths of his ambitious predecessors in the career of destruction.

If we examine the political limits of the great Getic nation in the time of Cyrus, six centuries before Christ, we shall find them little circumscribed in power on the rise of Timoor, though twenty centuries had elapsed.

At this period (A.D. 1330), under the last prince of Getic race, Togluc Timoor Khan, the kingdom of Chagitai [2] was bounded on the west by the Deshté Kipchak, and on the south by the Jihoon, on which river the Getic Khan, like Tomyris, had his capital. Kogend, Tashkant, Ootrar,[3] Cyropolis, and the most northern of the Alexandrias, were within the bounds of Chagitai.

The Gete, Jote, or Jit, and Takshac races, which occupy places amongst the thirty-six royal races of India, are all from the region of Sakatai. Regarding their earliest migrations, we shall endeavour to make the Poorāns contribute; but of their invasions in more modern times the histories of Mahmood of Ghizni, and Timoor, abundantly acquaint us.

From the mountains of Joud [4] to the shores of Mekran,[5] and along the Ganges, the Jit is widely spread; while the Takshac name is now confined to inscriptions or old writings.

Inquiries in their original haunts, and among tribes now under different names, might doubtless bring to light their original designation, now best known within the Indus; while the Takshac or Takiuk may probably be discovered in the Tajik, still in his ancient haunts, the Transoxiana and

[1] Mr. Pinkerton's research had discovered Sakitai, though he does not give his authority (D'Anville) for the Saca-dwipa of the Pooráns! "Sakitai, a region at the fountains of the Oxus and Jaxartes, styled Sakita from the Sacæ."—D'Anville, *Anc. Geog.*

The Yadus of Jessulmér, who ruled Zabulist'han and founded Guzni, claim the Chagitais as of their own *Indu* stock: a claim which, without deep reflection, appeared inadmissible; but which I now deem worthy of credit.

[2] Chagitai, or Sakatai, the Saca-dwipa of the Pooráns (corrupted by the Greeks to Scythia), "whose inhabitants worship the sun, and whence is the river Arverma."

[3] Ootrar, probably the Ottoracuræ of ancient geography: the ootroo (northern) cooru (race); a branch of Indu stock.

[4] Jiddoo Ca dang, the Joudes of Rennell's map; the Yadu hills high up in the Punjáb, where a colony of the Yadu race dwelt when expelled Saurashtra.

[5] The Noomri, or Loomri (foxes) of Balochist'han, are Jits. These are the Nomardies of Rennell.

Chorasmia of classic authors ; the Mawer-ool-nehr of the Persians ; the Turan, Turkist'han, or Tocharist'han of native geography ; the abode of the Tachari, Takshac, or Toorshka invaders of India, described in the Pooráns and existing inscriptions.

The Getes had long maintained their independence when Tomyris defended their liberty against Cyrus. Driven in successive wars across the Sutledge, we shall elsewhere show them preserving their ancient habits, as desultory cavaliers, under the Jit leader of Lahore, in pastoral communities in Bikanér, the Indian desert and elsewhere, though they have lost sight of their early history. The transition from pastoral to agricultural pursuits is but short, and the descendant of the nomadic Gete of Transoxiana is now the best husbandman on the plains of Hindust'han.

The invasion of these Indu-Scythic tribes, Getes, Takshacs, Asi, Catti, Rajpali,[1] Huns, Camari, introduced the worship of Boodha, the founder of the Indu or Lunar race.

Herodotus says the Getes were theists,[2] and held the tenets of the soul's immortality ; so with the Boodhists.

Before, however, touching on points of religious resemblance between the Asi, Gete, or Jut of Scandinavia (who gave his name to the Cimbric Chersonese) and the Gete of Scythia and India, let us make a few remarks on the Asi or Aswa.

To the Indu race of Aswa (the descendants of Deomida and Bajaswa), spread over the countries on both sides the Indus, do we probably owe the distinctive appellation of Asia.

Herodotus [3] says the Greeks denominated Asia from the wife of Prometheus ; while others deduce it from a grandson of Manes, indicating the Aswa descendants of the patriarch Menu.

Asa,[4] Sacambhari,[5] Mata,[6] is the divinity *Hope*, 'mother-protectress of the Sacæ,' or races.

Every Rajpoot adores Asapoorna, 'the fulfiller of desire' ; or, as Sacambhari Devi (goddess protectress), she is invoked previous to any undertaking.

The Aswas were chiefly of the Indu race ; yet a branch of the Sooryas also bore this designation. It appears to indicate their celebrity as horsemen.[7] All of them worshipped the horse, which they sacrificed to the sun. This grand rite, the Aswamedha, on the festival of the winter solstice, would alone go far to exemplify their common Scythic origin with the Getic Sacæ, authorising the inference of Pinkerton, "that a grand Scythic nation extended from the Caspian to the Ganges."

The Aswamedha was practised on the Ganges and Sarjoo by the

[1] Royal pastors.

[2] The sun was their 'great deity,' though they had in Xamolxis a lord of terror, with affinity to Yama, or the Hindu Pluto. "The chief divinity of the Fenns, a Scythic race, was Yammalu."—Pinkerton's *Hist. of the Goths*, vol. ii. p. 215.

[3] *Melpomene*, chap. xiv.

[4] Asa, 'hope.'

[5] Sacambhari : from *sacam*, the plural of *sachæ*, 'branch or race,' and *ambhar*, 'covering, protecting.'

[6] Mata, 'mother.'

[7] *Aswa* and *hya* are synonymous Sanscrit terms for 'horse' ; *asp* in Persian ; and as applied by the prophet Ezekiel to the Getic invasion of Scythia, A.C. 600 : "the sons of Togarmah riding on horses" ; described by Diodorus, the period the same as the Takshac invasion of India.

Solar princes, twelve hundred years before Christ, as by the Getes in the time of Cyrus; "deeming it right," says Herodotus, "to offer the swiftest of created to the chief of uncreated beings": and this worship and sacrifice of the horse has been handed down to the Rajpoot of the present day. A description of this grand ceremony shall close these analogies.

The Getic Asi carried this veneration for the steed, symbolic of their chief deity the sun, into Scandinavia: equally so of all the early German tribes, the Su, Suevi, Catti, Sucimbri, Getes, in the forests of Germany, and on the banks of the Elbe and Weser.

The milk-white steed was supposed to be the organ of the gods, from whose neighing they calculated future events; notions possessed also by the Aswa, sons of Boodha (Woden), on the Yamuna and Ganges, when the rocks of Scandinavia and the shores of the Baltic were yet untrod by man. It was this omen which gave Darius Hystaspes (*hysna*, 'to neigh,' *aspa*, 'a horse') a crown. The bard Chund makes it the omen of death to his principal heroes.

The steed of the Scandinavian god of battle was kept in the temple of Upsala, and always "found foaming and sweating after battle." "Money," says Tacitus, "was only acceptable to the German when bearing the effigies of the horse."

In the *Edda* we are informed that the Getes, or Jits, who entered Scandinavia, were termed Asi, and their first settlement As-gard.[1]

Pinkerton rejects the authority of the *Edda* and follows Torfæus, who "from Icelandic chronicles and genealogies concludes Odin to have come into Scandinavia in the time of Darius Hystaspes, five hundred years before Christ."

This is the period of the last Boodha, or Mahavira, whose era is four hundred and seventy-seven years before Vicrama, or five hundred and thirty-three before Christ.

The successor of Odin in Scandinavia was Gotama; and Gotama was the successor of the last Boodha, Mahavira,[2] who as Gotama, or Gaudama, is still adored from the Straits of Malacca to the Caspian Sea.

"Other antiquaries," says Pinkerton, "assert another Odin, who was put as the supreme deity one thousand years before Christ."

Mallet admits two Odins, but Mr. Pinkerton wishes he had abided by that of Torfæus, in 500 A.C.

It is a singular fact, that the periods of both the Scandinavian Odins should assimilate with the twenty-second Boodha, Naimnat'h, and twenty-fourth and last, Mahavira; the first the contemporary of Crishna, about 1000 or 1100 years, the last 533, before Christ. The Asi, Getes, etc., of Europe worshipped Mercury as founder of their line, as did the Eastern Asi, Takshacs, and Getes.

The Chinese and Tatar historians also say Boodha, or Fo, appeared 1027 years before Christ.

"The Yuchi, established in Bactria and along the Jihoon, eventually bore the name of Jeta or Yetan,[3] that is to say, Getes. Their empire subsisted a long time in this part of Asia, and extended even into India. These are the people whom the Greeks knew under the name of Indo-

[1] Asi-gur'h, 'fortress of the Asi.' [2] The great (*maha*) warrior (*vir*).

[3] Yeutland was the name given to the whole Cimbric Chersonese, or Jutland.—Pinkerton, *On the Goths*.

Scythes. Their manners are the same as those of the Turcs.[1] Revolutions occurred in the very heart of the East, whose consequences were felt afar."[2]

The period allowed by all these authorities for the migration of these Scythic hordes into Europe is also that for their entry into India.

The sixth century is that calculated for the Takshac from Sehesnagdésa; and it is on this event and reign that the Pooráns declare, that from this period "no prince of pure blood would be found, but that the Soodra, the Turshka, and the Yavan, would prevail."

All these Indu-Scythic invaders held the religion of Boodha: and hence the conformity of manners and mythology between the Scandinavian or German tribes and the Rajpoots increased by comparing their martial poetry.

Similarity of religious manners affords stronger proofs of original identity than language. Language is eternally changing—so are manners; but an exploded custom or rite traced to its source, and maintained in opposition to climate, is a testimony not to be rejected.

Personal Habits and Dress.—When Tacitus informs us that the first act of a German on rising was ablution, it will be conceded this habit was not acquired in the cold climate of Germany, but must have been of eastern[3] origin; as were "the loose flowing robe; the long and braided hair, tied in a knot at the top of the head"; with many other customs, personal habits, and superstitions of the Scythic Cimbri, Juts, Catti, Suevi, analagous to the Getic nations of the same name, as described by Herodotus, Justin, and Strabo, and which yet obtain amongst the Rajpoot Sachæ of the present day.

Let us contrast what history affords of resemblance in religion or manners. First, as to religion.

Theogony.—Tuisto (Mercury) and Ertha (the earth) were the chief divinities of the early German tribes.

Tuisto[4] was born of the Earth (Ella) and Manus (Menu). He is often confounded with Odin, or Woden, the Boodha of the eastern tribes, though they are the Mars and Mercury of these nations.

Religious Rites.—The Suiones or Suevi, the most powerful Getic nation of Scandinavia, was divided into many tribes, one of whom, the Su (Yuchi or Jit), made human sacrifices in their consecrated groves[5]

[1] Turc, Turshka, Takshac, or 'Taunak, fils de Turc.'—Abulgazi, *History of the Tatars.*

[2] *Histoire des Huns,* vol. i. p. 42.

[3] Though Tacitus calls the German tribes indigenous, it is evident he knew their claim to Asiatic origin, when he asks, "who would leave the softer abodes of Asia for Germany, where nature yields nothing but deformity."

[4] In an inscription of the Gete or Jit Prince of Salindrapoor (Sulpoor) of the fifth century, he is styled "of the race of Tusta" (*qu.* Tuisto?). It is in that ancient nail-headed character used by the ancient Boodhists of India, and still the sacred character of the Tatar Lamas: in short, the Pali. All the ancient inscriptions I possess of the branches of the Agniculas, as the Chohan, Pramara, Solanki, and Puriharu, are in this character. That of the Jit prince style him "Jit Cat'hi-da" (*qu.* of (da) Cathay?). From Tuisto and Woden we have our Tuesday and Wednesday. In India, Wednesday is Bud-war (Dies Mercurii), and Tuesday Mungul-war (Dies Martis), the *Mardi* of the French.

[5] Tacitus, xxxviii.

to Ertha (Ella), whom all worshipped, and whose chariot was drawn by a cow.[1]

The Suevi worshipped Isis (Isa, Gowri, the Isis and Ceres of Rajast'han), in whose rites the figure of a ship is introduced; "symbolic," observes Tacitus, "of its foreign origin." The festival of Isa, or Gowri, wife of Iswara, at Oodipoor, is performed on the lake, and appears to be exactly that of Isis and Osiris in Egypt, as described by Herodotus. On this occasion Iswara (Osiris), who is secondary to his wife, has a stalk of the onion in blossom in his hand; a root detested by the Hindus generally, though adored by the Egyptians.

Warlike Customs.—They sung hymns in praise of Hercules, as well as Tuisto or Odin, whose banners and images they carried to the field; and fought in clans, using the feram or javelin, both in close and distant combat. In all maintaining the resemblance to the Hericúla, descendants of Boodha, and the Aswa, offspring of Bajaswa, who peopled those regions west of the Indus, and whose redundant population spread both east and west.

The Suevi, or Suiones, erected the celebrated temple of Upsala, in which they placed the statues of Thor, Woden, and Freya, the triple divinity of the Scandinavian Asi, the Tri-murti of the Solar and Lunar races. The first (Thor, the thunderer, or god of war) is Har, or Mahadeva, the destroyer; the second (Woden) is Boodha,[2] the preserver; and the third (Freya) is Oomia, the creative power.

The grand festival to Freya was in spring, when all nature revived; then boars were offered to her by the Scandinavians, and even boars of paste were made and swallowed by the peasantry.

As Vassanti, or spring personified, the consort of Har is worshipped by the Rajpoot, who opens the season with a grand hunt,[3] led by the prince and his vassal chiefs, when they chase, slay, and eat the boar. Personal danger is disregarded on this day, as want of success is ominous that the *Great Mother* will refuse all petitions throughout the year.

Pinkerton, quoting Ptolemy (who was fifty years after Tacitus), says there were six nations in Yeutland or Jutland, the country of the Juts, of whom were the Sablingii (Suevi,[4] or Suiones), the Catti and Hermandri, who extended to the estuary of the Elbe and Weser. There they erected the pillar *Irmanseul* to "the god of war," regarding which Sammes[5] observes: "some will have it to be Mars his pillar, others *Hermes Saul*, or the pillar of Hermes or Mercury"; and he naturally asks, "how did the Saxons come to be acquainted with the Greek name of Mercury?"

Sacrificial pillars are termed *Sura* or *Sula* in Sanscrit; which, conjoined with Har,[6] the Indian god of war, would be Har-sula. The Rajpoot warrior invokes Har with his trident (tri-sula) to help him in battle, while his battle-shout is 'mar! mar!'

The Cimbri, one of the most celebrated of the six tribes of Yeutland, derive their name from their fame as warriors.[7]

[1] The gao, or cow, symbolic of Prit'hu, the earth. On this see note, p. 24.

[2] Crishna is the preserving deity of the Hindu triad. Crishna is of the Indu line of Boodha, whom he worshipped prior to his own deification.

[3] 'Muhoorut ca sikar.' [4] The Siebi of Tacitus.

[5] Sammes' *Saxon Antiquities*.

[6] Har is the Thor of Scandinavia; Heri is Boodha, Hermes, or Mercury.

[7] Mallet derives it from *kempfer*, 'to fight.'

Ku-mara [1] is the Rajpoot god of war. He is represented with seven heads in the Hindu mythology : the Saxon god of war has six.[2]

The six-headed Mars of the Cimbri Chersonese, to whom was raised the Irmanseul on the Weser, was worshipped by the Sacasenæ, the Catti, the Siebi or Suevi, the Jotæ or Gete, and the Cimbri, evincing in name, as in religious rites, a common origin with the martial warriors of Hindust'han.

The religion of the martial Rajpoot, and the rites of Har, the god of battle, are little analogous to those of the meek Hindus, the followers of the pastoral divinity, the worshippers of kine, and feeders on fruits, herbs, and water. The Rajpoot delights in blood : his offerings to the god of battle are sanguinary, blood and wine. The cup (cupra) of libation is the human skull. He loves them because they are emblematic of the deity he worships ; and he is taught to believe that Har loves them, who in war is represented with the skull to drink the foeman's blood, and in peace is the patron of wine and women. With Parbutti on his knee, his eyes rolling from the juice of the p'fool and opium, such is this Bacchanalian divinity of war. Is this Hinduism, acquired on the burning plains of India ? Is it not rather a perfect picture of the manners of the Scandinavian heroes ?

The Rajpoot slays buffaloes, hunts and eats the boar and deer, and shoots ducks and wild fowl (*cookru*) ; he worships his horse, his sword, and the sun, and attends more to the martial song of the bard than to the litany of the Brahmin. In the martial mythology and warlike poetry of the Scandinavians a wide field exists for assimilation, and a comparison of the poetical remains of the Asi of the east and west would alone suffice to suggest a common origin.

Bards.—In the sacred *Bardai* of the Rajpoot we have the bard of our Saxon ancestry ; those reciters of warlike poetry, of whom Tacitus says, " with their barbarous strains, they influence their minds in the day of battle with a chorus of military virtue."

A comparison, in so extensive a field, would include the whole of their manners and religious opinions, and must be reserved for a distinct work.[3] The Valkyrie, or fatal sisters of the Suevi or Siebi, would be the twin sisters of the Apsaras, who summon the Rajpoot warrior from the field of battle, and bear him to " the mansion of the sun," equally the object of attainment with the children of Odin in Scandinavia, and of Boodha and Soorya in the plains of Scythia and on the Ganges, like the Elysium [4] of the Heliadæ of Greece.

[1] *Cu* or *Ku* is a mere prefix, meaning ' evil ' ; ' the evil striker (*Már*).' Hence, probably, the Mars of Rome. The birth of Ku-mar, the general of the army of the gods, with the Hindus, is exactly that of the Grecians, born of the goddess Jahnuvi (Juno) without sexual intercourse. Kumara is always accompanied by the peacock, the bird of Juno.

[2] For a drawing of the Scandinavian god of battle, see Sammes.

[3] I have in contemplation to give to the public a few of the sixty-nine books of the poems of Chund, the last great bard of the last Hindu emperor of India, Pirthwirájá. They are entirely heroic : each book a relation of one of the exploits of this prince, the first warrior of his time. They will aid a comparison between the Rajpoot and Scandinavian bards, and show how far the Provençal Troubadour, the Neustrienne Trouveur, and Minnesinger of Germany, have anything in common with the Rajpoot Bardai.

[4] Ηλύσιὸς, from Ηλιος, ' the sun ' ; also a title of Apollo, the Heri of India.

In the day of battle we should see in each the same excitements to glory and contempt of death, and the *dramatis personæ* of the field, both celestial and terrestrial, move and act alike. We should see Thor, the thunderer, leading the Siebi, and Har (Siva) the Indian Jove, his own worshippers (Sivséba) ; in which Freya, or Bhavani, and even the preserver (Chrishna) himself, not unfrequently mingle.

WAR-CHARIOT.—The war-chariot is peculiar to the Indu-Scythic nations, from Désarat'ha,[1] and the heroes of the Mahabharat, to the conquest of Hindust'han by the Mahomedans, when it was laid aside. On the plains of Coorukhéta, Chrishna became charioteer to his friend Arjoon ; and the Getic hordes of the Jaxartes, when they aided Xerxes in Greece, and Darius on the plains of Arbela,[2] had their chief strength in the war-chariot.

The war-chariot continued to be used later in the south-west of India than elsewhere, and the Catti,[3] Comani, Comari of Saurashtra have to recent times retained their Scythic habits, as their monumental stones testify, expressing their being slain from their cars.

CONDUCT TO FEMALES.—In no point does resemblance more attach between the ancient German and Scandinavian tribes, and the martial Rajpoot or ancient Gete, than in their delicacy towards females.

" The Germans," says Tacitus, " deemed the advice of a woman in periods of exigence oracular." So does the Rajpoot, as the bard Chund often exemplifies ; and hence they append to her name the epithet *Devi* (or contracted *Dé*), ' godlike.' " To a German mind," says Tacitus, " the idea of a woman led into captivity is insupportable " ; and to prevent this the Rajpoot raises the poignard against the heart which beats only for him, though never to survive the dire necessity. It is then they perform the sacrifice ' johura,' when every sachæ (branch) is cut off : and hence the Rajpoot glories in the title of *Sacha-band*, from having performed the

[1] This title of the father of Rama denotes a ' charioteer.'

[2] The Indian satrapy of Darius, says Herodotus, was the richest of all the Persian provinces, and yielded six hundred talents of gold. Arrian informs us, that his Indo-Scythic subjects, in his wars with Alexander, were the élite of his army. Besides the Sacasenæ, we find tribes in name similar to those included in the thirty-six Rajcula ; especially the Dahæ (Dahya, one of the thirty-six races).

The Indo-Scythic contingent was two hundred war chariots and fifteen elephants, which were marshalled with the Parthii on the right, and also near Darius's person. By this disposition they were opposed to the cohort commanded by Alexander in person.

The chariots commenced the action, and prevented a manœuvre of Alexander to turn the left flank of the Persians. Of their horse, also, the most honourable mention is made ; they penetrated into the division where Parmenio commanded, to whom Alexander was compelled to send reinforcements. The Grecian historian dwells with pleasure on Indo-Scythic valour : " there were no equestrian feats, no distant fighting with darts, but each fought as if victory depended on his sole " arm." They fought the Greeks hand to hand.

But the loss of empire was decreed at Arbela, and the Sacæ and Indo-Scythæ had the honour of being slaughtered by the Yavans of Greece, far from their native land, in the aid of the king of kings.

[3] The Catti are celebrated in Alexander's wars. The Cattiawar Catti can be traced from Mool-t'han (*the ancient abode*). The Dahya (Dahæ), Johya (the latter Hunnish), and Catti, are amongst the thirty-six races. All dwelt, six centuries ago, within the five streams and in the deserts south of the Gara. The two last have left but a name.

sacha ; an awful rite, and with every appearance of being the *sacæa* of the Scythic Gete, as described by Strabo.[1]

GAMING.—In passion for play at games of chance, its extent and dire consequences, the Rajpoot, from the earliest times, has evinced a predilection, and will stand comparison with the Scythian and his German offspring.

The German staked his personal liberty, became a slave, and was sold as the property of the winner. To this vice the Pandus owed the loss of their sovereignty and personal liberty, involving at last the destruction of all the Indu races ; nor has the passion abated. Religion even consecrates the vice ; and once a year, on ' the Festival of Lamps ' (*Dewali*), all propitiate the goddess of wealth and fortune (Latchmi) by offering at her shrine.

Destitute of mental pursuits, the martial Rajpoot is often slothful or attached to sensual pleasures, and when roused, reckless on what he may wreak a fit of energy. Yet when order and discipline prevail in a wealthy chieftainship, there is much of that patriarchal mode of life, with its amusements, alike suited to the Rajpoot, the Gete of the Jihoon, or Scandinavian.

OMENS AND AUGURIES.—Divination by lots, auguries, and omens by flights of birds, as practised by the Getic nations described by Herodotus, and amongst the Germans by Tacitus, will be found amongst the Rajpoots, from whose works [2] on this subject might have been supplied the whole of the Augurs and Aruspices, German or Roman.

[1] The Sacæ had invaded the inhabitants on the borders of the Pontic sea : whilst engaged in dividing the booty, the Persian generals surprised them at night, and exterminated them. To eternise the remembrance of this event, the Persians heaped up the earth round a rock in the plain where the battle was fought, on which they erected two temples, one to the goddess Anaïtis, the other to the divinities Omanus and Anandate, and then founded the annual festival called *Sacæa*, still celebrated by the possessors of Zela. Such is the account by some authors of the origin of *Sacæa*. According to others it dates from the reign of Cyrus only. This prince, they say, having carried the war into the country of the Sacæ (Massagetæ of Herodotus) lost a battle. Compelled to fall back on his magazines, abundantly stored with provisions, but especially wine. and having halted some time to refresh his army, he departed before the enemy, feigning a flight, and leaving his camp standing full of provisions. The Sacæ, who pursued, reaching the abandoned camp stored with provisions, gave themselves up to debauch. Cyrus returned and surprised the inebriated and senseless barbarians. Some, buried in profound sleep, were easily massacred ; others occupied in drinking and dancing, without defence, fell into the hands of armed foes : so that all perished. The conqueror, attributing his success to divine protection, consecrated this day to the goddess honoured in his country, and decreed it should be called ' the day of the *Sacæa*.' [1]

Amongst the Rajpoot Sachæ, all grand battles attended with fatal results are termed *saca*. When besieged, without hope of relief, in the last effort of despair, the females are immolated, and the warriors, decorated in saffron robes, rush on inevitable destruction. This is to perform *saca*, where every branch (sacha) is cut off. Cheetore has to boast of having thrice (and a half) suffered saca. *Cheetore sac'ha ka páp*, ' by the sin of the sack of Cheetore,' the most solemn adjuration of the Gehlote Rajpoot.

If such the origin of the festival from the slaughter of the Sacæ of Tomyris, it will be allowed to strengthen the analogy contended for between the Sacæ east and west the Indus.

[2] I presented a work on this subject to the Royal Asiatic Society, as well as another on Palmistry, etc.

---

[1] This is the battle related by Herodotus, to which Strabo alludes, between the Persian monarch and Tomyris queen of the Getæ.

Love of Strong Drink.—Love of liquor, and indulgence in it to excess, were deep-rooted in the Scandinavian Asi and German tribes, and in which they showed their Getic origin; nor is the Rajpoot behind his brethren either of Scythia or Europe. It is the free use of this and similar indulgences, prohibited by ordinances which govern the ordinary Hindu, that first induced me to believe that these warlike races were little indebted to India.

The Rajpoot welcomes his guest with the *munwar peala*, or 'cup of request,' in which they drown ancient enmities. The heroes of Odin never relished a cup of mead more than the Rajpoot his *madhva*;[1] and the bards of Scandinavia and Rajwarra are alike eloquent in the praise of the bowl, on which the Bardai exhausts every metaphor, and calls it ambrosial, immortal.[2] "The bard, as he sipped the ambrosia, in which sparkled the ruby seed of the pomegranate, rehearsed the glory of the race of the fearless.[3] May the king live for ever, alike bounteous in gifts to the bard and the foe!"

Even in the heaven of Indra, the Hindu warrior's paradise, akin to Valhalla, the Rajpoot has his cup, which is served by the Apsara, the twin sister of the celestial Hebe of Scania. "I shall quaff full goblets amongst the gods," says the dying Getic warrior;[4] "I die laughing": sentiments which would be appreciated by a Rajpoot.

A Rajpoot inebriated is a rare sight: but a more destructive and recent vice has usurped much of the honours of the "invitation cup," which has been degraded from the pure "flower"[5] to an infusion of the poppy, destructive of every quality. Of this pernicious habit we may use the words which the historian of German manners applies to the tribes of the Weser and Elbe, in respect to their love of strong drink: "Indulge it, and you need not employ the terror of your arms; their own vices will subdue them."

The cup of the Scandinavian worshippers of Thor, the god of battle, was a human skull, that of the foe, in which they showed their thirst of blood; also borrowed from the chief of the Hindu Triad, Har, the god of battle, who leads his heroes in the "red field of slaughter" with the *cupra*[6] in his hand, with which he gorges on the blood of the slain.

Har is the patron of all who love war and strong drink, and is especially the object of the Rajpoot warrior's devotion: accordingly blood and wine form the chief oblations to the great god of the Indus. The goséns,[7] the

[1] *Madhva* is intoxicating drink, from *madhu*, 'a bee,' in Sanscrit. It is well known that mead is from honey. It would be curious if the German mead was from the Indian madhu (bee): then both cup (*cupra*) and beverage would be borrowed.

[2] *Imrita* (immortal), from the initial privative and *mrit*, 'death.' Thus the *Immurt'hal*, or 'vale of immortality,' at Neufchatel, is as good Sanscrit as German.

[3] Ubhye Sing, 'the fearless lion,' prince of Marwar, whose bard makes this speech at the festal board, when the prince presented with his own hand the cup to the bard.

[4] Regner Lodbrog, in his dying ode, when the destinies summon him.

[5] P'fool, the flower of the mahwa tree, the favourite drink of a Rajpoot. Classically, in Sanscrit it is *madhúca*, of the class Polyandria Monogynia.—See *As. Res.* vol. i. p. 300.

[6] A human skull; in the dialects pronounced *cupar*: *Qu. cup* in Saxon?

[7] The Kanfurra jogis, or goséns, are in great bodies, often in many thousands, and are sought as allies, especially in defensive warfare. In the grand military

peculiar priests of Har, or Bál, the sun, all indulge in intoxicating drugs, herbs and drinks. Seated on their lion, leopard, or deer-skins, their bodies covered with ashes, their hair matted and braided, with iron tongs to feed the penitential fires, their savage appearance makes them fit organs for the commands of the blood and slaughter. Contrary, likewise, to general practise, the minister of Har, the god of war, at his death is committed to the earth, and a circular tumulus is raised over him; and with some classes of goséns, small tumuli, whose form is the frustrum of a cone, with lateral steps, the apex crowned with a cylindrical stone.[1]

Funeral Ceremonies.—In the last rites for the dead, comparison will yield proofs of original similarity. The funeral ceremonies of Scandinavia have distinguished the national eras, and the 'age of fire' and 'the age of hills,'[2] designated the periods when the warrior was committed to mother earth or consumed on the pyre.

Odin (Boodha) introduced the latter custom, and the raising of tumuli over the ashes when the body was burned; as also the practice of the wife burning with her deceased lord. These manners were carried from Sacadwipa, or Saca Scythia, "where the Gete," says Herodotus, "was consumed on the pyre or burned alive with her lord."

With the Getæ, the Siebi or Suevi of Scandinavia, if the deceased had more than one wife, the elder claimed the privilege of burning.[3] Thus, "Nanna was consumed in the same fire with the body of her husband, Balder, one of Odin's companions." But the Scandinavians were anxious to forget this mark of their Asiatic origin, and were not always willing to burn, or to make "so cruel and absurd a sacrifice to the manes of their husbands, the idea of which had been picked up by their Scythian ancestors, when they inhabited the warmer climates of Asia, where they had their first abodes."[4]

"The Scythic Gete," says Herodotus, "had his horse sacrificed on his funeral pyre; and the Scandinavian Gete had his horse and arms buried with him, as they could not approach Odin on foot."[5] The Rajpoot warrior is carried to his final abode armed at all points as when alive, his shield on his back and brand in hand; while his steed, though not sacrificed, is often presented to the deity, and becomes a perquisite of the priest.

The burning of the dead warrior, and female immolation, or *Sati*, are well-known rites, though the magnificent cenotaphs raised on the spot of sacrifice are little known or visited by Europeans; than which there are no better memorials of the rise and decline of the states of the Rajpoot heptarchy. It is the son who raises the mausoleum to the memory of his father; which last token of respect, or laudable vanity, is only limited by the means of the treasury. It is commemorative of the splendour of

festivals at Oodipoor to the god of war, the scymitar, symbolic of Mars, worshipped by the Gehlotes, is entrusted to them.

[1] An entire cemetery of these, besides many detached, I have seen, and also the sacred rites to their manes by the disciples occupying these abodes of austerity, when the flowers of the *ák* and leaves of evergreen were strewed on the grave, and sprinkled with the pure element.

[2] Mallet's *Northern Antiquities*, chap. xii.

[3] Mallet, chap. xii. vol. i. p. 289.

[4] Edda.

[5] Mallet's *Northern Antiquities*, chap. xii. The Celtic Franks had the same custom. The arms of Chilperic, and the bones of the horse on which he was to be presented to Odin, were found in his tomb.

his reign that the dome of his father should eclipse that of his predecessor. In every principality of Rajwarra, the remark is applicable to chieftains as well as princes.

Each sacred spot, termed ' the place of great sacrifice ' (Maha-Sati), is the haunted ground of legendary lore. Almongst the altars on which have burned the beauteous and the brave, the harpy [1] takes up her abode, and stalks forth to devour the hearts of her victims. The Rajpoot never enters these places of silence but to perform stated rites, or anniversary offerings of flowers and water to the manes (pitri-iswars [2]) of his ancestors.

Odin [3] guarded his warriors' final abode from rapine by means of "wandering fires which played around the tombs"; and the tenth chapter of the Salic law is on punishments against "carrying off the boards or carpets of the tombs." Fire and water are interdicted to such sacrilegious spoliators.

The shahaba,[4] or wandering meteoric fires, on fields of battle and in the places of "great sacrifice," produce a pleasing yet melancholy effect; and are the source of superstitious dread and reverence to the Hindu, having their origin in the same natural cause as the "wandering fires of Odin"; the phosphorescent salts produced from animal decomposition.

The Scandinavian reared the tumulus over the ashes of the dead; so did the Gete of the Jaxartes, and the officiating priests of Har, the Hindu god of battle.

The noble picture drawn by Gibbon of the sepulture of the Getic Alaric, is parallelled by that of the great Jungheez Khan. When the lofty mound was raised, extensive forests were planted, to exclude for ever the footsteps of man from his remains.

The tumulus, the cairn, or the pillar, still rises over the Rajpoot who falls in battle; and throughout Rajwarra these sacrificial monuments are found, where are seen carved in relief the warrior on his steed, armed at all points; his faithful wife (*Sati*) beside him, denoting a sacrifice, and the sun and moon on either side, emblematic of never-dying fame.

In Saurashtra, amidst the Catti, Comani, Balla, and others of Scythic descent, the Palia, or Joojar (sacrificial pillars), are conspicuous under the walls of every town, in lines, irregular groups, and circles. On each is displayed in rude relief the warrior, with the manner of his death, lance

[1] The Dhakun (the Jigger Khor of Sinde) is the genuine vampire. Capt. W., after a long chase in the valley of Oodipoor, speared a hyena, whose abode was the tombs, and well known as the steed on which the witch of Ar sallied forth at night. Evil was predicted: and a dangerous fall, subsequently, in chasing an elk, was attributed to his sacrilegious slaughter of the weird sister's steed.

[2] Pitri-és, ' Father-lords.

[3] Mallet, chap. xii.

[4] At Gwalior, on the east side of that famed fortress, where myriads of warriors have fattened the soil, these phosphorescent lights often present a singular appearance. I have, with friends whose eyes this will meet, marked the procession of these lambent night-fires, becoming extinguished at one place and rising at another, which, aided by the unequal *locale*, have been frequently mistaken for the Mahratta prince returning with his numerous torch-bearers from a distant day's sport. I have dared as bold a Rajpoot as ever lived to approach them; whose sense of the levity of my desire was strongly depicted, both in speech and mien: "men he would encounter, but not the spirits of those erst slain in battle." It was generally about the conclusion of the rains that these lights were observed, when evaporation took place from these marshy grounds impregnated with salts.

in hand, generally on horseback, though sometimes in his car; and on the coast "the pirates of Boodha"[1] are depicted boarding from the shrouds.

Amidst the Comani of Tatary the Jesuits found stone circles, similar to those met with wherever the Celtic rites prevailed; and it would require no great ingenuity to prove an analogy, if not a common origin, between Druidic circles and the Indo-Scythic monumental remains.

The trilithon, or seat, in the centre of the judicial circle, is formed by a number sacred to Har, Bál, or the sun, whose priest expounds the law.

Worship of Arms. The Sword.—The devotion of the Rajpoot is still paid to his arms, as to his horse. He swears 'by the steel,' and prostrates himself before his defensive buckler, his lance, his sword, or his dagger.

The worship of the sword (*asi*) may divide with that of the horse (*aswa*) the honour of giving a name to the continent of Asia. It prevailed amongst the Scythic Getæ, and is described exactly by Herodotus. To Dacia and Thrace it was carried by Getic colonies from the Jaxartes, and fostered by these lovers of liberty when their hordes overran Europe.

The worship of the sword in the Acropolis of Athens by the Getic Atila, with all the accompaniments of pomp and place, forms an admirable episode in the history of the decline and fall of Rome; and had Gibbon witnessed the worship of the double-edged sword (*khanda*) by the prince of Méwar and all his chivalry, he might even have embellished his animated account of the adoration of the scymitar, the symbol of Mars.

Initiation to Arms.—Initiation to military fame was the same with the German as with the Rajpoot, when the youthful candidate was presented with the lance, or buckled with the sword; a ceremony which will be noticed when their feudal manners are described; many other traits of character will then be depicted. It would be easy to swell the list of analogous customs, which even to the objects of dislike in food[2] would furnish comparison between the ancient Celt and Rajpoot; but they shall close with the detail of the most ancient of rites.

Aswamedha, or Sacrifice of the Horse.—There are some things, animate and inanimate, which have been common objects of adoration amongst the nations of the earth, the sun, the moon, and all the host of heaven; the sword; reptiles, as the serpent; animals, as the noblest, the horse. This last was not worshipped as an abstract object of devotion, but as a type of that glorious orb which has had reverence from every child of nature. The plains of Tatary, the sands of Libya, the rocks of Persia, the valley of the Ganges, and the wilds of Orinoco, have each yielded votaries alike ardent in devotion to his effulgence,

"Of this great world both eye and soul."

His symbolic worship and offerings varied with clime and habit; and while the altars of Bál in Asia, of Belenus among the Celts of Gaul and Britain, smoked with human sacrifices, the bull[3] bled to Mithras in

[1] At Dwarica, the god of thieves is called Boodha Trivicrama, or of triple energy:—the Hermes Triplex, or three-headed Mercury of the Egyptians.

[2] Cæsar informs us that the Celts of Britain would not eat the hare, goose, or domestic fowl. The Rajpoot will hunt the first, but neither eats it, nor the goose, sacred to the god of battle (Har). The Rajpoot of Méwar eats the jungle fowl, but rarely the domestic.

[3] As he did also to Bál-nat'h (the god Bál) in the ancient times of India. The

Babylon, and the steed was the victim to Soorya on the Jaxartes and Ganges.

The father of history says, that the great Gete of Central Asia deemed it right to offer the swiftest of created to the swiftest of non-created beings. It is fair to infer that the sun's festival with the Gete and Aswa nations of the Jaxartes, as with those of Scandinavia, was the winter solstice, the Sacrant of the Rajpoot and Hindu in general.

Hi, *Hya*, *Hywor*, *Aswa*, denote the steed in Sanscrit and its dialects. In Gothic, *hyrsa* ; Teutonic, *hors* ; Saxon, *horse*.

The grand festival of the German tribes of the Baltic was the *Hi-ul*, or *Hi-el* (already commented on), the Aswa-Medha [1] of the children of Soorya, on the Ganges.

The ceremonies of the Aswamedha are too expensive, and attended with too great risk, to be attempted by modern princes. Of its fatal results we have many historical records, from the first dawn of Indian history to the last of its princes, Pirthwirájá. The *Ramayuna*, the *Mahabharata*, and the poems of Chund, all illustrate this imposing rite and its effects.[2]

The *Ramayuna* affords a magnificent picture of the Aswamedha. Désarat'ha, monarch of Ayodia, father of Rama, is represented as commanding the rite : " Let the sacrifice be prepared, and the horse [3] liberated from the north bank of the Sarjoo ! " [4]

A year being ended, and the horse having returned from his wanderings,[5] the sacrificial ground was prepared on the spot of liberation.

bul-dán, or gift of the bull to the sun, is well recorded. There are numerous temples in Rajast'han of Baalim ; and Balpoor (Mahadeo) has several in Saurashtra. All represent the sun—

" Peor his other name, when he enticed
Israel in Sittim, on their march from Nile."
—*Paradise Lost*, Book i.

The temple of Solomon was to Bál, and all the idolators of that day seem to have held to the grosser tenets of Hinduism.

[1] In *Aswa* (*medha* signifies ' to kill ') we have the derivation of the ancient races, sons of Bajaswa, who peopled the countries on both sides the Indus, and the probable etymon of *Asia*. The Assa-séni, the Ari-aspi of Alexander's historians, and Aspasianæ, to whom Arsaces fled from Seleucus, and whom Strabo terms a Getic race, have the same origin ; hence *Asi-gurh*, ' the fortress of the *Asi* ' (erroneously termed Hansi), and *As-gard* were the first settlements of the Getic Asi in Scandinavia.

Alexander received the homage of all these Getic races at ' the mother of cities,' Balk'h, ' seat of Cat'haian Khan ' (the Jit Cathi-da of my inscription), according to Marco Polo, from whom Milton took his geography.

[2] The last was undertaken by the celebrated Sowaie Jey Sing, of Ambér ; but the milk-white steed of the sun, I believe, was not turned out, or assuredly the Rahtores would have accepted the challenge.

[3] A milk-white steed is selected with peculiar marks. On liberation, properly guarded, he wanders where he listeth. It is a virtual challenge. Arjoona guarded the steed liberated by Yoodishtra ; but that sent round by Parikhita, his grandson, " was seized by the Takshac of the north." The same fate occurred to Sagara, father of Désarat'ha, which involved the loss of his kingdom.

[4] The Sarjoo, or Gunduk, from the Kemaon mountains, passes through Kosul-dés, the dominion of Désarat'ha.

[5] The horse's return after a year, evidently indicates an astronomical revolution, or the sun's return to the same point in the ecliptic. This return from his southern declination must have been always a day of rejoicing to the Scythic and Scandinavian nations, who could not, says Gibbon, fancy a worse hell than

Invitations were sent to all surrounding monarchs to repair to Ayodia. King Kykaya,[1] the king of Cassi,[2] Lompada of Ang-dés,[3] Coshula of Magad-dés,[4] with the kings of Sindha,[5] Soovira,[6] and Saurashtra.[7]

When the sacrificial pillars are erected, the rites commence. This portion of the ceremony, termed *Yuparchraya*, is thus minutely detailed: "There were twenty-one yupas, or pillars,[8] of octagonal shape, each twenty-one feet in height and four feet in diameter, the capitals bearing the figure of a man, an elephant, or a bull. They were of the various sorts of wood appropriated to holy rites, overlaid with plates of gold and ornamented cloth, and adorned with festoons of flowers. While the yupas were erecting, the Udhwaryoo, receiving his instructions from the Hotri, or sacrificing priest, recited aloud the incantations.

"The sacrificial pits were in triple rows, eighteen in number, and arranged in the form of the eagle. Here were placed the victims for immolation; birds, aquatic animals, and *the horse*.

"Thrice was the steed of King Désarat'ha led round the sacred fire by Coshula, and as the priests pronounced the incantations he was immolated[9] amidst shouts of joy.

"The king and queen, placed by the high priest near the horse, sat up all night watching the birds; and the officiating priest, having taken out the hearts, dressed them agreeably to the holy books. The sovereign of men smelled the smoke of the offered hearts, acknowledging his transgressions in the order in which they were committed.

"The sixteen sacrificing priests then placed (as commanded in the ordinances) on the fire the parts of the horse. The oblation of all the animals was made on wood, except that of the horse, which was on cane.

a large abode open to the cold wind of the north. To the south they looked for the deity; and hence, with the Rajpoots, a religious law forbids their doors being to the north.

[1] Kykaya is supposed by the translator, Dr. Carey, to be a king of Persia, the Ky-vansa preceding Darius. The epithet *Ky* not unfrequently occurs in Hindu traditional couplets. One, which I remember, is connected with the ancient ruins of Abhanér in Jeipoor, recording the marriage of one of its princes with a daughter of Ky Camb.

Tu béti Ky Camb *ca, nam Permála ho,* etc. 'Thou art the daughter of *Ky Camb*: thy name Fairy Garland.' *Ky* was the epithet of one of the Persian dynasties. *Qu. Cam-buksh*, the Cambyses of the Greeks?

[2] Benares. [3] Thibet or Ava. [4] Bahar.

[5] Sinde valley. [6] Unknown to me. [7] Peninsula of Cattiwar.

[8] I have seen several of these sacrificial pillars of stone of very ancient date. Many years ago, when all the Rajpoot states were suffering from the thraldom of the Mahrattas, a most worthy and wealthy banker of Surat, known by the family name of Tribeda, who felt acutely for the woes inflicted by incessant predatory foes on the sons of Rama and Crishna, told me, with tears in his eyes, that the evils which afflicted Jeipoor were to be attributed to the sacrilege of the prince, Jaggat Sing, who had dared to abstract the gold plates of the sacrificial pillars, and send them to his treasury. Worse than Rehoboam, who, when he took away from the temple "the shields of gold Solomon had made," had the grace to substitute others of brass. Whether, when turned into currency, it went as a war contribution to the Mahrattas, or was applied to the less worthy use of his concubine queen, "the essence of camphor," it was of a piece with the rest of this prince's unwise conduct. Jey Sing, who erected the pillars, did honour to his country, of which he was a second founder, and under whom it attained the height from which it has now fallen.

[9] On the Noroza, or festival of the new year, the great Mogul slays a camel with his own hand, which is distributed, and eaten by the court favourites.

"The rite concluded with gifts of land to the sacrificing priests and augurs; but the holy men preferring gold, ten millions of jambanuda [1] were bestowed on them."

Such is the circumstantial account of the Aswamedha, the most imposing and the earliest heathen rite on record. It were superfluous to point out the analogy between it and similar rites of various nations, from the chosen people to the Aurespex of Rome and the confessional rite of the Catholic church.

The Sacrant,[2] or Sivrát (night of Siva), is the winter solstice. On it the horse bled to the sun, or Bál-nat'h.

The Scandinavians termed the longest night the 'mother night,' [3] on which they held that the world was born. Hence the Beltane, the fires of Bál or Belenus; the Hi-ul of northern nations, the sacrificial fires on the Aswamedha, or worship of the sun, by the Sooryas on the Ganges, and the Syrians (Συροι) and Sauromatæ on the shores of the Mediterranean.

The altars of the Phœnician Heliopolis, Balbec [4] or Tadmor,[5] were sacred to the same divinity as on the banks of Sarjoo, or Balpoor, in Saurashtra, where "the horses of the sun ascended from his fountain (*Soorya-coond*)," to carry its princes to conquest.

From Syria came the instructors of the Celtic Druids, who made human sacrifices, and set up the pillar of Belenus on the hills of Cambria and Caledonia.

When "Judah did evil in the sight of the Lord, and built them high places, and images, and groves, on every high hill and under every tree," the object was Bál, and the pillar (the lingam) was his symbol. It was on his altar they burned incense, and "sacrificed unto the calf on the fifteenth [6] day of the month" (the sacred Amavus of the Hindus). The calf of Israel is the bull (*nandi*) of Bâlcésar or Iswara; the Apis of the Egyptian Osiris.

The ash was sacred to the sun-god in the west. The aswatat'ha (or peepul) [7] is the 'chief of trees,' say the books sacred to Bál in the East

[1] This was native gold, of a peculiarly dark and brilliant hue, which was compared to the fruit jamba (not unlike a damson). Everything forms an allegory with the Hindus; and the production of this metal is appropriated to the period of gestation of Jahnuvi, the river-goddess (Ganges), when by Agni, or fire, she produced Ku-mar, the god of war, the commander of the army of the gods. This was when she left the place of her birth, the Himaleh mountain (the great storehouse of metallic substances), whose daughter she is: and doubtless this is in allusion to some very remote period, when, bursting her rock-bound bed, Gunga exposed from "her side" veins of this precious metal.

[2] Little bags of brocade, filled with seeds of the sesamum or cakes of the same, are distributed by the chiefs to friends on this occasion. While the author writes, he has before him two of these, sent to him by the young Mahratta prince, Holkar.

[3] *Siv-rát* would be 'father night.' *Siva-Iswara* is the 'universal father.'

[4] Ferishta, the compiler of the imperial history of India, gives us a Persian or Arabic derivation of this, from *Bál* 'the sun,' and *bec*, 'an idol.'

[5] Corrupted to Palmyra, the etymon of which, I believe, has never been given, which is a version of Tadmor. In Sanscrit, *tal*, or *tar*, is the 'date-tree'; *mor* signifies 'chief.' We have more than one 'city of palms' (*Talpoor*) in India; and the tribe ruling in Hydrabad, on the Indus, is called *Talpoorie*, from the place whence they originated.

[6] Kings, chap. xxiii.

[7] *Ficus religiosa*. It presents a perfect resemblance to the popul (poplar) of Germany and Italy, a species of which is the aspen. So similar is it, that the specimen of the peepul from Carolina is called, in the Isola Bella of the Lago Maggiore, *populus angulata*; and another, in the *Jardin des Plantes* at Toulon,

and death, or loss of limb, is incurred by the sacrilegious mutilator of his consecrated groves,[1] where a pillar is raised bearing the inhibitory edict.

We shall here conclude the analogy between the Indo-Scythic Rajpoot races and those of early Europe. Much more might be adduced; the old Runic characters of Scandinavia, the Celtic, and the Osci or Etruscan, might, by comparison with those found in the cave temples and rocks in Rajast'han and Saurashtra, yield yet more important evidence of original similarity; and the very name of German (from wér, *bellum*)[2] might be found to be derived from the *feud* (*wér*) and *foe-man* (*wéri*) of the Rajpoot.

If these coincidences are merely accidental, then has too much been already said; if not, authorities are here recorded, and hypotheses founded, for the assistance of others.

is termed the *ficus populifolia, ou figuier à feuilles de peuplier*. The aspen, or ash, held sacred by the Celtic priests, is said to be the mountain-ash.

'The calf of Bál' is generally placed under the peepul; and Hindu tradition sanctifies a never-dying stem, which marks the spot where the Hindu Apollo, Heri (the sun), was slain by the savage Bhil on the shores of Saurashtra.

[1] The religious feelings of the Rajpoot, though outraged for centuries by Moguls and mercenary Pat'hans, will not permit him to see the axe applied to the noble peepul or umbrageous burr (*ficus indica*), without execrating the destroyer. Unhappy the constitution of mind which knowingly wounds religious prejudices of such ancient date! Yet is it thus with our countrymen in the East, who treat all foreign prejudices with contempt, shoot the bird sacred to the Indian Mars, slay the calves of Bál, and fell the noble peepul before the eyes of the native without remorse.

He is unphilosophic and unwise who treats such prejudices with contumely: prejudices beyond the reach of reason. He is uncharitable who does not respect them; impolitic, who does not use every means to prevent such offence by ignorance or levity. It is an abuse of our strength, and an ungenerous advantage over their weakness. Let us recollect who are the guardians of these fanes of Bál, his peepul, and sacred bird (the peacock); the children of Soorya and Chandra, and the descendants of the sages of yore, they who fill the ranks of our army, and are attentive, though silent, observers of all our actions: the most attached, the most faithful, and the most obedient of mankind! Let us maintain them in duty, obedience, and attachment, by respecting their prejudices and conciliating their pride. On the fulfilment of this depends the maintenance of our sovereignty in India: but the last fifteen years have assuredly not increased their devotion to us. Let the question be put to the unprejudiced, whether their welfare has advanced in proportion to the dominion they have conquered for us, or if it has not been in the inverse ratio of this prosperity? Have not their allowances and comforts decreased? Does the same relative standard between the currency and conveniences of life exist as twenty years ago? Has not the first depreciated twenty-five per cent., as half-batta stations and duties have increased? For the good of ruler and servant, let these be rectified. With the utmost solemnity, I aver, I have but the welfare of all at heart in these observations. I loved the service, I loved the native soldier. I have proved what he will do, where devoted, when, in 1817, thirty-two firelocks of my guard attacked, defeated, and dispersed, a camp of fifteen hundred men, slaying thrice their numbers.[1] Having quitted the scene for ever, I submit my opinion dispassionately for the welfare of the one, and with it the stability or reverse of the other.

[2] D'Anville's derivation of German, from *wer* (bellum) and *manus*.

---

[1] What says the Thermopylæ of India, Corygaum? Five hundred firelocks against twenty thousand men! Do the annals of Napoleon record a more brilliant exploit? Has a column been reared to the manes of the brave, European and native, of this memorable day, to excite to future achievement? What order decks the breast of the gallant Fitzgerald, for the exploit on the field of Nagpore? At another time and place his words, "At my peril be it! *Charge!*" would have crowned his crest! These things call for remedy!

CHAPTER VII

Catalogue of the thirty-six royal races.

HAVING discussed the ancient genealogies of the martial races of Rajast'han, as well as the chief points in their character and religion analogous to those of early Europe, we proceed to the catalogue of the *Chatees Raj-cúla*, or "thirty-six royal races."

The table before the reader presents, at one view, the authorities on which this list is given: they are as good as abundant. The first is from a detached leaf of an ancient work, obtained from a Yati of a Jain temple at the old city of Nadole in Marwar. The second is from the poems of Chund,[1] the bard of the last Hindu king of Dehli. The third is from an estimable work cotemporary with Chund's, the *Komarpal Charitra*,[2] or "History of the Monarchy of Anhulwarra Puttun." The fourth list is from the Kheechee bard.[3] The fifth, from a bard of Saurashtra.

From every one of the bardic profession, from all the collectors and collections of Rajast'han, lists have been received, from which the catalogue No. 6 has been formed, admitted by the genealogists to be more perfect than any existing document. From it, therefore, in succession, each race shall have its history rapidly sketched; though, as a text, a single name is sufficient to fill many pages.

The first list is headed by an invocation to 'Mata Sacambhari Devi,' or mother-goddess, protectress of the races (sachæ).

Each race (sacha) has its *Gotra Acharya*,[4] a genealogical creed, describing the essential peculiarities, religious tenets, and pristine locale of the clan. Every Rajpoot should be able to repeat this; though it is now confined to the family priest or the genealogist. Many chiefs, in these degenerate days, would be astonished if asked to repeat their 'gotra acharya,' and would refer to the bard. It is a touchstone of affinities, and guardian of the laws of intermarriage. When the inhibited degrees of propinquity have been broken, it has been known to rectify the mistake, where, however, "ignorance was bliss."[5]

[1] Of his works I possess the most complete copy existing.

[2] Presented to the Royal Asiatic Society.

[3] Mog-jee, one of the most intelligent bards of the present day; but, heart-broken, he has now but the woes of his race to sing. Yet has he forgot them for a moment to rehearse the deeds of Pursunga, who sealed his fidelity by his death on the Caggar. Then the invisible mantle of Bhavani was wrapt around him; and with the byrd (*furor poeticus*), flowing freely of their deeds of yore, their present degradation, time, and place, were all forgot. But the time is fast approaching when he may sing with the Cambrian bard:

> "Ye lost companions of my tuneful art,
> Where are ye fled?"

[4] One or two specimens shall be given in the proper place.

[5] A prince of Boondi had married a Rajpootni of the Malani tribe; a name now unknown: but a bard repeating the 'gotra acharya,' it was discovered to have been about eight centuries before a ramification (sacha) of the Chohan, to which the Hara of Boondi belonged—divorce and expiatory rites, with great unhappiness, were the consequences. What a contrast to the unhallowed doctrines of Polyandrism, as mentioned amongst the Pandus, the Scythic nations, the in-

LIST OF THE THIRTY-SIX ROYAL RACES OF RAJAST'HAN

OM! SACAMBARI MATA.

ANCIENT MSS.[1]	CHUND BARDAI.[2]	KOMAR PAL CHARITRA.[3]		KHEECHIE BARD.[4]	CORRECTED LIST BY THE AUTHOR
		Sanscrit Edition—MSS.	Guzzuratti Dialect—MSS.		
Icshwáca.	Ravya or Soorya.	Icshwáca.	Gotchar Gohil.	Gehlote.	Icshwáca, Cacoost'ha, or Soorya.
Soorya.	Suhsa or Soma.	Soma.	Uni Gohil	Pramara.	Unwye, Indu, Som, or Chandra.
Soma or Chandra.	Yadu.	Yadu.	Catti or Cat'hi.	Chohan.	Grahilote or Gehlote . 24 Sachæ.
Yadu.	Cacoostha.	Pramara.	Kisair.	Solanki.	Yadu 4
5 Chahuman (Chohan).	5 Pramara.	5 Chohan.	5 Nicoompa.	5 Rahtore.	5 Tuár 17
Pramara.	Chohan.	Chalook.	Burbeta.	Tuár.	Rahtore 13
Chalook or Solanki.	Chalook.	Chunduk.	Bawurea.	Birgoojur.	Cushwaha or Cutchwaha.
Purihara.	Chunduk.	Silar (*Raj Tilac*).	Maroo.	Purihara.	Pramara 35
Chawura.	Silar.	Chapotcut.	Macwahana.	Jhala.	Chahuman or Chohan 26
10 Dodia.	10 Abhira.	10 Pritihara.	10 Dahima.	10 Yadu.	10 Chalook or Solanki . 16
Rahtore.	Macwahana.	Sukrunka.	Dodia.	Cutchwaha.	Purihara 12
Gohil.	Gohil.	Coorpala.	Balla.	Gor.	Chawura. . . . . Single.
Dabi.	Chapotkut.	Chundail.	Bhagél.	These sub-divide: the following do not, and are called Yeka, or single.	Tâk, Tauk, or Takshac.
Macwahana.	Purihara.	Ohil.	Yadu.	Sengar.	Jit or Gete.
15 Norka.	15 Rahtore.	15 Paluka.	15 Jaitwa.	Balla.	15 Hun or Hoon.
Aswurea.	Deora.	Mori.	Jareja.	15 Khurwur.	Catti.
Salar or Silara.	Ták.	Macwahana.	Jit.	Chawura.	Balla.
Sinda.	Sindoo.	Dhunpala.	Solanki.	Dahima.	Jhala 2
Seput.	Anunga.	Rajpalica.	Pramara.	Dahya.	Jaitwa or Camari.
20 Hun or Hoon.	20 Patuk.	20 Dahya.	20 Kaba.	Byce.	20 Gohil.
Kirjal.	Pritihara.	Toorunduleeca.	Chawura.	20 Gherwal.	Sarweya.
Huraira.	Didiota.	Nicoompa.	Chourasima.	Nicoompa.	Silar.
Rajpali.	Karitpal.	Hoon.	Khant.	Dewut.	Dabi.
Dhunpali.	Kotpala.	Balla.	Khyera.	Johya.	Gor 5
25 Agnipali.	25 Hool.	25 Hureal.	25 Rawuli.	Sikerwal.	25 Doda or Dor.
Balla.	Gor.	Mokur.	Musania.	25 Dabia.	Gherwal.
Jhala.	Nicoompa.	Pokara.	Palani.	Doda.	Birgoojur 3
Bhagdola.	Rajpalica.		Halla.	Mori.	Sengar . . . . Single.
Motdan.	Kani.		Jhala.	Mokarra.	Sikerwal . . . . do.
30 Mohor.	30 Kalchoruk or Koorcurra.		30 Dahiria.	Abhira.	30 Byce . . . . do.
Kugair.			Bahuria.	30 Kalchoruk (Hya race).	Dahia.
Kurjeo.			Sarweya "*Chatrya tyn Sar.*"	Agnipala.	Johya.
Chadlea.			Purihara.	Aswaria or Sarja.	Mohil.
Pokara.			Chohan.	Hool.	Nicoompa.
Nicoompa.				Manutwal.	Rajpali.
36 Sulala.				Mallia.	36 Dahima . . . . do.
				36 Chahil.	Extra.
					Hool.
					Dahirya.

[1] The author, after the invocation to "the mother protectress," says, "I write the names of the thirty-six royal tribes."
[2] The bard Chund says, "of the thirty-six races, the four Agnipalus are the greatest—the rest are born of woman, but these from fire."
[3] As the work is chiefly followed with the exploits of Komarpal, who was of Chohan tribe, the author reserves it for a peroration to the last "of all the mightiest is the Chohan."
[4] By name Mogje.

Most of the cúla (races) are divided into numerous branches [1] (sacha), and these sacha subdivided into innumerable clans (gotra),[2] the most important of which shall be given.

A few of the cúla never ramified: these are termed *eka*, or 'single'; and nearly one-third are *eka*.

A table of the 'eighty-four' mercantile tribes, chiefly of Rajpoot origin, shall also be furnished, in which the remembrance of some races are preserved which would have perished. Lists of the aboriginal, the agricultural and the pastoral tribes are also given to complete the subject.

In the earlier ages there were but two races, Soorya and Chandra, to which were added the four Agnicúlas; [3] in all six. The others are subdivisions of Soorya and Chandra, or the sacha of Indo-Scythic origin, who found no difficulty in obtaining a place (though a low one), before the Mahomedan era, amongst the thirty-six regal races of Rajast'han. The former we may not unaptly consider as to the time, as the Celtic, the latter as the Gothic, races of India. On the generic terms Soorya and Chandra, I need add nothing.

GRAHILOTE OR GEHLOTE.—*Pedigree* [4] *of the Sooryavansi Rana, of royal race, Lord of Cheetore, the ornament of the thirty-six royal races.*

By universal consent, as well as by the gotra of this race, its princes are admitted to be the direct descendants of Rama, of the Solar line. The pedigree is deduced from him, and connected with Soomitra, the last prince mentioned in the genealogy of the Pooráns.

As the origin and progressive history of this family will be fully discussed in the "Annals of Méwar," we shall here only notice the changes which have marked the patronymic, as well as the regions which have been under their sway, from Kéneksén, who, in the second century, abandoned his native kingdom, Kosula, and established the race of Soorya in Saurashtra.

On the site of Virat, the celebrated abode of the Pandus during exile, the descendant of Icshwáca established his line, and his descendant Vijya, in a few generations, built Vijyapoor.[5]

They became sovereigns, if not founders, of Balabhi, which had a separate era of its own, called the *Balabhi Samvat*, according with S. Vicrama 375.[6] Hence they became the Balaca-raés, or kings of Balabhi;

habitants of Sirmor of the present day, and pertaining even to Britain in the days of Cæsar!—"Uxores habent deni duodenique inter se communes," says that accurate writer, speaking of the natives of this island; "et maximè fratres cum fratribus, parentesque cum liberis: sed si qui sint ex his nati, eorum habentur liberi, quo primum virgo quæque deducta est." A strange medley of polyandry and polygamy!

[1] *Aparam sacam*, 'of innumerable branches,' is inscribed on an ancient tablet of the Grahilote race.

[2] *Gote, kamp*, denote a clan; its subdivisions have the patronymic terminating with the syllable '*ote*,' '*awut*,' '*sote*,' in the use of which euphony alone is their guide: thus, *Suktawut*, 'sons of Sukta'; *Kurmasote*, 'of Kurma'; *Mair-awut*, or *mairote*, mountaineers, 'sons of the mountains.' Such is the Greek *Mainote*, from *maina*, a mountain, in the ancient Albanian dialect, of eastern origin.

[3] From *agni* (*qu. ignis?*) 'fire,' the sons of Vulcan, as the others of Sol and Luna, or Lunus, to change the sex of the parent of the Indu (moon) race.

[4] *Vansavuli, Sooryavansi Rajcúli Rana Cheetore ca Dhunni, Chatees Cúli Séngár.*—MSS. from the Rana's library, entitled *Khomán Rasa*.

[5] Always conjoined with Virat—"Vijyapoor Viratgurh."

[6] A.D. 319. The inscription recording this, as well as others relating to

a title maintained by successive dynasties of Saurashtra for a thousand years after this period, as can be satisfactorily proved by genuine history and inscriptions.

Gajni, or Gayni, was another capital, whence the last prince, Silladitya (who was slain), and his family, were expelled by Parthian invaders in the sixth century.

A posthumous son, called Grahaditya, obtained a petty sovereignty at Edur. The change was marked by his name becoming the patronymic, and 'Grahilote,' *vulgo* 'Gehlote,' designated the Sooryavansa of Rama.

With reverses and migration from the wilds of Edur to Ahar,[1] the Gehlote was changed to Aharya, by which title the race continued to be designated till the twelfth century, when the elder brother, Rahup, abandoned his claim to 'the throne of Cheetore,' obtained [2] by force of arms from the Mori,[3] and settled at Dongurpoor, which he yet holds, as well as the title 'Aharya'; while the younger, Mahup, established the seat of power at Seesoda, whence Seesodia set aside both Aharya and Gehlote.

Seesodia is now the common title of the race; but being only a subdivision, the Gehlote holds its rank in the cúla.

The Gehlote cúla is subdivided into twenty-four sacha, or ramifications, few of which exist—

1. Aharya	At Dongurpoor.
2. Mangulia	In the Deserts.
3. Seesodia	Méwar.
4. Peeparra	In Marwar.
5. Kalum	In few numbers, and mostly now unknown.
6. Gahor	
7. Dhornia	
8. Godah	
9. Mugrasah	
10. Bhimla	
11. Kamkotuc	
12. Kotecha	
13. Sorah	
14. Oohur	
15. Ooseba	
16. Nir-roop	
17. Nadoria	Almost extinct.
18. Nadhota	
19. Ojakra	
20. Kootchra	
21. Dosaud	
22. Batewara	
23. Paha	
24. Poorote	

Balahbi and this era, I discovered in Saurashtra, as well as the site of this ancient capital, occupying the position of "Byzantium" in Ptolemy's geography of India. They will be given in the *Transactions* of the Royal Asiatic Society.

[1] Anundpoor Ahar, or 'Ahar the city of repose.' By the tide of events, the family was destined to fix their last capital, Oodipoor, near Ahar.

[2] The middle of the eighth century.

[3] A Pramara prince.

YADU.—The Yadu was the most illustrious of all the tribes of Ind, and became the patronymic of the descendants of Boodha, progenitor of the Lunar (Indu) race.

Yoodishtra and Baladeva, on the death of Crishna and their expulsion from Dehli and Dwarica, the last stronghold of their power, retired by Mooltan across the Indus. The two first are abandoned by tradition; but the sons of Crishna, who accompanied them after an intermediate halt in the further Do-áb [1] of the five rivers, eventually left the Indus behind, and passed into Zabulist'han, founded Gajni, and peopled these countries even to Samarkhand.

The annals of Jessulmér, which give this early history of their founder, mix up in a confused manner [2] the cause of their being again driven back into India; so that it is impossible to say whether it was owing to the Greek princes who ruled all these countries for a century after Alexander, or to the rise of Islamism.

Driven back on the Indus, they obtained possession of the Punjáb and founded Salbhanpoor. Thence expelled, they retired across the Sutledge and Garah into the Indian deserts; whence expelling the Langahas, the Johyas, Mohilas, etc., they founded successively Tannote, Derrawal, and Jessulmér,[3] in S. 1212,[4] the present capital of the Bhattis, the lineal successors of Crishna.

BHATTI was the exile from Zabulist'han, and as usual with the Rajpoot races on any such event in their annals, his name set aside the more ancient patronymic, *Yadu*. The Bhattis subdued all the tracts south of the Garah; but their power has been greatly circumscribed since the arrival of the Rahtores. The Map defines their existing limits, and their annals will detail their past history.

JAREJA is the most important tribe of Yadu race next to the Bhatti. Its history is similar. Descended from Crishna, and migrating simultaneously with the remains of the Hericúlas, there is the strongest ground for believing that their range was not so wide as that of the elder branch, but that they settled themselves in the valley of the Indus, more especially on the west shore in Sewist'han; and in nominal and armorial distinctions, even in Alexander's time, they retained the marks of their ancestry.

Sambus, who brought on him the arms of the Grecians, was in all likelihood a Hericúla; and the Minagara of Greek historians, Samanagara ('city of Sama'), his capital.

The most common epithet of Crishna, or Heri, was Shama or Sama, from his dark complexion. Hence the Jareja bore it as a patronymic, and the whole race were Sama-pootras (children of Sama), whence the titular name Sambus of its princes.

The modern Jareja, who from circumstances has so mixed with the Mahomedans of Sinde as to have forfeited all pretensions to purity of blood, partly in ignorance and partly to cover disgrace, says that his origin is from Sham, or Syria, and of the stock of the Persian Jamsheed: conse-

[1] The place where they found refuge was in the cluster of hills still called *Yadu ca dang*, 'the Yadu hills':—the *Joudes* of Rennell's geography.

[2] The date assigned long prior to the Christian era, agrees with the Grecian, but the names and manners are Mahomedan.

[3] Lodurwa Puttun, whence they expelled an ancient race, was their capital before Jessulmér. There is much to learn of these regions.

[4] A.D. 1157.

quently, Sam has been converted into Jam;[1] which epithet designates one of the Jareja petty governments, the Jam Raj.

These are the most conspicuous of the Yadu race; but there are others who still bear the original title, of which the head is the prince of the petty state of Kerowli on the Chumbul.

This portion of the Yadu stock would appear never to have strayed far beyond the ancient limits of the Suraseni,[2] their ancestral abodes. They held the celebrated Biana; whence expelled, they established Kerowli west, and Subbulgurh east, of the Chumbul. The tract under the latter, called Yaduvati, has been wrested from the family by Sindia. Sri Mat'hoora [3] is an independent fief of Kerowli, held by a junior branch.

The Yadus, or as pronounced in the dialects Jadoon, are scattered over India, and many chiefs of consequence amongst the Mahrattas are of this tribe.

There are eight sachæ of the Yadu race:—

1. Yadu	Chief Kerowli.
2. Bhatti	Chief Jessulmér.
3. Jareja	Chief Cutch Bhooj.
4. Sumaitcha	Mahomedans in Sinde.
5. Mudaicha	Unknown.
6. Bidmun	
7. Budda	
8. Soha	

Tuár.—The Tuár, though acknowledged as a subdivision of the Yadu, is placed by the best genealogists as one of the 'thirty-six,' a rank to which its celebrity justly entitles it.

We have in almost every case the etymon of each celebrated race. For the Tuár we have none; and we must rest satisfied in delivering the dictum of the Bardai, who declares it of Pandu origin.

If it had to boast only of Vicramaditya, the paramount lord of India, whose era, established fifty-six years before the Christian, still serves as the grand beacon of Hindu chronology, this alone would entitle the Tuár to the highest rank. But it has other claims to respect. Dehli, the ancient Indraprest'ha, founded by Yoodishtra, and which tradition says lay desolate for eight centuries, was rebuilt and peopled by Anungpal Tuár, in S. 848 (A.D. 792), who was followed by a dynasty of twenty princes, which concluded with the name of the founder, Anungpal, in S. 1220 (A.D. 1164), when, contrary to the Salic law of the Rajpoots, he abdicated (having no issue) in favour of his grandchild, the Chohan Pirthwirájá.

The Tuár must now rest on his ancient fame; for not an independent possession remains to the race [4] which traces its lineage to the Pandus, boasts of Vicrama, and which furnished the last dynasty, emperors of Hindust'han.

[1] They have an infinitely better etymology for this, in being descendants of Jambuvati, one of Heri's eight wives.

[2] The Suraseni of Vrij, the tract so named, thirty miles around Mat'hoora.

[3] Its chief, Rao Munohur Sing, was well known to me, and was, I may say, my friend. For years letters passed between us, and he had made for me a transcript of a valuable copy of the *Mahabharat*.

[4] Several Mahratta chieftains deduce their origin from the Tuár race, as Ram Rao Falkia, a very gallant leader of horse in Sindia's state.

It would be a fact unparalleled in the history of the world, could we establish to conviction that the last Anungpal Tuár was the lineal descendant of the founder of Indraprest'ha ; that the issue of Yoodishtra sat on the throne which he erected, after a lapse of 2250 years. Universal consent admits it, and the fact is as well established as most others of a historic nature of such a distant period : nor can any dynasty or family of Europe produce evidence so strong as the Tuár, even to a much less remote antiquity.

The chief possessions left to the Tuárs are the district of Tuárgar, on the right bank of the Chumbul towards its junction with the Jumna, and the small chieftainship of Patun Tuárvati in the Jeipoor state, and whose head claims affinity with the ancient kings of Indraprest'ha.

RAHTORE.—A doubt hangs on the origin of this justly celebrated race. The Rahtore genealogies trace their pedigree to Cush, the second son of Rama ; consequently they would be Sooryavansa. But by the bards of this race they are denied this honour ; and although Cushite, they are held to be the descendants of Casyapa, of the Solar race, by the daughter of a Dyte (Titan). The progeny of Hirna Casyapa is accordingly stigmatised as being of demoniac origin.

It is rather singular that they should have succeeded to the Lunar race of Cushnaba, descendants of Ujamida, the founders of Canouj. Indeed, some genealogists maintain the Rahtores to be of Cusika race.

The pristine locale of the Rahtores is Gadhipoora, or Canouj, where they are found enthroned in the fifth century ; and though beyond that period they connect their line with the princes of Kosula or Ayodia, the fact rests on assertion only.

From the fifth century their history is cleared from the mist of ages, which envelops them all prior to this time ; and in the period approaching the Tatar conquest of India, we find them contesting with the last Tuár and Chohan kings of Dehli, and the Balića-raes of Anhulwarra, the right to paramount importance amidst the princes of Ind.

The combats for this phantom supremacy destroyed them all. Weakened by internal strife, the Chohan of Dehli fell, and his death exposed the north-west frontier. Canouj followed ; and while its last prince, Jychund, found a grave in the Ganges, his son sought an asylum in Maroost'hulli, " the regions of death."

Séôji was this son ; the founder of the Rahtore dynasty in Marwar, on the ruins of the Puriharas of Mundore. Here they brought their ancient martial spirit, and a more valiant being exists not than can be found amongst the sons of Séôji. The Mogul emperors were indebted for half their conquests to the *Lakh Turwar Rahtorán*, ' the 100,000 swords of the Rahtores ' ; for it is beyond a doubt that 50,000 of the blood of Séôji have been embodied at once. But enough of the noble Rahtores for the present.

The Rahtore has twenty-four sachæ :—Dhandul, Bhadail, Chackit, Doohuria, Khokra, Baddura, Chajira, Ramdeva, Kabria, Hatoondia, Malavat, Soondu, Kataicha, Muholi, Gogadeva, Mahaicha, Jeysinga, Moorsia, Jobsia, Jora, etc., etc.

Rahtore Gotra Acharya.—Gotama [1] Gotra (race),—Mardwunduni Sac'ha

[1] From this I should be inclined to pronounce the Rahtores descendants of a race (probably Scythic) professing the Boohdist faith, of which Gotama was the last great teacher, and disciple of the last Boodha Mahivira, in S. 477 (A.D. 533).

(branch),—Sookra-acharya Gooru (Regent of the planet Venus, Preceptor), —Garroopata Agni,[1]—Pankhani Devi (tutelary goddess, winged).

CUSHWAHA.—The Cushwaha race [2] is descended from Cush, the second son of Rama. They are the Cushites,[3] as the Rajpoots of Méwar are the Lavites of India.

Two branches migrated from Kosula : one founded Rotas on the Sone, the other established a colony amidst the ravines of the Cohari, at Lahar.[4]

In the course of time they erected the celebrated fortress of Nirwur, or Nirwar, the abode of the celebrated Raja Nala, whose descendants continued to hold possession throughout all the vicissitudes of the Tatar and Moghul domination, when they were deprived of it by the Mahrattas, and the abode of Nala is now a dependency of Sindia.

In the tenth century a branch emigrated and founded Ambér, dispossessing the aborigines, the Meenas, and adding from the Rajpoot tribe Birgoojur, who held Rajore and large possessions around. But even in the twelfth century the Cushwahas were but principal vassals to the Chohan king of Dehli ; and they have to date their greatness, as the other families (especially the Ranas of Méwar) of Rajast'han their decline, from the ascent of the house of Timoor to the throne of Dehli.

The map shows the limits of the sway of the Cushwahas, including their branches, the independent Nirookas of Macherri, and the tributary confederated Shekhavats.

The Cushwaha subdivisions have been mislaid ; but the present partition into Kotrees (chambers), of which there are twelve, shall be given in their annals.

AGNICÚLAS.—1st. *Pramara.* There are four races to whom the Hindu genealogists have given Agni, or the element of fire, as progenitor. The Agnicúlas are therefore the sons of Vulcan, as the others are of Sol,[5] Mercurius, and Terra.

The Agnicúlas are the Pramara, the Purihara, the Chalook or Solanki, and the Chohan.

That these races, the sons of Agni, were but regenerated, and converted

[1] Enigmatical—' Clay formation by fire' (*agni*).

[2] Erroneously written and pronounced Cutchwaha.

[3] The resemblance between the Cushite Ramesa of Ayodia and the Rameses of Egypt is strong. Each was attended by his army of satyrs, Anubis and Cynocephalus, which last is a Greek misnomer, for the animal bearing this title is of the Simian family, as his images (in the Turin museum) disclose, and the brother of the faithful Hanooman. The comparison between the deities within the Indus (called *Nil-áb*, ' blue waters ') and those of the Nile in Egypt, is a point well worth discussion.

[4] A name in compliment, probably, to the elder branch of their race, Lava.

[5] There is a captivating elegance thrown around the theogonies of Greece and Rome, which we fail to impart to the Hindu ; though that elegant scholar, Sir William Jones, could make even Sanscrit literature fascinating ; and that it merits the attempt intrinsically, we may infer from the charm it possesses to the learned chieftain of Rajast'han. That it is perfectly analogous to the Greek and Roman, we have but to translate the names to show. For instance :—

Solar.		Lunar.
Mireecha	(Lux) . . .	Atri.
Kasyapa	(Uranus) . . .	Samudra (Oceanus).
Vaivaswama or Soorya .	(Sol)	Soma, or Ind (Luna ; *qu.* Lunus ?).
Vaivaswamasoot Manoo .	(Filius Solis) .	Vrishpati (Jupiter).
Ella	(Terra) . . .	Boodha (Mercurius).

by the Brahmins to fight their battles, the clearest interpretation of their allegorical history will disclose; and, as the most ancient of their inscriptions are in the Pali character, discovered wherever the Boodhist religion prevailed, their being declared of the race of Tusta or Takshac,[1] warrants our asserting the Agnicúlas to be of this same race, which invaded India about two centuries before Christ. It was about this period that Parswa, the twenty-third Boodha,[2] appeared in India; his symbol, the serpent.

The legend of the snake (Takshac) escaping with the celebrated work *Pingal*, which was recovered by Garoora, the eagle of Crishna, is purely allegorical; and descriptive of the contentions between the followers of Parswa, figured under his emblem, the snake, and those of Crishna, depicted under his sign, the eagle.

The worshippers of Soorya probably recovered their power on the exterminating civil wars of the Lunar races, but the creation of the Agnicúlas is expressly stated to be for the preservation of the altars of Bál, or Iswara, against the Dytes, or Atheists.

The celebrated Aboo, or Ar-boodha, the Olympus of Rajast'han, was the scene of contention between the ministers of Soorya and these Titans, and their relation might, with the aid of imagination, be equally amusing with the Titanic war of the ancient poets of the west.

The Boodhists claim it for Ad-nat'h, their first Boodha; the Brahmins for Iswara, or, as the local divinity styled Achil-es.[3]

The Agnicoonda is still shown on the summit of Aboo, where the four races were created by the Brahmins to fight the battles of Achil-es and polytheism, against the monotheistic Boodhists, represented as the serpents or Takshacs.

The probable period of this conversion has been hinted at; but of the dynasties issuing from the Agnicúlas, many of the princes professed the Boodhist or Jain faith, to periods so late as the Mahomedan invasion.

The Pramara, though not, as his name implies, the 'chief warrior,' was the most potent of the Agnicúlas. He sent forth thirty-five sachæ, or branches, several of whom enjoyed extensive sovereignties. 'The world is the Pramar's,' is an ancient saying, denoting their extensive sway; and the *No-kote*[4] *Maroost'hulli* signified the nine divisions into which the country, from the Sutledge to the ocean, was partitioned amongst them.

Mahéswar, Dhar, Mandoo, Oojein, Chandrabhaga, Cheetore, Aboo,

[1] Figuratively, 'the serpent.'

[2] To me it appears that there were four distinguished Boodhas or wise men, teachers of monotheism in India, which they brought from Central Asia, with their science and its written character, the arrow or nail-headed, which I have discovered wherever they have been,—in the deserts of Jessulmér, in the heart of Rajast'han, and the shores of Saurashtra; which were their nurseries.

The first Boodha is the parent of the Lunar race, A.C. 2250.
The second (twenty-second of the Jains), Naimnat'h, A.C. 1120.
The third (twenty-third do.), Parswanat'h, A.C. 650.
The fourth (twenty-fourth do.), Mahivira, A.C. 533.

[3] *Achil*, 'immovable,' *Es*, contracted from *eswara*, 'lord.'

[4] It extended from the Indus almost to the Jumna, occupying all the sandy regions, Nokote, Arboodha or Aboo, Dhát. Mundodri, Khyraloo, Parkur, Lodurva, and Poogul.

Chandravati, M'how Maidana, Parmavati, Omrakote, Bekher, Lodurva, and Puttun, are the most conspicuous of the capitals they conquered or founded.

Though the Pramara family never equalled in wealth the famed Solanki princes of Anhulwarra, or shone with such lustre as the Chohan, it attained a wider range and an earlier consolidation of dominion than either, and far excelled in all, the Purihara, the last and least of the Agnicúlas, which it long held tributary.

Mahéswar, the ancient seat of the Hya kings, appears to have been the first seat of government of the Pramaras. They subsequently founded Dharanagar, and Mandoo on the crest of the Vindhya hills ; and to them is even attributed the city of Oojein, the first meridian of the Hindus, and the seat of Vicrama.

There are numerous records of the family, fixing eras in their history of more modern times ; and it is to be hoped that the interpretation of yet undeciphered inscriptions may carry us back beyond the seventh century.

The era [1] of Bhoj, the son of Moonj, has been satisfactorily settled ; and an inscription [2] in the nail-headed character, carries it back a step farther,[3] and elicits an historical fact of infinite value, giving the date of the last prince of the Pramaras of Cheetore, and the consequent accession of the Gehlotes.

The Nerbudda was no limit to the power of the Pramaras. About the very period of the foregoing inscription, Ram Pramar held his court in Telungana, and is invested by the Chohan Bard, Chund, with the dignity of paramount sovereign of India, and head of a splendid feudal [4] association, whose members became independent on his death. The Bard makes this a voluntary act of the Pramaras ; but coupled with the Gehlote's violent acquisition of Cheetore, we may suppose the successor of Ram was unable to maintain such supremacy.

While Hindu literature survives the name of Bhoj Pramara and " the nine gems " of his court cannot perish ; though it is difficult to say which of the three [5] princes of this name is particularly alluded to, as they all appear to have been patrons of science..

Chandragoopta, the supposed opponent of Alexander, was a Mori, and in the sacred genealogies is declared of the race of Takshac. The ancient inscriptions of the Pramars, of which the Mori is a principal branch, declare it of the race of Tusta and Takshac, as does that now given from the seat of their power, Cheetore.[6]

[1] See *Transactions of the Royal Asiatic Society*, vol. i. p. 227.

[2] Which will be given in the *Transactions of the Royal Asiatic Society.*

[3] S. 770, or A.D. 714.

[4] " When the Pramar of Telung took sanctuary with Har, to the thirty-six tribes he made gifts of land. To Kehur he gave Kuttair, to Rae Puhar the coast of Sinde, to the heroes of the shell the forest lands. Ram Pramar of Telung, the Chukwa lord of Oojein, made the gift. He bestowed Dehli on the Tuárs, and Puttun on the Chawuras ; Sambhur on the Chohans, and Canouj on the Kamdhuj ; Mar-dés on the Purihar, Sorat on the Jadoo, the Dekhan on Jawula, and Cutch on the Charun."—*Poems of Chund.*

[5] The inscription gives S. 1100 (A.D. 1044) for the third Bhoj : and this date agrees with the period assigned to this prince in an ancient Chronogrammatic Catalogue of reigns embracing all the Princes of the name of Bhoj, which may therefore be considered authentic. This authority assigns S. 631 and 721 (or A.D. 575 and 665) to the first and second Bhoj.

[6] Herbert has a curious story of Cheetore being called Taxila ; thence the

Salivahana, the conqueror of Vicramaditya, was a Takshac, and his era set aside that of the Tuár in the Dekhan.

Not one remnant of independence exists to mark the greatness of the Pramaras : ruins are the sole records of their power. The prince of Dhát,[1] in the Indian desert, is the last phantom of royalty of the race ; and the descendant of the prince who protected Hemayoon, when driven from the throne of Timoor, in whose capital, Omrakote, the great Akber was born, is at the foot of fortune's ladder ; his throne in the desert, the footstool of the Bulotch, on whose bounty he is dependent for support.

Among the thirty-five sachæ of the Pramaras the Vihil was eminent, the princes of which line appear to have been lords of Chandravati, at the foot of the Aravulli.

The Rao of Bijolli, one of the sixteen superior nobles of the Rana's court, is a Pramara of the ancient stock of Dhar, and perhaps its most respectable representative.

THIRTY-FIVE SACHÆ OF THE PRAMARAS.

Mori.—Of which was Chandragoopta, and the princes of Cheetore prior to the Gehlotes.

Soda.—Sogdi of Alexander, the princes of Dhát in the Indian desert.

Sankla.—Chiefs of Poogul, and in Marwar.

Khyr.—Capital Khyraloo.

Oomra and Soomra.—Anciently in the desert, now Mahomedans.

Vehil, or Bihil.—Princes of Chandravati.

Maipawut.—Present chief of Bijolli in Méwar.

Bulhar.—Northern desert.

Kaba.—Celebrated in Saurashtra in ancient times, a few yet in Sirowi.

Omuta.—The princes of Omutwarra in Malwa, there established for twelve generations. Omutwarra is the largest tract left to the Pramaras. Since the war in 1817, being under the British interference, they cannot be called independent.

Réhar . . . . }
Dhoonda . . . . } Grasia petty chiefs in Malwa.
Soruteah . . . . }
Hurair . . . . }

Besides others unknown ; as Chaonda, Khejur, Sugra, Burkota, Pooni, Sampal, Bheeba, Kalpoosur, Kulmoh, Kohila, Pupa, Kahoria, Dhund, Déba, Burhur, Jeepra, Posra, Dhoonta, Rikumva, and Tyka. Many of these are proselytes to Islamism, and several beyond the Indus.

CHAHUMAN OR CHOHAN.—On this race so much has been said elsewhere,[2]

story of the Ranas being sons of Porus. I have an inscription from a temple on the Chumbul, within the ancient limits of Méwar, which mentions Taksilanagara, 'the stone fort of the Tak,' but I cannot apply it. The city of Thoda (Tonk, or properly Tanka) is called in the Chohan chronicles, Tákatpoor.

[1] Of the Soda tribe, a grand division of the Pramaras, and who held all the desert regions in remote times. Their subdivisions, Oomra and Soomra, gave the names to Omrakote and Oomrasomra, in which was the insular Bekher on the Indus : so that we do not misapply etymology, when we say in Soda we have the Sogdi of Alexander.

[2] See *Transactions of the Royal Asiatic Society*, vol. i. p. 133, "Comments on a Sanscrit Inscription."

that it would be superfluous to give more than a rapid sketch of them here.

This is the most valiant of the Agnicúlas, and it may be asserted not of them only, but of the whole Rajpoot race. Actions may be recorded of the greater part of each of the Chatees-cúla, which would yield to none in the ample and varied pages of history ; and though the 'Tulwar Rhatorán' would be ready to contest the point, impartial decision, with a knowledge of their respective merits, must assign to the Chohan the van in the long career of arms.

Its branches (sachæ) have maintained all the vigour of the original stem ; and the Haras, the Kheechees, the Deoras, the Sonigurras, and others of the twenty-four, have their names immortalised in the song of the bard.

The derivation of Chohan is coeval with his fabulous birth : 'the four-handed warrior.' (*Chatoor bhooja Chatoor-baha Vira.*) All failed when sent against the demons, but the Chohan, the last creation of the Brahmins to fight their battles against infidelity.

A short extract may be acceptable from the original respecting the birth of the Chohan, to guard the rites of our Indian Jove on this Olympus, the sacred Aboo : " the Gooru of mountains, like Soomér or Kylas, which Achilés made his abode. Fast but one day on its summit, and your sins will be forgiven ; reside there for a year, and you may become the preceptor of mankind."

Notwithstanding the sanctity of Aboo, and the little temptation to disturb the anchorites of Bál, " the Moonis, who passed their time in devotion, whom desire never approached, who drew support from the cow, from roots, fruits, and flowers," yet did the Dytes, envying their felicity, render the sacrifice impure, and stop in transit the share of the gods.

" The Brahmins dug the pit for burnt-sacrifice to the south-west (nyrut) ; but the demons [1] raised storms which darkened the air and filled it with clouds of sand, showering ordure, blood, bones and flesh, with every impurity, on their rites. Their penance was of no avail."

Again they kindled the sacred fire ; and the priests, assembling round the *Agnicoonda*,[2] prayed for aid to Mahadeo.

" From the fire-fountain a figure issued forth, but he had not a warrior's mien. The Brahmins placed him as guardian of the gate, and thence his name, Prit'hiha-dwara.[3] A second issued forth, and being formed in the palm (*chaloo*) of the hand was named Chalooka. A third appeared and was named Pramara.[4] He had the blessing of the Rics, and with the others went against the demons, but they did not prevail.

" Again Vasishta, seated on the lotus, prepared incantations ; again he called the gods to aid : and, as he poured forth the libation, a figure arose, lofty in stature, of elevated front, hair like jet, eyes rolling, breast expanded, fierce, terrific, clad in armour, quiver filled, a bow in one hand

[1] Asoora-Dyte, which Titans were either the aboriginal Bhils or the Scythic hordes.

[2] I have visited this classic spot in Hindu mythology. An image of Ad-pal (the 'first-created'), in marble, still adorns its embankment, and is a piece of very fine sculpture. It was too sacred a relic to remove.

[3] 'Portal or door (*dwar*) of the earth'; contracted to Prit'hihara and Purihara.

[4] 'The first striker.'

and a brand in the other, quadriform (*Chatooranga*),[1] whence his name, *Chohan*.

"Vasishta prayed that his hope [2] might be at length fulfilled, as the Chohan was despatched against the demons. Sacti-devi [3] on her lion, armed with the trident, descended, and bestowed her blessing on the Chohan, and as Asapoorna, or Kalka, promised always to hear his prayer. He went against the demons; their leaders he slew. The rest fled, nor halted till they reached the depths of hell. Anhul slew the demons. The Brahmins were made happy; and of his race was Pirthwirájá."

The genealogical tree of the Chohans exhibits thirty-nine princes, from Anhul, the first created Chohan, to Pirthwirájá, the last of the Hindu emperors of India.[4] But whether the chain is entire we cannot say. The inference is decidedly against its being so; for this creation or regeneration is assigned to an age centuries anterior to Vicramaditya: and we may safely state these converts to be of the Takshac race, invaders of India at a very early period.

Ajipál is a name celebrated in the Chohan chronicles, as the founder of the fortress of Ajmér, one of the earliest establishments of Chohan power.

Sambhur,[5] on the banks of the extensive salt lake of the same name, was probably anterior to Ajmér, and yielded an epithet to the princes of this race, who were styled Sambri Rao. These continued to be the most important places of Chohan power, until the translation of Pirthwirájá to the imperial throne of Dehli threw a parting halo of splendour over the last of its independent kings. There were several princes whose actions emblazon the history of the Chohans. Of these was Manika Rae, who first opposed the progress of the Mahomedan arms. Even the history of the conquerors records that the most obstinate opposition which the arms of Mahmoud of Ghizni encountered was from the prince of Ajmér,[6] who forced him to retreat, foiled and disgraced, from this celebrated stronghold, in his destructive route to Saurashtra.

The attack on Manika Rae appears to have been by Kasim, the general of Walid, on the close of the first century of the Hegira. The second attack was at the end of the fourth century. A third was during the reign of Beesuldeva, who headed a grand confederacy of the Rajpoot princes against the foes of their religion. The celebrated Udya Dit Pramar is enumerated amongst the chiefs acting in subserviency to the Chohan prince on this occasion, and as his death has been fixed by unerring records in A.D. 1096, this combination must have been against the Islamite king Modud, the fourth from Mahmoud; and to this victory is the allusion in the inscription on the ancient pillar of Dehli. But these irruptions continued to the captivity and death of the last of the Chohans. whose reign exhibits a splendid picture of feudal manners.

The Chohans sent forth twenty-four branches, of whom the most

[1] *Chatoor* or *Cha*, 'four'; *Anga*, 'body.'

[2] *Asa*, 'hope,' *Poorna*, to 'fulfil'; whence the tutelary goddess of the Chohan race, Assapoorna.

[3] The goddess of energy (*Sacti*).

[4] Born in S. 1215, or A.D. 1159.

[5] A name derived from the goddess Sacambari, the tutelary divinity of the tribes, whose statue is in the middle of the lake.

[6] Dherma Dheraj, father of Beesuldeva, must have been the defender on this occasion

celebrated are the existing families of Boondi and Kotah, in the division termed Haravati. They have well maintained the Chohan reputation for valour. Six princely brothers shed their blood in one field, in the support of the aged Shah Jehan against his rebellious son Arungzéb, and of the six but one survived his wounds.

The Kheechees of Gagrown and Ragoogurh, the Deoras of Sirohi, the Sonagurras of Jhalore, the Chohans of Sooe Bah and Sanchore, and the Pawaitchas of Pawagurh, have all immortalised themselves by the most heroic and devoted deeds. Most of these families yet exist, brave as in the days of Pirthwirájá.

Many chiefs of the Chohan race abandoned their faith to preserve their lands, the Kaim-Khani,[1] the Surwanis, the Lowanis, the Kururwanis, and the Baidwanas, chiefly residing in Shekavati, are the most conspicuous. No less than twelve petty princes thus deserted their faith: which, however, is not contrary to the Rajpoot creed; for even Menu says, they may part with wife to preserve their land. Eesurdas, nephew of Pirthwirájá, was the first who set this example.

Twenty-four Sachæ of the Chohans.—Chohan, Hara, Kheechee, Sonigurra, Deora, Pabia, Sanchora, Goelwal, Bhadoria, Nurbhan, Malani, Poorbea, Soora, Madraetcha, Sankraetcha, B'hooraetcha, Balaetcha, Tussairah, Chachairah, Rosiah, Chundu, Nacoompa, Bhawur, and Bankut.

Chalook or Solanki.—Though we cannot trace the history of this branch of the Agnicúlas to such periods of antiquity as the Pramara or Chohan, it is from the deficiency of materials, rather than any want of celebrity, that we are unable to place it, in this respect, on a level with them. The tradition of the bard makes the Solankis important as princes of Sooru on the Ganges, ere the Rahtores obtained Canouj. The genealogical test[2] claims Lokote, said to be the ancient Lahore, as a residence, which makes them of the same Sacha (Madwuni) as the Chohans. Certain it is, that in the eighth century we find the Langahas[3] and Togras inhabiting Moolt'han and the surrounding country, the chief opponents of the Bhattis on their establishment in the desert. They were princes of Calian, on the Malabar coast,[4] which city still exhibits vestiges of ancient grandeur. It was from Calian that a scion of the Solanki tree was taken, and engrafted on the royal stem of the Chawuras of Anhulwarra Puttun.

It was in S. 987 (A.D. 931) that Bhojraj, the last of the Chawuras, and the Salic law of India were both set aside, to make way for the young Solanki, Moolraj,[5] who ruled Anhulwarra for the space of fifty-eight years. During the reign of his son and successor, Chaond Rae,[6] Mahmood of Ghizni carried his desolating arms into the kingdom of Anhulwarra. With

[1] About Futtehpoor Jhoon-joonee.

[2] Solanki Gotra Acharya is thus:—"Madwuni Sacha—Bardhwaj Gotra—Gur'h Lokote nékas—Sarasvati Nadi (river)—Sham Véda—Kapliswar Déva—Carduman Rikéswar—Teen Purwur Zénar (zone of three threads)—Keonj Devi—Maipal Pootra (one of the Penates)."

[3] Called Malkhani, being the sons of Mal Khan, the first apostate from his faith to Islamism. Whether these branches of the Solankis were compelled to quit their religion, or did it voluntarily, we know not.

[4] Near Bombay.

[5] Son of Jey Sing Solanki, the emigrant prince of Calian, who married the daughter of Bhojraj. These particulars are taken from a valuable little geographical and historical treatise, incomplete and without title.

[6] Called Jamund by Mahomedan historians.

its wealth he raised those magnificent trophies of his conquest, among which the "Celestial Bride" might have vied with any thing ever erected by man as a monument of folly. The wealth abstracted, as reported in the history of the conquerors, by this scourge of India, though deemed incredible, would obtain belief, if the commercial riches of Anhulwarra could be appreciated. It was to India what Venice was to Europe, the entrepôt of the products of both the eastern and western hemispheres. It fully recovered the shock given by Mahmood and the desultory wars of his successors; and we find Sid Rae Jey Sing,[1] the seventh from the founder, at the head of the richest, if not the most warlike, kingdom of India. Two and twenty principalities at one time owned his power, from the Carnatic to the base of the Himalaya Mountains; but his unwise successor drew upon himself the vengeance of the Chohan, Pirthwirájá, a slip of which race was engrafted, in the person of Komarpál, on the genealogical tree of the Solankis; and it is a curious fact that this dynasty of the Balica-raes alone gives us two examples of the Salic law of India being violated. Komarpál, installed on the throne of Anhulwarra, "tied round his head the turban of the Solanki." He became of the tribe into which he was adopted. Komarpál, as well as Sid Rae, was the patron of Boodhism; and the monuments erected under them and their successors claim our admiration, from their magnificence and the perfection of the arts; for, at no period, were they more cultivated than at the courts of Anhulwarra.

The lieutenants of Shabudin disturbed the close of Komarpál's reign; and his successor, Ballo Mooldeo, closed this dynasty in S. 1284 (A.D. 1228), when a new dynasty, called the Baghéla (descendants of Sid Rae) under Beesildeo, succeeded. The dilapidations from religious persecution were repaired; Somnat'h, renowned as Delphos of old, rose from its ruins, and the kingdom of the Balica-raes was attaining its pristine magnificence, when, under the fourth prince, Gehla Kurrun, the angel of destruction appeared in the shape of Alla-udin, and the kingdom of Anhulwarra was annihilated. The lieutenants of the Tatar despot of Dehli let loose the spirit of intolerance and avarice on the rich cities and fertile plains of Guzzerat and Saurashtra. In contempt of their faith, the altar of an Islamite Derveish was placed in contact with the shrine of Ad-nat'h, on the most accessible of their sacred mounts:[2] the statues of Boodha were thrown down, and the books containing the mysteries of their faith suffered the same fate as the Alexandrian library. The walls of Anhulwarra were demolished; its foundations excavated, and again filled up with the fragments of their ancient temples.[3]

The remnants of the Solanki dynasty were scattered over the land, and this portion of India remained for upwards of a century without any paramount head, until, by a singular dispensation of Providence, its splendour was renovated, and its foundations rebuilt, by an adventurer

[1] He ruled from S. 1150 to 1201. It was his court that was visited by El Edrisi, commonly called the Nubian geographer, who particularly describes this prince as following the tenets of Boodha.

[2] Satrunjya.

[3] In 1822 I made a journey to explore the remains of antiquity in Saurashtra. I discovered a ruined suburb of the ancient Puttun still bearing the name of *Anurwara*, the *Nehrwara*, which D'Anville had "fort à cœur de retrouver." I meditate a separate account of this kingdom, and the dynasties which governed it.

of the same race from which the Agnicúlas were originally converts, though Seharun the Ták hid his name and his tribe under his new epithet of Zuffir Khan, and as Mozuffir ascended the throne of Guzzerat, which he left to his son. This son was Ahmed, who founded Ahmedabad, whose most splendid edifices were built from the ancient cities around it.

Though the stem of the Solankis was thus uprooted, yet was it not before many of its branches (Sachæ), like their own indigenous burr-tree, had fixed themselves in other soils. The most conspicuous of these is the Bhagéla [1] family, which gave its name to an entire division of Hindust'han; and Bhagélkhund has now been ruled for many centuries by the descendants of Sid Rae.

Besides Bandoogurh, there are minor chieftainships still in Guzzerat of the Bhagéla tribe. Of these, Peetapoor and Theraud are the most conspicuous. One of the chieftains of the second class in Méwar is a Solanki, and traces his line immediately from Sid Rae: this is the chief of Roopnagurh,[2] whose stronghold commands one of the passes leading to Marwar, and whose family annals would furnish a fine picture of the state of border-feuds. Few of them, till of late years, have died natural deaths.

The Solanki is divided into sixteen branches.

1. Bhagéla—Raja of Bhagélkhund (capital Bandoogurh), Raos of Peetapoor, Theraud, and Adaluj, etc.
2. Beerpoora—Rao of Lunawarra.
3. Behila—Kulianpoor in Méwar, styled Rao, but serving the chief of Saloombra.
4. Bhoorta [3] } In Baroo, Tekra, and Chahir, in Jessulmér.
5. Kalacha [3] }
6. Langaha—Mooslims about Mooltan.
7. Togru—Mooslims in the Punjnud.
8. Briku. " "
9. Soorki—In Dekhan.
10. Sirwureah [4]—Girnar in Saurashtra.
11. Raoka—Thoda in Jeipoor.
12. Ranikia—Daisoori in Méwar.
13. Kharura—Allote and Jawura, in Malwa.
14. Tantia—Chandbhur Sakunbari.[5]
15. Almetcha—No land.
16. Kúlamor—Guzzerat.

Pritihara or Purihara.—Of this, the last and least of the Agnicúlas, we have not much to say. The Puriharas never acted a conspicuous part in the history of Rajast'han. They are always discovered in a subordinate capacity, acting in feudal subjection to the Tuárs of Dehli or the Chohans of Ajmér; and the brighest page of their history is the record of an abortive

[1] The name of this subdivision is from Bhag Rao, the son of Sid Rae; though the bards have another tradition for its origin.

[2] I knew this chieftain well, and a very good specimen he is of the race. He is in possession of the famous war-shell of Jey Sing, which is an heirloom.

[3] Famous robbers in the deserts, known as the Maldoots.

[4] Celebrated in traditional history.

[5] Desperate robbers. I saw this place fired and levelled in 1807, when the noted Kureem Pindarree was made prisoner by Sindia. It afterwards cost some British blood in 1817.

attempt of Nahur Rao to maintain his independence against Pirthwirájá. Though a failure, it has immortalised his name, and given to the scene of action,[1] one of the passes of the Aravulli, a merited celebrity.

Mundawur [1] (classically Mundodri) was the capital of the Purihars, and was the chief city of Marwar which owned the sway of this tribe prior to the invasion and settlement of the Rahtores. It is placed five miles northward of the modern Jodpoor, and preserves some specimens of the ancient Pali character, fragments of sculpture and Jain temples.

The Rahtore emigrant princes of Canouj found an asylum with the Purihars. They repaid it by treachery, and Chonda, a name celebrated in the Rahtore annals, dispossessed the last of the Purihars, and pitched the flag of the Rahtores on the battlements of Mundawur.

The power of the Purihars had, however, been much reduced previously by the princes of Méwar, who not only abstracted much territory from them, but assumed the title of its princes—Rana.[2]

The Purihara is scattered over Rajast'han, but I am unaware of the existence of any independent chieftainship there. At the confluence of the Cohari, the Sinde, and the Chumbul, there is a colony of this race, which has given its name to a commune of twenty-four villages, besides hamlets, situated amidst the ravines of these streams. They were nominally subjects of Sindia ; but it was deemed requisite for the line of defence along the Chumbul that it should be included within the British demarcation, by which we incorporated with our rule the most notorious body of thieves in the annals of T'hug history.

The Purihars had twelve subdivisions, of which the chief were the Indoh and Sindhil : a few of both are still to be found about the banks of the Loony.

CHAWURA OR CHAURA.—This tribe was once renowned in the history of India, though its name is now scarcely known, or only in the chronicles of the bard. Of its origin we are in ignorance. It belongs neither to the Solar nor Lunar race, and consequently we may presume it to be of Scythic origin. The name is unknown in Hindust'han, and is confined, with many others originating from beyond the Indus, to the peninsula of Saurashtra. If foreign to India proper, its establishment must have been at a remote period, as we find individuals of it intermarrying with the Sooryavansa ancestry of the present princes of Méwar, when this family were the lords of Balabhi.

The capital of the Chawuras was the insular Deobunder, on the coast of Saurashtra, and the celebrated temple of Somnat'h, with many others on this coast, dedicated to Bálnat'h, or the sun, is attributed to this tribe of the Sauras,[3] or worshippers of the sun ; most probably the generic name of the tribe as well as of the peninsula.[4]

[1] Though now desolate, the walls of this fortress attest its antiquity, and it is a work that could not be undertaken in this degenerate age. The remains of it bring to mind those of Volterra or Cortona, and other ancient cities of Tuscany : enormous squared masses of stone without any cement.

[2] This was in the thirteenth century, when Mundawur was captured, and its prince slain, by the *Rawul* of Cheetore.

[3] The Συροι of the Greek writers on Bactria, the boundary of the Bactrian kingdom under Apollodotus. On this see the paper on Grecian medals in the *Transactions of the Royal Asiatic Society*, vol. i.

[4] Many of the inhabitants of the south and west of India cannot pronounce

By a natural catastrophe, or as the Hindu superstitious chroniclers will have it, as a punishment for the piracies of the prince of Deo, the element whose privilege he abused rose and overwhelmed his capital. As all this coast is very low, such an occurrence is not improbable; though the abandonment of Deo might have been compelled by the irruptions of the Arabians, who at this period carried on a trade with these parts, and the plunder of some of their vessels may have brought this punishment on the Chawuras. That it was owing to some such political catastrophe, we have additional grounds for belief from the annals of Méwar, which state that its princes inducted the Chawuras into the seats of the power they abandoned on the continent and peninsula of Saurashtra.

At all events, the prince of Deo laid the foundation of Anhulwarra Puttun in S. 802 (A.D. 746), which henceforth became the capital city of this portion of India, in lieu of Balabhipoora, which gave the title of Balica-raes to its princes, the Balhara of the earlier Arabian travellers, and following them, the geographers of Europe.

Vena Raja (or, in the dialects, Bunraj), was this founder, and his dynasty ruled for one hundred and eighty-four years, when, as related in the sketch of the Solanki tribe, Bhoj Raj, the seventh from the founder, was deposed by his nephew. It was during this dynasty that the Arabian travellers [1] visited this court, of which they have left but a confused picture. We are not, however, altogether in darkness regarding the Chawura race, as in the Khoman Rassa, one of the chronicles of Méwar, mention is made of the auxiliaries under a leader named Chatunsi, in the defence of Cheetore against the first attack on record of the Mahomedans.

When Mahmood of Ghizni invaded Saurashtra and captured its capital, Anhulwarra, he deposed its prince, and placed upon the throne, according to Ferishta, a prince of the former dynasty, renowned for his ancient line and purity of blood, and who is styled Dabichalima; a name which has puzzled all European commentators. Now the Dabi was a celebrated tribe, said by some to be a branch of the Chawura, and this therefore may be a compound of Dabi Chawura, or the Chourasima, by some called a branch of the ancient Yadus.

This ancient connection between the Sooryavansi chiefs and the Chawuras, or Sauras, of Saurashtra, is still maintained after a lapse of more than one thousand years; for although an alliance with the Rana's family is deemed the highest honour that a Hindu prince can obtain, as being the first in rank in Rajast'han, yet is the humble Chawura sought out, even at the foot of fortune's ladder, whence to carry on the blood of Rama. The present heir-apparent of a line of 'one hundred kings,' the prince Jovana Sing, is the offspring of a Chawura mother, the daughter of a petty chieftain of Guzzerat.

It were vain to give any account of the present state of the families bearing this name. They must depend upon the fame of past days; to this we leave them.

TÂK OR TAKSHAC.—Takshac appears to be the generic term of the

the *ch*, and invariably substitute the *s*. Thus the noted Pindarrie leader Cheetoo was always called Seetoo by the Dekhanis. Again, with many of the tribes of the desert, the *s* is alike a stumbling-block, which causes many singular mistakes, when Jessulmér, the 'hill of Jessul,' becomes *Jehulmér*, 'the hill of *fools*.'

[1] *Rélations anciennes des Voyageurs*, par Remaudot.

race from which the various Scythic tribes, the early invaders of India, branched off. It appears of more ancient application than Gete, which was the parent of innumerable sachæ. It might not be judicious to separate them, though it would be speculative to say which was the primitive title of the races called Scythic, after their country, Sakatai or Saca-dwipa, the land of the great Gete.

Abulgazi makes Taunak,[1] the son of Turc or Targetai, who appears to be the Turishka of the *Pooráns* ; the Tukyuks of the Chinese historians, the nomadic Tochari of Strabo, who aided to overturn the Greek kingdom of Bactria, and gave their name to the grand division of Asia, Tocharistan[2] or Turkistan : and there is every appearance of that singular race, the Tajuk,[3] still scattered over these regions, and whose history appears a mystery, being the descendant of the Takshac.

It has been already observed, that ancient inscriptions in the Pali or Boodhist character have been discovered in various parts of Rajast'han, of the race called Tusta, Takshac, and Tâk, relating to the tribes, the Mori, Pramara, their descendants. *Naga* and *Takshac* are synonymous appellations in Sanscrit for the *snake*, and the Takshac is the celebrated Nagvansa of the early heroic history of India. The *Mahabharat* describes, in its usual allegorical style, the wars between the Pandus of Indraprest'ha and the Takshacs of the north. The assassination of Parikhita by the Takshac, and the exterminating warfare carried on against them by his son and successor, Janméja, who at last compelled them to sign tributary engagements, divested of its allegory,[4] is plain historical fact.

[1] Abulgazi says, when Noah left the ark he divided the earth amongst his three sons : Shem had Iran : Japhet, the country of " Kuttup Shamach," the name of the regions between the Caspian sea and India. There he lived two hundred and fifty years. He left eight sons, of whom Turc was the elder and the seventh Camari, supposed the Gomer of Scripture.

Turc had four sons ; the eldest of whom was Tanuk, the fourth from whom was Mogul, a corruption of Mungul, signifying *sad*, whose successors made the Jaxartes their winter abode. Under his reign no trace of the true religion remained : idolatry reigned everywhere. Oguz Khan succeeded.

The ancient Cimbri, who went west with Odin's horde of Jits, Cattis, and Su, were probably the tribes descended from Camari, the son of Turc.

[2] Tacash continued to be a proper name with the great Khans of Carazm (Chorasmia) until they adopted the faith of Mahomed. The father of Jellal, the foe of Jungheez Khan, was named Tacash. Tachkhund on the Jaxartes, the capital of Turkistan, may be derived from the name of the race.

Bayer says, " Tocharistan was the region of the Tochari, who were the ancient Τοχαροι (Tochari), or Ταχαροι (Tacharoi). Ammianus Marcellinus says, " many nations obey the Bactrians, whom the Tochari surpass."—*Hist. Reg. Bact.* p. 7.

[3] This singular race, the Tajuks, are repeatedly mentioned by Mr. Elphinstone, in his admirable account of the kingdom of Caubul. They are also particularly noticed as monopolising the commercial transactions of the kingdom of Bokhara, in that interesting work *Voyage d'Orenbourg à Bokhara*, the map accompanying which, for the first time, lays down authentically the sources and course of the Oxus and Jaxartes.

[4] The *Mahabharat* describes this warfare against the snakes literally : of which, in one attack, he seized and made a burnt-offering (hom) of twenty thousand. It is surprising that the Hindu will accept these things literally. It might be said he had but a choice of difficulties, and that it would be as impossible for any human being to make the barbarous sacrifice of twenty thousand of his species, as it would be difficult to find twenty thousand snakes for the purpose. The author's knowledge of what barbarity will inflict, leaves the fact of the human sacrifice, though not perhaps to this extent, not even improbable. In 1811 his duties called him to a survey amidst the ravines of the Chumbul,

When Alexander invaded India, he found the Parætakæ, the mountain (*pahar*) Tâk, inhabiting the Paropamisan range ; nor is it by any means unlikely that Taxiles,[1] the ally of the Macedonian king, was the chief (*es*) of the Tâks ; and in the early history of the Bhatti princes of Jessulmér, when driven from Zabulist'han, they dispossessed the Tâks on the Indus, and established themselves in their land, the capital of which was called Salbhanpoora ; and as the date of this event is given as 3008 of the Yoodishtra era, it is by no means unlikely that Salivahana, or Salbhan (who was a Takshac), the conqueror of the Tuár Vicrama, was of the very family dispossessed by the Bhattis, who compelled them to migrate to the south.

The calculated period of the invasion of the Takshacs, or Nag-vansa, under Sehesnag, is about six or seven centuries before the Christian era, at which very period the Scythic invasion of Egypt and Syria, " by the sons of Togarmah riding on horses " (the Aswas, or Asi), is alike recorded by the prophet Ezekiel and Diodorus. The Aboo Mahatma calls the Takshacs " the sons of Himachil," all evincing Scythic descent ; and it was only eight reigns anterior to this change in the Lunar dynasties of India, that Parswanat'h, the twenty-third Boodha, introduced his tenets into India, and fixed his abode in the holy mount Sarnet.[2]

Enough of the ancient history of the Tâk : we will now descend to more modern times, on which we shall be brief. We have already mentioned the Takshac Mori as being lords of Cheetore from a very early period ; and but a few generations after the Gehlotes supplanted the Moris, this palladium of Hindu liberty was assailed by the arms of Islam. We find amongst the numerous defenders who appear to have considered the cause of Cheetore their own, " the Tâk from Asérgurh." [3] This race appears to have retained possession of Asér for at least two centuries after this event, as its chieftain was one of the most conspicuous leaders in the array of Pirthwirájá. In the poems of Chund he is called the " standard-bearer, Tâk of Asér." [4]

This ancient race, the foe of Janméja and the friend of Alexander, closed its career in a blaze of splendour. The celebrity of the kings of

the tract call Goojurgar, a district inhabited by the Goojur tribe. Turbulent and independent, like the sons of Esau, their hand against every man and every man's hand against them, their nominal prince, Soorajmul, the Jit chief of Bhurtpore, pursued exactly the same plan towards the population of these villages, whom they captured in a night attack, that Janméja did to the Takshacs : he threw them into pits with combustibles, and actually thus consumed them ! This occurred not three quarters of a century ago.

[1] Arrian says that his name was Omphis, and that his father dying at this time, he did homage to Alexander, who invested him with the title and estates of his father Taxiles. Hence, perhaps (from *Tâk*), the name of the Indus, *Attac* ; not *Uttuc*, or ' forbidden,' according to modern signification, and which has only been given since the Mahomedan religion for a time made it the boundary between the two faiths.

[2] In Bahar, during the reign of Pradyota, the successor of Ripoonjya. Parswa's symbol is the serpent or Tackshac. His doctrines spread to the remotest parts of India, and the princes of Balabhipoora of Mundodri and Anhulwarra all held to the tenets of Boodha.

[3] This is the celebrated fortress in the Candeish, now in the possession of the British.

[4] In the list of the wounded at the battle of Canouj he is mentioned by name, as " Chatto the Tâk."

Guzzerat will make amends for the obscurity of the Tâks of modern times, of whom a dynasty of fourteen kings followed each other in succession, commencing and ending with the proud title of Mozuffir. It was in the reign of Mohammed,[1] son of the first Togluc, that an accident to his nephew Feroz proved the dawn of the fortunes of the Tâk; purchased, however, with the change of name and religion. Seharun the Tâk was the first apostate of his line, who, under the name of Wujeh ool Toolk concealed both his origin and tribe. His son, Zuffir Khan, was raised by his patron Feroz to the government of Guzzerat, about the period when Timoor invaded India. Zuffir availed himself of the weakness of his master and the distraction of the times, and mounted the throne of Guzzerat under the name of Mozuffir.[2] He was assassinated by the hand of his grandson, Ahmed, who changed the ancient capital, Anhulwarra, for the city founded by himself, and called Ahmedabad, one of the most splendid in the east.

With the apostasy of the Tâk,[3] the name appears to have been obliterated from the tribes of Rajast'han; nor has my search ever discovered one of this name now existing.

Jit.—In all the ancient catalogues of the thirty-six royal races of India the Jit has a place, though by none is he ever styled 'Rajpoot'; nor am I aware of any instance of a Rajpoot's intermarriage with a Jit. It is a name widely disseminated over India, though it does not now occupy a very elevated place amongst the inhabitants, belonging chiefly to the agricultural classes.

In the Punjâb they still retain their ancient name of *Jit.* On the Jumna and Ganges they are styled *Játs,* of whom the chief of Bhurtpoor is the most conspicuous. On the Indus and in Saurashtra they are termed *Juts.* The greater portion of the husbandmen in Rajast'han are Jits; and there are numerous tribes beyond the Indus, now proselytes to the Mahomedan religion, who derive their origin from this class.

Of its ancient history sufficient has been already said. We will merely add, that the kingdom of the great Gete, whose capital was on the Jaxartes, preserved its integrity and name from the period of Cyrus to the fourteenth century, when it was converted from idolatry to the faith of Islam. Herodotus informs us that the Getes were theists and held the tenet of the soul's immortality; and De Guignes,[4] from Chinese authorities, asserts that at a very early period they had embraced the religion of Fo or Boodha.

The traditions of the Jits claim the regions west of the Indus as the cradle of the race, and make them of Yadu extraction; thus corroborating the annals of the Yadus, which state their migration from Zabulist'han, and almost inducing as to dispense with the descent of this tribe from

[1] He reigned from A.D. 1325 to 1351. [2] 'The victorious.'

[3] The *Mirát Secundri* gives the ancestry of the apostate for twenty-three generations; the last of whom was Sehes, the same which introduced the Nagvansa, seven centuries before the Christian era, into India. The author of the work gives the origin of the name of Tâk, or Taunk, from *Tarka* 'expulsion,' from his caste, which he styles Khetri, evincing his ignorance of this ancient race.

[4] " The superiority of the Chinese over the Turks caused the great Khan to turn his arms against the Nomadic Getes of Mawer-ool-Nehr (Transoxiana), descended from the Yuchi, and bred on the Jihoon or Oxus, whence they had extended themselves along the Indus and even Ganges, and are there yet found. These Getes had embraced the religion of Fo."—*Hist. Gén. des Huns,* tom. i. p. 375.

Crishna, and to pronounce it an important colony of the Yuchi, Yuti, or Jits. Of the first migration from Central Asia of this race within the Indus, we have no record: it might have been simultaneous with the Takshac, from the wars of Cyrus or his ancestors.

It has been already remarked, that the Jit divided with the Takshac the claim of being the parent name of the various tribes called Scythic, invaders of India; and there is now before the author an inscription of the fifth century applying both epithets to the same prince,[1] who is invested moreover with the Scythic quality of worshipping the sun. It states, likewise, that the mother of this Jit prince was of Yadu race: strengthening their claims to a niche amongst the thirty-six Rajcúlas, as well as their Yadu descent.

The fifth century of the Christian era, to which this inscription belongs, is a period of interest in Jit history. De Guignes, from original authorities, states the Yuchi, or Jits, to have established themselves in the Punjáb in the fifth and sixth centuries, and the inscription now quoted applies to a prince whose capital is styled *Salindrapoora* in these regions; and doubtless the *Salivahanpoor* [2] where the Yadu Bhattis established themselves on the expulsion of the Tâk.

How much earlier than this the Jit penetrated into Rajast'han must be left to more ancient inscriptions to determine: suffice it, that in A.D. 440 we find him in power.[3]

When the Yadu was expelled from Salivahanpoora, and forced to seek refuge across the Sutledge among the Dahia and Johya Rajpoots of the Indian desert, where they founded their first capital, Derrawul, many from compulsion embraced the Mahomedan faith; on which occasion they assumed the name of *Ját*,[4] of which at least twenty different offsets are enumerated in the Yadu chronicles.

[1] "To my foe, salutation! This foe how shall I describe? Of the race of *Jit Cattida*, whose ancestor, the warrior Takshac, formed the garland on the neck of Mahadeva."

Though this is a figurative allusion to the snake necklace of the father of creation, yet it evidently pointed to the Jit's descent from the Takshac. But enough has been said elsewhere of the snake race, the parent of the Scythic tribes, which the divine Milton seems to have taken from Diodorus's account of the mother of the Scythæ:

> "Woman to the waist, and fair;
> But ended foul in many a scaly fold?"
> —*Paradise Lost*, Book ii.

Whether the *Jit Catti-da* is the Jit or Gete of Cathay (*da* being the mark of the genitive case) we will leave to conjecture.

[2] This place existed in the twelfth century as a capital; since an inscription of Komarpál, prince of Anhulwarra, declares that this monarch carried his conquests "even to Salpoor." There is Syal-kote in Rennell's geography, and Wilford mentions "Sangala, a famous city in ruins, sixty miles west by north of Lahore, situated in a forest, and said to be built by Pooru."

[3] At this time (A.D. 449) the Jut brothers, Hengist and Horsa, led a colony from Jutland and founded the kingdom of Kent (*qu. Cant'hi*, 'a coast,' in Sanscrit, as in Gothic *Konta* ?). The laws they there introduced, more especially the still prevailing one of gavelkind, where all the sons share equally, except the youngest who has a double portion, are purely Scythic, and brought by the original Goth from the Jaxartes.

Alaric had finished his career, and Theodoric and Genseric (*ric*, 'king,' in Sanscrit) were carrying their arms into Spain and Africa.

[4] Why should these proselytes, if originally Yadu, assume the name of Jit

That the Jits continued as a powerful community on the east bank of the Indus and in the Punjáb, fully five centuries after the period our inscription and their annals illustrate, we have the most interesting records in the history of Mahmoud, the conqueror of India, whose progress they checked in a manner unprecedented in the annals of continental warfare. It was in 416 of the Hegira (A.D. 1026) that Mahmoud marched an army against the Jits, who had harassed and insulted him on the return from his last expedition against Saurashtra. The interest of the account authorises its being given from the original.

"The Jits inhabited the country on the borders of Moolt'han, along the river that runs by the mountains of Joud.[1] When Mahmoud reached Moolt'han, finding the Jit country defended by great rivers, he built fifteen hundred boats,[2] each armed with six iron spikes projecting from their prows, to prevent their being boarded by the enemy, expert in this kind of warfare. In each boat he placed twenty arches, and some with fire-balls of naphtha to burn the Jit fleet. The monarch having determined on their extirpation, awaited the result at Moolt'han. The Jits sent their wives, children, and effects to Sind Sagur,[3] and launched four thousand, or, as others say, eight thousand boats well armed to meet the Guznians. A terrible conflict ensued, but the projecting spikes sunk the Jit boats while others were set on fire. Few escaped from this scene of terror; and those who did, met with the more severe fate of captivity."[4]

Many doubtless did escape; and it is most probable that the Jit communities, on whose overthrow the state of Bikanér was founded, were remnants of this very warfare.

Not long after this event the original empire of the Gete was overturned, when many fugitives found a refuge in India. In 1360, Togultash Timoor was the great Khan of the Gete nation; idolators even to this period. He had conquered Khorassan, invaded Transoxiana (whose prince fled, but whose nephew, Ameer Timoor, averted its subjugation), gained the friendship of Togultash, and commanded a hundred thousand Gete warriors. In 1369, when the Getic Khan died, such was the ascendancy obtained by Timoor over his subjects, that the Couraltai, or general assembly, transferred the title of Grand Khan from the Getic to the Chagitai Timoor. In 1370 he married a Getic princess, and added Kogend and Samarkand to his patrimony, Transoxiana. Rebellions and massacres almost depopulated this nursery of mankind, ere the Getes abandoned their independence; nor was it till 1388, after six invasions, in which he burnt

or Ját? It must be either that the Yadus were themselves the Scythic Yuti or Yuchi, or that the branches intermarried with the Jits, and consequently became degraded as Yadus, and the mixed issue bore the name of the mother.

[1] The Jiddoo ca Dang, 'or hills of Yadu,' mentioned in the sketch of this race as one of their intermediate points of halt when they were driven from India after the Mahabharat.

[2] Near the spot where Alexander built his fleet, which navigated to Babylon thirteen hundred years before.

[3] Translated by Dow, 'an island.' Sind Sagur is one of the Do-ábas of the Punjáb. I have compared Dow's translation of the earlier portion of the history of Ferishta with the original, and it is infinitely more faithful than the world gives him credit for. His errors are most considerable in numerals and in weights and measures; and it is owing to this that he has made the captured wealth of India appear so incredible.

[4] Ferishta, vol. i.

their towns, brought away their wealth, and almost annihilated the nation, that he felt himself secure.

In his expedition into India, having overrun great part of Europe, "taken Moscow, and slain the soldiers of the barbarous Ooroos," he encountered his old foes "the Getes, who inhabited the plains of Toheem, where he put two thousand to the sword, pursuing them into the desert and slaughtering many more near the Caggar." [1]

Still the Jit maintained himself in the Punjâb, and the most powerful and independent prince of India at this day is the Jit prince of Lahore, holding dominion over the identical regions where the Yuchi colonised in the fifth century. and where the Yadus, driven from Guzni, established themselves on the ruins of the Tâks. The Jit cavalier retains a portion of his Scythic manners, and preserves the use of the chukra or discus, the weapon of the Yadu Crishna in the remote age of the Bharat.

HUN OR HOON.—Amongst the Scythic tribes who have secured for themselves a niche with the thirty-six races of India, is the Hun. At what period this race, so well known by its ravages and settlement in Europe, invaded India, we know not. Doubtless it was in the society of many others yet found in the peninsula of Saurashtra, as the Catti, the Balla, the Macwahana, etc. It is, however, confined to the genealogies of that peninsula; for although we have mention of the Hun in the chronicles and inscriptions of India at a very early period, he failed to obtain a place in the catalogue of the northern bards.

The earliest notice of the tribe is in an inscription [2] recording the power of a prince of Behar, who, amidst his other conquests, "humbled the pride of the Huns." In the annals of the early history of Méwar, in the catalogue of princes who made common cause with this the chief of all the Rajpoots, when Cheetore was assailed in the first irruption of the Mahomedans, was Ungutsi, lord of the Huns, who led his quota on this occasion. De Guignes [3] describes *Ungut* as being the name of a considerable horde of Huns or Moguls; and Abulgazi says that the Tartar tribe who guarded the great wall of China were termed *Ungutti*, who had a distinct prince with high pay and honour. The countries inhabited by the Hiong-nou and the Ou-huon, the Turks and Moguls, called 'Tatar' from Tatan, the name of the country from the banks of the Irtish along the mountains of Altai to the shores of the Yellow Sea, are described at large by the historian of the Huns; following whom and other original sources, the historian of the Fall of Rome has given great interest to his narrative of their march into Europe. But those who are desirous to learn all that relates to the past history and manners of this people, must consult that monument of erudition and research, the Geography of Malte-Brun.[4]

[1] Abulgazi, vol. ii. chap. 16. After his battle with Sooltan Mahmoud of Dehli, Timoor gave orders, to use the word of his historian, "for the slaughter of a hundred thousand infidel slaves. The great mosque was fired, and the souls of the infidels were sent to the abyss of hell. Towers were erected of their heads, and their bodies were thrown as food to the beasts and birds of prey. At Mairta the infidel Guebres were flayed alive." This was by order of Tamerlane, to whom the dramatic historians of Europe assign every great and good quality!

[2] *Asiatic Researches*, vol. i. p. 136.

[3] *Hist Gén. des Huns*, tom. iii. p. 238.

[4] *Précis de Géographie universelle.* Malte-Brun traces a connection between the Hungarians and the Scandinavians, from similarity of language: "A ces

D'Anville,[1] quoting Cosmas the traveller, informs us, that the white Huns (λευκοὶ Οὔννοι)[2] occupied the north of India; and it is most probable a colony of these found their way into Saurashtra and Méwar.

It is on the eastern bank of the Chumbul, at the ancient Barolli, that tradition assigns a residence to the Hoon; and one of the celebrated temples at that place, called the Sengar Chaorie, is the marriage hall of the Hoon prince, who is also declared to have been possessed of a lordship on the opposite bank, occupying the site of the present town of Bhynsror. In the twelfth century the Huns must have possessed consequence, to occupy the place he holds in the chronicle of the princes of Guzzerat. The race is not extinct. One of the most intelligent of the living bards of India assured the author of their existence; and in a tour where he accompanied him, redeemed his pledge, by pointing out the residence of some in a village on the estuary of the Myhie, though degraded and mixed with other classes.[3]

We may infer that few convulsions occurred in Central Asia, which drove forth these hordes of redundant population to seek subsistence in Europe, without India participating in such overflow. The only singular circumstance is, by what means they came to be recognised as Hindus, even though of the lowest class. Soodra we cannot term them; for although the Catti and the Balla cannot be regarded as, or classed with Rajpoots, they would scorn the rank of Soodra.

Catti.—Of the ancient notices of this people much has been already said, and all the genealogists, both of Rajast'han and Saurashtra, concur in assigning it a place amongst the royal races of India. It is one of the most important tribes of the western peninsula, and which has effected the change of the name from Saurashtra to Cattiwar.

Of all its inhabitants the Catti retains most originality: his religion, his manners, and his looks, all are decidedly Scythic. He occupied, in the time of Alexander, that nook of the Punjab near the confluent five streams. It was against these Alexander marched in person, when he nearly lost his life, and where he left such a signal memorial of his vengeance. The Catti can be traced from these scenes to his present haunts. In the earlier portion of the annals of Jessulmér mention is made of their conflicts with the Catti; and their own traditions[4] fix their settlement in the Peninsula from the south-eastern part of the valley of the Indus, about the eighth century.

In the twelfth century the Catti were conspicuous in the wars with Pirthwirájá, there being several leaders of the tribe attached to his army, as well as to that of his rival, the monarch of Kanouj.[5] Though on this

siècles primitifs où les Huns, les Goths, les Jotes, les Ases, et bien d'autres peuples étaient réunis autour des anciens autels d'Odin." Several of the words which he affords us are Sanscrit in origin. Vol. vi. p. 370.

[1] *Eclaircissemens Géographiques sur la Carte de l'Inde*, p. 43.

[2] An orthography which more assimilates with the Hindu pronunciation of the name Huon, or Oun, than Hun.

[3] The same bard says that there are three or four houses of these Hoons at Tresaowee, three coss from Baroda; and the Kheechee bard, Mogjee, says their traditions record the existence of many powerful Hoon princes in India.

[4] The late Captain Macmurdo, whose death was a loss to the service and to literature, gives an animated account of the habits of the Catti. His opinions coincide entirely with my own regarding this race. See vol. i. p. 270, *Trans. Soc. of Bombay*.

[5] It is needless to particularise them here. In the poems of Chund, some

occasion they acted in some degree of subservience to the monarch of Anhulwarra, it would seem that this was more voluntary than forced.

The Catti still adores the sun, scorns the peaceful arts, and is much less contented with the tranquil subsistence of industry than the precarious earnings of his former predatory pursuits. The Catti was never happy but on horseback, collecting his *black mail*, lance in hand, from friend and foe.

We will conclude this brief sketch with Captain Macmurdo's character of this race. "The Catti differs in some respects from the Rajpoot. He is more cruel in his disposition, but far exceeds him in the virtue of bravery;[1] and a character possessed of more energy than a Catti does not exist. His size is considerably larger than common, often exceeding six feet. He is sometimes seen with light hair and blue-coloured eyes. His frame is athletic and bony, and particularly well adapted to his mode of life. His countenance is expressive, but of the worst kind, being harsh, and often destitute of a single mild feature."[2]

BALLA.—All the genealogists, ancient and modern, insert the Balla tribe amongst the Raj-culas. The *byrd*, or 'blessing,' of the bard is *Tatta Mooltan ca rao*,[3] indicative of their original abodes on the Indus. They lay claim, however, to descent from the Sooryavansi, and maintain that their great ancestor, Balla or Bappa, was the offspring of Lava, the eldest son of Ram; that their first settlement in Saurashtra was at the ancient Dhank, in more remote periods called Mongy Puttun; and that, in conquering the country adjacent, they termed it Baliakhetr (their capital Balabhipoora), and assumed the title of Balla-rae. Here they claim identity with the Gehlote race of Méwar: nor is it impossible that they may be a branch of this family, which long held power in Saurashtra. Before the Gehlotes adopted the worship of Mahadeo, which period is indicated in their annals, the chief object of their adoration was the sun, giving them that Scythic resemblance to which the Ballas have every appearance of claim.

The Ballas on the continent of Saurashtra, on the contrary, assert their origin to be Induvansa, and that they are the Balica-pootras who were the ancient lords of Arore on the Indus. It would be presumption to decide between these claims; but I would venture to surmise that they might be the offspring of Sehl, one of the princes of the Bharat, who founded Arore.

The Cattis claim descent from the Ballas: an additional proof of northern origin, and strengthening their right to the epithet of the bards, "Lords of Moolt'han and Tatta." The Ballas were of sufficient consequence in the thirteenth century to make incursions on Méwar, and the first exploit of the celebrated Rana Hamir was his killing the Balla chieftain of Choteela. The present chief of Dhank is a Balla, and the tribe yet preserves importance in the peninsula.

books of which I have translated and purpose giving to the public, the important part the Catti had assigned to them will appear.

[1] It is the Rajpoot of Cattiwar, not of Rajast'han, to whom Captain Macmurdo alludes.

[2] Of their personal appearance, and the blue eye indicative of their Gothic or Getic origin, the author will have occasion to speak more particularly in his personal narrative.

[3] 'Princes of Tatta and Mooltan.'

Jhala Macwahana.—This tribe also inhabits the Saurashtra peninsula. It is styled Rajpoot, though neither classed with the Solar, Lunar, nor Agni-cúla races; but though we cannot directly prove it, we have every right to assign to it a northern origin. It is a tribe little known in Hindust'han or even Rajast'han, into which latter country it was introduced entirely through the medium of the ancient lords of Saurashtra, the present family of Méwar: a sanction which covers every defect. A splendid act of self-devotion of the Jhala chief, when Rana Pertap was oppressed with the whole weight of Akbar's power, obtained, with the gratitude of this prince, the highest honours he could confer,—his daughter in marriage, and a seat on his right hand. That it was the act, and not his rank in the scale of the thirty-six tribes, which gained him this distinction, we have decided proof in later times, when it was deemed a mark of great condescension that the present Rana should sanction a remote branch of his own family bestowing a daughter in marriage on the Jhala ruler of Kotah.[1]

This tribe has given its name to one of the largest divisions of Saurashtra, Jhalawar, which possesses several towns of importance. Of these Bankanér, Hulwud, and Drangdra, are the principal.

Regarding the period of the settlement of the Jhalas tradition is silent, as also on their early history: but the aid of its quota was given to the Rana against the first attacks of the Mahomedans; and in the heroic history of Pirthwirájá we have ample and repeated mention of the Jhala chieftains who distinguished themselves in his service, as well as in that of his antagonist, and the name of one of these, as recorded by the bard Chund, I have seen inscribed on the granite rock of the sacred Girmar, near their primitive abodes, where we leave them.

There are several subdivisions of the Jhala, of which the Macwahana is the principal.

Jaitwa, Jétwa, or Camari.—This is an ancient tribe, and by all authorities styled Rajpoot; though, like the Jhala, little known out of Saurashtra, to one of the divisions of which it has given its name, Jaitwar. Its present possessions are on the western coast of the peninsula: the residence of its prince, who is styled Rana, is Poorbunder.

In remote times their capital was Goomlee, whose ruins attest considerable power, and afford singular scope for analogy, in architectural device, with the style termed Saxon of Europe. The bards of the Jaitwas run through a long list of one hundred and thirty crowned heads, and in the eighth century have chronicled the marriage of their prince with the Tuár refounder of Dehli. At this period the Jaitwa bore the name of Camar; and Sehl Camar is reported to be the prince who was driven from Goomlee, in the twelfth century, by invaders from the north. With this change the name of Camar was sunk, and that of Jaitwa assumed, which has induced the author to style them Camari; and as they, with the other inhabitants of this peninsula, have all the appearance of Scythic descent,

[1] His son, Madhu Sing, the present administrator, is the offspring of the celebrated Zalim and a Ranawut chieftain's daughter, which has entitled his (Madhu Sing's) issue to marry far above their scale in rank. So much does superiority of blood rise above all worldly considerations with a Rajpoot, that although Zalim Sing held the reins of the richest and best ordered state of Rajast'han, he deemed his family honoured by his obtaining to wife for his grandson the daughter of a Cutchwaha minor chieftain.

urging no pretensions to connection with the ancient races of India, they may be a branch of that celebrated race, the Cimmerii of higher Asia, and the Cimbri of Europe.

Their legends are as fabulous as fanciful. They trace their descent from the monkey-god Hanuman, and confirm it by alleging the elongation of the spine of their princes, who bear the epithet of *Pooncheria*, or the 'long-tailed,' Ranas of Saurashtra. But the manners and traditions of this race will appear more fully in the narrative of the author's travels amongst them.

GOHIL.[1]—This was a distinguished race: it claims to be Sooryavansi, and with some pretension. The first residence of the Gohils was Joonah Khérgurh, near the bend of the Loony in Marwar. How long they had been established here we know not. They took it from one of the aboriginal Bhil chiefs named Kherwo, and had been in possession of it for twenty generations when expelled by the Rahtores at the end of the twelfth century. Thence migrating to Saurashtra, they fixed at Perumgurh; which being destroyed, one branch settled at Bugwa, and the chief marrying the daughter of Nundun Nugger or Nandode, he usurped or obtained his father-in-law's estates; and twenty-seven generations are enumerated, from Sompál to Narsing, the present Raja of Nandode. Another branch fixed at Seehore, and thence founded Bhownugger and Gogo. The former town, on the gulf of the Myhie, is the residence of the Gohils, who have given their name, Gohilwar, to the eastern portion of the peninsula of Saurashtra.

The present chief addicts himself to commerce, and possesses ships which trade to the gold coast of Sofala.

SARWYA OR SARIASPA.—Of this race tradition has left us only the knowledge that it once was famous; for although, in the catalogues of the bard, it is introduced as the "essence of the Khetri race,"[2] we have only a few legends regarding its present degradation. Its name, as well as this epithet of the bard, induces a belief that it is a branch of the Aswas, with the prefix of *sár*, denoting 'essence,' or priority. But it is useless to speculate on a name.

SILAR OR SULAR.—Like the former, we have here but the shade of a name; though one which, in all probability, originated the epithet *Lariké*, by which the Saurashtra peninsula was known to Ptolemy and the geographers of early Europe. The tribe of Lar was once famous in Saurashtra, and in the annals of Anhulwarra mention is made of Sid Rae Jey Sing having extirpated them throughout his dominions. *Sular*, or *Silar*, would therefore be distinctively *the* Lar.[3] Indeed, the author of the *Komarpál Charitra* styles it *Raj-tilac*, or 'regal prince'; but the name only now exists amongst the mercantile classes professing the faith of Boodha: it is inserted as one of the eighty-four. The greater portion of these are of Rajpoot origin.

DABI.—Little can be said of this tribe, but that it was once celebrated in Saurashtra. By some it is called the branch of the Yadu, though all the genealogists give it distinct importance. It now possesses neither territory nor numbers.

[1] A compound word from Goh, 'strength'; Ela, 'the earth.'
[2] *Sarweya Khetrie tyn sár.*
[3] *Su*, as before observed, is a distinctive prefix, meaning 'excellent.'

Gor.—The Gor tribe was once respected in Rajast'han, though it never there attained to any considerable eminence. The ancient kings of Bengal were of this race, and gave their name to the capital, Luknowti.

We have every reason to believe that they were possessors of the land afterwards occupied by the Chohans, as they are styled in all the old chronicles the 'Gor of Ajmér.' Repeated mention is made of them in the wars of Pirthwirájá, as leaders of considerable renown, one of whom formed a small state in the centre of India, which survived through seven centuries of Mogul domination, till it at length fell a prey indirectly to the successes of the British over the Mahrattas, when Sindia, in 1809 annihilated the power of the Gor and took possession of his capital, Soopoor.[1] A petty district, yielding about £5000 annually, is all this rapacious head of a predatory government has left to the Gor, out of about twelve lacs of annual revenue. The Gor has five sacha: Ontahir, Silhala, Toor, Doosena, and Bodano.

Dor or Doda.—We have little to say of this race. Though occupying a place in all the genealogies, time has destroyed all knowledge of the past history of a tribe, to gain a victory over whom was deemed by Pirthwirájá worthy of a tablet.[2]

Gherwâl.—The Gherwál Rajpoot is scarcely known to his brethren in Rajast'han, who will not admit his contaminated blood to mix with theirs; though, as a brave warrior, he is entitled to their fellowship. The original country of the Gherwál is in the ancient kingdom of Cassi.[3] Their great ancestor was Khortaj Deva, from whom Jessonda, the seventh in descent, in consequence of some grand sacrificial rites performed at Bindabassi, gave the title of Boondéla to his issue. Boondéla has now usurped the name of Gherwál, and become the appellation of the immense tract which its various branches inhabit in Boondelkhund, on the ruins of the Chundailas, whose chief cities, Kalinjra, Mohini, and Mohoba, they took possession of.

The Chundaila, classed by some of the genealogists amongst the thirty-six tribes, were powerful in the twelfth century, possessing the whole of the regions between the Jumna and Nerbudda, now occupied by the Boondélas and Bhaghélas. Their wars with Pirthwirájá, forming one of the most interesting of his exploits, ended in the humiliation of the Chundéla, and prepared the way for their conquest by the Gherwáls; the date of the supremacy of the Boondéla Manvira was about A.D. 1200. Madhucar Sah, the thirteenth in descent from him, founded Orcha on the Bétwa, by whose son, Birsing Deva, considerable power was attained. Orcha became the chief of the numerous Boondéla principalities; but its

[1] In 1807 the author passed through this territory, in a solitary ramble to explore these parts, then little known; and though but a young *Sub.*, was courteously received and entertained both at Baroda and Soopoor. In 1809 he again entered the country under very different circumstances, in the suite of the British envoy with Sindia's court, and had the grief to witness the operations against Soopoor, and its fall, unable to aid his friends.

The Gor prince had laid aside the martial virtues. He became a zealot in the worship of Vishnu, left off animal food, was continually dancing before the image of the god, and was far more conversant in the mystical poetry of Crishna and his beloved Radha than in the martial song of the bard. His name was Radhaca-das, 'the slave of Radha'; and, as far as he is personally concerned, we might cease to lament that he was the last of his race.

[2] See *Transactions of Royal Asiatic Society*, vol. i. p. 133.

[3] Benares.

founder drew upon himself everlasting infamy, by putting to death the wise Abul Fuzil,[1] the historian and friend of the magnanimous Akbar, and the encomiast and advocate of the Hindu race.

From the period of Akbar the Boondélas bore a distinguished part in all the grand conflicts, to the very close of the monarchy: nor, amongst all the brave chiefs of Rajast'han, did any perform more gallant or faithful services than the Boondéla chieftains of Orcha and Duttea. Bagwan of Orcha commanded the advanced guard of the army of Shah Jehan. His son, Soopkurna, was Arungzebe's most distinguished leader in the Dekhan, and Dulput fell in the war of succession on the plains of Jajow. His descendants have not degenerated; nor is there anything finer in the annals of the chivalry of the West, than the dignified and heroic conduct of the father of the present chief.[2]

The Boondéla is now a numerous race, while the name Gherwál remains in their original haunts.

Birgoojur.—This race is Sooryavansi, and the only one, with the exception of the Gehlote, which claims from Lava, the elder son of Rama. The Birgoojur held considerable possessions in Dhoondar,[3] and their capital was the hill fortress of Rajore,[4] in the principality of Macherri. Rajgurh and Alwa were also their possessions. The Birgoojurs were expelled these abodes by the Cutchwahas. A colony found refuge and a new residence at Anopsher on the Ganges.

Sengar.—Of this tribe little is known, nor does it appear ever to have obtained great celebrity. The sole chieftainship of the Sengars is Jugmohunpoor on the Jumna.

Sikerwál.—This tribe, like the former, never appears to have claimed much notice amidst the princes of Rajast'han; nor is there a single independent chieftain now remaining, although there is a small district called after them, Sikerwár, on the right bank of the Chumbul, adjoining Jaduvati, and like it now incorporated in the province of Gwalior, in Sindia's dominions. The Sikerwál is therefore reduced to subsist by cultivation, or the more precarious employment of his lance, either as a follower of others, or as a common depredator.

They have their name from the town of Sikri (Futtehpoor), which was formerly an independent principality.

[1] Slain at the instigation of Prince Selim, son of Akbar, afterwards the Emperor Jehangir. See this incident stated in the emperor's own *Commentaries*.

[2] On the death of Madajee Sindia, the females of his family, in apprehension of his successor (Dowlut Rao), sought refuge and protection with the Raja of Duttea. An army was sent to demand their surrender, and hostility was proclaimed as the consequence of refusal. This brave man would not even await the attack, but at the head of a devoted band of three hundred horse, with their lances, carried destruction amongst their assailants, neither giving nor receiving quarter: and thus he fell in defence of the laws of sanctuary and honour. Even when grievously wounded, he would accept no aid, and refused to leave the field, but disdaining all compromise awaited his fate. The author has passed upon the spot where this gallant deed was performed; and from his son, the present Raja, had the annals of his house.

[3] Ambér or Jeipoor, as well as Macherri, were comprehended in Dhoondar, the ancient geographical designation.

[4] The ruins of Rajore are about fifteen miles west of Rajgurh. A person sent there by the author reported the existence of inscriptions in the temple of Nilkanta Mahadeo.

BYCE.—The Byce has obtained a place amongst the thirty-six races, though the author believes it but a subdivision of the Sooryavansi, as it is neither to be met with in the lists of Chund, nor in those of the *Komarpál Charitra*. It is now numerous, and has given its name to an extensive district, Bycewara in the Do-áb, or the land between the Ganges and Jumna.

DAHIA.—This is an ancient tribe, whose residence was the banks of the Indus, near its confluence with the Sutledge; and although they retain a place amongst the thirty-six royal races, we have not the knowledge of any as now existing. They are mentioned in the annals of the Bhattis of Jessulmér, and from name as well as from *locale*, we may infer that they were the Dahæ of Alexander.

JOYHA.—This race possessed the same haunts as the Dahia, and are always coupled with them. They, however, extended across the Garah into the northern desert of India, and in ancient chronicles are entitled "Lords of Jungul-Désa," a tract which comprehended Heriana, Bhatnair, and Nagore. The author possesses a work relative to this tribe, like the Dahia, now extinct.

MOHIL.—We have no mode of judging of the pretensions of this race to the place it is allowed to occupy by the genealogists. All that can be learned of its past history is, that it inhabited a considerable tract so late as the foundation of the present state of Bíkanér, the Rahtore founders of which expelled, if not extirpated, the Mohil. With the Malun, Malani, and Mallia, also extinct, it may claim the honour of descent from the ancient Malli, the foes of Alexander, whose abode was Moolt'han. (*Qu.* Mohil-t'han ?)

NICOOMPA.—Of this race, to which celebrity attaches in all the genealogies, we can only discover that they were proprietors of the district of Mandelgurh prior to the Gehlotes.

RAJ-PALI.—It is difficult to discover anything regarding this race, which, under the names of Raj-pali, Raj-palica, or simply Pala, are mentioned by all the genealogists; especially those of Saurashtra, to which in all probability it was confined. This tends to make it Scythic in origin; the conclusion is strengthened by the derivation of the name, meaning 'royal shepherd': it was probably a branch of the ancient Pali.[1]

DAHIRYA.—The *Komarpál Charitra* is our sole authority for classing this race with the thirty-six. Of its history we know nothing. Amongst the princes who came to the aid of Cheetore, when first assailed by the arms of Islam, was "the lord of Debeil, Dahir, *Despati*."[2] From the ignorance of the transcriber of the Gehlote annals, *Dehli* is written instead of *Debeil*; but we not only have the whole of the names of the Tuár race, but Dehli was not in existence at this time. Slight as is the mention of this prince in the Cheetore annals, it is nevertheless of high value, as stamping them with authenticity; for this Dahir was actually the *despot* of Sinde, whose tragical end in his capital Debeil is related by Abul Fuzil. It was in the ninety-ninth year of the Hegira that he was attacked by Cassim, the lieutenant of the Caliph of Bagdad, and treated with the greatest barbarity. Whether this prince used *Dahir* as a proper name, or as that of his tribe, must be left to conjecture.

[1] The final syllable *ca* is a mark of the genitive case.

[2] 'Chief of a country,' from *dés*, 'country,' and *pati*, 'chief.' (*Qu.* δεσπότης ?)

DAHIMA.—The Dahima has left but the wreck of a great name. Seven centuries have swept away all recollection of a tribe who once afforded one of the proudest themes for the song of the bard. The Dahima was the lord of Biana, and one of the most powerful vassals of the Chohan emperor, Pirthwirájá. Three brothers of this house held the highest offices under this monarch, and the period during which the elder, Kaimas, was his minister, was the brightest in the history of the Chohan: but he fell a victim to a blind jealousy. Poondir, the second brother, commanded the frontier at Lahore. The third, Chaond Rae, was the principal leader in the last battle, where Pirthwirájá fell, with the whole of his chivalry, on the banks of the Caggar. Even the historians of Shabudín have preserved the name of the gallant Dahima, Chaond Rae, whom they style Khandirai; and to whose valour, they relate, Shabudín himself nearly fell a sacrifice. With the Chohan, the race seems to have been extinguished. Rainsi, his only son, was by this sister of Chaond Rae, but he did not survive the capture of Dehli. This marriage forms the subject of one of the books of the bard, who never was more eloquent than in the praise of the Dahima.[1]

ABORIGINAL RACES.

Baugree, Mér, Kaba, Meena, Bhil, Sériah, T'hori, Khangar, Goand, Bhurr, Junwar, and Sarud.

AGRICULTURAL AND PASTORAL TRIBES.

Abhíra or Aheer, Goala, Koormi or Koolmbi, Goojur, and Jat.

RAJPOOT TRIBES TO WHICH NO SACHA IS ASSIGNED.

Jalia, Péshani, Sohagni, Chahira, Ran, Simala, Boteela, Gotchir, Malun, Ohir, Hool, Bachuk, Batur, Kéruch, Kotuk, Boosa, and Birgota.

CATALOGUE OF THE EIGHTY-FOUR MERCANTILE TRIBES.

Sri Sri Mal, Srimal, Oswal, Bhagairwal, Deendoo, Pooshkurwal, Mairtawal, Hursoruh, Soorurwal, Pilliwal, Bhumboo, Khundailwal, Dohilwal, Kehderwal, Deesawal, Goojurwal, Sohorwal, Uggurwal, Jaelwal, Manutwal, Kajotiwal, Kortawal, Chehtrawal, Soni, Sojutwal, Nagur, Mad, Julhéra, Lar, Kupole, Khuraita, Bururie, Dusora, Bamburwal, Nagudra, Kurbaira, Buttewura, Mewarra, Nursingpoora, Khaterwal, Punchumwal, Hunerwal, Sirkaira, Byce, Stukhi, Kumbowal, Jeerunwal, Bhagélwal, Orchitwal, Bamunwal, Sreegoor, Thakoorwal, Balmiwal, Tepora, Tilota, Atburgi, Ladisaka, Bednora, Kheecho, Gusora, Bahaohur, Jaimo, Pudmora,

[1] Chund, the bard, thus describes Biana, and the marriage of Pirthwirájá with the Dahimee: "On the summit of the hills of Druinadahar, whose awful load oppressed the head of Sehesnag, was placed the castle of Biana, resembling Kylas. The Dahima had three sons and two fair daughters: may his name be perpetuated throughout this iron age! One daughter was married to the Lord of Méwát, the other to the Chohan. With her he gave in dower eight beauteous damsels and sixty-three female slaves, one hundred chosen horses of the breed of Irak, two elephants, and ten shields, a pallet of silver for the bride, one hundred wooden images, one hundred chariots, and one thousand pieces of gold."

The bard, on taking leave, says: "the Dahima lavished his gold, and filled his coffers with the praises of mankind. The Dahimee produced a jewel, a gem without price, the Prince Rainsi."

The author here gives a fragment of the ruins of Biana, the ancient abode of the Dahima.

Meherea, Dhakurwal, Mungora, Goelwal, Mohorwal, Cheetora, Kakulea, Bharéja, Undora, Sachora, Bhoongrawal, Mundahulu, Bramunia, Bagria, Dindoria, Borwal, Sorbea, Orwal, Nufag, and Nagora. (One wanting.)

CHAPTER VIII

Reflections on the present political state of the Rajpoot tribes.

HAVING thus taken a review of the tribes which at various times inhabited and still inhabit Hindust'han, the subject must be concluded.

In so extensive a field it was impossible to introduce all that could have been advanced on the distinctive marks in religion and manners ; but this deficiency will be remedied in the annals of the most prominent races yet ruling, by which we shall prevent repetition.

The same religion governing the institutions of all these tribes operates to counteract that dissimilarity in manners, which would naturally be expected amidst so great a variety, from situation or climate ; although such causes do produce a material difference in external habit. Cross but the elevated range which divides upland Méwar from the low sandy region of Marwar, and the difference of costume and manners will strike the most casual observer. But these changes are only exterior and personal ; the mental character is less changed, because the same creed, the same religion (the principal former and reformer of manners), guides them all.

We have the same mythology, the same theogony, the same festivals, though commemorated with peculiar distinctions. There are niceties in thought, as in dress, which if possible to communicate would excite but little interest ; when the tie of a turban and the fold of a robe are, like Masonic symbols, distinguishing badges of tribes. But it is in their domestic circle that manners are best seen ; where restraint is thrown aside, and no authority controls the freedom of expression. But does the European seek access to this *sanctum* of nationality ere he gives his *debtor and creditor* account of character, his balanced catalogue of virtues and vices ? He may, however, with the Rajpoot, whose independence of mind places him above restraint, and whose hospitality and love of character will always afford free communication to those who respect his opinions and his prejudices, and who are devoid of that overweening opinion of self, which imagines that nothing can be learned from such friendly intercourse. The personal dissimilarity accordingly arises from *locale* ; the mental similarity results from a grand fixed principle, which, whatever its intrinsic moral effect, whatever its incompatibility with the elevated notions we entertain, has preserved to these races, as nations, the enjoyment of their ancient habits to this distant period. May our boasted superiority in all that exalts man above his fellows, ensure to our Eastern empire like duration ; and may these notions of our own peculiarly favoured destiny operate to prevent us from laying prostrate, in our periodical ambitious visitations, these the most ancient relics of civilisation on the face of the earth ! For the dread of their amalgamation with our empire will prevail, though such a result would be opposed not only to their happiness, but to our own stability.

With our present system of alliances, so pregnant with evil from their origin, this fatal consequence (far from desired by the legislative authorities at home) must inevitably ensue. If the wit of man had been taxed to devise a series of treaties with a view to an ultimate rupture, these would be entitled to applause as specimens of diplomacy.

There is a perpetual variation between the spirit and the letter of every treaty; and while the internal independence of each state is the groundwork, it is frittered away and nullified by successive stipulations, and these positive and negative qualities continue mutually repelling each other, until it is apparent that independence cannot exist under such conditions. Where discipline is lax, as with these feudal associations, and where each subordinate vassal is master of his own retainers, the article of military contingents alone, would prove a source of contention. By leading to interference with each individual chieftain, it would render such aid worse than useless. But this is a minor consideration to the tributary pecuniary stipulation, which unsettled and undetermined leaves a door open to a system of espionage into their revenue accounts—a system not only disgusting, but contrary to treaty, which leaves 'internal administration' sacred. These openings to dispute, and the general laxity of their governments coming in contact with our regular system, present dangerous handles for ambition; and who so blind as not to know that ambition to be distinguished must influence every vicegerent in the East? While deeds in arms and acquisition of territory outweigh the meek éclat of civil virtue, the periodical visitations to these kingdoms will ever be like the comet's,

"Foreboding change to princes."

Our position in the East has been, and continues to be, one in which conquest forces herself upon us. We have yet the power, however late, to halt, and not anticipate her further orders to march. A contest for a mud-bank has carried our arms to the *Aurea Chersonesus*, the limit of Ptolemy's geography. With the Indus on the left, the Brahmapootra to the right, the Himalayan barrier towering like a giant to guard the Tatarian ascent, the ocean and our ships at our back, such is our colossal attitude! But if misdirected ambition halts not at the Brahmapootra, but plunges in to gather laurels from the teak forest of Arracan, what surety have we for these Hindu states placed by treaty within the grasp of our control?

But the hope is cherished, that the same generosity which formed those ties that snatched the Rajpoots from degradation and impending destruction, will maintain the pledge given in the fever of success, "that their independence should be sacred"; that it will palliate faults we may not overlook, and perpetuate this oasis of ancient rule, in the desert of destructive revolution, of races whose virtues are their own, and whose vices are the grafts of tyranny, conquest, and religious intolerance.

To make them known is one step to obtain for them, at least, the boon of sympathy; for with the ephemeral power of our governors and the agents of government, is it to be expected that the rod will more softly fall when ignorance of their history prevails, and no kind association springs from a knowledge of their martial achievements and yet proud bearing, their generosity, courtesy, and extended hospitality? These are Rajpoot virtues yet extant amidst all their revolutions, and which have survived ages of Mahomedan bigotry and power; though to the honour of the virtuous and magnanimous few among the crowned heads of eight centuries, both Tatar and Mogul, there were some great souls; men of high worth, who appeared at intervals to redeem the oppression of a whole preceding dynasty.

The high ground we assumed, and the lofty sentiments with which we introduced ourselves amongst the Rajpoots, arrogating motives of purity, of disinterested benevolence, scarcely belonging to humanity, and to which their sacred writings alone yielded a parallel, gave such exalted notions of our right of exerting the attributes of divinity, justice, and mercy, that they expected little less than almighty wisdom in our acts; but circumstances have throughout occurred in each individual state, to show we were mere mortals, and that the poet's moral,

> "'Tis distance lends enchantment to the view,"

was true in politics. Sorrow and distrust were the consequences—anger succeeded; but the sense of obligation is still too powerful to operate a stronger and less generous sentiment. These errors may yet be redeemed, and our Rajpoot allies yet be retained as useful friends: though they can only be so while in the enjoyment of perfect internal independence, and their ancient institutions.

"No political institution can endure," observes the eloquent historian of the Middle Ages, "which does not rivet itself to the heart of men by ancient prejudices or acknowledged merit. The feudal compact had much of this character. In fulfilling the obligations of mutual assistance and fidelity by military service, the energies of friendship were awakened, and the ties of moral sympathy superadded to those of positive compact."

We shall throw out one of the assumed causes which give stability to political institutions; "acknowledged merit," which never belonged to the loose feudal compact of Rajwarra; but the absence of this strengthens the necessary substitute, "ancient prejudices," which supply many defects.

Our anomalous and inconsistent interference in some cases, and our non-interference in others, operate alike to augment the dislocation induced by long predatory oppression in the various orders of society, instead of restoring that harmony and continuity which had previously existed. The great danger, nay, the inevitable consequence of perseverance in this line of conduct, will be their reduction to the same degradation with our other allies, and their ultimate incorporation with our already too extended dominion.

It may be contended, that the scope and tenor of these alliances were not altogether unfitted for the period when they were formed, and our circumscribed knowledge; but was it too late, when this knowledge was extended, to purify them from the dross which deteriorated the two grand principles of mutual benefit, on which all were grounded, viz. "perfect internal independence" to them, and "acknowledged supremacy" to the protecting power? It will be said, that even these corner-stones of the grand political fabric are far from possessing those durable qualities which the contracting parties define, but that, on the contrary, they are the Ormuzd and Ahrimanes, the good and evil principles of contention. But when we have superadded pecuniary engagements of indefinite extent, increasing in the ratio of their prosperity, and armed quotas or contingents of their troops, whose loose habits and discipline would ensure constant complaint, we may certainly take credit for having established a system which must compel that direct interference, which the broad principle of each treaty professes to check.

The inevitable consequence is the perpetuation of that denationalising principle, so well understood by the Mahrattas, "*divide et impera.*" We are few; to use an Oriental metaphor, our agents must "use the eyes and ears of others." That mutual dependence, which would again have arisen, our interference will completely nullify. Princes will find they can oppress their chiefs, chiefs will find channels by which their sovereign's commands may be rendered nugatory, and irresponsible ministers must have our support to raise these undefined tributary supplies; and unanimity, confidence, and all the sentiments of gratitude which they owe, and acknowledge to be our due, will gradually fade with the national degradation. That our alliances have this tendency cannot be disputed. By their very nature they transfer the respect of every class of subjects from their immediate sovereign to the paramount authority and its subordinate agents. Who will dare to urge that a government, which cannot support its internal rule without restriction, can be national? that without power unshackled and unrestrained by exterior council or espionage, it can maintain self-respect, the corner-stone of every virtue with states as with individuals? This first of feelings these treaties utterly annihilate. Can we suppose such denationalised allies are to be depended upon in emergencies? or, if allowed to retain a spark of their ancient moral inheritance, that it will not be kindled into a flame against us when opportunity offers, instead of lighting up the powerful feeling of gratitude which yet exists towards us in these warlike communities?

Like us they were the natural foes of that predatory system which so long disturbed our power, and our preservation and theirs were alike consulted in its destruction. When we sought their alliance, we spoke in the captivating accents of philanthropy; we courted them to disunite from this Ahrimanes of political convulsion. The benevolent motives of the great mover of these alliances we dare not call in question, and his policy coincided with the soundest wisdom. But the treaties might have been revised, and the obnoxious parts which led to discord, abrogated, at the expense of a few paltry lacs of tribute and a portion of sovereign homage. It is not yet too late. True policy would enfranchise them altogether from our alliance; but till then let them not feel their shackles in the galling restraint on each internal operation. Remove that millstone to national prosperity, the poignant feeling that every increased bushel of corn raised in their long-deserted fields must send its tithe to the British granaries. Let the national mind recover its wonted elasticity, and they will again attain their former celebrity. We have the power to advance this greatness, and make it and its result our own; or, by a system unworthy of Britain, to retard and even quench it altogether.[1]

[1] If Lord Hastings' philanthropy, which rejoiced in snatching these ancient states from the degradation of predatory warfare, expected that in four short years order should rise out of the chaos of a century, and "was prepared to visit with displeasure all symptoms of internal neglect, arising from supineness, indifference, or concealed ill-will"; if *he* signified that "government would take upon itself the task of restoring order," and that "all changes" on this score "would

Never were their national characteristics so much endangered as in the seducing calm which followed the tempestuous agitations in which they had so long floated ; doubtful, to use their own figurative expression, whether " the gift of our friendship, or our arms," were fraught with greater evil. The latter they could not withstand ; though it must never be lost sight of, that, like ancient Rome when her glory was fading, we use " the arms of the barbarians " to defend our conquests against them ! Is the mind ever stationary ? are virtue and high notions to be acquired from contact and example ? Is there no mind above the level of £10 monthly pay in all the native legions of the three presidencies of India ? no Odoacer, no Sevaji, again to revive ? Is the book of knowledge and of truth, which we hold up, only to teach them submission and perpetuate their weakness ? Can we without fresh claims expect eternal gratitude, and must we not rationally look for reaction in some grand impulse, which, by furnishing a signal instance of the mutability of power, may afford a lesson for the benefit of posterity ?

Is the mantle of protection, which we have thrown over these warlike races, likely to avert such a result ? It might certainly, if embued with all those philanthropic feelings for which we took credit, act with soporific influence, and extinguish the embers of international animosity. "The lion and the lamb were to drink from the same fountain " ; they were led to expect the holy *Satya Yug*, when each man reposed under his own fig-tree, which neither strife nor envy dared approach.

When so many nations are called upon, in a period of great calamity and danger, to make over to a foreigner, their opposite in everything, their superior in most, the control of their forces in time of war, the adjudication of their disputes in time of peace, and a share in the fruits of their renovating prosperity, what must be the result ; when each Rajpoot may hang up his lance in the hall, convert his sword to a ploughshare, and make a basket of his buckler ? What but the prostration of every virtue ? It commences with the basis of the Rajpoot's,—the martial virtues ; extinguish these and they will soon cease to respect themselves. Sloth, low cunning and meanness will follow. What nation ever maintained its character that devolved on the stranger the power of protection ! To be great, to be independent, its martial spirit must be cherished ; happy if within the bounds of moderation. Led away by enthusiasm, the author experienced the danger of interference, when observing but one side of the picture—the brilliant lights which shone on their long days of darkness, not calculating the shade which would follow the sudden glare.

On our cessation from every species of interference alone depends their independence or their amalgamation—a crisis fraught with danger to our overgrown rule.

Let Alexander's speech to his veterans, tired of conquest and refusing to cross the Hyphasis, be applied, and let us not reckon too strongly on our empire of opinion : " Fame never represents matters truly as they are, but on the contrary magnifies everything. This is evident ; for our own

be demanded and rigidly exacted " : in fine, that " such arrangements would be made as would deprive them of the power of longer abusing the spirit of liberal forbearance, the motives of which they were incapable of understanding or appreciating " ; what have they to hope from those without his sympathies ?

reputation and glory, though founded on solid truth, is yet more obliged to rumour than reality." [1]

We may conclude with the Macedonian conqueror's reasons for showing the Persians and his other foreign allies so much favour : "The possession of what we got by the sword is not very durable, but the obligation of good offices is eternal. If we have a mind to keep Asia, and not simply pass through it, our clemency must extend to them also, and their fidelity will make our empire everlasting. As for ourselves, we have more than we know what to do with, and it must be an insatiable avaricious temper which desires to continue to fill what already runs over." [2]

[1] *Quintus Curtius.* lib. ix.

[2] *Ibid.* lib. viii.

SKETCH OF A FEUDAL SYSTEM IN RAJAST'HAN

CHAPTER I

Introduction—Existing condition of Rajast'han—General resemblance between the ancient systems of Asia and Europe—Noble origin of the Rajpoot race—Rahtores of Marwar—Cuchwahas of Ambér—Sesodias of Méwar—Gradation of ranks—Revenues and rights of the Crown—Burrar—Khur Lakur.

It is more than doubtful whether any code of civil or criminal jurisprudence ever existed in any of these principalities ; though it is certain that none is at this day discoverable in their archives. But there is a martial system peculiar to these Rajpoot states, so extensive in its operation as to embrace every object of society. This is so analogous to the ancient feudal system of Europe, that I have not hesitated to hazard a comparison between them, with reference to a period when the latter was yet imperfect. Long and attentive observation enables me to give this outline of a system, of which there exists little written evidence. Curiosity originally, and subsequently a sense of public duty (lest I might be a party to injustice), co-operated in inducing me to make myself fully acquainted with the minutiæ of this traditionary theory of government ; and incidents, apparently trivial in themselves, exposed parts of a widely extended system, which, though now disjointed, still continue to regulate the actions of extensive communities, and lead to the inference, that at one period it must have attained a certain degree of perfection.

Many years have elapsed since I first entertained these opinions, long before any connection existed between these states and the British government ; when their geography was little known to us, and their history still less so. At that period I frequently travelled amongst them for amusement, making these objects subservient thereto, and laying the result freely before my government. I had abundant sources of intelligence to guide me in forming my analogies ; Montesquieu, Hume, Millar, Gibbon :[1] but I sought only general resemblances and lineaments similar to those before me. A more perfect, because more familiar picture, has since appeared by an author,[2] who has drawn aside the veil of mystery which covered the subject, owing to its being till then but imperfectly understood. I compared the features of Rajpoot society with the finished picture of this eloquent writer, and shall be satisfied with having substantiated the claim of these tribes to participation in a system, hitherto deemed to belong exclusively to Europe. I am aware of the danger of

[1] *Miscellaneous Works*, vol. iii.

[2] Hallam's *Middle Ages*.

hypothesis, and shall advance nothing that I do not accompany by incontestible proofs.

The leading features of government amongst semi-barbarous hordes or civilised independent tribes must have a considerable resemblance to each other. In the same stages of society, the wants of men must everywhere be similar, and will produce the analogies which are observed to regulate Tatar hordes or German tribes, Caledonian clans, the Rajpoot Cúla (race), or Jhareja Bhyád (brotherhood). All the countries of Europe participated in the system we denominate feudal; and we can observe it, in various degrees of perfection or deterioration, from the mountains of Caucasus to the Indian ocean. But it requires a persevering toil, and more discriminating judgment than I possess, to recover all these relics of civilisation: yet though time, and still more oppression, have veiled the ancient institutions of Méwar, the mystery may be penetrated, and will discover parts of a system worthy of being rescued from oblivion.

Mahratta cunning, engrafted on Mahomedan intolerance, had greatly obscured these institutions. The nation itself was passing rapidly away: the remnant which was left had become a matter of calculation, and their records and their laws partook of this general decay. The nation may recover; the physical frame may be renewed; but the *morale* of the society must be recast. In this chaos a casual observer sees nothing to attract notice; the theory of government appears, without any of the dignity which now marks our regular system. Whatever does exist is attributed to fortuitous causes—to nothing systematic: no fixed principle is discerned, and none is admitted; it is deemed a mechanism without a plan. This opinion is hasty. Attention to distinctions, though often merely nominal, will aid us in discovering the outlines of a picture which must at some period have been more finished; when real power, unrestrained by foreign influence, upheld a system, the plan of which was original. It is in these remote regions, so little known to the Western world, and where original manners lie hidden under those of the conquerors, that we may search for the germs of the constitutions of European states.[1] A contempt for all that is Asiatic too often marks our countrymen in the East: though at one period on record the taunt might have been reversed.

In remarking the curious coincidence between the habits, notions, and governments of Europe in the Middle Ages, and those of Rajast'han, it is

[1] It is a high gratification to be supported by such authority as M. St. Martin, who, in his *Discours sur l'Origine et l'Histoire des Arsacides*, thus speaks of the system of government termed feudal, which I contend exists amongst the Rajpoots: "On pense assez généralement que cette sorte de gouvernement qui dominait il y a quelques siècles, et qu'on appelle *système féodal*, était particulière à l'Europe, et que c'est dans les forêts de la Germanie qu'il faut en chercher l'origine. Cependant, si au lieu d'admettre les faits sans les discuter, comme il arrive trop souvent, on examinait un peu cette opinion, elle disparaîtrait devant la critique, ou du moins elle se modifierait singulièrement; et l'on verrait que, si c'est des forêts de la Germanie que nous avons tiré le gouvernement féodal, il n'en est certainement pas originaire. Si l'on veut comparer l'Europe, telle qu'elle était au xiie. siècle, avec la monarchie fondée en Asie par les Arsacides trois siècles avant notre ère, partout on verra des institutions et des usages pareils. On y trouvera les mêmes dignités, et jusqu'aux mêmes titres, etc., etc. Boire, chasser, combattre, faire et défaire des rois, c'étaient là les nobles occupations d'un Parthe."—*Journal Asiatique*, vol. i. p. 65. It is nearly so with the Rajpoot.

not absolutely necessary we should conclude that one system was borrowed from the other ; each may, in truth, be said to have the patriarchal form for its basis. I have sometimes been inclined to agree with the definition of Gibbon, who styles the system of our ancestors the offspring of chance and barbarism. " Le système féodal, assemblage monstrueux de tant de parties que le tems et l'hazard ont réunies, nous offre un objet très compliqué : pour l'étudier il faut le décomposer." [1] This I shall attempt.

The form, as before remarked, is truly patriarchal in these states, where the greater portion of the vassal chiefs, from the highest of the sixteen peers to the holders of a *chursa* [2] of land, claim affinity in blood to the sovereign.[3]

The natural seeds are implanted in every soil, but the tree did not gain maturity except in a favoured aspect. The perfection of the system in England is due to the Normans, who brought it from Scandinavia, whither it was probably conveyed by Odin and the Sacasenæ, or by anterior migrations, from Asia ; which would coincide with Richardson's hypothesis, who contends that it was introduced from Tatary. Although speculative reasoning forms no part of my plan, yet when I observe analogy on the subject in the customs of the ancient German tribes, the Franks or Gothic races, I shall venture to note them. Of one thing there is no doubt—knowledge must have accompanied the tide of migration from the east : and from higher Asia emerged the Asi, the Catti, and the Cimbric Lombard, who spread the system in Scandinavia, Friesland, and Italy.

" It has been very common," says the enlightened historian of the Feudal System in the Middle Ages, " to seek for the origin of feuds, or at least for analogies to them, in the history of various countries : but though it is of great importance to trace the similarity of customs in different parts of the world, we should guard against seeming analogies, which vanish away when they are closely observed. It is easy to find partial resemblances to the feudal system. The relation of patron and client in the republic of Rome has been deemed to resemble it, as well as the barbarians and veterans who held frontier lands on the tenure of defending them and the frontier ; but they were bound not to an individual, but to the state. Such a resemblance of fiefs may be found in the Zemindars of Hindust'han and the Timariots of Turkey. The clans of the Highlanders and Irish followed their chieftain into the field : but their tie was that of imagined kindred and birth, not the spontaneous compact of vassalage." [4]

I give this at length to show, that if I still persist in deeming the Rajpoot system a pure relation of feuds, I have before my eyes the danger of seeming resemblances. By grants, deeds, charters, and traditions, copies of all of

[1] Gibbon, *Miscell.* vol. iii. Du governement féodal.

[2] A 'skin or hyde.' Millar (chap. v. p. 85) defines a 'hyde of land,' the quantity which can be cultivated by a single plough. A *chursa*, 'skin or hyde' of land, is as much as one man can water ; and what one can water is equal to what one plough can cultivate. If irrigation ever had existence by the founders of the system, we may suppose this the meaning of the term which designated a *knight's fee*. It may have gone westward with emigration.

[3] *Baupjée*, 'sire,' is the appellation of royalty, and, strange enough, whether to male or female ; while its offsets, which form a numerous branch of vassals, are called *bábás*, 'the infants.'

[4] Hallam's *Middle Ages*, vol. i. p. 200.

which will be found in the Appendix, will establish my opinions. I hope to prove that the tribes in the northern regions of Hindust'han did possess the system, and that it was handed down, and still obtains, notwithstanding seven centuries of paramount sway of the Mogul and Pat'han dynasties, altogether opposed to them except in this feature of government, where there was an original similarity. In some of these states—those least affected by conquest—the system remained freer from innovation. It is, however, from Méwar chiefly that I shall deduce my examples, as its internal rule was less influenced by foreign policy, even to the period at which the imperial power of Dehli was on the decline.

As in Europe, for a length of time, traditionary custom was the only regulator of the rights and tenures of this system, varying in each state, and not unfrequently (in its minor details) in the different provinces of one state, according to their mode of acquisition and the description of occupants when required. It is from such circumstances that the variety of tenure and customary law proceeds. To account for this variety, a knowledge of them is requisite; nor is it until every part of the system is developed that it can be fully understood. The most trifling cause is discovered to be the parent of some important result. If ever these were embodied into a code (and we are justified in assuming such to have been the case), the varied revolutions which have swept away almost all relics of their history were not likely to spare these. Mention is made of several princes of the house of Méwar who legislated for their country; but precedents for every occurring case lie scattered in formulas, grants, and traditionary sayings. The inscriptions still existing on stone would alone, if collected, form a body of laws sufficient for an infant community; and these were always first committed to writing, and registered ere the column was raised. The seven centuries of turmoil and disaster, during which these states were in continual strife with the foe, produced many princes of high intellect as well as valour. Sanga Rana, and his antagonist, Sultan Baber, were revived in their no less celebrated grandsons, the great Akber and Rana Pertáp: the son of the latter, Umra, the foe of Jehangír, was a character of whom the proudest nation might be vain.

The pen has recorded, and tradition handed down, many isolated fragments of the genius of these Rajpoot princes, as statesmen and warriors, touching the political division, regulations of the aristocracy, and commercial and agricultural bodies. Sumptuary laws, even, which append to a feudal system, are to be traced in these inscriptions: the annulling of monopolies and exorbitant taxes; the regulation of transit duties; prohibition of profaning sacred days by labour; immunities, privileges, and charters to trades, corporations, and towns; such as would, in climes more favourable to liberty, have matured into a league, or obtained for these branches a voice in the councils of the state. My search for less perishable documents than parchment when I found the cabinet of the prince contained them not, was unceasing; but though the bigotted Mahomedan destroyed most of the traces of civilisation within his reach, perseverance was rewarded with a considerable number. They are at least matter of curiosity. They will evince that monopolies and restraints on commerce were well understood in Rajwarra, though the doctrines of political economy never gained footing there. The setting up of these engraved tablets or pillars, called *Seoras*,[1] is of the highest antiquity. Every subject commences with invoking the sun and moon as witnesses, and concludes with a denunciation of the severest penalties on those who break the spirit of the imperishable bond. Tablets of an historical nature I have of twelve and fourteen hundred years' antiquity, but of grants of land or privileges about one thousand years is the oldest. Time has destroyed many, but man more. They became more numerous during the last three centuries, when successful struggles against their foes produced new privileges, granted in order to recall the scattered inhabitants. Thus one contains an abolition of the monopoly of tobacco;[2] another, the remission of tax on printed cloths, with permission to the country manufacturers to sell their goods free of duty at the neighbouring towns. To a third, a mercantile city, the abolition of war contributions,[3] and the establishment of its internal judicial authority. Nay, even where good manners alone are concerned, the lawgiver appears, and with an amusing simplicity:[4] "From the public feast none shall attempt to carry anything away." "None shall eat after sunset," shows that a Jain obtained the edict. To yoke the bullock or other animal for any work on the sacred Amavus,[5] is also declared punishable. Others contain revocations of vexatious fees to officers of the crown; "of beds and quilts;"[6] "the seizure of the carts, implements, or cattle of the husbandmen,"[7]—the sole boon in our own *Magna Charta* demanded for the husbandman. These and several others, of which copies are annexed, need not be repeated. If even from such memoranda a sufficient number could be collected of each prince's reign up to the olden time, what more could we desire to enable us to judge of the genius of their princes, the wants and habits of the people, their acts and occupations? The most ancient written customary law of France is A.D. 1088,[8] at which time Méwar was in high prosperity; opposing, at the head of a league far more powerful than France could form for ages after, the progress of revolution and foreign conquest. Ignorance, sloth, and all the vices which wait on and result from continual oppression in a perpetual struggle for existence of ages' duration, gradually diminished the reverence of the inhabitants themselves for these relics of the wisdom of their forefathers. In latter years, they so far forgot the ennobling feeling and respect for "the stone which told" their once exalted condition, as to convert the materials of the temple in which many of these stood into places of abode. Thus many a valuable relic is built up in the castles of their barons, or buried in the rubbish of the fallen pile.

We have, however, the books of grants to the chiefs and vassals, and also the grand rent-roll of the country. These are of themselves valuable documents. Could we but obtain those of remoter periods, they would serve as a commentary on the history of the country, as each contains the detail of every estate, and the stipulated service, in horse and foot, to be performed for it. In later times, when turbulence and disaffection

[1] Sanscrit, *Súla*.
[2] See Appendix, No. XII. [3] See Appendix, No. XIII.
[4] See Appendix, No. XIV. [5] 'Full moon.'—See Appendix, No. XIII.
[6] It is customary, when officers of the government are detached on service, to exact from the towns where they are sent both bed and board.
[7] Seized for public service, and frequently to exact a composition in money.
[8] Hallam, vol. i. p. 197.

went unpunished, it was useless to specify a stipulation of service that was nugatory; and too often the grants contained but the names of towns and villages, and their value; or if they had the more general terms of service, none of its details.[1] From all these, however, a sufficiency of customary rules could easily be found to form the written law of fiefs in Rajast'han. In France, in the sixteenth century, the variety of these customs amounted to two hundred and eighty-five, of which only sixty[2] were of great importance. The number of consequence in Méwar which have come to my observation is considerable, and the most important will be given in the Appendix. Were the same plan pursued there as in that ordinance which produced the laws of *Pays Coutumiers*[3] of France, viz. ascertaining those of each district, the materials are ready.

Such a collection would be amusing, particularly if the traditionary were added to the engraved laws. They would often appear *jéjune*, and might involve contradictions; but we should see the wants of the people; and if ever our connection (which God forbid!) should be drawn closer, we could then legislate without offending national customs or religious prejudices. Could this, by any instinctive impulse or external stimulus, be effected by themselves, it would be the era of their emersion from long oppression, and might lead to better notions of government, and consequent happiness to them all.

NOBLE ORIGIN OF THE RAJPOOT RACE.—If we compare the antiquity and illustrious descent of the dynasties which have ruled, and some which continue to rule, the small sovereignties of Rajast'han, with many of celebrity in Europe, superiority will often attach to the Rajpoot. From the most remote periods we can trace nothing ignoble, nor any vestige of vassal origin. Reduced in power, circumscribed in territory, compelled to yield much of their splendour and many of the dignities of birth, they have not abandoned an iota of the pride and high bearing arising from a knowledge of their illustrious and regal descent. On this principle the various revolutions in the Rana's family never encroached; and the mighty Jehangir himself, the Emperor of the Moguls, became, like Cæsar the commentator on the history of the tribe of Sesodia.[4] The potentate of the twenty-two Satrapies of Hind dwells with proud complacency on this Rajpoot king having made terms with him. He praises heaven, that what his immortal ancestor Baber, the founder of the Mogul dynasty, failed to do, the project in which Hemayoon had also failed, and in which the illustrious Akbar, his father, had but partial success was reserved for him. It is pleasing to peruse in the commentaries of these conquerors, Baber and Jehangir, their sentiments with regard to these princes. We have the evidence of Sir Thomas Roe, the ambassador of Elizabeth to Jehangir, as to the splendour of this race: it appears throughout their annals and those of their neighbours.

RAHTORES OF MARWAR.—The Rahtores can boast a splendid pedigree;

[1] Some of these, of old date, I have seen three feet in length.

[2] Hallam, vol. i. p. 199.

[3] Hallam notices these laws by this technical phrase.

[4] Sesodia is the last change of name which the Rana's race has undergone. It was first Sooryavansa, then Grahilote or Gehlote, Aharya, and Sesodia. These changes arise from revolutions and local circumstances.

and if we cannot trace its source with equal certainty to such a period of antiquity as the Rana's, we can, at all events, show the Rahtore monarch wielding the sceptre at Canouj, at the time the leader of an unknown tribe of the Franks was paving the way towards the foundation of the future kingdom of France. Unwieldy greatness caused the sudden fall of Canouj in the twelfth century, of which the existing line of Marwar is a renovated scion.

CUCHWAHAS OF AMBÉR.—Ambér is a branch of the once illustrious and ancient Nissida, now Nirwur, which produced the ill-fated prince whose story [1] is so interesting. Revolution and conquest compelled them to quit their ancestral abodes. Hindust'han was then divided into no more than four great kingdoms. By Arabian [2] travellers we have a confused picture of these states. But all the minor states, now existing in the west, arose about the period when the feudal system was approaching maturity in France and England.

The others are less illustrious, being the descendants of the great vassals of their ancient kings.

SESODIAS OF MÉWAR.—Méwar exhibits a marked difference from all the other states in her policy and institutions. She was an old-established dynasty when these renovated scions were in embryo. We can trace the losses of Méwar, but with difficulty her acquisitions; while it is easy to note the gradual aggrandisement of Marwar and Ambér, and all the minor states. Marwar was composed of many petty states, whose ancient possessions formed an allodial vassalage under the new dynasty. A superior independence of the control of the prince arises from the peculiarity of the mode of acquisition; that is, with rights similar to the allodial vassals of the European feudal system.

The poorest Rajpoot of this day retains all the pride of ancestry, often his sole inheritance; he scorns to hold the plough, or to use his lance but on horseback. In these aristocratic ideas he is supported by his reception amongst his superiors, and the respect paid to him by his inferiors. The honours and privileges, and the gradations of rank, amongst the vassals of the Rana's house, exhibit a highly artificial and refined state of society. Each of the superior rank is entitled to a banner, kettle-drums preceded by heralds and silver maces, with peculiar gifts and personal honours, in commemoration of some exploit of their ancestors.

The martial Rajpoots are not strangers to armorial bearings,[3] now so indiscriminately used in Europe. The great banner of Méwar exhibits a golden sun on a crimson field; those of the chiefs bear a dagger. Ambér

[1] Nala and Dumyanta.

[2] *Rélations anciennes des Voyageurs*, par Renaudot.

[3] It is generally admitted that armorial bearings were little known till the period of the Crusades, and that they belong to the east. The twelve tribes of Israel were distinguished by the animals on their banners, and the sacred writings frequently allude to the "Lion of Judah." The peacock was a favourite armorial emblem of the Rajpoot warrior; it is the bird sacred to their Mars (Kumara), as it was to Juno, his mother, in the west. The feather of the peacock decorates the turban of the Rajpoot and the warrior of the Crusade, adopted from the Hindu through the Saracens. "Le paon a toujours été l'emblême de la noblesse. Plusieurs chevaliers ornaient leurs casques des plumes de cet oiseau; un grand nombre de familles nobles le portaient dans leur blazon ou sur leur cimier; quelques uns n'en portaient que la queue."—Art. "Armoirie," *Dict. de l'ancien Régime*.

displays the *panchranga*, or five-coloured flag. The lion rampant on an argent field is extinct with the state of Chanderi.[1]

In Europe these customs were not introduced till the period of the Crusades, and were copied from the Saracens ; while the use of them amongst the Rajpoot tribes can be traced to a period anterior to the war of Troy. In the Mahabharat, or great war, twelve hundred years before Christ, we find the hero Bheesama exulting over his trophy, the banner of Arjoona, its field adorned with the figure of the Indian Hanuman.[2]

These emblems had a religious reference amongst the Hindus, and were taken from their mythology, the origin of all devices.

Every royal house has its palladium, which is frequently borne to battle at the saddle-bow of the prince. Rao Bhima Hara, of Kotah, lost his life and protecting deity together. The late celebrated Kheechee[3] leader, Jey Sing, never took the field without the god before him. "Victory to Bujrung" was his signal for the charge so dreaded by the Mahratta, and often has the deity been sprinkled with his blood and that of the foe.

Their ancestors, who opposed Alexander, did the same, and carried the image of Hercules (*Baldeva*) at the head of their array.

The custom (says Arrian) of presenting banners as an emblem of sovereignty over vassals, also obtained amongst the tribes of the Indus when invaded by Alexander. When he conquered the Sacæ and tribes east of the Caspian, he divided the provinces amongst the princes of the ancient families, for which they paid homage, engaged to serve with a certain quota of troops, and received from his own hand a banner ; in all of which he followed the customs of the country. But in these we see only the outline of the system ; we must descend to more modern days to observe it more minutely. A grand picture is drawn of the power of Méwar, when the first grand irruption of the Mahomedans occurred in the first century of their era ; when "a hundred[4] kings, its allies and dependents, had their thrones raised in Cheetore," for its defence and their own individually, when a new religion, propagated by the sword of conquest, came to enslave these realms. This invasion was by Sinde and Mekran ; for it was half a century later ere "the light" shone from the heights of Pámer[5] on the plains of the Jumna and Ganges.

From the commencement of this religious war in the mountains westward of the Indus, many ages elapsed ere the 'King of the Faith' obtained a seat on the throne of Yoodishtra. Chund, the bard, has left us various valuable memorials of this period, applicable to the subject historically as well as to the immediate topic. Visaldeva, the monarch whose name appears on the pillar of victory at Dehli, led an army against the invader, in which, according to the bard, "the banners of eighty-four princes were

[1] I was the first European who traversed this wild country, in 1807, not without some hazard. It was then independent : about three years after it fell a prey to Sindia.

[2] The monkey-deity.

[3] The Kheechees are a branch of the Chohans, and Kheechiwara lies east of Haravati.

[4] See annals of Méwar, and note from D'Anville.

[5] The Pámer range is a grand branch of the Indian Caucasus. Chund, the bard, designates them as the "Purbut Put Pámer," or Pámer Lord of Mountains. From Pahar and Pámer the Greeks may have compounded Paropamisan, in which was situated the most remote of the Alexandrias.

assembled." The bard describes with great animation the summons sent for this magnificent feudal levy from the heart of Anterbed [1] to the shores of the western sea, and it coincides with the record of his victory, which most probably this very army obtained for him. But no finer picture of feudal manners exists than the history of Pirthwirájá, contained in Chund's poems. It is surprising that this epic should have been allowed so long to sleep neglected: a thorough knowledge of it, and of others of the same character, would open many sources of new knowledge, and enable us to trace many curious and interesting coincidences.[2]

In perusing these tales of the days that are past, we should be induced to conclude that the *Couroltai* of the Tatars, the *Chougán* of the Rajpoot, and the *Champ de Mars* of the Frank, had one common origin.

Caste has for ever prevented the inferior classes of society from being incorporated with this haughty *noblesse*. Only those of pure blood in both lines can hold fiefs of the crown. The highest may marry the daughter of a Rajpoot, whose sole possession is a "skin of land": [3] the sovereign himself is not degraded by such alliance. There is no moral blot, and the operation of a law like the Salic would prevent any political evil resulting therefrom. Titles are granted, and even fiefs of office, to ministers and civil servants not Rajpoots; they are, however, but official, and never confer herditary right. These official fiefs may have originally arisen, here and in Europe, from the same cause; the want of a circulating medium to pay the offices. The Muntris [4] of Méwar prefer estates to pecuniary stipend, which gives more consequence in every point of view. All the higher offices—as cup-bearer, butler, stewards of the household, wardrobe, kitchen, master of the horse—all these are enumerated as ministerialists [5] at the court of Charlemagne in the dark ages of Europe, and of whom we have the duplicates. These are what the author of the Middle Ages designates as "improper feuds." [6] In Méwar the prince's architect, painter, physician, bard, genealogist, heralds, and all the generation of the foster-brothers, hold lands. Offices are hereditary in this patriarchal government; their services personal. The title even appends to the family, and if the chance of events deprive them of the substance, they are seldom left destitute. It is not uncommon to see three or four with the title of purdhan or premier.[7]

[1] The space between the grand rivers Ganges and Jumna, well known as the Do-áb.

[2] Domestic habits and national manners are painted to the life, and no man can well understand the Rajpoot of yore who does not read these.

Those were the days of chivalry and romance, when the assembled princes contended for the hand of the fair, who chose her own lord, and threw to the object of her choice, in full court, the *bur-mala*, or garland of marriage. Those were the days which the Rajpoot yet loves to talk of, when the glance of an eye weighed with a sceptre: when three things alone occupied him: his horse, his lance, and his mistress; for she is but the third in his estimation, after all: to the two first he owed her.

[3] Chursa, a 'hide or skin.'

[4] 'Ministers,' from *Muntera*, 'mystification.'

[5] It is probably of Teutonic origin, and akin to *Mantri*, which embraces all the ministers and councillors of loyalty (Hallam, p. 195).

[6] Hallam, p. 193.

[7] One I know, in whose family the office has remained since the period of Pirthwirájá, who transferred his ancestor to the service of the Rana's house seven hundred years ago. He is not merely a nominal hereditary minister, for his

But before I proceed further in these desultory and general remarks, I shall commence the chief details of the system as described in times past, and, in part, still obtaining in the principality of the Rana of Méwar. As its geography and distribution are fully related in their proper place, I must refer the reader to that for a preliminary understanding of its localities.

The local disposition of the estates was admirably contrived. Bounded on three sides, the south, east, and west, by marauding barbarous tribes of Bhils, Mérs, and Meenas, the circumference of this circle was subdivided into estates for the chiefs, while the *khalisa*, or fiscal land, the best and richest, was in the heart of the country, and consequently well protected.

It appears doubtful whether the khalisa lands amounted to one-fourth of those distributed in grant to the chiefs. The value of the crown demesne as the nerve and sinew of sovereignty, was well known by the former heads of this house. To obtain any portion thereof was the reward of important services; to have a grant of a few acres near the capital for a garden was deemed a high favour; and a village in the amphitheatre or valley, in which the present capital is situated, was the *ne plus ultra* of recompense. But the lavish folly of the present prince, out of this tract, twenty-five miles in circumference, has not preserved a single village in his khalisa.

By this distribution, and by the inroads of the wild tribes in the vicinity, or of Moguls and Mahrattas, the valour of the chiefs was kept in constant play.

The country was partitioned into districts, each containing from fifty to one hundred towns and villages, though sometimes exceeding that proportion. The great number of Chourasis[1] leads to the conclusion that portions to the amount of eighty-four had been the general subdivision. Many of these yet remain: as the 'Chourasi' of Jehazpoor and of Komulmér: tantamount to the old 'hundreds' of our Saxon ancestry. A circle of posts was distributed, within which the quotas of the chiefs attended, under "the Foujdar of the Símá" (*vulgo* Seem), or commander of the border. It was found expedient to appoint from court this lord of the frontier, always accompanied by a portion of the royal insignia, standard, kettle-drums, and heralds, and being generally a civil officer, he united to his military office the administration of justice.[2] The higher vassals never attended personally at these posts, but deputed a confidential branch of their family, with the quota required. For the government of the districts there were conjoined a civil and a military officer: the latter generally a vassal of the second rank. Their residence was the chief place of the district, commonly a stronghold.

The division of the chiefs into distinct grades, shows a highly artificial state of society.

uncle actually held the office; but in consequence of having favoured the views of a pretender to the crown, its active duties are not entrusted to any of the family.

[1] The numeral eighty-four.

[2] Now each chief claims the right of administering justice in his own domain, that is, in civil matters; but in criminal cases they ought not, without the special sanction of the crown. Justice, however, has long been left to work its own way, and the self-constituted tribunals, the punchaets, sit in judgment in all cases where property is involved.

First class.—We have the sixteen, whose estates were from fifty thousand to one hundred thousand rupees and upwards, of yearly rent. These appear in the presence only on special invitation, upon festivals and solemn ceremonies, and are the hereditary councillors of the crown.[1]

Second class, from five to fifty thousand rupees. Their duty is to be always in attendance. From these, chiefly, foujdars and military officers are selected.[1]

Third class is that of *Gole* [1] holding lands chiefly under five thousand rupees, though by favour they may exceed this limit. They are generally the holders of separate villages and portions of land, and in former times they were the most useful class to the prince. They always attended on his person, and indeed formed his strength against any combination or opposition of the higher vassals.

Fourth class.—The offsets of the younger branches of the Rana's own family, within a certain period, are called the *babas*, literally 'infants,' and have appanages bestowed on them. Of this class are Shapoora and Bunera ; too powerful for subjects. They hold on none of the terms of the great clans, but consider themselves at the disposal of the prince. These are more within the influence of the crown. Allowing adoption into these houses, except in the case of near kindred, is assuredly an innovation ; they ought to revert to the crown, failing immediate issue, as did the great estate of Bhynsrorgurh, two generations back.

From these to the holder of a *chursa*, or hide of land, the peculiarity of tenure and duties of each, will form a subject for discussion.

Revenues and Rights of the Crown.—I need not here expatiate upon the variety of items which constitute the revenues of the prince, the details of which will appear in their proper place. The land-tax in the khalisa demesne is, of course, the chief source of supply ; the transit duties on commerce and trade, and those of the larger towns and commercial marts, rank next. In former times more attention was paid to this important branch of income, and the produce was greater because less shackled. The liberality on the side of the crown was only equalled by the integrity of the merchant, and the extent to which it was carried would imply an almost Utopian degree of perfection in their mutual qualities of liberality and honesty ; the one, perhaps, generating the other. The remark of a merchant recently, on the vexatious train of duties and espionage attending their collection, is not merely figurative : "our ancestors tied their invoice to the horns of the oxen [2] at the first frontier post of customs, and no intermediate questions were put till we passed to the opposite or sold our goods, when it was opened and payment made accordingly ; but now every town has its rights." It will be long ere this degree of confidence is restored on either side ; extensive demand on the one is met by fraud and evasion on the other, though at least one-half of these evils have already been subdued.

The mines were very productive in former times, and yielded several lacs to the princes of Méwar. The rich tin mines of Jawara produced at one time a considerable proportion of silver. Those of copper are abundant,

[1] See Appendix, No. XX.

[2] Oxen and carts are chiefly used in the *Tandas*, or caravans, for transportation of goods in these countries ; camels further to the north.

as is also iron on the now alienated domain on the Chumbul; but lead least of all.[1]

The marble quarries also added to the revenue; and where there is such a multiplicity of sources, none are considered too minute to be applied in these necessitous times.

BURRÁR.—*Burrár* is an indefinite term for taxation, and is connected with the thing taxed: as *ganeem-burrár*,[2] 'war-tax'; *gurh geentee-burrár*,[3] 'house-tax'; *hal-burrár*, 'plough-tax'; *neauta-burrár*, 'marriage-tax'; and others, both of old and new standing. The war-tax was a kind of substitute for the regular mode of levying the rents on the produce of the soil; which was rendered very difficult during the disturbed period, and did not accord with the wants of the prince. It is also a substitute in those mountainous regions, for the *jareeb*,[4] where the produce bears no proportion to the cultivated surface; sometimes from poverty of soil, but often from the reverse, as in Komulmér, where the choicest crops are produced on the cultivated terraces, and on the sides of its mountains, which abound with springs, yielding the richest canes and cottons, and where experiment has proved that four crops can be raised in the same patch of soil within the year.

The offering on confirmation of estates (or fine on renewal) is now, though a very small, yet still one source of supply; as is the annual and triennial payment of the quit-rents of the Bhoomia chiefs. Fines in composition of offences may also be mentioned; and they might be larger, if more activity were introduced in the detection of offenders.

These governments are mild in the execution of the laws; and a heavy fine has more effect (especially on the hill tribes) than the execution of the offender, who fears death less than the loss of property.

KHUR-LAKUR.—The composition for 'wood and forage' afforded a considerable supply. When the princes of Méwar were oftener in the tented field than in the palace, combating for their preservation, it was the duty of every individual to store up wood and forage for the supply of the prince's army. What originated in necessity was converted into an abuse and annual demand. The towns also supplied a certain portion of provisions; where the prince halted for the day these were levied on the community; a goat or sheep from the shepherd, milk and flour from the farmer. The maintenance of these customs is observable in taxes, for the origin of which it is impossible to assign a reason without going into the history of the period; they scarcely recollect the source of some of these themselves. They are akin to those known under the feudal tenures of France, arising from exactly the same causes, and commuted for money payments; such as the *droit de giste et de chevauche*.[5] Many also originated

[1] The privilege of coining is a reservation of royalty. No subject is allowed to coin gold or silver, though the Saloombra chief has on sufferance a copper currency. The mint was a considerable source of income, and may be again when confidence is restored and a new currency introduced. The Cheetore rupee is now thirty-one per cent. inferior to the old Bhilara standard, and there was one struck at the capital even worse, and very nearly as bad as the *moneta nigra* of Philip the Fair of France, who allowed his vassals the privilege of coining it.

[2] Enemy. [3] Numbering of houses. [4] A measure of land.

[5] Hallam, vol. i. p. 232.

in the perambulations of these princes to visit their domains;[1] a black year in the calendar to the chief and the subject. When he honoured the chief by a visit, he had to present horses and arms, and to entertain his prince, in all which honours the cultivators and merchant had to share.

The duties on the sale of spirits, opium, tobacco, and even to a share of the garden-stuff, affords also modes of supply.[2]

CHAPTER II

Legislative authority—Rozina—Military service—Inefficiency of this form of government.

Legislative Authority.—During the period still called "the good times of Méwar," the prince, with the aid of his civil council, the four ministers of the crown and their deputies, promulgated all the legislative enactments in which the general rights and wants of the community were involved. In these the martial vassals or chiefs had no concern: a wise exclusion, comprehending also their immediate dependents, military, commercial, and agricultural. Even now, the little that is done in these matters is effected by the civil administration, though the Rajpoot Purdhans have been too apt to interfere in matters from which they ought always to be kept aloof, being ever more tenacious of their own rights than solicitous for the welfare of the community.

The neglect in the legislation of late years was supplied by the self-constituted tribunals, the useful punchaets, of which enough has been said to render further illustration unnecessary. Besides the resident ruler of the district, who was also a judicial functionary, there was, as already stated, a special officer of the government in each frontier t'hana, or garrison post. He united the triple occupation of embodying the quotas levying the transit duties, and administering justice, in which he was aided at the chabootra[3] or *court*, by assembling the Chotias or assessors of justice. Each town and village has its chotia, the members of which are elected by their fellow-citizens, and remain as long as they conduct themselves impartially in disentangling the intricacies of complaints preferred to them.

They are the aids to the Nagar Set'h, or chief magistrate, an hereditary office in every large city in Rajast'han. Of this chotia the Patél and Patwarri are generally members. The former of these, like the Dusondee of the Mahrattas, resembles in his duties the *décanus* of France and the tithing-man in England. The chotia and punchaet of these districts are analogous to the assessors of justice called *scabini*[4] in France, who held the office by election or the concurrence of the people. But these are the special and fixed council of each town; the general punchaets are formed

[1] Hume describes the necessity for our earlier kings making these tours to consume the produce, being in kind. So it is in Méwar; but I fancy the supply was always too easily convertible into circulating medium to be the cause there.

[2] See Appendix, No. X.

[3] Literally 'terrace,' or 'altar.'

[4] They were considered a sort of jury, bearing a close analogy to the *judices selecti*, who sat with the prætor in the tribunal of Rome.—Hallam.

from the respectable population at large, and were formerly from all classes of society.

The chabootras, or terraces of justice, were always established in the khalisa, or crown demesne. It was deemed a humiliating intrusion if they sat within the bounds of a chief. To 'erect the flag' within his limits, whether for the formation of defensive posts or the collection of duties, is deemed a gross breach of his privileged independence, as to establish them within the walls of his residence would be deemed equal to sequestration. It often becomes necessary to see justice enforced on a chief or his dependent, but it begets eternal disputes and disobedience, till at length they are worried to compliance by *rozina*.

Rozina.—When delay in these matters, or to the general commands of the prince, is evinced, an officer or herald is deputed with a party of four, ten, or twenty horse or foot, to the fief of the chief, at whose residence they take up their abode; and carrying, under the seal, a warrant to furnish them with specified daily (*rozina*) rations, they live at free quarters till he is quickened into compliance with the commands of the prince. This is the only accelerator of the slow movements of a Rajpoot chieftain in these days, whether for his appearance at court or the performance of an act of justice. It is often carried to a harassing excess, and causes much complaint.

In cases regarding the distribution of justice or the internal economy of the chief's estates, the government officers seldom interfere. But of their punchaets I will only remark, that their import amongst the vassals is very comprehensive; and when they talk of the '*punch*,' it means the 'collective wisdom.' In the reply to the remonstrance of the Deogurh vassals,[1] the chief promises never to undertake any measure without their deliberation and sanction.

On all grand occasions where the general peace or tranquillity of the government is threatened, the chiefs form the council of the sovereign. Such subjects are always first discussed in the domestic councils of each chief; so that when the *wittenagemote* of Méwar was assembled, each had prepared himself by previous discussion, and was fortified by abundance of advice.

To be excluded the council of the prince is to be in utter disgrace. These grand divans produce infinite speculation, and the ramifications which form the opinions are extensive. The council of each chief is, in fact, a miniature representation of the sovereign's. The greater sub-vassals, his civil purdhan, the mayor of the household, the purohit,[2] the bard, and two or three of the most intelligent citizens, form the minor councils, and all are separately deliberating while the superior court is in discussion. Thus is collected the wisdom of the magnates of Rajwarra.

Military Service.—In Méwar, during the days of her glory and prosperity, fifteen thousand horse, bound by the ties of fidelity and service, followed their prince into the field, all supported by lands held by grant; from the chief who headed five hundred of his own vassals, to the single horseman.

Knight's Fee or Single Horsemen.—A knight's fee in these states varies. For each thousand rupees of annual rent, never less than two, and generally three horsemen were furnished; and sometimes three horse and

[1] See Appendix, No. III. [2] Family priest.

three foot soldiers, according to the exigencies of the times when the grant was conferred. The different grants [1] appended will show this variety, and furnish additional proof that this, and all similar systems of policy, must be much indebted to chance for the shape they ultimately take. The knight's fee, when William the Conqueror partitioned England into sixty thousand such portions, from each of which a soldier's service was due, was fixed at £20. Each portion furnished its soldier or paid escuage. The knight's fee of Méwar may be said to be two hundred and fifty rupees, or about £30.

LIMITATIONS OF SERVICE.—In Europe, service was so restricted that the monarch had but a precarious authority. He could only calculate upon forty days' annual service from the tenant of a knight's fee. In Rajast'han it is very different: "at home and abroad, service shall be performed when demanded"; such is the condition of the tenure.

For state and show, a portion of the greater vassals [2] reside at the capital for some months, when they have permission to retire to their estates, and are relieved by another portion. On the grand military festival the whole attend for a given time; and when the prince took the field, the whole assembled at their own charge; but if hostilities carried them beyond the frontier they were allowed certain rations.

ESCUAGE OR SCUTAGE.—Escuage or scutage, the phrase in Europe to denote the amercement [3] for non-attendance, is also known and exemplified in deeds. Failure from disaffection, turbulence, or pride, brought a heavy fine; the sequestration of the whole or part of the estate.[4] The princes of these states would willingly desire to see escuage more general. All have made this first attempt towards an approximation to a standing army; but, though the chiefs would make compensation to get rid of some particular service, they are very reluctant to renounce lands, by which alone a fixed force could be maintained. The rapacity of the court would gladly fly to scutages, but in the present impoverished state of the fiefs, such if injudiciously levied would be almost equivalent to resumption; but this measure is so full of difficulty as to be almost impracticable.

INEFFICIENCY OF THIS FORM OF GOVERNMENT.—Throughout Rajast'han the character and welfare of the states depend on that of the sovereign: he is the mainspring of the system—the active power to set and keep in motion all these discordant materials; if he relax, each part separates, and moves in a narrow sphere of its own. Yet will the impulse of one great mind put the machine in regular movement, which shall endure during two or three imbecile successors, if no fresh exterior force be applied to check it. It is a system full of defects; yet we see them so often balanced by virtues, that we are alternately biased by these counteracting qualities; loyalty and patriotism, which combine a love of the institutions, religion, and manners of the country, are the counterpoise to systematic evil. In no country has the system ever proved efficient. It has been one of eternal excitement and irregular action; inimical to order, and the repose deemed necessary after conflict for recruiting the national strength. The absence of an external foe was but the signal for disorders

[1] See Appendix, Nos. IV., V., and VI.

[2] See Appendix, No. XX., art. 6; the treaty between the chiefs and his vassals defining service.

[3] Appendix, No. XVI.

[4] Both of which I have witnessed.

within, which increased to a terrific height in the feuds of the two great rival factions of Méwar, the clans of Chondawut [1] and Súktawut,[2] as the weakness of the prince augmented by the abstraction of his personal domain, and the diminution of the services of the third class of vassals (the Gole), the personal retainers of the crown; but when these feuds broke out, even with the enemy at their gates, it required a prince of great nerve and talent to regulate them. Yet is there a redeeming quality in the system, which, imperfect as it is, could render such perilous circumstances but the impulse to a rivalry of heroism.

When Jehangír had obtained possession of the palladium of Méwar, the ancient fortress of Cheetore, and driven the prince into the wilds and mountains of the west, an opportunity offered to recover some frontier lands in the plains, and the Rana with all his chiefs were assembled for the purpose. But the Suktawuts asserted an equal privilege with their rivals to form the vanguard; [3] a right which their indisputable valour (perhaps superior to that of the other party) rendered not invalid. The Chondawuts claimed it as an hereditary privilege, and the sword would have decided the matter but for the tact of the prince. "The *herole* to the clan which first enters Ontala," was a decision which the Suktawut leader quickly heard; while the other could no longer plead his right, when such a gauntlet was thrown down for its maintenance.

Ontala is the frontier fortress in the plains, about eighteen miles east of the capital, and covering the road which leads from it to the more ancient one of Cheetore. It is situated on a rising ground, with a stream flowing beneath its walls, which are of solid masonry, lofty, and with round towers at intervals.[4] In the centre was the governor's house, also fortified. One gate only gave admission to this castle.

The clans, always rivals in power, now competitors in glory, moved off at the same time, some hours before daybreak—Ontala the goal, the herole the reward! Animated with hope—a barbarous and cruel foe the object of their prowess—their wives and families spectators, on their return, of the meed of enterprise; the bard, who sang the praise of each race at their outset, demanding of each materials for a new wreath, supplied every stimulus that a Rajpoot could have to exertion.

The Suktawuts made directly for the gateway, which they reached as the day broke, and took the foe unprepared; but the walls were soon manned, and the action commenced. The Chondawuts, less skilled in topography, had traversed a swamp, which retarded them—but through which they dashed, fortunately meeting a guide in a shepherd of Ontala. With more foresight than their opponents, they had brought ladders. The chief led the escalade, but a ball rolled him back amidst his vassals; it was not his destiny to lead the herole! Each party was checked. The Suktawut depended on the elephant he rode, to gain admission by forcing the gate;

[1] A clan called after Chonda, eldest son of an ancient Rana, who resigned his birthright.

[2] Sukta was the son of Rana Udya Sing, founder of Udyapoora, or Oodipoor. The feuds of these two clans, like those of the Armagnacs and Bourguignons, "qui couvrirent la France d'un crêpe sanglant," have been the destruction of Méwar. It requires but a change of names and places, while reading the one, to understand perfectly the history of the other.

[3] Herole.

[4] It is now in ruins, but the towers and part of the walls are still standing.

but its projecting spikes deterred the animal from applying its strength. His men were falling thick around him, when a shout from the other party made him dread their success. He descended from his seat, placed his body on the spikes, and commanded the driver, on pain of instant death, to propel the elephant against him. The gates gave way, and over the dead body of their chief his clan rushed to the combat! But even this heroic surrender of his life failed to purchase the honour for his clan. The lifeless corpse of his rival was already in Ontala, and this was the event announced by the shout which urged his sacrifice to honour and ambition. When the Chondawut chief fell, the next in rank and kin took the command. He was one of those arrogant, reckless Rajpoots, who signalised themselves wherever there was danger, not only against men but tigers, and his common appellation was the *Bénda T'hacúr* ('mad chief') of Deogurh. When his leader fell, he rolled the body in his scarf; then tying it on his back, scaled the wall, and with his lance having cleared the way before him he threw the dead body over the parapet of Ontala, shouting, "The van-guard to the Chondawut! we are first in!" The shout was echoed by the clan, and the rampart was in their possession nearly at the moment of the entry of the Suktawuts. The Moguls fell under their swords: the standard of Méwar was erected in the castle of Ontala, but the leading of the vanguard remained with the Chondawuts.[1]

This is not the sole instance of such jealousies being converted into a generous and patriotic rivalry; many others could be adduced throughout the greater principalities, but especially amongst the brave Rahtores of Marwar.

It was a nice point to keep these clans poised against each other; their feuds were not without utility, and the tact of the prince frequently turned them to account. One party was certain to be enlisted on the side of the sovereign, and this alone counterbalanced the evil tendencies before described. To this day it has been a perpetual struggle for supremacy; and the epithets of "loyalist" and "traitor" have been alternating between them for centuries, according to the portion they enjoyed of the prince's favour, and the talents and disposition of the heads of the clans to maintain their predominance at court. The Suktawuts are weaker in numbers, but have the reputation of greater bravery and more genius than their rivals. I am inclined, on the whole, to assent to this opinion; and the very consciousness of this reputation must be a powerful incentive to its preservation.

When all these governments were founded and maintained on the same principle, a system of feuds, doubtless, answered very well; but it cannot exist with a well-constituted monarchy. Where individual will controls the energies of a nation, it must eventually lose its liberties. To preserve

[1] An anecdote appended by my friend Umra (the bard of the Sungawuts, a powerful division of the Chondawuts, whose head is Deogurh, often alluded to, and who alone used to lead two thousand vassals into the field) was well attested. Two Mogul chiefs of note were deeply engaged in a game of chess when the tumult was reported to them. Feeling confident of success, they continued their game; nor would they desist till the inner castle of this 'donjon keep' was taken, and they were surrounded by the Rajpoots, when they coolly begged they might be allowed to terminate their game. This the enemy granted; but the loss of their chiefs had steeled their breasts against mercy, and they were afterwards put to death.

their power, the princes of Rajast'han surrendered a portion of theirs to the emperors of Dehli. They made a nominal surrender to him of their kingdoms, receiving them back with a sunnud, or grant, renewed on each lapse: thereby acknowledging him as lord paramount. They received, on these occasions, the khelat of honour and investiture, consisting of elephants, horses, arms, and jewels; and to their hereditary title of 'prince' was added by the emperor, one of dignity, ***munsub***. Besides this acknowledgment of supremacy, they offered ***nuzzerana*** [1] and homage, especially on the festival of Noroza (the new year), engaging to attend the royal presence when required, at the head of a stipulated number of their vassals. The emperor presented them with a royal standard, kettle-drums, and other insignia, which headed the array of each prince. Here we have all the chief incidents of a great feudal sovereignty. Whether the Tatar sovereigns borrowed these customs from their princely vassals, or brought them from the highlands of Asia, from the Oxus and Jaxartes, whence, there is little doubt, many of these Sacha Rajpoots originated, shall be elsewhere considered.

The splendour of such an array, whether in the field or at the palace, can scarcely be conceived. Though Hemayoon had gained the services of some of the Rajpoot princes, their aid was uncertain. It was reserved for his son, the wise and magnanimous Akbar, to induce them to become at once the ornament and support of his throne. The power which he consolidated, and knew so well to wield, was irresistible; while the beneficence of his disposition, and the wisdom of his policy, maintained what his might conquered. He felt that a constant exhibition of authority would not only be ineffectual but dangerous, and that the surest hold on their fealty and esteem would be the giving them a personal interest in the support of the monarchy.

He determined to unite the pure Rajpoot blood to the scarcely less noble stream which flowed from Oguz Khan, through Jungheez, Timoor, and Baber, to himself, calculating that they would more readily yield obedience to a prince who claimed kindred with them, than to one purely Tatar; and that, at all events, it would gain the support of their immediate kin, and might in the end become general. In this supposition he did not err. We are less acquainted with the obstacles which opposed his first success, than those he subsequently encountered; *one* of which neither he nor his descendants *ever* overcame in the family of Méwar, who could never be brought to submit to such alliance.

Ambér, the nearest to Dehli and the most exposed, though more open to temptation, than to conquest, in its then contracted sphere, was the first to set the example.

Its Raja Bhagwandas gave his daughter to Hemayoon; and subsequently this practice became so common, that some of the most celebrated emperors were the offspring of Rajpoot princesses.

Of these, Selim, called after his accession, Jehangir; his ill-fated son, Khosroo; Shah Jehan; [2] Kambaksh,[3] the favourite of his father; Arungzéb, and his rebellious son Akbar, whom his Rajpoot kin would

[1] Fine of relief.

[2] The son of the Princess Jodh Bae, whose magnificent tomb still excites admiration at Secundra, near Agra.

[3] 'Gift of Love.'

have placed on the throne had his genius equalled their power, are the most prominent instances. Ferokhsér, when the empire began to totter, furnished the last instance of a Mogul sovereign marrying a Hindu princess,[1] the daughter of Raja Ajeet Sing, sovereign of Marwar.

These Rajpoot princes became the guardians of the minority of their imperial nephews, and had a direct stake in the empire, and in the augmentation of their estates.

Of the four hundred and sixteen Munsubdars, or military commanders of Akbar's empire, from leaders of two hundred to ten thousand men, forty-seven were Rajpoots, and the aggregate of their quotas amounted to fifty-three thousand horse: [2] exactly one-tenth of the united Munsubdars of the empire, or five hundred and thirty thousand horse.[3]

Of the forty-seven Rajpoot leaders, there were seventeen whose munsubs were from one thousand to five thousand horse, and thirty from two hundred to one thousand.

The princes of Ambér, Marwar, Bikanér, Boondi, Jessulmér, Boondelkhund, and even Shekawut, held munsubs of above one thousand; but Ambér only, being allied to the throne, had the dignity of five thousand.

The Raja Udya Sing of Marwar, surnamed the Fat, chief of the Rahtores, held but the munsub of one thousand, while a scion of his house, Rae Sing of Bikanér, had four thousand. This is to be accounted for by the dignity being thrust upon the head of that house. The independent princes of Chandéri, Kerowli, Duttea, with the tributary feudatories of the larger principalities, and members of the Shekawut federation, were enrolled on the other grades, from four to seven hundred. Amongst these we find the founder of the Suktawut clan, who quarrelling with his brother, Rana Pertap of Méwar, gave his services to Akbar. In short it became general, and what originated in force or persuasion, was soon coveted from interested motives; and as nearly all the states submitted in time to give queens to the empire, few were left to stigmatise this dereliction from Hindu principle.

Akbar thus gained a double victory, securing the good opinions as well as the swords of these princes in his aid. A judicious perseverance would have rendered the throne of Timoor immovable, had not the tolerant principles and beneficence of Akbar, Jehangir, and Shah Jehan been lost sight of by the bigoted and bloodthirsty Arungzéb; who, although while he lived his commanding genius wielded the destinies of this immense empire at pleasure, alienated the affections, by insulting the prejudices, of those who had aided in raising the empire to the height on which it stood. This affection withdrawn, and the weakness of Ferokhsér substituted for the strength of Arungzéb, it fell and went rapidly to pieces.

[1] To this very marriage we owe the origin of our power. When the nuptials were preparing, the emperor fell ill. A mission was at that time at Dehli from Surat, where we traded, of which Mr. Hamilton was the surgeon. He cured the king, and the marriage was completed. In the oriental style, he desired the doctor to name his reward; but instead of asking anything for himself, he demanded a grant of land for a factory on the Hoogly for his employers. It was accorded, and this was the origin of the greatness of the British empire in the East. Such an act deserved at least a column; but neither "trophied urn or monumental bust" marks the spot where his remains are laid.

[2] Abul Fuzil's Institutes of Akbar.

[3] The infantry, regulars, and militia, exceeded 4,000,000.

Predatory warfare and spoliation rose on its ruins. The Rajpoot princes, with a short-sighted policy, at first connived at, and even secretly invited the tumult; not calculating on its affecting their interests. Each looked to the return of ancient independence, and several reckoned on great accession of power. Old jealousies were not lessened by the part which each had played in the hour of ephemeral greatness; and the prince of Méwar, who preserved his blood uncontaminated, though with loss of land, was at once an object of respect and envy to those who had forfeited the first pretensions [1] of a Rajpoot. It was the only ovation the Sesodia [2] had to boast for centuries of oppression and spoliation, whilst their neighbours were basking in court favour. The great increase of territory of these princes nearly equalled the power of Méwar, and the dignities thus acquired from the sons of Timoor, they naturally wished should appear as distinguished as his ancient title. Hence, while one inscribed on his seal "The exalted in dignity, a prince amongst princes, and king of kings," [3] the prince of Méwar preserved his royal simplicity in 'Maha-Rana B'hima Sing, son of Ursi.' But this is digression.

It would be difficult to say what would be the happiest form of government for these states without reference to their neighbours. Their own feudal customs would seem to have worked well. The experiment of centuries has secured to them political existence, while successive dynasties of Afghans and Moguls, during eight hundred years, have left but the wreck of splendid names. Were they to become more monarchical, they would have everything to dread from unchecked despotism, over which even the turbulence of their chiefs is a salutary control.

Were they somewhat more advanced towards prosperity, the crown demesne redeemed from dissipation and sterility, and the chiefs enabled to bring their quotas into play for protection and police, recourse should never be had to bodies of mercenary troops, which practice, if persevered in, will inevitably change their present form of government. This has invariably been the result, in Europe as well as Rajast'han, else why the dread of standing armies?

Escuage is an approximating step. When Charles VII. of France [4] raised his companies of ordnance, the basis of the first national standing army ever embodied in Europe, a tax called '*taille*' was imposed to pay them, and Guienne rebelled. Kotah is a melancholy instance of subversion of the ancient order of society. Méwar made the experiment from necessity sixty years ago, when rebellion and invasion conjoined; and a body of Sindies were employed, which completed their disgust, and they fought with each other till almost mutually exterminated, and till all faith in their prince was lost. Jeipoor had adopted this custom to a greater extent; but it was an ill-paid band, neither respected at home nor feared abroad. In Marwar the feudal compact was too strong to tolerate it, till Pathan predatory bands, prowling amidst the ruins of

[1] See, in the annals of Méwar, the letter of Rae Sing of Bikanér (who had been compelled to submit to this practice), on hearing that Rana Pertap's reverses were likely to cause a similar result. It is a noble production, and gives the character of both.

[2] The tribe to which the princes of Méwar belonged.

[3] *Ráj Ráj éswara*, the title of the prince of Marwar: the prince of Ambér, *Ráj Ráj Indra*.

[4] Hallam, vol. i. p. 117.

Mogul despotism, were called in to partake in each family broil; the consequence was the weakening of all, and opening the door to a power stronger than any, to be the arbiter of their fate.

General Duties of the Puttawut, or Vassal Chief of Rajast'han.—"The essential principle of a fief was a mutual contract of support and fidelity. Whatever obligations it laid upon the vassal of service to his lord, corresponding duties of protection were imposed by it on the lord towards his vassal. If these were transgressed on either side, the one forfeited his land, the other his signiory or rights over it." [1]

In this is comprehended the very foundation of feudal policy, because in its simplicity we recognise first principles involving mutual preservation. The best commentary on this definition of simple truth will be the sentiments of the Rajpoots themselves in two papers: one containing the opinions of the chiefs of Marwar on the reciprocal duties of sovereign and vassal; [2] the other, those of the sub-vassals of Deogurh, one of the largest fiefs in Rajast'han, of their rights, the infringement of them, and the remedy.[3]

If, at any former period in the history of Marwar, its prince had thus dared to act, his signiory and rights over it would not have been of great value; his crown and life would both have been endangered by these turbulent and determined vassals. How much is comprehended in that manly, yet respectful sentence: "If he accepts our services, then he is our prince and leader; if not, but our equal, and we again his brothers, claimants of and laying claim to the soil."

In the remonstrance of the sub-vassals of Deogurh, we have the same sentiments on a reduced scale. In both we have the ties of blood and kindred, connected with and strengthening national policy. If a doubt could exist as to the principle of fiefs being similar in Rajast'han and in Europe, it might be set at rest by the important question long agitated by the feodal lawyers in Europe, "whether the vassal is bound to follow the standard of his lord against his own kindred or against his sovereign": which in these states is illustrated by a simple and universal proof. If the question were put to a Rajpoot to whom his service is due, whether to his chief or his sovereign, the reply would be, *Rájca malik weh pát* [4] *ca malik yeh*: 'He is the sovereign of the state, but this is my *head*': an ambiguous phrase, but well understood to imply that his own immediate chief is the only authority he regards.

This will appear to militate against the right of remonstrance (as in the case of the vassals of Deogurh), for they look to the crown for protection against injustice; they annihilate other rights by admitting appeal higher than this. Every class looks out for some resource against oppression. The sovereign is the last applied to on such occasions, with whom the sub-vassal has no bond of connection. He can receive no favour, nor perform any service, but through his own immediate superior; and presumes not to question (in cases not personal to himself) the propriety of his chief's actions, adopting implicitly his feelings and resentments. The daily familiar intercourse of life is far too engrossing to allow him to speculate, and with his lord he lives a patriot or dies a traitor. In proof of this,

[1] Hallam, vol. i. p. 173.
[2] See Appendix, No. I. [3] See Appendix, Nos. II. and III.
[4] *Pát* means 'head,' 'chief': also, 'board,' 'throne'—like *tukht*, in Persian.

numerous instances could be given of whole clans devoting themselves to the chief against their sovereign; [1] not from the ties of kindred, for many were aliens to blood; but from the ties of duty, gratitude, and all that constitutes clannish attachment, superadded to feudal obligation. The sovereign, as before observed, has nothing to do with those vassals not holding directly from the crown; and those who wish to stand well with their chiefs, would be very slow in receiving any honours or favours from the general fountain-head. The Deogurh chief sent one of his sub-vassals to court on a mission: his address and deportment gained him favour, and his consequence was increased by a seat in the presence of his sovereign. When he returned, he found this had lost him the favour of his chief, who was offended, and conceived a jealousy both of his prince and his servant. The distinction paid to the latter was, he said, subversive of his proper authority, and the vassal incurred by his vanity the loss of estimation where alone it was of value.

Obligations of a Vassal.—The attempt to define all the obligations of a vassal would be endless: they involve all the duties of kindred in addition to those of obedience. To attend the court of his chief; never to absent himself without leave; to ride with him a hunting; to attend him at the court of his sovereign or to war, and even give himself as a hostage for his release; these are some of the duties of a vassal.

CHAPTER III

Feudal incidents—Duration of grants.

Feudal Incidents.—I shall now proceed to compare the more general obligations of vassals, known under the term of 'Feudal Incidents' in Europe, and show their existence in Rajast'han. These were six in number:—1. Reliefs; 2. Fines of alienation; 3. Escheats; 4. Aids; 5. Wardship; 6. Marriage.

Relief.—The first and most essential mark of a feudal relation exists in all its force and purity here: it is a perpetually recurring mark of the source of the grant, and the solemn renewal of the pledge which originally obtained it. In Méwar it is a virtual and *bona fide* surrender of the fief and renewal thereof. It is thus defined in European polity: "A relief [2] is a sum of money due from every one of full age taking a fief by descent." It was arbitrary, and the consequent exactions formed a ground of discontent; nor was the tax fixed till a comparatively recent period.

[1] The death of the chief of Nimaj, in the annals of Marwar, and Seogurh Feud, in the Personal Narrative, vol. ii.

[2] "Plusieurs possesseurs de fiefs, ayant voulu en laisser perpétuellement la propriété à leurs descendans, prirent des arrangemens avec leur Seigneur; et, outre ce qu'ils donnèrent pour faire le marché, ils s'engagèrent, eux et leur postérité, à abandonner pendant une année, au Seigneur, la jouissance entière du fief, chaque fois que le dit fief changerait de main. C'est ce qui forma le droit de *relief*.

"Quand un gentilhomme avait dérogé, il pouvait effaçer cette tache moyennant finances, et ce qu'il payait s'appelait *relief*, il recevait pour quittance des lettres de *relief* ou de réhabilitation."—Art. "Relief," *Dict. de l'anc. Régime.*

By *Magna Charta* reliefs were settled at rates proportionate to the dignity of the holder.[1] In France the relief was fixed by the customary laws at one year's revenue.[2] This last has long been the settled amount of *nuzzerana*, or fine of relief, in Méwar.

On the demise of a chief, the prince immediately sends a party, termed the *zubti* (sequestrator), consisting of a civil officer and a few soldiers, who take possession of the state in the prince's name. The heir sends his prayer to court to be installed in the property, offering the proper relief. This paid, the chief is invited to repair to the presence, when he performs homage, and makes protestations of service and fealty; he receives a fresh grant, and the inauguration terminates by the prince girding him with a sword, in the old forms of chivalry. It is an imposing ceremony, performed in a full assembly of the court, and one of the few which has never been relinquished. The fine paid, and the brand buckled to his side, a steed, turban, plume, and dress of honour given to the chief, the investiture [3] is complete; the sequestrator returns to court, and the chief to his estate, to receive the vows and congratulations of his vassals.

In this we plainly perceive the original power (whether exercised or not) of resumption. On this subject more will appear in treating of the duration of grants. The *kharg bandai*, or 'binding of the sword,' is also performed when a Rajpoot is fit to bear arms; as amongst the ancient German tribes, when they put into the hands of the aspirant for fame a lance. Such are the substitutes for the *toga virilis* of the young Roman. The Rana himself is thus ordained a knight by the first of his vassals in dignity, the chief of Saloombra.

RENUNCIATION OF RELIEFS.—In the demoralisation of all those states, some of the chiefs obtained renunciation of the fine of relief, which was tantamount to making a grant in perpetuity, and annulling the most overt sign of paramount sovereignty. But these and many other important encroachments were made when little remained of the reality, or when it was obscured by a series of oppressions unexampled in any European state.

It is in Méwar alone, I believe, of all Rajast'han, that these marks of fealty are observable to such an extent. But what is remarked elsewhere upon the fiefs being movable, will support the doctrine of resumption though it might not be practised: a prerogative may exist without its being exercised.

FINE OF ALIENATION.—Rajast'han never attained this refinement

[1] Namely, " the heir or heirs of an earl, for an entire earldom, one hundred pounds; the heir or heirs of a baron, for an entire barony, one hundred marks; the heir or heirs of a knight, for a whole knight's fee, one hundred shillings at most."—Art. III. *Magna Charta*.

[2] " Le droit de rachat devoit se payer a chaque mutation d'héritier, et se paya même d'abord en ligne directe.—La coutume la plus générale l'avait fixé à une année du revenue."—*L'Esprit des Loix*," Liv. xxxi. chap. xxxiii.

[3] That symbolic species of investitute denominated 'improper investiture,' the delivery of a turf, stone, and wand, has its analogies amongst the mountaineers of the Aravulli. The old baron of Bednor, when the Mér villages were reduced, was clamorous about his feudal rights over those wild people. It was but the point of honour. From one he had a hare, from another a bullock, and so low as a pair of sticks which they use on the festivals of the *Holi*. These marks of vassalage come under the head of 'petite serjanteri' (petit serjeantry) in the feudal system of Europe. (See Art. XLI. of *Magna Charta*.)

indicative of the dismemberment of the system ; so vicious and self-destructive a notion never had existence in these states. Alienation does not belong to a system of fiefs : the lord would never consent to it, but on very peculiar occasions.

In Kutch, amongst the Jharéja [1] tribes, sub-vassals may alienate their estates ; but this privilege is dependent on the mode of acquisition. Perhaps the only knowledge we have in Rajast'han of alienation requiring the sanction of the lord paramount, is in donations for pious uses : but this is partial. We see in the remonstrance of the Deogurh vassals the opinion they entertained of their lord's alienation of their sub-fees to strangers, and without the Rana's consent ; which, with a similar train of conduct, produced sequestration of his fief till they were re-inducted.

Tenants of the Crown may Alienate.—The agricultural tenants, proprietors of land held of the crown, may alienate their rights upon a small fine, levied merely to mark the transaction. But the tenures of these non-combatants and the holders of fees are entirely distinct, and cannot here be entered on, further than to say that the agriculturist is, or was, the proprietor of the soil ; the chief, solely of the tax levied thereon. But in Europe the alienation of the *feudum paternum* was not good without the consent of the kindred in the line of succession.[2] This would involve sub-infeudation and frerage, which I shall touch on distinctly, many of the troubles of these countries arising therefrom.

Escheats and Forfeitures.—The fiefs which were only to descend in lineal succession, reverted to the crown on failure of heirs, as they could not be bequeathed by will. This answers equally well for England as for Méwar. I have witnessed escheats of this kind, and foresee more, if the pernicious practice of unlimited adoption do not prevent the Rana from regaining lands, alienated by himself at periods of contention. Forfeitures for crimes must, of course, occur, and these are partial or entire, according to the delinquency.

In Marwar, at this moment, nearly all the representatives of the great fiefs of that country are exiles from their homes : a distant branch of the same family, the prince of Edur, would have adopted a similar line of conduct but for a timely check from the hand of benevolence.[3]

There is, or rather was, a class of lands in Méwar appended to the crown, of which it bestowed life-rents on men of merit. These were termed *Chur-ootar*, and were given and taken back, as the name implies ; in contradistinction to grants which, though originating in good behaviour, not only continued for life but descended in perpetuity. Such places are still so marked in the rent-roll, but they are seldom applied to the proper purpose.

Aids.—Aids, implying 'free gifts,' or 'benevolences,' as they were termed in a European code, are well known. The *burrar* (war-tax) is well understood in Méwar, and is levied on many occasions for the neces-

[1] Jharéja is the title of the Rajpoot race in Kutch ; they are descendants of the Yadus, and claim from Crishna. In early ages they inhabited the tracts on the Indus and in Sewist'han.

[2] Wright on Tenures, *apud* Hallam, vol. i. p. 185.

[3] The Hon. Mr. Elphinstone, governor of Bombay. As we prevented the spoliation of Edur by the predatory powers, we are but right in seeing that the head does not become the spoliator himself, and make these brave men " wish any change but that which we have given them."

sities of the prince or the head of a clan. It is a curious fact, that the *dusoond*, or 'tenth,' in Méwar, as in Europe, was the stated sum to be levied in periods of emergency or danger. On the marriage of the daughters of the prince, a benevolence or contribution was always levied: this varied. A few years ago, when two daughters and a grand-daughter were married to the princes of Jessulmér, Bikanér, and Kishengurh, a schedule of one-sixth, to portion the three, was made out; but it did not realise above an eighth. In this aid the civil officers of government contribute equally with the others. It is a point of honour with all to see their sovereign's daughters married, and for once the contribution merited the name of benevolence.

But it is not levied solely from the coffers of the rich; by the chiefs it is exacted of their tenantry of all classes, who, of course, wish such subjects of rejoicing to be of as rare occurrence as possible.

"These feudal aids are deserving of our notice as the commencement of taxation, of which they long answered the purpose, till the craving necessities and covetous policy of kings established for them more durable and onerous burthens." [1]

The great chiefs, it may be assumed, were not backward, on like occasions, to follow such examples, but these gifts were more voluntary. Of the details of aids in France we find enumerated, "paying the relief to the suzerain on taking possession of his lands"; [2] and by *Magna Charta* our barons could levy them on the following counts: to make the baron's eldest son a knight, to marry his eldest daughter, or to redeem his person from captivity. The latter is also one occasion for the demand in all these countries. The chief is frequently made prisoner in their predatory invasions, and carried off as a hostage for the payment of a war contribution. Everything disposable is often got rid of on an occasion of this kind. *Cœur de Lion* would not have remained so long in the dungeons of Austria had his subjects been Rajpoots.

In Ambér the most extensive benevolence, or *burrar*,[3] is on the marriage of the Raj-Cumar, or heir apparent.

WARDSHIP.—This does exist, to foster the infant vassal during minority; but often terminating, as in the system of Europe, in the nefarious act of defrauding a helpless infant, to the pecuniary benefit of some court favourite. It is accordingly here undertaken occasionally by the head of the clan; but two strong recent instances brought the dark ages, and the purchase of wardships for the purpose of spoliation, to mind. The first was in the Deogurh chief obtaining by bribe the entire management of the lands of Singramgurh, on pretence of improving them for the infant, Nahar Sing, whose father was incapacitated by derangement. Nahar was a junior branch of the clan *Sangawut*, a subdivision of the Chondawut clan, both Sesodias of the Rana's blood. The object, at the time, was to unite them to Deogurh, though he pleaded duty as head of the clan. His nomination of young Nahar as his own heir gives a colouring of truth to his intentions; and he succeeded, though there were nearer of kin, who were set aside (at the wish of the vassals of Deogurh and with the concurrence of the sovereign) as unfit to head them or serve him.

Another instance of the danger of permitting wardships, particularly

[1] Hallam. [2] Ducange, *apud* Hallam.

[3] *Burrar* is the generic name for taxation.

where the guardian is the superior in clanship and kindred, is exemplified in the Kalianpoor estate in Méwar. That property had been derived from the crown only two generations back, and was of the annual value of ten thousand rupees. The mother having little interest at court, the Saloombra chief, by bribery and intrigue, upon paying a fine of about one year's rent, obtained possession—ostensibly to guard the infant's rights; but the falsehood of this motive was soon apparent. There were duties to perform on holding it which were not thought of. It was a frontier post, and a place of rendezvous for the quotas to defend that border from the incursions of the wild tribes of the south-west. The Saloombra chief, being always deficient in the quota for his own estate, was not likely to be very zealous in his muster-roll for his ward's, and complaints were made which threatened a change. The chief of Chaond was talked of as one who would provide for the widow and minor, who could not perform the duties of defence.

The sovereign himself often assumes the guardianship of minors; but the mother is generally considered the most proper guardian for her infant son. All others may have interests of their own; she can be actuated by his welfare alone. Custom, therefore, constitutes her the guardian; and with the assistance of the elders of the family, she rears and educates the young chief till he is fit to be girded with the sword.[1]

The Foujdar, or military manager, who frequently regulates the household as well as the subdivisions of the estate, is seldom of the kin or clan of the chief: a wise regulation, the omission of which has been known to produce, in these *maires du palais* on a small scale, the same results as will be described in the larger. This officer, and the civil functionary who transacts all the pecuniary concerns of the estate, with the mother and her family, are always considered to be the proper guardians of the minor. "Blood which could not inherit," was the requisite for a guardian in Europe,[2] as here; and when neglected, the results are in both cases the same.

MARRIAGE.—Refinement was too strong on the side of the Rajpoot to admit this incident, which, with that of wardship (both partial in Europe), illustrated the rapacity of the feudal aristocracy. Every chief, before he marries, makes it known to his sovereign. It is a compliment which is expected, and is besides attended with some advantage, as the prince invariably confers presents of honour, according to the station of the individual.

No Rajpoot can marry in his own clan; and the incident was originated in the Norman institutes, to prevent the vassal marrying out of his class, or amongst the enemies of his sovereign.

Thus, setting aside marriage (which even in Europe was only partial and local) and alienation, four of the six chief incidents marking the feudal system are in force in Rajast'han, viz. relief, escheats, aids, and wardships.

DURATION OF GRANTS.—I shall now endeavour to combine all the knowledge I possess with regard to the objects attained in granting lands, the nature and durability of these grants, whether for life and renewable, or in perpetuity. I speak of the rules as understood in Méwar. We ought

[1] The charter of Henry I. promises the custody of heirs to the mother or next of kin.—Hallam, vol. ii. p. 429.

[2] Hallam, vol. i. p. 190.

not to expect much system in what was devoid of regularity, even according to the old principles of European feudal law, which, though now reduced to some fixed principles, originated in, and was governed by, fortuitous circumstances; and after often changing its character, ended in despotism, oligarchy, or democracy.

There are two classes of Rajpoot landholders in Méwar, though the one greatly exceeds the other in number. One is the *Grásya t'hacoor*, or lord; the other the *Bhoomia*. The Grasya chieftain is he who holds (*grás*) by grant (*putta*) of the prince, for which he performs service with specified quotas at home and abroad, renewable at every lapse, when all the ceremonies of resumption,[1] the fine of relief,[2] and the investiture take place.

The Bhoomia does not renew his grant, but holds on prescriptive possession. He succeeds without any fine, but pays a small annual quit-rent, and can be called upon for local service in the district which he inhabits for a certain period of time. He is the counterpart of the allodial proprietor of the European system, and the real 'zemindar' of these principalities. Both have the same signification; from *bhoom* and *zemin*, 'land': the latter is an exotic of Persian origin.

GRASYA.—Grasya is from *grás*, 'a subsistence'; literally and familiarly 'a mouthful.' Whether it may have a like origin with the Celtic word *gwas*,[3] said to mean 'a servant,'[4] and whence the word vassal is derived, I shall leave to etymologists to decide, who may trace the resemblance to the *grásya*, the vassal chieftain of the Rajpoots. All the chartularies or puttas[5] commence, "To . . . *grás* has been ordained."

WHETHER RESUMABLE.—It has always been a subject of doubt whether grants were resumable at pleasure, or without some delinquency imputable to the vassal. Their duration in Europe was, *at least*, the life of the possessor, when they reverted[6] to the fisc. The whole of the ceremonies in cases of such lapse are decisive on this point in Méwar. The right to resume, therefore, may be presumed to exist; while the non-practice of it, the formalities of renewal being gone through, may be said to render the right a dead letter. But to prove its existence I need only mention, that so late as the reign of Rana Singram,[7] the fiefs of Méwar were actually movable; and little more than a century and a half has passed since this practice ceased. Thus a Rahtore would shift, with family, chattels, and retainers, from the north into the wilds of Chuppun;[8] while the Suktawut relieved would occupy the plains at the foot of the Aravulli;[9] or a Chondawut would exchange his abode on the banks of the Chumbul with a Pramara or Chohan from the table-mountain, the eastern boundary of Méwar.[10]

[1] *Zubti*, 'sequestration.' [2] *Nuzzerana*.

[3] It might not be unworthy of research to trace many words common to the Hindu and the Celt; or to inquire whether the Kimbri, the Juts or Getes, the Sacasenæ, the Catti of the Elbe and Cimbric Chersonese, and the ancient Britons, did not bring their terms with their bards and *vates* (the Bhats and Bardais) from the highland of Scythia east of the Caspian, which originated the nations common to both, improved beyond the Wolga and the Indus.

[4] Hallam, vol. i.

[5] *Patta*, a 'patent' or 'grant': *Pattawat*, 'holder of the fief or grant.'

[6] Montesquieu, chaps. xxv. liv. xxxi. [7] Ten generations ago.

[8] The mountainous and woody region to the south-west, dividing Méwar from Guzzerat.

[9] The grand chain dividing the western from the central states of Rajast'han.

[10] Such changes were triennial; and, as I have heard the prince himself say,

Since these exchanges were occurring, it is evident the fiefs (*puttas*) were not grants in perpetuity. This is just the state of the benefices in France at an early period, as described by Gibbon, following Montesquieu : " Les bénéfices étoient amovibles ; bientôt ils les rendirent perpétuels, et enfin héréditaires." [1] This is the precise gradation of fiefs in Méwar ; movable, perpetual, and then hereditary. The sons were occasionally permitted to succeed their fathers ; [2] an indulgence which easily grew into a right, though the crown had the indubitable reversion. It is not, however, impossible that these changes [3] were not of ancient authority, but arose from the policy of the times to prevent infidelity.

We ought to have a high opinion of princes who could produce an effect so powerful on the minds of a proud and turbulent nobility. The son was heir to the title and power over the vassals' personals and movables, and to the allegiance of his father, but to nothing which could endanger that allegiance.

A proper apportioning and mixture of the different clans was another good result to prevent their combinations in powerful families, which gave effect to rebellion, and has tended more than external causes to the ruin which the state of Méwar exhibits.

Throughout the various gradations of its nobility, it was the original policy to introduce some who were foreign in country and blood. Chiefs of the Rahtore, Chohan, Pramara, Solanki, and Bhatti tribes were intermingled. Of these several were lineal descendants of the most ancient races of the kings of Dehli and Anhulwarra Puttun ; [4] and from these, in order to preserve the purity of blood, the princes of Méwar took their wives, when the other princes of Hind assented to the degradation of giving daughters in marriage to the emperors of Dehli. The princes of Méwar never yielded in this point, but preserved their ancient manners amidst all vicissitudes. In like manner did the nobles of the Rana's blood take daughters from the same tribes ; the interest of this foreign race was therefore strongly identified with the general welfare, and on all occasions of internal turmoil and rebellion they invariably supported their prince. But when these wise institutions were overlooked, when the great clans increased and congregated together, and the crown demesne was impoverished by prodigality, rebellions were fostered by Mahratta rapacity, which were little known during the lengthened paramount sway of the kings of Dehli. This foreign admixture will lead us to the discussion of the different kinds

so interwoven with their customs was this rule that it caused no dissatisfaction ; but of this we may be allowed at least to doubt. It was a perfect check to the imbibing of local attachment ; and the prohibition against erecting forts for refuge or defiance, prevented its growth if acquired. It produced the object intended, obedience to the prince, and unity against the restless Mogul. Perhaps to these institutions it is owing that Méwar alone never was conquered by the kings during the protracted struggle of seven centuries ; though at length worried and worn out, her power expired with theirs, and predatory spoliation completed her ruin.

[1] Gibbon, *Misc. Works*, vol. iii. p. 189 ; *sur le système féodal surtout en France.*

[2] Hallam, quoting Gregory of Tours ; the picture drawn in A.D. 595.

[3] " Fiefs had partially become hereditary towards the end of the first race : in these days they had not the idea of an ' unalienable fief.' Montesquieu, vol. ii. p. 431. The historian of the Middle Ages doubts if ever they were resumable at pleasure, unless from delinquency.

[4] The Nehlvara of D'Anville and the Arabian travellers of the eighth century, the capital of the Balham kings.

of grants: a difference, perhaps, more nominal than real, but exhibiting a distinction so wide as to imply grants resumable and irresumable.

KALA PUTTAS.—It is elsewhere related that two great clans, descendants of the Ranas Rae Mul and Udya Sing, and their numerous scions, forming subdivisions with separate titles or patronymics, compose the chief vassalage of this country.

Chondawut and Suktawut are the stock; the former is subdivided into ten, the latter into about six clans. Rajpoots never intermarry with their own kin: the prohibition has no limit; it extends to the remotest degree. All these clans are resolvable into the generic term of 'the race' or Cúla Sesodia. A Sesodia man and woman cannot unite in wedlock—all these are therefore of the blood royal; and the essayists on population would have had a fine field in these quarters a century ago, ere constant misery had thinned the country, to trace the numerous progeny of Chonda and Sukta in the *Genesis*[1] of Méwar. The Bhat's genealogies would still, to a certain extent, afford the same means.

Descent gives a strength to the tenure of these tribes which the foreign nobles do not possess; for although, from all that has been said, it will be evident that a right of reversion and resumption existed (though seldom exercised, and never but in cases of crime), yet the foreigner had not this strength in the soil, even though of twenty generations' duration. The epithet of *kala putta*, or 'black grant,' attaches to the foreign grant, and is admitted by the holder, from which the kinsman thinks himself exempt. It is virtually a grant resumable; nor can the possessors feel that security which the other widely affiliated aristocracies afford. When, on a recent occasion, a revision of all the grants took place, the old ones being called in to be renewed under the sign-manual of the reigning prince, the minister himself visited the chief of Saloombra, the head of the Chondawuts, at his residence at the capital, for this purpose. Having become possessed of several villages in the confusion of the times, a perusal of the grant would have been the means of detection; and on being urged to send to his estate for it, he replied, pointing to the palace, "My grant is in the foundation of that edifice": an answer worthy of a descendant of Chonda, then only just of age. The expression marks the spirit which animates this people, and recalls to mind the well-known reply of our own Earl Warenne, on the very same occasion, to the *quo warranto* of Edward: "By their swords my ancestors obtained this land, and by mine will I maintain it."

Hence it may be pronounced that a grant of an estate is for the life of the holder, with inheritance for his offspring in lineal descent or adoption, with the sanction of the prince, and resumable for crime or incapacity:[2] this reversion and power of resumption being marked by the usual ceremonies on each lapse of the grantee, of sequestration (*zubti*), of relief (*nuzzerana*), of homage and investiture of the heir. Those estates held by foreign nobles differ not in tenure; though, for the reasons specified, they have not the same grounds of security as the others, in whose welfàre the whole body is

[1] *Jenem*, 'birth'; *es*, lord' or 'man.'

[2] "La loi des Lombards oppose les bénéfices à la propriété. Les historiens, les formules, les codes des différens peuples barbares, tous les monumens qui nous restent, sont unanimes. Enfin, ceux qui ont écrit le livre des fiefs, nous apprennent, que d'abord les Seigneurs purent les ôter à leur volonté, qu'ensuite ils les assurèrent pour un an, et après les donnerent pour la vie."—*L'Esprit des Loix*, chaps. xvi. liv. 30.

interested, feeling the case to be their own : and their interests, certainly, have not been so consulted since the rebellions of S. 1822,[1] and subsequent years. Witness the Chohans of Baidla and Kotario (in the Oodipoor valley), and the Pramar of the plateau of Méwar, all chiefs of the first rank.

The difficulty and danger of resuming an old-established grant in these countries are too great to be lightly risked. Though in all these estates there is a mixture of foreign Rajpoots, yet the blood of the chief predominates ; and these must have a leader of their own, or be incorporated in the estates of the nearest of kin. This increase might not be desirable for the crown, but the sub-vassals cannot be turned adrift ; a resumption therefore in these countries is widely felt, as it involves many. If crime or incapacity render it necessary, the prince inducts a new head of that blood ; and it is their pride, as well as the prince's interest, that a proper choice should be made. If, as has often occurred, the title be abolished, the sub-vassals retain their sub-infeudations, and become attached to the crown.

Many estates were obtained, during periods of external commotion, by threats, combination, or the avarice of the prince—his short-sighted policy, or that of his ministers,—which have been remedied in the late reorganisation of Méwar ; where, by retrograding half a century, and bringing matters as near as possible to the period preceding civil dissention, they have advanced at least a century towards order.

BHOOMIA, THE ALLODIAL PROPRIETOR.—It is stated in the historical annals of this country that the ancient clans, prior to Sanga Rana,[2] had ceased, on the rising greatness of the subsequent new division of clans, to hold the higher grades of rank ; and had, in fact, merged into the general military landed proprietors of this country under the term *bhoomia*, a most expressive and comprehensive name, importing absolute identity with the soil : *bhoom* meaning 'land,' and being far more expressive than the new-fangled word, unknown to Hindu India, of *zemindar*, the 'landholder' of Mahomedan growth. These Bhoomias, the scions of the earliest princes, are to be met with in various parts of Méwar ; though only in those of high antiquity, where they were defended from oppression by the rocks and wilds in which they obtained a footing ; as in Komulmér, the wilds of Chuppun, or plains of Mandelgurh, long under the kings, and where their agricultural pursuits maintained them.

Their clannish appellations, Kombawut, Loonawut, and Ranawut, distinctly show from what stem and when they branched off ; and as they ceased to be of sufficient importance to visit the court on the new and continually extending ramifications, they took to the plough. But while they disdained not to derive a subsistence from labouring as husbandmen, they never abandoned their arms ; and the Bhoomia, amid the crags of the alpine Aravulli where he pastures his cattle or cultivates his fields, preserves the erect mien and proud spirit of his ancestors, with more tractability, and less arrogance and folly, than his more courtly but now widely separated brethren, who often make a jest of his industrious but less refined qualifications.[3] Some of these yet possess entire villages, which are subject to the payment of a small quit-rent : they also constitute a local militia, to

[1] A.D. 1766. [2] Contemporary and opponent of Sultan Baber.

[3] Many of them taking wives from the degraded but aboriginal races in their neighbouring retreats, have begot a mixed progeny, who, in describing themselves, unite the tribes of father and mother.

be called in by the governor of the district, but for which service they are entitled to rations or *paiti*.[1] These, the allodial[2] tenantry of our feudal system, form a considerable body in many districts, armed with matchlock, sword, and shield. In Mandelgurh, when their own interests and the prince's unite (though the rapacity of governors, pupils of the Mahratta and other predatory schools, have disgusted these independents), four thousand Bhoomias could be collected. They held and maintained without support the important fortress of that district, during half a century of turmoil, for their prince. Mandelgurh is the largest district of Méwar, and in its three hundred and sixty towns and villages many specimens of ancient usage may be found. The Solanki held largely here in ancient days, and the descendant of the princes of Puttun still retains his Bhoom and title of Rao.[3]

All this feudal militia pay a quit-rent to the crown, and perform local but limited service on the frontier garrison ; and upon invasion,[4] when the *Khér* is called out, the whole are at the disposal of the prince on furnishing rations only. They assert that they ought not to pay this quit-rent and perform service also ; but this may be doubted, since the sum is so small. To elude it, they often performed service under some powerful chief, where faction or court interest caused it to be winked at. To serve without a *putta* is the great object of ambition. *Ma ca bhoom*, 'my land,' in their Doric tongue, is a favourite phrase.[5]

[1] Literally, 'a belly-full.'

[2] Allodial property is defined (Hallam, vol. i. p. 144) as "land which had descended by inheritance, subject to no burthen but public defence. It passed to all the children equally ; in failure of children, to the nearest kindred. Thus it is strictly the *Meeras* or *Bhoom* of the Rajpoots : inheritance, patrimony. In Méwar it is divisible to a certain extent ; but in Kutch, to infinity : and is liable only to local defence. The holder of bhoom calls it his *Adyapi, i.e.* of old, by prescriptive right ; not by written deed.

Montesquieu, describing the conversion of allodial estates into fiefs, says, "these lands were held by Romans or Franks (*i.e.* freemen) not the king's vassals," viz. lands exterior and anterior to the monarchy. We have Rahtore, Solanki, and other tribes, now holding bhoom in various districts, whose ancestors were conquered by the Sesodias, but left in possession of small portions insufficient to cause jealousy. Some of these may be said to have converted their lands into fiefs, as the Chohan lord of ——, who served the Saloombra chief.

[3] Amidst ruins overgrown with forest, I discovered on two tables of stone the genealogical history of this branch, which was of considerable use in elucidating that of Anhulwarra, and which corresponded so well with the genealogies of a decayed bard of the family, who travelled the country for a subsistence, that I feel assured they formerly made good use of these marble records.

[4] See Appendix, Nos. XVI. and XVII.

[5] I was intimately acquainted with, and much esteemed, many of these Bhoomia chiefs—from my friend Puharjee (the rock), Ranawut of Umurgurh, to the Kombawut of Sesodia on the highest point, lord of the pass of the Aravulli ; and even the mountain lion, Doonger Sing, who bore amongst us, from his old raids, the familiar title of Roderic Dhu. In each situation I have had my tents filled with them ; and it was one of the greatest pleasures I ever experienced, after I had taken my leave of them, perhaps for ever, crossed the frontiers of Méwar, and encamped in the dreary pass between it and Marwar, to find that a body of them had been my guards during the night. This is one of the many pleasing recollections of the past. Fortunately for our happiness, the mind admits their preponderance over opposite feelings. I had much to do in aiding the restoration of their past condition ; leaving, I believe, as few traces of error in the mode as could be expected, where so many conflicting interests were to be reconciled.

Circumstances have concurred to produce a resemblance even to the refined fiction of giving up their allodial property to have it conferred as a fief. But in candour it should be stated, that the only instances were caused by the desire of being revenged on the immediate superiors of the vassals. The Rahtore chief of Dabla held of his superior, the Raja of Bunéra, three considerable places included in the grant of Bunéra. He paid homage, an annual quit-rent, was bound to attend him personally to court, and to furnish thirty-five horse in case of an invasion. During the troubles, though perfectly equal to their performance, he was remiss in all these duties. His chief, with returning peace, desired to enforce the return to ancient customs, and his rights so long withheld; but the Rahtore had felt the sweets of entire independence, and refused to attend his summons. To the warrant he replied, "his head and Dabla were together"; and he would neither pay the quit-rent nor attend his court. This refractory spirit was reported to the Rana; and it ended in Dabla being added to the fisc, and the chief's holding the rest as a vassal of the Rana, but only to perform local service. There are many other petty free proprietors on the Bunéra estate, holding from small portions of land to small villages; but the service is limited and local in order to swell the chief's miniature court. If they accompany him, he must find rations for them and their steeds.

So cherished is this tenure of Bhoom, that the greatest chiefs are always solicitous to obtain it, even in the villages wholly dependent on their authority: a decided proof of its durability above common grants.

The various modes in which it is acquired, and the precise technicalities which distinguished its tenure, as well as the privileges attached to it, are fully developed in translations of different deeds on the subject.[1]

Rajas of Bunéra and Shapoora.—We have also, amongst the nobility of Méwar, two who hold the independent title of prince or raja, one of whom is by far too powerful for a subject. These are the Rajas of Bunéra and Shapoora, both of the blood royal. The ancestor of the first was the twin-brother of Rana Jey Sing; the other, a Ranawut, branched off from Rana Udya Sing.

They have their grants renewed, and receive the khelat of investiture; but they pay no relief, and are exempt from all but personal attendance at their prince's court, and the local service of the district in which their estates are situated. They have hitherto paid but little attention to their duties, but this defect arose out of the times. These lands lying most exposed to the imperial headquarters at Ajmér, they were compelled to bend to circumstances, and the kings were glad to confer rank and honour on such near relations of the Rana's house. He bestowed on them the titles of Raja, and added to the Shapoora chief's patrimony a large estate in Ajmér, which he now holds direct of the British Government, on payment of an annual tribute.

Form and Substance of Grant.—To give a proper idea of the variety of items forming these chartularies, I append several[2] which exhibit the rights, privileges, and honours, as well as the sources of income, while they also record the terms on which they are granted. Many royalties have been alienated in modern times by the thoughtless prodigality of the princes; even the grand mark of vassalage, the fine of relief,

[1] See Appendix.

[2] See Appendix, Nos. IV., V., VI.

has been forgiven to one or two individuals; portions of transit duties, tolls on ferries, and other seignorial rights; coining copper currency; exactions of every kind, from the levy of toll for night protection of merchandise and for the repairs of fortifications, to the share of the depredations of the common robber, will sufficiently show the demoralisation of the country.

Division of Puttas, or Sub-infeudation.—Many years ago, when the similarity of the systems first struck my attention, I took one of the grants or *puttas* of a great vassal of Jeipoor, and dissected it in all its minutiæ, with the aid of a very competent authority who had resided as one of the managers of the chief. This document, in which the subdivision of the whole clan is detailed, materially aided me in developing the system.

The court and the household economy of a great chieftain is a miniature representation of the sovereign's: the same officers, from the purdhan, or minister, to the cup-bearer (*panairie*), as well as the same domestic arrangements. He must have his *sheesh-mahl*,[1] his *bari-mahl*,[2] and his *mindur*,[3] like his prince. He enters the *durri-sala*, or carpet hall, the minstrel [4] preceding him rehearsing the praises of his family; and he takes his seat on his throne, while the assembled retainers, marshalled in lines on the right and left, simultaneously exclaim, "Health to our chief!" which salutation he returns by bowing to all as he passes them. When he is seated, at a given signal they all follow the example, and shield rattles against shield as they wedge into their places.

We have neither the kiss nor individual oaths of fidelity administered. It is sufficient, when a chief succeeds to his patrimony, that his '*án*' [5] is proclaimed within his *seem* or boundary. Allegiance is as hereditary as the land: "I am your child; my head and sword are yours, my service is at your command." It is a rare thing for a Rajpoot to betray his T'hacoor, while the instances of self-devotion for him are innumerable: many will be seen interspersed in these papers. Base desertion, to their honour be it said, is little known, and known only to be execrated. Fidelity to the chief, *Swam Dherma*, is the climax of all the virtues. The Rajpoot is taught from his infancy, in the song of the bard, to regard it as the source of honour here, and of happiness hereafter. The poet Chund abounds with episodes on the duty and beauty of fidelity; nor does it require a very fervid imagination to picture the affections which such a life is calculated to promote, when the chief is possessed of the qualities to call them forth. At the chase his vassals attend him: in the covert of the forest, the ground their social board, they eat their repast together, from the venison or wild boar furnished by the sport of the day; nor is the cup neglected. They are familiarly admitted at all times to his presence, and accompany him to the court of their mutual sovereign. In short, they are inseparable.[6]

[1] Mirror apartments. [2] Gardens on the terrace within the palace.

[3] Private temple of worship. [4] Dholi.

[5] *An* is the oath of allegiance. Three things in Méwar are royalties a subject cannot meddle with: 1, *An*, or oath of allegiance; 2, *Dán*, or transit dues on commerce; 3, *Kán*, or mines of the precious metals.

[6] I rather describe what they were, than what they are. Contentions and poverty have weakened their sympathies and affections; but the mind of philanthropy must hope that they will again become what they have been.

Their having retained so much of their ancient manners and customs, during centuries of misery and oppression, is the best evidence that those customs were riveted to their very souls. The Rajpoot of character is a being of the most acute sensibility; where honour is concerned, the most trivial omission is often ignorantly construed into an affront.

In all the large estates, the chief must provide for his sons or brothers, according to his means and the number of immediate descendants. In an estate of sixty to eighty thousand rupees of annual rent, the second brother might have a village of three to five thousand of rent. This is his patrimony (*bapota*): he besides pushes his fortune at the court of his sovereign or abroad. Juniors share in proportion. These again subdivide, and have their little circle of dependents. Each new family is known by the name of the founder conjoined to that of his father and tribe: *Mán Mégsingote Suktawut;* that is, 'Mán, family of Mégh, tribe Suktawut.' The subdivisions descend to the lowest denomination.

CHURSA.—*Chursa*, a 'hide of land,' or about sufficient to furnish an equipped cavalier. It is a singular coincidence that the term for the lowest subdivision of land for military service should be the same amongst the Rajpoots as in the English system. Besides being similar in name, it nearly corresponds in actual quantity. From the beginning of the Anglo-Saxon government the land was divided into hides, each comprehending what could be cultivated by a single plough.[1] Four hides constituted one knight's fee,[2] which is stated to be about forty acres. The Chursa may have from twenty-five to thirty beegas; which are equal to about ten acres—the Saxon hide.

For what these minor vassals held to be their rights on the great puttawuts, the reader is again referred to the letter of protest of the inferior puttawuts of the Deogurh estate—it may aid his judgment; and it is curious to observe how nearly the subject of their prayer to the sovereign corresponded with the edict of Conrad of Italy,[3] in the year 1037, which originated in disagreements between the great lords and their vassals on the subject of sub-infeudations.

The extent to which the subdivision before-mentioned is carried in some of the Rajpoot states, is ruinous to the protection and general welfare of the country. It is pursued in some parts till there is actually nothing left sufficiently large to share, or to furnish subsistence for one individual: consequently a great deprivation of services to the state ensues. But this does not prevail so much in the larger principalities as in the isolated tributary t'hacoorats or lordships scattered over the country; as amongst the Jharéjas of Kutch, the tribes in Cattiawar, and the small independencies of Guzzerat bordering on the greater western Rajpoot states. This error in policy requires to be checked by supreme

[1] Millar's *Historical View of the English Government*, p. 85.

[2] Hume, *History of England*, Appendix II. vol. ii. p. 291.

[3] "1. That no man should be deprived of his fief, whether held of the emperor or mesne lord, but by the laws of the empire and *judgment of his peers*. 2. That from such judgment the vassal might appeal to his sovereign. 3. That fiefs, should be inherited by sons and their children, or in their failure by brothers, provided they were *feuda paterna*, such as had descended from the father. 4. That the lord should not alienate the fief of his vassal without his consent."

authority, as it was in England by *Magna Charta*,[1] when the barons of those days took such precautions to secure their own seignorial rights.

The system in these countries of minute subdivision of fiefs is termed *bhyád*,[2] or brotherhood, synonymous to the tenure by frerage of France, but styled only an approximation to sub-infeudation.[3] "Give me my *bhut* (share)," says the Rajpoot, when he attains to man's estate, 'the bhut of the bhyad,' the portion of the frerage ; and thus they go on clipping and paring till all are impoverished. The 'customs' of France[4] preserved the dignities of families and the indivisibility of a feudal homage, without exposing the younger sons of a gentleman to beggary and dependence. It would be a great national benefit if some means could be found to limit this subdivision, but it is an evil difficulty of remedy. The divisibility of the Kutch and Cattiawar frerage, carried to the most destructive extent, is productive of litigation, crime, and misery. Where it has proper limits it is useful ; but though the idea of each rood supporting its man is very poetical, it does not and cannot answer in practice. Its limit in Méwar we would not undertake to assert, but the vassals are careful not to let it become too small ; they send the extra numbers to seek their fortunes abroad. In this custom, and the difficulty of finding *daijas*, or dowers, for their daughters, we have the two chief causes of infanticide amongst the Rajpoots, which horrible practice was not always confined to the female.

The author of the Middle Ages exemplifies ingeniously the advantages of sub-infeudation, by the instance of two persons holding one knight's fee ; and as the lord was entitled to the service of one for forty days, he could commute it for the joint service of the two for twenty days each. He even erects as a maxim on it, that "whatever opposition was made to the rights of sub-infeudation or frerage, would indicate decay in the military character, the living principle of feudal tenure" ;[5] which remark may be just where proper limitation exists, before it reaches that extent when the impoverished vassal would descend to mend his shoes instead of his shield. Primogeniture is the corner-stone of feudality, but this unrestricted sub-infeudation would soon destroy it.[6] It is strong in these states ; its rights were first introduced by the Normans from Scandinavia. But more will appear on this subject and its technicalities, in the personal narrative of the author.

[1] By the revised statute, *Qui emptores*, of Edw. I., which forbids it in excess, under penalty of forfeiture.—Hallam, vol. i. p. 184.

[2] *Bhyád*, 'frerage.'

[3] Hallam, vol. i. p. 186.

[4] *Ibid.*

[5] *Ibid.*

[6] "Le *droit d'aînesse* a causé, pendant l'existence du régime féodal, une multitude de guerres et de procès. Notre histoire nous présente, à chaque page, des cadets réduits à la mendicité, se livrant à toutes sortes de brigandages pour réparer les torts de la fortune ; des aînés, refusant la légitime à leurs frères ; des cadets, assassinant leur aîné pour lui succéder, etc."—See article, "Droit d'aînesse," *Dict. de l'Ancien Régime*.

CHAPTER IV

Rekwalee—Servitude—Bussie—Gola and Das—Private feuds and composition —Rajpoot Purdhans or Premiers.

REKWALEE.—I now proceed to another point of striking resemblance between the systems of the east and west, arising from the same causes—the unsettled state of society, and the deficiency of paramount protection. It is here called *rekwalee*,[1] or 'preservation'; the *salvamenta* of Europe.[2] To a certain degree it always existed in these states; but the interminable predatory warfare of the last half century increased it to so frightful an extent that superior authority was required to redeem the abuses it had occasioned. It originated in the necessity of protection; and the modes of obtaining it, as well as the compensation when obtained, were various. It often consisted of money or kind on the reaping of each harvest: sometimes in a multiplicity of petty privileges and advantages, but the chief object was to obtain *bhoom*: and here we have one solution of the constituted *bhoomia*,[3] assimilating, as observed, to the allodial proprietor. Bhoom thus obtained is irrevocable; and in the eager anxiety for its acquisition, we have another decided proof of every other kind of tenure being deemed resumable by the crown.

It was not unfrequent that application for protection was made to the nearest chief by the tenants of the fisc; a course eventually sanctioned by the government, which could not refuse assent where it could not protect. Here, then, we revert to first principles; and 'seignorial rights' may be forfeited when they cease to yield that which ought to have originated them, viz. benefit to the community. Personal service at stated periods, to aid in the agricultural[4] economy of the protector, was sometimes stipulated, when the husbandmen were to find implements and cattle,[5] and to attend whenever ordered. The protected calls the chief 'patron'; and the condition may not unaptly be compared to that of personal commendation,[6] like *salvamenta*, founded on the disturbed state of society. But what originated thus was often continued and multiplied by avarice, and the spirit of rapine, which disgraced the Rajpoot of the last half century, though he had abundance of apologies for 'scouring the country.' But all *salvamenta* and other marks of vassalage, obtained during these

[1] See Appendix, Nos. VII., VIII., and IX.

[2] This is the '*sauvement* ou *vingtain*' of the French system: there it ceased with the cause. " Les guerres (feudal) cessèrent avec le régime féodal, et les paysans n'eurent plus besoin de la protection du Seigneur; on ne les força pas moins de réparer son château, et de lui payer le droi qui se nommait de *sauvement* ou *vingtain*."—Art. " Château," *Dict. de l'Anc. Régime.*

[3] The chief might lose his *putta* lands, and he would then dwindle down into the *bhoomia* proprietor, which title only lawless force could take from him. See Appendix, No. IX.

[4] See Appendix, No. X., Art. II.

[5] This species would come under the distinct term of Hydages due by soccage vassals, who in return for protection supplies carriages and work.—Hume, vol. ii. p. 308.

[6] Hallam, vol. i. p. 169.

times of desolation, were annulled in the settlement which took place between the Rana and his chiefs, in A.D. 1818.[1]

But the crown itself, by some singular proceeding, possesses, or did possess, according to the *Putta Buhae*, or Book of Grants, considerable *salvamenta* right, especially in the districts between the new and ancient capitals, in sums of from twenty to one hundred rupees in separate villages.

To such an extent has this *rekwalee* [2] been carried when protection was desired, that whole communities have ventured their liberty, and become, if not slaves, yet nearly approaching the condition of slaves, to the protector. But no common visitation ever leads to an evil of this magnitude. I mention the fact merely to show that it does exist; and we may infer that the chief, who has become the arbiter of the lives and fortunes of his followers, must have obtained this power by devoting all to their protection. The term thus originated, and probably now (with many others) written for the first time in English letters in this sense, is *Bussie*.

BUSSIE.—Slavery is to be found in successive stages of society of Europe, but we have no parallel in Rajwarra (at least in name) to the agricultural serfs and *villains* of Europe; nor is there any intermediate term denoting a species of slavery between the *Gola* [3] of the Hindu chief's household and the free Rajpoot, but the singular one of *bussie*, which must be explained, since it cannot be translated. This class approximates closely to the *tributarii* and *coloni*, perhaps to the *servi*, of the Salic Franks, "who were cultivators of the earth, and subject to residence upon their master's estate, though not destitute of property or civil rights." [4] Precisely the

[1] In indulging my curiosity on this subject, I collected some hundred engagements, and many of a most singular nature. We see the chieftain stipulating for fees on marriages; for a dish of the good fare at the wedding feast, which he transfers to a relation of his district if unable to attend himself; portions of fuel and provender; and even wherewithal to fill the wassail cup in his days of merriment. The Rajpoot's religious notions are not of so strict a character as to prevent his even exacting his *rekwalee* dues from the church lands, and the threat of slaughtering the sacred flock of our Indian Apollo has been resorted to, to compel payment when withheld. Nay, by the chiefs it was imposed on things locomotive: on caravans, or Tandas of merchandise, wherever they halted for the day, *rekwalee* was demanded. Each petty chief through whose district or patch of territory they travelled, made a demand, till commerce was dreadfully shackled; but it was the only way in which it could be secured. It was astonishing how commerce was carried on at all; yet did the cloths of Dacca and the shawls of Cashmere pass through all such restraints, and were never more in request. Where there is demand no danger will deter enterprise; and commerce flourished more when these predatory armies were rolling like waves over the land, than during the succeeding halcyon days of pacification.

[2] The method by which the country is brought under this tax is as follows:—"When the people are almost ruined by continual robberies and plunders, the leader of the band of thieves, or some friend of his, proposes that, for a sum of money annually paid, he will keep a number of men in arms to protect such a tract of ground, or as many parishes as submit to the contribution. When the terms are agreed upon he ceases to steal, and thereby the contributors are safe: if anyone refuse to pay, he is immediately plundered. To colour all this villainy, those concerned in the robberies pay the tax with the rest; and all the neighbourhood must comply or be undone. This is the case (among others) with the whole low country of the shire of Ross."—Extract from Lord Lovat's Memorial to George I. on the State of the Highlands of Scotland, in A.D. 1724.

[3] In Persian *gholam*, literally 'slave'; evidently a word of the same origin with the Hindu *gola*.

[4] Hallam, vol. i. p. 217.

condition of the cultivator in Harouti, who now tills for a task-master the fields he formerly owned, degraded to the name of *hallee*,[1] a ploughman.

"When small proprietors," says Hallam, "lost their lands by mere rapine, we may believe their liberty was hardly less endangered." The *hallee* of Haravati knows the bitter truth of this inference, which applies to the subject immediately before us, the *bussie*. The portion of liberty the latter has parted with, was not originally lost through compulsion on the part of the protector, but from external violence, which made this desperate remedy necessary. Very different from the *hallee* of Kotah, who is servile though without the title—a serf in condition but without the patrimony; compelled to labour for subsistence on the land he once owned; chained to it by the double tie of debt and strict police; and if flight were practicable, the impossibility of bettering his condition from the anarchy around would render it unavailing. This is not the practice under the patriarchal native government, which, with all its faults, retains the old links of society, with its redeeming sympathies; but springs from a *maire du palais*, who pursued an unfeeling and mistaken policy towards this class of society till of late years. Mistaken ambition was the origin of the evil; he saw his error, and remedied it in time to prevent further mischief to the state. This octogenarian ruler, Zalim Sing of Kotah, is too much of a philosopher and politician to let passion overcome his interests and reputation; and we owe to the greatest despot a state ever had the only regular charter which at present exists in Rajast'han, investing a corporate body with the election of their own magistrates and the making of their own laws, subject only to confirmation; with all the privileges which marked in the outset the foundation of the free cities of Europe, and that of boroughs in England.

It is true that, in detached documents, we see the spirit of these institutions existing in Méwar, and it is as much a matter of speculation, whether this wise ruler promulgated this novelty as a trap for good opinions, or from policy and foresight alone: aware, when all around him was improving, from the shackles of restraint being cast aside, that his retention of them must be hurtful to himself. Liberality in this exigence answered the previous purpose of extortion. His system, even then, was good by comparison: all around was rapine, save in the little oasis kept verdant by his skill, where he permitted no other oppression than his own.

This charter is appended [2] as a curiosity in legislation, being given thirty years ago. Another, for the agriculturalists' protection, was set up in A.D. 1821. No human being prompted either; though the latter is modelled from the proceedings in Méwar, and may have been intended, as before observed, to entrap applause.

In every district of Haravati the stone was raised to record this ordinance.

GOLA—DAS (*Slaves*).—Famine in these regions is the great cause of loss of liberty: thousands were sold in the last great famine. The predatory system of the Pindarries and mountain tribes aided to keep it up. Here, as amongst the Franks, freedom is derived through the mother. The offspring of a *golee* [3] or *dasi* must be a slave. Hence the great number of

[1] From *hal*, 'a plough.' *Syl* is 'a plough' in Saxon (Turner's *Anglo-Saxons*). The *h* and *s* are permutable throughout Rajwarra. In Marwar, *Salim Sing* is pronounced *Halim Hing*.

[2] See Appendix, No XI.

[3] Female slave.

golas in Rajpoot families, whose illegitimate offspring are still adorned in Méwar, as our Saxon slaves were of old, with a silver ring round the left ankle, instead of the neck. They are well treated, and are often amongst the best of the military retainers; [1] but are generally esteemed in proportion to the quality of the mother, whether Rajpootnee, Moslem, or of the degraded tribes: they hold confidential places about the chiefs of whose blood they are. The great-grandfather of the late chief of Deogurh used to appear at court with three hundred *golas* [2] on horseback in his train, the sons of Rajpoots, each with a gold ring round his ankle: men whose lives were his own. This chief could then head two thousand retainers, his own vassals.[3]

Tacitus describes the baneful effects of gambling amongst the German tribes, as involving personal liberty; their becoming slaves, and being subsequently sold by the winner. The Rajpoot's passion for gaming, as remarked in the history of the tribes, is strong; and we can revert to periods long anterior to Tacitus, and perhaps before the woods of Germany were peopled with the worshippers of Tuisto, for the antiquity of this vice amongst the Rajpoot warriors, presenting a highly interesting picture of its pernicious effects. Yoodishtra having staked and lost the throne of India to Duryodhana, to recover it hazarded the beautiful and virtuous Droopdevi. By the loaded dice of his foe she became the *golee* of the Coorwa, who, triumphing in his pride, would have unveiled her in public; but the deity presiding over female modesty preserved her from the rude gaze of the assembled host; the miraculous scarf lengthened as he withdrew it, till tired, he desisted at the instance of superior interposition. Yoodishtra, not satisfied with this, staked twelve years of his personal liberty, and became an exile from the haunts of Kalindi, a wanderer in the wilds skirting the distant ocean.

The illegitimate sons of the Rana are called *das*, literally 'slave': they have no rank, though they are liberally provided for. *Bussie* signifies 'acquired slavery'; in contradistinction to *gola*, 'an hereditary slave.' The gola can only marry a golee: the lowest Rajpoot would refuse his daughter to a son of the Rana of this kind. The bussie can redeem [4] his liberty: the gola has no wish to do so, because he could not improve his condition nor overcome his natural defects. To the bussie nothing dishonourable attaches: the class retain their employments and caste, and

[1] See Appendix, No. XIX.

[2] The reader of Dow's translation of Ferishta may recollect that when Kootub Udin was left the viceroy of the conqueror, he is made to say, "He placed one *Gola* upon the throne of Ajmér"; mistaking this appellation of the natural brother of the last Hindu sovereign for a proper name. He is mentioned by the bard Chund in his exploits of Pirthwirájá.

[3] I have often received the most confidential messages, from chiefs of the highest rank, through these channels.

[4] The *das* or 'slave' may hold a fief in Rajast'han, but he never can rise above the condition in which this defect of birth has placed him. "L'affranchissement consistait à sortir de la classe des serfs, par l'acquisition d'un fief, ou seulement d'un fonds. La nécessité où s'étaient trouvés les seigneurs féodaux de vendre une partie de leurs terres, pour faire leurs équipages des croisades, avait rendu ces acquisitions communes; mais le fief n'anoblissait qu'à la troisième génération." Serfs who had twice or thrice been champions, or saved the lives of their masters, were also liberated. "Un evêque d'Auxerre déclara qu'il n'affranchirait gratuitement, qui que ce soit, s'il n'avait reçu quinze blessures à son service."—See Article "Affranchissement," *Dict. de l'ancien Régime*.

are confined to no occupation, but it must be exercised with the chief's sanction. Individuals reclaimed from captivity, in gratitude have given up their liberty: communities, when this or greater evils threatened, have done the same for protection of their lives, religion, and honour. Instances exist of the population of towns being in this situation. The greater part of the inhabitants of the estate of Bijolli are the bussie of its chief, who is of the Pramara tribe: they are his subjects; the Rana, the paramount lord, has no sort of authority over them. Twelve generations have elapsed since his ancestor conducted this little colony into Méwar, and received the highest honours and a large estate on the plateau of its border, in a most interesting country.[1]

The only badge denoting the bussie is a small tuft of hair on the crown of the head. The term interpreted has nothing harsh in it, meaning 'occupant, dweller, or settler.' The numerous towns in India called *Bussie* have this origin: chiefs abandoning their ancient haunts, and settling[2] with all their retainers and chattels in new abodes. From this, the town of Bussie near Tonk (Rampoora), derived its name, when the Solanki prince was compelled to abandon his patrimonial lands in Guzzerat; his subjects of all classes accompanying him voluntarily, in preference to submitting to foreign rule. Probably the foundation of Bijolli was similar; though only the name of Bussie now attaches to the inhabitants. It is not uncommon, in the overflowing of gratitude, to be told, "You may sell me, I am your bussie."[3]

Private Feuds—Composition.—In a state of society such as these sketches delineate, where all depends on the personal character of the sovereign, the field for the indulgence of the passions, and especially of that most incident to the uncontrollable habits of such races—revenge—must necessarily be great. Private feuds have tended, with the general distraction of the times, to desolate this country. Some account of their mode of prosecution, and the incidents thence arising, cannot fail to throw additional light on the manners of society, which during the last half-century were fast receding to a worse than semi-barbarous condition, and, aided by other powerful causes, might have ended in entire annihilation. The period was rapidly advancing, when this fair region of Méwar, the garden of Rajast'han, would have reverted to its primitive sterility. The tiger and the wild boar had already become inmates of the capital, and the bats flitted undisturbed in the palaces of her princes. The ante-courts, where the chieftains and their followers assembled to grace their prince's cavalcade, were overgrown with dank shrubs and grass, through which a mere footpath

[1] I could but indistinctly learn whether this migration, and the species of paternity here existing, arose from rescuing them from Tatar invaders or from the calamity of famine.

[2] *Bussna*, 'to settle.'

[3] I had the happiness to be the means of releasing from captivity some young chiefs, who had been languishing in Mahratta fetters as hostages for the payment of a war contribution. One of them, a younger brother of the Poorawut division, had a mother dying to see him; but though he might have taken her house in the way, a strong feeling of honour and gratitude made him forego this anxious visit: "I am your Rajpoot, your gola, your bussie." He was soon sent off to his mother. Such little acts, mingling with public duty, are a compensation for the many drawbacks of solitude, gloom, and vexation, attending such situations. They are no sinecures or beds of roses—ease, comfort, and health, being all subordinate considerations.

conducted the 'descendant of a hundred kings' to the ruins of his capital.

In these principalities the influence of revenge is universal. Not to prosecute a feud is tantamount to an acknowledgment of self-degradation; and, as in all countries where the laws are insufficient to control individual actions or redress injuries, they have few scruples as to the mode of its gratification. Hence feuds are entailed with the estates from generation to generation. To sheathe the sword till 'a feud is balanced' (their own idiomatic expression), would be a blot never to be effaced from the escutcheon.

In the Hindu word which designates a feud we have another of those striking coincidences in terms to which allusion has already been made: *wér* is 'a feud,' *wéree*, 'a foe.' The Saxon term for the composition of a feud, *wergeldt*, is familiar to every man. In some of these states the initial vowel is hard, and pronounced *bér*. In Rajast'han, *bér* is more common than *wér*, but throughout the south-west *wér* only is used. In these we have the original Saxon word *war*,[1] the French *guer*. The Rajpoot *wergeldt* is land or a daughter to wife. In points of honour the Rajpoot is centuries in advance of our Saxon forefathers, who had a legislative remedy for every bodily injury, when each finger and toe had its price.[2] This might do very well when the injury was committed on a hind, but the Rajpoot must have blood for blood. The monarch must be powerful who can compel acceptance of the compensation, or *moond-kuttie*.[3]

The prosecution of a feud is only to be stopped by a process which is next to impracticable; namely, by the party injured volunteering forgiveness, or the aggressor throwing himself as a suppliant unawares on the clemency of his foe within his own domains: a most trying situation for each to be placed in, yet not unexampled, and revenge in such a case would entail infamy. It was reserved for these degenerate days to produce such an instance.

The Raja of Shapoora, one of the most powerful of the chiefs of Méwar, and of the Rana's blood, had a feud with the Ranawut chief, the Bhoomia proprietor of Amergurh. Oméda,[4] the chief of Shapoora, held two estates: one was the grant of the kings of Dehli, the other of his own sovereign, and each amounting to £10,000 [5] of annual rent, besides the duties on com-

[1] Gilbert on *Tenures*, art. "Warranty," p. 169.

[2] "The great toe took rank as it should be, and held to double the sum of the others, for which ten scyllinga was the value without the nail, which was thirty scealta to boot."—Turner's *Anglo-Saxons*, vol. ii. p. 133.

[3] Appendix, No. XVIII. The laws of composition were carried to a much greater extent amongst the Hindu nations than even amongst those of the Anglo-Saxons, who might have found in Menu all that was ever written on the subject, from the killing of a Brahmin by design to the accidental murder of a dog. The Brahmin is four times the value of the soldier, eight of the merchant, and sixteen times of the Soodra. "If a Brahmin kill one of the soldier caste (without malice), a bull and one thousand cows is the fine of expiation. If he slays a merchant, a bull and one hundred cows is the fine. If a Soodra or lowest class, ten white cows and a bull to the priest is the expiation." Menu legislated also for the protection of the brute creation, and if the priest by chance kills a cat, a frog, a dog, a lizard, an owl, or a crow, he must drink nothing but milk for three days and nights, or walk four miles in the night.—Vide *Institutes of Menu*, edited by that able orientalist, Professor Haughton.

[4] *Omeda*, 'hope.'

[5] Together £20,000, equal to £100,000 of England, if the respective value of the necessaries of life be considered.

merce. His estate in Méwar was in the district of Mandelgurh, where also lay his antagonist's ; their bounds were in common and some of the lands were intermixed : this led to disputes, threats, and blows, even in the towns of their fathers, between their husbandmen. The Bhoomia Dellil was much less powerful ; he was lord of only ten villages, not yielding above £1200 a year ; but they were compact and well managed, and he was popular amongst his brethren, whose swords he could always command. His castle was perched on a rock, and on the towers facing the west (the direction of Shapoora) were mounted some swivels: moreover a belt of forest surrounded it, through which only two or three roads were cut, so that surprise was impossible. Dellil had therefore little to fear, though his antagonist could bring two thousand of his own followers against him. The feud burned and cooled alternately ; but the Raja's exposed villages enabled Dellil to revenge himself with much inferior means. He carried off the cattle, and sometimes the opulent subjects, of his foe, to his donjon-keep in Amergurh for ransom. Meanwhile the husbandmen of both suffered, and agriculture was neglected, till half the villages held by Oméda in Mandelgurh became deserted. The Raja had merited this by his arrogance and attempts to humble Dellil, who had deserved more of the sympathies of his neighbours than his rival, whose tenants were tired of the payments of *birchee-dohae*.[1]

Oméda was eccentric, if the term be not too weak to characterise acts which, in more civilised regions, would have subjected him to coercion. He has taken his son and suspended him by the cincture to the pinnacle of his little chapel at Shapoora, and then called on the mother to come and witness the sight. He would make excursions alone on horseback or on a swift camel, and be missing for days. In one of these moods he and his foe Dellil encountered face to face within the bounds of Amergurh. Dellil only saw a chief high in rank at his mercy. With courtesy he saluted him, invited him to his castle, entertained him, and pledged his health and forgiveness in the *munwár piala*:[2] they made merry, and in the cup agreed to extinguish the remembrance of the feud.

Both had been summoned to the court of the sovereign. The Raja proposed that they should go together, and invited him to go by Shapoora. Dellil accordingly saddled his twenty steeds, moved out his equipage, and providing himself with fitting raiment, and funds to maintain him at the capital, accompanied the Raja to receive the return of his hospitality. They ate from the same platter,[3] drank of the same cup and enjoyed the song and dance. They even went together to their devotions, to swear before their deity what they had pledged in the cup—oblivion of the past. But scarcely had they crossed the threshold of the chapel, when the head of the chief of Amergurh was rolling on the pavement, and the deity and the altar were sprinkled with his blood ! To this atrocious and unheard-of breach of the laws of hospitality, the Raja added the baseness of the pilferer, seizing on the effects of his now lifeless foe. He is said, also, with

[1] *Birchee* is 'a lance.' In these marauding days, when there was a riever in every village, they sallied out to 'run the country,' either to stop the passenger on the highway or the inhabitant of the city. The lance at his breast, he would call out '*dohae*,' an invocation of aid. During harvest time *birchee-dohae* used to be exacted.

[2] 'Cup of invitation.'

[3] This is a favourite expression, and a mode of indicating great friendship : "to eat of the same platter (*thali*), and drink of the same cup (*piala*)."

all the barbarity and malignity of long-treasured revenge, to have kicked the head with his foot, apostrophising it in the pitiful language of resentment. The son of Dellil, armed for revenge, collected all his adherents, and confusion was again commencing its reign. To prevent this, the Rana compelled restitution of the horses and effects ; and five villages from the estate of the Raja were the *moondkuttie* (wergeldt) or compensation to the son of Dellil. The rest of the estate of the murderer was eventually sequestrated by the crown.

The feuds of Arjah and Seogurh are elsewhere detailed, and such statements could be multiplied. Avowal of error and demand of forgiveness, with the offer of a daughter in marriage, often stop the progress of a feud, and might answer better than appearing as a suppliant, which requires great delicacy of contrivance.[1]

Border disputes [2] are most prolific in the production of feuds, and the Rajpoot lord-marchers have them entailed on them as regularly as their estates.

The border chiefs of Jessulmér and Bíkanér carry this to such extent that it often involved both states in hostilities. The *wér* and its composition in Mandelgurh will, however, suffice for the present to exemplify these things.

RAJPOOT PURDHANS OR PREMIERS.—It would not be difficult, amongst the *Majores Domûs Regiæ* of these principalities, to find parallels to the *Maires du Palais* of France. Imbecility in the chief, whether in the east or west, must have the same consequences ; and more than one state in India will present us with the joint appearance of the phantom and the substance of royalty. The details of personal attendance at court will be found elsewhere. When not absent on frontier duties, or by permission at their estates, the chiefs resided with their families at the capital ; but a succession of attendants was always secured, to keep up its splendour and perform personal service at the palace. In Méwar, the privileges and exemptions of the higher class are such as to exhibit few of the marks of vassalage observable at other courts. Here it is only on occasion of particular festivals and solemnities that they ever join the prince's cavalcade, or attend at court. If full attendance is required, on the reception of ambassadors, or in discussing matters of general policy, when they have a right to hear and advise as the hereditary council (*punchaet*) of the state, they are summoned by an officer, with the prince's *johar*,[3] and his request. On grand festivals the great *nakarras*, or kettle-drums, beat at three stated times ; the third is the signal for the chief to quit his abode and mount his

[1] The Boondí feud with the Rana is still unappeased, since the predecessor of the former slew the Rana's father. It was an indefensible act, and the Boondí prince was most desirous to terminate it. He had no daughter to offer, and hinted a desire to accompany me *incog.* and thus gain admission to the presence of the Rana. The benevolence and generosity of this prince would have insured him success ; but it was a delicate matter, and I feared some exposure from any arrogant hot-headed Rajpoot ere the scene could have been got up. The Raja Bishen Sing of Boondí is since dead ; a brave and frank Rajpoot ; he has left few worthier behind. His son, yet a minor, promises well. The protective alliance, which is to turn their swords into ploughshares, will prevent their becoming foes ; but they will remain sulky border-neighbours, to the fostering of disputes and the disquiet of the merchant and cultivator.

[2] Seem—Kankur.

[3] A salutation, only sent by a superior to an inferior.

steed. Amidst all these privileges, when it were almost difficult to distinguish between the prince and his great chiefs, there are occasions well understood by both, which render the superiority of the former apparent: one occurs in the formalities observed on a lapse; another, when at court in personal service, the chief once a week mounts guard at the palace with his clan. On these occasions the vast distance between them is seen. When the chief arrives in the grand court of the palace with his retainers, he halts under the balcony till intimation is given to the prince, who from thence receives his obeisance and duty. This over, he retires to the great *durrikhana*, or hall of audience, appropriated for these ceremonies, where carpets are spread for him and his retainers. At meals the prince sends his compliments, requesting the chief's attendance at the *rasorah* [1] or 'feasting hall,' where with other favoured chiefs he partakes of dinner with the prince. He sleeps in the hall of audience, and next morning with the same formalities takes his leave. Again, in the summons to the presence from their estates, instant obedience is requisite. But in this, attention to their rank is studiously shown by *roqqua*, written by the private secretary, with the sign-manual of the prince attached, and sealed with the private finger-ring. For the inferior grades, the usual seal of state entrusted to the minister is used.

But these are general duties. In all these states some great court favourite, from his talents, character, or intrigue, holds the office of premier. His duties are proportioned to his wishes, or the extent of his talents and ambition; but he does not interfere with the civil administration, which has its proper minister. They, however, act together. The Rajpoot premier is the military minister, with the political government of the fiefs; the civil minister is never of this caste. Local customs have given various appellations to this officer. At Oodipoor he is called *bhanjgurh*; at Jodpoor, *purdhan*; at Jeipoor (where they have engrafted the term used at the court of Dehli) *moosahib*; at Kotah, *kelladar*, and *dewan* or regent. He becomes a most important personage, as dispenser of the favours of the sovereign. Through him chiefly all requests are preferred, this being the surest channel to success. His influence, necessarily, gives him unbounded authority over the military classes, with unlimited power over the inferior officers of the state. With a powerful body of retainers always at his command, it is surprising we have not more frequently our 'mayors of Burgundy and Dagoberts,' [2] our 'Martels and Pepins,' in Rajast'han.

We have our hereditary Rajpoot premiers in several of these states:

[1] The kitchen is large enough for a fortress, and contains large eating halls. Food for seven hundred of the prince's court is daily dressed. This is not for any of the personal servants of the prince, or female establishments; all these are separate.

[2] Dagobert commended his wife and son Clovis to the trust of Æga, with whom she jointly held the care of the palace. On his death, with the aid of more powerful lords, she chose another mayor. He confirmed their grants for life. They made his situation hereditary; but which could only have held good from the crowd of imbeciles who succeeded Clovis, until the descendant of this mayor thrust out his children and seized the crown. This change is a natural consequence of unfitness; and if we go back to the genealogies (called sacred) of the Hindus, we see there a succession of dynasties forced from their thrones by their ministers. Seven examples are given in the various dynasties of the race of Chandra. (See Genealogical Tables, No. II.)

but in all the laws of succession are so regulated that they could not usurp the throne of their prince, though they might his functions.

When the treaty was formed between Méwar and the British Government, the ambassadors wished to introduce an article of guarantee of the office of purdhan to the family of the chief noble of the country, the Rawut of Saloombra. The fact was, as stated, that the dignity was hereditary in this family ; but though the acquisition was the result of an act of virtue, it had tended much towards the ruin of the country, and to the same cause are to be traced all its rebellions.

The ambassador was one of the elders of the same clan, being the grand uncle of the hereditary purdhan. He had taken a most active share in the political events of the last thirty years, and had often controlled the councils of his prince during this period, and actually held the post of premier himself when stipulating for his minor relative. With the ascendancy he exercised over the prince, it may be inferred that he had no intention of renouncing it during his lifetime ; and as he was educating his adopted heir to all his notions of authority, and initiating him in the intrigues of office, the guaranteed dignity in the head of his family would have become a nonentity,[1] and the Ranas would have been governed by the deputies of their mayors. From both those evils the times have relieved the prince. The crimes of Ajeet had made his dismissal from office a point of justice, but imbecility and folly will never be without 'mayors.'

When a Rana of Oodipoor leaves the capital, the Saloombra chief is invested with the government of the city and charge of the palace during his absence. By his hands the sovereign is girt with the sword, and from him he receives the mark of inauguration on his accession to the throne. He leads, by right, the van in battle ; and in case of the siege of the capital, his post is the *sooraj-pol*,[2] and the fortress which crowns it, in which this family had a handsome palace, which is now going fast to decay.

It was the predecessor of the present chief of Saloombra who set up a pretender and the standard of rebellion ; but when foreign aid was brought in, he returned to his allegiance and the defence of the capital. Similar sentiments have often been awakened in patriotic breasts, when roused by the interference of foreigners in their internal disputes. The evil entailed on the state by these hereditary offices will appear in its annals.

[1] So many sudden deaths had occurred in this family, that the branch in question (Ajeet Sing's) were strongly suspected of 'heaping these mortal murders on their crown,' to push their elders from their seats. The father of Padma, the present chief, is said to have been taken off by poison ; and Pahar Sing, one generation anterior, returning grievously wounded from the battle of Oojein, in which the southrons first swept Méwar, was not permitted to recover. The mother of the present young chief of the T'hala tribe of the house of Gogoonda, in the west, was afraid to trust him from her sight. She is a woman of great strength of mind and excellent character, but too indulgent to an only son. He is a fine bold youth, and, though impatient of control, may be managed. On horseback with his lance, in chase of the wild boar, a more resolute cavalier could not be seen. His mother, when he left the estate alone for court, which he seldom did without her accompanying him, never failed to send me a long letter, beseeching me to guard the welfare of her son. My house was his great resort : he delighted to pull over my books, or go fishing or riding with me.

[2] *Soorya*, 'sun' ; and *pol*, 'gate.' *Polia*, 'a porter.'

In Marwar the dignity is hereditary in the house of Ahwa ; but the last brave chief who held it became the victim of a revengeful and capricious sovereign,[1] who was jealous of his exploits ; and dying, he bequeathed a curse to his posterity who should again accept the office. It was accordingly transferred to the next in dignity, the house of Ausope. The present chief, wisely distrusting the prince whose reign has been a series of turmoils, has kept aloof from court. When the office was jointly held by the chiefs of Nimaj and Pokurna, the tragic end of the former afforded a fine specimen of the prowess and heroism of the Rahtore Rajpoot. In truth, these purdhans of Marwar have always been millstones round the necks of their princes ; an evil interwoven in their system when the partition of estates took place amidst the sons of Joda in the infancy of this state. It was, no doubt, then deemed politic to unite to the interests of the crown so powerful a branch, which when combined could always control the rest ; but this gave too much equality.

Deo Sing, the great-grandfather of the Pokurna chief alluded to, used to sleep in the great hall of the palace with five hundred of his clan around him. " The throne of Marwar is in the sheath of my dagger," was the repeated boast of this arrogant chieftain. It may be anticipated that either he or his sovereign would die a violent death. The lord of Pokurna was entrapped, and instant death commanded ; yet with the sword suspended over his head, his undaunted spirit was the same as when seated in the hall, and surrounded by his vassals. " Where, traitor, is now the sheath that holds the fortunes of Marwar ? " said the prince. The taunt recoiled with bitterness when he loftily replied, " With my son at Pokurna I have left it." No time was given for further insult ; his head rolled at the steps of the palace ; but the dagger of Pokurna still haunts the imagination of these princes, and many attempts have been made to get possessed of their stronghold on the edge of the desert.[2] The narrow escape of the present chief will be related hereafter, with the sacrifice of his friend and coadjutor, the chief of Nimaj.

In Kotah and Jessulmér the power of the ministers is supreme. We might describe their situation in the words of Montesquieu. " The Pepins kept their princes in a state of imprisonment in the palace, showing them once a year to the people. On this occasion they made such ordinances as were directed by the mayor ; they also answered ambassadors, but the mayor framed the answer." [3]

Like those of the Merovingian race, these puppets of royalty in the east are brought forth to the *Champ de Mars* once a year, at the grand military festival, the *Dusrewa.* On this day, presents provided by the minister are distributed by the prince. Allowances for every branch of expenditure are fixed, nor has the prince the power to exceed them. But at Kotah there is nothing parsimonious, though nothing superfluous. On the festival of the birth of Crishna, and other similar feasts, the prince likewise appears abroad, attended by all the insignia of royalty. Elephants with standards precede ; lines of infantry and guns are drawn up ; while

[1] " The *cur* can bite," the reply of this chief, either personally, or to the person who reported that his sovereign so designated him, was never forgiven.

[2] His son, Subbul Sing, followed in his footsteps, till an accidental cannon-shot relieved the terrors of the prince.

[3] *L'Esprit des Loix*, chaps. vi. liv. 31.

a numerous calvacade surrounds his person. The son of the minister sometimes condescends to accompany his prince on horseback ; nor is there anything wanting to magnificence, but the power to control or alter any part of it. This failing, how humiliating to a proud mind, acquainted with the history of his ancestors and imbued with a portion of their spirit, to be thus muzzled, enchained, and rendered a mere pageant of state ! This chain would have been snapped, but that each link has become adamantine from the ties this ruler has formed with the British Government. He has well merited our protection ; though we never contemplated to what extent the maintenance of these ties would involve our own character. But this subject is connected with the history of an individual who yields to none of the many extraordinary men whom India has produced, and who required but a larger theatre to have drawn the attention of the world. His character will be further elucidated in the Annals of Haravati.

CHAPTER V

Adoption—Reflections upon the subjects treated.

Adoption.—The hereditary principle, which perpetuates in these states their virtues and their vices, is also the grand preservative of their political existence and national manners : it is an imperishable principle, which resists time and innovation : it is this which made the laws of the Medes and Persians, as well as those of the Rajpoots, unalterable. A chief of Méwar, like his sovereign, never dies : he disappears to be regenerated. "*Le roi est mort, vive le roi!*" is a phrase, the precise virtue of which is there well understood. Neither the crown nor the greater fiefs are ever without heirs. Adoption is the preservative of honours and titles ; the great fiefs of Rajast'han can never become extinct. But, however valuable this privilege, which the law of custom has made a right, it is often carried to the most hurtful and foolish extent. They have allowed the limit which defined it to be effaced, and each family, of course, maintains a custom, so soothing to vanity, as the prospect of having their names revived in their descendants. This has resulted from the weakness of the prince and the misery of the times. Lands were bestowed liberally which yielded nothing to their master, who, in securing a nominal obedience and servitude, had as much as the times made them worth when given ; but with returning prosperity and old customs, these great errors have become too visible. Adoptions are often made during the life of the incumbent when without prospect of issue. The chief and his wife first agitate the subject in private ; it is then confided to the little council of the fief, and when propinquity and merit unite, they at once petition the prince to confirm their wishes, which are generally acceded to. So many interests are to be consulted on this occasion, that the blind partiality of the chief to any particular object is always counterpoised by the elders of the clan, who must have a pride in seeing a proper

T'hacoor [1] at their head, and who prefer the nearest of kin, to prevent the disputes which would be attendant on neglect in this point.

On sudden lapses, the wife is allowed the privilege, in conjunction with those interested in the fief, of nomination, though the case is seldom left unprovided for: there is always a presumptive heir to the smallest sub-infeudation of these estates. The wife of the deceased is the guardian of the minority of the adopted.

The chief of Deogurh, one of the sixteen Omras of Méwar, died without issue. On his death-bed he recommended to his wife and chiefs Nahar Sing for their adoption. This was the son of the independent chieftain of Singramgurh, already mentioned. There were nearer kin, some of the seventh and eighth degrees, and young Nahar was the eleventh. It was never contemplated that the three last gigantic [2] chieftains of Deogurh would die without issue, or the branches, now claimants from propinquity, would have been educated to suit the dignity; but being brought up remote from court, they had been compelled to seek employment where obtainable, or to live on the few acres to which their distant claim of birth restricted them. Two of these, who had but the latter resource to fly to, had become mere boors; and of two who had sought service abroad by arms, one was a cavalier in the retinue of the prince, and the other a hanger-on about court: both dissipated and unfitted, as the frerage asserted, "to be the chieftains of two thousand Rajpoots, the sons of one father." [3] Much interest and intrigue were carried on for one of these, and he was supported by the young prince and a faction. Some of the senior Puttawuts of Deogurh are men of the highest character, and often lamented the sombre qualities of their chief, which prevented the clan having that interest in the state to which its extent and rank entitled it. While these intrigues were in their infancy, they adopted a decided measure; they brought home young Nahar from his father's residence, and "bound round his head the turban of the deceased." In his name the death of the late chief was announced. It was added, that he hoped to see his friends after the stated days of '*matim*' or mourning; and he performed all the duties of the son of Deogurh, and lighted the funeral pyre.

When these proceedings were reported, the Rana was highly and justly incensed. The late chief had been one of the rebels of 1848; [4] and though pardon had been granted, yet this revived all the recollection of the past, and he felt inclined to extinguish the name of Sangawut. [5]

In addition to the common sequestration, he sent an especial one with commands to collect the produce of the harvest then reaping, charging the sub-vassals with the design of overturning his lawful authority. They replied very submissively, and artfully asserted that they had only given a son to Gokul Das, not an heir to Deogurh; that the sovereign alone could do this, and that they trusted to his nominating one who would be an efficient leader of so many Rajpoots in the service of the Rana. They urged the pretensions of young Nahar, at the same time leaving the

[1] As in Deogurh.

[2] Gokul Das, the last chief, was one of the finest men I ever beheld in feature and person. He was about six feet six, perfectly erect, and a Hercules in bulk. His father at twenty was much larger, and must have been nearly seven feet high. It is surprising how few of the chiefs of this family died a natural death. It has produced some noble Rajpoots.

[3] *Ek bap ca beta.* [4] A.D. 1792. [5] That of the clan of Deogurh.

decision to the sovereign. Their judicious reply was well supported by their ambassador at court, who was the bard of Deogurh, and had recently become, though *ex officio*, physician to the prince.[1] The point was finally adjusted, and Nahar was brought to court, and invested with the sword by the hand of the sovereign, and he is now lord of Deogurh Madaria, one of the richest and most powerful fiefs[2] of Méwar. Madaria was the ancient name of the estate; and Singramgurh, of which Nahar was the heir, was severed from it, but by some means had reverted to the crown, of which it now holds. The adoption of Nahar by Gokul Das leaves the paternal estate without an immediate heir; and his actual father being mad, if more distant claims are not admitted, it is probable that Singramgurh will eventually revert to the fisc.

Reflections.—The system of feuds must have attained considerable maturity amongst the Rajpoots, to have left such traces, notwithstanding the desolation that has swept the land: but without circumspection these few remaining customs will become a dead letter. Unless we abstain from all internal interference, we must destroy the links which connect the prince and his vassals; and, in lieu of a system decidedly imperfect, we should leave them none at all, or at least not a system of feuds, the only one they can comprehend. Our friendship has rescued them from exterior foes, and time will restore the rest. With the dignity and establishments of their chiefs, ancient usages will revive; and *nuzzerana* (relief), *kurg bundaï* (investiture), *dussoond* (aids or benevolence, literally 'the tenth'), and other incidents, will cease to be mere ceremonies. The desire of every liberal mind, as well as the professed wish of the British Government, is to aid in their renovation, and this will be best effected by not meddling with what we but imperfectly understand.[3]

We have nothing to apprehend from the Rajpoot States if raised to their ancient prosperity. The closest attention to their history proves beyond contradiction that they were never capable of uniting, even for their own preservation: a breath, a scurrilous stanza of a bard, has severed their closest confederacies. No national head exists amongst them as amongst the Mahrattas; and each chief being master of his own house and followers, they are individually too weak to cause us any alarm.

No feudal government can be dangerous as a neighbour; for defence

[1] Apollo is the patron both of physicians and poets; and though my friend Umra does not disgrace him in either calling, it was his wit, rather than his medical degree, that maintained him at court. He said it was not fitting that the sovereign of the world should be served by clowns or opium-eaters; and that young Nahar, when educated at court under the Rana's example, would do credit to the country: and what had full as much weight as any of the bard's arguments was, that the fine of relief on the *Yulwar bundai* (or girding on of the sword) of a lack of rupees, should be immediately forthcoming.

[2] Putta.

[3] Such interference, when inconsistent with past usage and the genius of the people, will defeat the very best intentions. On the grounds of policy and justice, it is alike incumbent on the British Government to secure the maintenance of their present form of government, and not to repair, but to advise the repairs of the fabric, and to let their own artists alone be consulted. To employ ours would be like adding a Corinthian capital to a column of Ellora, or replacing the mutilated statue of Buldeva with a limb from the Hercules Farnese.

To have a chain of prosperous independent states on our only exposed frontier, the north-west, attached to us from benefits, and the moral conviction that we do not seek their overthrow, must be a desirable policy.

it has in all countries been found defective; and for aggression, totally inefficient. Let there exist between us the most perfect understanding and identity of interests; the foundation-step to which is to lessen or remit the galling, and to us contemptible tribute, now exacted, enfranchise them from our espionage and agency, and either unlock them altogether from our dangerous embrace, or let the ties between us be such only as would ensure grand results: such as general commercial freedom and protection, with treaties of friendly alliance. Then, if a Tatar or a Russian invasion threatened our eastern empire, fifty thousand Rajpoots would be no despicable allies.

Let us call to mind what they did when they fought for Aurungzéb: they are still unchanged, if we give them the proper stimulus. Gratitude, honour, and fidelity, are terms which at one time were the foundation of all the virtues of a Rajpoot. Of the theory of these sentiments he is still enamoured; but, unfortunately, for his happiness, the times have left him but little scope for the practice of them. Ask a Rajpoot which is the greatest of crimes? he will reply, '*goonchor*,' 'forgetfulness of favours.' This is his most powerful term for ingratitude. Gratitude with him embraces every obligation of life, and is inseparable from *swamdherma*, 'fidelity to his lord.' He who is wanting in these is not deemed fit to live, and is doomed to eternal pains in Pluto's [1] realm hereafter.[2]

"It was a powerful feeling," says an historian [3] who always identifies his own emotions with his subject, "which could make the bravest of men put up with slights and ill-treatment at the hand of their sovereign, or call forth all the energies of discontented exertion for one whom they never saw, and in whose character there was nothing to esteem. Loyalty has scarcely less tendency to refine and elevate the heart than patriotism itself." That these sentiments were combined, the past history of the Rajpoots will show; [4] and to the strength of these ties do they owe their political existence, which has outlived ages of strife. But for these, they would have been converts and vassals to the Tatars, who would still have been enthroned in Dehli. Neglect, oppression, and religious interference, sunk one of the greatest monarchies of the world; [5] made Sévaji a hero, and

[1] *Yamaloca.*

[2] The *goonchor* (ungrateful) and *satchor* (violator of his faith) are consigned, by the authority of the bard, to sixty-thousand years' residence in hell. Europeans, in all the pride of mastery, accuse the natives of want of gratitude, and say their language has no word for it. They can only know the *nimmuk-haram* of the Ganges. *Goonchor* is a compound of powerful import, as ingratitude and infidelity are the highest crimes. It means, literally, "abandoner (from *chorna*, 'to quit') of virtue (*goon*)."

[3] Hallam, vol. i. p. 323.

[4] Of the effects of loyalty and patriotism combined, we have splendid examples in Hindu history and tradition. A more striking instance could scarcely be given than in the recent civil distractions at Kotah, where a mercenary army raised and maintained by the Regent, either openly or covertly declared against him, as did the whole feudal body to a man, the moment their young prince asserted his subverted claims, and in the cause of their rightful lord abandoned all consideration of self, their families and lands, and with their followers offered their lives to redeem his rights or perish in the attempt. No empty boast, as the conclusion testified. God forbid that we should have more such examples of Rajpoot devotion to their sense of fidelity to their lords!

[5] See statement of its revenues during the last emperor, who had preserved the empire of Dehli united.

converted the peaceful husbandman of the Kistna and Godavery into a brave but rapacious soldier.

We have abundant examples, and I trust need not exclaim with the wise minister of Akber, "who so happy as to profit by them?"[1]

The Rajpoot, with all his turbulence, possesses in an eminent degree both loyalty and patriotism; and though he occasionally exhibits his refractory spirit to his father and sovereign,[2] we shall see of what he is capable when his country is threatened with dismemberment, from the history of Méwar, and the reign of Ajeet Sing of Marwar. In this last we have one of the noblest examples history can afford of unbounded devotion. A prince, whom not a dozen of his subjects had ever seen, who had been concealed from the period of his birth throughout a tedious minority to avoid the snares of a tyrant,[3] by the mere magic of a name kept the discordant materials of a great feudal association in subjection, till, able to bear arms, he issued from his concealment to head these devoted adherents, and reconquer what they had so long struggled to maintain. So glorious a contest, of twenty years' duration, requires but an historian to immortalise it. Unfortunately we have only the relation of isolated encounters, which, though exhibiting a prodigality of blood and acts of high devotion, are deficient in those minor details which give unity and interest to the whole.

Let us take the Rajpoot character from the royal historians themselves, from Akber, Jehangir, Aurungzéb. The most brilliant conquests of these monarchs were by their Rajpoot allies; though the little regard the latter had for opinion alienated the sympathies of a race, whom when rightly managed, encountered at command the Afghan amidst the snows of Caucasus, or made the furthest Chersonese tributary to the empire. Assam, where the British arms were recently engaged, and for the issue of which such anxiety was manifested in the metropolis of Britain, was conquered by a Rajpoot prince,[4] whose descendant is now an ally of the British Government.

But Englishmen in the east, as elsewhere, undervalue everything not national. They have been accustomed to conquest, not reverses: though it is only by studying the character of those around them that the latter can be avoided and this superiority maintained. Superficial observers imagine that from lengthened predatory spoliation the energy of the Rajpoot has fled: an idea which is at once erroneous and dangerous. The vices now manifest from oppression will disappear with the cause, and with reviving prosperity new feelings will be generated, and each national tie and custom be strengthened. The Rajpoot would glory in putting on

[1] Abul Fuzil uses this expression when moralising on the fall of Shabudin, king of Ghizni and first established monarch of India, slain by Pirthwirájá, the Hindu sovereign of Dehli.

[2] The Rajpoot, who possesses but an acre of land, has the proud feeling of common origin with his sovereign, and in styling him *bapjee* (sire), he thinks of him as the common father or representative of the race. What a powerful incentive to action!

[3] Aurungzéb.

[4] Raja Maun of Jeipoor, who took Aracan, Orissa, and Assam. Raja Jeswunt Sing of Marwar retook Caubul for Aurungzéb, and was rewarded by poison. Raja Ram Sing Hara, of Kotah, made several important conquests; and his grandson, Raja Essuree Sing, and his five brothers, were left on one field of battle.

his saffron robes [1] to fight for such a land, and for those who disinterestedly laboured to benefit it.

Let us, then, apply history to its proper use. We need not turn to ancient Rome for illustration of the dangers inseparable from wide dominion and extensive alliances. The twenty-two Satrapies of India, the greater part of which are now the appanage of Britain, exhibited, even a century ago, one of the most splendid monarchies history has made known, too extensive for the genius of any single individual effectually to control. Yet was it held together, till encroachment on their rights, and disregard to their habits and religious opinions, alienated the Rajpoots, and excited the inhabitants of the south to rise against their Mogul oppressors. Then was the throne of Aurungzéb at the mercy of a Brahmin, and the grandson [2] of a cultivator in the province of Candeish held the descendants of Timoor pensioners on his bounty!

[1] When a Rajpoot is determined to hold out to the last in fighting, he always puts on a robe dyed in saffron.

[2] Sindia.

APPENDIX

PAPERS REFERRED TO IN THE SKETCH OF A FEUDAL SYSTEM IN RAJAST'HAN

BEING

LITERAL TRANSLATIONS *from* INSCRIPTIONS *and* ORIGINAL DOCUMENTS, *most of which are in the* AUTHOR'S POSSESSION

No. I

Translation of a Letter from the expatriated Chiefs [1] *of Marwar to the Political Agent of the British Government, Western Rajpoot States.*

After compliments.

We have sent to you a confidential person, who will relate what regards us. The Sirkar company are sovereigns of Hindust'han, and you know well all that regards our condition. Although there is nothing which respects either ourselves or our country hid from you, yet is there matter immediately concerning us which it is necessary to make known.

Sri Maharaja and ourselves are of one stock, all Rahtores. He is our head, we his servants: but now anger has seized him, and we are dispossessed of our country. Of the estates, our patrimony and our dwelling, some have been made khalisa,[2] and those who endeavour to keep aloof expect the same fate. Some under the most solemn pledge of security have been inveigled and suffered death, and others imprisoned. Mootsuddies,[3] officers of state, men of the soil and those foreign to it, have been seized, and the most unheard-of deeds and cruelties inflicted, which we cannot even write. Such a spirit has possessed his mind as never was known to any former prince of Jodpoor. His forefathers have reigned for generations; our forefathers were their ministers and advisers, and whatever was performed was by the collective wisdom of the council of our chiefs. Before the face of his ancestors, our own ancestors have slain and been slain; and in performing services to the kings,[4] they made the state of Jodpoor what it is. Wherever Marwar was concerned, there our fathers were to be found, and with their lives preserved the land. Sometimes our head was a minor; even then by the wisdom of our fathers and their services, the land was kept firm under our feet, and thus has it descended from generation to generation. Before his eyes (Raja Maun's) we have performed good service: when at that perilous time the host of Jeipoor [5] surrounded Jodpoor, on the field we attacked it; our lives and fortunes were at stake, and God granted us success; the witness is God

[1] The names omitted to prevent any of them falling a sacrifice to the blind fury of their prince. The brave chief of Nímaj has sold his life, but dearly. In vain do we look in the annals of Europe for such devotion and generous despair as marked his end, and that of his brave clan. He was a perfect gentleman in deportment, modest and mild, and head of a powerful clan.

[2] Fiscal, that is, sequestrated.

[3] Clerks, and inferior officers of government.

[4] Alluding to the sovereigns of Dehli. In the magnificent feudal assemblage at this gorgeous court, where seventy-six princes stood in the Divan (*Dewan Khas*) each by a pillar covered with plates of silver, the Marwar prince had the right hand of all. I have an original letter from the great-grandfather of Raja Maun to the Rana, elate with this honour.

[5] In 1806.

Almighty. Now, men of no consideration are in our prince's presence; hence this reverse. *When our services are acceptable, then is he our lord; when not, we are again his brothers and kindred, claimants and laying claim to the land.*

He desires to dispossess us; but can we let ourselves be dispossessed? The English are masters of all India. The chief of —— sent his agent to Ajmér; he was told to go to Dehli. Accordingly T'hacoor —— went there, but no path was pointed out. If the English chiefs will not hear us, who will? The English allow no one's lands to be usurped, and our birthplace is Marwar—from Marwar we must have bread. A hundred thousand Rahtores—where are they to go to? From respect to the English alone have we been so long patient, and without acquainting your government of our intentions, you might afterwards find fault; therefore we make it known, and we thereby acquit ourselves to you. What we brought with us from Marwar we have consumed, and even what we could get on credit; and now, when want must make us perish, we are ready and can do anything.[1]

The English are our rulers, our masters. Sri Maun Sing has seized our lands; by your government interposing these troubles may be settled, but without its guarantee and intervention we can have no confidence whatever. Let us have a reply to our petition. We will wait it in patience; but if we get none, the fault will not be ours, having given everywhere notice. Hunger will compel man to find a remedy. For such a length of time we have been silent from respect to your government alone: our own Sirkar is deaf to complaint. But to what extreme shall we wait? Let our hopes be attended to. Sumbut 1878, Sawun sood dooj. (August 1821.)

True Translation:

(Signed) JAMES TOD.

No. II.

Remonstrance of the Sub-Vassals of Deogurh against their chief, Rawut Gokul Das.

1. He respects not the privileges or customs established of old.
2. To each Rajpoot's house a churras[2] or hide of land was attached: this he has resumed.
3. Whoever bribes him is a true man: who does not, is a thief.
4. Ten or twelve villages established by his puttaéts[3] he has resumed, and left their families to starve.
5. From time immemorial sanctuary (*sirnah*) has been esteemed sacred: this he has abolished.
6. On emergencies he would pledge his oath to his subjects (*ryots*), and afterwards plunder them.
7. In old times, it was customary when the presence of his chiefs and kindred was required, to invite them by letter: a fine is now the warrant of summons: thus lessening their dignity.
8. Such messengers, in former times, had a tacka[4] for their ration (*bhatta*); now he imposes two rupees.

[1] The historian of the Middle Ages justly remarks, that "the most deadly hatred is that which men, exasperated by proscription and forfeitures, bear their country."

[2] Hide or skin, from the vessel used in irrigation being made of leather.

[3] The vassals, or those holding fiefs (putta) of Deogurh.

[4] A copper coin, equal to twopence.

9. Formerly, when robberies occurred in the mountains within the limits of Deogurh, the loss was made good : now all complaint is useless, for his foujdar [1] receives a fourth of all such plunder. The Mérs [2] range at liberty ; but before they never committed murder : now they slay as well as rob our kin ; nor is there any redress, and such plunder is even sold within the town of Deogurh.

10. Without crime, he resumes the lands of his vassals for the sake of imposition of fines ; and after such are paid, he cuts down the green crops, with which he feeds his horses.

11. The cultivators [3] on the lands of the vassals he seizes by force, extorts fines, or sells their cattle to pay them. Thus cultivation is ruined and the inhabitants leave the country.

12. From oppression the town magistrates [4] of Deogurh have fled to Raepoor. He lays in watch to seize and extort money from them.

13. When he summons his vassals for purposes of extortion and they escape his clutches, he seizes on their wives and families. Females, from a sense of honour, have on such occasions thrown themselves into wells.

14. He interferes to recover old debts, distraining the debtor of all he has in the world : half he receives.

15. If any one have a good horse, by fair means or foul he contrives to get it.

16. *When Deogurh was established, at the same time were our allotments : as is his patrimony, so is our patrimony.*[5] Thousands have been expended in establishing and improving them, yet our rank, privileges, and rights he equally disregards.

17. From these villages, founded by our forefathers, he, at will, takes four or five skins of land and bestows them on foreigners ; and thus the ancient proprietors are reduced to poverty and ruin.

18. From of old, all his Rajpoot kin had daily rations, or portions of grain : for four years these rights have been abolished.

19. From ancient times the puttaéts formed his council ; now he consults only foreigners. What has been the consequence ? the whole annual revenue derived from the mountains is lost.

20. From the ancient Bhoom [6] of the Frerage [7] the mountaineers carry off the cattle, and instead of redeeming them, this foujdar sets the plunderers up to the trick of demanding rekwalee.[8]

21. Money is justice, and there is none other : whoever has money may be heard. The bankers and merchants have gone abroad for protection, but he asks not where they are.

22. When cattle are diven off to the hills, and we do ourselves justice and recover them, we are fined, and told that the mountaineers have his pledge. Thus our dignity is lessened. Or if we seize one of these marauders, a party is sent to liberate him, for which the foujdar receives a bribe. Then a feud ensues at the instigation of the liberated Mér, and the unsupported Rajpoot is obliged to abandon his patrimony.[9] There is

[1] Military commander ; a kind of inferior *maire du palais*, on every Rajpoot chieftain's estate, and who has the military command of the vassals. He is seldom of the same family, but generally of another tribe.

[2] Mountaineers. [3] Of the Jit and other labouring tribes.

[4] Chohutias, from *chohut*, 'civil jurisdiction.' In every town there is an unpaid magistracy, of which the head is the Nuggur Sét'h, or chief citizen, and the four Chotias, tantamount to the Lord Mayor and Aldermen, who hold their courts and decide in all civil cases.

[5] Here are the precise sentiments embodied in the remonstrances of the great feudal chiefs of Marwar to their prince ; see Appendix, No. I.

[6] The old allodial allotments. [7] Bhyád.

[8] The *salvamenta* of our feudal writers ; the *black-mail* of the north.

[9] 'Wuttun.'

neither protection nor support. The chief is supine, and so regardless of honour, that he tells us to take money to the hills and redeem our property. Since this foujdar had power, 'poison has been our fate.' Foreigners are all in all, and the home-bred are set aside. Dekhanis and plunderers enjoy the lands of his brethren. Without fault, the chiefs are deprived of their lands, to bring which into order time and money have been lavished. Justice there is none.

Our rights and privileges in his family are the same as his in the family of the Presence.[1] Since you [2] entered Méwar, lands long lost have been recovered. What crimes have we committed that at this day we should lose ours?

We are in great trouble.[3]

No. III.

Maharaja Sri Gokul Das to the four ranks (*char misal*) of Puttaćts of Deogurh, commanding. Peruse.

Without crime no vassal shall have his estate or chursas disseized. Should any individual commit an offence, it shall be judged by the *four ranks* (chár misal), my brethren, and then punished. Without consulting them on all occasions I shall never inflict punishment.[4] To this I swear by Sri Nat'hjee. No departure from this agreement shall ever occur. S. 1874; the 6th Paush.

No. IV.

Grant from Maharana Ur Sing, Prince of Méwar, to the Sindie Chief, Abdool Ruhím Beg.

Ramji![5]

Gunésji![5] Eklingji![5]

Sri Maharaja Dhéraj Maharana Ur Sing to Mirza Abdool Ruhím Beg Adilbégote, commanding.

Now some of our chiefs having rebelled and set up the impostor Rutna Sing, brought the Dekhany army and erected batteries against Oodipoor, in which circumstances your services have been great and tended to the preservation of our sovereignty: therefore, in favour towards you, I have made this grant, which your children and children's children shall continue to enjoy. You will continue to serve faithfully; and whoever of

[1] The Rana. [2] The Author.

[3] With the articles of complaint of the vassals of Deogurh and the short extorted charter, to avoid future cause for such, we may contrast the following:— " Pour avoir une idée du brigandage que les nobles exerçaient à 'l'époque où les premières *chartes* furent accordées, il suffit d'en lire quelques-unes, et l'on verra que le seigneur y disait:— Je promets de ne point *voler*, *extorquer* les biens et les meubles des habitans, de les délivrer des *totes* ou *rapines*, et autres *mauvaises coutumes*, et de ne plus commettre envers eux d'exactions.'—En effet, dans ces tems malheureux, vivres, meubles, chevaux, voitures, dit le savant Abbé de Mably, tout était enlevé par l'insatiable et aveugle avidité des seigneurs."—Art. " Chartes," *Dict. de l'anc. Régime*.

[4] This reply to the remonstrance of his vassals is perfectly similar in point to the 43rd article of *Magna Charta*.

[5] Invocations to Ram, Gunés (god of wisdom), and Eklinga, the patron-divinity of the Sesodia Gehlotes.

my race shall dispossess you or yours, on him be Eklingji and the sin of the slaughter of Cheetore.

Particulars.

1st. In estates, 200,000 rupees.
2nd. In cash annually, 25,000.
3rd. Lands outside the Debarri gate, 10,000.
4th. As a residence, the dwelling-house called Bharat Sing's.
5th. A hundred beegas of land outside the city for a garden.
6th. The town of Mittoon in the valley, to supply wood and forage.
7th. To keep up the tomb of Ajméri Bég, who fell in action, one hundred beegas of land.

Privileges and Honours.

8th. A seat in Durbar and rank in all respects equal to the chieftain of Sadree.[1]

9th. Your kettle-drums (Nakarra) to beat to the exterior gate, but with one stick only.

10th. Umr Bulaona,[2] and a dress of honour on the Dusréwa [3] festival.

11th. Drums to beat to Ahar. All other privileges and rank like the house of Saloombra.[4] Like that house, yours shall be from generation to generation; therefore according to the valuation of your grant you will serve.

12th. Your brothers or servants, whom you may dismiss, I shall not entertain or suffer my chief to entertain.

13th. The Chaours [5] and Kirnia [6] you may use at all times when alone, but never in the presence.

14th. Munowur Bég, Unwur Bég, Chumun Bég, are permitted seats in front of the throne; Umr Bulaona, and honorary dresses on Dusréwa, and seats for two or three other relatives who may be found worthy the honour.

15th. Your agent (*Vakeel*) shall remain at court with the privileges due to his rank.

By command:
SAH MOOTIE RAM BOLIA,
S. 1826 (A.D. 1770) Bhadoon (August) sood 11 Somwar (Monday).

No. V.

Grant of the Putta of Bhynsrore to Rawut Lal Sing, one of the sixteen great vassals of Méwar.

Maharaja Juggut Sing to Rawut Lal Sing Kesurisingote,[7] commanding. Now to you the whole Pergunna of Bhynsrore [8] is granted as *Gras*, viz.:

Town of Bhynsrore	3,000	1,500
Fifty-two others (names uninteresting), besides one in the valley of the capital. Total value . . .	62,000	31,000 [9]

[1] The first of the foreign vassals of the Rana's house.

[2] A horse furnished by the prince, always replaced when he dies, therefore called *Umr*, or immortal.

[3] The grand military festival, when a muster is made of all the Rajpoot quotas.

[4] The first of the home-chieftains.

[5] The tail of the wild ox, worn across the saddle-bow.

[6] An umbrella or shade against the sun; from *kirn*, 'a ray.'

[7] Clan (*gote*) of Kesuri Sing, one of the great branches of the Chondawuts.

[8] On the left bank of the Chumbul.

[9] To explain these double *rékhs*, or estimates, one is the full value, the other the deteriorated rate.

With two hundred and forty-eight horse and two hundred and forty-eight foot, good horse and good Rajpoots, you will perform service. Of this, forty-eight horse and forty-eight foot are excused for the protection of your fort; therefore with two hundred foot and two hundred horse you will serve when and wherever ordered. The first grant was given in Pos, S. 1798, when the income inserted was over-rated. Understanding this, the presence (t'huzoor) ordered sixty thousand of annual value to be attached to Bhynsrore.

No. VI.

Grant from Maharana Singram Sing of Méwar to his Nephew, the Prince Madhú Sing, heir apparent to the principality of Jeipoor.

SRI RAMJEYTI.
(*Victory to Rama*).

SRI GUNÉS PRESAD (*By favour of Gunés*). SRI EKLING PRESAD (*By favour of Eklinga*).

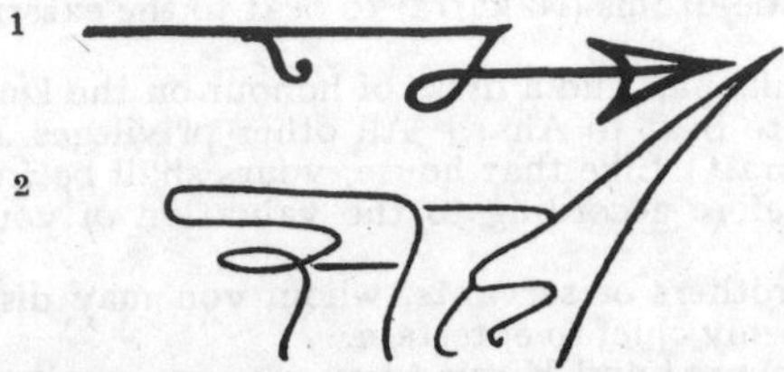

Maharaja Dhéraj Maharana Sri Singram Sing, Adesatoo, commanding. To my nephew, Komar Madhú Sing-ji, *gras* (a fief) has been granted, viz.:

The fief (*putta*) of Rampoora; therefore, with one thousand horse and two thousand foot, you will perform service during six months annually; and when foreign service is required, three thousand foot and three thousand horse.

While the power of the presence is maintained in these districts you will not be dispossessed.

By command:
PANCHOULI RAECHUND amd MEHTA MUL DAS.
S. 1785 (A.D. 1729); Cheit-sood 7th (   ); Mungulwar (Tuesday).

Addressed in the Rana's own hand.

To my nephew Madhú Sing.[3] My child, I have given you Rampoora: while minc, you shall not be deprived of it. Done.

No. VII.

Grant of Bhom Rekwali (Salvamenta) from the village of Dongla to Maharaja Khooshial Sing.

S. 1806 (A.D. 1750), *the first of Sawun* (*July*).

1st. A field of one hundred and fifty-one beegas, of which thirty-six are irrigated.

2nd. One hundred and two beegas of waste and unirrigated, viz.:

Six beegas cultivated by Govinda the oilman.
Three, under Heera and Tara the oilmen.
Seventeen cultivated by the mason Hunso, and Lal the oilman.

[1] The b'hala, or lance, is the sign-manual of the Saloombra chieftain, as hereditary premier of the state.

[2] Is a monogram forming the word *Suhaie*, being the sign-manual of the prince.

[3] *Bhanaij* is sister's son; as *Bhatija* is brother's son. It will be seen in the Annals, that to support this prince to the succession of the Jeipoor Gadi, both Méwar and Jeipoor were ruined, and the power of the Dekhanys established in both countries.

Four beegas of waste and forest land (*purte, aryana*) which belonged to Govinda and Heera, etc., etc.; and so on enumerating all the fields composing the above aggregate.

Dues and Privileges.

Pieces of money . . 12
Grain . . . . 24 maunds.
On the festivals of Rakhi, Dewalee, and Hooli, one copper coin from each house.
Seeranoh . . . at harvest.
Sookrie from the Brahmins.
Transit duties for protection of merchandise, viz., a pice on every cart-load, and half a pice for each bullock.
Two platters on every marriage feast.

No. VIII.

Grant of Bhom by the Inhabitants of Amlee to Rawut Futteh Sing of Amait. S. 1814 (A.D. 1758).

The Ranawuts Sawunt Sing and Sobagh Sing had Amlee in grant; but they were oppressive to the inhabitants, slew the patéls Joda and Bhaggi, and so ill-treated the Brahmins, that Koosul and Nat'hoo sacrificed themselves on the pyre. The inhabitants demanded the protection of the Rana, and the puttaéts were changed; and now the inhabitants grant in rekwalee one hundred and twenty-five beegas as bhom to Futteh Sing.[1]

No. IX.

Grant of Bhom by the Inhabitants of the Town of Dongla to Maharaja Zoorawur Sing, of Bheendir.

To Sri Maharaja Zoorawur Sing, the patéls, traders, merchants, brahmins, and united inhabitants of Dongla, make agreement.

Formerly the "runners" in Dongla were numerous: to preserve us from whom we granted bhom to the Maharaja. To wit:

One well, that of Heera the oilman.
One well, that of Deepa the oilman.
One well, that of Déwa the oilman.

In all, three wells, being forty-four beegas of irrigated (*peewul*), and one hundred and ninety-one beegas of unirrigated (*mál*) land. Also a field for jooar.

Customs or Dignities (Murjád) attached to the Bhom.

1st. A dish (*khansa*) on every marriage.
2nd. Six hundred rupees ready cash annually.
3rd. All bhomias, grasias, the high roads, passes from raids and "runners," and all disturbances whatsoever, the Maharaja must settle.

[1] This is a proof of the value attached to bhom, when granted by the inhabitants, as the first act of the new proprietor though holding the whole town from the crown, was to obtain these few beegas as bhom. After having been sixty years in that family, Amlee has been resumed by the crown: the bhom has remained with the chief.

When the Maharaja is pleased to let the inhabitants of Dongla reinhabit their dwellings, then only can they return to them.[1]

Written by the accountant Kutchia, on the full moon of Jeit, S. 1858, and signed by all the traders, brahmins, and towns-people.

No. X.

Grant of Bhom by the Prince of Méwar to an inferior Vassal.

Maharana Bheem Sing to Baba Ram Sing, commanding.

Now a field of two hundred and twenty-five beegas in the city of Jehajpoor, with the black orchard (*sham bagh*) and a farm-house (*nohara*) for cattle, has been granted you in bhom.

Your forefathers recovered for me Jehajpoor and served with fidelity; on which account this bhom is renewed. Rest assured no molestation shall be offered, nor shall any puttaét interfere with you.

Privileges.

One seeranoh.[2]
Two hulmohs.[3]
Offerings of cocoa-nuts on the Holi and Dusréwa festivals.
From every hundred bullock-loads[4] of merchandise, twelve annas.
From every hundred and twenty-five ass-loads, six annas.
From each horse sold within Jehajpoor, two annas.
From each camel sold, one anna.
From each oil-mill, one puloh.
From each iron mine (*madri*), a quarter rupee.
From each distillation of spirits, a quarter rupee.
From each goat slain, one pice.
On births and marriages,[5] five platters (*khansa*).

[1] This shows how bhom was extorted in these periods of turbulence, and that this individual gift was as much to save them from the effects of the Maharaja's violence as to gain protection from that of others.

[2] A seer on each maund of produce.

[3] The labour of two ploughs (*húl*). *Hulmoh* is the personal service of the husbandman with his plough for such time as is specified. *Hulmoh* is precisely the detested *corvée* of the French régime. " Les *corvées* sont tout ouvrage ou service, soit de corps ou de charrois et bêtes, pendant le jour, qui est dû à un seigneur. Il y avait deux sortes de *corvées* : les réelles et les personelles, etc. Quelquefois le nombre des *corvées* était fixé : mais, le plus souvent, elles étaient à volonté du seigneur, et c'est ce qu'on appelait *corvées à merci*."—Art. " Corvée," *Dict. de l'anc. Régime*. Almost all the exactions for the last century in Méwar may come under this latter denomination.

[4] A great variety of oppressive imposts were levied by the chiefs during these times of trouble, to the destruction of commerce and all facility of travelling. Everything was subject to tax, and a long train of vexatious dues exacted for " repairs of forts, boats at ferries, night-guards, guards of passes," and other appellations, all having much in common with the " Droit de *Péage* " in France. " Il n'y avait pas de ponts, de gués, de chaussées, d'écluses, de défilés, de portes, etc., où les féodaux ne fissent payer un droit à ceux que leurs affaires ou leur commerce forçaient de voyager."—*Dict. de l'anc. Régime*.

[5] The privileges of our Rajpoot chieftains on the marriages of their vassals and cultivating subjects are confined to the best dishes of the marriage feast or a pecuniary commutation. This is, however, though in a minor degree, one of the vexatious claims of feudality of the French system, known under the term *noçages*, where the seigneur or his deputy presided, and had the right to be placed in front of the bride, "et de chanter à la fin du répas, une chanson guillerette." But they even carried their insolence further, and " poussèrent leur mépris

The handful (*eech*) from every basket of greens.
With every other privilege attached to bhom.

Irrigated land (*peewul*)	. . .	51 beegas.
Unirrigated „ (*mál*)	. . .	110 „
Mountain „ (*mugro*)	. . .	40 „
Meadow „ (*beera*)	. . .	25 „
		226 beegas.

Asar (June) S. 1853 (A.D. 1797).

No. XI.

Charter of Privileges and Immunities granted to the town of Jhalra Patun, engraved on a Pillar in that City.

S. 1853 (A.D. 1797), corresponding with the Saka 1718, the sun being in the south, the season of cold, and the happy month of Kartika,[1] the enlightened half of the month, being Monday the full moon.

Maharaja Dheraj Sri Omeid Sing Deo,[2] the Foujdar [3] Raj Zalim Sing and Komar Madhu Sing, commanding. To all the inhabitants of Jhalra Patun, Patéls,[4] Putwarries,[5] Mahajins,[6] and to all the thirty-six castes, it is written.

At this period entertain entire confidence, build and dwell.

Within this abode all forced contributions and confiscations are for ever abolished. The taxes called Bulmunsie,[7] Annie,[8] and Rék Burrar,[9] and likewise all Bhét-Bégar,[10] shall cease.

To this intent is this stone erected, to hold good from year to year, now and evermore. There shall be no violence in this territory. This is sworn by the cow to the Hindu and the hog to the Mussulman : in the presence of Captain Dellil Khan, Choudree Saroop Chund, Patél Lallo, the Mahésri Patwarri Balkishen, the architect Kaloo Ram, and the stone-mason Balkishen.

Purmoh [11] is for ever abolished. Whoever dwells and traffics within the town of Patun, one half of the transit duties usually levied in Haravati are remitted ; and all mauppa (meter's) duties are for ever abolished.

No. XII.

Abolitions, Immunities, Prohibitions, etc., etc. Inscription in the Temple of Latchmi Narrain at Akola.

In former times tobacco was sold in one market only. Rana Raj Sing commanded the monopoly to be abolished. S. 1645.

pour les villains (the agricultural classes of the Rajpoot system) jusqu'à exiger que leurs chiens eussent *leur couvert* auprès de la mariée, et qu'on les laissât manger sur la table."—Art. " Noçages," *Dict. de l'anc. Régime.*

[1] December.
[2] The Raja of Kotah.
[3] Commander of the forces and regent of Kotàh.
[4] Officers of the land revenue.
[5] Land accountants.
[6] The mercantile class.
[7] Literally 'good behaviour.'
[8] An agricultural tax.
[9] Tax for registering.
[10] This includes in one word the forced labour exacted from the working classes : the *corvée* of the French system.
[11] Grain thrown on the inhabitants at an arbitrary rate ; often resorted to at Kotah, where the regent is farmer general.

Rana Juggut Sing prohibited the seizure of the cots and quilts by the officers of his government from the printers of Akola.

No. XIII.

Privileges and Immunities granted to the Printers of Calico and Inhabitants of the Town of Great Akola in Méwar.

Maharana Bheem Sing, commanding, to the inhabitants of Great Akola.

Whereas the village has been abandoned from the assignments levied by the garrison of Mandelgurh, and it being demanded of its population how it could again be rendered prosperous, they unanimously replied : " Not to exact beyond the dues and contributions (*dind dor*) established of yore ; to erect the pillar promising never to exact above half the produce of the crops, or to molest the persons of those who thus paid their dues."

The Presence agreed, and this pillar has been erected. May Eklinga look to him who breaks this command. The hog to the Mussulman and the cow to the Hindu.

Whatever contributions (*dind*) purmoh,[1] poolee,[2] heretofore levied shall be paid.

All crimes committed within the jurisdiction of Akola to be tried by its inhabitants, who will sit in justice on the offender and fine him according to his faults.

On Amavus [3] no work shall be done at the well [4] or at the oil-mill, nor printer put his dye-pot on the fire.[5]

Whoever breaks the foregoing, may the sin of the slaughter of Cheetore be upon him.

This pillar was erected in the presence of Mehta Sirdar Sing, Sawul Das, the Choudries Bhoput Ram and Doulut Ram, and the assembled Punch of Akola.

Written by the Choudrie Bhopji, and engraved by the stone-cutter Bheema.

S. 1856 (A.D. 1800).

No. XIV.

Prohibition against Guests carrying away Provisions from the Public Feast.[6]

Sri Maharana Singram Sing to the inhabitants of Mirmi.

On all feasts of rejoicing, as well as those on the ceremonies for the

[1] Grain, the property of the government, thrown on the inhabitants for purchase at an arbitrary valuation.

[2] The handful from each sheaf at harvest.

[3] A day sacred to the Hindu, being that which divides the month.

[4] Meaning, they shall not irrigate the fields.

[5] This part of the edict is evidently the instigation of the Jains, to prevent the destruction of life, though only that of insects.

[6] The cause of this sumptuary edict was a benevolent motive, and to prevent the expenses on these occasions falling too heavily on the poorer classes. It was customary for the women to carry away under their petticoats (*ghagra*) sufficient sweetmeats for several days' consumption. The great Jey Sing of Ambér had an ordinance restricting the number of guests to fifty-one on these occasions, and prohibited to all but the four wealthy classes the use of sugar-candy : the others were confined to the use of molasses and brown sugar. To the lower vassals and the cultivators these feasts were limited to the coarser fare ; to joar flour, greens and oil. A dyer who on the Hooli feasted his friends with sweetmeats of fine

dead, none shall carry away with them the remains of the feast. Whoever thus transgresses shall pay a fine to the crown of one hundred and one rupees. S. 1769 (A.D. 1713), Cheit Sood 7th.

No. XV.

Maharana Singram Sing to the merchants and bankers of Bákrole.

The custom of furnishing quilts (*see-rak*) [1] of which you complain, is of ancient date. Now when the collectors of duties, their officers, or those of the land revenue stop at Bákrole, the merchants will furnish them with beds and quilts. All other servants will be supplied by the other inhabitants.

Should the dam of the lake be in any way injured, whoever does not aid in its repair shall, as a punishment, feed one hundred and one Brahmins. Asar 1715, or June A.D. 1659.

No. XVI.

Warrant of the Chief of Bijollí to his Vassal, Gopal Das Suktawut.

Maharaja Mandhata to Suktawut Gopal Das, be it known.

At this time a daily fine of four rupees is in force against you. Eighty are now due ; Gunga Ram having petitioned in your favour, forty of this will be remitted. Give a written declaration to this effect—that with a specified quota you will take the field ; if not, you will stand the consequences.

Viz. : One good horse and one matchlock, with appurtenances complete, to serve at home and abroad (*dés purdés*), and to run the country [2] with the Khér.

sugar and scattered about balls made of brown sugar, was fined five thousand rupees for setting so pernicious an example. The *sád*, or marriage present, from the bridegroom to the bride's father, was limited to fifty-one rupees. The great sums previously paid on this score were preventives of matrimony. Many other wholesome regulations of a much more important kind, especially those for the suppression of infanticide, were instituted by this prince.

[1] 'Defence against the cold weather' (*see*). This in the ancient French régime came under the denomination of "*Albergie* ou Hébergement, un droit royal. Par exemple, ce ne fut qu'après le règne de Saint Louis, et moyennant finances, que les habitans de Paris et de Corbeil s'affranchirent, les premiers de fournir au roi et à sa suite de bons oreillers et d'excellens lits de plumes, tant qu'il séjournait dans leur ville, et les seconds de le régaler quand it passait par leur bourg."

[2] The '*douraéts*' or runners, the term applied to the bands who swept the country with their forays in those periods of general confusion, are analogous to the armed bands of the Middle Ages, who in a similar manner desolated Europe under the term *routiers*, tantamount to our *raburs* (on the road), the *laburs* of the Pindarries in India. The Rajpoot *douraét* has as many epithets as the French *routier*, who were called *escorcheurs*, *tard veneurs* (of which class Gopal Das appears to have been), *mille-diables*, *Guilleries*, etc.

From the Crusades to the sixteenth century, the nobles of Europe, of whom these bands were composed (like our Rajpoots), abandoned themselves to this sort of life ; who, to use the words of the historian, " préférèrent la vie vagabonde à laquelle ils s'étoient accoutumés dans le camp, à retourner cultiver leurs champs. C'est alors que se formèrent ces bandes qu'on vit parcourir le royaume et étendre sur toutes les provinces le fléau de leurs inclinations destructives, répandre partout léffroi, la misère, le deuil et le désespoir ; mettre les villes à contribution, piller et incendier les villages, égorger les laboureurs, et se livrer à des accès de cruanté qui font frémir."—*Dict. de l'ancien régime et des abus féodaux*, art. " Routier," p. 422.

We have this apology for the Rajpoot *routiers*, that the nobles of Europe had

When the levy (*khér*) takes the field, Gopal Das must attend in person. Should he be from home, his retainers must attend, and they shall receive rations from the presence.

Sawun sood dos (August 10) S. 1782.

No. XVII.

Maharaja Odykurn to the Suktawut Simboo Sing. Be it known.

I had annexed Gooroh to the fisc, but now, from favour, restore it to you. Make it flourish, and serve me at home and abroad, with one horse, and one foot soldier.

When abroad you shall receive rations (*bhatta*) as follows :—

Flour	3 lb.
Pulse	4 ounces.
Butter (*ghee*)	2 pice weight.
Horses' feed	4 seers at 22 takas each seer, of daily allowance.

If for defence of the fort you are required, you will attend with all your dependents, and bring your wife, family, and chattels ; for which, you will be exempted from two years of subsequent service.

Asar 14, S. 1834.

No. XVIII.

Bhoom in Moond-kati, or Compensation for Blood, to Jait Sing Chondawut.

The Patél's son went to bring home his wife with Jait's Rajpoots as a guard. The party was attacked, the guard killed, and there having been no redress for the murder, twenty-six beegas have been granted in moond-kati [1] (compensation).

No. XIX.

Rawut Megh Sing to his natural brother, Jumna Das, a putta (*fief*) has been granted, viz. :

The village of Rajpoora, value	Rupees 401
A garden of mogra flower	11
Rupees	412

Serve at home and abroad with fidelity : contributions and aids pay according to custom, and as do the rest of the vassals. Jait 14th, S. 1874.

No. XX.

Charter given by the Rana of Méwar, accepted and signed by all his Chiefs ; defining the duties of the contracting Parties. A.D. 1818.

Sid Sri Maharana Dhéraj, Maharana Bheem Sing, to all the nobles my brothers and kin, Rajas, Patéls, Jhalas, Chohans, Chondawuts, Powars, Sarangdeots, Suktawuts, Rahtores, Ranawuts, etc., etc.

not ; they were driven to it by perpetual aggressions of invaders. I invariably found that the reformed *routier* was one of the best subjects : it secured him from indolence, the parent of all Rajpoot vices.

[1] *Moond*, 'the head' ; *kati*, 'cut.'

Now, since S. 1822 (A.D. 1776), during the reign of Sri Ur Sing-ji,[1] when the troubles commenced, laying ancient usages aside, undue usurpations of the land have been made: therefore on this day, Bysák badi 14th, S. 1874 (A.D. 1818), the Maharana assembling all his chiefs, lays down the path of duty in new ordinances.

1st. All lands belonging to the crown obtained since the troubles, and all lands seized by one chief from another, shall be restored.

2nd. All Rekwali,[2] Bhom, Lagut,[3] established since the troubles, shall be renounced.

3rd. Dhan,[4] Biswo,[5] the right of the crown alone, shall be renounced.

4th. No chiefs shall commit thefts or violence within the boundaries of their estates. They shall entertain no Thugs,[6] foreign thieves or thieves of the country, as Mogees,[6] Baories,[6] Thories:[6] but those who shall adopt peaceful habits may remain; but should any return to their old pursuits, their heads shall instantly be taken off. All property stolen shall be made good by the proprietor of the estate within the limits of which it is plundered.

5th. Home or foreign merchants, traders, Kaffilas,[7] Bunjarries,[8] who enter the country, shall be protected. In no wise shall they be molested or injured, and whoever breaks this ordinance, his estate shall be confiscated.

6th. According to command, at home or abroad service must be performed. Four divisions (*chokies*) shall be formed of the chiefs, and each division shall remain three months in attendance at court, when they shall be dismissed to their estates. Once a year, on the festival of the Dosérra,[9] all the chiefs shall assemble with their quotas ten days previous thereto, and twenty days subsequent they shall be dismissed to their estates. On urgent occasions, and whenever their services are required, they shall repair to the Presence.

7th. Every Puttawut holding a separate putta from the Presence, shall perform separate service. They shall not unite or serve under the greater Puttawuts: and the sub-vassals of all such chiefs shall remain with and serve their immediate Puttawut.[10]

8th. The Maharana shall maintain the dignities due to each chief according to his degree.

9th. The Ryots shall not be oppressed: there shall be no new exactions or arbitrary fines. This is ordained.

10th. What has been executed by Thacoor Ajeet Sing and sanctioned by the Rana, to this all shall agree.[11]

11th. Whosoever shall depart from the foregoing, the Maharana shall punish. In doing so the fault will not be the Rana's. Whoever fails, on him be the oath (*an*) of Eklinga and the Maharana.

[Here follow the signatures of all the chieftains of rank in Méwar, which it is needless to insert.]

1 The rebellion broke out during the reign of this prince.

2 Salvamenta.

3 Dues.

4 Transit duty.

5 *Ibid.*

6 Different descriptions of thieves.

7 Caravans of merchandise, whether on camels, bullocks or in carts.

8 Caravans of bullocks, chiefly for the transport of grain and salt.

9 On this festival the muster of all the feudal retainers is taken by the Rana in person, and honorary dresses and dignities are bestowed.

10 This article had become especially necessary, as the inferior chiefs, particularly those of the third class, had amalgamated themselves with the head of their clans, to whom they had become more accountable than to their prince.

11 This alludes to the treaty which this chief had formed, as the ambassador of the Rana, with the British Government.

ANNALS OF MÉWAR

CHAPTER I

Origin of the Gehlote princes of Méwar—Authorities—Keneksén the founder of the present dynasty—His descent from Rama—He emigrates to Saurashtra —Balabhipoora—Its sack and destruction by the Huns or Parthians.

WE now proceed to the history of the states of Rajpootana, and shall commence with the annals of Méwar, and its princes.

These are styled *Ranas*, and are the elder branch of the Sooryavansi, or 'children of the sun.' Another patronymic is Raghoovansi, derived from a predecessor of Rama, the focal point of each scion of the solar race. To him, the conqueror of Lanka,[1] the genealogists endeavour to trace the solar lines. The titles of many of these claimants are disputed ; but the Hindu tribes yield unanimous suffrage to the prince of Méwar as the legitimate heir to the throne of Rama, and style him *Hindua Sooraj*, or 'Sun of the Hindus.'[2] He is universally allowed to be the first of the 'thirty-six royal tribes' ; nor has a doubt ever been raised respecting his purity of descent. Many of these tribes[3] have been swept away by time ; and the genealogist, who abhors a vacuum in his mystic page, fills up their place with others, mere scions of some ancient but forgotten stem.

With the exception of Jessulmér, Méwar is the only dynasty of these races[3] which has outlived eight centuries of foreign domination, in the same lands where conquest placed them. The Rana still possesses nearly the same extent of territory which his ancestors held when the conqueror from Guzni first crossed the 'blue waters'[4] of the Indus to invade India ; while the other families now ruling in the north-west of Rajast'han are the relics of ancient dynasties driven from their pristine seats of power, or their junior branches, who have erected their own fortunes. This circumstance adds to the dignity of the Ranas, and is the cause of the general homage which they receive, notwithstanding the diminution of their power. Though we cannot give the princes of Méwar an ancestor in the Persian Noshirwan, nor assert so confidently as Sir Thomas Roe his

[1] Said to be Ceylon ; an idea scouted by the Hindus, who transfer Lanka to a very distant region.

[2] This descendant of one hundred kings shows himself in cloudy weather from the *soorya-gokra*, or 'balcony of the sun.'

[3] See *History of the Tribes*.

[4] *Niláb*, from *nil*, 'blue,' and *áb*, 'water' ; hence the name of the Nile in Egypt and in India. *Sinde*, or *Sind'hu*, appears to be a Scythian word : *Sin* in the Tatar, *t'sin* in Chinese, 'river.' Hence the inhabitants of its higher course termed it *aba sin*, 'parent stream' ; and thus, very probably, *Abyssinia* was formed by the Arabians ; 'the country on the Nile,' or *aba sin*.

claims to descent from the celebrated Porus,[1] the opponent of Alexander, we can carry him into the regions of antiquity more remote than the Persian, and which would satisfy the most fastidious in respect to ancestry.

In every age and clime we observe the same eager desire after distinguished pedigree, proceeding from a feeling which, though often derided, is extremely natural. The Rajapootras are, however, scarcely satisfied with discriminating their ancestors from the herd of mankind. Some plume themselves on a celestial origin, whilst others are content to be demi-celestial; and those who cannot advance such lofty claims, rather than acknowledge the race to have originated in the ordinary course of nature, make their primeval parent of demoniac extraction; accordingly, several of the dynasties who cannot obtain a niche amongst the children of the sun or moon, or trace their descent from some royal saint, are satisfied to be considered the offspring of some Titan (*Dyte*). These puerilities are of modern fabrication, in cases where family documents have been lost, or emigration has severed branches from the parent stock; who, increasing in power, but ignorant of their birth, have had recourse to fable to supply the void. Various authors, borrowing from the same source, have assigned the seat of Porus to the Rana's family; and coincidence of name has been the cause of the family being alternately elevated and depressed. Thus the incidental circumstance of the word *Rhanæ* being found in Ptolemy's geography, in countries bordering on Méwar, furnishes our ablest geographers[2] with a reason for planting the family there in the second century; while the commentators[3] on the geography of the Arabian travellers of the ninth and tenth centuries[4] discover sufficient evidence in "the kingdom of Rahmi, always at war with the Balhara sovereign," to consider him (notwithstanding Rahmi is expressly stated "not to be much considered for his birth or the antiquity of his kingdom") as the prince of Cheetore, celebrated in both these points.

The translator of the *Periplus of the Erythrean Sea*, following D'Anville,[5] makes Ozene (Oojein) the capital of a Porus,[6] who sent an embassy to Augustus to regulate their commercial intercourse, and whom he asserts to be the ancestor of the Rana. But to show how guarded we should be in admitting verbal resemblance to decide such points, the title of Rana is of modern adoption, even so late as the twelfth century; and was assumed in consequence of the victorious issue of a contest with the Purihara prince of Mundore, who bore the title of Rana, and who surrendered it with his life and capital to the prince of Méwar. The latter substituted it for the more ancient appellation of *Rawul*;[7] but it was not till the thirteenth century that the novel distinction was generally recognised by neighbouring powers. Although we cannot for a moment admit

[1] See p. 35. [2] D'Anville and Rennell. [3] Maurice and others.

[4] *Rélations Anciennes des Voyageurs*, par Renaudot.

[5] D'Anville (*Antiquités de l'Inde*) quotes Nicolas of Damascus as his authority, who says the letter written by Porus, prince of Ozene, was in the Greek character.

[6] This *Porus* is a corruption of *Púar*, once the most powerful and conspicuous tribe in India; classically written Pramara, the dynasty which ruled at Oojein for ages.

[7] *Rawul*, or *Raoul*, is yet borne as a princely title by the Aharya prince of Dongurpoor, and the Yadu prince of Jessulmér, whose ancestors long ruled in the heart of Scythia. *Raoul* seems to have been titular to the Scandinavian chiefs of Scythic origin. The invader of Normandy was *Raoul*, corrupted to *Rollon* or *Rollo*.

the *Rahmi*, or even the *Rhanæ* of Ozene, to be connected with this family, yet Ptolemy appears to have given the real ancestor in his *Baleocuri*, the Balhara monarchs of the Arabian travellers, the Balabhi-raes of Saurashtra, who were the ancestors of the princes of Méwar.[1]

Before we proceed, it is necessary to specify the sources whence materials were obtained for the Annals of Méwar, and to give some idea of the character they merit as historical data.

For many years previous to sojourning at the court of Oodipoor, sketches were obtained of the genealogy of the family from the rolls of the bards. To these was added a chronological sketch, drawn up under the eye of Raja Jey Sing of Ambér, with comments of some value by him, and which served as a ground-work. Free access was also granted to the Rana's library, and permission obtained to make copies of such MSS. as related to his history. The most important of these was the *Khomán Rásá*,[2] which is evidently a modern work founded upon ancient materials, tracing the genealogy to Rama, and halting at conspicuous beacons in this long line of crowned heads, particularly about the period of the Mahomedan irruption in the tenth century, the sack of Cheetore by Alla-oo-din in the thirteenth century, and the wars of Rana Pertáp with Akber, during whose reign the work appears to have been recast.

The next in importance were the *Raj Vulas*, in the Vrij Bakha, by Mán Kubéswara;[3] and the *Raj Rutnakur*,[4] by Sudasheo Bhut; both written in the reign of Rana Raj Sing, the opponent of Arungzéb: also the *Jey Vulas*, written in the reign of Jey Sing, son of Raj Sing. They all commence with the genealogies of the family, introductory to the military exploits of the princes whose names they bear.

The *Mamadéva Prasist'ha* is a copy of the inscriptions[5] in the temple of 'the Mother of the Gods' at Komulmér. Genealogical rolls of some antiquity were obtained from the widow of an ancient family bard, who had left neither children nor kindred to follow his profession. Another roll was procured from a priest of the Jains residing in Sanderai, in Marwar, whose ancestry had enjoyed from time immemorial the title of *Gooru*, which they held at the period of the sack of Balabhipoora in the fifth century, whence they emigrated simultaneously with the Rana's ancestors. Others were obtained from Jain priests at Jawud in Malwa. Historical documents possessed by several chiefs were readily furnished, and extracts were made from works, both Sanscrit and Persian, which incidentally mention the family. To these were added traditions or biographical anecdotes furnished in conversation by the Rana, or men of intellect amongst his chiefs, ministers, or bards, and inscriptions calculated to reconcile dates; in short, every corroborating circumstance was treasured

[1] The Balhara kings, and their capital Nehrwalla, or Anhulwarra Putun, have given rise to much conjecture amongst the learned. We shall, before this work is closed, endeavour to condense what has been said by ancient and modern authorities on the subject; and from manuscripts, ancient inscriptions, and the result of a personal visit to this ancient domain, to set the matter completely at rest.

[2] *Khoman* is an ancient title of the earlier princes, and still used. It was borne by the son of *Bappa*, the founder, who retired to Transoxiana, and there ruled and died: the very country of the ancient Scythic *Khomani*.

[3] Lord of rhyme.

[4] Sea of gems.

[5] These inscriptions will be described in the Personal Narrative.

up which could be obtained by incessant research during sixteen years. The Commentaries of Baber and Jehangír, the Institutes of Akber, original grants, public and autograph letters of the emperors of Dehli and their ministers, were made to contribute more or less; yet, numerous as are the authorities cited, the result may afford but little gratification to the general reader, partly owing to the unpopularity of the subject, partly to the inartificial mode of treating it.

At least ten genealogical lists, derived from the most opposite sources, agree in making Keneksén the founder of this dynasty; and assign his emigration from the most northern of the provinces of India to the peninsula of Saurashtra in S. 201, or A.D. 145. We shall, therefore, make this the point of outset; though it may be premised that Jey Sing, the royal historian and astronomer of Ambér, connects the line with Soomitra (the fifty-sixth descendant from the deified Rama), who appears to have been the contemporary of Vicramaditya, A.C. 56.

The country of which Ayodia (now Oude) was the capital, and Rama monarch, is termed, in the geographical writings of the Hindus, *Koshula*; doubtless from the mother of Rama, whose name was *Koshulya*. The first royal emigrant from the north is styled, in the Rana's archives, *Koshula-pootra*, 'son of Koshula.'

Rama had two sons, Loh and Cush: from the former the Rana's family claim descent. He is stated to have built Lahore, the ancient Loh-kote; and the branch from which the princes of Méwar are descended resided there until Keneksén emigrated to Dwarica. The difficulty of tracing these races through a long period of years is greatly increased by the custom of changing the appellation of the tribe, from conquest, locality, or personal celebrity. *Sén*[1] seems to have been the martial termination for many generations: this was followed by *Dit*, or *Aditya*, a term for the 'sun.' The first change in the name of the tribe was on their expulsion from Saurashtra, when for the generic term of *Sooryavansi* was substituted the particular appellation of *Gehlote*. This name was maintained till another event dispersed the family, and when they settled in Ahar,[2] *Aharya* became the appellative of the branch. This continued till loss of territory and new acquisitions once more transferred the dynasty to Seesoda,[3] a temporary capital in the western mountains. The title of *Ranawut*, borne by all descendants of the blood royal since the eventful change which removed the seat of government from Cheetore to Oodipoor, might in time have superseded that of *Seesodia*, if continued warfare had not checked the increase of population; but the Gehlote branch of the Sooryavansi still retain the name of *Seesodia*.

Having premised thus much, we must retrograde to the darker ages, through which we shall endeavour to conduct this celebrated dynasty, though the clue sometimes nearly escapes from our hands in these labyrinths of antiquity.[4] When it is recollected to what violence this family

[1] *Sén*, 'army'; *kenk*, 'war.'

[2] *Ahar*, or *Ar*, is in the valley of the present capital, Oodipoor.

[3] The origin of this name is from the trivial occurrence of the expelled prince of Cheetore having erected a town to commemorate the spot, where after an extraordinarily hard chase he killed a hare (*sussoo*).

[4] The wild fable which envelops or adorns the cradle of every illustrious family is not easily disentangled. The bards weave the web with skill, and it clings like ivy round each modern branch, obscuring the aged stem, in the time-worn

has been subjected during the last eight centuries, often dispossessed of all but their native hills and compelled to live on their spontaneous produce, we could scarcely expect that historical records should be preserved. Cheetore was thrice sacked and destroyed, and the existing records are formed from fragments, registers of births and marriages, or from the oral relations of the bards.

By what route Keneksén, the first emigrant of the solar race, found his way into Saurashtra from Loh-kote, is uncertain: he, however, wrested dominion from a prince of the Pramara race, and founded Birnagara in the second century (A.D. 144). Four generations afterwards, Vijya Sén, whom the prince of Ambér calls *Noshirwan*, founded Vijyapoor, supposed to be where Dholka now stands, at the head of the Saurashtra peninsula. Vidurba was also founded by him, the name of which was afterwards changed to Seehore. But the most celebrated was the capital, Balabhipoora, which for years baffled all search, till it was revealed in its now humbled condition as Balbhi, ten miles north-west of Bhownugger. The existence of this city was confirmed by a celebrated Jain work, the *Satroonjya Mahatma*.[1] The want of satisfactory proof of the Rana's emigration from thence was obviated by the most unexpected discovery of an inscription of the twelfth century, in a ruined temple on the table-land forming the eastern boundary of the Rana's present territory, which appeals to the 'walls of Balabhi' for the truth of the action it records. And a work written to commemorate the reign of Rana Raj Sing opens with these words: "In the west is Sooratdés,[2] a country well known: the *barbarians* invaded it, and conquered *Bhal-ca-nat'h*; [3] all fell in the sack of Balabhipoora, except the daughter of the Pramara." And the Sanderai roll thus commences: "When the city of Balabhi was sacked, the inhabitants fled and founded Balli, Sanderai, and Nadole in Mordur dés." [4] These are towns yet of consequence, and in all the Jain religion is still maintained, which was the chief worship of Balabhipoora when sacked by the '*barbarian*.' The records preserved by the Jains give S.B. 205 (A.D. 524) as the date of this event.

The tract about Balabhipoora and northward is termed *Bhal*, probably from the tribe of *Balla*, which might have been the designation of the Rana's tribe prior to that of Grahilote; and most probably Moolt'han, and all these regions of the Catti, Balla, etc., were dependent on Lokkote, whence emigrated Keneksén; thus strengthening the surmise of the Scythic descent of the Ranas, though now installed in the seat of Rama. The sun was the deity of this northern tribe, as of the Rana's ancestry, and the remains of numerous temples to this grand object of Scythic homage are still to be found scattered over the peninsula; whence its name, *Saurashtra*, the country of the *Sauras*, or *Sun-worshippers*; the *Surostrene* or *Syrastrene* of ancient geographers; its inhabitants, the *Suros* (Σύρων) of Strabo.

branches of which monsters and demi-gods are perched, whose claims of affinity are held in high estimation by these 'children of the sun,' who would deem it criminal to doubt that the *loin-robe* (*dhoti*) of their great founder, Bappa Rawul, was less than five hundred cubits in circumference, that his two-edged sword (*khanda*), the gift of the Hindu Proserpine, weighed an ounce less than sixty-four pounds, or that he was an inch under twenty feet in height.

[1] Presented to the Royal Asiatic Society of London.

[2] Soorat or Saurashtra. [3] The 'lord of Bhal.' [4] Marwar.

Besides these cities, the MSS. give Gayni [1] as the last refuge of the family when expelled Saurashtra. One of the poetic chronicles thus commences : "The *barbarians* had captured Gajni. The house of Silladitya was left desolate. In its defence his heroes fell ; of his seed but the name remained."

These invaders were Scythic, and in all probability a colony from the Parthian kingdom, which was established in sovereignty on the Indus in the second century, having their capital at *Saminagara*, where the ancient Yadu ruled for ages : the *Minagara* [2] of Arrian, and the *Mankir* of the Arabian geographers. It was by this route, through the eastern portion of the valley of the Indus, that the various hordes of Getes or Jits, Huns, Camari, Catti, Macwahana, Balla and Aswaria, had peopled this peninsula, leaving traces still visible. The period is also remarkable when these and other Scythic hordes were simultaneously abandoning higher Asia for the cold regions of Europe and the warm plains of Hindust'han. From the first to the sixth century of the Christian era, various records exist of these irruptions from the north. Gibbon, quoting De Guignes, mentions one in the second century, which fixed permanently in the Saurashtra peninsula ; and the latter, from original authorities, describes another of the Getes or Jits, styled by the Chinese *Yu-chi*, in the north of India.[3] But the

[1] Gayni, or Gajni, is one of the ancient names of Cambay (the port of Balabhipoora), the ruins of which are about three miles from the modern city. Other sources indicate that these princes held possessions in the southern continent of India, as well as in the Saurashtra peninsula. Tilatilpoor Putun, on the Godavery, is mentioned, which tradition asserts to be the city of Deogir ; but which, after many years' research, I discovered in Saurashtra, it being one of the ancient names of Kundala. In after times, when succeeding dynasties held the title of Bhal-ca-rae, though the capital was removed inland to Anhulwarra Putun, they still held possession of the western shore, and Cambay continued the chief port.

[2] The position of Minagara has occupied the attention of geographers from D'Anville to Pottinger. Sinde being conquered by Omar, general of the caliph Al-Mansoor (Abbasi), the name of *Minagara* was changed to *Mansoora*, "une ville célébre sur le rivage droit du Sind ou Mehran." "Ptolémée fait aussi mention de cette ville ; mais en la déplaçant," etc. D'Anville places it about 26°, but not so high as Ulug Bég, whose tables make it 26° 40′. I have said elsewhere that I had little doubt that Minagara, handed down to us by the author of the *Periplus* as the μετρόπολις τῆς Σκυθιας, was the *Saminagara* of the Yadu Jharéjas, whose chronicles claim Sewisthan as their ancient possession, and in all probability was the stronghold (*nagara*) of Sambus, the opponent of Alexander. On every consideration, I am inclined to place it on the site of Sehwan. The learned Vincent, in his translation of the *Periplus*, enters fully and with great judgment upon this point, citing every authority, Arrian, Ptolemy, Al-Biruni, Edrisi, D'Anville, and De la Rochette. He has a note (26, p. 386, vol. i.) which is conclusive, could he have applied it : "Al-Birun [equi-distant] between Debeil and Mansura." D'Anville also says : "de Mansora à la ville nommée Birun, la distance est indiquée de quinze parasanges dans Abulféda," who fixes it, on the authority of Abu-Rehan (surnamed Al-Biruni from his birthplace), at 26° 40′.

The ancient name of Hydrabad, the present capital of Sinde, was Neroon (نير ون) or Nirun, and is almost equi-distant, as Abulfeda says, between Dabul (Dewul or Tatta) and Mansoora, Sehwan, or Minagara, the latitude of which, according to my construction, is 26° 11′. Those who wish to pursue this may examine the *Eclaircissemens sur la Carte de l'Inde*, p. 37 et seq., and Dr. Vincent's estimable translation, p. 386.

[3] See *History of the Tribes*, p. 107, and translation of Inscription No. I. *Vide* Appendix.

authority directly in point is that of Cosmas, surnamed Indopleustes, who was in India during the reign of Justinian, and that of the first monarch of the Chinese dynasty of Leam.[1] Cosmas had visited Callian, included in the Balḥara kingdom; and he mentions the *Abtelites*, or white Huns, under their king Golas, as being established on the Indus at the very period of the invasion of Balabhipoora.

Arrian, who resided in the second century at Barugaza (Baroach), describes a Parthian sovereignty as extending from the Indus to the Nerbudda. Their capital has already been mentioned, Minagara. Whether these, the Abtelites[2] of Cosmas, were the Parthian dynasty of Arrian, or whether the Parthians were supplanted by the Huns, we must remain in ignorance, but to one or the other we must attribute the sack of Balabhipoora. The legend of this event affords scope for speculation, both as regards the conquerors and the conquered, and gives at least a colour of truth to the reputed Persian ancestry of the Rana: a subject which will be distinctly considered. The solar orb, and its type, fire, were the chief objects of adoration of Silladitya of Balabhipoora. Whether to these was added that of the lingam, the symbol of Bálnat'h (the sun), the primary object of worship with his descendants, may be doubted. It was certainly confined to these, and the adoption of 'strange gods' by the Sooryavansi Gehlote is comparatively of modern invention.[3]

There was a fountain (*Sooryacoonda*) 'sacred to the sun' at Balabhipoora, from which arose, at the summons of Silladitya (according to the legend) the seven-headed horse Septaswa, which draws the car of Soorya, to bear him to battle. With such an auxiliary no foe could prevail; but a wicked minister revealed to the enemy the secret of annulling this aid, by polluting the sacred fountain with blood. This accomplished, in vain did the prince call on Septaswa to save him from the strange and barbarous foe: the charm was broken, and with it sunk the dynasty of Balabhi. Who the 'barbarian' was that defiled with blood of kine the fountain of the sun,[4] whether Gete, Parthian, or Hun, we are left to conjecture. The

[1] Considerable intercourse was carried on between the princes of India and China from the earliest periods; but particularly during the dynasties of Sum, Leam and Tám, from the fourth to the seventh centuries, when the princes from Bengal and Malabar to the Punjáb sent embassies to the Chinese monarchs. The diminions of these Hindu princes may yet be identified.

[2] D'Herbelot (vol. i. p. 179) calls them the *Haiathelah* or *Indoscythæ*, and says that they were apparently from Thibet, between India and China. De Guignes (tome i. p. 325) is offended with this explanation, and says: "Cette conjecture ne peut avoir lieu, les Euthélites n'ayant jamais demeuré dans le Thibet." A branch of the Huns, however, did most assuredly dwell in that quarter, though we will not positively assert that they were the Abtelites. The Hya was a great branch of the Lunar race of Yayat, and appears early to have left India for the northern regions, and would afford a more plausible etymology for the *Haiathelah* than the *Te-le*, who dwelt on the waters (*áb*) of the Oxus. This branch of the Hunnish race has also been termed Nephthalite, and fancied one of the lost tribes of Israel.

[3] Ferishta, in the early part of his history, observes that, some centuries prior to Vicramaditya, the Hindus abandoned the simple religion of their ancestors, made idols, and worshipped the host of heaven, which faith they had from Cashmere, the foundry of magic superstition.

[4] Divested of allegory, it means simply that the supply of water was rendered impure, and consequently useless to the Hindus, which compelled them to abandon their defences and meet death in the open field. Alla-o-din practised the same *ruse* against the celebrated Achil, the Kheechie prince of Gagrown,

Persian, though he venerated the bull, yet sacrificed him on the altar of Mithras ;[1] and though the ancient Guebre purifies with the urine[2] of the cow, he will not refuse to eat beef ; and the iniquity of Cambyses, who thrust his lance into the flank of the Egyptian Apis, is a proof that the bull was abstractedly no object of worship. It would be indulging a legitimate curiosity, could we by any means discover how these 'strange' tribes obtained a footing amongst the Hindu races ; for so late as seven centuries ago we find Getes, Huns, Catti, Ariaspas, Dahæ, definitively settled, and enumerated amongst the Chatées rajcúla.[3] How much earlier the admission, no authority states ; but mention is made of several of them aiding in the defence of Cheetore, on the first appearance of the faith of Islam upwards of eleven hundred years ago.

CHAPTER II

Birth of Goha—He acquires Edur—Derivation of the term 'Gehlote'—Birth of Bappa—Early religion of the Gehlotes—Bappa's history—Oguna Panora—Bappa's initiation into the worship of Síva—He gains possession of Cheetore—Remarakable end of Bappa—Four epochs established, from the second to the eleventh century.

Of the prince's family, the queen Pooshpavati alone escaped the sack of Balabhi, as well as the funeral pyre, upon which, on the death of Silladitya, his other wives were sacrificed. She was a daughter of the Pramara prince of Chandravati, and had visited the shrine of the universal mother, Amba-Bhavani, in her native land, to deposit upon the altar of the goddess a votive offering consequent to her expectation of offspring. She was on her return, when the intelligence arrived which blasted all her future hopes, by depriving her of her lord, and robbing him, whom the goddess had just granted to her prayers, of a crown. Excessive grief closed her pilgrimage. Taking refuge in a cave in the mountains of Mallia, she was delivered of a son. Having confided the infant to a Brahminee of Birnugger named Camlavati, enjoining her to educate the young prince as a Brahmin, but to marry him to a Rajpootnee, she mounted the funeral pile to join her

which caused the surrender of this impregnable fortress. "It matters not," observes an historian whose name I do not recollect, "whether such things are true, it is sufficient that they were believed. We may smile at the mention of the ghost, the evil genius of Brutus, appearing to him before the battle of Pharsalia ; yet it never would have been stated, had it not assimilated with the opinions and prejudices of the age." And we may deduce a simple moral from 'the parent orb refusing the aid of his steed to his terrestrial offspring,' viz. that he was deserted by the deity. Fountains sacred to the sun and other deities were common to the Persians, Scythians, and Hindus, and both the last offered steeds to him in sacrifice. Vide *History of the Tribes*, article "Aswamedha," p. 76.

[1] The Bul-dan, or sacrifice of the bull to Bál-nat'h, is on record, though now discontinued amongst the Hindus.

[2] Pinkerton, who is most happy to strengthen his aversion for the Celt, seizes on a passage in Strabo, who describes him as having recourse to the same mode of purification as the Guebre. Unconscious that it may have had a religious origin, he adduces it as a strong proof of the uncleanliness of their habits.

[3] See Table, p. 69.

lord. Camlavati, the daughter of the priest of the temple, was herself a mother, and she performed the tender offices of one to the orphan prince, whom she designated Goha, or 'cave-born.' The child was a source of perpetual uneasiness to its protectors: he associated with Rajpoot children, killing birds, hunting wild animals, and at the age of eleven was totally unmanageable: to use the words of the legend, "How should they hide the ray of the sun?"

At this period Edur was governed by a chief of the savage race of Bhil; his name, Mandalica. The young Goha frequented the forests in company with the Bhils, whose habits better assimilated with his daring nature than those of the Brahmins. He became a favourite with the Vena-pootras, or 'children of the forest,' who resigned to him Edur with its woods and mountains. The fact is mentioned by Abul Fuzil, and is still repeated by the bards, with a characteristic version of the incident, of which doubtless there were many. The Bhils having determined in sport to elect a king, the choice fell on Goha; and one of the young savages, cutting his finger, applied the blood as the teeka of sovereignty to his forehead. What was done in sport was confirmed by the old forest chief. The sequel fixes on Goha the stain of ingratitude, for he slew his benefactor, and no motive is assigned in the legend for the deed. Goha's name became the patronymic of his descendants, who were styled *Gohilote*, classically *Grahilote*, in time softened to *Gehlote*.

We know very little concerning these early princes but that they dwelt in this mountainous region for eight generations; when the Bhils, tired of a foreign rule, assailed Nagadit, the eighth prince, while hunting, and deprived him of life and Edur. The descendants of Camlavati (the Birnuggur Brahmin), who retained the office of priest in the family, were again the preservers of the line of Balabhi. The infant Bappa, son of Nagadit, then only three years old, was conveyed to the fortress of Bhandere,[1] where he was protected by a Bhil of Yadu descent. Thence he was removed for greater security to the wilds of Parassur. Within its impervious recesses rose the three peaked (*tri-cúta*) mountain, at whose base was the town of Nagindra,[2] the abode of Brahmins, who performed the rites of the 'great god.' In this retreat passed the early years of Bappa, wandering through these Alpine valleys, amidst the groves of Bál and the shrines of the brazen calf.

The most antique temples are to be seen in these spots—within the dark gorge of the mountain, or on its rugged summit—in the depths of the forest, and at the sources of streams, where sites of seclusion, beauty, and sublimity alternately exalt the mind's devotion. In these regions the creative power appears to have been the earliest, and at one time the sole, object of adoration, whose symbols, the serpent-wreathed phallus (lingam), and its companion, the bull, were held sacred even by the 'children of the forest.' In these silent retreats Mahadeva continued to rule triumphant, and the most brilliant festivities of Oodipoor were those where his rites are celebrated in the nine days sacred to him, when the Jains and Vaishnus mix

[1] Fifteen miles south-west of Jarrole, in the wildest region in India.

[2] Or Nagda, still a place of religious resort, about ten miles north of Oodipoor. Here I found several very old inscriptions relative to the family, which preserve the ancient denomination *Gohil* instead of *Gehlote*. One of these is about nine centuries old.

with the most zealous of his votaries ; but the strange gods from the plains of the Yamuna and Ganges have withdrawn a portion of the zeal of the Gehlotes from their patron divinity Eklinga, whose deewan,[1] or vicegerent, is the Rana. The temple of Eklinga, situated in one of the narrow defiles leading to the capital, is an immense structure, though more sumptuous than elegant. It is built entirely of white marble, most elaborately carved and embellished ; but lying in the route of a bigoted foe, it has undergone many dilapidations. The brazen bull, placed under his own dome, facing the sanctuary of the phallus, is nearly of the natural size, in a recumbent posture. It is cast (hollow) of good shape, highly polished and without flaw, except where the hammer of the Tatar had opened a passage in the hollow flank in search of treasure.[2]

Tradition has preserved numerous details of Bappa's [3] infancy, which resembles the adventures of every hero or founder of a race. The young prince attended the sacred kine, an occupation which was honourable even to the 'children of the sun,' and which they still pursue : possibly a remnant of their primitive Scythic habits. The pranks of the royal shepherd are the theme of many a tale. On the Jul Jhoolni, when swinging is the amusement of the youth of both sexes, the daughter of the Solanki chief of Nagda and the village maidens had gone to the groves to enjoy this festivity, but they were unprovided with ropes. Bappa happened to be at hand, and was called by the Rajpoot damsels to forward their sport. He promised to procure a rope if they would first have a game at marriage. One frolic was as good as another, and the scarf of the Solankini was united to the garment of Bappa, the whole of the village lassies joining hands with his as the connecting link ; and thus they performed the mystical number of revolutions round an aged tree. This frolic caused his flight from Nagda, and originated his greatness, but at the same time burthened him with all these damsels ; and hence a heterogeneous issue, whose descendants still ascribe their origin to the prank of Bappa round the old mango-tree of Nagda. A suitable offer being shortly after made for the young Solankini's hand, the family priests of the bridegroom, whose duty it was, by his knowledge of palmistry, to investigate the fortunes of the bride, discovered that she was already married : intelligence which threw the family into the greatest consternation. Though Bappa's power over his brother shepherds was too strong to create any dread of disclosure as to his being the principal in this affair, yet was it too much to expect that a secret, in which no less than six hundred of the daughters of Eve were concerned, could long remain such ? Bappa's mode of swearing his companions to secrecy is preserved. Digging a small pit, and taking a pebble in his hand, "Swear," cried he, "secrecy and obedience to me in good and in evil ; that you will reveal to me all that you hear, and failing, desire that the good deeds of your forefathers may, like this pebble

[1] Ekling-ca-Deewan is the common title of the Rana.

[2] Amongst the many temples where the brazen calf forms part of the establishment of Bal-Çésar, there is one sacred to Nanda alone, at Naen in the valley. This lordly bull has his shrine attended as devoutly as was that of Apis at Memphis ; nor will Eklinga yield to his brother Serapis. The changes of position of the Apis at Naen are received as indications of the fruitfulness of the seasons, though it is not apparent how such are contrived.

[3] *Bappa* is not a proper name, it signifies merely a 'child.' He is frequently styled *Syeel*, and in inscriptions *Syeel Ahdes*, 'the mountain lord.'

(dropping it into the pit) fall into the Washerman's well."[1] They took the oath. The Solanki chief, however, heard that Bappa was the offender, who, receiving from his faithful scouts intimation of his danger, sought refuge in one of the retreats which abound in these mountains, and which in after-times proved the preservation of his race. The companions of his flight were two Bhils: one of Oondree, in the valley of the present capital; the other of Solanki descent, from Oguna Panora, in the western wilds. Their names, Baleo and Dewa, have been handed down with Bappa's; and the former had the honour of drawing the teeka of sovereignty with his own blood on the forehead of the prince, on the occasion of his taking the crown from the Mori.

It is pleasing to trace, through a series of ages, the knowledge of a custom still 'honoured in the observance.' The descendants of Baleo of Oguna and the Oondree Bhil still claim the privilege of performing the teeka on the inauguration of the descendants of Bappa.

OGUNA PANORA is the sole spot in India which enjoys a state of natural freedom. Attached to no state, having no foreign communications, living under its own patriarchal head, its chief, with the title of Rana, whom one thousand hamlets scattered over the forest-crowned valleys obey, can, if requisite, appear at 'the head of five thousand bows.' He is a Bhoomia Bhil of mixed blood, from the Solanki Rajpoot, on the old stock of pure (*oojla*) Bhils, the autochthones (if such there be of any country) of Méwar. Besides making the teeka of blood from an incision in the thumb, the Oguna chief takes the prince by the arm and seats him on the throne, while the Oondree Bhil holds the salver of spices and sacred grains of rice[2] used in making the teeka.

But the solemnity of being seated on the throne of Méwar is so expensive, that many of these rites have fallen into disuse. Juggut Sing was the last prince whose coronation was conducted with the ancient magnificence of this princely house. It cost the sum of ninety lacks of rupees (£1,125,000), nearly one entire year's revenue of the state in the days of its prosperity, and which, taking into consideration the comparative value of money, would amount to upwards of *four millions sterling*.[3]

To resume the narrative: though the flight of Bappa and its cause are perfectly natural, we have another episode; when the bard assuming a

[1] Deemed in the East the most impure of all receptacles. These wells are dug at the sides of streams, and give a supply of pure water filtering through the sand.

[2] Hence, perhaps, the name *kúshkeh* for teeka. Grains of ground rice in curds is the material of the primitive teeka, which the author has had applied to him by a lady in Goojurgar, one of the most savage spots in India, amidst the *levy en masse*, assembled hostilely against him, but separated amicably.

[3] Such the pride of these small kingdoms in days of yore, and such their resources, till reduced by constant oppression! But their public works speak what they could do, and have done; witness the stupendous work of marble, and its adjacent causeway, which dams the lake of Rajsumund at Kankerowli, and which cost upwards of a million. When the spectator views this expanse of water, this 'royal sea' (*rajsumund*) on the borders of the plain; the pillar of victory towering over the plains of Malwa, erected on the summit of Cheetore by Rana Mokul; their palaces and temples in this ancient abode; the regal residence erected by these princes when ejected, must fill the observer with astonishment at the resources of the state. They are such as to explain the metaphor of my ancient friend Zalim Sing, who knew better than we the value of this country: 'Every pinch of the soil of Méwar contains gold.'

higher strain has recourse to celestial machinery for the *dénouement* of this simple incident : but "an illustrious race must always be crowned with its proper mythology." Bappa, who was the founder of a line of a 'hundred kings,' feared as a monarch, adored as more than mortal, and, according to the legend, 'still living (*chernjíva*),' deserves to have the source of his pre-eminent fortune disclosed, which, in Méwar, it were sacrilege to doubt. While he pastured the sacred kine in the valleys of Nagindra, the princely shepherd was suspected of appropriating the milk of a favourite cow to his own use. He was distrusted and watched, and although indignant, the youth admitted that they had reason to suspect him, from the habitual dryness of the brown cow when she entered the pens at even.[1] He watched, and traced her to a narrow dell, when he beheld the udder spontaneously pouring its stores amidst the shrubs. Under a thicket of cane a hermit was reposing in a state of abstraction, from which the impetuosity of the shepherd soon roused him. The mystery was revealed in the phallic symbol of the 'great God,' which daily received the lacteal shower, and raised such doubts of the veracity of Bappa.

No eye had hitherto penetrated into this natural sanctuary of the rites of the Hindu Creator, except the sages and hermits of ancient days (of whom this was the celebrated Harita),[2] whom this bounteous cow also fed.

Bappa related to the sage all he knew of himself, received his blessing, and retired ; but he went daily to visit him, to wash his feet, carry milk to him, and gather such wild flowers as were acceptable offerings to the deity. In return he received lessons of morality, and was initiated into the mysterious rites of Síva : and at length he was invested with the triple cordon of faith (*teen purwa zinár*) by the hands of the sage, who became his spiritual guide, and bestowed on his pupil the title of 'Regent (Déwan) of Eklinga.' Bappa had proofs that his attentions to the saint and his devotions to Eklinga were acceptable, by a visit from his consort, 'the lion-born goddess.' From her hand he received the panoply of celestial fabrication, the work of Viswacarma (the Vulca of Eastern mythology), which outvies all the arms ever forged for Greek or Trojan. The lance, bow, quiver, and arrows ; a shield and sword (more famed than Balisarda) which the goddess girded on him with her own hand : the oath of fidelity and devotion was the 'relief' of this celestial investiture. Thus initiated into the mysteries of 'the first' (*ad*), admitted under the banners of Bhavani, Harita resolved to leave his pupil to his fortunes, and to quit the worship of the symbol for the presence of the deity in the mansions above. He informed Bappa of his design, and commanded him to be at the sacred spot early on the following morn ; but Bappa showed his materiality by oversleeping himself, and on reaching the spot the sage had already made some progress in his car, borne by the Apsaras, or celestial messengers. He checked his aerial ascent to give a last token of affection to his pupil ; and desiring him to reach up to receive his blessing, Bappa's stature was extended to twenty cubits ; but as he did not reach the car,

[1] *Gaoda-luk*, the time when the cows come home.

[2] On this spot the celebrated temple of Eklinga was erected, and the present high priest traces sixty-six descents from Harita to himself. To him (through the Rana) I was indebted for the copy of the Sheo (*Siva*) Pooran presented to the Royal Asiatic Society.

he was commanded to open his mouth, when the sage did what was recorded as performed, about the same period, by Mahomed, who spat into the mouth of his favourite nephew, Hussein, the son of Ali. Bappa showed his disgust and aversion by blinking, and the projected blessing fell on his foot, by which squeamishness he obtained only invulnerability by weapons instead of immortality: the saint was soon lost in the cerulean space. Thus marked as the favourite of heaven, and having learned from his mother that he was nephew to the Mori prince of Cheetore, he 'disdained a shepherd's slothful life,' and with some companions from these wilds quitted his retreat, and for the first time emerged into the plains. But, as if the brand of Bhavani was insufficient, he met with another hermit in the forest of the Tiger Mount,[1] the famed Goruknat'h, who presented to him the double-edged sword,[2] which, with the proper incantation, could 'sever rocks.' With this he opened the road to fortune leading to the throne of Cheetore.

Cheetore was at this period held by the Mori prince of the Pramar race, the ancient lords of Malwa, then paramount sovereigns of Hindust'han: but whether this city was then the chief seat of power is not known. Various public works, reservoirs, and bastions, yet retain the name of this race.

Bappa's connection with the Mori[3] obtained him a good reception; he was enrolled amongst the samunts or leaders, and a suitable estate conferred upon him. The inscription of the Mori prince's reign, so often alluded to, affords a good idea of his power, and of the feudal manners of his court. He was surrounded by a numerous nobility, holding estates on the tenure of military service, but whom he had disgusted by his neglect, and whose jealousy he had provoked by the superior regard shown to Bappa. A foreign foe appearing at this time, instead of obeying the summons to attend, they threw up their grants, and tauntingly desired him to call on his favourite.[4]

Bappa undertook the conduct of the war, and the chiefs, though dispossessed of their estates, accompanied him from a feeling of shame. The foe was defeated and driven out of the country; but instead of returning to Cheetore, Bappa continued his course to the ancient seat of his family, Gajni, expelled the 'barbarian' called Selím, placed on the throne a chief of the Chawura tribe, and returned with the discontented nobles. Bappa, on this occasion, is said to have married the daughter of his enemy. The nobles quitted Cheetore, leaving their defiance with their prince. In vain

[1] The *Nahra Mugra*, seven miles from the eastern pass leading to the capital, where the prince has a hunting seat surrounded by several others belonging to the nobles, but all going to decay. The tiger and wild boar now prowl unmolested, as none of the 'unlicensed' dare shoot in these royal preserves.

[2] They surmise that this is the individual blade which is yet annually worshipped by the sovereign and chiefs on its appropriate day, one of the nine sacred to the god of war; a rite completely Scythic. I had this relation from the chief genealogists of the family, who gravely repeated the incantation: "By the preceptor, Goruknat'h and the great god, Eklinga; by Takyac the serpent, and the sage Haríta; by Bhavani (Pallas), strike!"

[3] Bappa's mother was a Pramar, probably from Aboo or Chandravati, near to Edur; and consequently Bappa was nephew to every Pramar in existence.

[4] We are furnished with a catalogue of the tribes which served the Mori prince, which is extremely valuable, from its acquainting us with the names of tribes no longer existing.

were the spiritual preceptor (*Gooru*) and foster-brother (*Dabhae*) sent as ambassadors : their only reply was, that as they had 'eaten his salt,' they would forbear their vengeance for twelve months. The noble deportment of Bappa won their esteem, and they transferred to him their service and homage. With the temptation of a crown, the gratitude of the Grahilote was given to the winds. On return they assaulted and carried Cheetore, and, in the words of the chronicle, " Bappa took Cheetore from the Mori and became himself the mor (crown) of the land " : he obtained by universal consent the title of 'sun of the Hindus (*Hindua sooraj*), preceptor of princes (*Raj Gooru*), and universal lord (*Chukwa*).'

He had a numerous progeny, some of whom returned to their ancient seats in Saurashtra, whose descendants were powerful chieftains in that tract so late as Akber's reign.[1] Five sons went to Marwar, and the ancient Gohils 'of the land of Kheir,' expelled and driven to Gohilwal,[2] have lost sight of their ancestry, and by a singular fatality are in possession of the wreck of Balabhipoora, ignorant of its history and their connection with it, mixing with Arabs and following marine and mercantile pursuits ; and the office of the bard having fallen into disrepute, they cannot trace their forefathers beyond Kheirdhur.[3]

The close of Bappa's career is the strangest part of the legend, and which it might be expected they would be solicitous to suppress. Advanced in years, he abandoned his children and his country, carried his arms west to Khorassan, and there established himself, and married new wives from among the 'barbarians,' by whom he had a numerous offspring.[4]

Bappa had reached the patriarchal age of one hundred when he died. An old volume of historical anecdotes, belonging to the chief of Dailwara, states that he became an ascetic at the foot of Méru, where he was buried alive after having overcome all the kings of the west, as in Ispahan, Kandahar, Cashmere, Irak, Iran, Tooran, and Cafferist'han ; all of whose daughters he married, and by whom he had one hundred and thirty sons, called the Nosheyra Pathans. Each of these founded a tribe, bearing the name of the mother. His Hindu children were ninety-eight in number, and were called *Agni-oopasi Sooryavansi*, or 'sunborn fire-worshippers.' The chronicles also record that (in like manner as did the subjects of the Bactrian king Menander, though from a different motive) the subjects of Bappa quarrelled for the disposal of his remains. The Hindu wished the fire to consume them ; the 'barbarian' to commit them to earth ; but on raising the pall while the dispute was raging, innumerable flowers of the lotus were found in the place of the remains of mortality : these were conveyed and planted in the lake. This is precisely what is related of the end of the Persian Noshirwan.

Having thus briefly sketched the history of the founder of the Gehlote dynasty in Méwar, we must now endeavour to establish the epoch of

[1] See *Ayen Akberi*, who states fifty thousand Gehlotes in Sorat.

[2] Peparra Gohilotes.

[3] The 'land of Kheir,' on the south-west frontier of Marwar, near the Loony river.

[4] The reigning prince told the author that there was no doubt of Bappa having ended his days among 'the Toorks' : a term now applied to all Mahomedans by the Hindu, but at that time confined to the inhabitants of Toorkistan, the Toorushka of the Poorans, and the Takshac of early inscriptions.

this important event in its annals. Although Bappa Rawul was nine generations after the sack of Balabhipoora, the domestic annals give S. 191 (A.D. 135) for his birth; which the bards implicitly following, have vitiated the whole chronology. An important inscription[1] in a character little known, establishes the fact of the Mori dynasty being in possession of Cheetore in S. 770 (A.D. 714). Now the annals of the Rana's house expressly state Bappa Rawul to be the nephew of the Mori prince of Cheetore; that at the age of fifteen he was enrolled amongst the chieftains of his uncle, and that the vassals (before alluded to), in revenge for the resumption of their grants by the Mori, dethroned him and elevated as their sovereign the youthful Bappa. Notwithstanding this apparently irreconcilable anachronism, the family traditions accord with the inscription, except in date. Amidst such contradictions the development of the truth seemed impossible. Another valuable inscription of S. 1024 (A.D. 968), though giving the genealogy from Bappa to Sacti Komar and corroborating that from Cheetore, and which furnished convincing evidence, was not sanctioned by the prince or his chroniclers, who would admit nothing as valid that militated against their established era 191 for the birth of their founder. After six years' residence and unremitting search amid ruins, archives, inscriptions, traditions, and whatever could throw light upon this point, the author quitted Oodipoor with all these doubts in his mind, for Saurashtra, to prosecute his inquiries in the pristine abodes of the race. Then it was that he was rewarded, beyond his most sanguine expectations, by the discovery of an inscription which reconciled these conflicting authorities and removed every difficulty. This marble, found in the celebrated temple of Somnat'h,[2] made mention of a distinct era, viz. the *Balabhi Samvat*, as being used in Saurashtra; which era was three hundred and seventy-five years subsequent to Vicramaditya.

On the sack of Balabhi thirty thousand families abandoned this 'city of a hundred temples,' and led by their priests found a retreat for themselves and their faith in Mordur-dés (Marwar), where they erected the towns of Sanderai and Balhi, in which latter we recognise the name of the city whence they were expelled. The religion of Balabhi, and consequently of the colonists, was the Jain; and it was by a priest descended from the survivors of this catastrophe, and still with their descendants inhabiting those towns, that these most important documents were furnished to the author. The Sanderai roll assigns the year 305 (Balabhi era) for the destruction of Balabhi: another, also from Jain authority, gives 205; and as there were but nine princes from Vijya Sén, the founder, to its fall, we can readily believe the first a numerical error. Therefore 205 + 375 = 580 S. Vicrama (A.D. 524), for the invasion of Saurashtra by 'the barbarians from the north,' and sack of Balabhipoora.

Now if from 770, the date of the Mori tablet, we deduct 580, there remains 190; justifying the pertinacity with which the chroniclers of Méwar adhered to the date given in their annals for the birth of Bappa, viz., 191: though they were ignorant that this period was dated from the flight from Balabhipoora.

Bappa, when he succeeded to the Mori prince, is said to have been fifteen years old; and his birth being one year anterior to the Mori in-

[1] *Vide* Appendix, Translation, No. II. [2] See Translation, No. III.

scription of 770+14=S.V. 784 (A.D. 728),[1] is the period for the foundation of the Gehlote dynasty in Méwar: since which, during a space of eleven hundred years, fifty-nine princes lineally descended from Bappa have sat on the throne of Cheetore.

Though the bards and chroniclers will never forgive the temerity which thus curtails the antiquity of their founder, he is yet placed in the dawn of chivalry, when the Carlovingian dynasty was established in the west, and when Walid, whose bands planted 'the green standard' on the Ebro, was 'commander of the faithful.'

From the deserted and now forgotten 'city of the sun,' Aitpoor, the abode of wild beasts and savage Bhils, another memorial[2] of the princes of Méwar was obtained. It relates to the prince Sacti Komar. Its date is S. 1024 (A.D. 968), and it contains the names of fourteen of his ancestors in regular succession. Amongst these is Bappa, or Syeel. When compared with the chronicles and family archives, it was highly gratifying to find that, with the exception of one superfluous name and the transposition of others, they were in perfect accordance.

Hume says, "Poets, though they disfigure the most certain history by their fictions, and use strange liberties with truth, when they are the sole historians, as among the Britons, have commonly some foundation for their wildest exaggerations." The remark is applicable here; for the names which had been mouldering for nine centuries, far from the abode of man, are the same they had worked into their poetical legends. It was at this exact epoch that the arms of Islam, for the first time, crossed the Indus. In the ninety-fifth year of the Hegira,[3] Mahomed Bin Kasim, the general of the Caliph Walid, conquered Sinde, and penetrated (according to early Arabian authors) to the Ganges; and although Elmacin mentions only Sinde, yet other Hindu states were at this period convulsed from the same cause: witness the overthrow of Manik-raé of Ajmér, in the middle of the eighth century, by a foe 'coming in ships,' Anjar specified as the point where they landed. If any doubt existed that it was Kasim who advanced to Cheetore[4] and was defeated by Bappa, it was set at rest by finding at this time in Cheetore 'Dahir,[5] the Prince of Debeil.' Abul Fuzil records, from Arabian authorities, that Dahir was lord of Sinde, and resided at his capital, Debeil, the first place captured by Kasim in 95. His miserable end, and the destruction of his house, are mentioned by the historian, and account for the son being found with the Mori prince of Cheetore.

Nine princes intervened between Bappa and Sacti Komar, in two centuries (twenty-two years to each reign): just the time which should

[1] This will make Bappa's attainment of Cheetore fifteen years posterior to Kasim's invasion. I have observed generally a discrepancy of ten years between the Ṣamvat and Hegira; the Hegira reckoned from the sixteenth year of Mohamed's mission, and would if employed reconcile this difficulty.

[2] See Translation of Inscription, No. IV.

[3] A.D. 713, or S. 769: the Inscription 770 of Maun Mori, against whom came the 'barbarian.'

[4] I was informed by a friend, who had seen the papers of Captain Macmurdo, that he had a notice of Kasim's having penetrated to Dongerpoor. Had this gentleman lived, he would have thrown much light on these Western antiquities.

[5] By an orthographical error, the modern Hindu, ignorant of Debeil, has written Dehli. But there was no lord of Dehli at this time: he is styled Dahir, Désput (lord) of Debeil, from *dés*, 'a country,' and *put*, 'the head.'

elapse from the founder, who 'abandoned his country for Iran,' in S. 820, or A.D. 764. Having thus established four epochs in the earlier history of the family, viz.—1, Keneksen, A.D. 144; 2, Silladitya, and sack of Balabhi, A.D. 524; 3, Establishment in Cheetore and Méwar, A.D. 720; 4, Sacti Komar, A.D. 1068; we may endeavour to relieve this narrative by the notices which regard their Persian descent.

CHAPTER III

Alleged Persian extraction of the Ranas of Méwar—Authorities for it—Implied descent of the Ranas from a Christian princess of Byzantium—The Author's reflections upon these points.

HISTORIC truth has, in all countries, been sacrificed to national vanity: to its gratification every obstacle is made to give way; fictions become facts, and even religious prejudices vanish in this *mirage* of the imagination. What but this spurious zeal could for a moment induce any genuine Hindu to believe that, only twelve centuries ago, 'an eater of beef' occupied the chair of Rama, and enjoyed by universal acclaim the title of 'Sun of the Hindus'; or that the most ancient dynasty in the world could owe its existence to the last of the Sassanian kings:[1] that a slip from such a tree could be surreptitiously grafted on that majestic stem, which has flourished from the golden to the iron age, covering the land with its branches? That there existed a marked affinity in religious rites between the Rana's family and the Guebres, or ancient Persians, is evident. With both, the chief object of adoration was the sun; each bore the image of the orb on their banners. The chief day in the seven[2] was dedicated to the sun; to it is sacred the chief gate of the city, the principal bastion of every fortress. But though the faith of Islam has driven away the fairy inhabitants from the fountains of Mithras, that of Soorya has still its devotees on the summit of Cheetore, as at Balabhi: and could we trace with accuracy their creeds to a distant age, we might discover them to be of one family, worshipping the sun at the fountains of the Oxus and Jaxartes.

The darkest period of Indian history is during the six centuries following Vicramaditya, which are scarcely enlightened by a ray of knowledge: but India was undergoing great changes, and foreign tribes were pouring in from the north. To this period, the sixth century, the genealogies of the *Pooráns* are brought down, which expressly declare (adopting the prophetic spirit to conceal the alterations and additions they then underwent) that at this time the genuine line of princes would be extinct, and that a mixed race would rule conjointly with foreign barbarians; as the Turshka,[3] the Mauna,[3] the Yavan,[4] the Gor-ind, and Gardha-bin. There is much of

[1] Yezdegird died A.D. 651.

[2] *Sooraj-war*, or *Adit-war*, Sun-day; and the other days of the week, from the other planets, which Western nations have taken from the East.

[3] See *History of the Tribes*, pp. 103, 113, articles "Takshac," and "J'hala," or *Macwahana*, in all probability the *Mauna* of the *Poorâns*.

[4] The *Yavan*, or Greek princes, who apparently continued to rule within the Indus after the Christian era, were either the remains of the Bactrian dynasty

truth in this; nor is it to be doubted that many of the Rajpoot tribes entered India from the north-west regions about this period. *Gor* and *Gardha* have the same signification; the first is Persian; the second its version in Hinduí, meaning the 'wild ass,' an appellation of the Persian monarch Bahram, surnamed *Gor* from his partiality to hunting that animal. Various authorities state Byramgor being in India in the fifth century, and his having there leftp rogeny by a princess of Kanouj. A passage extracted by the author from an ancient Jain MS., indicates that "in S. 523, Raja Gardha-bhéla, of Cacoost'ha, or Sooryavansa, ruled in Balabhipoora." If has been surmised that Gardha-bhéla was the son of Byramgor, a son of whom is stated to have obtained dominion at Putun; which may be borne in mind when the authorities for the Persian extraction of the Rana's family are given.

The Hindus, when conquered by the Mahomedans, naturally wished to gild the chains they could not break. To trace a common, though distant, origin with the conquerors, was to remove some portion of the taint of dishonour which arose from giving their daughters in marriage to the Tatar emperors of Dehli; and a degree of satisfaction was derived from assuming that the blood thus corrupted once flowed from a common fountain.[1]

Further to develop these claims of Persian descent, we shall commence with an extract from the *Oopdês Presád*, a collection of historic

or the independent kingdom of Demetrius or Apollodotus, who ruled in the Panjáb, having as their capital *Sagala*, changed by Demetrius to Euthymedia. Bayer says, in his *Hist. Reg. Bact.*; p. 84: "I find from Claudius Ptolemy, that there was a city within the Hydaspes yet nearer the Indus, called Sagala, also Euthymedia; but I scarcely doubt that Demetrius called it Euthy*demia*, from his father, after his death and that of Menander. Demetrius was deprived of his patrimony A.U.C. 562."

On this ancient city, Sagala, I have already said much; conjecturing it to be the *Salbhanpoora* of the Yadus when driven from Zabulist'han, and that of the *Yuchi* or *Yuti*, who were fixed there from Central Asia in the fifth century, and if so early as the second century, when Ptolemy wrote, may have originated the change to *Yuti-media*, the 'Central Yuti.' The numerous medals which I possess, chiefly found within the probable limits of the Greek kingdom of Sagala, either belong to these princes or the Parthian kings of Minagara on the Indus. The legends are in Greek on one side, and in the Sassanian character on the reverse. Hitherto I have not deciphered the names of any but those of Apollodotus and Menander; but the titles of 'Great King,' 'Saviour,' and other epithets adopted by the Arsacidæ, are perfectly legible. The devices, however, all incline me to pronounce them Parthian. It would be curious to ascertain how these Greeks and Parthians gradually merged into the Hindu population.

[1] The Hindu genealogist, in ignorance of the existence of Oguz Khan, the Tatar patriarch, could not connect the chain of Chagitai with Chandra. The Brahmin, better read, supplied the defect, and with his doctrine of the metempsychosis animated the material frame of the beneficent Akber with the 'good genius' of a Hindu; and that of their mortal foe, Arungzéb, with one of evil destiny, being that of Kal-jumun, the foe of Crishna. They gravely assert that Akber visited his ancient hermitage at the confluence of the Ganges and Jumna, and excavated the implements of penance used by him in his former shape, as one of the sages of ancient times; while such is their aversion to Arungzéb, that they declare the final avatar, Time (*Kal*), on his white steed, will appear in his person.

The Jessulmér annals affirm that the whole Turkish (*Toorshka*) race of Chagitai are of Yadu stock; while the Jam Jharéja of Kutch traces his descent from the Persian Jamshid, contemporary with Solomon. These are curious claims, but the Rana's family would consider such vanity criminal.

fragments in the Magadhi dialect. "In Goojur-dés (Guzzerat) there are eighty-four cities. In one of these, Kaira, resided the Brahmin Devadit, the expounder of the Vedas. He had an only child, Soobhagna (*of good fortune*) by name, at once a maiden and a widow. Having learned from her preceptor the solar incantation, incautiously repeating it, the sun appeared and embraced her, and she thence became pregnant. The affliction of her father was diminished when he discovered the parent; nevertheless [as others might be less charitable] he sent her with a female attendant to Balabhipoora, where she was delivered of twins, male and female. When grown up the boy was sent to school; but being eternally plagued about his mysterious birth, whence he received the nickname of *Gybie* ('concealed'), in a fit of irritation he one day threatened to kill his mother if she refused to disclose the author of his existence. At this moment the sun revealed himself: he gave the youth a pebble, with which it was sufficient to touch his companions in order to overcome them. Being carried before the Balhara prince, who menaced Gybie, the latter slew him with the pebble, and became himself sovereign of Saurashtra, taking the name of Silladitya [1] (from *silla*, 'a stone or pebble,' and *aditya*, 'the sun'): his sister was married to the Rajah of Baroach." Such is the literal translation of a fragment totally unconnected with the history of the Rana's family, though evidently bearing upon it. The father of Silladitya, according to the Sanderai roll and other authorities of that period, is Sooraj (the sun) Rao, though two others make a Somaditya intervene.[2]

Let us see what Abul Fuzil says of the descent of the Ranas from Noshirwan: "The Rana's family consider themselves to be descendants of Noshirwan. They came to Berar (Berat), and became chiefs of Pernalla, which city being plundered eight hundred years prior to the writing of this book,[3] his mother fled to Méwar, and was protected by Mandalica Bhil, whom the infant Bappa slew, and seized his territory." [4]

The work which has furnished all the knowledge which exists on the Persian ancestry of the Méwar princes is the *Maaser-al-Omra*, or that (in the author's posesssion) founded on it, entitled *Bisat-al-Ganaém*, or

[1] This is probably the Silladitya of the Satroonja Mahatma, who repaired the temple on Satroonja in S. 477 (A.D. 421).

[2] In perusing this fragment we are struck by the similarity of production of these Hindu Heliadæ and that of the celebrated Tatar dynasty from which Jungheez Khan was descended. The *Nooranyon*, or 'children of light,' were from an amour of the sun with Elancua, from which Jungheez was the ninth in descent. Authorities quoted by Petis de la Croix, in his life of this conqueror, and likewise by Marigny, in his *History of the Saracens*, affirm Jungheez Khan to be a descendant of Yezdegird, the last Sassanian prince. Jungheez was an idolater, and hated the very name of Mahomedan.

A courtier telling Arungzéb of his celestial ancestry, gravely quoting the affair of the mother of the race of Timoor with the sun, the bigoted monarch coarsely replied, "Mama cába bood," which we will not translate.

[3] Akber commenced his reign A.D. 1555, and had been forty years on the throne when the 'Institutes' were composed by Abul Fuzil.

[4] Orme was acquainted with this passage, and shows his knowledge of the Hindu character by observing, that it was a strange pedigree to assign a Hindu prince, for Khoosru, of the religion of Zoroaster, though compelled to many abstinences, was not restrained from eating beef: and Anquetil du Perron says of the Parsees, their descendants, that they have refrained since their emigration from slaying the cow merely to please the Hindu.

'Display of the Foe,' written in A.H. 1204.[1] The writer of this work styles himself *Latchmi Narrain Shufeek Arungabadi*, or 'the rhymer of Arungabad.' He professes to give an account of Sevaji, the founder of the Mahratta empire; for which purpose he goes deep into the lineage of the Ranas of Méwar, from whom Sevaji was descended,[2] quoting at length the *Maaser-al-Omra*, from which the following is a literal translation: "It is well known that the Rajahs of Oodipoor are exalted over all the princes of Hind. Other Hindu princes, before they can succeed to the throne of their fathers, must receive the khushka, or tiluk of regality and investiture, from them. This type of sovereignty is received with humility and veneration. The khushka of these princes is made with human blood: their title is Rana, and they deduce their origin from Noshirwan-i-Adil (*i.e.* the Just), who conquered the countries of ———,[3] and many parts of Hindust'han. During his life-time his son Noshizad, whose mother was the daughter of Késar of Room,[4] quitted the ancient worship and embraced the 'faith[5] of the Christians,' and with numerous followers entered Hindust'han. Thence he marched a great army towards Iran, against his father Noshirwan; who despatched his general, Rambarzeen,[6] with numerous forces to oppose him. An action ensued, in which Noshizad was slain; ***but his issue remained in Hindust'han, from whom are descended the Ranas of Oodipoor.*** Noshirwan had a wife from the

[1] The cryptographic date is contained in the numerical value of the letters which compose the title:

B.	S.	A.	T.	a.	l.	G.	N.	A.	E.	M.	As the total is only 1183, either the date is wrong, or a deficient value given to the numerals.
2.	60.	1.	9.	1.	9.	1000.	50.	1.	10.	40.	

[2] Wilford, who by his indefatigable research and knowledge of Sanscrit had accumulated extensive materials, unhappily deteriorated by a too credulous imagination, yet containing much valuable matter available to those sufficiently familiar with the subject to select with safety, has touched on this, and almost on every other point in the circle of Hindu antiquities. Ali Ibrahim, a learned native of Benares, was Wilford's authority for asserting the Rana's Persian descent, who stated to him that he had seen the original history, which was entitled, *Origin of the Peishwas from the Ranas of Méwar.* (Ibrahim must have meant the Satarra princes, whose ministers were the Peishwas.) From this authority three distinct emigrations of the Guebres, or ancient Persians, are recorded, from Persia into Guzzerat. The first in the time of Abu Beker, A.D. 631; the second on the defeat of Yezdegird, A.D. 651; and the third when the descendants of Abbas began to prevail, A.D. 749. Also that a son of Noshirwan landed near Surat with eighteen thousand of his subjects, from Larist'han, and were well received by the prince of the country.

Abul Fuzil confirms this account by saying, "the followers of Zerdesht (Zoroaster), when they fled from Persia, settled in *Surat*, the contracted term for the peninsular of Saurashtra, as well as the city of this name."

[3] The names are obliterated in the original. Ferishta informs us that Ramdeo Rahtore, sovereign of Kanouj, was made tributary by Feroz 'Sassan'; and that Pertap Chund, who usurped the throne of Ramdeo, neglecting to pay this tribute, Noshirwan marched into India to recover it, and in his progress subdued Caubul and the Punjáb. From the striking coincidence of these original and decisive authorities, we may rest assured that they had recourse to ancient records, both of the Guebres and the Hindus, for the basis of their histories, which research may yet discover.

[4] Maurice, emperor of Byzantium.

[5] *Deen-i-Tersár.* See Ebn Haukal, art. "Serir," or Russia; whose king, a son of Byram Chassin, whom he styles a *Tersár* or Christian, first possessed it about the end of the sixth century.

[6] The *Verames* of Western historians.

Khakhan[1] of China, by whom he had a son called Hormuz, declared heir to the throne shortly before his death. As according to the faith of the fire-worshippers[2] it is not customary either to bury or to burn the dead, but to leave the corpse exposed to the rays of the sun, so it is said the body of Noshirwan has to this day suffered no decay, but is still fresh."

I now come to the account of Yezd, "the son of Shariar, the son of Khoosru Purves, the son of Hormuz, the son of Noshirwan.

"Yezd was the last king of Ajim. It is well known he fought many battles with the Mahomedans. In the fifteenth year of the caliphat, Roostum, son of Ferock, a great chief, was slain in battle by Said-ul-kas, who commanded for Omar, which was the death-blow to the fortunes of the house of Sassan: so that a remnant of it did not remain in A.H. 31, when Iran was seized by the Mahomedans. This battle had lasted four days when Roostum Ferock Zad was slain by the hand of Hillal, the son of Il Kumna, at Said's command; though Ferdusi asserts by Said himself. Thirty thousand Moslems were slain, and the same number of the men of Ajim. To count the spoils was a torment. During this year (the thirty-first), the sixteenth of the prophet,[3] the era of the Hegira was introduced. In A.H. 17, Abu Musa of Ashur seized Hormuz, the son of the uncle of Yezdegird, whom he sent with Yezdegird's daughter to Imam Hosein, and another daughter to Abubeker.

"Thus far have I[4] extracted from the history of the fire-worshippers. He who has a mind to examine these, let him do so. The people of the religion of Zerdusht have a full knowledge of all these events, with their dates; for the pleasure of their lives is the obtaining accounts of antiquity and astronomical knowledge, and their books contain information of two and three thousand years. It is also told, that when the fortunes of Yezdegird were on the wane, his family dispersed to different regions. The second daughter, Shehr Banoo, was married to Imam Hosein, who when he fell a martyr (*shuheed*), an angel carried her to heaven. The third daughter, Banoo, was seized by a plundering Arab and carried into the wilds of Chichik, thirty coss from Yezd. Praying to God for deliverance, she instantly disappeared; and the spot is still held sacred by the Parsees, and named 'the secret abode of perfect purity.' Hither, on the twenty-sixth of the month Bahman, the Parsees yet repair to pass a month in pilgrimage, living in huts under indigenous vines skirting the rock, out of whose fissures water falls into a fountain below: but if the unclean approach the spring, it ceases to flow.

"Of the eldest daughter of Yezdegird, Maha Banoo, the Parsees have no accounts; but the books of Hind give evidence to her arrival in that country, and that from her issue is the tribe Sesodia. *But, at all events,*

[1] *Khakhan* was the title of the kings of Chinese Tartary. It was held by the leader of the Huns, who at this period held power on the Caspian: it was also held by the Ooroos, Khozr, Bulgar, Serir, all terms for Russia, before its *Késar* was cut down into *Czar*, for the original of which, the kings of Rome, as of Russia, were indebted to the Sanscrit *Késar*, a 'lion.'—*Vide* Ebn Haukal, art. "Khozr."

[2] *Deen-i-Majoosa*; literally, 'faith of the Magi.'

[3] Mahomed, born A.D. 578; the Hegira, or flight, A.D. 622.

[4] It must be borne in mind that it is the author of the *Maaser-al-Omra*, not the rhymer of Arungabad, who is speaking.

this race is either of the seed of Noshizad, the son of Noshirwan, or of that of the daughter of Yezdegird." [1]

Thus have we adduced, perhaps, all the points of evidence for the supposed Persian origin of the Rana's family. The period of the invasion of Saurashtra by Noshizad, who mounted the throne A.D. 531, corresponds well with the sack of Balabhi, A.D. 524. The army he collected in Larist'han to depose his father might have been from the Parthians, Getes, Huns, and other Scythic races then on the Indus, though it is unlikely, with such an object in view as the throne of Persia, that he would waste his strength in Saurashtra. Khoosru Purves, grandson of Noshirwan the great, and who assumed this title according to Ferdusi, married Marian, the daughter of Maurice, the Greek emperor of Byzantium. She bore him *Shirooeh* (the *Siroes* of the early Christian writers), who slew his father. It is difficult to separate the actions of the two Noshirwans, and still more to say which of them merited the epithet of *adil*, or 'just.'

According to the 'Tables' in Moréri,[2] Noshizad, son of Khoosru the great, reigned from A.D. 531 to 591. This is opposed to the *Maaser-al-Omra*, which asserts that he was slain during his rebellion. Siroes, son of Khoosru (the second Noshirwan) by his wife Marian, alternately called the friend and foe of the Christians, did raise the standard of revolt, and met the fate attributed to Noshizad; on which Yezdegird, his nephew, was proclaimed. The crown was intended for Shirooeh's younger brother, which caused the revolt, during which the elder sought refuge in India.

These revolutions in the Sassanian house were certainly simultaneous with those which occurred in the Rana's, and no barrier existed to the political intercourse at least between the princely worshippers of Soorya and Mithras. It is, therefore, curious to speculate even on the possibility of such a pedigree to a family whose ancestry is lost in the mists of time; and it becomes interesting when, from so many authentic sources, we can raise testimonies which would furnish, to one even untinctured with the love of hypothesis, grounds for giving ancestors to the Ranas in Maurice of Byzantium and Cyrus (Khoosru) of Persia. We have a singular support to these historic relics in a geographical fact, that places on the site of the ancient Balabhi a city called Byzantium, which almost affords conclusive proof that it must have been the son of Noshirwan who captured Balabhi and Gajni, and destroyed the family of Silladitya; for it would be a legitimate occasion to name such conquest after the city where his Christian mother had had birth. Whichever of the propositions we adopt at the command of the author of *The Annals of Princes*, namely, " that the Sesodia race is of the seed of Noshizad, son of Noshirwan, or of that of Maha-Banoo, daughter of Yezdegird," we arrive at a singular and startling conclusion, viz. that the 'Hindua Sooraj, descendant of a hundred kings,' the undisputed possessor of the honours of Rama, the patriarch of the Solar race, is the issue of a Christian princess: that the chief prince amongst the nations of Hind can claim affinity with the

[1] For the extract from "The Annals of Princes (*Maaser-al-Omra*)' let us laud the memory of the rhymer of Arungabad. An original copy, which I in vain attempted to procure in India, is stated by Sir William Ouseley to be in the British Museum. We owe that country a large debt, for we have robbed her of all her literary treasures, leaving them to sleep on the shelves of our public institutions.

[2] Vide *Grand Dictionnaire Historique.*

emperors of 'the mistress of the world,' though at a time when her glory had waned, and her crown had been transferred from the Tiber to the Bosphorus.

But though I deem it morally impossible that the Ranas should have their lineage from any *male* branch of the Persian house, I would not equally assert that Maha-Banoo, the fugitive daughter of Yezdegird, may not have found a husband, as well as sanctuary, with the prince of Saurashtra ; and she may be the Soobhagna (mother of Silladitya), whose mysterious amour with the 'sun'[1] compelled her to abandon her native city of Kaira. The *son* of Marian had been in Saurashtra, and it is therefore not unlikely that her grandchild should there seek protection in the reverses of her family.

The Salic law is here in full force, and honours, though never acquired by the female, may be stained by her ; yet a daughter of the noble house of Sassan might be permitted to perpetuate the line of Rama without the reproach of taint.[2]

We shall now abandon this point to the reader, and take leave of Yezdegird,[3] the last of the house of Sassan, in the words of the historian of Rome : "Avec lui, on voit périr pour jamais la gloire et l'empire des Perses. Les rochers du Mazendaran et las sables du Kerman, furent les seuls[4] asiles que les vainqueurs laissèrent aux sectateurs de Zoroastre."[5]

[1] It will be recollected that the various authorities given state Raja Sooraj (*sun*), of Cacoost'ha race, to be the father of Silladitya. *Cacoost'ha* is a term used synonymously with *Sooryavansa*, according to the Solar genealogists. Those who may be inclined to the Persian descent may trace it from *Kai-caous*, a well-known epithet in the Persian dynasties. I am unacquainted with the etymology of Cacoost'ha ; but it may possibly be from *ca*, 'of or belonging to,' *Coosa* (Cush), the second son of Rama. I have already hinted that the Assyrian Medes might be descendants of Hyaspa, a branch of the Indu-Mede of the family of Yayat which bore the name of *Causika*.

[2] "The moral consequence of a pedigree," says Hume, "is differently marked by the influence of law and custom. The male sex is deemed more noble than the female. The association of our ideas pursues the regular descent of honour and estates from father to son, and their wives, however essential, are considered only in the light of foreign auxiliaries" (*Essays*, vol. ii. p. 192). Not unlike the Rajpoot axiom, though more coarsely expressed : "It is, who planted the tree, not where did it grow," that marks his idea of the comparative value of the side whence honours originate ; though purity of blood in both lines is essential.

[3] A new era had commenced, not of Yezdegird's accession, as is supposed, which would have been vain indeed, when the throne was tottering under him, but consequent to the completion of the grand cycle of 1440 years. He was slain at Murve in A.D. 651, the 31st of the Hegira ; on the eleventh year of which, or A.D. 632 (according to Moreri), he commenced his reign.

[4] Gibbon was wrong. India afforded them an asylum, and their issue constitutes the most wealthy, the most respected, and the most enlightened part of the native community of Bombay and the chief towns of that presidency.

[5] Gibbon, *Miscellaneous Works*, "Sur la Monarchie des Médes," vol. iii.

CHAPTER IV

Intervening sovereigns between Bappa and Samarsi—Bappa's descendants—Irruptions of the Arabians into India—Catalogue of Hindu princes who defended Cheetore.

HAVING established Bappa on the throne of Cheetore S. 784 (A.D. 728), we will proceed to glean from the annals, from the period of his departure for Iran, S. 820 (A.D. 764) to another halting point—the reign of Samarsi, S. 1249 (A.D. 1193); an important epoch, not only in the history of Méwar, but to the whole Hindu race; when the diadem of sovereignty was torn from the brow of the Hindu to adorn that of the Tatar. We shall not, however, overleap the four intervening centuries, though we may not be able to fill up the reigns of the eighteen princes [1] whose "banner at this time was a golden sun on a crimson field," [2] and several of whose names yet live recorded "with an iron pen on the rock" of their native abodes.

An intermediate period, from Bappa to Samarsi, that of *Sacti Komar*, is fixed by the Aítpoor inscription in S. 1024 (A.D. 968); and from the more perishable yet excellent authority of an ancient Jain MS. the era of Ullut, the ancestor of Sacti Komar, was S. 922 (A.D. 866), four generations anterior. From Bappa's departure for Iran in A.D. 764, to the subversion of Hindu dominion in the reign of Samarsi, in A.D. 1193, we find recorded an intermediate Islamite invasion. This was during the reign of Khomán, between A.D. 812 and 836, which event forms the chief subject of the *Khomán-Rásá*, the most ancient of the poetic chronicles of Méwar.

As the history of India at this period is totally dark, we gladly take advantage of the lights thus afforded. By combining these facts with what is received as authentic, though scarcely less obscure or more exact than these native legends, we may furnish materials for the future historian. With this view, let us take a rapid sketch of the irruptions of the Arabians into India, from the rise of Islamism to the foundation of the Gaznivid empire, which sealed the fate of the Hindus. The materials are but scanty. El-Makin, in his history of the Caliphs, passes over such intercourse almost without notice. Abul Fuzil, though not diffuse, is minute in what he does say, and we can confide in his veracity. Ferishta has a chapter devoted to this subject, which merits a better translation than yet exists.[3] We shall, however, in the first place, touch on Bappa's descendants, till we arrive at the point proper for the introduction of the intended sketch.

[1] See Genealogical Table.

[2] This, according to the roll, was the standard of Bappa.

[3] Amongst the passages which Dow has slurred over in his translation, is the interesting account of the origin of the Afghans; who, when they first came in contact with those of the new faith, in A.H. 62, dwelt around the Koh-i-Sooliman. Ferishta, quoting authority, says: "The Afghans were Copts, ruled by Pharaoon, many of whom were converted to the laws and religion of Moses; but others, who were stubborn in their worship to their gods, fled towards Hindust'han, and took possession of the country adjoining the Koh-i-Sooliman. They were visited by Kasim from Sinde, and in the 143rd year of the Hegira had possessed themselves of the provinces of Kirman, Peshawur, and all within their bounds (*sinoran*)," which Dow has converted into a province. The whole geographical description of the Kohistan, the etymology of the term *Rohilla*, and other important matter, is omitted by him.

Of the twenty-four tribes of Gehlote, several issued from the founder, Bappa. Shortly after the conquest of Cheetore, Bappa proceeded to Saurashtra and married the daughter of Esupgole, prince of the island of Bunderdhíva.[1] With his bride he conveyed to Cheetore the statue of Vyánmata, the tutelary goddess of her race, who still divides with Eklinga the devotion of the Gehlote princes. The temple in which he enshrined this islandic goddess yet stands on the summit of Cheetore, with many other monuments assigned by tradition to Bappa. This princess bore him Aprajeet, who from being born in Cheetore was nominated successor to the throne, to the exclusion of his less fortunate elder brother, Asil (born of the daughter of the Kaba (Pramara) prince of Kalibao near Dwarica), who, however, obtained possessions in Saurashtra, and founded a race called the *Asila Gehlotes*,[2] whose descendants were so numerous, even in Akber's reign, as to be supposed able to bring into the field fifty thousand men at arms. We have nothing important to record of the actions of Aprajeet, who had two sons, Khalbhoj [3] and Nundkomar. Khalbhoj succeeded Aprajeet, and his warlike qualities are extolled in an inscription discovered by the author in the valley of Nagda. Nundkomar slew Bhimsén Dor (*Doda*), and possessed himself of Deogurh in the Dekhan.

Khoman succeeded Khalbhoj. His name is remarkable in the history of Méwar. He came to the throne at the beginning of the ninth century, when Cheetore was assailed by another formidable invasion of Mahomedans. The chief object of the *Khomán Rásá* is to celebrate the defence made on this occasion, and the value of this *rasa* consists in the catalogue of the princes who aided in defending this bulwark of the Hindu faith. The bard, in an animated strain, makes his sovereign on this occasion successfully defend the 'crimson standard' of Méwar, treat with contempt the demand for tribute, and after a violent assault, in which the 'barbarian' is driven back, follow and discomfit him in the plain, carrying back the hostile leader, *Mahmood*, captive. With this event, which introduces the name of Mahmood two centuries before the conqueror of Gazni, we will pause, and resume the promised sketch of the intercourse of Arabia and Hindust'han at this period.

The first intimation of the Moslems attempting the invasion of India is during the caliphat of Omar, who built the port of Bassorah at the mouth of the Tigris, chiefly to secure the trade of Guzzerat and Sinde ; into which

[1] Esupgole is stated to have held Chowal on the main land. He was most probably the father of *Venraj* Chawura, the founder of Putun Anhulwara, whose ancestors, on the authority of the *Komarpal Charitra*, were princes of Bunderd'hiva, held by the Portuguese since the time of Albuquerque, who changed its name to Deo.

[2] The ancient roll from which this is taken mentions Asil giving his name to a fortress, called Asilgurh. His son, Beejy Pal, was slain in attempting to wrest Khumbayet (Cambay) from Singram Dabi. One of his wives, from a violent death, was prematurely delivered of a boy, called Setoo ; and as, in such cases, the Hindu supposes the deceased to become a discontented spirit (*choorail*) Chooraila became the name of the tribe. Beeja, the twelfth from Asil, obtained Sonul from his maternal uncle, Khengar Dabi, prince of Girnar, but was slain by Jey Sing Deo, prince of Surat. From these names compounded, *Dabi* and *Chooraila*, we may have the *Dabisalima* of Mahmood.

[3] Also called Kurna. He it was who excavated the Boraila lake, and erected the grand temple of Eklinga on the site of the hermitage of Harita, whose descendant, the present officiating priest, reckons sixty-six descents, while the princes of Méwar amount to seventy-two in the same period.

latter country a powerful army penetrated under Abul Aas, who was killed in battle at Arore. The Caliph Oosman, who succeeded Omar, sent to explore the state of India, while he prepared an army to invade it in person: a design which he never fulfilled. The generals of the Calpih Ali made conquests in Sinde, which they abandoned at Ali's death. While Yezid was governor of Khorassan several attempts were made on India, as also during the caliphat of Abdool Melek, but without any lasting results. It was not till the reign of Walid [1] that any successful invasion took place. He not only finally conquered Sinde and the adjoining continent of India, but rendered tributary all that part of India on this side the Ganges.[2] What an exalted idea must we not form of the energy and rapidity of such conquests, when we find the arms of Islam at once on the Ganges and the Ebro, and two regal dynasties simultaneously cut off, that of Roderic, the last of the Goths of Andaloos, and Dahir Despati in the valley of the Indus. It was in A.H. 99 (A.D. 718, S. 774) that Mahomed bin Kasim vanquished and slew Dahir prince of Sinde, after numerous conflicts. Amongst the spoils of victory sent to the caliph on this occasion were the

[1] GEHLOTE AND CONTEMPORARY PRINCES.

Gehlote Princes.	Eras.		Caliphs of Bagdad and Kings of Gazni.	Eras.		Remarks.
	Samvat.	Christian.		A.H.	A.D.	
			Caliphs of Bagdad.			
Bappa, born	769	713	Walid (11th Caliph)	86 to 96	705 to 715	Conquered India to the Ganges.
—— obtained Cheetore	784	728	Omar II. (13th do.)	99 to 102	718 to 721	Sindi conquered. The Mori prince of Cheetore attacked by Mahomed (son of Kasim), the General of Omar.
—— governs Méwar.	—	—	Husham (15th do.)	104 to 125	723 to 742	Battle of Tours, A.D. 732, and defeat of the Caliph's army, under Abdulrahman, by Charles Martel.
—— abandons Cheetore	820	764	Al-Mansoor (21st do.)	136 to 158	754 to 775	Final conquest of Sinde, and the name of its capital, Arore, changed to Mansoora. Bappa, founder of the Gehlote race in Mewar, retires to Iran.
Aprajeet.						
Khalbhoj . .	—	—	Haroon al Rashid (24th do.)	170 to 193	786 to 809	Partition of the caliphat amongst Haroon's sons. The second, Al-Mamoon, obtains Zabulist'han, Sinde, and India, and ruled them till A.D. 813, when he became Caliph.
Khoman .	868 to 892	812 to 836	Al-Mamoon (26th do.)	198 to 218	813 to 833	Invasion and attack on Cheetore from Zabulist'han.
Bhartribhat.						
Sing-ji.						
Ullut.						
Nurbahan.						
Salbahan.			*Kings of Gazni.*			
Sacti Komar .	1024	968	Aleptegin . .	350	957	Inscription of Sacti-komar from ruins of Aítpoor.
Umba Pussao.						
Narvarma	—	—	Soobektegin . .	367	977	Invasion of India.
Jussoovarma .	—	—	Mahmood . .	387 to 418	997 to 1027	Invasions of India, destruction of Aítpoor.

[2] Marigny (quoting El-Makin), *Hist. of the Arabians*, vol. ii. p. 283; *Mod. Univ. Hist.*, vol. ii. p. 47.

daughters of the subjugated monarch, who were the cause of Kasim's destruction,[1] when he was on the eve of carrying the war against Raja Harchund of Kanouj. Some authorities state that he actually prosecuted it ; and as Sinde remained a dependency of the caliphat during several successive reigns, the successor of Kasim may have executed his plans. Little is said of India from this period to the reign of Al-Mansoor, except in regard to the rebellion of Yezid in Khorassan, and the flight of his son to Sinde. The eight sovereigns, who rapidly followed, were too much engaged with the Christians of the west and the Huns on the Caspian to think of India. Their armies were then in the heart of France, which was only saved from the Koran by their overthrow at Tours by Charles Martel.

Al-Mansoor, when only the lieutenant of the Caliph Abbas, held the government of Sinde and of India, and made the island of Bekher on the Indus, and the adjacent Arore,[2] the ancient capital, his residence, naming it Mansoora ; and it was during his government that Bappa Rawul abandoned Cheetore for Iran.

The celebrated Haroon al Rashid, contemporary of Charlemagne, in apportioning his immense empire amongst his sons, gave to the second, Al - Mamoon, Khorassan, Zabulist'han, Cabulist'han, Sinde, and Hindust'han.[3] Al-Mamoon, on the death of Haroon, deposed his brother, and became caliph in A.H. 198 or A.D. 813, and ruled to 833, the exact period of the reign of Khoman, prince of Cheetore. The domestic history brings the enemy assailant of Cheetore from Zabulist'han ; and as the leader's name is given *Mahmood Khorasan Put*, there can be little doubt that it is an error arising from ignorance of the copyist, and should be *Mahmoon*.

Within twenty years after this event, the sword of conquest and conversion was withdrawn from India, and Sinde was the only province left to Motawekel (A.D. 850), the grandson of Haroon, for a century after whom the throne of Bagdad, like that of ancient Rome, was sold by her prætorians to the highest bidder. From this time we find no mention whatever of Hindust'han, or even of Sinde, until Soobektegin,[4] governor of Khorassan, hoisted the standard of independent sovereignty at Gazni. In A.H. 365 (A.D. 975) he carried his arms across the Indus, forcing the inhabitants to abandon the religion of their ancestors, and to read the Koran from the altars of Bal and Crishna. Towards the close of this century he made his last invasion, accompanied by his son, the celebrated Mahmood, destined to be the scourge of the Hindu race, who early imbibed the paternal lesson inculcating the extirpation of infidels. Twelve several visitations did Mahmood make with his Tatar hordes, sweeping India of her riches, de-

[1] " The two young princesses, in order to revenge the death of their father, represented falsely to the Khalif that Mahommed Kasim had been connected with them. The Khalif, in a rage, gave order for Mahommed Kasim to be sewed up in a raw hide, and sent in that condition to court. When the mandate arrived at Tatta, Kasim was prepared to carry an expedition against Harchund, monarch of Kanouj. When he arrived at court, the Khalif showed him to the daughters of Dahir, who expressed their joy upon beholding their father's murderer in such a condition" (Ayeen Akbery, vol. ii. p. 119).

[2] Arore is seven miles east of Bekher.

[3] Marigny, vol. iii. p. 83 ; *Univ. Hist.*, vol. ii. p. 162.

[4] His father's name was Aleptegin, termed a slave by Ferishta and his authorities ; though El-Makin gives him an ancestor in Yesdegird.

stroying her temples and architectural remains, and leaving the country plunged in poverty and ignorance. From the effect of these incursions she never recovered; for though she had a respite of a century between Mahmood and the final conquest, it was too short to repair what it had cost ages to rear: the temples of Somnat'h, of Cheetore, and Girnar are but types of the magnificence of past times. The memorial of Sacti Komar proves him to have been the contemporary of Soobektegin, and to one of his son's visitations is attributed the destruction of the 'city of the sun' (Aítpoor),[1] his capital.

Having thus condensed the little information afforded by Mahomedan historians of the connection between the caliphs of Badgad and princes of Hind, from the first to the end of the fourth century of the Hegira, we shall revert to the first recorded attack on the Mori prince of Cheetore, which brought Bappa into notice. This was either by Yezid or Mahomed bin Kasim from Sinde. Though in the histories of the caliphs we can only expect to find recorded those expeditions which were successful, or had some lasting results, there are inroads of their revolted lieutenants or their frontier deputies, which frequently, though indistinctly, alluded to in Hindu annals, have no place in Mahomedan records. Throughout the period mentioned there was a stir amongst the Hindu nations, in which we find confusion and dethronement from an unknown invader, who is described as coming sometimes by Sinde, sometimes by sea, and not unfrequently as a demon and magician; but invariably as *m'lectcha*, or 'barbarian.'[2] From S. 750 to S. 780 (A.D. 694 to 724), the annals of the Yadus, the Chohans, the Chawuras, and the Gehlotes, bear evidence to simultaneous convulsions in their respective houses at this period. In S. 750 (A.H. 75), the Yadu Bhatti was driven from his capital Salpoora in the Punjáb, across the Sutledge into the Indian desert; the invader named

[1] *Ait*, contracted from *Aditya*: hence *Ait-wár*, 'Sun-day.'

[2] Even from the puerilities of Hindu legends something may be extracted. A mendicant derveish, called Roshun Ali (*i.e.* the '*light* of Ali'), had found his way to Gur'h Beetli (the ancient name of the Ajmér fortress), and having thrust his hand into a vessel of curds destined for the Rajah, had his finger cut off. The disjointed member flew to Mecca, and was recognised as belonging to the saint. An army was equipped in the disguise of horse-merchants, which invaded Ajmér, whose prince was slain. May we not gather from this incident, that an insult to the first Islamite missionary in the person of Roshun Ali, brought upon the prince the arms of the Caliph? The same Chohan legends state that Ajipal was prince of Ajmér at this time; that in this invasion by sea he hastened to Anjar (on the coast of Cutch), where he held the 'guard of the ocean' (*Samoodra ca Choky*), where he fell in opposing the landing. An altar was erected on the spot, on which was sculptured the figure of the prince on horseback, with his lance at rest, and which still annually attracts multitudes at the 'fair (Méla) of Ajipal.'

The subsequent invasion alluded to in the text, of S. 750 (A.D. 694), is marked by a curious anecdote. When the 'Assoors' had blockaded Ajmér, Lot, the infant son of Manika Rae, was playing on the battlements, when an arrow from the foe killed the heir of Ajmér, who has ever since been worshipped amongst the lares and penates of the Chohans; and as he had on a silver chain anklet at the time, this ornament is forbid to the children of the race. In all these Rajpoot families there is a pootra (*adolescens*) amongst the penates, always one who has come to an untimely end, and chiefly worshipped by females; having a strong resemblance to the rites in honour of Adonis. We have traced several Roman and Grecian terms to Sanscrit origin; may we add that of *lares*, from *larla*, 'dear' or 'beloved?'

Ferid. At the same period, Manika Rae, the Chohan prince of Ajmér, was assailed and slain.

The first of the Keechie princes who occupied the Do-ábeh of Sind-sagur in the Punjáb, as well as the ancestor of the Haras established in Golcoonda, was expelled at the same time. The invader is treated in the genuine Hindu style as a danoo, or demon, and is named 'Gyraram' (*i.e.* restless), from *Gujlibund*,[1] a term geographically given to a portion of the Himalaya mountains about the glaciers of the Ganges. The ancestor of the founder of Putun was expelled from his petty islandic dominion on the coast of Saurashtra at the same time. This is the period when Yezid was the caliph's lieutenant in Khorassan, and when the arms of Walid conquered to the Ganges; nor is there a doubt that Yezid or Kasim was the author of all these revolutions in the Hindu dynasties. We are supported in this by the names of the princes contained in the catalogue, who aided to defend Cheetore and the Mori prince on this occasion. It is evident that Cheetore was, alternately with Oojein, the seat of sovereignty of the Pramara at this period, and, as it became the rallying point of the Hindus, that this race was the first in consequence.[2] We find the prince of Ajmér, and the quotas of Saurashtra and Guzzerat; Ungutsi, lord of the Huns; Boosa, the lord of the North; Seo, the prince of the Jharéjas; the Johya, lord of Junguldés; the Aswuria, the Seput, the Koolhur, the Malun, the Ohir, the Hool, and many others, having nothing of the Hindu in name, now extinct. But the most conspicuous is "Dahir

[1] Signifying 'Elephant forests,' and described in a Hindu map (stamped on cloth and painted) of India from Gujlibund to Lanka, and the provinces west of the Indus to Calcutta; presented by me to the Royal Asiatic Society.

[2] The list of the vassal princes at the court of the Mori confirms the statement of the bard Chund, of the supremacy of Ram Pramara, and the partition of his dominion, as described (see p. 44, note) amongst the princes who founded separate dynasties at this period; hitherto in vassalage or subordinate to the Pramara. We can scarcely suppose the family to have suffered any decay since their ancestor, Chandragoopta, connected by marriage with as well as the ally of the Grecian Seleucus, and who held Greeks in his pay. From such connection, the arts of sculpture and architecture may have derived a character hitherto unnoticed. Amidst the ruins of Barolli are seen sculptured the Grecian helmet; and the elegant ornament, the *Camcoomp*, or 'vessel of desire,' on the temple of *Anapoorna* (*i.e.* 'giver of food'), the Hindu Ceres, has much affinity to the Grecian device.

From the inscription (see No. 2) it is evident that Cheetore was an appanage of Oojein, the seat of Pramar empire. Its monarch, Chandragoopta (Mori), degraded into the barber (maurya) tribe, was the descendant of Srenica, prince of Rajgraha, who, according to the Jain work, *Calpoodrum Calka*, flourished in the year 477 before Vicramaditya, and from whom Chandragoopta was the thirteenth in descent. The names as follows: Konika, Oodsén, and nine in succession of the name of Nanda, thence called the *No-nanda*. These, at twenty-two years to a reign (see p. 45), would give 286 years, which—477=191 S.V.+56=247 A.C. Now it was in A.C. 260, according to Bayer, that the treaty was formed between Seleucus and Chandragoopta; so that this scrap of Jain history may be regarded as authentic and valuable. Asoca (a name of weight in Jain annals) succeeded Chandragoopta. He by Koonāl, whose son was Sumpriti, with whose name ends the line of Srenica, according to the authority from which I made the extract. The name of Sumpriti is well known from Ajmér to Saurashtra, and his era is given in a valuable chronogrammatic catalogue in an ancient Jain manuscript from the temple of Nadole, at 202 of the Virat Samvat. He is mentioned both traditionally and by books, as the great supporter of the Jain faith, and the remains of temples dedicated to Mahavira, erected by this prince, yet exist at Ajmér, on Aboo, Komulmér, and Girnar.

Déspáti from Deweil." This is erroneously written Dehli, the seat of the Túars; whereas we recognise the name of the prince of Sinde, slain by Kasim, whose expatriated son doubtless found refuge in Cheetore.

This attack on the Mori prince was defeated chiefly through the bravery of the youthful Gehlote. The foe from Gujlibund, though stated to have advanced by Mat'hoora, retreated by Saurashtra and Sinde, pursued by Bappa. He found the ancient seat of his ancestors, Gajni,[1] still in the possession of the 'Assoor': a term as well as *m'letcha*, or 'barbarian,' always given to the Islamite at this period. Selim, who held Gajni, was attacked and forced to surrender, and Bappa inducted into this stronghold of his ancestors a nephew of his own. It is no less singular than honourable to their veracity, that the annals should record the fact, so contrary to their religion, of Bappa having married the daughter of the conquered Selim; and we have a right to infer that it was from the influence acquired by this union, that he ultimately abandoned the sovereignty of Méwar and the title of 'Hindua Sooraj,' to become the founder of the 'one hundred and thirty tribes of Nosheyra Pat'hans' of the west. It is fair to conclude from all these notices regarding the founder of the Gehlote race in Cheetore, that he must have abjured his faith for that of Islam; and it is probable (though the surmise must ever remain unproved), that, under some new title applicable to such change, we may have, in one of the early distinguished leaders of 'the Faith,' the ancestor of the Gehlotes.

Let us now proceed to the next irruption of the Islamite invaders in the reign of Khoman, from A.D. 812 to 836. Though the leader of this attack is styled 'Mahmood Khorasan Put,' it is evident from the catalogue of Hindu princes who came to defend Cheetore, that this 'lord of Khorassan' was at least two centuries before the son of Soobektegin; and as the period is in perfect accordance with the partition of the caliphat by Haroon amongst his sons, we can have no hesitation in assigning such invasion to Mahmoon, to whose share was allotted Khorassan, Sinde, and the Indian dependencies. The records of this period are too scanty to admit of our passing over in silence even a barren catalogue of names, which, as texts, with the aid of collateral information, may prove of some benefit to the future antiquarian and historian.

"From Gajuni came the Gehlote; the Tâk from Asér; from Nadolaye the Chohan; the Chalook from Rahirgurh; from Sét-Bunder the Jirkéra; from Mundore the Khairávi; from Mangrole the Macwahana; from Jeitgurh the Joria; from Taragurh the Réwur; the Cutchwaha from Nirwur; from Sanchore the Kalum; from Joengurh the Dussanoh; from Ajmér the Gor; from Lohadurgurh the Chundano; from Kasoondi the Dor; from Dehli the Túar; from Patun the Chawura, preserver of royalty (*Rijdhur*); from Jhalore the Sonigurra; from Sirohi the Deora; from Gagrown the Keechie; the Jadoo from Joonagurh; the J'hala from Patri; from Kanouj the Rahtore; from Chotiala the Balla; from Perun-

[1] It has already been stated that the ancient name of Cambay was Gayni or Gajni, whose ruins are three miles from the present city. There is also a Gajni on the estuary of the Myhie, and Abul Fuzil incidently mentions a *Gujnagur* as one of the most important fortresses of Guzzerat, belonging to Ahmed Shah; in attempting to obtain which by stratagem, his antagonist, Hoshung, king of Malwa, was made prisoner. I am unaware of the site of this place, though there are remains of an extensive fortress near the capital, founded by Ahmed, and which preserves no name. It may be the ancient Gujnagur.

gurh the Gohil ; from Jesulgurh the B'hatti ; the Boosa from Lahore ; the Sankla from Ronéja ; the Sehut from Kherligurh ; from Mandelgurh the Nacoompa ; the Birgoojur from Rajore ; from Kurrungurh the Chundail ; from Sikur the Sikurwal ; from Omergurh the Jaitwa ; from Palli the Birgota ; from Khunturgurh the Jaréja ; from Jirgah the Kherwur ; from Cashmér the Purihara."

Of the Gehlote from Gajuni we have said enough ; nor shall we comment on the Tâk, or his capital, Asér, which now belongs to the British government. The Chohan, who came from Nadolaye, was a celebrated branch of the Ajmér house, and claims the honour of being the parent of the Sonigurras of Jhalore and the Deoras of Sirohi. Nadole [1] is mentioned by Ferishta as falling a prey to one of Mahmood's invasions, who destroyed its ancient temples ; but from erroneous punctuation it is lost in the translation as Bazule. Of Rahirgurh and the Jirkhéra from Sétbunder (on the Malabar coast) nothing is known. Of the Kheiravi from Mundore we can only say that it appears to be a branch of the Pramaras (who reckoned Mundore one of the nine strongholds, '*No-kote*,' under its dominion), established anterior to the Puriharas, who at this period had sovereignty in Cashmér. Both the Dor and his capital, Dussoondi, are described in ancient books as situated on the Ganges below Kanouj.

It is a subject of regret that the annals do not mention the name of the Túar prince of Dehli, which city could not have been re-founded above a century, when this call was made upon its aid. Abul Fuzil, Ferishta, their translators, and those who have followed them, have been corrected by the *Edinburgh Review*, whose critical judgment on this portion of ancient history is eminently good. I possess the original Hindu record used by Abul Fuzil, which gives S. 829 for the first Anungpal instead of S. 429 ; and as there were but nineteen princes who intervened until his dynasty was set aside by the Chohan, it requires no argument to support the *four* instead of *eight* centuries. The former will give the just average of twenty-one years to a reign. The name of Anungpal was titular in the family, and the epithet was applied to the last as to the first of the race.

The name of the Chawura prince of Putun (Anhulwara) being recorded amongst the auxiliaries of Khoman, is another satisfactory proof of the antiquity of this invasion ; for this dynasty was extinct, and succeeded by the Solankis, in S. 998 (A.D. 942), fifty years prior to Mahmood of Gazni, who captured Putun during the reign of Chaond, the second Solanki prince.

The Sonigurra, who came from Jhalore, is a celebrated branch of the Chohan race, but we are ignorant of the extent of time that it held this fortress : and as nothing can invalidate the testimonies afforded by the names of the Chawura of Putun, the Cutchwaha of Nirwur, the Túar of Dehli, and the Rahtore from Kanouj, there can be no hesitation at pointing out the anachronisms of the chronicle, which states the Deora from Sirohi, the Keechie from Gagrown, or the Bhatti from Jessulgurh, amongst the

[1] I presented to the Royal Asiatic Society two inscriptions from Nadole, one dated S. 1024, the other 1039. They are of Prince Lakha, and state as instances of his power, that he collected the transit duties at the further barrier of Putun, and levied tribute from the prince of Cheetore. He was the contemporary of Mahmood, who devastated Nadole. I also discovered inscriptions of the twelfth century relative to this celebrated Chohan family, in passing from Oodipoor to Jodpoor.

levies on this occasion ; and which we must affirm to be decided interpolations, the two first being at that period in possession of the Pramara, and the latter not erected for three centuries later. That the Deoras, the Keechies, and the Bhattis, came to the aid of Khoman, we cannot doubt ; but the copyist, ignorant even of the names of the ancient capitals of these tribes, Chotun, Sind-Sagur, and Tannote, substituted those which they subsequently founded.

The Jadu (Yadu) from Joonagurh (Girnar), was of the race of Chrishna, and appeared long to have held possession of this territory ; and the names of the Khengars, of this tribe, will remain as long as the stupendous monuments they reared on this sacred hill. Besides the Jadu, we find Saurashtra sending forth the J'halas, the Ballas, and the Gohils, to the aid of the descendant of the lord of Balabhipoora, whose paramount authority they once all acknowledged, and who appeared to have long maintained influence in that distant region.

Of the tribe of Boosa, who left their capital, Lahore, to succour Cheetore, we have no mention, further than the name being enumerated amongst the unassigned tribes of Rajpoots.[1] Ferishta frequently notices the princes of Lahore in the early progress of Islamism, though he does not tell us the name of the tribe. In the reign of the caliph Al-Mansoor, A.H. 143 (A.D. 761), the Afghans of Kirman and Peshawur, who according to this authority were a Coptic colony expelled from Egypt, had increased in such numbers as to abandon their residence about the 'hill of Suliman,' and crossing the Indus, wrested possessions from the Hindu princes of Lahore. This frontier warfare with a tribe which, though it had certainly not then embraced the faith of Islam, brought to their succour the forces of the caliph in Zabilust'han, so that in five months seventy battles were fought with varied success ; but the last, in which the Lahore prince carried his arms to Peshawur,[2] produced a peace. Hence arose a union of interests between them and the hill tribe of Ghiker, and all the Kohistan west of the Indus was ceded to them, on the condition of guarding this barrier into Hindust'han against invasion. For this purpose the fortress of Khyber was erected in the chief pass of the Koh-i-Damaun. For two centuries after this event Ferishta is silent on this frontier warfare, stating that henceforth Hindust'han was only accessible through Sinde. When Aliptegin first crossed the Indus, the prince of Lahore and the Afghans still maintained this alliance and united to oppose him. Jeipal was then prince of Lahore ; and it is on this event that Ferishta, for the first time, mentions the tribe of Bhatti,[3] "at the advice of whose prince he conferred the command of the united forces on an Afghan chief," to whom he assigned the provinces of Mooltan and Limgham. From this junction of interests the princes of Lahore enjoyed comparative security, until Soobektegin and Mahmood compelled the Afghans to serve them : then Lahore was captured. The territory dependent upon Lahore, at this period, extended from Sirhind to Limgham, and from Cashmér to Mooltan. Bhatinda divided with Lahore the residence of its princes. Their first encounter was at Limgham, on which occasion young Mahmood first distinguished

[1] See p. 99.

[2] The scene of action was between Peshawur and Kirman, the latter lying ninety miles south-west of the former.

[3] Dow omits this in his translation.

himself, and as the historian says, "the eyes of the heavens were obscured at seeing his deeds."[1] A tributary engagement was the result, which Jeipal soon broke; and being aided by levies from all the princes of Hindust'han, marched an army of one hundred thousand men against Soobektegin, and was again defeated on the banks of the Indus. He was at length invested and taken in Bhatinda by Mahmood, when he put himself to death. The successors of Jeipal are mentioned merely as fugitives, and always distinct from the princes of Dehli. It is most probable that they were of the tribe termed Boosa in the annals of Méwar, possibly a subdivision of another; though Ferishta calls the prince of Lahore a Brahmin.

The Sankla from Ronéja. Both tribe and abode are well known: it is a subdivision of the Pramara. Hurba Sankla was the Paladin of Marwar, in which Ronéja was situated.

The Sehat from Kherligurh was a northern tribe, dwelling about the Indus, and though entirely unknown to the modern genealogists of India, is frequently mentioned in the early history of the Bhattis, when their possessions extended on both sides of the Hyphasis. As intermarriages between the Bhattis and Sehats are often spoken of, it must have been Rajpoot. It most probably occupied the province of Séwad, the *Suvat* of D'Anville, a division of the province of Ash-nagar, where dwelt the Assacani of Alexander; concerning which this celebrated geographer says, "Il est mention de Suvat comme d'un canton du pays d'Ash-nagar dans la même géographie Turque" (*Ecl.* p. 25). The whole of this ground was sacred to the Jadu tribe from the most remote antiquity, from Mooltan, the hills of Joud, to Aswini-kote (the *Tshehin-kote* of D'Anville) which, built on the point of confluence of the Choaspes of the Greeks with the Indus, marks the spot where dwelt the Asaséni, corroborated by the Pooráns, which mention the partition of all these territories amongst the sons of Baj-aswa, the lord of Kampilnagara, the grand subdivision of the Yadu race. In all likelihood, the Sehat, who came to the aid of Khoman of Cheetore, was a branch of these Asaséni, the opponents of Alexander. The modern town of Deenkote appears to occupy the site of Aswini-kote, though D'Anville feels inclined to carry it into the heart of Bijore and place it on the rock (*silla*) Aornus. Such the Sehat; not improbably the *Soha*, one of the eight subdivisions of the Yadu.[2] When, in S. 785, the Bhatti chief Rao Tannoo was driven across the Sutledge, the Sehats are mentioned with other tribes as forming the army of Hussein Shah, with the Barahas, the Joudis, and Johyas (the Juds and Jinjohyas of Baber), the Bootas, and the 'men of Doode.'

The Chundail, from Kurrungurh, occupied the tracts now termed Boondélkhund.

We shall pass over the other auxiliary tribes and conclude with the Purihar, who came from Cashmér on this occasion: a circumstance entirely overlooked in the dissertation on this tribe;[3] nor does this isolated fact afford room for further discussion on a race which expelled the Pramaras from Mundore.

Such aids, who preserved Khoman when assailed by the 'Khorasan Put,' fully demonstrate the antiquity of the annals, which is further attested by inscriptions. Khoman fought twenty-four great battles,

[1] The sense of this passage has been quite perverted by Dow.

[2] See p. 73. [3] See p. 83.

and his name, like that of Cæsar, became a family distinction. At Oodipoor, if you make a false step, or even sneeze, you hear the ejaculation of 'Khoman aid you!' Khoman, by the advice of the Brahmins, resigned the Gadi to his younger son, Jograz; but again resumed it, slaying his advisers and execrating the name of Brahmin, which he almost exterminated in his own dominions. Khoman was at length slain by his own son, Mangul; but the chiefs expelled the parricide, who seized upon Lodurwa in the northern desert, and there established the Mangulia Gehlotes.

Bhartribhut (familiarly Bhatto) succeeded. In his reign, and in that of his successor, the territory dependent on Cheetore was greatly increased. All the forest tribes, from the banks of the Myhie to Aboo, were subjugated, and strongholds erected, of which D'horungurh and Ujargurh still remain to maintain them. He established no less than thirteen [1] of his sons in independent possessions in Malwa and Guzzerat, and these were distinguished as the Bhatéwra Gehlotes.

We shall now leap over fifteen generations; which, though affording a few interesting facts to the antiquarian, would not amuse the general reader. We will rest satisfied with stating that the Chohans of Ajmér and the Gehlotes of Cheetore were alternately friends and foes; that Doorlub Chohan was slain by Bérsi Raoul in a grand battle fought at Kowario, of which the Chohan annals state 'that their princes were now so powerful as to oppose the chief of Cheetore.' Again, in the next reign, we find the renowned Beesuldeo, son of Doorlub, combining with Raoul Téjsi of Cheetore to oppose the progress of Islamite invasion: facts recorded by inscriptions as well as by the annals. We may close these remarks on the fifteen princes, from Khoman to Samarsi, with the words of Gibbon on the dark period of Guelphic annals: "It may be presumed that they were illiterate and valiant; that they plundered in their youth, and reared churches in their old age; that they were fond of arms, horses, and hunting"; and, we may add, continued bickering with their vassals within, when left unemployed by the enemy from without.

CHAPTER V

Historical facts furnished by the bard Chund—Anungpal—Pirthi Raj—Samarsi—Overthrow of the Chohan monarch by the Tatars—Posterity of Samarsi—Rahup—Changes in the title and the tribe of its prince—Successors of Rahup.

ALTHOUGH the whole of this chain of ancestry, from Keneksén in the second, Vijya the founder of Balabhi in the fourth, to Samarsi in the thirteenth century, cannot be discriminated with perfect accuracy, we may affirm, to borrow a metaphor, that "the two extremities of it are riveted in truth": and some links have at intervals been recognised as equally valid. We will now extend the chain to the nineteenth century.

Samarsi was born in S. 1206. Though the domestic annals are not silent on his acts, we shall recur chiefly to the bard of Dehli [2] for his charac-

[1] By name, Koolanugger, Champanair, Choréta, Bhojpoor, Loonara, Neemthore, Sodaru, Jodghur, Sandpoor, Aetpoor, and Gungabhéva. The remaining two are not mentioned.

[2] The work of Chund is a universal history of the period in which he wrote.

ter and actions, and the history of the period. Before we proceed, however, a sketch of the political condition of Hindust'han during the last of the Túar sovereigns of Dehli, derived from this authority and in the bard's own words, may not be unacceptable. " In Putun is Bhola Bheem the Chalook, of iron frame. On the mountain Aboo, Jeit Pramara, in battle immovable as the star of the north. In Méwar is Samar Sing, who takes tribute from the mighty, a wave of iron in the path of Dehli's foe. In the midst of all, strong in his own strength, Mundore's prince, the arrogant Nahar Rao, the might of Maroo, fearing none. In Dehli the chief of all Anunga, at whose summons attended the princes of Mundore, Nagore, Sinde, Julwut [1] and others on its confines, Peshawur, Lahore, Kangra and its mountain chiefs, with Kasi,[2] Priag,[3] and Gurh Deogir. The lords of Seemar [4] were in constant danger of his power." The Bhatti, since their expulsion from Zabulist'han, had successively occupied as capitals, Salbahana in the Punjáb, Tannote, Derawul, which last they founded, and the ancient Lodurwa, which they conquered in the desert ; and at the period in question were constructing their present residence, Jessulmér. In this nook they had been fighting for centuries with the lieutenants of the Caliph at Arore, occasionally redeeming their ancient possessions as far as the city of the Tâk on the Indus. Their situation gave them little political interest in the affairs of Hindust'han until the period of Pirthi Raj, one of whose principal leaders, Achilés, was the brother of the Bhatti prince. Anungpal, from this description, was justly entitled to be termed the paramount sovereign of Hindust'han ; but he was the last of a dynasty of nineteen princes, who had occupied Dehli nearly four hundred years, from the time of the founder Beelun Deo, who, according to a manuscript in the author's possession, was only an opulent Thacoor when he assumed the ensigns of royalty in the then deserted Indraprest'ha, taking the name of Anungpal,[5] ever after titular in the family. The Chohans of Ajmér owed at least homage to Dehli at this time, although Beesildeo had rendered it almost nominal ; and to Soméswar, the fourth in descent,

In the sixty-nine books, comprising one hundred thousand stanzas, relating to the exploits of Pirthi Raj, every noble family of Rajast'han will find some record of their ancestors. It is accordingly treasured amongst the archives of each race having any pretensions to the name of Rajpoot. From this he can trace his martial forefathers who 'drank of the wave of battle' in the passes of Kirman, when 'the cloud of war rolled from Himachil' to the plains of Hindust'han. The wars of Pirthi Raj, his alliances, his numerous and powerful tributaries, their abodes and pedigrees, make the works of Chund invaluable as historic and geographical memoranda, besides being treasures in mythology, manners, and the annals of the mind. To read this poet well is a sure road to honour, and my own *Gooru* was allowed, even by the professional bards, to excel therein. As he read I rapidly translated about thirty thousand stanzas. Familiar with the dialects in which it is written, I have fancied that I seized occasionally the poet's spirit ; but it were presumption to suppose that I embodied all his brilliancy, or fully comprehended the depth of his allusions. But I knew for whom he wrote. The most familiar of his images and sentiments I heard daily from the mouths of those around me, the descendants of the men whose deeds he rehearses. I was enabled thus to seize his meaning, where one more skilled in poetic lore might have failed, and to make my prosaic version of some value.

[1] Unknown, unless the country on the 'waters' (*jul*) of Sinde.

[2] Benares. [3] Allahabad. [4] The cold regions (see 'cold').

[5] *Anunga* is a poetical epithet of the Hindu Cupid, literally 'incorporeal': but, according to good authority, applicable to the founder of the desolate abode, *palna* being 'to support,' and *unga*, with the primitive *an*, 'without body.'

Anungpal was indebted for the preservation of this supremacy against the attempts of Kanouj, for which service he obtained the Túar's daughter in marriage, the issue of which was Pirthi Raj, who when only eight years of age was proclaimed successor to the Dehli throne. Jychund of Kanouj and Pirthi Raj bore the same relative situation to Anungpal; Beejipal, the father of the former, as well as Soméswar, having had a daughter of the Túar to wife. This originated the rivalry between the Chohans and Rahtores, which ended in the destruction of both. When Pirthi Raj mounted the throne of Dehli, Jychund not only refused to acknowledge his supremacy, but set forth his own claims to this distinction. In these he was supported by the prince of Putun Anhulwara (the eternal foe of the Chohans), and likewise by the Purihars of Mundore. But the affront given by the latter, in refusing to fulfil the contract of bestowing his daughter on the young Chohan, brought on a warfare, in which this first essay was but the presage of his future fame. Kanouj and Putun had recourse to the dangerous expedient of entertaining bands of Tatars, through whom the sovereign of Gazni was enabled to take advantage of their internal broils.

Samarsi, prince of Cheetore, had married the sister of Pirthi Raj, and their personal characters, as well as this tie, bound them to each other throughout all these commotions, until the last fatal battle on the Caggar. From these feuds Hindust'han never was free. But unrelenting enmity was not a part of their character: having displayed the valour of the tribe, the bard or Nestor of the day would step in, and a marriage would conciliate and maintain in friendship such foes for two generations. From time immemorial such has been the political state of India, as represented by their own epics, or in Arabian or Persian histories: thus always the prey of foreigners, and destined to remain so. Samarsi had to contend both with the princes of Putun and Kanouj; and although the bard says, "he washed his blade in the Jumna," the domestic annals slur over the circumstance of Sid Rae Jey Sing having actually made a conquest of Cheetore; for it is not only included in the eighteen capitals enumerated as appertaining to this prince, but the author discovered a tablet [1] in Cheetore, placed there by his successor, Komarpal, bearing the date S. 1206, the period of Samarsi's birth. The first occasion of Samarsi's aid being called in by the Chohan emperor was on the discovery of treasure at Nagore, amounting to seven millions of gold, the deposit of ancient days. The princes of Kanouj and Putun, dreading the influence which such sinews of war would afford their antagonist, invited Shabudín to aid their designs of humiliating the Chohan, who in this emergency sent an embassy to Samarsi. The envoy was Chund Poondir, the vassal chief of Lahore, and guardian of that frontier. He is conspicuous from this time to the hour "when he planted his lance at the ford of the Ravee," and fell in opposing the passage of Shabudín. The presents he carries, the speech with which he greets the Cheetore prince, his reception, reply, and dismissal, are all preserved by Chund. The style of address and the apparel of Samarsi betoken that he had not laid aside the office and ensigns of a 'Regent of Mahadeva.' A simple necklace of the seeds of the lotus adorned his neck; his hair was braided, and he is addressed as Jogindra, or chief of ascetics. Samarsi proceeded to Dehli; and it was arranged,

[1] See Inscription No. 5.

as he was connected by marriage with the prince of Putun, that Pirthi Raj should march against this prince, while he should oppose the army from Gazni. He (Samarsi) accordingly fought several indecisive battles, which gave time to the Chohan to terminate the war in Guzzerat and rejoin him. United, they completely discomfited the invaders, making their leader prisoner. Samarsi declined any share of the discovered treasure, but permitted his chiefs to accept the gifts offered by Chohan. Many years elapsed in such subordinate warfare, when the prince of Cheetore was again constrained to use his buckler in defence of Dehli and its prince, whose arrogance and successful ambition, followed by disgraceful inactivity, invited invasion with every presage of success. Jealousy and revenge rendered the princes of Putun, Kanouj, D'har, and the minor courts, indifferent spectators of a contest destined to overthrow them all.

The bard gives a good description of the preparations for his departure from Cheetore, which he was destined never to see again. The charge of the city was entrusted to a favourite and younger son, Kurna : which disgusted the elder brother, who went to the Dekhan to Biedur, where he was well received by an Abyssinian chief,[1] who had there established himself in sovereignty. Another son, either on this occasion or on the subsequent fall of Cheetore, fled to the mountains of Nepal, and there spread the Gehlote line. It is in this, the last of the books, of Chund, termed *The Great Fight*, that we have the character of Samarsi fully delineated. His arrival at Dehli is hailed with songs of joy as a day of deliverance. Pirthi Raj and his court advance seven miles to meet him, and the description of the greeting of the king of Dehli and his sister, and the chiefs on either side who recognise ancient friendships, is most animated. Samarsi reads his brother-in-law an indignant lecture on his unprincely inactivity, and throughout the book divides attention with him.

In the planning of the campaign, and march towards the Caggar to meet the foe, Samarsi is consulted, and his opinions are recorded. The bard represents him as the Ulysses of the host : brave, cool, and skilful in the fight ; prudent, wise, and eloquent in council ; pious and decorous on all occasions ; beloved by his own chiefs, and reverenced by the vassals of the Chohan. In the line of march no augur or bard could better explain the omens, none in the field better dress the squadrons for battle, none guide his steed or use his lance with more address. His tent is the principal resort of the leaders after the march or in the intervals of battle, who were delighted by his eloquence or instructed by his knowledge. The bard confesses that his precepts of government are chiefly from the lips of Khoman ;[2] and of his best episodes and allegories, whether on morals, rules for the guidance of ambassadors, choice of ministers, religious or social duties (but especially those of the Rajpoot to the sovereign), the wise prince of Cheetore is the general organ.

On the last of three days' desperate fighting Samarsi was slain, together with his son Calian, and thirteen thousand of his household troops and most renowned chieftains. His beloved Pirtha, on hearing the fatal issue, her husband slain, her brother captive, the heroes of Dehli and Cheetore

[1] Styled Hubshee Padsha.

[2] I have already mentioned, that Khoman became a patronymic and title amongst the princes of Cheetore.

" asleep on the banks of the Caggar, in the wave of the steel," joined her lord through the flame, nor waited the advance of the Tatar king, when Dehli was carried by storm, and the last stay of the Chohans, prince Rainsi, met death in the assault. The capture of Dehli and its monarch, the death of his ally of Cheetore, with the bravest and best of their troops, speedily ensured the further and final success of the Tatar arms ; and when Canouj fell, and the traitor to his nation met his fate in the waves of the Ganges, none were left to contend with Shabudín the possession of the regal seat of the Chohan. Scenes of devastation, plunder, and massacre commenced, which lasted through ages ; during which nearly all that was sacred in religion or celebrated in art was destroyed by these ruthless and barbarous invaders. The noble Rajpoot, with a spirit of constancy and enduring courage, seized every opportunity to turn upon his oppressor. By his perseverance and valour he wore out entire dynasties of foes, alternately yielding ' to his fate,' or restricting the circle of conquest. Every road in Rajast'han was moistened with torrents of blood of the spoiled and the spoiler. But all was of no avail ; fresh supplies were ever pouring in, and dynasty succeeded dynasty, heir to the same remorseless feeling which sanctified murder, legalised spoliation, and deified destruction. In these desperate conflicts entire tribes were swept away, whose names are the only memento of their former existence and celebrity.

What nation on earth would have maintained the semblance of civilisation, the spirit or the customs of their forefathers, during so many centuries of overwhelming depression, but one of such singular character as the Rajpoot ? Though ardent and reckless, he can, when required, subside into forbearance and apparent apathy, and reserve himself for the opportinity of revenge. Rajast'han exhibits the sole example in the history of mankind, of a people withstanding every outrage barbarity can inflict, or human nature sustain, from a foe whose religion commands annihilation, and bent to the earth, yet rising buoyant from the pressure, and making calamity a whetstone to courage. How did the Britons at once sink under the Romans, and in vain strive to save their groves, their druids, or the altars of Bal from destruction ! To the Saxons they alike succumbed ; they, again, to the Danes ; and this heterogeneous breed to the Normans. Empire was lost and gained by a single battle, and the laws and religion of the conquered merged in those of the conquerors. Contrast with these the Rajpoots ; not an iota of their religion or customs have they lost, though many a foot of land. Some of their states have been expunged from the map of dominion ; and, as a punishment of national infidelity, the pride of the Rahtore, and the glory of the Chalook, the overgrown Canouj and gorgeous Anhulwarra, are forgotten names ! Méwar alone, the sacred bulwark of religion, never compromised her honour for her safety, and still survives her ancient limits ; and since the brave Samarsi gave up his life, the blood of her princes has flowed in copious streams for the maintenance of this honour, religion, and independence.

Samarsi had several sons ; [1] but Kurna was his heir, and during his minority his mother, Korumdevi, a princess of Putun, nobly maintained what his father left. She headed her Rajpoots and gave battle [2] in person

[1] Calianraé, slain with his father ; Koomkurna, who went to Biedur ; a third, the founder of the Gorkas.

[2] This must be the battle mentioned by Ferishta. See Dow, p. 169, vol. ii.

to Kootub-o-din, near Ambér, when the viceroy was defeated and wounded. Nine Rajas, and eleven chiefs of inferior dignity with the title of Rawut, followed the mother of their prince.

Kurna (the radiant) succeeded in S. 1249 (A.D. 1193); but he was not destined to be the founder of a line in Méwar.[1] The annals are at variance with each other on an event which gave the sovereignty of Cheetore to a younger branch, and sent the elder into the inhospitable wilds of the west, to found a city [2] and perpetuate a line. It is stated generally that Kurna had two sons, Mahup and Rahup; but this is an error: Samarsi and Soorajmul were brothers: Kurna was the son of the former and *Mahup* was his son, whose mother was a Chohan of Bhagur. Soorajmul had a son named Bharut, who was driven from Cheetore by a conspiracy. He proceeded to Sinde, obtained Arore from its prince, a Moosulman, and married the daughter of the Bhatti chief of Poogul, by whom he had a son named *Rahup*. Kurna died of grief for the loss of Bharut and the unworthiness of Mahup, who abandoned him to live entirely with his maternal relations, the Chohans.

The Sonigurra chief of Jhalore had married the daughter of Kurna, by whom he had a child named Rindhole,[3] whom by treachery he placed on the throne of Cheetore, slaying the chief Gehlotes. Mahup being unable to recover his rights, and unwilling to make any exertion, the chair of Bappa Rawul would have passed to the Chohans but for an ancient bard of the house. He pursued his way to Arore, held by old Bharut as a fief of Çabul. With the levies of Sinde he marched to claim the right abandoned by Mahup and at Palli encountered and defeated the Sonigurras. The retainers of Méwar flocked to his standard, and by their aid he enthroned himself in Cheetore. He sent for his father and mother, Ranungdevi, whose dwelling on the Indus was made over to a younger brother, who bartered his faith for Arore, and held it as a vassal of Cabul.

Rahup obtained Cheetore in S. 1257 (A.D. 1201), and shortly after sustained the attack of Shemsudin, whom he met and overcame in a battle at Nagore. Two great changes were introduced by this prince; the first in the title of the tribe, to Sesodia; the other in that of its prince, from Rawul to Rana. The puerile reason for the former has already been noticed;[4] the cause of the latter is deserving of more attention. Amongst the foes of Rahup was the Purihar prince of Mundore: his name Mokul, with the title of Rana. Rahup seized him in his capital and brought him to Sesodia, making him renounce the rich district of Godwar, and his title of Rana, which he assumed himself, to denote the completion of his feud. He ruled thirty-eight years in a period of great distraction, and appears to have been well calculated, not only to uphold the fallen fortunes of the state, but to rescue them from utter ruin. His reign is the more remarkable by contrast with his successors, nine of whom are "pushed from their stools" in the same or even a shorter period than that during which he upheld the dignity.

From Rahup to Lakumsi, in the short space of half a century, nine princes of Cheetore were crowned, and at nearly equal intervals of time

[1] He had a son, Sírwan, who took to commerce. Hence the mercantile Sesodia caste, Sirwanea.

[2] Dongurpoor, so named from *dongra*, 'a mountain.'

[3] So pronounced, but properly written Rin-dhaval, 'the standard of the field.'

[4] See note, p. 176.

followed each other to 'the mansions of the sun.' Of these nine, six fell in battle. Nor did they meet their fate at home, but in a chivalrous enterprise to redeem the sacred Gya from the pollution of the barbarian. For this object these princes successively fell, but such devotion inspired fear, if not pity or conviction, and the bigot renounced the impiety which Pirthimull purchased with his blood, and until Alla-o-din's reign, this outrage to their prejudices was renounced. But in this interval they had lost their capital, for it is stated as the only occurrence in Bhonsi's [1] reign, that he "recovered Cheetore" and made the name of Rana be acknowledged by all. Two memorials are preserved of the nine princes from Rahup to Lakumsi, and of the same character: confusion and strife within and without. We will, therefore, pass over these to another grand event in the vicissitudes of this house, which possesses more of romance than of history, though the facts are undoubted.

CHAPTER VI

Rana Lakumsi—Attack of Cheetore by Alla-o-din—Treachery of Alla—Ruse of the Cheetore chiefs to recover Bheemsi—Devotion of the Rana and his sons—Sack of Cheetore by the Tatars—Its destruction—Rana Ajeysi—Hamir—He gains possession of Cheetore—Renown and prosperity of Méwar—Khaitsi—Lakha.

LAKUMSI succeeded his father in S. 1331 (A.D. 1275), a memorable era in the annals, when Cheetore, the repository of all that was precious yet

[1] His second son, Chandra, obtained an appanage on the Chumbul, and his issue, well known as Chanderawuts, constituted one of the most powerful vassal clans of Méwar. Rampoora (Bhanpoora) was their residence, yielding a revenue of nine lakhs (£110,000), held on the tenure of service which, from an original grant in my possession from Rana Juggut Sing to his nephew Madhú Sing, afterwards prince of Ambér, was two thousand horse and foot (see p. 164), and the fine of investiture was seventy-five thousand rupees. Madhú Sing, when prince of Ambér, did what was invalid as well as ungrateful; he made over this domain, granted during his misfortunes, to Holkar, the first limb lopped off Méwar. The Chanderawut proprietor continued, however, to possess a portion of the original estate with the fortress of Amud, which it maintained throughout all the troubles of Rajwarra till A.D. 1821. It shows the attachment to custom, that the young Rao applied and received 'the sword' of investiture from his old lord paramount, the Rana, though dependent on Holkar's forbearance. But a minority is proverbially dangerous in India. Disorder from party plots made Amud troublesome to Holkar's government, which as his ally and preserver of tranquillity we suppressed by blowing up the walls of the fortress. This is one of many instances of the harsh, uncompromising nature of our power, and the anomalous description of our alliances with the Rajpoots. However necessary to repress the disorder arising from the claims of ancient proprietors and the recent rights of Holkar, or the new proprietor, Guffoor Khan, yet surrounding princes, and the general population, who know the history of past times, lament to see a name of five hundred years' duration thus summarily extinguished, which chiefly benefits an upstart Pat'han. Such the vortex of the ambiguous, irregular, and unsystematic policy, which marks many of our alliances, which protect too often but to injure, and gives to our office of general arbitrator and high constable of Rajast'han a harsh and unfeeling character.

Much of this arises from ignorance of the past history; much from disregard of the peculiar usages of the people; or from that expediency which too often comes in contact with moral fitness, which will go on until the day predicted by the Nestor of India, when "*one sicca* (seal) alone will be used in Hisdust'han."

untouched of the arts of India, was stormed, sacked, and treated with remorseless barbarity, by the Pathan emperor, Alla-o-din. Twice it was attacked by this subjugator of India. In the first siege it escaped spoliation, though at the price of its best defenders: that which followed is the first successful assault and capture of which we have any detailed account.

Bheemsi was the uncle of the young prince, and protector during his minority. He had espoused the daughter of Hamir Sank (Chohan) of Ceylon, the cause of woes unnumbered to the Sesodias. Her name was Pudmani, a title bestowed only on the superlatively fair, and transmitted with renown to posterity by tradition and the song of the bard. Her beauty, accomplishments, exaltation, and destruction, with other incidental circumstances, constitute the subject of one of the most popular traditions of Rajwarra. The Hindu bard recognises the fair, in preference to fame and love of conquest, as the motive for the attack of Alla-o-din, who limited his demand to the possession of Pudmani; though this was after a long and fruitless siege. At length he restricted his desire to a mere sight of this extraordinary beauty, and acceded to the proposal of beholding her through the medium of mirrors. Relying on the faith of the Rajpoot, he entered Cheetore slightly guarded, and having gratified his wish, returned. The Rajpoot, unwilling to be outdone in confidence, accompanied the king to the foot of the fortress, amidst many complimentary excuses from his guest at the trouble he thus occasioned. It was for this that Alla risked his own safety, relying on the superior faith of the Hindu. Here he had an ambush; Bheemsi was made prisoner, hurried away to the Tatar camp, and his liberty made dependent on the surrender of Pudmani.

Despair reigned in Cheetore when this fatal event was known, and it was debated whether Pudmani should be resigned as a ransom for their defender. Of this she was informed, and expressed her acquiescence. Having provided wherewithal to secure her from dishonour, she communed with two chiefs of her own kin and clan of Ceylon, her uncle Gorah, and his nephew Badul, who devised a scheme for the liberation of their prince without hazarding her life or fame. Intimation was despatched to Alla, that on the day he withdraw from his trenches the fair Pudmani would be sent, but in a manner befitting her own and his high station, surrounded by her females and handmaids; not only those who would accompany her to Dehli, but many others who desired to pay her this last mark of reverence. Strict commands were to be issued to prevent curiosity from violating the sanctity of female decorum and privacy. No less than seven hundred covered litters proceeded to the royal camp. In each was placed one of the bravest of the defenders of Cheetore, borne by six armed soldiers disguised as litter-porters. They reached the camp. The royal tents were enclosed with *kanats* (walls of cloth); the litters were deposited, and half an hour was granted for a parting interview between the Hindu prince and his bride. They then placed their prince in a litter and returned with him, while the greater number (the supposed damsels) remained to accompany the fair to Dehli. But Alla had no intention to permit Bheemsi's return, and was becoming jealous of the long interview he enjoyed, when, instead of the prince and Pudmani, the devoted band issued from their litters: but Alla was too well guarded. Pursuit was ordered, while these covered the retreat till they perished to a man. A fleet horse was in reserve for Bheemsi, on which he was placed, and in safety ascended the fort, at whose outer gate the host of Alla was encountered. The choicest of the heroes of Cheetore met the assault. With Gorah and Badul at their head, animated by the noblest sentiments, the deliverance of their chief and the honour of their queen, they devoted themselves to destruction, and few were the survivors of this slaughter of the flower of Méwar. For a time Alla was defeated in his object, and the havoc they had made in his ranks, joined to the dread of their determined resistance, obliged him to desist from the enterprise.

Mention has already been made of the adjuration, "by the sin of the sack of Cheetore." Of these sacks they enumerate *three and a half*. This is the 'half'; for though the city was not stormed, the best and bravest were cut off (*saka*). It is described with great animation in the *Khoman Rásá*. Badul was but a stripling of twelve, but the Rajpoot expects wonders from this early age. He escaped, though wounded, and a dialogue ensues between him and his uncle's wife, who desires him to relate how her lord conducted himself ere she joins him. The stripling replies: "He was the reaper of the harvest of battle; I followed his steps as the humble gleaner of his sword. On the gory bed of honour he spread a carpet of the slain; a barbarian prince his pillow, he laid him down, and sleeps surrounded by the foe." Again she said: "Tell me, Badul, how did my love (*peeár*) behave?" "Oh! mother, how further describe his deeds, when he left no foe to dread or admire him?" She smiled farewell to the boy, and adding, "My lord will chide my delay," sprung into the flame.

Alla-o-din, having recruited his strength, returned to his object, Cheetore. The annals state this to have been in S. 1346 (A.D. 1290), but Ferishta gives a date thirteen years later. They had not yet recovered the loss of so many valiant men who had sacrificed themselves for their prince's safety, and Alla carried on his attacks more closely, and at length obtained the hill at the southern point, where he entrenched himself. They still pretend to point out his trenches; but so many have been formed by subsequent attacks that we cannot credit the assertion. The poet has found in the disastrous issue of this siege admirable materials for his song. He represents the Rana, after an arduous day, stretched on his pallet, and during a night of watchful anxiety, pondering on the means by which he might preserve from the general destruction one at least of his twelve sons; when a voice broke on his solitude, exclaiming "*Myn bhooka hó*";[1] and raising his eyes, he saw, by the dim glare of the cheragh,[2] advancing between the granite columns, the majestic form of the guardian goddess of Cheetore. "Not satiated," exclaimed the Rana, "though eight thousand of my kin were late an offering to thee?" "I must have regal victims; and if twelve who wear the diadem bleed not for Cheetore, the land will pass from the line." This said, she vanished.

On the morn he convened a council of his chiefs, to whom he revealed the vision of the night, which they treated as the dream of a disordered fancy. He commanded their attendance at midnight; when again the form appeared, and repeated the terms on which alone she would remain amongst them. "Though thousands of barbarians strew the earth, what are they to me? On each day enthrone a prince. Let the

[1] 'I am hungry.' [2] Lamp.

kirnia,[1] the chehtra and the chamra,[1] proclaim his sovereignty, and for three days let his decrees be supreme: on the fourth let him meet the foe and his fate. Then only may I remain."

Whether we have merely the fiction of the poet, or whether the scene was got up to animate the spirit of resistance, matters but little, it is consistent with the belief of the tribe; and that the goddess should openly manifest her wish to retain as her tiara the battlements of Cheetore on conditions so congenial to the warlike and superstitious Rajpoot, was a gage readily taken up and fully answering the end. A generous contention arose amongst the brave brothers, who should be the first victim to avert the denunciation. Ursi urged his priority of birth: he was proclaimed, the umbrella waved over his head, and on the fourth day he surrendered his short-lived honours and his life. Ajeysi, the next in birth, demanded to follow; but he was the favourite son of his father, and at his request he consented to let his brothers precede him. Eleven had fallen in turn, and but one victim remained to the salvation of the city, when the Rana, calling his chiefs around him, said, "Now I devote myself for Cheetore." But another awful sacrifice was to precede this act of self-devotion, in that horrible rite, the *Johur,* where the females are immolated to preserve them from pollution or captivity. The funeral pyre was lighted within the 'great subterranean retreat,' in chambers impervious to the light of day, and the defenders of Cheetore beheld in procession the queens, their own wives and daughters, to the number of several thousands. The fair Pudmani closed the throng, which was augmented by whatever of female beauty or youth could be tainted by Tatar lust. They were conveyed to the cavern, and the opening closed upon them, leaving them to find security from dishonour in the devouring element.

A contest now arose between the Rana and his surviving son; but the father prevailed, and Ajeysi, in obedience to his commands, with a small band passed through the enemy's lines, and reached Kailwarra in safety. The Rana, satisfied that his line was not extinct, now prepared to follow his brave sons; and calling around him his devoted clans, for whom life had no longer any charms, they threw open the portals and descended to the plains, and with a reckless despair carried death, or met it, in the crowded ranks of Alla. The Tatar conqueror took possession of an inanimate capital, strewed with brave defenders, the smoke yet issuing from the recesses where lay consumed the once fair object of his desire; and since this devoted day the cavern has been sacred: no eye has penetrated its gloom, and superstition has placed as its guardian a huge serpent, whose "venomous breath" extinguishes the light which might guide intruders [2] to "the place of sacrifice."

Thus fell, in A.D. 1303, this celebrated capital, in the round of conquest of Alla-o-din, one of the most vigorous and warlike sovereigns who have

[1] These are the insignia of royalty. The *kirnia* is a parasol, from *keren,* 'a ray': the *chehtra* is the umbrella, always red; the *chamra,* the flowing tail of the wild ox, set in a gold handle, and used to drive away the flies.

[2] The author has been at the entrance of this retreat, which, according to the *Khomán Rásá* conducts to a subterranean palace, but the mephitic vapours and venomous reptiles did not invite to adventure, even had official situation permitted such slight to these prejudices. The author is the only Englishman admitted to Cheetore since the days of Herbert, who appears to have described what he saw.

occupied the throne of India. In success, and in one of the means of attainment, a bigoted hypocrisy, he bore a striking resemblance to Arungzéb; and the title of 'Secunder Sani,' or the second Alexander, which he assumed and impressed on his coins, was no idle vaunt. The proud Anhulwara, the ancient D'har and Avanti, Mundore and Deogir, the seats of the Solankis, the Pramaras, the Puriharas and Tâks, the entire Agnicúla race, were overturned for ever by Alla. Jessulmér, Gagrown, Boondí, the abodes of the Bhatti, the Keechee, and the Hara, with many of minor importance, suffered all the horrors of assault from this foe of the race, though destined again to raise their heads. The Rahtores of Márwar and the Cutchwahas of Ambér were yet in a state of insignificance: the former were slowly creeping into notice as the vassals of the Puriharas, while the latter could scarcely withstand the attacks of the original Meena population. Alla remained in Cheetore some days, admiring the grandeur of his conquest; and having committed every act of barbarity and wanton dilapidation which a bigoted zeal could suggest, overthrowing the temples and other monuments of art, he delivered the city in charge to Maldeo, the chief of Jhalore, whom he had conquered and enrolled amongst his vassals. The palace of Bheem and the fair Pudmani alone appears to have escaped the wrath of Alla; it would be pleasing could we suppose any kinder sentiment suggested the exception, which enables the author of these annals to exhibit the abode of the fair of Ceylon.

The survivor of Cheetore, Rana Ajéysi, was now in security at Kailwarra, a town situated in the heart of the Aravulli mountains, the western boundary of Méwar, to which its princes had been indebted for twelve centuries of dominion. Kailwarra is at the highest part of one of its most extensive valleys, termed the Shero Nalla, the richest district of this Alpine region. Guarded by faithful adherents, Ajeysi cherished for future occasion the wrecks of Méwar. It was the last behest of his father, that when he attained 'one hundred years' (a figurative expression for dying) the son of Ursi, the elder brother, should succeed him. This injunction, from the deficiency of the qualities requisite at such a juncture in his own sons, met a ready compliance. Hamir was this son, destined to redeem the promise of the genius of Cheetore and the lost honours of his race, and whose birth and early history fill many a page of their annals. His father, Ursi, being out on a hunting excursion in the forest of Ondwa, with some young chiefs of the court, in pursuit of the boar entered a field of maize, when a female offered to drive out the game. Pulling one of the stalks of maize, which grows to the height of ten or twelve feet, she pointed it, and mounting the platform made to watch the corn, impaled the hog, dragged him before the hunters, and departed. Though accustomed to feats of strength and heroism from the nervous arms of their countrywomen, the act surprised them. They descended to the stream at hand, and prepared the repast, as is usual, on the spot. The feast was held, and comments were passing on the fair arm which had transfixed the boar, when a ball of clay from a sling fractured a limb of the prince's steed. Looking in the direction whence it came, they observed the same damsel, from her elevated stand,[1] preserving her fields from aerial depredators;

[1] A stand is fixed upon four poles in the middle of a field, on which a guard is placed armed with a sling and clay balls, to drive away the ravens, peacocks, and other birds that destroy the corn.

but seeing the mischief she had occasioned she descended to express her regret, and then returned to her pursuit. As they were proceeding homewards after the sports of the day, they again encountered the damsel, with a vessel of milk on her head, and leading in either hand a young buffalo. It was proposed, in frolic, to overturn her milk, and one of the companions of the prince dashed rudely by her; but without being disconcerted, she entangled one of her charges with the horse's limbs, and brought the rider to the ground. On inquiry the prince discovered that she was the daughter of a poor Rajpoot of the Chundano tribe.[1] He returned the next day to the same quarter and sent for her father, who came and took his seat with perfect independence close to the prince, to the merriment of his companions, which was checked by Ursi asking his daughter to wife. They were yet more surprised by the demand being refused. The Rajpoot, on going home, told the more prudent mother, who scolded him heartily, made him recall the refusal, and seek the prince. They were married, and Hamir was the son of the Chundano Rajpootnee. He remained little noticed at the maternal abode till the catastrophe of Cheetore. At this period he was twelve years of age, and had led a rustic life, from which the necessity of the times recalled him.

Méwar was now occupied by the garrisons of Dehli, and Ajeysi had besides to contend with the mountain chiefs, amongst whom Moonja Balaitcha was the most formidable, who had, on a recent occasion, invaded the Shero Nalla, and personally encountered the Rana, whom he wounded on the head with a lance. The Rana's sons, Sujunsi and Ajimsi, though fourteen and fifteen, an age at which a Rajpoot ought to indicate his future character, proved of little aid in the emergency. Hamir was summoned, and accepted the feud against Moonja, promising to return successful or not at all. In a few days he was seen entering the pass of Kailwarra with Moonja's head at his saddle-bow. Modestly placing the trophy at his uncle's feet, he exclaimed: "Recognise the head of your foe!" Ajeysi "kissed his beard,"[2] and observing that fate had stamped empire on his forehead, impressed it with a teeka of blood from the head of the Balaitcha. This decided the fate of the sons of Ajeysi; one of whom died at Kailwarra, and the other, Sujunsi, who might have excited a civil war, was sent from the country.[3] He departed for the Dekhan, where his issue was destined to avenge some of the wrongs the parent country had sustained, and eventually to overturn the monarchy of Hindust'han; for Sujunsi was the ancestor of Sevaji, the founder of the Satarra throne, whose lineage[4] is given in the chronicles of Méwar.

Hamir succeeded in S. 1357 (A.D. 1301), and had sixty-four years granted to him to redeem his country from the ruins of the past century,

[1] One of the branches of the Chohan.

[2] This is an idiomatic phrase; Hamir could have had no beard.

[3] *Dés désá.*

[4] Ajeysi, Sujunsi, Duleepji, Seoji, B'horaji, Deoraj, Oogursén, Mahoolji, Khailooji, Junkoji, Suttooji, Sambaji, Sevaji (the founder of the Mahratta nation), Sambaji, Ramraja, usurpation of the Peishwas. The Satarra throne, but for the jealousies of Oodipoor, might on the imbecility of Ramraja have been replenished from Méwar. It was offered to Nathji, the grandfather of the present chief Sheodan Sing, presumptive heir to Cheetore. Two noble lines were reared from princes of Cheetore expelled on similar occasions; those of Sevaji and the Ghorkas of Nepal.

which period had elapsed since India ceased to own the paramount sway of her native princes. The day on which he assumed the ensigns of rule he gave, in the *teeka dowr*, an earnest of his future energy, which he signalised by a rapid inroad into the heart of the country of the predatory Balaitcha, and captured their stronghold Possalio. We may here explain the nature of this custom of a barbaric chivalry. The teeka dowr signifies the foray of inauguration, which obtained from time immemorial on such events, and is yet maintained where any semblance of hostility will allow its execution. On the morning of installation, having previously received the teeka of sovereignty, the prince at the head of his retainers makes a foray into the territory of anyone with whom he may have a feud, or with whom he may be indifferent as to exciting one; he captures a stronghold or plunders a town, and returns with the trophies. If amity should prevail with all around, which the prince cares not to disturb, they have still a mock representation of the custom. For many reigns after the Jeipoor princes united their fortunes to the throne of Dehli, their frontier town, Malpoora, was the object of the teeka dowr of the princes of Méwar.

"When Ajmal [1] went another road," as the bard figuratively describes the demise of Rana Ajeysi, "the son of Ursi unsheathed the sword, thence never stranger to his hand." Maldeo remained with the royal garrison at Cheetore, but Hamir desolated their plains, and left to his enemies only the fortified towns which could safely be inhabited. He commanded all who owned his sovereignty either to quit their abodes, and retire with their families to the shelter of the hills on the eastern and western frontiers, or share the fate of the public enemy. The roads were rendered impassable from his parties, who issued from their retreats in the Aravulli, the security of which baffled pursuit. This destructive policy of laying waste the resources of their own country, and from this asylum attacking their foes as opportunity offered, has obtained from the time of Mahmood of Gazni in the tenth, to Mahomed, the last who merited the name of Emperor of Dehli, in the eighteenth century.

Hamir made Kailwarra [2] his residence, which soon became the chief retreat of the emigrants from the plains. The situation was admirably chosen, being covered by several ranges, guarded by intricate defiles, and situated at the foot of a pass leading over the mountain into a still more inaccessible retreat (where Komulmér now stands),[3] well watered and wooded, with abundance of pastures and excellent indigenous fruits and roots. This tract, above fifty miles in breadth, is twelve hundred feet above the level of the plains and three thousand above the sea, with a considerable quantity of arable land, and free communication to obtain supplies by the passes of the western declivity from Marwar, Guzzerat, or the friendly Bhils of the west, to whom this house owes a large debt of gratitude. On various occasions, the communities of Oguna and Panora furnished the princes of Méwar with five thousand bowmen, supplied them with provisions, or guarded the safety of their families when they

[1] This is a poetical version of the name of Ajeysi; a liberty frequently taken by the bards for the sake of rhyme.

[2] The lake he excavated here, the '*Hamir-tallao*,' and the temple of the protecting goddess on its bank, still bear witness of his acts while confined to this retreat.

[3] See Plate, view of Komulmér.

had to oppose the foe in the field. The elevated plateau of the eastern frontier presented in its forests and dells many places of security; but Alla[1] traversed these in person, destroying as he went: neither did they possess the advantages of climate and natural productions arising from the elevation of the other. Such was the state of Méwar: its places of strength occupied by the foe, cultivation and peaceful objects neglected from the persevering hostility of Hamir, when a proposal of marriage came from the Hindu governor of Cheetore, which was immediately accepted, contrary to the wishes of the prince's advisers. Whether this was intended as a snare to entrap him, or merely as an insult, every danger was scouted by Hamir which gave a chance to the recovery of Cheetore. He desired that '*the cocoa-nut*[2] *might be retained,*' coolly remarking on the dangers pointed out, "My feet shall at least tread in the rocky steps in which my ancestors have moved. A Rajpoot should always be prepared for reverses; one day to abandon his abode covered with wounds, and the next to reascend with the *mor* (crown) on his head." It was stipulated that only five hundred horse should form his suite. As he approached Cheetore, the five sons of the Chohan advanced to meet him, but on the portal of the city no torun,[3] or nuptial emblem, was suspended. He, however, accepted the unsatisfactory reply to his remark on this indication of treachery, and ascended for the first time the ramp of Cheetore. He was received in the ancient halls of his ancestors by Rao Maldeo, his son Bunbeer, and other chiefs, *with folded hands.* The bride was brought forth, and presented by her father without any of the solemnities practised on such occasions; 'the knot of their garments tied and their hands united,' and thus they were left. The family priest recommended patience, and Hamir retired with his bride to the apartments allotted for them. Her kindness and vows of fidelity overcame his sadness upon learning that he had married a widow. She had been wedded to a chief of the Bhatti tribe, shortly afterwards slain, and when she was so young as not to recollect even his appearance. He ceased to lament the insult when she herself taught him how it might be avenged, and that it might even lead to the recovery of Cheetore. It is a privilege

[1] I have an inscription, and in *Sanscrit,* set up by an apostate chief or bard in his train, which I found in this tract.

[2] This is the symbol of an offer of marriage.

[3] The *torun* is the symbol of marriage. It consists of three wooden bars, forming an equilateral triangle; mystic in shape and number, and having the apex crowned with the effigies of a peacock, it is placed over the portal of the bride's abode. At Oodipoor, when the princes of Jusselmér, Bikanér, and Kishengurh simultaneously married the two daughters and granddaughter of the Rana, the toruns were suspended from the battlements of the tripolia, or *three-arched portal,* leading to the palace. The bridegroom on horseback, lance in hand, proceeds to break the torun (*torun toorna*), which is defended by the damsels of the bride, who from the parapet assail him with missiles of various kinds, especially with a crimson powder made from the flowers of the *palasa,* at the same time singing songs fitted to the occasion, replete with *double-entendres.* At length the torun is broken amidst the shouts of the retainers; when the fair defenders retire.

The similitude of these ceremonies in the north of Europe and in Asia, increases the list of common affinities, and indicates the violence of rude times to obtain the object of affection; and the lance, with which the Rajpoot chieftain breaks the torun, has the same emblematic import as the spear, which, at the marriage of the nobles in Sweden, was a necessary implement in the furniture of the marriage chamber. Vide *Northern Antiquities.*

possessed by the bridegroom to have one specific favour complied with as a part of the dower (*daeja*), and Hamir was instructed by his bride to ask for Jal, one of the civil officers of Cheetore, and of the Mehta tribe. With his wife so obtained, and the scribe whose talents remained for trial, he returned in a fortnight to Kailwarra. Kaitsi was the fruit of this marriage, on which occasion Maldeo made over all the hill tracts to Hamir. Kaitsi was a year old when one of the penates (Kaitr Pal) was found at fault, on which she wrote to her parents to invite her to Cheetore, that the infant might be placed before the shrine of the deity. Escorted by a party from Cheetore, with her child she entered its walls ; and instructed by the Mehta, she gained over the troops who were left, for the Rao had gone with his chief adherents against the Mérs of Madarai. Hamir was at hand. Notice that all was ready reached him at Bagore. Still he met opposition that had nearly defeated the scheme ; but having forced admission, his sword overcame every obstacle, and the oath of allegiance (*án*) was proclaimed from the palace of his fathers.

The Sonigurra on his return was met with 'a salute of arabas,' [1] and Maldeo himself carried the account of his loss to the Ghilji king Mahmood, who had succeeded Alla. The 'standard of the sun' once more shone refulgent from the walls of Cheetore, and was the signal for return to their ancient abodes from their hills and hiding-places to the adherents of Hamir. The valleys of Komulmér and the western highlands poured forth their 'streams of men,' while every chief of true Hindu blood rejoiced at the prospect of once more throwing off the barbarian yoke. So powerful was this feeling, and with such activity and skill did Hamir follow up this favour of fortune, that he marched to meet Mahmood, who was advancing to recover his lost possessions. The king unwisely directed his march by the eastern plateau, where numbers were rendered useless by the intricacies of the country. Of the three steppes which mark the physiognomy of this tract, from the first ascent from the plain of Méwar to the descent at the Chumbul, the king had encamped on the central, at Singolli, where he was attacked, defeated, and made prisoner by Hamir, who slew Hari Sing, brother of Bunbeer, in single combat. The king suffered a confinement of three months in Cheetore, nor was liberated till he had surrendered Ajmér, Rinthumbore, Nagore, and Sooe Sopoor, besides paying fifty lakhs of rupees and one hundred elephants. Hamir would exact no promise of cessation from further inroads, but contented himself with assuring him that from such he should be prepared to defend Cheetore, not within, but without the walls.[2]

Bunbeer, the son of Maldeo, offered to serve Hamir, who assigned the districts of Neemutch, Jeerun, Ruttunpoor, and the Kairar, to maintain the family of his wife in becoming dignity ; and as he gave the grant he remarked : "Eat, serve, and be faithful. You were once the servant of a Toork, but now of a Hindu of your own faith ; for I have but taken back my own, the rock moistened by the blood of my ancestors, the gift of the deity I adore, and who will maintain me in it ; nor shall I endanger it by the worship of a fair face, as did my predecessor." Bunbeer shortly after

[1] A kind of arquebuss.

[2] Ferishta does not mention this conquest over the Ghilji emperor ; but as Méwar recovered her wonted splendour in this reign, we cannot doubt the truth of the native annals.

carried Bhynsrore by assault, and this ancient possession guarding the Chumbul was again added to Méwar. The chieftains of Rajast'han rejoiced once more to see a Hindu take the lead, paid willing homage, and aided him with service when required.

Hamir was the sole Hindu prince of power now left in India : all the ancient dynasties were crushed, and the ancestors of the present princes of Marwar and Jeipoor brought their levies, paid homage, and obeyed the summons of the prince of Cheetore, as did the chiefs of Boondí, Gwalior, Chanderi, Raeseen, Sicri, Calpee, Aboo, etc.

Extensive as was the power of Méwar before the Tatar occupation of India, it could scarcely have surpassed the solidity of sway which she enjoyed during the two centuries following Hamir's recovery of the capital. From this event to the next invasion from the same Cimmerian abode, led by Baber, we have a succession of splendid names recorded in her annals, and though destined soon to be surrounded by new Mahomedan dynasties, in Malwa and Guzzerat as well as Dehli, yet successfully opposing them all. The distracted state of affairs when the races of Ghilji, Lodi, and Soor alternately struggled for and obtained the seat of dominion, Dehli, was favourable to Méwar, whose power was now so consolidated that she not only repelled armies from her territory, but carried war abroad, leaving tokens of victory at Nagore, in Saurashtra, and to the walls of Dehli. The subjects of Méwar must have enjoyed not only a long repose, but high prosperity during this period, judging from their magnificent public works, when a triumphal column must have cost the income of a kingdom to erect, and which ten years' produce of the crown-lands of Méwar could not at this time defray. Only one of the structures prior to the sack of Cheetore was left entire by Alla, and is yet existing, and this was raised by private and sectarian hands. It would be curious if the unitarian profession of the Jain creed was the means of preserving this ancient relic from Alla's wrath. The princes of this house were great patrons of the arts, and especially of architecture ; and it is a matter of surprise how their revenues, derived chiefly from the soil, could have enabled them to expend so much on these objects and at the same time maintain such armies as are enumerated. Such could be effected only by long prosperity, and a mild, paternal system of government ; for the subject had his monuments as well as the prince, the ruins of which may yet be discovered in the more inaccessible or deserted portions of Rajast'han. Hamir died full of years, leaving a name still honoured in Méwar, as one of the wisest and most gallant of her princes, and bequeathing a well-established and extensive power to his son.

KHAITSI succeeded in S. 1421 (A.D. 1365) to the power and to the character of his father. He captured Ajmér and Jehajpoor from Lilla Patan, and reannexed Mandelgurh, Dussore, and the whole of Chuppun (for the first time) to Méwar. He obtained a victory over the Dehli monarch Hemayoon at Bakrole ; but unhappily his life terminated in a family broil with his vassal, the Hara chief of Bumâóda, whose daughter he was about to espouse.

LAKHA RANA, by this assassination, mounted the throne in Cheetore in S. 1439 (A.D. 1373). His first act was the entire subjugation of the mountainous region of Mérwarra, and the destruction of its chief stronghold, Bérâtgurh, where he erected Bednore. But an event of much greater importance than settling his frontier, and which most powerfully tended to the prosperity of the country, was the discovery of the tin and silver mines of Jawura, in the tract wrested by Khaitsi from the Bhils of Chuppun. Lakha Rana has the merit of having first worked them, though their existence is superstitiously alluded to so early as the period of the founder. It is said the "seven metals (*heft-dhat*)" [1] were formerly abundant; but this appears figurative. We have no evidence for the gold; though silver, tin, copper, lead, and antimony, were yielded in abundance (the first two from the same matrix), but the tin that has been extracted for many years past yields but a small portion of silver.[2] Lakha Rana defeated the Sankla Rajpoots of Nagarchal,[3] at Ambér. He encountered the emperor Mahomed Shah Lodi, and on one occasion defeated a royal army at Bednore; but he carried the war to Gya, and in driving the barbarian from this sacred place was slain. Lakha is a name of celebrity, as a patron of the arts and benefactor of his country. He excavated many reservoirs and lakes, raised immense ramparts to dam their waters, besides erecting strongholds. The riches of the mines of Jawura were expended to rebuild the temples and palaces levelled by Alla. A portion of his own palace yet exists, in the same style of architecture as that, more ancient, of Rutna and the fair Pudmani; and a minster (*mundir*) dedicated to the creator (Brimha), an enormous and costly fabric, is yet entire. Being to "the one," and consequently containing no idol, it may thus have escaped the ruthless fury of the invaders.

Lakha had a numerous progeny, who have left their clans called after them, as the Loonawuts and Doolawuts, now the sturdy allodial proprietors of the Alpine regions bordering on Oguna, Panora, and other tracts in the Aravulli.[4] But a circumstance which set aside the rights of primogeniture, and transferred the crown of Cheetore from his eldest son, Chonda, to the younger, Mokul, had nearly carried it to another line. The consequences of making the elder branch a powerful vassal clan with claims to the throne, and which have been the chief cause of its subsequent prostration, we will reserve for another chapter.

[1] *Heft-dhat*, corresponding to the planets, each of which ruled a metal: hence *Mohar*, 'the sun,' for gold; *Chandra*, 'the moon,' for silver.

[2] They have long been abandoned, the miners are extinct, and the protecting deities of mines are unable to get even a flower placed on their shrines, though some have been reconsecrated by the Bhils, who have converted Latchmi into Seetlamata (Jung Lucina), whom the Bhil females invoke to pass them through danger.

[3] Jhoonjoonoo, Singhana, and Nurbana, formed the ancient Nagarchal territory.

[4] The Sarungdeote chief of Kanorh (on the borders of Chuppun), one of the sixteen lords of Méwar, is also a descendant of Lakha, as are some of the tribes of Sondwara, about Firfurah and the ravines of the Cali Sinde.

CHAPTER VII

Delicacy of the Rajpoots—The occasion of changing the rule of primogeniture in Méwar—Succession of the infant Mokulji, to the prejudice of Chonda, the rightful heir—Disorders in Méwar through the usurpations of the Rahtores—Chonda expels them from Cheetore and takes Mundore—Transactions between Méwar and Marwar—Reign of Mokulji—His assassination.

If devotion to the fair sex be admitted as a criterion of civilisation, the Rajpoot must rank high. His susceptibility is extreme, and fires at the slightest offence to female delicacy, which he never forgives. A satirical impromptu, involving the sacrifice of Rajpoot prejudices, dissolved the coalition of the Rahtores and Cutchwahas, and laid each prostrate before the Mahrattas, whom when united they had crushed: and a jest, apparently trivial, compromised the right of primogeniture to the throne of Cheetore, and proved more disastrous in its consequences than the arms either of Moguls or Mahrattas.

Lakha Rana was advanced in years, his sons and grandsons established in suitable domains, when "the cocoa-nut came" from Rinmull prince of Marwar, to affiance his daughter with Chonda, the heir of Méwar. When the embassy was announced, Chonda was absent, and the old chief was seated in his chair of state surrounded by his court. The messenger of Hymen was courteously received by Lakha, who observed that Chonda would soon return and take the gage; "for," added he, drawing his fingers over his moustaches, "I don't suppose you send such playthings to an old greybeard like me." This little sally was of course applauded and repeated; but Chonda, offended at delicacy being sacrificed to wit, declined accepting the symbol which his father had even in jest supposed might be intended for him: and as it could not be returned without gross insult to Rinmull, the old Rana, incensed at his son's obstinacy, agreed to accept it himself, provided Chonda would swear to renounce his birthright in the event of his having a son, and be to the child but the "first of his Rajpoots." He swore by Eklinga to fulfil his father's wishes.

Mokulji was the issue of this union, and had attained the age of five when the Rana resolved to signalise his finale, by a raid against the enemies of their faith, and to expel the 'barbarian' from the holy land of Gya. In ancient times this was by no means uncommon, and we have several instances in the annals of these states of princes resigning 'the purple' on the approach of old age, and by a life of austerity and devotion, pilgrimage and charity, seeking to make their peace with heaven 'for the sins inevitably committed by all who wield a sceptre.' But when war was made against their religion by the Tatar proselytes to Islam, the Sutledge and the Caggar were as the banks of the Jordan—Gya, their Jerusalem, their holy land; and if there destiny filled his cup, the Hindu chieftain was secure of beatitude,[1] exempted from the troubles of 'second birth'; [2] and borne from the scene of probation in celestial cars by the

[1] *Mookt.*

[2] This is a literal phrase, denoting further transmigration of the soul, which is always deemed a punishment. The soldier, who falls in battle in the faithful performance of his duty, is alone exempted, according to their martial mythology, from the pains of 'second birth.'

Apsaras,[1] was introduced at once into the 'realm of the sun.'[2] Ere, however, the Rana of Cheetore journeyed to this bourne, he was desirous to leave his throne unexposed to civil strife. The subject of succession had never been renewed; but discussing with Chonda his warlike pilgrimage to Gya, from which he might not return, he sounded him by asking what estates should be settled on Mokul. "The throne of Cheetore," was the honest reply; and to set suspicion at rest, he desired that the ceremony of installation should be performed previous to Lakha's departure. Chonda was the first to pay homage and swear obedience and fidelity to his future sovereign: reserving, as the recompense of his renunciation, the first place in the councils, and stipulating that in all grants to the vassals of the crown, his symbol (the lance) should be superadded to the autograph of the prince. In all grants the lance of Saloombra[3] still precedes the monogram of the Rana.[4]

The sacrifice of Chonda to offended delicacy and filial respect was great, for he had all the qualities requisite for command. Brave, frank, and skilful, he conducted all public affairs after his father's departure and death, to the benefit of the minor and the state. The queen-mother, however, who is admitted as the natural guardian of her infant's rights on all such occasions, felt umbrage and discontent at her loss of power; forgetting that, but for Chonda, she would never have been mother to the Rana of Méwar. She watched with a jealous eye all his proceedings; but it was only through the medium of suspicion she could accuse the integrity of Chonda, and she artfully asserted that, under colour of directing state affairs, he was exercising absolute sovereignty, and that if he did not assume the title of Rana, he would reduce it to an empty name. Chonda, knowing the purity of his own motives, made liberal allowance for maternal solicitude; but upbraiding the queen with the injustice of her suspicions, and advising a vigilant care to the rights of Sesodias, he retired to the court of Mandoo, then rising into notice, where he was received with the highest distinctions, and the district of Hallar was assigned to him by the king.

His departure was the signal for an influx of the kindred of the queen from Mundore. Her brother Joda (who afterwards gave his name to Jodpoor) was the first, and was soon followed by his father, Rao Rinmull, and numerous adherents, who deemed the arid region of Maroo-dés, and its rabri, or maize porridge, well exchanged for the fertile plains and wheaten bread of Méwar.

With his grandson on his knee, the old Rao "would sit on the throne of Bappa Rawul, on whose quitting him for play, the regal ensigns of Méwar waved over the head of Mundore." This was more than the Sesodia nurse[5] (an important personage in all Hindu governments) could bear, and bursting with indignation, she demanded of the queen if her kin was to defraud her own child of his inheritance. The honesty of the nurse was greater than her prudence. The creed of the Rajpoot is to "obtain

[1] The fair messengers of heaven. [2] *Sooraj Mandal.*

[3] The abode of the chief of the various clans of Chondawut.

[4] *Vide* p. 164.

[5] The *Dhaé.* The *Dhabhdes*, or 'foster-brothers,' often hold lands in perpetuity, and are employed in the most confidential places; on embassies, marriages, etc.

sovereignty," regarding the means as secondary, and this avowal of her suspicions only hastened their designs. The queen soon found herself without remedy, and a remonstrance to her father produced a hint which threatened the existence of her offspring. Her fears were soon after augmented by the assassination of Ragoodeva, the second brother of Chonda, whose estates were Kailwarra and Kowaria. To the former place, where he resided aloof from the court, Rao Rinmull sent a dress of honour, which etiquette requiring him to put on when presented, the prince was assassinated in the act. Ragoodeva was so much beloved for his virtues, courage, and manly beauty, that his murder became martyrdom, and obtained for him divine honours, and a place amongst the *Di Patres* (*Pitri-déva*) of Méwar. His image is on every hearth, and is daily worshipped with the Penates. Twice in the year his altars receive public homage from every Sesodia, from the Rana to the serf.[1]

In this extremity the queen-mother turned her thoughts to Chonda, and it was not difficult to apprise him of the danger which menaced the race, every place of trust being held by her kinsmen, and the principal post of Cheetore by a Bhatti Rajpoot of Jessulmér. Chonda, though at a distance, was not inattentive to the proverbially dangerous situation of a minor amongst the Rajpoots. At his departure he was accompanied by two hundred Ahaireas or huntsmen, whose ancestors had served the princes of Cheetore from ancient times. These had left their families behind, a visit to whom was the pretext for their introduction to the fort. They were instructed to get into the service of the keepers of the gates, and, being considered more attached to the place than to the family, their object was effected. The queen-mother was counselled to cause the young prince to descend daily with a numerous retinue to give feasts to the surrounding villages, and gradually to increase the distance, but not to fail on the "festival of lamps"[2] to hold the feast (*gote*) at Gosoonda.[3]

These injunctions were carefully attended to. The day arrived, the feast was held at Gosoonda; but the night was closing in, and no Chonda appeared. With heavy hearts the nurse, the Purohit,[4] and those in the secret, moved homeward, and had reached the eminence called Chitoree, when forty horsemen passed them at the gallop, and at their head Chonda in disguise, who by a secret sign paid homage as he passed to his younger brother and sovereign. Chonda and his band had reached the *Rampol*,[5]

[1] On the 8th day of the *dusserah*, or 'military festival,' when the levies are mustered at the *Chaogán*, or 'Champ de Mars,' and on the 10th of Cheit, his altars are purified, and his image is washed and placed thereon. Women pray for the safety of their children; husbands, that their wives may be fruitful. Previously to this, a son of Bappa Rawul was worshipped; but after the enshrinement of Ragoodeva, the adoration of Kulés-pootra was gradually abolished. Nor is this custom confined to Méwar: there is a deified *Pootra* in every Rajpoot family—one who has met a violent death. Besides Eklinga, the descendants of Bappa have adopted numerous household divinities: the destinies of life and death, Byen-mata the goddess of the Chawuras, Nagnaitcha the serpent divinity of the Rahtores, and Khétra-pal, or 'fosterer of the field,' have with many others obtained a place on the Sesodia altars. This festival may not unaptly be compared to that of Adonis amongst the Greeks, for the *Pootra* is worshipped chiefly by women.

[2] The *Dewalli*, from *dewa*, 'a lamp.' This festival is in honour of Latchmi, goddess of wealth.

[3] Seven miles south of Cheetore, on the road to Malwa.

[4] The family priest and instructor of youth.

[5] *Ram-pol*, 'the gate of Ram.'

or upper gate, unchecked. Here, when challenged, they said they were neighbouring chieftains, who, hearing of the feast at Gosoonda, had the honour to escort the prince home. The story obtained credit; but the main body, of which this was but the advance, presently coming up, the treachery was apparent. Chonda unsheathed his sword, and at his well-known shout the hunters were speedily in action. The Bhatti chief, taken by surprise, and unable to reach Chonda, launched his dagger at and wounded him, but was himself slain; the guards at the gates were cut to pieces, and the Rahtores hunted out and killed without mercy.

The end of Rao Rinmull was more ludicrous than tragical. Smitten with the charms of a Sesodia handmaid of the queen, who was compelled to his embrace, the old chief was in her arms, intoxicated with love, wine, and opium, and heard nothing of the tumult without. A woman's wit and revenge combined to make his end afford some compensation for her loss of honour. Gently rising, she bound him to his bed with his own Marwari turban:[1] nor did this disturb him, and the messengers of fate had entered ere the opiate allowed his eyes to open to a sense of his danger. Enraged, he in vain endeavoured to extricate himself; and by some tortuosity of movement he got upon his legs, his wallet at his back like a shell or shield of defence. With no arms but a brass vessel of ablution, he levelled to the earth several of his assailants, when a ball from a matchlock extended him on the floor of the palace. His son Joda was in the lower town, and was indebted to the fleetness of his steed for escaping the fate of his father and kindred, whose bodies strewed the *terre-pleine* of Cheetore, the merited reward of their usurpation and treachery.

But Chonda's revenge was not yet satisfied. He pursued Rao Joda, who, unable to oppose him, took refuge with Hurba Sankla, leaving Mundore to its fate. This city Chonda entered by surprise, and holding it till his sons Kontotji and Munjaji arrived with reinforcements, the Rahtore treachery was repaid by their keeping possession of the capital during twelve years. We might here leave the future founder of Jodpoor, had not this feud led to the junction of the rich province of Godwar to Méwar, held for three centuries and again lost by treachery. It may yet involve a struggle between the Sesodias and Rahtores.

'Sweet are the uses of adversity.' To Joda it was the first step in the ladder of his eventual elevation. A century and a half had scarcely elapsed since a colony, the wreck of Kanouj, found an asylum, and at length a kingdom, taking possession of one capital and founding another, abandoning Mundore and erecting Jodpoor. But even Joda could never have hoped that his issue would have extended their sway from the valley of the Indus to within one hundred miles of the Jumna, and from the desert bordering on the Sutledge to the Aravulli mountains: that one hundred thousand swords should at once be in the hands of Rahtores, 'the sons of one father (*ék Bap ca Bétan*).'

If we slightly encroach upon the annals of Marwar, it is owing to its history and that of Méwar being here so interwoven, and the incidents these events gave birth so illustrative of the national character of each, that it is, perhaps, more expedient to advert to the period when Joda was shut out from Mundore, and the means by which he regained that city, previous to relating the events of the reign of Mokul.

[1] Often sixty cubits in length.

Hurba Sankla, at once a soldier and a devotee, was one of those Rajpoot cavaliers '*sans peur et sans reproche*,' whose life of celibacy and perilous adventure was mingled with the austere devotion of an ascetic; by turns aiding with his lance the cause which he deemed worthy, or exercising an unbounded hospitality towards the stranger. This generosity had much reduced his resources when Joda sought his protection. It was the eve of the *Sudda Birt*, one of those hospitable rites which, in former times, characterised Rajwarra. This 'perpetual charity' supplies food to the stranger and traveller, and is distributed not only by individual chiefs and by the government, but by subscriptions of communities. Even in Méwar, in her present impoverished condition, the offerings to the gods in support of their shrines and the establishment of the *Sudda Birt* were simultaneous. Hospitality is a virtue pronounced to belong more peculiarly to a semi-barbarous condition. Alas! for refinement and ultra-civilisation, strangers to the happiness enjoyed by Hurba Sankla. Joda, with one hundred and twenty followers, came to solicit the 'stranger's fare': but unfortunately it was too late, the *Sudda Birt* had been distributed. In this exigence, Hurba recollected that there was a wood called *mujd*,[1] used in dyeing, which among other things in the desert regions is resorted to in scarcity. A portion of this was bruised, and boiled with some flour, sugar, and spices, making altogether a palatable pottage; and with a promise of better fare on the morrow, it was set before the young Rao and his followers, who, after making a good repast, soon forgot Cheetore in sleep. On waking, each stared at his fellow, for their mustachios were dyed with their evening's meal; but the old chief, who was not disposed to reveal his expedient, made it minister to their hopes by giving it a miraculous character, and saying "that as the grey of age was thus metamorphosed into the tint of morn [2] and hope, so would their fortunes become young, and Mundore again be theirs."

Elevated by this prospect, they enlisted Hurba on their side. He accompanied them to the chieftain of Méwoh, "whose stables contained one hundred chosen steeds." Pabooji, a third independent of the same stamp, with his 'coal-black steed,' was gained to the cause, and Joda soon found himself strong enough to attempt the recovery of his capital. The sons of Chonda were taken by surprise: but despising the numbers of the foe, and ignorant who were their auxiliaries, they descended sword in hand to meet the assailants. The elder [3] son of Chonda with many adherents was slain; and the younger, deserted by the subjects of Mundore, trusted to the swiftness of his horse for escape; but being pursued, was overtaken and killed on the boundary of Godwar. Thus Joda, in his turn, was revenged, but the "feud was not balanced." Two sons of Cheetore had fallen for one chief of Mundore. But wisely reflecting on the original aggression, and the superior power of Méwar, as well as his being indebted for his present success to foreign aid, Joda sued for peace, and offered as the *moondkati*, or 'price of blood,' and "to quench the feud," that the

[1] The wood of Solomon's temple is called *al-mug*; the prefix *al* is merely the article. This is the wood also mentioned in the annals of Guzzerat, of which the temple to 'Adnath' was constructed. It is said to be indestructible even by fire. It has been surmised that the fleets of Tyre frequented the Indian coast: could they thence have carried the *Al-Mujd* for the temple of Solomon?

[2] This wood has a brownish red tint.

[3] This is related with some variation in other annals of the period.

spot where Manja fell should be the future barrier of the two states. The entire province of Godwar was comprehended in the cession, which for three centuries withstood every contention, till the internal dissensions of the last half century, which grew out of the cause by which it was obtained, the change of succession in Méwar severed this most valuable acquisition.[1]

Who would imagine, after such deadly feuds between these rival states, that in the very next succession these hostile frays were not only buried in oblivion, but that the prince of Marwar abjured "his turban and his bed" till he had revenged the assassination of the prince of Cheetore, and restored his infant heir to his rights? The annals of these states afford numerous instances of the same hasty, overbearing temperament governing all; easily moved to strife, impatient of revenge, and steadfast in its gratification. But this satisfied, resentment subsides. A daughter of the offender given to wife banishes its remembrance, and when the bard joins the lately rival names in the couplet, each will complacently curl his mustachio over his lip as he hears his "renown expand like the lotus," and thus "the feud is extinguished."

Thus have they gone on from time immemorial, and will continue, till what we may fear to contemplate. They have now neither friend nor foe but the British. The Tatar invader sleeps in his tomb, and the Mahratta depredator is muzzled and enchained. To return.

MOKUL, who obtained the throne by Chonda's surrender of his birthright, was not destined long to enjoy the distinction, though he evinced qualities worthy of heading the Sesodias. He ascended the throne in S. 1454 (A.D. 1398), at an important era in the history of India; when Timoor, who had already established the race of Chagitai in the kingdoms of Central Asia, and laid prostrate the throne of Byzantium, turned his arms towards India. But it was not a field for his ambition; and the event is not even noticed in the annals of Méwar: a proof that it did not affect their repose. But they record an attempted invasion by the king of Dehli, which is erroneously stated to have been by Feroz Shah. A grandson of this prince had indeed been set up, and compelled to fly from the arms of Timoor, and as the direction of his flight was Guzzerat, it is not unlikely that the recorded attempt to penetrate by the passes of Méwar may have been his. Be this as it may, the Rana Mokul anticipated and met him beyond the passes of the Aravulli, in the field of Raepoor, and compelled him to abandon his enterprise. Pursuing his success, he took possession of Sambur and its salt lakes, and otherwise extended and strengthened his territory, which the distracted state of the empire consequent to Timoor's invasion rendered a matter of little difficulty. Mokul finished the palace commenced by Lakha, now a mass of ruins; and erected the shrine of Chatoor-bhooja, 'the four-armed deity,' in the western hills.

Besides three sons, Rana Mokul had a daughter, celebrated for her

[1] There is little hope, while British power acts as high constable and keeper of the peace in Rajwarra, of this being recovered: nor, were it otherwise, would it be desirable to see it become an object of contention between these states. Marwar has attained much grandeur since the time of Joda, and her resources are more unbroken than those of Méwar; who, if she could redeem, could not, from its exposed position, maintain the province against the brave Rahtore.

beauty, called Lal Bae, or 'the ruby.' She was betrothed to the Keechie chieftain of Gagrown, who at the *Hatléva* [1] demanded the pledge of succour on foreign invasion. Dheruj, the son of the Keechie, had come to solicit the stipulated aid against Hoshung of Malwa, who had invested their capital. The Rana's headquarters were then at Madaria, and he was employed in quelling a revolt of the mountaineers, when Dheruj arrived and obtained the necessary aid. Madaria was destined to be the scene of the termination of Mokul's career: he was assassinated by his uncles, the natural brothers of his father, from an unintentional offence, which tradition has handed down in all its details.

Chacha and Maira were the natural sons of Kaitsi Rana (the predecessor of Lakha); their mother a fair handmaid of low descent, generally allowed to be a carpenter's daughter. 'The fifth sons of Méwar' (as the natural children are figuratively termed) possess no rank, and though treated with kindness, and entrusted with confidential employments, the sons of the chiefs of the second class take precedence of them, and 'sit higher on the carpet.' These brothers had the charge of seven hundred horse in the train of Rana Mokul at Madaria. Some chiefs at enmity with them, conceiving that they had overstepped their privileges, wished to see them humiliated. Chance procured them the opportunity: which, however, cost their prince his life. Seated in a grove with his chiefs around him, he inquired the name of a particular tree. The Chohan chief, feigning ignorance, whispered him to ask either of the brothers; and not perceiving their scope, he artlessly did so. "Uncle, what tree is this?" The sarcasm thus prompted, they considered as reflecting on their birth (being sons of the carpenter's daughter), and the same day, while Mokul was at his devotions, and in the act of counting his rosary, one blow severed his arm from his body, while another stretched him lifeless. The brothers, quickly mounting their steeds, had the audacity to hope to surprise Cheetore, but the gates were closed upon them.

Though the murder of Mokul is related to have no other cause than the sarcasm alluded to, the precautions taken by the young prince Koombho, his successor, would induce a belief that this was but the opening of a deep-laid conspiracy. The traitors returned to the stronghold near Madaria, and Koombho trusted to the friendship and good feeling of the prince of Marwar in this emergency. His confidence was well repaid. The prince put his son at the head of a force, and the retreat of the assassins being near his own frontier, they were encountered and dislodged. From Madaria they fled to Paye, where they strengthened a fortress in the mountains named Ratakote; a lofty peak of the compound chain which encircles Oodipoor, visible from the surrounding country, as are the remains of this stronghold of the assassins. It would appear that their lives were dissolute, for they had carried off the virgin daughter of a Chohan, which led to their eventual detection and punishment. Her father, Sooja, had traced the route of the ravishers, and, mixing with the workmen, found that the approaches to the place of their concealment were capable of being scaled. He was about to lay his complaint before his prince, when he met the cavalcade of Koombho and the Rahtore. The distressed father "covering his face," disclosed the story of his own and daughter's dishonour. They encamped till night at Dailwara, when, led by the Chundanah, they issued

[1] The ceremony of joining hands.

forth to surprise the authors of so many evils. Arrived at the base of the rock, where the parapet was yet low, they commenced the escalade, aided by the thick foliage. The path was steep and rugged, and in the darkness of the night each had grasped his neighbour's skirt for security. Animated by a just revenge, the Chohan (Sooja) led the way, when on reaching a ledge of the rock the glaring eye-balls of a tigress flashed upon him. Undismayed, he squeezed the hand of the Rahtore prince who followed him, and who on perceiving the object of terror instantly buried his poignard in her heart. This omen was superb. They soon reached the summit. Some had ascended the parapet; others were scrambling over, when the minstrel slipping, fell, and his drum, which was to have accompanied his voice in singing the conquest, awoke by its crash the daughter of Chacha. Her father quieted her fears by saying it was only "the thunder and the rains of Bhadoon": to fear God only and go to sleep, for their enemies were safe at Kailwa. At this moment the Rao and his party rushed in. Chacha and Maira had no time to avoid their fate. Chacha was cleft in two by the Chundanah, while the Rahtore prince laid Maira at his feet, and the spoils of Ratakote were divided among the assailants.

CHAPTER VIII

Succession of Koombho—He defeats and takes prisoner Mahmood of Malwa—Splendour of Koombho's reign—Assassinated by his son—The murderer dethroned by Raemul—Méwar invaded by the imperial forces—Raemul's successes—Feuds of the family—Death of Raemul.

KOOMBHO succeeded his father in S. 1475 (A.D. 1419); nor did any symptom of dissatisfaction appear to usher in his reign, which was one of great success amidst no common difficulties. The bardic historians [1] do as much honour to the Marwar prince, who had made common cause with their sovereign in revenging the death of his father, as if it had involved the security of his crown; but this was a precautionary measure of the prince, who was induced thus to act from several motives, and, above all, in accordance with usage, which stigmatises the refusal of aid when demanded: besides "Koombho was the nephew of Marwar."

It has rarely occurred in any country to have possessed successively so many energetic princes as ruled Méwar through several centuries. She was now in the middle path of her glory, and enjoying the legitimate triumph of seeing the foes of her religion captives on the rock of her power. A century had elapsed since the bigot Alla had wreaked his vengeance on the different monuments of art. Cheetore had recovered the sack, and new defenders had sprung up in the place of those who had fallen in their 'saffron robes,' a sacrifice for her preservation. All that was wanting to augment her resources against the storms which were collecting on the brows of Caucasus and the shores of the Oxus, and were destined to burst on the head of his grandson Sanga, was effected by Koombho; who with Hamir's energy, Lakha's taste for the arts, and a genius comprehensive

[1] The *Raj Ruttuna*, by Rinchor B'hut, says: "The Mundore Rao was purdhan, or premier, to Mokul, and conquered Nowah and Deedwana for Méwar."

as either and more fortunate, succeeded in all his undertakings, and once more raised the ' crimson banner ' of Méwar upon the banks of the Caggar, the scene of Samarsi's defeat. Let us contrast the patriarchal Hindu governments of this period with the despotism of the Tatar invader.

From the age of Shabudín, the conqueror of India, and his contemporary Samarsi, to the time we have now reached, two entire dynasties, numbering twenty-four emperors and one empress, through assassination, rebellion, and dethronement, had followed in rapid succession, yielding a result of only nine years to a reign. Of Méwar, though several fell in defending their altars at home or their religion abroad, eleven princes suffice to fill the same period.

It was towards the close of the Ghilji dynasty that the satraps of Dehli shook off its authority and established subordinate kingdoms: Beejipoor and Golconda in the Dekhan; Malwa, Guzzerat, Joinpoor in the east; and even Calpee had its king. Malwa and Guzzerat had attained considerable power when Koombho ascended the throne. In the midst of his prosperity these two states formed a league against him, and in S. 1496 (A.D. 1440) both kings, at the head of powerful armies, invaded Méwar. Koombho met them on the plains of Malwa bordering on his own state, and at the head of one hundred thousand horse and foot and fourteen hundred elephants, gave them an entire defeat, carrying captive to Cheetore Mahmood, the Ghilji sovereign of Malwa.

Abul Fuzil relates this victory, and dilates on Koombho's greatness of soul in setting his enemy at liberty, not only without ransom but with gifts. Such is the character of the Hindu: a mixture of arrogance, political blindness, pride, and generosity. To spare a prostrate foe is the creed of the Hindu cavalier, and he carries all such maxims to excess. The annals, however, state that Mahmood was confined six months in Cheetore; and that the trophies of conquest were retained we have evidence from Baber, who mentions receiving from the son of his opponent, Sanga, the crown of the Malwa king. But there is a more durable monument than this written record of victory: the triumphal pillar in Cheetore, whose inscriptions detail the event, "when, shaking the earth, the lords of Goojur-khund and Malwa, with armies overwhelming as the ocean, invaded Médpat." Eleven years after this event Koombho laid the foundations of this column, which was completed in ten more: a period apparently too short to place "this ringlet on the brow of Cheetore, which makes her look down upon Méru with derision." We will leave it, with the aspiration that it may long continue a monument of the fortune of its founders.

It would appear that the Malwa king afterwards united his arms with Koombho, as, in a victory gained over the imperial forces at Jhoonjoonoo, when "he planted his standard in Hissar," the Malwa troops were combined with those of Méwar. The imperial power had at this period greatly declined: the Khootba was read in the mosques in the name of Timoor, and the Malwa king had defeated, single-handed, the last Ghorian sultan of Dehli.

Of eighty-four fortresses for the defence of Méwar, thirty-two were erected by Koombho. Inferior only to Cheetore is that stupendous work called after him Koombhomér,[1] ' the hill of Khoombho,' from its natural position, and the works he raised, impregnable to a native army. These

[1] Pronounced *Komulmér*.

works were on the site of a more ancient fortress, of which the mountaineers long held possession. Tradition ascribes it to Sumprit Raja, a Jain prince in the second century, and a descendant of Chandragoopta; and the ancient Jain temples appear to confirm the tradition. When Koombho captured Nagore he brought away the gates, with the statue of the god Hanuman, who gives his name to the gate which he still guards. He also erected a citadel on a peak of Aboo, within the fortress of the ancient Pramara, where he often resided. Its magazine and alarm-tower still bear Koombho's name; and in a rude temple the bronze effigies of Koombho and his father still receive divine honours. Centuries have passed since the princes of Méwar had influence here, but the incident marks the vivid remembrance of their condition. He fortified the passes between the western frontier and Aboo, and erected the fort Vasunti near the present Sirohi, and that of Macheen, to defend the Shero Nalla and Deogurh against the *Mairs* of Aravulli. He re-established Ahore and other smaller forts to overawe the Bhoomia [1] Bhil of Jarole and Panora, and defined the boundaries of Marwar and Méwar.

Besides these monuments of his genius, two consecrated to religion have survived: that of "Koombho Sham," on Aboo, which, though worthy to attract notice elsewhere, is here eclipsed by a crowd of more interesting objects; the other, one of the largest edifices existing, cost upwards of a million sterling, towards which Koombho contributed eighty thousand pounds. It is erected in the Sadri pass leading from the western descent of the highlands of Méwar, and is dedicated to Rishub-deva.[2] Its secluded position has preserved it from bigoted fury, and its only visitants now are the wild beasts who take shelter in its sanctuary. Koombho Rana was also a poet: but in a far more elevated strain than the troubadour princes, his neighbours, who contented themselves with rehearsing their own prowess or celebrating their lady's beauty. He composed a *tika*, or appendix to the "Divine Melodies," [3] in praise of Crishna. We can pass no judgment on these inspirations of the royal bard, as we are ignorant whether any are preserved in the records of the house: a point his descendant, who is deeply skilled in such lore, might probably answer.

Koombho married a daughter of the Rahtore of Mairta, the first of the clans of Marwar. Meera Bae was the most celebrated princess of her time for beauty and romantic piety. Her compositions were numerous, though better known to the worshippers of the Hindu Apollo than to the ribald bards. Some of her odes and hymns to the deity are preserved and

[1] A powerful phrase, indicating 'possessor of the soil.'

[2] The Rana's minister, of the Jain faith, and of the tribe Porwar (one of the *twelve and a half* divisions), laid the foundation of this temple in A.D. 1438. It was completed by subscription. It consists of three stories, and is supported by numerous columns of granite, upwards of forty feet in height. The interior is inlaid with mosaics of cornelian and agate. The statues of the Jain saints are in its subterranean vaults. We could not expect much elegance at a period when the arts had long been declining, but it would doubtless afford a fair specimen of them, and enable us to trace their gradual descent in the scale of refinement. This temple is an additional proof of the early existence of the art of inlaying. That I did not see it is now to me one of the many vain regrets which I might have avoided.

[3] *Gita Govinda*.

admired. Whether she imbibed her poetic piety from her husband, or whether from her he caught the sympathy which produced the "sequel to the songs of Govinda," we cannot determine. Her history is a romance, and her excess of devotion at every shrine of the favourite deity with the fair of Hind, from the Yamuna to "the world's end,"[1] gave rise to many tales of scandal. Koombho mixed gallantry with his warlike pursuits. He carried off the daughter of the chief of Jhalawar, who had been betrothed to the prince of Mundore: this renewed the old feud, and the Rahtore made many attempts to redeem his affianced bride. His humiliation was insupportable, when through the purified atmosphere of the periodical rains "the towers of Khoombhomér became visible from the castle of Mundore, and the light radiated from the chamber of the fair through the gloom of a night in Bhadoon,[2] to the hall where he brooded o'er his sorrows." It was surmised that this night-lamp was an understood signal of the Jhalani, who pined at the decree which ambition had dictated to her father, in consigning her to the more powerful rival of her affianced lord. The Rahtore exhausted every resource to gain access to the fair, and had once nearly succeeded in a surprise by escalade, having cut his way in the night through the forest in the western and least guarded acclivity: but, as the bard equivocally remarks, "though he cut his way through the *jhal* (brushwood), he could not reach the *Jhalani*."

Koombho had occupied the throne half a century; he had triumphed over the enemies of his race, fortified his country with strongholds, embellished it with temples, and with the superstructure of her fame had laid the foundation of his own—when, the year which should have been a jubilee was disgraced by the foulest blot in the annals; and his life, which nature was about to close, terminated by the poignard of an assassin—that assassin, his son!

This happened in S. 1525 (A.D. 1469). Ooda was the name of the parricide, whose unnatural ambition, and impatience to enjoy a short lustre of sovereignty, bereft of life the author of his existence. But such is the detestation which marks this unusual crime that, like that of the Venetian traitor, his name is left a blank in the annals, nor is Ooda known but by the epithet *Hatiaro*, 'the murderer.' Shunned by his kin, and compelled to look abroad for succour to maintain him on the throne polluted by his crime, Méwar in five years of illegitimate rule lost half the consequence which had cost so many to acquire. He made the Deora prince independent in Aboo, and bestowed Sambhur, Ajmér, and adjacent districts on the prince of Jodpoor[3] as the price of his friendship. But, a prey to remorse, he felt that he could neither claim regard from, nor place any dependence upon, these princes, though he bribed them with provinces. He humbled himself before the king of Dehli, offering him a daughter in marriage to obtain his sanction to his authority; "but heaven manifested its vengeance to prevent this additional iniquity, and preserve the house of Bappa Rawul from dishonour." He had scarcely quitted the divan (*dewankhaneh*), on taking leave of the king, when a flash of lightning struck the *Hatiaro* to the earth, whence he never arose. The bards pass over this period cursorily, as one of their race was the instrument of Ooda's crime.

[1] *Juggut Koont*, or Dwarica. [2] The darkest of the rainy months.

[3] Joda laid the foundation of his new capital in S. 1515, ten years anterior to the event we are recording.

There has always been a jealousy between the *Mangtas*, as they term all classes 'who extend the palm,' whether Brahmins, Yatis, Charuns, or B'hats; but since Hamir, the Charun influence had far eclipsed the rest. A Brahmin astrologer predicted Koombho's death through a Charun, and as the class had given other cause of offence, Koombho banished the fraternity his dominions, resuming all their lands: a strong measure in those days, and which few would have had nerve to attempt or firmness to execute. The heir-apparent, Raemul, who was exiled to Eidur for what his father deemed an impertinent curiosity,[1] had attached one of these bards to his suite, whose ingenuity got the edict set aside, and his race restored to their lands and the prince's favour. Had they taken off the Brahmin's head, they might have falsified the prediction which unhappily was too soon fulfilled.[2]

RAEMUL succeeded in S. 1530 (A.D. 1474) by his own valour to the seat of Koombho. He had fought and defeated the usurper, who on this occasion fled to the king of Dehli and offered him a daughter of Méwar. After his death in the manner described, the Dehli monarch, with Sehesmul and Soorajmul, sons of the parricide, invaded Méwar, encamping at Siarh, now Nat'hdwara. The chiefs were faithful to their legitimate prince, Raemul, and aided by his allies of Aboo and Girnar, at the head of fifty-eight thousand horse and eleven thousand foot, he gave battle to the pretender and his imperial ally at Ghassa. The conflict was ferocious. "The streams ran blood," for the sons of the usurper were brave as lions, but the king was so completely routed that he never again entered Méwar.

Raemul bestowed one daughter on Soorji (Yadu), the chief of Girnar; and another on the Deora, Jeymul of Sirohi, confirming his title to Aboo as her dower. He sustained the warlike reputation of his predecessors, and carried on interminable strife with Gheas-o-din of Malwa, whom he defeated in several pitched battles, to the success of which the valour of his nephews, whom he had pardoned, mainly contributed. In the last of these encounters the Ghilji king sued for peace, renouncing the pretensions he had formerly urged. The dynasty of Lodi next enjoyed the imperial bauble, and with it Méwar had to contest her northern boundary.

[1] He had observed that his father, ever since the victory over the king at Jhoonjoonu, before he took a seat, thrice waved his sword in circles over his head, pronouncing at the same time some incantation. Inquiry into the meaning of this was the cause of his banishment.

[2] During the rains of 1820, when the author was residing at Oodipoor, the Rana fell ill; his complaint was an intermittent (which for several years returned with the monsoon), at the same time that he was jaundiced with bile. An intriguing Brahmin, who managed the estates of the Rana's eldest sister, held also the twofold office of physician and astrologer to the Rana. He had predicted that year as one of evil in his horoscope, and was about to verify the prophecy, since, instead of the active medicines requisite, he was administering the *Héft d'hat*, or 'seven metals,' compounded. Having a most sincere regard for the Rana's welfare, the author seized the opportunity of a full court being assembled on the distribution of swords and coco-nuts preparatory to the military festival, to ask a personal favour. The Rana, smiling, said that it was granted, when he was entreated to leave off the poison he was taking. He did so; the amendment was soon visible, and, aided by the medicines of Dr. Duncan, which he readily took, his complaint was speedily cured. The 'man of fate and physic' lost half his estates, which he had obtained through intrigue. He was succeeded by Umra the bard, who is not likely to ransack the pharmacopœia for such poisonous ingredients; his ordinary prescription being the 'amrit.'

Raemul had three sons, celebrated in the annals of Rajast'han. Sanga, the competitor of Baber, Pirthi Raj, the Rolando of his age, and Jeimal. Unhappily for the country and their father's repose, fraternal affection was discarded for deadly hate, and their feuds and dissensions were a source of constant alarm. Had discord not disunited them, the reign of Raemul would have equalled any of his predecessors. As it was, it presented a striking contrast to them: his two elder sons banished; the first, Sanga, self-exiled from perpetual fear of his life, and Pirthi Raj, the second, from his turbulence; while the youngest, Jeimal, was slain through his intemperance. A sketch of these feuds will present a good picture of the Rajpoot character, and their mode of life when their arms were not required against their country's foes.

Sanga [1] and Pirthi Raj were the offspring of the Jhali queen; Jeimal was by another mother. What moral influence the name he bore had on Pirthi Raj we can surmise only from his actions, which would stand comparison with those of his prototype, the Chohan of Dehli, and are yet the delight of the Sesodia. When they assemble at the feast after a day's sport, or in a sultry evening spread the carpet on the terrace to inhale the leaf or take a cup of kusoomba, a tale of Pirthi Raj recited by the bard is the highest treat they can enjoy. Sanga, the heir-apparent, was a contrast to his brother. Equally brave, his courage was tempered by reflection; while Pirthi Raj burned with a perpetual thirst for action, and often observed "that fate must have intended him to rule Méwar." The three brothers, with their uncle, Soorajmul, were one day discussing these topics, when Sanga observed that, though heir to 'the ten thousand towns' of Méwar, he would waive his claims, and trust them, as did the Roman brothers, to the omen which should be given by the priestess of Charuni Devi at Nahra Mugro,[2] the 'Tiger's Mount.' They repaired to her abode. Pirthi Raj and Jeimal entered first, and seated themselves on a pallet: Sanga followed and took possession of the panther hide of the prophetess; his uncle, Soorajmul, with one knee resting thereon. Scarcely had Pirthi Raj disclosed their errand, when the sybil pointed to the panther-hide [3] as the decisive omen of sovereignty to Sanga, with a portion to his uncle. They received the decree as did the twins of Rome. Pirthi Raj drew his sword and would have falsified the omen, had not Soorajmul stepped in and received the blow destined for Sanga, while the prophetess fled from their fury. Soorajmul and Pirthi Raj were exhausted with wounds, and Sanga fled with five sword-cuts and an arrow in his eye, which destroyed the sight for ever. He made for the sanctuary of Chutturb'hooja, and passing Sevantee, took refuge with Beeda (Oodawut), who was accoutred for a journey, his steed standing by him. Scarcely had he assisted the wounded heir of Méwar to alight when Jeimal galloped up in pursuit. The Rahtore guarded the sanctuary, and gave up his life in defence of his guest, who meanwhile escaped.

Pirthi Raj recovered from his wounds; and Sanga, aware of his implacable enmity, had recourse to many expedients to avoid discovery.

[1] His name classically is *Singram Sing*, 'the lion of war.'

[2] About ten miles east of Oodipoor.

[3] *Singasun* is the ancient term for the Hindu throne, signifying 'the lion-seat.' Charuns, bards, who are all *Maharajas*, 'great princes,' by courtesy, have their seats of the hide of the lion, tiger, panther, or black antelope.

He, who at a future period leagued a hundred thousand men against the descendant of Timoor, was compelled to associate with goat-herds, expelled the peasant's abode as too stupid to tend his cattle, and, precisely like our Alfred the Great, having in charge some cakes of flour, was reproached with being more desirous of eating than tending them. A few faithful Rajpoots found him in this state, and, providing him with arms and a horse, they took service with Rao Kurimchund, Pramar, chief of Sreenugger,[1] and with him "ran the country." After one of these raids, Sanga one day alighted under a banian tree, and placing his dagger under his head, reposed, while two of his faithful Rajpoots, whose names are preserved,[2] prepared his repast, their steeds grazing by them. A ray of the sun penetrating the foliage, fell on Sanga's face, and discovered a snake, which, feeling the warmth, had uncoiled itself and was rearing its crest over the head of the exile: a bird of omen[3] had perched itself on the crested serpent, and was chattering aloud. A goat-herd named Maroo, "versed in the language of birds," passed at the moment Sanga awoke. The prince repelled the proffered homage of the goat-herd, who, however, had intimated to the Pramara chief that he was served by "royalty."[4] The Pramara kept the secret, and gave Sanga a daughter to wife, and protection till the tragical end of his brother called him to the throne.

When the Rana heard of the quarrel which had nearly deprived him of his heir, he banished Pirthi Raj, telling him that he might live on his bravery and maintain himself with strife. With but five horse[5] Pirthi Raj quitted the paternal abode, and made for Baleoh in Godwar. These dissensions following the disastrous conclusion of the last reign, paralysed the country, and the wild tribes of the west and the mountaineers of the Aravulli so little respected the garrison of Nadole (the chief town of Godwar), that they carried their depredations to the plains. Pirthi Raj halted at Nadole, and having to procure some necessaries pledged a ring to the merchant who had sold it to him, the merchant recognised the prince, and learning the cause of his disguise, proffered his services in the scheme which the prince had in view for the restoration of order in Godwar, being determined to evince to his father that he had resources independent of birth. The Meenas were the aboriginal proprietors of all these regions; the Rajpoots were interlopers and conquerors. A Rawut of this tribe had regained their ancient haunts, and held his petty court at the town of Nadolaye in the plains, and was even served by Rajpoots. By the advice of Ojah, the merchant, Pirthi Raj enlisted himself and his band among the adherents of the Meena. On the *Ahairea*, or 'hunter's festival,' the vassals have leave to rejoin their families. Pirthi Raj, who had also obtained leave, rapidly retraced his steps, and despatching his Rajpoots to dislodge the Meena, awaited the result in ambush at the gate of the town. In a short time the Meena appeared on horseback, and in full flight to the mountains for security. Pirthi Raj pursued, overtook, and transfixed him with his lance to a kesoola tree, and setting fire to the village, he slew the Meenas as they sought to escape the flames. Other towns shared the

[1] Near Ajmér.
[2] Jey Sing Baleo and Jeimoo Sindil.
[3] Called the *devi*, about the size of the wagtail, and like it, black and white.
[4] Chut'burd'hari.
[5] The names of his followers were, Jessa Sindil, Singum (Dabi), Abho, Junoh, and a Bhadail Rahtore.

same fate, and all the province of Godwar, with the exception of Daisoori, a stronghold of the Madraicha Chohans, fell into his power. At this time Sadda Solanki, whose ancestor had escaped the destruction of Putun and found refuge in these mountainous tracts, held Sodgurh. He had espoused a daughter of the Madraicha, but the grant of Daisoori and its lands [1] in perpetuity easily gained him to the cause of Pirthi Raj.

Pirthi Raj having thus restored order in Godwar, and appointed Ojah and the Solanki to the government thereof, regained the confidence of his father; and his brother Jeimal being slain at this time, accelerated his forgiveness and recall. Ere he rejoins Raemul we will relate the manner of this event. Jeimal was desirous to obtain the hand of Tarra Bhaé, daughter of Rao Soortan,[2] who had been expelled Thoda by the Pathans. The price of her hand was the recovery of this domain: but Jeimal, willing to anticipate the reward, and rudely attempting access to the fair, was slain by the indignant father. The quibbling remark of the bard upon this event is that "Tarra was not the star (*tarra*) of his destiny." At the period of this occurrence Sanga was in concealment, Pirthi Raj banished, and Jeimal consequently looked to as the heir of Méwar. The Rana, when incited to revenge, replied with a magnanimity which deserves to be recorded, "that he who had thus dared to insult the honour of a father, and that father in distress, richly merited his fate"; and in proof of his disavowal of such a son he conferred on the Solanki the district of Bednore.

This event led to the recall of Pirthi Raj, who eagerly took up the gage disgraced by his brother. The adventure was akin to his taste. The exploit which won the hand of the fair Amazon, who, equipped with bow and quiver, subsequently accompanied him in many perilous enterprises, will be elsewhere related.

Soorajmul (the uncle), who had fomented these quarrels, resolved not to belie the prophetess if a crown lay in his path. The claims acquired from his parricidal parent were revived when Méwar had no sons to look to. Pirthi Raj on his return renewed the feud with Soorajmul, whose "vaulting ambition" persuaded him that the crown was his destiny, and he plunged deep into treason to obtain it. He joined as partner in his schemes Sarungdeo, another descendant of Lakha Rana, and both repaired to Mozuffir, the sultan of Malwa. With his aid they assailed the southern frontier, and rapidly possessed themselves of Sadri, Baturo, and a wide tract extending from Nye to Neemutch, attempting even Cheetore. With the few troops at hand Raemul descended to punish the rebels, who met the attack on the river Gumbeeree. The Rana, fighting like a common soldier, had received two and twenty wounds, and was nearly falling through faintness, when Pirthi Raj joined him with one thousand fresh horse, and reanimated the battle. He selected his uncle Soorajmul, whom he soon covered with wounds. Many had fallen on both sides, but

[1] The grant in the preamble denounces a curse on any of Pirthi Raj's descendants who should resume it. I have often conversed with this descendant, who held Sodgurh and its lands, which were never resumed by the princes of Cheetore, though they reverted to Marwar. The chief still honours the Rana, and many lives have been sacrificed to maintain his claims, and with any prospect of success he would not hesitate to offer his own.

[2] This is a genuine Hindu name, 'the Hero's refuge,' from *Soor*, 'a warrior,' and *T'han*, 'an abode.'

neither party would yield ; when worn out they mutually retired from the field, and bivouacked in sight of each other.

It will show the manners and feelings so peculiar to the Rajpoot, to describe the meeting between the rival uncle and nephew,—unique in the details of strife, perhaps, since the origin of man. It is taken from a MS. of the J'hala chief who succeeded Soorajmul in Sadri. Pirthi Raj visited his uncle, whom he found in a small tent reclining on a pallet, having just had " the barber " (*náe*) to sew up his wounds. He rose, and met his nephew with the customary respect, as if nothing unusual had occurred ; but the exertion caused some of the wounds to open afresh, when the following dialogue ensued :—

Pirthi Raj—" Well, uncle, how are your wounds ? "

Soorajmul—" Quite healed, my child, since I have the pleasure of seeing you."

Pirthi Raj—" But, uncle (*kaka*), I have not yet seen the Déwánji.[1] I first ran to see you, and I am very hungry ; have you anything to eat? "

Dinner was soon served, and the extraordinary pair sat down and " ate off the same platter " ; [2] nor did Pirthi Raj hesitate to eat the *pán*,[3] presented on his taking leave.

Pirthi Raj—" You and I will end our battle in the morning, uncle."

Soorajmul—" Very well, child ; come early ! "

They met ; but Sarungdeo bore the brunt of the conflict, receiving thirty-five wounds. During " four gurries [4] swords and lances were plied, and every tribe of Rajpoot lost numbers that day " ; but the rebels were defeated and fled to Sadri, and Pirthi Raj returned in triumph, though with seven wounds, to Cheetore. The rebels, however, did not relinquish their designs, and many personal encounters took place between the uncle and nephew : the latter saying he would not let him retain " as much land of Méwar as would cover a needle's point " ; and Soojoh [5] retorting, that " he would allow his nephew to redeem only as much " as would suffice to lie upon." But Pirthi Raj gave them no rest, pursuing them from place to place. In the wilds of Baturro they formed a stockaded retreat of the dho tree, which abounds in these forests. Within this shelter, horses and men were intermingled : Soojoh and his coadjutor communing by the night-fire in their desperate plight, when their cogitations were checked by the rush and neigh of horses. Scarcely had the pretender exclaimed " This must be my nephew ! " when Pirthi Raj dashed his steed through the barricade and entered with his troops. All was confusion, and the sword showered its blows indiscriminately. The young prince reached his uncle, and dealt him a blow which would have levelled him, but for the support of Sarungdeo, who upbraided him, adding that " a buffet now was more than a score of wounds in former days " : to which Soojoh rejoined, " only when dealt by my nephew's

[1] ' Regent ' ; the title the Rana is most familiarly known by.

[2] *T'hali*, ' a brass platter.' This is the highest mark of confidence and friendship.

[3] This compound of the betel or areca-nut, cloves, mace, terra japonica, and prepared lime, is always taken after meals, and has not unfrequently been a medium for administering poison.

[4] Hours of twenty-two minutes each.

[5] Familiar contraction of Soorajmul.

hand." Soojoh demanded a parley; and calling on the prince to stop the combat, he continued: "If I am killed, it matters not—my children are Rajpoots, they will run the country to find support; but if you are slain, what will become of Cheetore? My face will be blackened, and my name everlastingly reprobated."

The sword was sheathed, and as the uncle and nephew embraced, the latter asked the former, "What were you about, uncle, when I came?"—"Only talking nonsense, child, after dinner." "But with me over your head, uncle, as a foe how could you be so negligent?"—"What could I do? you had left me no resource, and I must have some place to rest my head!" There was a small temple near the stockade, to which in the morning Pirthi Raj requested his uncle to accompany him to sacrifice to Cali,[1] but the blow of the preceding night prevented him. Sarungdeo was his proxy. One buffalo had fallen, and a goat was about to follow, when the prince turned his sword on Sarungdeo. The combat was desperate; but Pirthi Raj was the victor, and the head of the traitor was placed as an offering on the altar of Time. The Gooda[2] was plundered, the town of Baturro recovered, and Soorajmul fled to Sadri, where he only stopped to fulfil his threat, "that if he could not retain its lands he would make them over to those stronger than the king";[3] and having distributed them amongst Brahmins and bards, he finally abandoned Méwar. Passing through the wilds of Khant'hul, he had an omen which recalled the Charuni's prediction: 'a wolf endeavouring in vain to carry off a kid defended by maternal affection.' This was interpreted as 'strong ground for a dwelling.' He halted, subdued the aboriginal tribes, and on this spot erected the town and stronghold of Deola, becoming lord of a thousand villages, which have descended to his offspring, who now enjoy them under British protection. Such was the origin of Pertabgurh Deola.

Pirthi Raj was poisoned by his brother-in-law, of Aboo, whom he had punished for maltreating his sister, and afterwards confided in. His death was soon followed by that of Rana Raemul, who, though not equal to his predecessors, was greatly respected, and maintained the dignity of his station amidst no ordinary calamities.[4]

[1] The Hindu Proserpine, or Calligenia. Is this Grecian handmaid of Hecate also Hindu, 'born of time' (*Cali-jenema*)?

[2] Gooda, or Goora, is the name of such temporary places of refuge; the origin of towns bearing this name.

[3] Such grants are irresumable, under the penalty of sixty thousand years in hell. This fine district is eaten up by these mendicant Brahmins. One town alone, containing 52,000 beegas (about 15,000 acres) of rich land, is thus lost; and by such follies Méwar has gradually sunk to her present extreme poverty.

[4] The walls of his palace are still pointed out.

CHAPTER IX

Accession of Rana Sanga—State of the Mahomedan power—Grandeur of Méwar—Sanga's victories—Invasions of India—Baber's invasion—Defeats and kills the King of Dehli—Opposed by Sanga—Battle of Kanúa—Defeat of Sanga—His death and character—Accession of Rana Rutna—His death—Rana Bickramajeet—His character—Disgusts his nobles—Cheetore invested by the King of Malwa—Storm of Cheetore—Saca or immolation of the females—Fall and plunder of Cheetore—Hemayoon comes to its aid—He restores Cheetore to Bickramajeet, who is deposed by the nobles—Election of Bunbeer—Bickramajeet assassinated.

SINGRAM, better known in the annals of Méwar as Sanga (called Sinka by the Mogul historians), succeeded in S. 1565 (A.D. 1509). With this prince Méwar reached the summit of her prosperity. To use their own metaphor, "he was the kullus [1] on the pinnacle of her glory." From him we shall witness this glory on the wane; and though many rays of splendour illuminated her declining career, they served but to gild the ruin.

The imperial chair, since occupied by the Túar descendant of thePandus, and the first and last of the Chohans, and which had been filled successively by the dynasties of Gazni and Ghor, the Ghilji and Lodi, was now shivered to pieces, and numerous petty thrones were constructed of its fragments. Méwar little dreaded these imperial puppets, 'when Amurath to Amurath succeeded,' and when four kings reigned simultaneously between Dehli and Benares.[2] The kings of Malwa, though leagued with those of Guzzerat, conjoined to the rebels, could make no impression on Méwar when Sanga led her heroes. Eighty thousand horse, seven Rajas of the highest rank, nine Raos, and one hundred and four chieftains bearing the titles of Rawul and Rawut, with five hundred war elephants, followed him into the field. The princes of Marwar and Ambér [3] did him homage, and the Raos of Gwalior, Ajmér, Sikri, Raésen, Kalpee, Chandéri, Boondi, Gagrown, Rampoora, and Aboo, served him as tributaries or held of him in chief.

Sanga did not forget those who sheltered him in his reverses. Kurimchund of Sreenuggur had a grant of Ajmér and the title of Rao for his son Jugmal, the reward of his services in the reduction of Chandéri.

In a short space of time, Sanga entirely allayed the disorders occasioned by the intestine feuds of his family; and were it permitted to speculate on the cause which prompted a temporary cession of his rights and his dignities to his more impetuous brother, it might be discerned in a spirit of forecast, and of fraternal and patriotic forbearance, a deviation from which would have endangered the country as well as the safety of his family. We may assume this, in order to account for an otherwise pusillanimous surrender of his birthright, and being in contrast to all the subsequent heroism of his life, which, when he resigned, was contained

[1] The ball or urn which crowns the pinnacle (*sikr*).

[2] Dehli, Biana, Kalpee, and Joinpoor.

[3] Pirthi Raj was yet but Rao of Ambér, a name now lost in Jeipoor. The twelve sons of this prince formed the existing subdivisions or clans of the Cutchwahas, whose political consequence dates from Hemayoon, the son and successor of Baber.

within the wreck of a form. Sanga organised his forces, with which he always kept the field, and ere called to contend with the descendant of Timoor, he had gained eighteen pitched battles against the kings of Dehli and Malwa. In two of these he was opposed by Ibrahim Lodi in person, at Bakrole and Ghatolli, in which last battle the imperial forces were defeated with great slaughter, leaving a prisoner of the blood royal to grace the triumph of Cheetore. The Peela-khal (yellow rivulet) near Biana became the northern boundary of Méwar, with the Sinde river to the east,—touching Malwa to the south, while his native hills were an impenetrable barrier to the west. Thus swaying, directly or by control, the greater part of Rajast'han, and adored by the Rajpoots for the possession of those qualities they hold in estimation, Sanga was ascending to the pinnacle of distinction ; and had not fresh hordes of Usbecs and Tatars from the prolific shores of the Oxus and Jaxartes again poured down on the devoted plains of Hindust'han, the crown of the *Chacraverta* [1] might again have encircled the brow of a Hindu, and the banner of supremacy been transferred from Indraprest'ha to the battlements of Cheetore. But Baber arrived at a critical time to rally the dejected followers of the Koran, and to collect them around his own victorious standard.

From the earliest recorded periods of her history, India has been the prey of the more hardy population from the central regions of Asia. From this fact we may infer another, namely, that its internal form of government was the same as at the present day, partitioned into numerous petty kingdoms, of tribes and clans, of a feudal federation, a prey to all the jealousies inseparable from such a condition. The historians of Alexander bear ample testimony to such form of government, when the Punjâb alone possessed many sovereigns, besides the democracies of cities. The Persians overran it, and Darius the Mede accounted India the richest of his satrapies. The Greeks, the Parthians, who have left in their medals the best proofs of their power ; the Getes or Yuti followed ; and from the Gori Shabudín to the Chagitai Baber, in less than three centuries, five invasions are recorded, each originating a dynasty. Sanga's opponent was the last, and will continue so until the rays of knowledge renovate the ancient nursery of the human race,—then, may end the anomaly in the history of power, of a handful of Britons holding the succession to the Mede, the Parthian, and the Tatar. But, however surprise may be excited at witnessing such rapidity of change, from the physical superiority of man over man, it is immeasurably heightened at the little moral consequence which in every other region of the world has always attended such concussions. Creeds have changed, races have mingled, and names have been effaced from the page of history ; but in this corner of civilisation we have no such result, and the Rajpoot remains the same singular being, concentrated in his prejudices, political and moral, as in the days of Alexander, desiring no change himself, and still less to cause any in others. Whatever be the conservative principle, it merits a philosophic analysis ; but more, a proper application and direction, by those to whom the destinies of this portion of the globe are confided ; for in this remote spot there is a nucleus of energy, on which may accumulate a mass for our support or our destruction.

To return : a descendant of the Toorshka of the Jaxartes, the ancient

[1] Universal potentate : the Hindus reckon only six of these in their history.

foe of the children of Soorya and Chandra, was destined to fulfil the prophetic pooran which foretold dominion "to the Toorshka, the Yavan," and other foreign races in Hind; and the conquered made a right application of the term Toork, both as regards its ancient and modern signification, when applied to the conquerors from Toorkist'han. Baber, the opponent of Sanga, was king of Ferghana, and of Toorki race. His dominians were on both sides the Jaxartes, a portion of ancient Sakatai, or Saca-dwipa (Scythia), where dwelt Tomyris the Getic queen immortalised by Herodotus, and where her opponent erected Cyropolis, as did in after-times the Macedonian his most remote Alexandria. From this region did the same Gete, Jit, or Yuti, issue, to the destruction of Bactria, two centuries before the Christian era, and also five subsequent thereto to found a kingdom in Northern India. Again, one thousand years later, Baber issued with his bands to the final subjugation of India. As affecting India alone, this portion of the globe merits deep attention; but as the *officina gentium*, whence issued those hordes of Asi, Jits, or Yeuts (of whom the Angles were a branch), who peopled the shores of the Baltic, and the precursors of those Goths who, under Attila and Alaric, altered the condition of Europe, its importance is vastly enhanced. But on this occasion it was not redundant population which made the descendant of Timoor and Jungheez abandon the Jaxartes for the Ganges, but unsuccessful ambition: for Baber quitted the delights of Samarcand as a fugitive, and commenced his enterprise, which gave him the throne of the Pandús, with less than two thousand adherents.

The Rajpoot prince had a worthy antagonist in the king of Ferghana. Like Sanga, he was trained in the school of adversity, and like him, though his acts of personal heroism were even romantic, he tempered it with that discretion which looks to its results. In A.D. 1494, at the tender age of twelve, he succeeded to a kingdom; ere he was sixteen he defeated several confederacies and conquered Samarcand, and in two short years again lost and regained it. His life was a tissue of successes and reverses; at one moment hailed lord of the chief kingdoms of Transoxiana; at another flying, unattended, or putting all to hazard in desperate single combats, in one of which he slew five champions of his enemies. Driven at length from Ferghana, in despair he crossed the Hindu-Coosh, and in 1519 the Indus. Between the Punjâb and Cabul he lingered seven years, ere he advanced to measure his sword with Ibrahim of Dehli. Fortune returned to his standard; Ibrahim was slain, his army routed and dispersed, and Dehli and Agra opened their gates to the fugitive king of Ferghana. His reflections on success evince it was his due: "Not to me, oh God! but to thee, be the victory!" says the chivalrous Baber. A year had elapsed in possession of Dehli, ere he ventured against the most powerful of his antagonists, Rana Sanga of Cheetore.

With all Baber's qualities as a soldier, supported by the hardy clans of the 'cloud mountains (*Belut Tag*)' of Karatagin,[1] the chances were

[1] The literary world is much indebted to Mr. Erskine for his *Memoirs of Baber*, a work of a most original stamp and rare value for its extensive historical and geographical details of a very interesting portion of the globe. The king of Ferghana, like Cæsar, was the historian of his own conquests, and unites all the qualities of the romantic troubadour to those of the warrior and statesman. It is not saying too much when it is asserted, that Mr. Erskine is the only person

many that he and they terminated their career on the 'yellow rivulet' of Biana. Neither bravery nor skill saved him from this fate, which he appears to have expected. What better proof can be desired than Baber's own testimony to the fact, that a horde of invaders from the Jaxartes, without support or retreat, were obliged to entrench themselves to the teeth in the face of their Rajpoot foe, alike brave and overpowering in numbers? To ancient jealousies he was indebted for not losing his life instead of gaining a crown, and for being extricated from a condition so desperate that even the frenzy of religion, which made death martyrdom in "this holy war," scarcely availed to expel the despair which so infected his followers, that in the bitterness of his heart he says, "not a single person who uttered a manly word, nor an individual who delivered a courageous opinion."

Baber advanced from Agra and Sikri to oppose Rana Sanga, in full march to attack him at the head of almost all the princes of Rajast'han. Although the annals state some points which the imperial historian has not recorded, yet both accounts of the conflict correspond in all the essential details. On the 5th of Kartik, S. 1584 [1] (A.D. 1528), according to the annals, the Rana raised the siege of Biana, and at Kanúa encountered the advanced guard of the Tatars, amounting to fifteen hundred men, which was entirely destroyed; the fugitives carrying to the main body the accounts of the disaster, which paralysed their energies, and made them entrench for security, instead of advancing with the confidence of victory. Reinforcements met the same fate, and were pursued to the camp. Accustomed to reverses, Baber met the check without dismay, and adopted every precaution that a mind fertile in expedients could suggest to re-assure the drooping spirits of his troops. He threw up entrenchments, in which he placed his artillery, connecting his guns by chains, and in the more exposed parts *chevaux de frise*, united by leather ropes: a precaution continued in every subsequent change of position. Everything seemed to aid the Hindu cause: even the Tatar astrologer asserted that as Mars was in the west, whoever should engage coming from the opposite quarter should be defeated. In this state of total inactivity, blockaded in his encampment, Baber remained near a fortnight, when he determined to renounce his besetting sin, and merit superior aid to extricate himself from his peril: the *naïvete* of his vow must be given in his own words.[2] But the destruction of the wine flasks would appear

existing who could have made such a translation, or preserved the great charm of the original—its elevated simplicity; and though his modesty makes him share the merit with Dr. Leyden, it is to him the public thanks are due. Mr. Erskine's introduction is such as might have been expected from his well-known erudition and research, and with the notes interspersed adds immensely to the value of the original. With his geographical materials, those of Mr. Elphinstone, and the journal of the *Voyage d'Orenbourg à Bokhara*, full of merit and modesty, we now possess sufficient materials for the geography of the nursery of mankind. I would presume to amend one valuable geographical notice (Introd. p. 27), and which only requires the permutation of a vowel, Kas-*mér* for Kas-*mir*; when we have, not 'the country of the Kas,' but the *Kasia Montes* (mér) of Ptolemy: the Kho (*mér*) Kas, or *Caucasus*. *Mir* has no signification, *Mér* is 'mountain' in Sanscrit, as is *Kho* in Persian. *Kas* was the race inhabiting these: and *Kasgar*, the Kasia Regio of Ptolemy. *Gar* is a Sanscrit word still in use for a 'region,' as *Cutchwaha-gár, Goojur-gár*.

[1] According to the *Memoirs of Baber*, 11th February 1527.

[2] "On Monday, the 23rd of the first Jemâdi, I had mounted to survey my

only to have added to the existing consternation, and made him, as a last resort, appeal to their faith. Having addressed them in a speech of manly courage, though bordering on despair, he seized the happy moment that his exhortation elicited, to swear them on the Koran to conquer or perish.[1] Profiting by this excitement, he broke up his camp, to which

posts, and in the course of my ride was seriously struck with the reflection, that I had always resolved, one time or another, to make an effectual repentance, and that some traces of a hankering after the renunciation of forbidden works had ever remained in my heart: I said to myself, 'O, my soul.'

(*Persian Verse*).

"'How long wilt thou continue to take pleasure in sin?
Repentance is not unpalatable—taste it.

(*Tûrki Verse*).

"'How great has been thy defilement from sin!
How much pleasure thou didst take in despair!
How long hast thou been the slave of thy passions!
How much of thy life hast thou thrown away!
Since thou hast set out on a holy war,
Thou hast seen death before thine eyes for thy salvation.
He who resolves to sacrifice his life to save himself,
Shall attain that exalted state which thou knowest.
Keep thyself far away from all forbidden enjoyments;
Cleanse thyself from all thy sins.'

"Having withdrawn myself from such temptation, I vowed never more to drink wine. Having sent for the gold and silver goblets and cups, with all the other utensils used for drinking parties, I directed them to be broken, and renounced the use of wine, purifying my mind. The fragments of the goblets and other utensils of gold and silver I directed to be divided among derwîshes and the poor. The first person who followed me in my repentance was Asas, who also accompanied me in my resolution of ceasing to cut the beard, and of allowing it to grow. That night and the following, numbers of Amirs and courtiers, soldiers, and persons not in the service, to the number of nearly three hundred men, made vows of reformation. The wine which we had with us we poured on the ground. I ordered that the wine brought by Bâba Dost should have salt thrown into it, that it might be made into vinegar. On the spot where the wine had been poured out I directed a wâîn to be sunk and built of stone, and close by the wâîn an almshouse to be erected. In the month of Moharrem in the year 935, when I went to visit Guâliâr, in my way from Dholpûr to Sikri, I found this wâîn completed. I had previously made a vow, that if I gained the victory over Rana Sanka the Pagan, I would remit the Temgha (or stamp-tax) levied from Musulmans. At the time when I made my vow of penitence, Derwîsh Muhammed Sârbân and Sheikh Zîn put me in mind of my promise. I said, 'You did right to remind me of this: I renounce the temgha in all my dominions, so far as concerns 'Musulmans'; and I sent for my secretaries, and desired them to write and send to all my dominions firmâns conveying intelligence of the two important incidents that had occurred."—*Memoirs of Baber*, p. 354.

[1] "At this time, as I have already observed, in consequence of preceding events, a general consternation and alarm prevailed among great and small. There was not a single person who uttered a manly word, nor an individual who delivered a courageous opinion. The Vazîrs, whose duty it was to give good counsel, and the Amirs, who enjoyed the wealth of kingdoms, neither spoke bravely, nor was their counsel or deportment such as became men of firmness. During the whole course of this expedition, Khalîfeh conducted himself admirably, and was unremitting and indefatigable in his endeavours to put everything in the best order. At length, observing the universal discouragement of my troops, and their total want of spirit, I formed my plan. I called an assembly of all the Amirs and officers, and addressed them: 'Noblemen and soldiers! Every man that comes into the world is subject to dissolution. When we are passed away and gone, God only survives, unchangeable. Whoever comes to the feast of life must, before it is over, drink from the cup of death. He who arrives at the inn of mortality, must one day inevitably take his departure from

he had been confined nearly a month, and marched in order of battle to a position two miles in advance, the Rajpoots skirmishing up to his guns. Without a regular circumvallation, his movable pallisadoes and guns chained, he felt no security. The inactivity of Sanga can scarcely escape censure, however we may incline to palliate it by supposing that he deemed his enemy in the toils, and that every day's delay brought with it increased danger to him. Such reasoning would be valid, if the heterogeneous mass by which the prince of Méwar was surrounded had owned the same patriotic sentiments as himself: but he ought to have known his countrymen, nor overlooked the regulating maxim of their ambition, *get land*. Delay was fatal to this last coalition against the foes of his race. Baber is silent on the point to which the annals ascribe their discomfiture, a negotiation pending his blockade at Kanúa; but these have preserved it, with the name of the traitor who sold the cause of his country. The negotiation [1] had reached this point, that on condition of Baber being left Dehli and its dependencies, the Peela-khal at Biana should be the boundary of their respective dominions, and even an annual tribute was offered to the Rana. We can believc that in the position Baber then was, he would not scruple to promise anything. The chief of Rayseen, by name Sillaidi, of the Túar tribe, was the medium of communication, and though the arrangement was negatived, treason had effected the salvation of Baber.

On the 16th March the attack commenced by a furious onset on the centre and right wing of the Tatars, and for several hours the conflict was tremendous. Devotion was never more manifest on the side of the Rajpoot, attested by the long list of noble names amongst the slain as well as the bulletin of their foe, whose artillery made dreadful havoc in the close ranks of the Rajpoot cavalry, which could not force the entrenchments, nor reach the infantry which defended them. While the battle was still doubtful, the Túar traitor who led the van (*herole*) went over to Baber, and Sanga was obliged to retreat from the field, which in the onset promised a glorious victory, himself severely wounded and the choicest of his chieftains slain: Rawul Udi [2] Sing of Dongerpoor, with two hundred of his clan; Rutna

that house of sorrow, the world. How much better it is to die with honour than to live with infamy!

"'With fame, even if I die, I am contented;
Let fame be mine, since my body is death's.

"'The most high God has been propitious to us, and has now placed us in such a crisis, that if we fall in the field we die the death of martyrs; if we survive, we rise victorious, the avengers of the cause of God. Let us, then, with one accord, swear on God's holy word, that none of us will even think of turning his face from this warfare, nor desert from the battle and slaughter that ensues, till his soul is separated from his body.'

"Master and servant, small and great, all with emulation, seizing the blessed Koran in their hands, swore in the form that I had given. My plan succeeded to admiration, and its effects were instantly visible far and near, on friend and foe."—*Memoirs of Baber*, p. 357.

[1] Baber says, "although Rana Sanka (Sanga) the Pagan, when I was at Cabul, sent me ambassadors, and had arranged with me that if I would march upon Dehli he would on Agra; but when I took Dehli and Agra, the Pagan did not move."—*Memoirs of Baber*, p. 339.

[2] In the translation of Baber's *Memoirs*, Udi Sing is styled "Wali of the country," confounding him with Udi Sing, successor of Sanga. He was Wali (sovereign) of Dongerpoor, not "Oodipoor," which was not then in existence.

of Saloombra, with three hundred of his Chondawut kin ; Raemul Rahtore, son of the prince of Marwar, with the brave Mairtea leaders Khaitsi and Rutna ; Ramdas the Sonigurra Rao ; Ujo the J'hala ; Gokuldas Pramara ; Manikchund and Chundrbhan, Chohan chiefs of the first rank in Méwar ; besides a host of inferior names. Husein Khan of Mewat, and a son of the last Lodi king of Dehli, who coalesced with Sanga, were amongst the killed. Triumphal pyramids were raised of the heads of the slain, and on a hillock which overlooked the field of battle a tower of skulls was erected ; and the conqueror assumed the title of *Ghazi*, which has ever since been retained by his descendants.

Sanga retreated towards the hills of Mewat, having announced his fixed determination never to re-enter Cheetore but with victory. Had his life been spared to his country, he might have redeemed the pledge ; but the year of his defeat was the last of his existence, and he died at Buswa, on the frontier of Mewat, not without suspicion of poison. It is painful to record the surmise that his ministers prompted the deed, and the cause is one which would fix a deep stain on the country ; namely, the purchase by regicide of inglorious ease and stipulated safety, in preference to privations and dangers, and to emulating the manly constancy of their prince, who resolved to make the heavens his canopy till his foe was crushed,—a determination which was pursued with the most resolute perseverance by some of his gallant successors.

Polygamy is the fertile source of evil, moral as well as physical, in the east. It is a relic of barbarism and primeval necessity, affording a proof that ancient Asia is still young in knowledge. The desire of each wife,[1] that her offspring should wear a crown, is natural ; but they do not always wait the course of nature for the attainment of their wishes, and the love of power too often furnishes instruments for any deed, however base. When we see, shortly after the death of Sanga, the mother of his second son intriguing with Baber, and bribing him with the surrender of Rinthumbor and the trophy of victory, the crown of the Malwa king, to supplant the lawful heir, we can easily suppose she would not have scrupled to remove any other bar. On this occasion, however, the suspicion rests on the ministers alone. That Baber respected and dreaded his foe we have the best proof, in his not risking another battle with him ; and the blame which he bestows on himself for the slackness of his pursuit after victory is honourable to Sanga, who is always mentioned with respect in the commentaries of the conqueror : and although he generally styles him the Pagan, and dignifies the contest with the title of "the holy war," yet he freely acknowledges his merit, when he says, "Rana Sanga attained his present high eminence by his own valour and his sword."

Sanga Rana was of the middle stature, but of great muscular strength ; fair in complexion, with unusually large eyes, which appear to be peculiar to his descendants.[2] He exhibited at his death but the fragments of a

[1] The number of queens is determined only by state necessity and the fancy of the prince. To have them equal in number to the days of the week is not unusual, while the number of *handmaids* is unlimited. It will be conceded that the prince who can govern such a household, and maintain equal rights when claims to pre-eminence must be perpetually asserted, possesses no little tact. The government of the kingdom is but an amusement compared with such a task, for it is within the *Rawula* that intrigue is enthroned.

[2] I possess his portrait, given to me by the present Rana, who has a collection

warrior: one eye was lost in the broil with his brother; an arm in an action with the Lodi king of Dehli, and he was a cripple owing to a limb being broken by a cannon-ball in another; while he counted eighty wounds from the sword or the lance on various parts of his body. He was celebrated for energetic enterprise, of which his capture of Mozuffur, king of Malwa, in his own capital, is a celebrated instance; and his successful storm of the almost impregnable Rinthumbor, though ably defended by the imperial general Ali, gained him great renown. He erected a small palace at Kanúa, on the line which he determined should be the northern limit of Méwar; and had he been succeeded by a prince possessed of his foresight and judgment, Baber's descendants might not have retained the sovereignty of India. A cenotaph long marked the spot where the fire consumed the remains of this celebrated prince. Sanga had seven sons, of whom the two elder died in non-age. He was succeeded by the third son,

RUTNA (S. 1586, A.D. 1530), who possessed all the arrogance and martial virtue of his race. Like his father, he determined to make the field his capital, and commanded that the gates of Cheetore never should be closed, boasting that 'its portals were Dehli and Mandoo.' Had he been spared to temper by experience the exuberance of youthful impetuosity, he would have well seconded the resolution of his father, and the league against the enemies of his country and faith. But he was not destined to pass the age always dangerous to the turbulent and impatient Rajpoot, ever courting strife if it would not find him. He had married by stealth the daughter of Pirthi Raj of Ambér, probably before the death of his elder brothers made him heir to Cheetore. His double-edged sword, the proxy of the Rajpoot cavalier, represented Rutna on this occasion. Unfortunately it was kept but too secret; for the Hara prince of Boondí,[1] in ignorance of the fact, demanded and obtained her to wife, and carried her to his capital. The consequences are attributable to the Rana alone, for he ought, on coming to the throne, to have espoused her; but his vanity was flattered at the mysterious transaction, which he deemed would prevent all application for the hand of his "affianced" (*manga*). The bards of Boondí are rather pleased to record the power of their princes, who dared to solicit and obtain the hand of the "bride" of Cheetore. The princes of Boondí had long been attached to the Sesodia house: and from the period when their common ancestors fought together on the banks of the Caggar against Shabudín, they had silently grown to power under the wing of Méwar, and often proved a strong plume in her pinion. The Hara inhabited the hilly tract on her eastern frontier, and though not actually incorporated with Méwar, they yet paid homage to her princes, bore her ensigns and titles, and in return often poured forth their blood. But at the tribunal of *Anunga*,[2] the Rajpoot scattered all other homage and allegiance to the winds. The maiden of Ambér saw no necessity for disclosing her secret, or refusing the brave Hara, of whom fame spoke loudly, when Rutna

of full-lengths of all his royal ancestors, from Samarsi to himself, of their exact heights and with every bodily peculiarity, whether of complexion or form. They are valuable for the costume. He has often shown them to me while illustrating their actions.

[1] Soorajmul.

[2] The Hindu Cupid, implying 'incorporeal,' from *anga*, 'body,' with the privative prefix '*an*.'

delayed to redeem his proxy. The unintentional offence sank deep into the heart of the Rana, and, though he was closely connected with the Hara, having married his sister, he brooded on the means of revenge, in the attainment of which he sacrified his own life as well as that of his rival. The festival of the *Ahairéa* [1] (the spring hunt), which has thrice been fatal to the princes of Méwar, gave the occasion, when they fell by each other's weapons. Though Rutna enjoyed the dignity only five years, he had the satisfaction to see the ex-king of Ferghana, now founder of the Mogul dynasty of India, leave the scene before him, and without the diminution of an acre of land to Méwar since the fatal day of Biana. Rana Rutna was succeeded by his brother,

BIKRAMAJEET,[2] in S. 1591 (A.D. 1535). This prince had all the turbulence, without the redeeming qualities of character, which endeared his brother to his subjects; he was insolent, passionate, and vindictive, and utterly regardless of that respect which his proud nobles rigidly exacted. Instead of appearing at their head, he passed his time amongst wrestlers and prize-fighters, on whom and a multitude of 'pâéks,' or foot soldiers, he lavished those gifts and that approbation, to which the aristocratic Rajpoot, the equestrian order of Rajast'han, arrogated exclusive right. In this innovation he probably imitated his foes, who had learned the superiority of infantry, despised by the Rajpoot, who, except in sieges, or when "they spread the carpet and hamstrung their steeds," held the foot-soldier very cheap. The use of artillery was now becoming general, and the Moslems soon perceived the necessity of foot for their protection: but prejudice operated longer upon the Rajpoot, who still curses "those vile guns," which render of comparatively little value the lance of many a gallant soldier; and he still prefers falling with dignity from his steed, to descending to an equality with his mercenary antagonist.

An open rupture was the consequence of such innovation, and (to use the figurative expression for misrule) "Pappa Baé ka Raj" [3] was triumphant; the police were despised; the cattle carried off by the mountaineers from under the walls of Cheetore; and when his cavaliers were ordered in pursuit, the Rana was tauntingly told to send his pâéks.

Buhadoor, sultan of Guzzerat, determined to take advantage of the Rajpoot divisions, to revenge the disgrace of the defeat and captivity of his predecessor Mozuffur.[4] Reinforced by the troops of Mandoo, he marched against the Rana, then encamped at Loeecha, in the Boondí territory. Though the force was overwhelming, yet with the high courage which belonged to his house, Bikramajeet did not hesitate to give battle; but he found weak defenders in his mercenary pâéks, while his vassals and kin not only kept aloof, but marched off in a body to defend Cheetore, and the posthumous son of Sanga Rana, still an infant.

There is a sanctity in the very name of Cheetore, which from the

[1] I have given the relation of this duel in the narrative of my journeys on my visit to the cenotaph of Rutna, erected where he fell. It was the pleasure of my life to listen to the traditional anecdotes illustrative of Rajpoot history on the scenes of their transactions.

[2] The Bhakha orthography for Vicramaditya.

[3] The government of Poppa Baé, a princess of ancient time, whose mismanaged sovereignty has given a proverb to the Rajpoot.

[4] Taken by Pirthi Raj and carried to Rana Raemul, who took a large sum of money and seven hundred horses as his ransom.

earliest times secured her defenders ; and now, when threatened again by "the barbarian," such the inexplicable character of the Rajpoot, we find the heir of Soorajmul abandoning his new capital of Deola, to pour out the few drops which yet circulated in his veins in defence of the abode of his fathers.

"The son of Boondí," with a brave band of five hundred Haras, also came; as did the Sonigurra and Deora Raos of Jhalore and Aboo, with many auxiliaries from all parts of Rajwarra. This was the most powerful effort hitherto made by the sultans of Central India, and European artillerists [1] are recorded in these annals as brought to the subjugation of Cheetore. The engineer is styled 'Labri Khan of Frengán,' and to his skill Buhadoor was indebted for the successful storm which ensued. He sprung a mine at the "Beeka rock," which blew up forty-five cubits of the rampart, with the bastion where the brave Haras were posted. The Boondí bards dwell on this incident, which destroyed their prince and five hundred of his kin. Rao Doorga, with the Chondawut chieftains Sutto and Doodoo and their vassals, bravely defended the breach and repelled many assaults ; and, to set an example of courageous devotion, the queen-mother Jawahir Bae, of Rahtore race, clad in armour, headed a sally in which she was slain. Still the besiegers gained ground, and the last council convened was to concert means to save the infant son of Sanga from this imminent peril. But Cheetore can only be defended by royalty, and again they had recourse to the expedient of crowning a king, as a sacrifice to the dignity of the protecting deity of Cheetore. Bágh-ji, prince of Deola, courted the insignia of destruction ; the banner of Méwar floated over him, and the golden sun from its sable field never shone more refulgent than when the changi [2] was raised amidst the shouts of her defenders over the head of the son of Soorajmul. The infant, Oody Sing, was placed in safety with Soortan, prince of Boondí,[3] the garrison put on their saffron robes, while materials for the *johur* were preparing. There was little time for the pyre. The bravest had fallen in defending the breach, now completely exposed. Combustibles were quickly heaped up in reservoirs and magazines excavated in the rock, under which gunpowder was strewed. Kurnavati, mother of the prince, and sister to the gallant Arjoon Hara, led the procession of willing victims to their doom, and thirteen thousand

[1] We have, in the poems of Chund, frequent indistinct notices of firearms, especially the 'nal-gola' or *tube*-ball ; but whether discharged by percussion or the expensive force of gunpowder is dubious. The poet also repeatedly speaks of "the volcano of the field," giving to understand great guns ; but these may be interpolations, though I would not check a full investigation of so curious a subject by raising a doubt. Baber was the first who introduced field guns in the Mohamedan wars, and Buhadoor's invasion is the first notice of their application in sieges, for in Alla-o-din's time, in the thirteenth century, he used the catapult or battering-ram, called 'munjaníka.' To these guns Baber was indebted for victory over the united cavalry of Rajast'han. They were served by Roomi Khan, probably a Roumeliot, or Syrian Christian. The Franks (Feringees), with Buhadoor, must have been some of Vasco di Gama's crew.

[2] The *Changi*, the chief insignia of regality in Méwar, is a sun of gold in the centre of a disc of black ostrich feathers or felt, about three feet in diameter, elevated on a pole, and carried close to the prince. It has something of a Scythic cast about it. What *changi* imports I never understood.

[3] The name of the faithful Rajpoot who preserved Oody Sing, Chuka Sén Dhoondéra, deserves to be recorded.

females were thus swept at once from the record of life. The gates were thrown open, and the Deola chief, at the head of the survivors, with a blind and impotent despair, rushed on his fate.

Buhadoor must have been appalled at the horrid sight on viewing his conquest ;[1] the mangled bodies of the slain, with hundreds in the last agonies from the poniard or poison, awaiting death as less dreadful than dishonour and captivity.[2] To use the emphatic words of the annalist, "the last day of Cheetore had arrived." Every clan lost its chief, and the choicest of their retainers ; during the siege and in the storm thirty-two thousand Rajpoots were slain. This is the second *saka* of Cheetore.

Buhadoor had remained but a fortnight, when the tardy advance of Hemayoon with his succours warned him to retire. According to the annals, he left Bengal at the solicitation of the queen Kurnavati ; but instead of following up the spoil-encumbered foe, he commenced a pedantic war of words with Buhadoor, punning on the word 'Cheetore.' Had Hemayoon not been so distant, this catastrophe would have been averted, for he was bound by the laws of chivalry, the claims of which he had acknowledged, to defend the queen's cause, whose knight he had become. The relation of the peculiarity of a custom analogous to the taste of the chivalrous age of Europe may amuse. When her Amazonian sister the Rahtore queen was slain, the mother of the infant prince took a surer method to shield him in demanding the fulfilment of the pledge given by Hemayoon when she sent the *Rakhi* to that monarch.

'The festival of the bracelet (*Rakhi*)' is in spring, and whatever its origin, it is one of the few when an intercourse of gallantry of the most delicate nature is established between the fair sex and the cavaliers of Rajast'han. Though the bracelet may be sent by maidens, it is only on occasions of urgent necessity or danger. The Rajpoot dame bestows with the Rakhi the title of adopted brother ; and while its acceptance secures to her all the protection of a *cavaliere servente*, scandal itself never suggests any other tie to his devotion. He may hazard his life in her cause, and yet never receive a smile in reward, for he cannot even see the fair object who, as brother of her adoption, has constituted him her defender. But there is a charm in the mystery of such connection, never endangered by close observation, and the loyal to the fair may well attach a value to the public recognition of being the *Rakhi-bund Bháe*, the 'bracelet-bound brother' of a princess. The intrinsic value of such pledge is never looked to, nor is it requisite it should be costly, though it varies with the means and rank of the donor, and may be of flock silk and spangles, or gold chains and gems. The acceptance of the pledge and its return is by the *katchli*, or corset, of simple silk or satin, of gold brocade and pearls. In shape or application there is nothing similar in Europe, and as defending the most delicate part of the structure of the fair, it is peculiarly appropriate as an emblem of devotion. A whole province has often accompanied the Katchli, and the monarch of India was so pleased with this

[1] The date, "Jeit sood 12th, S. 1589," A.D. 1533, and according to Ferishta A.H. 949, A.D. 1532-3.

[2] From ancient times, leading the females captive appears to have been the sign of complete victory. Rajpoot inscriptions often allude to "a conqueror beloved by the wives of his conquered foe," and in the early parts of Scripture the same notion is referred to. The mother of Sisera asks, "Have they not divided the prey ; to every man a damsel or two ?"—*Judges* v. 30.

courteous delicacy in the customs of Rajast'han, on receiving the bracelet of the princess Kurnavati, which invested him with the title of her brother, and uncle and protector to her infant Oody Sing, that he pledged himself to her service, "even if the demand were the castle of Rinthumbor." Hemayoon proved himself a true knight, and even abandoned his conquests in Bengal when called on to redeem his pledge and succour Cheetore, and the widows and minor sons of Sanga Rana.[1] Hemayoon had the highest proofs of the worth of those courting his protection; he was with his father Baber in all his wars in India, and at the battle of Biana his prowess was conspicuous, and is recorded by Baber's own pen. He amply fulfilled his pledge, expelled the foe from Cheetore, took Mandoo by assault, and, as some revenge for her king's aiding the king of Guzzerat, he sent for the Rana Bikramajeet, whom, following their own notions of investitute, he girt with a sword in the captured citadel of his foe.

The Mahomedan historians, strangers to their customs, or the secret motives which caused the emperor to abandon Bengal, ascribe it to the Rana's solicitation; but we may credit the annals, which are in unison with the chivalrous notions of the Rajpoots, into which succeeding monarchs, the great Akber, his son Jehangír, and Shah Jehan, entered with delight; and even Arungzéb, two of whose original letters to the queen-mother of Oodipoor are now in the author's possession, and are remarkable for their elegance and purity of diction, and couched in terms perfectly accordant with Rajpoot delicacy.[2]

Bikramajeet, thus restored to his capital, had gained nothing by adversity; or, to employ the words of the annalist, "experience had yielded no wisdom." He renewed all his former insolence to his chiefs, and so entirely threw aside his own dignity, and, what is of still greater consequence, the reverence universally shown to old age, as to strike in open court Keremchund of Ajmér, the protector of his father Sanga in his misfortunes. The assembly rose with one accord at this indignity to their order; and as they retired, the Chondawut leader Kanji, the first of the nobles, exclaimed, "Hitherto, brother chiefs, we have had but a smell of the blossom, but now we shall be obliged to eat the fruit"; to which the insulted Pramara added, as he hastily retired, "to-morrow its flavour will be known."

Though the Rajpoot looks up to his sovereign as to a divinity, and is

[1] Many romantic tales are founded on "the gift of the Rakhi." The author, who was placed in the enviable situation of being able to do good, and on the most extensive scale, was the means of restoring many of these ancient families from degradation to affluence. The greatest reward he could, and the only one he would, receive, was the courteous civility displayed in many of these interesting customs. He was the *Rakhi-bund Bháe* of, and received 'the bracelet' from, three queens of Oodipoor, Boondí, and Kotah, besides Chund-Bae, the maiden sister of the Rana; as well as many ladies of the chieftains of rank, with whom he interchanged letters. The sole articles of 'barbaric pearl and gold,' which he conveyed from a country where he was six years supreme, are these testimonies of friendly regard. Intrinsically of no great value, they were presented and accepted in the ancient spirit, and he retains them with a sentiment the more powerful, because he can no longer render them any service.

[2] He addresses her as "dear and virtuous sister," and evinces much interest in her welfare. We are in total ignorance of the refined sentiment which regulates such a people—our home-bred prejudices deem them beneath inquiry; and thus indolence and self-conceit combine to deprive the benevolent of a high gratification.

enjoined implicit obedience by his religion, which rewards him accordingly hereafter, yet this doctrine has its limits, and precedents are abundant for deposal, when the acts of the prince may endanger the realm. But there is a bond of love as well as of awe which restrains them, and softens its severity in the paternity of sway; for these princes are at once the father and king of their people: not in fiction, but reality—for he is the representative of the common ancestor of the aristocracy,—the sole lawgiver of Rajast'han.

Sick of these minors (and they had now a third in prospect), which in a few years had laid prostrate the throne of Méwar, her nobles on leaving their unworthy prince repaired to Bunbeer, the natural son of the heroic Pirthi Raj, and offered "to seat him on the throne of Cheetore." He had the virtue to resist the solicitation; and it was only on painting the dangers which threatened the country, if its chief at such a period had not their confidence, that he gave his consent. The step between the deposal and death of a king is necessarily short, and the cries of the females, which announced the end of Bikramajeet, were drowned in the acclamations raised on the elevation of the *changi* over the head of the bastard Bunbeer.

CHAPTER X

The bastard Bunbeer rules Méwar—Attempted assassination of the posthumous son of Sanga—Oody Sing's escape and long concealment—Acknowledged as Rana—The Doonah described—Oody Sing gains Cheetore—Deposal of Bunbeer—Origin of the Bhonslas of Nagpoor—Rana Oody Sing—His unworthiness—Hemayoon expelled the throne of India—Birth of Akber—Hemayoon recovers his throne—His death—Accession of Akber—Characters of Akber and Oody Sing contrasted—Akber besieges Cheetore, which is abandoned by the Rana—Its defence—Jeimul and Putto—Anecdotes of Rajpoot females—Saka or Johur—General assault—Cheetore taken—Massacre of the inhabitants—Oody Sing founds the new capital Oodipoor—His death.

A FEW hours of sovereignty sufficed to check those "compunctious visitings" which assailed Bunbeer ere he assumed its trappings, with which he found himself so little encumbered that he was content to wear them for life. Whether this was the intention of the nobles who set aside the unworthy son of Sanga, there is abundant reason to doubt; and as he is subsequently branded with the epithet of "usurper" it was probably limited, though unexpressed, to investing him with the executive authority during the minority of Oody Sing. Bunbeer, however, only awaited the approach of night to remove with his own hands the obstacle to his ambition. Oody Sing was about six years of age. "He had gone to sleep after his rice and milk," when his nurse was alarmed by screams from the rawula,[1] and the Bari[2] coming in to take away the remains of the dinner, informed her of the cause, the assassination of the Rana. Aware that one murder was the precursor of another, the faithful nurse put her charge into a fruit basket and, covering it with leaves, she delivered it to the Bari, enjoining him to escape with it from the fort. Scarcely had she time to

[1] The seraglio, or female palace.

[2] Bari, Naé, are names for the barbers, who are the *cuisiniers* of the Rajpoots.

substitute her own infant in the room of the prince, when Bunbeer, entering, inquired for him. Her lips refused their office; she pointed to the cradle, and beheld the murderous steel buried in the heart of her babe. The little victim to fidelity was burnt amidst the tears of the rawula, the inconsolable household of their late sovereign, who supposed that their grief was given to the last pledge of the illustrious Sanga. The nurse (*Dhaé*) was a Rajpootnee of the Kheechee tribe, her name *Punna*, or 'the Diamond.' Having consecrated with her tears the ashes of her child, she hastened after that she had preserved. But well had it been for Méwar had the poniard fulfilled its intention, and had the annals never recorded the name of Oody Sing in the catalogue of her princes.

The faithful barber was awaiting the nurse in the bed of the Béris River, some miles west of Cheetore, and fortunately the infant had not awoke until he descended the city. They departed for Deola, and sought refuge with Sing Rao, the successor to Bagh-ji, who fell for Cheetore; who dreading the consequence of detection, they proceeded to Dongerpoor. Rawul Aiskurn then ruled this principality, which, as well as Deola, was not only a branch, but the elder branch, of Cheetore. With every wish to afford a shelter, he pleaded the danger which threatened himself and the child in such a feeble sanctuary. Pursuing a circuitous route through Edur, and the intricate valleys of the Aravulli, by the help and with the protection of its wild inmates, the Bhils, she gained Komulmér. The resolution she had formed was bold as it was judicious. She demanded an interview with the governor, Assa Sah his name, of the mercantile tribe of Dépra, and a follower of the theistical tenets of the Jains. The interview being granted, she placed the infant in his lap, and bid him "guard the life of his sovereign." He felt perplexed and alarmed: but his mother, who was present, upbraided him for his scruples. "Fidelity," said she, "never looks at dangers or difficulties. He is your master, the son of Sanga, and by God's blessing the result will be glorious." Having thus fulfilled her trust, the faithful Punna withdrew from Komulmér to avoid the suspicion which a Rajpootnee about a Srawuk's [1] child would have occasioned, as the heir of Cheetore was declared to be the nephew of the Dépra.

Suspicions were often excited regarding Assa's nephew; once, especially, on the anniversary (*samvatsiri*) of the governor's father, when "the Rajpoot guests being in one rank, and the men of wealth in another, young Oody seized a vessel of curds, which no intreaty could prevail on him to relinquish, deriding their threats." Seven years elapsed before the secret transpired; at length self-revealed, from the same independent bearing. On occasion of a visit from the Sonigurra chief, Oody was sent to receive him, and the dignified manner in which he performed the duty convinced the chief "he was no nephew to the Sah." Rumour spread the tale, and brought not only the nobles of Méwar, but adjacent chiefs, to hail the son of Sanga Rana. Sahidas of Saloombra, the representative of Chonda, Juggo of Kailwa, Sanga of Bagore, all chiefs of the clans of Chondawut; the Chohans of Kotario and Baidla, the Pramar of Bijolli Akhiraj (Sonigurra), Pirthi Raj of Sanchore, and Loonkurn Jaitawut, repaired to Komulmér, when all doubt was removed by the testimony of the nurse, and of her coadjutor in the preservation of the child.

[1] The laity of the Jain persuasion are so called.

A court was formed, when the faithful Assa Sah resigned his trust and placed the prince of Cheetore "in the lap of the Kotario Chohan," as the "great ancient"[1] among the nobles of Méwar, who was throughout acquainted with the secret, and who, to dissipate the remaining scruples which attached to the infant's preservation, "ate off the same platter with him." The Sonigurra Rao did not hesitate to affiance to him his daughter, and it was accepted by his advisers, notwithstanding the interdict of Hamir to any intermarriage with the Sonigurra, since the insult of giving the widow to his bed.[2] Oody received the teeka of Cheetore in the castle of Koombho, and the homage of nearly all the chiefs of Méwar.

The tidings soon reached the usurper, who had not borne his faculties meekly since his advancement; but having seized on the dignity, he wished to ape all the customs of the legitimate monarchs of Cheetore, and even had the effrontery to punish as an insult the refusal of one of the proud sons of Chonda to take the *doonah* from his bastard hand.

The *doonah*, or *dooah*, is a portion of the dish of which the prince partakes, sent by his own hand to whomsoever he honours at the banquet. At the russora, or refectory, the chiefs who are admitted to dine in the presence of their sovereign are seated according to their rank. The repast is one of those occasions when an easy familiarity is permitted, which, though unrestrained, never exceeds the bounds of etiquette, and the habitual reverence due to their father and prince. When he sends, by the steward of the kitchen, a portion of the dish before him, or a little from his own *khansa*, or plate, all eyes are guided to the favoured mortal, whose good fortune is the subject of subsequent conversation. Though, with the diminished lustre of this house, the *doonah* may have lost its former estimation, it is yet received with reverence; but the extent of this feeling, even so late as the reign of Ursi Rana, the father of the reigning prince, the following anecdote will testify. In the rebellion during this priuce's reign, amongst the ancient customs which became relaxed, that of bestowing the *doonah* was included; and the Rana conferring it on the Rahtore prince of Kishengurh, the Bijolli chief, one of the sixteen superior nobles of Méwar, rose and left the presence, observing, "Neither the Kutchwaha or the Rahtore has a right to this honour, nor can we, who regard as sanctified even the leavings of your repast, witness this degradation; for the Thakoor of Kishengurh is far beneath me." To such extent is this privilege even yet carried, and such importance is attached from habit to the personal character of the princes of Méwar, that the test of regal legitimacy in Rajast'han is admission to eat from the same plate (*khansa*) with the Rana: and to the refusal of this honour to the great Maun Sing of Ambér, may be indirectly ascribed the ruin of Méwar.

It may, therefore, be conceived with what contempt the haughty nobility of Cheetore received the mockery of honour from the hand of this "fifth son of Méwar"; and the Chondawut chief had the boldness to add to his refusal, "that an honour from the hand of a true son of Bappa Rawul became a disgrace when proffered by the offspring of the handmaid Seetulséni." The defection soon became general, and all repaired to the valley of Komulmér to hail the legitimate son of Méwar. A caravan of

[1] *Burra* 'great,' *boora* 'aged'; the 'wise elder' of Rajast'han, where old age and dignity are synonymous.

[2] See p. 219.

five hundred horses and ten thousand oxen, laden with merchandise from Kutch, the dower of Bunbeer's daughter, guarded by one thousand Gherwal Rajpoots, was plundered in the passes ; a signal intimation of the decay of his authority, and a timely supply to the celebration of the nuptials of Oody Rana with the daughter of the Rao of Jhalore. Though the interdict of Hamir was not forgotten, it was deemed that the insult given by Bunbeer *Sonigurra*, was amply effaced by his successor's redemption of the usurpation of Bunbeer *Seesodia*. The marriage was solemnised at Balhi, within the limits of Jhalore, and the customary offerings were sent or given by all the princes of Rajast'han. Two chiefs only, of any consequence, abstained from attending on their lawful prince on this occasion, the Solanki of Maholi and Maloji of Tanah. In attacking them, the bastard was brought into conflict ; but Maloji was slain and the Solanki surrendered. Deserted by all, Bunbeer held out in the capital ; but his minister admitted, under the garb of a reinforcement with supplies, a thousand resolute adherents of the prince : the keepers of the gates were surprised and slain, and the *án* of Oody Sing was proclaimed. Bunbeer was even permitted to retire with his family and his wealth. He sought refuge in the Dekhan, and the Bhonslas of Nagpoor are said to derive their origin from this spurious branch of Cheetore.

Rana Oody Sing ascended the throne in S. 1597 (A.D. 1541–2). Great were the rejoicings on the restoration of this prince. 'The song of joy,' [1] which was composed on the occasion, is yet a favourite at Oodipoor, and on the festival of Isáni (the Ceres of Rajast'han), the females still chant in chorus the 'farewell to Komulmér.' [2] But the evil days of Méwar which set in with Sanga's death, and were accelerated by the fiery valour of Rutna and the capricious conduct of Bikramajeet, were completed by an anomaly in her annals : a coward succeeding a bastard to guide the destinies of the Seesodias. The vices of Rutna and his brother were virtues compared to this physical defect, the consequences of which destroyed a great national feeling, the opinion of its invincibility.

"Woe to the land where a minor rules or a woman bears sway !" exclaims the last of the great bards [3] of Rajast'han ; but where both were united, as in Méwar, the measure of her griefs was full. Oody Sing had not one quality of a sovereign ; and wanting martial virtue, the common heritage of his race, he was destitute of all. Yet he might have slumbered life away in inglorious repose during the reign of Hemayoon, or the contentions of the Pat'han usurpation ; but, unhappily for Rajast'han, a prince was then rearing who forged fetters for the Hindu race which enthralled them for ages ; and though the corroding hand of time left but their fragments, yet even now, though emancipated, they bear the indelible marks of the manacle ; not like the galley slave's, physical and exterior, but deep mental scars, never to be effaced. Can a nation which has run its long career of glory be regenerated ? Can the soul of the Greek or the Rajpoot be reanimated with the spark divine which defended the kangras [4] of Cheetore or the pass of Thermopylæ ? Let history answer the question.

In the same year that the song of joy was raised in the cloud-capped [5] palace of Komulmér for the deliverance of Oody Sing, the note of woe was

[1] Sohuloh. [2] Komulmér biddaona.
[3] Chund, the heroic bard of the last Hindu emperor.
[4] Battlements. [5] *Badul Mahl.*

pealed through the walls of Amerkote, and given to the winds of the desert, to proclaim the birth [1] of an infant destined to be the greatest monarch who ever swayed the sceptre of Hindust'han. In an oasis of the Indian desert, amidst the descendants of the ancient Sogdi [2] of Alexander, Akber first saw the light ; his father a fugitive, the diadem torn from his brows, its recovery more improbable than was its acquisition by Baber. The ten years which had elapsed since Hemayoon's accession were passed in perpetual strife with his brothers, placed according to custom in subordinate governments. Their selfish ambition met its reward ; for with the fall of Hemayoon their own was ensured, when Shere Shah displaced the dynasty of Chagitai for his own, the Pat'han.

From the field of battle at Kanouj, where Hemayoon left his crown, his energetic opponent gave him no respite, driving him before him from Agra to Lahore. Thence, with his family and a small band of adherents, alternately protected and repelled by Hindu chieftains, he reached the valley of Sinde, where he struggled to maintain himself amidst the greatest privations, attempting in succession each stronghold on the Indus, from Mooltan to the ocean. Foiled in every object, his associates made rebels by distress, he abandoned them for the more dubious shelter of the foes of his race. Vain were his solicitations to Jessulmér and Jodpoor ; and though it cannot be matter of wonder that he found no commiseration from either Bhatti or Rahtore, we must reprobate the unnational conduct of Maldeo, who, the Mogul historian says, attempted to make him captive. From such inhospitable treatment the royal exile escaped by again plunging into the desert, where he encountered, along with the tender objects of his solicitude, hardships of the most appalling description, until sheltered by the Soda prince of Amerkote. The high courage and the virtues of this monarch increase that interest in his sufferings which royalty in distress never fails to awaken by its irresistible influence upon our sympathies ; and they form an affecting episode in the history of Ferishta.[3] Hemayoon,

[1] A.D. 1542. [2] The Sodas, a branch of the Pramars, see p. 78.

[3] "Humaioon mounted his horse at midnight and fled towards Amercot, which is about one hundred coss from Tatta. His horse, on the way, falling down dead with fatigue, he desired Tirdi Beg, who was well mounted, to let him have his ; but so ungenerous was this man, and so low was royalty fallen, that he refused to comply with his request. The troops of the raja being close to his heels, he was necessitated to mount a camel, till one Nidim Koka, dismounting his own mother, gave the king her horse, and, placing her on the camel, ran himself on foot by her side.

"The country through which they fled being an entire sandy desert, the troop began to be in the utmost distress for water. Some ran mad, others fell down dead ; nothing was heard but dreadful screams and lamentations. To add, if possible, to this calamity, news arrived of the enemy's near approach. Humaioon ordered all those who could fight to halt, and let the women and baggage move forward. The enemy not making their appearance, the king rode on in front to see how it fared with his family.

"Night, in the meantime, coming on, the rear lost their way, and in the morning were attacked by a party of the enemy. Shech Ali, with about twenty brave men, resolved to sell his life dear. Having repeated the creed of martyrdom, he rushed upon the enemy, and the first arrow having reached the heart of the chief of the party, the rest were by the valour of this handful put to flight. The other Moguls joined in the pursuit, and took many of the camels and horses. They then continued their march, found the king sitting by a well which he had fortunately found, and gave him an account of their adventure.

"Marching forward the next day from this well, they were more distressed

though more deeply skilled in the mysteries of astrology than any professed seer of his empire, appears never to have enjoyed that prescience which, according to the initiated in the science, is to be obtained from accurate observation :

"And coming events cast their shadows before ;"

for, could he, by any prophetic power, have foreseen that the cloud which then shaded his fortunes, was but the precursor of glory to his race, he would have continued his retreat from the sheltering sand-hills of Amerkote with very different sentiments from those which accompanied his flight into Persia.

Hemayoon educated the young Akber in the same school of adversity in which he had studied under Baber. Between the Persian court and his ancient patrimony in Transoxiana, Candahar, and Cashmere, twelve years were passed in every trial of fortune. During this short period, India, always the prize of valour, had witnessed in succession six kings descended from the Pat'han 'Lion' (*shere*), of whom the last, Secunder, was involved in the same civil broils which brought the crown to his family. Hemayoon, then near Cashmere, no sooner observed the tide of events set counter to his foe, than he crossed the Indus and advanced upon Sirhind, where the Pat'han soon appeared with a tumultuous array. The impetuosity of young Akber brought on a general engagement, which the veterans deemed madness. Not so Hemayoon, who gave the command to his boy, whose heroism so excited all ranks, that they despised the numbers of the enemy, and gained a glorious victory. This was the presage of his future fame ; for Akber was then but twelve years of age,[1] the same period of life at which his grandfather, Baber, maintained himself on the throne of Ferghana. Hemayoon, worthy of such a son and such a sire, entered Dehli in triumph ; but he did not long enjoy his recovered crown. His death will appear extraordinary, according to the erroneous estimate formed of Eastern

than before, there being no water for two days' journey. On the fourth day of their retreat they fell in with another well, which was so deep, that the only bucket they had took a great deal of time in being wound up, and therefore a drum was beat to give notice to the cassilas when the bucket appeared, that they might repair by turns to drink. The people were so impatient for the water, that as soon as the first bucket appeared, ten or twelve of them threw themselves upon it before it quite reached the brim of the well, by which means the rope broke, and the bucket was lost, and several fell headlong after it. When this fatal accident happened, the screams and lamentations of all became loud and dreadful. Some lolling out their tongues, rolled themselves in agony on the hot sand ; while others, precipitating themselves into the well, met with an immediate, and consequently an easier death. What did not the unhappy king feel, when he saw this terrible situation of his few faithful friends !

"The next day, though they reached water, was not less fatal than the former. The camels, who had not tasted water for several days, now drank so much that the greatest part of them died. The people, also, after drinking, complained of an oppression of the heart, and in about half an hour a great part of them expired.

"A few, with the king, after this unheard-of distress, reached Amercote. The raja, being a humane man, took compassion on their misfortunes : he spared nothing that could alleviate their miseries, or express his fidelity to the king.

"At Amercote, upon Sunday the fifth of Rigib, in the year nine hundred and forty-nine, the prince Akber was brought forth by Hamida Banu Begum. The king, after returning thanks to God, left his family under the protection of Raja Rana, and, by the aid of that prince, marched against Bicker."—Dow's *Ferishta*.

[1] A.D. 1554.

princes : its cause was a fall from the terrace of his library ; for, like every individual of his race, he was not merely a patron of literature, but himself a scholar. Were we to contrast the literary acquirements of the Chagitai princes with those of their contemporaries of Europe, the balance of lore would be found on the side of the Asiatics, even though Elizabeth and Henry IV. of France were in the scale. Amongst the princes from the Jaxartes are historians, poets, astronomers, founders of systems of government and religion, warriors, and great captains, who claim our respect and admiration.

Scarcely had Akber been seated on the throne, when Dehli and Agra were wrested from him, and a nook of the Punjâb constituted all his empire : but by the energetic valour of the great Byrám Khan, his lost sovereignty was regained with equal rapidity, and established by the wisdom of this Sully [1] of Hindust'han on a rock. Calpee, Chandéri, Callinger, all Boondelkhund and Malwa, were soon attached to the empire, and at the early age of eighteen Akber assumed the uncontrolled direction of the state. He soon turned his attention towards the Rajpoots ; and whether it was to revenge the inhospitality of Maldeo towards his father, he advanced against the Rahtores, and stormed and took Mairtea, the second city in Marwar. Raja Bharmul of Ambér anticipated the king, enrolled himself and son Bhagwandas amongst his vassals, gave the Chagitai a daughter to wife, and held his country as a fief of the empire. But the rebellions of the Usbec nobles, and the attempts of former princes to regain their lost power, checked for a time his designs upon Rajast'han. These matters adjusted, and the petty sovereigns in the East (to whom the present monarch of Oude is as Alexander) subjected to authority, he readily seized upon the provocation which the sanctuary given to Baz Bahadoor of Malwa and the ex-prince of Nirwur afforded, to turn his arms against Cheetore.[2]

Happy the country where the sovereignty is in the laws, and where the monarch is but the chief magistrate of the state, unsubjected to those vicissitudes, which make the sceptre in Asia unstable as a pendulum, kept in perpetual oscillation by the individual passions of her princes ; where the virtues of one will exalt her to the summit of prosperity, as the vices of a successor will plunge her into the abyss of degradation. Akber and Oody Sing furnish the corollary to this self-evident truth.

The Rana was old enough to philosophise on " the uses of adversity " ; and though the best of the " great ancients " had fallen in defence of Cheetore, there were not wanting individuals capable of instilling just and noble sentiments into his mind : but it was of that common character which is formed to be controlled by others ; and an artful and daring concubine stepped in, to govern Oody Sing and Méwar.

Akber was not older when he came to the throne [3] of Dehli than Oody Sing when he ascended that of Méwar. Nor were his hopes much brighter ; but the star which beamed upon his cradle in the desert, conducted to his

[1] There are excellent grounds for a parallel between Akber and Henry IV. and between Byrám and Sully, who were, moreover, almost contemporaries. The haughty and upright Byrám was at length goaded from rebellion to exile, and died by assassination only four years after Akber's accession. The story is one of the most useful lessons of history.

[2] A.H. 975, or A.D. 1567.

[3] A.D. 1555 ; both were under thirteen years of age.

aid such counsellors as the magnanimous Byrám, and the wise and virtuous Abul Fuzil. Yet it may be deemed hardly fair to contrast the Rajpoot with the Mogul: the one disciplined into an accurate knowledge of human nature, by experience of the mutability of fortune; the other cooped up from infancy in a valley of his native hills, his birth concealed, and his education restricted.[1]

Akber was the real founder of the empire of the Moguls, the first successful conqueror of Rajpoot independence: to this end his virtues were powerful auxiliaries, as by his skill in the analysis of the mind and its readiest stimulant to action, he was enabled to gild the chains with which he bound them. To these they became familiarised by habit, especially when the throne exerted its power in acts gratifying to national vanity, or even in ministering to the more ignoble passions. But generations of the martial races were cut off by his sword, and lustres rolled away ere his conquests were sufficiently confirmed to permit him to exercise the beneficence of his nature, and obtain by the universal acclaim of the conquered, the proud epithet of *Juggat Goor*, or 'guardian of mankind.' He was long ranked with Shabudín, Alla, and other instruments of destruction, and with every just claim; and, like these, he constructed a Mumba [2] for the Koran from the altars of Eklinga. Yet he finally succeeded in healing the wounds his ambition had inflicted, and received from millions that meed of praise which no other of his race ever obtained.

The absence of the kingly virtues in the sovereign of Méwar filled to the brim the bitter cup of her destiny. The guardian goddess of the Seesodias had promised never to abandon the rock of her pride while a descendant of Bappa Rawul devoted himself to her service. In the first assault by Alla, twelve crowned heads defended the 'crimson banner' to the death. In the second, when conquest led by Bajazet[3] came from the south, the chieftain of Deola, a noble scion of Méwar, 'though severed from her stem,' claimed the crown of glory and of martyrdom. But on this, the third and grandest struggle, no regal victim appeared to appease the Cybele of Cheetore, and win her to retain its 'kangras'[4] as her coronet. She fell! the charm was broken; the mysterious tie was severed for ever which connected Cheetore with perpetuity of sway to the race of Ghelote. With Oody Sing fled the "fair face" which in the dead of night unsealed the eyes of Samarsi, and told him "the glory of the Hindu was departing":[5] with him, that opinion, which for ages esteemed her walls the sanctuary of the race, which encircled her with a halo of glory, as the palladium of the religion and the liberties of the Rajpoots.

To traditions such as these, history is indebted for the noblest deeds recorded in her page; and in Méwar they were the covert impulse to national glory and independence. For this the philosopher will value the relation; and the philanthropist as being the germs or nucleus of resistance against tyrannical domination. Enveloped in a wild fable, we see the

[1] If we argue this according to a Rajpoot's notions, he will reject the compromise, and say that the son of Sanga should have evinced himself worthy of his descent, under whatever circumstances fortune might have placed him.

[2] The pulpit or platform of the Islamite preachers.

[3] Bayazeed was the name of the Malwa sovereign ere he came to the throne, corrupted by Europeans to Bajazet. He is always styled "Baz Buhadoor" in the annals of Méwar.

[4] Battlements.

[5] The last book of *Chund* opens with this vision.

springs of their prejudices and their action : batter down these adamantine walls of national opinion, and all others are but glass. The once invincible Cheetore is now pronounced indefensible. "The abode of regality, which for a thousand years reared her head above all the cities of Hindust'han," is become the refuge of wild beasts, which seek cover in her temples ; and this erst sanctified capital is now desecrated as the dwelling of evil fortune, into which the entrance of her princes is solemnly interdicted.

Ferishta mentions but one enterprise against Cheetore, that of its capture ; but the annals record another, when Akber was compelled to relinquish the undertaking. The successful defence is attributed to the masculine courage of the Rana's concubine queen, who headed the sallies into the heart of the Mogul camp, and on one occasion to the emperor's headquarters. The imbecile Rana proclaimed that he owed his deliverance to her ; when the chiefs, indignant at this imputation on their courage, conspired and put her to death. Internal discord invited Akber to re-invest Cheetore ; he had just attained his twenty-fifth year, and was desirous of the renown of capturing it. The site of the royal Oordoo,[1] or camp, is still pointed out. It extended from the village of Pandowly [2] along the high road to Bussie, a distance of ten miles. The headquarters of Akber are yet marked by a pyramidal column of marble, to which tradition has assigned the title of *Akber cá dėwá*, or 'Akber's lamp.' [3] Scarcely had Akber sat down before Cheetore, when the Rana was compelled (say the annals) to quit it ; but the necessity and his wishes were in unison. It lacked not, however, brave defenders. Sahidás, at the head of a numerous band of the descendants of Chonda, was at his post, 'the gate of the sun' ; there he fell resisting the entrance of the foe, and there his altar stands, on the brow of the rock which was moistened with his blood. Rawut Dooda of Madaria led "the sons of Sanga." [4] The feudatory chiefs of Baidla and Kotario, descended from Pirthiraj of Dehli—the Pramar of Bijollí—the Jhala of Sadri—inspired their contingents with their brave example : these were all home chieftains. Another son of Deola again combated for Cheetore, with the Sonigurra Rao of Jhalore—Esuridas Rahtore, Kurumchund Cutchwaha,[5] with Dooda Sadani,[6] and the Túar

[1] Of which *horde* is a corruption.

[2] There are two villages of this name. This is on the lake called "Mánsurwur," on whose bank I obtained that invaluable inscription (see No. 2) in the nail-headed character, which settled the establishment of the Ghelotes in Cheetore, at a little more than (as Orme has remarked) one thousand years. To the eternal regret of my Yati Gúrú and myself, a barbarian Brahmin servant, instead of having it copied, broke the venerable column to bring the inscription to Oodipoor.

[3] It is as perfect as when constructed, being of immense blocks of compact white limestone, closely fitted to each other ; its height thirty feet, the base a square of twelve, and summit four feet, to which a staircase conducts. A huge concave vessel was then filled with fire, which served as a night-beacon to this ambulatory city, where all nations and tongues were assembled, or to guide the foragers. Akber, who was ambitious of being the founder of a new faith as well as kingdom, had tried every creed, Jewish, Hindu, and even made some progress in the doctrines of Christianity, and may have in turn affected those of Zerdusht, and assuredly this pyramid possesses more of the appearance of a pyreum than a "déwa" ; though either would have fulfilled the purport of a beacon.

[4] The Sangawuts, not the sons of Rana Sanga, but of a chieftain of Chonda's kin, whose name is the patronymic of one of its principal subdivisions, of whom the chief of Deogurh is now head. See p. 131.

[5] Of the Punchaénote branch.

[6] One of the Shekhavat subdivisions.

prince of Gwalior, were distinguished amongst the foreign auxiliaries on this occasion.

But the names which shine brightest in this gloomy page of the annals of Méwar, which are still held sacred by the bard and the true Rajpoot, and immortalised by Akber's own pen, are Jeimul of Bednore and Putta of Kailwa, both of the sixteen superior vassals of Méwar. The first was a Rahtore of the Mairtea house, the bravest of the brave clans of Marwar; the other was head of the Jugawuts, another grand shoot from Chonda. The names of 'Jeimul and Putta' are 'as household words,' inseparable in Méwar, and will be honoured while the Rajpoot retains a shred of his inheritance or a spark of his ancient recollections. Though deprived of the stimulus which would have been given had their prince been a witness of their deeds, heroic achievements such as those already recorded were conspicuous on this occasion; and many a fair form threw the buckler over the scarf, and led the most desperate sorties.

When Saloombra [1] fell at the gate of the sun, the command devolved on Putta of Kailwa. He was only sixteen: his father had fallen in the last shock, and his mother had survived but to rear this the sole heir of their house. Like the Spartan mother of old, she commanded him to put on the 'saffron robe,' and to die for Cheetore: but surpassing the Grecian dame, she illustrated her precept by example; and lest any soft 'compunctious visitings' for one dearer than herself might dim the lustre of Kailwa, she armed the young bride with a lance, with her descended the rock, and the defenders of Cheetore saw her fall, fighting by the side of her Amazonian mother. When their wives and daughters performed such deeds, the Rajpoots became reckless of life. They had maintained a protracted defence, but had no thoughts of surrender, when a ball struck Jeimul, who took the lead on the fall of the kin of Méwar. His soul revolted at the idea of ingloriously perishing by a distant blow. He saw there was no ultimate hope of salvation, the northern defences being entirely destroyed, and he resolved to signalise the end of his career. The fatal Johur was commanded, while eight thousand Rajpoots ate the last 'beera' [2] together, and put on their saffron robes; the gates were thrown open, the work of destruction commenced, and few survived 'to stain the yellow mantle' by inglorious surrender. Akber entered Cheetore, when thirty thousand of its inhabitants became victims to the ambitious thirst of conquest of this 'guardian of mankind.' All the heads of clans, both home and foreign, fell, and seventeen hundred of the immediate kin of the prince sealed their duty to their country with their lives. The Túar chief of Gwalior appears to have been the only one of note who was reserved for another day of glory. Nine queens, five princesses (their daughters), with two infant sons, and the families of all the chieftains not at their estates, perished in the flames or in the assault of this ever memorable day. Their divinity had indeed deserted them; for it was on 'Aditwar,' the day of the sun,[3] he shed for the last time a ray of glory on Cheetore. The rock of their

[1] The abode of the Chondawut leader. It is common to call them by the name of their estates.

[2] The beera, or pán, the aromatic leaf so called, enveloping spices, terra japonica, calcined shell-lime, and pieces of the areca nut, is always presented on taking leave.

[3] "Cheit sood egárus, S. 1624," 11th Cheit, or May, A.D. 1568.

strength was despoiled; the temples, the palaces dilapidated: and, to complete her humiliation and his triumph, Akber bereft her of all the symbols of regality; the nakaras,[1] whose reverberations proclaimed, for miles around, the entrance and exit of her princes; the candelabras from the shrine of the 'great mother,' who girt Bappa Rawul with the sword with which he conquered Cheetore; and, in mockery of her misery, her portals, to adorn his projected capital, Akberabad.[2]

Akber claimed the honour of the death of Jeimul by his own hand: the fact is recorded by Abul Fuzil, and by the emperor Jehangír, who conferred on the matchlock which aided him to this distinction the title of *Singram*.[3] But the conqueror of Cheetore evinced a more exalted sense, not only of the value of his conquest, but of the merits of his foes, in erecting statues to the names of Jeimul and Putta at the most conspicuous entrance of his palace at Dehli; and they retained that distinction even when Bernier was in India.[4]

When the Carthaginian gained the battle of Cannæ, he measured his success by the bushels of rings taken from the fingers of the equestrian Romans who fell in that memorable field. Akber estimated his, by the quantity of cordons (*zinár*) of distinction taken from the necks of the

[1] Grand kettle-drums, about eight or ten feet in diameter.

[2] The *teejo saca Cheetore ra*, or 'third sack of Cheetore,' was marked by the most illiterate atrocity, for every monument spared by Alla or Bayazeed was defaced, which has left an indelible stain on Akber's name as a lover of the arts, as well as of humanity. Alla's assault was comparatively harmless, as the care of the fortress was assigned to a Hindu prince; and Bayazeed had little time to fulfil this part of the Mosaic law, maintained with rigid severity by the followers of Islamism. Besides, at those periods, they possessed both the skill and the means to reconstruct: not so after Akber, as the subsequent portion of the annals will show but a struggle for existence. The arts do not flourish amidst penury: the principle to construct cannot long survive, when the means to execute are fled; and in the monumental works of Cheetore we can trace the gradations of genius, its splendour and decay.

[3] "He (Akber) named the matchlock with which he shot Jeimul *Singram*, being one of great superiority and choice, and with which he had slain three or four thousand birds and beasts."—*Jehangír-nameh.*

[4] "I find nothing remarkable at the entry but two great elephants of stone, which are in the two sides of one of the gates. Upon one of them is the statue of Jamel (Jeimul), that famous raja of Cheetore, and upon the other Potter (Putta) his brother. These are two gallant men that, together with their mother, who was yet braver than they, cut out so much work for Ekbar; and who, in the sieges of towns which they maintained against him, gave such extraordinary proofs of their generosity, that at length they would rather be killed in the out-falls (sallies) with their mother, than submit; and for this gallantry it is, that even their enemies thought them worthy to have these statues erected to them. These two great elephants, together with the two resolute men sitting on them, do at the first entry into this fortress make an impression of I know not what greatness and awful terror."—*Letter written at Dehli, 1st July* 1663, *from edition printed in London in* 1684, in the author's possession.

Such the impression made on a Parisian a century after the event: but far more powerful the charm to the author of these annals, as he pondered on the spot where Jeimul received the fatal shot from Singram, or placed flowers on the cenotaph that marks the fall of the son of Chonda and the mansion of Putta, whence issued the Seesodia matron and her daughter. Every foot of ground is hallowed by ancient recollections.

Rajpoots, and seventy-four máns and a half[1] are the recorded amount. To eternise the memory of this disaster, the numerals '74½' are *tilác*, or accursed. Marked on the banker's letter in Rajast'han it is the strongest of seals, for 'the sin of the slaughter of Cheetore'[2] is thereby invoked on all who violate a letter under the safeguard of this mysterious number. He would be a fastidious critic who stopped to calculate the weight of these cordons of the Rajpoot cavaliers, probably as much over-rated as the trophies of the Roman rings, which are stated at three and a half bushels. It is for the moral impression that history deigns to note such anecdotes, in themselves of trivial import. So long as '74½' shall remain recorded, some good will result from the calamity, and may survive when the event which caused it is buried in oblivion.

When Oody Sing abandoned Cheetore, he found refuge with the Gohil in the forests of Rajpiplee. Thence he passed to the valley of the Girwo in the Aravulli, in the vicinity of the retreat of his great ancestor Bappa, ere he conquered Cheetore. At the entrance of this valley, several years previous to this catastrophe, he had formed the lake, still called after him 'Oody Sagur,' and he now raised a dyke between the mountains which dammed up another mountain stream. On the cluster of hills adjoining he raised the small palace called 'Nochoki,' around which edifices soon arose, and formed a city to which he gave his own name, Oodipoor,[3] henceforth the capital of Méwar.

Four years had Oody Sing survived the loss of Cheetore, when he expired at Gogoonda, at the early age of forty-two; yet far too long for his country's honour and welfare. He left a numerous issue of twenty-five legitimate sons, whose descendants, all styled Ranawut, pushed aside the more ancient stock, and form that extensive clan distinctively termed the *Babas*, or 'infants,' of Méwar, whether Ranawuts, Poorawuts, or Kanawuts. His last act was to entail with a barren sceptre contention upon his children; for, setting aside the established laws of primogeniture, he proclaimed his favourite son Jugmal his successor. In Méwar there is no interregnum: even the ceremony of *malim* (mourning) is held at the house of the family priest while the palace is decked out for rejoicing. On the full moon of the spring month of Falgoon, while his brothers and the nobles attended the funeral pyre, Jugmal took possession of the throne in the infant capital, Oodipoor: but even while the trumpets sounded, and the heralds called aloud 'may the king live for ever!' a cabal was formed round the bier of his father. It will be borne in mind, that Oody Sing espoused the Sonigurra princess; and the Jhalore Rao, desirous to see his sister's son have his right, demanded of Kistna, the 'great ancient' of Méwar and the leader of the Chondawuts, how such injustice was sanctioned by him. "When a sick man has reached the last extreme and asks for milk to drink, why refuse it?" was the reply;—with the addition: "The Sonigurra's nephew is my choice, and my stand by Pertáp." Jugmal had just entered the Russora, and Pertáp was

[1] The *mán* is of four seers: the maund is forty, or seventy-five pounds. Dow, calculating all the captured wealth of India by the latter, has rendered many facts improbable.

[2] '*Cheetore marya ra páp*': *ra* is the sign of the genitive, in the Doric tongue of Méwar, the *ca* of the refined.

[3] Classically '*Udya-poora*,' the city of the East; from *udya* (*oriens*), the point of sunrise, as *usht* (west) is of sunset.

saddling for his departure, when Rawut Kistna entered, accompanied by the ex-prince of Gwalior. Each chief took an arm of Jugmal, and with gentle violence removed him to a seat in front of the 'cushion' he had occupied; the hereditary premier remarking, "You had made a mistake, Mahraj; that place belongs to your brother": and girding Pertáp with the sword (the privilege of this house), thrice touching the ground, hailed him king of Méwar. All followed the example of Saloombra. Scarcely was the ceremony over, when the young prince remarked, it was the festival of the Ahairea, nor must ancient customs be forgotten: "Therefore to horse, and slay a boar to Gouri,[1] and take the omen for the ensuing year." They slew abundance of game, and in the mimic field of war, the nobles who surrounded the gallant Pertáp anticipated happier days for Méwar.

CHAPTER XI

Accession of Pertáp—The Rajpoot princes unite with Akber—Depressed condition of Pertáp—He prepares for war—Maldeo submits to Akber—Pertáp denounces connection with the Rajpoot princes—Raja Maun of Ambér—Prince Selim invades Méwar—Battle of Huldighat—Pertáp encounters Selim, is wounded, and saved by the Jhala chief—Assisted in his flight by his brother Sukta—Komulmér taken by Akber—Oodipoor occupied by the Moguls—Pertáp cuts off Ferid and his army—Pertáp's family saved by the Bhils—The Khankhanan—Aggravated hardships of Pertáp—He negotiates with Akber—Pirthi Raj of Bikanér—The Khooshroz described—Pertáp abandons Méwar—Departure for the Indus—Fidelity of his minister—Returns—Surprises the Moguls—Regains Komulmér and Oodipoor—His successes—His sickness and death.

PERTÁP succeeded to the titles and renown of an illustrious house, but without a capital, without resources, his kindred and clans dispirited by reverses: yet possessed of the noble spirit of his race, he meditated the recovery of Cheetore, the vindication of the honour of his house, and the restoration of its power. Elevated with this design, he hurried into conflict with his powerful antagonist, nor stooped to calculate the means which were opposed to him. Accustomed to read in his country's annals the splendid deeds of his forefathers, and that Cheetore had more than once been the prison of their foes, he trusted that the revolutions of fortune might co-operate with his own efforts to overturn the unstable throne of Dehli. The reasoning was as just as it was noble; but whilst he gave loose to those lofty aspirations which meditated liberty to Méwar, his crafty opponent was counteracting his views by a scheme of policy which, when disclosed, filled his heart with anguish. The wily Mogul arrayed against Pertáp his kindred in faith as well as blood. The princes of Marwar, Ambér, Bikanér, and even Boondí, late his firm ally, took part with Akber and upheld despotism. Nay, even his own brother, Sagarji,[2] deserted

[1] Ceres—The Ahairea, or *Muhoorut ca Sikár*, will be explained in the Personal Narrative, as it would here break the connection of events.

[2] Sagarji held the fortress and lands of Kandhar. His descendants formed an extensive clan called *Sagarawuts*, who continued to hold Kandhar till the time of Sowaé Jey Sing of Ambér, whose situation as one of the great satraps of the Mogul court enabled him to wrest it from Sagarji's issue, upon their refusal to intermarry with the house of Ambér. The great Mohabet Khan, the most intrepid

him, and received, as the price of his treachery, the ancient capital of his race, and the title which that possession conferred.

But the magnitude of the peril confirmed the fortitude of Pertáp, who vowed, in the words of the bard, 'to make his mother's milk resplendent'; and he amply redeemed his pledge. Single-handed, for a quarter of a century did he withstand the combined efforts of the empire; at one time carrying destruction into the plains, at another flying from rock to rock, feeding his family from the fruits of his native hills, and rearing the nursling hero Umra, amidst savage beasts and scarce less savage men, a fit heir to his prowess and revenge. The bare idea that 'the son of Bappa Rawul should bow the head to mortal man,' was insupportable; and he spurned every overture which had submission for its basis, or the degradation of uniting his family by marriage with the Tatar, though lord of countless multitudes.

The brilliant acts he achieved during that period live in every valley; they are enshrined in the heart of every true Rajpoot, and many are recorded in the annals of the conquerors. To recount them all, or relate the hardships he sustained, would be to pen what they would pronounce a romance who had not traversed the country where tradition is yet eloquent with his exploits, or conversed with the descendants of his chiefs, who cherish a recollection of the deeds of their forefathers, and melt, as they recite them, into manly tears.[1]

Pertáp was nobly supported; and though wealth and fortune tempted the fidelity of his chiefs, not one was found base enough to abandon him. The sons of Jeimul shed their blood in his cause, along with the successors of Putta—the house of Saloombra redoubled the claims of Chonda to fidelity; and these five lustres of adversity are the brightest in the chequered page of the history of Méwar. Nay, some chiefs, attracted by the very desperation of his fortunes, pressed to his standard, to combat and die with Pertáp. Amongst these was the Dailwarra chief, whose devotion gained him the prince's 'right hand.'

To commemorate the desolation of Cheetore, which the bardic historian represents as a 'widow' despoiled of the ornaments to her loveliness, Pertáp interdicted to himself and his successors every article of luxury or pomp, until the insignia of her glory should be redeemed. The gold and silver dishes were laid aside for *pateras*[2] of leaves; their beds henceforth of straw, and their beards left untouched. But in order more distinctly to mark their fallen fortune and stimulate to its recovery, he commanded that the martial *nakaras*, which always sounded in the van of battle or processions, should follow in the rear. This last sign of the depression of Méwar still survives; the beard is yet untouched by the

of Jehangír's generals, was an apostate Sagarawut. They established many chieftainships in Central India, as Omri Bhadora, Gunésgunge, Digdolli; places better known to Sindia's officers than to the British.

[1] I have climbed the rocks, crossed the streams, and traversed the plains which were the theatre of Pertáp's glory, and conversed with the lineal descendants of Jeimul and Putta on the deeds of their forefathers, and many a time has the tear started in their eye at the tale they recited.

[2] The first invented drinking cup or eating vessel being made from the leaf (*pát*) of particular trees, especially the palasa (*butea frondosa*) and burr (*ficus religiosa*). The cups of a beautiful brown earthenware, made at Kotario, are chiefly *pateras*, of a perfectly classical shape. Query, the Roman *patera*, or the Greek ποτηρ, or Saxon *pot*?

shears ; and even in the subterfuge by which the patriot king's behest is set aside, we have a tribute to his memory : for though his descendant eats off gold and silver, and sleeps upon a bed, he places the leaves beneath the one and straw under the other.

Often was Pertáp heard to exclaim, "Had Oody Sing never been, or none intervened between him and Sanga Rana, no Toork should ever have given laws to Rajast'han." Hindu society had assumed a new form within the century preceding : the wrecks of dominion from the Jumna and Ganges had been silently growing into importance ; and Ambér and Marwar had attained such power, that the latter single-handed coped with the imperial Shere Shah ; while numerous minor chieftainships were attaining shape and strength on both sides the Chumbul. A prince of commanding genius alone was wanting, to snatch the sceptre of dominion from the Islamite. Such a leader they found in Sanga, who possessed every quality which extorts spontaneous obedience, and the superiority of whose birth, as well as dignity, were admitted without cavil, from the Himalaya to Ramaiser.[1] These states had powerful motives to obey such a leader, in the absence of whom their ancient patrimony was lost ; and such they would have found renewed in Sanga's grandson, Pertáp, had Oody Sing not existed, or had a less gifted sovereign than Akber been his contemporary.

With the aid of some chiefs of judgment and experience, Pertáp remodelled his government, adapting it to the exigencies of the times and to his slender resources. New grants were issued, with regulations defining the service required. Komulmér, now the seat of government, was strengthened, as well as Gogoonda and other mountain fortresses ; and, being unable to keep the field in the plains of Méwar, he followed the system of his ancestors, and commanded his subjects, on pain of death, to retire into the mountains. During the protracted contest, the fertile tracts watered by the Bunas and the Béris, from the Aravulli chain west to the eastern tableland, were *bé cherágh*, 'without a lamp.'

Many tales are related of the unrelenting severity with which Pertáp enforced obedience to this stern policy. Frequently, with a few horse, he issued forth to see that his commands were obeyed. The silence of the desert prevailed in the plains ; grass had usurped the place of the waving corn ; the highways were choked with the thorny babool,[2] and beasts of prey made their abode in the habitations of his subjects. In the midst of this desolation, a single goatherd, trusting to elude observation, disobeyed his prince's injunction, and pastured his flock in the luxuriant meadows of Ontalla, on the banks of the Bunas. After a few questions, he was killed and hung up *in terrorem*. By such patriotic severity, Pertáp rendered 'the garden of Rajast'han' of no value to the conqueror, and the commerce already established between the Mogul court and Europe, conveyed through Méwar from Surat and other ports, was intercepted and plundered.

Akber took the field against the Rajpoot prince, establishing his headquarters at Ajmér. This celebrated fortress, destined ultimately to be one of the twenty-two soubahs of his empire and an imperial residence, had admitted for some time a royal garrison. Maldeo of Marwar, who had

[1] The bridge of Ram, the southern point of the peninsula.

[2] *Mimosa Arabica.*

so ably opposed the usurper Shere Shah, was compelled to follow the example of his brother prince, Bagwandas of Ambér, and to place himself at the footstool of Akber: only two years subsequent to Pertáp's accession, after a brave but fruitless resistance in Mairta and Jodpoor, he sent his son, Oodi Sing, to pay homage to the king.[1] Akber received him at Nagore, on his route to Ajmér, on which occasion the Raos of Mundore were made Rajas; and as the heir of Marwar was of uncommon bulk, the title by which he was afterwards known in Rajast'han was 'Moota Rajah,'[2] and henceforth the descendants of the kings of Canouj had the 'right hand' of the emperor of the Moguls. But the Rahtore was greater in his native pride than with all the accession of dignity or power which accrued on his sacrifice of Rajpoot principles. Oodi 'le gros' was the first of his race who gave a daughter in marriage to a Tatar. The bribe for which he bartered his honour was splendid; for four provinces,[3] yielding £200,000 of annual revenue, were given in exchange for Jod Baé,[4] at once doubling the fisc of Marwar. With such examples as Ambér and Marwar, and with less power to resist the temptation, the minor chiefs of Rajast'han, with a brave and numerous vassalage, were transformed into satraps of Dehli, and the importance of most of them was increased by the change. Truly did the Mogul historian designate them 'at once the props and the ornaments of the throne.'

But these were fearful odds against Pertáp: the arms of his countrymen thus turned upon him, derived additional weight from their self-degradation, which kindled into jealousy and hatred against the magnanimous resolution they wanted the virtue to imitate. When Hindu prejudice was thus violated by every prince in Rajast'han (that of Boondí alone excepted[5]), the Rana renounced all alliance with those who were thus degraded; and in order to carry on the line, he sought out and incorporated with the first class of nobles of his own kin the descendants of the ancient princes of Dehli, of Puttun, of Marwar, and of Dhar. To the eternal honour of Pertáp and his issue be it told, that to the very close of the monarchy of the Moguls, they not only refused such alliance with the throne, but even with their brother princes of Marwar and Ambér. It is a proud triumph of virtue to record, from the autograph letters of the most powerful of their princes, Bukhta Sing and Jey Sing, that whilst they had risen to greatness from the surrender of principle, as Méwar had decayed from her adherence to it, they should, even while basking in court favour, solicit, and that humbly, to be re-admitted to the honour of matrimonial intercourse—'to be purified,' 'to be regenerated,' 'to be made Rajpoots':—and that this was granted only on condition of their abjuring the contaminating practice which had disunited them for more than a century; with the additional stipulation, that the issue of

[1] A.H. 977, A.D. 1569.

[2] There is less euphony in the English than in the French designation, Oody "*le Gros.*"

[3] Godwar, Rs. 900,000; Oojein, 249,914; Debalpoor 182,500; Budnawur, 250,000.

[4] The magnificent tomb of Jod Baé, the mother of Shah Jehán, is at Secundra, near Agra, and not far from that in which Akber's remains are deposited.

[5] The causes of exemption are curious, and are preserved in a regular treaty with the emperor, a copy of which the author possesses, which will be given in *The Annals of Boondi.*

marriage with the house of Méwar should be the heirs to those they entered: conditions which the decline of the empire prevented from being broken.

An anecdote illustrative of the settled repugnance of this noble family to sully the purity of its blood may here be related, as its result had a material influence on its subsequent condition. Raja Maun, who had succeeded to the throne of Ambér, was the most celebrated of his race, and from him may be dated the rise of his country. This prince exemplified the wisdom of that policy which Baber adopted to strengthen his conquest; that of connecting his family by ties of marriage with the Hindus. It has been already related, that Hemayoon espoused a daughter of Bagwandas, consequently Raja Maun was brother-in-law to Akber. His courage and talents well seconded this natural advantage, and he became the most conspicuous of all the generals of the empire. To him Akber was indebted for half his triumphs. The Cutchwaha bards find a delightful theme in recounting his exploits, from the snow-clad Caucasus to the shores of the 'golden Chersonese.'[1] Let the eye embrace these extremes of his conquests, Cabul and the Paropamisan of Alexander, and Arracan (a name now well known) on the Indian ocean; the former reunited, the latter subjugated, to the empire by a Rajpoot prince and a Rajpoot army. But Akber knew the master-key to Hindu feeling, and by his skill overcame prejudices deemed insurmountable, and many are the tales yet told of their blind devotion to their favourite emperor.

Raja Maun was returning from the conquest of Sholapoor to Hindust'han when he invited himself to an interview with Pertáp, then at Komulmér, who advanced to the Oody-Sagur to receive him. On the mound which embanks this lake a feast was prepared for the prince of Ambér. The board was spread, the Raja summoned, and Prince Umra appointed to wait upon him; but no Rana appeared, for whose absence apologies alleging headache were urged by his son, with the request that Raja Maun would wave all ceremony, receive his welcome, and commence. The prince, in a tone at once dignified and respectful, replied: "Tell the Rana I can divine the cause of his headache; but the error is irremediable, and if he refuses to put a plate (*khansa*) before me, who will?" Further subterfuge was useless. The Rana expressed his regret; but added, that "He could not eat with a Rajpoot who gave his sister to a Toork, and who probably ate with him." Raja Maun was unwise to have risked this disgrace: and if the invitation went from Pertáp, the insult was ungenerous as well as impolitic; but of this he is acquitted. Raja Maun left the feast untouched, *save the few grains of rice he offered to Undéva,*[2] *which he placed in his turban*, observing as he withdrew: "It

[1] When Raja Maun was commanded to reduce the revolted province of Cabul, he hesitated to cross the Indus, the Rubicon of the Hindu, and which they term *Uttuc*, or 'the barrier,' as being the limit between their faith and the barbarian. On the Hindu prince assigning this as his reason for not leading his Rajpoots to the snowy Caucasus, the accomplished Akber sent him a couplet in the dialect of Rajast'han:—

"Sub hyn bhúm Gopal ca	"The whole earth is of God,
Jis mi Uttuc kaha	In which he has placed the Uttuc.
Jis ca mun myn Uttuc hy	The mind that admits *impediments*
So een Uttuc hoéga."	Will always find an Uttuc."

This delicate irony succeeded when stronger language would have failed.

[2] The Hindus, as did the Greeks and other nations of antiquity, always made

was for the preservation of your honour that we sacrificed our own, and gave our sisters and our daughters to the Toork; but abide in peril, if such be your resolve, for this country shall not hold you"; and mounting his horse he turned to the Rana, who appeared at this abrupt termination of his visit, "If I do not humble your pride, my name is not Maun": to which Pertáp replied, "He should always be happy to meet him"; while some one, in less dignified terms, desired he would not forget to bring his '*Phoopa*,' Akber. The ground was deemed impure where the feast was spread: it was broken up and lustrated with the water of the Ganges, and the chiefs who witnessed the humiliation of one they deemed apostate, bathed and changed their vestments, as if polluted by his presence. Every act was reported to the emperor, who was exasperated at the insult thus offered to himself, and who justly dreaded the revival of those prejudices he had hoped were vanquished; and it hastened the first of those sanguinary battles which have immortalised the name of Pertáp: nor will Huldighat be forgotten while a Seesodia occupies Méwar, or a bard survives to relate the tale.

Prince Selim, the heir of Dehli, led the war, guided by the councils of Raja Maun and the distinguished apostate son of Sagurji, Mohabet Khan. Pertáp trusted to his native hills and the valour of twenty-two thousand Rajpoots to withstand the son of Akber. The divisions of the royal army encountered little opposition at the exterior defiles by which they penetrated the western side of the Aravulli, concentrating as they approached the chief pass which conducted to the vulnerable part of this intricate country.

The range to which Pertáp was restricted was the mountainous region around, though chiefly to the west of the new capital. From north to south, Komulmér to Ricumnat'h, about eighty miles in length; and in breadth, from Meerpoor west to Satolla east, about the same. The whole of this space is mountain and forest, valley and stream. The approaches to the capital from every point to the north, west, and south, are so narrow as to merit the term of defile; on each side lofty perpendicular rocks, with scarcely breadth for two carriages abreast, across which are those ramparts of nature termed *Col* in the mountain scenery of Europe, which occasionally open into spaces sufficiently capacious to encamp a large force. Such was the plain of Huldighat, at the base of a neck of mountain which shut up the valley and rendered it almost inaccessible.[1] Above and below the Rajpoots were posted, and on the cliffs and pinnacles overlooking the field of battle, the faithful aborigines, the Bhil, with his natural weapon the bow and arrow, and huge stones ready to roll upon the combatant enemy.

At this pass Pertáp was posted with the flower of Méwar, and glorious was the struggle for its maintenance. Clan after clan followed with desperate intrepidity, emulating the daring of their prince, who led the crimson banner into the hottest part of the field. In vain he strained every nerve to encounter Raja Maun; but though denied the luxury of revenge

offering of the first portion of each meal to the gods. Un-déva, 'the god of food.'

[1] Whoever has travelled through the Oberhasli of Meyringen, in the Oberland Bernois, requires no description of the alpine Aravulli. The *Col de Balme*, in the vale of Chamouni, is, on a larger scale, the Huldighat of Méwar.

on his Rajpoot foe, he made good a passage to where Selim commanded. His guards fell before Pertáp, and but for the steel plates which defended his howda, the lance of the Rajpoot would have deprived Akber of his heir. His steed, the gallant Chytuc, nobly seconded his lord, and is represented in all the historical drawings of this battle with one foot raised upon the elephant of the Mogul, while his rider has his lance propelled against his foe. The conductor, destitute of the means of defence, was slain, when the infuriated animal, now without control, carried off Selim. On this spot the carnage was immense: the Moguls eager to defend Selim; the heroes of Méwar to second their prince, who had already received seven wounds.[1] Marked by the 'royal umbrella,' which he would not lay aside, and which collected the might of the enemy against him, Pertáp was thrice rescued from amidst the foe, and was at length nearly overwhelmed, when the Jhala chief gave a signal instance of fidelity, and extricated him with the loss of his own life. Manah seized upon the insignia of Méwar, and rearing the 'gold sun' over his own head, made good his way to an intricate position, drawing after him the brunt of the battle, while his prince was forced from the field. With all his brave vassals the noble Jhala fell; and in remembrance of the deed his descendants have, since the day of Huldighat, borne the regal ensigns of Méwar, and enjoyed 'the right-hand of her princes.'[2] But this desperate valour was unavailing against such a force, with a numerous field artillery and a dromedary corps mounting swivels; and of twenty-two thousand Rajpoots assembled on that day for the defence of Huldighat, only eight thousand quitted the field alive.

Pertáp, unattended, fled on the gallant Chytuc, who had borne him through the day, and who saved him now by leaping a mountain stream when closely pursued by two Mogul chiefs, whom this impediment momentarily checked. But Chytuc, like his master, was wounded; his pursuers gained upon Pertáp, and the flash from the flinty rock announced them at his heels, when, in the broad accents of his native tongue, the salutation *Ho! nila ghora ra aswár*, 'ho! rider of the blue horse,' made him look back, and he beheld but a single horseman: that horseman his brother.

Sukta, whose personal enmity to Pertáp had made him a traitor to Méwar, beheld from the ranks of Akber the 'blue horse' flying unattended. Resentment was extinguished, and a feeling of affection, mingling with sad and humiliating recollections, took possession of his bosom. He joined in the pursuit, but only to slay the pursuers, who fell beneath his lance; and now, for the first time in their lives, the brothers embraced in friendship. Here Chytuc fell, and as the Rana unbuckled his caparison to place it upon Unkarro, presented to him by his brother, the noble steed expired. An altar was raised, and yet marks the spot, where Chytuc[3] died; and the entire scene may be seen painted on the walls of half the houses of the capital.

The greeting between the brothers was necessarily short; but the merry Sukta, who was attached to Selim's personal force, could not let

[1] Three from the spear, one shot, and three by the sword.

[2] The descendants of Manah yet hold Sadri and all the privileges obtained on this occasion. Their kettle-drums beat to the gate of the palace, a privilege allowed to none besides, and they are addressed by the title of *Raj*, or royal.

[3] 'Chytuc ca Chabootra' is near to Jarrole.

it pass without a joke; and inquiring "how a man felt when flying for his life?" he quitted Pertáp with the assurance of reunion the first safe opportunity. On rejoining Selim, the truth of Sukta was greatly doubted when he related that Pertáp had not only slain his pursuers, but his own steed, which obliged him to return on that of the Khorasani. Prince Selim pledged his word to pardon him if he related the truth; when Sukta replied, "The burthen of a kingdom is on my brother's shoulders, nor could I witness his danger without defending him from it." Selim kept his word, but dismissed the future head of the Suktawuts. Determined to make a suitable 'nuzzur' on his introduction, he redeemed Bhynsror by a *coup de main*, and joined Pertáp at Oodipoor, who made him a grant of the conquest, which long remained the chief abode of the Suktawuts;[1] and since the day when this, their founder, preserved the life of his brother and prince against his Mogul pursuers, the byrd of the bard to all of his race is *Khorasani Mooltani ca Aggul*, 'the barrier to Khorasan and Mooltan,' from which countries were the chiefs he slew.

On the 7th of Sawun, S. 1632 (July, A.D. 1576), a day ever memorable in her annals, the best blood of Méwar irrigated the pass of Huldighat. Of the nearest kin of the prince five hundred were slain: the exiled prince of Gwalior, Ramsah, his son Khandirao, with three hundred and fifty of his brave Túar clan, paid the debt of gratitude with their lives. Since their expulsion by Baber they had found sanctuary in Méwar, whose princes diminished their feeble revenues to maintain inviolable the rites of hospitality.[2] Manah, the devoted Jhala, lost one hundred and fifty of his vassals, and every house of Méwar mourned its chief support.

Elate with victory, Selim left the hills. The rainy season had set in, which impeded operations, and obtained for Pertáp a few months of repose; but with the spring the foe returned, when he was again defeated,[3] and took post in Komulmér, which was invested by the Koka, Shabaz Khan. He here made a gallant and protracted resistance, and did not retire till insects rendered the water of the Nogun' well, their sole resource, impure. To the treachery of the Deora chief of Aboo, who was now with Akber, this deed is imputed. Pertáp thence withdrew to Chaond,[4] while Bhan, the Sonigurra chief, defended the place to the last, and was slain in the assault. On this occasion also fell the chief bard of Méwar, who inspired by his deeds, as well as by his song, the spirit of resistance to the 'ruthless king,' and whose laudatory couplets on the deeds of his lord are still in every mouth. But the spirit of poesy died not with him, for princes and nobles, Hindu and Toork, vied with each other in exalting the patriot Pertáp, in strains replete with those sentiments which elevate the mind of the martial Rajpoot, who is inflamed into action by this national excitement.

On the fall of Komulmér, the castles of Dhurmeti and Gogoonda were

[1] The mother of Sukta was the *Báe-ji Raj*, 'Royal Mother' (Queen Dowager) of Méwar. She loved this son, and left Oodipoor to superintend his household at Bhynsror: since which renunciation of rank to affection, the mothers of the senior branch of Suktawut are addressed 'Báe-ji Ráj.'

[2] 800 rupees, or £100 daily, is the sum recorded for the support of this prince.

[3] The date of this battle is Maug Sood 7, S. 1633, A.D. 1577.

[4] A town in the heart of the mountainous tract on the south-west of Méwar, called Chuppun, containing about three hundred and fifty towns and villages, peopled chiefly by the aboriginal Bhils.

invested by Raja Maun. Mohabet Khan took posssession of Oodipoor; and while a prince of the blood [1] cut off the resources furnished by the inhabitants of Oguna Panora, Khan Ferid invaded Chuppun, and approached Chaond from the south. Thus beset on every side, dislodged from the most secret retreats, and hunted from glen to glen, there appeared no hope for Pertáp: yet, even while his pursuers deemed him panting in some obscure lurking-place, he would by mountain signals reassemble his bands, and assail them unawares and often unguarded. By a skilful manœuvre, Ferid, who dreamed of nothing less than making the Rajpoot prince his prisoner, was blocked up in a defile and his force cut off to a man. Unaccustomed to such warfare, the mercenary Moguls became disgusted in combating a foe seldom tangible; while the monsoon swelled the mountain streams, filling the reservoirs with mineral poisons and the air with pestilential exhalations. The periodical rains accordingly always brought some respite to Pertáp.

Years thus rolled away, each ending with a diminution of his means and an increase to his misfortunes. His family was his chief source of anxiety: he dreaded their captivity, an apprehension often on the point of being realised. On one occasion they were saved by the faithful Bhils of Cavah, who carried them in wicker baskets and concealed them in the tin mines of Jawura, where they guarded and fed them. Bolts and rings are still preserved in the trees about Jawura and Chaond, to which baskets were suspended, the only cradles of the royal children of Méwar, in order to preserve them from the tiger and the wolf. Yet amidst such complicated evils the fortitude of Pertáp remained unshaken, and a spy sent by Akber represented the Rajpoot and his chiefs seated at a scanty meal, maintaining all the etiquette observed in prosperity, the Rana bestowing the *doonah* to the most deserving, and which, though only of the wild fruit of the country, was received with all the reverence of better days. Such inflexible magnanimity touched the soul of Akber, and extorted the homage of every chief in Rajast'han; nor could those who swelled the gorgeous train of the emperor withhold their admiration. Nay, these annals have preserved some stanzas addressed by the Khankhanan, the first of the satraps of Dehli, to the noble Rajpoot, in his native tongue, applauding his valour and stimulating his perseverance: "All is unstable in this world: land and wealth will disappear, but the virtue of a great name lives for ever. Putto [2] abandoned wealth and land, but never bowed the head: alone, of all the princes of Hind, he preserved the honour of his race."

But there were moments when the wants of those dearer than his own life almost excited him to frenzy. The wife of his bosom was insecure, even in the rock or the cave; and his infants, heirs to every luxury, were weeping around him for food: for with such pertinacity did the Mogul myrmidons pursue them, that "five meals have been prepared and abandoned for want of opportunity to eat them." On one occasion his queen and his son's wife were preparing a few cakes from the flour of the meadow grass,[3] of which one was given to each; half for the present, the rest for a future meal. Pertáp was stretched beside them pondering on his misfortunes, when a piercing cry from his daughter roused him from reflection: a wild cat had darted on the reserved portion of food, and the agony

[1] Called Ami Shah in the Annals.
[2] A colloquial contraction for Pertáp.
[3] Called *Mol*.

of hunger made her shrieks insupportable. Until that moment his fortitude had been unsubdued. He had beheld his sons and his kindred fall around him on the field without emotion—"For this the Rajpoot was born"; but the lamentation of his children for food "unmanned him." He cursed the name of royalty, if only to be enjoyed on such conditions, and he demanded of Akber a mitigation of his hardships.

Overjoyed at this indication of submission, the emperor commanded public rejoicings, and exultingly showed the letter to Pirthi Raj, a Rajpoot compelled to follow the victorious car of Akber. Pirthi Raj was the younger brother of the prince of Bikanér, a state recently grown out of the Rahtores of Marwar, and which, being exposed in the flats of the desert, had no power to resist the example of its elder, Maldeo. Pirthi Raj was one of the most gallant chieftains of the age, and like the Troubadour princes of the west, could grace a cause with the soul-inspiring effusions of the muse, as well as aid it with his sword: nay, in an assembly of the bards of Rajast'han, the palm of merit was unanimously awarded to the Rahtore cavalier. He adored the very name of Pertáp, and the intelligence filled him with grief. With all the warmth and frankness of his nature, he told the king it was a forgery of some foe to the fame of the Rajpoot prince. "I know him well," said he; "for your crown he would not submit to your terms." He requested and obtained permission from the king to transmit by his courier a letter to Pertáp, ostensibly to ascertain the fact of his submission, but really with the view to prevent it. On this occasion he composed those couplets, still admired, and which for the effect they produced will stand comparison with any of the *sirventes* of the Troubadours of the west.[1]

"The hopes of the Hindu rest on the Hindu; yet the Rana forsakes them. But for Pertáp, all would be placed on the same level by Akber; for our chiefs have lost their valour and our females their honour. Akber is the broker in the market of our race: all has he purchased but the son of Oodoh; he is beyond his price. What true Rajpoot would part with honour for nine days (*Noroza*); yet how many have bartered it away? Will Cheetore come to this market, when all have disposed of the chief article of the Khetri? Though Putto has squandered away wealth, yet this treasure has he preserved. Despair has driven many to this mart, to witness their dishonour: from such infamy the descendant of Hamir alone has been preserved. The world asks, whence the concealed aid of Pertáp? None but the soul of manliness and his sword: with it, well has he maintained the Khetri's pride. This broker in the market of men will one day be overreached; he cannot live for ever: then will our race come to Pertáp, for the seed of the Rajpoot to sow in our desolate lands. To him all look for its preservation, that its purity may again become resplendent."

This effusion of the Rahtore was equal to ten thousand men; it nerved the drooping mind of Pertáp, and roused him into action: for it was a noble incentive to find every eye of his race fixed upon him.

The allusion of the princely poet in the phrase, "bartering their honour on the 'Noroza,'" requires some explanation. The *Noroza*, or 'New

[1] It is no affectation to say that the spirit evaporates in the lameness of the translation. The author could feel the force, though he failed to imitate the strength, of the original.

Year's Day,' when the sun enters Aries, is one of great festivity among the Mahomedan princes of the East ; but of that alluded to by Pirthi Raj we can form an adequate idea from the historian Abul Fuzil.

It is not New Year's Day, but a festival especially instituted by Akber, and to which he gave the epithet *Khooshroz*, ' day of pleasure,' held on the ninth day (*no-roza*), following the chief festival of each month. The court assembled, and was attended by all ranks. The queen also had her court, when the wives of the nobles and of the Rajpoot vassal princes were congregated. But the Khooshroz was chiefly marked by a fair held within the precincts of the court, attended only by females. The merchants' wives exposed the manufactures of every clime, and the ladies of the court were the purchasers.[1] " His majesty is also there in disguise, by which means he learns the value of merchandise, and hears what is said of the state of the empire and the character of the officers of government." The ingenuous Abul Fuzil thus softens down the unhallowed purpose of this day ; but posterity cannot admit that the great Akber was to obtain these results amidst the *Pushto* jargon of the dames of Islam, or the mixed *Bhaka* of the fair of Rajast'han. These ' ninth day fairs ' are the markets in which Rajpoot honour was bartered, and to which the brave Pirthi Raj makes allusion.

It is scarcely to be credited that a statesman like Akber should have hazarded his popularity or his power, by the introduction of a custom alike appertaining to the Celtic races of Europe as to these the Goths of Asia ; [2]

[1] At these royal fairs were also sold the productions of princely artisans, male and female, and which, out of compliment to majesty, made a bounteous return for their industry. It is a fact but little known, that most Asiatic princes profess a trade : the great Arungzéb was a cap-maker, and sold them to such advantage on these ' ninth day ' fairs, that his funeral expenses were by his own express command defrayed from the privy purse, the accumulation of his personal labour. A delightful anecdote is recorded of the Ghilji king Mahmood, whose profession was literary, and who obtained good prices from his Omrahs for his specimens of caligraphy. While engaged in transcribing one of the Persian poets, a professed scholar, who with others attended the *conversazione*, suggested an emendation, which was instantly attended to, and the supposed error remedied. When the Moolah was gone, the monarch erased the emendation and re-inserted the passage. An Omrah had observed and questioned the action, to which the king replied : " It was better to make a blot in the manuscript than wound the vanity of a humble scholar."

[2] This laxity, as regards female delicacy, must have been a remnant of Scythic barbarism, brought from the banks of the Jaxartes, the land of the Gete, where now, as in the days of Tomyris, a shoe at the door is a sufficient barrier to the entrance of many Tatar husbands. It is a well-known fact, also, that the younger son in these regions inherited a greater share than the elder, which is attributed to their pastoral habits, which invited early emigration in the elder sons. This habit prevailed with the Rajpoot tribes of very early times, and the annals of the Yadus, a race allied to the Yuti-Gete, or Jit, afford many instances of it. Modified it yet exists amongst the Jarejas (of the same stock), with whom the sons divide equally ; which custom was transmitted to Europe by these Getic hordes, and brought into England by the *Jut* brothers, who founded the kingdom of Kent,[1] where it is yet known as *Gavelkind*. In English law it is termed *borough English*. In Scotland it existed in barbarous times, analogous to those when the Noroza was sanctioned ; and the lord of the manor had privileges, which rendered it more than doubtful whether the first-born was natural heir : hence, the youngest was the heir. So in France, in ancient times ; and though the *'droit de Jambage'* no longer exists, the term sufficiently denotes the extent of privilege, in com-

[1] *Canthi*, ' a coast ' in Gothic and Sanscrit.

and that he should seek to degrade those whom the chances of war had made his vassals, by conduct so nefarious and repugnant to the keenly cherished feelings of the Rajpoot. Yet there is not a shadow of doubt that many of the noblest of the race were dishonoured on the 'Noroza'; and the chivalrous Pirthi Raj was only preserved from being of the number by the high courage and virtue of his wife, a princess of Méwar, and daughter of the founder of the Suktawuts. On one of these celebrations of the Khooshroz, the monarch of the Moguls was struck with the beauty of the daughter of Méwar, and he singled her out from amidst the united fair of Hind as the object of his passion. It is not improbable that an ungenerous feeling united with that already impure, to despoil the Seesodias of their honour, through a princess of their house under the protection of the sovereign. On retiring from the fair, she found herself entangled amidst the labyrinth of apartments by which egress was purposely ordained, when Akber stood before her: but instead of acquiescence, she drew a poniard from her corset, and held it to his breast, dictating, and making him repeat, the oath of renunciation of the infamy to all her race. The anecdote is accompanied in the original with many dramatic circumstances. The guardian goddess of Méwar, the terrific '*Mata*,' appears on her tiger in the subterranean passage of this palace of pollution, to strengthen her mind by a solemn denunciation, and her hand with a weapon to protect her honour. Raé Sing, the elder brother of the princely bard, had not been so fortunate; his wife wanted either courage or virtue to withstand the regal tempter, and she returned to their dwelling in the desert despoiled of her chastity, but loaded with jewels; or, as Pirthi Raj expresses it: "She returned to her abode, tramping to the tinkling sound of the ornaments of gold and gems on her person; but where, my brother, is the moustache [1] on thy lip?"

It is time to return to the Aravulli, and to the patriot prince Pertáp. Unable to stem the torrent, he had formed a resolution worthy of his character; he determined to abandon Méwar and the blood-stained Cheetore (no longer the stay of his race), and to lead his Seesodias to the Indus, plant 'the crimson banner' on the insular capital of the Sogdi, and leave a desert between him and his inexorable foe. With his family, and all that was yet noble in Méwar, his chiefs and vassals, a firm and intrepid band, who preferred exile to degradation, he descended the Aravulli, and had reached the confines of the desert, when an incident occurred which made him change his measures, and still remain a dweller in the land of his forefathers. If the historic annals of Méwar record acts of unexampled severity, they are not without instances of unparalleled devotion. The minister of Pertáp, whose ancestors had for ages held the office, placed at his prince's disposal their accumulated wealth, which, with other resources, is stated to have been equivalent to the maintenance of twenty-five thousand men for twelve years. The name of Bhama Sah is preserved as the saviour of Méwar. With this splendid proof of gratitude, and the *sirvente* of Pirthi Raj as incitements, he again "screwed his courage to the sticking-place," collected his bands, and while his foes imagined that he

parison with which the other rights of '*Noçages*,' the seigneur's feeding his greyhounds with the best dishes and insulting the bride's blushes with ribald songs, were innocent.

[1] The loss of this is the sign of mourning.

was endeavouring to effect a retreat through the desert, surprised Shabaz in his camp at Deweir, whose troops were cut in pieces. The fugitives were pursued to Amait, the garrison of which shared the same fate. Ere they could recover from their consternation, Komulmér was assaulted and taken; Abdoola and his garrison were put to the sword, and thirty-two fortified posts in like manner carried by surprise, the troops being put to death without mercy. To use the words of the annals: "Pertáp made a desert of Méwar; he made an offering to the sword of whatever dwelt in its plains": an appalling but indispensable sacrifice. In one short campaign (S. 1586, A.D. 1530), he had recovered all Méwar, except Cheetore, Ajmér, and Mandelgurh; and determining to have a slight ovation in return for the triumph Raja Maun had enjoyed (who had fulfilled to the letter his threat, that Pertáp should "live in peril"), he invaded Ambér, and sacked its chief mart of commerce, Malpoora.

Oodipoor was also regained; though this acquisition was so unimportant as scarcely to merit remark. In all likelihood it was abandoned from the difficulty of defending it, when all around had submitted to Pertáp; though the annals ascribe it to a generous sentiment of Akber, prompted by the great Khankhanan, whose mind appears to have been captivated by the actions of the Rajpoot prince. An anecdote is appended to account for Akber's relaxation of severity, but it is of too romantic a nature even for this part of their annals.

Pertáp was indebted to a combination of causes for the repose he enjoyed during the latter years of his life; and though this may be ascribed principally to the new fields of ambition which occupied the Mogul arms, we are authorised also to admit the full weight of the influence that the conduct of the Hindu prince exerted upon Akber, together with the general sympathy of his fellow-princes, who swelled the train of the conqueror, and who were too powerful to be regarded with indifference.

Repose was, however, no boon to the noblest of his race. A mind like Pertáp's could enjoy no tranquillity, while from the summit of the pass which guarded Oodipoor, his eye embraced the Kangras of Cheetore, to which he must ever be a stranger. To a soul like his, burning for the redemption of the glory of his race, the mercy thus shown him, in placing a limit to his hopes, was more difficult of endurance than the pangs of fabled Tantalus. Imagine the warrior, yet in manhood's prime, broken with fatigues and covered with scars, from amidst the fragments of basaltic ruin [1] (fit emblem of his own condition!), casting a wistful eye to the rock stained with the blood of his fathers; whilst in the 'dark chamber' of his mind the scenes of glory enacted there appeared with unearthly lustre. First, the youthful Bappa, on whose head was the 'mor

[1] These mountains are of granite and close-grained quartz; but on the summit of the pass there is a mass of columnar rocks, which, though the author never examined them very closely, he has little hesitation in calling basaltic. Were it permitted to intrude his own feelings on his reader, he would say, he never passed the portals of Dubari, which close the pass leading from Cheetore to Oodipoor, without throwing his eye on this fantastic pinnacle and imagining the picture he has drawn. Whoever, in rambling through the 'eternal city,' has had his sympathy awakened in beholding at the *Porta Salaria* the stone seat where the conqueror of the Persians and the Goths, the blind Belisarius, begged his daily dole,—or pondered at the unsculptured tomb of Napoleon upon the vicissitudes of greatness, will appreciate the feeling of one who, in sentiment, had identified himself with the Rajpoots, of whom Pertáp was justly the model.

he had won from the Mori': the warlike Samarsi, arming for the last day of Rajpoot independence, to die with Pirthi Raj on the banks of the Caggar: again, descending the steep of Cheetore, the twelve sons of Ursi, the crimson banner floating around each, while from the embattled rock the guardian goddess looked down on the carnage which secured a perpetuity of sway. Again, in all the pomp of sacrifice, the Deola chiefs, Jeimul and Putta; and like the Pallas of Rajast'han, the Chondawut dame, leading her daughter into the ranks of destruction: examples for their sons' and husbands' imitation. At length clouds of darkness dimmed the walls of Cheetore: from her battlements 'Kangra Ranee'[1] had fled; the tints of dishonour began to blend with the visions of glory; and lo! Oody Sing appeared flying from the rock to which the honour of his house was united. Aghast at the picture his fancy had portrayed, imagine him turning to the contemplation of his own desolate condition, indebted for a cessation of persecution to the most revolting sentiment that can assail an heroic mind—compassion; compared with which scorn is endurable, contempt even enviable: these he could retaliate; but for the high-minded, the generous Rajpoot, to be the object of that sickly sentiment, pity, was more oppressive than the arms of his foe.

A premature decay assailed the pride of Rajast'han; a mind diseased preyed on an exhausted frame, and prostrated him in the very summer of his days. The last moments of Pertáp were an appropriate commentary on his life, which he terminated, like the Carthaginian, swearing his successor to eternal conflict against the foes of his country's independence. But the Rajpoot prince had not the same joyful assurance that inspired the Numidian Hamilcar; for his end was clouded with the presentiment that his son Umra would abandon his fame for inglorious repose. A powerful sympathy is excited by the picture which is drawn of this final scene. The dying hero is represented in a lowly dwelling; his chiefs, the faithful companions of many a glorious day, awaiting round his pallet the dissolution of their prince, when a groan of mental anguish made Saloombra inquire, "What afflicted his soul that it would not depart in peace?" He rallied: "It lingered," he said, "for some consolatory pledge that his country should not be abandoned to the Toork"; and with the death-pang upon him, he related an incident which had guided his estimate of his son's disposition, and now tortured him with the reflection, that for personal ease he would forego the remembrance of his own and his country's wrongs.

On the banks of the Péshola, Pertáp and his chiefs had constructed a few huts[2] (the site of the future palace of Oodipoor), to protect them during the inclemency of the rains in the day of their distress. Prince Umra, forgetting the lowliness of the dwelling, a projecting bamboo of the roof caught the folds of his turban and dragged it off as he retired. A hasty emotion, which disclosed a varied feeling, was observed with pain by Pertáp, who thence adopted the opinion that his son would never withstand the hardships necessary to be endured in such a cause. "These sheds," said the dying prince, "will give way to sumptuous dwellings, thus generating the love of ease; and luxury with its concomitants will

[1] 'The queen of battlements,' the turreted Cybele of Rajast'han.

[2] This magnificent lake is now adorned with marble palaces. Such was the wealth of Méwar even in her decline.

ensue, to which the independence of Méwar, which we have bled to maintain, will be sacrificed: and you, my chiefs, will follow the pernicious example." They pledged themselves, and became guarantees for the prince, "by the throne of Bappa Rawul," that they would not permit mansions to be raised till Méwar had recovered her independence. The soul of Pertáp was satisfied, and with joy he expired.

Thus closed the life of a Rajpoot whose memory is even now idolised by every Seesodia, and will continue to be so, till renewed oppression shall extinguish the remaining sparks of patriotic feeling. May that day never arrive! yet if such be her destiny, may it, at least, not be hastened by the arms of Britain!

It is worthy the attention of those who influence the destinies of states in more favoured climes, to estimate the intensity of feeling which could arm this prince to oppose the resources of a small principality against the then most powerful empire of the world, whose armies were more numerous and far more efficient than any ever led by the Persian against the liberties of Greece. Had Méwar possessed her Thucydides or her Xenophon, neither the wars of the Peleponnesus nor the retreat of the 'ten thousand' would have yielded more diversified incidents for the historic muse, than the deeds of this brilliant reign amid the many vicissitudes of Méwar. Undaunted heroism, inflexible fortitude, that which "keeps honour bright," perseverance,—with fidelity such as no nation can boast, were the materials opposed to a soaring ambition, commanding talents, unlimited means, and the fervour of religious zeal; all, however, insufficient to contend with one unconquerable mind. There is not a pass in the alpine Aravulli that is not sanctified by some deed of Pertáp,—some brilliant victory or, oftener, more glorious defeat. Huldighat is the Thermopylæ of Méwar; the field of Deweir her Marathon.

CHAPTER XII

Umra mounts the throne—Akber's death through an attempt to poison Raja Maun—Umra disregards the promise given to his father—Conduct of the Saloombra chief—Umra defeats the Imperial armies—Sugraji installed as Rana in Cheetore—Resigns it to Umra—Fresh successes—Origin of the Suktawuts—The Emperor sends his son Purvéz against the Rana, who is defeated—Mohabet Khan defeated—Sultan Khoorum invades Méwar—Umra's despair and submission—Embassy from England—Umra abdicates the throne to his son—Umra's seclusion—His death—Observations.

Of the seventeen sons of Pertáp, Umra, who succeeded him, was the eldest. From the early age of eight to the hour of his parent's death, he had been his constant companion and the partner of his toils and dangers. Initiated by his noble sire in every act of mountain strife, familiar with its perils, he entered on his career [1] in the very flower of manhood, already attended by sons able to maintain whatever his sword might recover of his patrimony.

Akber, the greatest foe of Méwar, survived Pertáp nearly eight years.

[1] S. 1653, A.D. 1597.

The vast field in which he had to exert the resources of his mind, necessarily withdrew him from a scene where even success ill repaid the sacrifices made to attain it. Umra was left in perfect repose during the remainder of this monarch's life, which it was not wisdom to disturb by the renewal of a contest against the colossal power of the Mogul. An extended reign of more than half a century permitted Akber to consolidate the vast empire he had erected, and to model the form of his government, which displays, as handed down by Abul Fuzil, an incontestable proof of his genius as well as of his natural beneficence. Nor would the Mogul lose, on being contrasted with the contemporary princes of Europe; with Henry IV. of France, who, like himself, ascended a throne weakened by dissension; with Charles V., alike aspiring to universal sway; or the glorious queen of our own isle, who made advances to Akber and sent him an embassy.[1] Akber was fortunate as either Henry or Elizabeth in the choice of his ministers. The lofty integrity, military genius, and habits of civil industry, for which Sully was distinguished, found their parallel in Byram; and if Burleigh equalled in wisdom, he was not superior in virtue to Abul Fuzil, nor possessed of his excessive benevolence. Unhappily for Méwar, all this genius and power combined to overwhelm her. It is, however, a proud tribute to the memory of the Mogul, that his name is united with that of his rival Pertáp in numerous traditionary couplets honourable to both; and if the Rajpoot bard naturally emblazons first on his page that of his own hero, he admits that none other but Akber can stand a comparison with him; thereby confirming the eulogy of the historian of his race, who, in summing up his character, observes that, "if he sometimes did things beneath the dignity of a great king, he never did any thing unworthy of a good man." But if the annalist of the Boondí state can be relied upon, the very act which caused Akber's death will make us pause ere we subscribe to these testimonies to the worth of departed greatness; and, disregarding the adage of only speaking good of the dead, compel us to institute, in imitation of the ancient Egyptians, a posthumous inquest on the character of the monarch of the Moguls. The Boondí records are well worthy of belief, as diaries of events were kept by her princes, who were of the first importance in this and the succeeding reigns: and they may be more likely to throw a light upon points of character of a tendency to disgrace the Mogul king, than the historians of his court, who had every reason to withhold such. A desire to be rid of the great Raja Maun of Ambér, to whom he was so much indebted, made the emperor descend to act the part of the assassin. He prepared a *majoom*, or confection, a part of which contained poison; but caught in his own snare, he presented the innoxious portion to the Rajpoot and ate that drugged with death himself. We have a sufficient clue to the motives which influenced Akber to a deed so unworthy of him, and which were more fully developed in the reign of his successor; namely, a design on the part of Raja Maun to alter the succession, and that Khoosru, his nephew, should succeed instead of Selim. With such a motive, the aged emperor might have admitted with less scruple the advice which prompted an act he dared not openly undertake, without

[1] The embassy under Sir Thomas Roe was prepared by Elizabeth, but did not proceed till the accession of James. He arrived just as Méwar had bent her head to the Mogul yoke, and speaks of the Rajpoot prince Kurrun, whom he saw at court as a hostage for the treaty, with admiration.

exposing the throne in his latter days to the dangers of civil contention, as Raja Maun was too powerful to be openly assaulted.

Let us return to Méwar. Umra remodelled the institutions of his country, made a new assessment of the lands and distribution of the fiefs, apportioning the service to the times. He also established the gradation of ranks such as yet exists, and regulated the sumptuary laws even to the tie of a turban,[1] and many of these are to be seen engraved on pillars of stone in various parts of the country.

The repose thus enjoyed realised the prophetic fears of Pertáp, whose admonitions were forgotten. Umra constructed a small palace on the banks of the lake, named after himself "the abode of immortality,"[2] still remarkable for its Gothic contrast to the splendid marble edifice erected by his successors, now the abode of the princes of Méwar. Jehangír had been four years on the throne, and having overcome all internal dissension, resolved to signalise his reign by the subjugation of the only prince who had disdained to acknowledge the paramount power of the Moguls; and assembling the royal forces, he put them in motion for Méwar.

Umra, between the love of ease and reputation, wavered as to the conduct he should adopt; nor were sycophants wanting who

> "Counselled ignoble ease and peaceful sloth,
> Not peace:"

and dared to prompt his following the universal contagion, by accepting the imperial firmán. In such a state of mind the chiefs found their prince, when they repaired to the new abode to warn him, and prepare him for the emergency. But the gallant Chondawut, recalling to their remembrance the dying behest of their late glorious head, demanded its fulfilment. All resolved to imitate the noble Pertáp.

> ". . . preferring
> Hard liberty before the easy yoke
> Of servile pomp."

A magnificent mirror of European fabrication adorned the embryo palace. Animated with a noble resentment at the inefficacy of his appeal to the better feelings of his prince, the chieftain of Saloombra hurled 'the slave of the carpet'[3] against the splendid bauble, and starting up, seized his sovereign by the arm and moved him from the throne. "To horse, chiefs!" he exclaimed, "and preserve from infamy the son of Pertáp." A burst of passion followed the seeming indignity, and the patriot chief was branded with the harsh name of traitor; but with his sacred duty in view, and supported by every vassal of note, he calmly disregarded the insult. Compelled to mount his steed, and surrounded by the veterans and all the chivalry of Méwar, Umra's passion vented itself in tears of indignation. In such a mood the cavalcade descended the ridge, since studded with palaces, and had reached the spot where the temple of Juggernat'h now stands, when he recovered from this fit of passion; the

[1] The '*Umrasahi pagri*,' or turban, is still used by the Rana and some nobles on court days, but the foreign nobility have the privilege, in this respect, of conforming to their own tribes.

[2] *Umra mahl.*

[3] A small brass ornament placed at the corners of the carpet to keep it steady.

tear ceased to flow, and passing his hand over his moustache,[1] he made a courteous salutation to all, entreating their forgiveness for this omission of respect; but more especially expressing his gratitude to Saloombra, he said, "Lead on, nor shall you ever have to regret your late sovereign." Elevated with every sentiment of generosity and valour, they passed on to Deweir, where they encountered the royal army led by the brother of the Khankhanan, as it entered the pass, and which, after a long and sanguinary combat, they entirely defeated.[2]

The honours of the day are chiefly attributed to the brave Kana, uncle to the Rana, and ancestor of that numerous clan called after him Kanawuts. A truce followed this battle, but it was of short duration; for another and yet more murderous conflict took place in the spring of 1666, in the pass of the sacred Ranpoor, where the imperial army, under its leader Abdoolla, was almost exterminated;[3] though with the loss of the best and bravest of the chiefs of Méwar, whose names, however harsh, deserve preservation.[4] A feverish exultation was the fruit of this victory, which shed a hectic flush of glory over the declining days of Méwar, when the crimson banner once more floated throughout the province of Godwar.

Alarmed at these successive defeats, Jehangír, preparatory to equipping a fresh army against Méwar, determined to establish a new Rana, and to instal him in the ancient seat of power, Cheetore, thus hoping to withdraw from the standard of Umra many of his adherents. The experiment evinced at least a knowledge of their prejudices; but, to the honour of Rajpoot fidelity, it failed. Sugra, who abandoned Pertáp and went over to Akber, was selected; the sword of investiture was girded on him by the emperor's own hands, and under the escort of a Mogul force he went to reign amidst the ruins of Cheetore. Her grandeur, even in desolation, is beautifully depicted at this very period by the chaplain to the embassy from Elizabeth to Jehangír, the members composing which visited the capital of the Seesodias in their route to Ajmér.[5]

For seven years Sugra had a spurious homage paid to him amidst this

[1] This is a signal both of defiance and self-gratulation.

[2] S. 1664, A.D. 1608.

[3] Falgoon 7th, S. 1666, the spring of A.D. 1610. Ferishta misplaces this battle, making it immediately precede the invasion under Khoorum. The defeats of the Mogul forces are generally styled 'recalls of the commander.'

[4] Doodo Sangawut of Deogurh, Narrayn-das, Soorajmull, Aiskurn, all Seesodias of the first rank; Poorun Mull, son of Bhan, the chief of the Suktawuts; Hurridas Rahtore, Bhoput the Jhala of Sadri, Kahirdas Cutchwaha, Késoodas Chohan of Baidla, Mokund-das Rahtore, Jeimulote, or of the blood of Jeimul.

[5] "Chitor, an ancient great kingdom, the chief city so called, which standeth upon a mighty hill flat on the top, walled about at the least ten English miles. *There appear to this day above a hundred ruined churches and divers fair palaces, which are lodged in like manner among their ruins, beside many exquisite pillars of carved stone; and the ruins likewise of one hundred thousand stone houses, as many English by the observation have guessed.* There is but one ascent to it, cut out of a firm rock, to which a man must pass through four (sometime very magnificent) gates. *Its chief inhabitants at this day are Züm and Ohim, birds and wild beasts; but the stately ruins thereof give a shadow of its beauty while it flourished in its pride.* It was won from Ranas, an ancient Indian prince, who was forced to live himself ever after on high mountainous places adjoining to that province, and his posterity to live there ever since. Taken from him it was by Achabar Podsha (the father of that king who lived and reigned when I was in these parts) after a very long siege, which famished the besieged, without which it could never have been gotten."

desolation, the ruined pride of his ancestors. But it is gratifying to record, that not even by this recreant son of Cheetore could the impressions formed in contemplating such scenes be resisted; and Sugra, though flinty as the rock to a brother and nephew, could not support the silent admonition of the altars of the heroes who had fallen in her defence. The triumphal column raised for victory over a combination of kings, was a perpetual memento of his infamy; nor could he pass over one finger's breadth of her ample surface, without treading on some fragment which reminded him of their great deeds and his own unworthiness. We would be desirous of recording, that a nobler remembrancer than 'coward conscience,' animated the brother of Pertáp to an act of redeeming virtue; but when the annals tell us, that "the terrific Bhiroo (the god of battle) openly manifested his displeasure," it is decisive that it was not less the wish for greatness, than the desire to be "without the illness should attend it"; and sending for his nephew, he restored to him Cheetore, retiring to the isolated Kandhar.[1] Some time after, upon going to court, and being upbraided by Jehangír, he drew his dagger and slew himself in the emperor's presence: an end worthy of such a traitor.[2]

Umra took possession of the seat of his ancestors; but wanting the means to put it in defence, the acquisition only served to increase the temporary exultation. The evil resulting from attaching so much consequence to a capital had been often signally manifested; as to harass the enemy from their mountains, and thereby render his conquests unavailing, was the only policy which could afford the chance of independence. With Cheetore the Rana acquired, by surrender or assault, possession of no less than eighty of the chief towns and fortresses of Méwar: amongst them Ontalla, at whose capture occurred the patriotic struggle between the clans of Chondawut and Suktawut for the leading of the vanguard, elsewhere related.[3] On this memorable storm, besides the leaders of the rival bands, five of the infant clan Suktawut, consisting but of sixteen brave brothers, with three of the house of Saloombra, perished, struggling for the immortality promised by the bard. We may here relate the rise of the Suktawuts, with which is materially connected the future history of Méwar.

Sukta was the second of the twenty-four sons of Oody Sing. When only five years of age, he discovered that fearless temperament which marked his manhood. The armourer having brought a new dagger to try its edge by the usual proof on thinly spread cotton, the child asked the Rana "if it was not intended to cut bones and flesh," and seizing it, tried it on his own little hand. The blood gushed on the carpet, but he betrayed no symptom of pain or surprise. Whether his father admitted the tacit reproof of his own want of nerve, or that it recalled the prediction of the

[1] An isolated rock in the plain between the confluence of the Parbutty and Chumbul, and the famous Rint'humbor. The author has twice passed it in his travels in these regions.

[2] It was one of his sons who apostatised from his faith, who is well known in the imperial history as Mohabet Khan, beyond doubt the most daring chief in Jehangír's reign. This is the secret of his bond of union with prince Khoorum (Shah Jehan), himself half a Rajpoot. It was with his Rajpoots Mohabet did that daring deed, making Jehangír prisoner in his own camp, in the zenith of his power.

[3] P. 122.

astrologers, who, in casting Sukta's horoscope, had announced that he was to be "the bane of Méwar," he was incontinently commanded to be put to death, and was carried off for this purpose, when saved by the Saloombra chief, who arrested the fiat, sped to the Rana, and begged his life as a boon, promising, having no heirs, to educate him as the future head of the Chondawuts. The Saloombra chief had children in his old age, and while wavering between his own issue and the son of his adoption, the young Sukta was sent for to court by his brother Pertáp. The brothers for a considerable time lived on the most amicable footing, unhappily interrupted by a dispute while hunting, which in time engendered mutual dislike. While riding in the ring, Pertáp suddenly proposed to decide their quarrel by single combat, "to see who was the best lancer." Not backward, Sukta replied, "Do you begin"; and some little time was lost in a courteous struggle for the first spear, when, as they took their ground and agreed to charge together, the Purohit [1] rushed between the combatants and implored them not to ruin the house. His appeal, however, being vain, there was but one way left to prevent the unnatural strife: the priest drew his dagger, and plunging it in his breast, fell a lifeless corpse between the combatants. Appalled at the horrid deed, "the blood of the priest on their head," they desisted from their infatuated aim. Pertáp, waving his hand, commanded Sukta to quit his dominions, who bowing retired, and carried his resentments to Akbér. Pertáp performed with the obsequies of this faithful servant many expiatory rites, and made an irrevocable grant of Salaira to his son, still enjoyed by his descendants, while a small column yet identifies the spot of sacrifice to fidelity. From that hour to the memorable day when the founder of the Suktawuts gained the byrd of the race '*Khorasan Mooltán ca Aggul,*' on the occasion of his saving his sovereign flying from the field, the brothers had never beheld each other's face.

Sukta had seventeen sons, all of whom, excepting the heir of Bhynsror,[2] attended his obsequies. On return from this rite they found the gates barred against them by Bhánji, now chief of the Suktawuts, who told them "there were too many mouths," and that they must push their fortunes elsewhere while he attended his sovereign with the quota of Bhynsror. They demanded their horses and their arms, if such were his pleasure; and electing Achil as their head (whose wife was then pregnant), they took the route to Edur, which had recently been acquired by a junior branch of the Rahtores of Marwar. They had reached Palode when the pangs of childbirth seized the wife of Achil; and being rudely repulsed by the Sonigurra vassal of Palode, who refused her shelter at such a moment, they sought refuge amidst the ruins of a temple.[3] It was the shrine of *Mata Januvi*, 'the mother of births,' the *Juno Lucina* of the Rajpoots. In a corner of the sanctuary they placed the mother of a future race; but the rain, which fell in torrents, visibly affected the ruin. A beam of

[1] Family priest.

[2] I have visited the cenotaphs of Sukta and his successors at the almost insulated Bhynsror on the Chumbul. The castle is on a rock at the confluence of the *black Bamuni* and the Chumbul.

[3] Probably the identical temple to *the Mother*, in which I found a valuable inscription of Komarpal of Anhulwarra Puttun, dated S. 1207. Palode is in the district of Neemahaira, now alienated from Méwar, and under that upstart Pat'han, Meer Khan.

stone gave way, which but for Ballo would have crushed her: he supported the sinking roof on his head till the brothers cut down a babool tree, with which they propped it and relieved him. In this retreat Assa (*Hope*) was born, who became the parent of an extensive branch known as the Achilés Suktawuts.

The 'Great Mother' was propitious. The parent of '*Hope*' was soon enabled to resume her journey for Edur, whose chief received them with open arms, and assigned lands for their support. Here they had been some time when the Rana's prime minister passed through Edur from a pilgrimage to Satrunja.[1] A violent storm would have thrown down the tent in which was his wife, but for the exertion of some of the brothers; and the minister, on learning that it was to the near kin of his sovereign he was indebted for this kindness, invited them to Oodipoor, taking upon him to provide for them with their own proper head, which they declined without a special invitation. This was not long wanting; for Umra was then collecting the strength of his hills against the king, and the services of the band of brothers, his kinsmen, were peculiarly acceptable. The first act of duty, though humble, is properly recorded, as ennobled by the sentiment which inspired it, and the pictured scene is yet preserved of Ballo and Joda collecting logs of wood for a night fire in the mountain bivouac for their kinsman and sovereign. In the more brilliant exploit which followed Ballo took the lead, and though the lord of Bhynsror was in camp, it was Ballo who obtained the leading of the vanguard: the commencement of that rivalry of clanship from whence have resulted some of the most daring, and many of the most merciless deeds in the history of Méwar. The right to lead in battle belonged to the Chondawuts, and the first intimation the chieftain had of his prince's inconsiderate insult was from the bard incessantly repeating the '*byrd*' of the clan, until "the portal of the ten thousand" of Méwar deemed him mad. "Not so," replied he; "but it is, perhaps, the last time your ears may be gratified with the watchword of Chonda, which may to-morrow be given as well as the Herole to the Suktawuts." An explanation followed, and the assault of Ontalla ensued, which preserved the rights of the Chondawuts, though nobly contested by their rivals. The vassal of Bakrole carried the tidings of the successful assault to the Rana, who arrived in time to receive the last obeisance of Ballo, whose parting words to his prince were seized on by the bard and added to the byrd of the clan: and although, in sloth and opium, they now "lose and neglect the creeping hours of time," yet whenever a Suktawut chief enters the court of his sovereign, or takes his seat amongst his brother chiefs, the bards still salute him with the dying words of Ballo:

"*Doonoh dátár.*
Chaôgoona joojár,
Khorasan Mooltán ca aggul."[2]

---

[1] One of the *five sacred mounts* of the Jains, of whose faith was the minister. Of these I shall speak at length in the Personal Narrative.

[2] "Double gifts, fourfold sacrifice." Meaning, with increase of their prince's favour the sacrifice of their lives would progress; and which, for the sake of euphony probably, preceded the byrd won by the founder, "*the barrier to Khorasan and Mooltán.*"

The *Byrd* of the Chondawuts is: *Dos sehés Méwár ca bur Kéwár,* "the portal of the ten thousand [towns] of Méwar." It is related that Sukta, jealous of so

Then passing the hand over his moustache, for a moment the escalade of Ontalla flits before his vision, where Ballo, Achilés, Joda, Dilla, and Chut'-harbhan, five of the seventeen sons of Sukta, fell for the maintenance of the post of honour. Bhánji soon after performed a service which obtained him the entire favour of his prince, who, returning from Rutlam, was insulted by the Rahtores of Bheendir, which was punished by the Suktawut, who took the town by assault, expelling the aggressors. Umra added it to his fief of Bhynsror, and since the latter was bestowed on the rival clan, Bheendir has continued the chief residence of the leader of the Suktawuts. Ten chiefs [1] have followed in regular succession, whose issue spread over Méwar, so that in a few generations after Sukta, their prince could muster the swords of ten thousand Suktawuts ; but internal feuds and interminable spoliation have checked the progress of population, and it might be difficult now to assemble half that number of the 'children of Sukta' fit to bear arms.

To return. These defeats alarmed Jehangír, who determined to equip an overwhelming force to crush the Rana. To this end he raised the imperial standard at Ajmér, and assembled the expedition under his immediate inspection, of which he appointed his son Purvéz commander, with instructions on departure "that if the Rana or his elder son Kurrun should repair to him, to receive them with becoming attention, and to offer no molestation to the country." [2] But the Seesodia prince little thought of submission : on the contrary, flushed with success, he gave the royal army the meeting at a spot oft moistened with blood, the pass of Khamnor,[3] leading into the heart of the hills. The imperial army was disgracefully beaten, and fled, pursued with great havoc, towards Ajmér. The Mogul historian admits it to have been a glorious day for Méwar. He

sweeping a byrd, complained that nothing was left for him : when the master bard replied, he was *Kéwár ca Aggul*, the bar which secures the door (*Kéwár*).

[1] Sukta.—17 sons.

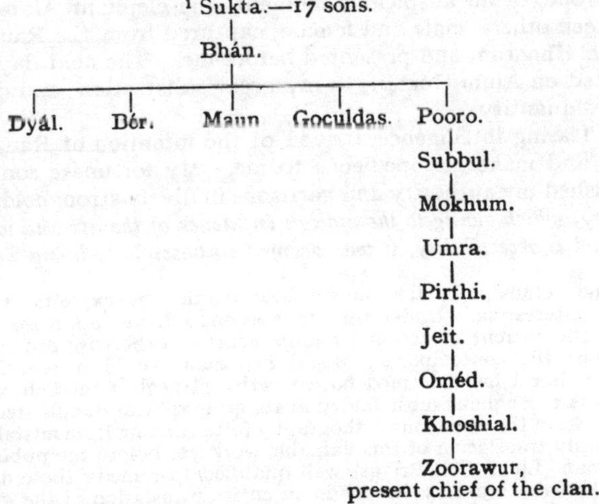

[2] A.D. 1611.

[3] Translated 'Brampoor' in Dow's *Ferishta*, and transferred to the Deccan ; and the *pass* (*bala-ghat*) rendered *the* Balaghat mountains of the south. There are numerous similar errors.

describes Purvéz entangled in the passes, dissensions in his camp, his supplies cut off, and under all these disadvantages attacked; his precipitate flight and pursuit, in which the royal army lost vast numbers of men.[1] But Jehangír in his diary slurs it over, and simply remarks: "I recalled Purvéz to join me at Lahore, and directed his son with some chiefs to be left to watch the Rana."

This son, tutored by the great Mohabet Khan, fared no better than Purvéz; he was routed and slain. But the Hydra was indestructible; for every victory, while it cost the best blood of Méwar, only multiplied the number of her foes. Seventeen pitched battles had the illustrious Rajpoot fought since the death of his father: but the loss of his experienced veterans withered the laurels of victory, nor had he sufficient repose either to husband his resources, or to rear his young heroes to replace them. Another, and yet more mighty army, was assembled under prince Khoorum, the ablest of the sons of Jehangír, and better known in history as Shah Jehán, when emperor of the Moguls.

Again did the Rana with his son Kurrun collect the might of their hills; but a handful of warriors was all their muster to meet the host of Dehli, and 'the crimson banner,' which for more than eight hundred years had waved in proud independence over the heads of the Gehlotes, was now to be abased to the son of Jehangír. The Emperor's own pen shall narrate the termination of this strife.

"Eighth year of my reign, A.H. 1022,[2] I determined to move [3] to Ajmér and send my fortunate son Khoorum before me; and having fixed the moment of departure, I dismissed him with magnificent khelats, an elephant, horse, sword, shield, and dagger, and besides his usual force added twelve thousand horse under Azim Khan, and presented to all the officers of his army suitable gratifications.

"On the commencement of the ninth year (A.D. 1614), while seated on my throne, in an auspicious moment, the elephant Alum Gomán,[4] with seventeen others, male and female, captured from the Rana, were sent by my son Khoorum and presented before me. The next day I went abroad mounted on Alum Gomán, to my great satisfaction, and distributed gold in great quantity.

"Pleasing intelligence arrived of the intention of Rana Umra Sing to repair and make his obedience to me. My fortunate son Khoorum had established my authority and garrisons in divers strongholds of the Rana's country, *which owing to the malign influence of the air and water, its barrenness and inaccessibility, it was deemed impossible to bring under subjection*;

[1] The details of battles, unless accompanied by exploits of individuals, are very uninteresting. Under this impression, I have suppressed whatever could impair the current of action by amplification, otherwise not only the Rajpoot bard, but the contemporary Mogul historian, would have afforded abundant matter; but I have deemed both worthy of neglect in such cases. Ferishta's history is throughout most faulty in its geographical details, rendered still more obscure from the erroneous orthography (often arising from mistaken punctuation) of the only translation of this valuable work yet before the public. There is one gentleman (Lieut.-Col. Briggs) well qualified to remedy these defects, and who, with a laudable industry, has made an entire translation of the works of Ferishta, besides collating the best MSS. of the original text. It is to be hoped he will present his performance to the public.

[2] A.D. 1613. [3] See p. 42. Dow gives in a note a description of his camp.

[4] 'The Arrogant of the earth.'

yet, from the perpetual overrunning of the country, without regard to the heats or the rains, by my armies, the capture and imprisonment of the wives and children of many of the men of rank of the country, the Rana was at length reduced to acknowledge the despair to which he was driven, and that a further continuance of such distress would be attended with utter ruin, with the choice of captivity or being forced to abandon the country. He therefore determined to make his submission, and sent two of his chiefs, Soopkurrun and Heridás Jhala, to my son Khoorum, to represent that if he would forgive and take him by the hand, he would pay his respects to him, and would send his eldest son Kurrun to attend and to serve the emperor, as did other Hindu princes ; but that, *on account of his years, he would hold himself*[1] *excused from attending in person.* Of these events my son sent a full relation by Shukur Oolah Afzul Khanee.

"I was greatly rejoiced at this event happening under my own reign, and I commanded that these ancient possessors of the country should not be driven from it. The fact is, Rana Umra Sing and his ancestors were proud, and confident in the strength and inaccessibility of their mountainous country and its strongholds, *and had never beheld a king of Hindustan, nor made submission to any one. I was desirous, in my own fortunate time, the opportunity should not slip my hands ; instantly, therefore, on the representation of my son, I forgave the Rana, and sent a friendly firmaun that he might rest assured of my protection and care, and imprinted thereon, as a solemn testimony of my sincerity, my 'five fingers'* (punja[2]) *; I also wrote my son, that by any means by which it could be brought about, to treat this illustrious one according to his own heart's wishes.*

"My son despatched the letter and firmaun by the chiefs Soopkurrun and Heridás Jhala, accompanied by Shukur Oolla and Soonderdás, with assurances to the Rana that he might rely on my generosity and esteem, to receive my firmaun and *impress of my hand* : and it was agreed that on the 26th of the month he should repair to my son.

"Having gone out of Ajmér to hunt, Mahmood Bég, a servant of my son Khoorum, arrived, and presented a letter from him, and stated to me verbally the Rana having met my son.

"On receiving this news, I presented Mahmood Bég with an elephant, horse, and dagger, and gave him the title of Zoolfecar Khan.

"*Account of the meeting of Rana Umra Sing with Sultan Khoorum and of Khoorum's visit to prince Kurrun, with all the Omras, and of the rank bestowed on prince Kurrun in the household of the emperor, on the part of the empress Noor Jehán.*"

"On Sunday the 26th the Rana, with respect and due attention to

[1] "He would hold himself excused." In these few words, to which the emperor has nobly given a place in his diary, we have the Rajpoot's prince's feelings depicted on this painful occasion.

[2] The giving the hand amongst all nations has been considered as a pledge for the performance or ratification of some act of importance, and the custom amongst the Scythic or Tatar nations, of transmitting its impress as a substitute, is here practically described. I have seen the identical Firmán in the Rana's archives. The hand being immersed in a compost of sandal-wood, is applied to the paper, and the palm and five fingers (*punja*) are yet distinct. In a masterly delineation of Oriental manners (*Carne's Letters from the East*) is given an anecdote of Mahommed, who, unable to sign his name to a convention, dipped his hand in ink, and made an impression therewith. It is evident the prophet of Islám only followed an ancient solemnity, of the same import as that practised by Jehangír.

etiquette, as other vassals of the empire, paid his respects to my son, and presented a celebrated ruby, well known in possession of this house, and various arms inlaid with gold ; with seven elephants of great price, which alone remained after those formerly captured ; and also nine horses as tribute. My son received him with princely generosity and courtesy ; when the Rana taking my son by the knee, requested to be forgiven. He raised his head, and gave him every kind assurance of countenance and protection, and presented him with suitable khelats, an elephant, horses, and a sword. Though he had not above one hundred persons in his train worthy to be dignified with khelats, yet one hundred and twenty khelats, fifty horses, and twelve jewelled aigrettes, were bestowed on them. The custom, however, of these princes being that the heir and the father never visit together,[1] he observed this usage, and Kurrun, his declared successor, did not accompany the Rana. Sultan Khoorum, the same day, gave Umra Sing his leave, promising forthwith to send his son Kurrun, who was introduced, and khelats, with elephant, sword, and dagger, were bestowed ; and that same day he repaired with him to me.

"In my interview with Sultan Khoorum on his arrival at Ajmér, he represented that if it was my pleasure he would present the prince Kurrun, whom I accordingly desired him to bring. He arrived, paid his respects, *and his rank was commanded to be, at the request of my son, immediately on my right hand,* and I rewarded him with suitable khelats. As Kurrun, owing to the rude life he had led in his native hills, was extremely shy, and unused to the pageantry and experience of a court, in order to reconcile and give him confidence I daily gave him some testimonies of my regard and protection, and in the second day of his service I gave him a jewelled dagger, and on the third a choice steed of Irak with rich caparisons ; and on the same day, I took him with me to the queen's court, when the queen, Noor Jehán, made him splendid khelats, elephant and horse caparisoned, sword, etc. The same day I gave him a rich necklace of pearls, another day an elephant, and it was my wish to give him rarities and choice things of every kind. I gave him three royal hawks and three gentle falcons trained to the hand,[2] a coat of mail, chain and plate armour, and two rings of value ; and, on the last day of the month, carpets, state cushions, perfumes, vessels of gold, and a pair of the bullocks of Guzzerat.

"10th year.[3] At this time I gave prince Kurrun leave to return to his jagheer ;[4] when I bestowed on him an elephant, horse, and a pearl necklace valued at 50,000 rupees (£5000) ; and from the day of his repairing to my court to that of his departure, the value of the various gifts I presented him exceeded ten lakhs of rupees (£125,000), exclusive of one hundred and ten horses, five elephants, or what my son Khoorum gave him. I sent Mabarick Khan along with him, by whom I sent an elephant, horse, etc., and various confidential messages to the Rana.

"On the 8th Suffur of the 10th year of the H. 1024, Kurrun was

[1] This was to avoid treachery. I have often had the honour to receive the descendant princes, father and son, "of these illustrious ones" together.

[2] Baz and Toora.

[3] Of his reign.

[4] Such was now the degraded title of the ancient, independent, sovereign Méwar. Happy Pertáp, whose ashes being mingled with his parent earth, was spared his country's humiliation !

elevated to the dignity of a Munsubdar [1] of five thousand, when I presented him with a bracelet of pearls, in which was a ruby of great price.

"24th Mohurrum, 10th year (A.D. 1615), Juggut Sing, son of Kurrun, aged twelve years, arrived at court and paid his respects, and presented the arzees of his father and grandfather, Rana Umra Sing. *His countenance carried the impression of his illustrious extraction,*[2] *and I delighted his heart with presents and kindness.*

[1] With this the annals state the restoration of many districts: the Kheirár, Phoolia, Bednore, Mandelgurh, Jeerun, Neemutch, and Bhynsror, with supremacy over Deola and Dongerpoor.

[2] It must have been this grandson of Umra of whom Sir Thomas Roe thus writes: "The right issue of Porus is here a king in the midst of the Mogul's dominions, never subdued till last year; and, to say the truth, he is rather bought than conquered: won to own a superior by gifts and not by arms. The pillar erected by Alexander is yet standing at Dehli, the ancient seat of Rama, the successor of Porus."—*Extract of a letter to the Archbishop of Canterbury, dated at Ajmere, January 29th,* 1615.

"Copy of a letter written by the great Mogul unto King James, in the Persian tongue, here faithfully translated, which was as follows:—

"Unto a king rightly descended from his ancestors, bred in military affairs, clothed with honour and justice, a commander worthy of all command, strong and constant in the religion which the great prophet Christ did teach, King James, whose love hath bred such an impression in my thoughts as shall never be forgotten; but as the smell of amber, or as a garden of fragrant flowers, whose beauty and odour is still increasing, so, be assured, my love shall still grow and increase with yours.

"The letters which you sent me in the behalf of your merchants I have received, whereby I rest satisfied of your tender love towards me, desiring you not to take it ill, that I have not wrote to you heretofore: this present letter I send to you to renew our loves, and herewith do certifie you, that I have sent forth my firmaunes throughout all my countries to this effect, that if any English ships or merchants shall arrive in any of my ports, my people shall permit and suffer them to do what they please, freely in their merchandising causes, aiding and assisting them in all occasion of injuries that shall be offered them, that the least cause of discourtesie be not done unto them; that they may be as free, or freer than my own people.

"And as now, and formerly, I have received from you divers tokens of your love; so I shall still desire your mindfulness of me by some novelties from your countries, as an argument of friendship betwixt us, for such is the custom of princes here.

"And for your merchants, I have given express order through all my dominions, to suffer them to buy, sell, transport, and carry away at their pleasure, without the lett or hinderance of any person whatsoever, all such goods and merchandises as they shall desire to buy; and let this my letter as fully satisfie you in desired peace and love, as if my own son had been messenger to ratifie the same.

"And if any in my countries, not fearing God, nor obeying their king, or any other void of religion, should endeavour to be an instrument to break this league of friendship, I would send my son Sultan Caroom, a souldier approved in the wars, to cut him off, that no obstacle may hinder the continuance and increase of our affections.

"When your majesty shall open this letter, let your royal heart be as fresh as a small garden, let all people make reverence at your gate. Let your throne be advanced higher. Amongst the greatness of the kings of the prophet Jesus, let your majesty be the greatest; and all monarchs derive their wisdom and counsel from your breast, as from a fountain, that the law of the majesty of Jesus may receive, and flourish under your protection.

"The letters of love and friendship which you sent me, the present tokens of your good affection towards me, I have received by the hands of your ambassadour, Sir Thomas Row, who well deserveth to be your trusty servant, delivered to me in an acceptable and happy hour; upon which mine eyes were so

"On the 10th Shaban, Juggut Sing had permission to return to his house. At his departure I presented him with 20,000 rupees, a horse, elephant, and khelats; and to Heridás Jhala, preceptor of Prince Kurrun, 5000 rupees, a horse, and khelat; and I sent by him six golden images [1] to the Rana.

"28th Rubee ool Akber, 11th year. *The statues of the Rana and Kurrun, sculptured in white marble, I desired should have inscribed the date in which they were prepared and presented, and commanded they should be placed in the gardens at Agra.*

"In the 11th year of my reign, an arzee from Etimad Khan acquainted me that Sultan Khoorum had entered the Rana's country, and that prince and his son had both exchanged visits with my son; and that from the tribute, consisting of seven elephants, twenty-seven saddle horses, trays of jewels, and ornaments of gold, my son took three horses and returned all the rest, and engaged that Prince Kurrun and fifteen hundred Rajpoot horse should remain with him in the wars.

"In the 13th year Prince Kurrun repaired to my court, then at Sindla, to congratulate me on my victories and conquest of the Dukhun, and presented 100 mohors,[2] 1000 rupees, nuzzerana, and effects in gold and jewels to the amount of 21,000 rupees, hardy elephants and horses; the last I returned, but kept the rest, and next day presented him a dress of honour; and from Futehpoor gave him his leave, with elephant, horse, sword, and dagger, and a horse for his father.

"14th year of my reign. On the 17th Rubbee-ool-awal, 1029 H., I received intelligence of the death of Rana Umra Sing. To Juggut Sing, his grandson, and Bheem Sing, his son, in attendance, I gave khelats, and dispatched Raja Kishoredás [3] with the firmán conferring benefits and with the dignity of Rana, the khelat of investiture, choice horses, and a letter of condolence suitable to the occasion to Prince Kurrun. 7th Shuval. Beharri dás Bramin I dispatched with a firmán to Rana Kurrun, desiring that his son with his contingent should attend me."

To have generalised this detail of the royal historian would have been to lessen the interest of this important period in the annals of Méwar. Jehangír merits to have his exultation, his noble and unostentatious conduct, described by his own pen, the extreme minuteness of which description but increases the interest. With his self-gratulation, he bears full testimony to the gallant and long-protracted resistance of the Rajpoots;

fixed, that I could not easily remove them unto any other objects, and have accepted them with great joy and delight, etc."

The last letter had this beginning:—"How gracious is your majesty, whose greatness God preserve. As upon a rose in a garden, so are mine eyes fixed upon you. God maintain your estate, that your monarchy may prosper and be augmented; and that you may obtain all your desires worthy the greatness of your renown; and as the heart is noble and upright, so let God give you a glorious reign, because you strongly defend the law of the majesty of Jesus, which God made yet more flourishing, for that it was confirmed by miracles, etc."—*Della Valle*, p. 473.

[1] There are frequent mention of such images (*pootlis*), but I know not which they are.

[2] Golden suns, value £1. 12s.

[3] Increasing the respect to the Ranas by making a prince the bearer of the firmán

and while he impartially, though rather erroneously, estimates their motives and means of opposition, he does Umra ample justice in the declaration, that he did not yield until he had but the alternative of captivity or exile; and with a magnanimity above all praise, he records the Rajpoot prince's salvo for his dignity, "that he would hold himself excused from attending in person." The simple and naïve declaration of his joy, "his going abroad on Alum Gomán," the favourite elephant of the Rana which had been captured, on learning his submission, is far stronger than the most pompous testimony of public rejoicing. But there is a heart-stirring philanthropy in the conduct of the Mogul which does him immortal honour; and in commanding his son "to treat the illustrious one according to his heart's wishes," though he so long and so signally had foiled the royal armies, he proved himself worthy of the good fortune he acknowledges, and well shows his sense of the superiority of the chief of all the Rajpoots, by placing the heir of Méwar, even above all the princes of his own house, "immediately on *his right hand.*" Whether he attempts to relieve the shyness of Kurrun, or sets forth the princely appearance of Juggut Sing, we see the same amiable feeling operating to lighten the chains of the conquered. But the shyness of Kurrun deserved a worthier term: he felt the degradation which neither the statues raised to them, the right hand of the monarch, the dignity of a 'commander of five thousand,' or even the restoration of the long-alienated territory could neutralise, when the kingdom to which he was heir was called a fief (*jagheer*), and himself, 'the descendant of a hundred kings,' a vassal (*jagheerdar*) of the empire, under whose banner, which his ancestors had so signally opposed, he was now to follow with a contingent of fifteen hundred Rajpoot horse.

Seldom has subjugated royalty met with such consideration; yet, to a lofty mind like Umra's, this courteous condescension but increased the severity of endurance. In the bitterness of his heart he cursed the magnanimity of Khoorum, himself of Rajpoot blood[1] and an admirer of Rajpoot valour, which circumstance more than the force of his arms had induced him to surrender; for Khoorum demanded but the friendship of the Rajpoot as the price of peace, and to withdraw every Mahomedan from Méwar if the Rana would but receive the emperor's firmán outside of his capital. This his proud soul rejected; and though he visited Prince Khoorum as a friend, he spurned the proposition of acknowledging a superior, or receiving the rank and titles awaiting such an admission. The noble Umra, who—

"Rather than be less,
Cared not to be at all"—

took the resolution to abdicate[2] the throne he could no longer hold but at the will of another. Assembling his chiefs, and disclosing his determination, he made the *teeka* on his son's forehead; and observing that the honour of Méwar was now in his hands, forthwith left the capital

[1] Khoorum was son of a Rajpoot princess of Ambér, of the *Cutchwaha* tribe, and hence his name was probably *Koorm*, synonymous to cutchwa, *a tortoise.* The bards are always punning upon it.

[2] Surrendered S. 1672, A.D. 1616 (according to Dow, S. 1669, A.D. 1613); died 1621.

and secluded himself in the *No-choki*:[1] nor did he from that hour cross its threshold, but to have his ashes deposited with those of his fathers.

All comment is superfluous on such a character as Rana Umra. He was worthy of Pertáp and his race. He possessed all the physical as well as mental qualities of a hero, and was the tallest and strongest of all the princes of Méwar. He was not so fair as they usually are, and he had a reserve bordering upon gloominess, doubtless occasioned by his reverses, for it was not natural to him; he was beloved by his chiefs for the qualities they most esteem, generosity and valour, and by his subjects for his justice and kindness, of which we can judge from his edicts, many of which yet live on the column or the rock.

CHAPTER XIII

Rana Kurrun fortifies and embellishes Oodipoor—The Ranas of Méwar excused attendance at court—Bheem commands the contingent of Méwar—Leagues with Sultan Khoorum against Purvéz—Jehangír attacks the insurgents—Bheem slain—Khoorum flies to Oodipoor—His reception by the Rana—Death of Kurrun—Rana Juggut Sing succeeds—Death of Jehangír and accession of Khoorum as Shah Jehán—Méwar enjoys profound peace—The island palaces erected by Juggut Sing—Repairs Cheetore—His death—Rana Raj Sing—Deposal of Shah Jehán and accession of Arungzéb—Causes for attachment to the Hindus of Jehangír and Shah Jehán—Arungzéb's character; imposes the Jezeya or capitation tax on the Rajpoots—Raj Sing abducts the intended wife of the emperor and prepares for war—Arungzéb marches—The valley of Girwo—Prince Akber surprised—Defeated—Blockaded in the mountains—Liberated by the heir of Méwar—Delhire Khan defeated—Arungzéb defeated by the Rana and his Rahtore allies—Arungzéb quits the field—Prince Bheem invades Guzzerat—The Rana's minister ravages Malwa—United Rajpoots defeat Azím and drive him from Cheetore—Méwar freed from the Moguls—War carried into Marwar—Seesodias and Rahtores defeat Sultan Akber—Rajpoot stratagem—Design to depose Arungzéb and elevate Akber to the throne—Its failure—The Mogul makes overtures to the Rana—Peace—Terms—The Rana dies of his wounds—His character, contrasted with that of Arungzéb—Lake Rajsumund—Dreadful famine and pestilence.

KURRUN, or Kurna (*the radiant*), succeeded to the last independent king of Méwar, S. 1677, A.D. 1621. Henceforth we shall have to exhibit these princely 'children of the sun' with diminished lustre, moving as satellites round the primary planet; but, unaccustomed to the laws of its attraction, they soon deviated from the orbit prescribed, and in the eccentricity of their movements occasionally displayed their unborrowed effulgence. For fifteen hundred years we have traced each alternation of the fortune of this family, from their establishment in the second, to their expulsion in the fifth century from Saurashtra by the Parthians; the acquisition and loss of Edur; the conquest and surrender of Cheetore; the rise of Oodipoor and abasement of the red flag to Jehangír; and we shall conclude with

[1] It must have been here that Sultan Khoorum visited the Rana. The remains of this palace, about half a mile without the city wall (north), on a cluster of hills, are yet in existence. It was built by Oody Sing on the banks of a lake, under which are gardens and groves, where the author had the Rana's permission to pitch his tents in the hottest months.

not the least striking portion of their history, their unity of interests with Britain.

Kurrun was deficient neither in courage nor conduct ; of both he had given a decided proof, when, to relieve the pecuniary difficulties of his father, with a rapidity unparalleled, he passed through the midst of his foes, surprised and plundered Surat, and carried off a booty which was the means of protracting the evil days of his country. But for the exercise of the chief virtue of the Rajpoot, he had little scope throughout his reign, and fortunately for his country the powerful esteem and friendship which Jehangír and Prince Khoorum evinced for his house, enabled him to put forth the talents he possessed to repair past disasters. He fortified the heights round the capital, which he strengthened with a wall and ditch, partly enlarged the noble dam which retains the waters of the Péshola, and built that entire portion of the palace called the Rawula, still set apart for the ladies of the court.

When Rana Umra made terms with Jehangír, he stipulated, as a salvo for his dignity and that of his successors, exemption from all personal attendance ; and confined the extent of homage to his successors receiving, on each lapse of the crown, the firmaun or imperial decree in token of subordination, which, more strongly to mark their dependent condition, the Rana was to accept without the walls of his capital ; accordingly, though the heirs-apparent of Méwar [1] attended the court, they never did as Rana. Partly to lessen the weight of this sacrifice to independence, and partly to exalt the higher grade of nobles, the princes of the blood-royal of Méwar were made to rank below the *sixteen*, a fictitious diminution of dignity which, with similar acts peculiar to this house, enhanced the self-estimation of the nobles, and made them brave every danger to obtain such sacrifices to the ruling passion of the Rajpoot, a love of distinction.[2] It is mentioned by the emperor that he placed the heir-apparent of Méwar immediately on his right hand, over all the princes of Hindust'han ; consequently the superior nobles of Méwar, who were all men of royal descent,

[1] The contingent of Méwar was one thousand horse.

[2] During the progress of my mediation between the Rana and his nobles, in 1818, the conduct of the lineal representative of Jeimul, the defender of Cheetore against Akber, was striking. Instead of surrendering the lands which he was accused of usurping, he placed himself at the door of the threshold of the palace, whence he was immovable. His claims were left to my adjudication : but he complained with great heat of the omission of ceremonials, and especially of the prostration of honours by the prince. I incautiously remarked that these were trivial compared with the other objects in view, and begged him to disregard it. "Disregard it ! why, it was for these things my ancestors sacrificed their lives ; when such a band [1] as this on my turban was deemed ample reward for the most distinguished service, and made them laugh at wounds and hardships !" Abashed at the inconsiderate remark which provoked this lofty reproof, I used my influence to have the omission rectified : the lands were restored, and the enthusiastic reverence with which I spoke of Jeimul would have obtained even greater proof of the Bednore chief's regard for the fame of his ancestors than the surrender of them implied. Who would not honour this attachment to such emblems in the days of adversity ?

[1] *Bala-bund*, a fillet or band, sometimes embroidered ; often, as in the present case, of silk or gold thread knotted, and tassels tied round the turban. *Bala-bund* is synonymous with *diadem*.

deemed themselves, and had their claims admitted, to rank above their peers at other courts, and to be seated almost on an equality with their princes.[1]

The Seesodia chieftains were soon distinguished amongst the Rajpoot vassals of the Mogul, and had a full share of power. Of these Bheem, the younger brother of Kurrun, who headed the quota of Méwar, was conspicuous, and became the chief adviser and friend of Sultan Khoorum, who well knew his intrepidity. At his son's solicitation, the emperor conferred upon him the title of Raja, and assigned a small principality on the Bunas for his residence, of which Thoda was the capital. Ambitious of perpetuating a name, he erected a new city and palace on the banks of the river, which he called Rajmahl, and which his descendants held till about forty years ago. The ruins of Rajmahl[2] bear testimony to the architectural taste of this son of Méwar, as do the fallen fortunes of his descendant to the instability of power: the lineal heir of Raja Bheem serves the chief of Shahpoora on half a crown a day!

Jehangír, notwithstanding his favours, soon had a specimen of the insubordinate spirit of Bheem. Being desirous to separate him from Sultan Khoorum, who aspired to the crown in prejudice to his elder brother Purvéz, he appointed Bheem to the government of Guzzerat, which was distinctly refused. Detesting Purvéz, who, it will be recollected, invaded Méwar, and was foiled for his cruelty on this occasion, Bheem advised his friend at once to throw off the mask, if he aspired to reign. Purvéz was slain, and Khoorum manifested his guilt by flying to arms. He was secretly supported by a strong party of the Rajpoot interest, at the head of which was Guj Sing of Marwar, his maternal grandfather, who cautiously desired to remain neutral. Jehangír advanced to crush the incipient revolt; but dubious of the Rahtore (Guj Sing), he gave the van to Jeipoor, upon which the prince furled his banners and determined to be a spectator. The armies approached and were joining action, when the impetuous Bheem sent a message to the Rahtore either to aid or oppose them. The insult provoked him to the latter course, and Bheem's party was destroyed, him-

[1] This was conceded, as the following anecdote will attest. When the first Péshwa appeared at the Jeipoor court he was accompanied by the Saloombra chieftain. The Jeipoor prince divided his gadi (*cushion*) with the Péshwa, and the latter made room for the Saloombra chief upon it, observing that their privileges and rank were similar. The same Péshwa had the address to avoid all discussion of rank at Oodipoor, by alleging the prerogative of his order to '*spread his cloth in front of the throne*,' a distinction to which every priest is entitled.

[2] There are many picturesque scenes of this nature on the Bunas. Doonee made a celebrated defence against Sindia's army in 1808, and held out several months, though the Mahratta prince had an army of forty thousand men and a park of eighty pieces of cannon to oppose two hundred Rajpoots. They made sorties, captured his foragers, cut his batteries to pieces, and carried off his guns (of which they had none), and, placing them on their walls, with his own shot made the whole army change position, beyond matchlock range. At last their inexpertness rendered them useless, and they obtained honourable terms. On one occasion the foragers of our escort were returning, and met Sindia's coming away without their guns and cattle, which had just been taken from them. Our lads, from fellowship, volunteered to recover them, and returned on the captors, who gave them up (if my memory deceive me not) without a struggle, and from respect to the *red coat*!

self slain,[1] and Khoorum and Mohabet Khan compelled to seek refuge in Oodipoor. In this asylum he remained undisturbed : apartments in the palace were assigned to him ; but his followers little respecting Rajpoot prejudices, the island became his residence, on which a sumptuous edifice was raised, adorned with a lofty dome crowned with the crescent. The interior was decorated with mosaic, in onyx, cornelian, jaspers, and agates, rich Turkey carpets, etc. ; and that nothing of state might be wanting to the royal refugee, a throne was sculptured from a single block of serpentine, supported by quadriform female Caryatidæ. In the court a little chapel was erected to the Mahomedan saint Madar, and here the prince with his court resided, every wish anticipated, till a short time before his father's death, when he retired into Persia.[2]

Such was Rajpoot gratitude to a prince who, when the chances of war made him victor over them, had sought unceasingly to mitigate the misery attendant on the loss of independence ! It is pleasing to record to the honour of this calumniated race, that these feelings on the part of Kurrun were not transient ; and that so far from expiring with the object,

"The debt immense of endless gratitude"

was transmitted as an heirloom to his issue ; and though two centuries have fled, during which Méwar had suffered every variety of woe, pillaged by Mogul, Pat'han, and Mahratta, yet the turban of Prince Khoorum, the symbol of fraternity,[3] has been preserved, and remains in the same folds as when transferred from the head of the Mogul to that of the Rajpoot prince. The shield is yet held as the most sacred of relics, nor will the lamp which illumines the chapel of Madar want oil while the princes of Oodipoor have wherewithal to supply it.[4]

[1] Maun Sing, chief of the Suktawuts, and his brother Gokuldas, were Bheem's advisers, and formed with Mohabet Khan the junta who ruled the Mogul heir-apparent. Maun held Sanwar in the Khairár, and was celebrated in Umra's wars as the great champion of the Seesodias. He counted above eighty wounds, and had at various times "sent a *seer* (two pounds) of exfoliated bone to the Ganges." Such was the affection between Maun and Bheem, that they concealed the death of the latter, sending him food in Bheem's name ; but he no sooner learned the truth than he tore away the bandages and expired. Of Gokuldas the bard says, in allusion to the peaceful reign of Kurrun, "The wreath of Kurrun's renown was fading, but Gokul revived it with his blood." It was with the Seesodia Rajpoots and the Suktawuts that Mohabet performed the most daring exploit in Mogul history, making Jehangír prisoner in his own camp : but it is too long for insertion in a note.

[2] Contemporary historians say to Golconda.

[3] An exchange of turbans is the symbol of fraternal adoption.

[4] It is an affecting proof of the perpetuity of true gratitude,

"Which owing, owes not,"

as well as of religious toleration, to find the shrine of the Mahomedan saint maintained in this retreat of the Seesodias, and the priest and establishment kept up, though the son of their benefactor persecuted them with unrelenting barbarity. Are these people worth conciliating ? or does the mist of ignorance and egotism so blind us that we are to despise the minds hidden under the cloak of poverty and long oppression ? The orange-coloured turban, and the shield of Shah Jehán, have been brought from their sacred niche for my view : that I looked on them with sentiments of reverence, as relics consecrated by the noblest feeling of the mind, will be credited. I bowed to the turban with an irresistible impulse, and a fervour as deep as ever did pilgrim before the most hallowed shrine.

Rana Kurrun had enjoyed eight years of perfect tranquillity when he was gathered to his fathers. The sanctuary he gave Prince Khoorum had no apparent effect on Jehangír, who doubtless believed that the Rana did not sanction the conduct of his brother Bheem. He was succeeded by his son Juggut Sing, 'the lion of the world,' in S. 1684 (A.D. 1628).

The Emperor Jehangír died shortly after his accession, and while Khoorum was in exile. This event, which gave the throne to the friend of his house, was announced to him by the Rana, who sent his brother and a band of Rajpoots to Surat to form the cortège of the emperor, who repaired directly to Oodipoor; and it was in the Bádul Mahl ('the cloud saloon') of his palace that he was first saluted by the title of 'Shah Jehán,' by the satraps and tributary princes of the empire.[1] On taking leave, the new monarch restored five alienated districts, and presented the Rana with a ruby of inestimable value, giving him also permission to reconstruct the fortifications of Cheetore.

The twenty-six years during which Juggut Sing occupied the throne passed in uninterrupted tranquillity: a state unfruitful to the bard, who flourishes only amidst agitation and strife. This period was devoted to the cultivation of the peaceful arts, especially architecture; and to Juggut Sing Oodipoor is indebted for those magnificent works which bear his name, and excite our astonishment, after all the disasters we have related, at the resources he found to accomplish them.

The palace on the lake (covering about four acres), called the Jugnewás, is entirely his work, as well as many additions to its sister isle, on which is the Jugmunder.[2] Nothing but marble enters into their composition; columns, baths, reservoirs, fountains, all are of this material, often inlaid with mosaics, and the uniformity pleasingly diversified by the light passing through glass of every hue. The apartments are decorated with historical paintings in water-colours, almost meriting the term fresco from their deep absorption in the wall, though the darker tints have blended with and in part obscured the more delicate shades, from atmospheric causes. The walls, both here and in the grand palace, contain many medallions, in considerable relief, in gypsum, portraying the principal historical events of the family, from early periods even to the marriage pomp of the present Rana. Parterres of flowers, orange and lemon groves, intervene to dispel the monotony of the buildings, shaded by the wide-spreading tamarind and magnificent evergreen kheenee; while the graceful palmyra and cocoa wave their plume-like branches over the dark cypress or cooling plantain. Detached colonnaded refectories are placed on the water's edge for the chiefs, and extensive baths for their use. Here they listened to the tale of the bard, and slept off their noonday opiate amidst the cool breezes of the lake, wafting delicious odours from myriads of the lotus-flower which covered the surface of the waters; and as the fumes of the potion evaporated, they opened their eyes on a landscape to which not even its inspirations could frame an equal: the broad waters of the Péshola, with its indented and well-wooded margin receding to the terminating

[1] Ferishta, whose geography is often quite unintelligible, omits this in his history, and passes the king direct to Ajmér: but the annals are fuller, and describe the royal insignia conveyed by Mohabet, Abdoola, Khan Jehán, and his secretary Sadoola.

[2] 'The *minster* of the world.'

point of sight, at which the temple of Brimpoori opened on the pass of the gigantic Aravulli, the field of the exploits of their forefathers. Amid such scenes did the Seesodia princes and chieftains recreate during two generations, exchanging the din of arms for voluptuous inactivity.

Juggut Sing was a highly respected prince, and did much to efface the remembrance of the rude visitations of the Moguls. The dignity of his character, his benevolence of address and personal demeanour, secured the homage of all who had access to him, and are alike attested by the pen of the emperor, the ambassador of England, and the chronicles of Méwar. He had the proud satisfaction of redeeming the ancient capital from ruin; rebuilding the "chaplet bastion,[1] restoring the portals, and replacing the pinnacles on the temples of Chutterkote." By a princess of Marwar he left two sons, the eldest of whom succeeded.

Raj Sing (the royal lion) mounted the throne in S. 1710 (A.D. 1654). Various causes over which he had no control, combined, together with his personal character, to break the long repose his country had enjoyed. The emperor of the Moguls had reached extreme old age, and the ambition of his sons to usurp his authority involved every Rajpoot in support of their individual pretensions. The Rana inclined to Dara,[2] the legitimate heir to the throne, as did nearly the whole Rajpoot race; but the battle of Futtehbad silenced every pretension, and gave the lead to Arungzéb, which he maintained by the sacrifice of whatever opposed his ambition. His father, brothers, nay, his own offspring, were in turn victims to that thirst for power which eventually destroyed the monarchy of the Moguls.

The policy introduced by their founder, from which Akber, Jehangír, and Shah Jehán had reaped so many benefits, was unwisely abandoned by the latter, who of all had the most powerful reasons for maintaining those ties which connected the Rajpoot princes with his house. Historians have neglected to notice the great moral strength derived from this unity of the indigenous races with their conquerors; for during no similar period was the empire so secure, nor the Hindu race so cherished, as during the reigns of Jehangír and Shah Jehán: the former born from a Rajpoot princess of Ambér, and the latter from the house of Marwar. Arungzéb's unmixed Tatar blood brought no Rajpoot sympathies to his aid; on the contrary, every noble family shed their best blood in withstanding his accession, and in the defence of Shah Jehán's rights, while there was a hope of success. The politic Arungzéb was not blind to this defect, and he tried to remedy it in his successor; for both his declared heir, Shah Allum, and Azím, as well as his favourite grandson,[3] were the offspring of Rajpootnis; but, uninfluenced himself by such predilections, his bigotry outweighed his policy, and he visited the Rajpoots with an unrelenting and unwise persecution.

We shall pass the twice-told tale of the struggle for power which ended in the destruction of the brothers, competitors with Arungzéb: this belongs to general history, not to the annals of Méwar; and that history

[1] The *Mala Boorj*, a 'chaplet bastion' blown up by Akber, is a small fortress of itself.

[2] I have copies of the original letters written by Dara, Sujah, Morad, and Arungzéb on this occasion, each soliciting the Rana's aid.

[3] Kám-buksh (son of Jodpoori, not Udipoori), *the gift of Cupid*. Of this the Greeks made Cambyses.

is in every hand,[1] in which the magnanimity of Dara, the impetuosity of Morad, and the activity of Sujah met the same tragical end.

It has seldom occurred that so many distinguished princes were contemporary as during the reign of Arungzéb. Every Rajpoot principality had a head above mediocrity in conduct as in courage. Jey Sing of Ambér, surnamed 'the Mirza Raja'; Jeswunt Sing of Marwar, with the Haras of Boondí and Kotah; the Rahtores of Bikanér, and Boondélas of Orcha and Duttea, were men whose prejudices, properly consulted, would have rendered the Mogul power indissoluble: but he had but one measure of contumely for all, which inspired Sevaji with designs of freedom to Mahrashtra, and withdrew every sentiment of support from the princes of Rajast'han. In subtlety and the most specious hypocrisy, in that concentration of resolve which confides its deep purpose to none, in every qualification of the warrior or scholar,[2] Arungzéb had no superior amongst

[1] Bernier, who was an eye-witness of these transactions, describes them far better than the Mogul historians, and his accounts tally admirably with the Rajpoot annals.

[2] We possess a most erroneous idea of the understanding of Asiatic princes, and the extent of its cultivation. Arungzéb's rebuke to his tutor *Moolla Salé*, who beset him with a sycophantic intrusion on his coming to the throne, may correct this, and, with the letter of Rana Raj Sing, give the European world juster notions of the powers of mind both of Hindu and Mahomedan. It is preserved by Bernier, who had ample opportunity to acquire a knowledge of them. (*From an edition in the author's possession, printed* A.D. 1684, *only three years after these events.*)

"'What is it you would have of me, Doctor? Can you reasonably desire I should make you one of the chief *Omrahs* of my court? Let me tell you, if you had instructed me as you should have done, nothing would be more just; for I am of this persuasion, that a child well educated and instructed is as much, at least, obliged to his master as to his father. But where are those good documents you have given me? In the first place, you have taught me that all that Frangistan (so it seems they call Europe) was nothing, but I know not what little island, of which the greatest king was he of Portugal, and next to him he of Holland, and after him he of England: and as to the other kings, as those of France and Andalusia, you have represented them to me as our petty Rajas; telling me that the kings of Indostan were far above them all together, and that they were the true and only Houmajons, the Ekbars, the Jehan-Guyres, the Chah-Jehans, the fortunate ones, the great ones, the conquerors and kings of the world; and that Persia and Usbec, Kachguer, Tartar and Catay, Pegu, China and Matchina did tremble at the name of the kings of Indostan. Admirable geography! You should rather have taught me exactly to distinguish all those different states of the world, and well to understand their strength, their way of fighting, their customs, religions, governments, and interests; and, by the perusal of solid history, to observe their rise, progress, decay, and whence, how, and by what accidents and errors those great changes and revolutions of empires and kingdoms have happened. I have scarce learnt of you the name of my grandsires, the famous founders of this empire: so far were you from having taught me the history of their life, and what course they took to make such great conquests. You had a mind to teach me the Arabian tongue, to read and to write. I am much obliged to you, forsooth, for having made me lose so much time upon a language that requires ten or twelve years to attain to its perfection; as if the son of a king should think it to be an honour to him to be a grammarian or some doctor of the law, and to learn other languages than those of his neighbours, when he cannot well be without them; he, to whom time is so precious for so many weighty things, which he ought by times to learn. As if there were any spirit that did not with some reluctancy, and even with a kind of debasement, employ itself in so sad and dry an exercise, so longsom and tedious, as is that of learning words.'

"Thus did Arung-Zebe resent the pedantic instructions of his tutor; to

the many distinguished of his race ; but that sin by which 'angels fell' had steeped him in an ocean of guilt, and not only neutralised his natural capacities, but converted the means for unlimited power into an engine of self-destruction. "This hypocrisy," says the eloquent Orme, "increased with his power, and in order to palliate to his Mahomedan subjects the crimes by which he had become their sovereign, he determined to enforce the conversion of the Hindus by the severest penalties, and even by the sword: as if the blood of his subjects were to wash away the stains from his hands, already encrimsoned with that of his family. Labour left the field and industry the loom, until the decrease of the revenues induced Arungzéb to substitute a capitation tax [1] as the balance of account between the two religions." The same historian justly characterises this enactment as one so contrary to all notions of sound policy, as well as of the feelings of humanity, that "reflection seeks the motive with amazement." In this amazement we might remain, nor seek to develop the motive, did not the ample page of history in all nations disclose that in the name of religion more blood has been shed, and more atrocity committed, than by

which 'tis affirmed in that court, that after some entertainment which he had with others, he further added the following reproof :—

"'Know you not, that childhood well govern'd, being a state which is ordinarily accompanied with an happy memory, is capable of thousands of good precepts and instructions, which remain deeply impressed the whole remainder of a man's life, and keep the mind always raised for great actions ? The law, prayers, and science, may they not as well be learned in our mother-tongue as in Arabick ? You told my father, *Chah Jehan*, that you would teach me philosophy. 'Tis true, I remember very well, that you have entertain'd me for many years with airy questions of things that afford no satisfaction at all to the mind, and are of no use in humane society, empty notions and mere phancies, that have only this in them, that they are very hard to understand and very easie to forget, which are only capable to tire and spoil a good understanding, and to breed an opinion that is insupportable. I still remember, that after you had thus amused me, I know not how long, with your fine philosophy, all I retained of it was a multitude of barbarous and dark words, proper to bewilder, perplex, and tire out the best wits, and only invented the better to cover the vanity and ignorance of men like yourself, that would make us believe that they know all, and that under those obscure and ambiguous words are hid great mysteries which they alone are capable to understand. If you had season'd me with that philosophy which formeth the mind to ratiocination, and insensibly accustoms it to be satisfied with nothing but solid reasons, if you had given me those excellent precepts and doctrines which raise the soul above the assaults of fortune, and reduce her to an unshakeable and always equal temper, and permit her not to be lifted up by prosperity nor debased by adversity ; if you had taken care to give me the knowledge of what we are and what are the first principles of things, and had assisted me in forming in my mind a fit idea of the greatness of the universe, and of the admirable order and motion of the parts thereof ; if, I say, you had instilled into me this kind of philosophy, I should think myself incomparably more obliged to you than Alexander was to his Aristotle, and believe it my duty to recompense you otherwise than he did him. Should not you, instead of your flattery, have taught me somewhat of that point so important to a king, which is, what the reciprocal duties are of a sovereign to his subjects and those of subjects to their sovereign ; and ought not you to have considered, that one day I should be obliged with the sword to dispute my life and the crown with my brothers ? Is not that the destiny almost of all the sons of Indostan ? Have you ever taken any care to make me learn, what 'tis to besiege a town or to set an army in array ? For these things I am obliged to others, not at all to you. Go, and retire to the village whence you are come, and let no body know who you are or what is become of you.'"

[1] The Jezeya.

the united action of the whole catalogue of the passions. Mahomed's creed was based on conversion, which, by whatever means effected, was a plenary atonement for every crime. In obedience thereto Arungzéb acted ; but though myriads of victims who clung to their faith were sacrificed by him at the fiat of this gladiatorial prophet, yet nor these, nor the scrupulous fulfilment of fanatic observances, could soothe at the dread hour the perturbations of the 'still small voice' which whispered the names of father, brother, son, bereft by him of life. Eloquently does he portray these terrors in his letters to his grandson on his death-bed, wherein he says, "Whichever way I look, I see only the divinity"—and that an offended divinity.[1]

[1] I deem it right, in order further to illustrate the cultivated understanding of Arungzéb, to annex the letters written to his sons a few days before his death. With such talents, with so just a conception as these and the rebuke to his tutor evince of his knowledge of the right, what might he not have been had not fell ambition misguided him !

"To Shaw Azim Shaw.

"Health to thee ! my heart is near thee. Old age is arrived : weakness subdues me, and strength has forsaken all my members. I came a stranger into this world, and a stranger I depart. I know nothing of myself, what I am, and for what I am destined. The instant which passed in power, hath left only sorrow behind it. I have not been the guardian and protector of the empire. My valuable time has been passed vainly. I had a patron in my own dwelling (conscience), but his glorious light was unseen by my dim sight. Life is not lasting, there is no vestige of departed breath, and all hopes from futurity are lost. The fever has left me, but nothing of me remains but skin and bone. My son (Kaum Buksh), though gone towards Beejapore, is still near ; and thou, my son, are yet nearer. The worthy of esteem, Shaw Aulum, is far distant ; and my grandson (Azeem Ooshaun), by the orders of God, is arrived near Hindostan. The camp and followers, helpless and alarmed, are like myself, full of affliction, restless as the quicksilver. Separated from their lord, they know not if they have a master or not.

"I brought nothing into this world, and, except the infirmities of man, carry nothing out. I have a dread for my salvation, and with what torments I may be punished. Though I have strong reliance on the mercies and bounty of God, yet, regarding my actions, fear will not quit me ; but when I am gone, reflection will not remain. Come then what may, I have launched my vessel to the waves. Though Providence will protect the camp, yet, regarding appearances, the endeavours of my sons are indispensably incumbent. Give my last prayers to my grandson (Bedar Bukht), whom I cannot see, but the desire affects me. The Begum (his daughter) appears afflicted ; but God is the only judge of hearts. The foolish thoughts of women produce nothing but disappointment. Farewell ! farewell ! farewell !"

"To the Prince Kaum Buksh.

"My son, nearest to my heart. Though in the height of my power, and by God's permission, I gave you advice, and took with you the greatest pains, yet, as it was not the divine will, you did not attend with the ears of compliance. Now I depart a stranger, and lament my own insignificance, what does it profit me ? I carry with me the fruits of my sins and imperfections. Surprising Providence ! I came here alone, and alone I depart. The leader of this caravan hath deserted me. The fever which troubled me for twelve days has left me. Wherever I look, I see nothing but the divinity. My fears for the camp and followers are great : but, alas ! I know not myself. My back is bent with weakness, and my feet have lost the powers of motion. The breath which rose is gone, and left not even hope behind it. I have committed numerous crimes, and know not with what punishments I may be seized. Though the protector of mankind will guard the camp, yet care is incumbent also on the faithful and my sons. When I was alive, no care was taken ; and now I am gone, the consequence may be guessed. The guardianship of a people is the trust by God committed to my sons. Azim Shaw is near. Be cautious that none of the faithful are slain, or

Raj Sing had signalised his accession by the revival of the warlike *Teeka-dowr*, and plundered Malpoora, which though on the Ajmér frontier, Shah Jehán, when advised to vengeance, replied "it was only a folly of his nephew."[1] An appeal to his gallantry made him throw down the gauntlet to Arungzéb in the plentitude of his power, when the valour of the Seesodias again burst forth in all the splendour of the days of Pertáp; nor did the contest close till after a series of brilliant victories, and with the narrow escape from captivity of the Xerxes of Hindust'han. The Mogul demanded the hand of the princess of Roopnagurh, a junior branch of the Marwar house, and sent with the demand (a compliance with which was contemplated as certain) a cortège of two thousand horse to escort the fair to court. But the haughty Rajpootni, either indignant at such precipitation or charmed with the gallantry of the Rana, who had evinced his devotion to the fair by measuring his sword with the head of her house, rejected with disdain the proffered alliance, and, justified by brilliant precedents in the romantic history of her nation, she entrusted her cause to the arm of the chief of the Rajpoot race, offering herself as the reward of protection. The family priest (her preceptor) deemed his office honoured by being the messenger of her wishes, and the billet he conveyed is incorporated in the memorial of this reign. "Is the swan to be the mate of the stork: a Rajpootni, pure in blood, to be wife to the monkey-faced barbarian!" concluding with a threat of self-destruction if not saved from dishonour. This appeal, with other powerful motives, was seized on with avidity by the Rana as a pretext to throw away the scabbard, in order to illustrate the opening of a warfare, in which he determined to put all to the hazard in defence of his country and his faith. The issue was an omen of success to his warlike and superstitious vassalage. With a chosen band he rapidly passed the foot of the Aravulli and appeared before Roopnagurh, cut up the imperial guards, and bore off the prize to his capital. The daring act was applauded by all who bore the name of Rajpoot, and his chiefs with joy gathered their retainers around the 'red standard,' to protect the queen so gallantly achieved.

their miseries fall upon my head. I resign you, your mother and son, to God, as I myself am going. The agonies of death come upon me fast. Behadur Shaw is still where he was, and his son is arrived near Hindostan. Bedar Bukht is in Guzarat. Hyaut al Nissa, who has beheld no afflictions of time till now, is full of sorrows. Regard the Begum as without concern. *Odiporee,[1] your mother, was a partner in my illness, and wishes to accompany me in death; but every thing has its appointed time.*

"The domestics and courtiers, however deceitful, yet must not be ill-treated. It is necessary to gain your views by gentleness and art. Extend your feet no lower than your skirt. The complaints of the unpaid troops are as before. Dara Shekkoh, though of much judgment and good understanding, settled large pensions on his people, but paid them ill and they were ever discontented. I am going. Whatever good or evil I have done, it was for you. Take it not amiss, nor remember what offences I have done to yourself; that account may not be demanded of me hereafter. No one has seen the departure of his own soul; but I see that mine is departing."—*Memoirs of Eradut Khan.* See Scott's *Hist. of the Dekhan.*

[1] The emperor was the adopted brother of Rana Kurrun.

---

[1] Orme calls her a Cashmerian; certainly she was not a daughter of the Rana's family, though it is not impossible she may have been of one of the great families of Shahpoora or Bunéra (then acting independently of the Rana), and her desire to burn shows her to have been Rajpoot.

The annalist of Rajpootana is but an indifferent chronologist, and leaves us doubtful of the exact succession of events at this period. It was not, however, till the death of those two powerful princes, Jeswunt Sing of Marwar and Jey Sing of Ambér, both poisoned by command of the tyrant, the one at his distant government of Cabul, the other in the Dekhan, that he deemed himself free to put forth the full extent of his long-concealed design, the imposition of the *jezeya* or capitation tax, on the whole Hindu race. But he miscalculated his measures, and the murder of these princes, far from advancing his aim, recoiled with vengeance on his head. Foiled in his plot to entrap the infant sons of the Rahtore by the self-devotion of his vassals,[1] the compound treachery evinced that their only hope lay in a deadly resistance. The mother of Ajít, the infant heir of Marwar, a woman of the most determined character, was a princess of Méwar, and she threw herself upon the Rana as the natural guardian of his rights, for sanctuary (*sirna*) during the dangers of his minority. This was readily yielded, and Kailwa assigned as his residence, where under the immediate safeguard of the brave Doorga-das Ajít resided,[2] while she nursed the spirit of resistance at home. A union of interests was cemented between these the chief states of Rajpootana, for which they never before had such motive, and but for repeated instances of an ill-judged humanity, the throne of the Moguls might have been completely overturned.

On the promulgation of that barbarous edict, the *jezeya*, the Rana remonstrated by letter, in the name of the nation of which he was the head, in a style of such uncompromising dignity, such lofty yet temperate resolve, so much of soul-stirring rebuke mingled with a boundless and tolerating benevolence, such elevated ideas of the Divinity with such pure philanthropy, that it may challenge competition with any epistolary production of any age, clime, or condition.[3] In this are contained the true principles

[1] Two hundred and fifty Rajpoots opposed five thousand of the Imperialists at a pass, till the family of Jeswunt escaped.

[2] The Rana received the young Rahtore with the most princely hospitality, and among other gifts a diamond worth ten thousand dinárs is enumerated.

[3] This letter, first made known to Europe by Orme, has by him been erroneously attributed to Jeswunt Sing of Marwar, who was dead before the promulgation of the edict, as the mention of *Ramsing* sufficiently indicates, whose father, Jy Sing, was contemporary with Jeswunt, and ruled nearly a year after his death. My Moonshee obtained a copy of the original letter at Oodipoor, where it is properly assigned to the Rana. It were superfluous to give a translation after the elegant production of Sir W. B. Rouse.

"Letter from Rana Raj Sing to Arungzéb.

"All due praise be rendered to the glory of the Almighty, and the munificence of your majesty, which is conspicuous as the sun and moon. Although I, your well-wisher, have separated from your sublime presence, I am nevertheless zealous in the performance of every bounden act of obedience and loyalty. My ardent wishes and strenuous services are employed to promote the prosperity of the Kings, Nobles, Mirzas, Rajahs, and Roys of the provinces of Hindostan, and the chiefs of Æraun, Turaun, Room, and Shawn, the inhabitants of the seven climates, and all persons travelling by land and by water. This my inclination is notorious, nor can your royal wisdom entertain a doubt thereof. Reflecting therefore on my former services, and your majesty's condescension, I presume to solicit the royal attention to some circumstances, in which the public as well as private welfare is greatly interested.

"I have been informed that enormous sums have been dissipated in the prosecution of the designs formed against me, your well-wisher; and that you

of Christianity, and to the illustrious Gentile, and such as acted as he did, was pointed that golden sentence of toleration, "Those who have not the law, yet do by nature the things contained in the law, shall be a law unto themselves."

This letter, the sanctuary afforded Ajít, and (what the historical

have ordered a tribute to be levied to satisfy the exigencies of your exhausted treasury.

"May it please your majesty, your royal ancestor Mahomed Jelaul ul Deen Akbar, whose throne is now in heaven, conducted the affairs of this empire in equity and firm security for the space of fifty-two years, preserving every tribe of men in ease and happiness, whether they were followers of Jesus or of Moses, of David or Mahomed ; were they Brahmins, were they of the sect of Dharians, which denies the eternity of matter, or of that which ascribes the existence of the world to chance, they all equally enjoyed his countenance and favour : insomuch that his people, in gratitude for the indiscriminate protection he afforded them, distinguished him by the appellation of *Juggut Gooroo* (Guardian of Mankind).

"His majesty Mahomed Noor ul Deen Jehangheer, likewise, whose dwelling is now in paradise, extended, for a period of twenty-two years, the shadow of his protection over the heads of his people ; successful by a constant fidelity to his allies, and a vigorous exertion of his arm in business.

"Nor less did the illustrious Shâh Jehán, by a propitious reign of thirty-two years, acquire to himself immortal reputation, the glorious reward of clemency and virtue.

"Such were the benevolent inclinations of your ancestors. Whilst they pursued these great and generous principles, wheresoever they directed their steps, conquest and prosperity went before them ; and then they reduced many countries and fortresses to their obedience. During your majesty's reign, many have been alienated from the empire, and farther loss of territory must necessarily follow, since devastation and rapine now universally prevail without restraint. Your subjects are trampled under foot, and every province of your empire is impoverished ; depopulation spreads, and difficulties accumulate. When indigence has reached the habitation of the sovereign and his princes, what can be the condition of the nobles ? As to the soldiery, they are in murmurs ; the merchants complaining, the Mahomedans discontented, the Hindoos destitute, and multitudes of people, wretched even to the want of their nightly meal, are beating their heads throughout the day in rage and desperation.

"How can the dignity of the sovereign be preserved who employs his power in exacting heavy tributes from a people thus miserably reduced ? At this juncture it is told from east to west, that the emperor of Hindostan, jealous of the poor Hindoo devotee, will exact a tribute from Brahmins, Sanorahs, Joghies, Berawghies, Sanyasees ; that, regardless of the illustrious honour of his Timurean race, he condescends to exercise his power over the solitary inoffensive anchoret. If your majesty places any faith in those books, by distinction called divine, you will there be instructed that God is the God of all mankind, not the God of Mahomedans alone. The Pagan and the Mussulman are equally in His presence. Distinctions of colour are of His ordination. It is He who gives existence. In your temples, to His name the voice is raised in prayer; in a house of images, where the bell is shaken, still He is the object of adoration. To vilify the religion or customs of other men is to set at naught the pleasure of the Almighty. When we deface a picture, we naturally incur the resentment of the painter ; and justly has the poet said, presume not to arraign or scrutinise the various works of power divine.

"In fine, the tribute you demand from the Hindoos is repugnant to justice : it is equally foreign from good policy, as it must impoverish the country : moreover, it is an innovation and an infringement of the laws of Hindostan. But if zeal for your own religion hath induced you to determine upon this measure, the demand ought, by the rules of equity, to have been made first upon Ramsing, who is esteemed the principal amongst the Hindoos. Then let your well-wisher be called upon, with whom you will have less difficulty to encounter ; but to torment ants and flies is unworthy of an heroic or generous mind. It is wonderful that the ministers of your government should have neglected to instruct your majesty in the rules of rectitude and honour."

parasite of the Mogul's life dared not indite [1]) the carrying off of his betrothed, made him pour out all the phials of his wrath against the devoted Méwar, and his preparations more resembled those for the conquest of a potent kingdom than the subjugation of a Rajpoot *zemindar*,[2] a vassal of that colossal empire, on whose surface his domain was but a speck. In the very magnitude of these, the Suzerain of Hindust'han paid the highest tribute of praise to the tributary Rajpoot, for he denuded the very extremities of his empire to assemble a host which he deemed must prove irresistible. Akber was recalled from his province, Bengal; Azím from the distant Cabul; and even Mauzum (the Mogul's heir) from the war in the Dekhan. With this formidable array [3] the emperor entered Méwar, and soon reduced the low countries, which experience had taught them were indefensible, the inhabitants previously retiring with their effects to the hills. Cheetore, Mandelgurh, Mundisor, Jeerun, and many other strongholds were obtained after the usual form of opposition, and garrisoned by the Moguls. Meanwhile the Rana was animating the might of the Aravulli, where he meditated a resistance proportioned to the peril which threatened every cherished prejudice of his race: not the mere defence of dominion or dignity, but a struggle, *pro aris et focis*, around which rallied every Rajpoot with the most deadly determination. Even the primitive races of the western wilds, "the Palindas [4] and Palipats [4] (*lord of the passes*), with thousands of bows, and hearts devoted in the cause of Hinduput," [5] assembled round the red banner of Méwar. The Rana divided his forces into three bodies. His eldest son, Jey Sing, was posted on the crest of the Aravulli, ready to act on the invaders from either side of the mountains. Prince Bheem was to the west, to keep up the communications with the outlets to Guzzerat; while the Rana, with the main body, took post in the Naén defile, unassailable by the enemy, and hanging on his left flank, ready to turn it, and cut off all retreat the moment the Imperialists entered the mountains. Arungzéb advanced to Dobarri, but instead of entering the valley of which it was the gorge, he halted, and by the advice of Tyber Khan sent on Prince Akber with fifty thousand men to the capital. This caution of the wily monarch saved him from the ably planned scheme of the Rajpoot prince, who evinced a thorough knowledge [6] of the topography of this intricate and romantic portion of his domain. The *Girwo*, emphatically '*the Circle*,' from which the valley of the capital is named, has this form to the eye when viewing it from thence as a centre. It is, however,

[1] It is well known that Arungzéb forbade the continuation of the history of his life, subsequent to that portion comprehending the first ten years.

[2] The epithet by which these Tatar sovereigns affected to call the indigenous (*blúmia*) princes.

[3] There were no such field trains in Europe as those of the Moguls. Seventy pieces of heavy ordnance, sixty of *horse artillery*, and a dromedary corps three hundred strong, mounting swivels, accompanied the emperor on an *excursion* to Cashmere. Bernier, who gives this detail, describes what he saw.

[4] *Pāl* is the local term for these long defiles, the residence of the mountaineers: their *chiefs* are called *Indras*, *Pati*, in bhaka, *Put*.

[5] Chief of the Hindus.

[6] The Suktawut leader, Gureeb Dás, has the merit of having prompted this plan. His speech on the advance of Arungzéb is given in the Annals; and his advice, "Let the king have free entrance through the passes, shut him in, and make famine his foe," was literally followed, with the hard knocks, which being a matter-of-course accompaniment, the gallant Suktawut deemed it unnecessary to specify.

an irregular ellipse of about fourteen miles in length from south to north, and about eleven in breadth from east to west, the capital being situated towards the extremity of the transverse axis, having only the lake Péshola between it and the base of the Aravulli. The mountains of this circular (*girwo*) valley, ranging from eight to twelve hundred feet in height, are of primitive formation, and raise their fantastic pinnacles in every diversity of shape over each other. To the westward the grand chain rises two thousand feet above the plains, and might be termed the chord, of which the Girwo is an irregular segment of a circle, less in height, and far less compound in character. Towards the plains east, it has three practicable passes; one, the more northern, by Dailwarra; the other (central), by Dobarri; a third, leading to the intricacies of Chuppun, that of Naén. Of these three passes the emperor chose the most practicable, and encamped near the Oody-sagur lake, on the left of its entrance.

Prince Akber advanced. "Not a soul interrupted his progress to the city. "Palaces, gardens, lakes, and isles met his eye, but no living thing: all was silence." Akber encamped. Accustomed to this desertion from the desire of the people to avoid a licentious soldiery, and lulled into a hardy security, he was surprised by the heir of Méwar. Some were praying, some feasting, some at chess: "they came to steal and yet fell asleep," says the annalist, and were dispersed with terrific and unrelenting slaughter. Cut off from the possibility of a junction with the emperor by a movement of a part of the Rana's personal force, Akber attempted a retreat to the plains of Marwar by the route of Gogoonda. It was a choice of evils, and he took the worst. The allodial vassals of the mountains, with the Bhil auxiliaries, outstripped his retreat, and blocked up farther egress in one of those long-extended valleys termed *Nal*, closed by a natural rampart or *Col*, on which they formed *abbatis* of trees, and manning the crests on each side, hurled destruction on the foe; while the prince, in like manner, blocked up the entrance and barred retrogression. Death menaced them in every form. For several days they had only the prospect of surrender to save them from famine and a justly incensed foe, when an ill-judged humanity on the part of Jey Sing saved them from annihilation. He admitted overtures, confided in protestations to renounce the origin of the war, and gave them guides to conduct them by the defile of Jilwarra, nor did they halt till protected by the walls of Cheetore.[1]

[1] Orme, who has many valuable historical details of this period, makes Arungzéb in person to have been in the predicament assigned by the annals to his son, and to have escaped from the operation of those high and gallant sentiments of the Rajpoot, which make him no match for a wily adversary.

"In the meantime Aurengzebe was carrying on the war against the Rana of Cheetore, and the Raja of Marwar, who on the approach of his army at the end of the preceding year, 1678, had abandoned the accessible country, and drew their herds and inhabitants into the vallies, within the mountains; the army advanced amongst the defiles with incredible labour, and with so little intelligence, that the division which moved with Aurengzebe himself was unexpectedly stopped by insuperable defences and precipices in front; whilst the Rajpoots in one night closed the streights in his rear, by felling the overhanging trees; and from their stations above prevented all endeavours of the troops, either within or without, from removing the obstacle. Udeperri, the favourite and Circassian wife of Aurengzebe, accompanied him in this arduous war, and with her retinue and escort was enclosed in another part of the mountains; her conductors, dreading to expose her person to danger or public view, surrendered. She was carried to the Rana, who received her with homage and every attention. Meanwhile the

Another body of the Imperialists, under the celebrated Delhire Khan, who entered by the Daisoori Pass from Marwar (probably with a view of extricating Prince Akber), were allowed to advance unopposed, and when in the long intricate gorge were assailed by Bikram Solanki [1] and Gopinath Rahtore [2] (both nobles of Méwar), and after a desperate conflict entirely destroyed. On each occasion a vast booty fell into the hands of the Rajpoots.

So ably concerted was this mountain warfare, that these defeats were the signal for a simultaneous attack by the Rana on Arungzéb, who, with his son Azím, watched at Dobarri the result of the operations under Akber and Delhire. The great home-clans had more than their wonted rivalry to sustain them, for the gallant Doorga-das with the Rahtore swords (*tulwár Rahtorán*) whetted by an accumulation of wrongs, were to combat with them against their common oppressor ; and nobly did they contest the palm of glory. The tyrant could not withstand them : his guns, though manned by *Franks*, could not protect him against the just cause and avenging steel of the Rajpoot, and he was beaten and compelled to disgraceful flight, with an immense loss in men and equipment. The Rana had to lament many brave leaders, home and auxiliary ; and the imperial standard, elephants, and state equipage fell into his hands, the acquisition of Mohkim and the Suktawuts. This glorious encounter occurred in the spring month of Falgoon, S. 1737.[3]

The discomfited forces formed a junction under the walls of Cheetore, whence the emperor dictated the recall of his son, Prince Mauzum, from the Dekhan, deeming it of greater moment to regain lost importance in the north than to prevent the independence of Sevaji. Meanwhile the activity of Sawuldás (descended from the illustrious Jeimul) cut off the communication between Cheetore and Ajmér, and alarmed the tyrant for his personal safety. Leaving, therefore, this perilous warfare to his sons Azím and Akber, with instructions how to act till reinforced,—foiled in his vengeance and personally disgraced, he abandoned Méwar, and at the head of his guards repaired to Ajmér. Thence he detached Khan Rohilla, with twelve thousand men, against Sawuldás, with supplies and equipments for

emperor himself might have perished by famine, of which the Rana let him see the risque, by a confinement of two days ; when he ordered his Rajpoots to withdraw from their stations, and suffer the way to be cleared. As soon as Aurengzebe was out of danger, the Rana sent back his wife, accompanied by a chosen escort, who only requested in return that he would refrain from destroying the sacred animals of their religion which might still be left in the plains ; but Aurengzebe, who believed in no virtue but self-interest, imputed the generosity and forbearance of the Rana to the fear of future vengeance, and continued the war. Soon after he was again well-nigh enclosed in the mountains. This second experience of difficulties beyond his age and constitution, and the arrival of his sons, Azím and Acbar, determined him not to expose himself any longer in the field, but to leave its operations to their conduct, superintended by his own instructions from Azmir ; to which city he retired with the households of his family, the officers of his court, and his bodyguard of four thousand men, dividing the army between his two sons, who each had brought a considerable body of troops from their respective governments. They continued the war each in a different part of the country, and neither at the end of the year had forced the ultimate passes of the mountains."

[1] Chief of Roopnagurh.

[2] Chief of Ganora, in Godwar, now alienated from Méwar.

[3] March 1681, A.D.

his sons. The Rahtore, joined by the troops of Marwar, gave him the meeting at Poorh Mandel, and defeated the Imperialists with great loss, driving them back on Ajmér.

While the Rana, his heir and auxiliaries, were thus triumphant in all their operations, Prince Bheem with the left division was not idle, but made a powerful diversion by the invasion of Guzzerat, captured Edur, expelling Hussun and his garrison, and proceeding by Birnuggur, suddenly appeared before Puttun, the residence of the provincial satrap, which he plundered. Sidpoor, Mhourasso, and other towns shared the same fate; and he was in full march to Surat, when the benevolence of the Rana, touched at the woes of the fugitives, who came to demand his forbearance, caused him to recall Bheem in the midst of his career.

Contrary to the Rajpoot character, whose maxim is *parcere subjectis*, they were compelled by the utter faithlessness of Arungzéb (chiefly vulnerable through his resources) to retaliate his excesses; and Dyal Sah, the civil minister, a man of high courage and activity, headed another flying force, which ravaged Malwa to the Nerbudda and Bétwa. Sarangpoor, Déwás, Saronj, Mandoo, Oojein, and Chandéri were plundered, and numerous garrisons put to the sword; and, to use the words of the Chronicle, "husbands abandoned their wives and children, and whatever could not be carried off was given to the flames." For once they avenged themselves, in imitation of the tyrant, even on the religion of their enemies: "the Kazees were bound and shaved, and the Korans thrown into wells." The minister was unrelenting and made Malwa a desert, and from the fruits of his incursions repaired the resources of his master. Flushed with success, he formed a junction with the heir of Méwar, and gave battle to Azím near Cheetore. On this occasion the flower of Méwar, with the Rahtore and Kheetchee auxiliaries,[1] were engaged, and obtained a glorious victory, the Mogul prince being defeated and pursued with great slaughter to Rinthumbor, which he entered. This was a just revenge, for it was Azím who surprised Cheetore the year preceding. In Méwar the contest terminated with the expulsion of the Imperialists from the country; when the Rana, in support of the rights of the minor prince of Marwar, united his arms to the forces of that state, and opened the campaign at Ganora, the chief town of Godwar. The heroic mother of the infant Rahtore prince, a daughter of Méwar, had, since the death of her husband, well supported his rights, having resisted every aggression and regained many lost advantages over their antagonist. Prince Bheem commanded the Seesodias, who formed a junction with the Rahtores, and gave battle to the royal forces led by Akber and Tyber Khan, whom they entirely defeated. The victory is chiefly attributed to a stratagem of a Rajpoot chief, who, having carried off five hundred camels from the Imperialists, conceived the idea of fixing torches to them and letting them loose in the royal camp; and, in the confusion produced by the charge of such a body, the Rajpoots assaulted them. On their continued successes, the Rana and his allies meditated the project of dethroning the tyrant and setting up his son Akber. The pernicious example of his

[1] Mokhim and Gunga Suktawuts, Rutten Chondawut of Saloombra, Chandrasén Jhala of Sadri, Subbul Sing Chohan of Baidla, Berri-Sal Pūar of Bijollí. Four of the chiefs made speeches on the eve preceding the battle, which are recorded in the Chronicle.

father towards Shah Jehán was not lost upon Akber, who favourably received the overture ; but he wanted the circumspection which characterised Arungzéb, whose penetration defeated the scheme when on the eve of execution. Already had the Rajpoot armies united with Akber, and the astrologer had fixed the day which was to exalt him ; but the revealer of secrets baffled his own prediction by disclosing it to the emperor. Arungzéb, attended only by his guards at Ajmér, had recourse to the same artifice which raised him to empire, in order to ward off this danger. Akber was but one day's march distant ; his elder sons, Mauzum and Azím, yet far off. Not a moment was to be lost : he penned a letter to his son, which by a spy was dropped in the tent of the Rajpoot leader Doorga-Das. In this he applauded a pretended scheme by which Akber was to fall upon them when they engaged the emperor. The same scheme had saved Shere Shah in this country from Maldeo, and has more recently been put in practice, and with like success, in the war with Sevaji. It succeeded. The Rajpoots detached themselves from the prince who had apparently betrayed them. Tyber Khan, in despair, lost his life in an attempt to assassinate the emperor, and before the artifice was discovered, the reinforcements under Mauzum and Azím arrived, and Arungzéb was saved. The Rajpoots still offered *sirna* (refuge) to Akber ; but aware of his father's vigour of character, he deemed himself unsafe in his vicinage, and accepted the escort of five hundred Rajpoots led by Doorga-Das,[1] who cut their way through every opposition by the defiles of Méwar and Dongerpoor, and across the Nerbudda, to the Mahratta leader Sambaji, at Palergurh, whence he was shortly after conveyed in an English ship to Persia.

"The escape of Akber" (observes an historian,[2] who appreciated the importance of the transactions of this period) "to Sambaji, oppressed Arungzéb with as much anxiety, as formerly the phantom of his brother Sujah amongst the Pat'hans ; and the consequence of their alliance became a nearer care than the continuance of the war against the Rajpoots, whose gallant activity prevented a speedy decision by the sword ; but the dignity of the throne precluded any overtures of peace to a resistance which had attempted the deposal, if not the life, of the monarch. A Rajpoot officer, who had long served with distinction under Delhír Khan, solved the difficulty : he quitted the army under pretence of retiring to his own country and visited the Rana as from courtesy on his journey.

[1] A portrait of this Rahtore hero was given to the author of the present work by his descendants. He was chief of Droonara, on the Looni. He saved his young sovereign's life from the tyrant, and guarded him during a long minority, heading the Rahtores in all the wars for the independence of his country. A bribe of forty thousand *gold suns* was sent to him by Azím *without stipulation*, when conveying Akber out of danger. The object was obvious, yet the Mogul prince dared not even specify his wishes. It is needless to say that Doorga spurned the offer.

[2] "We are not without hopes that some of the many in India who have the means will supply the portions of information which are deficient in these fragments, and must otherwise always continue out of our reach. The knowledge is well worth the inquiry ; for, besides the magnitude of the events and the energy of the characters which arise within this period, there are no states or powers on the continent of India, with whom our nation has either connexion or concern, which do not owe the origin of their present condition to the reign of Aurungzebe, or to its influence on the reigns of his successors."—Orme's *Fragments*, p. 165.

The conversation turned on the war, which the Rajpoot perhaps really lamented, and he persuaded the Rana that though Arungzéb would never condescend to make, he might accept overtures of peace: upon which he was empowered by the Rana to tender them." The domestic annals confirm this account, and give the name of this mediator, Raja Shiam Sing of Bíkanér; but the negotiation was infamously protracted to the rains, the period when operations necessarily cease, and by which time Arungzéb had recruited his broken forces, and was again enabled to take the field; and it was concluded "without assertion or release of the capitation tax, but with the surrender of the districts taken from Cheetore, and the state of Jodpoor was included in the treaty." How correctly this elegant historian had obtained a knowledge of those events, a translation of the treaty evinces.[1] But these occurrences belong to the succeeding reign, for the Rana died about this period,[2] from wounds and vexation.

Once more we claim the reader's admiration on behalf of another patriot prince of Méwar, and ask him to contrast the indigenous Rajpoot with the emperor of the Moguls; though to compare them would be manifestly unjust, since in every moral virtue they were antipodes to each other. Arungzéb accumulated on his head more crimes than any prince who ever sat on an Asiatic throne. With all the disregard of life which marks his nation, he was never betrayed, even in the fever of success, into a single generous action; and, contrary to the prevailing principle of our nature, the moment of his foe's submission was that chosen for the malignant completion of his revenge: witness his scourging the prostrate King of Golconda. How opposite to the beneficence of the Rajpoot prince, who, when the most efficient means of self-defence lay in the destruction of the resources of his enemy, feeling for the miseries of the suffering population of his persecutor, recalled his son in the midst of victory! As a skilful

[1] "*Jowab-sowal*[1] *of Soor Sing and Nurhur Bhut (uncle of Rana Raj Sing) with the Emperor.*

Punja, or impress of the Emperor's hand, with the word '*Munzoori*,' written by himself. *Munzoori* ('agreed').

"Your servants, according to your royal pleasure and summons, have been sent by the Rana to represent what is written underneath. We hope you will agree to these requests, besides others which will be made by Puddum Sing.

"1. Let Cheetore, with the districts adjacent appertaining thereto when it was inhabited, be restored.

"2. In such temples and places of Hindu religious resort as have been converted into mosques, the past cannot be recalled, but let this practice be abolished.

"3. The aid hitherto afforded to the empire by the Rana shall be continued, but let no additional commands be imposed.

"4. The sons and dependants of the deceased Raja Jeswunt Sing, so soon as enabled to perform their duties, we hope will have their country restored to them.[2]

"Respect prevents inferior demands. May the splendour of your fortune, like the sun illuminating the world, be for ever increasing and never set.

"The Arzi (requests) of your servants, Soor Sing and Nurhur Bhut."

[2] S. 1737, A.D. 1681.

---

[1] Treaties or engagements are thus designated; literally *stipulations* and *answers*.

[2] It was to defend the rights of the heir of Marwar, as well as to oppose the odious *jezeya*, that the Rana took to arms. Ajít was still under the Rana's safeguard.

general and gallant soldier, in the defence of his country, he is above all praise. As a chivalrous Rajpoot, his braving all consequences when called upon to save the honour of a noble female of his race, he is without parallel. As an accomplished prince and benevolent man, his dignified letter of remonstrance to Arungzéb on the promulgation of the capitation edict, places him high in the scale of moral as well as intellectual excellence; and an additional evidence of both, and of his taste for the arts, is furnished by the formation of the inland lake, the Rajsumund, with a slight account of which, and the motives for its execution, we shall conclude the sketch of this glorious epoch in the annals of Méwar.

LAKE RAJSUMUND.—This great national work is twenty-five miles north of the capital, and is situated on the declivity of the plain about two miles from the base of the Aravulli. A small perennial stream, called the *Gomtee* or 'serpentine,' flowing from these mountains, was arrested in its course, and confined by an immense embankment, made to form the lake called after himself, *Rajsumund*, or 'royal sea.' The *bund* or dam forms an irregular segment of a circle, embracing an extent of nearly three miles, and encircling the waters on every side except the space between the north-west and north-east points. This barrier, which confines a sheet of water of great depth, and about twelve miles in circumference, is entirely of white marble, with a flight of steps of the same material, throughout this extent, from the summit to the water's edge; the whole buttressed by an enormous rampart of earth, which, had the projector lived, would have been planted with trees to form a promenade. On the south side are the town and fortress built by the Rana, and bearing his name, Rajnuggur; and upon the embankment stands the temple of Kunkeraoli, the shrine of one of the seven forms (*saroop*) of Crishna. The whole is ornamented with sculpture of tolerable execution for the age; and a genealogical sketch of the founder's family is inscribed in conspicuous characters. One million one hundred and fifty thousand pounds sterling,[1] contributed by the Rana, his chiefs and opulent subjects, was expended on this work, of which the material was from the adjacent quarries. But, magnificent, costly, and useful as it is, it derives its chief beauty from the benevolent motive to which it owes its birth: to alleviate the miseries of a starving population, and make their employment conducive to national benefit, during one of those awful visitations of providence, famine, and pestilence with which these states are sometimes afflicted.

It was in S. 1717,[2] only seven years after the accession of Raj Sing, that these combined evils reached Méwar, less subject to them, owing to its natural advantages, than any other state in India;[3] and on Tuesday the 8th of Pos, *Hasti Nakhetra* (constellation of the elephant), as fixed by the astrologer, the first stone was laid. "The chief of Méwar, deeply meditating on this extreme distress, determined to raise a monument, by which the wretched might be supported and his own name perpetuated.

[1] Ninety-six lakhs of rupees. [2] A.D. 1661.

[3] From all I could learn, it was the identical pestilence which has been ravaging India for the last ten years, erroneously called *cholera morbus*. About thirty-five years ago the same disease carried off multitudes in these countries. Orme gives notice of something similar in A.D. 1684, in the imperial camp near Goa, when five hundred victims daily fell its prey. Méwar was not free from the last visitation of 1818, and the only son of the Rana was the first person attacked.

This was seven years in constructing, and at its commencement and termination all the rites of sacrifice and oblation were observed.

"The Rana went to implore favour at the temple of the '*four-armed*'; for though Asár [1] was over, not a drop of rain fell from the heavens; and, in like manner, the months of Sawun [1] and Bhadoon [1] passed away. For want of water the world was in despair, and people went mad with hunger. Things unknown as food were eaten. The husband abandoned the wife, the wife the husband—parents sold their children—time increased the evil; it spread far and wide: even the insects died: they had nothing to feed on. Thousands of all ages became victims to hunger. Those who procured food to-day, ate twice what nature required. The wind was from the west, a pestilential vapour. The constellations were always visible at night, nor was there a cloud in the sky by day, and thunder and lightning were unknown. Such portents filled mankind with dread. Rivers, lakes, and fountains were dried up. Men of wealth meted out the portions of food. The ministers of religion forgot their duties. There was no longer distinction of caste, and the Soodra and Brahmin were undistinguishable. Strength, wisdom, caste, tribe, all were abandoned, and food alone was the object. The *Charburrun* [2] threw away every symbol of separation; all was lost in hunger. Fruits, flowers, every vegetable thing, even trees were stripped of their bark, to appease the cravings of hunger: nay, *man ate man*! Cities were depopulated. The seed of families was lost, the fishes were extinct, and the hope of all extinguished." [3]

Such is the simple yet terrific record of this pestilence, from which Méwar was hardly freed, when Arungzéb commenced the religious warfare narrated, with all its atrocities, still further to devastate this fair region. But a just retribution resulted from this disregard to the character and prejudices of the Rajpoots, which visited the emperor with shame, and his successors with the overthrow of their power.

CHAPTER XIV

Rana Jey Sing—Anecdote regarding him and his twin brother—The Rana and Prince Azím confer—Peace—Rupture—The Rana forms the Lake Jeysumund—Domestic broils—Umra, the heir-apparent, rebels—The Rana dies—Accession of Umra—His treaty with the heir of Arungzéb—Reflections on the events of this period—Imposition of the Jezeya or capitation tax—Alienation of the Rajpoots from the empire—Causes—Arungzéb's death—Contests for empire—Buhadoor Shah, emperor—The Siks declare for independence—Triple alliance of the Rajpoot states of Méwar, Marwar, and Ambér—They commence hostilities—Death of the Mogul Buhadoor Shah—Elevation of Ferochsér—He marries the daughter of the Prince of Marwar—Origin of the British power in India—The Rana treats with the emperor—The Jâts declare their independence—Rana Umra dies—His character.

RANA JEY SING took possession of the *Gadi* [4] in S. 1737 (A.D. 1681). A circumstance occurred at his birth, which as descriptive of manners may

[1] The three months of rain, termed the *Bursát*.
[2] The four castes, sacerdotal, military, mercantile, and servile.
[3] From the *Raj Vulas*, the chronicle of the reign of Raj Sing.
[4] "*The Cushion,*" by which a Rajpoot throne is designated.

deserve notice. A few hours only intervened between his entrance into the world and that of another son called Bheem. It is customary for the father to bind round the arm of the new-born infant a root of that species of grass called the *ámirdhob*, the 'imperishable' *dhob*, well known for its nutritive properties and luxuriant vegetation under the most intense heat. The Rana first attached the ligature round the arm of the youngest, apparently an oversight, though in fact from superior affection for his mother. As the boys approached to manhood, the Rana, apprehensive that this preference might create dissension, one day drew his sword, and placing it in the hand of Bheem (the elder), said, it was better to use it at once on his brother, than hereafter to endanger the safety of the state. This appeal to his generosity had an instantaneous effect, and he not only ratified, "*by his father's throne*,"[1] the acknowledgment of the sovereign rights of his brother, but declared, to remove all fears, "he was not his son if he again drank water within the pass of Dobari"; and, collecting his retainers, he abandoned Oodipoor to court Fortune where she might be kinder. The day was sultry, and on reaching the barrier he halted under the shade of a sacred fig-tree to bestow a last look upon the place of his birth. His cup-bearer (*Panairi*) brought his silver goblet filled from the cool fountain, but as he raised it to his lips, he recollected that his vow was incomplete while within the portal; he poured the libation on the earth in the name of the Supreme, and casting the cup as an offering to the deity of the fountain, the huge gates closed upon the valley. He proceeded to Buhadoor Shah, who conferred upon him the dignity (*munsub*) of a leader of three thousand five hundred horse, with the *Bawuna*, or fifty-two districts for their support: but quarrelling with the imperial general, he was detached with his contingent west of the Indus, where he died.[2]

Let us return to Jey Sing (*the lion of victory*). He concluded a treaty with Arungzéb, conducted by Prince Azím and Delhír Khan, who took every occasion to testify his gratitude for the clemency of Rana Raj Sing, when blockaded in the defiles of the Aravulli. At this conference, the Rana was attended by ten thousand horse and forty thousand foot, besides the multitude collected from the mountains to view the ceremony, above one hundred thousand souls, who set up a shout of joy at the prospect of revisiting the plains, which disconcerted Azím, while Delhír expatiated on the perils from which the Rana's generosity had liberated him. Azím, who said he was no stranger to the Rana's illustrious house, concluded a treaty on the spot, in which, as a salvo for the imperial dignity, a nominal fine and surrender of three districts were inserted for aiding Akber's rebellion, and a hint that the regal colour (*crimson*) of his

[1] *Gádi ca Án.*

[2] I give these anecdotes as related to me by his descendant and representative the Raja of Bunéra, while seated in a balcony of his castle overlooking the plains of Méwar. Often have I quenched my thirst at the fountain, and listened to their traditionary tales. It is a spot consecrated to recollections: every altar which rises around it is a text for the '*great ancients*' of the clans to expatiate on; and it is, moreover, a grand place of rendezvous, whether for the traveller or sportsman.

Bheem dislocated his spine in a feat of strength. He was celebrated for activity, and could, while his steed was urged to his speed, disengage and suspend himself by the arms from the bough of a tree; and to one of these experiments he owed his death.

tents and umbrella should be discontinued. That advantages were gained by the Rana, we may infer from Delhír's sons being left as hostages for Azím's good faith; a fact we learn from his farewell address to the Rana: "Your nobles are rude, and my children are the hostages of your safety; but if at the expense of their lives I can obtain the entire restoration of your country, keep your mind at ease, for there was friendship between your father and me."

But all other protection than what his sword afforded was futile; and though Delhír's intentions were noble, he had little control over events: in less than five years after his accession, the Rana was again forced to fly the plains for the inaccessible haunts of Kamori. Yet, in spite of these untoward circumstances and uninterrupted warfare, such were the resources of this little state that the Rana completed a work which perpetuates his name. He threw a dam across a break in the mountains, the channel of an ever-flowing stream, by which he formed the largest lake in India, giving it his own name, the Jeysumund, or *sea of victory.* Nature had furnished the hint for this undertaking, for there had always existed a considerable volume of water; but the Rana had the merit of uniting these natural buttresses, and creating a little sea from the *Dheybur pool*, its ancient appellation. The circumference cannot be less than thirty miles, and the benefits to cultivation, especially in respect to the article of rice, which requires perpetual irrigation, were great. On this huge rampart he erected a palace for his favourite queen, Comálá-devi, a princess of the Pramara race, familiarly known as the *Roota Ranee*, or "testy queen."

Domestic unhappiness appears to have generated in the Rana inaptitude to state affairs; and, unluckily, the favoured queen estranged him from his son. Umra, a name venerated in Méwar, was that of the heir of Jey Sing. His mother was of the Boondí house, a family which has performed great services to, and brought great calamities upon, the ancient sovereigns of Méwar. To the jealousies of the rival queens, one of them mother to the heir, the other the favourite of the sovereign, are attributed dissensions, which at such a juncture were a greater detriment than the loss of a battle, and which afford another illustration, if any were wanting, of the impolicy of polygamy. The annals of Méwar seldom exhibit those unnatural contentions for power, from which no other Hindu state was exempt; this was owing to the wholesome regulation of not investing the princes of the blood with any political authority; and establishing as a counterpoise to natural advantages an artificial degradation of their rank, which placed them beneath the sixteen chief nobles of the state; which, while it exalted these in their own estimation, lessened the national humiliation, when the heirs-apparent were compelled to lead their quota in the *arrière-ban* of the empire.

Rana Jey Sing, who had evinced such gallantry and activity in the wars of Arungzéb, now secluded himself with Comálá in the retreat of Jeysumund, leaving Umra under the guidance of the Pancholi minister, at the capital. But he having personally insulted this chief officer of the state, in consequence of receiving a rebuke for turning loose an infuriated elephant in the town, the Rana left his retreat, and visiting Cheetore in his tour, arrived at Oodipoor. Umra awaited not his father's arrival, but adding his mother's resentments to a feeling of patriotic indignation at the abasement his indolence produced, fled to Boondí, took up arms, and, joined by many of his own nobles and Hara auxiliaries, returned at the head of ten thousand men. Desirous of averting civil war, the Rana retired to Godwar beyond the Aravulli, whence he sent the Ganora chieftain, the first feudatory of that department, to expostulate with his son. But Umra, supported by three-fourths of the nobles, made direct for Komulmér to secure the state treasure, saved by the Dépra governor for his sovereign. A failure in this project, the knowledge that the Rahtores fostered the quarrel with a view to obtain Godwar, and the determination of the few chiefs yet faithful [1] to the Rana, to defend the Jilwarra pass to the last, made the prince listen to terms, which were ratified at the shrine of Eklinga, whereby the Rana was to return to the capital, and the prince to abide in exile at the new palace during the life of his father, which closed twenty years after his accession. Had he maintained the reputation he established in his early years, the times were well calculated for the redemption of his country's independence; but documents which yet exist afford little reason to doubt that in his latter years a state of indolence, having all the effects of imbecility, supervened, and but for the formation of 'the victorious sea,' would have left his name a blank in the traditional history of Méwar.

Umra II., who succeeded in S. 1756 (A.D. 1700), had much of the gallantry and active turn of mind of his illustrious namesake; but the degrading conflict with his father had much impaired the moral strength of the country, and counteracted the advantages which might have resulted from the decline of the Mogul power. The reigns of Raj Sing and Jey Sing illustrate the obvious truth, that on the personal character of the chief of a feudal government everything depends. The former, infusing by his talent and energy patriotic sentiments into all his subordinates, vanquished in a series of conflicts the vast military resources of the empire, led by the emperor, his sons, and chosen generals; while his successor, heir to this moral strength, and with every collateral aid, lowered her to a stage of contempt from which no talent could subsequently raise her.

Umra early availed himself of the contentions amongst the sons of Arungzéb to anticipate events, and formed a private treaty [2] with the

[1] Béri Sál of Bijollí, Kandul of Saloombra, Gopinat'h of Ganora, and the Solanki of Daisoori.

[2] "*Private Treaty between the Rana and Shah Alum Buhadoor Shah, and bearing his sign-manual.*

"Six articles of engagement, just, and tending to the happiness of the people, have been submitted by you, and by me accepted, and with God's blessing shall be executed without deviation—

"1. The re-establishment of Cheetore as in the time of Shah Jehan.

"2. Prohibition of kine-killing.[1]

[1] From the second of these articles, which alternate between stipulations of a temporal and spiritual nature, we may draw a lesson of great political importance. In all the treaties which have come under my observation, the insertion of an article against the slaughter of kine was prominent. This sacrifice to their national prejudices was the subject of discussion with every ambassador when the states of Rajast'han formed engagements with the British government in 1817–8, "the prohibition of kine-killing within their respective limits." From the construction of our armies we could not guarantee this article, but assurances were given that every practical attention would be paid to their wishes; and kine are not absolutely slain within the jurisdiction of any of these Rajpoot princes. But even long habit, though it has familiarised, has not

Mogul heir-apparent, Shah Alum, when commanded to the countries west of the Indus, on which occasion the Méwar contingent [1] accompanied him, and fought several gallant actions under a Suktawut chieftain.

It is important to study the events of this period, which involved the overthrow of the Mogul power, and originated that form of society which paved the way to the dominion of Britain in these distant regions. From such a review a political lesson of great value may be learned, which will show a beacon warning us against the danger of trusting to mere physical power, unaided by the latent, but more durable support of moral influence. When Arungzéb neglected the indigenous Rajpoots, he endangered the key-stone of his power; and in despising opinion, though his energetic mind might for a time render him independent of it, yet long before his death the enormous fabric reared by Akber was tottering to its foundation: demonstrating to conviction that the highest order of talent, either for government or war, though aided by unlimited resources, will not suffice for the maintenance of power, unsupported by the affections of the governed. The empire of Arungzéb was more extensive than that of Britain at this day—the elements of stability were incomparably more :enacious: he was associated with the Rajpoots by blood, which seemed o guarantee a respect for their opinions; he possessed the power of disributing the honours and emoluments of the state, when a service could be ewarded by a province,[2] drawing at will supplies of warriors from the

" 3. The restoration of all the districts held in the reign of Shah Jehan.
" 4. Freedom of faith and religious worship, as during the government of him ·hose *nest is Paradise* (Akber).
" 5. Whoever shall be dismissed by you shall receive no countenance from ie king.
" 6. The abrogation of the contingent for the service of the Dekhan." [1]

[1] It consisted of twenty-two *Nagarbund* chiefs, *i.e.* each entitled to a kettle-rum, and fifteen *Toorées*, or chiefs, entitled to brass trumpets.

[2] In lieu of all, what reward does Britain hold out to the native population o be attached? Heavy duties exclude many products of their industry from

---

·econciled them to this revolting sacrifice; nor would the kine-killer in Méwar ɔe looked upon with less detestation than was Cambyses by the Egyptians, when he thrust his lance into the flank of Apis. But in time this will be overlooked, and the verbal assurance will become a dead letter; men of good intention will be lulled into the belief that, because not openly combated, the prejudice is extinct, and that homage to our power has obliterated this article of their creed. Thus Arungzéb thought, but he avowedly and boldly opposed the religious opinions of his tributaries; we only hold them in contempt, and even protect them when productive of no sacrifice. Yet if we look back on the early page of history, we shall find both policy and benevolence combined to form this legislative protection to one of the most useful of domestic animals, and which would tempt the belief that Triptolemus, the lawgiver of Sparta, had borrowed from Menu, or rather from the still greater friends of dumb creatures, the Jains, in the law which exempted not only the lordly bull from the knife, but " every living thing."

[1] The Méwar contingent had been serving under Azím in the south, as the following letter from him to the Rana discloses:—

" Be it known to Rana Umra Sing, your arzee arrived, and the accounts of your mother gave me great grief, but against the decrees of God there is no struggling. Pray for my welfare. Raja Raé Sing made a request for you; you are my own; rest in full confidence and continue in your obedience. The lands of your illustrious ancestors shall all be yours—but this is the time to evince your duty—the rest learn from your own servants—continue to think of me."

" Your Rajpoots have behaved well."

mountains of the west, as a check on his indigenous subjects, while these left the plains of India to control the Afghan amidst the snows of Caucasus. But the most devoted attachment and most faithful service were repaid by insults to their habits, and the imposition of an obnoxious tax; and to the *jezeya*, and the unwise pertinacity with which his successors adhered to it, must be directly ascribed the overthrow of the monarchy. No condition was exempted from this odious and impolitic assessment, which was deemed by the tyrant a mild substitute for the conversion he once meditated of the entire Hindu race to the creed of Islam.

An abandonment of their faith was the Rajpoot's surest road to the tyrant's favour, and an instance of this dereliction in its consequences powerfully contributed to the annihilation of the empire. Rao Gopâl, a branch of the Rana's family, held the fief of Rampoora, on the Chumbul,[1] and was serving with a select quota of his clan in the wars of the Dekhan, when his son, who had been left at home, withheld the revenues, which he applied to his own use instead of remitting them to his father. Rao Gopâl complained to the emperor; but the son discovered that he could by a sacrifice not only appease Arungzéb, but attain the object of his wishes: he apostatised from his faith, and obtained the emperor's forgiveness, with the domain of Rampoora. Disgusted and provoked at such infurious conduct, Rao Gopal fled the camp, made an unsuccessful attempt to redeem his estate, and took refuge with Rana Umra, his suzerain. This natural asylum granted to a chief of his own kin was construed by the tyrant into a signal of revolt, and Azím was ordered to Malwa to watch the Rana's motions: conduct thus characterised in the memoirs of a Rajpoot chieftain,[2] one of the most devoted to Arungzéb, and who died fighting for his son. "The emperor showed but little favour to his faithful and most useful subjects the Rajpoots, which greatly cooled their ardour in his service." The Rana took up arms, and Malwa joined the tumult; while the first irruption of the Mahrattas across the Nerbudda,[3] under Neema Sindia, compelled the emperor to detach Raja Jey Sing to join Prince Azím. Amidst these accumulated troubles, the Mahrattas rising into importance, the Rajpoot feudatories disgusted and alienated, his sons and grandsons ready to commit each individual pretension to the decision of the sword, did Arungzéb, after a reign of terror of half a century's duration, breathe his last on the 28th Zekaud, A.D. 1707, at the city bearing his name—Arungabad.

At his death his second son Azím assumed the imperial dignity, and aided by the Rajpoot princes of Duttea and Kotah,[4] who had always served in his division, he marched to Agra to contest the legitimate claims of his eldest brother Mauzum, who was advancing from Cabul supported by the contingents of Méwar and Marwar, and all western Rajwarra. The

the home market. The rates of pay to civil officers afford no security to integrity; and the faithful soldier cannot aspire to higher reward than £120 per annum, were his breast studded with medals. Even their prejudices are often too little considered, prejudices, the violation of which lost the throne of India, in spite of every local advantage, to the descendants of Arungzéb.

[1] Rampoora *Bhânpoora* (city of the sun) to distinguish it from Rampoora *Tonk*. Rao Gopâl was of the Chanderawut clan. See note, p. 212.

[2] Rao Dulput Boondéla of Duttea, a portion of whose memoirs were presented to me by the reigning prince, his descendant.

[3] A.D. 1706–7.

[4] Rao Dulput (Boondéla), and Rao Ram Sing (Hara).

battle of Jajow was fatal to Azím, who with his son Bedar-bukt and the princes of Kotah and Duttea was slain, when Mauzum ascended the throne under the title of Shah Alum Buhadoor Shah. This prince had many qualities which endeared him to the Rajpoots, to whom his sympathies were united by the ties of blood, his mother being a Rajpoot princess. Had he immediately succeeded the beneficent Shah Jehan, the race of Timoor, in all human probability, would have been still enthroned at Dehli, and might have presented a picture of one of the most powerful monarchies of Asia. But Arungzéb had inflicted an incurable wound on the mind of the Hindu race, which for ever estranged them from his successors; nor were the virtues of Buhadoor, during the short lustre of his sway, capable of healing it. The bitter fruit of a long experience had taught the Rajpoots not to hope for amelioration from any graft of that stem, which, like the deadly Upas, had stifled the vital energies of Rajast'han, whose leaders accordingly formed a league for mutual preservation, which it would have been madness to dissolve merely because a fair portion of virtue was the inheritance of the tyrant's successor. They had proved that no act of duty or subserviency could guarantee them from the infatuated abuse of power, and they were at length steeled against every appeal to their loyalty, replying with a trite adage, which we may translate "*quem Deus vult perdere, prius dementat*,"—of common application with the Rajpoot in such a predicament.

The emperor was soon made to perceive the little support he had in future to expect from the Rajpoots. Scarcely had he quashed the pretensions of Kambuksh, his youngest brother, who proclaimed himself emperor in the Dekhan, than he was forced to the north, in consequence of an insurrection of the Siks of Lahore. This singular race, the disciples (*siks*) of a teacher called Nanuk, were the descendants of the Scythic Gete,[1] or Jit, of Transoxiana, who so early as the fifth century were established in the tract watered by the five arms (*Punjâb*) of the Indus. Little more than a century has elapsed since their conversion from a spurious Hinduism to the doctrines of the sectarian Nanuk, and their first attempt to separate themselves, in temporal as well as spiritual matters, from all control, and they are now the sole independent power within the limits of the Mogul monarchy. On this occasion[2] the princes of Ambér and Marwar visited the emperor, but left his camp without permission, and, as the historian[3] adds, manifested a design to struggle for independence. Such was the change in their mutual circumstances that the Mogul sent the heir-apparent to conciliate and conduct them to him; but they came at the head of all their native bands, when "they were gratified with whatever their insolence demanded":[4] a splenetic effusion of the historian, which well paints their altered position. From the royal *oordoo*,[5] or camp, they repaired to Rana Umra at Oodipoor, where a triple league was formed, which once more united them to the head of their nation. This treaty of unity of interests against the common foe was solemnised by nuptial engagements, from which those princes had been excluded since

[1] See *History of the Tribes*, article "Jits," p. 88.

[2] A.D. 1709–10.

[3] *Memoirs of Eradut Khan*, p. 58; also autograph letters of all those princes, with files of the regular newspapers (*akbars*) of the day, in my possession, dated from the emperor's camp.

[4] *Memoirs of Eradut Khan.*

[5] Hence the corruption of *horde*.

the reigns of Akber and Pertáp. To be readmitted to this honour was the basis of this triple alliance, in which they ratified on oath the renunciation of all connection, domestic or political, with the empire. It was, moreover, stipulated that the sons of such marriage should be heirs, or if the issue were females, that they should never be dishonoured by being married to a Mogul.

But this remedy, as will be seen, originated a worse disease; it was a sacrifice of the rights of primogeniture (clung to by the Rajpoots with extreme pertinacity), productive of the most infurious effects, which introduced domestic strife, and called upon the stage an umpire not less baneful than the power from whose iron grasp they were on the point of freeing themselves: for although this treaty laid prostrate the throne of Baber, it ultimately introduced the Mahrattas as partisans in their family disputes, who made the bone of contention their own.

The injudicious support afforded by the emperor to the apostate chief of Rampoora first brought the triple federation into action. The Rana, upholding the cause of Himmut Sing, made an attack on Rampoora, which the apostate usurper Ruttun Sing, now *Raj Mooslim Khan*, defeated, and was rewarded for it by the emperor.[1] But the same report conveyed to the king "*that the Rana determined to lay waste his country, and retire to the hills,*"[2] which was speedily confirmed by the unwelcome intelligence that Sawuldás, an officer of the Rana's, had attacked Feeroz Khan, the governor of Poorh Mandel, who was obliged to retreat with great loss to Ajmér;[3] on which occasion this loyal descendant of the illustrious Jeimul lost his life.[4] The brave Doorga-Das, who conveyed the rebellious Akber through all opposition to a place of refuge, again appeared upon the stage—his own prince being unable to protect him, he had found a safe asylum at Oodipoor, and had the sum of five hundred rupees daily paid for his expenditure—a princely liberality. But the result of this combination was reserved for the following reigns, Shah Alum being carried off by poison,[5] ere he could correct the disorders which were rapidly breaking up the empire from the Hindu-Koosh to the ocean. Had his life been spared, his talents for business, his experience, and courteous manners might have retarded the ruin of the monarchy, which the utter unworthiness of his successor sunk beyond the power of man to redeem. Every subsequent succession was through blood; and the sons of Shah Alum performed the part for which they had so many great examples. Two brothers,[6] Syeds, from the town of Bareh in the Doáb, were long the Warwicks of Hindust'han, setting up and plucking down its puppet kings at their pleasure; they had elevated Ferochsér when the triumvirs of Rajast'han commenced their operations.

Giving loose to long-suppressed resentment, the Rajpoots abandoned the spirit of toleration which it would have been criminal to preserve;

[1] Newspapers, dated 3rd Rejib, Sun. 3—(3rd year of his reign).

[2] Newspapers, 10th Rejib, Sun. 3.

[3] Newspapers, 5th Shaval, Sun. 3.

[4] The following edict, which caused this action, I translated from the archives; it is addressed to the son of Sawuldás:—

"Mahrana Umra Sing to Rahtore Raé Sing *Sawuldasote* (race of Sawuldás)—

"Lay waste your villages and the country around you—your families shall have other habitations to dwell in—for particulars consult Dowlut Sing Chondawut: obey these."—Asoj, S. 1764 (Dec. A.D. 1708).

[5] A.D. 1712.

[6] Husein Alli and Abdoolla Khan.

and profiting by the lessons of their tyrants, they overthrew the mosques built on the sites of their altars, and treated the civil and religious officers of the government with indignity. Of these every town in Rajast'han had its *moolâh* to proclaim the name of Mahomed, and its *câzi* for the administration of justice,—branches of government entirely wrested from the hands of the native princes,[1] abusing the name of independence. But for a moment it was redeemed, especially by the brave Rahtores, who had made a noble resistance, contesting every foot of land since the death of Jeswunt Sing, and now his son Ajít entirely expelled the Moguls from Marwar. On this occasion the native forces of the triple alliance met at the salt lake of Sambur, which was made the common boundary of their territory, and its revenues were equally divided amongst them.

The pageant of an emperor, guided by the Syeds, or those who intrigued to supplant their ministry, made an effort to oppose the threatening measures of the Rajpoots; and one of them, the Ameer-ool Omra,[2] marched against Raja Ajít, who received private instructions from the emperor to resist his commander-in-chief, whose credit was strengthened by the means taken to weaken it, which engendered suspicions of treachery. Ajít leagued with the Syeds, who held out to the Rahtore an important share of power at court, and agreed to pay tribute and give a daughter in marriage to Ferochsér.

This marriage yielded most important results, which were not confined to the Moguls or Rajpoots, for to it may be ascribed the rise of the British power in India. A dangerous malady,[3] rendering necessary a surgical operation upon Ferochsér, to which the faculty of the court were unequal, retarded the celebration of the nuptials between the emperor and the Rajpoot princess of Marwar, and even threatened a fatal termination. A mission from the British merchants at Surat was at that time at court, and, as a last resource, the surgeon attached to it was called in, who cured the malady, and made the emperor happy in his bride.[4] His gratitude was displayed with oriental magnificence. The emperor desired Mr. Hamilton to name his reward, and to the disinterested patriotism of this individual did the British owe the first royal grant or *firmân*, conferring territorial possession and great commercial privileges. These were the objects of the mission, which till this occurrence had proved unsuccessful.

This gorgeous court ought to have been, and probably was, impressed with a high opinion of the virtuous self-denial of the inhabitants of Britain;

[1] Next to kine-killing was the article inhibiting the introduction of the *Adawlet*, or British courts of justice, into the Rajpoot states, in all their treaties with the British government in A.D. 1817–8, the very name of which is abhorrent to a native.

[2] The title of Hussein Alli,—as Kootub-ool Moolk (*the axis of the state*), was that of his brother Abdoolla.

[3] A white swelling or tumour on the back.

[4] The ceremony is described, as it was celebrated, with true Asiatic pomp. "The Ameer-ool Omra conducted the festivities on the part of the bride, and the marriage was performed with a splendour and magnificence till then unseen among the princes of Hindust'han. Many pompous insignia were added to the royal cortège upon this occasion. The illuminations rivalled the planets, and seemed to upbraid the faint lustre of the stars. The nuptials were performed at the palace of the Ameer-ool Omra, whence the emperor conveyed his bride with the highest splendour of imperial pomp to the citadel, amidst the resoundings of musical instruments and the acclamations of the people."—Scott's *History of Arungzéb's Successors*, p. 132, vol. i.

and if history has correctly preserved the transaction, some mark of public gratitude should have been forthcoming from those who so signally benefited thereby. But to borrow the phraseology of the Italian historian, "Obligations which do not admit of being fully discharged are often repaid with the coin of ingratitude": the remains of this man rest in the churchyard of Calcutta, without even a stone to mark the spot!

This marriage, which promised a renewal of interests with the Rajpoots, was soon followed by the revival of the obnoxious *jezeya*. The character of this tax, though much altered from its original imposition by Arungzéb, when it was at once financial and religious, was held in unmitigated abhorrence by the Hindus from the complex association; and although it was revived chiefly to relieve pecuniary wants, it kindled a universal feeling of hatred amongst all classes, and quenched the little zeal which the recent marriage had inspired in the Rajpoots of the desert. The mode and channel of its introduction evinced to them that there was no hope that the intolerant spirit which originally suggested it would ever be subdued. The weak Ferochsér, desirous of snapping the leading-strings of the Syeds, recalled to his court Enayet Oolla Khan, the minister of Arungzéb, and restored to him his office of *Déwán*, who, to use the words of the historian of the period, "did not consult the temper of the times, so very different from the reign of Arungzéb, and the revival of the *jezeya* came with him." Though by no means severe in its operation, not amounting to three-quarters per cent. on annual income,[1]—from which the lame, the blind, and very poor were exempt,—it nevertheless raised a general spirit of hostility, particularly from its retaining the insulting distinction of a "*tax on infidels.*" Resistance to taxation appears to be a universal feeling, in which even the Asiatic forgets the divine right of sovereignty, and which throws us back on the pervading spirit of selfishness which governs human nature. The *temgha*, or stamp tax, which preceded the *jezeya*, would appear to have been as unsatisfactory as it was general, from the solemnity of its renunciation by Baber on the field of battle after the victory *over infidels*, which gave him the crown of India; and though we have no record of the jezeya being its substitute, there are indications which authorise the inference.

Rana Umra was not an idle spectator of these occurrences; and although the spurious thirst for distinction so early broke up the alliance by detaching Ajít, he redoubled his efforts for personal independence, and with it that of the Rajpoot nation. An important document attests this solicitude, namely, a treaty [2] with the emperor, in which the second article

[1] 13 rupees on every 2000 rupees.

[2] "*Memorandum of Requests.*

"1. The *Munsub* [1] of 7000.

"2. Firmán of engagement under the *punja* private seal and sign that the jezeya shall be abolished—that it shall no longer be imposed on the Hindu nation; at all events, that none of the Chagitai race shall authorise it in Méwar. Let it be annulled.

"3. The contingent of one thousand horse for service in the Dekhan to be excused.

"4. All places of Hindu faith to be rebuilt, with perfect freedom of religious worship.

[1] The dignity (*munsub*) of commander of a legion of 7000 horse, the highest grade of rank.

stipulates emancipation from the galling *jezeya*. It may be well to analyse this treaty, which attests the altered condition of both parties. Its very title marks the subordination of the chief of the Rajpoots; but while this is headed a "Memorandum of Requests," the eighth article discloses the effective means of the Rána, for there he assumes an air of protection towards the emperor. In the opening stipulation for the *munsub* of 7000, the mind reverts to the great Umra, who preferred abdication to acknowledgment of a superior; but opinion had undergone a change as great as the mutual relations of the Rajpoots. In temporal dignities other states had risen to an equality with Méwar, and all had learned to look on the Mogul as he fountain of honour. The abolition of the jezeya, freedom from religious restraint, control over the ancient feudatories of his house, and the restoration of all sequestrations, distinguish the other articles, and amply attest the improving attitude of Méwar, and the rapid decay of the Mogul empire. The Mahrattas under Raja Sahoo were successfully prosecuting their peculiar system in the south, with the same feelings which characterised the early Gothic invaders of Italy; strangers to settled government, they imposed the taxes of *chout'h* and *desmookie*, the *fourth* and *tenth* of all territorial income, in the countries they overran. The Jât tribes west of the Chumbul likewise bearded their oppressors in this reign, by hoisting the standard of independence at the very threshold of their capital; and from the siege of Sinsini (mentioned in this treaty) to the last storm of Bhurtpoor, they maintained the consequence thus assumed.

This treaty was the last act of Rana Umra's life; he died in A.D. 1716, leaving the reputation of an active and high-minded prince, who well upheld his station and the prosperity of his country, notwithstanding the anarchy of the period. His encouragement of agriculture and protection

"5. If my uncles, brothers, or chiefs, repair to the presence, to meet no encouragement.

"6. The Bhomias of Deola, Banswarra, Dongerpoor, and Sirohi, besides other zemindars over whom I am to have control, they shall not be admitted to the presence.

"7. The forces I possess are my chiefs—what troops you may require for a given period, you must furnish with rations (*paiti*), and when the service is over, their accounts will be settled.

"8. Of the Hukdars, Zemindars, Munsubdars, who serve you with zeal and from the heart, let me have a list—and those who are not obedient I will punish; but in effecting this no demand is to be made for *Páemáli*." [1]

"List of the districts attached to the *Punj-hazari*,[2] at present under sequestration, to be restored—Phoolia, Mandelgurh, Bednore, Poorh, Bassar, Ghiaspoor, Purdhar, Banswarra, Dongerpoor. Besides the 5000 of old, you had on ascending the throne granted an increase of 1000, and on account of the victory at Sinsini 1000 more, of two and three horse." [3]

"Of three crones of *dams*[4] in gift (*enám*), namely, two according to firman, and one for the payment of the contingent in the Dekhan, and of which two are immediately required, you have given me in lieu thereof Sirohi.

"Districts now desired—Eidur, Kekri, Mandel, Jehajpoor, Malpoor (and another illegible).

---

[1] Destruction of property, alluding to the crops which always suffered in the movements of disorderly troops.

[2] Munsub of 5000.

[3] It was usual to allow two and three horses to each cavalier when favour was intended.

[4] 40 dams to the rupee.

of manufactures are displayed in the edicts engraved on pillars, which will hand down his name to posterity. His memory is held in high veneration; nor do the Rajpoots admit the absolute degradation of Méwar till the period of the second prince in succession to Umra.

CHAPTER XV

Rana Sangram—Dismemberment of the Mogul Empire—Nizam-ool Moolk establishes the Hydrabad state—Murder of the Emperor Ferochsér—Abrogation of the Jezeya—Mahomed Shah, Emperor of Dehli—Saadut Khan obtains Oude—Repeal of the Jezeya confirmed—Policy of Méwar—Rana Sangram dies—Anecdotes regarding him—Rana Juggut Sing II. succeeds—Treaty of triple alliance with Marwar and Ambér—The Mahrattas invade and gain footing in Malwa and Guzzerat—Invasion of Nadir Shah—Sack of Dehli—Condition of Rajpootana—Limits of Méwar—Rajpoot alliances—Bajerow invades Méwar—Obtains a cession of annual tribute—Contest to place Madhú Sing on the throne of Ambér—Battle of Rajmahl—The Rana defeated—He leagues with Mulhar Holkar—Esuri Sing of Ambér takes poison—The Rana dies—His character.

SANGRAM SING (*the lion of battle*) succeeded; a name renowned in the annals of Méwar, being that of the opponent of the founder of the Moguls. He ascended the throne about the same time with Mahomed Shah, the last of the race of Timoor who deserved the name of emperor of India. During the reign of Sangram, from A.D. 1716 to 1734, this mighty empire was dismembered; when, in lieu of one paramount authority, numerous independent governments started up, which preserved their uncertain existence until the last revolution, which has given a new combination to these discordant materials—Mahomedan, Mahratta, and Rajpoot, in the course of one century under the dominion of a handful of Britons! Like the Satraps of the ancient Persian, or the Lieutenants of Alexander, each chief proclaimed himself master of the province, the government of which was confided to his loyalty and talents; and it cannot fail to diminish any regret at the successive prostration of Bengal, Oude, Hydrabad, and other less conspicuous states, to remember that they were founded in rebellion, and erected on ingratitude; and that their rulers were destitute of those sympathies, which could alone give stability to their ephemeral greatness, by improving the condition of their subjects. With the Mahrattas the case is different: their emergence to power claims our admiration, when tyranny transformed the industrious husbandman, and the minister of religion, into a hardy and enterprising soldier, and a skilful functionary of government. Had their ambition been restrained within legitimate bounds, it would have been no less gratifying than politically and morally just that the family of Sevaji should have retained its authority in countries which his active valour wrested from Arungzéb. But the genius of conquest changed their natural habits; they devastated instead of consolidating; and in lieu of that severe and frugal simplicity, and that energy of enterprise, which were their peculiar characteristics, they became distinguished for mean parsimony, low cunning, and dastardly depredation. Had they, retaining their original character, been content with their proper sphere of action, the Dekhan, they might yet have held the sovereignty of that vast region, where their habits and language assimilated them with the people. But as they spread over the north they encountered national antipathies, and though professing the same creed, a wider difference in sentiment divided the Mahratta from the Rajpoot, than from the despots of Dehli, whose tyrannical intolerance was more endurable, because less degrading, than the rapacious meanness of the Southron. Rajast'han benefited by the demolition of the empire : to all but Méwar it yielded an extension of power. Had the national mind been allowed to repose, and its energies to recruit, after so many centuries of demoralisation, all would have recovered their strength, which lay in the opinions and industry of the people, a devoted tenantry and brave vassalage, whom we have so often depicted as abandoning their habitations and pursuits to aid the patriotic views of their princes.

The short reign of Ferochsér was drawing to a close ; its end was accelerated by the very means by which that monarch hoped to emancipate himself from the thraldom of the Syeds, against whose authority the faction of Enayet Oolla was but a feeble counterpoise, and whose arbitrary habits, in the re-establishment of the jezeya, lost him even the support of the father of his queen. It was on this occasion that the celebrated Nizam-ool Moolk, the founder of the Hydrabad state, was brought upon the stage : he then held the unimportant charge of the district of Moradabad ; but possessed of high talents, he was bought over, by the promise of the government of Malwa, to further the views of the Syeds. Supported by a body of ten thousand Mahrattas, these makers of kings soon manifested their displeasure by the deposal of Ferochsér, who was left without any support but that of the princes of Ambér and Boondí. Yet they would never have abandoned him had he hearkened to their counsel to take the field, and trust his cause to them : but, cowardly and infatuated, he refused to quit the walls of his palace, and threw himself upon the mercy of his enemies, who made him dismiss the faithful Rajpoots and " admit a guard of honour of their troops into the citadel." [1]

[1] Amongst the archives of the Rana to which I had access, I discovered an autograph letter of Raja Jey Sing, addressed at this important juncture to the Rana's prime minister, Beharri-dás.

" The Ameer-ool Omra has arrived, and engagements through Ballajee Pundit have been agreed to : he said that he always had friendship for me, but advised me *to march*, a measure alike recommended by Kishen Sing and Jewa Loll. On this I presented an *arzee* to his Majesty, stated the advice, but desired to have his Majesty's commands ; when the king sanctioning my leave, such being the general desire, on Thursday the 9th of Falgoon I moved, and pitched my tents at Serbul Serai. I told the Rao Rajah (of Boondí) to accompany me, but it did not reach his mind, and he joined Kootub-ool Moolk, who gave him some horse, and made him encamp with Ajít Sing. Bheem Sing's (of Kotah) army arrived, and an engagement took place, in which Jaet Sing Hara was killed, and the Rao Raja fled to Aliverdi Khan's serai. I sent troops to his aid ; the king has made over the baths and wardrobe to the Syeds, who have everything their own way. *You know the Syeds* ; I am on my way back to my own country, and have much to say *vivâ voce* to the *Huzoor* : [1] come and meet me. Falgoon, S. 19, 1775 (A.D. 1719)."

" Sid Sri Mahraja dheraj Sri Singram Sing ji ; receive the *moojra* [2] of Raja

[1] *Huzoor* signifies *the Presence*. Such was the respectful style of the Ambér prince to the Rana ; to illustrate which I shall add another letter from the same prince, though merely complimentary, to the Rana.

[2] *Moojra* is a salutation of respect used to a superior.

Ferochsér hoped for security in the inviolability of the harem—but he found no sanctuary even there: to use the words of the Mogul memoir, "night advanced, and day, like the fallen star of the emperor, sunk in darkness. The gates of the citadel were closed upon his friends: the Vizier and Ajít Sing remained within. This night was dreadful to the inhabitants of the city; no one knew what was passing in the palace, and the troops under the Ameer-ool Omra, with ten thousand Mahrattas, remained under arms: morning came, and all hope was extinguished by the royal band (*Nobut*) announcing the deposal of Ferochsér, in the proclamation of Rufféh-ool Dirjat, his successor." The interval between the deposal and the death of an Asiatic prince is short, and even while the heralds vociferated "long live the king!" to the new puppet, the bowstring was on the neck of the contemptible Ferochsér.

The first act of the new reign (A.D. 1719) was one of conciliation towards Ajít Sing and the Rajpoots, namely, the abrogation of the *jezeya*; and the Syeds further showed their disposition to attach them by conferring the important office of *Déwán* on one of their own faith: Raja Ruttun Chund was accordingly inducted into the ministry in lieu of Enayet Oolla. Three phantoms of royalty flitted across the scene in a few months, till Roshun Akter, the eldest son of Buhadoor Shah, was enthroned with the title of Mahomed Shah (A.D. 1720), during whose reign of nearly thirty years the empire was completely dismembered, and Mahrattas from the south disputed its spoils with the Afghan mountaineers. The haughty demeanour of the Syeds disgusted all who acted with them, especially their coadjutor the Nizam,[1] of whose talents, displayed in restoring Malwa to prosperity, they entertained a dread. It was impossible to cherish any abstract loyalty for the puppets they established, and treason lost its name, when the Nizam declared for independence, which the possession of the fortresses of Asér and Boorhanpoor enabled him to secure. The brothers had just cause for alarm. The Rajpoots were called upon for their contingents,[2] and the princes of Kotah and Nirwur

Sawaie Jey Sing. Here all is well; your welfare is desired; you are the chief, nor is there any separation of interests: my horses and Rajpoots are at your service; command when I can be of use. It is long since I have seen the royal mother (*Sri Baeji Raj*); if you come this way, I trust she will accompany you. For news I refer you to Deep Chund Pancholi. Asoj 6, S. 1777."

[1] Raja Jey Sing to Beharridás, the Rana's minister:—"You write that your Lord despatches money for the troops—I have no accounts thereof; put the treasure on camels and send it without delay. The Nawab Nizam-ool Moolk is marching rapidly from Oojein, and Jubeela Ram is coming hither, and according to accounts from Agra he has crossed at Calpee. Let the Déwan's army form a speedy junction. Make no delay; in supplies of cash everything is included."—Bhadoon, 4th, S. 1776 (A.D. 1720).

[2] Letter from Raja Bukhta Sing of Nagore to Beharri-das, the Rana's prime minister:—"Your letter was received, and its contents made me happy. Sri *Déwán's roqqua* reached me and was understood. You tell me both the Nawabs (*Syeds*) had taken the field, that both the Mahrajas attended, and that your own army was about to be put in motion, for how could ancient friendships be severed? All was comprehended. But neither of the Nawabs will take the field, nor will either of the Mahrajas proceed to the Dekhan: they will sit and enjoy themselves quietly in talking at home. But should by some accident the Nawabs take the field, espouse their cause; if you cling to any other you are lost; of this you will be convinced ere long, so guard yourself—*if you can wind up our own thread, don't give it to another to break*—you are wise, and can anticipate intentions. Where there is such a servant as you, that house can be in no danger."

gallantly interposed their own retainers to cut off the Nizam from the Nerbudda, on which occasion the Kotah prince was slain. The independence of the Nizam led to that of Oude. Saadut Khan was then but the commandant of Biana, but he entered into the conspiracy to expel the Syeds, and was one of those who drew lots to assassinate the Ameer-ool Omra. The deed was put into execution on the march to reduce the Nizam, when Hyder Khan buried his poniard in the Ameer's heart. The emperor then in camp, being thus freed, returned against the Vizier, who instantly set up Ibrahim and marched against his opponents. The Rajpoots wisely remained neutral, and both armies met. The decapitation of Ruttun Chund was the signal for the battle, which was obstinate and bloody; the Vizier was made prisoner, and subjected to the bowstring. For the part Saadut Khan acted in the conspiracy he was honoured with the title of Buhadoor Jung, and the government of Oude. The Rajpoot princes paid their respects to the conqueror, who confirmed the repeal of the *jezeya*, and as the reward of their neutrality the Rajas of Ambér and Jodpoor, Jey Sing and Ajít, were gratified, the former with the government of the province of Agra, the last with that of Guzzerat and Ajmér, of which latter fortress he took possession. Gheerdir-dás [1] was made governor of Malwa to oppose the Mahrattas, and the Nizam was invited from his government of Hydrabad to accept the office of vizier of the empire.

The policy of Méwar was too isolated for the times; her rulers clung to forms and unsubstantial homage, while their neighbours, with more active virtue, plunged into the tortuous policy of the imperial court, and seized every opportunity to enlarge the boundaries of their states: and while Ambér appropriated to herself the royal domains almost to the Jumna; while Marwar planted her banner on the battlements of Ajmér, dismembered Guzzerat, and pushed her clans far into the desert, and even to "the world's end"; [2] Méwar confined her ambition to the control of her ancient feudatories of Aboo, Edur, and the petty states which grew out of her, Dongerpoor and Banswarra. The motive for this policy was precisely the same which had cost such sacrifices in former times; she dreaded amalgamating with the imperial court, and preferred political inferiority to the sacrifice of principle. The internal feuds of her two great clans also operated against her aggrandisement; and while the brave Suktawut, Jeit Sing, expelled the Rahtore from Edur, and subdued the wild mountaineers even to Koliwarra, the conquest was left incomplete by the jealousy of his rival, and he was recalled in the midst of his success. From these and other causes an important change took place in the internal policy of Méwar, which tended greatly to impair her energies. To this period none of the vassals had the power to erect places of strength within their domains, which, as already stated, were not fixed, but subject to triennial change; their lands were given for subsistence, their native hills were their fortresses, and the frontier strongholds defended their families in time of invasion. As the Mogul power waned, the general defensive system was abandoned, while the predatory warfare which succeeded compelled them to stud their country with castles, in order

[1] Gheerdir-dás was a Nagar Bramin, son of Jubeela Ram, the chief secretary of Ruttun Chund.

[2] *Juggut coont*, the *Jigat point*, of our maps, at Dwarica, where the *Bhadails*, a branch of the Rahtores, established themselves.

to shelter their effects from the Mahratta and Pat'han, and in later times to protect rebels.

Rana Sangram ruled eighteen years ; under him Méwar was respected, and the greater portion of her lost territory was regained. His selection of Beharri-das Pancholi evinced his penetration, for never had Méwar a more able or faithful minister, and numerous autograph letters of all the princes of his time attest his talent and his worth as the oracle of the period. He retained his office during three reigns : but his skill was unable to stem the tide of Mahratta invasion, which commenced on the death of Sangram.

Tradition has preserved many anecdotes of Sangram, which aid our estimate of Rajpoot character, whether in the capacity of legislators or the more retired sphere of domestic manners. They uniformly represent this Rana as a patriarchal ruler, wise, just, and inflexible,[1] steady in his application to business, regulating public and private expenditure, and even the sumptuary laws, which were rigidly adhered to, and on which the people still expatiate, giving homely illustrations of the contrast between them and the existing profusion. The Chohan of Kotario, one of the highest class of chieftains, had recommended an addition to the folds of the court robe, and as courtesy forbids all personal denial, his wish was assented to, and he retired to his estate pluming himself on his sovereign's acquiescence. But the Rana, sending for the minister, commanded the sequestration of two villages of Kotario, which speedily reaching the ears of the chief, he repaired to court, and begged to know the fault which had drawn upon him this mark of displeasure. "None, Raoji ; but on a minute calculation I find the revenue of these two villages will just cover the expense of the superfluity of garment which obedience to your wishes will occasion me, and as every iota of my own income is appropriated, I had no other mode of innovating on our ancient costume than by making you bear the charge attending a compliance with your suggestion." It will readily be believed, that the Chohan prayed the revocation of this edict, and that he was careful for the future of violating the sumptuary laws of his sovereign.

On another occasion, from lapse of memory or want of consideration, he broke the laws he had established, and alienated a village attached to the household. Each branch had its appropriate fund, whether for the kitchen, the wardrobe, the privy purse, the queens ; these lands were called *thooa*, and each had its officer, or *thooa-dar*, all of whom were made accountable for their trust to the prime minister ; it was one of these he had alienated. Seated with his chiefs in the *russorah*, or banqueting-hall, there was no sugar forthcoming for the curds, which has a place in the dinner *carte* of all Rajpoots, and he chid the superintendent for the omission. "*Andata*" (giver of food), replied the officer, "the minister says you have given away the village set apart for sugar."—"Just," replied the Rana, and finished his repast without further remark, and without sugar to his curds.

Another anecdote will show his inflexibility of character, and his resistance to that species of interference in state affairs which is the bane of Asiatic governments. Sangram had recently emancipated him-

[1] In the dialect, "churri muzboot t'ha," *his rod was strong*—a familiar phrase, which might be rendered "sceptre"—a long rod with an iron spike on it, often placed before the *gadi*, or throne.

self from the trammels of a tedious minority, during which his mother, according to custom, acted a conspicuous part in the guardianship of her son and the state. The chieftain of Deriavud had his estate confiscated: but as the Rana never punished from passion or pardoned from weakness, none dared to plead his cause, and he remained proscribed from court during two years, when he ventured a petition to the queen-mother through the *Bindarins*,[1] for the reversion of the decree, accompanied with a note for two lacks of rupees,[2] and a liberal donation to the fair mediators. It was the daily habit of the Rana to pay his respects to his mother before dinner, and on one of these visits she introduced the Ranawut's request, and begged the restoration of the estate. It was customary, on the issue of every grant, that eight days should elapse from the mandate to the promulgation of the edict, to which eight official seals[3] were attached; but on the present occasion the Rana commanded the execution of the deed at once, and to have it ere he left the *Rawula*. On its being brought, he placed it respectfully in his mother's hands, begging her to return the note to the Ranawut; having made this sacrifice to duty, he bowed and retired. The next day he commanded dinner an hour earlier, without the usual visit to the Rawula: all were surprised, but none so much as the queen-mother—the day passed—another came—still no visit, and to a confidential message, she received a ceremonious reply. Alarmed for the loss of her son's affections, she pondered on the cause, but could find none, except the grant—she entreated the minister's interference; he respectfully intimated that he was interdicted from the discussion of state affairs but with his sovereign—she had recourse to other expedients, which proving alike fruitless, she became sullen, punished her damsels without cause, and refused food: Sangram still remained obdurate. She talked of a pilgrimage to the Ganges, and befitting equipage and escort were commanded to attend her—the moment of departure was at hand, and yet he would not see her. She repaired by Ambér on her route to Muttra, to worship the Apollo of Vrij, when the great Raja Jey Sing (married to the Rana's sister)[4] advanced, and

[1] The dames attendant on the queens,—the Lady Mashams of every female court in Rajast'han. [2] £25,000.

[3] There were eight ministers; from this the Mahrattas had their *usht purdhans*, the number which formed the ministry of Rama.

[4] I discovered the following letter from one of the princesses of Ambér to Rana Sangram, written at this period; it is not evident in what relation she stood to him, but I think she must have been his wife, and the sister of Jey Sing:

"To *Sid Sri Singrám Sing*, happiness! the Cutchwaha Ranee (*queen*) writes, read her *asees*[1] (blessing). Here all is well; the welfare of the *Sri Déwán-ji* is desired. You are very dear to me; you are great, the sun of Hindust'han; if you do not thus act, who else can? the action is worthy of you; with your house is my entire friendship. From ancient times we are the Rajpoots of your house, from which both Rajas[2] have had their consequence increased, and I belong to it of old, and expect always to be fostered by it, nor will the Sri Déwán-ji disappoint us. My intention was to proceed to the feet of the Sri Déwán-ji, but the wet weather has prevented me; but I shall soon make my appearance."—S. 1778 (A.D. 1722).

[1] *Asees* is benediction, which only ladies and holy men employ in epistolary writing or in verbal compliment.

[2] Ambér and Marwar; this expression denotes the letter to have been written on intermarriage with the Rana's house, and shows her sense of such honour.

conducted her to his new city of Jeipoor, and to evince his respect "put his shoulder to the travelling litter or palkee," and promised to return with her and be a suppliant to his brother-in-law for the restoration of his regard. She made a tour of the sacred places, and on return accepted the escort of the Prince of Ambér. The laws of hospitality amongst the Rajpoots are rigid: the Rana could not refuse to his guest the request for which he had left his capital: but averse to owing reconciliation to external intercession, and having done enough for the suppression of intrigue, he advanced to meet the cortège when within one march of Oodipoor, as if to receive the Ambér prince; but proceeding direct to his mother's tents, he asked her blessing, and having escorted her to the palace, returned to greet and conduct his brother prince; all the allusion he made to the subject was in the simple but pithy expression, "family quarrels should be kept in the family."

Another anecdote shows him as the vigilant shepherd watching over the safety of his flock. As he sat down to dinner, tidings arrived of an invasion of the Malwa Pat'hans, who had rifled several villages at Mundisore, carrying the inhabitants into captivity. Pushing the platter from him, he ordered his armour, and the *nakara* to beat the assemblage of his chieftains. With all speed a gallant band formed on the terrace below, but they prevailed on the Rana to leave the punishment of the desultory aggression to them, as unworthy of his personal interference. They departed: several hours after, the chief of Kanorh arrived, having left a sick bed, and with a tertian come in obedience to his sovereign's summons. Vain was his prince's dissuasion to keep him back, and he joined the band as they came up with the invaders. The foe was defeated and put to flight, but the sick chieftain fell in the charge, and his son was severely wounded by his side. On the young chief repairing to court he was honoured with a *beera* [1] from the Rana's own hand, a distinction which he held to be an ample reward for his wounds, and testimonial of the worth of his father. The existence of such sentiments are the strongest tests of character.

On another occasion, some parasite had insinuated suspicions against the chief of the nobles, the Rawut of Saloombra, who had just returned victorious in action with the royal forces at Malwa, and had asked permission to visit his family on his way to court. The Rana spurned the suspicion, and to show his reliance on the chief, he despatched a messenger for Saloombra to wait his arrival and summon him to the presence. He had reached his domain, given leave to his vassals as they passed their respective abodes, dismounted, and reached the door of the *Rawula*, when the herald called aloud, "The Rana salutes you, Rawut-ji, and commands this letter." With his hand on the door where his wife and children awaited him, he demanded his horse, and simply leaving his "duty for his mother," he mounted, with half a dozen attendants, nor loosed the rein until he reached the capital. It was midnight; his house empty; no servants; no dinner; but his sovereign had foreseen and provided, and when his arrival was announced, provender for his cattle, and vessels

[1] The *beera* is the beetle or pan-leaf folded up, containing aromatic spices, and presented on taking leave. The Kanorh chieftain, being of the second grade of nobles, was not entitled to the distinction of having it from the sovereign's own hand.

of provision prepared in the royal kitchen, were immediately sent to his abode. Next morning, Saloombra attended the court. The Rana was unusually gracious, and not only presented him with the usual tokens of regard, a horse and jewels, but moreover a grant of land. With surprise he asked what service he had performed to merit such distinction, and from a sentiment becoming the descendant of Chonda solemnly refused to accept it ; observing, that even if he had lost his head, the reward was excessive ; but if his prince would admit of his preferring a request, it would be, that in remembrance of his sovereign's favour, when he, or his, in after times, should on the summons come from their estate to the capital, the same number of dishes from the royal kitchen should be sent to his abode : it was granted, and to this day his descendants enjoy the distinction. These anecdotes paint the character of Sangram far more forcibly than any laboured effort. His reign was as honourable to himself as it was beneficial to his country, in whose defence he had fought eighteen actions ; but though his policy was too circumscribed, and his country would have benefited more by a surrender of some of those antique prejudices which kept her back in the general scramble for portions of the dilapidated monarchy of the Moguls, yet he was respected abroad, as he was beloved by his subjects, of whose welfare he was ever watchful, and to whose wants ever indulgent. Rana Sangram was the last prince who upheld the dignity of the *gadi* of Bappa Rawul ; with his death commenced Mahratta ascendancy, and with this we shall open the reign of his son and successor.

Juggut Sing II., the eldest of the four sons of Sangram, succeeded S. 1790 (A.D. 1734). The commencement of his reign was signalised by a revival of the triple alliance formed by Rana Umra, and broken by Raja Ajít's connection with the Syeds and the renewal of matrimonial ties with the empire, the abjuration whereof was the basis of the treaty. The present engagement, which included all the minor states, was formed at Hoorlah, a town in Méwar on the Ajmér frontier, where the confederate princes met at the head of their vassals. To insure unanimity, the Rana was invested with paramount control, and headed the forces which were to take the field after the rains, already set in.[1] Unity of interests was the

[1] Treaty.

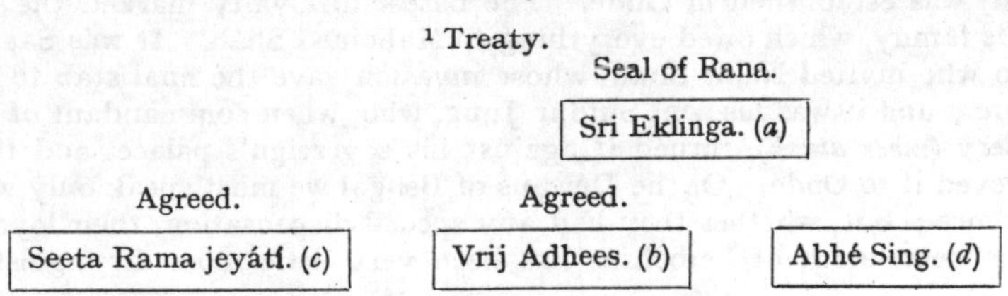
Seal of Rana.

Sri Eklinga. (*a*)

Agreed. Agreed.

Seeta Rama jeyáti. (*c*) | Vrij Adhees. (*b*) | Abhé Sing. (*d*)

Swesta Sri ! By the united chiefs the under-written has been agreed to, from which no deviation can take place. Sawun sood 13, S. 1791 (A.D. 1735), Camp Hoorlah.

1. All are united, in good and in evil, and none will withdraw therefrom,

(*a*) (*b*) (*c*). All these seals of Méwar, Marwar, and Ambér, bear respectively the names of the tutelary divinity of each prince and his tribe :—(*a*) Eklinga, or Mahadeva of the Seesodias of Méwar ; (*b*) Vrij Adhees, the lord of Vrij, the country round Mat'hoora ; the epithet of Crishna ; seal of the Hara prince ; (*c*) Victory to Seeta and Rama, the demi-god, ancestor of the princes of Ambér ; (*d*) Abhé Sing, prince of Marwar.

chief character of the engagement, had they adhered to which, not only the independence, but the aggrandisement, of Rajast'han, was in their power, and they might have alike defied the expiring efforts of Mogul tyranny, and the Parthian-like warfare of the Mahratta. They were indeed the most formidable power in India at this juncture ; but difficult as it had ever proved to coalesce the Rajpoots for mutual preservation, even when a paramount superiority of power, both temporal and spiritual, belonged to the Ranas, so now, since Ambér and Marwar had attained an equality with Méwar, it was found still less practicable to prevent the operation of the principles of disunion. In fact, a moment's reflection must discover that the component parts of a great feudal federation, such as that described, must contain too many discordant particles—too many rivalries and national antipathies—ever cordially to amalgamate. Had it been otherwise, the opportunities were many and splendid for the recovery of Rajpoot freedom ; but though individually enamoured of liberty, the universality of the sentiment prevented its realisation : they never would submit to the control required to work it out, and this, the best opportunity which had ever occurred, was lost. A glance at the disordered fragments of the throne of Akber will show the comparative strength of the Rajpoots.

Nizam-ool Moolk had completely emancipated himself from his allegiance, and signalised his independence, by sending the head of the imperial general, who ventured to oppose it, as that of a traitor, to the emperor. He leagued with the Rajpoots, and instigated Bajerow to plant the Mahratta standard in Malwa and Guzzerat. In defending the former, Dya Buhadoor fell ; and Jey Sing of Ambér, being nominated to the trust, delegated it to the invader, and Malwa was lost. The extensive province of Guzzerat soon shared the same fate ; for in the vacillating policy of the court, the promise of that government to the Rahtores had been broken, and Abhé Sing, son of Ajít, who had expelled Sirbullund Khan after a severe contest, following the example of his brother prince of Ambér, connived with the invaders, while he added its most northern districts to Marwar. In Bengal, Behar, and Orissa, Shuja ud Dowlah, and his deputy Aliverdi Khan, were supreme, and Sufdur Jung (son of Saadut Khan) was established in Oude. The basest disloyalty marked the rise of this family, which owed everything to Mahomed Shah. It was Saadut Khan who invited Nadir Shah, whose invasion gave the final stab to the empire ; and it was his son, Sufdur Jung, who, when commandant of the artillery (*meer atush*), turned it against his sovereign's palace, and then conveyed it to Oude. Of the Déwans of Bengal we must speak only with reverence ; but, whether they had any special dispensation, their loyalty to the descendant of Ferochsér has been very little more distinguished

on which oaths have been made, and faith pledged, which will be lost by whoever acts contrary thereto. The honour and shame of one is that of all, and in this everything is contained.

2. No one shall countenance the traitor of another.
3. After the rains the affair shall commence, and the chiefs of each party assemble at Rampoora ; and if from any cause the head cannot come, he will send his *Konwar* (heir), or some personage of weight.
4. Should from inexperience such *Konwar* commit error, the Rana alone shall interfere to correct it.
5. In every enterprise, all shall unite to effect it.

than that of the satraps enumerated, though the original tenure of Bengal is still apparent, and the feudal obligation to the suzerain of Dehli manifested, in the homage of *petite serjanterie,* in transmitting with the annual fine of relief (one hundred mohors) the spices of the eastern archipelago. Yet of all those who gloried in the title of *fidooé padshaé ghazi*, the only '*slave of the victorious king,*' who has been generous to him in the day of his distress, is the Déwan of Bengal, better known as the English East India Company. In the hour of triumph, they rescued the blind and aged descendants of the illustrious Baber from a state of degradation and penury, and secured to him all the dignity and comfort which his circumstances could lead him to hope ; and the present state of his family, contrasted with the thraldom and misery endured while fortune favoured the Mahratta, is splendid. Yet perhaps the most acute stroke of fortune to this fallen monarch was when the British governor of India lent his aid to the descendant of the rebellious Sufdur Jung to mount the throne of Oude, and to assume, in lieu of the title of vizier of the empire, that of king. We can appreciate and commiserate the feeling ; for the days of power were yet too recent [1] for Akber *Sani* (the second) to receive such intelligence without a shock, or without comparing his condition with him whose name he bore. It is well to pause upon this page of eastern history, which is full of instruction ; since by weighing the abuses of power, and its inevitable loss through placing a large executive trust in the hands of those who exercised it without sympathy towards the governed, we may at least retard the day of our decline.

The Mahratta establishments in Malwa and Guzzerat constituted a nucleus for others to form upon, and like locusts, they crossed the Nerbudda in swarms ; when the Holkars, the Sindias, the Púars, and other less familiar names, emerged from obscurity ; when the plough [2] was deserted for the sword, and the goat-herd [3] made a lance of his crook. They devastated, and at length settled upon, the lands of the indigenous Rajpoots. For a time, the necessity of unity made them act under one standard, and hence the vast masses under the first Bajerow, which bore down all opposition, and afterwards dispersed themselves over those long-oppressed regions. It was in A.D. 1735 that he first crossed the Chumbul [4] and appeared before Dehli, which he blockaded, when his retreat was purchased by the surrender of the *chout'h,* or fourth of the gross revenues of the empire. The Nizam, dreading the influence such pusillanimous concession might exert upon his rising power, determined to drive the Mahrattas from Malwa, where, if once fixed, they would cut off his communications with the north. He accordingly invaded Malwa, defeated Bajerow in a pitched battle, and was only prevented from following it up by Nadir Shah's advance, facilitated by the Afghans, who, on becoming independent in Cabul, laid open the frontiers of Hindust'han.[5] In this emergency, " great hopes were placed on the valour of the Rajpoots " ; but the spirit of devotion in this brave race, by whose aid the Mogul power

[1] I have conversed with an aged sheikh who recollected the splendour of Mahomed Shah's reign before Nadir's invasion. He was *darogah* (superintendent) to the Dooáb canal, and described to me the fête on its opening.

[2] Sindia's family were husbandmen.

[3] Holkar was a goat-herd.

[4] The ford near Dhalpoor still is called Bhow-ghát.

[5] A.D. 1740.

was made and maintained, was irretrievably alienated, and not one of those high families, who had throughout been so lavish of their blood in its defence, would obey the summons to the royal standard, when the fate of India was decided on the plains of Kurnal. A sense of individual danger brought together the great home feudatories, when the Nizam and Saadut Khan (now Vizier) united their forces under the imperial commander; but their demoralised levies were no match for the Persian and the northern mountaineer. The Ameer-ool Omra was slain, the Vizier made prisoner, and Mahomed Shah and his kingdom were at Nadir's disposal. The disloyalty of the Vizier filled the capital with blood, and subjected his sovereign to the condition of a captive. Jealous of the Nizam, whose diplomatic success had obtained him the office of Ameer-ool Omra, he stimulated the avarice of the conqueror by exaggerating the riches of Dehli, and declared that he alone could furnish the ransom negotiated by the Nizam. Nadir's love of gold overpowered his principle; the treaty was broken, the keys of Dehli were demanded, and its humiliated emperor was led in triumph through the camp of the conqueror, who, on the 8th March A.D. 1740, took possession of the palace of Timoor, and coined money bearing this legend:

> "King over the kings of the world
> Is Nadir, king of kings, and lord of the period."

The accumulated wealth of India contained in the royal treasury, notwithstanding the lavish expenditure during the civil wars, and the profuse rewards scattered by each competitor for dominion, was yet sufficient to gratify even avarice itself, amounting in gold, jewels, and plate to forty millions sterling, exclusive of equipages of every denomination. But this enormous spoil only kindled instead of satiating the appetite of Nadir, and a fine of two millions and a half was exacted, and levied with such unrelenting rigour and cruelty on the inhabitants, that men of rank and character could find no means of escape but by suicide. A rumour of this monster's death excited an insurrection, in which several Persians were killed. The provocation was not lost: the conqueror ascended a mosque,[1] and commanded a general massacre, in which thousands were slain. Pillage accompanied murder; whilst the streets streamed with blood, the city was fired, and the dead were consumed in the conflagration of their late habitations. If a single ray of satisfaction could be felt amidst such a scene of horror, it must have been when Nadir commanded the minister of the wretch who was the author of this atrocity, the infamous Saadut Khan, to send, on pain of death, an inventory of his own and his master's wealth; demanding meanwhile the two millions and a half, the original composition settled by the Nizam, from the Vizier alone. Whether his "coward conscience" was alarmed at the mischief he had occasioned, or mortification at discovering that his ambition had "o'erleaped itself," and recoiled with vengeance on his own head, tempted the act, it is impossible to discover, but the guilty Saadut became his own executioner. He swallowed poison; an example followed by his déwan, Raja Mujlis Rae, in order to escape the rage of the offended Nadir. By the new treaty, all the western provinces, Cabul, Tatta, Sinde, and Mooltan, were surrendered and united to Persia, and on the vernal equinox, Nadir, gorged

[1] It is yet pointed out to the visitor of this famed city.

with spoil, commenced his march from the desolated Dehli.[1] The philosophic comment of the native historian on these events is so just, that we shall transcribe it verbatim. "The people of Hindust'han at this period thought only of personal safety and gratification; misery was disregarded by those who escaped it, and man, centred wholly in self, felt not for his kind. This selfishness, destructive of public and private virtue, was universal in Hindust'han at the invasion of Nadir Shah; nor have the people become more virtuous since, and consequently neither more happy nor more independent."

At this eventful era in the political history of India, the Rajpoot nation had not only maintained their ground amidst the convulsions of six centuries under the paramount sway of the Islamite, but two of the three chief states, Marwar and Ambér, had by policy and valour created substantial states out of petty principalities, junior branches[2] from which had established their independence, and still enjoy it under treaty with the British Government. Méwar at this juncture was defined by nearly the same boundaries as when Mahmood of Ghizni invaded her in the tenth century, though her influence over many of her tributaries, as Boondí, Aboo, Edur, and Deola, was destroyed. To the west, the fertile district of Godwar carried her beyond her natural barrier, the Aravulli, into the desert; while the Chumbul was her limit to the east. The Khary separated her from Ajmér, and to the south she adjoined Malwa. These limits comprehended one hundred and thirty miles of latitude and one hundred and forty of longitude, containing 10,000 towns and villages, with upwards of a million sterling of revenue, raised from a fertile soil by an excellent

[1] As the hour of departure approached, the cruelties of the ruthless invaders increased, to which the words of the narrator, an eye-witness, can alone do justice: "A type of the last day afflicted the inhabitants of this once happy city; hitherto it was a general massacre, but now came the murder of individuals. In every house was heard the cry of affliction. Bussunt Rae, agent for pensions, killed his family and himself; Khalik Yár Khan stabbed himself; many took poison. The venerable chief magistrate was dishonoured by stripes; sleep and rest forsook the city. The officers of the court were beaten without mercy, and a fire broke out in the imperial *ferásh-khana*, and destroyed effects to the amount of a crore (a million sterling). There was a scarcity of grain, two seers of coarse rice sold for a rupee, and from a pestilential disorder crowds died daily in every street and lane. The inhabitants, like the affrighted animals of the desert, sought refuge in the most concealed corners. Yet four or five crores (millions) more were thus extracted." On the 5th April, Nadir's seals were taken off the imperial repositories, and his firmans sent to all the feudatories of the empire to notify the peace and to inculcate obedience "to his dear brother," which as a specimen of eastern diplomatic phraseology is worth insertion. It was addressed to the Rana, the Rajas of Marwar and Ambér, Nagore, Sitarra, the Peshwa Bajerow, etc. "Between us and our dear brother, Mahomed Shah, in consideration of the regard and alliances of the two sovereignties, the connections of regard and friendship have been renewed, so that we may be esteemed as one soul in two bodies. Now our dear brother has been replaced on the throne of this extensive empire, and we are moving to the conquest of other regions, it is incumbent that ye, like your forefathers, walk in the path of submission and obedience to our dear brother, as they did to former sovereigns of the house of Timoor. God forbid it; but if accounts of your rebelling should reach our ears, we will blot you out of the pages of the book of creation."—"Memoirs of Eradut Khan,"—*Scott's History of Dekhan*, vol. ii. p. 213.

[2] Bikanér and Kishengurh arose out of Marwar, and Machéri from Ambér; to which we might add Shekhavati, which, though not separate, is tributary to Ambér (now Jeipoor).

agricultural population, a wealthy mercantile community, and defended by a devoted vassalage. Such was this little patriarchal state after the protracted strife which has been related ; we shall have to exhibit her, in less than half a century, on the verge of annihilation from the predatory inroads of the Mahrattas.

In order to mark with exactitude the introduction of the Mahrattas into Rajast'han, we must revert to the period [1] when the dastardly intrigues of the advisers of Mahomed Shah surrendered to them as tribute the *chout'h*, or fourth of his revenues. Whether in the full tide of successful invasion, these spoilers deemed any other argument than force to be requisite in order to justify their extortions, they had in this surrender a concession of which the subtle Mahrattas were well capable of availing themselves ; and as the Mogul claimed sovereignty over the whole of Rajast'han, they might plausibly urge their right of *chout'h*, as applicable to all the territories subordinate to the empire.

The rapidity with which these desultory bands flew from conquest to conquest appears to have alarmed the Rajpoots, and again brought about a coalition, which, with the characteristic peculiarity of all such contracts, was commenced by matrimonial alliances. On this occasion, Beejy Sing, the heir of Marwar, was affianced to the Rana's daughter, who at the same time reconciled the princes of Marwar and Ambér, whose positions at the court of the Mogul often brought their national jealousies into conflict, as they alternately took the lead in his councils : for it was rare to find both in the same line of politics. These matters were arranged at Oodipoor.[2]

[1] A.D. 1735.

[2] These documents are interesting, if merely showing the high respect paid by every Rajpoot prince to the Ranas of Méwar, and illustrating what is recorded in the reign of Pertáp, who abjured all intercourse with them.

No. 1.

" From Konwar Beejy Sing of Marwar to the Mah-Rana Sri-Sri-Sri.

" Juggut Sing's *Presence*—let my *moojra* (obedience) be known. You honoured me by sending Rawut Kesuri Sing and Beharri-das, and commanding a marriage connection. Your orders are on your child's head. You have made me a servant. To every thing I am agreed, and now I am your child ; while I live I am yours. If a true Rajpoot, my head is at your disposal. You have made 20,000 Rahtores your servants. If I fail in this, the Almighty is between us. Whoever is of my blood will obey your commands, and the *fruit of this marriage shall be sovereign, and if a daughter, should I bestow her on the Toorkana, I am no true Rajpoot*. She shall be married to a proper connection, and not without your advice ; and even should *Sri Bhahoji* (an epithet of respect to his father), or others of our elders, recommend such proceeding, I swear by God I shall not agree. I am the Déwans, let others approve or disapprove.—Assar Sood Poonum, Full Moon, Thursday, S. 1791 (A.D. 1735–6)."

" *N.B.*—This deed was executed in the balcony of the Kishen-bulas by Rawut Kesuri Sing and Pancholi Beharri-das, and written by Pancholi Laljee—namely, marriage-deed of Konwar Beejy Sing, son of Bukt Sing."

No. 2.

" From Beejy Sing to Rana Juggut Sing.

" Here all is well. Preserve your friendship and favour for me, and give me tidings of your welfare. That day I shall behold you will be without price (*amoluc*). *You have made me a thorough Rajpoot*—never shall I fail in whatever service I can perform. You are the father of all the tribes, and bestow gifts on each according to his worth—the support and preservation of all around you—to your enemy destruction ; great in knowledge, and wise like Brimha. May the Lord of the world keep the Rana happy.—Asar 13."

But, as we have often had occasion to observe, no public or general benefit ever resulted from these alliances, which were obstructed by the multitude of petty jealousies inseparable from clanship ; even while this treaty was in discussion, the fruit of the triple league formed against the tyranny of Arungzéb was about to show its baneful influence, as will presently appear.

When Malwa was acquired by the Mahrattas, followed by the cession of the *chout'h*, their leader, Bajerow, repaired to Méwar, where his visit created great alarm.[1] The Rana desired to avoid a personal interview,

No. 3.

" Raja Bukt Sing to the Rana.

" To Mahrana Sri-Sri-Sri Juggut Sing, let Bukt Sing's respects (*moojra*) be made known. *You have made me a thorough Rajpoot*, and by such your favour is known to the world. What service I can perform, you will never find me backward. The day I shall see you I shall be happy, my heart yearns to be with you.—Asar 11."

No. 4.

" Sawaie Jey Sing to the Rana.

" May the respects of Sawaie Jey Sing be known to the Mahrana. According to the Sri Déwan's *commands* (*hooqm*), I have entered into terms of friendship with you (Abhí Sing of Marwar). For neither Hindu nor Mussulman shall I swerve therefrom. To this engagement God is between us, and the Sri Déwan-ji is witness.—Asar Sood 7."

No. 5.

" Raja Bukt Sing to the Rana.

" Your *Khas roqqua* (note in the Rana's own hand) I received, read, and was happy. Jey Sing's engagement you will have received, and mine also will have reached you. At your commands I entered into friendship with him, and as to my preserving it have no doubts, for having given you as my guarantee, no deviation can occur ; do you secure his. Whether you may be accounted my father, brother, or friend, I am yours ; besides you I care for neither connection nor kin.—Asar 6."

No. 6.

" From Raja Abhí Sing to the Rana.

" To the Presence of Mahrana Juggut Sing, Mahraja Abhí Sing writes—read his respects (*moojra*). God is witness to our engagement, whoever breaks it may he fare ill. In good and in evil we are joined ; with one mind let us remain united, and let no selfishness disunite us. Your chiefs are witnesses, and the true Rajpoot will not deviate from his engagement.—Asoj 3, Thursday."

Abhí Sing and Bukt Sing were brothers, sons of Raja Ajít of Marwar, to whom the former succeeded, while Bukt Sind held Nagore independently. His son was Beejy Sing, with whom this marriage was contracted. He ultimately succeeded to the government of Marwar or Jodpoor. He will add another example of political expediency counteracting common gratitude, in seizing on domestic convulsions to deprive the Rana's grandson of the province of Godwar. Zalim Sing was the fruit of this marriage, who resided during his elder brother's (Futteh Sing) lifetime at Oodipoor. He was brave, amiable, and a distinguished poet. The *Yati* (priest), who attended me during twelve years, my assistant in these researches, was brought up under the eye of this prince as his amanuensis, and from him he imbibed his love of history and poetry, in reading which he excelled all the bards of Rajwarra.

[1] Letters from Rana Juggut Sing to Beharri-das Pancholi.

No. 1.

" Swesta Sri, chief of ministers, Pancholi-ji, read my *Johâr*.[1] The remembrance of you never leaves me. The Dekhany question you have settled well but if a meeting is to take place,[2] let it be beyond Deola—nearer is not advisable. Lessen the number of your troops, by God's blessing there will be no want of

[1] A compliment used from a superior to any inferior.

[2] To the Peshwa is the allusion.

and sent as his ambassadors, the chief of Saloombra and his prime minister, Beharri-das. Long discussions followed as to the mode of Bajerow's

funds. Settle for Rampoora according to the preceding year, and let Dowlut Sing know the opportunity will not occur again. The royal mother is unwell. Garrarow and Guj Manik fought nobly, and Soondur Guj played a thousand pranks.[1] I regretted your absence. How shall I send Sobharam?—Asoj 6, S. 1791 (A.D. 1735)."

No. 2.—*To the Same.*

"I will not credit it, therefore send witnesses and a detail of their demands. Bajerow is come, and he will derive reputation from having compelled a contribution from me, besides his demand of land. He has commenced with my country, and will take twenty times more from me than other Rajas—if a proportionate demand, it might be complied with. Mulhar came last year, but this was nothing—Bajerow this, and he is powerful. But if God hears me he will not get my land. From Devichund learn particulars.

"Thursday. S. 1792.

"At the *Holi* all was joy at the Jugmundur,[2] but what is food without salt? what Oodipoor without Beharri-das?"

No. 3.—*Same to the Same.*

"With such a man as you in my house I have no fears for its stability; but why this appearance of poverty? perhaps you will ask, what fault have you committed, that you sit and move as I direct? The matter is thus: money is all in all, and the troubles on foot can only be settled by you, and all other resolutions are useless. You may say, you have got nothing, and how can you settle them—but already two or three difficulties have occurred, in getting out of which, both your pinions and mine, as to veracity, have been broken, so that neither scheming nor wisdom is any longer available. Though you have been removed from me for some time, I have always considered you at hand; but now it will be well if you approach nearer to me, that we may raise supplies, for in the act of hiding you are celebrated, and the son[3] (*bétà*) hides none: therefore your hoarding is useless, and begets suspicions. Therefore, unless you have a mind to efface all regard for your master and your own importance at my court, you will got ready some jewels and bonds under good security and bring them to me. There is no way but this to allay these troubles: but should you think you have got ever so much time, and that I will send for you at all events, then have I thrown away mine in writing you this letter. You are wise—look to the future, and be assured I shall write no second letter.—S. 1792."

This letter will show that the office of prime minister is not a bed of roses. The immediate descendants of Beharri-das are in poverty like their prince, though some distant branches of the family are in situations of trust; his ambassador to Dehli, and who subsequently remained with me as medium of communication with the Rana, was a worthy and able man—Kishen-das Pancholi.

I shall subjoin another letter from the Sitarra prince to Rana Juggut Sing, though being without date it is doubtful whether it is not addressed to Juggut Sing the First; this is, however, unimportant, as it is merely one of compliment, but showing the high respect paid by the sovereign of the Peshwas to the house whence they originally sprung.

"Swesta Sri, worthy of all praise (*opma*), from whose actions credit results; the worshipper of the remover of troubles; the ambrosia of the ocean of the Rajpoot race[4] (*imrita rutnácára khétri cula*); resplendent as the sun; who has

---

[1] As the Rana never expected his confidential notes to be translated into English, perhaps it is illiberal to be severe on them; or we might say, his elephants are mentioned more *con amore* than his sick mother or state affairs. I obtained many hundreds of these autograph notes of this prince to his prime minister.

[2] The Hindu saturnalia held in the island, "The Minster of the world."

[3] The Rana always styled him 'father.'

[4] The ocean has the poetical appellation of *rutnácára*, or "house of gems";

reception, which was settled to be on the same footing as the Raja of Bunéra,[1] and that he should be seated in front of the throne. A treaty followed, stipulating an annual tribute, which remained in force during ten years,[2] when grasping at the whole they despised a part, and the treaty became a nullity.[3] The dissensions which arose soon after, in consequence of the Rajpoot engagements, afforded the opportunity sought for to mix in their internal concerns. It may be recollected that in the family engagements formed by Rana Umra there was an obligation to invest the issue of such marriage with the rights of primogeniture ; and the death of Sawaie Jey Sing [4] of Ambér, two years after Nadir's invasion, brought that stipulation into effect. His eldest son, Esuri Sing, was proclaimed Raja, but a strong party supported Madhú Sing, the Rana's nephew, and the stipulated, against the natural order of succession. We are left in doubt as to the real designs of Jey Sing in maintaining his guarantee, which was doubtless inconvenient ; but that Madhú Sing was not brought up to the expectation is evident, from his holding a fief of the Rana Sangram, who appropriated the domain of Rampoora for his support, subject to the service of one thousand horse and two thousand foot, formally sanctioned by his father, who allowed the transfer of his services. On the other hand, the letter of permission entitles him *Cheema*, an epithet only applied to the heir-apparent of Jeipoor. Five years, however, elapsed before any extraordinary exertions were made to annul the rights of Esuri Sing, who led his vassals to the Sutledge in order to oppose the first invasion of the Dooranees.[5] It would be tedious to give even an epitome of the intrigues for the development of this object, which properly belong to the annals of Ambér, and whence resulted many of the troubles of Rajpootana.

made a river of tears from the eyes of the wives of your warlike foes ; in deeds munificent. *Sriman Mahraja dheraj Mahrana Sri Juggut Sing-ji*, of all the princes chief, *Sriman Sahoo Chut'hurpáti Rahja* writes, read his Ram, Ram ! Here all is well ; honour me by good accounts, which I am always expecting, as the source of happiness.

"Your favour was received by the Pundhit Purdhan) [1] with great respect ; and from the period of the arrival of Raj Sri Rawut Oody Sing to this time my good-will has been increasing towards him : let your favour between us be enlarged : what more can I write ?"

[1] The descendant of Bheem, son of Rana Raj Sing. The seat assigned to Bajerow was made the precedent for the position of the representative of the British government.

[2] The amount was 160,000 rupees, divided into three shares of 53,333 0 4½, assigned to Holkar, Sindia, and the Púar. The management was entrusted to Holkar ; subsequently Sindia acted as receiver-general. This was the only regular tributary engagement Méwar entered into.

[3] See letter No. 2, in note, p. 336. [4] A.D. 1743.

[5] A.D. 1747.

---

the fable of the churning of the ocean is well known, when were yielded many bounties, of which the *imrita* or 'immortal food' of the gods was one, to which the Rana, as head of all the Rajpoot tribes, is likened.

[1] This expression induces the belief that the letter is written by the Peshwa in his sovereign's name, as they had at this time commenced their usurpation of his power. It was to the second Juggut Sing that an offer was made to fill the Sitarra throne by a branch of his family, then occupied by an imbecile. A younger brother of the Rana, the ancestor of the present heir presumptive, Sheodan Sing, was chosen, but intrigues prevented it, the Rana dreading a superior from his own family.

The Rana took the field with his nephew, and was met by Esuri Sing,[1] supported by the Mahrattas; but the Seesodias did not evince in the battle of Rajmahl that gallantry which must have its source in moral strength: they were defeated and fled. The Rana vented his indignation in a galling sarcasm; he gave the sword of state to a common courtesan to carry in procession, observing "it was a woman's weapon in these degenerate times": a remark, the degrading severity of which made a lasting impression in the decline of Méwar. Elated with this success, Esuri Sing carried his resentments and his auxiliaries, under Sindia, against the Haras of Kotah and Boondí, who supported the cause of his antagonist. Kotah stood a siege and was gallantly defended, and Sindia (Appajee) lost an arm: on this occasion both the states suffered a diminution of territory, and were subjected to tribute. The Rana, following the example of the Cutchwahas, called in as auxiliary Mulhar Rao Holkar, and engaged to pay sixty-four lakhs of rupees (£800,000) on the deposal of Esuri Sing. To avoid degradation this unfortunate prince resolved on suicide, and a dose of poison gave Madhú Sing the *gadi*, Holkar his bribe, and the Mahrattas a firm hold upon Rajast'han. Such was the cause of Rajpoot abasement; the moral force of the vassals was lost in a contest unjust in all its associations, and from this period we have only the degrading spectacle of civil strife and predatory spoliation till the existing treaty of A.D. 1817.

In S. 1808 (A.D. 1752) Rana Juggut Sing died. Addicted to pleasure, his habits of levity and profusion totally unfitted him for the task of governing his country at such a juncture; he considered his elephant fights[2] of more importance than keeping down the Mahrattas. Like all his family, he patronised the arts, greatly enlarged the palace, and expended £250,000 in embellishing the islets of the Péshola. The villas scattered over the valley were all erected by him, and many of those festivals devoted to idleness and dissipation, and now firmly rooted at Oodipoor, were instituted by Juggut Sing II.

CHAPTER XVI

Rana Pertáp II.—Rana Raj Sing II.—Rana Ursi—Holkar invades Méwar, and levies contributions—Rebellion to depose the Rana—A Pretender set up by the rebel chiefs—Zalim Sing of Kotah—The Pretender unites with Sindia—Their combined force attacked by the Rana, who is defeated—Sindia invades Méwar and besieges Oodipoor—Umra Chund made minister by the Rana—His noble conduct—Negotiates with Sindia, who withdraws—Loss of territory to Méwar—Rebel chiefs return to their allegiance—Province of Godwar lost—Assassination of the Rana—Rana Hamír succeeds—Contentions between the Queen Regent and Umra—His noble conduct, death, and character—Diminution of the Méwar territory.

Pertáp II. succeeded in A.D. 1752. Of the history of this prince, who renewed the most illustrious name in the annals of Méwar, there is nothing to record beyond the fact, that the three years he occupied the throne were

[1] The great Jey Sing built a city which he called after himself, and henceforth Jeipoor will supersede the ancient appellation, Ambér.

[2] See letters from Rana Juggut Sing to Beharri-das, p. 336.

marked by so many Mahratta invasions [1] and war contributions. By a daughter of Raja Jey Sing of Ambér he had a son, who succeeded him.

Rana Raj Sing II. was as little entitled to the name he bore as his predecessor. During the seven years he held the dignity, at least seven shoals of the Southrons overran Méwar,[2] and so exhausted this country, that the Rana was compelled to ask pecuniary aid from the Brahmin collector of the tribute, to enable him to marry the Rahtore chieftain's daughter. On his death the order of succession retrograded, devolving on his uncle,

Rana Ursi, in S. 1818, A.D. 1762. The levity of Juggut Sing, the inexperience of his successors Pertáp and Raj Sing, with the ungovernable temper of Rana Ursi, and the circumstances under which he succeeded to power, introduced a train of disorders which proved fatal to Méwar. Until this period not a foot of territory had been alienated. The wisdom of the Pancholi ministers, and the high respect paid by the organ of the Sitarra government, for a while preserved its integrity; but when the country was divided by factions, and the Mahrattas, ceasing to be a federate body, prowled in search of prey under leaders, each having an interest of his own, they formed political combinations to suit the ephemeral purposes of the former, but from which they alone reaped advantage. An attempt to depose Pertáp and set up his uncle Nat'hji introduced a series of rebellions, and constituted Mulhar Rao Holkar, who had already become master of a considerable portion of the domain of Méwar, the umpire in their family disputes.

The ties of blood or of princely gratitude are feeble bonds if political expediency demands their dissolution; and Madhú Sing, when firmly established on the throne of Ambér, repaid the immense sacrifices by which the Rana had effected it by assigning his fief of Rampoora, which he had not a shadow of right to alienate, to Holkar: this was the first limb severed from Méwar.[3] Holkar had also become the assignee of the tribute imposed by Bajerow, but from which the Rana justly deemed himself exempt, when the terms of all further encroachment in Méwar were set at nought. On the plea of recovering these arrears, and the rent of some districts [4] on the Chumbul, Mulhar, after many threatening letters, invaded Méwar, and his threats of occupying the capital were only checked by draining their exhausted resources of six hundred thousand pounds.[5] In the same year [6] a famine afflicted them, when flour and tamarinds were equal in value, and were sold at the rate of a rupee for one pound and a half. Four years subsequent to this, civil war broke out

[1] The leaders of these invasions were Sutwaji, Jankoji, and Raganaut Rao.

[2] In S. 1812, Raja Buhadoor; in 1813, Mulhar Rao Holkar and Vitul Rao; in 1814, Ranaji Boortea: in 1813 *three* war contributions were levied, namely, by Sudasheo Rao, Govind Rao, and Kunaje Jadoon.

[3] This was in S. 1808 (A.D. 1752); portions, however, remained attached to the fisc of Méwar for several years, besides a considerable part of the feudal lands of the Chanderawut chief of Amud. Of the former, the Rana retained Hinglazgurh and the Tuppas of Jarda Kinjerra, and Boodsoo. These were surrendered by Raj Sing, who rented Boodsoo under its new appellation of Mulhargurh.

[4] Boodsoo, etc.

[5] Holkar advanced as far as Ontala, where Urjoon Sing of Korabur and the Rana's foster-brothers met him, and negotiated the payment of fifty-one lakhs of rupees.

[6] S. 1820, A.D. 1764.

and continued to influence all posterior proceedings, rendering the inhabitants of this unhappy country a prey to every invader until 1817, when they tasted repose under British protection.

The real cause of this rebellion must ever remain a secret: for while some regard it as a patriotic effort on the part of the people to redeem themselves from foreign domination, others discover its motive in the selfishness of the hostile clans, who supported or opposed the succession of Rana Ursi. This prince is accused of having unfairly acquired the crown, by the removal of his nephew Raj Sing; but though the traditional anecdotes of the period furnish strong grounds of suspicion, there is nothing which affords a direct confirmation of the crime. It is, however, a public misfortune when the line of succession retrogrades in Méwar: Ursi had no right to expect the inheritance he obtained, having long held a seat below the sixteen chief nobles; and as one of the 'infants' (*babas*) he was incorporated with the second class of nobles with an appanage of only £3000 per annum. His defects of character had been too closely contemplated by his compeers, and had kindled too many enmities, to justify expectation that the adventitious dignity he had attained would succeed in obliterating the memory of them; and past familiarity alone destroyed the respect which was exacted by sudden greatness. His insolent demeanour estranged the first of the home nobility, the Sadri chieftain,[1] whose ancestor at Huldighat acquired a claim to the perpetual gratitude of the Seesodias, while to an unfeeling pun on a personal defect of Jeswunt Sing of Deogurh is attributed the hatred and revenge of this powerful branch of the Chondawuts. These chiefs formed a party which eventually entrained many of lesser note to depose their sovereign, and immediately set up a youth called Rutna Sing, declared to be the posthumous son of the last Rana by the daughter of the chief of Gogoonda, though to this hour disputes run high as to whether he was really the son of Raj Sing, or merely the puppet of a faction. Be the fact as it may, he was made a rallying point for the disaffected, who soon comprehended the greater portion of the nobles, while out of the 'sixteen' greater chiefs five[2] only withstood the defection: of these, Saloombra, the hereditary premier, at first espoused, but soon abandoned, the cause of the Pretender; not from the principle of loyalty which his descendants take credit for, but from finding the superiority of intellect of the heads of the rebellion[3] (which now counted the rival Suktawuts) too powerful

[1] An autograph letter of this chief's to the minister of the day I obtained, with other public documents, from the descendant of the Pancholi:

"To Jeswunt Rao Pancholi, Raj Rinna Raghoodeo writes. After compliments. I received your letter—from old times you have been my friend, and have ever maintained faith towards me, for I am of the loyal to the Rana's house. I conceal nothing from you, therefore I write that my heart is averse to longer service, and it is my purpose in Asar to go to *Gya*.[1] When I mentioned this to the Rana, he sarcastically told me I might go to *Dwarica*.[2] If I stay, the Rana will restore the villages in my fief, as during the time of Jaetji. My ancestors have performed good service, and I have served since I was fourteen. If the Durbar intends me any favour, this is the time."

[2] Saloombra (*Chondawut*), Bijolli, Amait, Ganora, and Bednore.

[3] Bheendir (*Suktawut*), Deogurh, Sadri, Gogoonda, Dailwarra, Baidla, Kotario, and Kanorh.

---

[1] Gya is esteemed the proper pilgrimage for the Rajpoots.

[2] Dwarica, the resort for religious and unwarlike tribes.

for the supremacy he desired. Bussut Pal, of the Depra tribe, was invested with the office of *Purdhan* to the Pretender. The ancestor of this man accompanied Samarsi in the twelfth century from Dehli, where he held a high office in the household of Pirthi Raj, the last emperor of the Hindus, and it is a distinguished proof of the hereditary quality of official dignity to find his descendant, after the lapse of centuries, still holding office with the nominal title of Purdhan. The *Fitoori*[1] (by which name the court still designates the Pretender) took post with his faction in Komulmér; where he was formally installed, and whence he promulgated his decrees as Rana of Méwar. With that heedlessness of consequences and the political debasement which are invariable concomitants of civil dissension, they had the meanness to invite Sindia to their aid, with a promise of a reward of more than one million sterling[2] on the dethronement of Ursi.

This contest first brought into notice one of the most celebrated Rajpoot chiefs of India, Zalim Sing of Kotah, who was destined to fill a distinguished part in the annals of Rajast'han, but more especially in Méwar, where his political sagacity first developed itself. Though this is not the proper place to delineate his history, which will occupy a subsequent portion of the work, it is impossible to trace the events with which he was so closely connected without adverting slightly to the part he acted in these scenes. The attack on Kotah, of which his father was military governor (during the struggle to place Madhú Sing on the throne of Ambér), by Esuri Sing, in conjunction with Sindia, was the first avenue to his distinguished career, leading to an acquaintance with the Mahratta chiefs, which linked him with their policy for more than half a century. Zalim having lost his prince's favour, whose path in love he had dared to cross, repaired, on his banishment from Kotah, to the Rana, who, observing his talents, enrolled him amongst his chiefs, and conferred on him, with the title of Raj Rinna, the lands of Cheeturkhaira for his support. By his advice the Mahratta leaders, Raghoo Paigawalla and Dowla Meea, with their bands, were called in by the Rana, who, setting aside the ancient Pancholi ministry, gave the seals of office to Uggurji Mehta. At this period (S. 1824, A.D. 1768), Madhaji Sindia was at Oojein, whither the conflicting parties hastened, each desirous of obtaining the chieftain's support. But the Pretender's proposals had been already entertained, and he was then encamped with Sindia on the banks of the Sippra.

The Rana's force, conducted by the chief of Saloombra, the Rajas of Shapoora and Bunéra, with Zalim Sing and the Mahratta auxiliaries, did not hesitate to attack the combined camp, and for a moment they were victorious, driving Madhaji and the Pretender from the field, with great loss, to the gates of Oojein. Here, however, they rallied, and being joined by a fresh body of troops, the battle was renewed with great disadvantage to the Rajpoots, who, deeming the day theirs, had broken and dispersed to plunder. The chiefs of Saloombra, Shapoora, and Bunéra were slain, and the auxiliary Dowla Meea, Raja Maun (ex-prince of Nirwur), and Raj Kullian, the heir of Sadri, severely wounded. Zalim Sing had his horse killed under him, and being left wounded on the field, was made prisoner, but hospitably treated by Trimbuck Rao, father to the celebrated Umbaji. The discomfited troops retreated to Oodipoor

[1] Agitator, or disturber. [2] One crore and twenty-five lakhs.

while the Pretender's party remained with Sindia, inciting him to invest that capital and place Rutna on the throne. Some time, however, elapsed before he could carry this design into execution; when at the head of a large force the Mahratta chief gained the passes and besieged the city. The Rana's cause now appeared hopeless. Bheem Sing of Saloombra, uncle and successor to the chief slain at Oojein, with the Rahtore chief of Bednore (descendant of Jeimul), were the only nobles of high rank who defended their prince and capital in this emergency; but the energies of an individual saved both.

Umra Chund Burwa, of the mercantile class, had held office in the preceding reigns, when his influence retarded the progress of evils which no human means could avert. He was now displaced, and little solicitous of recovering his transient power, amidst hourly increasing difficulties, with a stubborn and unpopular prince, a divided aristocracy, and an impoverished country. He was aware also of his own imperious temper, which was as ungovernable as his sovereign's, and which experienced no check from the minor Pertáp, who regarded him as his father. During the ten years he had been out of office, mercenaries of Sind had been entertained and established on the forfeited lands of the clans, perpetuating discontent and stifling every latent spark of patriotism. Even those who did not join the Pretender remained sullenly at their castles, and thus all confidence was annihilated. A casual incident brought Umra forward at this critical juncture. Oodipoor had neither ditch nor walls equal to its defence. Ursi was engaged in fortifying Eklingurh, a lofty hill south of the city, which it commanded, and attempting to place thereon an enormous piece of ordnance, but it baffled their mechanical skill to get it over the scraggy ascent. Umra happened to be present when the Rana arrived to inspect the proceedings. Excuses were made to avert his displeasure, when turning to the ex-minister, he inquired what time and expense ought to attend the completion of such an undertaking. The reply was, "a few rations of grain and some days": and he offered to accomplish the task, on condition that his orders should be supreme in the valley during its performance. He collected the whole working population, cut a road, and in a few days gave the Rana a salute from Eklingurh. The foster-brother of the Rana had succeeded the Jhala chieftain, Raghoo Deo, in the ministerial functions. The city was now closedy invested on every side but the west, where communications were still kept open by the lake, across which the faithful mountaineers of the Aravulli, who in similar dangers never failed, supplied them with provisions. All defence rested on the fidelity of the mercenary Sindies, and they were at this very moment insolent in their clamours for arrears of pay. Nor were the indecisive measures daily passing before their eyes calculated to augment their respect, or stimulate their courage. Not satisfied with demands, they had the audacity to seize the Rana by the skirt of his robe as he entered the palace, which was torn in the effort to detain him. The haughtiness of his temper gave way to this humiliating proof of the hopelessness of his condition; and while the *D'habhae* (foster-brother) counselled escape by water to the mountains, whence he might gain Mandelgurh, the Saloombra chief confessed his inability to offer any advice save that of recourse to Umra Chund. He was summoned, and the uncontrolled charge of their desperate affairs offered to his guidance. He replied that it was a task of which no man could be covetous, more especially himself, whose administration had formerly been marked by the banishment of corruption and disorder, for that he must now call in the aid of these vices, and assimilate the means to the times. "You know also," he added, "my defect of temper, which admits of no control. Wherever I am, I must be absolute—no secret advisers, no counteraction of measures. With finances ruined, troops mutinous, provisions expended, if you desire me to act, swear that no order, whatever its purport, shall be countermanded, and I may try what can be done: but recollect, Umra 'the just,' will be the unjust, and reverse his former character." The Rana pledged himself by the patron deity to comply with all his demands, adding this forcible expression: "Should you even send to the queen's apartment and demand her necklace or *nutna*,[1] it shall be granted." The advice of the *D'habhae* encountered the full flood of Umra's wrath. "The counsel is such as might be expected from your condition. What will preserve your prince at Mandelgurh if he flies from Oodipoor, and what hidden resources have you there for your support? The project would suit you, who might resume your original occupation of tending buffaloes and selling milk, more adapted to your birth and understanding than state affairs; but these pursuits your prince has yet to learn." The Rana and his chiefs bent their heads at the bold bearing of Umra. Descending to the terrace, where the Sindie leaders and their bands were assembled, he commanded them to follow him, exclaiming, "look to me for your arrears, and as for your services, it will be my fault if you fail." The mutineers, who had just insulted their sovereign, rose without reply, and in a body left the palace with Umra, who calculated their arrears and promised payment the next day. Meanwhile he commanded the *bundars* (repositories) to be broken open, as the keeper of each fled when the keys of their trust were demanded. All the gold and silver, whether in bullion or in vessels, were converted into money—jewels were pledged—the troops paid and satisfied, ammunition and provisions laid in—a fresh stimulus supplied, the enemy held at defiance, and the siege prolonged during six months.

The Pretender's party had extended their influence over a great part of the crown domain, even to the valley of Oodipoor; but unable to fulfil the stipulation to Sindia, the baffled Mahratta, to whom time was treasure, negotiated with Umra to raise the siege, and abandon the Pretender on the payment of seventy lakhs. But scarcely was the treaty signed, when the reported disposition of the auxiliaries, and the plunder expected on a successful assault, excited his avarice and made him break his faith, and twenty lakhs additional were imposed. Umra tore up the treaty, and sent back the fragments to the faithless Mahratta with defiance. His spirit increased with his difficulties, and he infused his gallantry into the hearts of the most despairing. Assembling the Sindies and the home-clans who were yet true to their prince, he explained to them the transaction, and addressed them in that language which speaks to the souls of all mankind, and to give due weight to his exhortation, he distributed amongst the most deserving, many articles of cumbrous ornament lying useless in the treasury. The stores of grain in the city and neigh-

[1] The nose-jewel, which even to mention is considered a breach of delicacy.

bourhood, whether public or private, were collected and sent to the market, and it was proclaimed by beat of drum that every fighting man should have six months' provision on application. Hitherto grain had been selling at little more than a pound for the rupee, and these unexpected resources were matter of universal surprise, more especially to the besiegers.[1] The Sindies, having no longer cause for discontent, caught the spirit of the brave Umra, and went in a body to the palace to swear in public never to abandon the Rana, whom their leader, Adil Beg,[2] thus addressed: "We have long eaten your salt and received numerous favours from your house, and we now come to swear never to abandon you. Oodipoor is our home, and we will fall with it. We demand no further pay, and when our grain is exhausted, we will feed on the beasts, and when these fail we will thin the ranks of the Southrons and die sword in hand." Such were the sentiments that Umra had inspired, the expression of which extorted tears from the Rana—a sight so unusual with this stern prince, as to raise frantic shouts from the Sindies and his Rajpoots. The enthusiasm spread and was announced to Sindia with all its circumstances by a general discharge of cannon on his advanced posts. Apprehensive of some desperate display of Rajpoot valour, the wary Mahratta made overtures for a renewal of the negotiation. It was now Umra's turn to triumph, and he replied that he must deduct from the original terms the expense they had incurred in sustaining another six months' siege. Thus outwitted, Sindia was compelled to accept sixty lakhs, and three and a half for official expenses.[3]

Thirty-three lakhs in jewels and specie, gold and silver plate, and assignments on the chiefs, were immediately made over to Sindia, and lands mortgaged for the liquidation of the remainder. For this object the districts of Jawud, Jeerun, Neemutch, and Morwun were set aside to be superintended by joint officers of both governments, with an annual investigation of accounts. From S. 1825 to S. 1831 no infringement took place of this arrangement; but in the latter year Sindia dismissed the Rana's officers from the management, and refused all further settlement; and with the exception of a temporary occupation on Sindia's reverse of fortune in S. 1851, these rich districts have remained severed from Méwar. In S. 1831 the great officers of the Mahratta federation began to shake off the trammels of the Peshwa's authority; and Sindia retained for the state of which he was the founder, all these lands except Morwun, which was made over to Holkar, who the year after the transaction demanded of the Rana the surrender of the district of Neembahaira, threatening, in the event of non-compliance, to repeat the part his predatory coadjutor Sindia had just performed. The cession was unavoidable.

Thus terminated, in S. 1826, the siege of Oodipoor, with the dislocation of these fine districts from Méwar. But let it be remembered that they were only mortgaged:[4] and although the continued degradation of the

[1] To Umra's credit it is related, that his own brother-in-law was the first and principal sufferer, and that to his remonstrance and hope that family ties would save his grain pits, he was told, that it was a source of great satisfaction that he was enabled through him to evince his disinterestedness.

[2] See grant to this chief's son, p. 162.

[3] *Mootsuddi kurch*, or douceur to the officers of government, was an authorised article of every Mahratta *mŏámla*, or war contribution.

[4] Little Maloni, now Gungapoor, with its lands, was the only place decidedly

country from the same causes has prevented their redemption, the claim to them has never been abandoned. Their recovery was stipulated by the ambassadors of the Rana in the treaty of A.D. 1817 with the British government; but our total ignorance of the past transactions of these countries, added to our amicable relations with Sindia, prevented any pledge of the reunion of these districts; and it must ever be deeply lamented that, when the teacherous and hostile conduct of Sindia gave a noble opportunity for their restoration, it was lost, from policy difficult to understand, and which must be subject to the animadversions of future historians of that important period in the history of India. It yet remains for the wisdom of the British government to decide whether half a century's abeyance, and the inability to redeem them by the sword, render the claim a dead letter. At all events, the facts here recorded from a multiplicity of public documents, and corroborated by living actors[1] in the scene, may be useful at some future day, when expedience may admit of their being reannexed to Méwar.

Umra's defence of the capital, and the retreat of the Mahrattas, was a deathblow to the hopes of the Pretender, who had obtained not only many of the strongholds, but a footing in the valley of the capital. Rajnuggur, Raepoor, and Ontala were rapidly recovered; many of the nobles returned to the Rana and to their allegiance; and Rana was left in Komulmér with the Dépra minister, and but three of the sixteen principal nobles, namely Deogurh, Bheendir, and Amait. These contentions lasted till S. 1831, when the chiefs above named also abandoned him, but not until their rebellion had cost the feather in the crown of Méwar. The rich province of Godwar, the most fruitful of all her possessions, and containing the most loyal of her vassalage, the Ranawuts, Rahtores, and Solankis, was nearly all held on tenure of feudal service, and furnished three thousand horse besides foot, a greater number than the aggregate of the Chondawuts. This district, which was won with the title of Rana from the Purihara prince of Mundore, before Jodpoor was built, and whose northern boundary was confirmed by the blood of the Chondawut chief in the reign of Joda, was confided by the Rana to the care of Raja Beejy Sing of Jodpoor, to prevent its resources being available to the Pretender, whose residence, Komulmér, commanded the approach to it: and the original treaty yet exists in which the prince of Marwar binds himself to provide and support a body of three thousand men for the Rana's service, from its revenues. This province might have been recovered; but the evil genius of Ursi Rana at this time led him to Boondí to hunt at the spring festival (the *Ahairea*), with the Hara prince, in spite of the prophetic warning of the suttee, who from the funeral pile denounced a practice which had already thrice proved fatal to the princes of Méwar. Rana Ursi fell by the hand of the Boondí prince, and Godwar, withheld from his minor successor, has since remained severed. The Boondí heir, who perpetrated this atrocious assassination, was said to be prompted by the Méwar nobles, who detested their sovereign, and with whom, since the late events, it was impossible they could ever unite in confidence. Implacable in his disposition, he brooded over injuries, calmly awaiting the moment to avenge

alienated, being a voluntary gift to Sindia, to endow the establishment of his wife, Gunga Baé, who died there.

[1] Zalim Sing of Kotah, and Lallaji Bellal, both now dead.

them. A single instance will suffice to evince this, as well as the infatuation of Rajpoot devotion. The Saloombra chief, whose predecessor had fallen in support of the Rana's cause at the battle of Oojein, having incurred his suspicions, the Rana commanded him to eat the *pan* (leaf) presented on taking leave. Startled at so unusual an order, he remonstrated, but in vain; and with the conviction that it contained his death-warrant he obeyed, observing to the tyrant, "my compliance will cost you and your family dear": words fulfilled with fearful accuracy, for to this and similar acts is ascribed the murder of Ursi, and the completion of the ruin of the country. A colour of pretext was afforded to the Boondí chief in a boundary dispute regarding a patch of land yielding only a few good mangoes; but, even admitting this as a palliative, it could not justify the inhospitable act, which in the mode of execution added cowardice to barbarity: for while both were pursuing the boar, the Boondí heir drove his lance through the heart of the Rana. The assassin fell a victim to remorse, the deed being not only disclaimed, but severely reprobated by his father, and all the Hara tribe. A cenotaph still stands on the site of the murder, where the body of Ursi was consumed, and the feud between the houses remains unappeased.

Rana Ursi left two sons, Hamir and Bheem Sing. The former, a name of celebrity in their annals, succeeded in S. 1828 (A.D. 1772) to the little enviable title of Rana. With an ambitious mother, determined to control affairs during his minority, a state pronounced by the bard peculiarly dangerous to a Rajpoot dynasty,—and the vengeful competition of the Saloombra chief (successor to the murdered noble), who was equally resolved to take the lead, combined with an unextinguishable enmity to the Suktawuts, who supported the policy of the queen-mother, the demoralisation of Méwar was complete: her fields were deluged with blood, and her soil was the prey of every paltry marauder.

The mercenary Sindies, who, won by the enthusiasm of Umra, had for a moment assumed the garb of fidelity, threw it off at their prince's death, taking possession of the capital, which it will be remembered had been committed to the charge of the Saloombra chief, whom they confined and were about to subject to the torture of the hot iron [1] to extort their arrears of pay, when he was rescued from the indignity by the unlooked-for return of Umra from Boondí. This faithful minister determined to establish the rights of the infant prince against all other claimants for power. But he knew mankind, and had attained, what is still more difficult, the knowledge of himself. Aware that his resolution to maintain his post at all hazards, and against every competitor, would incur the imputation of self-interest, he, like our own Wolsey, though from far different motives, made an inventory of his wealth, in gold, jewels, and plate, even to his wardrobe, and sent the whole in trays to the queen-mother. Suspicion was shamed and resentment disarmed by this proceeding; and to repeated entreaties that he would receive it back he was inflexible, with the exception of articles of apparel that had already been in use. This imperious woman was a daughter of Gogoonda. She possessed considerable talents, but was ruled by an artful *intriguante*, who, in her turn, was governed by a young *homme d'affaires*, then holding an inferior office, but who subsequently acted a conspicuous part; slew and was slain, like almost all who entered into the

[1] A heated platter used for baking bread, on which they place the culprit.

politics of this tempestuous period. The queen-mother, now supported by the Chondawuts, opposed the minister, who maintained himself by aid of the Sindies, kept the Mahrattas from the capital, and protected the crown land; but the ungrateful return made to his long-tried fidelity rendered his temper ungovernable. Rampearie [1] (such the name of the *intriguante*) repaired on one occasion to the office of the minister, and in the name of the regent queen reviled him for some supposed omission. Umra, losing all temper at this intrusion, applied to the fair abigail the coarsest epithets used to her sex, bidding her begone as a *Kootee ca Rand* (a phrase we shall not translate), which was reported with exaggeration to the queen, who threw herself into a litter and set off to the Saloombra chief. Umra, anticipating an explosion, met the cavalcade in the street, and enjoined her instant return to the palace. Who dared disobey? Arrived at the door of the Rawula, he made his obeisance, and told her it was a disgrace to the memory of her lord that she should quit the palace under any pretext; that even the potter's wife did not go abroad for six months after her husband's death, while she, setting decorum at defiance, had scarcely permitted the period of mourning to elapse. He concluded by saying he had a duty to perform, and that he would perform it in spite of all obstacles, in which, as it involved her own and her children's welfare, she ought to co-operate, instead of thwarting him. But Baeji Raj (the royal mother) was young, artful, and ambitious, and persevered in her hostility till the demise of this uncompromising minister shortly after, surmised to be caused by poison. His death yielded a flattering comment on his life: he left not funds sufficient to cover the funeral expenses, and is, and will probably continue, the sole instance on record in Indian history of a minister having his obsequies defrayed by subscription among his fellow-citizens.

The man who thus lived and thus died would have done honour to any, even the most civilised, country, where the highest incentives to public virtue exist. What, therefore, does not his memory merit, when amongst a people who, through long oppression, were likely to hold such feelings in little estimation, he pursued its dictates from principle alone, his sole reward that which the world could not bestow, the applause of the monitor within? But they greatly err who, in the application of their own overweening standard of merit, imagine there is no public opinion in these countries; for recollections of actions like this (of which but a small portion is related) they yet love to descant upon, and an act of vigour and integrity is still designated *Umrachunda*; [2] evincing that if virtue has few imitators in this country, she is not without ardent admirers.

In S. 1831 (A.D. 1775) the rebellion of the Beygoo chief, head of a grand division of the Chondawuts, the *Megawut*, obliged the queen-mother to call upon Sindia for his reduction, who recovered the crown lands he had usurped, and imposed on this refractory noble a fine of twelve lakhs of rupees, or £100,000 sterling. [3] But instead of confining himself to punish-

[1] 'The beloved of Rama.'

[2] *Umra Chund*, it will be recollected, was the name of the minister.

[3] The treaty by which Sindia holds these districts yet exists, which stipulates their surrender on the liquidation of the contribution. The Rana still holds this as a responsible engagement, and pleaded his rights in the treaty with the British government in A.D. 1817–18. But half a century's possession is a strong bond, which we dare not break; though the claim now registered may hereafter prove of service to the family.

ing the guilty, and restoring the lands to the young Rana, he inducted his own son-in-law Bérji Táp into the districts of Ruttengurh Khérí and Singolli; and at the same time made over those of Irnia, Jaut'h, Beechore, and Nuddowye to Holkar, the aggregate revenue of which amounted to six lakhs annually. Besides these alienations of territory, the Mahrattas levied no less than four grand war contributions in S. 1830–31,[1] while in S. 1836[2] their rapacity exacted three more. Inability to liquidate these exorbitant demands, was invariably a signal for further sequestration of land. Amidst such scenes of civil strife and external spoliation, one Mahratta following another in the same track of rapine, Hamir died before he had attained even Rajpoot majority,[3] in S. 1834 (A.D. 1778).

We may here briefly recapitulate the diminution of territory and wealth in Méwar from the period of the first Mahratta visitation in A.D. 1736, to the death of Hamir. It were a waste of time to enumerate the rapacious individuals who shared in the spoils of this devoted country. We may be content to say their name was "legion." These forty years were surcharged with evil. The Mogul princes observed at least the forms of government and justice, which occasionally tempered their aggressions; the Mahrattas were associations of vampires, who drained the very life-blood wherever the scent of spoil attracted them. In three payments we have seen the enormous sum of one crore and eighty-one lakhs,[4] upwards of two millions English money, exacted from Méwar, exclusive of individual contributions levied on chiefs, ministers, and the Pretender's party: and a schedule drawn up by the reigning prince of contributions levied up to his own time, amounts to £5,000,000 sterling. Yet the land would eventually have reimbursed these sums, but the penalty inflicted for deficiencies of payment renders the evil irremediable; for the alienated territory which then produced an annual revenue of twenty-eight lakhs,[5] or £323,000 sterling, exceeds in amount the sum-total now left, whether fiscal or feudal, in the present impoverished state of the country.

[1] 1830, Madajee Sindia's contribution (*móámla*) on account of Beygoo; 1831, Bérji Táp's *móámla* through Govind and Gunput Rao; 1831, Umbaji Inglia, Bapoo Holkar, and Dadooji Pundit's joint *móámla*.

[2] 1. Appaji and Makaji Getea, on Holkar's account; 2. Tukooji Holkar's, through Somji; 3. Alli Buhadoor's, through Somji.

[3] The age of eighteen.

[4] Namely,

S. 1808, by Rana Juggut Sing to Holkar	. .	Lakhs 66
1820, Pertáp and Ursi Rana to Holkar	. .	51
1826, Ursi Rana to Madajee Sindia	. . .	64
	Total .	181

[5]

S. 1808, Rampoora, Bhanpoora	. .	Lakhs 9
1826, Jawud, Jeerun, Neemutch, Neembahaira	. .	4½
1831, Ruttungurh Khérí, Singolli, Irnia, Jaut'h, Nuddowye, etc. etc.		6
1831, Godwar	. . . . .	9
	Total .	28½

CHAPTER XVII

Rana Bheem—Feud of Seogurh—The Rana redeems the alienated lands—Ahelia Bae attacks the Rana's army—Which is defeated—Chondawut rebellion—Assassination of the Minister Somji—The rebels seize on Cheetore—Madhaji Sindia called in by the Rana—Invests Cheetore—The rebels surrender—Designs of Zalim Sing for power in Méwar—Counteracted by Umbaji, who assumes the title of Soobadar, contested by Lukwa—Effects of these struggles—Zalim obtains Jehajpoor—Holkar invades Méwar—Confines the priests of Nat'hdwara—Heroic conduct of the Chief of Kotario—Lukwa dies—The Rana seizes the Mahratta leaders—Liberated by Zalim Sing—Holkar returns to Oodipoor—Imposes a heavy contribution—Sindia's invasion—Reflections on their contest with the British—Umbaji projects the partition of Méwar—Frustrated—Rivalry for Kishna Komari, the Princess of Méwar, produces war throughout Rajast'han—Immolation of Kishna—Meer Khan and Ajít Sing—Their villainy—British Embassy to Sindia's Court at Oodipoor—Umbaji is disgraced, and attempts suicide—Meer Khan and Bapoo Sindia desolate Méwar—The Rana forms a treaty with the British.

RANA BHEEM SING (the reigning prince), who succeeded his brother in S. 1834 (A.D. 1778), was the fourth minor in the space of forty years who inherited Méwar; and the half-century during which he has occupied the throne has been as fruitful in disaster as any period of her history already recorded. He was but eight years of age on his accession, and remained under his mother's tutelage long after his minority had expired. This subjection fixed his character; naturally defective in energy, and impaired by long misfortune, he continued to be swayed by faction and intrigue. The cause of the Pretender, though weakened, was yet kept alive; but his insignificance eventually left him so unsupported, that his death is not even recorded.

In S. 1840 (A.D. 1784) the Chondawuts reaped the harvest of their allegiance and made the power thus acquired subservient to the indulgence of ancient animosities against the rival clan of Suktawut. Saloombra with his relatives Oorjun Sing[1] of Korabur and Pertáp Sing[2] of Amait, now ruled the councils, having the Sindie mercenaries under their leaders Chundun and Sadik at their command. Mustering therefore all the strength of their kin and clans, they resolved on the prosecution of the feud, and invested Bheendir, the castle of Mokhim the chief of the Suktawuts, against which they placed their batteries.

Sangram Sing, a junior branch of the Suktawuts, destined to play a conspicuous part in the future events of Méwar, was then rising into notice, and had just completed a feud with his rival the Poorawut, whose abode, Lawah,[3] he had carried by escalade; and now, determined to make a diversion in favour of his chief, he invaded the estate of Korabur, engaged against Bheendir, and was driving off the cattle, when Salim Sing the heir of Korabur intercepted his retreat, and an action ensued in which Salim[4]

[1] Brother of Ajít, the negotiator of the treaty with the British.

[2] Chief of the Juggawut clan, also a branch of the Chondawuts; he was killed in a battle with the Mahrattas.

[3] It is yet held by the successor of Sangram, whose faithful services merited the grant he obtained from his prince, and it was in consequence left unmolested in the arrangement of 1817, from the knowledge of his merits.

[4] The father of Rawut Jowan Sing, whom I found at Oodipoor as military minister, acting for his grand-uncle Ajít the organ of the Chondawuts, whose

was slain by the lance of Sangram. The afflicted father, on hearing the fate of his son, " threw the turban off his head," swearing never to replace it till he had tasted revenge. Feigning a misunderstanding with his own party he withdrew from the siege, taking the road to his estate, but suddenly abandoned it for Seogurh, the residence of Lalji the father of Sangram. The castle of Seogurh, placed amidst the mountains and deep forests of Chuppun, was from its difficulty of access deemed secure against surprise ; and here Sangram had placed the females and children of his family. To this point Oorjun directed his revenge, and found Seogurh destitute of defenders save the aged chief ; but though seventy summers had whitened his head, he bravely met the storm, and fell in opposing the foe ; when the children of Sangram were dragged out and inhumanly butchered, and the widow [1] of Lalji ascended the pyre. This barbarity aggravated the hostility which separated the clans, and together with the minority of their prince and the yearly aggressions of the Mahrattas, accelerated the ruin of the country. But Bheem Sing, the Chondawut leader, was governed by insufferable vanity, and not only failed in respect to his prince, but offended the queen regent. He parcelled out the crown domain from Cheetore to Oodipoor amongst the Sindie bands, and whilst his sovereign was obliged to borrow money to defray his marriage at Edur, this ungrateful noble had the audacity to disburse upwards of £100,000 on the marriage of his own daughter. Such conduct determined the royal mother to supplant the Chondawuts, and calling in the Suktawuts to her aid, she invested with power the chiefs of Bheendir and Lawah. Aware, however, that their isolated authority was insufficient to withstand their rivals, they looked abroad for support, and made an overture to Zalim Sing of Kotah, whose political and personal resentments to the Chondawuts, as well as his connection by marriage with their opponents, made him readily listen to it. With his friend the Mahratta, Lallaji Bellal, he joined the Suktawuts with a body of 10,000 men. It was determined to sacrifice the Saloombra chief, who took post in the ancient capital of Cheetore, where the garrison was composed chiefly of Sindies, thus effacing his claim to his prince's gratitude, whom he defied, while the pretender still had a party in the other principal fortress, Komulmér.

Such was the state of things, when the ascendancy of Madhaji Sindia received a signal check from the combined forces of Marwar and Jeipoor ; and the battle of Lalsont, in which the Mahratta chief was completely defeated, was the signal for the Rajpoots to resume their alienated territory. Nor was the Rana backward on the occasion, when there appeared a momentary gleam of the active virtue of past days. Maldas Mehta was civil minister, with Mouzee Ram as his deputy, both men of talent and energy. They first effected the reduction of Neembahaira and the smaller garrisons of Mahrattas in its vicinity, who from a sense of common danger assembled their detachments in Jawud, which was also invested. Sevaji Nana, the governor, capitulated, and was allowed

head, Puddum Sing, was just emerging from his minority. It was absolutely necessary to get to the very root of all these feuds, when as envoy and mediator I had to settle the disputes of half a century, and make each useful to detect their joint usurpations of the crown domain.

[1] She was the grandmother of Maun Sing, a fine specimen of a Suktawut cavalier.

to march out with his effects. At the same time, the "sons of the black cloud"[1] assembling, drove the Mahrattas from Beygoo, Singolli, etc., and the districts on the plateau; while the Chondawuts redeemed their ancient fief of Rampoora, and thus for a while the whole territory was recovered. Elated by success, the united chiefs advanced to Churdoo on the banks of the Rirkia, a streamlet dividing Méwar from Malwa, preparatory to further operations. Had these been confined to the maintenance of the places they had taken, and which had been withheld in violation of treaties, complete success might have crowned their efforts; but in including Neembahaira in their capture they drew upon them the energetic Ahelia Bae, the regent-queen of the Holkar state, who unluckily for them was at hand and who coalesced with Sindia's partisans to check this reaction of the Rajpoots. Toolaji Sindia and Sri Bhae, with five thousand horse, were ordered to support the discomfited Seva Nana, who had taken refuge in Mundisore, where he rallied all the garrisons whom the Rajpoots had unwisely permitted to capitulate. On Tuesday, the 4th of Magh S. 1844,[2] the Rana's troops were surprised and defeated with great slaughter, the minister slain, the chiefs of Kanorh and Sadri with many others severely wounded, and the latter made prisoner.[3] The newly made conquests were all rapidly lost, with the exception of Jawud, which was gallantly maintained for a month by Deep Chund, who, with his guns and rockets, effected a passage through the Mahrattas, and retired with his garrison to Mandelgurh. Thus terminated an enterprise which might have yielded far different results but for a misplaced security. All the chiefs and clans were united in this patriotic struggle except the Chondawuts, against whom the queen-mother and the new minister, Somji, had much difficulty to contend for the establishment of the minor's authority. At length overtures were made to Saloombra, when the fair Rampearie was employed to conciliate the obdurate chief, who condescended to make his appearance at Oodipoor and to pay his respects to the prince. He pretended to enter into the views of the minister and to coalesce in his plans; but this was only a web to ensnare his victim, whose talent had diminished his authority, and was a bar to the prosecution of his ambitious views. Somji was seated in his bureau when Oorjun Sing of Korabur and Sirdar Sing[4] of Bhadaisser entered, and the latter, as he demanded how he dared to resume his fief, plunged his dagger into the minister's breast. The Rana was passing the day at one of the villas in the valley called the *Suhailea Bari*, 'the garden of nymphs,' attended by Jait Sing of Bednore, when the brothers[5] of the minister suddenly

[1] Meg'h Sing was the chief of Beygoo, and founder of that subdivision of the Chondawuts called after him *Meghawut*, and his complexion being very dark (*kala*), he was called "kala megh," the "black cloud." His descendants were very numerous and very refractory.

[2] A.D. 1788.

[3] He did not recover his liberty for two years, nor till he had surrendered four of the best towns in his fief.

[4] Father of the present Hamir Sing, the only chief with whom I was compelled to use severity: but he was incorrigible. He was celebrated for his raids in the troubles, and from his red whiskers bore with us the name of the 'Red Riever' of Bhadaisser—more of him by and by.

[5] Sheodas and Suttidas, with their cousin Jychund. They revenged their brother's death by that of his murderer, and were both in turn slain. Such were

rushed into the presence to claim protection against the murderers. They were followed by Oorjun of Korabur, who had the audacity to present himself before his sovereign with his hands yet stained with the blood of Somji. The Rana, unable to punish the insolent chief, branding him as a traitor, bade him begone; when the whole of the actors in this nefarious scene, with their leader Saloombra, returned to Cheetore. Sheodas and Suttidas, brothers to the murdered minister, were appointed to succeed him, and with the Suktawuts fought several actions against the rebels, and gained one decisive battle at Akola, in which Oorjun of Korabur commanded. This was soon balanced by the defeat of the Suktawuts at Khyroda. Every triumph was attended with ruin to the country. The agriculturist, never certain of the fruits of his labour, abandoned his fields, and at length his country; mechanical industry found no recompense, and commerce was at the mercy of unlicensed spoliation. In a very few years Méwar lost half her population, her hands lay waste, her mines were unworked, and her looms, which formerly supplied all around, forsaken. The prince partook of the general penury; instead of protecting, he required protection; the bonds which united him with his subjects were snapped, and each individual or petty community provided for itself that defence which he could not give. Hence arose a train of evils: every cultivator, whether fiscal or feudal, sought out a patron, and entered into engagements as the price of protection. Hence every Rajpoot who had a horse and lance, had his clients; and not a camel-load of merchandise could pass the abode of one of these cavaliers without paying fees. The effects of such disorder were felt long after the cause ceased to exist, and claims difficult to adjust arose out of these licentious times, for the having prescriptive right was deemed sufficient to authorise their continuance.[1] Here were displayed the effects of a feudal association, where the powers of government were enfeebled. These feuds alone were sufficient to ruin the country; but when to such internal ills shoals of Mahratta plunderers were added, no art is required to describe the consequences.

The Rana and his advisers at length determined to call in Sindia to expel the rebellious Chondawuts from the ancient capital; a step mainly prompted by Zalim Sing (now Regent of Kotah), who with the Rana's ministers was deputed to the Mahratta chieftain, then enjoying himself at the sacred lake of Poshkur.[2] Since the overthrow of Lalsont he had reorganised his brigades under the celebrated De Boigne, through whose conduct he had redeemed his lost influence in Rajpootana by the battles

these times! The author more than once, when resuming the Chondawut lands, and amongst them Bhadaisser, the fief of the son of Sirdar, was told to recollect the fate of Somji; the advice, however, excited only a smile; he was deemed more of a Suktawut than a Chondawut, and there was some truth in it, for he found the good actions of the former far outweigh the other, who made a boast and monopoly of their patriotism. It was a curious period in his life; the stimulus to action was too high, too constant, to think of self; and having no personal views, being influenced solely by one feeling, the prosperity of all, he despised the very idea of danger, though it was said to exist in various shapes, even in the hospitable plate put before him! But he deemed none capable of such treachery, though once he was within a few minutes' march to the other world; but the cause, if the right one, came from his own *cuisinier*, or rather *boulanger*, whom he discharged.

[1] See the Essay on a Feudal System. [2] S. 1847 (A.D. 1791).

of Mairta and Patun, in which the brave Rahtores, after acts of the most devoted gallantry, were completely overthrown. Sindia's plans coincided entirely with the object of the deputation, and he readily acquiesced in the Rana's desire. This event introduced on the political stage some of the most celebrated men of that day, whose actions offer a fair picture of manners, and may justify our entering a little into details.[1]

Zalim Sing had for some years become regent of Kotah, and though to maintain himself in power, and the state he controlled in an attitude to compel the respect of surrounding foes, was no slight task, yet he found the field too contracted for his ambition, and his secret views had long been directed to permanent influence in Méwar. His skill in reading character convinced him that the Rana would be no bar to his wishes, the attainment of which, by giving him the combined resources of Haroutí and Méwar, would bestow the lead in Rajast'han. The Jeipoor court he disregarded, whose effeminate army he had himself defeated single-handed with the Kotah troops, and the influence he established amongst the leading chiefs of Marwar held out no fear of counteraction from that quarter. The stake was high, the game sure, and success would have opened a field to his genius which might have entirely altered the fate of Hindust'han; but one false move was irretrievable, and instead of becoming the arbitrator of India, he left only the reputation of being the Nestor of Rajpootana.

The restriction of the Rana's power was the cloak under which he disguised all his operations, and it might have been well for the country had his plans succeeded to their full extent. To re-establish the Rana's authority, and to pay the charges of the reduction of Cheetore, he determined that the rebels chiefly should furnish the means, and that from them and the fiscal lands, mostly in their hands, sixty-four lakhs should be levied, of which three-fifths should be appropriated to Sindia, and the remainder to replenish the Rana's treasury. Preliminaries being thus arranged, Zalim was furnished with a strong corps under Umbaji Inglia; while Sindia followed, hanging on the Marwar frontier, to realise the contributions of that state. Zalim Sing and Umbaji moved towards Cheetore, levying from the estates of those obnoxious to Zalim's views. Hamirgurh, whose chief, Dheruj Sing, a man of talent and courage, was the principal adviser of Bheem Sing, the Saloombra chief, was besieged, and stood several assaults during six weeks' vigorous operations, when the destruction of the springs of the wells from the concussion of the guns compelled its surrender, and the estate was sequestrated. The force continued their progress, and after a trifling altercation at Bussee, a Chondawut fief, also taken, they took up a position at Cheetore, and were soon after joined by the main body under Sindia.

Zalim, to gratify Madhaji's vanity, who was desirous of a visit from the Rana, which even the Peshwa considered an honour, proceeded to Oodipoor to effect this object; when the Rana, placing himself under his guidance, marched for this purpose, and was met at the Tiger Mount, within a few miles of his capital, by Sindia, who received the Rana, and escorted him to the besieging army. But in this short interval, Umbaji, who remained with the army at Cheetore, intrigued with the rebel

[1] Acquired from the actors in those scenes: the prince, his ministers, Zalim Sing, and the rival chiefs have all contributed.

Chondawut to supplant the predominant influence of his friend Zalim Sing, and seized the opportunity of his absence to coûnteract him, by communicating his plans to Saloombra; aware that, unless he broke with Zalim, he could only hope to play a secondary part under him. Though the ulterior views of Zalim were kept to his own breast, they could not escape the penetration of the crafty Mahratta; his very anxiety to hide them furnished Umbaji with the means of detection. Had Zalim possessed an equal share of meanness with his political antagonist, he might have extricated himself from the snare; but once overreached, he preferred sinking to grasping at an unworthy support. Bheem Sing (Saloombra) privately negotiated with Umbaji the surrender of Cheetore, engaging to humble himself before the Rana, and to pay a contribution of twenty lakhs, levied on the clans, provided Zalim Sing was ordered to retire. This suggestion, apparently founded on the rebellious chief's antipathy to Zalim, but in reality prompted by Umbaji, ensured the approbation, as it suited the views, of all parties, but especially Sindia, who was desirous of repairing to Poonah. Zalim, the sole obstacle to this arrangement, furnished to his enemies the means of escape from the dilemma, and lost the opportunity of realising his long-cherished scheme of wielding the united resources of Méwar and Haroutí. Zalim had always preserved a strict amity with Umbaji wherever their interests did not clash, and his regard had the cement of gratitude to the Mahratta, whose father Trimbukji had saved Zalim's life and procured his liberty, when left wounded and a prisoner at the battle of Oojein. On Zalim's return with the Rana, Umbaji touched on the terms of Bheem Sing's surrender, hinting that Zalim's presence was the sole obstacle to this desirable result; who, the more to mask his views, which any expressed reluctance to the measure might expose, went beyond probability in asseverations of readiness to be no bar to such arrangement, even so far as to affirm that, besides being tired of the business from the heavy expense it entailed on him, he had his prince's wish for his return to Kotah. There is one ingredient in Zalim's character, which has never been totally merged in the vices acquired from the tortuous policy of a long life, and which in the vigour of youth had full sway—namely, pride, one of the few virtues left to the Rajpoot, defrauded of many others by long oppression. But Zalim's pride was legitimate, being allied to honour, and it has retained him an evident superiority through all the mazes of ambition. Umbaji skilfully availed himself of this defect in his friend's political character. "A pretty story, indeed!—you tell this to me: it might find credit with those who did not know you." The sarcasm only plunged him deeper into asseveration. "Is it then really your wish to retire?" "Assuredly." "Then," retorted the crafty Umbaji, "your wish shall be gratified in a few minutes." Giving him no time to retract, he called for his horse and galloped to Sindia's tent. Zalim relied on Sindia not acceding to the proposition; or if he did, that the Rana, over whom he imagined he had complete influence, would oppose it. His hopes of Sindia rested on a promise privately made to leave troops under his authority for the restoration of order in Méwar; and a yet stronger claim, the knowledge that without Zalim he could not realise the stipulated sums for the expulsion of the Chondawut from Cheetore. Umbaji had foreseen and prepared a remedy for these difficulties, and upon their being urged offered himself to advance the amount by bills on the Dekhan. This argument was irresistible; money, and the consequent prosecution of his journey to Poonah, being attained, Sindia's engagements with Zalim and the Rana ceased to be a matter of importance. He nominated Umbaji his lieutenant, with the command of a large force, by whose aid he would reimburse himself for the sums thus advanced. Having carried his object with Sindia, Umbaji proceeded direct from his tent to that of the Rana's ministers, Sheodas and Suttidas, with whom, by the promise of co-operation in their views, and perfect subserviency to the Rana's interests, he was alike successful. Umbaji, with the rapidity necessary to ensure success, having in a few hours accomplished his purpose, hastened back to Zalim, to acquaint him that his wish to retire had met with general acquiescence; and so well did he manage, that the Rana's mace-bearer arrived at the same moment to announce that the *khelat of leave* awaited his acceptance. Zalim being thus outwitted; the Saloombra chief descended from Cheetore, and *touched the Rana's feet.* Sindia pursued his march to the Dekhan, and Umbaji was left sole arbiter of Méwar. The Suktawuts maintained the lead at court, and were not backward in consigning the estates of their rivals to the incubus now settled on the country: while the mortified Zalim, on his retreat, recorded his expenses, to be produced on some fitting occasion.

Umbaji remained eight years in Méwar, reaping its revenues and amassing those hoards of wealth which subsequently gave him the lead in Hindust'han, and enabled him nearly to assert his independence. Yet, although he accumulated £2,000,000 sterling from her soil,[1] exacting one-half of the produce of agricultural industry, the suppression of feuds and exterior aggressions gave to Méwar a degree of tranquillity and happiness to which she had long been a stranger. The instructions delivered to Umbaji were—

1. The entire restoration of the Rana's authority and resumption of the crown-lands from rebellious chiefs and mercenary Sindies.
2. The expulsion of the pretender from Komulmér.
3. The recovery of Godwar from the Raja of Marwar.
4. To settle the Boondí feud for the murder of Rana Ursi.

A schedule (*pandri*) for the twenty lakhs stipulated was made and levied; twelve from the Chondawut estates and eight from the Suktawuts; and the sum of sixty lakhs was awarded, besides the expense of Umbaji's army, when the other specified objects should be attained. Within two years the pretender was expelled Komulmér, Jehajpoor was

[1] It was levied as follows:—

Saloombra	Lakhs	3
Deogurh	,,	3
Singingir Gosén, their adviser	,,	2
Kositul	,,	1
Amait	,,	2
Korabur	,,	1
	Lakhs	12

recovered from a rebellious Ranawut, and the crown-lands[1] were redeemed from the nobles; the personal domain of the Rana, agricultural and commercial, still realised nearly fifty lakhs of rupees. After these services, though Godwar was still unredeemed, the Boondí feud unappeased, and the lands mortgaged to the Mahrattas were not restored, Umbaji assumed the title of Soobadar of Méwar, and identified himself with the parties of the day. Yet so long as he personally upheld the interests of the Rana, his memory is done justice to, notwithstanding he never conformed to the strict letter of his engagements. The Rana's ministers, fearing lest their brother's fate should be theirs in the event of the Chondawuts again attaining power, and deeming their own and their sovereign's security dependent on Umbaji's presence, made a subsidiary engagement with him, and lands to the amount of 75,000 rupees monthly, or eight lakhs annually, were appropriated for his force; but so completely were the resources of the country diverted from their honest use, that when, in S. 1851, a marriage was negotiated between the Rana's sister and the prince of Jeipoor, the Rana was obliged to borrow £50,000 from the Mahratta commander to purchase the nuptial presents. The following year was marked by a triple event—the death of the queen-mother, the birth of a son and heir to the Rana, and the bursting of the embankment of the lake, which swept away a third of the city and a third of its inhabitants. Superstition attributed this catastrophe to the Rana's impiety, in establishing a new festival[2] to Gowrie, the Isis of Rajast'han.

Umbaji, who was this year nominated by Sindia his viceroy in Hindust'han, left Gunés Punt as his lieutenant in Méwar, with whom acted the Rana's officers, Sowaie and Sheerji Mehta;[3] who applied themselves to make the most of their ephemeral power with so rapacious a spirit, that Umbaji was compelled to displace Gunés Punt and appoint the celebrated Rae Chund. To him they would not yield, and each party formed a nucleus for disorder and misrule. It would be uninteresting and nauseating to the reader to carry him through all the scenes of villainy which gradually desolated this country; for whose spoil pilfering Mahrattas, savage Rohillas, and adventurous Franks were all let loose. The now humbled Chondawuts, many of whose fiefs were confiscated, took to horse, and in conjunction with lawless Sindies scoured the country. Their estates were attacked, Korabur was taken, and batteries were placed against Saloombra, whence the Sindies fled and found refuge in Deogurh. In this exigence, the Chondawuts determined to send an envoy to Umbaji, who was then engaged in the siege of Duttea; and Ajít Sing, since prominent in the intrigues of Méwar, was the organ of his clan on this occasion. For the sum of ten lakhs the avaricious Mahratta agreed to recall his deputy from Méwar,[4] to renounce Sheodas and the Suktawuts, and lend his

[1] Raepoor Rajnuggur from the Sindies; Goorlah and Gadermala from the Poorawuts; Hamirgurh from Sirdar Sing, and Koorj Kowario from Saloombra.

[2] In Bhadoon, the third month of the rainy season. An account of this festival will hereafter be given.

[3] The first of these is now the manager of Prince Jowan Sing's estates, a man of no talent; and the latter, his brother, was one of the ministers on my arrival at Oodipoor. He was of invincible good humour, yet full of the spirit of intrigue, and one of the bars to returning prosperity. The cholera carried off this Falstaff of the court, not much to my sorrow.

[4] S. 1853, A.D. 1797.

support to the Chondawuts. The Saloombra chief again took the lead at court, and with Aggurji Mehta [1] as minister, the Suktawuts were attacked,

[1] This person was nominated the chief civil minister on the author's arrival at Oodipoor, an office to which he was every way unequal. The affairs of Méwar had never prospered since the faithful Pancholis were deprived of power. Several productions of the descendants of Beharri-das have fallen into my hands; their quaint mode of conveying advice may authorise their insertion here.

The Pancholis who had performed so many services to the country, had been for some time deprived of the office of prime minister, which was disposed of as it suited the views of the factious nobles who held power for the time being; and who bestowed it on the Mehtas, Dépras, or D'habhaes. Amongst the papers of the Pancholis, several addressed to the Rana and to Uggurji Mehta, the minister of the day, are valuable for the patriotic sentiments they contain, as well as for the general light they throw upon the period. In S. 1853 (A.D. 1797) Imrit Rao devised a plan to remedy the evils that oppressed the country. He inculcated the necessity of dispensing with the interference of the Suktawuts and Chondawuts in the affairs of government, and strengthening the hands of the civil administration by admitting the foreign chieftains to the power he proposed to deprive the former of. He proceeds in the following quaint style :—

"Disease fastened on the country from the following causes, envy and party spirit. With the *Toorks* disease was introduced; but then the prince, his ministers, and chiefs, were of one mind, and medicine was ministered and a cure effected. During Rana Jey Sing's time the disorder returned, which his son Umra put down. He recovered the affairs of government from confusion, gave to everyone his proper rank and dignity, and rendered all prosperous. But Maharana Sangram Sing put from under his wing the Chunderawut of Rampoora, and thus a pinion of Méwar was broken. The calamity of Beharri-das, whose son committed suicide, increased the difficulties. The arrival of the Dekhanis under Baji Rao, the Jeipoor affair [1] and the defeat at Rajmahl, with the heavy expenditure thereby occasioned, augmented the disorder. Add to this in Juggut Sing's time the enmity of the D'habhaes towards the Pancholis, which lowered their dignities at home and abroad, and since which time every man has thought himself equal to the task of government. Juggut Sing was also afflicted by the rebellious conduct of his son Pertáp, when Shama Solanki and several other chiefs were treacherously cut off. Since which time the minds of the nobles have never been loyal, but black and not to be trusted. Again, on the accession of Pertáp, Maharaja Nat'hji allowed his thoughts to aspire, from which all his kin suffered. Hence animosities, doubts, and deceits, arose on all sides. Add to this the haughty proceeding of Umra Chund now in office; and besides the strife of the Pancholis with each other, their enmity to the Dépras. Hence parties were formed which completely destroyed the credit of all. Yet, notwithstanding, they abated none of their strife, which was the acme to the disease. The feud between Koman Sing and the Suktawuts for the possession of Heet'ha, aggravated the distresses. The treacherous murder of Maharaja Nat'hji, and the consequent disgust and retreat of Jeswunt Sing of Deogurh; the setting up the impostor Rutna Sing, and J'hala Raghoo Deo's struggle for office, with Umra Chund's entertaining the mercenaries of Sind, brought it to a crisis. The negligence arising out of luxury, and the intrigues of the D'habhaes of Rana Ursi, made it spread so as to defeat all attempt at cure. In S. 1829, on the treacherous murder of the Rana by the Boondí prince, and the accession of the minor Hamir, everyone set up his own authority, so that there was not even the semblance of government. And now you (to the Rana), listening to the advice of Bheem Sing (Saloombra), and his brother, Urjoon, have taken foreigners [2] into pay, and thus riveted all the former errors. You and *Sri Baeji Raj* (the royal mother), putting confidence in foreigners and Dekhanis, have rendered the disease contagious; besides, your mind is gone. What can be done? Medicine may yet be had. Let us unite and struggle to restore the duties of the minister and we

[1] The struggle to place the Rana's nephew, Madhú Sing, on the throne of Jeipoor.

[2] The Pancholi must allude to the Mahratta subsidiary force under Umbaji.

the stipulated ten lakhs raised from their estates, and two fiefs of note, Heeta and Saimari, confiscated.

The death of Madhaji Sindia, and the accession of his nephew Dowlut Rao, his murder of the Sainowee Brahmins, and his quarrels with the Báes ('princesses,' wives of the deceased Sindia), all occurred at this time, and materially influenced the events in Méwar. The power of Umbaji as Soobadar of Hindust'han was strengthened by the minority of Sindia, although contested by Lukwa and the Baes, supported by the Kheechie prince, Doorjun Sal, and the Duttea Raja, who fought and died for the princesses. Lukwa wrote to the Rana to throw off Umbaji's yoke and expel his lieutenant; while Umbaji commanded his deputy to eject the Sainowee [1] Brahmins, supporters of Lukwa, from all the lands in Méwar. To this end Gunés Punt called on the Rana's ministers and chiefs, who, consulting thereon, determined to play a deep game; and while they apparently acquiesced in the schemes of Gunés, they wrote the Sainowees to advance from Jawud and attack him, promising them support. They met at Sawah; Nana was defeated with the loss of his guns, and retired on Cheetore. With a feint of support, the Chondawuts made him again

may conquer, or at least check its progress. If now neglected, it will hereafter be beyond human power. The Dekhanis are the great sore. Let us settle their accounts, and at all events get rid of them, or we lose the land for ever. At this time there are treaties and engagements in every corner. I have touched on every subject. Forgive whatever is improper. Let us look the future in the face, and let chiefs, ministers, and all unite. With the welfare of the country all will be well. But this is a disease which, if not now conquered, will conquer us."

A second paper as follows :—

"The disease of the country is to be considered and treated as a remittent.

"Umra Sing cured it and laid a complete system of government and justice.

"In Sangram's time it once more gained ground.

"In Juggut Sing's time the seed was thrown into the ground thus obtained.

"In Pertáp's time it sprung up.

"In Raj Sing's time it bore fruit.

"In Rana Ursi's time it was ripe.

"In Hamir's time it was distributed, and all have had a share.

"And you, Bheem Sing (the present Rana), have eaten plentifully thereof. Its virtues and flavour you are acquainted with, and so likewise is the country; and if you take no medicine you will assuredly suffer much pain, and both at home and abroad you will be lightly thought of. Be not therefore negligent, or faith and land will depart from you."

A third paper to Uggurji Mehta (then minister):

"If the milk is curdled it does not signify. Where there is sense butter may yet be extracted; and if the butter-milk (*chauch*) is thrown away it matters not. But if the milk be curdled and black it will require wisdom to restore its purity. This wisdom is now wanted. The foreigners are the black in the curdled milk of Méwar. At all hazards remove them. Trust to them and the land is lost.

"In moonlight what occasion for a blue light? (*Chundra jote*).[1]

"Who looks to the false coin of the juggler?

"Do not credit him who tells you he will make a pigeon out of a feather.

"Abroad it is said there is no wisdom left in Méwar, which is a disgrace to her reputation."

[1] There are three classes of Mahratta Brahmins: Sainowee, Purbo, and Mahrat. Of the first was Lukwa, Balabha Tantia, Jewa Dada, Sewaji Nana, Lallaji Pundit, and Jeswunt Rao Bhow, men who held the mortgaged lands of Méwar.

---

[1] Literally, a "moonlight." The particular kind of firework which we call a "blue light."

call in his garrison and try another battle, which he also lost and fled to Hamirgurh ; then, uniting with his enemies, they invested the place with 15,000 men. Nana bravely maintained himself, making many sallies, in one of which both the sons of D'heruj Sing, the chief of Hamirgurh, were slain. Shortly after, Nana was relieved by some battalions of the new raised regulars sent by Umbaji under Golaub Rao Kudum, upon which he commenced his retreat on Ajmér. At Moosa-Moosi he was forced to action, and success had nearly crowned the efforts of the clans, when a horseman, endeavouring to secure a mare, calling out, "*Bhaga ! bhaga !*" "She flies ! she flies !" the word spread, while those who caught her, exclaiming "*Milgya ! milgya !*" "She is taken !" but equally significant with 'going over' to the enemy, caused a general panic, and the Chondawuts, on the verge of victory, disgraced themselves, broke and fled. Several were slain, among whom was the Sindie leader Chundun. Shapoora opened its gates to the fugitives led by the Goliath of the host, the chief of Deogurh.[1] It was an occasion not to be lost by the bards of the rival clan, and many a ribald stanza records this day's disgrace. Umbaji's lieutenant, however, was so roughly handled that several chiefs redeemed their estates, and the Rana much of the fisc, from Mahratta control. Méwar now became the arena on which the rival satraps Umbaji and Lukwa contested the exalted office of Sindia's lieutenancy in Hindust'han. Lukwa was joined by all the chiefs of Méwar, his cause being their own ; and Hamirgurh, still held by Nana's party, was reinvested. Two thousand shot had made a practicable breach, when Bala Rao Inglia, Bapoo Sindia, Eswunt Rao Sindia, a brigade under the European 'Mutta field,' with the auxiliary battalions of Zalim Sing of Kotah, the whole under the command of Umbaji's son, arrived to relieve the lieutenant. Lukwa raised the siege, and took post with his allies under the walls of Cheetore ; whilst the besieged left the untenable Hamirgurh, and joined the relief at Gosoonda. The rival armies were separated only by the Béris river, on whose banks they raised batteries and cannonaded each other, when a dispute arose in the victor camp regarding the pay of the troops, between Bala Rao (brother of Umbaji) and Nana, and the latter withdrew and retreated to Sanganér. Thus disunited, it might have been expected that these congregated masses would have dissolved, or fallen upon each other, when the Rajpoots might have given the *coup de grâce* to the survivors ; but they were Mahrattas, and their politics were too complicated to end in simple strife : almost all the actors in these scenes lived to contest with, and be humiliated by, the British.

The defection of Nana equalised the parties ; but Bala Rao, never partial to fighting, opportunely recollected a debt of gratitude to Lukwa, to whose clemency he owed his life when taken by storm in Googul Chupra. He also wanted money to pay his force, which a private overture to Lukwa secured. They met, and Bala Rao retired boasting of his gratitude, to which, and the defection of Nana, soon followed by that of Bapoo Sindia, the salvation of Lukwa was attributed. Sutherland with a brigade was detached by Umbaji to aid Nana : but a dispute depriving him of this

[1] I knew him well. He stood six feet six inches, and was bulky in proportion. His limbs rivalled those of the Hercules Farnese. His father was nearly seven feet, and died at the early age of twenty-two, in a vain attempt to keep down, by regimen and medicine, his enormous bulk.

reinforcement, he called in a partisan of more celebrity, the brave George Thomas. Umbaji's lieutenant and Lukwa were once more equal foes, and the Rana, his chiefs and subjects being distracted between these conflicting bands, whose leaders alternately paid their respects to him, were glad to obtain a little repose by espousing the cause of either combatant, whose armies during the monsoon encamped for six weeks within sight of each other.[1]

Doorjun Sal (Kheechie), with the nobles of Méwar, hovered round Nana's camp with five thousand horse to cut off his supplies; but Thomas escorted the convoys from Shapoora with his regulars, and defied all their efforts. Thomas at length advanced his batteries against Lukwa, on whose position a general assault was about taking place, when a tremendous storm, with torrents of rain which filled the stream, cut off his batteries from the main body, burst the gates of Shapoora, his *point d'appui*, and laid the town in ruins.[2] Lukwa seized the moment, and with the Méwar chiefs stormed and carried the isolated batteries, capturing fifteen pieces of cannon; and the Shapoora Raja, threatened at once by his brother-nobles and the vengeance of heaven, refused further provision to Nana, who was compelled to abandon his position and retreat to Sanganér. The discomfited lieutenant vowed vengeance against the estates of the Méwar chieftains, and after the rains, being reinforced by Umbaji, again took the field. Then commenced a scene of carnage, pillage, and individual defence. The whole of the Chondawut estates under the Aravulli range were laid waste, their castles assaulted, some taken and destroyed, and heavy sums levied on all. Thomas besieged Deogurh and Amait, and both fought and paid. Kossitul and Lusani were captured, and the latter razed for its gallant resistance. Thus they were proceeding in the work of destruction, when Umbaji was dispossessed of the government of Hindust'han, to which Lukwa was nominated,[3] and Nana was compelled to surrender all the fortresses and towns he held in Méwar.

From this period must be dated the pretensions of Sindia to consider Méwar as tributary to him. We have traced the rise of the Mahrattas, and the progress of their baneful influence in Méwar. The abstractions of territory from S. 1826 to 1831, as pledges for contributions, satisfied their avarice till 1848, when the Saloombra rebellion brought the great Sindia to Cheetore, leaving Umbaji as his lieutenant, with a subsidiary force, to recover the Rana's lost possessions. We have related how these conditions were fulfilled; how Umbaji, inflated with the wealth of Méwar, assumed almost regal dignity in Hindust'han, assigning the devoted land to be governed by his deputies, whose contest with other aspirants made this unhappy region the stage for constant struggles for supremacy; and while the secret policy of Zalim Sing stimulated the Suktawuts to cling to

[1] Both camps were on the right bank of the Bunas: Lukwa's at Amlee, about ten miles south of Shapoora, and Nana's at Kadaira, between these towns.

[2] Lukwa at this time[1] put the Shapoora Raja in possession of the important fortress and district of Jehajpoor, which, although the Rana consented to it, covertly receiving from the Raja two lakhs of rupees, disgusted the nobles with Lukwa.

[3] Balabha Tantia and Bukshu Narrain Rao were Sindia's ministers at this period, of the same tribe (the Sainowee) as Lukwa.

[1] S. 1856 (A.D. 1800).

Umbaji, the Chondawuts gave their influence and interest to his rival Lukwa. The unhappy Rana and the peasantry paid for this rivalry; while Sindia, whose power was now in its zenith, fastened one of his desultory armies on Méwar, in contravention of former treaties, without any definite views, or even instructions to its commander. It was enough that a large body should supply itself without assailing him for prey, and whose services were available when required.

Lukwa, the new viceroy, marched to Méwar: Aggurji Mehta was appointed minister to the Rana, and the Chondawuts again came into power. For the sum of six lakhs Lukwa dispossessed the Shapoora of Jehajpoor, for the liquidation of which thirty-six of its towns were mortgaged. Zalim Sing, who had long been manœuvring to obtain Jehajpoor, administered to the necessities of the Mahratta, paid the note of hand, and took possession of the city and its villages. A contribution of twenty-four lakhs was imposed throughout the country, and levied by force of arms, after which first act of the new viceroy he quitted Méwar for Jeipoor, leaving Jeswunt Rao Bhow as his deputy. Moujee Ram, the deputy of Aggurji (the Rana's minister), determined to adopt the European mode of discipline, now become general amongst all the native powers of India. But when the chiefs were called upon to contribute to the support of mercenary regulars and a field-artillery, they evinced their patriotism by confining this zealous minister. Suttidas was once more placed in power, and his brother Sheodas recalled from Kotah, whither he had fled from the Chondawuts, who now appropriated to themselves the most valuable portions of the Rana's personal domain.

The battle of Indore, in A.D. 1802, where at least 150,000 men assembled to dispute the claim to predatory empire, wrested the ascendancy from Holkar, who lost his guns, equipage, and capital, from which he fled to Méwar, pursued by Sindia's victorious army led by Sudasheo and Bala Rao. In his flight he plundered Rutlam, and passing Bheendir, the castle of the Suktawut chief, he demanded a contribution, from which and his meditated visit to Oodipoor, the Rana and his vassal were saved by the activity of the pursuit. Failing in these objects, Holkar retreated on Nat'hdwarra, the celebrated shrine of the Hindu Apollo. It was here this active soldier first showed symptoms of mental derangement. He upbraided Crishna, while prostrate before his image, for the loss of his victory; and levied three lakhs of rupees on the priests and inhabitants, several of whom he carried to his camp as hostages for the payment. The portal (*dwarra*) of the god (*Nat'h*) proving no bar either to Toork or equally impious Mahratta, Damodurji, the high priest, removed the God of Vrij from his pedestal and sent him with his establishment to Oodipoor for protection. The Chohan chief of Kotario (one of the sixteen nobles), in whose estate was the sacred fane, undertook the duty, and with twenty horsemen, his vassals, escorted the shepherd god by intricate passes to the capital. On his return he was intercepted by a band of Holkar's troops, who insultingly desired the surrender of their horses. But the descendant of the illustrious Pirthi Raj preferred death to dishonour: dismounting, he ham-strung his steed, commanding his vassals to follow his example; and sword in hand courted his fate in the unequal conflict, in which he fell, with most of his gallant retainers. There are many such isolated exploits in the records of this eventful period, of which the Chohans of Kotario had their full share. Spoil, from whatever source, being welcome to these depredators, Nat'hdwarra [1] remained long abandoned; and Apollo, after six months' residence at Oodipoor, finding insufficient protection, took another flight to the mountains of Gassyar, where the high priest threw up fortifications for his defence; and spiritual thunders being disregarded, the pontiff henceforth buckled on the armour of flesh, and at the head of four hundred cavaliers, with lance and shield, visited the minor shrines in his extensive diocese.

To return to Holkar. He pursued his route by Bunéra and Shapoora, levying from both, to Ajmér, where he distributed a portion of the offerings of the followers of Crishna amongst the priests of Mahomed at the mosque of Khwaja Peer. Thence he proceeded towards Jeipoor. Sindia's leaders on reaching Méwar renounced the pursuit, and Oodipoor was cursed with their presence, when three lakhs of rupees were extorted from the unfortunate Rana, raised by the sale of household effects and the jewels of the females of his family. Jeswunt Rao Bhow, the Soobadar of Méwar, had prepared another schedule (*pandri*), which he left with Tantia, his deputy, to realise. Then followed the usual scene of conflict—the attack of the chieftain's estates, distraining of the husbandman, seizure of his cattle, and his captivity for ransom, or his exile.

The celebrated Lukwa, disgraced by his prince, died at this time [2] in sanctuary at Saloombra; and Bala Rao, brother to Umbaji, returned, and was joined by the Suktawuts and the minister Suttidas, who expelled the Chondawuts for their control over the prince. Zalim Sing, in furtherance of his schemes and through hatred of the Chondawuts, united himself to this faction, and Devi Chund, minister to the Rana, set up by the Chondawuts, was made prisoner. Bala Rao levied and destroyed their estates with unexampled ferocity, which produced a bold attempt at deliverance. The Chondawut leaders assembled at the Chougan (the *Champ de Mars*) to consult on their safety. The insolent Mahratta had preceded them to the palace, demanding the surrender of the minister's deputy, Moujee Ram. The Rana indignantly refused them—the Mahratta importuned, threatened, and at length commanded his troops to advance to the palace, when the intrepid minister pinioned the audacious plunderers, and secured his adherents (including their old enemy, Nana Gunés), Jumalkur, and Ooda Kooer. The latter, a notorious villain, had an elephant's chain put round his neck, while Bala Rao was confined in a bath. The leaders thus arrested, the Chondawuts sallied forth and attacked their camp in the valley, which surrendered; though the regulars under Hearsay retreated in a hollow square, and reached Gadermala in safety. Zalim Sing determined to liberate his friend Bala Rao from peril; and aided by the Suktawuts under the chiefs of Bheendir and Lawah, advanced to the Chaija pass, one of the defiles leading to the capital. Had the Rana put these chiefs to instant death, he would have been justified, although he would have incurred the resentment of the whole Mahratta nation. Instead of this, he put himself at the head of a motley levy of six thousand Sindies, Arabs, and Goseins, with the brave Jey Sing and a band of his gallant Kheechies, ever ready to poise the lance against a

[1] Five-and-twenty miles north of Oodipoor. On this subject we shall have much to say hereafter.

[2] S. 1859 (A.D. 1803).

Mahratta. They defended the pass for five days against a powerful artillery. At length the Rana was compelled to liberate Bala Rao, and Zalim Sing obtained by this interference possession of the fortress and entire district of Jehajpoor. A schedule of war contribution, the usual finale to these events, followed Bala's liberation, and no means were left untried to realise the exaction, before Holkar, then approaching, could contest the spoil.

This chief recruited his shattered forces, again left the south.[1] Bheendir felt his resentment for non-compliance with his demands on his retreat after the battle of Indore ; the town was nearly destroyed, but spared for two lakhs of rupees, for the payment of which villages were assigned. Thence he repaired to Oodipoor, being met by Ajít Sing, the Rana's ambassador, when the enormous sum of forty lakhs, or £500,000, was demanded from the country, of which one-third was commanded to be instantly forthcoming. The palace was denuded of everything which could be converted into gold ; the females were deprived of every article of luxury and comfort : by which, with contributions levied on the city, twelve lakhs were obtained ; while hostages from the household of the Rana and chief citizens were delivered as security for the remainder, and immured in the Mahratta camp. Holkar then visited the Rana. Lawah and Bednore were attacked, taken, and restored on large payments. Deogurh alone was mulcted four and a half lakhs. Having devastated Méwar during eight months, Holkar marched to Hindust'han,[2] Ajít Sing accompanying him as the Rana's representative ; while Bala Ram Set'h was left to levy the balance of the forty lakhs. Holkar had reached Shapoora when Sindia entered Méwar, and their camps formed a junction to allow the leaders to organise their mutual plans of hostility to the British government. These chieftains, in their efforts to cope with the British power, had been completely humiliated, and their resources broken. But Rajast'han was made to pay the penalty of British success, which riveted her chains, and it would be but honest, now we have the power, to diminish that penalty.

The rainy season of A.D. 1805 found Sindia and Holkar encamped in the plains of Bednore, desirous, but afraid, to seek revenge in the renewal of war. Deprived of all power in Hindust'han, and of the choicest territory north and south of the Nerbudda, with numerous discontented armies now let loose on these devoted countries, their passions inflamed by defeat, and blind to every sentiment of humanity, they had no alternative to pacify the soldiery and replenish their own ruined resources but indiscriminate pillage. It would require a pen powerful as the pencil of Salvator Rosa to paint the horrors which filled up the succeeding ten years, to which the author was an eye-witness, destined to follow in the train of rapine, and to view in the traces of Mahratta camps the desola-

[1] In S. 1860 (A.D. 1804).

[2] At this juncture an officer of Holkar's, Hurnát Chéla, on passing through Bansein, had some camels carried off by the Bhils of the Satola estate. Hurnát summoned Golab Sing Chondawut, who came with eight of his relatives, when he was told he should be detained till the cattle were restored ; and in the morning, as the Mahratta mounted his elephant, he commanded the Raghaut chieftain to be seized. Golab drew his sword and made at Hurnát, but his sword broke in the howda, when he plunged his dagger into the elephant ; but at length he and all his relations, who nobly plied their swords on the Mahrattas, were cut to pieces.

tion and political annihilation of all the central states of India,[1] several of which aided the British in their early struggles for dominion, but were now allowed to fall without a helping hand, the scape-goats of our successes. Peace between the Mahrattas and British was, however, doubtful, as Sindia made the restoration of the rich provinces of Gohud and Gwalior a *sine qua non*: and unhappily for their legitimate ruler, who had been inducted into the seat of his forefathers, a Governor-General (Lord Cornwallis) of ancient renown, but in the decline of life, with views totally unsuited to the times, abandoned our allies, and renounced all for peace, sending an ambassador[2] to Sindia to reunite the bonds of "perpetual friendship."

The Mahratta leaders were anxious, if the war should be renewed, to shelter their families and valuables in the strongholds of Méwar, and their respective camps became the rendezvous of the rival factions. Sirdar Sing, the organ of the Chondawuts, represented the Rana at Sindia's court, at the head of whose councils Umbaji had just been placed.[3] His rancour to the Rana was implacable, from the support given in self-defence to his political antagonist, Lukwa, and he agitated the partition of Méwar amongst the great Mahratta leaders. But whilst his baneful influence was preparing this result, the credit of Sangram Suktawut with Holkar counteracted it. It would be unfair and ungallant not to record that a fair suitor, the Baéza Bae, Sindia's wife, powerfully contributed to the Rana's preservation on this occasion. This lady, the daughter of the notorious Surji Rao, had unbounded power over Sindia. Her sympathies were awakened on behalf of the supreme head of the Rajpoot nation, of which blood she had to boast, though she was now connected with the Mahrattas. Even the hostile clans stifled their animosities on this occasion, and Sirdar Sing Chondawut left Sindia's camp to join his rival Sangram with Holkar, and aided by the upright Kishen-das Pancholi, united in their remonstrances, asking Holkar if he had given his consent to sell Méwar to Umbaji. Touched by the picture of the Rana's and their country's distresses, Holkar swore it should not be; advised unity amongst themselves, and caused the representatives of the rival clans "to eat opium together." Nor did he stop here, but with the envoys repaired to Sindia's tents, descanted on the Rana's high descent, "the master of their master's master,"[4] urging that it did not become them to overwhelm him, and that they should even renounce the mortgaged lands which their

[1] The Rana of Gohud and Gwalior, the Kheechie chiefs of Ragoogurh and Buhadoorgurh, and the Nabob of Bhopal, made common cause with us in Warren Hastings' time. The three first possess not a shadow of independence; the latter fortunately formed a link in our own policy, and Lord Hastings, in 1818, repaid with liberal interest the services rendered to the government of Warren Hastings in 1782. It was in his power, with equal facility, to have rescued all the other states, and to have claimed the same measure of gratitude which Bhopal is proud to avow. But there was a fatality in the desire to maintain terms with Sindia, whose treachery to our power was overlooked.

[2] The author, then a subaltern, was attached to the suite of the ambassador, Mr. Græme Mercer. He left the subsidiary force at Gwalior in December 1805, and the embassy reached Sindia's court in the spring of 1806, then encamped amidst the ruins of Méwar.

[3] The ministers of Sindia were Umbaji, Bapoo Chitnavees, Madhuba Huzooria, and Anaji Bhasker.

[4] That is, chief of the race from which issued the Sitarra sovereigns, whose minister, the Péshwa, accounted Sindia and Holkar his feudatories.

fathers had too long unjustly held, himself setting the example by the restitution of Neembahaira. To strengthen his argument, he expatiated with Sindia on the policy of conciliating the Rana, whose strongholds might be available in the event of a renewal of hostilities with the British. Sindia appeared a convert to his views, and retained the envoys in his camp. The Mahratta camps were twenty miles apart, and incessant torrents of rain had for some days prevented all intercourse. In this interim, Holkar received intelligence that Bhiroo Bux, as envoy from the Rana, was in Lord Lake's camp negotiating for the aid of British troops, then at Tonk, to drive the Mahrattas from Méwar. The incensed Holkar sent for the Rana's ambassadors, and assailed them with a torrent of reproach; accusing them of treachery, he threw the newspaper containing the information at Kishen-das, asking if that were the way in which the Méwarries kept faith with him? "I cared not to break with Sindia in support of your master, and while combating the Fringies (Franks), when all the Hindus should be as brothers, your sovereign the Rana, who boasts of not acknowledging the supremacy of Dehli, is the first to enter into arms with them. Was it for this I prevented Umbaji being fastened on you?" Kishen-das here interrupted and attempted to pacify him, when Alikur Tantia, Holkar's minister, stopped him short, observing to his prince, "You see the faith of these *Rangras*;[1] they would disunite you and Sindia, and ruin both. Shake them off: be reconciled to Sindia, dismiss Surji Rao, and let Umbaji be Soobadar of Méwar, or I will leave you and take Sindia into Malwa." The other councillors, with the exception of Bhow Bhasker, seconded this advice: Surji Rao was dismissed; and Holkar proceeded northward, where he was encountered and pursued to the Punjâb by the British under the intrepid and enterprising Lake, who dictated terms to the Mahratta at the altars of Alexander.

Holkar had the generosity to stipulate, before his departure from Méwar, for the security of the Rana and his country, telling Sindia he should hold him personally amenable to him if Umbaji were permitted to violate his guarantee. But in his misfortunes this threat was disregarded, and a contribution of sixteen lakhs was levied immediately on Méwar; Sudasheo Rao, with Baptiste's brigade, was detached from the camp in June 1806, for the double purpose of levying it, and driving from Oodipoor a detachment of the Jeipoor prince's troops, bringing proposals and preliminary presents for this prince's marriage with the Rana's daughter.

It would be imagined that the miseries of Rana Bheem were not susceptible of aggravation, and that fortune had done her worst to humble him; but his pride as a sovereign and his feelings as a parent were destined to be yet more deeply wounded. The Jeipoor cortège had encamped near the capital, to the number of three thousand men, while the Rana's acknowledgments of acceptance were despatched, and had reached Shapoora. But Raja Maun of Marwar also advanced pretensions, founded on the princes having been actually betrothed to his predecessor; and urging that the throne of Marwar, and not the individual occupant, was the object, he vowed resentment and opposition if his claims were disregarded. These were suggested, it is said, by his nobles to cloak their own views; and promoted by the Chondawuts (then in favour with the

[1] Rangra is an epithet applied to the Rajpoots, implying turbulent, from '*ring*,' strife.

Rana), whose organ, Ajít, was bribed to further them, contrary to the decided wishes of their prince.

Kishna Komari (the *Virgin* Kishna) was the name of the lovely object, the rivalry for whose hand assembled under the banners of her suitors (Juggut Sing of Jeipoor and Raja Maun of Marwar), not only their native chivalry, but all the predatory powers of India; and who like Helen of old, involved in destruction her own and the rival houses. Sindia having been denied a pecuniary demand by Jeipoor, not only opposed the nuptials, but aided the claims of Raja Maun, by demanding of the Rana the dismissal of the Jeipoor embassy: which being refused, he advanced his brigades and batteries, and after a fruitless resistance, in which the Jeipoor troops joined, forced the pass, threw a corps of eight thousand men into the valley, and following in person, encamped within cannon-range of the city. The Rana had now no alternative but to dismiss the nuptial cortège, and agree to whatever was demanded. Sindia remained a month in the valley, during which an interview took place between him and the Rana at the shrine of Eklinga.[1]

The heralds of Hymen being thus rudely repulsed and its symbols intercepted, the Jeipoor prince prepared to avenge his insulted pride and disappointed hopes, and accordingly arrayed a force such as had not assembled since the empire was in its glory. Raja Maun eagerly took up the gauntlet of his rival, and headed "the swords of Maroo." But dissension prevailed in Marwar, where rival claimants for the throne had divided the loyalty of the clans, introducing there also the influence of the Mahrattas. Raja Maun, who had acquired the sceptre by party aid, was obliged to maintain himself by it, and to pursue the demoralising policy of the period by ranging his vassals against each other. These nuptials gave the malcontents an opportunity to display their long-curbed resentments, and following the example of Méwar, they set up a pretender, whose interests were eagerly espoused, and whose standard was erected in the array of Jeipoor; the prince at the head of 120,000 men advancing against his rival, who with less than half the number met him at Purbutsir, on their mutual frontier. The action was short, for while a heavy cannonade opened on either side, the majority of the Marwar nobles went over

[1] To increase his importance, Sindia invited the British envoy and suite to be present on the occasion, when the princely demeanour of the Rana and his sons was advantageously contrasted with that of the Mahratta and his suite. It was in this visit that the regal abode of this ancient race, its isles and palaces, acted with irresistible force on the cupidity of this *scion of the plough*, who aspired to, yet dared not seat himself in, "the halls of the Cæsars." It was even surmised that his hostility to Jeipoor was not so much from the refused war-contribution, as from a mortifying negative to an audacious desire to obtain the hand of this princess himself.

The impression made on the author upon this occasion by the miseries and noble appearance of "this descendant of a hundred kings," was never allowed to weaken, but kindled an enthusiastic desire for the restoration of his fallen condition, which stimulated his perseverance to obtain that knowledge by which alone he might be enabled to benefit him. Then a young *Sub.*, his hopes of success were more sanguine than wise; but he trusted to the rapid march of events, and the discordant elements by which he was surrounded, to effect the redemption of the prince from thraldom. It was a long dream—but after ten years of anxious hope, at length realised—and he had the gratification of being instrumental in snatching the family from destruction, and subsequently of raising the country to comparative prosperity.

to the pretender. Raja Maun turned his poniard against himself: but some chiefs yet faithful to him wrested the weapon from his hand, and conveyed him from the field. He was pursued to his capital, which was invested, besieged, and gallantly defended during six months. The town was at length taken and plundered, but the castle of Joda "laughed a siege to scorn"; in time with the aid of finesse, the mighty host of Jeipoor, which had consumed the forage of these arid plains for twenty miles around, began to crumble away; intrigue spread through every rank, and the siege ended in pusillanimity and flight. The Xerxes of Rajwarra, the effeminate Cutchwaha, alarmed at length for his personal safety, sent on the spoils of Purbutsir and Jodpoor to his capital: but the brave nobles of Marwar, drawing the line between loyalty and patriotism, and determined that no trophy of Rahtore degradation should be conveyed by the Cutchwahas from Marwar, attacked the cortège and redeemed the symbols of their disgrace. The colossal array of the invader was soon dismembered, and the "lion of the world" (Juggut Sing) humbled and crestfallen, skulked from the desert retreat of his rival, indebted to a partisan corps for safety and convoy to his capital, around whose walls the wretched remnants of this ill-starred confederacy long lagged in expectation of their pay, while the bones of their horses and the ashes of their riders whitened the plain, and rendered it a Golgotha.[1]

By the aid of one of the most notorious villains India ever produced, the Nawab Ameer Khan, the pretender's party was treacherously annihilated. This man with his brigade of artillery and horse was amongst the most efficient of the foes of Raja Maun; but the *auri sacra fames* not only made him desert the side on which he came for that of the Raja, but for a specific sum offer to rid him of the pretender and all his associates. Like Judas, he kissed whom he betrayed, took service with the pretender, and at the shrine of a saint of his own faith exchanged turbans with their leaders; and while the too credulous Rajpoot chieftains celebrated this acquisition to their party in the very sanctuary of hospitality, crowned by the dance and the song, the tents were cut down, and the victims thus enveloped, slaughtered in the midst of festivity by showers of grape.

Thus finished the under-plot; but another and more noble victim was demanded before discomfited ambition could repose, or the curtain drop on this eventful drama. Neither party would relinquish his claim to the fair object of the war; and the torch of discord could be extinguished only in her blood. To the same ferocious Khan is attributed the unhallowed suggestion, as well as its compulsory execution. The scene was now changed from the desert castle of Joda to the smiling valley of Oodipoor, soon to be filled with funereal lamentation.

Kishna Komari Baé, the "Virgin Princess Kishna," was in her sixteenth year: her mother was of the Chawura race, the ancient kings of Anhulwara. Sprung from the noblest blood of Hind, she added beauty of face and person to an engaging demeanour, and was justly proclaimed the "flower of

[1] I witnessed the commencement and the end of this drama, and have conversed with actors in all the intermediate scenes. In June 1806 the passes of Oodipoor were forced; and in January 1808, when I passed through Jeipoor in a solitary ramble, the fragments of this contest were scattered over its sandy plains.

Rajast'han." When the Roman father pierced the bosom of the dishonoured Virginia, appeased virtue applauded the deed. When Iphigenia was led to the sacrificial altar, the salvation of her country yielded a noble consolation. The votive victim of Jephtha's success had the triumph of a father's fame to sustain her resignation, and in the meekness of her sufferings we have the best parallel to the sacrifice of the lovely Kishna: though years have passed since the barbarous immolation, it is never related but with a faltering tongue and moistened eyes, "albeit unused to the melting mood."

The rapacious and blood-thirsty Pat'han, covered with infamy, repaired to Oodipoor, where he was joined by the pliant and subtle Ajít. Meek in his demeanour, unostentatious in his habits; despising honours, yet covetous of power,—religion, which he followed with the zeal of an ascetic, if it did not serve as a cloak, was at least no hindrance to an immeasurable ambition, in the attainment of which he would have sacrificed all but himself. When the Pat'han revealed his design, that either the princess should wed Raja Maun, or by her death seal the peace of Rajwarra, whatever arguments were used to point the alternative, the Rana was made to see no choice between consigning his beloved child to the Rahtore prince, or witnessing the effects of a more extended dishonour from the vengeance of the Pat'han, and the storm of his palace by his licentious adherents—the fiat passed that Kishna Komari should die.

But the deed was left for women to accomplish—the hand of man refused it. The Rawula [1] of an eastern prince is a world within itself; it is the labyrinth containing the strings that move the puppets which alarm mankind. Here intrigue sits enthroned, and hence its influence radiates to the world, always at a loss to trace effects to their causes. Maharaja Dowlut Sing,[2] descended four generations ago from one common ancestor with the Rana, was first sounded "to save the honour of Oodipoor"; but, horror-struck, he exclaimed, "Accursed the tongue that commands it! Dust on my allegiance, if thus to be preserved!" The Maharaja Jowandás, a natural brother, was then called upon; the dire necessity was explained, and it was urged that no common hand could be armed for the purpose. He accepted the poniard, but when in youthful loveliness Kishna appeared before him, the dagger fell from his hand, and he returned more wretched than the victim. The fatal purpose thus revealed, the shrieks of the frantic mother reverberated through the palace, as she implored mercy, or execrated the murderers of her child, who alone was resigned to her fate. But death was arrested, not averted. To use the phrase of the narrator, "she was excused the steel—the cup was prepared,"—and prepared by female hands! As the messenger presented it in the name of her father, she bowed and drank it, sending up a prayer for his life and prosperity. The raving mother poured imprecations on his head, while the lovely victim, who shed not a tear, thus endeavoured to console her: "Why afflict yourself, my mother, at this shortening of the sorrows of life? I fear not to die! Am I not your daughter? Why should I fear death? We are marked out for sacrifice [3] from our birth; we scarcely enter the world but to be sent out again;

[1] Harem.

[2] I knew him well—a plain honest man.

[3] Alluding to the custom of infanticide—here, very rare; indeed, almost unknown.

let me thank my father that I have lived so long!"[1] Thus she conversed till the nauseating draught refused to assimilate with her blood. Again the bitter potion was prepared. She drained it off, and again it was rejected; but, as if to try the extreme of human fortitude, a third was administered; and, for the third time, Nature refused to aid the horrid purpose. It seemed as if the fabled charm, which guarded the life of the founder of her race,[2] was inherited by the Virgin Kishna. But the bloodhounds, the Pat'han and Ajít, were impatient till their victim was at rest; and cruelty, as if gathering strength from defeat, made another and a fatal attempt. A powerful opiate was presented—*the kasoomba draught*.[3] She received it with a smile, wished the scene over, and drank it. The desires of barbarity were accomplished. "She slept!"[4] a sleep from which she never awoke.

The wretched mother did not long survive her child; nature was exhausted in the ravings of despair; she refused food; and her remains in a few days followed those of her daughter to the funeral pyre.

Even the ferocious Khan, when the instrument of his infamy, Ajít, reported the issue, received him with contempt, and spurned him from his presence, tauntingly asking "if this were the boasted Rajpoot valour?" But the wily traitor had to encounter language far more bitter from his political adversary, whom he detested. Sangram Suktawut reached the capital only four days after the catastrophe—a man in every respect the reverse of Ajít; audaciously brave, he neither feared the frown of his sovereign nor the sword of his enemy. Without introduction he rushed into the presence, where he found seated the traitor Ajít. "Oh dastard! who hast thrown dust on the Seesodia race, whose blood which has flowed in purity through a hundred ages has now been defiled! this sin will check its course for ever; a blot so foul in our annals that

[1] With my mind engrossed with the scenes in which I had passed the better part of my life, I went two months after my return from Rajpootana, in 1823, to York Cathedral, to attend the memorable festival of that year. The sublime recitations of Handel in "Jephtha's Vow," the sonorous woe of Sapio's "Deeper and deeper still," powerfully recalled the sad exit of the Rajpootni; and the representation shortly after of Racine's tragedy of "Iphigénie," with Talma as Achille, Duchesnois as Clytemnestre, and a very interesting personation of the victim daughter of Agamemnon, again served to waken the remembrance of this sacrifice. The following passage, embodying not only the sentiments, but couched in the precise language in which the "Virgin Kishna" addressed her father—proving that human nature was but one mode of expression for the same feelings—I am tempted to transcribe:

"Mon père,
"Cessez de vous troubler, vous n'êtes point trahi.
Quand vous commanderez, vous serez obéi:
Ma vie est votre bien. Vous voulez le reprendre,
Vos ordres, sans détour, pouvaient se faire entendre;
D'un œil aussi content, d'un cœur aussi soumis,
Que j'acceptais l'époux que vous m'aviez promis,
Je saurai, s'il le faut, victime obéissante
Tendre au fer de Calchas une tête innocente;
Et respectant le coup par vous-même ordonné,
Vous rendre tout le sang que vous m'avez donné."

[2] Bappa Rawul.

[3] The kasoomba draught is made of flowers and herbs of a cooling quality; into this an opiate was introduced.

[4] The simple but powerful expression of the narrator.

no Seesodia[1] will ever again hold up his head! A sin to which no punishment were equal. But the end of our race is approaching! The line of Bappa Rawul is at an end! Heaven has ordained this, a signal of our destruction." The Rana hid his face with his hands, when turning to Ajít, he exclaimed, "Thou stain on the Seesodia race, thou impure of Rajpoot blood, dust be on thy head as thou hast covered us all with shame. May you die childless, and your name die with you![2] Why this indecent haste? Had the Pat'han stormed the city? Had he attempted to violate the sanctity of the Rawula? And though he had, could you not die as Rajpoots, like your ancestors? Was it thus they gained a name? Was it thus our race became renowned—thus they opposed the might of kings? Have you forgotten the Sakas of Cheetore? But whom do I address—not Rajpoots? Had the honour of your females been endangered, had you sacrificed them all and rushed sword in hand on the enemy, your name would have lived, and the Almighty would have secured the seed of Bappa Rawul. But to owe preservation to this unhallowed deed! You did not even await the threatened danger. Fear seems to have deprived you of every faculty, or you might have spared the blood of Sreejee,[3] and if you did not scorn to owe your safety to deception, might have substituted some less noble victim! But the end of our race approaches!"

The traitor to manhood, his sovereign, and humanity, durst not reply. The brave Sangram is now dead, but the prophetic anathema has been fulfilled. Of *ninety-five* children, sons and daughters, but one son (the brother of Kishna)[4] is left to the Rana; and though his two remaining daughters have been recently married to the princes of Jessulmér and Bikanér, the Salic law, which is in full force in these states, precludes all honour through female descent. His hopes rest solely on the prince, Juvana Sing,[5] and though in the flower of youth and health, the marriage bed (albeit boasting no less than four young princesses) has been blessed with no progeny.[6]

The elder brother of Juvana[7] died two years ago. Had he lived he would have been Umra the Third. With regard to Ajít, the curse has been fully accomplished. Scarcely a month after, his wife and two sons were numbered with the dead; and the hoary traitor has since been wandering from shrine to shrine, performing penance and alms in

[1] The tribe of the Rana.

[2] That is, without adoption even to perpetuate it.

[3] A respectful epithet to the prince—*sire*. [4] By the same mother.

[5] He was nearly carried off by that awful scourge, the cholera, and, singular to remark, was the first person attacked at Oodipoor. I remained by his bedside during the progress of this terrible visitation, and never shall I forget his grateful exclamation of surprise, when after a salutary sleep he opened his eyes to health. Sheerjee Mehta, his chief adviser and manager of his estates, merry as ever, though the heir of Méwar was given over, was seized with the complaint as his master recovered—was dead and his ashes blanching on the sands of the streamlet of Ar within twelve hours! Jovial and good-humoured as he was, "we could have better spared a better man." He was an adept in intrigue; of Umbaji's school; and till death shall extinguish the whole of this, and better morals are born, the country will but slowly improve.

[6] Since this work has gone to press, the author has been rejoiced to find that an heir has been born from the last marriage by a princess of Réwah of the Bhagéla tribe.

[7] See genealogical descendants of Rana Juggut Sing. Appendix, No. VIII.

expiation of his sins, yet unable to fling from him ambition; and with his beads in one hand, *Rama! Rama!* ever on his tongue, and subdued passion in his looks, his heart is deceitful as ever. Enough of him: let us exclaim with Sangram, "Dust on his head,"[1] which all the waters of the Ganges could not purify from the blood of the virgin Kishna, but

"rather would the multitudinous sea incarnadine."

His coadjutor, Ameer Khan, is now linked by treaties "in amity and unity of interests" with the sovereigns of India; and though he has carried mourning into every house of Rajast'han, yet charity might hope forgiveness would be extended to him, could he cleanse himself from this deed of horror—"throwing this pearl away, richer than all his tribe!" His career of rapine has terminated with the caresses of the blind goddess, and placed him on a pinnacle to which his sword would never have traced the path. Enjoying the most distinguished post amongst the foreign chieftains of Holkar's state, having the regulars and park under his control, with large estates for their support, he added the epithet of traitor to his other titles, when the British government, adopting the leading maxim of Asiatic policy, *divide et impera*, guaranteed to him the sovereignty of these districts on his abandoning the Mahrattas, disbanding his legions, and surrendering the park. But though he personally fulfilled not, nor could fulfil, one single stipulation, this man, whose services were not worth the pay of a single sepoy,—who fled from his camp[2] unattended, and sought personal protection in that of the British commander,—claimed and obtained the full price of our pledge, the sovereignty of about one-third of his master's dominions; and the districts of Seronge, Tonk, Rampoora, and Neembahaira, form the domain of the *Nawab Ameer Khan*, etc., etc., etc.!! This was in the fitful fever of success, when our arms were everywhere triumphant. But were the viceroy of Hind to summon the forty tributaries[3] now covered by the ægis of British protection to a meeting, the murderer of Kishna would still occupy a place (though low) in this illustrious divan. Let us hope that his character being known, he would feel himself ill at ease; and let us dismiss him likewise in the words of Sangram, "Dust on his head!"

The mind sickens at the contemplation of these unvarying scenes of atrocity; but this unhappy state had yet to pass through two more lustres of aggravated sufferings (to which the author of these annals was an eye-witness) before their termination, upon the alliance of Méwar with Britain. From the period of the forcing of the passes, the dismissal of the Jeipoor embassy by Sindia, and the murder of Kishna Komari,

[1] This was written at Oodipoor in 1820. This old intriguer then attempted to renew the past, as the organ of the Chondawuts, but his scheme ended in exile to the sacred city of Benares; and there he may now be seen with his rosary on the consecrated *ghat* of the Ganges.

[2] Brigadier-General Alexander Knox had the honour of dissolving these bands in the only way worthy of us. He marched his troops to take their guns and disperse their legions; and, when in order of battle, the gallant General taking out his watch, gave them half an hour to reflect, their commander Jamshid, second only in villainy to his master, deeming "discretion the better part of valour," surrendered.

[3] There are full this number of princes holding under the British.

the embassy of Britain was in the train of the Mahratta leader, a witness of the evils described—a most painful predicament—when the hand was stretched out for succour in vain, and the British flag waved in the centre of desolation, unable to afford protection. But this day of humiliation is past, thanks to the predatory hordes who goaded us on to their destruction; although the work was incomplete, a nucleus being imprudently left in Sindia for the scattered particles again to form.

In the spring of 1806, when the embassy entered the once-fertile Méwar, from whose native wealth the monuments the pencil will portray were elected, nothing but ruin met the eye—deserted towns, roofless houses, and uncultured plains. Wherever the Mahratta encamped, annihilation was ensured; it was a habit; and twenty-four hours sufficed to give to the most flourishing spot the aspect of a desert. The march of destruction was always to be traced for days afterwards by burning villages and destroyed cultivation. Some satisfaction may result from the fact, that there was scarcely an actor in these unhallowed scenes whose end was not fitted to his career. Umbaji was compelled to disgorge the spoils of Méwar, and his personal sufferings made some atonement for the ills he had inflicted upon her. This satrap, who had almost established his independence in the fortress and territory of Gwalior, suffered every indignity from Sindia, whose authority he had almost thrown off. He was confined in a mean tent, manacled, suffered the torture of small lighted torches applied to his fingers, and even attempted suicide to avoid the surrender of his riches; but the instrument (an English penknife) was inefficient: the surgeon to the British embassy sewed up the wounds, and his coffers were eased of fifty-five lakhs of rupees! Méwar was, however, once more delivered over to him; he died shortly after. If report be correct, the residue of his treasures was possessed by his ancient ally, Zalim Sing. In this case, the old politician derived the chief advantage of the intrigues of S. 1848, without the crimes attendant on the acquisition.

Sindia's father-in-law, when expelled that chief's camp, according to the treaty, enjoyed the ephemeral dignity of minister to the Rana, when he abstracted the most valuable records, especially those of the revenue.

Komulmér was obtained by the minister Suttidas from Jeswunt Rao Bhow for seventy thousand rupees, for which assignments were given on this district, of which he retained possession. Meer Khan in A.D. 1809 led his myrmidons to the capital, threatening the demolition of the temple of Eklinga if refused a contribution of eleven lakhs of rupees. Nine were agreed to, but which by no effort could be raised, upon which the Rana's envoys were treated with indignity, and Kishen-das [1] wounded. The passes were forced, Meer Khan entering by Dobarri, and his coadjutor and son-in-law, the notorious Jamshid, by the Cheerwa, which made but a feeble resistance. The ruffian Pat'hans were billeted on the city,

[1] This veteran attended me during all these troubles, as the medium of communication with the Rana. Though leagued with the Chondawuts, he was a loyal subject and good servant. I saw him expire, and was of opinion, as well as the doctor who accompanied me, that his death was caused by poison. The general burst of sorrow from hundreds collected around his house, when the event was announced, is the best encomium on his public character.

subjecting the Rana to personal humiliation, and Jamshid [1] left with his licentious Rohillas in the capital. The traces of their barbarity are to be seen in its ruins. No woman could safely venture abroad, and a decent garment or turban was sufficient to attract their cupidity.

In S. 1867 (A.D. 1811) Bapoo Sindia arrived with the title of Soobadar, and encamped in the valley, and from this to 1814 these vampires, representing Sindia and Meer Khan, possessed themselves of the entire fiscal domain, with many of the fiefs, occasionally disputing for the spoils; to prevent which they came to a conference at the *Dhola Mugra* (the white hill), attended by a deputation [2] from the Rana, when the line of demarcation was drawn between the spoilers. A schedule was formed of the towns and villages yet inhabited, the amount to be levied from each specified, and three and a half lakhs adjudged to Jamshid, with the same sum to Sindia; but this treaty was not better kept than the former ones. Méwar was rapidly approaching dissolution, and every sign of civilisation fast disappearing; fields laid waste, cities in ruins, inhabitants exiled, chieftains demoralised, the prince and his family destitute of common comforts. Yet had Sindia the audacity to demand compensation for the loss of his tribute stipulated to Bapoo Sindia,[3] who rendered Méwar a desert, carrying her chiefs, her merchants, her farmers, into captivity and fetters in the dungeons of Ajmér, where many died for want of ransom, and others languished till the treaty with the British, in A.D. 1817, set them free.

CHAPTER XVIII

Overthrow of the predatory system—Alliances with the Rajpoot states—Envoy appointed to Méwar—Arrives at Oodipoor—Reception—Description of the Court—Political geography of Méwar—The Rana—His character—His ministers—Plans—Exiles recalled—Merchants invited—Bhilwara established—Assembly of the nobles—Charter ratified—Resumptions of land—Anecdotes of the Chiefs of Arjah—Bednore, Bhadaiser, and Amait—Landed tenures in Méwar—Village rule—Freehold (*bápóta*) of Méwar—Bhomia, or allodial vassals: Character and privileges—Great Register of Patents—Traditions exemplifying right in the soil—The Patél; his origin; character—Assessment of land-rents—General results.

THE history of the Rana's family has now been traced through all the vicissitudes of its fortunes, from the second to the nineteenth century, whilst contending for existence, alternately with Parthians, Bhils, Tartars, and Mahrattas, till at length it has become tributary to Britain.

[1] This monstrous villain (for he was a Goliath) died soon after Méwar was rescued, from a cancer in his back.

[2] Suttidas, Kishen-das, and Roop Ram.

[3] Bapoo Sindia shortly outlived his expulsion from Ajmér, and as he had to pass through Méwar in his passage to his future residence, he was hooted by the population he had plundered. While I was attending the Rana's court, some one reporting Bapoo Sindia's arrival at his destination, mentioned that some pieces of ordnance formerly taken from Oodipoor had, after saluting him, *exuded a quantity of water*, which was received with the utmost gravity by the court, until I remarked they were crying because they should never again be employed in plunder: an idea which caused a little mirth.

The last chapter portrays the degraded condition of their princes, and the utter desolation of their country, in a picture which embodied the entire Rajpoot race. An era of repose at length dawned upon them. The destruction of that vast predatory system, under the weight of which the prosperity of these regions had so long been repressed, was effected by one short campaign in 1817; which if less brilliant than that of 1803, is inferior to none in political results. The tardy policy of the last-named period, at length accomplished, placed the power of Britain in the East on an expugnable position, and rescued the Rajpoots from a progressing destruction.

To prevent the recurrence of this predatory system it was deemed politic to unite all these settled states, alike interested with ourselves in its overthrow, in one grand confederation. Accordingly the Rajpoot states were invited to shelter under our protecting alliance; and with one exception (*Jeipoor*), they eagerly embraced the invitation. The ambassadors of the various governments followed each other in quick succession to Dehli, where the treaties were to be negotiated, and in a few weeks all Rajpootana was united to Britain by compacts of one uniform character;[1] insuring to them external protection with internal independence, as the price of acknowledged supremacy, and a portion of revenue to the protecting government. By this comprehensive arrangement, we placed a most powerful barrier between our territories and the strong natural frontier of India; and so long as we shall respect their established usages, and by contributing to the prosperity of the people preserve our motives from distrust, it will be a barrier impenetrable to invasion.

Of all the princes who obtained succour at this momentous crisis in the political history of India, none stood more in need of it than the Rana of Oodipoor. On the 16th January 1818 the treaty was signed, and in February an envoy was nominated; who immediately proceeded to the Rana's court, to superintend and maintain the newly-formed relations.[2] The right wing of the grand army[3] had already preceded him to compel the surrender of such territory as was unjustly held by the lawless partisans of Sindia, and to reduce to obedience the refractory nobles, to whom anarchy was endeared from long familiarity. The strongholds in the plains as Raepoor, Rajnuggur, etc., soon surrendered; and the payment of the arrears of the garrison of Komulmér put this important fortress in our possession.

In his passage from Jehajpoor, which guards the range on the east to Komulmér on the Aravulli west, a space of 140 miles, the limits of Méwar, only two thinly-peopled towns were seen which acknowledged the Rana's authority. All was desolate; even the traces of the footsteps

[1] See Appendix, No. VI., for treaty with the Rana.

[2] Commanded by Major-General Sir R. Donkin, K.C.B.

[3] The author had the honour to be selected by the Marquis of Hastings to represent him at the Rana's court, with the title of "Political Agent to the Western Rajpoot States." During the campaign of 1817–18, he was placed as the point of communication to the various divisions of the northern army; at the same time being intrusted with the negotiations with Holkar (previous to the rupture), and with those of Kotah and Boondí. He concluded the treaty with the latter state *en route* to Oodipoor, where, as at the latter, there were only the benefits of moral and political existence to confer.

of man were effaced. The babool (*mimosa Arabica*), and gigantic reed. which harboured the boar and the tiger, grew upon the highways; and every rising ground displayed a mass of ruin. Bhilwara, the commercial *entrepôt* of Rajpootana, which ten years before contained six thousand families, showed not a vestige of existence. All was silent in her streets —no living thing was seen except a solitary dog, that fled in dismay from his lurking-place in the temple, scared at the unaccustomed sight of man.[1]

An envoy was despatched by the Rana to congratulate the Agent, who joined him in the British camp at Nat'hdwara; and while he returned to arrange the formalities of reception, the Agent obtained the cession of Komulmér; which, with the acquisitions before mentioned, paved the way for a joyful reception. The prince, Juvan Sing, with all the state insignia, and a numerous cortège, advanced to receive the mission, and conduct it to the capital. A spot was fixed on in a grove of palmyras, about two miles from the city, where carpets were spread, and where the prince received the Agent and suite in a manner at once courteous and dignified.[2] Of him it might have been said, in the language applied by Jehangír to the son of Rana Umra—"His countenance carried the impression of his illustrious extraction."

We entered the city [3] by the gate of the sun; and through a vista of ruin the mission was inducted into its future residence, once the abode of the fair Rampearie.[4] Like all the mansions of Rajpootana, it was a quadrangular pile, with an open paved area, the suites of apartments carried round the sides, with latticed or open corridors extending parallel to each suite. Another deputation with the *méjmani*, consisting of a hundred trays of sweetmeats, dried fruits, and a purse of one thousand rupees for distribution amongst the domestics, brought the Rana's welcome upon our arrival in his capital, and fixed the next day for our introduction at court.

At four in the afternoon, a deputation, consisting of the officiating prime minister, the representative of the Chondawuts, with mace-bearers and a numerous escort, came to announce the Rana's readiness to receive the mission; which, with all the "pomp and circumstance" peculiar to these countries, was marshalled in front of the residency, thronged by crowds of well-dressed inhabitants, silently gazing at the unusual sight.[5] The grand Nakarras having announced the Rana in court, the mission proceeded through streets which everywhere presented marks of rapine, hailed by the most enthusiastic greetings. "Jy! jy! Frengi ca Raj!" *Victory, victory to the English government!* resounded from every tongue.

[1] The author had passed through Bhilwara in May 1806, when it was comparatively flourishing. On this occasion (Feb. 1818) it was entirely deserted. It excited a smile, in the midst of regrets, to observe the practical wit of some of the soldiers, who had supplied the naked representative of *Ád-nath* with an apron—not of leaves, but scarlet cloth.

[2] The Agent had seen him when a boy, at a meeting already described; but he could scarcely have hoped to find in one, to the formation of whose character the times had been so unfavourable, such a specimen as this descendant of Pertáp.

[3] A description of the city and valley will be more appropriate elsewhere.

[4] See p. 346.

[5] The escort consisted of two companies of foot, each of one hundred men, with half a troop of cavalry. The gentlemen attached to the mission were Captain Waugh (who was secretary and commandant of the escort), with Lieutenant Carey as his subaltern. Dr. Duncan was the medical officer.

The bards were not idle ; and the unpoetic name of the Agent was hitched into rhyme. Groups of musicians were posted here and there, who gave a passing specimen of the *tuppas* of Méwar ; and not a few of the fair, with brazen ewers of water on their heads, welcomed us with the *suhailea*, or song of joy. Into each of these vessels the purse-bearer dropped a piece of silver ; for neither the songs of the suhailea, the tuppas of the minstrel, nor encomiastic stave of the bard, are to be received without some acknowledgment that you appreciate their merit and talents, however you may doubt the value they put upon your own. As we ascended the main street leading to the TRIPOLIA, or triple portal, which guards the sacred enclosure, dense masses of people obstructed our progress, and even the walls of the temple of Juggernat'h were crowded. According to etiquette, we dismounted at the *Porte*, and proceeded on foot across the ample terrace ; on which were drawn up a few elephants and horse, exercising for the Rana's amusement.

The palace is a most imposing pile, of a regular form, built of granite and marble, rising at least a hundred feet from the ground, and flanked with octagonal towers, crowned with cupolas. Although built at various periods, uniformity of design has been very well preserved ; nor is there in the East a more striking or majestic structure. It stands upon the very crest of a ridge running parallel to, but considerably elevated above, the margin of the lake. The terrace, which is at the east and chief front of the palace, extends throughout its length, and is supported by a triple row of arches from the declivity of the ridge. The height of this arcaded wall is fully fifty feet ; and although all is hollow beneath, yet so admirably is it constructed, that an entire range of stables is built on the extreme verge of the terrace, on which the whole personal force of the Rana, elephants, horse, and foot, are often assembled. From this terrace the city and the valley lay before the spectator, whose vision is bounded only by the hills shutting out the plains ; while from the summit of the palace nothing obstructs its range over lake and mountain.

A band of Sindies guarded the first entrance to the palace ; and being Saturday, the Suktawuts were on duty in the great hall of assembly. Through lines of Rajpoots we proceeded till we came to the marble staircase, the steps of which had taken the form of the segment of an ellipse, from the constant friction of the foot ; an image of *Ganésa* guarded the ascent to the interior of the palace, and the apartment, or landing, is called *Ganésa deori*, from the Rajpoot *Janus*. After proceeding through a suite of saloons, each filled with spectators, the herald's voice announced to " the lord of the world " that the English envoy was in his presence ; on which he arose and advanced a few paces in front of the throne, the chieftains standing to receive the mission. Everything being ruled by precedent, the seat allotted for the envoy was immediately in front and touching the *royal cushion* (gadi) : being that assigned to the Péshwa in the height of Mahratta prosperity, the arrangement, which was a subject of regular negotiation, could not be objected to. The apartment chosen for the initiatory visit was the *Surya mahl*, or " hall of the sun," so called from a medallion of the orb in basso-rilievo which decorates the wall. Close thereto is placed the Rana's throne, above which, supported by slender silver columns, rises a velvet canopy. The *Gadi*, or throne, in the East is but a huge cushion, over which is thrown an embroidered velvet mantle. The chiefs of the higher grade, or "*the sixteen*," were seated, according to their rank, on the right and left of the Rana ; next and below these were the princes Umra and Juvan Sing ; and at right angles (by which the court formed three sides of a square), the chiefs of the second rank. The civil officers of the state were near the Rana in front, and the seneschal, butler, keeper of the wardrobe, and other confidential officers and inferior chieftains, formed a group standing on the extreme edge of the carpet.

The Rana's congratulations were hearty and sincere : in a few powerful expressions he depicted the miseries he had experienced, the fallen condition of his state, and the gratitude he felt to the British Government which had interposed between him and destruction ; and which for the first moment of his existence allowed him to sleep in peace. There was an intense earnestness in every word he uttered, which, delivered with great fluency of speech and dignity of manner, inspired deep respect and sympathy. The Agent said that the Governor-General was no stranger to the history of his illustrious family, or to his own immediate sufferings ; and that it was his earnest desire to promote, by every means in his power, the Rana's personal dignity and the prosperity of his dominions. After conversing a few minutes, the interview was closed with presents to the Agent and suite : to the former a caparisoned elephant and horse, jewelled aigrette, and pearl necklace, with shawls and brocades ; and with the customary presentation of essence of rose and the pan leaf the Rana and court rising, the envoy made his *salaam* and retired. In a short time the Rana, attended by his second son, ministers, and a select number of the chiefs, honoured the envoy with a visit. The latter advanced beyond his residence to meet the prince, who was received with presented arms by the guard, the officers saluting, and conducted to his throne, which had been previously arranged. Conversation was now unrestrained, and questions were demanded regarding everything which appeared unusual. After sitting half an hour, the Agent presented the Rana with an elephant and two horses, caparisoned with silver and gilt ornaments and velvet embroidered housings, with *twenty-one shields* [1] of shawls, brocades, muslins, and jewels ; to prince Umra, unable from sickness to attend his father, a horse and *eleven shields* ; and to his brother, the second prince, Juvan Sing, a horse and *nine shields* ; to the ministers and chiefs according to rank : the whole entertainment costing about 20,000 rupees, or £2000. Amidst these ceremonials, receiving and returning visits of the Rana, his chiefs, his ministers, and men of influence and information commercial and agricultural, some weeks passed in silent observation, and in the acquisition of materials for action.[2]

[1] The buckler is the tray in which gifts are presented by the Rajpoots.

[2] If we dare compare the moral economy of an entire people to the physical economy of the individual, we should liken this period in the history of Méwar to intermittent pulsation of the heart—a pause in moral as in physical existence ; a consciousness thereof, inertly awaiting the propelling power to restore healthful action to a state of languid repose ; or what the Rajpoot would better comprehend, his own condition when the opiate stimulant begins to dissipate, and mind and body are alike abandoned to helpless imbecility. Who has lived out of the circle of mere vegetation, and not experienced this temporary deprivation of moral vitality ? for no other simile would suit the painful pause in the sympathies of the inhabitants of this once fertile region, where experience could point out but one page in their annals, one period in their history, when the clangour of the war trumpet was suspended, or the sword shut up in its scabbard. The

For the better comprehension of the internal relations, past and present, of Méwar, a sketch is presented, showing the political divisions of the tribes and the fiscal domain, from which a better idea may be formed of Rajpoot feudal economy than from a chapter of dissertation. The princes of Méwar skilfully availed themselves of their natural advantages in the partition of the country. The mountain-barriers east and west were allotted to the chiefs to keep the mountaineers and foresters in subjection, whose leading passes were held by a *lord-marcher*, and the quotas of his quarter; and while strong forts guarded the exposed northern and southern entrances, the crown-land lay in the centre, the safest and the richest. The exterior, thus guarded by a cordon of feudal levies composed of the quotas of the greater fiefs; the minor and most numerous class of vassals, termed *gole*, literally "the mass," and consisting of ten thousand horse, each holding directly of the crown independent of the greater chiefs, formed its best security against both external aggression and internal commotions.

Such is a picture of the feudal economy of Méwar in the days of her renown; but so much had it been defaced through time and accident, that with difficulty could the lineaments be traced with a view to their restoration: her institutions a dead letter, the prince's authority despised, the nobles demoralised and rebellious, internal commerce abandoned, and the peasantry destroyed by the combined operation of war, pestilence, and exile. Expression might be racked for phrases which could adequately delineate the miseries all classes had endured. It is impossible to give more than a sketch of the state of the *dos sches Méwar*, 'the ten thousand townships' which once acknowledged her princes, and of which above three thousand still exist. All that remained to them was the valley of the capital; and though Cheetore and Mandelgurh were maintained by the fidelity of the Rana's servants, their precarious revenues scarcely sufficed to maintain their garrisons. The Rana was mainly indebted to Zalim Sing of Kotah for the means of subsistence; for in the struggle for existence his chiefs thought only of themselves, of defending their own estates, or buying off their foes; while those who had succumbed took to horse, scoured the country, and plundered without distinction. Inferior clanships declared themselves independent of their superiors, who in their turn usurped the crown domain, or by bribing the necessities of their prince, obtained his patent for lands, to which, as they yielded him nothing, he became indifferent. The crown-tenants purchased of these chiefs the protection (*rekwalee*) which the Rana could not grant, and made alienations of the *crown taxes*, besides private rights of the community, which were often extorted at the point of the lance. Feuds multiplied, and the name

portals of Janus at Rome were closed but twice in a period of seven hundred years; and in exactly the same time from the conquest by Shabudín to the great pacification, but twice can we record peace in Méwar—the reign of Numa has its type in Shah Jehan, while the more appropriate reign of Augustus belongs to Britain. Are we to wonder then that a chilling void now occupied (if the solecism is admissible) the place of interminable action? when the mind was released from the anxiety of daily, hourly, devising schemes of preservation, to one of perfect security,—that enervating calm, in which, to use their own homely phrase, *Bhér aur bakri iki thâli sa pia*, 'the wolf and the goat drank from the same vessel.' But this unruffled torpidity had its limit: the Agrarian laws of Méwar were but mentioned, and the national pulse instantly rose.

of each clan became the watchword of alarm or defiance to its neighbour: castles were assaulted, and their inmates, as at Seogurh and Lawah, put to the sword; the Méras and Bhils descended from their hills, or emerged from their forests, and planted ambuscades for the traveller or merchant, whom they robbed or carried to their retreats, where they languished in durance till ransomed. Marriage processions were thus intercepted, and the honeymoon was passed on a cliff of the Aravulli, or in the forests on the Myhie. The Rajpoot, whose moral energies were blunted, scrupled not to associate and to divide the spoil with these lawless tribes, of whom it might be said, as of the children of Ishmael, "Their hands were against every man, and every man's hand against them." Yet notwithstanding such entire disorganisation of society, external commerce was not stagnant; and in the midst of this rapine, the produce of Europe and Cashmere would pass each other in transit through Méwar, loaded it is true by a multiplicity of exactions, but guarded by those who scorned all law but the *point of honour*, which they were paid for preserving.

The capital will serve as a specimen of the country. Oodipoor, which formerly reckoned fifty thousand houses within the walls, had not now three thousand occupied, the rest were in ruin, the rafters being taken for fire-wood. The realisation of the spring harvest of 1818, from the entire fiscal land, was about £4000! Grain sold for seven seers the rupee, though thrice the quantity was procurable within the distance of eighty miles. Insurance from the capital to Nat'hdwara (twenty-five miles) was eight per cent. The Kotario chief, whose ancestors are immortalised for fidelity, had not a horse to conduct him to his prince's presence, though his estates were of fifty thousand rupees annual value. All were in ruins; and the Rana, the descendant of those patriot Rajpoots who opposed Baber, Akber, and Arungzéb, in the days of Mogul splendour, had not fifty horse to attend him, and was indebted for all the comforts he possessed to the liberality of Kotah.

Such was the chaos from which order was to be evoked. But the elements of prosperity, though scattered, were not extinct; and recollections of the past deeply engraved in the national mind, became available to reanimate their moral and physical existence. To call these forth demanded only the exertion of moral interference, and every other was rejected. The lawless freebooter, and even the savage Bhil, felt awed at the agency of a power never seen. To him moral opinion (compared with which the strength of armies is nought) was inexplicable, and he substituted in its stead another invisible power—that of magic: and the belief was current throughout the intricate region of the West, that a single individual could carry an army in his pocket, and that our power could animate slips of paper cut into the figures of armed men, from which no precaution could guard their retreats. Accordingly, at the mere name of the British power, rapine ceased, and the inhabitants of the wilds of the West, the "forest lords," who had hitherto laughed at subjection, to the number of seven hundred villages, put each the sign of the dagger to a treaty, promising abstinence from plunder and a return to industrious life—a single individual of no rank the negotiator. Moreover, the treaty was religiously kept for twelve months; when the peace was broken, not by them, but against them.

To the Rajpoot, the moral spectacle of a Péshwa marched into exile with all the quietude of a pilgrimage, effected more than twenty thousand bayonets, and no other auxiliary was required than the judicious use of the impressions from this and other passing events, to relay the foundations of order and prosperity—by never doubting the issue, success was insured. The British force, therefore, after the reduction of the plans enumerated, was marched to cantonments ; the rest was left for time and reason to accomplish.

Before proceeding further, it may be convenient to sketch the form of civil government in Méwar, and the characters of its most conspicuous members : the former we shall describe as it was when the machine was in regular action ; it will be found simple, and perfectly suited to its object.

There are four grand officers of the government :—

1. The Purdhan, or prime minister.
2. Bukshee, commander of the forces.
3. Soorutnama, keeper of the records.
4. Suhaie, keeper of the signet.[1]

The first, the Purdhan, or civil premier, must be of the non-militant tribe. The whole of the territorial and financial arrangements are vested in him. He nominates the civil governors of districts, and the collectors of the revenue and custom ; and has fourteen *thoás*, or departments, under him, which embrace all that relates to expenditure.

2. The Bukshee must also be of a non-militant tribe, and one different from the Purdhan. His duties are mixed civil and military. He takes the musters, and pays mercenaries, or rations, to the feudal tenants when on extra service, and he appoints a deputy to accompany all expeditions, or to head frontier-posts, with the title of *foujdar*, or commander. The royal insignia, the standard, and kettle-drums accompany him, and the highest nobles assemble under the general control of this civil officer, never under one of their own body. From the Bukshee's bureau all patents are issued, as also all letters of sequestration of feudal land.

The Bukshee has four secretaries :—

1. Draws out deeds.
2. Accountant.
3. Recorder of all patents or grants.
4. Keeps duplicates.

3. The Soorutnama is the auditor and recorder of all the household expenditure and establishments, which are paid by his cheques. He has four assistants also, who make a daily report, and give a daily balance of accounts.

4. The Suhaie. He is secretary both for home and foreign correspondence. He draws out the royal grants or patents of estates, and superintends the deeds of grant on copper-plate to religious establishments. Since the privilege appertaining to Saloombra, of confirming all royal grants with his signet *the lance*, has fallen into desuetude, the *Suhaie* executes this military autograph.[2]

[1] Or rather, who makes the monogrammatic signet "*Suhaie*," to all deeds, grants, etc.

[2] The Saloombra chief had his deputy, who resided at court for this sole duty, for which he held a village. See p. 164.

To all decrees, from the daily stipend to the *putta*, or patent of an estate, each minister must append his seal, so that there is a complete system of check. Besides these, the higher officers of government, there are thirty-six *karkhanas*, or inferior officers, appointed directly by the Rana, the most conspicuous of which are the justiciary,[1] the keepers of the register-office, of the mint, of the armoury, of the regalia, of the jewels, of the wardrobe, of the statutes, of the kitchen, of the band, of the seneschalsy, and of the seraglio.

There was no want of aspirants to office, here hereditary; but it was vain to look amongst the descendants of the virtuous Pancholi, or the severe Umrachund, and the prediction of the former, " Dust will cover the head of Méwar when virtue wanders in rags," was strictly fulfilled. There appeared no talent, no influence, no honesty; yet the deficiency was calculated to excite sorrow rather than surprise; to stimulate exertion on their behalf, rather than damp the hope of improvement; though all scope for action, save in the field of intrigue, was lost, and talent was dormant for want of exercise.

The Rana's character was little calculated to supply his minister's deficiencies. Though perfectly versed in the past history of his country, its resources, and their management; though able, wise, and amiable, his talents were nullified by numerous weak points. Vain shows, frivolous amusements, and an ill-regulated liberality alone occupied him; and so long as he could gratify these propensities, he trusted complacently to the exertions of others for the restoration of order and his proper authority. He had little steadiness of purpose, and was particularly obnoxious to female influence. It is scarcely to be wondered that he coveted repose, and was little desirous to disturb the only moment his existence had presented of enjoying it, by inviting the turmoils of business. No man, however, was more capable of advising: his judgment was good, but he seldom followed its dictates; in short, he was an adept in theory, and a novice in practice. The only man about the court at once of integrity and efficiency was Kishen-das, who had long acted as ambassador, and to whose assiduity the sovereign and the country owed much; but his services were soon cut off by death.

Such were the materials with which the work of reform commenced. The aim was to bring back matters to a correspondence with an era of their history, when the rights of the prince, the vassal, and the cultivator, were alike well defined—that of Umra Sing.

The first point to effect was the recognition of the prince's authority by his nobles; the surest sign of which was their presence at the capital, where some had never been, and others only when it suited their convenience or their views. In a few weeks the Rana saw himself surrounded by a court such as had not been known for half a century. It created no small curiosity to learn by what secret power they were brought into each other's presence. Even the lawless Hamira, who but a short while before had plundered the marriage dower of the Hari queen coming from Kotah, and the chief of the Sungawut clan, who had sworn " he might bend his head to woman, but never to his sovereign," left their castles of Bhadaiser and Deogurh, and " placing the royal rescript on their heads," hastened to

[1] Neeyao, Duftur, Taksala, Silleh, Gadi, Gyna, Kapra-bindár, Ghora, Rusora, Nákár-khaneh, Julaib, Rawula.

his presence ; and in a few weeks the whole feudal association of Méwar was embodied in the capital.

To recall the exiled population was a measure simultaneous with the assembling of the nobles ; but this was a work requiring time : they had formed ties, and incurred obligations to the societies which had sheltered them, which could not at once be disengaged or annulled. But wherever a subject of Méwar existed, proclamations penetrated, and satisfactory assurances were obtained, and realised to an extent which belied in the strongest manner the assertion that patriotism is unknown to the natives of Hindust'han. The most enthusiastic and cheering proofs were afforded that neither oppression from without, nor tyranny within, could expel the feeling for the '*bápóta*,' the land of their fathers. Even now, though time has chastened the impressions, we should fear to pen but a tithe of the proofs of devotion of the husbandman of Méwar to the *solum natale* : it would be deemed romance by those who never contemplated humanity in its reflux from misery and despair to the 'sweet influences' of hope ; he alone who had witnessed the day of trouble, and beheld the progress of desolation—the standing corn grazed by Mahratta horse—the rifled towns devoted to the flames—the cattle driven to the camp, and the chief men seized as hostages for money never to be realised—could appreciate their deliverance. To be permitted to see these evils banished, to behold the survivors of oppression congregated from the most distant provinces, many of them strangers to each other, and the aged and the helpless awaiting the *lucky day* to take possession of their ruined abodes, was a sight which memory will not part with. Thus on the 3rd of Sawun (*July*), a favourite day with the husbandman, three hundred of all conditions, with their waggons and implements of labour, and preceded by banners and music, marched into Kupasun ; and *Ganésa* was once again invoked as they reconsecrated their dwellings, and placed his portrait as the Janus of the portals. On the same day, and within eight months subsequent to the signature of the treaty, above three hundred towns and villages were *simultaneously* reinhabited ; and the land, which for many years had been a stranger to the plough-share, was broken up. Well might the superstitious fancy that miracles were abroad ; for even to those who beheld the work in progression it had a magical result, to see the waste covered with habitations, and the verdant corn growing in the fields where lately they had roused the boar from his retreat ! It was a day of pride for Britain ! By such exertions of her power in these distant lands her sway is hallowed. By Britain alone can this fair picture be defaced ; the tranquillity and independence she has conferred, by her alone may be disturbed !

To these important preliminary measures, the assembly of the nobles and recall of the population, was added a third, without which the former would have been nugatory. There was no wealth, no capital, to aid their patriotism and industry. Foreign merchants and bankers had abandoned the devoted land ; and those who belonged to it partook of her poverty and her shame. Money was scarce, and want of faith and credit had increased the usury on loans to a ruinous extent. The Rana borrowed at thirty-six per cent. ; besides twenty-five to forty per cent. discount for his *báráts*, or patents empowering collection on the land ; a system pursued for some time even after his restoration to authority. His profusion exceeded even the rapidity of renovation ; and the husbandman had scarcely broken up his long-waste fields, when a call was made by the harpies of the state for an advance on their produce, while he himself had been compelled to borrow at a like ruinous rate for seed and the means of support, to be paid by expectations. To have hoped for the revival of prosperity amidst such destitution, moral and pecuniary, would have been visionary. It was as necessary to improve the one as to find the other ; for poverty and virtue do not long associate, and certainly not in Méwar. Proclamations were therefore prepared by the Rana, inviting foreign merchants and bankers to establish connections in the chief towns throughout the country ; but as in the days of demoralisation little faith was placed in the words of princes, similar ones were prepared by the Agent, guaranteeing the stipulations, and both were distributed to every commercial city in India. The result was as had been foreseen : branch banks were everywhere formed, and mercantile agents fixed in every town in the country, whose operations were only limited by the slow growth of moral improvement. The shackles which bound external commerce were at once removed, and the multifarious posts for the collections of transit duties abolished ; in lieu of which chain of stations, all levies on goods in transit were confined to the frontiers. The scale of duties was revised ; and by the abolition of intermediate posts, they underwent a reduction of from thirty to fifty per cent. By this system, which could not for some time be comprehended, the transit and custom duties of Méwar made the most certain part of the revenue, and in a few years exceeded in amount what had ever been known.

The chief commercial mart, Bhilwara, which showed not a vestige of humanity, rapidly rose from ruin, and in a few months contained twelve hundred houses, half of which were occupied by foreign merchants. Bales of goods, the produce of the most distant lands, were piled up in the streets lately overgrown with grass, and a weekly fair was established for the home manufactures. A charter of privileges and immunities was issued, exempting them from all taxation for the first year, and graduating the scale for the future ; calculated with the same regard to improvement, by giving the mind the full range of enjoying the reward of its exertions. The right of electing their own chief magistrates and the assessors of justice, was above all things indispensable, so as to render them as independent as possible of the needy servants of the court. A guard was provided by the government for their protection, and a competent authority nominated to see that the full extent of their privileges, and the utmost freedom of action, were religiously maintained. The entire success of this plan may at once be recorded to prevent repetition. In 1822, Bhilwara contained nearly three thousand dwellings, which were chiefly inhabited by merchants, bankers, or artisans. An entire new street had been constructed in the centre of the town, from the duties levied, and the shops and houses were rented at a moderate rate ; while many were given up to the proprietors of their sites, returning from exile, on their paying the price of construction. But as there is no happiness without alloy, so even this pleasing picture had its dark shades to chasten the too sanguine expectation of imparting happiness to all. Instead of a generous emulation, a jealous competition checked the prosperity of Bhilwara : the base spirit of exclusive monopoly desired a distinction between the native and the stranger-merchant, for which they had a precedent in the latter paying an addition to the town-duty of metage (*mápá*). The unreasonableness of this was discussed, and it was shown to be more consonant to justice that he who came from Jessulmér, Surát, Benares, or Dehli, should pay less than the merchant whose domicile was on the spot. When at length the parties acquiesced in this opinion, and were intreated and promised to know none other distinction than that of "inhabitant of Bhilwara," sectarian differences, which there was less hope of reconciling, became the cause of disunion. All the Hindu merchants belong either to the Vishnu or Jain sects; consequently each had a representative head, and "*the five*" for the adjudication of their internal arrangements; and these, the wise men of both parties, formed the general council for the affairs of Bhilwara. But they carried their religious differences to the judgment-seat, where each desired pre-eminence. Whether the point in dispute hinged on the interpretation of law, which with all these sects is of divine origin, or whether the mammon of unrighteousness was the lurking cause of their bickerings, they assuredly did much harm, for their appeals brought into play what of all things was least desired, the intrigues of the profligate dependents of the court. It will be seen hereafter,[1] in visits to Bhilwara, how these disputes were in some degree calmed. The leaders on both sides were distinctly given to understand they would be made to leave the place. Self-interest prevented this extremity; but from the withdrawing of that active interference (which the state of the alliance did not indeed warrant, but which humanity interposed for their benefit) together with the effect of appeals to the court, it is to be apprehended that Bhilwara may fail to become what it was intended to be, the chief commercial mart of Central India.[2]

Of the three measures simultaneously projected and pursued for the restoration of prosperity, the industrious portion has been described. The feudal interest remains, which was found the most difficult to arrange. The agricultural and commercial classes required only protection and stimulus, and we could repay the benefits their industry conferred by the lowest scale of taxation, which, though in fact equally beneficial to the government, was constructed as a boon. But with the feudal lords there was no such equivalent to offer in return for the sacrifices many had to make for the re-establishment of society. Those who were well inclined, like Kotario, had everything to gain, and nothing left to surrender; while those who, like Deogurh, Saloombra, or Bednore, had preserved their power by foreign aid, intrigue, or prowess, dreaded the high price they might be called upon to pay for the benefit of security which the new alliance conferred. All dreaded the word 'restitution,' and the audit of half a century's political accounts; yet the adjustment of these was the corner-stone of the edifice,

[1] In the Personal Narrative.

[2] Although Bhilwara has not attained that high prosperity my enthusiasm anticipated, yet the philanthropic Heber records that in 1825 (three years after I had left the country) it exhibited "a greater appearance of trade, industry, and moderate but widely diffused wealth and comfort, than he had witnessed since he left Dehli." The record of the sentiments of the inhabitants towards me, as conveyed by the bishop, was gratifying, though their expression could excite no surprise in any one acquainted with the characters and sensibilities of these people.

which anarchy and oppression had dismantled. Feuds were to be appeased, a difficult and hazardous task; and usurpations, both on the crown and each other, to be redeemed. "To bring the wolf and the goat to drink from the same vessel," was a task of less difficulty than to make the Chondawut and Suktawut labour in concert for the welfare of the prince and the country. In fine, a better idea cannot be afforded of what was deemed the hopelessness of success than the opinion of Zoorawur Sing, the chief of the latter clan, who had much to relinquish: "Were *Purmeswara* (the Almighty) to descend, he could not reform Méwar." We judged better of them than they did of each other.

It were superfluous to detail all the preparatory measures for the accomplishment of this grand object; the meetings and adjournments, which only served to keep alive discontent. On the 27th of April, the treaty with the British government was read, and the consequent change in their relations explained. Meanwhile, a charter, defining the respective rights of the crown and of the chiefs, with their duties to the community, was prepared, and a day named for a general assembly of the chieftains to sanction and ratify this engagement. The 1st of May was fixed: the chiefs assembled; the articles, ten in number, were read and warmly discussed; when with unmeaning expressions of duty, and objections to the least prominent, they obtained through their speaker, Goculdas of Deogurh, permission to re-assemble at his house to consider them, and broke up with the promise to attend next day. The delay, as apprehended, only generated opposition, and the 2nd and 3rd passed in intercommunications of individual hope and fear. It was important to put an end to speculation. At noon, on the 4th of May, the grand hall was again filled, when the Rana, with his sons and ministers, took their seats. Once more the articles were read, objections raised and combatted, and midnight had arrived without the object of the meeting being advanced, when an adjournment, proposed by Goculdas, till the arrival of the Rana's plenipotentiary from Dehli, met with a firm denial; and the Rana gave him liberty to retire, if he refused his testimony of loyalty. The Beygoo chief, who had much to gain, at length set the example, followed by the chiefs of Amait and Deogurh, and in succession by all the sixteen nobles, who also signed as the proxies of their relatives, unable from sickness to attend. The most powerful of the second grade also signed for themselves and the absent of their clans, each, as he gave in his adhesion, retiring; and it was three in the morning of the 5th of May ere the ceremony was over. The chief of the Suktawuts, determined to be conspicuous, was the last of his own class to sign. During this lengthened and painful discussion of fifteen hours' continuance, the Rana conducted himself with such judgment and firmness, as to give sanguine hopes of his taking the lead in the settlement of his affairs.

This preliminary adjusted, it was important that the stipulations of the treaty [1] should be rigidly if not rapidly effected. It will not be a matter of surprise, that some months passed away before the complicated arrangements arising out of this settlement were completed; but it may afford just

[1] A literal translation of this curious piece of Hindu legislation will be found at p. 170. If not drawn up with all the dignity of the legal enactments of the great governments of the West, it has an important advantage in conciseness; the articles cannot be misinterpreted, and require no lawyer to expound them.

grounds for gratulation, that they were finally accomplished without a shot being fired, or the exhibition of a single British soldier in the country, nor, indeed, within one hundred miles of Oodipoor. " Opinion " was the sole and all-sufficient ally effecting this political reform. The Rajpoots, in fact, did not require the demonstration of our physical strength ; its influence had reached far beyond Méwar. When the few firelocks defeated hundreds of the foes of public tranquillity, they attributed it to *"the strength of the Company's salt,"* [1] the moral agency of which was proclaimed the true basis of our power. " *Sach'ha Raj* " was the proud epithet applied by our new allies to the British government in the East ; a title which distinguished the immortal Alfred, " the upright."

It will readily be imagined that a reform, which went to touch the entire feudal association, could not be accomplished without harassing and painful discussions, when the object was the renunciation of lands, to which in some cases the right of inheritance could be pleaded, in others, the cognisance of successful revenge, while to many prescriptive possession could be asserted. It was the more painful, because although the shades which marked the acquisition of such lands were varied, no distinction could be made in the mode of settlement, namely, unconditional surrender. In some cases, the Rana had to revoke his own grants, wrung either from his necessities or his weakness ; but in neither predicament could arguments be adduced to soften renunciation, or to meet the powerful and pathetic, and often angry appeals to justice or to prejudice. Counter-appeals to their loyalty, and the necessity for the re-establishment of their sovereign's just weight and influence in the social body, without which their own welfare could not be secured, were adduced ; but individual views and passions were too absorbing to bend to the general interest. Weeks thus passed in interchange of visits, in soothing pride, and in flattering vanity by the revival of past recollections, which gradually familiarised the subject to the mind of the chiefs, and brought them to compliance. Time, conciliation, and impartial justice, confirmed the victory thus obtained ; and when they were made to see that no interest was overlooked, that party views were unknown, and that the system included every class of society in its beneficial operation, cordiality followed concession. Some of these cessions were alienations from the crown of half a century's duration. Individual cases of hardship were unavoidable without incurring the imputation of favouritism, and the

[1] " *Compani Saheb ca nimuk ca zoor sa* " is a common phrase of our native soldiery ; and " *Dowahi ! Compani ca !* " is an invocation or appeal against injustice ; but I never heard this watch-word so powerfully applied as when a *Sub.* with the Resident's escort in 1812. One of our men, a noble young Rajpoot about nineteen years of age, and six feet high, had been sent with an elephant to forage in the wilds of Nirwur. A band of at least fifty predatory horsemen assailed him, and demanded the surrender of the elephant, which he met by pointing his musket and giving them defiance. Beset on all sides, he fired, was cut down, and left for dead, in which state he was found, and brought to camp upon a litter. One sabre-cut had opened the back entirely across, exposing the action of the viscera, and his arms and wrists were barbarously hacked : yet he was firm, collected, and even cheerful ; and to a kind reproach for his rashness, he said, " What would you have said, Captain Sahib, had I surrendered the Company's musket (*compani ca bandooq*) without fighting ? " From their temperate habits, the wound in the back did well ; but the severed nerves of the wrists brought on a lockjaw of which he died. The Company have thousands who would alike die for their *bandooq*. It were wise to cherish such feelings.

dreaded revival of ancient feuds, to abolish which was indispensable, but required much circumspection. Castles and lands in this predicament could therefore neither be retained by the possessor nor returned to the ancient proprietor without rekindling the torch of civil war. The sole alternative was for the crown to take the object of contention, and make compensation from its own domain. It would be alike tedious and uninteresting to enter into the details of these arrangements, where one chief had to relinquish the levy of transit duties in the most important outlet of the country, asserted to have been held during seven generations, as in the case of the chief of Deogurh. Of another (the Bheendir chief) who held *forty-three towns and villages,* in addition to his grant ; of Amait, of Bhadaiser, of Dabla, of Lawah, and many others who held important fortresses of the crown independent of its will ; and other claims, embracing every right and privilege appertaining to feudal society ; suffice it, that in six months the whole arrangements were effected.

In the painful and protracted discussions attendant on these arrangements, powerful traits of national character were developed. The castle and domain of Arjah half a century ago belonged to the crown, but had been usurped by the Poorawuts, from whom it was wrested by storm about fifteen years back by the Suktawuts, and a patent sanctioning possession was obtained, on the payment of a fine of £1000 to the Rana. Its surrender was now required from Futteh Sing, the second brother of Bheendir, the head of this clan ; but being regarded as the victorious completion of a feud, it was not easy to silence their prejudices and objections. The renunciation of the forty-three towns and villages by the chief of the clan caused not half the excitation, and every Suktawut seemed to forego his individual losses in the common sentiment expressed by their head : "Arjah is the price of blood, and with its cession our honour is surrendered." To preserve the point of honour, it was stipulated that it should not revert to the Poorawuts, but be incorporated with the fisc, which granted an equivalent ; when letters of surrender were signed by both brothers, whose conduct throughout was manly and confiding.

The Bednore and Amait chiefs, both of the superior grade of nobles, were the most formidable obstacles to the operation of the treaty of the 4th of May. The first of these, by name Jeyt Sing (*the victorious lion*), was of the Mairtea clan, the bravest of the brave race of Rahtore, whose ancestors had left their native abodes on the plains of Marwar, and accompanied the celebrated Meera Bae on her marriage with Rana Koombho. His descendants, amongst whom was Jeimul, of immortal memory, enjoyed honour in Méwar equal to their birth and high deserts. It was the more difficult to treat with men like these, whose conduct had been a contrast to the general license of the times, and who had reason to feel offended, when no distinction was observed between them and those who had disgraced the name of Rajpoot. Instead of the submission expected from the Rahtore, so overwhelmed was he from the magnitude of the claims, which amounted to a virtual extinction of his power, that he begged leave to resign his estates and quit the country. In prosecution of this design, he took post in the chief hall of the palace, from which no entreaties could make him move ; until the Rana, to escape his importunities, and even restraint, obtained his promise to abide by the decision of the Agent. The forms of the Rana's court, from time immemorial, prohibit all personal communication between the sovereign and his chiefs in matters of individual interest, by which indecorous altercation is avoided. But the ministers, whose office it was to obtain every information, did not make a rigid scrutiny into the title-deeds of the various estates previous to advancing the claims of the crown. This brave man had enemies, and he was too proud to have recourse to the common arts either of adulation or bribery to aid his cause. It was a satisfaction to find that the two principal towns demanded of him were embodied in a grant of Singram Sing's reign; and the absolute rights of the fisc, of which he had become possessed, were cut down to about fifteen thousand rupees of annual revenue. But there were other points on which he was even more tenacious than the surrender of these. Being the chief noble of the fine district of Bednore, which consisted of three hundred and sixty towns and villages, chiefly of feudal allotments (many of them of his own clan), he had taken advantage of the times to establish his influence over them, to assume the right of wardship of minors, and secure those services which were due to the prince, but which he wanted the power to enforce. The holders of these estates were of the third class of vassals or *gole* (the mass), whose services it was important to reclaim, and who constituted in past times the most efficient force of the Ranas, and were the preponderating balance of their authority when mercenaries were unknown in these patriarchal states. Abundant means towards a just investigation had been previously procured; and after some discussion, in which all admissible claims were recognised, and argument was silenced by incontrovertible facts, this chieftain relinquished all that was demanded, and sent in, as from himself, his written renunciation to his sovereign. However convincing the data by which his proper rights and those of his prince were defined, it was to feeling and prejudice that we were mainly indebted for so satisfactory an adjustment. An appeal to the name of Jeimul, who fell defending Cheetore against Akber,[1] and the contrast of his ancestor's loyalty and devotion with his own contumacy, acted as a talisman, and wrung tears from his eyes and the deed from his hand. It will afford some idea of the difficulties encountered, as well as the invidiousness of the task of arbitrating such matters, to give his own comment verbatim: "I remained faithful when his own kin deserted him, and was one of four chiefs who alone of all Méwar fought for him in the rebellion; but the son of Jeimul is forgotten, while the '*plunderer*' is his boon companion, and though of inferior rank, receives an estate which elevates him above me;" alluding to the chief of Bhadaiser, who plundered the queen's dower. But while the brave descendant of Jeimul returned to Bednore with the marks of his sovereign's favour, and the applause of those he esteemed, the '*runner*' went back to Bhadaiser in disgrace, to which his prince's injudicious favour further contributed.

Hamira of Bhadaiser was of the second class of nobles, a Chondawut by birth. He succeeded to his father Sirdar Sing, the assassin of the prime minister even in the palace of his sovereign;[2] into whose presence he had the audacity to pursue the surviving brother, destined to avenge

[1] See p. 262. [2] See p. 351 and note.

him.[1] Hamira inherited all the turbulence and disaffection, with the estates, of his father; and this most conspicuous of the many lawless chieftains of the times was known throughout Rajast'han as Hamira '*the runner*' (*douraet*). Though not entitled to hold lands beyond thirty thousand annually, he had become possessed to the amount of eighty thousand, chiefly of the fisc or *khalisa*, and nearly all obtained by violence, though since confirmed by the prince's patent. With the chieftain of Lawah (precisely in the same predicament), who held the fortress of Khyroda and other valuable lands, Hamira resided entirely at the palace, and obtaining the Rana's ear by professions of obedience, kept possession, while chiefs in every respect his superiors had been compelled to surrender; and when at length the Suktawut of Lawah was forbid the court until Khyroda and all his usurpations were yielded up, the son of Sirdar displayed his usual turbulence, "curled his moustache" at the minister, and hinted at the fate of his predecessor. Although none dared to imitate him, his stubbornness was not without admirers, especially among his own clan; and as it was too evident that fear or favour swayed the Rana, it was a case for the Agent's interference, the opportunity for which was soon afforded. When forced to give letters of surrender, the Rana's functionaries, who went to take possession, were insulted, refused admittance, and compelled to return. Not a moment could be lost in punishing this contempt of authority; and as the Rana was holding a court when the report arrived, the Agent requested an audience. He found the Rana and his chiefs assembled in "the balcony of the sun," and amongst them the notorious Hamira. After the usual compliments, the Agent asked the minister if his master had been put in possession of Sianoh. It was evident from the general constraint, that all were acquainted with the result of the deputation; but to remove responsibility from the minister, the Agent, addressing the Rana as if he were in ignorance of the insult, related the transaction, and observed that his government would hold him culpable if he remained at Oodipoor while his highness's commands were disregarded. Thus supported, the Rana resumed his dignity, and in forcible language signified to all present his anxious desire to do nothing which was harsh or ungracious; but that, thus compelled, he would not recede from what became him as their sovereign. Calling for a *beera*, he looked sternly at Hamira, and commanded him to quit his presence instantly, and the capital in an hour; and, but for the Agent's interposition, he would have been banished the country. Confiscation of his whole estate was commanded, until renunciation was completed. He departed that

[1] It will fill up the picture of the times to relate the revenge. When Jamshid, the infamous lieutenant of the infamous Meer Khan, established his headquarters at Oodipoor, which he daily devastated, Sirdar Sing, then in power, was seized and confined as a hostage for the payment of thirty thousand rupees demanded of the Rana. The surviving brothers of the murdered minister Somji "*purchased their foe*" with the sum demanded, and anticipated his clansmen, who were on the point of effecting his liberation. The same sun shone on the head of Sirdar, which was placed as a signal of revenge over the gateway of Rampearie's palace. I had the anecdotes from the minister Scaloll, one of the actors in these tragedies, and a relative of the brothers, who were all swept away by the dagger. A similar fate often seemed to him, though a brave man, inevitable during these resumptions; which impression, added to the Rana's known inconstancy of favour, robbed him of half his energies.

night; and, contrary to expectation, not only were all the usurpations surrendered, but, what was scarcely contemplated by the Agent, the Rana's flag of sequestration was quietly admitted into the fortress of Bhadaiser.[1]

One more anecdote may suffice. The lands and fortress of Amlee had been in the family of Amait since the year 27, only five years posterior to the date to which these arrangements extended; their possession verged on half a century. The lords of Amait were of the sixteen, and were chiefs of the clan Jugawat. The present representative enjoyed a fair character: he could, with the chief of Bednore, claim the succession of the loyal; for Pertáp and Jeimul, their respective ancestors, were rivals and martyrs on that memorable day when the genius of Cheetore abandoned the Seesodias. But the heir of Amait had not this alone to support his claims; for his predecessor Pertáp had lost his life in defending his country against the Mahrattas, and Amlee had been his acquisition. Futteh Sing (such was his name) was put forward by the more artful of his immediate kin, the Chondawut interest; but his disposition, blunt and impetuous, was little calculated to promote their views: he was an honest Rajpoot, who neither could nor cared to conceal his anger, and at a ceremonious visit paid him by the Agent, he had hardly sufficient control over himself to be courteous, and though he said nothing, his eyes, inflamed with opium and disdain, spoke his feelings. He maintained a dogged indifference, and was inaccessible to argument, till at length, following the example of Bednore, he was induced to abide by the Agent's mediation. He came attended by his vassals, who anxiously awaited the result, which an unpremeditated incident facilitated. After a long and fruitless expostulation, he had taken refuge in an obstinate silence; and seated in a chair opposite to the envoy, with his shield in front, placed perpendicularly on his knees, and his arms and head reclined thereon, he continued vacantly looking on the ground. To interrupt this uncourteous silence in his own house, the envoy took a picture, which with several others was at hand, and placing it before him, remarked, "*That* chief did not gain his reputation for *swamdherma*[2] (loyalty) by conduct such as yours." His eyes suddenly recovered their animation and his countenance was lighted with a smile, as he rapidly uttered, "How did you come by this—why does this interest you?" A tear started in his eye as he added, "This is my father!"—"Yes," said the Agent, "it is the loyal Pertáp on the day he went forth to meet his death; but his name yet lives, and a stranger does homage to his fame."—"Take Amlee, take Amlee," he hurriedly repeated, with a suppressed tone of exultation and sorrow, "but forget not the extent of the sacrifice." To prolong the visit would have been painful to both, but as it might have been trusting too much

[1] Nearly twelve months after this, my public duty called me to Neembahaira *en route* to Kotah. The castle of Hamira was within an hour's ride, and at night he was reported as having arrived to visit me, when I appointed the next day to receive him. Early next morning, according to custom, I took my ride, with four of Skinner's horse, and galloped past him, stretched with his followers on the ground not far from my camp, towards his fort. He came to me after breakfast, called me his greatest friend, "swore by his dagger he was my Rajpoot," and that he would be in future obedient and loyal; but this, I fear, can never be.

[2] Literally faith (*dherma*) to his lord (*swama*).

to humanity to delay the resumption, the Agent availed himself of the moment to indite the *choorchitti* [1] of surrender for the lands.

With these instances, characteristic of individuals and the times, this sketch of the introductory measures for improving the condition of Méwar may be closed. To enter more largely in detail is foreign to the purpose of the work; nor is it requisite for the comprehension of the unity of the object, that a more minute dissection of the parts should be afforded. Before, however, we exhibit the general results of these arrangements, we shall revert to the condition of the more humble, but a most important part of the community, the peasantry of Méwar; and embody, in a few remarks, the fruits of observation or inquiry, as to their past and present state, their rights, the establishment of them, their infringement, and restitution. On this subject much has been necessarily introduced in the sketch of the feudal system, where landed tenures were discussed; but it is one on which such a contrariety of opinion exists, that it may be desirable to show the exact state of landed tenures in a country, where Hindu manners should exist in greater purity than in any other part of the vast continent of India.

The ryot (*cultivator*) is the proprietor of the soil in Méwar. He compares his right therein to the *a'khye d'hooba*,[2] which no vicissitudes can destroy. He calls the land his *bápóta*, the most emphatic, the most ancient, the most cherished, and the most significant phrase his language commands for *patrimonial* [3] *inheritance*. He has nature and Menu in support of his claim, and can quote the text, alike compulsory on prince and peasant, "*cultivated* land is the property of him who cut away the wood, or *who cleared and tilled it*." [4] an ordinance binding on the whole Hindu race, and which no international wars, or conquest, could overturn. In accordance with this principle is the ancient adage, not of Méwar only but all Rajpootana, *Bhóg ra dhanni Raj ho: bhom rá dhanni ma cho*: 'the government is owner of the rent, but I am the master of the land.' With the toleration and benevolence of the race the conqueror is commanded "to respect the deities adored by the conquered, also their virtuous priests, and *to establish the laws of the conquered nation as declared in their books*." [5] If it were deemed desirable to recede to the system of pure Hindu agrarian law, there is no deficiency of materials. The customary laws contained in the various reports of able men, superadded to the general ordinances of Menu, would form a code at once simple and efficient: for though innovation from foreign conquest has placed many principles in abeyance, and modified others, yet he has observed to little purpose who does not trace a uniformity of design,

[1] Paper of relinquishment.

[2] The *d'hooba* grass flourishes in all seasons, and most in the intense heats; it is not only *amara* or 'immortal,' but *a'khye*, 'not to be eradicated'; and its tenacity to the soil deserves the distinction.

[3] From *bap* 'father,' and the termination *ot*, or *belonging to*, and by which clans are distinguished; as *Kurrunsote*, 'descended of Kurrun'; *Mansingote*, 'descended of Mansing.' It is curious enough that the mountain clans of Albania, and other Greeks, have the same distinguishing termination, and the Mainote of Greece and the Mairote of Rajpootana alike signify *mountaineer*, or 'of the mountain,' *maina* in Albanian; *maira* or *méra* in Sanscrit.

[4] Text 44. On the *Servile Classes*, Menu; Haughton's edition.

[5] On Government, text 201–3.

which at one time had ramified wherever the name of Hindu prevailed: language has been modified, and terms have been corrupted or changed, but the primary pervading principle is yet perceptible; and whether we examine the systems of Candeish, the Carnatic, or Rajast'han, we shall discover the elements to be the same.

If we consider the system from the period described by Arrian, Curtius, and Diodorus, we shall see in the government of townships each commune an '*imperium in imperio*'; a little republic, maintaining its municipal legislation independent of the monarchy, on which it relies for general support, and to which it pays the *bhóg*, or *tax in kind*, as the price of this protection; for though the prescribed duties of kings are as well defined by Menu [1] as by any jurisconsult in Europe, nothing can be more lax than the mutual relations of the governed and governing in Hindu monarchies, which are resolved into unbounded liberty of action. To the artificial regulation of society, which leaves all who depend on manual exertion to an immutable degradation, must be ascribed these multitudinous governments, unknown to the rest of mankind, which, in spite of such dislocation, maintain the bonds of mutual sympathies. Strictly speaking, every state presents the picture of so many hundred or thousand minute republics, without any connection with each other, giving allegiance (*án*) and rent (*bhóg*) to a prince, who neither legislates for them, nor even forms a police for their internal protection. It is consequent on this want of paramount interference that, in matters of police, of justice, and of law, the communes act for themselves; and from this want of paternal interference only have arisen those courts of equity, or arbitration, the '*punchaets*.'

But to return to the *freehold* ryot of Méwar, whose *bápóta* is the *wuttun* and the *meerás* of the peninsula,—words of foreign growth, introduced by the Mahomedan conquerors; the first (Persian) is of more general use in Candeish; the other (Arabic) in the Carnatic. Thus the great Persian moralist Sadi exemplifies its application: "If you desire to succeed to your father's inheritance (*meerás*), first obtain his wisdom."

While the term *bápóta* thus implies the inheritance or patrimony, its holder, if a military vassal, is called 'Bhomia,' a term equally powerful, meaning one actually identified with the soil (*bhom*), and for which the Mahomedan has no equivalent but in the possessive compound *wuttun-dár*, or *meeras-dár*. The *Caniatchi* [2] of Malabar is the *Bhomia* of Rajast'han.

The emperors of Dehli, in the zenith of their power, bestowed the epithet 'zemindar' upon the Hindu tributary sovereigns: not out of disrespect, but in the true application of their own term '*Bhomia Raj*,'

[1] "Let the king receive his annual revenue through his collectors; but let him observe the divine ordinances, and *act as a father* to his people." Text 80.—"*To protect the people*, and to honour the priests, are the highest duties of kings, and ensures them felicity." 88.—"*From the people* he must learn the theory of agriculture, commerce, and practical arts." 43.—To those who imagine that these ancient monarchies are simply despotic, instead of patriarchal, their divine legislator expressly declares, that "a king addicted to vices (which tend to misrule) may lose even his life *from the public resentment*." 46.—"*The Duties of Kings*."

[2] *Cani* 'land,' and *atchi* 'heritage': *Report*, p. 289.—I should be inclined to imagine the *atchi*, like the *ote* and *awut*, Rajpoot terminations, implying clanship.

expressive of their tenacity to the soil; and this fact affords additional evidence of the proprietary right being in the cultivator (*ryot*), namely, that he alone can confer the freehold *land*, which gives the title of *Bhomia*, and of which both past history and present usage will furnish us with examples. When the tenure of land obtained from the cultivator is held more valid than the grant of the sovereign, it will be deemed a conclusive argument of the proprietary right being vested in the ryot. What should induce a chieftain, when inducted into a perpetual fief, to establish through the ryot a right *to a few acres in bhom*, but the knowledge that although the vicissitudes of fortune or of favour may deprive him of his aggregate signiorial rights, his claims, derived from the spontaneous favour of the commune, can never be set aside; and when he ceases to be the lord, he becomes a member of the commonwealth, merging his title of Thacoor, or Signior, into the more humble one of Bhomia, the allodial tenant of the Rajpoot feudal system, elsewhere discussed.[1] Thus we have touched on the method by which he acquires this distinction, for protecting the community from violence; and if left destitute by the negligence or inability of the government, he is vested with the rights of the crown, in its share of the *bhóg* or rent. But when their own land is in the predicament called '*gult'has*,' or reversions from lapses to the commune, he is '*seised*' in all the rights of the former proprietor; or, by internal arrangements, they can convey such right by cession of the commune.

The privilege attached to the *bhom*,[1] and acquired from the community by the protection afforded to it, is the most powerful argument for the recognition of its original rights. The bhomia, thus vested, may at pleasure drive his own plough, the right to the soil. His *bhom* is exempt from the *jureeb* (measuring rod); it is never assessed, and his only sign of allegiance is a quit-rent, in most cases triennial, and the tax of *khur-lakur*,[2] a war imposition, now commuted for money. The state, however, indirectly receives the services of these allodial tenants, the yeomen of Rajast'han, who constitute, as in the districts of Komulmér and Mandelgurh, the *landwehr*, or local militia. In fact, since the days of universal repose set in, and the townships required no protection, an arrangement was made with the Bhomias of Méwar, in which the crown, foregoing its claim of quit-rent, has obtained their services in the garrisons and frontier stations of police at a very slight pecuniary sacrifice.

Such are the rights and privileges derived from the ryot cultivator alone. The Rana may dispossess the chiefs of Bednore, or Saloombra, of their estates, the grant of the crown—he could not touch the rights emanating from the community; and thus the descendants of a chieftain, who a few years before might have followed his sovereign at the head of one hundred cavaliers, would descend into the humble foot militia of a district. Thousands are in this predicament: the Kanawuts, Loonawuts, Koombhawuts, and other clans, who, like the Celt, forget not their claims of birth in the distinctions of fortune, but assert their propinquity as "brothers in the nineteenth or thirtieth degree to the prince" on the throne. So sacred was the tenure derived from the ryot, that even monarchs held lands in *bhom* from their subjects, for an instance of which we are indebted to the great poetic historian of the last Hindu king. Chund relates, that

[1] See p. 170.

[2] See Sketch of Feudal System.

when his sovereign, the Chohan, had subjugated the kingdom of Anhulwarra [1] from the Solanki, he returned to the nephew of the conquered prince several districts and seaports, and *all the bhom held by the family.* In short, the Rajpoot vaunts his aristocratic distinction derived from the land; and opposes the title of '*Bhomia Raj*,' or government of the soil, to the '*Bania Raj*,' or commercial government, which he affixes as an epithet of contempt to Jeipoor: where "wealth accumulates and men decay."

In the great "register of patents" (*putta buhye*) of Méwar, we find a species of *bhom* held by the greater vassals on particular crown lands; whether this originated from inability of ceding entire townships to complete the estate to the rank of the incumbent, or whether it was merely in confirmation of the grant of the commune, could not be ascertained. The benefit from this *bhom* is only pecuniary, and the title is 'bhom rekwalee' [2] or *land* [in return for] 'preservation.' Strange to say, the crown itself holds '*bhom rekwalee*' on its own fiscal demesnes consisting of small portions in each village, to the amount of ten thousand rupees in a district of thirty or forty townships. This species, however, is so incongruous that we can only state it does exist: we should vainly seek the cause for such apparent absurdity, for since society has been unhinged, the oracles are mute to much of antiquated custom.

We shall close these remarks with some illustrative traditions and yet existing customs, to substantiate the ryot's right in the soil of Méwar. After one of those convulsions described in the annals, the prince had gone to espouse the daughter of the Raja of Mundore, the (then) capital of Marwar. It is customary at the moment of "*hátléva*," or the junction of hands, that any request preferred by the bridegroom to the father of the bride should meet compliance, a usage which has yielded many fatal results; and the Rana had been prompted on this occasion to demand a body of ten thousand Jat cultivators to repeople the deserted fisc of Méwar. An assent was given to the unprecedented demand, but when the inhabitants were thus despotically called on to migrate, they denied the power and refused. "Shall we," said they, "abandon the lands of our inheritance (*bápóta*), the property of our children, to accompany a stranger into a foreign land, there to labour for him? Kill us you may, but never shall we relinguish our inalienable rights." The Mundore prince, who had trusted to this reply, deemed himself exonerated from his promise, and secured from the loss of so many subjects: but he was deceived. The Rana held out to them the enjoyment of the proprietary rights escheated to the crown in his country, with the lands left without occupants by the sword, and to all, increase of property. When equal and absolute power was thus conferred, they no longer hesitated to exchange the arid soil of Marwar for the garden of Rajwarra; and the descendants of these Jats still occupy the flats watered by the Béris and Bunas.

In those districts which afforded protection from innovation, the proprietary right of the ryot will be found in full force; of this the populous and extensive district of Jehajpoor, consisting of one hundred and six

[1] Nehrwala of D'Anville; the Balhara sovereignty of the Arabian travellers of the eighth and ninth centuries. I visited the remains of this city on my last journey, and from original authorities shall give an account of this ancient emporium of commerce and literature.

[2] *Salvamenta* of the European system.

townships, affords a good specimen. There are but two pieces of land throughout the whole of this tract the property of the crown, and these were obtained by force during the occupancy of Zalim Sing of Kotah. The right thus unjustly acquired was, from the conscientiousness of the Rana's civil governor, on the point of being annulled by sale and reversion, when the court interfered to maintain its proprietary right to the tanks of Lohario and Etounda, and the lands which they irrigate, now the *bhom* of the Rana.[1] This will serve as an illustration how *bhom* may be acquired, and the annals of Kotah will exhibit, unhappily for the Ryots of that country, the almost total annihilation of their rights, by the same summary process which originally attached Lohario to the fisc.

The power of alienation being thus proved, it would be superfluous to insist further on the proprietary right of the cultivator of the soil.

Besides the ability to alienate as demonstrated, all the overt symbols which mark the proprietary right in other countries are to be found in Méwar; that of entire conveyance by sale, or temporary by mortgage; and numerous instances could be adduced, especially of the latter. The fertile lands of Horlah, along the banks of the Khary, are almost all mortgaged, and the registers of these transactions form two considerable volumes, in which great variety of deeds may be discovered: one extended for one hundred and one years; [2] when redemption was to follow, without regard to interest on the one hand, or the benefits from the land on the other, but merely by repayment of the sum borrowed. To maintain the interest during abeyance, it is generally stipulated that a certain portion of the harvest shall be reserved for the mortgagee—a fourth, a fifth, or '*googri*,'—a share so small as to be valued only as a mark of proprietary recognition.[3] The mortgagees were chiefly of the commercial classes of the large frontier towns; in many cases the proprietor continues to cultivate for another the lands his ancestor mortgaged four or five generations ago, nor does he deem his right at all impaired. A plan had been sketched to raise money to redeem these mortgages, from whose complex operation the revenue was sure to suffer. No length of time or absence can affect the claim to the *bápóta*, and so sacred is the right of absentees, that land will lay sterile and unproductive from the penalty which Menu denounces on all who interfere with their neighbour's rights: "for unless there be an especial agreement between the owner of the land and the seed, the fruits belongs clearly to the land-owner"; even "if seed conveyed by water or by wind should germinate, the plant belongs to the land-owner, *the mere sower* takes not the fruit."[4] Even crime and the extreme sentence of the law will not alter succession to property, either to the military or cultivat-

[1] The author has to acknowledge with regret, that he was the cause of the Meena proprietors not re-obtaining their *bápóta*: this arose, partly from ignorance at the time, partly from the individual claimants being dead, and more than all, from the representation that the intended sale originated in a bribe to Sudda-Ram the governor, which, however, was not the case.

[2] Claims to the *bápóta* appear to be maintainable if not alienated longer than one hundred and one years; and undisturbed possession (no matter how obtained) for the same period appears to confer this right. The *meeras* of Candeish appears to have been on the same footing. See Mr. Elphinstone's *Report*.

[3] The *sawmy begum* of the peninsula in *Fifth Report*, pp. 356–57; correctly *swami bhoga*, 'lord's rent,' in Sanscrit.

[4] Menu, 52–54, on the *Servile Classes*.

ing vassal ; and the old Kentish adage, probably introduced by the Jats from Scandinavia, who under Hengist established that kingdom of the heptarchy, namely—

"The father to the bough,
And the son to the plough."

is practically understood by the Jats and Bhomias [1] of Méwar, whose treason is not deemed hereditary, nor a chain of noble acts destroyed because a false link was thrown out. We speak of the military vassals—the cultivator cannot aspire to so dignified a crime as treason.

The officers of the townships are the same as have been so often described, and are already too familiar to those interested in the subject to require illustration. From the Patél, the Cromwell of each township, to the village gossip, the ascetic Sanyasi, each deems his office, and the land he holds in virtue thereof in perpetuity, free of rent to the state, except a small triennial quit-rent,[2] and the liability, like every other branch of the state, to two war taxes.[3]

Opinions are various as to the origin and attributes of the Patél, the most important personage in village sway, whose office is by many deemed foreign to the pure Hindu system, and to which language even his title is deemed alien. But there is no doubt that both office and title are of ancient growth, and even etymological rule proves the Patél to be head (*páti*) of the community.[4] The office of Patél of Méwar was originally elective ; he was "*primus inter pares,*" the constituted attorney or representative of the commune, and as the medium between the cultivator and the government, enjoyed benefits from both. Besides his *bápóta*, and the *seerano*, or one-fortieth of all produce from the ryot, he had a remission of a third or fourth of the rent from such extra lands as he might cultivate in addition to his patrimony. Such was the Patél, the link connecting the peasant with the government, ere predatory war subverted all order : but as rapine increased, so did his authority. He became the plenipotentiary of the community, the security for the contribution imposed, and often the hostage for its payment, remaining in the camp of the predatory hordes till they were paid off. He gladly undertook the liquidation of such contributions as these perpetual invaders imposed. To indemnify himself, a schedule was formed of the share of each ryot, and mortgage of land, and sequestration of personal effects followed till his avarice was satisfied. Who dared complain against a Patél, the intimate of Pat'han and Mahratta commanders, his adopted patrons ? He thus became the master of his fellow-citizens ; and, as power corrupts all men, their tyrant instead of their mediator. It was a system necessarily involving its own decay ; for a while glutted with plenty, but failing with the supply, and

[1] Patél. [2] Patél *burrar.*

[3] The Ghur-geenti *burrar,* and Khur-lakur, or *wood and forage,* explained in the Feudal System.

[4] In copper-plate grants dug from the ruins of the ancient Oojein (presented to the Royal Asiatic Society), the prince's patents (*putta*) conferring gifts are addressed to the *Patta-cilas* and Ryots. I never heard an etymology of this word, but imagine it to be from *patta* 'grant,' or '*patent,*' and *cila,* which means a nail, or sharp instrument ; metaphorically, that which binds or unites these patents ; all, however, having *páti,* or chief, as the basis.—See *Transactions of the Royal Asiatic Society,* vol. i. p. 237.

ending in desolation, exile, and death. Nothing was left to prey on but the despoiled carcase ; yet when peace returned, and in its train the exile ryot to reclaim the *bápóta*, the vampire Patél was resuscitated, and evinced the same ardour for supremacy, and the same cupidity which had so materially aided to convert the fertile Méwar to a desert. The Patél accordingly proved one of the chief obstacles to returning prosperity ; and the attempt to reduce this corrupted *middle-man* to his original station in society was both difficult and hazardous, from the support they met in the corrupt officers at court, and other influences " behind the curtain." A system of renting the crown lands being deemed the most expedient to advance prosperity, it was incumbent to find a remedy for this evil. The mere name of some of these petty tyrants inspired such terror, as to check all desire of return to the country ; but the origin of the institution of the office and its abuses being ascertained, it was imperative, though difficult, to restore the one and banish the other. The original elective right in many townships was therefore returned to the ryot, who nominated new Patéls, his choice being confirmed by the Rana, in whose presence investiture was performed by binding a turban on the elected, for which he presented his *nuzzur*. Traces of the sale of these offices in past times were observable ; and it was deemed of primary importance to avoid all such channels for corruption, in order that the ryot's election should meet with no obstacle. That the plan was beneficial there could be no doubt ; that the benefit would be permanent, depended, unfortunately, on circumstances which those most anxious had not the means to control : for it must be recollected, that although " personal aid and advice might be given when asked," all internal interference was by treaty strictly, and most justly, prohibited.

After a few remarks on the mode of levying the crown-rents, we shall conclude the subject of village economy in Méwar, and proceed to close this too extended chapter with the results of four years of peace and the consequent improved prosperity.

There are two methods of levying the revenues of the crown on every description of corn—*kunkoot* and *bhuttaie* , for on sugar-cane, poppy, oil, hemp, tobacco, cotton, indigo, and garden stuffs, a money payment is fixed, varying from two to six rupees per beegah. The *kunkoot* is a conjectural assessment of the standing crop, by the united judgment of the officers of government, the Patél, the Patwarri, or registrar, and the owner of the field. The accuracy with which an accustomed eye will determine the quantity of grain on a given surface is surprising : but should the owner deem the estimate overrated, he can insist on *bhuttaie*, or division of the corn after it is threshed ; the most ancient and only infallible mode by which the dues either of the government or the husbandman can be ascertained. In the *bhuttaie* system, the share of the government varies from one-third to two-fifths of the spring harvest, as wheat and barley ; and sometimes even half, which is the invariable proportion of the autumnal crops. In either case, *kunkoot* or *bhuttaie*, when the shares are appropriated, those of the crown may be commuted to a money payment at the average rate of the market. The *koot* is the most liable to curruption. The ryot bribes the collector, who will underrate the crop ; and when he betrays his duty, the *shanah*, or watchman, is not likely to be honest : and as the *mukhee*, or Indian corn, the grand autumnal crop of Méwar, is eaten green, the crown may be defrauded of half its dues. The system is one of uncertainty, from which eventually the ryot derives no advantage, though it fosters the cupidity of patéls and collectors; but there was a *burrar*, or tax, introduced to make up for this deficiency, which was in proportion to the quantity cultivated, and its amount at the mercy of the officers. Thus the ryot went to work with a mill-stone round his neck; instead of the exhilarating reflection that every hour's additional labour was his own, he saw merely the advantage of these harpies, and contented himself with raising a scanty subsistence in a slovenly and indolent manner, by which he forfeited the ancient reputation of the Jat cultivator of Méwar.

Notwithstanding these and various other drawbacks to the prosperity of the country, in an impoverished court, avaricious and corrupt officers, discontented patéls, and bad seasons, yet the final report in May 1822 could not but be gratifying when contrasted with that of February 1818. In order to ascertain the progressive improvement, a census had been made at the end of 1821, of the three central fiscal districts [1] watered by the Béris and Bunas. As a specimen of the whole, we may take the *tuppa* or sub-division of Sahara. Of its twenty-seven villages, six were inhabited in 1818, the number of families being *three hundred* and sixty-nine, three-fourths of whom belonged to the resumed town of Amlee. In 1821 *nine hundred* and twenty-six families were reported, and every village of the twenty-seven was occupied, so that population had almost trebled. The number of ploughs was more than trebled, and cultivation quadrupled; and though this, from the causes described, was not above one-third of what real industry might have effected, the contrast was abundantly cheering. The same ratio of prosperity applied to the entire crown demesne of Méwar. By the recovery of Komulmér, Raepoor, Rajnuggur, and Sadi-Kunéro from the Mahrattas; of Jehajpoor from Kotah; of the usurpations of the nôbles; together with the resumption of all the estates of the females of his family, a task at once difficult and delicate; [2] and by the subjugation of the mountain districts of Mairwarra, a thousand towns and villages were united to form the fiscal demesne of the Rana, composing twenty-four districts of various magnitudes, divided, as in ancient times, and with the primitive appellations, into portions tantamount to the tithings and hundreds of England, the division from time immemorial amongst the Hindus.[3] From these and the commercial duties [4] a revenue was derived sufficient for the comforts, and even the dignities of the prince and his court, and promising an annual increase in the ratio of good government: but profusion scattered all that industry and ingenuity could collect; the artificial wants of the prince perpetuated the real necessities of the

[1] Mooé, Burruk, and Kupassun.

[2] To effect this, indispensable alike for unity of government and the establishment of a police, the individual statements of their holders were taken for the revenues they had derived from them, and money payments three times the amount were adjudged to them. They were gainers by this arrangement, and were soon loaded with jewels and ornaments, but the numerous train of harpies who cheated them and abused the poor ryot, were eternally at work to defeat all such beneficial schemes; and the counteraction of the intrigues was painful and disgusting.

[3] Menu ordains the division into tens, hundreds, and thousands.

[4] Farmed for the ensuing three years from 1822, for seven lakhs of rupees.

peasant, and this, it is to be feared, will continue till the present generation shall sleep with their forefathers.

Abstract of the Fiscal Revenues of Méwar in the years 1818–19–20–21–22.

Spring harvest of 1818	. .	Rs. 40,000	
,, 1819	. .	451,281	
,, 1820	. .	659,100	
,, 1821	. .	1,018,478	
,, 1822	. .	936,640	The active superintendence of the British Agent being almost entirely withdrawn.

Abstract of Commercial Duties included in the above.

In 1818	. . .	*Nominal*	
1819	. . .	Rs. 96,683	
1820	. . .	165,108	
1821	. . .	220,000	Farmed for three years from 1822, for 750,000 rupees, which was assigned by the Rana for the liquidation of tribute fallen in arrear.
1822	. . .	217,000	

There are sources of wealth in Méwar yet untouched, and to which her princes owe much of their power. The tin mines of Jawura and Dureeba alone, little more than half a century ago, yielded above three lakhs annually;[1] besides rich copper mines in various parts. From such, beyond a doubt, much of the wealth of Méwar was extracted, but the miners are now dead, and the mines filled with water. An attempt was made to work them, but it was so unprofitable that the design was soon abandoned.

Nothing will better exemplify the progress of prosperity, than the comparative population of some of the chief towns before, and after, four years of peace:—

	No. of houses in 1818.	No. of houses in 1822.
Oodipoor	3,500	10,000
Bhilwara	*not one*	2,700
Poorh	200	1,200
Mandel	80	400
Gosoonda	60	350

The feudal lands, which were then double the fiscal, did not exhibit the like improvement, the merchant and cultivator residing thereon not having the same certainty of reaping the fruits of their industry; still great amelioration took place, and few were so blind as not to see their account in it.[2] The earnestness with which many requested the Agent to back their expressed intentions with his guarantee to their communities of the same measure of justice and protection as the fiscal tenants enjoyed, was proof that they well understood the benefits of reciprocal confidence; but this could not be tendered without danger. Before the Agent left

[1] In S. 1816, Jawara yielded Rs. 222,000 and Dureeba Rs. 80,000. The tin of these mines contains a portion of silver.

[2] There are between two and three thousand towns, villages, and hamlets, besides the fiscal land of Méwar; but the tribute of the British government is derived only from the fiscal; it would have been impossible to collect from the feudal lands, which are burthened with service, and form the army of the state.

the country he greatly withdrew from active interference, it being his constant, as it was his last impressive lesson, that they should rely upon themselves if they desired to retain a shadow of independence. To give an idea of the improved police, insurance which has been described as amounting to eight per cent. in a space of twenty-five miles, became almost nominal, or cne-fourth of a rupee per cent. from one frontier to the other. It would, however, have been quite Utopian to have expected that the lawless tribes would remain in that stupid subordination which the unexampled state of society imposed for a time (as described in the opening of these transactions), when they found that real restraints did not follow imaginary terrors. Had the wild tribes been under the sole influence of British power, nothing would have been so simple as effectually, not only to control, but to conciliate and improve them; for it is a mortifying truth, that the more remote from civilisation, the more tractable and easy was the object to manage, more especially the Bhil.[1] But these children of nature were incorporated in the demesnes of the feudal chiefs, who when they found our system did not extend to perpetual control, returned to their old habits of oppression: this provoked retaliation, which to subdue requires more power than the Rana yet possesses, and, in the anomalous state of our alliances, will always be an embarrassing task to whosoever may exercise political control.

In conclusion, it is to be hoped that the years of oppression that have swept the land will be held in remembrance by the protecting power, and that neither petulance nor indolence will lessen the benevolence which restored life to Méwar, or mar the picture of comparative happiness it created.

[1] Sir John Malcolm's wise and philanthropic measures for the reclamation of this race in Malwa will support my assertions.

The Sixteen chief Nobles of Méwar, their Titles, Names, Clans, Tribes, Estates, number of Villages in each, and their Value.

Title.	Names.	Clan.	Tribe.	Estate.	Number of Villages.	Value, A.D. 1760.	REMARKS.
Raj	Chundun Sing	Jhala	Jhala	Sadri	127	100,000	These estates are all diminished one-half in nominal amount; and their revenues still more.
Rao	Pertáp Sing	Chohan	Chohan	Baidla	80	100,000	
Rao	Mokim Sing	Chohan	Chohan	Kotario	65	80,000	
Rawut	Pudma Sing	Chondawut	Seesodia	Saloombra	85	84,000	Would realise this if cultivated.
Thacoor	Zorawur Sing	Mairtea	Rahtore	Ganora	100	100,000	This chief ceases to be one of the 16 since the Rana lost the province of Godwar.
Rao	Késudás	—	Pramar	Bijollí	40	45,000	Would realise this if cultivated.
Rawut	Gokuldás	Sangawut	Seesodia	Deogurh	125	80,000	Would realise more if cultivated.
Rawut	Maha Sing	Mégawut	Seesodia	Beygoo	150	200,00	This includes usurpations —now seized by Sindia. The estate would realise 70,000 if cultivated.
Raj	Kalian Sing	Jhala	Jahla	Dailwarra	125	100,000	Would realise two-thirds if cultivated.
Rawut	Salim Sing	Jugawut	Seesodia	Amait	60	60,000	Do., do.
Raj	Chutter Sál	Jhala	Jhala	Gogoonda	50	50,000	Would realise this if cultivated.
Rawut	Futteh Sing	Sarangdéote	Seesodia	Kanorh	50	95,000	Would realise half if cultivated.
Mahraja	Zorawur Sing	Suktawut	Seesodia	Bheendir	64	64,000	Would realise this if cultivated.
Thacoor	Jeyt Sing	Mairtea	Rahtore	Bednore	80	80,000	Do., do.
Rawut	Salim Sing	Suktawut	Seesodia	Bansi	40	40,000	These chiefs have lost all their influence and half their estates.
Rao	Soorajmul	Chohan	Chohan	Parsoli	40	40,000	
Rawut	Kesuri Sing	Kishenawut	Seesodia	Bhynsror	60	60,000	These chiefs have taken rank on the depression of the above — they never appear at court on the same day.
Rawut	Jowan Sing	Kishenawut	Seesodia	Korabur	35	35,000	
Total number and estimated value of their estates sixty years ago, omitting Bhynsror and Korabur, then enrolled in the second grade of chieftains.					1,181	1,310,000	

Note.—The inferior grades possessed estates to a still larger amount, conjointly yielding a revenue of thirty lakhs of rupees; and as each thousand rupees of estate furnished on emergency three horses completely equipped, the feudal interest could supply nine thousand horse besides foot, of which they make little account.

RELIGIOUS ESTABLISHMENTS, FESTIVALS, AND CUSTOMS OF MÉWAR

CHAPTER XIX

Influence of the hierarchy in Rajpootana—Emulation of its princes in grants to the priesthood—Analogy between the customs of the Hindus, in this respect, and those of the ancient people—Superstition of the lower orders—Secret influence of the Brahmins on the higher classes—Their frauds—Ecclesiastical dues from the land, etc.—The Saivas of Rajast'han—The worship and shrine of Eklinga—The Jains—Their numbers and extensive power—The temple of Nat'hdwara, and worship of Kaniya—The privilege of Sanctuary—Predominance of the doctrines of Kaniya beneficial to Rajpoot society.

In all ages the ascendancy of the hierarchy is observable ; it is a tribute paid to religion through her organs. Could the lavish endowments and extensive immunities of the various religious establishments in Rajast'han be assumed as criteria of the morality of the inhabitants, we should be authorised to assign them a high station in the scale of excellence. But they more frequently prove the reverse of their position ; especially the territorial endowments, often the fruits of a death-bed repentance,[1] which, prompted by superstition or fear, compounds for past crimes by posthumous profusion, although vanity not rarely lends her powerful aid. There is scarcely a state in Rajpootana in which one-fifth of the soil is not assigned for the support of the temples, their ministers, the secular Brahmins, bards, and genealogists. But the evil was not always so extensive ; the abuse is of modern growth.

An anecdote related of the Rajas of Marwar and Ambér, always rivals in war, love, and folly, will illustrate the motives of these dismemberments. During the annual pilgrimage to the sacred lake of Poshkur, it is the custom for these lords of the earth to weigh their persons against all that is rare, in gold, gems, and precious cloths ; which are afterwards distributed to the priests. The Ambér chief had the advantage of a full treasury and a fertile soil, to which his rival could oppose a more extended sway over a braver race ; but his country was proverbially poor, and at Poshkur, the weight of the purse ranks above the deeds of the sword. As these princes were suspended in the scale, the Ambér Raja, who was balanced against the more costly material,

[1] Menu commands, " Should the king be near his end through some incurable disease, he must bestow on the priests all his riches accumulated from legal fines : and having duly committed his kingdom to his son, let him seek death in battle, or, if there be no war, by abstaining from food."—Chap. ix. p. 337, Haughton's edition. The annals of all the Rajpoot States afford instances of obedience to this text of their divine legislator.

indirectly taunted his brother-in-law on the poverty of his offerings, who would gladly, like the Roman, have made up the deficiency with his sword. But the Marwar prince had a minister of tact, at whose suggestion he challenged his rival (of Ambér) to equal him in the magnitude of his gift to the Brahmins. On the gage being accepted, the Rahtore exclaimed, "Perpetual charity (*sahsuna*) of all the lands held by the Brahmins in Marwar!" His unreflecting rival had commenced the redemption of his pledge, when his minister stopped the half-uttered vow, which would have impoverished the family for ever; for there were ten Brahmins in Ambér who followed secular employments, cultivating or holding lands in usufruct, to one in Marwar. Had these lords of the earth been left to their misguided vanity, the fisc of each state would have been seriously curtailed.

The Brahmins, Sanyasis, and Gosaéns are not behind those professional flatterers, the Bards; and many a princely name would have been forgotten but for the record of the gift of land. In Méwar, the lands in *sahsun*, or religious grants, amount in value to *one-fifth* of the revenue of the state, and the greater proportion of these has arisen out of the prodigal mismanagement of the last century. The dilapidated state of the country, on the general pacification in A.D. 1818, afforded a noble opportunity to redeem in part these alienations, without the penalty of denunciation attached to the resumer of sacred charities. But death, famine, and exile, which had left but few of the grantees in a capacity to return and re-occupy the lands, in vain coalesced to restore the fisc of Méwar. The Rana dreaded a "*sixty thousand years' residence in hell*," and some of the finest land of his country is doomed to remain unproductive. In this predicament is the township of Mynâr, with 50,000 bígahs (16,000 acres), which with the exception of a nook where some few have established themselves, claiming to be descendants of the original holders, are condemned to sterility, owing to the agricultural proprietors and the rent-receiving Brahmins being dead; and apathy united to superstition admits their claims without inquiry.

The antiquary, who has dipped into the records of the dark period in European church history, can have ocular illustration in Rajast'han of traditions which may in Europe appear questionable. The vision of the Bishop of Orleans,[1] who saw Charles Martel in the depths of hell, undergoing the tortures of the damned, for having stripped the churches of their possessions, "thereby rendering himself guilty of the sins of all those who had endowed them," would receive implicit credence from every Hindu, whose ecclesiastical economy might both yield and derive illustration from a comparison, not only with that of Europe, but with

[1] Saint Eucher, évêque d'Orléans, eut une vision qui étonna les princes. Il faut que je rapporte à ce sujet la lettre que les évêques, assemblés à Reims, écrivent à Louis-le-Germanique, qui étoit entré dans les terres de Charles-le-chauve, parcequ'elle est très-propre à nous faire voir quel étoit, dans ces temps-là, l'état des choses, et la situation des esprits. Ils disent que "Saint Eucher ayant été ravi dans le ciel, il vit Charles Martel tourmenté dans l'enfer inférieur par l'ordre des saints qui doivent assister avec Jésus-Christ au jugement dernier; qu'il avoit été condamné à cette peine avant le temps pour avoir dépouillé les églises de leurs biens, et s'être par là rendu coupable des péchés de tous ceux qui les avoient dotées."—Montesquieu, *l'Esprit des Lois*, livre xxxi. chap. xi. p. 460.

the more ancient Egyptian and Jewish systems, whose endowments, as explained by Moses and Ezekiel, bear a strong analogy to his own. The disposition of landed property in Egypt, as amongst the ancient Hindus, was immemorially vested in the cultivator; and it was only through Joseph's ministry in the famine, that "the land became Pharaoh's, as the Egyptians sold every man his field." [1] And the coincidence is manifest even in the tax imposed on them as occupants of their *inheritance*, being *one-fifth* of the crops to the king, while the maximum rate among the Hindus is a *sixth*.[2] The Hindus also, in visitations such as that which occasioned the dispossession of the *ryots* of Egypt, can mortgage or sell their patrimony (*bápóta*). Joseph did not attempt to infringe the privileges of the sacred order when the whole of Egypt became crown-land, "except the lands of the priests, which became not Pharaoh's;" and these priests, according to Diodorus, held for themselves and the sacrifices no less than *one-third* of the lands of Egypt. But we learn from Herodotus, that Sesostris, who ruled after Joseph's ministry, restored the lands to the people, reserving the customary tax or tribute.[3]

The prelates of the middle ages of Europe were often completely feudal nobles, swearing fealty and paying homage as did the lay lords.[4] In Rajast'han, the sacerdotal caste not bound to the altar may hold lands and perform the duties of vassalage: [5] but of late years, when land has been assigned to religious establishments, no reservation has been made of fiscal rights, territorial or commercial. This is, however, an innovation; since, formerly, princes never granted, along with territorial assignments, the prerogative of dispensing justice, of levying transit duties, or exemption from personal service of the feudal tenant who held on the land thus assigned. Well may Rajpoot heirs exclaim with the grandson of Clovis, "our exchequer is impoverished, and our riches are transferred to the clergy." [6] But Chilperic had the courage to recall the grants of his predecessors, which, however, the pious Gontram re-established. Many Gontrams could be found, though but few Chilperics, in Rajast'han: we have, indeed, one in Jograz, the Rana's ancestor, almost a contemporary of the Merovingian king, who not only resumed all the lands of the Brahmins, but put many of them to death, and expelled the rest his dominions.[7]

It may be doubted whether vanity and shame are not sufficient in themselves to prevent a resumption of the lands of the *Mangtas* or mendicants, as they style all those "who extend the palm," without the dreaded penalty, which operates very slightly on the sub-vassal or cultivator, who, having no superfluity, defies their anathemas when they attempt to wrest from him, by virtue of the crown-grant, any of his long-established rights. By these, the threat of impure transmigration

[1] Genesis, chap. xlvii. 20. [2] Menu, chap. vii.

[3] *Origin of Laws and Government*, vol. i. p. 54, and vol. ii. p. 13.

[4] Hallam's *Middle Ages*, vol. ii. p. 212.

[5] " A Brahmin unable to subsist by his duties just mentioned (sacerdotal), may live by the duty of a soldier."—Menu, chap. x.

[6] Montesquieu.

[7] " Le clergé recevoit tant, qu'il faut que, dans les trois races, on lui ait donné plusieurs fois tous les biens du royaume. Mais si les rois, la noblesse, et le peuple, trouvèrent le moyen de leur donner tous leurs biens, ils ne trouvèrent pas moins celui de les leur ôter."—Montesquieu, *l'Esprit des Lois*, livre xxxi. chap. x.

is despised ; and the Brahmin may spill his blood on the threshold of his dwelling or in the field in dispute, which will be relinquished by the owner but with his life. The *Pat Raní*, or chief queen, on the death of prince Umra, the heir-apparent, in 1818, bestowed a grant of fifteen bígahs of land, in one of the central districts, on a Brahmin who had assisted in the funeral rites of her son. With grant in hand, he hastened to the Jat proprietor, and desired him to make over to him the patch of land. The latter coolly replied that he would give him all the prince had a right to, namely the tax. The Brahmin threatened to spill his own blood if he did not obey the command, and gave himself a gash in a limb ; but the Jat was inflexible, and declared that he would not surrender his patrimony (*bápóta*) even if he slew himself.[1] In short, the *ryot* of Méwar would reply, even to his sovereign, if he demanded his field, in the very words of Naboth to Ahab, king of Israel, when he demanded the vineyard contiguous to the palace : "The Lord forbid it me that I should give the *inheritance of my fathers* unto thee."

But the tithes, and other small and legally established rights of the hierarchy, are still religiously maintained. The village temple and the village priest are always objects of veneration to the industrious husbandman, on whom superstition acts more powerfully than on the bold marauding Rajpoot, who does not hesitate to demand *salvamenta* (*rekwalee*) from the lands of Kaniya or Eklinga. But the poor *ryot* of the nineteenth century of Vicrama has the same fears as the peasants of Charlemagne, who were made to believe that the ears of corn found empty had been devoured by infernal spirits, reported to have said they owed their feast to the non-payment of tithes.[2]

The political influence of the Brahmins is frequently exemplified in cases alike prejudicial to the interests of society and the personal welfare of the sovereign. The latter is often surrounded by lay-Brahmins as confidential servants, in the capacities of butler, keeper of the wardrobe, or seneschal,[3] besides the *Gúrú* or domestic chaplain, who to the duty of

[1] These worshippers of God and Mammon, when threats fail, have recourse to maiming, and even destroying themselves, to gain their object. In 1820, one of the confidential servants of the Rana demanded payment of the petty tax called *gǔgri*, of one rupee on each house, from some Brahmins who dwelt in the village, and which had always been received from them. They refused payment, and on being pressed, four of them stabbed themselves mortally. Their bodies were placed upon biers, and funeral rites withheld till punishment should be inflicted on the priest-killer. But for once superstition was disregarded, and the rights of the Brahmins in this community were resumed. See Appendix to this Part, No. I.

[2] Mais le bas peuple n'est guère capable d'abandonner ses intérêsts par des exemples. Le synode de Francfort lui présenta un motif plus pressant pour payer les dîmes. On y fit un capitulaire dans lequel il est dit que, dans la dernière famine, on avoit trouvé les épis de blé vides, qu'ils avoient été dévorés par les démons, et qu'on avoit entendu leurs voix qui reprochoient de n'avoir pas payé la dîme : et, en conséquence, il fut ordonné à tous ceux qui tenoient les biens ecclésiastiques de payer la dîme, et, en conséquence encore, on l'ordonna à tous. *L'Esprit des Lois*, livre XXXI. chap. XII.

[3] These lay Brahmins are not wanting in energy or courage ; the sword is as familiar to them as the *mala* (chaplet). The grandfather of Ramnat'h, the present worthy seneschal of the Rana, was governor of the turbulent district of Jehajpoor, which has never been so well ruled since. He left a curious piece of advice to his successors, inculcating vigorous measures. "With two thousand men you may eat *khitchri* ; with one thousand *dalb'hat* ; with five hundred *júti*

ghostly comforter sometimes joins that of astrologer and physician, in which case God help the prince ! [1] These *Gúrús* and *Purohits*, having the education of the children, acquire immense influence, and are not backward in improving " the greatness thrust upon them." They are all continually importuning their prince for grants of land for themselves and the shrines they are attached to ; and every chief, as well as every influential domestic, takes advantage of ephemeral favour to increase the endowments of his tutelary divinity. The Péshwas of Satarra are the most striking out of numerous examples.

In the dark ages of Europe the monks are said to have prostituted their knowledge of writing to the forging of charters in their own favour: a practice not easily detected in the days of ignorance.[2] The Brahmins, in like manner, do not scruple to employ this method of augmenting the wealth of their shrines ; and superstition and indolence combine to support the deception. There is not a doubt that the grand charter of Nat'hdwara was a forgery, in which the prince's butler was bribed to aid ; and report alleges that the Rana secretly favoured an artifice which regard to opinion prevented him from overtly promulgating. Although the copper-plate had been buried under ground, and came out disguised with a coating of verdigris, there were marks which proved the date of its execution to be false. I have seen charters which, it has been gravely asserted, were granted by Rama upwards of three thousand years ago ! Such is the origin assigned to one found in a well at the ancient Brimpoori, in the valley of the capital. If there be sceptics as to its validity, they are silent ones ; and this copper-plate of the brazen age is worth gold

(the *shoe*)." *Khitchri* is a savoury mess of pulse, rice, butter, and spices ; *dalb'hat* is simple rice and pulse ; *the shoe* is indelible disgrace.

[1] Menu, in his rules on government, commands the king to impart his momentous counsel and entrust all transactions to a learned and distinguished Brahmin. Chap. vii. p. 195.

There is no being more aristocratic in his ideas than the secular Brahmin or priest, who deems the bare name a passport to respect. The *Koolun* Brahmin of Bengal piques himself upon *this* title of nobility granted by the last Hindu king of Canouj (whence they migrated to Bengal), and in virtue of which his alliance in matrimony is courted. But although Menu has imposed obligations towards the Brahmin little short of adoration, these are limited to the " learned in the *Védas* " : he classes the unlearned Brahmin with " an elephant made of wood, or an antelope of leather " ; nullities, save in name. And he adds further, that " as liberality to a fool is useless, so is a Brahmin useless if he read not the holy texts " : comparing the person who gives to such an one, to a husbandman " who, sowing seed in a barren soil, reaps no gain ; " so the Brahmin " obtains no reward in heaven." These sentiments are repeated in numerous texts, holding out the most powerful inducements to the sacerdotal class to cultivate their minds, since their power consists solely in their wisdom. For such, there are no privileges too extensive, no homage too great. " A king, even though dying *with want*, must not receive any tax from a Brahmin learned in the *Védas*." His person is sacred. " Never shall the king slay a Brahmin, though convicted of all possible crimes," is a premium at least to unbounded insolence, and unfits them for members of society, more especially for soldiers : banishment, with person and property untouched, is the declared punishment for even the most heinous crimes. " A Brahmin may seize without hesitation, if he be distressed for a subsistence, the goods of his *Súdra* slave." But the following text is the climax : " What prince could gain wealth by oppressing these [Brahmins], who, if angry, could frame other worlds, and regents of worlds, and could give birth to new gods and mortals ? "—Menu, chaps. ii. iii. vii. viii. ix.

[2] Hallam's *Middle Ages*, vol. i. p. 204.

to the proprietor.[1] A census [2] of the three central districts of Méwar, discovered that more than twenty thousand acres of these fertile lands, irrigated by the Béris and Bunas rivers, were distributed in isolated portions, of which the mendicant castes had the chief share, and which proved fertile sources of dispute to the husbandman and the officers of the revenue. From the mass of title-deeds of every description by which these lands were held, one deserves to be selected, on account of its being pretended to have been written and bestowed on the incumbent's ancestor by the deity upwards of three centuries ago, and which has been maintained as a *bona-fide* grant of Crishna [3] ever since. By such credulity and apathy are the Rajpoot states influenced: yet let the reader check any rising feeling of contempt for Hindu legislation, and cast a retrospective glance at the page of European church history, where he will observe in the time of the most potent of our monarchs that the clergy possessed *one-half* of the soil: [4] and the chronicles of France will show him Charlemagne on his death-bed, bequeathing *two-thirds* of his domains to the church, deeming the remaining third sufficient for the ambition of four sons. The same dread of futurity, and the hope to expiate the sins of a life, at its close, by gifts to the organs of religion, is the motive for these unwise alienations, whether in Europe or in Asia. Some of these establishments, and particularly that at Nat'hdwara, made a proper use of their revenues in keeping up the *Sudda Birt*, or perpetual charity, though it is chiefly distributed to religious pilgrims: but among the many complaints made of the misapplication of the funds, the diminution of this hospitable right is one; while, at other shrines, the avarice of the priests is observable in the coarseness of the food dressed for sacrifice and offering.

Besides the crown-grants to the greater establishments, the Brahmins received petty tithes from the agriculturist, and a small duty from the trader, as *mappa* or metage, throughout every township, corresponding with the scale of the village-chapel. An inscription found by the author at the town of Palode,[5] and dated nearly seven centuries back, affords a good specimen of the claims of the village priesthood. The following are among the items. The *seerano*, or a *seer*, in every *maund*, being the fortieth part of the grain of the *oonálú*, or summer-harvest; the *kirpa*, or a bundle from every sheaf of the autumnal crops, whether *mukhi* (Indian corn), *bajra* or *joár* (maize), or the other grains peculiar to that season.[6]

They also derive a tithe from the oil-mill and sugar-mill, and receive a *khansa* or platter of food on all rejoicings, as births, marriages, etc., with *churaie*, or the right of pasturage on the village common; and where they have become possessed of landed property they have *hulmoh*, or

[1] These forgeries of charters cannot be considered as invalidating the arguments drawn from them, as we may rest assured nothing is introduced foreign to custom, in the items of the deeds.

[2] Suggested by the author, and executed under his superintendence, who waded through all these documents, and translated upwards of a hundred of the most curious.

[3] See the Appendix to this Part, No. II.

[4] Hallam.

[5] See Appendix to this Part, No. III.

[6] Each bundle consists of a specified number of ears, which are roasted and eaten in the unripe state with a little salt.

unpaid labour in man and beasts, and implements, for its culture: an exaction well known in Europe as one of the detested *corvées* of the feudal system of France,[1] the abolition of which was the sole boon the English husbandman obtained by the charter of Runymede. Both the chieftain and the priest exact *hulmoh* in Rajast'han; but in that country it is mitigated, and abuse is prevented, by a sentiment unknown to the feudal despot of the middle ages of Europe, and which, though difficult to define, acts imperceptibly, having its source in accordance of belief, patriarchal manners, and clannish attachments.

I shall now briefly consider the privileges of the Saivás and Jains—the orthodox and heterodox sects of Méwar; and then proceed to those of Vishnu, whose worship is the most prevalent in these countries, and which I am inclined to regard as of more recent origin.

Mahadeva, or Iswara, is the tutelary divinity of the Rajpoots in Méwar; and from the early annals of the dynasty appears to have been, with his consort Isani, the sole object of *Gehlote* adoration. Iswara is adored under the epithet of Eklinga,[2] and is either worshipped in his monolithic symbol, or as Iswara Chaomûkhi, the quadriform divinity, represented by a bust with four faces. The sacred bull, Nanda, has his altar attached to all the shrines of Iswara, as was that of Mneves or Apis to those of the Egyptian Osiris. Nanda has occasionally his separate shrines, and there is one in the valley of Oodipoor which has the reputation of being oracular as regards the seasons. The bull was the steed of Iswara, and carried him in battle; he is often represented upon it, with his consort Isa, at full speed. I will not stop to inquire whether the Grecian fable of the rape of Europa[3] by the tauriform Jupiter, may not be derived, with much more of their mythology, from the Hindu pantheon; whether that pantheon was originally erected on the Indus, or the Ganges, or the more central scene of early civilisation, the banks of the Oxus. The bull was offered to Mithras by the Persian, and opposed as it now appears to Hindu faith, he formerly bled on the altars of the Sun-god, on which not only the Buld-dan,[4] '*offering of the bull*,' was made, but human sacrifices.[5]

[1] *Dict. de l'Ancien Régime*, p. 131, art. "Corvée."

[2] That is, with *one* (*ek*) *lingam* or *phallus*—the symbol of worship being a single cylindrical or conical stone. There are others, termed *Seheslinga* and *Kot-iswara*, with a thousand or a million of phallic representatives, all minutely carved on the monolithic emblem, having then much resemblance to the symbol of Bacchus, whose orgies, both in Egypt and Greece, are the counterpart of those of the Hindu *Bagh-es*, thus called from being clad in a tiger's or leopard's hide: Bacchus had the panther's for his covering. There is a very ancient temple to Kotiswara at the *embouchure* of the eastern arm of the Indus; and here are many to Seheslinga in the peninsula of Saurashtra.

[3] It might have appeared fanciful, some time ago, to have given a Sanscrit derivation to a Greek proper name: but *Europa* might be derived from *Súrúpa*, 'of the beautiful face'—the initial syllable *su* and *eu* having the same signification in both languages, namely, *good*—*Rupa* is 'countenance.'

[4] "In this sacrifice four altars are erected, for offering the flesh to the four gods, Lacshmi-Narayana, U'mia-Mechéswar, Brimha, and Anunta. The nine planets, and Prit'hu, or the earth, with her ten guardian-deities, are worshipped. Five *Vilwú*, five *Khudiru*, five *Pulashu*, and five *Udumburu* posts are to be erected, and a bull tied to each post. Clarified butter is burnt on the altar, and pieces of the flesh of the slaughtered animals placed thereon. This sacrifice was very common."—Ward, *On the Religion of the Hindus*, vol. ii. p. 263.

[5] "First a covered altar is to be prepared; sixteen posts are then to be erected of various woods; a golden image of a man, and an iron one of a goat,

We do not learn that the Egyptian priesthood presented the kindred of Apis to Osiris, but as they were not prohibited from eating beef, they may have done so.

The shrine of Eklinga is situated in a defile about six miles north of Oodipoor. The hills towering around it on all sides are of the primitive formation. and their scarped summits are clustered with honeycombs.[1] There are abundant small springs of water, which keep verdant numerous shrubs, the flowers of which are acceptable to the deity; especially the *kinér* or oleander, which grows in great luxuriance on the Aravulli. Groves of bamboo and mango were formerly common, according to tradition; but although it is deemed sacrilege to thin the groves of Bál,[2] the bamboo has been nearly destroyed: there are, however, still many trees sacred to the deity scattered around. It would be difficult to convey a just idea of a temple so complicated in its details. It is of the form commonly styled pagoda, and, like all the ancient temples of Síva, its *sikra*, or pinnacle, is pyramidal. The various orders of Hindu sacred architecture are distinguished by the form of the *sikra*, which is the portion springing from and surmounting the perpendicular walls of the body of the temple. The *sikra* of those of Síva is invariably pyramidal, and its sides vary with the base, whether square or oblong. The apex is crowned with an ornamental figure, as a sphynx, an urn, a ball, or a lion, which is called the *kullus*. When the *sikra* is but the frustrum of a pyramid, it is often surmounted by a row of lions, as at Bijollí. The fane of Eklinga is of white marble and of ample dimensions. Under an open-vaulted temple supported by columns, and fronting the four-faced divinity, is the brazen bull Nanda, of the natural size; it is cast, and of excellent proportions. The figure is perfect, except where the shot or hammer of an infidel invader has penetrated its hollow flank in search of treasure. Within the quadrangle are miniature shrines, containing some of the minor divinities.[3]

with golden images of Vishnu and Lacshmi, a silver one of Síva, with a golden bull, and a silver one of Garuda 'the eagle,' are placed upon the altar. Animals, as goats, sheep, etc., are tied to the posts, and to one of them, of the wood of the *mimosa*, is to be tied the human victim. Fire is to be kindled by means of a burning glass. The sacrificing priest, '*hota*,' strews the grass called *d'hub* or immortal, round the sacred fire. Then follows the burnt sacrifice to the ten guardian deities of the earth—to the nine planets, and to the Hindu Triad, to each of whom clarified butter is poured on the sacred fire one thousand times. Another burnt-sacrifice, to the sixty-four inferior gods, follows, which is succeeded by the sacrifice and offering of all the other animals tied to the posts. The human sacrifice concludes, the sacrificing priest offering pieces of the flesh of the victim to each god as he circumambulates the altar."—*Ibid.* 260.

[1] This is to be taken in its literal sense; the economy of the bee being displayed in the formation of extensive colonies which inhabit large masses of black comb adhering to the summits of the rocks. According to the legends of these tracts, they were called in as auxiliaries on Mahommedan invasions, and are said to have thrown the enemy more than once into confusion.

[2] See Appendix to this Part, No. IV.

[3] In June 1806 I was present at a meeting between the Rana and Sindia at the shrine of Eklinga. The rapacious Mahratta had just forced the passes to the Rana's capital, which was the commencement of a series of aggressions involving one of the most tragical events in the history of Méwar—the immolation of the Princess Kishna and the subsequent ruin of the country. I was then an *attaché* of the British embassy to the Mahratta prince, who carried the ambassador to the meeting to increase his consequence. In March 1818 I again visited the shrine, on my way to Oodipoor, but under very different circumstances—to

The high-priest of Eklinga, like all his order, is doomed to celibacy, and the office is continued by adopted disciples. Of such spiritual descents they calculate sixty-four since the Sage Harita, whose benediction obtained for the Gehlote Rajpoot the sovereignty of Cheetore, when driven from Saurashtra by the Parthians.

The priests of Eklinga are termed Gosaén or Goswámi, which signifies "control over the senses!" The distinguishing mark of the faith of Síva is the crescent on the forehead:[1] the hair is braided and forms a tiara round the head, and with its folds a chaplet of the lotus-seed is often entwined. They smear the body with ashes, and use garments dyed of an orange hue. They bury their dead in a sitting posture, and erect tumuli over them, which are generally conical in form.[2] It is not uncommon for priestesses to officiate in the temple of Síva. There is a numerous class of Gosaéns who have adopted celibacy, and who yet follow secular employments both in commerce and arms. The mercantile Gosaéns[3] are amongst the richest individuals in India, and there are several at Oodipoor who enjoy high favour, and who were found very useful when the Mahrattas demanded a war-contribution, as their privileged character did not prevent their being offered and taken as hostages for its payment. The Gosaéns who profess arms, partake of the character of the knights of St. John of Jerusalem. They live in monasteries scattered over the country, possess lands, and beg, or serve for pay when called upon. As defensive soldiers, they are good. Síva, their patron, is the god of war, and like him they make great use of intoxicating herbs, and even of spirituous liquors. In Méwar they can always muster many hundreds of the Kanfera Jogi, or 'split-ear ascetics,' so called from the habit of piercing the ear and placing therein a ring of the conch-shell, which is their battle-trumpet. Both Brahmins and Rajpoots, and even Goojers, can belong to this order, a particular account of whose internal discipline and economy could not fail to be interesting. The poet Chund gives an animated description of the body-guard of the King of Canouj, which was composed of these monastic warriors.

The Ranas of Méwar, as the *dewans*, or vicegerents of Síva, when they

announce the deliverance of the family from oppression, and to labour for its prosperity. While standing without the sanctuary, looking at the quadriform divinity, and musing on the changes of the intervening twelve years, my meditations were broken by an old Rajpoot chieftain, who, saluting me, invited me to enter and adore Baba Adam, 'Father Adam,' as he termed the phallic emblem. I excused myself on account of my boots, which I said I could not remove, and that with them I would not cross the threshold: a reply which pleased them, and preceded me to the Rana's court.

[1] Síva is represented with three eyes: hence his title of Trinitra and Trilochun, the Tri-ophthalmic Jupiter of the Greeks. From the fire of the central eye of Síva is to proceed Pralaya, or the final destruction of the universe: this eye placed vertically, resembling the flame of a taper, is a distinguishing mark on the foreheads of his votaries.

[2] I have seen a cemetery of these, each of very small dimensions, which may be described as so many concentric rings of earth, diminishing to the apex, crowned with a cylindrical stone pillar. One of the disciples of Síva was performing rites to the manes, strewing leaves of an evergreen and sprinkling water over the graves.

[3] For a description of this, vide *Transactions of the Royal Asiatic Society*, vol. i. p. 217.

visit the temple supersede the high priest in his duties, and perform the ceremonies, which the reigning prince does with peculiar correctness and grace.[1]

The shrine of Eklinga is endowed with twenty-four large villages from the fisc, besides parcels of land from the chieftains; but the privileges of the tutelary divinity have been waning since Kaniya fixed his residence amongst them: and as the priests of Apollo complained that the god was driven from the sacred mount Girdhana, in Vrij, by the influence of those of Jupiter[2] with Shah Jehan, the latter may now lament that the day of retribution has arrived, when propitiation to the Preserver is deemed more important than to the Destroyer. This may arise from the personal character of the high priests, who, from their vicinity to the court, can scarcely avoid mingling in its intrigues, and thence lose in character: even the Ranees do not hesitate to take mortgages on the estates of B'hola Nat'h.[3] We shall not further enlarge on the immunities to Eklinga, or the forms in which they are conveyed, as these will be fully discussed in the account of the shrine of Crishna; but proceed to notice the privileges of the heterodox Jains—the Védíaván[4] or Magi of Rajast'han. The numbers and power of these sectarians are little known to Europeans, who take it for granted that they are few and dispersed. To prove the extent of their religious and political power, it will suffice to remark, that the pontiff of the Khartra-gatcha,[5] one of the many branches of this

[1] The copy of the *Síva Púrana* which I presented to the Royal Asiatic Society, was obtained for me by the Rana from the temple of Eklinga.

[2] Jíva-pitri, the 'Father of Life,' would be a very proper epithet for Mahadéva, the creative 'power,' whose Olympus is Kailás.

[3] B'hola Nat'h, or the 'Simple God,' is one of the epithets of Síva, whose want of reflection is so great, that he would give away his own divinity if asked.

[4] Védíaván, the 'Man of Secrets or Knowledge,' is the term used by way of reproach to the Jains, having the import of *magician*. Their opponents believe them to be possessed of supernatural skill; and it is recorded of the celebrated Umara, author of the *Cos'a* or dictionary called after him, that he miraculously "made the full moon appear on Amavus"—the ides of the month, when the planet is invisible.

[5] Khartra signifies 'true,' an epithet of distinction which was bestowed by that great supporter of the Buddhists or Jains, Sidraj, king of Anhulwarra Putun, on one of the branches (*gatcha*), in a grand religious disputation (*badha*) at that capital in the eleventh century. The celebrated Hemachandra Acharya was head of the *Khartra-gatchas*; and his spiritual descendant honoured Oodipoor with his presence in his visit to his dioceses in the desert in 1821. My own *Yati* tutor was a disciple of Hemachandra, and his *patravali*, or pedigree, registered his descent by spiritual successions from him.

This pontiff was a man of extensive learning and of estimable character. He was versed in all the ancient inscriptions, to which no key now exists, and deciphered one for me which had been long unintelligible. His travelling library was of considerable extent, though chiefly composed of works relating to the ceremonies of his religion: it was in the charge of two of his disciples remarkable for talent, and who, like himself, were perfectly acquainted with all these ancient characters. The pontiff kindly permitted my *Yati* to bring for my inspection some of the letters of invitation written by his flocks in the desert. These were rolls, some of them several feet in length, containing pictured delineations of their wishes. One from Bikanér represented that city, in one division of which was the school or college of the Jains, where the *Yatis* were all portrayed at their various studies. In another part, a procession of them was quitting the southern gate of the city, the head of which was in the act of delivering a scroll to a messenger, while the pontiff was seen with his cortège advancing in the distance. To

faith, has 11,000 clerical disciples scattered over India; that a single community, the Ossi or Oswal,[1] numbers 100,000 families; and that more than half of the mercantile wealth of India passes through the hands of the Jain laity. Rajast'han and Saurashtra are the cradles of the Buddhist or Jain faith, and three out of their five sacred mounts, namely, Abu, Pali-t'hana,[2] and Girna, are in these countries. The officers of the state and revenue are chiefly of the Jain laity, as are the majority of the bankers, from Lahore to the ocean. The chief magistrate and assessors of justice, in Oodipoor and most of the towns of Rajast'han, are of this sect; and as their voluntary duties are confined to civil cases, they are as competent in these as they are the reverse in criminal cases, from their tenets forbidding the shedding of blood. To this leading feature in their religion they owe their political debasement: for Komarpal, the last king of Anhulwara of the Jain faith, would not march his armies in the rains, from the unavoidable sacrifice of animal life that must have ensued. The strict Jain does not even maintain a lamp during that season, lest it should attract moths to their destruction.

The period of sectarian intolerance is now past; and as far as my observation goes, the ministers of Vishnu, Síva, and Budha, view each other without malignity; which feeling never appears to have influenced the laity of either sect, who are indiscriminately respectful to the ministers of all religions, whatever be their tenets. It is sufficient that their office is one of sanctity, and that they are ministers of the Divinity, who, they say, excludes the homage of none, in whatever tongue, or whatever manner he is sought; and with this spirit of entire toleration, the devout missionary, or Moolla, would in no country meet more security or hospitable courtesy than among the Rajpoots. They must, however, adopt the toleration they would find practised towards themselves, and not exclude, as some of them do, the races of Súrya and Chundra from divine mercy, who, with less arrogance, and more reliance on the compassionate nature of the Creator, say, he has established a variety of paths by which the good may attain beatitude.

Méwar has, from the most remote period, afforded a refuge to the followers of the Jain faith, which was the religion of Balabhi, the first capital of the Rana's ancestors, and many monuments attest the support this family has granted to its professors in all the vicissitudes of their fortunes. One of the best preserved monumental remains in India is a column most elaborately sculptured, full seventy feet in height, dedicated

show the respect in which these high priests of the Jains are held, the princes of Rajpootana invariably advance outside the walls of their capital to receive and conduct them to it—a mark of respect paid only to princes. On the occasion of the high priest of the *Khartras* passing through Oodipoor, as above alluded to, the Rana received him with every distinction.

[1] So called from the town of Ossa, in Marwar.

[2] Pali-t'hana, or 'the abode of the Pali,' is the name of the town at the foot of the sacred mount Satrunjya (signifying 'victorious over the foe'), on which the Jain temples are sacred to Budhiswara, or the 'Lord of the Budhists.' I have little doubt that the name of Pali-t'hana is derived from the pastoral (*pali*) Scythic invaders bringing the Budhist faith in their train—a faith which appears to me not indigenous to India. Palestine, which, with the whole of Syria and Egypt, was ruled by the Yksos or Shepherd kings, who for a season expelled the old Coptic race, may have had a similar import to the *Pali-t'hana* founded by the Indo-Scythic Pali. The author visited all these sacred mounts.

to Parswa-na'th, in Cheetore. The noblest remains of sacred architecture, not in Méwar only, but throughout Western India, are Budhist or Jain: and the many ancient cities where this religion was fostered, have inscriptions which evince their prosperity in these countries, with whose history their own is interwoven. In fine, the necrological records of the Jains bear witness to their having occupied a distinguished place in Rajpoot society; and the privileges they still enjoy, prove that they are not overlooked. It is not my intention to say more on the past or present history of these sectarians, than may be necessary to show the footing on which their establishments are placed; to which end little is required beyond copies of a few simple warrants and ordinances in their favour.[1] Hereafter I may endeavour to add something to the knowledge already possessed of these deists of Rajast'han, whose singular communities contain mines of knowledge hitherto inaccessible to Europeans. The libraries of Jessulmér in the desert, of Anhulwara, the cradle of their faith, of Cambay, and other places of minor importance, consist of thousands of volumes These are under the control, not of the priests alone, but of communities of the most wealthy and respectable amongst the laity, and are preserved in the crypts of their temples, which precaution ensured their preservation, as well as that of the statues of their deified teachers, when the temples themselves were destroyed by the Mahomedan invaders, who paid more deference to the images of Budha than those of Síva or Vishnu. The preservation of the former may be owing to the natural formation of their statues; for while many of Adnath, of Nemi, and of Parswa, have escaped the hammer, there is scarcely an Apollo or a Venus, of any antiquity, entire, from Lahore to Ram-iswara. The two arms of these theists sufficed for their protection; while the statues of the polytheists have met with no mercy.

No. V.[2] is the translation of a grant by the celebrated Rana Raj Sing, the gallant and successful opponent of Arungzéb in many a battle. It is at once of a general and special nature, containing a confirmation of the old privileges of the sect, and a mark of favour to a priest of some distinction, called Manoh. It is well known that the first law of the Jains, like that of the ancient Athenian lawgiver Triptolemus, is, "Thou shalt not kill," a precept applicable to every sentient thing. The first clause of this edict, in conformity thereto, prohibits all innovation upon this cherished principle; while the second declares that even the life which is forfeited to the laws is immortal (*amra*) if the victim but passes near their abodes. The third article defines the extent of *sirna*, or sanctuary, the dearest privilege of the races of these regions. The fourth article sanctions the tithes, both on agricultural and commercial produce; and makes no distinction between the Jain priests and those of Síva and Vishnu in this source of income, which will be more fully detailed in the account of Nat'hdwara. The fifth article is the particular gift to the priest; and the whole closes with the usual anathema against such as may infringe the ordinance.

The edicts Nos. VI. and VII.,[3] engraved on pillars of stone in the towns of Rasmi and Bakrole, further illustrate the scrupulous observances of the Rana's house towards the Jains; where, in compliance with their peculiar

[1] See Appendix to this Part. [2] *Ibid.*
[3] See Appendix to this article.

doctrine, the oil-mill and the potter's wheel suspend their revolutions for the four months in the year when insects most abound. Many others of a similar character could be furnished, but these remarks may be concluded with an instance of the influence of the Jains on Rajpoot society, which passed immediately under the author's eye. In the midst of a sacrifice to the god of war, when the victims were rapidly falling by the scymitar, a request preferred by one of them for the life of a goat or a buffalo on the point of immolation, met instant compliance, and the animal, become *amra* or immortal, with a garland thrown round his neck, was led off in triumph from the blood-stained spot.

NAT'HDWARA.—This is the most celebrated of the fanes of the Hindu Apollo. Its etymology is 'the portal (*dwára*) of the god' (*nat'h*), of the same import as his more ancient shrine of Dwarica[1] at the 'world's end.' Nat'hdwara is twenty-two miles N.N.E. of Oodipoor, on the right bank of the Bunas. Although the principal resort of the followers of Vishnu, it has nothing very remarkable in its structure or situation. It owes its celebrity entirely to the image of Crishna, said to be the same that has been worshipped at Mat'hura ever since his deification, between eleven and twelve hundred years before Christ.[2] As containing the representative of the mildest of the gods of Hind, Nat'hdwara is one of the most frequented places of pilgrimage, though it must want that attraction to the classical Hindu which the caves of Gaya, the shores of the distant Dwarica, or the pastoral Vrij,[3] the place of the nativity of Crishna, present to his imagination; for though the groves of Vindra,[4] in which Kaniya disported with the Gopis, no longer resound to the echoes of his flute; though the waters of the Yamuna[5] are daily polluted with the blood of the sacred kine, still it is the holy land of the pilgrim, the sacred Jordan of his fancy, on whose banks he may sit and weep, as did the banished Israelite of old, the glories of Mat'hura, his Jerusalem!

It was in the reign of Arungzéb that the pastoral divinity was exiled from Vrij, that classic soil which, during a period of two thousand eight hundred years, had been the sanctuary of his worshippers. He had been compelled to occasional flights during the visitations of Mahmood and the first dynasties of Afghan invaders; though the more tolerant of the

[1] Dwarica is at the point called Juggut Koont, of the Saurashtra peninsula. *Ca* is the mark of the genitive case: *Dwarca-nat'h* would be the 'gate of the god.'

[2] Fifty-seven descents are given, both in their sacred and profane genealogies, from Crishna to the princes supposed to have been contemporary with Vicramaditya. The *Yadu Bhatti* or *Shamah Bhatti* (the *Asham Betti* of Abul Fusil), draw their pedigree from Crishna or Yadunat'h, as do the *Jharéjas* of Kutch.

[3] With Mat'hura, as a centre and a radius of eighty miles, describe a circle: all within it is Vrij, which was the seat of whatever was refined in Hinduism, and whose language, the Vrij-basha, was the purest dialect of India. *Vrij* is tantamount to the land of the Suraseni, derived from Súrsén, the ancestor of Crishna, whose capital, Súrpúri, is about fifty miles south of Mat'hura on the Yamuna (Jumna). The remains of this city (Súrpúri) the author had the pleasure of discovering. The province of the Surséni, or Suraseni, is defined by Menu, and particularly mentioned by the historians of Alexander.

[4] *Vindra-vana*, or the 'forests of Vindra,' in which were placed many temples sacred to Kaniya, is on the Yamuna, a few miles above Mat'hura. A pilgrimage to this temple is indispensable to the true votary of Crishna.

[5] This river is called the *Kal* Yamuna, or *black* Yamuna, and *Kali-dé* or the 'black pool,' from Kaniya having destroyed the hydra Kaliya which infested it. Jydéva calls the Yamuna 'the blue daughter of the sun.'

Mogul kings not only reinstated him, but were suspected of dividing their faith between Kaniya and the prophet. Akber was an enthusiast in the mystic poetry of Jydéva, which paints in glowing colours the loves of Kaniya and Radha, in which lovely personification the refined Hindu abjures all sensual interpretation, asserting its character of pure spiritual love.[1]

Jehangír, by birth half a Rajpoot, was equally indulgent to the worship of Kaniya: but Shah Jehan, also the son of a Rajpoot princess, inclined to the doctrines of Síva, in which he was initiated by Sid-rup the Sanyasi. Sectárian animosity is more virulent than faiths totally dissimilar. Here we see Hindu depressing Hindu: the followers of Síva oppressing those of Kaniya; the priests of Jupiter driving the pastoral Apollo from the Parnassus of Vrij. At the intercession, however, of a princess of Oodipoor, he was replaced on his altar, where he remained till Arungzéb became emperor of the Moguls. In such detestation did the Hindus hold this intolerant king, that in like manner as they supposed the beneficent Akber to be the devout Mokund in a former birth, so they make the tyrant's body enclose the soul of Kal-Yamun the foe of Crishna, ere his apotheosis, from whom he fled to Dwarica, and thence acquired the name of Rinchor.[2]

When Arungzéb proscribed Kaniya, and rendered his shrines impure throughout Vrij, Rana Raj Sing "offered the heads of one hundred thousand Rajpoots for his service," and the god was conducted by the route of Kotah and Rampoora to Méwar. An omen decided the spot of his future residence. As he journeyed to gain the capital of the Seesodias the chariot-wheel sunk deep into the earth and defied extrication; upon which the *Sookuni* (augur) interpreted the pleasure of the god, that he desired to dwell there. This circumstance occurred at an inconsiderable village called Siarh, in the fief of Dailwara, one of the sixteen nobles of Méwar. Rejoiced at this decided manifestation of favour, the chief hastened to make a perpetual gift of the village and its lands, which was speedily confirmed by the patent of the Rana.[3] Nat'hji (*the* god) was removed from his car, and in due time a temple was erected for his reception, when the hamlet of Siarh became the town of Nat'hdwara, which now contains many thousand inhabitants of all denominations, who, reposing under the especial protection of the god, are exempt from every mortal tribunal. The site is not uninteresting, nor devoid of the means of defence. To the east it is shut in by a cluster of hills, and to the westward flows the Bunas, which nearly bathes the extreme points of the hills. Within these bounds is the sanctuary (*sirna*) of Kaniya, where the criminal is free from pursuit; nor dare the rod of justice appear on the mount, or the foot of

[1] It affords an example of the Hindu doctrine of the Metempsychosis, as well as of the regard which Akber's toleration had obtained him, to mention, that they held his body to be animated by the soul of a celebrated Hindu gymnosophist: in support of which they say he (Akber) went to his accustomed spot of penance (*tapasya*) at the confluence of the Yamuna and Ganges, and excavated the implements, namely, the tongs, gourd, and deer-skin, of his anchorite existence.

[2] *Rin*, the 'field of battle,' *Chor*, from *chorna*, 'to abandon.' Hence Rinchor, one of the titles under which Crishna is worshipped at Dwarica, is most unpropitious to the martial Rajpoot. Kal-Yamun, the foe from whom he fled, and who is figured as a serpent, is doubtless the Tâk, the ancient foe of the Yadús, who slew Janméja, emperor of the Pandús.

[3] See Appendix to this Part, No. VIII.

the pursuer pass the stream ; neither within it can blood be spilt, for the pastoral Kaniya delights not in offerings of this kind. The territory contains within its precincts abundant space for the town, the temple, and the establishments of the priests, as well as for the numerous resident worshippers, and the constant influx of votaries from the most distant regions,

> "From Samarcand, by Oxus, Temir's throne,
> Down to the golden Chersonese,"

who find abundant shelter from the noontide blaze in the groves of tamarind, peepul, and semul,[1] where they listen to the mystic hymns of Jydéva. Here those whom ambition has cloyed, superstition unsettled, satiety disgusted, commerce ruined, or crime disquieted, may be found as ascetic attendants on the mildest of the gods of India. Determined upon renouncing the world, they first renounce the ties that bind them to it, whether family, friends, or fortune, and placing their wealth at the disposal of the deity, stipulate only for a portion of the food dressed for him, and to be permitted to prostrate themselves before him till their allotted time is expired. Here no blood-stained sacrifice scares the timid devotee ; no austerities terrify, or tedious ceremonies fatigue him ; he is taught to cherish the hope that he has only to ask for mercy in order to obtain it ; and to believe that the compassionate deity who guarded the lapwing's nest [2] in the midst of myriads of combatants, who gave beautitude to the courtesan [3] who as the wall crushed her pronounced the name of "Rama," will not withhold it from him who has quitted the world and its allurements that he may live only in his presence, be fed by the food prepared for himself, and yield up his last sigh invoking the name of Heri. There have been two hundred individuals at a time, many of whom, stipulating

[1] The cotton tree, which grows to an immense height.

[2] Whoever has unhooded the falcon at a lapwing, or even scared one from her nest, need not be told of its peculiarly distressing scream, as if appealing to sympathy. The allusion here is to the lapwing scared from her nest, as the rival armies of the Curus and Pandus joined in battle, when the compassionate Crishna, taking from an elephant's neck a war-bell (*vira-gunt'ha*), covered the nest, in order to protect it. When the majority of the feudal nobles of Marwar became self-exiled, to avoid the almost demoniac fury of their sovereign, since his alliance with the British Government, Anar Sing, the chief of Ahore, a fine specimen of the Rahtore Rajpoot, brave, intelligent, and amiable, was one day lamenting, that while all India was enjoying tranquillity under the shield of Britain, they alone were suffering from the caprice of a tyrant ; concluding a powerful appeal to my personal interposition with the foregoing allegory, and observing on the beauty of the office of mediator : "You are all powerful," added he, "and we may be of little account in the grand scale of affairs ; but Crishna condescended to protect even the lapwing's egg in the midst of battle." This brave man knew my anxiety to make their peace with their sovereign, and being acquainted with the allegory, I replied with some fervour, in the same strain, "Would to God, Thakoor Sahib, I had the *vira-gunt'ha* to protect you." The effect was instantaneous, and the eye of this manly chieftain, who had often fearlessly encountered the foe in battle, filled with tears as, holding out his hand, he said, "At least you listen to our griefs, and speak the language of friendship. Say but the word, and you may command the services of twenty thousand Rahtores." There is, indeed, no human being more susceptible of excitement, and, under it, of being led to any desperate purpose, whether for good or for evil, than the Rajpoot.

[3] Chund, the bard, gives this instance of the compassionate nature of Crishna, taken, as well as the former, from the *Mahabharat*.

merely for food, raiment, and funeral rites, have abandoned all to pass their days in devotion at the shrine: men of every condition, Rajpoot, merchant, and mechanic; and where sincerity of devotion is the sole expiation, and gifts outweigh penance, they must feel the road smooth to the haven of hope.

The dead stock of Crishna's shrine is augmented chiefly by those who hold life "unstable as the dew-drop on the lotus"; and who are happy to barter "the wealth of Ormuz and of Ind" for the intercessional prayers of the high priest, and his passport to *Heri-púr*, the heaven of Heri. From the banks of the Indus to the mouths of the Ganges, from the coasts of the Peninsula to the shores of the Red Sea, the gifts of gratitude or of fear are lavishly poured in; and though the unsettled aspect of the last half century curtailed the transmission of the more bulky, but least valuable benefactions, it less affected the bills of exchange from the successful sons of commerce, or the legacies of the dead. The safe arrival of a galleon from Sofala or Arabia produced as much to the shrine as to the insurance office, for Kaniya is the Saint Nicholas of the Hindu navigator, as was Apollo to the Grecian and Celtic sailors, who purchased the charmed arrows of the god to calm the troubled sea.[1] A storm accordingly yields in proportion to its violence, or to the nerve of the owner of the vessel. The appearance of a long-denied heir might deprive him of half his patrimony, and force him to lament his parent's distrust in natural causes; while the accidental mistake of touching forbidden food on particular fasts requires expiation, not by flagellation or seclusion, but by the penance of the purse.

There is no donation too great or too trifling for the acceptance of Crishna, from the baronial estate to a patch of meadow-land; from the gemmed coronet to adorn his image, to the widow's mite; nor, as before observed, is there a principality in India which does not diminish its fisc to add to his revenues. What effect the milder rites of the shepherd-god has produced on the adorers of Síva we know not, but assuredly Eklinga, the tutelary divinity of Méwar, has to complain of being defrauded of half his dues since Kaniya transferred his abode from the Yamuna to the Bunas; for the revenues assigned to Kaniya, who under the epithet of "Yellow mantle," has a distinguished niche in the domestic chapel of the Rana, far exceed those of the Avenger. The grants or patents of *Hindu-*

[1] Near the town of Avranches, on the coast of Normandy, is a rock called Mont St. Michel, in ancient times sacred to the Gallic or Celtic Apollo, or Belenus; a name which the author from whom we quote observes, "certainly came from the East, and proves that the littoral provinces of Gaul were visited by the Phœnicians."—"A college of Druidical priestesses was established there, who sold to seafaring men certain arrows endowed with the peculiar virtue of allaying storms, if shot into the waves by a young mariner. Upon the vessel arriving safe, the young archer was sent by the crew to offer thanks and rewards to the priestesses. His presents were accepted in the most graceful manner; and at his departure the fair priestesses, who had received his embraces, presented to him a number of shells, which afterwards he never failed to use in adorning his person."—*Tour through France.*

When the early Christian warrior consecrated this mount to his protector St. Michel, its name was changed from *Mons Jovis* (being dedicated to Jupiter) to *Tumba*, supposed from *tumulus*, a mound; but as the Saxons and Celts placed pillars on all these mounts, dedicated to the Sun-god Belenus, Bal, or Apollo, it is not unlikely that *Tumba* is from the Sanscrit *t'humba*, or *st'humbsa*, 'a pillar.'

páti,[1] defining the privileges and immunities of the shrine, are curious documents.[2]

The extension of the sanctuary beyond the vicinage of the shrine became a subject of much animadversion ; and in delegating judicial authority over the whole of the villages in the grant to the priests, the Rana committed the temporal welfare of his subjects to a class of men not apt to be lenient in the collection of their dues, which not unfrequently led to bloodshed. In alienating the other royalties, especially the transit duties, he was censured even by the zealots. Yet, however important such concessions, they were of subordinate value to the rights of sanctuary, which were extended to the whole of the towns in the grant, thereby multiplying the places of refuge for crime, already too numerous.

In all ages and countries the rights of sanctuary have been admitted, and however they may be abused, their institution sprung from humane motives. To check the impulse of revenge and to shelter the weak from oppression are noble objects, and the surest test of a nation's independence is the extent to which they are carried. From the remotest times *sirna* has been the most valued privilege of the Rajpoots, the lowest of whom deems his house a refuge against the most powerful. But we merely propose to discuss the sanctuary of holy places, and more immediately that of the shrine of Kaniya. When Moses, after the Exodus, made a division of the lands of Canaan amongst the Israelites, and appointed "six cities to be the refuge of him who had slain unwittingly, from the avenger of blood," [3] the intention was not to afford facilities for eluding justice, but to check the hasty impulse of revenge ; for the slayer was only to be protected "until he stood before the congregation for judgment, or until the death of the high-priest," which event appears to have been considered as the termination of revenge.[4] The infraction of political sanctuary (*sirna toorna*) often gives rise to the most inveterate feuds ; and its abuse by the priests is highly prejudicial to society. Moses appointed but six cities of refuge to the whole Levite tribe ; but the Rana has assigned more to one shrine than the entire possessions of that branch of the Israelites who had but forty-two cities, while Kaniya has forty-six. The motive of sanctuary in Rajast'han may have been originally the same as that of the divine legislator ; but the privilege has been abused, and the most notorious criminals deem the temple their best safeguard. Yet some

[1] *Hindupáti*, vulgò *Hinduput*, 'chief of the Hindu race,' is a title justly appertaining to the Ranas of Méwar. It has, however, been assumed by chieftains scarcely superior to some of his vassals, though with some degree of pretension by Sevaji, who, had he been spared, might have worked the redemption of his nation, and of the Rana's house, from which he sprung.

[2] See Appendix to this paper, Nos. IX. and X.

[3] Numbers, chap. xxxv. 11, 12.

[4] Numbers, chap. xxxv. 25, and Joshua, chap. xx. 6. There was an ancient law of Athens analogous to the Mosaic, by which he who committed "*chance-medley*" should fly the country for a year, during which his relatives made satisfaction to the relatives of the deceased. The Greeks had *asyla* for every description of criminals, which could not be violated without infamy. Gibbon gives a memorable instance of disregard to the sanctuary of St. Julian in Auvergne, by the soldiers of the Frank king Theodoric, who divided the spoils of the altar, and made the priests captives : an impiety not only unsanctioned by the son of Clovis, but punished by the death of the offenders, the restoration of the plunder, and the extension of the right of sanctuary five miles around the sepulchre of the holy martyr.

princes have been found hardy enough to violate, though indirectly, the sacred *sirna*. Zalim Sing of Kotah, a zealot in all the observances of religion, had the boldness to draw the line when selfish priestcraft interfered with his police; and though he would not demand the culprit, or sacrilegiously drag him from the altar, he has forced him thence by prohibiting the admission of food, and threatening to build up the door of the temple. It was thus the Greeks evaded the laws, and compelled the criminal's surrender by kindling fires around the sanctuary. The towns of Kaniya did not often abuse their privilege; but the author once had to interpose, where a priest of Eklinga gave asylum to a felon who had committed murder within the bounds of his domain of Pahona. As this town, of eight thousand rupees annual revenue belonging to the fisc, had been gained by a forged charter, the author was glad to seize on the occasion to recommend its resumption, though he thereby incurred the penalty for seizing church land, namely "sixty thousand years in hell." The unusual occurrence created a sensation, but it was so indisputably just that not a voice was raised in opposition.

Let us revert to the endowments of Nat'hdwara. Herodotus furnishes a powerful instance of the estimation in which sacred offerings were held by the nations of antiquity. He observes that these were transmitted from the remotest nations of Scythia to Delos in Greece; a range far less extensive than the offerings to the Dewul of Apollo in Méwar. The spices of the isles of the Indian archipelago; the balmy spoils of Araby the blest; the nard or frankincense of Tartary; the raisins and pistachios of Persia; every variety of saccharine preparation, from the *sacar-cand* (sugar-candy) of the celèstial empire, with which the god sweetens his evening repast, to that more common sort which enters into the *péras* of Mat'hura, the food of his infancy; the shawls of Cashmér, the silks of Bengal, the scarfs of Benares, the brocades of Guzzerat,

> . . ." the flower and choice
> Of many provinces from bound to bound,"

all contribute to enrich the shrine of Nat'hdwara. But it is with the votaries of the maritime provinces of India that he has most reason to be satisfied; in the commercial cities of Surat, Cambay, Muscat-mandavi, etc., etc., where the Mookhias, or comptrollers deputed by the high-priest, reside, to collect the benefactions, and transmit them as occasion requires. A deputy resides on the part of the high priest at Mooltan, who invests the distant worshippers with the initiative cordon and necklace. Even from Samarcand the pilgrims repair with their offerings; and a sum, seldom less than ten thousand rupees, is annually transmitted by the votaries from the Arabian ports of Muscat, Mocha, and Jidda; which contribution is probably augmented not only by the votaries who dwell at the mouths of the Wolga,[1] but by the

[1] Pallas gives an admirable and evidently faithful account of the worship of Crishna and other Hindu divinities in the city of Astracan, where a Hindu mercantile colony is established. They are termed *Mooltani*, from the place whence they migrated—Mooltan, near the Indus. This class of merchants of the Hindu faith is disseminated over all the countries, from the Indus to the Caspian: and it would have been interesting had the professor given us any account of their period of settlement on the western shore of the Caspian sea. In costume and feature, as represented in the plate given by that author, they have nothing to

Samoyede [1] of Siberia. There is not a petty retailer professing the Vishnu creed who does not carry a tithe of his trade to the stores: and thus

denote their origin; though their divinities might be seated on any altar on the Ganges. The Mooltanis of Indeskoi Dvor, or '*Indian court*,' at Astracan, have erected a pantheon, in which Crishna, the god of all Vishnuë merchants, is seated in front of Juggernath, Rama, and his brothers, who stand in the background; while Síva and his consort Ashta-bhooja '*the eight-armed*,' form an intermediate line, in which is also placed a statue which Pallas denominates *Moorli*; but Pallas mistook the flute (*moorali*) of the divine Crishna for a rod. The principal figure we shall describe in his own words. "In the middle was placed a small idol with a very high bonnet, called *Gupaledshi*. At its right there was a large black stone, and on the left two smaller ones of the same colour, brought from the Ganges, and regarded by the Hindus as sacred. These fossils were of the species called *Sankara*, and appeared to be an impression of a bivalve muscle." Minute as is the description, our judgment is further aided by the plate. *Gupaledshi* is evidently Gopalji, the pastoral deity of Vrij (from *gao*, a cow, and *pali*, a herdsman). The head-dress worn by him and all the others is precisely that still worn by Crishna, in the sacred dance at Muttra: and so minute is the delineation that even the *péra* or sugar-ball is represented, although the professor appears to have been ignorant of its use, as he does not name it. He has likewise omitted to notice the representation of the sacred mount of Girdhana, which separates him from the Hindu Jove and the turreted Cybele (Doorga), his consort. The black stones are the *Saligramas*, worshipped by all *Vishnuës*. In the names of "N'handigana and Gori," though the first is called a lion saddled, and the other a male divinity, we easily recognise Nanda, the bull-*attendant* (*Gana*) of Síva and his consort Gouri. Were all travellers to describe what they see with the same accuracy as Pallas, they would confer important obligations on society, and might defy criticism.

It is with heartfelt satisfaction I have to record, from the authority of a gentleman who has dwelt amongst the *Hindikis* of Astracan, that distance from their ancient abodes has not deteriorated their character for uprightness. Mr. Mitchell, from whose knowledge of Oriental languages the Royal Asiatic Society will some day derive benefit, says, that the reputation of these Hindu colonists, of whom there are about five hundred families, stands very high, and that they bear a preference over all the merchants of other nations settled in this great commercial city.

[1] Other travellers besides Pallas have described Hinduism as existing in the remote parts of the Russian empire, and if nominal resemblances may be admitted, we would instance the strong analogy between the *Samoyedes* and *Tchoudes* of Siberia and Finland and the *Sama Yadús* and *Joudes* of India. The languages of the two former races are said to have a strong affinity, and are classed as *Hindu-Germanic* by M. Klaproth, on whose learned work, *Asia Polyglotta*, M. Rémusat has given the world an interesting *critique*, in his *Mélanges Asiatiques* (tome i. p. 267), in which he traces these tribes to Central Asia; thus approaching the land of the *Gete* or *Yuti*. Now the *Yutis* and *Yadús* have much in their early history to warrant the assertion of more than nominal analogy. The annals of the *Yadús* of Jessulmér state, that long anterior to Vicrama they held dominion from Guzni to Samarcand: that they established themselves in those regions after the Mahabharat, or great war; and were again impelled, on the rise of Islamism, within the Indus. As *Yadús* of the race of Shám or Sam (a title of Crishna), they would be *Sama-Yadús*; in like manner as the *B'hatti* tribe are called *Shama-b'hatti*, the *Ashambétti* of Abulfuzil. The race of *Joude* was existing near the Indus in the Emperor Baber's time, who describes them as occupying the mountainous range in the first Do-áb, the very spot mentioned in the annals of the *Yadús* as their place of halt, on quitting India twelve centuries before Christ, and thence called *Jadu* or *Yadu-ca-dang*, the 'hills of *Jadu* or *Yadu*.' The peopling of all these regions, from the Indus to remote Tartary, is attributed to the race of *Ayu* or *Indu*, both signifying the moon, of which are the *Hyas*, *Aswas* (*Asi*), *Yadús*, etc., who spread a common language over all Western Asia. Amongst the few words of *Hindu-Germanic* origin which M. Rémusat gives to prove affinity between the Finnish and Samoyede languages is "*Miel, Mod*, dans le dialecte Caucasien, et *Méd*, en Slave," and which, as well as *mead*, the

caravans of thirty and forty cars, double-yoked, pass twice or thrice annually by the upper road to Nat'hdwara. These pious bounties are not allowed to moulder in the *bindars* : the apparel is distributed with a liberal hand as the gift of the deity to those who evince their devotion; and the edibles enter daily into the various food prepared at the shrine.

It has been remarked by the celebrated Goguet,[1] that the custom of offering food to the object of divine homage had its origin in a principle of gratitude, the repast being deemed hallowed by presenting the first portion to him who gave it, since the devotee was unable to conceive aught more acceptable than that whereby life is sustained. From the earliest period such offerings have been tendered; and in the burnt-offering (*hom*) of Abel, of the firstling of the flock, and the first portion of the repast presented by the Rajpoot to Anadeva[2] '*the nourisher*,' the motive is the same. But the *pursad* (such is the denomination of the food sacred to Kaniya) is deemed unlucky, if not unholy; a prejudice arising from the heterogeneous sources whence it is supplied—often from bequests of the dead. The Mookhias of the temple accordingly carry the sacred food to wheresoever the votaries dwell, which proves an irresistible stimulus to backward zeal, and produces an ample return. At the same time are transmitted, as from the god, dresses of honour corresponding in material and value with the rank of the receiver: a diadem, or fillet of satin and gold, embroidered; a *dugla*, or quilted coat of gold or silver brocade for the cold weather; a scarf of blue and gold; or if to one who prizes the gift less for its intrinsic worth than as a mark of special favour, a fragment of the garland worn on some festival by the god; or a simple necklace, by which he is inaugurated amongst the elect.[3]

It has been mentioned that the lands of Méwar appropriated to the shrine are equal in value to a baronial appanage, and, as before observed, there is not a principality in India which does not assign a portion of its domain or revenue to this object. The Hara princes of Kotah and Boondí are almost exclusive worshippers of Kaniya, and the regent Zalim Sing is devoted to the maintenance of the dignity of the establishment. Everything at Kotah appertains to Kaniya. The prince has but the usufruct of the palace, for which £12,000 are annually transmitted to the shrine. The grand lake east of the town, with all its finny tenants, is under his especial protection;[4] and the extensive suburb adjoining, with its rents, lands, and transit duties, all belong to the god. Zalim Sing moreover transmits to the high priest the most valuable shawls, broadcloths, and horses; and throughout the long period of predatory warfare he maintained two Néshans[5] of a hundred firelocks each, for

drink of the Scandinavian warrior, is from the Sanscrit *Madhu*, a bee. Hence intoxicating beverage is terned *Madhva*, which supplies another epithet for Crishna, *Madhú* or *Madhava*.

[1] *Origin of Laws and Government*.

[2] Literally "the giver of food."

[3] *Kaniya ca canti band'hna*, 'to bind on [the neck] the chaplet of Kaniya,' is the initiatory step.

[4] I had one day thrown my net into this lake, which abounded with a variety of fish, when my pastime was interrupted by a message from the regent, Zalim Sing: "Tell Captain Tod that Kotah and all around it are at his disposal; but these fish belong to Kaniya." I, of course, immediately desisted, and the fish were returned to the safeguard of the deity.

[5] A Néshan, or standard, is synonymous with a company.

the protection of the temple. His favourite son also, a child of love, is called Gordhun-das, the 'slave of Gordhun,' one of the many titles of Kaniya. The prince of Marwar went mad from the murder of the high priest of Jalindra, the epithet given to Kaniya in that state; and the Raja of Sheopúr,[1] the last of the Gores, lost his sovereignty by abandoning the worship of Hur for that of Heri. The '*slave*' of Radha[2] (such was the name of this prince) almost lived in the temple, and used to dance before the statue. Had he upheld the rights of him who wields the trident, the tutelary deity of his capital, Síva-púr, instead of the unwarlike divinity whose unpropitious title of Rinchor should never be borne by the martial Rajpoot, his fall would have been more dignified, though it could not have been retarded when the overwhelming torrent of the Mahrattas under Sindia swept Rajwarra.[3]

A distinction is made between the grants to the temple and those for the personal use of the pontiff, who at least affects never to apply any portion of the former to his own use, and he can scarcely have occasion to do so; but when from the stores of Apollo could be purchased the spices of the isles, the fruits of Persia, and the brocades of Guzzerat, we may indulge our scepticism in questioning this forbearance: but the abuse has been rectified, and traffic banished from the temple. The personal grant (Appendix, No. XI.) to the high priest ought alone to have sufficed for his household expenditure, being twenty thousand rupees per annum, equal to £10,000 in Europe. But the ten thousand towns of Méwar, from each of which he levied a crown, now exist only in the old rent-roll, and the heralds of Apollo would in vain attempt to collect their tribute from two thousand villages.

The Appendix, No. XII., being a grant of privileges to a minor shrine of Kaniya, in his character of *moorali* or 'flute-player,' contains much information on the minutiæ of benefactions, and will afford a good idea of the nature of these revenues.

The predominance of the mild doctrines of Kaniya over the dark rites of Síva, is doubtless beneficial to Rajpoot society. Were the prevention of female immolation the sole good resulting from their prevalence, that alone would conciliate our partiality; a real worshipper of Vishnu should forbid his wife following him to the pyre, as did recently the Boondí prince. In fact, their tenderness to animal life is carried to nearly as great an excess as with the Jains, who shed no blood. Celibacy is not imposed upon the priests of Kaniya, as upon those of Síva: on the contrary, they are enjoined to marry, and the priestly office is hereditary by descent. Their wives do not burn, but are committed, like themselves, to the earth. They inculcate tenderness towards all beings; though whether this feeling influences the mass, must depend on the soil which receives the seed, for the outward ceremonies of religion cost far less effort than the practice or essentials. I have often smiled

[1] Sheopúr or Síva-púr, the city of Sheo or Síva, the god of war, whose battle-shout is *Hur*; and hence one of his epithets, as Heri, is that of Crishna or Kaniya.

[2] Radha was the name of the chief of the *Gopis* or nymphs of Vrij, and the beloved of Kaniya.

[3] In October 1807 I rambled through all these countries, then scarcely known by name to us. At that time Sheopúr was independent, and its prince treated me with the greatest hospitality. In 1809 I witnessed its fall, when following with the embassy in the train of the Mahratta leader.

at the incessant aspirations of the Macchiavelli of Rajast'han, Zalim Sing, who, while he ejaculated the name of the god as he told his beads, was inwardly absorbed by mundane affairs; and when one word would have prevented a civil war, and saved his reputation from the stain of disloyalty to his prince, he was, to use his own words, "at fourscore years and upwards, laying the foundation for another century of life." And thus it is with the prince of Marwar, who esteems the life of a man or a goat of equal value when prompted by revenge to take it. Hope may silence the reproaches of conscience, and gifts and ceremonies may be deemed atonement for a deviation from the first principle of their religion—a benevolence which should comprehend every animated thing. But fortunately the princely worshippers of Kaniya are few in number: it is to the sons of commerce we must look for the effects of these doctrines; and it is my pride and duty to declare that I have known men of both sects, Vishnue and Jain, whose integrity was spotless, and whose philanthropy was unbounded.

CHAPTER XX

The origin of Kaniya or Crishna—Sources of a plurality of gods among the Hindus—Allegories respecting Crishna elucidated—Songs of Jydéva celebrating the loves of Kaniya—The Rasmandel, a mystic dance—Girdhana—Crishna anciently worshipped in caves—His conquest of the 'Black serpent' allegorical of the contests between the Buddhists and Vishnués—Analogies between the legends of Crishna and western mythology—Festivals of Crishna—Pilgrimage to Nat'hdwara—The seven gods of that temple—Its Pontiff.

HERI, Crishna, familiarly Kaniya, was of the celebrated tribe of Yadu, the founder of the fifty-six tribes [1] who obtained the universal sovereignty of India, and descended from Yayat, the third son [2] of Swayambhuma Manu,[3] or "The Man, Lord of the earth," whose daughter Ella [4] (*Terra*) was espoused by Budha (*Mercury*), son of Chandra [5] (*the Moon*), whence the Yadus are styled Chandravansi, or "children of the moon." Budha was therefore worshipped as the great ancestor (*Pitriswara*) of the lunar race; and previous to the apotheosis of Crishna, was adored by all the Yadu race. The principal shrine of Budha was at Dwarica, where he still receives adoration as Budha Trivicrama.[6] Kaniya lived towards the conclusion of the brazen age, calculated to have been about 1100 to 1200 years before Christ.[7] He was born to the inheritance of Vrij,

[1] *Chappun cula Yadu.* [2] *Qu.* Japhet?

[3] Also called *Vaiva-swata Manú*—'the man, son of the sun.'

[4] Ella, the earth—the Saxon *Ertha*. The Germans chiefly worshipped Tuisco or Teutates and Ertha, who are the Buddha and Ella of the Rajpoots.

[5] A male divinity with the Rajpoots, the Tatars, and ancient Germans.

[6] 'Triple Energy,' the *Hermes Triplex* of the Egyptians.

[7] I shall here subjoin an extract of the rise and progress of Vishnúism as written at my desire by the Múkhia of the temple:

"Twenty-five years of the *Dwapur* (the brazen age) were yet unexpired, the country of the Suraséni, comprehending the territory round Mat'hura for a space of eighty miles, of which he was unjustly deprived in his infancy by his relative Kansa. From its vicinity to Dehli we may infer either that there was no lord paramount amongst the Yadus of this period, or that Crishna's family held as vassals of Hastinapoor, then, with Indraprestha or Dehli, the chief seat of Yadu power. There were two princes named Súrasen amongst the immediate predecessors of Crishna: one, his grandfather, the other eight generations anterior. Which of these was the founder of Súrapoor on the Yamuna, the capital of the Yadus,[1] we know not, but we may assume that the first gave his name to the region around Mat'hura, described by Arrian as the country of the Suraseni. Alexander was in India probably about eight centuries after the deification of Crishna, and it is satisfactory to find that the inquiries he instituted into the genealogy of the dynasty then ruling on the Yamuna correspond very closely with those of the Yadus of this distant period; and combined with what Arrian says of the origin of the Pandus, it appears indisputable that the descendants of this powerful branch of the Yadus ruled on the Yamuna when the Macedonian erected the altars of Greece on the Indus. That the personage whose epithets of Crishna-Sham designate his colour as '*the Black Prince*,' was in fact a distinguished chief of the Yadus, there is not a shadow of doubt; nor that, after his death, they placed him among the gods as an incarnation of Vishnu or the Sun; and from this period we may induce the Hindu notion of their Trinity. Arrian enumerates the names of Budæus (Βυδύας) and Cradévas (Κραδεύας) amongst the early ancestors of the tribe

when the incarnation (*avatar*) of Sri Crishna took place. Of these, eleven were passed at Gokul,[1] and fourteen at Mat'hura. There he used to manifest himself personally, especially at Goverdhun. But when the *Kaliyúg* (the iron age) commenced, he retired to Dwarica, an island separated by the ocean from Barat-khund,[2] where he passed a hundred years before he went to heaven. In Samvat 937 (A.D. 881) God decreed that the Hindu faith should be overturned, and that the Túrishka[3] should rule. Then the *jézéya*, or capitation tax, was inflicted on the head of the Hindu. Their faith also suffered much from the Jains and the various infidel (*assúra*) sects which abounded. The Jains were so hostile, that Brimha manifested himself in the shape of Sancara Acharya who destroyed them and their religion at Benares. In Guzzerat, by their magic, they made the moon appear at Amavus.[4] Sancara foretold to its prince, Sid Raj,[5] the flood then approaching, who escaped in a boat and fled to T'hoda, on which occasion all the Vedyas[6] (magicians) in that country perished."

[1] For an account of the discovery of the remains of this ancient city, see *Transactions of the Royal Asiatic Society*, vol. i. p. 314.

---

[1] A small town and island in the Jumna, below Mat'hura. Hence one of Crishna's titles is Gokul Nath, 'Lord of Gokul.'

[2] The channel which separates the island of Dwarica from the mainland is filled up, except in spring tides. I passed it when it was dry.

[3] We possess no record of the invasion of India in A.D. 881, by the Túrki tribes, half a century after Mahmoun's expedition from Zabulist'han against Cheetore, in the reign of Rawul Khoman.

[4] The ides of the month, when the moon is obscured.

[5] He ruled Samvat 1151 (A.D. 1095) to S. 1201 (A.D. 1145).

[6] Still used as a term of reproach to the Jains and Buddhists, in which, and other points, as *Ari* (the foe, qu. *Aria*?) they bear a strong resemblance to the followers of the Arian Zerdusht, or Zoroaster. Amongst other peculiarities, the ancient Persian fire-worshipper, like the present Jain, placed a bandage over the mouth while worshipping.

then in power, which would alone convince us that Alexander had access to the genealogies of the *Púranas*; for we can have little hesitation in affirming these to be Budha and Croshtdeva, ancestors of Crishna; and that "Mathoras and Clisobaras, the chief cities of the Suraséni," are the Mat'hura and Súrpoor occupied by the descendants of Súrsén. Had Arrian afforded as many hints for discussing the analogy between the Hindu and Grecian Apollos as he has for the Hercules of Thebes and India, we might have come to a conclusion that the three chief divinities [1] of Egypt, Greece, and India, had their altars first erected on the Indus, Ganges, and Jumna.

The earliest objects of adoration in these regions were the sun and moon, whose names designated the two grand races, Surya and Chandra or Indu. Budha, son of Indu, married Ella, a grand-child of Surya, from which union sprung the Indu race. They deified their ancestor Budha, who continued to be the chief object of adoration until Crishna: hence the worship of Bal-nath [2] and Budha [3] were coeval. That the Nomadic tribes of Arabia, as well as those of Tartary and India, adored the same objects, we learn from the earliest writers; and Job, the probable contemporary of Hasti, the founder of the first capital of the Yadus on the Ganges, boasts in the midst of his griefs that he had always remained uncorrupted by the Sabeïsm which surrounded him. "If I beheld the sun when it shined, or the moon walking in brightness, and my mouth has kissed my hand, this also were an iniquity to be punished by the judge, for I should have denied the God that is above." [4] That there were many Hindus who, professing a pure monotheism like Job, never kissed the hand either to Surya or his herald Budha, we may easily credit from the sublimity of the notions of the 'One God,' expressed both by the ancients and moderns, by poets and by princes, of both races; [5] but more especially by the sons of Budha, who for ages bowed not before graven images, and deemed it impious to raise a temple to

"The Spirit in whose honour shrines are weak."

Hence the Jains, the chief sect of the Budhists, so called from adoring the spirit (Jin), were untinctured with idolatry until the apotheosis of Crishna,[6] whose mysteries superseded the simpler worship of Budha. Némnáth (*the deified Némi*) was the pontiff of Budha, and not only the contemporary of Crishna, but a Yadu, and his near relation; and both had epithets denoting their complexion; for *Arishta*, the surname of Némi, has the same import as Shám or Crishna, '*the black*,' though the latter is of a less Ethiopic hue than Némí. It was anterior to this schism amongst the sons of Budha that the creative power was degraded under

[1] Hercules, Mercury, and Apollo; *Bala-ram, Budha,* and *Kaniya.*

[2] The 'God Bal,' the Vivifier, the Sun.

[3] Budha signifies 'wisdom.'

[4] Job, chap. xxxi. 26, 27, 28.

[5] Chund, the bard, after having separately invoked the three persons of the Hindu triad, says, that he who believes them distinct, "hell will be his portion."

[6] A very curious cause was assigned by an eminent Jain priest for the innovation of enshrining and worshipping the forms of the twenty-four pontiffs: namely, that the worship of Kaniya, before and after the apotheosis, became quite a rage amongst the women, who crowded his shrines, drawing after them all the youth of the Jains; and that, in consequence, they made a statue of Némí to counteract a fervour that threatened the existence of their faith. It is seldom we are furnished with such rational reasons for religious changes.

sensual forms, when the pillar rose to Bal or Surya in Syria and on the Ganges: and the serpent, "subtlest beast of all the field," worshipped as the emblem of wisdom (Budha), was conjoined with the symbol of the creative power, as at the shrine of Eklinga, where the brazen serpent is wreathed round the lingam.[1] Budha's descendants, the Indus, preserved the Ophite sign of their race, when Crishna's followers adopted the eagle as his symbol. These, with the adorers of Surya, form the three idolatrous classes of India, not confined to its modern restricted definition, but that of antiquity, when Indu-st'han or Indu-Scythia extended from the Ganges to the Caspian. In support of the position that the existing polytheism was unknown on the rise of Vishnuism, we may state, that in none of the ancient genealogies do the names of such deities appear as proper names in society, a practice now common; and it is even recorded that the rites of magic, the worship of the host of heaven, and of idols, were introduced from Cashmér, between the periods of Crishna and Vicrama. The powers of nature were personified, and each quality, mental and physical, had its emblem, which the Brahmins taught the ignorant to adopt as realities, till the pantheon became so crowded that life would be too short to acquire even the nomenclature of their "thirty-three millions of gods."[2] No object was too high or too base, from the glorious Orb to the Rampi, or paring-knife of the shoemaker. In illustration of the increase of polytheism, I shall describe the seven forms under which Crishna is worshipped, whose statues are established in the various capitals of Rajast'han, and are occasionally brought together at the festival of Anacuta at Nat'hdwara.

The international wars of the Suryas and the Yadu races, as described in the *Ramayuna* and *Mahabharat*, are lost between allegory and literal interpretation. The Suryas, or Saivas, were depressed; and the Indus, who counted "fifty-six" grand tribes, under the appellations of takshac, '*serpent*,' aswa, '*horse*,' sassu, '*hare*,' etc., etc., had paramount sway. Crishna's schism produced a new type, that of the eagle, and the wars of the schismatics were depicted under their respective emblems, the eagle and serpent, of which latter were the Curus and Takshacs,[3] the

[1] It was the serpent (Budha) who ravished Ella, daughter of Icshwaca, the son of Manu, whence the distinctive epithet of his descendants in the East, *Manús*, or men, the very tradition on an ancient sculptured column in the south of India, which evidently points to the primeval mystery. In Portici there is an exact *lingam* entwined with a brazen serpent, brought from the temple of Isis at Pompeii: and many of the same kind, in mosaic, decorate the floors of the dwelling-houses. But the most singular coincidence is in the wreaths of *lingams* and the *yoni* over the door of the minor temple of Isis at Pompeii; while on another front is painted the rape of Venus by Mercury (Budha and Ella). The Lunar race, according to the *Purans*, are the issue of the rape of Ella by Budha.

Aphah is a serpent in Hebrew. *Ahe* and *Serp* are two of its many appellations in Sanscrit.

[2] *Tyntees crore devota.*

[3] The *Mahabharat* records constant wars from *ancient times* amongst the children of *Surya* (the sun), and the *Tak* or *Takshac* (serpent races). The horse of the sun, liberated preparatory to sacrifice, by the father of Rama, was seized by the *Takshac Anunta*; and Janméja, king of Dehli, grandson of Pandu, was killed by one of the same race. In both instances the *Takshac* is literally rendered the *snake*.

The successor of Janméja carried war into the seats of this *Tâk* or serpent race, and is said to have sacrificed 20,000 of them in revenge; but although it

political adversaries of the Pandus, the relatives of Crishna. The allegory of Crishna's eagle pursuing the serpent Budha, and recovering the books of science and religion with which he fled, is an historical fact disguised : namely, that of Crishna incorporating the doctrines of Budha with his own after the expulsion of the sect from India. Dare we further attempt to lift the veil from this mystery, and trace from the seat of redemption of lost science its originals source ? [1] The gulf of Kutch, the point where the serpent attempted to escape, has been from time immemorial to the present day the entrepôt for the commerce of Sofala, the Red Sea, Egypt, and Arabia. There Budha Trivicrama, or Mercury, has been and is yet invoked by the Indian mariners, especially the pirates of Dwarica. Did Budha or Mercury come from, or escape to the Nile ? Is he the *Hermes* of Egypt to whom the "four books of science," like the four *Védas* [2] of the Hindus, were sacred ? The statues of Némí,[3] the representative of Budha, exactly resemble in feature the bust of young Memnon.

I have already observed that Crishna, before his own deification, worshipped his great ancestor Budha ; and his temple at *Dwarica* rose over the ancient shrine of the latter, which yet stands. In an inscription from the cave of Gaya their characters are conjoined ; "*Heri who is Budha.*" According to western mythology, Apollo and Mercury exchanged symbols, the *caduceus* for the *lyre* ; so likewise in India their characters intermingle : and even the *Sáivá* propitiates Heri as the mediator and disposer of the 'divine spark' (*jote*) to its reunion with the 'parent-flame': —thus, like Mercury, he may be said to be the conveyer of the souls of the dead. Accordingly in funeral lamentation his name only is invoked, and *Heri-bol* ! *Heri-bol* ! is emphatically pronounced by those conveying the corpse to its final abode. The *vahan* (*qu.* the Saxon *van* ?) or celestial car of Crishna, in which the souls (*ansa*) of the just are conveyed to *Surya-Mandal*, the 'mansion of the sun,' is painted like himself, blue (indicative of space, or as *Ouranos*), with the eagle's head ; and here he partakes of the Mercury of the Greeks, and of *Oulios*, the preserver or saviour, one of the titles of Apollo at Delos.[4]

is specifically stated that he subsequently compelled them to sign tributary engagements (*paénameh*), the Brahmins have nevertheless distorted a plain historical fact by a literal and puerile interpretation.

The *Parætacæ* (*Mountain-Tâk*) of Alexander were doubtless of this race, as was his ally Taxiles, which appellation was titular, as he was called Omphis till his father's death. It is even probable that this name is the Greek ΟΦΙΣ, in which they recognised the tribe of the *Tâk* or *Snake*.

Taxiles may be compounded of *es*, 'lord or chief,' *silla*, 'rock or mountain,' and *Tâk*, 'lord of the mountain Tàk,' whose capital was in the range west of the Indus. We are indebted to the Emperor Baber for the exact position of the capital of this celebrated race, which he passed in his route of conquest. We have, however, an intermediate notice of it between Alexander and Baber, in the early history of the *Yadu Bhatti*, who came in conflict with the *Tâks* on their expulsion from Zabulist'han and settlement in the Punjâb.

[1] The Budhists appeared in this peninsula and the adjacent continent was the cradle of Budhism, and here are three of the "*five*" sacred mounts of their faith, *i.e.* Girnar, Satrunja, and Abu. The author purposes giving, hereafter, an account of his journey through these classic regions.

[2] The Budhists and Jains are stigmatised as *Védyavan*, which, signifying 'possessed of science,' is interpreted 'magician.'

[3] He is called *Arishta-Némí*, 'the *black* Némí,' from his complexion.

[4] The Sun-god (Kan, according to Diodorus) is the Minos of the Egyptians. The hieroglyphics at Turin represent him with the head of an ibis, or eagle, with

The Tatar nations, who are all of *Indu* race, like the Rajpoots and German tribes, adored the moon as a male divinity, and to his son, Budha, they assign the same character of mediator. The serpent is alike the symbol of the Budha of the Hindus, the Hermes of the Egyptians, and the Mercury of Greece : and the allegory of the *dragon's teeth*, the origin of letters, brought by Cadmus from Egypt, is a version of the Hindu fable of Kaniya (Apollo) wresting the *Védas* (*secrets*) from Budha or wisdom (*Hermes*), under his sign, the serpent or dragon. We might still further elucidate the resemblance, and by an analysis of the titles and attributes of the Hindu Apollo, prove that from the Yamuna may have been supplied the various incarnations of this divinity, which peopled the pantheons of Egypt, Greece, and Rome. As Nomios, who attended the herds of Admetus, we have Nonita,[1] the infantine appellation of Kaniya, when he pastured the kine of Cesava in the woods of Vindra, whence the ceremony of the sons of princes assuming the crook, and on particular days tending the flocks.[2] As Muralidhara, or the 'flute-holder,' Kaniya is the god of music ; and in giving him the shepherd's reed instead of the *vina* or lyre, we may conjecture that the simple bamboo (*bhans*) which formed the first flute (*bhansli*) was in use before the *chatàra*,[3] the Grecian *cithara*,[4] the first invented lyre of Apollo. Thus from the *six-wired* instrument of the Hindus we have the Greek *cithara*, the English *cithern*, and the Spanish *guitar* of modern days. The Greeks, following the Egyptians, had but six notes, with their lettered symbols ; and it was reserved for the Italians to add a seventh. Guido Aretine, a monk in the thirteenth century, has the credit of this. I, however, believe the Hindus numbered theirs from the heavenly bodies—the Sun, Moon, Mercury, Venus, Mars, Jupiter, Saturn,—hence they had the regular octave, with its semi-tones : and as, in the pruriency of their fancy, they converted the ascending and descending notes into *grahas*, or planetary

an altar before him, on which a shade places his offerings, namely, a goose, cakes of bread, and flowers of the lotus, and awaits in humble attitude his doom. In Sanscrit the same word means *soul*, *goose*, and *swan*, and the Hindu poet is always punning upon it ; though it might be deemed a levity to represent the immaterial portion under so unclassical an emblem. The lotus flowers are alike sacred to the Kan of the Egyptians as to Kaniya the mediator of the Hindus, and both are painted blue and bird-headed. The claims of Kaniya (contracted Kan) as the sun divinity of the Hindus, will be abundantly illustrated in the account of the festivals.

[1] I do not mean to derive any aid from the resemblance of names, which is here merely accidental.

[2] When I heard the octogenarian ruler of Kotah ask his grandson, "Bappa-lal, have you been tending the cows to-day ? " my surprise was converted into pleasure on the origin of the custom being thus classically explained.

[3] From *cha*, 'six' ; and *tar*, 'a string or wire.'

[4] Strabo says, the Greeks consider music as originating from Thrace and Asia, of which countries were Orpheus, Musæus, etc. ; and that others "who regard *all Asia, as far as India*, as a country sacred to *Dionysius* (Bacchus), attribute to that country the invention of nearly all the science of music. We perceive them sometimes describing the *cithara* of the Asiatic, and sometimes applying to flutes the epithet of Phrygian. The names of certain instruments, such as the *nabla*, and others likewise, are taken from barbarous tongues." This *nabla* of Strabo is possibly the *tabla*, the small tabor of India. If Strabo took his orthography from the Persian or Arabic, a single point would constitute the difference between the *N* (ن) and the *T* (ت).

bodies, so they may have added them to the harmonious numbers, and produced the *no-ragini*, their *nine* modes of music.[1] Could we affirm that the hymns composed and set to music by Jydéva, nearly three thousand years ago, and still chanted in honour of the Apollo of Vrij, had been handed down with the sentiments of these mystic compositions (and Sir W. Jones sanctions the idea), we should say, from their simplicity, that the musicians of that age had only the diatonic scale; but we have every reason to believe, from the very elaborate character of their written music, which is painful and discordant to the ear from its minuteness of subdivision, that they had also the chromatic scale, said to have been invented by Timotheus in the time of Alexander, who might have carried it from the banks of the Indus. In the mystic dance, the *Rasmandel*, yet imitated on the annual festival sacred to the sun-god Heri, he is represented with a radiant crown in a dancing attitude, playing on the flute to the nymphs encircling him, each holding a musical instrument.

> " In song and dance about the sacred hill;
> Mystical dance, which yonder starry sphere
> Of planets, and of fixed, in all her wheels
> Resembles nearest, mazes intricate,
> Eccentric, intervolved, yet regular
> Then most, when most irregular they seem;
> And in their motions harmony divine
> So smooths her charming tones, that God's own ear
> Listens delighted."
>
> —MILTON, Book v. 155.

These nymphs are also called the *no-ragini*, from *rága*, a mode of song over which each presides, and *no-rasa*, or 'nine passions,' excited by the powers of harmony. May we not in this trace the origin of Apollo and the sacred nine? In the manner described above, the *rasmandel* is typical of the zodiacal phenomena; and in each sign a musical nymph is sculptured in *alto-relievo*, in the vaulted temples dedicated to the god,[2] or in secular edifices by way of ornament, as in the triumphal column of Cheetore. On the festival of the Jenem, or 'birth-day,' there is a scenic representation of Kaniya and the Gopis: when are rehearsed in the mellifluous accents of the Ionic land of Vrij, the songs of Jydéva, as addressed by Kaniya to Radha and her companions. A specimen of these, as translated by that elegant scholar, Sir W. Jones, may not be considered inappropriate here.

I have had occasion to remark elsewhere,[3] that the Rajpoot bards, like

[1] An account of the state of musical science amongst the Hindus of early ages, and a comparison between it and that of Europe, is yet a desideratum in Oriental literature. From what we already know of the science, it appears to have attained a theoretical precision yet unknown to Europe, and that, at a period when even Greece was little removed from barbarism. The inspirations of the bards of the first ages were all set to music; and the children of the most powerful potentates sang the episodes of the great epics of Valmika and Vyasu. There is a distinguished member of the Royal Asiatic Society, and perhaps the only one, who could fill up this *hiatus*; and we may hope that the leisure and inclination of the Right Honourable Sir Gore Ousely will tempt him to enlighten us on this most interesting point.

[2] I have often been struck with a characteristic analogy in the sculptures of the most ancient Saxon cathedrals in England and on the Continent, to Kaniya and the *Gopis*. Both may be intended to represent divine harmony. Did the Asi and Jits of Scandinavia, the ancestors of the Saxons, bring them from Asia?

[3] *Trans. Royal Asiatic Society*, vol. i. p. 146.

the heroic Scalds of the north, lose no opportunity of lauding themselves; of which Jydéva, the bard of the Yadus, has set an eminent example in the opening of "the songs of Govinda."

"If thy soul be delighted with the remembrance of Heri, or sensible to the raptures of love, listen to the voice of Jydéva, whose notes are both sweet and brilliant."

The poet opens the first interview of Crishna and Radha with an animated description of a night in the rainy season, in which Heri is represented as a wanderer, and Radha, daughter of the shepherd Nanda, is sent to offer him shelter in their cot. Nanda thus speaks to Radha: "The firmament is obscured by clouds; the woodlands are black with Tamála trees; that youth who roves in the forest will be fearful in the gloom of night; go, my daughter, bring the wanderer to my rustic mansion. Such was the command of Nanda the herdsman, and hence arose the love of Radha and Madhava." [1]

The poet proceeds to apostrophise Heri, which the Hindu bard terms *rúpaca*, or 'personal description':

"Oh thou who reclinest on the bosom of Camala, whose ears flame with gems, and whose locks are embellished with sylvan flowers; thou, from whom the day-star derived his effulgence, who slewest the venom-breathing Caliya, who beamedst like a sun on the tribe of Yadu, that flourished like a lotus; thou, who sittest on the plumage of Garura, who sippest nectar from the radiant lips of Pédema, as the fluttering chacora drinks the moon-beams; be victorious, O Heri."

Jydéva then introduces Heri in the society of the pastoral nymphs of Vrij, whom he groups with admirable skill, expressing the passion by which each is animated towards the youthful prince with great warmth and elegance of diction. But Radha, indignant that he should divide with them the affection she deemed exclusively her own, flies his presence. Heri, repentant and alarmed, now searches the forest for his beloved, giving vent at each step to impassioned grief. "Woe is me! she feels a sense of injured honour, and has departed in wrath. How will she conduct herself? How will she express her pain in so long a separation? What is wealth to me? What are numerous attendants? What the pleasures of the world? How can I invite thee to return? Grant me but a sight of thee, oh! lovely Radha, for my passion torments me. O God of love! mistake me not for Síva. Wound me not again. I love already but too passionately; yet have I lost my beloved. Brace not thy bow, thou conqueror of the world! My heart is already pierced by arrows from Radha's eyes, black and keen as those of the antelope."

Radha relents and sends a damsel in quest of Heri, whom she finds in a solitary arbour on the banks of the Yamuna. She describes her mistress as animated by the same despair which controls him:

"Her face is like a water-lily veiled in the dew of tears, and her eyes are as moons eclipsed. She draws thy picture and worships it, and at the close of every sentence exclaims, 'O Madhava, at thy feet am I fallen!' Then she figures thee standing before her: she sighs, she smiles, she mourns, she weeps. Her abode, the forest—herself through thy absence is become a timid roe, and love is the tiger who springs on her, like Yama, the genius of death. So emaciated is her beautiful body, that

[1] *Madhu* in the dialect of Vrij.

even the light garland which waves o'er her bosom is a load. The palm of her hand supports her aching temple, motionless as the crescent rising at eve. Thus, O divine healer, by the nectar of thy love must Radha be restored to health; and if thou refusest, thy heart must be harder than the thunder-stone."[1]

The damsel returns to Radha and reports the condition of Heri, mourning her absence: "Even the hum of the bee distracts him. Misery sits fixed in his heart, and every returning night adds anguish to anguish." She then recommends Radha to seek him. "Delay not, O, loveliest of women; follow the lord of thy heart. Having bound his locks with forest flowers, he hastens to yon arbour, where a soft gale breathes over the banks of Yamuna, and there pronouncing thy name, *he modulates his divine reed.* Leave behind thee, O friend, the ring which tinkles on thy delicate ankle when thou sportest in the dance. Cast over thee thy azure mantle and run to the shady bower."

But Radha, too weak to move, is thus reported to Heri by the same fair mediator: "She looks eagerly on all sides in hope of thy approach: she advances a few steps and falls languid to the ground. She weaves bracelets of fresh leaves, and looking at herself in sport, exclaims, behold the vanquisher of Madha! Then she repeats the name of Heri, and catching at a dark blue cloud,[2] strives to embrace it, saying, 'It is my beloved who approaches.'"

Midnight arrives, but neither Heri nor the damsel returns, when she gives herself up to the frenzy of despair, exclaiming: "The perfidy of my friend rends my heart. Bring disease and death, O gale of Malaya! receive me in thy azure wave, O sister of Yama,[3] that the ardour of my heart may be allayed."

The repentant Heri at length returns, and in speech well calculated to win forgiveness, thus pleads his pardon:

"Oh! grant me a draught of honey from the lotus of thy mouth: or if thou art inexorable, grant me death from the arrows of thine eyes; make thy arms my chains: thou art my ornament; thou art the pearl in the ocean of my mortal birth! Thine eyes, which nature formed like blue water-lilies, are become through thy resentment like petals of the crimson lotus! Thy silence affects me; oh! speak with the voice of music, and let thy sweet accents allay my ardour."

"Radha with timid joy, darting her eyes on Govinda while she musically sounded the rings of her ankles and *the bells of her zone*,[4] entered the mystic bower of her beloved. His heart was agitated by her sight, as the waves of the deep are affected by the lunar orb.[5] From his graceful

[1] We meet with various little philosophical phenomena used as similies in this rhapsody of Jydéva. These *aërolites*, mentioned by a poet the contemporary of David and Solomon, are but recently known to the European philosopher.

[2] This is, in allusion to the colour of Crishna, a dark blue.

[3] The Indian Pluto; she is addressing the Yamuna.

[4] Thus the ancient statues do not present merely the sculptor's fancy in the zone of bells with which they are ornamented.

[5] This is a favourite metaphor with the bards of India, to describe the alternations of the exciting causes of love; and it is yet more important as showing that Jydéva was the philosopher as well as the poet of nature, in making the action of the moon upon the tides the basis of this beautiful simile.

waist flowed a pale yellow robe,[1] which resembled the golden dust of the water-lily scattered over its blue petals.[2] His locks interwoven with blossoms, were like a cloud variegated by the moonbeam. Tears of transport gushed in a stream from the full eyes of Radha, and their watery glances beamed on her best beloved. Even shame, which had before taken its abode in their dark pupils, was itself ashamed,[3] and departed when the fawn-eyed Radha gazed on the bright face of Crishna."

The poet proceeds to describe Apollo's bower on the sable Yamuna, as "Love's recess"; and sanctifies it as

. . . "The ground
Where early Love his Psyche's zone unbound."[4]

In the morning the blue god aids in Radha's simple toilet. He stains her eye with antimony "which would make the blackest bee envious," places "a circle of musk on her forehead," and intertwines "a chaplet of flowers and peacock's feathers in her dark tresses," replacing "the zone of golden bells." The bard concludes as he commenced, with an eulogium on the inspirations of his muse, which it is evident were set to music. "Whatever is delightful in the modes of music, whatever is graceful in the fine strains of poetry, whatever is exquisite in the sweet art of love, let the happy and wise learn from the songs of Jydéva."

This mystic dance, the ***rasmandel***, appears analogous to the Pyhrric dance, or the *fire*-dance of the Egyptians. The movements of those who personate the deity and his fair companions are full of grace, and the dialogue is replete with harmony.[5] The Chobis[6] of Mat'hura and Vindravana have considerable reputation as vocalists; and the effect of the modulated and deep tones of the adult blending with the clear treble of the juvenile performers, while the time is marked by the cymbal or the soothing monotony of the tabor, accompanied occasionally by the ***múrali*** or flute, is very pleasing.

We have a Parnassus in Girdhana, from which sacred hill the god derives one of his principal epithets, Girdhun or Gordhun-nath, 'God of the mount of wealth.' Here he first gave proofs of miraculous power, and a cave in this hill was the first shrine, on his apotheosis, whence his miracles and oracles were made known to the Yadus. From this cave (*gopha*) is derived another of his titles—*Goph-nath*, 'Lord of the cave,' distinct from his epithet Gopi-nath, 'Lord of the Gopis,' or pastoral

[1] This *yellow robe* or mantle furnishes another title of the Sun-god, namely *Pit-ambra*, typical of the resplendence which precedes his rising and setting.

[2] It will be again necessary to call to mind the colour of Crishna, to appreciate this elegant metaphor.

[3] This idea is quite new.

[4] *Childe Harold*, Canto iii.

[5] The anniversary of the birth of Kaniya is celebrated with splendour at Sindia's court, where the author frequently witnessed it, during a ten year's residence.

[6] The priests of Kaniya, probably so called from the *chob* or club with which, on the annual festival, they assault the castle of Kansa, the tyrant usurper of Crishna's birthright, who, like Herod, ordered the slaughter of all the youth of Vrij, that Crishna might not escape. These *Chobis* are most likely the *Sobii* of Alexander, who occupied the chief towns of the Punjab, and who, according to Arrian, worshipped Hercules (*Heri-cul-és*, chief of the race of Heri), and were armed with clubs. The mimic assault of Kansa's castle by some hundreds of these robust church militants, with their long clubs covered with iron rings, is well worth seeing.

nymphs. On the annual festival held at Girdhana, the sacred mount is purified with copious oblations of milk, for which all the cows of the district are in requisition.

The worship of Crishna in ancient days, like that of Apollo amongst the Greeks, was chiefly celebrated in caves, of which there were many scattered over India. The most remarkable were those of Girdhana in Vrij; Gaya in Bahar; Goph-nath on the shores of Saurashtra; and Jalindra[1] on the Indus. In these dark and mysterious retreats superstition had her full influence over the votaries who sought the commands and deprecated the wrath of the deity: but, as the Mookhia told the author, "the age of oracles and miracles is past"; and the new wheel, which was miraculously furnished each revolving year to supply the place of that which first indicated his desire to abide at Nat'hdwara, is no longer forthcoming. The old one, which was the signal of his wish, is, however, preserved as a relic, and greatly reverenced. The statue now worshipped at Nat'hdwara, as the representative of 'the god of the mount,' is said to be the identical image raised in the cave of Girdhana, and brought thence by the high priest Balba.

As the destroyer of Kali-nag, 'the *black* serpent,' which infested the waters of the Yamuna, Kaniya has the character of the Pythic Apollo. He is represented dragging the monster from the 'black stream,' and bruising him with his foot. He had, however, many battles with his hydra-foe ere he vanquished him, and he was once driven by Kalyamun from Vrij to Dwarica, whence his title of Rinchor. Here we have the old allegory of the schismatic wars of the Budhists and Vishnués.

Diodorus informs us that *Kan* was one of the titles of the Egyptian Apollo as the sun; and this is the common contraction for Kaniya, whose colour is a dark cerulean blue (*nila*): and hence his name Nila-nath, who, like the Apollo of the Nile, is depicted with the human form and eagle-head, with a lotus in his hand. S and H are permutable letters in the Bhakka, and Sám or Sham, the god of the Yamuna, may be the *Ham* or Hammon of Egypt. Heri accompanied Ramesa to Lanka, as did the Egyptian Apollo, Rameses-Sesostris, on his expedition to India: both were attended in their expedition by an army of Satyrs, or tribes bearing the names of different animals: and as we have the *Aswas*, the *Takshacs*, and the *Sassus* of the *Yadu* tribes, typified under the horse, the serpent, and the hare, so the races of *Surya*, of which Rama was the head, may have been designated *Rishi* and *Hanuman*, or bears and monkeys. The distance of the Nile from the Indian shore forms no objection; the sail spread for Ceylon, could waft the vessel to the Red Sea, which the fleets of Tyre, of Solomon, and Hiram covered about this very time. That the Hindus navigated the ocean from the earliest ages, the traces of their religion in the isles of the Indian archipelago sufficiently attest; but on this subject we have already said enough.

The coincidence between the most common epithets of the Apollos of Greece and India, as applied to the sun, are peculiarly striking. Heri, as Bhan-nat'h, 'the lord of beams,' is Phœbus, and his heaven is *Heripúr*

[1] Jalindra on the Indus is described by the Emperor Baber as a very singular spot, having numerous caves. The deity of the caves of Jalindra is the tutelary deity of the Prince of Marwar.

(Heliopolis), or 'city of Heri.' [1] Helios (Ηλιος) was a title of Apollo, whence the Greeks had their Elysium, the Heripúr or *Bhan-t'han* (the abode of the sun), the highest of the heavens or abodes of bliss of the martial Rajpoot. Hence the eagle (the emblem of Heri as the sun) [2] was adopted by the western warrior as the symbol of victory.

The *Di Majores* of the Rajpoot are the same in number and title as amongst the Greeks and Romans, being the deities who figuratively preside over the planetary system. Their grades of bliss are therefore in unison with the eccentricity of orbit of the planet named. On this account Chandra or Indu, the moon, being a mere satellite of Ella, the earth, though probably originating the name of the *Indu* race, is inferior in the scale of blissful abodes to that of his son Budha or Mercury, whose heliacal appearance gave him importance even with the sons of Vaiva, the sun. From the poetic seers of the martial races we learn that there are two distinct places of reward; the one essentially spiritual, the other of a material nature. The bard inculcates that the warrior who falls in battle in the fulfilment of his duty, "who abandons life through the wave of steel," will know no "second birth," but that the unconfined spark (*jote*) will reunite to the parent orb. The doctrine of transmigration through a variety of hideous forms, may be considered as a series of purgatories.

The Greeks and Celts worshipped Apollo under the title of Carneios, which "selon le scholiaste de Théocrite" is derived from Carnos, "qui ne prophétisoit que des malheurs aux Héraclides lors de leur incursion dans le Péloponnèse. Un d'eux appelé *Hippotés, le tua d'un coup de flèche.*" Now one of the titles of the Hindu Apollo is Carna, 'the radiant'; from *carna*, 'a ray': and when he led the remains of the *Hericúlas* in company with Baldéva (*the god of strength*), and Yudishtra, after the great international war, into the Peloponnesus of Saurashtra, they were attacked by the aboriginal Bhils, *one of whom slew the divine Carna with an arrow.* The Bhils claim to be of *Hyvansa*, or the race of *Hya*, whose chief seat was at Mahéswar on the Nerbudda: the assassin of Carna would consequently be Hipúta, or *descendant* of *Hya.*[3]

The most celebrated of the monuments commonly termed Druidic, scattered throughout Europe, is at Carnac in Brittany, on which coast the Celtic Apollo had his shrines, and was propitiated under the title of Carneus, and this monument may be considered at once sacred to the manes of the warriors and the sun-god Carneus. Thus the Roman Saturnalia, the

[1] "In Hebrew *heres* signifies the sun, but in Arabic the meaning of the radical word is to guard, preserve; and of *haris*, guardian, preserver."—Volney's *Ruins of Empires*, p. 316.

[2] The heaven of *Vishnu, Vaicûnt'ha,* is entirely of gold, and 80,000 miles in circumference. Its edifices, pillars, and ornaments are composed of precious stones. The crystal waters of the Ganges form a river in Vaicûnt'ha, where are lakes filled with blue, red, and white water-lilies, each of a hundred and even a thousand petals. On a throne glorious as the meridian sun resting on water-lilies, is Vishnu, with Lacshmi or *Sri*, the goddess of abundance (the Ceres of the Egyptians and Greeks), on his right hand, surrounded by spirits who constantly celebrate the praise of Vishnu and Lacshmi, who are served by his votaries, and to whom the eagle (*garûda*) is door-keeper.—Extract from the *Mahabharat.*—See Ward on the *History and Religion of the Hindus*, vol. ii. p. 14.

[3] Supposing these coincidences in the fabulous history of the ancient nations of Greece and Asia to be merely fortuitous, they must excite interest; but conjoined with various others in the history of the *Hericúlas* of India and the *Heraclidæ* of Greece, I cannot resist the idea that they were connected.

carnivale, has a better etymology in the festival to Carneus, as the sun, than in the "adieu to flesh" during the fast. The character of this festival is entirely oriental, and accompanied with the licentiousness which belonged to the celebration of the powers of nature. Even now, although Christianity has banished the grosser forms, it partakes more of a Pagan than a Christian ceremony.

Of the festivals of Crishna the *Anacúta* is the most remarkable; when the seven statues were brought from the different capitals of Rajast'han, and mountains (*cúta*) of food (*ana*) piled up for their repast, at a given signal are levelled by the myriads of votaries assembled from all parts. About eighty years ago, on a memorable assemblage at the Anacúta, before warfare had devastated Rajast'han, and circumscribed the means of the faithful disciples of Heri, amongst the multitude of *Vishnués* of every region were almost all the Rajpoot princes; Rana Ursi of Méwar, Raja Beejy Sing of Marwar, Raja Guj Sing of Bíkanér, and Buhadoor Sing of Kishengurh. Rana Ursi presented to the god a *tora*, or massive golden anklet-chain set with emeralds: Beejy Sing a diamond necklace worth twenty-five thousand rupees: the other princes according to their means. They were followed by an old woman of Surat, with infirm step and shaking head, who deposited four coppers in the hand of the high-priest, which were received with a gracious smile, not vouchsafed to the lords of the earth. "The Ránd is in luck," whispered the chief of Kishengurh to the Rana. Soon afterwards the statue of Heri was brought forth, when the same old woman placed at its feet a bill of exchange for seventy thousand rupees. The mighty were humbled, and the smile of the *Gosaén* was explained. Such gifts, and to a yet greater amount, are, or were, by no means uncommon from the sons of commerce, who are only known to belong to the flock from the distinguishing necklace of the sect.[1]

The predatory system which reduced these countries to a state of the most degraded anarchy, greatly diminished the number of pilgrimages to Nat'hdwara; and the gods of Vrij had sufficient prescience to know that they could guard neither their priests nor followers from the Pat'han and Mahratta, to whom the crown of the god, or the *nutna* (nose-jewel) of Radha, would be alike acceptable: nor would they have scrupled to retain both the deities and priests as hostages for such imposition as they might deem within their means. Accordingly, of late years, there had been no congress of the gods of Vrij, who remained fixtures on their altars till the halcyon days of A.D. 1818 permitted their liberation.[2]

The *seven statues* of Kaniya were brought together by the high-priest

[1] Gibbon records a similar offering of 200,000 sesterces to the Roman church, by a stranger, in the reign of Decius.

[2] I enjoyed no small degree of favour with the supreme pontiff of the shrine of Apollo and all his votaries, for effecting a meeting of the seven statues of Vishnu in 1820. In contriving this I had not only to reconcile ancient animosities between the priests of the different shrines, in order to obtain a free passport for the gods, but to pledge myself to the princes in whose capitals they were established, for their safe return: for they dreaded lest bribery might entice the priests to fix them elsewhere, which would have involved their loss of sanctity, dignity, and prosperity. It cost me no little trouble, and still more anxiety, to keep the assembled multitudes at peace with each other, for they are as outrageous as any sectarians in contesting the supreme power and worth of their respective forms (*rúpa*). Yet they all separated, not only without violence, but without even any attempt at robbery, so common on such occasions.

Balba, who established the festival of the Anacúta. They remained in the same sanctuary until the time of Girdharí, the grandson of Balba, who having seven sons, gave to each a *rúpa* or statue, and whose descendants continue in the office of priest. The names and present abodes of the gods are as follows :—

Nath-ji, *the* god, or Gordan-Nath, god of the mount . Nat'hdwara.

1. Nonita . . . . . . Nat'hdwara.
2. Mat'hura-Nath . . . . Kotah.
3. Dwar-ca-Nath . . . . . Kankerowli.
4. Gokul-Nath, or Gokul-Chandrama . Jeipoor.
5. Yadu-Nath . . . . . . Surat.
6. Vital-Nath . . . . . . Kotah.
7. Mudhun Mohuna . . . . . Jeipoor.

Nath-ji is not enumerated amongst the forms ; he stands supreme.

Nonita, or Nonanda, the juvenile Kaniya, has his altar separate, though close to Nath-ji. He is also styled Bala-mokund, 'the blessed child,' and is depicted as an infant with a *pêra* [1] or comfit-ball in his hand. This image, which was one of the *penates* of a former age, and which, since the destruction of the shrines of Crishna by the Islamites, had lain in the Yamuna, attached itself to the sacerdotal zone (*zunu*) of the high-priest Balba, while he was performing his ablutions, who, carrying it home, placed it in a niche of the temple and worshipped it : and Nonanda yet receives the peculiar homage of the high-priest and his family as their household divinity. Of the second image, Mat'hura Nath, there is no particular mention : it was at one time at Kamnorh in Méwar, but is now at Kotah.

Balcrishna, the third son, had Dwar-ca Nath, which statue, now at Kankerowli in Méwar, is asserted to be the identical image that received the adoration of Raja Umríka, a prince of the solar race who lived in the *Satya Yuga*, or silver age. The 'god of the mount' revealed himself in a dream to his high-priest, and told him of the domicile of this his representative at Kanouj. Thither Balba repaired, and having obtained it from the *Brahmin*, appointed Damodur-das Khetri to officiate at his altar.

The fourth statue, that of Gokul-Nath, or Gokul Chandrama (*i.e.* the *moon* of Gokul), had an equally mysterious origin, having been discovered in a deep ravine on the banks of the river ; Balba assigned it to his brother-in-law. Gokul is an island on the Jumna, a few miles below Mat'hura, and celebrated in the early history of the pastoral divinity. The residence of this image at Jeipoor does not deprive the little island of its honours as a place of pilgrimage ; for the '*god of Gokul*' has an altar on the original site, and his rites are performed by an aged priestess, who disowns the jurisdiction of the high-priest of Nat'hdwara, both in the spiritual and temporal concerns of her shrine ; and who, to the no small scandal of all who are interested in Apollo, appealed from the fiat of the high-priest to the British court of justice. The royal grants of the Mogul emperors were produced, which proved the right to lay in the high-priest, though a

[1] The *pêra* of Mat'hura can only be made from the waters of the Yamuna, from whence it is still conveyed to Nonanda at Nat'hdwara, and with curds forms his evening repast.

long period of almost undisturbed authority had created a feeling of independent control in the family of the priestess, which they desired might continue. A compromise ensued, when the author was instrumental in restoring harmony to the shrines of Apollo.

The fifth, Yadu-Nath, is the deified ancestor of the whole *Yadu* race. This image, now at Surat, formerly adorned the shrine of Mahavan near Mat'hura, which was destroyed by Mahmud.

The sixth, Vitul-Nath, or Pandurang, was found in the Ganges at Benares, *Samvat* 1572 (A.D. 1516), from which we may judge of their habit of multiplying divinities.

The seventh, Mudhun Mohuna, " he who intoxicates with desire," the seductive lover of Radha and the *Gopis*, has his rites performed by a female. The present priestess of Mohuna is the mother of Damodra, the supreme head of all who adore the Apollo of Vrij.

I am not aware of the precise period of Balba Acharya, who thus collected the seven images of Crishna now in Rajast'han ; but he must have lived about the time of the last of the Lodi kings, at the period of the conquest of India by the Moguls (A.D. 1526). The present pontiff, Damodra, as before said, is his lineal descendant ; and whether in addressing him verbally or by letter, he is styled *Maharaja* or 'great prince.' [1]

As the supreme head of the Vishnu sect, his person is held to be *Ansa*, or " a portion of the divinity " ; and it is maintained that so late as the father of the present incumbent, the god manifested himself and conversed with the high-priest. The present pontiff is now about thirty years of age. He is of a benign aspect, with much dignity of demeanour : courteous, yet exacting the homage due to his high calling : meek, as becomes the priest of Govinda, but with the finished manners of one accustomed to the first society. His features are finely moulded, and his complexion good. He is about the middle size, though as he rises to no mortal, I could not exactly judge of his height. When I saw him he had one only daughter, to whom he is much attached. He has but one wife, nor does Crishna allow polygamy to his priest. In times of danger, like some of his prototypes in the dark ages of Europe, he poised the lance, and found it more effective than spiritual anathemas, against those who would first adore the god, and then plunder him. Such were the Mahratta chiefs, Jeswunt Rao Holkar and Bapoo Sindia. Damodra accordingly made the tour of his extensive diocese at the head of four hundred horse, two standards of foot, and two field-pieces. He rode the finest mares in the country ; laid aside his pontificals for the quilted *dugla*, and was summoned to matins by the kettle-drum instead of the bell and cymbal. In this he only imitated Kaniya, who often mixed in the ranks of battle, and " dyed

[1] *Gosáen* is a title more applicable to the *célibataire* worshippers of Hari than of Heri—of Jupiter than of Apollo. It is alleged that the Emperor Akber first bestowed this epithet on the high-priest of Crishna, whose rites attracted his regard. They were previously called *Dikhit*, 'one who performs sacrifice,' a name given to a very numerous class of Brahmins.

The *Gotra Acharya*, or genealogical creed of the high-priest, is as follows : " *Tylung Brahmin, Bhardhwaja gotra*,[1] *Gûracûla*,[2] *Tyturi sac'ha ; i.e.* Brahmin of Telingana, of the tribe of Bhardhwaja, of the race of Gúr, of the branch Tyturi."

[1] *Bhardhwaja* was a celebrated founder of a sect in the early ages.
[2] *Gúr* is an epithet applied to Vrishpati, " Lord of the Bull," the Indian Jupiter, who is called the *Gúr*, preceptor or guardian of the gods.

his saffron robe in the red-stained field." Had Damodra been captured on one of these occasions by any marauding Pat'han, and incarcerated, as he assuredly would have been, for ransom, the marauder might have replied to the Rana, as did the Plantagenet king to the Pope, when the surrender of the captive church-militant bishop was demanded, "Is this thy son Joseph's coat ?" But, notwithstanding this display of martial principle, which covered with a helmet the shaven crown, his conduct and character are amiable and unexceptionable, and he furnishes a striking contrast to the late head of the Vishnu establishments in Marwar, who commenced with the care of his master's conscience, and ended with that of the state ; meek and unassuming till he added temporal [1] to spiritual power, which developed unlimited pride, with all the qualities that too often wait on "a little brief authority," and to the display of which he fell a victim. Damodra,[2] similarly circumstanced, might have evinced the same failings, and have met the same end ; but though endeavours were made to give him political influence at the Rana's court, yet, partly from his own good sense, and partly through the dissuasion of the Nestor of Kotah (Zalim Sing), he was not entrained in the vortex of its intrigues, which must have involved the sacrifice of wealth and the proper dignity of his station.

APPENDIX

No. I.

Grant of the Rahtore Rani, the Queen-Mother of Oodipoor, on the death of her Son, the Heir-Apparent, Prince Umra.

Sid Sri Burra [3] *Rahtor-ji* to the *Patéls* and inhabitants of *Giroh.* The four *bígahs* of land, belonging to the Jat Rogga, have been assigned to the Brahmin Kishna on the *Anta Samya* (final epoch) of *Lalji.*[4] *Let him possess*

[1] The high priest of Jalindra-nath used to appear at the head of a cavalcade far more numerous than any feudal lord of Marwar. A sketch of this personage will appear elsewhere. These Brahmins were not a jot behind the ecclesiastical lords of the Middle Ages, who are thus characterised : "Les seigneurs ecclésiastiques, malgré l'humilité chrétienne, ne se sont pas montrés moins orgueilleux que les nobles laïcs. Le doyen du chapitre de Notre Dame du Port, à Clermont, pour montrer sa grande noblesse, officiait avec toute la pompe féodale. Etant à l'autel, il avait l'oiseau sur la perche gauche, et on portait devant lui la hallebarde ; on la lui portait aussi de la même manière pendant qu'on chantait l'évangile, et aux processions il avait lui-même l'oiseau sur le poing, et il marchait à la tête de ses serviteurs, menant ses chiens de chasse."—*Dict. de l'Anc. Régime,* p. 380.

[2] The first letter I received on reaching England after my long residence in India was from this priest, filled with anxious expressions for my health, and speedy return to protect the lands and sacred kine of Apollo.

[3] The *great Rahtore* queen. There were two of this tribe ; she was the queen-mother.

[4] An endearing epithet, applied to children, from *larla,* beloved.

the rents thereof.[1] The dues for wood and forage (*khur lákur*) contributions (*burar*) are renounced by the state in favour of the Brahmins.

Samvat 1875, *Amavus* 15*th of Asoj*, A.D. 1819.

No. II.

Grant held by a Brahmin of Birkhairah.

"A Brahmin's orphan was compelled by hunger to seek sustenance in driving an oil-mill; instead of oil the receptacle was filled with blood. The frightened oilman demanded of the child who he was; 'A Brahmin's orphan,' was the reply. Alarmed at the enormity of his guilt in thus employing the son of a priest, *he covered the palm of his hand with earth, in which he sowed the túlasi seed*, and went on a pilgrimage to Dwarica. He demanded the presence (*dursuna*) of the god; the priests pointed to the ocean, when he plunged in, and had an interview with Dwarica Nath, who presented him with a written order on the *Rana* for forty-five *bígahs* of land. He returned and threw the writing before the *Rana*, on the steps of the temple of Juggernat'h. The *Rana* read the writing of the god, placed it on his head, and immediately made out the grant. This is three hundred and fifty years ago, as recorded by an inscription on stone, and his descendant, Koshala, yet enjoys it."

(A true Translation.) J. Tod.

No. III.

The Palode inscription is unfortunately mislaid; but in searching for it, another was discovered from Unair, four miles south-west of the ancient Morwan, where there is a temple to the four-armed divinity (Chathurbhuja), endowed in *Samvat* 1570, by *Rana* Juggut Sing.

On one of the pillars of the temple is inscribed a voluntary gift made in *Samvat* 1845, and signed by the village *Panch*, of the first-fruits of the harvest, namely, *two seers and a-half* (five pounds weight) from each *khal*[2] of the spring, and the same of the autumnal harvests.

No. IV.

Sri Umra Sing (II.) etc., etc.

Whereas the shrine of Sri Pratap-Iswara (*the God of Fortune*) has been erected in the meadows of Rasmi, all the groves and trees are sacred to

[1] It is customary to call these grants to religious orders "grants of land," although they entitle only the rents thereof; for there is no *seizin* of the land itself, as numerous inscriptions testify, and which, as well as the present, prove the proprietary right to be in the cultivator only. The *tamba-patra*,[1] or copper-plate *patent* (by which such grants are properly designated) of Yasóvarma, the *Pramara* prince of Oojein, seven hundred years ago, is good evidence that the rents only are granted; he commands the crown tenants of the two villages assigned to the temple "to pay all dues as they arise—money-rent—first share of produce," not a word of *seizin* of the soil.—See *Transactions of the Royal Asiatic Society*, vol. i. p. 223.

[2] A *khal* is one of the heaps after the corn is thrashed out, about *five maunds*.

---

[1] To distinguish them from grants of land to *feudal tenants*, which patents (*putta*) are manuscript.

him; whoever cuts down any of them is an offender to the state, and shall pay a fine of three hundred rupees, and the *ass* [1] shall be the portion of the officers of government who suffer it.

Pos. 14, *Samvat* 1712 (A.D. 1656).

No. V.

Mahrana Sri Raj Sing, commanding.

To the *Nobles, Ministers, Patéls,*[2] *Putwaris,*[2] of the ten thousand [villages] of Méwar (*dossehés Méwar-ra*), according to your stations—read!

1. From remote times, the temples and dwellings of the *Jains* have been authorised; let none therefore within their boundaries carry animals to slaughter—this is their ancient privilege.

2. Whatever life, whether man or animal, passes their abode for the purpose of being killed, is saved (*amra*).[3]

3. Traitors to the state, robbers, felons escaped confinement, who may fly for sanctuary (*sirna*) to the dwellings (*upasrá*) [4] of the *Yatis,*[5] shall not there be seized by the servants of the court.

4. The *kúnchi* [6] (handful) at harvest, the *múti* (handful) of *keranoh*, the charity lands (*doli*), grounds, and houses, established by them in the various towns, shall be maintained.

5. This ordinance is issued in consequence of the representation of the *Ric* [7] Manoh, to whom is granted fifteen *bígahs* of *adhán* [8] land, and twenty-five of *malaiti.*[8] The same quantity of each kind in each of the districts of Nímutch and Nímbahaira.—Total in three districts, forty-five *bígahs* of *adhán*, and seventy-five of *mal.*[9]

On seeing this ordinance, let the land be measured and assigned, and let none molest the *Yatis*, but foster their privileges. Cursed be he who infringes them—the *cow* to the Hindu—the *hog* and *corpse* to the Musulman.

(By command)

Samvat 1749, *Mahsud* 5th, A.D. 1693. SAH DYAL (Minister).

No. VI.

Maharaja Chuttur Sing (one of the Rana's sons), commanding.

In the town of Rasmi, whoever slays sheep, buffaloes, goats, or other living thing, is a criminal to the state; his house, cattle, and effects shall be forfeited, and himself expelled the village.

(By command)

Pos Sud 14, *Samvat* 1705, A.D. 1649. The *Pancholi* DUMICA DAS.

[1] The *gadda-ghál* is a punishment unknown in any but the Hindu code; the hieroglyphic import appears on the pillar, and must be seen to be understood.

[2] Revenue officers.

[3] Literally 'immortal,' from *mura*, 'death,' and the privative prefix.

[4] Schools or colleges of the *Yatis*.

[5] Priests of the *Jains*.

[6] *Kúnchi* and *múti* are both a 'handful'; the first is applied to grain in the stalk at harvest time; the other to such edibles in merchandise as sugar, raisins, etc., collectively termed *keranoh*.

[7] *Ric* is an ancient title applied to the highest class of priests; *Ric-Ricsha-Riciswára*, applied to royalty in old times.

[8] *Adhán* is the richest land, lying under the protection of the town walls; *mal* or *malaiti* land is land not irrigated from wells.

[9] In all a hundred and twenty *bígahs*, or about forty acres.

No. VII.

Mahrana Jey Sing to the inhabitants of Bakrole; printers, potters, oilmen, etc., etc., commanding.

From the 11th *Asar* (June) to the full moon of *Asoj* (September), none shall drain the waters of the lake; no oil-mill shall work, or earthen vessel be made, during these the four rainy months.

No. VIII.

Mahrana Sri Juggut Sing II., commanding

The village of Síarh in the hills, of one thousand rupees yearly rent, having been chosen by Nat'h-ji (*the* God) for his residence, and given up by Rinna Raghudé,[1] I have confirmed it. The *Gosaén*[2] and his heirs shall enjoy it for ever.

Samvat 1793, A.D. 1737.

No. IX.

Sid Sri Mahraja Dheraj, Mahrana Sri Bhím Sing-ji, commanding.

The undermentioned towns and villages were presented to Sri-ji[3] by copper-plate. The revenues (*hasil*),[4] contributions (*burar*), taxes, dues (*lagut-bé-lagut*), trees, shrubs, *foundations* and *boundaries* (*ním sím*), shall all belong to Sri-ji. If of my seed, none will ever dispute this.

The ancient copper-plate being lost, I have thus renewed it.

Here follows a list of *thirty-four* entire towns and villages, many from the fisc, or confirmations of the grants of the chiefs, besides various parcels of arable land, from twenty to one hundred and fifty *bígahs*, in forty-six more villages, from chiefs of every class, and patches of meadow-land (*bíra*) in twenty more.

No. X.

Sri Mahrana Bhíma Sing-ji, commanding.

To the towns of Sri-ji, or to the [*personal*] lands of the *Gosaén-ji*,[5] no molestation shall be offered. No warrants or exactions shall be issued

[1] The chief of Délwara.

[2] There are other grants later than this, which prove that all grants were renewed in every new reign. This grant also proves that no chief has the power to alienate without his sovereign's sanction.

[3] Epithet indicative of the greatness of the deity.

[4] Here is another proof that the sovereign can only alienate the revenues (*hasil*); and though everything upon and about the grant, yet *not the soil.* The *ním-sím* is almost as powerful an expression as the old grant to the Rawdons—

"From earth to heaven,
From heaven to hell,
For thee and thine
Therein to dwell."

[5] The high-priest.

or levied upon them. All complaints, suits, or matters, in which justice is required, originating in Na'thdwara, shall be settled there; none shall interfere therein, and the decisions of the *Gosaén-ji* I shall invariably confirm. The town and transit duties[1] (of Nat'hdwara and villages pertaining thereto), the assay (*purkhaye*)[1] fees from the public markets, duties on precious metals (*kasoti*),[1] all brokerage (*dulali*), and dues collected at the four gates; all contributions and taxes of whatever kind, are presented as an offering to Sri-ji; let the income thereof be placed in Sri-ji's coffers.

All the products of foreign countries imported by the *Vaishnuvas*,[2] whether domestic or foreign, and intended for consumption at Nat'hdwara,[3] shall be exempt from duties. The right of sanctuary (*sirna*) of Sri-ji, both in the town and in all his other villages,[4] will be maintained: the Almighty will take cognisance of any innovation. Wherefore, let all chiefs, farmers of duties, beware of molesting the goods of Nat'h-ji (*the* god), and wherever such may halt, let guards be provided for their security, and let each chief convey them through his bounds in safety. If of my blood, or if my servants, this warrant will be obeyed for ever and for ever. Whoever resumes this grant will be a caterpillar in hell during 60,000 years.

By command—through the chief butler (*Panairi*) Eklingdas: written by Surut Sing, son of Nat'hji Pancholi, *Mah-sud* 1st, *Samvat* 1865; A.D. 1809.

No. XI.

Personal grant to the high-priest, Damodurji Mahraj.

Swesta Sri, from the abode at Udyapúr, Mahrana Sri Bhím Sing-ji, commanding.

To all the chieftains, landholders, managers of the crown and *dori*[5] lands, to all *Patéls*, etc., etc., etc. As an offering to the *Sri Gosaén-ji* two rupees have been granted in every village throughout *Méwar*, one in each harvest—let no opposition be made thereto. If of my kin or issue, none will revoke this—the *ân* (oath of allegiance) be upon his head. By command, through Purihara Myaram, *Samvat* 1860, *Jaet sud* 5th *Munlgulwar*; A.D. 1804.

At one side of the patent, in the Rana's own hand, "An offering to Sri Girdhari-ji[6] Mahraj—If of my issue none will disobey—who dares, may the Almighty punish!"

[1] All these are royalties, and the Rana was much blamed, even by his *Vishnuva* ministers, for sacrificing them even to Kaniya.

[2] Followers of Vishnu, Crishna, or Kaniya, chiefly mercantile.

[3] Many merchants, by the connivance of the conductors of the caravans of Nat'h-ji's goods, contrived to smuggle their goods to Nat'hdwara, and to the disgrace of the high priest or his underlings, this traffic was sold for their personal advantage. It was a delicate thing to search these caravans, or to prevent the loss to the state from the evasion of the duties. The Rana durst not interfere lest he might incur the penalty of his own anathemas. The author's influence with the high-priest put a stop to this.

[4] This extent of sanctuary is an innovation of the present Rana's, with many others equally unwise.

[5] Lands for the queens or others of the immediate household.

[6] Father of the present high-priest, Damodurji.

No. XII.

Mahrana Bhím Sing, commanding.

To the Mindra (*minister*) of Sri Murli Munohur (*flute delighting*), situated on the dam of the lake at Mandelgurh, the following grant has been made, with all the dues, income, and privileges, viz.:

1. The hamlet called Kotwal-khéra, with all thereto appertaining.
2. Three rupees worth of saffron monthly from the transit duty *chábútra*.
3. From the police-office of Mandelgurh:
   Three tunics (*bagha*) for the idol on each festival, *viz. Ushtumí, Jul-jatra*, and *Vassunt Panchama*.
   Five rupees worth of oil [1] on the *Jul-jatra*, and two and a half in the full moon of *Kartik*.
4. Both gardens under the dam of the lake, with all the fruits and flowers thereof.
5. The *Inch* [2] on all the vegetables appertaining to the prince.
6. *Kúnchí* and *dalali*, or the handful at harvest, and all brokerage.
7. The income arising from the sale of the estates is to be applied to the repairs of the temple and dam.

Megsir Sud 1, *Samvat* 1866; A.D. 1810.

CHAPTER XXI

Importance of mythological history—Aboriginal tribes of India—The Rajpoots are conquerors—Solar year of the Hindus—Opened at the winter solstice—The Vassant, or spring festival—Birth of the Sun—Common origin assumed of the Rajpoots and Getic tribe of Scandinavia—Surya, the sun-god of all nations, Thor, Syrus, Sol—Sun-worship—The Ahairea, or spring-hunt, described—Boar-feast—Phalgun festival—The Rajpoot Saturnalia—Games on horseback—Rites to the Manes—Festival of Sítla as guardian of children—Rana's birthday—Phûladóla, the Rajpoot Floralia—Festival of Gouri—Compared with the Diana of Egypt—The Isis or Ertha of the Suevi—And the Phrygian Cybele—Anniversary of Rama—Fête of Camdéva or Cupid—Little Gangore—Inundation of the capital—Festival of Rembha or Venus—Rajpoot and Druiditic rites—Their analogy—Serpent worship—Rakhi, or Festival of the bracelet.

It has been observed by that philosophical traveller, Dr. Clarke, that, "by a proper attention to the vestiges of ancient superstition, we are sometimes enabled to refer a whole people to their original ancestors, with as much, if not more certainty, than by observations made upon their language; because the superstition is engrafted upon the stock, but the language is liable to change." [3] Impressed with the justness, as well as the originality of the remark, I shall adopt it as my guide in the observations I propose to make on the religious festivals and superstitions of Méwar. However important may be the study of military,

[1] Amongst the items of the Chartulary of Dumfermline, is the tithe of the oil of the Greenland whale fisheries.

[2] A handful of every basket of vegetables sold in the public markets.

[3] *Travels in Scandinavia*, vol. i. p. 33.

civil, and political history, the science is incomplete without mythological history; and he is little imbued with the spirit of philosophy, who can perceive in the fables of antiquity nothing but the extravagance of a fervid imagination. Did no other consequence result from the study of mythology, than the fact, that, in all ages and countries, man has desecrated his reason, and voluntarily reduced himself below the level of the brutes that perish, it must provoke inquiry into the cause of this degradation. Such an investigation would develop, not only the source of history, the handmaid of the arts of sciences, but the origin and application of the latter, in a theogony typical of the seasons, their changes, and products. Thus mythology may be considered the parent of all history.

With regard, however, to the rude tribes who still inhabit the mountains and fastnesses of India, and who may be regarded as the aborigines of that country, the converse of this doctrine is more probable. Not their language only, but their superstitions, differ from those of the Rajpoots: though, from a desire to rise above their natural condition, they have engrafted upon their own the most popular mythologies of their civilised conquerors, who from the north gradually spread themselves over the continent and peninsula, even to the remote isles of the Indian ocean. Of the primitive inhabitants we may enumerate the Meenas, the Méras, the Goands, the Bhils, the Séryas, the Sarjas, the Ahiras, the Goojurs, and those who inhabit the forests of the Nerbudda, the Sone, the Mahanadi, the mountains of Sargooja, and the lesser Nagpore; many of whom are still but little removed from savage life, and whose dialects are as various as their manners. These are content to be called the 'sons of the earth,' [1] or 'children of the forest,' [2] while their conquerors, the Rajpoots, arrogate celestial descent.[3] How soon after the flood the Suryas, or sun-worshippers, entered India Proper, must ever remain uncertain. It is sufficient that they were anterior in date to the Indus, or races tracing their descent from the moon (*Ind*); as the migration of the latter from the central lands of Indo-Scythia was antecedent to that of the Agnicûlas, or fire-worshippers, of the Snake race, claiming Takshac as their original progenitor. The Suryas,[4] who migrated both to the East and West, as population became redundant in these fertile regions, may be considered the *Celtic*, as the Indu-Getæ may be accounted the *Gothic*, races of India. To attempt to discriminate these different races, and mark the shades which once separated them, after a system of priestcraft has amalgamated the mass, and identified their superstitions, would be fruitless; but the observer of ancient customs may, with the imperfect guidance of peculiar rites, discover things, and even names, totally incongruous with the Brahminical system, and which could never have originated within the Indus or Uttuc,—the Rubicon of Gangetic antiquarians, who fear to look beyond that stream for the origin of tribes.

[1] *Bhomapûtra.* [2] *Venapûtra.* [3] *Sûryás* and *Indupûtrás.*

[4] The Sauromatia, or Sarmatians of early Europe, as well as the Syrians, were most probably colonies of the same Sûryavansi, who simultaneously peopled the shores of the Caspian and Mediterranean, and the banks of the Indus and Ganges. Many of the tribes described by Strabo as dwelling around the Caspian, are enumerated amongst the thirty-six royal races of India. One of these, the *Sacaseni*, supposed to be the ancestors of our own Saxon race, settled themselves on the Araxes in Armenia, adjoining Albania.

A residence amongst the Rajpoots would lead to a disregard of such boundaries, either to the moral or physical man, as the annals of Méwar abundantly testify.

Sir Wm. Jones remarks, "If the festivals of the old Greeks, Persians, Romans, Egyptians, and Goths could be arranged with exactness in the same form with the Indian, there would be found a striking resemblance among them ; and an attentive comparison of them all might throw great light on the religion, and perhaps on the history, of the primitive world."

In treating of the festivals and superstitions of the Rajpoots, wherever there may appear to be a fair ground for supposing an analogy with those of other nations of antiquity, I shall not hesitate to pursue it. The proper names of many of the martial Rajpoots would alone point out the necessity of seeking for a solution of them out of the explored paths ; and where Sanscrit derivation cannot be assigned, as it happens in many instances, we are not, therefore, warranted in the hasty conclusion that the names must have been adopted since the conquests of Mahmoud or Shabudín, events of comparatively modern date. Let us at once admit the hypothesis of Pinkerton,—the establishment of an original Indu-Getic or Indo-Scythic empire, "extending from the Caspian to the Ganges" ; or if this conjecture be too extensive or too vague, let us fix the centre of this *Media-Bhúmi* in the fertile region of Sogdiana ;[1] and from the lights which modern history affords on the many migrations from this nursery of mankind, even since the time of Mahomed, let us form an opinion of those which have not been recorded, or have been conveyed by the Hindus only in imperfect allegory ; and with the aid of ancient customs, obsolete words, and proper names, trace them to Indo-Scythic colonies grafted on the parent stock. The *Poorans* themselves bear testimony to the incorporation of Scythic tribes with the Hindus, and to the continual irruptions of the Sacæ, the Pelavi, the Yavans,[2] the Túrshkas, names conspicuous amongst the races of Central Asia, and recorded in the pages of the earliest Western historians. Even so early as the period of Rama, when furious international wars were carried on between the military and sacerdotal classes for supremacy, we have the names of these tribes recorded as auxiliaries to the priesthood ; who, while admitting them to fight under the banners of Síva, would not scruple to stamp them with the seal of Hinduism. In this manner, beyond a doubt, at a much later period than the events in the *Ramayuna*, these tribes from the North either forced themselves among, or were incorporated with, 'the races of the sun.' When, therefore, we meet

[1] Long after the overthrow of the Greek kingdom of Bactria by the Yuti or Getes, this region was populous and flourishing. In the year 120 before Christ, De Guignes says : "Dans ce pays on trouvait d'excellens grains, du vin de vigne, plus de cent villes, tant grandes que petites. Il est aussi fait mention du Tahia situé au midi du Gihon, et où il y a de grandes villes murées. Le général Chinois y vit des toiles de l'Inde et autres marchandises, etc., etc."—*Hist. Gen. des Huns*, vol. i. p. 51.

[2] Yavan or Javan is a celebrated link of the Indu (*lunar*) genealogical chain ; nor need we go to Ionia for it, though the Ionians may be a colony descended from Javan, the ninth from Yayat, who was the third son of Ayú, the ancestor of the Hindu as well as of the Tatar Indu-vansi. The *Asuras*, who are so often described as invaders of India, and which word has ordinarily a mere irreligious acceptation, I firmly believe to mean the Assyrians.

with rites in Rajpootana and in ancient Scandinavia, such as were practised amongst the Getic nations on the Oxus, why should we hesitate to assign the origin of both to this region of earliest civilisation ? When we see the ancient Asi, and the Yeuts, or Juts, taking omens from the white steed of Thor, shut up in the temple at Upsala ; and in like manner, the Rajpoot of past days offering the same animal in sacrifice to the sun, and his modern descendant taking the omen from his neigh, why are we to refuse our assent to the common origin of the superstition practised by the Gete of the Oxus ? Again, when we find the "homage to the sword" performed by all the Getic races of antiquity in Dacia, on the Baltic, as well as by the modern Rajpoot, shall we draw no conclusion from this testimony of the father of history, who declares that such rites were practised on the Jaxartes in the very dawn of knowledge ? Moreover, why hesitate to give Eastern etymologies for Eastern rites, though found on the Baltic ? The antiquarian of the North (Mallet) may thus be assisted to the etymon of '*Tir-sing*,' the enchanted sword of Angantyr, in *tir*, 'water,' and *sing*, 'a lion' ; *i.e.* in water or spirit like a lion ; for even *pani*, the common epithet for water, is applied metaphorically to 'spirit.'

It would be less difficult to find Sanscrit derivations for many of the proper names in the *Edda*, than to give a Sanscrit analysis of many common amongst the Rajpoots, which we must trace to an Indo-Scythic root : [1] such as Eyvorsél, Udila, Attitai, Pujoon, Hamira,[2] and numerous other proper names of warriors. Of tribes : the Cat'hi, Rajpali, Mohila, Sariaspah, Aswaria (*qu.* Assyrian ?), Binâfur, Camari, Silara, Dahima, etc. Of mountains : Drúnádhâr, Arabûdha, Aravulli, Aravind'-ha (the root *ara*, or mountain, being Scythic, and the expletive adjunct Sancrit), 'the hill of Budha,' 'of strength,' 'of limit.' To all such as cannot be resolved into the cognate language of India, what origin can we assign but Scythic ? [3]

In a memoir prepared for me by a well-informed public officer in the

[1] See Turner's *History of Anglo-Saxons* for Indo-Scythic words.

[2] There were no less than four distinguished leaders of this name amongst the vassals of the last Rajpoot emperor of Dehli ; and one of them, who turned traitor to his sovereign and joined Shabudín, was actually a Scythian, and of the Ghiker race, which maintained their ancient habits of polyandrism even in Baber's time. The *Haoli Rao* Hamíra was lord of Kangra and the Ghikers of Pamer.

[3] Turner, when discussing the history of the *Sakai*, or *Sacaseni*, of the Caspian, whom he justly supposes to be the Saxons of the Baltic, takes occasion to introduce some words of Scythic origin (preserved by ancient writers), to almost every one of which, without straining etymology, we may give a Sanscrit origin.

	Scythic.	Sanscrit, or Bakha.
Exampaios	sacred ways	*Agham* is the sacred book ; *pâi* and *páda*, a foot ; *pante*, a path.
Arimu	one	*Ad* is *the first ;* whence *Adima*, or man.
Spou	an eye.	
Oior	a man.	
Pata	to kill	*Badha*, to kill.
Tahiti	the chief deity is Vesta	Tâpi is heat or flame ; the type of Vesta.
Papaios	,, Jupiter	Baba, or Bapa, the universal father. The Hindu Jíva-pitri, or *Father* of Life.

Rana's court, on the chief festivals celebrated in Méwar, he commenced with those following the autumnal equinox, in the month Asoj or Aswini, opening with the *Noratri*, sacred to the god of war. Their fasts are in general regulated by the moon; although the most remarkable are solar, especially those of the equinoxes and solstices, and the *Sancrantis*, or days on which the sun enters a new sign. The Hindu solar year anciently commenced on the winter solstice, in the month Posha, and was emphatically called "the morning of the gods"; also Sivrát, or night of Síva, analogous, as has been before remarked, to the 'mother night,' which ushered in the new year of the Scandinavian Asi, and other nations of Asiatic origin dwelling in the north.

They term the summer solstice in the month of Asar, 'the night of the Gods,' because Vishnu (as the sun) reposes during the four rainy months on his serpent couch. The lunar year of 360 days was more ancient than the solar, and commenced with the month of Asoj or Aswini: "the moon being at the full when that name was imposed on the first lunar station of the Hindu ecliptic." [1]

According to another authority, the festivals commenced on Amavus, or the '*ides*' of Cheyt, near which the vernal equinox falls, the opening of the modern solar year; when, in like manner as at the commencement of the lunar year in Asoj, they dedicate the first nine days of Cheyt (also called Noratri) to Iswara and his consort Isa.

Having thus specified both modes of reckoning for the opening of the solar and lunar years, I shall not commence the abstract of the festivals of Méwar with either, but follow the more ancient division of time, when the year closed with the winter solstice in the month of Posh, consequently opening the new year with Magh. By this arrangement, we shall commence with the spring festivals, and let the days dedicated to mirth and gaiety follow each other; preferring the natural to the astrological year, which will enable us to preserve the analogy with the northern nations of Europe, who also reckoned from the winter solstice. The Hindu divides the year into six seasons, each of two months; namely, Vassanta, Greeshma, Varsha, Sharati, Shîshíra, Sheeta; or spring, summer, rainy, sultry, dewy, and cold.

It is not, however, my intention to detail all the fasts and festivals which the Rajpoot of Méwar holds in common with the Hindu nation,

	Scythic.	Sanscrit, or Bakha.
Oitosuros . .	the chief deity is Apollo .	Aitiswara, or *Sun-God*, applicable to Vishnu, who has every attribute of Apollo; from *ait* contraction of *aditya*, the sun.
Artimpasa, or Aripasa	,, Venus .	Apsára, because born from the froth or essence, '*sara*,' of the waters, '*ap*.'
Thamimasadus .	,, Neptune .	Thoéna'tha; or *God of the Waters*.
Apia . . .	wife of Papaios, or Earth .	Ambá, Amá, Omia, is the *universal mother*; wife of "Baba Adam," as they term the universal father.

—See Turner's *History of the Anglo-Saxons*, vol. i. p. 35.

[1] Sir W. Jones, 'On the Lunar Year of the Hindus,' *Asiatic Researches*, vol. iii. p. 257.

but chiefly those restricted to that state, or such as are celebrated with local peculiarity, or striking analogies to those of Egypt, Greece, or Scandinavia. The goddess who presides over mirth and idleness, preferred holding her court amidst the ruins of Oodipoor, to searching elsewhere for a dwelling. This determination to be happy amidst calamity, individual and national, has made the court proverbial in Rajwarra, in the adage, "*sat'h bára, aur no tahwara*," i.e. *nine* holidays out of *seven* days. Although many of these festivals are common to India, and their maintenance is enjoined by religion, yet not only the prolongation and repetition of some, but the entire institution of others, as well as the peculiar splendour of their solemnisation, originate with the prince; proving how much individual example may influence the manners of a nation.

By the arrangement we have adopted, the lovely VASSANTI, goddess of the spring, will usher in the festivals of Méwar. In 1819 her rites were celebrated in the kalends of January, and even then, on the verge of the tropic, her birth was premature.

The opening of the spring being on the 5th of the month Magha, is thence called the Vassant *panchami*, which in 1819 fell on the 30th of January; consequently the first of Posh (the antecedent month), the beginning of the old Hindu year, or "*the morning of the gods*," fell on the 25th of December. The Vassant continues forty days after the *panchami*, or initiative fifth, during which the utmost license prevails in action and in speech; the lower classes regale even to intoxication on every kind of stimulating confection and spirituous beverage, and the most respectable individuals, who would at other times be shocked to utter an indelicate allusion, roam about with the groups of bacchanals, reciting stanzas of the warmest description in praise of the powers of nature, as did the conscript fathers of Rome during the Saturnalia. In this season, when the barriers of rank are thrown down, and the spirit of democracy is let loose, though never abused, even the wild Bhil, or savage Mér, will leave his forest or mountain shade to mingle in the revelries of the capital; and decorating his ebon hair or tattered turban with a garland of jessamine, will join the clamorous parties which perambulate the streets of the capital. These orgies are, however, reserved for the conclusion for the forty days sacred to the goddess of nature.

Two days following the initiative fifth, is the *bhán septimi* or 'seventh [day] of the sun,' also called 'the birth of the sun,' with various other metaphorical denominations.[1] On this day there is a grand procession of the Rana, his chiefs and vassals, to the Chougan, where the sun is worshipped. At the Jeipoor court, whose princes claim descent from CUSH, the second son of RAMA, the *bhán septimi* is peculiarly sacred. The chariot of the sun, drawn by eight horses, is taken from the temple dedicated to that orb, and moves in procession: a ceremony otherwise never observed but on the inauguration of a new prince.

In the mythology of the Rajpoots, of which we have a better idea from their heroic poetry than from the legends of the Brahmins, the sun-god is the deity they are most anxious to propitiate; and in his honour they fearlessly expend their blood in battle, from the hope of being received

[1] *Bhascara septimi*, in honour of the sun, as a form of Vishnu.—*Varaha Púrana. Macari*, from the sun entering the constellation *Macara* (Pisces), the first of the solar Mágha.—See *Asiatic Researches*, vol. iii. p. 273.

into his mansion. Their highest heaven is accordingly the *Bhan-t'han* or *Bhánuloca*, the 'region of the sun': and like the Indu-Scythic Gete, the Rajpoot warrior of the early ages sacrificed the horse in his honour,[1] and dedicated to him the first day of the week, namely, *Aditwár*, contracted to *Aitwar*, also called T'hawara.[2]

The more we attend to the warlike mythology of the north, the more apparent is its analogy with that of the Rajpoots, and the stronger ground is there for assuming that both races inherited their creed from the common land of the *Yuti* of the Jaxartes. What is a more proper etymon for Scandinavian, the abode of the warriors who destroyed the Roman power, than *Scanda*, the Mars or Ku-mara of the Rajpoots? perhaps the origin of the *Kimbri*, derived by Mallet from *Kæmpfer*, 'to fight.'

Thor, in the eleventh fable of the *Edda*, is denominated Asa-Thor,[3] the 'lord Thor,' called the Celtic Mars by the Romans. The chariot of Thor is ignobly yoked compared with the car of Surya; but in the substitution of the *he-goats* for the seven-headed horse *Septaswa*, we have but the change of an adjunct depending on clime, when the *Yuti* migrated from the plains of Scythia, of which the horse is a native, to *Yutland*, of whose mountains the goat was an inhabitant prior to any of the race of *Asi*. The northern warrior makes the palace of the sun-god Thor the most splendid of the celestial abodes, "in which are five hundred and forty halls": vying with the *Surya-Mandala*, the supreme heaven of the Rajpoot. Whence such notions of the *Aswa* races of the Ganges, and the *Asi* of Scandinavia, but from the Scythic Sacæ, who adored the solar divinity under the name of "*Gæto-Syrus*," [4] the *Surya* of the *Sacha* Rajpoot; and as, according to the commentator on the *Edda*, "the ancient people of the north pronounced the "*th* as the English now do *ss*," the sun-god *Thor* becomes *Sor*, and is identified still more with *Surya* whose worship no doubt gave the name to that extensive portion of Asia called Συρια, as it did to the small peninsula of the *Sauras*, still peopled by tribes of Scythic origin. The *Sol* of the Romans has probably the same Celto-Etrurian origin; with those tribes the sun was the great object of adoration, and their grand festival, the winter solstice, was called *Yule*, *Hiul*, *Houl*, "which even at this day signifies the SUN, in the language of Bas-Bretagne and Cornwall." [5] On the conversion of the descendants of these Scythic Yeuts, who, according to Herodotus, sacrificed the horse (*Hi*) to the sun (*El*), the name of the Pagan jubilee of the solstice was transferred to the day of Christ's nativity, which is thus still held in remembrance by their descendants of the north.

At Oodipoor the sun has universal precedence; his portal (*Surya-pol*)

[1] See p. 63.

[2] This word appears to have the same import as Thor, the sun-god and war divinity of the Scandinavians.

[3] Odin is also called *As* or 'lord'; the Gauls also called him *Œs* or *Es*, and with a Latin termination *Hesus*, whom Lucan calls *Esus*; *Edda*, vol. ii. pp. 45–6. The celebrated translator of these invaluable remnants of ancient superstitions, by which alone light can be thrown on the origin of nations, observes that *Es* or *Œs* is the name for *God* with all the Celtic races. So it was with the Tuscans, doubtless from the Sanscrit, or rather from a more provincial tongue, the common contraction of *Eswúr*, the Egyptian *Osiris*, the Persian *Syr*, the sun-god.

[4] Which Mallet, from Hesychius, interprets 'good star.'

[5] Mallet's *Northern Antiquities*, vol. ii. p. 42.

is the chief entrance to the city ; his name gives dignity to the chief apartment or hall (*Surya-mahal*) of the palace ; and from the balcony of the sun (*Surya-gokra*) the descendant of Rama shows himself in the dark monsoon as the sun's representative. A huge painted sun of gypsum in high relief, with gilded rays, adorns the hall of audience, and in front of it is the throne. As already mentioned, the sacred standard bears his image, as does that Scythic part of the regalia called the *changi*, a disc of black felt or ostrich feathers, with a plate of gold to represent the sun in its centre, borne upon a pole. The royal parasol is termed *kirnia*, in allusion to its shape, like a ray (*carna*) of the orb. The last day but one of the month of Magha is called *Sivrat* (night of Síva), and is held peculiarly sacred by the Rana, who is styled the Regent of Síva. It is a rigid fast, and the night is passed in vigils, and rites to the phallic representative of Síva.

The merry month of Phalgun is ushered in with the *Ahairea*, or spring-hunt.[1] The preceding day the Rana distributes to all his chiefs and servants either a dress of green, or some portion thereof, in which all appear habited on the morrow, whenever the astrologer has fixed the hour for sallying forth to slay the boar to *Gouri*, the Ceres of the Rajpoots : the *Ahairea* is therefore called the *Muhoorut ca sikar*, or *the chase* fixed astrologically. As their success on this occasion is ominous of future good, no means are neglected to secure it, either by scouts previously discovering the lair, or the desperate efforts of the hunters to slay the boar when roused. With the sovereign and his sons all the chiefs sally forth, each on his best steed, and all animated by the desire to surpass each other in acts of prowess and dexterity. It is very rare that in some one of the passes or recesses of the valley the hog is not found ; the spot is then surrounded by the hunters, whose vociferations soon start the *d'hokra*,[2] and frequently a drove of hogs. Then each cavalier impels his steed, and with lance or sword, regardless of rock, ravine, or tree, presses on the bristly foe, whose knowledge of the country is of no avail when thus circumvented, and the ground soon reeks with gore, in which not unfrequently is mixed that of horse or rider. On the last occasion, there occurred fewer casualties than usual ; though the Chondawut Hamíra, whom we nicknamed the "*Red Riever*," had his leg broken, and the second son of Sheodan Sing, a near relation of the Rana, had his neighbour's lance driven through his arm. The young chief of Saloombra was amongst the distinguished of this day's sport. It would appal even an English fox-hunter to see the Rajpoot driving their steeds at full speed, bounding like the antelope over every barrier,—the thick jungle covert, or rocky steep bare of soil or vegetation, —with their lances balanced in the air, or leaning on the saddle-bow slashing at the boar.

The royal kitchen moves out on this occasion, and in some chosen spot

[1] In his delight for this diversion, the Rajpoot evinces his Scythic propensity. The grand hunts of the last Chohan emperor often led him into warfare, for Pirthi Raj was a *poacher* of the first magnitude, and one of his battles with the Tatars was while engaged in field sports on the *Raví*.

The heir of Gengis Khan was chief huntsman, the highest office of the state amongst the Scythic Tatars ; as Ajânbahu, alike celebrated in either field, of war and sport, was chief huntsman to the Chohan emperor of Dehli, whose bard enters minutely into the subject, describing all the variety of dogs of chase.

[2] A hog in Hindué ; in Persian *hooq*, nearly our *hog*.

the repast is prepared, of which all partake, for the hog is the favourite food of the Rajpoot, as it was of the heroes of Scandinavia. Nor is the *munwár piála*, or invitation cup, forgotten ; and having feasted, and thrice slain their bristly antagonist, they return to the capital, where fame had already spread their exploits,—the deeds done by the *birchi* (lance) of Pudma,[1] or the *khanda* (sword) blow of Hamíra,[2] which lopped the head of the foe of *Gouri*. Even this martial amusement, the *Ahairea*, has a religious origin. The boar is the enemy of Gouri of the Rajpoots ; it was so held of Isis by the Egyptians, of Ceres by the Greeks, of Freya by the north-man, whose favourite food was the hog : and of such importance was it deemed by the Franks, that the second chapter of the Salic law is entirely penal with regard to the stealers of swine. The heroes of the *Edda*, even in Valhalla, feed on the fat of the wild boar Serimner, while " the illustrious father of armies fattens his wolves *Geri* and *Freki*, and takes no other nourishment himself than the interrupted quaffing of wine " : quite the picture of Hur, the Rajpoot god of war, and his sons the Bhyrûs, Gora, and Kala, metaphorically called the " *sons of slaughter*." We need hardly repeat that the cup of the Scandinavian god of war, like that of the Rajpoots, is the human skull (*cupra*).

As Phalgun advances, the bacchanalian mirth increases ; groups are continually patrolling the streets, throwing a crimson powder at each other, or ejecting a solution of it from syringes, so that the garments and visages of all are one mass of crimson. On the 8th, emphatically called the *Phág*, the Rana joins the queens and their attendants in the palace, when all restraint is removed and mirth is unlimited. But the most brilliant sight is the playing of the *holi* on horseback, on the terrace in front of the palace. Each chief who chooses to join has a plentiful supply of missiles, formed of thin plates of mica or talc, enclosing this crimson powder, called *abíra*, which with the most graceful and dextrous horsemanship they dart at each other, pursuing, caprioling, and jesting. This part of it much resembles the Saturnalia of Rome of this day, when similar missiles are scattered at the *Carnivâle*. The last day or *Poonum* ends the *holi*, when the Nakarras from the *Tripolia* summon all the chiefs with their retinues to attend their prince, and accompany him in procession to the Chougan, their *Champ de Mars*. In the centre of this is a long *sala* or hall, the ascent to which is by a flight of steps : the roof is supported by square columns without any walls, so that the court is entirely open. Here, surrounded by his chiefs, the Rana passes an hour, listening to the songs in praise of *Holica*, while a scurrilous *cavya* or couplet from some wag in the crowd reminds him, that exalted rank is no protection against the license of the spring Saturnalia ; though " the Dewan of Eklinga " has not to reproach himself with a failure of obedience to the rites of the goddess, having fulfilled the command " to multiply," more than any individual in his kingdom.[3] While the Rana and his chiefs are thus amused above, the buffoons and itinerant groups mix with the cavalcade, throw powder in their eyes, or deluge their garments with the crimson solution. To resent it would only expose the sensitive party to be laughed at, and draw upon him a host of these bacchanals :

[1] Chief of Saloombra. [2] Chief of Hamirgur'h.

[3] He has been the father of more than one hundred children, legitimate and illegitimate, though very few are living.

so that no alternative exists between keeping entirely aloof or mixing in the fray.[1]

On the last day, the Rana feasts his chiefs, and the camp breaks up with the distribution of *khanda nareal*, or swords and coco-nuts, to the chiefs and all "whom the king delighteth to honour." These *khandas* are but "of lath," in shape like the Andrea Ferrara, or long cut-and-thrust, the favourite weapon of the Rajpoot. They are painted in various ways, like Harlequin's sword, and meant as a burlesque, in unison with the character of the day, when war is banished, and the multiplication,[2] not the destruction, of man is the behest of the goddess who rules the spring. At nightfall, the forty days conclude with "*the burning of the holí*," when they light large fires, into which various substances, as well as the crimson *abíra*, are thrown, and around which groups of children are dancing and screaming in the streets like so many infernals. Until three hours after sunrise of the new month of Cheyt, these orgies are continued with increased vigour, when the natives bathe, change their garments, worship, and return to the rank of sober citizens; and princes and chiefs receive gifts from their domestics.[3]

CHEYT.—The first of this month is the Samvatsiri (vulg. *Chamchari*), or anniversary of the death of the Rana's father, to whose memory solemn rites are performed both in the palace and at *Ara*, the royal cemetery, metaphorically termed 'Maha-Sati,' or place of '*great faith*.' Thither the Rana repairs, and offers oblations to the *manes* of his father; and after purifying in the *Gangabheva*, a rivulet which flows through the middle of "the abode of silence," he returns to the palace.

On the 3rd, the whole of the royal insignia proceeds to Baidla, the residence of the Chohan chief (one of the *sixteen*), within the valley of the capital, in order to convey the *Rao* to court. The Rana advances to the *Ganésa Deori* [4] to receive him; when, after salutation, the sovereign and his chief return to the great hall of assembly, hand in hand, but that of the *Chohan above or upon his sovereign's*. In this ceremony we have another singular memorial of the glorious days of Méwar, when almost every chieftain established by deeds of devotion a right to the eternal gratitude of their princes; the decay of whose power but serves to hallow such reminiscences. It is in these little acts of courteous condescension, deviations from the formal routine of reception, that we recognise the traces of Rajpoot history; for inquiry into these customs will reveal the incident which gave birth to each, and curiosity will be amply repaid, in a lesson at

[1] That this can be done without any loss of dignity by the *Sahib log* (a name European gentlemen have assumed) is well known to those who may have partaken of the hospitalities of that honourable man, and brave and zealous officer, Colonel James Skinner, C.B., at Hansi. That his example is worthy of imitation in the mode of commanding, is best evinced by the implicit and cheerful obedience his men pay to his instructions when removed from his personal control. He has passed through the ordeal of nearly thirty years of unremitted service, and from the glorious days of Delhi and Laswari under Lake, to the last siege of Bhurtpore, James Skinner has been second to none. In obtaining for this gallant and modest officer the order of the Bath, Lord Combermere must have been applauded by every person who knows the worth of him who bears it, which includes the whole army of Bengal.

[2] Evinced in the presentation of the *sri-phala*, the fruit of *Sri*, which is the coco-nut, emblematic of fruitfulness.

[3] Another point of resemblance to the Roman Saturnalia.

[4] A hall so called in honour of Ganésa, or Janus, whose effigies adorn the entrance.

once of political and moral import. For my own part, I never heard the kettledrum of my friend Raj Kulian strike at the sacred barrier, the *tripolia*, without recalling the glorious memory of his ancestor at the Thermopylæ of Méwar ; [1] nor looked on the autograph lance, the symbol of the Chondawuts, without recognising the fidelity of the founder of the clan ; [2] nor observed the honours paid to the Chohans of Baidlu and Kotario, without the silent tribute of applause to the manes of their sires.

Cheyt badi sath, or '7th of Cheyt,' is in honour of the goddess *Sítla*, the protectress of children : all the matrons of the city proceed with their offerings to the shrine of the goddess, placed upon the very pinnacle of an isolated hill in the valley. In every point of view, this divinity is the twin-sister of the *Mater Montana*, the guardian of infants amongst the Romans, the Grecian or Phrygian Cybele.

This is also the Rana's birthday,[3] on which occasion all classes flock with gifts and good wishes that "the king may live for ever" ; but it is in the penetralia of the *Rawula*, where the profane eye enters not, that the greatest festivities of this day are kept.

Cheyt *Sudi* 1st (15th of the month) is the opening of the *luni-solar* year of Vicramaditya. Ceremonies, which more especially appertain to the *Noratri* of Asoj, are performed on this day ; and the sword is worshipped in the palace. But such rites are subordinate to those of the fair divinity, who still rules over this the smiling portion of the year. Vassanti has ripened into the fragrant Flora, and all the fair of the capital, as well as the other sex, repair to the gardens and groves, where parties assemble, regale, and swing, adorned with chaplets of roses, jessamine, or oleander, when the Nolakhu gardens may vie with the Tivoli of Paris. They return in the evening to the city.

"*The Festival of Flowers.*"—The Rajpoot Floralia ushers in the rites of the beneficent Gouri, which continue nine days, the number sacred to the creative power. These vie with the *Cerealia* of Rome, or the more ancient rites of the goddess of the Nile : I shall therefore devote some space to a particular account of them.

GANGORE.—Among the many remarkable festivals of Rajast'han, kept with peculiar brilliancy at Oodipoor, is that in honour of *Gouri*, or Isani, the goddess of abundance, the Isis of Egypt, the Ceres of Greece. Like the Rajpoot Saturnalia, which it follows, it belongs to the vernal equinox, when nature in these regions proximate to the tropic is in the full expanse of her charms, and the matronly Gouri casts her golden mantle over the beauties of the verdant Vassanti.[4] Then the fruits exhibit their promise to the eye ; the kohil fills the ear with melody ; the air is impregnated with aroma, and the crimson poppy contrasts with the spikes of golden grain, to form a wreath for the beneficent Gouri.

Gouri is one of the names of Isa or Parvati, wife of the greatest of the gods, Mahadéva or Iswara, who is conjoined with her in these rites, which almost exclusively appertain to the women. The meaning of *gouri* is 'yellow,' emblematic of the ripened harvest, when the votaries of the goddess adore her effigies, which are those of a matron painted the colour of ripe corn ; and though her image is represented with only two hands, in

[1] See p. 270.
[2] See p. 224.
[3] It fell on the 18th March 1819.
[4] Personification of spring.

one of which she holds the lotos, which the Egyptians regarded as emblematic of reproduction, yet not unfrequently they equip her with the warlike conch, the discus, and the club, to denote that the goddess, whose gifts sustain life, is likewise accessary to the loss of it: uniting, as Gouri and Cali, the characters of life and death, like the Isis and Cybele of the Egyptians. But here she is only seen as *Ana-púrana*, the benefactress of mankind. The rites commence when the sun enters Aries (the opening of the Hindu year), by a deputation to a spot beyond the city, "to bring *earth* for the image of Gouri."[1] When this is formed, a smaller one of Iswara is made, and they are placed together; a small trench is then excavated, in which barley is sown; the ground is irrigated and artificial heat supplied till the grain germinates, when the females join hands and dance round it, invoking the blessings of Gouri on their husbands. The young corn is then taken up, distributed, and presented by the females to the men, who wear it in their turbans. Every wealthy family has its image, or at least every poorwa or subdivision of the city. These and other rites known only to the initiated, having been performed for several days within doors, they decorate the images, and prepare to carry them in procession to the lake. During these days of preparation, nothing is talked of but Gouri's departure from the palace; whether she will be as sumptuously apparelled as in the year gone by; whether an additional boat will be launched on the occasion; though not a few forget the goddess altogether in the recollection of the gazelle eyes (*mirg-náeni*) and serpentine locks (*nágni-zoolf*)[2] of the beauteous handmaids who are selected to attend her. At length the hour arrives, the martial nakaras give the signal "to the cannonier without," and speculation is at rest when the guns on the summit of the castle of Eklinggurh announce that Gouri has commenced her excursion to the lake.

The cavalcade assembles on the magnificent terrace, and the Rana, surrounded by his nobles, leads the way to the boats, of a form as primitive as that which conveyed the Argonauts to Colchis. The scenery is admirably adapted for these fêtes, the ascent being gradual from the margin of the lake, which here forms a fine bay, and gently rising to the crest of the ridge on which the palace and dwellings of the chiefs are built. Every turret and balcony is crowded with spectators, from the palace to the water's edge; and the ample flight of marble steps which intervene from the *Tripolia*, or triple portal, to the boats, is a dense mass of females in variegated robes, whose scarfs but half conceal their ebon tresses adorned with the rose and the jessamine. A more imposing or more exhilarating sight cannot be imagined than the entire population of a city thus assembled for the purpose of rejoicing; the countenance of every individual, from the prince to the peasant, dressed in smiles. Carry the eye to heaven, and it rests on "a sky without a cloud": below is a magnificent lake, the even surface of the deep blue waters broken only by palaces of marble, whose arched piazzas are seen through the foliage of orange groves, plantain, and tamarind; while the vision is bounded by noble mountains, their peaks towering over each other, and composing an immense amphitheatre. Here the deformity of vice intrudes not; no object is degraded by inebriation: no tumultuous disorder or deafening clamour, but all await patiently, with

[1] Here we have *Gouri* as the type of the earth.
[2] Here the Hindu mixes Persian with his Sanscrit, and produces the mongrel dialect *Hindee*.

eyes directed to the *Tripolia*, the appearance of Gouri. At length the procession is seen winding down the steep, and in the midst, borne on a *pat'h*,[1] or throne, gorgeously arrayed in yellow robes, and blazing with "barbaric pearl and gold," the goddess appears; on either side the two beauties wave the silver *chamra* over her head, while the more favoured damsels act as harbingers, preceding her with wands of silver: the whole chanting hymns. On her approach, the Rana, his chiefs and ministers rise and remain standing till the goddess is seated on her throne close to the water's edge, when all bow, and the prince and court take their seats in the boats. The females then form a circle around the goddess, unite hands, and with a measured step and various graceful inclinations of the body, keeping time by beating the palms at particular cadences, move round the image singing hymns, some in honour of the goddess of abundance, others on love and chivalry; and embodying little episodes of national achievements, occasionally sprinkled with *double entendre*, which excites a smile and significant nod from the chiefs, and an inclination of the head of the fair choristers. The festival being entirely female, not a single male mixed in the immense groups, and even Iswara himself, the husband of Gouri, attracts no attention, as appears from his ascetic or mendicant form begging his dole from the bounteous and universal *mother*. It is taken for granted that the goddess is occupied in bathing all the time she remains, and ancient tradition says death was the penalty of any male intruding on these solemnities; but the present prince deems them so fitted for amusement, that he has even instituted a second *Gangore*. Some hours are thus consumed, while easy and good-humoured conversation is carried on. At length, the ablutions over, the goddess is taken up, and conveyed to the palace with the same forms and state. The Rana and his chiefs then unmoor their boats, and are rowed round the margin of the lake, to visit in succession the other images of the goddess, around which female groups are chanting and worshipping, as already described, with which ceremonies the evening closes, when the whole terminates with a grand display of fireworks, the *finale* of each of the three days dedicated to Gouri.

Considerable resemblance is to be discerned between this festival of *Gouri* and that in honour of the Egyptian Diana[2] at Bubastis, and Isis at Busiris, within the Delta of the Nile, of which Herodotus says: "They who celebrate those of Diana embark in vessels; the women strike their tabors, the men their flutes; the rest of both sexes clap their hands, and join in chorus. Whatever city they approach, the vessels are brought on shore; the women use ungracious language, dance, and indelicately

[1] Tukht, Pat'h, Persian and Sanscrit, alike meaning *board*.

[2] The Ephesian Diana is the twin sister of Gouri, and can have a Sanscrit derivation in *Devi-ana*, 'the goddess of food,' contracted *Dé-ana*, though commonly Aña-dé or Ana-devi, and Anapûrna, 'filling with food,' or the nourisher, the name applied by "the mother of mankind," when she places the repast before the messenger of heaven:

"Heavenly stranger, please to taste
These bounties, which our Nourisher, from whom
All perfect good, unmeasured out, descends,
To us for food and for delight, hath caused
The earth to yield."

Paradise Lost, bk. v, v. 397–401.

throw about their garments."[1] Wherever the rites of Isis prevailed, we find the boat introduced as an essential emblem in her worship, whether in the heart of Rajast'han, on the banks of the Nile, or in the woods of Germany. Bryant[2] furnishes an interesting account from Diodorus and Curtius, illustrated by drawings from Pocock, from the temple of Luxor, near Carnac, in the Thebaid, of "the ship of Isis," carrying an ark; and from a male figure therein, this learned person thinks it bears a mysterious allusion to the deluge. I am inclined to deem the personage in the ark *Osiris*, husband of Isis, the type of the sun arrived in the sign of Aries (of which the rams' heads ornamenting both the prow and stem of the vessel are typical), the harbinger of the annual fertilising inundation of the Nile: evincing identity of origin as an equinoctial festival with that of *Gouri* (Isis) of the *Indu-Scythic* races of Rajast'han.

The German Suevi adored Isis, and also introduced a ship in her worship, for which Tacitus is at a loss to account, and with his usual candour says, he has no materials whence to investigate the origin of a worship denoting the foreign origin of the tribe. This Isis of the Suevi was evidently a form of Ertha, the chief divinity of all the Saxon races, who, with her consort Teutates or Hesus[3] (*Mercury*), were the chief deities of both the Celtic and early Gothic races: the Búdha and Ella of the Rajpoots; in short, *the earth*,[4] the prolific mother, the Isis of Egypt, the Ceres of Greece, the Ana-purana (*giver of food*) of the Rajpoots. On some ancient temples dedicated to this Hindu Ceres, we have sculptured on the frieze and pedestal of the columns the emblem of abundance, termed the *cámácúmpa*, or *vessel of desire*, a vase of elegant form, from which branches of the palm are gracefully pendent. Herodotus says that similar water-vessels, filled with wheat and barley, were carried in the festival of Isis; and all who have attended to Egyptian antiquities are aware, that the god Canopus is depicted under the form of a *water-jar*, or Nilometer, whose covering bears the head of Osiris.

To render the analogy perfect between the vessels emblematic of the Isis of the Nile and the Ganges, there is a festival sacred to the sage *Agastya*, who presides over the star Canopus, when the sun enters Virgo (*Kaniya*). The *cámácúmpa* is then personified under the epithet *cúmbháyóní*, and the votary is instructed to pour water into a sea-shell, in which having placed *white flowers and unground rice*, turning his face to *the south*, he offers it with this incantation: "Hail, CUMBHAYONI, born in the sight of MITRA and VARUNA (the sun and water divinities); bright as the blossom of the *cusa* (grass), who sprung from *Agni* (fire) and Maruta." By the prefix of

[1] Euterpe, 283. [2] *Analysis of Ancient Mythology*, p. 312.

[3] Hesus is probably derived from Eswara, or Esa, *the* god. Toth was the Egyptian, and Teutates the Scandinavian, Mercury. I have elsewhere attempted to trace the origin of the Suevi, Su, or Yeuts of Yeutland (Jutland), to Yute, Gete, or Jit, of Central Asia, who carried thence the religion of Búdha into India as well as to the Baltic. There is little doubt that the races called Jotner, Jæter, Jotuns, Jæts, and Yeuts, who followed the *Asi* into Scandinavia, migrated from the Jaxartes, the land of *the great Gete* (Massagetæ); the leader was supposed to be endued with supernatural powers, like the Budhist, called *Védianán*, or magician, whose haunts adjoined Aria, the cradle of the Magi. They are designated *Ari-punta*, under the sign of a serpent, the type of Búdha; or Ari-mánús, 'the foe of man.'

[4] The German *Ertha*, to show her kindred to the *Ella* of the Rajpoots, had her car drawn by a cow, under which form the Hindus typify the earth (*prithwi*).

Ganga (*the* river) to *Gouri*, we see that the *Gangore* festival is essentially sacred to a river-goddess, affording additional proof of the common origin of the rites of the Isis of Egypt and India.

The Egyptians, according to Plutarch, considered the Nile as flowing from Osiris, in like manner as the Hindu poet describes the fair Ganga flowing from the head of Iswara, which Sir W. Jones thus classically paints in his hymn to Ganga :—

> " Above the reach of mortal ken,
> On blest Coilasa's top, where every stem
> Glowed with a vegetable gem,
> Mahesa stood, the dread and joy of men ;
> While Parvati, to gain a boon,
> Fixed on his locks a beamy moon,
> And hid his frontal eye in jocund play,
> With reluctant sweet delay ;
> All nature straight was locked in dim eclipse,
> Till Brahmins pure, with hallowed lips
> And warbled prayers, restored the day,
> When Ganga from his brow, with heavenly fingers prest,
> Sprang radiant, and descending, graced the caverns of the west."

Ganga, *the* river goddess, like the Nile, is the type of fertility, and like that celebrated stream, has her source amidst the eternal glaciers of Chundrágíri or Somadri (the mountains of the moon) ; the higher peaks of the gigantic Himalya, where Parvati is represented as ornamenting the tiara of Iswara " with a beamy moon." In this metaphor, and in his title of Somanát'ha (*lord of the moon*), we again have evidence of Iswara, or Síva, after representing the sun, having the satellite moon as his ornament.[1] His Olympus, Cailása, is studded with that majestic pine, the *cedar* ; thence he is called *Cédár-nat'h*, ' lord of the cedar-trees.' The mysteries of Osiris and those of Eleusis [2] were of the same character, commemorative of the first germ of civilisation, the culture of the *earth*, under a variety of names, Ertha, Isis, Diana, Ceres, Ella. It is a curious fact, that in the terra-cotta images of Isis, frequently excavated about her temple at Pæstum,[3] she holds in her right hand an exact representation of the Hindu lingam and yoni combined ; and on the Indian expedition to Egypt, our Hindu soldiers deemed themselves amongst the altars of their own god Iswara (*Osiris*), from the abundance of his emblematic representatives.

In the festival of *Gangore*, as before mentioned, Iswara yields to his consort Gouri, and occupies an unimportant position near her at the water's edge, meanly clad, smoking intoxicating herbs, and, whether by accident or design, holding the stalk of an onion in full blossom as a mace or club—a plant regarded by some of the Egyptians with veneration, and held by the Hindus generally in detestation : and why they should on such an occasion thus degrade Iswara, I know not. Onion-juice is reluctantly taken when prescribed medicinally, as a powerful stimulant, by those who would reject spirituous liquors ; and there are classes, as the *Aghori*, that worship

[1] Let it be borne in mind that *Indu, Chundra, Soma*, are all epithets for ' the moon,' or as *he* is classically styled (in an inscription of the famous Komarpal, which I discovered in Cheetore), " *Nissa Nat'h*," the ruler of darkness (*Nissa*).

[2] I have before remarked that a Sanscrit etymology might be given to this word in *Ella* and *Isa*, i.e. ' the goddess of the earth.'

[3] I was informed at Naples that four thousand of these were dug out of one spot, and I obtained while at Pæstum many fragments and heads of this goddess.

Iswara in his most degraded form, who will not only devour raw flesh, but that of man ; and to whom it is a matter of perfect indifference whether the victim was slaughtered or died a natural death. For the honour of humanity, such monsters are few in number ; but that they practise these deeds I can testify, from a personal visit to their haunts, where I saw the cave of one of these Troglodyte monsters, in which by his own command he was inhumed ; and which will remain closed, until curiosity and incredulity greater than mine may disturb the bones of the *Aghori* of Aboo.

The ὠμοφαγία, or eating raw flesh with the blood, was a part of the secret mysteries of Osiris, in commemoration of the happy change in the condition of mankind from savage to civilised life, and intended to deter by disgust the return thereto.[1]

The Budhists pursued this idea to excess ; and in honour of *Ad-Iswara*, the *First*, who from his abode of Méru taught them the arts of agriculture, they altogether abandoned that type of savage life, the eating of the flesh of animals,[2] and confined themselves to the fruits of the earth. With these sectarian anti-idolaters, *who are almost all of Rajpoot descent*, the beneficent *Lacshmi*, *Sri*, or *Gouri*, is an object of sincere devotion.

But we must close this digression ; for such is the affinity between the mythology of India, Greece, and Egypt, that a bare recapitulation of the numerous surnames of the Hindu goddess of abundance would lead us beyond reasonable limits ; all are forms of *Parvati* or *Doorga Mata*, the *Mater Montana* of Greece and Rome, an epithet of Cybele or Vesta (according to Diodorus), as the guardian goddess of children, one of the characters of the Rajpoot "Mother of the Mount," whose shrine crowns many a pinnacle in Méwar ; and who, with the prolific Gouri, is amongst the amiable forms of the universal mother, whose functions are more varied and extensive than her sisters of Egypt and of Greece. Like the Ephesian Diana, Doorga wears the crescent on her head. She is also "the turreted Cybele," the guardian goddess of all places of strength (*doorga*),[3] and like her she is drawn or carried by the lion. As Mata Janávi, '*the Mother of Births*,' she is *Juno Lucina* : as Pudma, '*whose throne is the lotos*,' she is the fair Isis of the Nile : as Tri-poora,[4] '*governing the three worlds*,' and Atmá-devi, '*the Goddess of Souls*,' she is the *Hecate Triformis* of the Greeks. In short, her power is manifested under every form from the birth, and all the intermediate stages until death ; whether Janávi, Gouri, or the terrific Cali, the Proserpine or Calligenia of the West.

Whoever desires to witness one of the most imposing and pleasing of Hindu festivals, let him repair to Oodipoor, and behold the rites of the lotos-queen Pudma, the Gouri of Rajast'han.

Cheyt (*Súdi*) 8th, which, being after the *ides*, is the 23rd of the month, is sacred to *Dévi, the* goddess of every tribe ; she is called *Asócashtami*, and being the ninth night (*noratri*) from the opening of their Floralia, they perform the *homa*, or sacrifice of fire. On this day, a grand procession

[1] Prichard's *Researches into the Physical History of Man*, p. 369.

[2] The Baudhas of Tartary make no scruple of eating flesh.

[3] *Doorga*, 'a fort' ; as *Suverna-doorg*, 'the golden castle,' etc. etc.

[4] Literally *Tripoli* 'the three cities,' *poora*, *polis*.

takes place to the *Chougan*, and every Rajpoot worships his tutelary divinity.

Cheyt (*Súdi*) 9th is the anniversary of Rama, the grand beacon of the solar race, kept with great rejoicings at Oodipoor. Horses and elephants are worshipped, and all the implements of war. A procession takes place to the Chougan, and the succeeding day, called the *Dusséra* or tenth, is celebrated in Asoj.

The last days of spring are dedicated to *Camdéva*, the god of love. The scorching winds of the hot season are already beginning to blow, when Flora droops her head, and "the god of love turns anchorite"; yet the rose continues to blossom, and affords the most fragrant chaplets for the Rajpootnis, amidst all the heats of summer. Of this the queen of flowers, the jessamine (*chaméli*), white and yellow, the magra, the champaca, that flourish in extreme heat, the ladies form garlands, which they twine in their dark hair, weave into bracelets, or wear as pendent collars. There is no city in the East where the adorations of the sex to *Camdéva* are more fervent than in "the city of the rising sun" (*Udyápûra*). On the 13th and 14th of Cheyt they sing hymns handed down by the sacred bards :—

"Hail, god of the flowery bow ![1] hail, warrior with a fish on thy banner ! hail, powerful divinity, who causeth the firmness of the sage to forsake him !"

"Glory to MADANA, to Cáma,[2] the god of gods ; to HIM by whom BRAHMA, VISHNU, SíVA, and INDRA are filled with emotions of rapture !" —*Bhavishya Púrána.*[3]

Vysakh.—There is but one festival in this month of any note, when the grand procession denominated the "*Nakarra ca aswari*" (from the equestrians being summoned, as already described, by the grand kettle-drums from the Tripolia), takes place ; and this is against the canons of the Hindu church, being instituted by the present Rana in S. 1847, a memorable year in the calendar. It was in this year, on the 2nd of Vysakh, that he commanded a repetition of the rites of GOURI, by the name of the *Little Gangore* ; but this act of impiety was marked by a sudden rise of the waters of the Péshola, the bursting of the huge embankment, and the inundation of the lake's banks, to the destruction of one-third of the capital : life, property, mansions, trees, all were swept away in the tremendous rush of water, whose ravages are still marked by the site of streets and bazaars now converted into gardens or places of recreation, containing thousands of acres within the walls, subdivided by hedges of the *cactus*, the natural fence of Méwar, which alike thrives in the valley or covers the most barren spots of her highest hills. But although the superstitious look grave, and add that a son was also taken from him on this very day, yet the Rana persists in maintaining the fête he established ; the barge is manned, he and his chiefs circumnavigate the Péshola, regale on majaom, and terrify Varûná (the water-god) with the pyrotechnic exhibitions.

[1] Cupid's bow is formed of a garland of flowers.

[2] *Madana*, he who intoxicates with desire (*cáma*), both epithets of the god of love. The festivals on the 13th and 14th are called *Madana triodasi* (the tenth) and *chaturdasi* (fourteenth).

[3] *Asiatic Researches*, vol. iii. p. 278.

Although the court calendar of Oodipoor notices only those festivals on which state processions occur, yet there are many minor fêtes, which are neither unimportant nor uninteresting. We shall enumerate a few, both in Vyshak, Jeyt, and Asar, which are blank as to the "*Nakarra Aswari.*"

On the 29th Vyshak, there is a fast common to India peculiar to the women, who perform certain rites under the sacred fig-tree (the *vata* or *peepul*), to preserve them from widowhood; and hence the name of the fast *Savítri-vata.*

On the second of Jeyt, when the sun is in the zenith, the Rajpoot ladies commemorate the birth of the sea-born goddess *Rembha*, the queen of the naiads or *Apsárás*,[1] whose birth, like that of Venus, was from the froth of the waters; and hence the Rajpoot bards designate all the fair messengers of heaven by the name of Apsaras, who summon the "chosen" from the field of battle, and convey him to the "mansion of the sun."[2]

On the 6th of Jeyt, the ladies have another festival called the *Aranya shashti*, because on this day those desirous of offspring walk in the woods (*aranya*) to gather and eat certain herbs. Sir W. Jones has remarked the analogy between this and the *Druidic* ceremony of gathering the mistletoe (also on the *shashti*, or *6th day of the moon*), as a preservative against sterility.

Asar, the initiative month of the periodical rains, has no particular festivity at Oodipoor, though in other parts of India the *Rat'ha yatra*, or procession of the car of Vishnu or *Jaganat'ha* (lord of the universe) is well known: this is on the 2nd and the 11th, "the *night of the gods*," when Vishnu (the sun) reposes four months.

Sawun, classically *Srávana.* There are two important festivals, with processions, in this month.

The third, emphatically called "*the* teej" (*third*), is sacred to the mountain goddess *Parvati*, being the day on which, after long austerities, she was reunited to Síva: she accordingly declared it holy, and proclaimed that whoever invoked her on that day should possess whatever was desired. The *teej* is accordingly reverenced by the women, and the husbandman of Rajast'han, who deems it a most favourable day to take possession of land, or to reinhabit a deserted dwelling. When on the expulsion of the predatory powers from the devoted lands of Méwar, proclamations were disseminated far and wide, recalling the expatriated inhabitants, they showed their love of country by obedience to the summons. Collecting their goods and chattels, they congregated from all parts, but assembled at a common rendezvous to make their entry to the *bápóta*, 'land of their sires,' on the *teej* of Sawun. On this fortunate occasion, a band of three hundred men, women, and children, with colours flying, drums beating, the females taking precedence with brass vessels of water on their heads, and chanting the *suhailéa* (song of joy), entered the town of Kapasan, to revisit their desolate dwellings, and

[1] *Ap*, 'water,' and *sara*, 'froth or essence.'

[2] The Romans held the calends of June (generally Jeyt) sacred to the goddess CARNA, significant of the sun. Carneus was the sun-god of the Celts, and a name of Apollo at Sparta, and other Grecian cities. The Carneia was a festival in honour of Apollo.

return thanks on their long-abandoned altars to *Parvati* [1] for a happiness they had never contemplated.

Red garments are worn by all classes on this day, and at Jeipoor clothes of this colour are presented by the Raja to all the chiefs. At that court the teej is kept with more honour than at Oodipoor. An image of Parvati on the teej, richly attired, is borne on a throne by women chanting hymns, attended by the prince and his nobles. On this day, fathers present red garments and stuffs to their daughters.

The 5th is the *Nagpanchami*, or day set apart for the propitiation of the chief of the reptile race, the Naga or serpent. Few subjects have more occupied the notice of the learned world than the mysteries of Ophite worship, which are to be traced wherever there existed a remnant of civilisation, or indeed of humanity; among the savages of the savannahs [2] of America, and the magi of Fars, with whom it was the type of evil,—their Ahrimanes.[3] The *Nagas*, or serpent-genii of the Rajpoots, have a semi-human structure, precisely as Diodorus describes the snake-mother of the Scythæ, in whose country originated this serpent-worship, engrafted on the tenets of Zerdusht, of the *Purans* of the priesthood of Egypt, and on the fables of early Greece. Dupuis, Volney, and other expounders of the mystery, have given an astronomical solution to what they deem a varied ramification of an ancient fable, of which that of Greece, "the dragon guarding the fruits of Hesperides," may be considered the most elegant version. Had these learned men seen those ancient sculptures in India, which represent "the fall," they might have changed their opinion. The traditions of the Jains or Budhists (originating in the land of the Takyacs,[4] or Turkist'han) assert the creation of the human species in pairs, called *joogal*, who fed off the ever-fructifying *calpa-vrisha*, which possesses all the characters of the Tree of Life, like it bearing

> "Ambrosial fruit of vegetable gold";

which was termed *amrita*, and rendered them immortal. A drawing, brought by Colonel Coombs, from a sculptured column in a cave temple in the south of India, represents the first pair at the foot of this ambrosial tree, and a serpent entwined among the heavily laden boughs, presenting to them some of the fruit from his mouth. The tempter appears to be at that part of his discourse, when

> ". . . his words, replete with guile,
> Into her heart too easy entrance won:
> Fixed on the fruit she gazed."

This is a curious subject to be engraved on an ancient pagan temple; if Jain or Budhist, the interest would be considerably enhanced. On this festival, at Oodipoor, as well as throughout India, they strew

[1] The story of the vigils of Parvati, preparatory to her being reunited to her lord, consequent to her sacrifice as *Sati*, is the counterpart of the Grecian fable of Cybele, her passion for, and marriage with, the youth Atys or *Papas*, the *Babu*, or universal father, of the Hindus.

[2] How did a word of Persian growth come to signify "the boundless brake" of the new world?

[3] *Ari*, 'a foe'; *manoos*, 'man.'

[4] This is the snake-race of India, the foes of the Pandus.

particular plants about the threshold, to prevent the entrance of reptiles.

RAKHI.—This festival, which is held on the last day of Sawun, was instituted in honour of the good genii, when Durvasa the sage instructed Salone (the genius or nymph presiding over the month of Sawun) to bind on *rakhis*, or bracelets, as charms to avert evil. The ministers of religion and females alone are privileged to bestow these charmed wrist-bands. The ladies of Rajast'han, either by their handmaids or the family priests, send a bracelet as the token of their esteem to such as they adopt as brothers, who return gifts in acknowledgment of the honour. The claims thus acquired by the fair are far stronger than those of consanguinity: for illustration of which I may refer to an incident already related in the annals of this house.[1] Sisters also present their brothers with clothes on this day, who make an offering of gold in return.[2]

This day is hailed by the Brahmins as indemnifying them for their expenditure of silk and spangles, with which they decorate the wrists of all who are likely to make a proper return.

Bhadoon.—On the 3rd there is a grand procession to the Chougan; and *the* 8th, or Ashtami, is the birth of Crishna, which will be described at large in an account of Nat'hdwara. There are several holidays in this month, when the periodical rains are in full descent; but that on the last but one (*súdi* 14, or 29th) is the most remarkable.

On this day[3] commences the worship of the ancestorial manes (the Pitri-iswara, or *father-gods*) of the Rajpoots, which continues for fifteen days. The Rana goes to the cemetery at Ara, and performs at the cenotaph of each of his forefathers the rites enjoined, consisting of ablutions, prayers, and the hanging of garlands of flowers, and leaves sacred to the dead, on their monuments. Every chieftain does the same amongst the altars of the "great ancients" (*burra boora*); or, if absent from their estates, they accompany their sovereign to Ara.

[1] See p. 250.

[2] I returned from three to five pieces of gold for the *rakhis* sent by my adopted sisters; from one of whom, the sister of the Rana, I annually received this pledge by one of her handmaids; three of them I have yet in my possession, though I never saw the donor, who is now no more. I had, likewise, some presented through the family priest, from the Boondí queen-mother, with whom I have conversed for hours, though she was invisible to me; and from the ladies of rank of the chieftains' families, but one of whom I ever beheld, though they often called upon me for the performance of brotherly offices in consequence of such tie. There is a delicacy in this custom, with which the bond uniting the cavaliers of Europe to the service of the fair, in the days of chivalry, will not compare.

[3] Sacred to Vishnu, with the title of *Ananta*, or infinite—*Bhavishattara*. (See *Asiatic Researches*, vol. iii. p. 291.) Here Vishnu appears as 'lord of the manes.'

CHAPTER XXII

Festivals continued—Adoration of the sword : its Scythic origin—The Dusséra, or military festival : its Scythic origin—Toruns or triumphal arcs—Ganésa of the Rajpoots and Janus of the Romans—Worship of arms : of the magic brand of Méwar, compared with the enchanted sword, Tirsing, of the Edda—Birth of Ku-mára, the Rajpoot Mars, compared with the Roman divinity—Birth of Ganga : her analogy to Pallas—Adoration of the moon—Worship of Lacshmí, or Fortune ; of Yama, or Pluto—Déwali, or festival of lamps, in Arabia, in China, in Egypt, and in India—Anacúta and Julyatra—Festivals sacred to the Ceres and Neptune of the Hindus—Festival of the autumnal equinox—Reflections on the universal worship of the elements, Fire, Light, Water—Festival sacred to Mithras or Vishnu, as the sun—The Phallus : its etymology—Rajpoot doctrine of the Triad—Symbols Vishnu, as the sun-god : his messenger Garúda, the eagle : his charioteer Arûná, or the dawn—Sons of Arûná—Fable analogous to that of Icarus—Rites of Vishnu on the vernal equinox and summer solstice—Dolayátra, or festival of the ark, compared with the ark of Osiris, and Argonautic expedition of the Greeks—Etymology of *Argonaut*—Ethiopia the Lanka of the Hindus—Their sea-king, Sagara—Rama, or Ramesa, chief of the Cushite races of India—Ramesa of the Rajpoots and Rameses of Egypt compared—Reflections.

KARGA S'HAPNA, *Worship of the Sword*.—The festival in which this imposing rite occurs is the *Noratri*,[1] sacred to the god of war, commencing on the first of the month Asoj. It is essentially martial, and confined to the Rajpoot, who on the departure of the monsoon finds himself at liberty to indulge his passion whether for rapine or revenge, both which in these tropical regions are necessarily suspended during the rains. Arguing from the order of the passions, we may presume that the first objects of emblematic worship were connected with war, and we accordingly find the highest reverence paid to arms by every nation of antiquity. The Scythic warrior of Central Asia, the intrepid Gete, admitted no meaner representative of the god of battle than his own scimitar.[2] He worshipped it, he swore by it ; it was buried with him, in order that he might appear before the martial divinity in the other world as became his worshipper on earth : for the Gete of Transoxiana, from the earliest ages, not only believed in the soul's immortality, and in the doctrine of rewards and punishments hereafter, but, according to the father of history, he was a monotheist ; of which fact he has left a memorable proof in the punishment of the celebrated Anacharsis, who, on his return from a visit to Thales and his brother philosophers of Greece, attempted to introduce into the land of the Sacæ (*Sakatai*) the corrupted polytheism of Athens.

[1] *Noratri* may be interpreted the *nine days*' festival, or the '*new night*.'

[2] "It was natural enough," says Gibbon, "that the Scythians should adore with peculiar devotion the god of war ; but as they were incapable of forming either an abstract idea, or a corporeal representation, they worshipped their tutelar deity under the symbol of an iron cimeter. If the rites of Scythia were practised on this solemn occasion,[1] a lofty altar, or rather pile of faggots, three hundred yards in length and in breadth, was raised in a spacious plain ; and the sword of Mars was placed erect on the summit of this rustic altar, which was annually consecrated by the blood of sheep, horses, and of the hundredth captive."—Gibbon's *Roman Empire*, vol. vi. p. 43.

---

[1] Attila dictating the terms of peace with the envoys of Constantinople, at the city of Margus, in Upper Mœsia.

If we look westward from this the central land of earliest civilisation, to Dacia, Trace, Pannonia, the seats of the Thyssagetæ or western Getes, we find the same form of adoration addressed to the emblem of Mars, as mentioned by Xenophon in his memorable *retreat*, and practised by Alaric and his Goths, centuries afterwards, in the Acropolis of Athens. If we transport ourselves to the shores of Scandinavia, amongst the Cimbri and Getes of Jutland, to the *Ultima Thule*, wherever the name of Gete prevails, we shall find the same adoration paid by the Getic warrior to his sword.

The Frisian Frank, also of Gothic race, adhered to this worship, and transmitted it with the other rites of the Getic warrior of the Jaxartes; such as the adoration of the steed, sacred to the sun, the great god of the Massagetæ, as well as of the Rajpoot, who sacrificed it at the annual feast, or with his arms and wife burnt it on his funeral pile. Even the kings of the '*second race*' kept up the religion of their Scythic sires from the Jaxartes, and the bones of the war-horse of Chilperic were exhumed with those of the monarch. These rites, as well as those long-cherished chivalrous notions, for which the Salian Franks have ever been conspicuous, had their birth in Central Asia; for though contact with the more polished Arab softened the harsh character of the western warrior, his thirst for glory, the romantic charm which fed his passion, and his desire to please the fair, he inherited from his ancestors on the shores of the Baltic, which were colonised from the Oxus. Whether Charlemagne addressed his sword as *Joyeuse*,[1] or the Scandinavian hero Angantyr as the enchanted blade *Tirsing* (*Híalmar's bane*), each came from one common origin, the people which invented the custom of *Karga S'hapna*, or 'adoration of the sword.' But neither the faulchion "made by the dwarfs for Suafurlama," nor the redoubted sword of Bayard with which he dubbed the first Francis, —not even the enchanted brand of Ariosto's hero, can for a moment compare with the double-edged *khanda* (scimitar) annually worshipped by the chivalry of Méwar. Before I descant on this monstrous blade, I shall give an abstract of the ceremonies on each of the *nine days* sacred to the god of war.

On the 1st of Asoj, after fasting, ablution, and prayer on the part of the prince and his household, the double-edged *khanda* is removed from the hall of arms (*áwadsálá*), and having received the homage (*pooja*) of the court, it is carried in procession to the *Kishenpól* (gate of Kishen), where it is delivered to the *Raj Jogi*,[2] the *Mehunts*, and band of *Jogis* assembled in front of the temple of Déví '*the* goddess,' adjoining the portal of Kishen.[3] By these, the monastic militant adorers of Heri, *the god of battle*, the brand emblematic of the divinity is placed[4] on the altar before the image of his divine consort. At three in the afternoon the *nakarras*, or grand kettledrums, proclaim from the Tripólia[5] the signal for the assemblage of the chiefs with their retainers; and the Rana and his cavalcade proceed

[1] St. Palaye, *Memoirs of Ancient Chivalry*, p. 305.

[2] *Raj Jogi* is the chief of the ascetic warriors; the *Mehunts* are commanders. More will be said of this singular society when we discuss the religious institutions of Méwar.

[3] The god CRISHNA is called *Kishen* in the dialects.

[4] This is the *t'hapna* of the sword, literally its *inauguration* or *induction*, for the purposes of *adoration*.

[5] *Tripo-lia*, or triple portal.

direct to the stables, when a buffalo is sacrificed in honour of the war-horse. Thence the procession moves to the temple of Dévi, where the Raja Crishen (*Godi*) has preceded. Upon this, the Rana seats himself close to the *Raj Jogi*, presents two pieces of silver and a coco-nut, performs homage to the sword (*karga*), and returns to the palace.

Asoj 2nd. In similar state he proceeds to the Chougan, their *Champ de Mars*, where a buffalo is sacrificed ; and on the same day another buffalo victim is felled by the nervous arm of a Rajpoot, near the *Torun-pol*, or triumphal gate. In the evening the Rana goes to the temple of AMBA MATÁ, the universal mother, when several goats and buffaloes bleed to the goddess.

The 3rd. Procession to the Chougan, when another buffalo is offered ; and in the afternoon five buffaloes and two rams are sacrificed to *Harsid Matá*.

On the 4th, as on every one of the nine days, the first visit is to the *Champ de Mars* : the day opens with the slaughter of a buffalo. The Rana proceeds to the temple of Dévi, when he worships the sword, and the standard of the *Raj Jogi*, to whom, as the high-priest of Síva, *the god of war*, he pays homage, and makes offering of sugar, and a garland of roses. A buffalo having been previously fixed to a stake near the temple the Rana sacrifices him with his own hand, by piercing him from his travelling throne (raised on men's shoulders and surrounded by his vassals) with an arrow. In the days of his strength, he seldom failed almost to bury the feather in the flank of the victim ; but on the last occasion his enfeebled arm made him exclaim with Pirthi Raj, when, captive and blind, he was brought forth to amuse the Tatar despot, " I draw not the bow as in the days of yore."

On the 5th, after the usual sacrifice at the Chougan, and an elephant fight, the procession marches to the temple of *Asapúrná* (Hope) ; a buffalo and a ram are offered to the goddess adored by all the Rajpoots, and the tutelary divinity of the Chohans. On this day, the lives of some victims are spared at the intercession of the Nuggur-Sét'h, or chief-magistrate, and those of his faith, the Jains.

On the 6th, the Rana visits the Chougan, but makes no sacrifice. In the afternoon, prayers and victims to Dévi ; and in the evening the Rana visits *Bikhiári Nat'h*, the chief of the *Kanfárá Jogis*, or split-ear ascetics.

The 7th. After the daily routine at the Chougan, and sacrifices to Dévi (the goddess of destruction), the chief equerry is commanded to adorn the steeds with their new caparisons, and lead them to be bathed in the lake. At night, the sacred fire (*hom*) is kindled, and a buffalo and a ram are sacrificed to Dévi ; the Jogis are called up and feasted on boiled rice and sweetmeats. On the conclusion of this day, the Rana and his chieftains visit the hermitage of Súkria Baba, an anchorite of the Jogi sect.

8th. There is the *homá*, or fire-sacrifice in the palace. In the afternoon, the prince, with a select cavalcade, proceeds to the village of Sameena, beyond the city walls, and visits a celebrated Gosaén.[1]

9th. There is no morning procession. The horses from the royal

[1] On this day sons visit and pay adoration to their fathers. The diet is chiefly of vegetables and fruits. Brahmins with their unmarried daughters are feasted, and receive garments called *choonduree* from their chiefs.

stables, as well as those of the chieftains, are taken to the lake, and bathed by their grooms, and on returning from purification they are caparisoned in their new housings, led forth, and receive the homage of their riders, and the Rana bestows a largess on the master of the horse, the equerries, and grooms. At three in the afternoon, the nakarras having thrice sounded, the whole state insignia, under a select band, proceed to Mount Matachil, and bring home the sword. When its arrival in the court of the palace is announced, the Rana advances and receives it with due homage from the hands of the *Raj Jogi*, who is presented with a khelat; while the *mehunt*, who has performed all the austerities during the nine days, has his *patera* [1] filled with gold and silver coin. The whole of the Jogis are regaled, and presents are made to their chiefs. The elephants and horses again receive homage, and the sword, the shield, and spear are worshipped within the palace. At three in the morning the prince takes repose.

The 10th, or *Dusséra*,[2] is a festival universally known in India, and respected by all classes, although entirely military, being commemorative of the day on which the deified Rama commenced his expedition to Lanka for the redemption of Seeta; [3] the "tenth of Asoj" is consequently deemed by the Rajpoot a fortunate day for warlike enterprise. The day commences with a visit from the prince or chieftain to his spiritual guide. Tents and carpets are prepared at the Chougan or Matachil mount, where the artillery is sent; and in the afternoon the Rana, his chiefs, and their retainers repair to the *field of Mars*, worship the *kaijri* tree, liberate the *niltach* or jay (sacred to Rama), and return amidst a discharge of guns.

11th. In the morning, the Rana, with all the state insignia, the kettle-drums sounding *in the rear*, proceeds towards the Matachil mount, and takes the muster of his troops, amidst discharges of cannon, tilting, and display of horsemanship. The spectacle is imposing even in the decline of this house. The hilarity of the party, the diversified costume, the various forms, colours, and decorations of the turbans, in which some have the heron plume, or sprigs from some shrub sacred to the god of war; the clusters of lances, shining matchlocks, and black bucklers, the scarlet housings of the steeds, and waving pennons, recall forcibly the glorious days of the devoted Sanga, or the immortal Pertáp, who on such occasions collected round the black *changi* and crimson banner of Méwar a band of sixteen thousand of his own kin and clan, whose lives were their lord's and their country's. The shops and bazaars are ornamented with festoons of flowers and branches of trees, while the costliest cloths and brocades are extended on screens, to do honour to their prince; the *torun* (or triumphal arch) is placed before the tent, on a column of which he places one hand as he alights, and before entering makes several circumambula-

[1] The Jogi's *patera* is not so revolting as that of their divinity Hari (the god of war), which is the human *cranium*; this is a hollow gourd.

[2] From *dus* or *dos*, the numeral *ten*; *the* tenth.

[3] In this ancient story we are made acquainted with the distant maritime wars which the princes of India carried on. Even supposing Ravana's abode to be the insular Ceylon, he must have been a very powerful prince to equip an armament sufficiently numerous to carry off from the remote kingdom of *Koshula* the wife of the great king of the Súryás. It is most improbable that a petty king of Ceylon could wage equal war with a potentate who held the chief dominion of India; whose father, *Désárát'ha*, drove his victorious car (*rat'ha*) over every region (*désa*), and whose intercourse with the countries beyond the Brahmapútra is distinctly to be traced in the *Ramayuna*.

tions. All present offer their *nuzzurs* to the prince, the artillery fires, and the bards raise "the song of praise," celebrating the glories of the past; the fame of Samra, who fell with thirteen thousand of his kin on the Caggar; of Ursi and his twelve brave sons, who gave themselves as victims for the salvation of Cheetore; of Koombho, Lakha, Sanga, Pertáp, Umra, Raj, all descended of the blood of Rama, whose exploits, three thousand five hundred years before, they are met to celebrate. The situation of Matachil is well calculated for such a spectacle, as indeed is the whole ground from the palace through the Dehli portal to the mount, on which is erected one of the several castles commanding the approaches to the city. The fort is dedicated to *Mata,* though it would not long remain stable (*áchil*) before a battery of thirty-six pounders. The guns are drawn up about the termination of the slope of the natural glacis; the Rana and his court remain on horseback half up the ascent; and while every chief or vassal is at liberty to leave his ranks, and "witch the world with noble horsemanship," there is nothing tumultuous, nothing offensive in their mirth.

The steeds purchased since the last festival are named, and as the cavalcade returns, their grooms repeat the appellations of each as the word is passed by the master of the horse; as *Baj Raj,* 'the royal steed'; *Hymór,* 'the chief of horses'; *Manika,* 'the gem'; *Bujra,* 'the thunder-bolt,' etc. etc. On returning to the palace, gifts are presented by the Rana to his chiefs. The Chohan chief of Kotario claims the apparel which his prince wears on this day, in token of the fidelity of his ancestor to the minor, Oody Sing, in Akber's wars. To others, a fillet or *bala-bund* for the turban is presented; but all such compliments are regulated by precedent or immediate merit.

Thus terminates the *noratri* festival sacred to the god of war, which in every point of view is analogous to the autumnal festival of the Scythic warlike nations, when these princes took the muster of their armies, and performed the same rites to the great celestial luminary.[1] I have presented to the antiquarian reader these details, because it is in minute particulars that analogous customs are detected. Thus the temporary *torun,* or triumphal arch, erected in front of the tent at *Mount Machila,* would scarcely claim the least notice, but that we discover even in this emblem the origin of the triumphal arches of antiquity, with many other rites which may be traced to the Indo-Scythic races of Asia. The *torun* in its original form consisted of two columns and an architrave, constituting the number *three,* sacred to Hari, the god of war. In the progress of the arts the architrave gave way to the Hindu arch, which consisted of two or more ribs without the keystone, the apex being the perpendicular junction of the archivaults; nor is the arc of the *torun* semicircular, or

[1] "A la première lune de chaque année, tous ces officiers, grands et petits, tenoient une assemblée générale à la cour du Tanjou, et y faisoient un sacrifice solemnel: à la cinquième lune, ils s'assembloient à Lumtching, où ils sacrifioient au ciel, à la terre, aux esprits, et aux ancêtres. Il se tenoit encore une grande assemblée à Tai-lin dans l'automne, parce qu' alors les chevaux étoient plus gras, et on y faisoit en même-tems le denombrement des hommes et des troupeaux; mais tous les jours le Tanjou sortoit de son camp, le matin pour adorer le soleil, et le soir la lune. Sa tente étoit placée à gauche, comme le côté le plus honorable chez ces peuples, et regardoit le couchant."—*Avant J. C.* 209.—*L'Histoire Générale des Huns,* vol. i. p. 24.

any segment of a circle, but with that graceful curvature which stamps with originality one of the arches of the Normans, who may have brought it from their ancient seats on the Oxus, whence it may also have been carried within the Indus. The cromlech, or trilithic altar in the centre of all those monuments called druidic, is most probably a *toruń*, sacred to the Sun-god Belenus, like Hur, or Bál-síva, the god of battle, to whom as soon as a temple is raised the *toruп* is erected, and many of these are exquisitely beautiful.

An interesting essay might be written on *portes* and *toruns*, their names and attributes, and the genii presiding as their guardians. Amongst all the nations of antiquity, the portal has had its peculiar veneration : to pass it was a privilege regarded as a mark of honour. The Jew Haman, in the true oriental style, took post at the king's gate as an inexpugnable position. The most pompous court in Europe takes its title from its *porte*, where, as at Oodipoor, all alight. The *tripolia*, or triple portal, the entry to the magnificent terrace in front of the Rana's palace, consists, like the Roman arcs of triumph, of three arches, still preserving the numeral sacred to the god of battle, one of whose titles is TRIPOORI, which may be rendered *Tripoli*, or lord of the *three places of abode*, or cities, but applied in its extensive sense to the three worlds, heaven, earth, and hell. From the Sanscrit *Póla*, we have the Greek πυλης, *a gate*, or pass ; and in the guardian or *Polioh*, the πυλωρος or *porter* ; while to this *langue mère* our own language is indebted, not only for its portes and porters, but its doors (*dwára*). Pylos signified also a pass ; so in Sanscrit these natural barriers are called *Palas*, and hence the poetical epithet applied to the aboriginal mountain tribes of Rajast'han, namely, Páli-pati and Pal-indra, '*lords of the pass*.'

One of the most important of the Roman divinities was Janus, whence *Januæ*, or portals, of which he was the guardian.[1] A resemblance between the Ganésa of the Hindu pantheon and the Roman Janus has been pointed out by Sir W. Jones, but his analogy extended little beyond nominal similarity. The fable of the birth of *Ganésa* furnishes us with the origin of the worship of Janus, and as it has never been given, I shall transcribe it from the bard Chund. Ganésa is the chief of the genii [2] attendant on the god of war, and was expressly formed by Oomia, the Hindu Juno, to guard the entrance of her caverned retreat in the Caucasus, where she took refuge from the tyranny of the lord of *Cailása* (Olympus), whose throne is fixed amidst eternal snows on the summit of this peak of the gigantic Caucasus (*Khô-kása*).[3]

" Strife arose between Mahadeo and the faithful Parvati : she fled to the mountains and took refuge in a cave. A crystal fountain tempted her to bathe, but shame was awakened ; she dreaded being seen. Rubbing her frame, she made an image of man ; with her nail she sprinkled it with the water of life, and placed it as guardian at the entrance of the cave."

[1] Hence may be found a good etymology of *janizary*, the guardian of the *serai*, a title left by the lords of Eastern Rome for the Porte.

[2] In Sanscrit *gén* (pronounced as *gun*), the *jin* of the Persians, transmuted to *genii* ; here is another instance in point of the alternation of the initial, and softened by being transplanted from Indo-Scythia to Persia, as *Ganés* was *Janus* at Rome.

[3] The *Casia Montes* of Ptolemy.

Engrossed with the recollection of Parvati,[1] Síva went to *Kartika* [2] for tidings of his mother, and together they searched each valley and recess, and at length reached the spot where a figure was placed at the entrance of a cavern. As the chief of the gods prepared to explore this retreat, he was stopped by the *Polioh.* In a rage he struck off his head with his discus (*chukra*), and in the gloom discovered the object of his search. Surprised and dismayed, she demanded how he obtained ingress : " Was there no guardian at the entrance ? " The furious Síva replied that he had cut off his head. On hearing this, the mountain-goddess was enraged, and weeping, exclaimed, "You have destroyed my child." The god, determined to recall him to life, decollated a young elephant, replaced the head he had cut off, and naming him *Ganésa,* decreed that in every resolve his name should be the first invoked

Invocation of the Bard to Ganésa.

" Oh, Ganésa ! thou art a mighty lord ; thy single tusk [3] is beautiful, and demands the tribute of praise from the Indra of song.[4] Thou art the chief of the human race ; the destroyer of unclean spirits ; the remover of fevers, whether daily or tertian. Thy bard sounds thy praise ; let my work be accomplished ! "

Thus Ganésa is the chief of the *Di minores* of the Hindu pantheon, as the etymology of the word indicates,[5] and like Janus, was intrusted with the gates of heaven ; while of his right to preside over peace and war, the fable related affords abundant testimony. Ganésa is the first invoked and propitiated [6] on every undertaking, whether warlike or pacific. The warrior implores his counsel ; the banker indites his name at the commencement of every letter ; the architect places his image in the foundation of every edifice ; and the figure of Ganésa is either sculptured or painted at the door of every house as a protection against evil. Our Hindu Janus is represented as four-armed, and holding the disk (*chukra*), the war-shell, the club, and the lotos. Ganésa is not, however, *bifrons,* like the Roman guardian of portals. In every transaction he is *ad,* or the first, though the Hindu does not, like the Roman, open the year with his name. I shall conclude with remarking that one of the portes of every Hindu city is named the *Ganésa Pol,* as well as some conspicuous entrance to the palace : thus Oodipoor has its Ganésa *dwara,* who also gives a name to the hall, the Ganésa *deori* ; and his shrine will be found on the ascent of every sacred mount, as at Aboo, where it is placed close to a fountain on

[1] *Parvati,* ' the mountain goddess,' was called Sati, or ' the faithful ' in her former birth. She became the mother of *Januvi,* the river (*gunga*) goddess.

[2] Kartika, the son of Síva and Parvati, the Jupiter and Juno of the Hindu theogony, has the leading of the armies of the gods, delegated by his father ; and his mother has presented to him her peacock, which is the steed of this warlike divinity. He is called Kartika (*Carticeya*) from being nursed by six females called *Krittiku,* who inhabit six of the seven stars composing the constellation of the Wain, or Ursa Major. Thus the Hindu Mars, born of Jupiter and Juno, and nursed by Ursa Major, is, like all other theogonies, an astronomical allegory. There is another legend of the birth of Mars, which I shall give in the text.

[3] This elephant-headed divinity has but one tusk.

[4] The bard thus modestly designates himself.

[5] Chief (*esa, ísa,* or *iswara*) of the gana (*genii*) or *attendants* on Síva.

[6] So he was at Rome, and his statue held the keys of heaven in his right hand, and, like Ganésa, a rod (*the unkoos*) in his left.

the abrupt face about twelve hundred feet from the base. There is likewise a hill sacred to him in Méwar called *Ganésa Gir*, tantamount to the *mons janiculum* of the eternal city. The companion of this divinity is a rat, who indirectly receives a portion of homage, and with full as much right as the bird emblematic of Minerva.

We have abandoned the temple of the warlike divinity (*Dévi*), the sword of Mars, and the triumphal *torun*, to invoke Ganésa. It will have been remarked that the Rana aids himself to dismount by placing his hand on one of the columns of the *torun*, an act which is pregnant with a martial allusion, as are indeed the entire ceremonials of the "worship of the sword."

It might be deemed folly to *trace* the rites and superstitions of so remote an age and nation to Central Asia; but when we find the superstitions of the Indo-Scythic Gete prevailing within the Indus, in Dacia, and on the shores of the Baltic, we may assume their common origin; for although the worship of arms has prevailed among all warlike tribes, there is a peculiar respect paid to the sword amongst the Getic races. The Greeks and and Romans paid devotion to their arms, and swore by them. The Greeks brought their habits from ancient Thrace, where the custom existed of presenting as the greatest gift that peculiar kind of sword called *acinaces*, which we dare not derive from the Indo-Scythic or Sanscrit *asi*, a sword. When Xenophon, on his retreat, reached the court of Seuthes, he agreed to attach his corps to the service of the Thracian. His officers on introduction, in the true oriental style, presented their *nuzzurs*, or gifts of homage, excepting Xenophon, who, deeming himself too exalted to make the common offering, presented his sword, probably only to be touched in recognition of his services being accepted. The most powerful oath of the Rajpoot, next to his sovereign's throne (*gádi ca án*), is by his arms, *ya sil ca án*, 'by this weapon!' as, suiting the action to the word, he puts his hand on his dagger, never absent from his girdle. *Dhál, turwár, ca án*, 'by my sword and shield!' The shield is deemed the only fit vessel or salver on which to present gifts; and accordingly at a Rajpoot court, shawls, brocades, scarfs, and jewels are always spread before the guest on bucklers.[1]

In the Runic "incantation of Hervor," daughter of Angantyr, at the tomb of her father, she invokes the dead to deliver the enchanted brand *Tirsing*, or "*Hialmar's bane*," which, according to Getic custom, was buried in his tomb; she adjures him and his brothers "*by all their arms, their shields, etc.*" It is depicted with great force, and, translated, would deeply interest a Rajpoot, who might deem it the spell by which the *Khanda* of Hamíra, which he annually worships, was obtained.

Incantation.

Hervor—"Awake, Angantyr! Hervor, the only daughter of thee and Suafú, doth awaken thee. Give me out of the tomb the tempered sword which the dwarfs made for Suafurlama.

"Can none of Eyvors'[2] sons speak with me out of the habitations of the dead? Hervardur,[2] Hurvardur?"[2]

[1] The Gothic invaders of Italy inaugurated their monarch by placing him upon a shield, and elevating him on their shoulders in the midst of his army.

[2] All these proper names might have Oriental etymologies assigned to them;

The tomb at length opens, the inside of which appears on fire, and a reply is sung within :

Angantyr—"Daughter Hervor, full of spells to raise the dead, why dost thou call so ? I was not buried either by father or friends ; two who lived after me got *Tirsing*, one of whom is now in possession thereof."

Hervor—"The dead shall never enjoy rest unless Angantyr deliver me Tirsing, that cleaveth shields, and killed Hialmar." [1]

Angantyr—"Young maid, thou art of manlike courage, who dost rove by night to tombs, with spear engraven with magic spells,[2] with helm and coat of mail, before the door of our hall."

Hervor—"It is not good for thee to hide it."

Angantyr—"The *death of Hialmar* [3] lies under my shoulders ; it is all wrapt up in fire : I know no maid that dares to take this sword in hand."

Hervor—"I shall take in hand the sharp sword, if I may obtain it. I do not think *that* fire will burn which plays about the site of deceased men." [4]

Angantyr—"Take and keep *Hialmar's bane* : touch but the edges of it, there is poison in them both ; [5] it is a most cruel devourer of men." [6]

Tradition has hallowed the two-edged sword (*khanda*) of Méwar, by investing it with an origin as mysterious as "the bane of Hialmar." It is supposed to be the enchanted weapon fabricated by *Viswacarma*,[7] with which the Hindu Proserpine girded the founder of the race, and led him forth to the conquest of Cheetore.[8] It remained the great heirloom of her princes till the sack of Cheetore by the Tatar Alla, when Rana Ursi and eleven of his brave sons devoted themselves at the command of the guardian goddess of their race, and their capital falling into the hands of the invader, the last scion of Bappa became a fugitive amidst the mountains of the west. It was then the Tatar inducted the Sonigurra Maldeo, as his lieutenant, into the capital of the Gehlotes. The most celebrated of the

Eyvor-sail is the name of a celebrated Rajpoot hero of the Bhatti tribe, who were driven at an early period from the very heart of Scythia, and are of Yadu race.

[1] This word can have a Sanscrit derivation from *hia*, 'a horse' ; *marna*, 'to strike or kill' ; *Hialmar*, 'the horse-slayer.'

[2] The custom of engraving incantations on weapons is also from the East, and thence adopted by the Mahomedan, as well as the use of phylacteries. The name of the goddess guarding the tribe is often inscribed, and I have had an entire copy of the *Bhagvat Gita* taken from the turban of a Rajpoot killed in action : in like manner the Mahomedans place therein the *Korán*.

[3] The metaphorical name of the sword Tirsing.

[4] I have already mentioned these fires (see p. 62), which the northern nations believed to issue from the tombs of their heroes, and which seemed to guard their ashes ; them they called *Hauga Elldr*, or 'the sepulchral fires,' and they were supposed more especially to surround tombs which contained hidden treasures. These supernatural fires are termed *Shahaba* by the Rajpoots. When the intrepid Scandinavian maiden observes that she is not afraid of the flame burning her, she is bolder than one of the boldest Rajpoots, for *Sri-Kishen*, who was shocked at the bare idea of going near these sepulchral lights, was one of the three non-commissioned officers who afterwards led thirty-two firelocks to the attack and defeat of 1500 Pindarries.

[5] Like the Rajpoot *Khanda*, Tirsing was double-edged ; the poison of these edges is a truly Oriental idea.

[6] This poem is from the *Hervarer Saga*, an ancient Icelandic history. See *Edda*, vol. ii. p. 192.

[7] The Vulcan of the Hindus.

[8] For an account of the initiation to arms of Bappa, the founder of the Gehlotes, see p. 184.

poetic chronicles of Méwar gives an elaborate description of the subterranean palace in Cheetore, in one of whose entrances the dreadful sacrifice was perpetuated to save the honour of Pudmani and the fair of Cheetore from the brutalised Tatars.[1] The curiosity of Maldeo was more powerful than his superstition, and he determined to explore these hidden abodes, though reputed to be guarded by the serpent genii attendant on *Nagnécha*, the ancient divinity of its *Takshac* founders.[2] Whether it was through the identical caverned passage, and over the ashes of those martyred *Kámunis*, that he made good his way into those rock-bound abodes, the legend says not ; but though

> " In darkness, and with dangers compassed round,
> And solitude,"

the intrepid Maldeo paused not until he had penetrated to the very bounds of the abyss, where in a recess he beheld the snaky sorceress and her sister crew seated round a cauldron, in which the materials of their incantation were solving before a fire that served to illume this abode of horror. As he paused, the reverberation of his footsteps caused the infernal crew to look athwart the palpable obscure of their abode, and beholding the audacious mortal, they demanded his intent. The valiant Sonigurra replied that he did not come as a spy,

> " With purpose to explore or to disturb
> The secrets of their realm,"

but in search of the enchanted brand of the founder of the Gehlotes. Soon they made proof of Maldeo's hardihood. Uncovering the cauldron, he beheld a sight most appalling : amidst divers fragments of animals was the arm of an infant. A dish of this horrid repast was placed before him, and a silent signal made for him to eat. He obeyed, and returned the empty platter : it was proof sufficient of his worth to wear the enchanted blade, which, drawn forth from its secret abode, was put into the hand of Maldeo, who bowing, retired with the trophy.

Rana Hamíra recovered this heirloom of his house, and with it the throne of Cheetore, by his marriage with the daughter of the Sonigurra, as related in the annals.[3] Another version says it was Hamíra himself who obtained the enchanted sword, by his incantations to Charuni Déví, or the goddess of the bards, whom he worshipped.

We shall conclude this account of the military festival of Méwar with the birth of *Kumara*, the god of war, taken from the most celebrated of their mythological poems, the *Ramayuna*, probably the most ancient book in the world. " Mérá, daughter of Mérú, became the spouse of Himavati,

[1] See p. 215.

[2] The *Mori* prince, from whom Bappa took Cheetore, was of the *Ták* or *Takshac* race, of whom *Nágnéchá*, or *Nágáni Mata* was the mother, represented as half woman and half serpent ; the sister of the mother of the Scythic race, according to their legends ; so that the deeper we dive into these traditions, the stronger reason we shall find to assign a Scythic origin to all these tribes. As *Bappa*, the founder of the Gehlotes, retired into Scythia and left his heirs to rule in India, I shall find fault with no antiquary, who will throw overboard all the connection between Kenéksen, the founder of the Balabhi empire, and Sumitra, the last of Rama's line. Many rites of the Rana's house are decidedly Scythic.

[3] See p. 219.

from whose union sprung the beauteous Ganga, and her sister Ooma. Ganga was sought in marriage by all the celestials ; while Ooma, after a long life of austerity, was espoused by *Roodra.*" [1] But neither sister was fortunate enough to have offspring, until Ganga became pregnant by HUTASHNA (regent of fire), and " KUMARA, resplendent as the sun, illustrious as the moon, was produced from the side of Ganga." The gods, with Indra at their head, carried him to the *Krittikees* [2] to be nursed, and he became their joint care. " As he resembled the fire in brightness, he received the name of Scanda, when the immortals, with AGNI (fire) at their head, anointed him as *general of the armies of the gods.*" [3]—" Thus (the bard Valmíka speaks), oh ! Rama, have I related the story of the production of *Kúmár.*"

This is a very curious relic of ancient mythology, in which we may trace the most material circumstances of the birth of the Roman divinity of war. Kumara (Mars) was the son of Januvi (Juno), and born, like the Romans, without sexual intercourse, but by the agency of Vulcan (regent of fire). Kumara has the peacock (sacred to Juno likewise) as his companion ; and as the Grecian goddess is feigned to have her car drawn by peacocks, so *Ku-mara* (the evil-striker) has a peacock for his steed.

Ganga, ' the river goddess,' has some of the attributes of Pallas, being like the Athenian maid (Ganga never married) born from the head of Jove. The bard of the silver age makes her fall from a glacier of Kailas (Olympus) on the head of the father of the gods, and remain many years within the folds of his tiara (*jit'ha*), until at length being liberated, she was precipitated into the plains of Aryaverta. It was in this escape that she burst her rocky barrier (the Himaleh), and on the birth of Kumara exposed those veins of gold called *jambunadi*, in colour like the jambu fruit, probably alluding to the veins of gold discovered in the rocks of the Ganges in those distant ages.

The last day of the month Asoj ushers in the Hindu winter (*surd rit*).

[1] One of the names of the divinity of war, whose images are covered with vermilion in imitation of blood. (*Qy.* the German *roodur*, ' red.')

[2] The Pleiades.

[3] The festival of the birth of this son of Ganga, or *Januvi*, is on the 10th of *Jeyt.* Sir W. Jones gives the following couplet from the *Sancha* : ' On the 10th of *Jyaisht'ha*, on the bright half of the month, on the day of MANGALA,[1] son of the earth, when the moon was in Hasta, this daughter of *Jahnu* brought from the rocks, and ploughed over the land inhabited by mortals."

[1] MANGALA is one of the names (and perhaps one of the oldest) of the Hindu Mars (*Kumara*), to whom the *Wodens-dag* of the Northmen, the *Mardi* of the French, the *dies Martis* of the Romans, are alike sacred. *Mangala* also means ' happy,' the reverse of the origin of *Mongul*, said to mean ' sad.' The juxtaposition of the Rajpoot and Scandinavian days of the week will show that they have the same origin ;

Rajpoot.	Scandinavian and Saxon.	Rajpoot.	Scandinavian and Saxon.
Surya-war .	. Sun-day.	Vrishpát-war (*a*) .	Thors-day.
Som, or Indu-war	. Moon-day.	Sucra-war (*b*)	. Frey-day.
Búd-war .	. Tuſs-day.	Sani, or Sanichra }-war	. Satur-day.
Mangal-war .	. Wodens-day.		

(*a*) *Vrishut-pati*, ' he who rides on the bull ' ; the steed of the Rajpoot god of war.

(*b*) Sucra is a Cyclop, regent of the planet Venus.

On this day, nothing but white vestments and silver (*chandi*) ornaments are worn, in honour of the moon (*Chandra*), who gives *his* [1] name to the

> "Pale and common drudge
> 'Tween man and man."

This year there was an entire intercalary month: such are called *Lúna*. There is a procession of all the chiefs to the Chougan; and on their return, a full court is held in the great hall, which breaks up with "obeisance to the lamp" (*jote ca moojra*), whose light each reverences; when the candles are lit at home, every Rajpoot, from the prince to the owner of a "skin (*chursa*) of land," seated on a white linen cloth, should worship his tutelary divinity, and feed the priests with sugar and milk.

CARTICA.—This month is peculiarly sacred to *Lacshmí*, the goddess of wealth, the *Juno Moneta* of the Romans. The 13th is called the *Dhuntérus*, or thirteenth [day] of wealth, when gold and silver coin are worshipped, as the representatives of the goddess, by her votaries of all classes, but especially by the mercantile. On the 14th, all anoint with oil, and make libations thereof to *Yama*, the judge of departed spirits. Worship (*pooja*) is performed to the lamp, which represents the god of hell, and is thence called *Yama-déwa*, 'the lamp of Pluto'; and on this day partial illumination takes place throughout the city.

DÉWALI, or *Festival of Lamps*.—On the Amavus, or *ides* of Cartic, is one of the most brilliant fêtes of Rajast'han, called the *Déwali*, when every city, village, and encampment exhibits a blaze of splendour. The potters' wheels revolve for weeks before solely in the manufacture of lamps (*déwa*), and from the palace to the peasant's hut every one supplies himself with them, in proportion to his means, and arranges them according to his fancy. Stuffs, pieces of gold, and sweetmeats are carried in trays and consecrated at the temple of Lacshmí, the *goddess of wealth*, to whom the day is consecrated. The Rana on this occasion honours his prime minister with his presence to dinner; and this chief officer of the state, who is always of the mercantile caste, pours oil into a terra-cotta lamp, which his sovereign holds; the same libation of oil is permitted by each of the near relations of the minister. On this day, it is incumbent upon every votary of Lacshmí to try the chance of the dice, and from their success in the *déwali*, the prince, the chief, the merchant, and the artisan foretell the state of their coffers for the ensuing year.

Lacshmí, though on this festival depicted under by the type of riches, is evidently the beneficent *Anupûrna* in another garb, for the agricultural community place a corn-measure filled with grain and adorned with flowers as her representative; or, if they adorn her effigies, they are those of *Padma*, the water-nymph, with a lotos in one hand, and the *pashu* (or fillet for the head) in the other. As Lacshmí was produced at "*the Churning of the Ocean*," and hence called one of the "fourteen gems," she is confounded with *Rembha*, chief of the *apsaras*, the Venus of the Hindus. Though both were created from the froth (*sara*) of the waters (*ap* or *up*), they are as distinct as the representations of *riches* and *beauty* can be. Lacshmí became the wife of Vishnu, or Kaniya, and is placed at the feet

[1] It will be recollected that the moon with the Rajpoots as with the Scandinavians is a male divinity. The Tatars, who also consider him a male divinity, pay him especial adoration in this autumnal month.

of his marine couch when he is floating on the chaotic waters. As his consort, she merges into the character of Sarasvati, the goddess of eloquence, and here we have the combination of Minerva and Apollo. As of Minerva, the owl is the attendant of Lacshmí; and when we reflect that the Egyptians, who furnished the Grecian pantheon, held these solemn festivals, also called "*the feast of lamps*," in honour of Minerva at Sais, we may deduce the origin of this grand Oriental festival from that common mother-country in Central Asia, whence the *Déwali* radiated to remote China, the Nile, the Ganges, and the shores of the Tigris; for the *shebrát* of Islám is but "the feast of lamps" of the Rajpoots. In all these there is a mixture of the attributes of Ceres and Proserpine, of Plutus and Pluto. Lacshmí partakes of the attributes of both the first, while *Cuvéra*,[1] who is conjoined with her, is Plutus: as Yama is Pluto, the infernal judge. The consecrated lamps and the libations of oil are all dedicated to him; and "torches and flaming brands are likewise kindled and consecrated, to burn the bodies of kinsmen who may be dead in battle in a foreign land, and light them through the shades of death to the mansion of Yama."[2]

To the infernal god Yama, who is "the son of the sun," the second day following the Amavus, or *ides* of Cartica, is also sacred; it is called the *Bhrátri divitya*, or 'the brothers,' because the river goddess *Yamuna* on this day entertained her brother (*bhrátri*) Yama, and is therefore consecrated to fraternal affection. At the hour of curfew (*gaódaluk*,[3] when the cattle return from the fields), the cow is worshipped, the herd having been previously tended. From this ceremony no rank is exempted on the preceding day, dedicated to Crishna: prince and peasant all become pastoral attendants on the cow, as the form of Prithwi,[4] or the earth.

The 1st (*Súdi*), or 16th of Cartica, is the grand festival of ANACÚTA, sacred to the Hindu Ceres, which will be described with its solemnities at Nat'hdwara. There is a state procession, horse-races, and elephant-fights at the Chougan; the evening closes with a display of fireworks.

The 14th (*Súdi*), or 29th, is another solemn festival in honour of Vishnu. It is called the *Jul-jatra*, from being performed on the water (*jul*). The Rana, chiefs, ministers, and citizens go in procession to the lake, and adore the "spirit of the waters," on which floating lights are placed, and the whole surface is illuminated by a grand display of pyrotechny. On this day, "*Vishnu rises from his slumber of four months*";[5] a figurative expression to denote the sun's emerging from the cloudy months of the periodical flood.

The next day (the *poonum*, or last day of Cartica), being the *macara sancranti*, or autumnal equinox, when the sun enters the zodiacal sign *Macara*, or Pisces, the Rana and chiefs proceed in state to the Chougan, and play at ball on horseback. The entire last half of the month Cartica, from Amavus (the *ides*) to the Poonum, is sacred to Vishnu; who is declared by the *Puranas* to represent the sun, and whose worship, that of

[1] The Hindu god of riches.
[2] Yamala is the great god of the Finlanders.—(*Clarke.*)
[3] From *gao*, 'a cow.'
[4] See anecdote in chap. xxi., which elucidates this practice of princes becoming herdsmen.
[5] Matsyu Purana.

water, and the floating-lights placed thereon—all objects emblematic of fecundity—carry us back to the point whence we started—the adoration of the powers of nature: clearly proving all mythology to be universally founded on an astronomical basis.

In the remaining months of *Aghun*, or *Magsir*, and *Posh*, there are no festivals in which a state procession takes place, though in each there are marked days, kept not only by the Rajpoots, but generally by the Hindu nation; especially that on the 7th of Aghun, which is called *Mitra Septimi*, or seventh of *Mithras*, and like the *Bháscara Septimi* or the 7th of Magha, is sacred to the sun as a form of Vishnu. On this seventh day occurred the descent of the river-goddess (*Ganga*) from the foot of Vishnu; or the genius of fertilisation, typified under the form of the river goddess, proceeding from the sun, the vivifying principle, and impended over the head of Iswara, the divinity presiding over generation, in imitation of which his votary pours libations of water (if possible from the sacred river *Ganga*) over his emblem, the lingam or phallus: a comparison which is made by the bard Chund in an invocation to this god, for the sake of contrasting his own inferiority "to the mighty bards of old."

"The head of Ees [1] is in the skies; on his crown falls the ever-flowing stream (*Ganga*); but on his statue below, does not his votary pour the fluid from his *patera*?"

No satisfactory etymology has ever been assigned for the *phallic* emblem of generation, adored by Egyptian, Greek, Roman, and even by the *Christian*, which may be from the same primeval language that formed the Sanscrit.

Phalísa is the 'fructifier,' from *phala*, 'fruit,' and *Isa*, 'the god.' Thus the type of Osiris can have a definite interpretation, still wanting to the *lingam* of Iswara. Both deities presided over the streams which fertilised the countries in which they received divine honours: Osiris over the *Nile*, from 'the mountains of the moon,' in Æthiopia,[2] Iswara over the Indus,[3] (also called the Nil), and the Ganges from *Chandragiri*, 'the mountains of the moon,' on a peak of whose glaciers he has his throne.

Síva occasionally assumes the attributes of the sun-god; they especially appertain to Vishnu, who alone is styled "*immortal*, the *one*, *creator*, and *uncreated*"; and in whom centre all the qualities (*goonân*), which have peopled the Hindu pantheon with their ideal representatives. The bard Chund, who has embodied the theological tenets of the Rajpoots in his prefatory invocation to every divinity who can aid his intent, apostrophises Ganésa, and summons the goddess of eloquence (Sarasvati) "to make his tongue her abode"; deprecates the destroying power, "him whom wrath inhabits," lest he should be cut off ere his book was finished; and lauding distinctly each member of the triad (*tri-múrti*), he finishes by declaring them *one*, and that "*whoever believes them separate, hell will be his portion.*" Of this *One* the sun is the great visible type, adored under a variety of names, as *Surya*, *Mitra*, *Bháscar*, *Viava*, *Vishnu*, *Carña*, or *Kana*, likewise an Egyptian epithet for the sun.[4]

[1] Iswara, Isa, or as pronounced, *Ees*.
[2] "The land of the sun" (*aët*).
[3] Ferishta calls the Indus the *Nil-ab*, or 'blue waters'; it is also called *Abá-sin*, the 'father of streams.'
[4] According to Diodorus Siculus.

The emblem of Vishnu is *Garúda*, or the eagle,[1] and the Sun-god both of the Egyptians and Hindus is typified with the bird's head. *Arûná* (the dawn), brother of Garúda, is classically styled the charioteer of Vishnu, whose two sons, *Sumpati* and *Jutayoo*, attempting in imitation of their father to reach the sun, the wings of the former were burnt and he fell to the earth: of this the Greeks may have made their fable of Icarus.[2]

In the chief zodiacal phenomena, observation will discover that Vishnu is still the object of worship. The *Phúla-dola*,[3] or Floralia, in the vernal equinox, is so called from the image of Vishnu being carried in a *dola*, or ark, covered with garlands of flowers (*phúla*). Again, in the month of Asár, the commencement of the periodical rains, which date from the summer solstice, the image of Vishnu is carried on a car, and brought forth on the first appearance of the moon, the 11th of which being the solstice, is called "*the night of the gods.*" Then Vishnu reposes on his serpent-couch until the cessation of the flood on the 11th of Bhadoon, when "he turns on his side."[4]

The 4th is also dedicated to Vishnu under his infantine appellation *Heri* (Ηλιος), because when a child "*he hid himself in the moon.*" We must not derogate from Sir W. Jones the merit of drawing attention to the analogy between these Hindu festivals on the equinoxes, and the Egyptian, called the *entrance of Osiris into the moon*, and *his confinement in an ark*. But that distinguished writer merely gives the hint, which the learned Bryant aids us to pursue, by bringing modern travellers to corroborate the ancient authorities: the drawings of Pocock from the *sun* temple of Luxor to illustrate Plutarch, Curtius, and Diodorus. Bryant comes to the same conclusion with regard to Osiris enclosed in the ark, which we adopt regarding *Vishnu's* repose during the four months of inundation, the period of fertilisation. I have already, in the rites of *Anapûrna*, the Isis of the Egyptians, noticed the *crescent* form of the ark of Osiris, as well as the *ram's-head* ornaments indicative of the vernal equinox, which the Egyptians called *Phaménoth*, being the birthday of Osiris, or the sun; the *Phág*, or *Phalgoon* month of the Hindus; the *Phagesia* of the Greeks, sacred to Dionysius.

The expedition of Argonauts in search of the golden fleece is a version of the arkite worship of Osiris, the *Dolayatra* of the Hindus: and Sanscrit etymology, applied to the vessel of the Argonauts, will give the sun (*argha*) god's (*nat'ha*) entrance into the sign of the *Ram*.

The Tauric and Hydra foes, with which Jason had to contend before he obtained the fleece of *Aries*, are the symbols of the sun-god, both of the Ganges, and the Nile; and this fable, which has occupied almost every pen of antiquity, is clearly astronomical, as the names alone of the *Argha-Nat'h*, sons of *Apollo*, *Mars*, *Mercury*, *Sol*, *Arcus or Argus*,[5] *Jupiter*, *Bacchus*, etc., sufficiently testify, whose voyage is entirely celestial.

[1] The vulture and crane, which soar high in the heavens, are also called *garúda*, and vulgarly *geed*. The ibis is of the crane or heron kind.

[2] Phaëton was the son of Cephalus and Aurora. The former answers to the Hindu bird-headed messenger of the sun. *Arûná* is the Aurora of the Greeks, who with more taste have given the *dawn* a female character.

[3] Also called *Dola-yatra*.

[4] *Bhagvat* and *Matsya Puranas*. See Sir W. Jones on the lunar year of the Hindus, *Asiatic Researches*, vol. iii. p. 286.

[5] *Argha*, 'the sun,' in Sanscrit.

If it be destined that any portion of the veil which covers these ancient mysteries, connecting those of the Ganges with the Nile, shall be removed, it will be from the interpretation of the expedition of Rama, hitherto deemed almost as allegorical as that of the *Arghanat'hs*. I shall at once assume an opinion I have long entertained, that the western coast of the Red Sea was the *Lanka* of the memorable exploit in the history of the Hindus. If Alexander from the mouths of the Indus ventured to navigate those seas with his frail fleet of barks constructed in the Punjâb, what might we not expect from the resources of the King of Cushala, the descendant of Sagara, emphatically called the *sea-king*, whose " 60,000 *sons* " were so many mariners, and who has left his name as a memorial of his marine power at the island (*Sagur*) at the embouchure of the main arm of *the* Ganges, and to the ocean itself, also called *Sagara*. If the embarkation of Ramésa and his heroes for the redemption of Síta had been from the Gulph of Cutch, the grand emporium from the earliest ages, the voyage of Rama would have been but the prototype of that of the Macedonians ; but local tradition has sanctified *Ramiswara*, the southern part of the peninsula, as the rendezvous of his armament. The currents in the Straits of Manar, curiosity, or a wish to obtain auxiliaries from this insular kingdom, may have prompted the visit to Ceylon ; and hence the vestiges there found of this event. But even from this " *utmost isle, Taprobane*," the voyage across the Erythrean Sea is only twenty-five degrees of longitude, which with a flowing sail they would run down in ten or twelve days. The only difficulty which occurs is in the synchronical existence of Rama and the Pharaoh [1] of Moses, which would tend to the opposite of my hypothesis, and show that India received her Phallic rites, her architecture, and symbolic mythology from the Nile, instead of planting them there.

" Est-ce, l'Inde, la Phénicie, l'Ethiopie, la Chaldée, ou l'Egypte, qui a vu naitre ce culte ? ou bien le type en a-t-il été fourni aux habitans de ces contrées, *par une nation plus ancienne encore* ? " asks an ingenious but anonymous French author, on the origin of the Phallic worship.[2] *Ramésa*, chief of the *Suryas*, or sun-born race, was king of the city designated from his mother, *Cusháli*, of which *Ayodhia* was the capital. His sons were Lava and Cush, who originated the races we may term the *Lavites* and *Cushites*, or *Cushwas* of India.[3] Was then *Cusháli* the mother of Ramésa, a native of Æthiopia,[4] or *Cusha-dwipa*, 'the land of Cush ?' Rama and Crishna are both painted blue (*nila*), holding the lotus, emblematic of the Nile. Their names are often identified. Ram-Crishna, the bird-headed divinity, is painted as the messenger of each, and the historians of both were contemporaries. That both were real princes there is no doubt, though Crishna assumed to be an incarnation of Vishnu, as Rama was of the sun. Of Rama's family was *Trisankha*, mother of the great apostle of Budha, whose symbol was the serpent ; and the followers of Budha assert that Crishna and this apostle, whose statues are *facsimiles* of those of Memnon, were cousins. Were the *Hermetic* creed and Phallic

[1] *Pha-ra* is but a title, ' the king.'

[2] " Des Divinités génératives ; ou du culte du Phallus chez les anciens et les modernes."—*Paris*.

[3] Of the former race the ranas of Méwar, of the latter the princes of Nirwar and Ambér, are the representatives.

[4] Æthiopia, ' the country of the sun ' ; from *Aët*, contraction of *Aditya*. Ægypt may have the same etymology, *Aëtia*.

rites therefore received from the Ethiopic Cush? Could emblematic relics be discovered in the caves of the Troglodytes, who inhabited the range of mountains on the Cushite shore of the Arabian straits, akin to those of Ellora and Elephanta,[1] whose style discloses physical, mythological, as well as architectural affinity to the Egyptian, the question would at once be set at rest.

I have derived the Phallus from *Phalisa*, the *chief fruit*. The Greeks, who either borrowed it from the Egyptians or had it from the same source, typified the *Fructifier* by a *pineapple*, the form of which resembles the *Sitaphala*,[2] or fruit of Síta, whose rape by Ravana carried Rama from the Ganges over many countries ere he recovered her.[3] In like manner *Gouri*, the Rajpoot Ceres, is typified under the coco-nut, or sriphala,[4] the *chief of fruit*, or *fruit* sacred to *Sri*, or *Isa* (Isis), whose other elegant emblem of abundance, the *camacumpa*, is drawn with branches of the *palmyra*,[5] or coco-tree, gracefully pendent from the vase (*cumbha*).

The *Sriphala*[6] is accordingly presented to all the votaries of Iswara and Isa on the conclusion of the spring-festival of *Phúlguna*, the *Phagesia* of the Greeks, the *Phamenoth* of the Egyptian, and the Saturnalia of antiquity; a rejoicing at the renovation of the powers of nature; the empire of heat over cold—of light over darkness.[7]

The analogy between the goddess of the spring Saturnalia, *Phalgúní*, and the Phagesia of the Greeks, will excite surprise; the word is not derived from (φαγειν) *eating*, with the Rajpoot votaries of *Holica*, as with those of the *Dionysia* of the Greeks; but from *phalgúní*, compounded of *gúna*, 'quality, virtue, or characteristic,' and *phala* 'fruit'; in short, the *fructifier*. From

[1] It is absurd to talk of these being modern; decipher the characters thereon, and then pronounce their antiquity.

[2] Vulg. *Sureefa*.

[3] Rama subjected her to the fiery ordeal, to discover whether her virtue had suffered while thus forcibly separated.

[4] Vulg. *Naryal*.

[5] *Palmyra* is Sanscrit corrupted, and affords the etymology of Solomon's city of the desert, *Tadmor*. The ث p, by the retrenchment of a single diacritical point, becomes ت t; and the ل (*l*) and د (*d*) being permutable, *Pal* becomes *Tad*, or *Tal*—the *Palmyra*, which is the *Mor*, or chief of trees; hence *Tadmor*, from its date-trees.

[6] The *Jayaphala*, 'the fruit of victory,' is the nutmeg; or, as a native of Java, *Javuphala*, 'fruit of Java,' is most probably derived from *Jayadíva*, 'the victorious isle.'

[7] The Camari of the *Saura* tribes, or sun-worshippers of Saurashtra, claims descent from the *bird-god* of Vishnu (who aided Rana[1] to the discovery of Sita), and the *Macara*[2] or crocodile, and date the monstrous conception from that event, and their original abode from *Sancodra* Bate, or island of Sancodra. Whether to the *Dioscorides* at the entrance of the Arabian Gulf this name was given, evidently corrupted from *Sanc'ha-dwara* to Socotra, we shall not stop to inquire. Like the isle in the entrance of the gulf of Cutch, it is the *dwara* or portal to the *Sinus Arabicus*, and the pearl-shell (*sanc'ha*) there abounds. This tribe deduce their origin from Rama's expedition, and allege that their Icthyiopic mother landed them where they still reside. Wild as is this fable, it adds support to this hypothesis.

[1] Rama and Vishnu interchange characters.

[2] It is curious that the designation of the tribe *Camar* is a transposition of *Macar*, for the final letter of each is mute.

φαλλος,[1] to which there is no definite meaning, the Egyptian had the festival *Phallica*, the *Holica* of the Hindus. *Phûla* [1] and *phala*, flower and fruit, are the roots of all, Floralia and Phalária, the Phallus of Osiris, the Thyrsus of Bacchus, or Lingam of Iswara, symbolised by the *Sriphala*, or *Ananas*, the 'food of the gods,' [2] or the *Síta-phala* of the Helen of Ayodhia.

From the existence of this worship in Congo at this day, the author already quoted asks if it may not have originated in ETHIOPIA: "qui comme le témoignent plusieurs écrivains de l'antiquité, a fourni ses dieux à l'Egypte." On the first of the five complementary days called "*epagomenes*," preceding New-Year's Day, the Egyptians celebrated *the birth of the sun-god Osiris*, in a similar manner as the Hindus do their solstitial festival, "*the morning of the gods*," the Hiul of Scandinavia; on which occasion, "on prominait en procession une figure d'Osiris, dont le Phallus était triple;" a number, he adds, expressing "la pluralité indéfinée." The number *three* is sacred to Iswara, chief of the *Tri-múrti* or Triad, whose statue adorns the junction (*sangum*) of all triple streams; hence called *Trivêni*, who is *Trinêtra*, or 'three-eyed,' and *Tridenta*, or 'god of the trident'; *Trilóca*, 'god of the *triple abode*, heaven, earth, and hell'; *Tripúra*, of the triple city, to whom the *Tripoli* or triple gates are sacred, and of which he has made *Ganés* the Janitor, or guardian. The grotesque figure placed by the Hindus during the Saturnalia in the highways, and called *Nat'ha-Rama* (the god Rama), is the counterpart of the figure described by Plutarch as representing Osiris, "*ce soleil printanier*," in the Egyptian Saturnalia or *Phamenoth*. Even Ram-isa and Ravana may, like Osiris and Typhon, be merely the ideal representatives of light and darkness; and the chaste *Síta*, spouse of the *Surya* prince, the astronomical Virgo, only a zodiacal sign.

That a system of Hinduism pervaded the whole Babylonian and Assyrian empires, Scripture furnishes abundant proofs, in the mention of the various types of the sun-god *Bálnát'h*, whose pillar adorned "every mount" and "every grove"; and to whose other representative, the brazen calf (*nanda*), the 15th of each month (*amavus*) [3] was especially sacred. It was not confined to these celebrated regions of the East, but was disseminated throughout the earth; because from the Aral to the Baltic, colonies were planted from that central region,[4] the cradle of the Suryas and the Indus, whose branches (*sachæ*) [5] the Yavan, the Aswa, and the Méda, were the progenitors of the Ionians, the Assyrians, and the

[1] See Lempriere, arts. *Phagesia* and *Phallica*. "L'Abbé Mignot pense que le *Phallus* est originaire de l'Assyrie et de la Chaldeé, et que c'est de ce pays que l'usage de consacrer ce symbole de la génération a passé en Egypte. Il croit d'après le savant Le Clerc, que le nom de ce symbole est Phénicien: qu'il dérive de *Phalou*, qui, dans cette langue, signifie une *chose secrète* et *cachée*, et du verbe *phala*, qui veut dire *être tenu secret*." [1]

[2] *Ana*, 'food,' and *asa* or *ísa*, 'the god.'

[3] The Hindus divide the month into two portions called *pukhs* or fortnights. The first is termed *badi*, reckoning from the 1st to the 15th, which day of partition is called *amavus*, answering to the *ides* of the Romans, and held by the Hindus as it was by the Jews in great sanctity. The last division is termed *Súdi*, and they recommence with the initial numeral, thence to the 30th or completion, called *poonum*; thus instead of the 16th, 17th, etc., of the month, they say *Súdi ékum* (1st), *Súdi doag* (3rd).

[4] Sogdiana and Transoxiana.

[5] Hence the word Sacæ.

---

[1] Des Divinités Génératives.

Medes;[1] while in latter times, from the same teeming region, the *Galati* and *Getæ*,[2] the Kelts and Goths, carried modifications of the system to the shores of Armorica and the Baltic, the cliffs of Caledonia, and the remote isles of the German Ocean. The monumental circles sacred to the sun-god Belenus at once existing in that central region,[3] in India,[4] and throughout Europe, is conclusive. The apotheosis of the patriarch Noah, whom the Hindu styles "*Manú-Vaivaswata*, '*the* man, son of the sun,' may have originated the *Dolayatra* of the Hindus, the ark of Osiris, the ship of Isis amongst the Suevi, in memory of "*the forty days*" noticed in the traditions of every nation of the earth.

The time may be approaching when this worship in the East like the Egyptian, shall be only matter of tradition; although this is not likely to be effected by such summary means as were adopted by Cambyses, who slew the sacred Apis and whipped his priests, while their Greek and Roman conquerors adopted and embellished the Pantheon of the Nile.[5] But when Christianity reared her severe yet simple form, the divinities of the Nile, the Pantheon of Rome, and the Acropolis of Athens, could not abide her awful majesty. The temples of the Alexandrian Serapis were levelled by Theophilus,[6] while that of Osiris at Memphis became a church of Christ. "Muni de ses pouvoirs, et escorté d'une foule de moines, il mit en fuite les prêtres, brisa les idoles, démolit les temples, ou y établit des monastères.[7]" The period for thus subverting idolatry is passed: the religion of Christ is not of the sword, but one enjoining peace and good-will on earth. But as from him "to whom much is given," much will be required, the good and benevolent of the Hindu nations may have ulterior advantages over those Pharisees who would make a monopoly even of the virtues; who "see the mote in their neighbour's eye, but cannot discern the beam in their own." While, therefore, we strive to impart a purer taste and better faith, let us not imagine that the minds of those we would reform are the seats of impurity, because, in accordance with an idolatry coeval with the flood, they continue to worship mysteries opposed to our own modes of thinking.

[1] See Genealogical Table No. 2, for these names. The sons of the three *Midas*, pronounced *Mede*, founded kingdoms at the precise point of time, according to calculation from the number of kings, that Assyria was founded.

[2] The former were more *pastoral*, and hence the origin of their name, corrupted to Keltoi. The Gete or Jits pursued the hunter's occupation, living more by the chase, though these occupations are generally conjoined in the early stages of civilisation.

[3] Rubruquais and other travellers.

[4] Colonel Mackenzie's invaluable and gigantic collection.

[5] Isis and Osiris, Serapis and Canopus, Apis and Ibis, adopted by the Romans, whose temples and images, yet preserved, will allow full scope to the Hindu antiquary for analysis of both systems. The temple of Serapis at Pozzouli is quite Hindu in its ground plan.

[6] In the reign of Theodosius.

[7] *Du Culte*, etc. etc., p. 47.

CHAPTER XXIII

The nicer shades of character difficult to catch—Morals more obvious and less changeable than manners—Dissimilarity of manners in the various races of Rajast'han—Rajpoots have deteriorated in manners, as they declined in power—Regard and deference paid to Women in Rajast'han—Seclusion of the Females, no mark of their degradation—High spirit of the Rajpoot princesses—Their unbounded devotion to their husbands—Examples from the chronicles and bardic histories—Anecdotes in more recent times—Their magnanimity—Delicacy—Courage and presence of mind—Anecdote of Sadoo of Poogul and Korumdévi, daughter of the Mohil chief—The seclusion of the Females increases their influence—Historical evidences of its extent.

THE manners of a nation constitute the most interesting portion of its history, but a thorough knowledge of them must be the fruit of long and attentive observation: an axiom which applies to a people even less inaccessible than the Rajpoots. The importance and necessity of such an illustration of the Rajpoot character, in a work like the present, calls for and sanctions the attempt, however inadequate the means. Of what value to mankind would be the interminable narrative of battles, were their moral causes and results passed by unheeded? Although both the Persian and Hindu annalists not unfrequently unite the characters of moralist and historian, it is in a manner unsuitable to the subject, according to the more refined taste of Europe. In the poetic annals of the Rajpoot, we see him check his war-chariot, and when he should be levelling his javelin, commence a discourse upon ethics; or when the battle is over, the Nestor or Ulysses of the host converts his tent into a lyceum, and delivers lectures on morals or manners. But the reflections which should follow, and form the corollary to each action, are never given; and even if they were, though we might comprehend the moral movements of a nation, we should still be unable to catch the minute shades of character that complete the picture of domestic life, and which are to be collected from those familiar sentiments uttered in social intercourse, when the mind unbends and nature throws aside the trammels of education and of ceremony. Such a picture would represent the *manners*, which are continually undergoing modifications, in contradistinction to the *morals* of society; the latter, having a fixed creed for their basis, are definite and unchangeable. The *chál* of the Rajpoot, like the *mores* of the Romans, or *costumi* of modern Italy, is significant alike of mental and external habit. In the moral point of view, it is the path chalked out for him by the sages of antiquity; in the personal, it is that which custom has rendered immutable. *Kea boora chál chalta*, 'in what a bad path does he march!' says the moralist: *Báp, Dádá ca chál choora*, 'he abandons the usages of his ancestors,' says the stickler for custom, in Rajast'han.

The grand features of morality are few, and nearly the same in every nation not positively barbarous. The principles contained in the Decalogue form the basis of every code—of Menu and of Mahomed, as well as of Moses. These are grand landmarks of the truth of divine history; and are confirmed by the less important traits of personal customs and religious rites, which nations the most remote from each other continue to hold in common. The *Koran* we know to have been founded on the Mosaic law;

the *Sastra* of Menu, unconsciously, approaches still more to the Jewish Scriptures in spirit and intention ; and from its pages might be formed a manual of moral instruction, which, if followed by the disciples of the framer, might put more favoured societies to the blush.

As it has been observed in a former part of this work, the same religion governing all must tend to produce a certain degree of mental uniformity. The shades of *moral* distinction which separate these races are almost imperceptible : while you cannot pass any grand natural barrier without having the dissimilarity of customs and manners forced upon your observation. Whoever passes from upland Méwar, the country of the Seesodias, into the sandy flats of Marwar, the abode of the Rahtores, would feel the force of this remark. Innovations proceeding from external causes, such as conquest by irreligious foes, and the birth of new sects and schisms, operate important changes in manners and customs. We can only pretend, however, to describe facts which are obvious, and those which history discloses, whence some notions may be formed of the prevailing traits of character in the Rajpoot ; his ideas of virtue and vice, the social intercourse and familiar courtesies of Rajast'han, and their recreations, public and private.

"The manners of a people," says the celebrated Goguet, "always bear a proportion to the progress they have made in the arts and sciences." If by this test we trace the analogy between past and existing manners amongst the Rajpoots, we must conclude at once that they have undergone a decided deterioration. Where can we look for sages like those whose systems of philosophy were the prototypes of those of Greece : to whose works Plato, Thales, and Pythagoras were disciples ? Where shall we find the astronomers, whose knowledge of the planetary system yet excites wonder in Europe, as well as the architects and sculptors, whose works claim our admiration, and the musicians, "who could make the mind oscillate from joy to sorrow, from tears to smiles, with the change of modes and varied intonation." [1] The manners of those days must have corresponded with this advanced stage of refinement, as they must have suffered from its decline : yet the homage paid by Asiatics to precedent, has preserved many relics of ancient customs, which have survived the causes that produced them.

It is universally admitted that there is no better criterion of the refinement of a nation than the condition of the fair sex therein. As it is elegantly expressed by Comte Ségur, "Leur sort est un boussole sûr pour le premier regard d'un étranger qui arrive dans un pays inconnu." [2] Unfortunately, the habitual seclusion of the higher classes of females in the East contracts the sphere of observation in regard to their influence on society ; but, to borrow again from our ingenious author, "les hommes font les lois, les femmes font les mœurs" ; and their incarceration in Rajast'han by no means lessens the application of the adage to that country. Like the magnetic power, however latent, their attraction is not the less certain. "C'est aux hommes à faire des grandes choses, c'est aux femmes à les inspirer," is a maxim to which every Rajpoot cavalier would subscribe, with whom the age of chivalry is not fled, though ages of oppression have passed over him. He knows there is no retreat into which the report of a

[1] So says Valmika, the author of the oldest epic in existence, the *Ramayuna*.

[2] *Les Femmes, leur Condition et leur Influence dans l'Ordre Social*, vol. i. p. 10.

gallant action will not penetrate, and set fair hearts in motion to be the object of his search. The bards, those chroniclers of fame, like the *jongleurs* of old, have everywhere access, to the palace as to the hamlet; and a brilliant exploit travels with all the rapidity of a comet, and clothed with the splendid decorations of poetry, from the Indian desert to the valley of the Jumna. If we cannot paint the Rajpoot dame as invested with all the privileges which Ségur assigns to the first woman, "compagne de l'homme et son égale, vivant par lui, pour lui, associée, à son bonheur, à ses plaisirs, à la puissance qu'il exerçait sur ce vaste univers"; she is far removed from the condition which demands commiseration.

Like the ancient German or Scandinavian, the Rajpoot consults her in every transaction; from her ordinary actions he draws the omen of success, and he appends to her name the epithet of *dévi*, or 'godlike.' The superficial observer, who applies his own standard to the customs of all nations, laments with an affected philanthropy, the degraded condition of the Hindu female, in which sentiment he would find her little disposed to join. He particularly laments her want of liberty, and calls her seclusion imprisonment. Although I cordially unite with Ségur, who is at issue with his compatriot Montesquieu on this part of discipline, yet from the knowledge I do possess of the freedom, the respect, the happiness, which Rajpoot women enjoy, I am by no means inclined to deplore their state as one of captivity. The author of the *Spirit of Laws*, with the views of a closet philosopher, deems seclusion necessary from the irresistible influence of climate on the passions; while the chivalrous Ségur, with more knowledge of human nature, draws the very opposite conclusion, asserting all restraints to be injurious to morals. Of one thing we are certain, seclusion of females could only originate in a moderately advanced stage of civilisation. Amongst hunters, pastors, and cultivators, the women were required to aid in all external pursuits, as well as internal economy. The Jews secluded not their women, and the well, where they assembled to draw water, was the place where marriages were contracted, as with the lower classes in Rajpootana. The inundations of the Nile, each house of whose fertile valleys was isolated, is said to have created habits of secluding women with the Egyptians; and this argument might apply to the vast valleys of the Indus and Ganges first inhabited, and which might have diffused example with the spread of population. Assuredly, if India was colonised from the cradle of nations, Central Asia, they did not thence bring these notions within the Indus; for the Scythian women went to the opposite extreme, and were polyandrists.[1] The desire of eradicating those impure habits, described by Herodotus, that the slipper at the tent-door should no longer be a sign, may have originated the opposite extreme in a life of entire seclusion. Both polygamy and polyandrism originated in a mistaken view of the animal economy, and of the first great command to people the earth: the one was general amongst all the nations of antiquity; the other rare, though to be found in Scythia, India, and even amongst the Natches, in the new world; but never with the Rajpoot, with whom monogamy existed during the patriarchal ages of India, as amongst the Egyptians. Of all the nations of the world who have habitu-

[1] So are some of the Hindu races in the mountainous districts about the Himalaya, and in other parts of India. This curious trait in ancient manners is deserving of investigation: it might throw some light on the early history of the world.

ated the female to a restricted intercourse with society, whether Grecian, Roman, Egyptian, or Chinese, the Rajpoot has given least cause to provoke the sentiment of pity ; for if deference and respect be proofs of civilisation, Rajpootana must be considered as redundant in evidence of it. The uxoriousness of the Rajpoot might be appealed to as indicative of the decay of national morals ; " chez les barbares (says Ségur) les femmes ne sont rien : les mœurs de ces peuples s'adoucissent-t'elles, on compte les femmes pour quelque-chose : enfin, se corrompent-elles, les femmes sont tout" ; and whether from this decay, or the more probable and amiable cause of seeking, in their society, consolation for the loss of power and independence, the women are nearly everything with the Rajpoot.

It is scarcely fair to quote Menu as an authority for the proper treatment of the fair sex, since many of his dicta by no means tend to elevate their condition. In his lengthened catalogue of things pure and impure he says, however, "The mouth of a woman is constantly pure,"[1] and he ranks it with the running waters, and the sun-beam ; he suggests that their names should be "agreeable, soft, clear, captivating the fancy, auspicious, ending in long vowels, resembling words of benediction."[2]

"Where females are honoured" (says Menu), "there the deities are pleased ; but where dishonoured, *there all religious rites become useless*": and he declares, "that in whatever house a woman not duly honoured pronounces an imprecation, that house, with all that belongs to it, shall utterly perish."[3] "Strike not, even with a blossom, a wife guilty of a hundred faults,"[4] says another sage : a sentiment so delicate, that Reginald de Born, the prince of troubadours, never uttered any more refined.

However exalted the respect of the Rajpoot for the fair, he nevertheless holds that

"—— Nothing lovelier can be found
In woman, than to study household good."

In the most tempestuous period of the history of Méwar, when the Ranas

[1] Chap. v. 130. [2] Chap. ii. 33.

[3] *Digest of Hindu Law*, Colebrooke, vol. ii. p. 209.

[4] Of all the religions which have diversified mankind, whatever man might select, woman should chose the Christian. This alone gives her just rank in the scale of creation, whether arising from the demotic principle which pervades our faith, or the dignity conferred on the sex in being chosen to be the mother of the Saviour of man. In turning over the pages of Menu, we find many mortifying texts, which I am inclined to regard as interpolations ; as the following, so opposed to the beautiful sentiment above quoted :—" A wife, a son, a servant, a pupil, and a *younger brother*, may be corrected when they commit faults with a rope, or the small thong of a cane."[1] Such texts might lead us to adopt Ségur's conclusions, that ever since the days of the patriarchs women were only brilliant slaves—victims, who exhibited, in the wreaths and floral coronets which bedecked them, the sacrifices to which they were destined. In the patriarchal ages their occupations were to season the viands, and bake the bread, and weave cloth for the tents : their recreations limited to respire the fresh evening air under the shade of a fig tree, and sing canticles to the Almighty. Such a fate, indeed, must appear to a Parisian dame, who passes her time between the *Feydeau* and *Tivoli*, and whose daily promenade is through the *Champs Elysées*, worse than death : yet there is no positive hardship in these employments, and it was but the fair division of labour in the primitive ages, and that which characterises the Rajpootni of the present day.

[1] *On Judicature*, p. 268.

broke asunder the bonds which united them to the other chiefs of Rajast'han, and bestowed their daughters on the foreign nobles incorporated with the higher class of their own kin, the chief of Sadri, so often mentioned, had obtained a princess to wife. There was a hazard to domestic happiness in such unequal alliance, which the lord of Sadri soon experienced. To the courteous request, "Ranawut-jí, fill me a cup of water," he received a contemptuous refusal, with the remark, that "The daughter of a hundred kings would not become cup-bearer to the chieftain of Sadri."—"Very well," replied the plain soldier, "you may return to your father's house, if you can be of no use in mine." A messenger was instantly sent to the court, and the message, with every aggravation, was made known; and she followed on the heels of her messenger. A summons soon arrived for the Sadri chief to attend his sovereign at the capital. He obeyed; and arrived in time to give his explanation just as the Rana was proceeding to hold a full court. As usual, the Sadri chief was placed on his sovereign's right hand, and when the court broke up, the heir-apparent of Méwar, at a preconcerted sign, stood at the edge of the carpet, performing the menial office of holding the slippers of the chief. Shocked at such a mark of extreme respect, he stammered forth some words of homage, his unworthiness, etc.; to which the Rana replied, "As my son-in-law, no distinction too great can be conferred: take home your wife, she will never again refuse you a cup of water." [1]

Could authority deemed divine ensure obedience to what is considered a virtue in all ages and countries, the conjugal duties of the Rajpoots are comprehended in the following simple text: "*Let mutual fidelity* continue to death; this, in few words, may be considered as the supreme law between husband and wife." [2]

That this law governed the Rajpoots in past ages, as well as the present, in as great a degree as in other stages of society and other countries, we cannot doubt. Nor will the annals of any nation afford more numerous or more sublime instances of female devotion, than those of the Rajpoots; and such would never have been recorded, were not the incentive likely to be revered and followed. How easy would it be to cite examples for every passion which can actuate the human mind! Do we desire to see a model of unbounded devotion, resignation, and love, let us take the picture of Síta, as painted by the Milton of their silver age, than which nothing more beautiful or sentimental may be culled even from *Paradise Lost*. Rama was about to abandon his faithful wife for the purpose of becoming a *Vena-*

[1] Menu lays down some plain and wholesome rules for the domestic conduct of the wife; above all, he recommends her to "preserve a cheerful temper," and "frugality in domestic expenses." Some of his texts savour, however, more of the anchorite than of a person conversant with mankind; and when he commands the husband to be reverenced as a god by the virtuous wife, even though enamoured of another woman, it may be justly doubted if ever he found obedience thereto; or the scarcely less difficult ordinance, "for a whole year let a husband bear with his wife who treats him with aversion," after which probation he is permitted to separate. It is very likely the Rajpoots are more in the habit of quoting the first of these texts than of hearing the last: for although they have a choice at home, they are not ashamed to be the avowed admirers of the Aspasias and Phrynes of the capital; from the same cause which attracted Socrates and made Pericles a slave. and which will continue until the united charms of the dance and the song are sanctioned to be practised by the *légitimes* within.

[2] Menu, chap. ix. p. 302, text 101, *Haughton's edition.*

prest'ha or hermit, when she thus pours out her ardent desire to partake of his solitude.

" A woman's bliss is found, not in the smile
Of father, mother, friend, nor in herself:
Her husband is her only portion here,
Her heaven hereafter. If thou indeed
Depart this day into the forest drear,
I will precede, and smooth the thorny way.

A gay recluse
On thee attending, happy shall I feel
Within the honey-scented grove to roam,
For thou e'en here canst nourish and protect;
And therefore other friend I cannot need.
To-day most surely with thee will I go,
And thus resolved, I must not be deny'd.
Roots and wild fruit shall be my constant food;
Nor will I near thee add unto thy cares,
Nor lag behind, nor forest-food refuse,
But fearless traverse every hill and dale.

Thus could I sweetly pass a thousand years;
But without thee e'en heaven would lose its charms.

Pleased to embrace thy feet, I will reside
In the rough forest as my father's house.
Void of all other wish, supremely thine,
Permit me this request—I will not grieve,
I will not burden thee—refuse me not.
But shouldst thou, Raghŭvŭ, this prayer deny
Know, I resolve on death."

—*Vide* Ward, *On the History, Literature, and Mythology of the Hindus*, vol. ii. p. 408.

The publication of Mr. Wilson's specimens of the Hindu drama has put the English public in possession of very striking features of ancient Hindu manners, amongst which conjugal fidelity and affection stand eminently conspicuous. The *Uttara Rama Cheritra*, the *Vikrama and Urvasi*, and the *Mudra Rákshasa*, contain many instances in point. In the latter piece occurs an example, in comparatively humble life, of the strong affection of a Hindu wife. Chandana Das, like Antonio in the *Merchant of Venice*, is doomed to die, to save his friend. His wife follows him to the scene of execution, with their only child, and the succeeding dialogue ensues:—

Chand. Withdraw, my love, and lead our boy along.
Wife. Forgive me, husband,—to another world
Thy steps are bound, and not to foreign realms,
Whence in due time thou homeward wilt return;
No common farewell our leave-taking now
Admits, nor must the partner of thy fate
Leave thee to trace thy solitary way.
Chand. What dost thou mean?
Wife. To follow thee in death.
Chand. Think not of this—our boy's yet tender years
Demand affectionate and guardian care.
Wife. I leave him to our household gods, nor fear
They will desert his youth:—come, my dear boy,
And bid thy sire a long and last farewell.

The annals of no nation on earth record a more ennobling or more magnanimous instance of female loyalty than that exemplified by Dewuldé, mother of the Binafur brothers, which will at once illustrate the manners of the Rajpoot fair, and their estimation and influence in society.

The last Hindu emperor of Dehli, the chivalrous Pirthiraj of the Chohan race, had abducted the daughter of the prince of Saméta. Some of the wounded who had covered his retreat were assailed and put to death by Purmal, the Chundail prince of Mahoba. In order to avenge this insult, the emperor had no sooner conveyed his bride to Dehli than he invaded the territory of the Chundail, whose troops were cut to pieces at Sirswah,[1] the advanced post of his kingdom. While pursuing his success, the Chundail called a council, and by the advice of his queen Malundevi demanded a truce of his adversary, on the plea of the absence of his chieftains Ala and Udila. The brother of the bard of Mahoba was the envoy, who found the Chohan ready to cross the Pahouj. He presented his gifts, and adjured him, "as a true Rajpoot, not to take them at such disadvantage." The gifts were accepted, and the Chohan pledged himself, "albeit his warriors were eager for the fight," to grant the truce demanded ; and having dismissed the herald, he inquired of his own bard, the prophetic Chund, the cause of the disaffection which led to the banishment of the Binafurs ; to which he thus replies : "Jessraj was the leader of the armies of Mahoba when his sovereign was defeated and put to flight by the wild race of Goands ; Jessraj repulsed the foe, captured Gurra their capital, and laid his head at his sovereign's feet. Purmal returning with victory to Mahoba, in gratitude for his service, embraced the sons of Jessraj, and placed them in his honours and lands, while Malundevi the queen made no distinction between them and her son." The fief of the young Binafur chieftains was at the celebrated fortress Kalinjer, where their sovereign happening to see a fine mare belonging to Ala, desired to possess her, and being refused, so far forgot past services as to compel them to abandon the country. On retiring they fired the estates of the Purihara chief who had instigated their disgrace. With their mother and families they repaired to Canouj, whose monarch received them with open arms, assigning lands for their maintenance. Having thus premised the cause of banishment, Chund conducts us to Canouj, at the moment when Jagnuk the bard was addressing the exiles on the dangers of Mahoba.

"The Chohan is encamped on the plains of Mahoba ; Nursing and Birsing have fallen, Sirswah is given to the flames, and the kindgom of Purmal laid waste by the Chohan. For one month a truce has been obtained : while to you I am sent for aid in his griefs. Listen, oh sons of Binafur ; sad have been the days of Malundevi since you left Mahoba ! Oft she looks towards Canouj ; and while she recalls you to mind, tears gush from her eyes and she exclaims, 'The fame of the Chundail is departing' ; but when gone, oh sons of Jessraj, great will be your self-accusing sorrow : yet, think of Mahoba."

"Destruction to Mahoba ! Annihilation to the Chundail who, without fault, expelled us our home : in whose service fell our father, by whom his kingdom was extended. Send the slanderous Purihara—let him lead your armies against the heroes of Dehli. Our heads were the pillars of Mahoba ; by us were the Goands expelled, and their strongholds Deogurh and Chandbari added to his sway. We maintained the field against the Jadoon,

[1] On the Pahouj, and now belonging to the Boondela prince of Duttea. The author has been over this field of battle.

sacked Hindown,[1] and planted his standard on the plains of Kuttair. It was I (continued Ala) who stopped the sword of the conquering Cutchwaha[2] —The amirs of the Sooltan fled before us.—At Gya we were victorious, and added Rewah[3] to his kingdom. Antérved[4] I gave to the flames, and levelled to the ground the towns of Méwat.[5] From ten princes did Jessraj bring spoil to Mahoba. This have we done ; and the reward is exile from our home ! Seven times have I received wounds in his service, and since my father's death gained forty battles ; and from seven has Udila conveyed the *record of victory*[6] to Purmal. Thrice my death seemed inevitable. The honour of his house I have upheld—yet exile is my reward ! "

The bard replies—" The father of Purmal left him when a child to the care of Jessraj. Your father was in lieu of his own ; the son should not abandon him when misfortune makes him call on you. The Rajpoot who abandons his sovereign in distress will be plunged into hell. Then place on your head the loyalty of your father. Can you desire to remain at Canouj while he is in trouble, who expended thousands in rejoicings for your birth ? Malundevi (the queen), who loves you as her own, presses your return. She bids me demand of Dewuldé fulfilment of the oft-repeated vow, that your life and Mahoba, when endangered, were inseparable. The breaker of vows, despised on earth, will be plunged into hell, there to remain while sun and moon endure."

Dewuldé heard the message of the queen. " Let us fly to Mahoba," she exclaimed. Ala was silent, while Udila said aloud, " May evil spirits seize upon Mahoba !—Can we forget the day when, in distress, he drove us forth ?—Return to Mahoba—let it stand or fall, it is the same to me ; Canouj is henceforth my home."

" Would that the gods had made me barren," said Dewuldé, " that I had never borne sons who thus abandon the paths of the Rajpoot, and refuse to succour their prince in danger ! " Her heart bursting with grief, and her eyes raised to heaven, she continued : " Was it for this, O universal lord, thou mad'st me feel a mother's pangs for these destroyers of Binafur's fame ? Unworthy offspring ! the heart of the true Rajpoot dances with joy at the mere name of strife—but ye, degenerate, cannot be the sons of Jessraj—some carl must have stolen to my embrace, and from such ye must be sprung." The young chiefs arose, their faces withered in sadness. " When we perish in defence of Mahoba, and covered with wounds, perform deeds that will leave a deathless name ; when our heads roll in the field—when we embrace the valiant in fight, and treading in the footsteps of the brave, make resplendent the blood of both lines, even in the presence of the heroes of the Chohan, then will our mother rejoice."

[1] Hindown was a town dependent on Biana, the capital of the Jadoons, whose descendants still occupy Kerowli and Sri Mat'hura.

[2] Rao Pùjaon of Ambér, one of the great vassals of the Chohan, and ancestor of the present Raja of Jeipoor.

[3] In the original, " the land of the Bhagél to that of the Chundail." Rewah is capital of Bhagélkhund, founded by the Bhagela Rajpoots, a branch of the Solanki kings of Anhulwarra.

[4] Antérved, the Do-áb, or Mesopitamia of the Jumna and Ganges.

[5] A district S.W. of Dehli, notorious for the lawless habits of its inhabitants : a very ancient Hindu race, but the greater part forced proselytes to the faith of Islam. In the time of Pirthiraj the chief of Mewat was one of his vassals.

[6] *Jeytpatra*, or ' bulletin of victory.'

The envoy having, by this loyal appeal of Dewuldé, attained the object of his mission, the brothers repair to the monarch of Canouj,[1] in order to ask permission to return to Mahoba ; this is granted, and they are dismissed with magnificent gifts, in which the bardic herald participated ;[2] and the parting valediction was "*preserve the faith of the Rajpoots.*" The omens during the march were of the worst kind : as Jugnuk expounded them, Ala with a smile replied, " O bard, though thou canst dive into the dark recesses of futurity, to the brave all omens are happy, even though our heroes shall fall, and the fame of the Chundail must depart ; thus in secret does my soul assure me." The sarus [3] was alone on the right—the eagle as he flew dropped his prey—the chukwa [4] separated from his mate—drops fell from the eyes of the warlike steed—the shíal [5] sent forth sounds of lamentation ; spots were seen on the disc of the sun." The countenance of Lakhun fell ; [6] these portents filled his soul with dismay : but Ala said, " though these omens bode death, yet death to the valiant, to the pure in faith, is an object of desire not of sorrow. The path of the Rajpoot is beset with difficulties, rugged, and filled with thorns ; but he regards it not, so it but conducts to battle."—" To carry joy to Purmala alone occupied their thoughts : the steeds bounded over the plain like the swift-footed deer." The brothers, ere they reached Mahoba, halted to put on the *saffron robe*, the sign of "*no quarter*" with the Rajpoot warrior. The intelligence of their approach filled the Chundaila prince with joy, who advanced to embrace his defenders, and conduct them to Mahoba ; while the queen Malundevi came to greet Dewuldé, who with the herald bard paid homage, and returned with the queen to the city. Rich gifts were presented, gems resplendent with light. The queen sent for Ala, and extending her hands over his head, bestowed the *asees* [7] (blessing), as kneeling he swore his head was with Mahoba, and then waved a vessel filled with pearls over his head, which were distributed to his followers.[8]

The bardic herald was rewarded with four villages. We are then introduced to the Chohan camp and council, where Chund the bard is expatiating on the return of the Binafurs with the succours of Canouj. He recommends his sovereign to send a herald to the Chundail to announce the expiration of the truce, and requiring him to meet him in the field, or abandon Mahoba. According to the bard's advice, a despatch was transmitted to Purmal, in which the cause of war was recapitulated—the

[1] Jeichund was then king of this city, only second to Dehli. He was attacked in 1193 (A.D.) by Shabudin, after his conquest of the Chohan, driven from his kingdom, and found a watery grave in the Ganges.

[2] Jugnuk had two villages conferred upon him, besides an elephant and a dress.

[3] The phenicopteros.

[4] A large red duck, the emblem of fidelity with the Rajpoots.

[5] The jackal.

[6] Commander of the succours of Canouj.

[7] *Asees* is a form of benediction only bestowed by females and priests : it is performed by clasping both hands over the person's head, and waving a piece of silver or other valuable over him, which is bestowed in charity.

[8] This is a very ancient ceremony, and is called *Nachravali*. The author has frequently had a large salver filled with silver coin waved over his head, which was handed for distribution amongst his attendants. It is most appropriate from the fair, from whom also he has had this performed by their proxies, the family priest or female attendants.

murder of the wounded ; and stating that, according to Rajpoot faith, he had granted seven days beyond the time demanded, " and although so many days had passed since succour had arrived from Canouj, the lion-horn had not yet sounded (*sing-nád*) " : adding, " if he abandon all desire of combat, let him proclaim his vassalage to Dehli, and abandon Mahoba."

Purmal received the hostile message in despair ; but calling his warriors around him, he replied to the herald of the chohan, that "on the day of the sun, the first of the month, he would join him in strife."

" On the day sacred to *Sucra* (Friday), Pirthiraj sounded the shell, while the drums thrice struck proclaimed the truce concluded.[1] The standard was brought forth, around which the warriors gathered ; the cup circulated, the prospect of battle filled their souls with joy. They anointed their bodies with fragrant oils, while the celestial apsaras with ambrosial oils and heavenly perfumes anointed their silver forms, tinged their eyelids, and prepared for the reception of heroes.[2] The sound of the war-shell reached Kylâs ; the abstraction of Iswara was at an end—joy seized his soul at the prospect of completing his chaplet of skulls (*roonda-mala*). The Yoginis danced with joy, their faces sparkled with delight, as they seized their vessels to drink the blood of the slain. The devourers of flesh, the *Palcharas*, sung songs of triumph at the game of battle between the Chohan and Chundail."

In another measure, the bard proceeds to contrast the occupations of his heroes and the celestials preparatory to the combat, which descriptions are termed *roopaca*. " The heroes gird on their armour, while the heavenly fair deck their persons. They place on their heads the helm crowned with the war-bell (*vîrá-gantha*), these adjust the corset ; they draw the girths of the war-steed, the fair of the world of bliss bind the anklet of bells ; nets of steel defend the turban's fold, they braid their hair with golden flowers and gems ; the warrior polishes his falchion—the fair tints the eyelid with *unjum* ; the hero points his dagger, the fair paints a heart on her forehead ; he braces on his ample buckler—she places the resplendent orb in her ear ; he binds his arms with a gauntlet of brass—she stains her hands with the *henna*. The hero decorates his hand with the tiger-claw [3]—the Apsara ornaments with rings and golden bracelets ; the warrior shakes the ponderous lance—the heavenly fair the garland of love [4] to decorate those who fall in the fight ; she binds on a necklace of pearls, he a *mala* of the túlasi.[5] The warrior strings his bow—the fair assume their killing glances. Once more the heroes look to their girths, while the celestial fair prepare their cars."

After the bard has finished his *roopaca*, he exclaims, " Thus says Chund, the lord of verse ; with my own eyes have I seen what I describe." It is important to remark, that the national faith of the Rajpoot never questions

[1] The lankh, or war-shell, is thrice sounded, and the nakarras strike thrice, when the army is to march ; but should it after such proclamation remain on its ground, a scape-goat is slain in front of the imperial tent.

[2] This picture recalls the remembrance of Hacon and the heroes of the north ; with the Valkyrias or choosers of the slain ; the celestial maids of war of Scandinavia.

[3] Bágh-nuk, or Nahar-nuk.

[4] Burmala.

[5] *Mala*, a necklace. The *túlasi* or *rudraca* had the same estimation amongst the Hindus that the mistletoe had amongst the ancient Britons, and was always worn in battle as a charm.

the prophetic power of their chief bard, whom they call *Tricála*, or cognoscent of the past, the present, and the future—a character which the bard has enjoyed in all ages and climes ; but Chund was the last whom they admitted to possess supernatural vision.

We must now return to Mahoba, where a grand council had assembled at a final deliberation ; at which, shaded by screens, the mother of the Binafurs, and the queen Malundevi, were present. The latter thus opens the debate : " O mother of Ala, how may we succeed against the lord of the world ? [1] If defeated, lost is Mahoba ; if we pay tribute, we are loaded with shame." Dewuldé recommends hearing *seriatim* the opinions of the chieftains, when Ala thus speaks : " Listen, O mother, to your son ; he alone is of pure lineage who, placing loyalty on his head, abandons all thoughts of self, and lays down his life for his prince ; my thoughts are only for Purmal. *If she lives* she will show herself a woman, or emanation of Parvati.[2] The warriors of Sambhur shall be cut in pieces. I will so illustrate the blood of my fathers, that my fame shall last for ever. My son Eendal, O prince ! I bequeath to you, and the fame of Dewuldé is in your keeping."

The queen thus replies : " The warriors of the Chohan are fierce as they are numerous ; pay tribute, and save Mahoba." The soul of Udila inflamed, and turning to the queen, " Why thought you not thus when you slew the defenceless ? but then I was unheard. Whence now your wisdom ? thrice I beseeched you to pardon. Nevertheless, Mahoba is safe while life remains in me, and in your cause, O Purmal ! we shall espouse celestial brides."

" Well have you spoken, my son," said Dewuldé, " nothing now remains but to make thy parent's milk resplendent by thy deeds. The call of the peasant driven from his home meets the ear, and while we deliberate, our villages are given to the flames." But Purmal replied : " Saturn [3] rules the day, to-morrow we shall meet the foe." With indignation Ala turned to the king : " He who can look tamely on while the smoke ascends from his ruined towns, his fields laid waste, can be no Rajpoot—he who succumbs to fear when his country is invaded, his body will be plunged into the hell of hells, his soul a wanderer in the world of spirits for sixty thousand years ; but the warrior who performs his duty will be received into the mansion of the sun, and his deeds will last for ever."

But cowardice and cruelty always accompany each other, nor could all the speeches of the brothers " screw his courage to the sticking place " Purmal went to his queen, and gave fresh vent to his lamentation. She upbraided his unmanly spirit, and bid him head his troops and go forth to the fight. The heroes embraced their wives for the last time, and with the dawn performed their pious rites. The Binafur offered oblations to the nine planets, and having adored the image of his tutelary god, he again put the chain round his neck ; [4] then calling his son Eendal, and Udila his brother, he once more poured forth his vows to the universal

[1] *Pirthiraj.*

[2] A Rajpoot never names his wife. Here it is evidently optional to the widow to live or die, though Ala shows his wish for her society above. See chapter on *Satis*, which will follow.

[3] Sanichur.

[4] It was a *juntur* or phylactery of Hanooman the monkey deity ; probably a magical stanza, with his image.

mother "that he would illustrate the name of Jessraj, and evince the pure blood derived from Dewuldé, whene'er he met the foe."—"Nobly have you resolved," said Udila, "and shall not my *kirban*[1] also dazzle the eyes of Sambhur's lord? shall he not retire from before me?"—"Farewell, my children," said Dewuldé, "*be true to your salt*, and should you lose your heads for your prince, doubt not you will obtain the celestial crown." Having ceased, the wives of both exclaimed, "What virtuous wife survives her lord? for thus says Gori-ji,[2] 'the woman, who survives her husband who falls in the field of battle, will never obtain bliss, but wander a discontented ghost in the region of unhallowed spirits.'"

This is sufficient to exhibit the supreme influence of women, not only on, but also in society.

The extract is taken from the Bardic historian, when Hindu customs were pure, and the Chohan was paramount sovereign of India. It is worth while to compare it with another written six centuries after the conquest by the Mahomedans; although six dynasties—namely, Ghizni, Gor, Khillij, Seyed, Lodi, and Mogul, numbering more than thirty kings, had intervened, yet the same uncontrollable spirit was in full force, unchangeable even in misfortune. Both Hindu and Persian historians expatiate with delight on the anecdote; but we prefer the narrative of the ingenuous Bernier, under whose eye the incident occurred.

In the civil war for empire amongst the sons of Shah Jehan, when Arungzéb opened his career by the deposal of his father and the murder of his brothers, the Rajpoots, faithful to the emperor, determined to oppose him. Under the intrepid Rahtore Jeswunt Sing, thirty thousand Rajpoots, chiefly of that clan, advanced to the Nerbudda, and with a magnanimity amounting to imprudence, they permitted the junction of Morad with Arungzéb, who, under cover of artillery served by Frenchmen, crossed the river almost unopposed. Next morning the action commenced, which continued throughout the day. The Rajpoots behaved with their usual bravery; but were surrounded on all sides, and by sunset left ten thousand dead on the field.[3] The Mahraja retreated to his own country, but his wife, a daughter of the Rana of Oodipoor, "disdained (says Ferishta) to receive her lord, and shut the gates of the castle."

Bernier, who was present, says, "I cannot forbear to relate the fierce reception which the daughter of the Rana gave to her husband Jeswunt Sing, after his defeat and flight. When she heard he was nigh, and had understood what had passed in the battle; that he had fought with all possible courage; that he had but four or five hundred men left; and at last, no longer able to resist the enemy, had been forced to retreat; instead of sending some one to condole him in his misfortunes, she commanded in a dry mood to shut the gates of the castle, and not to let this infamous man enter; that he was not her husband; that the son-in-law of the great Rana could not have so mean a soul; that he was to remember, that being grafted into so illustroius a house, he was to imitate its virtue;

[1] A crooked scimitar.

[2] One of the names of Méra or Parvati. This passage will illustrate the subject of *Satis* in a future chapter.

[3] "'Tis a pleasure (says Bernier) to see them with the fume of opium in their heads, embrace each other when the battle is to begin, and give their mutual farewells, as men resolved to die."

in a word, he was to vanquish, or to die. A moment after, she was of another humour; she commands a pile of wood to be laid, that she might burn herself; that they abused her; that her husband must needs be dead; that it could not be otherwise. And a little while after, she was seen to change countenance, to fall into a passion, and break into a thousand reproaches against him. In short, she remained thus transported eight or nine days, without being able to resolve to see her husband, till at last her mother coming, brought her in time to herself, composed by assuring her that as soon as the Raja had but refreshed himself he would raise another army to fight Arungzéb, and repair his honour. By which story one may see," says Bernier, " a pattern of the courage of the women in that country"; and he adds this philosophical corollary on this and the custom of suttees, which he had witnessed: "*There is nothing which opinion, prepossession, custom, hope, and the point of honour, may not make men do or suffer.*" [1]

The romantic history of the Chohan emperor of Dehli abounds in sketches of female character; and in the story of his carrying off Sunjogta, the princess of Canouj, we have not only the individual portrait of the Helen of her country, but in it a faithful picture of the sex. We see her, from the moment when, rejecting the assembled princes, she threw the "garland of marriage" round the neck of her hero, the Chohan abandon herself to all the influences of passion—mix in a combat of five days' continuance against her father's array, witness his overthrow, and the carnage of both armies, and subsequently, by her seductive charms, lulling her lover into a neglect of every princely duty. Yet when the foes of his glory and power invade India, we see the enchantress at once start from her trance of pleasure, and exchanging the softer for the sterner passions, in accents not less strong because mingled with deep affection, she conjures him, while arming him for the battle, to die for his fame, declaring that she will join him in "the mansions of the sun." Though it is difficult to extract, in passages sufficiently condensed, what may convey a just idea of this heroine, we shall attempt it in the bard's own language, rendered into prose. He announces the tidings of invasion by the medium of a dream, which the Chohan thus relates :—

" 'This night, while in the arms of sleep, a fair, beautiful as Rembha, rudely seized my arm; then she assailed you, and while you were struggling, a mighty elephant,[2] infuriated, and hideous as a demon, bore down upon me. Sleep fled—nor Rembha nor demon remained—but my heart was panting, and my quivering lips muttering *Hur! Hur!*[3] What is decreed the gods only know.'

" Sunjogta replied, 'Victory and fame to my lord! O, sun of the Chohans, in glory, or in pleasure, who has tasted so deeply as you? To die is the destiny not only of man but of the gods: all desire to throw off the old garment; but to die well is to live for ever. Think not of self, but of immortality; let your sword divide your foe, and I will be your *ardhanga*[4] hereafter.'

[1] Bernier's *History of the Late Revolution of the Empire of the Mogul*, fol. p. 13, ed. 1684.

[2] It is deemed unlucky to see this emblem of Ganésa in sleep.

[3] The battle-shout of the Rajpoot.

[4] 'Half-body,' which we may render, in common phraseology, "*other half.*"

The king sought the bard, who expounded the dream, and the Gúrú wrote an incantation, which he placed in his turban. A thousand brass vessels of fresh milk were poured in libations to the sun and moon. Ten buffaloes were sacrificed to the supporters of the globe, and gifts were made to all. But will offerings of blood or libations of milk arrest what is decreed? If by these man could undo what is ordained, would Nala or the Pandus have suffered as they did?"

While the warriors assemble in council to consult on the best mode of opposing the Sultan of Ghizni, the king leaves them to deliberate, in order to advise with Sunjogta. Her reply is curious:

"Who asks woman for advice? The world deems their understanding shallow; even when truths issue from their lips, none listen thereto. Yet what is the world without woman? We have the forms of Sacti with the fire of Síva; we are at once thieves and sanctuaries; we are vessels of virtue and of vice—of knowledge and of ignorance. The man of wisdom, the astrologer, can from *the books* calculate the motion and course of the planets; but in the book of woman he is ignorant: and this is not a saying of to-day, it ever has been so: our book has not been mastered, therefore, to hide their ignorance, they say, in woman there is no wisdom! Yet woman shares your joys and your sorrows. Even when you depart from the mansion of the sun, we part not. Hunger and thirst we cheerfully partake with you; we are as the lakes, of which you are the swans; what are you when absent from our bosoms?"

The army having assembled, and all being prepared to march against the Islamite, in the last great battle which subjugated India, the fair Sunjogta armed her lord for the encounter. "In vain she sought the rings of his corslet; her eyes were fixed on the face of the Chohan, as those of the famished wretch who finds a piece of gold. The sound of the drum reached the ear of the Chohan; it was as a death-knell on that of Sunjogta: and as he left her to head Dehli's heroes, she vowed that henceforward water only should sustain her. "I shall see him again in the region of Surya, but never more in Yoginipoor."[1] Her prediction was fulfilled: her lord was routed, made captive and slain; and, faithful to her vow, she mounted the funeral pyre.

Were we called upon to give a pendant for Lucretia, it would be found in the queen of Ganore. After having defended five fortresses against the foe, she retreated to her last stronghold on the Nerbudda, and had scarcely left the bark, when the assailants arrived in pursuit. The disheartened defenders were few in number, and the fortress was soon in possession of the foe, the founder of the family now ruling in Bhopal. The beauty of the queen of Ganore was an allurement only secondary to his desire for her country, and he invited her to reign over it and him. Denial would have been useless, and would have subjected her to instant coercion, for the Khan awaited her reply in the hall below; she therefore sent a message of assent, with a complimentary reflection on his gallant conduct and determination of pursuit; adding, that he merited her hand for his bravery, and might prepare for the nuptials, which should be celebrated on the terrace of the palace. She demanded two hours for unmolested preparation, that she might appear in appropriate attire, and with the distinction her own and his rank demanded.

[1] Dehli.

Ceremonials, on a scale of magnificence equal to the shortness of the time, were going on. The song of joy had already stifled the discordant voice of war, and at length the Khan was summoned to the terrace. Robed in the marriage garb presented to him by the queen, with a necklace and aigrette of superb jewels from the coffers of Ganore, he hastened to obey the mandate, and found that fame had not done justice to her charms. He was desired to be seated, and in conversation full of rapture on his side, hours were as minutes while he gazed on the beauty of the queen. But presently his countenance fell—he complained of heat; punkas and water were brought, but they availed him not, and he began to tear the bridal garments from his frame, when the queen thus addressed him: "Know, Khan, that your last hour is come; our wedding and our death shall be sealed together. The vestments which cover you are poisoned; you had left me no other expedient to escape pollution." While all were horror-struck by this declaration, she sprung from the battlements into the flood beneath. The Khan died in extreme torture, and was buried on the road to Bhopal; and, strange to say, a visit to his grave has the reputation of curing the tertian of that country.

We may give another anecdote illustrative of this extreme delicacy of sentiment, but without so tragical a conclusion. The celebrated Raja Jey Sing of Ambér had espoused a princess of Haravati, whose manners and garb, accordant with the simplicity of that provincial capital, subjected her to the *badinage* of the more refined court of Ambér, whose ladies had added the imperial costume to their own native dress. One day being alone with the prince, he began playfully to contrast the sweeping *jupe* of Kotah with the more scanty robe of the belles of his own capital; and taking up a pair of scissors, said he would reduce it to an equality with the latter. Offended at such levity, she seized his sword, and assuming a threatening attitude, said, "that in the house to which she had the honour to belong, they were not habituated to jests of this nature; that mutual respect was the guardian, not only of happiness but of virtue;" and she assured him, that if he ever again so insulted her, he would find that the daughter of Kotah could use a sword more effectively than the prince of Ambér the scissors; adding, that she would prevent any future scion of her house from being subjected to similar disrespect, by declaring such intermarriages '*tilac*,' or forbidden, which interdict I believe yet exists.[1]

I will append an anecdote related by the celebrated Zalim Sing, characteristic of the presence of mind, prowess, and physical strength of the Rajpoot women. To attend and aid in the minutiæ of husbandry is by no means uncommon with them, as to dress and carry the meals of their husbands to the fields is a general practice. In the jungle which skirts the knolls of Puchpahar, a huge bear assaulted a Rajpootní as she was carrying her husband's dinner. As he approached with an air of gallantry upon his hind-legs, doubting whether the food or herself were the intended prey, she retreated behind a large tree, round the trunk of which Bruin, still in his erect attitude, tried all his powers of circumvention to seize her. At length, half exhausted, she boldly grasped his paws, and with so vigorous

[1] The physician (unless he unite with his office that of ghostly comforter) has to feel the pulse of his patient with a curtain between them, through a rent, in which the arm is extended.

a hold that he roared with pain, while in vain, with his short neck, did he endeavour to reach the powerful hand which fixed him. While she was in this dilemma, a *purdêsi* (a foreign soldier of the state) happened to be passing to the garrison of Gagrown, and she called out to him in a voice of such unconcern to come and release her for a time, that he complied without hesitation. She had not retired, however, above a dozen yards ere he called loudly for her return, being scarcely able to hold his new friend; but laughingly recommending perseverance, she hastened on, and soon returned with her husband, who laid the monster prostrate with his matchlock, and rescued the purdési from his unpleasing predicament.

Such anecdotes might be multiplied *ad infinitum*; but I will conclude with one displaying the romantic chivalry of the Rajpoot, and the influence of the fair in the formation of character; it is taken from the annals of Jessulmér, the most remote of the states of Rajast'han, and situated in the heart of the desert, of which it is an oasis.

Raningdeo was lord of Poogul, a fief of Jessulmér; his heir, named Sadoo, was the terror of the desert, carrying his raids even to the valley of the Indus, and on the east to Nagore. Returning from a foray, with a train of captured camels and horses, he passed by Aureent, where dwelt Manik Rao, the chief of the Mohils, whose rule extended over 1440 villages. Being invited to partake of the hospitality of the Mohil, the heir of Poogul attracted the favourable regards of the old chieftain's daughter:

"She loved him for the dangers he had passed";

for he had the fame of being the first riever of the desert. Although betrothed to the heir of the Rahtore of Mundore, she signified her wish to renounce the throne to be the bride of the chieftain of Poogul; and in spite of the dangers he provoked, and contrary to the Mohil chief's advice, Sadoo, as a gallant Rajpoot, dared not reject the overture, and he promised "*to accept the coco*,"[1] if sent in form to Poogul. In due time it came, and the nuptials were solemnised at Aureent. The dower was splendid; gems of high price, vessels of gold and silver, a golden bull, and a train of thirteen *déwádháris*,[2] or damsels of wisdom and penetration.

Irrinkowal, the slighted heir of Mundore, determined on revenge, and with four thousand Rahtores planted himself in the path of Sadoo's return, aided by the Sankla Mehraj, whose son Sadoo had slain. Though entreated to add four thousand Mohils to his escort, Sadoo deemed his own gallant band of seven hundred Bhattis sufficient to convey his bride to his desert abode, and with difficulty accepted fifty, led by Megraj, the brother of the bride.

The rivals encountered at Chondun, where Sadoo had halted to repose; but the brave Rahtore scorned the advantage of numbers, and a series of single combats ensued, with all the forms of chivalry. The first who entered the lists was Jeytanga, of the Pahoo clan, and of the kin of Sadoo. The enemy came upon him by surprise while reposing on the ground, his saddle-cloth for his couch, and the bridle of his steed twisted round his arm; he was soon recognised by the Sankla, who had often encountered his

[1] Sriphala.

[2] Literally 'lamp-holders'; such is the term applied to these handmaids; who invariably form a part of the *daeja* or 'dower.'

prowess, on which he expatiated to Irrinkowal, who sent an attendant to awake him ; but the gallant *Panch Kalyan* for such was the name of his steed) had already performed this service, and they found him upbraiding *white-legs* [1] for treading upon him. Like a true Rajpoot, "*toujours prêt*," he received the hostile message, and sent the envoy back with his compliments, and a request for some *uml* or opium, as he had lost his own supply. With all courtesy this was sent, and prepared by the domestics of his antagonist ; after taking which he lay down to enjoy the customary *siesta*. As soon as he awoke, he prepared for the combat, girt on his armour, and having reminded Panch Kalyan of the fields he had won, and telling him to bear him well that day, he mounted and advanced. The son of Chonda admiring his *sang froid*, and the address with which he guided his steed, commanded Joda Chohan, the leader of his party, to encounter the Pahoo. "Their two-edged swords soon clashed in combat ;" but the gigantic Chohan fell beneath the Bhatti, who, warmed with the fight, plunged amidst his foes, encountering all he deemed worthy of his assault.

The fray thus begun, single combats and actions of equal parties followed, the rivals looking on. At length Sadoo mounted : twice he charged the Rahtore ranks, carrying death on his lance ; each time he returned for the applause of his bride, who beheld the battle from her car. Six hundred of his foes had fallen, and nearly half his own warriors. He bade her a last adieu, while she exhorted him to the fight, saying, "she would witness his deeds, and if he fell, would follow him even "in death." Now he singled out his rival Irrinkowal,[2] who was alike eager to end the strife, and blot out his disgrace in his blood. They met : some seconds were lost in a courteous contention, each yielding to his rival the first blow, at length dealt out by Sadoo on the neck of the disappointed Rahtore. It was returned with the rapidity of lightning, and the daughter of the Mohil saw the steel descend on the head of her lover. Both fell prostrate to the earth : but Sadoo's soul had sped ; the Rahtore had only swooned. With the fall of the leaders the battle ceased ; and the fair cause of strife, Korumdévi, at once a virgin, a wife, and a widow, prepared to follow her affianced. Calling for a sword, with one arm she dissevered the other, desiring it might be conveyed to the father of her lord—"tell him such was his daughter." The other she commanded to be struck off, and given, with her marriage jewels thereon, to the bard of the Mohils. The pile was prepared on the field of battle ; and taking her lord in her embrace, she gave herself up to the devouring flames. The dissevered limbs were disposed of as commanded ; the old Rao of Poogul caused the one to be burnt, and a tank was excavated on the spot, which is still called after the heroine, "the lake of Korumdévi."

This encounter took place in S. 1462, A.D. 1406. The brunt of the battle fell on the Sanklas, and only twenty-five out of three hundred and fifty left the field with their leader, Mehraj, himself severely wounded. The rejected lover had four brothers dangerously hurt ; and in six months the wounds of Irrinkowal opened afresh : he died, and the rites to the

[1] Panch Kalyan is generally, if not always, a chestnut, having four white legs, with a white nose and list or star.

[2] *Arânkowal*, 'the lotos of the desert,' from *aranya* (Sanscrit), 'a waste,' and *comala* (pronounced *kowal*), 'a lotos' ; classically it should be written *arancomala* ; I write it as pronounced.

manes of these rivals in love, the *chaomassa* [1] of Sadoo, and the *dúádasa* [2] of Irrinkowal, were celebrated on the same day.

Without pausing to trace the moral springs of that devotion which influenced the Mohila maiden, we shall relate the sequel to the story (though out of place) [3] in illustration of the prosecution of feuds throughout Rajast'han. The fathers now took up the quarrel of their sons; and as it was by the prowess of the Sankia vassal of Mundore that the band of Sadoo was discomfited, the old Roa, Raningdeo, drew together the lances of Poogul, and carried destruction into the fief of Mehraj. The Sanklas yield in valour to none of the brave races who inhabit the "*region of death*"; and Mehraj was the father of Harba Sankla, the Palladin of Maroodés, whose exploits are yet the theme of the erratic bards of Rajast'han. Whether he was unprepared for the assault, or overcome by numbers, three hundred of his kin and clan moistened the sand-hills of the Looni with their blood. Raningdeo, flushed with revenge and laden with spoil, had reached his own frontier, when he was overtaken by Chonda of Mundore, alike eager to avenge the loss of his son Irrinkowal, and this destructive inroad on his vassal. A desperate conflict ensued, in which the Rao of Poogul was slain; and the Rahtore returned in triumph to Mundore.

Unequal to cope with the princes of Mundore, the two remaining sons of Raningdeo, Tunno and Mairah, resolved to abandon their faith, in order to preserve the point of honour, and "to take up *their father's feud.*" [4] At this period the king, Khizer Khan, was at Mooltan; to him they went, and by offers of service and an open apostacy, obtained a force to march against Chonda, who had recently added Nagore to his growing dominions. While the brothers were thus negotiating, they were joined by Keelun, the third son of their common sovereign, the Rawul of Jessulmér, who advised the use of *chul*, which with the Rajpoot means indifferently stratagem or treachery, so that it facilitates revenge. With the ostensible motive of ending their feuds, and restoring tranquillity to their borderers, whose sole occupation was watching, burning, and devastating, Keelun offered a daughter in marriage to Chonda, and went so far as to say, that if he suspected aught unfair, he would, though contrary to custom and his own dignity, send the Bhatti princess to Nagore. This course being deemed the wisest, Chonda acquiesced in his desire "to extinguish the feud (*wér bujâona*)."

Fifty covered chariots were prepared as the nuptial *cortége*, but which, instead of the bride and her handmaids, contained the bravest men of Poogul. These were preceded by a train of horses led by Rajpoots, of whom seven hundred also attended the camels laden with baggage, provisions, and gifts, while a small armed retinue brought up the rear. The king's troops, amounting to one thousand horse, remained at a cautious distance behind. Chonda left Nagore to meet the cavalcade and his bride, and had reached the chariots ere his suspicions were excited. Observing, however, some matters which little savoured of festivity, the Rahtore commenced his retreat. Upon this the chiefs rushed from their chariots

[1] The rites to the manes on the completion of the 'sixth month.'
[2] The rites to the manes on the 'twelfth day.'
[3] The greater portion of these anecdotes, the foundation of national character, will appear in the respective annals.
[4] Bap ra wér léná.

and camels, and the royal auxiliaries advancing, Chonda was assailed and fell at the gate of Nagore ; and friend and foe entering the city together, a scene of general plunder commenced.

Once more the feud was balanced ; a son and a father had fallen on each side, and the petty Rao of Poogul had bravely maintained the *wér* against the princes of Mundore. The point of honour had been carried to the utmost bound by both parties, and an opportunity of reconciliation was at hand, which prevented the shadow of disgrace either to him who made or him who accepted the overture. The Rahtores dreaded the loss of the recent acquisition, Nagore, and proposed to the Bhattis to seal their pacification with the blood of their common foe. United, they fell on the spoil-encumbered Tatars, whom they slew to a man.[1] Their father's feud thus revenged, the sons of Raningdeo (who, as apostates from their faith, could no longer hold Poogul in fief, which was retained by Keelun, who had aided their revenge) retired amongst the *Abhoria* Bhattis, and their descendants are now styled *Moomun Músulmân Bhatti.*

From such anecdotes, it will be obvious wherein consists the point of honour with the Rajpoots ; and it is not improbable that the very cause which has induced an opinion that females can have no influence on the lords of the creation,. namely, their seclusion, operates powerfully in the contrary way.

In spite of this seclusion, the knowledge of their accomplishments and of their personal perfections, radiates wherever the itinerant bard can travel. Though invisible themselves, they can see ; and accident often favours public report, and brings the object of renown within the sphere of personal observation : as in the case of Sadoo and the Mohila maiden. Placed behind screens, they see the youths of all countries, and there are occasions when permanent impressions are made, during tournaments and other martial exercises. Here we have just seen that the passion of the daughter of the Mohil was fostered at the risk of the destruction not only of her father's house, but also that of her lover ; and as the fourteen hundred and forty towns, which owned the sway of the former, were not long after absorbed into the accumulating territory of Mundore, this insult may have been the cause of the extirpation of the Mohils, as it was of the Bhattis of Poogul.

The influence of women *on* Rajpoot society is marked in every page of Hindu history, from the most remote periods. What led to the wars of Rama ? the rape of Sítá. What rendered deadly the feuds of the Yadus ? the insult to Drupdévi. What made prince Nala an exile from Nirwur ? his love for Damyanta. What made Raja Bhirtri abandon the throne of Awinti ? the loss of Pingani. What subjected the Hindu to the dominion of the Islamite ? the rape of the princess of Canouj. In fine, the cause which overturned kingdoms, commuted the sceptre to the pilgrim's staff, and formed the groundwork of all their grand epics, is woman. In ancient, and even in modern times, she had more than a negative in the choice of a husband, and this choice fell on the gallant and the gay. The fair Drupdévi was the prize of the best archer, and the Pandu Bhima established his fame, and bore her from all the suitors of Kampila. The princess of Canouj, when led through ranks of the princes of Hind, each

[1] Khizer Khan succeeded to the throne of Dehli in A.D. 1414, and according to the Jessulmér annals, the commencement of these feuds was in A.D. 1406.

hoping to be the object of her choice, threw the marriage-garland (*burmala*) over the neck of the effigy of the Chohan, which her father in derision had placed as porter at the gate. Here was incense to fame and incentive to gallantry ! [1]

In the same manner, as related in another part of this work, did the princess of Kishengurh invite Rana Raj Sing to bear her from the impending union with the emperor of the Moguls ; and abundant other instances could be adduced of the free agency of these invisibles.

It were superfluous to reason on the effects of traditional histories, such as these, on the minds and manners of the females of Rajast'han. They form the amusement of their lives, and the grand topic in all their conversaziones ; they read them with the *Purohit*, and they have them sung by the itinerant bard or Dholi minstrel, who disseminates them wherever the Rajpoot name extends. The Rajpoot mother claims her full share in the glory of her son, who imbibes at the maternal fount his first rudiments of chivalry ; and the importance of this parental instruction cannot be better illustrated than in the ever-recurring simile, " make thy mother's milk resplendent " ; the full force of which we have in the powerful, though over-strained expression of the Boondí queen's joy on the announcement of the heroic death of her son : " the long-dried fountain at which he fed, jetted forth as she listened to the tale of his death, and the marble pavement, on which it fell, rent asunder." Equally futile would it be to reason on the intensity of sentiment thus implanted in the infant Rajpoot, of whom we may say without metaphor, the shield is his cradle, and daggers his playthings ; and with whom the first commandment is, " avenge thy father's feud " ; on which they can heap text upon text, from the days of the great Pandu moralist Vyasu, to the not less influential bard of their nation, the Tricala Chund.

CHAPTER XXIV

Origin of female immolation—The sacrifice of Sati, the wife of Iswara—The motive to it considered—Infanticide—Its causes among the Rajpoots, the Rajkoomars, and the Jarejas—The rite of Johur—Female captives in war enslaved—Summary of the Rajpoot character—Their familiar habits—The use of Opium—Hunting—The use of weapons—Jaitis, or wrestlers—Armouries—Music—Feats of dexterity—Maharaja Sheodan Sing—Literary qualifications of the princes—Household economy—Furniture—Dress, etc.

WE now proceed to consider another trait of Rajpoot character, exemplified in the practice of female immolation, and to inquire whether religion,

[1] The Samnite custom, so lauded by Montesquieu as the reward of youthful virtue, was akin in sentiment to the Rajpoot, except that the fair Rajpootni made herself the sole judge of merit in her choice. It was more calculated for republican than aristocratic society :—" On assembloit tous les jeunes gens, et on les jugeoit ; celui qui était déclaré le meilleur de tout prenoit pour sa femme la fille qu'il vouloit : l'amour, la beauté, la chasteté, la vertu, la naissance, les richesses même, tout cela était, pour ainsi dire, la dot de la vertu." It would be difficult, adds Montesquieu, to imagine a more noble recompense, or one less expensive to a petty state, or more influential on the conduct of both sexes.—*L'Esprit des Lois*, chap. xvi. livre vii.

custom, or affection, has most share in such sacrifice. To arrive at the origin of this rite, we must trace it to the recesses of mythology, where we shall discover the precedent in the example of *Sati*, who to avenge an insult to Iswara, in her own father's omission to ask her lord to an entertainment, consumed herself in the presence of the assembled gods. With this act of fealty (*sati*) the name of Dacsha's daughter has been identified; and her regeneration and reunion to her husband, as the mountain-nymph *Mérá*, or 'Párvati,' furnish the incentive to similar acts. In the history of these celestial beings, the Rajpootni has a memorable lesson before her, that no domestic differences can afford exemption from this proof of faith: for Jupiter and Juno were not more eminent examples of connubial discord than Mérá and Siva, who was not only alike unfaithful, but more cruel, driving Mérá from his Olympus (Kylas), and forcing her to seek refuge in the murky caverns of Caucasus. Female immolation, therefore, originated with the sun-worshipping *Saivas*, and was common to all those nations who adored this the most splendid object of the visible creation. Witness the Scythic Gete or Jut warrior of the Jaxartes, who devoted his wife, horse, arms, and slaves, to the flames; the "giant Gete" of Scandinavia, who forgot not on the shores of the Baltic his Transoxianian habits; and the Frisian Frank and Saxon descended from him, who ages after omitted only the female. Could we assign the primary cause of a custom so opposed to the first law of nature with the same certainty that we can prove its high antiquity, we might be enabled to devise some means for its abolition. The chief characteristic of *satiism* is its expiating quality: for by this act of *faith*, the Sati not only makes atonement for the sins of her husband, and secures the remission of her own, but has the joyful assurance of reunion to the object whose beatitude she procures. Having once imbibed this doctrine, its fulfilment is powerfully aided by that heroism of character inherent to the Rajpootni; though we see that the stimulant of religion requires no aid even in the timid female of Bengal, who, relying on the promise of regeneration, lays her head on the pyre with the most philosophical composure.

Nothing short of the abrogation of the doctrines which pronounce such sacrifices exculpatory can be effectual in preventing them; but this would be to overturn the fundamental article of their creed, the notion of metempsychosis. Further research may disclose means more attainable, and the sacred Sastras are at once the surest and the safest. Whoever has examined these, is aware of the conflict of authorities for and against cremation; but a proper application of them (and they are the highest who give it not their sanction) has, I believe, never been resorted to. Vyasu, the chronicler of the Yadus, a race whose manners were decidedly Scythic, is the great advocate for female sacrifice: he (in the *Mahabharat*) pronounces the expiation perfect. But Menu inculcates no such doctrine; and although the state of widowhood he recommends might be deemed onerous by the fair sex of the west, it would be considered little hardship in the east. "Let her emaciate her body, by living *voluntarily* on pure flowers, roots, and fruit; but let her not, when her lord is deceased, even pronounce the name of another man." Again he says, "A virtuous wife ascends to heaven, if, after the decease of her lord, she devote herself to pious austerity; but a widow, who slights her deceased husband by *marrying again*, brings disgrace on herself here below, and shall be excluded from the seat of her lord."[1]

These and many other texts, enjoining purity of life and manners to the widow, are to be found in this first authority, but none demanding such a cruel pledge of affection. Abstinence from the common pursuits of life, and entire self-denial, are rewarded by "high renown in this world, and in the next the abode of her husband"; and procure for her the title of "*sáddwi*, or the *virtuous*." These are deemed sufficient pledges of affection by the first of sages.[2] So much has been written on this subject, that we shall not pursue it further in this place; but proceed to consider a still more inhuman practice, infanticide.

Although custom sanctions, and religion rewards, a Sati, the victim to marital selfishness, yet, to the honour of humanity, neither traditionary adage nor religious text can be quoted in support of a practice so revolting as infanticide. Man alone, of the whole animal creation, is equal to the task of destroying his offspring: for instinct preserves what reason destroys. The wife is the sacrifice to his egotism, and the progeny of her own sex to his pride; and if the unconscious infant should escape the influence of the latter, she is only reserved to become the victim of the former at the period when life is most desirous of extension. If the female reasoned on her destiny, its hardships are sufficient to stifle all sense of joy, and produce indifference to life. When a female is born, no anxious inquiries await the mother—no greetings welcome the new-comer, who appears an intruder on the scene, which often closes in the hour of its birth. But the very silence with which a female birth is accompanied, forcibly expresses

[1] Menu, *On Women*, chap. v. text 157, 160, 161.

[2] Were all Menu's maxims on this head collected, and with other good authorities, printed, circulated, and supported by Hindu missionaries, who might be brought to advocate the abolition of Satiism, some good might be effected. Let every text tending to the respectability of widowhood be made prominent, and degrade the opponents by enumerating the weak points they abound in. Instance the polyandrism which prevailed among the Pandus, whose high priest Vyasu was an illegitimate branch; though above all would be the efficacy of the abolition of polygamy, which in the lower classes leaves women destitute, and in the higher condemns them to mortification and neglect. Whatever result such a course might produce, there can be no danger in the experiment. Such sacrifices must operate powerfully on manners; and, barbarous as is the custom, yet while it springs from the same principle, it ought to improve the condition of women, from the fear that harsh treatment of them might defeat the atonement hereafter. Let the advocate for the abolition of this practice by the hand of power, read attentively Mr. Colebrooke's essay, "On the Duties of a faithful Hindu Widow," in the fourth volume of the *Asiatic Researches*, to correct the notion that there is no adequate religious ordinance for the horrid sacrifice. Mr. C. observes (p. 220): "Though an alternative be allowed, the Hindu legislators have shown themselves disposed to encourage widows to burn themselves with their husband's corpse." In this paper he will find too many authorities deemed sacred for its support; but it is only by knowing the full extent of the prejudices and carefully collecting the conflicting authorities, that we can provide the means to overcome it. Jehangír legislated for the abolition of this practice by successive ordinances. At first he commanded that no woman, being mother of a family, should under any circumstances be permitted, however willing, to immolate herself; and subsequently the prohibition was made entire when the slightest compulsion was required, "whatever the assurances of the people might be." The royal commentator records no reaction. We might imitate Jehangír, and adopting the partially prohibitive ordinance, forbid the sacrifice where there was a family to rear.

sorrow; and we dare not say that many compunctious visitings do not obtrude themselves on those who, in accordance with custom and imagined necessity, are thus compelled to violate the sentiments of nature. Families may exult in the *Satis* which their cenotaphs portray, but none ever heard a Rajpoot boast of the destruction of his infant progeny.

What are the causes, we may ask, sufficiently powerful to induce the suppression of a feeling which every sentient being has in common for its offspring? To suppose the Rajpoot devoid of this sentiment would argue his deficiency in the ordinary attributes of humanity: often is he heard to exclaim, "Accursed the day when a woman child was born to me!" The same motive which studded Europe with convents, in which youth and beauty were immured until liberated by death, first prompted the Rajpoot to infanticide: and, however revolting the policy, it is perhaps kindness compared to incarceration. There can be no doubt that monastic seclusion, practised by the Frisians in France, the Langobardi in Italy, and the Visigoths in Spain, was brought from Central Asia, the cradle of the Goths.[1] It is, in fact, a modification of the same feeling, which characterises the Rajpoot and the ancient German warrior,—the dread of dishonour to the fair: the former raises the poniard to the breast of his wife rather than witness her captivity, and he gives the opiate to the infant, whom, if he cannot portion and marry to her equal, he dare not see degraded.

Although religion nowhere authorises this barbarity, the laws which regulate marriage amongst the Rajpoots powerfully promote infanticide. Not only is intermarriage prohibited between families of the same clan (*campa*), but between those of the same tribe (*gote*); and though centuries may have intervened since their separation, and branches thus transplanted may have lost their original patronymic, they can never be regrafted on the original stem: for instance, though eight centuries have separated the two grand subdivisions of the Gehlotes, and the younger, the Seesodia, has superseded the elder, the Aharya, each ruling distinct states, a marriage between any of the branches would be deemed incestuous: the Seesodia is yet brother to the Aharya, and regards every female of the race as his sister. Every tribe has therefore to look abroad, to a race distinct from its own, for suitors for the females. Foreign war, international feuds, or other calamities affect tribes the most remote from each other; nor can war or famine thin the clans of Marwar, without diminishing the female population of Ambér: thus both suffer in a twofold degree. Many virtuous and humane princes have endeavoured to check or mitigate an evil, in the eradication of which every parental feeling would co-operate. Sumptuary edicts alone can control it; and the Rajpoots were never sufficiently enamoured of despotism to permit it to rule within their private dwellings. The plan proposed, and in some degree followed by the great Jey Sing of Ambér, might with caution be pursued,

[1] The Ghikers, a Scythic race inhabiting the banks of the Indus, at an early period of history were given to infanticide. "It was a custom," says Ferishta, "as soon as a female child was born, to carry her to the market-place and there proclaim aloud, holding the child in one hand and a knife in the other, that any one wanting a wife might have her; otherwise she was immolated." By this means they had more men than women, which occasioned the custom of several husbands to one wife. When any one husband visited her, she set up a mark at the door, which being observed by the others, they withdrew till the signal was removed.

and with great probability of success. He submitted to the prince of every Rajpoot state a decree, which was laid before a convocation of their respective vassals, in which he regulated the *daeja* or dower, and other marriage expenditure, with reference to the property of the vassal, limiting it to one year's income of the estate. This plan was, however, frustrated by the vanity of the Chondawut of Saloombra, who expended on the marriage of his daughter a sum even greater than his sovereign could have afforded; and to have his name blazoned by the bards and genealogists, he sacrificed the beneficent views of one of the wisest of the Rajpoot race. Until vanity suffers itself to be controlled, and the aristocratic Rajpoot submit to republican simplicity,[1] the evils arising from nuptial profusion will not cease. Unfortunately, those who could check it, find their interest in stimulating it, namely, the whole class of *mangtas* (mendicants), bards, minstrels, jugglers, Brahmins who assemble on these occasions, and pour forth their epithalamiums in praise of the virtue of liberality. The *bardais* are the grand recorders of fame, and the volume of *precedent* is always recurred to, in citing the liberality of former chiefs; while the dread of their satire (*viserva*, literally 'poison') shuts the eyes of the chiefs to consequences, and they are only anxious to maintain the reputation of their ancestors, though fraught with future ruin. "The Dahima emptied his coffers" (says Chund, the pole-star of the Rajpoots) "on the marriage of his daughter with Pirthiraj; but he filled them with the praises of mankind." The same bard retails every article of these *daejas* or 'dowers,' which thus become precedents for future ages; and the "*lakh passao*," then established for the chief bardai, has become a model to posterity. Even now the Rana of Oodipoor, in his season of poverty, at the recent marriage of his daughters bestowed "the gift of a lakh" on the chief bard; though the articles of gold, horses, clothes, etc., were included in the estimate, and at an undue valuation, which rendered the gift not quite so precious as in the days of the Chohan. Were bonds taken from all the feudal chiefs, and a penal clause inserted, of forfeiture of their fief by all who exceeded a fixed nuptial expenditure, the axe would be laid to the root, the evil would be checked, and the heart of many a mother (and we may add father) be gladdened, by preserving at once the point of honour and their child. When ignorance declaims against the gratuitous love of murder amongst these brave men, our contempt is excited equally by its short-sighted conclusions, and the affected philanthropy which overlooks all remedy but the "*sic volo*." Sir John Shore, when acting on the suggestions of the benevolent Duncan for the suppression of this practice amongst the Rajkoomars, judged more wisely as a politician, and more charitably in his estimate of human motives. "A prohibition," says he, "enforced by the denunciation of the severest temporal penalties, would have had little efficacy in abolishing a custom which existed in opposition to the feelings of humanity and natural affection;" but "the sanction of that religion which the Rajkoomars professed was appealed to in aid of the ordinances of civil authority; and an engagement binding themselves to desist from the barbarous practice was prepared, and circulated for signature amongst

[1] Could they be induced to adopt the custom of the ancient Marsellois, infanticide might cease: "Marseille fut la plus sage des républiques de son temps: les dots ne pourraient passer cents écus en argent, et cinq en habits, dit Strabon."—*De l'Esprit des Loix*, chap. xv. liv. v. 21.

the Rajkoomars." It may well be doubted how far this influence could extend, when the root of the evil remained untouched, though not unseen, as the philanthropic Duncan pointed out in the confession of the Rajkoomars: "all unequivocally admitted it, but all did not fully acknowledge its atrocity; and the only reason they assigned for the inhuman practice was the great expense of procuring suitable matches for their daughters, if they allowed them to grow up." The Rajkoomar is one of Chohan *sachæ*, chief of the *Agnicúlas*, and in proportion to its high and well-deserved pretensions on the score of honour, it has more infanticides than any other of the "*thirty-six royal races*." Amongst those of this race out of the pale of feudalism, and subjected to powers not Rajpoot, the practice is fourfold greater, from the increased pressure of the cause which gave it birth, and the difficulty of establishing their daughters in wedlock. Raja Jey Sing's enactment went far to remedy this. Conjoin his plan with Mr. Duncan's, provide dowers, and infanticide will cease. It is only by removing the cause that the consequences can be averted.

As to the almost universality of this practice amongst the Jarejas, the leading cause, which will also operate to its continuance, has been entirely overlooked. The Jarejas were Rajpoots, a subdivision of the Yadus; but by intermarriage with the Mahomedans, to whose faith they became proselytes, they lost their caste. Political causes have disunited them from the Mahomedans, and they desire again to be considered as pure Rajpoots; but having been contaminated, no Rajpoot will intermarry with them. The owner of a *hyde* of land, whether Seesodia, Rahtore, or Chohan, would scorn the hand of a Jareja princess. Can the "*sic volo*" be applied to men who think in this fashion?

Having thus pointed out the causes of the sacrifice of widows and of infants, I shall touch on the yet more awful rite of *Johur*, when a whole tribe may become extinct, of which several instances have been recorded in the annals of Méwar. To the fair of other lands the fate of the Rajpootni must appear one of appalling hardship. In each stage of life, death is ready to claim her; by the poppy at its dawn, by the flames in riper years; while the safety of the interval depending on the uncertainty of war, at no period is her existence worth a twelvemonth's purchase. The loss of a battle, or the capture of a city, is a signal to avoid captivity and its horrors, which to the Rajpootni are worse than death. To the doctrines of Christianity Europe owes the boon of protection to the helpless and the fair, who are comparatively safe amidst the vicissitudes of war; to which security the chivalry of the Middle Ages doubtless contributed. But it is singular that a nation so refined, so scrupulous in its ideas with regard to females, as the Rajpoot, should not have entered into some national compact to abandon such proof of success as the bondage[1] of the sex. We can enter into the feeling, and applaud the deed, which ensured the preservation of their honour by the fatal *johur*, when the foe was the brutalised Tatar. But the practice was common in the international wars of the Rajpoots; and I possess numerous inscriptions (on stone and on brass) which record as the first token of victory the captive wives of the foeman. When "the mother of Sisera looked out of the window, and cried *through the lattice*, Why tarry the wheels of his chariot—have they not sped? have

[1] *Bunda* is 'a bondsman' in Persian; *Bandi*, 'a female slave' in Hindí.

they not divided the prey; to every man a damsel or two?" [1] we have a perfect picture of the Rajpoot mother expecting her son from the foray.

The Jewish law with regard to female captives was perfectly analogous to that of Menu; both declare them "lawful prize," and both Moses and Menu establish rules sanctioning the marriage of such captives with the captors. "When a girl is made captive by her lover, after a victory over her kinsman," marriage "is permitted by law." [2] That forcible marriage in the Hindu law termed *Rachasa*, namely, "the seizure of a maiden by force from her house while she weeps and calls for assistance, after her kinsman and friends have been slain in battle," [3] is the counterpart of the ordinance regarding the usage of a captive in the *Pentateuch*,[4] excepting the "*shaving of the head*," which is the sign of complete slavery with the Hindu. When Hector, anticipating his fall, predicts the fate which awaits Andromache, he draws a forcible picture of the misery of the Rajpoot; but the latter, instead of a lachrymose and enervating harangue as he prepared for the battle with the same chance of defeat, would have spared her the pain of plying the "Argive loom" by her death. To prevent such degradation, the brave Rajpoot has recourse to the *johur*, or immolation of every female of the family: nor can we doubt that, educated as are the females of that country, they gladly embrace such a refuge from pollution. Who would not be a Rajpoot in such a case? The very term widow (*rand*) is used in common parlance as one of reproach.[5]

Menu commands that whoever accosts a woman shall do so by the title of "sister," [6] and that "way must be made for her, even as for the aged, for a priest, a prince, or a bridegroom"; and in the admirable text on the laws of hospitality, he ordains that "pregnant women, brides, and damsels shall have food [7] before all the other guests"; which, with various other texts, appears to indicate a time when women were less than now objects of restraint; a custom attributable to the paramount dominion of the Mahomedans, from whose rigid system the Hindus have borrowed. But so many conflicting texts are to be found in the pages

[1] Jud. v. 28–30. [2] Menu, on Marriage, art. 26.

[3] Menu, on Marriage, art. 33.

[4] "When thou goest forth to war against thine enemies, and the Lord thy God hath delivered them into thine hands, and thou hast taken them captive, and seest among the captives a beautiful woman, and hast a desire unto her, that thou wouldest have her to thy wife; then thou shalt bring her home to thine house, and she shall shave her head, and pare her nails; and she shall put the raiment of her captivity from off her, and shall remain in thine house, and bewail her father and her mother a full month: and after that thou shalt go in unto her, and be her husband, and she shall be thy wife."—Deut. xxi. 10, 11, 12, 13.

[5] I remember in my subaltern days, and wanderings through countries then little known, one of my Rajpoot soldiers at the well, impatient for water, asked a woman for the rope and bucket by the uncivil term of *rand*: "*Myn Rajpútni ché*," 'I am a Rajputni,' she replied in the Hara dialect, to which tribe she belonged, "*aur Rajpoot ca ma cho*," 'and the mother of Rajpoots.' At the indignant reply the hands of the brave Kulian were folded, and he asked her forgiveness by the endearing and respectful epithet of "mother." It was soon granted, and filling his brass vessel, she dismissed him with the epithet of "son," and a gentle reproof. Kulian was himself a Rajpoot, and a bolder lives not, if he still exists; this was in 1807, and in 1817 he gained his sergeant's knot, as one of the thirty-two firelocks of my guard, who led the attack, and defeated a camp of fifteen hundred Pindarries.

[6] On Education, art. 129. [7] On Marriage, art. 114.

of Menu, that we may pronounce the compilation never to have been the work of the same legislator: from whose dicta we may select with equal facility texts tending to degrade as to exalt the sex. For the following he would meet with many plaudits: "Let women be constantly supplied with ornaments at festivals and jubilees, for if the wife be not elegantly attired, she will not exhilarate her husband. A wife gaily adorned, the whole house is embellished."[1] In the following text he pays an unequivocal compliment to her power: "A female is able to draw from the right path in this life, not a fool only, but even a sage, and can lead him in subjection to desire or to wrath." With this acknowledgment from the very fountain of authority, we have some ground for asserting that *les femmes font les mœurs*, even in Rajpootana; and that though immured and invisible, their influence *on* society is not less certain than if they moved in the glare of open day.

Most erroneous ideas have been formed of the Hindu female from the pictures drawn by those who never left the banks of the Ganges. They are represented as degraded beings, and that not one in many thousands can even read. I would ask such travellers whether they know the name of Rajpoot, for there are few of the lowest chieftains whose daughters are not instructed both to read and write; though the customs of the country requiring much form in epistolary writing, only the signature is made to letters. But of their intellect, and knowledge of mankind, whoever has had to converse with a Rajpootni guardian of her son's rights, must draw a very different conclusion.[2] Though excluded by the Salic law of India from governing, they are declared to be fit regents during minority; and the history of India is filled with anecdotes of able and valiant females in this capacity.[3]

The more prominent traits of character will be found disseminated throughout the annals; we shall therefore omit the customary summaries of nationalities, those fanciful debtor and creditor accounts, with their balanced amount, favourable or unfavourable according to the disposition of the observer; and from the anecdotes through these pages leave the reader to form his own judgment of the Rajpoot. High courage, patriotism, loyalty, honour, hospitality, and simplicity are qualities which must at once be conceded to them; and if we cannot vindicate them from charges to which human nature in every clime is obnoxious;

[1] On Marriage, arts. 57, 60, 61, 62, 63.

[2] I have conversed for hours with the Boondí queen-mother on the affairs of her government and welfare of her infant son, to whom I was left guardian by his dying father. She had adopted me as her brother; but the conversation was always in the presence of a third person in her confidence, and a curtain separated us. Her sentiments showed invariably a correct and extensive knowledge, which was equally apparent in her letters, of which I had many. I could give many similar instances.

[3] Ferishta in his history gives an animated picture of Durgavati, queen of Gurrah, defending the rights of her infant son against Akber's ambition. Like another Boadicea, she headed her army, and fought a desperate battle with Asoph Khan, in which she was wounded and defeated; but scorning flight, or to survive the loss of independence, she, like the antique Roman in such a predicament, slew herself on the field of battle.

Whoever desires to judge of the comparative fidelity of the translations of this writer, by Dow and Briggs, cannot do better than refer to this very passage. The former has clothed it in all the trappings of Ossianic decoration: the latter gives "a plain unvarnished tale," which ought to be the aim of every translator.

if we are compelled to admit the deterioration of moral dignity, from the continual inroads of, and their consequent collision with, rapacious conquerors ; we must yet admire the quantum of virtue which even oppression and bad example have failed to banish. The meaner vices of deceit and falsehood, which the delineators of national character attach to the Asiatic without distinction, I deny to be universal with the Rajpoots, though some tribes may have been obliged from position to use these shields of the weak against continuous oppression. Every court in Rajast'han has its characteristic epithet ; and there is none held more contemptible than the affix of *joot'ha durbar*, 'the lying court,' applied to Jeipoor ; while the most comprehensive measure of praise is the simple epithet of *sacha*,[1] 'the truth-teller.' Again, there are many shades between deceit and dissimulation : the one springs from natural depravity ; the other may be assumed, as with the Rajpoot, in self-defence. But their laws, the mode of administering them, and the operation of external causes, must be attentively considered before we can form a just conclusion of the springs which regulate the character of a people. We must examine the opinions of the competent of past days, when political independence yet remained to the Rajpoots, and not found our judgment of a nation upon a superficial knowledge of individuals. To this end I shall avail myself of the succinct but philosophical remarks of Abulfuzil, the wise minister of the wise Akber, which are equally applicable to mankind at large, as to the particular people we are treating of. "If," he says, speaking of the Hindus, "a diligent investigator were to examine the temper and disposition of the people of each tribe, he would find every individual differing in some respect or other. Some among them are virtuous in the highest degree, and others carry vice to the greatest excess. They are renowned for wisdom, disinterested friendship, obedience to their superiors, and many other virtues : but, at the same time, there are among them men whose hearts are obdurate and void of shame, turbulent spirits, who for the merest trifle will commit the greatest outrages."

Again : "The Hindus are religious, affable, courteous to strangers, cheerful, *enamoured of knowledge*, lovers of justice, able in business, grateful, *admirers of truth*, and of unbounded fidelity in all their dealings. Their character shines brightest in adversity. Their soldiers (the Rajpoots) know not what it is to fly from the field of battle ; but when the success of the combat becomes doubtful, they dismount from their horses, and throw away their lives in payment of the debt of valour."

I shall conclude this chapter with a sketch of their familiar habits, and a few of their indoor and outdoor recreations.

To Baber, the founder of the Mogul dynasty, India is indebted for the introduction of its melons and grapes ; and to his grandson Jehangír for tobacco.[2] For the introduction of opium we have no date, and it is not even mentioned in the poems of Chund. This pernicious plant has robbed the Rajpoot of half his virtues ; and while it obscures these, it heightens

[1] *Sach'ha* is very comprehensive ; in common parlance it is the opposite of 'untrue' ; but it means 'loyal, upright, just.'

[2] The autobiography of both these noble Tatar princes are singular compositions, and may be given as standards of Eastern intellectual acquirement. They minutely note the progress of refinement and luxury.

his vices, giving to his natural bravery a character of insane ferocity, and to the countenance, which would otherwise beam with intelligence, an air of imbecility. Like all stimulants, its effects are magical for a time; but the reaction is not less certain: and the faded form or amorphous bulk too often attest the debilitating influence of a drug which alike debases mind and body. In the more ancient epics we find no mention of the poppy-juice as now used, though the Rajpoot has at all times been accustomed to his *madhava ra-peala*, or 'intoxicating cup.' The essence,[1] whether of grain, of roots, or of flowers, still welcomes the guest, but is secondary to the opiate. *Umul lar kana*, 'to eat opium together,' is the most inviolable pledge; and an agreement ratified by this ceremony is stronger than any adjuration. If a Rajpoot pays a visit, the first question is, *umul kya?* 'have you had your opiate?'—*umul kao*, 'take your opiate.' On a birthday, when all the chiefs convene to congratulate their brother on another 'knot to his years,' the large cup is brought forth, a lump of opiate put therein, upon which water is poured, and by the aid of a stick a solution is made, to which each helps his neighbour, not with a glass, but with the hollow of his hand held to his mouth. To judge by the wry faces on this occasion, none can like it, and to get rid of the nauseous taste, comfit-balls are handed round. It is curious to observe the animation it inspires; a Rajpoot is fit for nothing without his *umul*, and I have often dismissed their men of business to refresh their intellects by a dose, for when its effects are dissipating they become mere logs.[2] Opium to the Rajpoot is more necessary than food, and a suggestion to the Rana to tax it highly was most unpopular. From the rising generation the author exacted promises that they would resist initiation in this vice, and many grew up in happy ignorance of the taste of opium. He will be the greatest friend to Rajast'han who perseveres in eradicating the evil. The valley of Oodipoor is a poppy garden, of every hue and variety, whence the Hindu Sri may obtain a coronet more variegated than ever adorned the Isis of the Nile.

A pledge once given by the Rajpoot, whether ratified by the "eating opium together," "an exchange of turbans," or the more simple act of "giving the right hand," is maintained inviolable under all circumstances.

[1] *Arac*, 'essence'; whence *arrack* and *rack*.

[2] Even in the midst of conversation, the eye closes and the head nods as the exciting cause is dissipating, and the countenance assumes a perfect vacuity of expression. Many a chief has taken his siesta in his chair while on a visit to me: an especial failing of my good friend Raj Kulian of Sadri, the descendant of the brave Shama, who won "*the right hand*" of the prince at Huldighat. The lofty turban worn by the Raj, which distinguishes this tribe (*the Jhala*), was often on the point of tumbling into my lap, as he unconsciously nodded. When it is inconvenient to dissolve the opium, the chief carries it in his pocket, and presents it, as we would a pinch of snuff in Europe. In my subaltern days, the chieftain of Sent'hal, in Jeipoor, on paying me a visit, presented me with a piece of opium, which I took and laid on the table. Observing that I did not eat it, he said he should like to try the *Frangi ca umul*, 'the opiate of the Franks.' I sent him a bottle of powerful *Schedam*, and to his inquiry as to the quantity of the dose, I told him he might take from an eighth to the half, as he desired exhilaration or oblivion. We were to have hunted the next morning; but having no sign of my friend, I was obliged to march without ascertaining the effect of the barter of *apheem* for the waters of Friesland; though I have no doubt that he found them quite Lethean.

Their grand hunts have been described. The Rajpoot is fond of his dog and his gun. The former aids him in pulling down the boar or hare, and with the stalking-horse he will toil for hours after the deer. The greater chieftains have their *rumnas* or preserves, where poaching would be summarily punished, and where the slaughter of all kinds of beasts, elk, hog, hyena, tiger, boar, deer, wild-dog, wolf, or hare, is indiscriminate. Riding in the ring with the lance in tournaments, without the spike, the point being guarded ; defence of the sword against the lance, with every variety of "noble horsemanship," such as would render the most expert in Europe an easy prey to the active Rajpoot, are some of the chief exercises. Firing at a mark with a matchlock, in which they attain remarkable accuracy of aim ; and in some parts of the country throwing a dart or javelin from horseback, are favourite amusements. The practice of the bow is likewise a main source of pastime, and in the manner there adopted it requires both dexterity and strength. The Rajpoot is not satisfied if he cannot bury his arrow either in the earthern target, or in the buffalo, to the feather. The use of the bow is hallowed ; Arjuna's bow in the "great war," and that of the Chohan king, Pirthiraj, with which the former gained Droopdeví and the latter the fair Sunjogta, are immortalised like that of Ulysses. In these martial exercises, the youthful Rajpoot is early initiated, and that the sight of blood may be familiar, he is instructed, before he has strength to wield a sword, to practise with his boy's scimitar on the heads of lambs and kids. His first successful essay on the animals '*feræ naturæ*' is a source of congratulation to his whole family.[1] In this manner the spirit of chivalry is continually fed, for everything around him speaks of arms and strife. His very amusements are warlike ; and the dance and the song, the burthen of which is the record of his successful gallantry, so far from enervating, serve as fresh incitements to his courage.

The exhibition of the *jaitis*, or wrestlers, is another mode of killing time. It is a state concern for every prince or chief to entertain a certain number of these champions of the glove. Challenges are sent by the most celebrated from one court to another ; and the event of the *akarra*, as the arena is termed, is looked to with great anxiety.

No prince or chief is without his *silleh-khaneh*, or armoury, where he passes hours in viewing and arranging his arms. Every favourite weapon, whether sword, matchlock, spear, dagger, or bow, has a distinctive epithet. The keeper of the armoury is one of the most confidential officers about the person of the prince. These arms are beautiful and costly. The *sirohi*, or slightly-curved blade, is formed like that of Damascus, and is the greatest favourite of all the variety of sabres throughout Rajpootana. The long cut-and-thrust, like the *Andrea Ferrara*, is not uncommon ; nor the *khanda*, or double-edged sword. The matchlocks both of Lahore and the country are often highly finished and inlaid with mother-of-pearl and gold : those of Boondí are the best. The shield of the rhinoceros-hide offers the best resistance, and is often ornamented with animals, beautifully painted, and enamelled in gold and silver. The bow is of buffalo-

[1] The author has now before him a letter written by the queen-mother of Boondí desiring his rejoicings on *Lalji*, the beloved's, *coup d'essai* on a deer, which he had followed most pertinaciously to the death. On this occasion a court was held, and all the chiefs presented offerings and congratulations.

horn, and the arrows of reed, and barbed in a variety of fashions, as the crescent, the trident, the snake's tongue, and other fanciful forms.

The Maharaja Sheodan Sing (whose family are heirs presumptive to the throne) was one of my constant visitors ; and the title of 'adopted brother,' which he conferred upon me, allowed him to make his visits unreasonably long. The Maharaja had many excellent qualities. He was the best shot in Méwar ; he was well read in the classic literature of his nation ; deeply versed in the secrets of the chronicles, not only of Méwar but of all Rajwarra ; conversant with all the mysteries of the bard, and could *improvise* on every occasion. He was a proficient in musical science, and could discourse most fluently on the whole theory of Sangíta, which comprehends vocal and instrumental harmony. He could explain each of the *ragas*, or musical modes, which issued from the five mouths of Síva and his consort Méra, together with the almost endless variations of the *ragas*, to each of which are allotted six consorts or *raginis*. He had attached to his suite the first vocalists of Méwar, and occasionally favoured me by letting them sing at my house. The chief *cantatrice* had a superb voice, a *contr' alto* of great extent, and bore the familiar appellation of 'Catalani.' Her execution of all the *bussunt* or 'spring-songs,' and the *megh* or 'cloud-songs' of the monsoon, which are full of melody, was perfect. But she had a rival in a singer from Oojein, and we made a point of having them together, that emulation might excite to excellence. The chieftain of Saloombra, the chief of the Suktawuts, and others, frequently joined these parties, as well as the Maharaja : for all are partial to the dance and the song, during which conversation flows unrestrained. Sadoola, whose execution on the guitar would have secured applause even at the Philharmonic, commanded mute attention when he played a *tan* or symphony, or when, taking any of the simple *tuppas* of Oojein as a theme, he wandered through a succession of voluntaries. In summer, these little parties were held on the terrace or the house-top, where carpets were spread under an awning, while the cool breezes of the lake gave life after the exhaustion of a day passed under 96° of Fahrenheit. The subjects of their songs are various, love, glory, satire, etc. I was invited to similar assemblies by many of the chiefs ; though none were so intellectual as those of the Maharaja. On birthdays or other festivals, the chief bardai often appears, or the bard of any other tribe who may happen to be present. Then all is mute attention, broken only by the emphatic "*wah, wah !*" the measured nod of the head, or fierce curl of the moustache, in token of approbation or the reverse.[1]

The Maharaja's talents for amplification were undoubted, and by more than one of his friends this failing was attributed to his long residence at the court of Jeipoor, whose cognomen will not have been forgotten. He had one day been amusing us with feats of his youth, his swimming from island to island, and bestriding the alligators for an excursion.[2]

[1] Poetic impromptus pass on these occasions unrestricted by the fear of the critic, though the long yawn now and then should have given the hint to my friend the Maharaja that his verses wanted Attic. But he had certainly talent, and he did not conceal his light, which shone the stronger from the darkness that surrounded him : for poverty is not the school of genius, and the trade of the schoolmaster has ever been the least lucrative in a capital where rapine has ruled.

[2] There are two of these alligators quite familiar to the inhabitants of Oodipoor, who come when called "from the vasty deep" for food ; and I have often ex-

Like Tell, he had placed a mark on his son's head and hit it successfully. He could kill an eagle on the wing, and divide a ball on the edge of a knife, the knife itself unseen. While running on in this manner, my features betraying some incredulity, he insisted on redeeming his word. A day was accordingly appointed, and though labouring under an ague, he came with his favourite matchlocks. The more dangerous experiment was desisted from, and he commenced by dividing the ball on the knife. This he placed perpendicularly in the centre of an earthen vessel filled with water; and taking his station at about twenty paces, perforated the centre of the vessel, and allowed you to take up the fragments of the ball; having previously permitted you to load the piece, and examine the vessel, which he did not once approach himself. Another exhibition was striking an orange from a pole without perforating it. Again, he gave the option of loading to a bystander, and retreating a dozen paces, he knocked an orange off untouched by the ball, which, according to a preliminary proviso, could not be found: the orange was not even discoloured by the powder. He was an adept also at chess [1] and choupan, and could carry on a conversation by stringing flowers in a peculiar manner. If he plumed himself upon his pretensions, his vanity was always veiled under a demeanour full of courtesy and grace; and Maharaja Sheodan Sing would be esteemed a well-bred and well-informed man at the most polished court of Europe.

Every chief has his band, vocal and instrumental; but Sindia, some years since, carried away the most celebrated vocalists of Oodipoor. The Rajpoots are all partial to music. The tuppa is the favourite measure. Its chief character is plaintive simplicity; and it is analogous to the Scotch, or perhaps still more to the Norman. [2]

The Rana, who is a great patron of the art, has a small band of musicians, whose only instrument is the *shehna*, or hautboy. They played their national tuppas with great taste and feeling; and these strains, wafted from the lofty terrace of the palace in the silence of the night, produced a sensation of delight not unmixed with pain, which its peculiarly melancholy character excites. The Rana has also a few flute or flageolet players, who discourse most eloquent music. Indeed, we may enumerate this among the principal amusements of the Rajpoots; and although it would be deemed indecorous to be a performer, the science forms a part of education. [3]

asperated them by throwing an inflated bladder, which the monsters greedily received, only to dive away in angry disappointment. It was on these that my friend affirmed he had ventured.

[1] *Chatranga*, so called from imitating the formation of an army. The 'four' *chatur* 'bodied' *anga* array; or elephants, chariots, horse, and foot. His chief antagonist at chess was a blind man of the city.

[2] The *tuppa* belongs to the very extremity of India, being indigenous as far as the Indus and the countries watered by its arms; and though the peculiar measure is common in Rajast'han, the prefix of *punjábi* shows its origin. I have listened at Caen to the viola or hurdy-gurdy, till I could have fancied myself in Méwar.

[3] Chund remarks of his hero, the Chohan, that he was "master of the art," both vocal and instrumental. Whether profane music was ever common may be doubted; but sacred music was a part of early education with the sons of kings. Rama and his brothers were celebrated for the harmonious execution of episodes from the grand epic, the *Ramayuna*. The sacred canticles of Jydeva were set to music, and apparently by himself, and are yet sung by the Chobis.

Who that has marched in the stillness of night through the mountainous regions of Central India, and heard the warder sound the *tooraye* from his turreted abode, perched like an eyrie on the mountain-top, can ever forget its graduated intensity of sound, or the emphatic *hem ! hem !* 'all's well,' which follows the lengthened blast of the cornet reverberating in every recess.[1]

A species of bagpipe, so common to all the Celtic races of Europe, is not unknown to the Rajpoots. It is called the *mêshek*, but is only the rudiment of that instrument whose peculiar influence on the physical, through the moral agency of man, is described by our own master-bard. They have likewise the double flageolet ; but in the same ratio of perfection to that of Europe as the *mêshek* to the heart-stirring pipe of the north. As to their lutes, guitars, and all the varieties of tintibulants (as Dr. Johnson would call them), it would fatigue without interesting the reader to enumerate them.

We now come to the literary attainments of the lords of Rajast'han, of whom there is none without sufficient clerkship to read his grant or agreement for *rekwalee* or blackmail ; and none either so ignorant, or so proud, as the boasted ancestral wisdom of England, whose barons could not even sign their names to the great charter of their liberties. The Rana of Oodipoor has unlimited command of his pen, and his letters are admirable ; but we may say of him nearly what was remarked of Charles the Second—" he never wrote a foolish thing, and seldom did a wise one." The familiar epistolary correspondence of the princes and nobles of Rajast'han would exhibit abundant testimony of their powers of mind : they are sprinkled with classical allusions, and evince that knowledge of mankind which constant collision in society must produce. A collection of these letters, which exist in the archives of every principality, would prove that the princes of this country are upon a par with the rest of mankind, not only in natural understanding, but, taking their opportunities into account, even in its cultivation. The prince who in Europe could quote Hesiod and Homer with the freedom that the Rana does on all occasions Vyasa and Valmika, would be accounted a prodigy ; and there is not a divine who could make application of the ordinances of Moses with more facility than the Rana of those of their great lawgiver Menu. When they talk of the wisdom of their ancestors, it is not a mere figure of speech. The instruction of their princes is laid down in rules held sacred, and must have been far more onerous than any system of European university education, for scarcely a branch of human knowledge is omitted. But the cultivation of the mind, and the arts of polished life, must always flourish in the ratio of a nation's prosperity, and from the decline of the one, we may date the deterioration of the other with the Rajpoot. The astronomer has now no

The inhabitants of the various monastic establishments chant their addresses to the deity ; and I have listened with delight to the modulated cadences of the hermits, singing the praises of Pataliswara from their pinnacled abode of Aboo. It would be injustice to touch incidentally on the merits of the minstrel Dholi, who sings the warlike compositions of the sacred Bardai of Rajast'han.

[1] The *tooraye* is the sole instrument of the many of the trumpet kind which is not dissonant. The Kotah prince has the largest band, perhaps, in these countries ; instruments of all kinds—stringed, wind, and percussion. But as it is formed by rule, in which the sacred and shrill conch-shell takes precedence, it must be allowed that it is anything but harmonious.

patron to look to for reward ; there is no Jey Sing to erect such stupendous observatories as he built at Dehli, Benares, Oojein, and at his own capital ; to construct globes and armillary spheres, of which, according to their own and our system, the Kotah prince has two, each three feet in diameter. The same prince (Jey Sing) collated De la Hire's tables with those of Ulug Bég, and presented the result to the last emperor of Dehli, worthy the name of the Great Mogul. To these tables he gave the name of *Zeej Mohamed Shahé*. It was Jey Sing who, as already mentioned, sought to establish sumptuary laws throughout the nation, to regulate marriages, and thereby prevent infanticide ; and who left his name to the capital he founded, the first in Rajast'han.

But we cannot march over fifty miles of country without observing traces of the genius, talent, and wealth of past days : though—whether the more abstruse sciences, or the lighter arts which embellish life—all are now fast disappearing. Whether in the tranquillity secured to them by the destruction of their predatory foes, these arts and sciences may revive, and the nation regain its elevated tone, is a problem which time alone can solve.

In their household economy, their furniture and decorations, they remain unchanged during the lapse of a thousand years. No chairs, no couches adorn their sitting apartments, though the painted and gilded ceiling may be supported by columns of serpentine, and the walls one mass of mirrors, marble, or china ;—nothing but a soft carpet, hidden by a white cloth, on which the guests seat themselves according to rank. In fine, the quaint description of the chaplain to the first embassy which England sent to India, more than two hundred years ago, applies now, as it probably will two hundred years hence. " As for the furniture the greatest men have, it is *curta supellex*, very little ; they (the rooms) being not beautified with hangings, nor with anything besides to line their walls ; for they have no chairs, no stools, nor couches, nor tables, nor beds enclosed with canopies, nor curtains, in any of their rooms. And the truth is, that if they had them, the extreme heat would forbid the use of many of them ; all their bravery is upon their floors, on which they spread most excellent carpets." [1]

[1] Those who wish for an opinion " of the most excellent moralities which are to be observed amongst the people of these nations," cannot do better than read the 14th section of the observant, intelligent, and tolerant chaplain, who is more just, at least on one point, than the modern missionary, who denies to the Hindu filial affection. " And here I shall insert another most needful particular, which deserves a most high commendation to be given unto that people in general, how poor and mean soever they be ; and that is, the great exemplary care they manifest in their piety to their parents, that, notwithstanding they serve for very little, but five shillings a moon for their whole livelihood and subsistence, yet if their parents be in want, they will impart, at the least, half of that little towards their necessaries, choosing rather to want themselves than that their parents should suffer need." It is in fact one of the first precepts of their religion. The Chaplain thus concludes his chapter " On the Moralities of the Hindu " : " O ! what a sad thing is it for Christians to come short of Indians, even in moralities ; come short of those, who themselves believe to come short of heaven ! "

The Chaplain closes his interesting and instructive work with the subject of Conversion, which is as remote from accomplishment at this day, as it was at that distant period. " Well known it is that the Jesuits there, who, like the Pharisees that would ' compass sea and land to make one proselyte ' (Matt. xxiii. 15), have sent into Christendom many large reports of their great

It were useless to expatiate on dress, either male or female, the fashion varying in each province and tribe, though the texture and materials are everywhere the same: cotton in summer, and quilted chintz or broad-cloth in winter. The ladies have only three articles of *parure*; the *ghagra*, or 'petticoat'; the *kanchli*, or 'corset'; and the *dopati*, or 'scarf,' which is occasionally thrown over the head as a veil. Ornaments are without number. For the men, trousers of every shape and calibre, a tunic girded with a ceinture, and a scarf, form the wardrobe of every Rajpoot. The turban is the most important part of the dress, and is the unerring mark of the tribe; the form and fashion are various, and its decorations differ according to time and circumstances. The *balabund*, or 'silken fillet,' was once valued as the mark of the sovereign's favour, and was tantamount to the courtly "orders" of Europe. The colour of the turban and tunic varies with the season; and the changes are rung upon crimson, saffron, and purple, though white is by far the most common. Their shoes are mere slippers, and sandals are worn by the common classes. Boots are yet used in hunting or war, made of chamois leather, of which material the warrior often has a doublet, being more commodious, and less oppressive, than armour. The dagger or poniard is inseparable from the girdle.

The culinary art will be discussed elsewhere, together with the medical, which is very low, and usurped by empyrics, who waste alike the purse and health of the ignorant by the sale of aphrodisiacs, which are sought after with great avidity. Gums, metals, minerals, all are compounded, and for one preparation, while the author was at Oodipoor, 7000 rupees (nearly £1000) were expended by the court-physician.

Their superstitions, incantations, charms, and phylacteries against danger, mental or bodily, will appear more appropriately where the subject is incidently introduced.

conversions of infidels in East India. But all these boastings are but reports; the truth is, that they have there spilt the precious water of Baptism upon some few faces, working upon the necessity of some poor men, who for want of means, which they give them, are contented to wear crucifixes; but for want of knowledge in the doctrine of Christianity are only in name Christians." [1]

[1] "A Voyage to East India" (*Della Valle*), pp. 402, 417, 419, 480.

PERSONAL NARRATIVE OF THE AUTHOR

CHAPTER XXV

JOURNEY TO MARWAR

Valley of Oodipoor—Departure for Marwar—Encamp on the heights of Toos—Resume the march—Distant view of Oodipoor—Deopoor—Zalim Sing—Reach Pulanoh—Ram Sing Mehta—Manikchund—Ex-raja of Nursingurh—False policy pursued by the British Government in 1817–18—Departure from Pulanoh—Aspect and geological character of the country—Nat'h-dwara ridge—Arrival at the city of Nat'hdwara—Visit from the Mookhia of the temple—Departure for the village of Oosurwas—Benighted—Elephant in a bog—Oosurwas—A Sanyasi—March to Sumaicha—The Shero Nullah—Locusts—Coolness of the air—Sumaicha—March to Kailwarra, the capital—Elephant's pool—Moorcho—Kheyrlee—Mahraja Dowlut Sing—Komulmér—Its architecture, remains, and history—March to the 'Region of Death,' or Marwar—The difficult nature of the country—A party of native horsemen—Bivouac in the glen.

October 11, 1819.—Two years had nearly sped since we entered the valley of Oodipoor, the most diversified and most romantic spot on the continent of India. In all this time, none of us had penetrated beyond the rocky barrier which formed the limit of our horizon, affording the vision a sweep of six miles radius. Each hill and dale, tower and tree, had become familiar to us; every altar, cenotaph, and shrine, had furnished its legend, till tradition was exhausted. The ruins were explored, their inscriptions deciphered, each fantastic pinnacle had a name, and the most remarkable chieftains and servants of the court had epithets assigned to them, expressive of some quality or characteristic. We had our 'Red Reaver,' our 'Roderic Dhu,' and a 'Falstaff,' at the court; our 'Catalani,' our 'Vestris,' in the song or the ballet. We had our palace in the city, our cutter on the lake, our villa in the woods, our fairy-islands in the waters; streams to angle in, deer to shoot, much, in short, to please the eye and gratify the taste:—yet did *ennui* intrude, and all panted to escape from the "happy valley," to see what was in the world beyond the mountains. In all these twenty moons, the gigantic portals of Dobarri, which guard the entrance of the Gírwoh,[1] had not once creaked on their hinges for our egress; and though from incessant occupation I had where-withal to lessen the *tedium vitæ*, my companions not having such resources, it was in vain that, like the sage Imlac, I urged them not to feel dull in this "blissful captivity": the scenery had become hideous, and I verily believe had there been any pinion-maker in the capital of the Seesodias, they would have essayed a flight, though it might have terminated in the lake. Never did Rasselas sigh more for escape. At length the day arrived,

[1] The amphitheatre, or *circle*.

and although the change was to be from all that constitutes the enchantments of vision, from wood and water, dale and mountain, verdure and foliage, to the sterile plains of the sandy desert of Marwar, it was sufficient that it was *change*. Our party was composed of Captain Waugh, Lieutenant Carey, and Dr. Duncan, with the whole of the escort, consisting of two companies of foot and sixty of Skinner's Horse, all alike delighted to quit the valley where each had suffered more or less from the prevalent fevers of the monsoon, during which the valley is peculiarly unhealthy, especially to foreigners, when the wells and reservoirs overflow from the springs which break in, impregnated with putrid vegetation and mineral poisons, covering the surface with a bluish oily fluid. The art of filtrating water to free it from impurities is unknown to the Rajpoots, and with some shame I record that we did not make them wiser, though they are not strangers to the more simple process, adopted throughout the desert, of using potash and alum; the former to neutralise the salt and render the water more fit for culinary purposes; the latter to throw down the impurities held suspended. They also use an alkaline nut in washing, which by simply steeping emits a froth which is a good substitute for soap.[1]

On the 12th *October*, at five a.m. our trumpet sounded to horse, and we were not slow in obeying the summons; the "yellow boys" with their old native commandant looking even more cheerful than usual as we joined them. Skinner's Horse wear a jamah or tunic of yellow broadcloth, with scarlet turbans and cincture. Who does not know that James Skinner's men are the most orderly in the Company's service, and that in every other qualification constituting the efficient soldier, they are second to none? On another signal which reverberated from the palace, where the drums announced that the descendant of Surya was no sluggard, we moved on through the yet silent capital towards the gate of the sun, where we found drawn up the quotas of Bheendir, Dailwarra, Amait, and Bansi, sent as an honorary guard by the Rana, to escort us to the frontiers. As they would have been an incumbrance to me and an inconvenience to the country, from their laxity of discipline, after chatting with their leader, during a sociable ride, I dismissed them at the pass, with my respects to the Rana and their several chieftains. We reached the camp before eight o'clock, the distance being only thirteen miles. The spot chosen (and where I afterwards built a residence) was a rising ground between the villages of Mairta and Toos, sprinkled with trees, and for a space of four miles clear of the belt of forest which fringes the granite barriers of the valley. It commanded an entire view of the plains in the direction of Cheetore, still covered, excepting a patch of cultivation here and there, with jungle. The tiger-mount, its preserves of game, and the smouldering hunting-seats of the Rana and his chieftains, were three miles to the north; to the south, a mile distant, we had the Béris River, abounding in trout; and the noble lake whence it issues, called after its founder the Oody Sagur, was not more than three to the west. For several reasons it was deemed advisable to choose a spot out of the valley; the health of the party, though not an unimportant, was not a principal motive for choosing such a distance from the court. The wretchedness in which we found it rendered a certain degree of interference requisite, and it was necessary that they should shake this off, in order to preserve their independence. It was dreaded

[1] *Sabon*, in the *lingua franca* of India, signifies 'soap.'

lest the aid requested by the Rana, from the peculiar circumstances on our first going amongst them, might be construed as a precedent for the intrusion of advice on after occasions. The distance between the court and the agent of the British Government was calculated to diminish this impression, and obliged them also to trust to their own resources, after the machine was once set in motion. On the heights of Toos our tents were pitched, the escort paraded, and St. George's flag displayed. Here camels, almost wild, were fitted for the first time with the pack-saddle, lamenting in discordant gutturals the hardship of their fate, though luckily ignorant of the difference between grazing whither they listed in the happy valley, and carrying a load in " the region of death," where they would only find the thorny *mimosa* or prickly *phok* to satisfy their hunger.

PULANOH, *October* 13.—There being no greater trial of patience, than the preparations for a march after a long halt, we left the camp at daybreak amidst the most discordant yells from the throats of a hundred camels, which drowned every attempt to be heard, while the elephants squeaked their delight in that peculiar treble which they emit when happy. There was one little fellow enjoying himself free from all restraints of curbs or pack-saddles, and inserting his proboscis into the sepoy's baggage, whence he would extract a bag of flour, and move off, pursued by the owner; which was sure to produce shouts of mirth to add to the discord. This little representative of Ganésa was only eight years old, and not more than twelve hands high. He was a most agreeable pet, though the proofs he gave of his wisdom in trusting himself amidst the men when cooking their dinners, were sometimes disagreeable to them, but infinitely amusing to those who watched his actions. The rains having broken up unusually late, we found the boggy ground, on which we had to march, totally unable to bear the pressure of loaded cattle; even the ridges, which just showed their crests of quartz above the surface, were not safe. Our route was over a fine plain well wooded and watered, soil excellent, and studded with numerous large villages; yet all presenting uniformly the effects of warfare and rapine. The landscape, rendered the more interesting by our long incarceration in the valley, was abstractedly pleasing. On our left lay the mountains enclosing the capital, on one of whose elevated peaks are the ruins of Ratakote, overlooking all around; while to the east the eye might in vain seek for a boundary. We passed Deopoor, once a township of some consequence, and forming part of the domain of the *Bhanaij*,[1] Zalim Sing, the heir of Marwar, whose history, if it could be given here, would redeem the nobles of Rajpootana from the charge of being of uncultivated intellect. In listening to his biography, both time and place were unheeded; the narrator, my own venerable *Gúrú*,[2] had imbibed much of his varied knowledge from this accomplished chieftain, to whom arms and letters were alike familiar. He was the son of Raja Beejy Sing and a princess of Méwar: but domestic quarrels made it necessary to abandon the paternal for the maternal mansion, and a domain was assigned by the Rana, which put him on a footing with his own children. Without neglect-

[1] *Bhanaij*, or 'nephew,' a title of courtesy enjoyed by every chieftain who marries a daughter or immediate kinswoman of the Rana's house.

[2] My guide or instructor, Yati Gyan Chandra, a priest of the Jain sect, who had been with me ten years. To him I owe much, for he entered into all my antiquarian pursuits with zeal.

ing any of the martial amusements and exercises of the Rajpóot, he gave up all those hours, generally devoted to idleness, to the cultivation of letters. He was versed in philosophical theology, astronomy, and the history of his country; and in every branch of poesy, from the sacred canticles of Jydéva to the couplets of the modern bard, he was an adept. He composed and *improvised* with facility, and his residence was the rendezvous for every bard of fame. That my respected tutor did not over-rate his acquirements, I had the best proof in his own, for all which (and he rated them at an immeasurable distance compared with the subject of his eulogy) he held himself indebted to the heir of Marwar, who was at length slain in asserting his right to the throne in the desert.

After a four hours' march, picking our way amidst swamps and treacherous bogs, we reached the advanced tents at Pulanoh. Like Deopoor, it presented the spectacle of a ruin, a corner of which held all its inhabitants; the remains of temples and private edifices showed what it had once been. Both towns formerly belonged to the fisc of the Rana, who, with his usual improvidence, on the death of his nephew included them in the grant to the temple of Kaniya. I found at my tents the minister's right hand, Ram Sing Mehta; Manikchund, the *dewan* or *factotum* of the chieftain of Bheendir; and the ex-Raja of Nursingurh, now an exile at Oodipoor, The first was a fine specimen of the non-militant class of these countries, and although he had seldom passed the boundaries of Méwar, no country could produce a better specimen of a courteous gentleman: his figure tall, deportment easy, features regular and handsome, complexion fair, with a fine slightly-curled beard and mustachios jet black. Ram Sing, without being conceited, is aware that nature has been indulgent to him, and without any foppery he pays great attention to externals. He is always elegantly attired, and varies with good taste the colours of his turban and ceinture, though his loose tunics are always white; the aroma of the *uttur* is the only mark of the dandy about him: and this forms no criterion, as our red coats attest, which receive a sprinkling at every visit. With his dagger and pendant tassel, and the *balabund* or purple cordon (the Rana's gift) round his turban, behold the servant "whom the king delighteth to honour." As he has to support himself by paying court to the Rana's sister, the queens, and other fair influentials behind the curtain, his personal *attraits* are no slight auxiliaries. He is of the Jain faith, and of the tribe of Osi, which now reckons one hundred thousand families, all of Rajpoot origin, and descendants of the Agnicúla stock. They proselytised in remote antiquity, and settling at the town of Osi in Marwar, retain this designation, or the still more common one of Oswal. It was from the Pramara and Solanki branches of the Agnicúla race that these assumed the doctrines of Budha or Jaina: not however from the ranks of the Brahmins, but, as I firmly believe, from that faith, whatever it was, which these Scythic or Takshac tribes brought from beyond the Indus. In like manner we found the Chohan (also an Agnicúla) regenerated by the Brahmins on Mount Aboo; while the fourth tribe, the Purihara (ancient sovereigns of Cashmere), have left traces in the monuments of their capital, Mundore, that they espoused the then prevailing faith of Rajast'han, namely, that of Budha.

Manikchund, also of the Jain faith, but of a different tribe (the Sambri), was in all the reverse of Ram Sing. He was tall, thin, rather bent, and of swarthy complexion, and his tongue and his beads were in perpetual motion. He had mixed in all the intrigues of the last quarter of a century, and, setting Zalim Sing of Kotah aside, had more influenced events than any individual now alive. He was the organ of the Suktawuts, and the steward and counsellor of the head of this clan, the Bheendir chief; and being accordingly the irreconcilable foe of the Chondawuts, had employed all the resources of his talents and his credit to effect their humiliation. To this end, he has leagued with Sindies, Pat'hans, and Mahrattas, and would not have scrupled to coalesce with his Satanic majesty, could he thereby have advanced their revenge: in pursuance of which he has been detained in confinement as a hostage, put to torture from inability to furnish the funds he would unhesitatingly promise for aid, and all the while sure of death if he fell into the hands of his political antagonists. His talent and general information made him always a welcome guest: which was wormwood to the Chondawuts, who laid claim to a monopoly of patriotism, and stigmatised the Suktawuts as the destroyers of Méwar, though in truth both were equally blind to her interests in their contests for supremacy. He was now beyond fifty, and appeared much older; but was cheerful, good-humoured, and conversant in all the varied occurrences of the times. He at length completely established himself in the Rana's good graces, who gave his elder son a confidential employment. Had he lived, he would have been conspicuous, for he had all the talent of his father, with the personal adjuncts possessed by Ram Sing; but being sensitive and proud, he swallowed poison, in consequence it was said of the severity of an undeserved rebuke from his father, and died generally regretted. I may here relate the end of poor Manika. It was on the ground we had just quitted that he visited me for the last time, on my return from the journey just commenced. He had obtained the contract for the whole transit duties of the state, at the rate of 250,000 rupees per annum. Whether from the corruption of his numerous deputy collectors, his own cupidity, or negligence, he professed his inability to fulfil the contract by nearly a sixth of the amount, though from his talents and promises, a perfect establishment of this important department, which had been taken from others on his account, was expected. It was difficult to judge charitably of his assertions, without giving occasion to his enemies to put a wrong construction on the motives. He pitched his tent near me, and requested an interview. He looked very disconsolate, and remarked, that he had seven several times left his tent, and as often turned back, the bird of omen having each time passed him on the adverse side; but that at length he had determined to disregard it, as having forfeited confidence, he was indifferent to the future. He admitted the profligacy of his inferiors, whom he had not sufficiently superintended, and took his leave, promising by assiduity to redeem his engagements, though his past character for intrigue made his asseverations doubtful. Again failing to make good his promises, or, as was surmised, having applied the funds to his own estate, he took *sirna* with the Raja of Shahpoora; where, mortified in all probability by the reflection of the exultation of his rivals over his disgrace, and having lost the confidence of his own chief when he obtained that of the Rana, he had recourse to the usual expedient of these countries when " perplexed in the extreme," —took poison and died.

The last of the trio of visitors on this occasion, the Raja of Nursingurh, is now, as before stated, in exile. He is of the tribe of Omúta, one of thirty-six divisions of the Pramaras,[1] settled during fifteen generations in Central India, and giving the name of Omutwarra to the petty sovereignty of which Nursingurh is the capital. Placed in the very heart of the predatory hordes, the Pindarries and Mahrattas occupied almost every village that owned their sway, and compelled him to the degradation of living under Holkar's orange standard, which waved over the battlements of his abode. To one or other of the great Mahratta leaders, Sindia and Holkar, all the petty princes were made tributary dependents, and Omutwarra had early acknowledged Holkar, paying the annual sum of eighty thousand rupees : but this vassalage did not secure the Raja from the ravages of the other spoliators, nor from the rapacity of the myrmidons of his immediate lord paramount. In 1817, when these countries, for the first time in many centuries, tasted the blessings of peace, Omutwarra was, like Méwar, a mass of ruins, its fertile lands being overgrown with the thorny *mimosa* or the useful *kesoola*. The Raja partook of the demoralisation around him ; he sought refuge in opium and *urruc* from his miseries, and was totally unfitted to aid in the work of redemption when happier days shone upon them. His son Chyne Sing contrived to escape these snares, and was found in every respect competent to co-operate in the work of renovation, and through the intervention of the British agent (Major Henley), an arrangement was effected by which the Raja retired on a stipend and the son carried on the duties of government in his name.

It was unfortunate for these ancient races, that on the fortunate occasion presented in 1817–18, when both Sindia and Holkar aimed at the overthrow of our power (the one treacherously cloaking his views, the other disclosing them in the field), our policy did not readily grasp it, to rescue all these states from ruin and dependence. Unfortunately, their peculiar history was little known, or it would have been easily perceived that they presented the exact materials we required between us, and the entire occupation of the country. But there was then a strong notion afloat of a species of balance of power, and it was imagined that these demoralised, and often humiliated Mahrattas, were the fittest materials to throw into the scale—against I know not what, except ourselves : for assuredly the day of our reverses will be a jubilee to them, and will level every spear that they can bring against our existence. They would merit contempt if they acted otherwise. Can they cease to remember that the orange flag which waved in triumph from the Sutledge to the Kistna, has been replaced by the cross of St. George ? But the snake which flutters in tortuous folds thereon, fitting crest for the wily Mahratta, is only scathed, and may yet call forth the lance of the red cross knight to give the *coup de grace.*[2] Let it then be remembered that, both as regards good policy and justice, we owe to these states—independence.

To what does our interference with Omutwarra tend, but to realise the tribute of Holkar ; to fix a millstone round their necks, which, notwithstanding the comparative happiness they enjoy, will keep them always repining, and to secure which will make our interference eternal. Had

[1] One of the four Agnicúlas.

[2] Sindia's flag is a snake *argent* on an *orange* field.

a due advantage been taken of the hostilities in 1817, it might have obviated these evils by sending the predatory sovereign of half a century's duration to a more restricted sphere. It may be said that it is easy to devise plans years after the events which immediately called for them: these not only were mine at the time, but were suggested to the proper authorities; and I am still disposed to think my views correct.

After chatting some time with the two chiefs described, and presenting them with *uttr* and *pán*,[1] they took leave.

NAT'HDWARA—*October* 14.—Marched at day-break, and found the route almost impracticable for camels, from the swampy nature of the soil. The country is much broken with irregular low ridges of micaceous schist, in the shape of a chine or hog's back, the crest of which has throughout all its length a vein of quartz piercing the slate, and resembling a back-bone; the direction of these veins is uniformly N.N.E., and the inclination about 75° to the east. Crossed the Nat'hdwara ridge, about four hundred feet in height, and, like the hills encircling the valley, composed of a brown granite intersected with protruding veins of quartz, incumbent on blue compact slate. The ascent was a mile and a half east of the town, and on the summit, which is table-land, there are two small lakes, whence water-courses conduct streams on each side of the road to supply the temple and the town. There are noble trees planted on either side of these rivulets, forming a delightful shade. As we passed through the town to our encampment on the opposite side of the Bunas River, the inhabitants crowded the streets, shouting their grateful acknowledgments to the power which had redeemed the sacred precincts of Kaniya from the scenes of turpitude amidst which they had grown up. They were all looking forward with much pleasure to the approaching festival of Anacúta.

October 15.—Halted to allow the baggage to join, which, partly from the swamps and partly from the intractable temper of the cattle, we have not seen since we parted company at Mairta. Received a visit from the mookhia of the temple, accompanied by a pilgrim in the person of a rich banker of Surat. A splendid quilted cloak of gold brocade, a blue scarf with a deep border of gold, and an embroidered band for the head, were brought to me as the gift of the god through his high-priest, in testimony of my zeal. I was also honoured with a tray of the sacred food, which consisted of all the dried fruits, spices, and aromatics of the East. In the evening I had a portion of the afternoon repast, consisting of a preparation of milk; but the days of simplicity are gone, and the Apollo of Vrij has his curds adultered with rose-water and amber. Perhaps, with the exception of Lodi, where is fabricated the far-famed *Parmasan*, whose pastures maintain forty thousand kine, there is no other place known which possesses more than the city of the Hindu Apollo, though but a tenth of that of Lodi. But from the four thousand cows, the expenditure of milk and butter for the votaries of Kaniya may be judged. I was entertained with the opinions of the old banker on the miraculous and oracular power

[1] *Pán*, 'the leaf'; *pan* and *pat*, the Sanscrit for 'a leaf'; and hence *panna*, 'a leaf or sheet of paper'; and *patera* 'a plate of metal or sacrificial cup,' because these vessels were first made of leaves. I was amused with the coincidence between the Sanscrit and Tuscan *panna*. That lovely subject by Raphael, the "Madonna impannata," in the Pitti palace at Florence, is so called from the subdued light admitted through the window, the *panes* of which are of *paper*.

of the god of Nat'hdwara. He had just been permitted to prostrate himself before the car which conveyed the deity from the Yamuna, and held forth on the impiety of the age, in withholding the transmission of the miraculous wheels from heaven, which in former days came once in six months. The most devout alone are permitted to worship the chariot of Kaniya. The garments which decorate his representative are changed several times a day, to imitate the different stages of his existence, from the youthful Bala to the conqueror of Kansa; or, as the Surat devotee said in broken English, "Oh, sir, he be much great god; he first of all; and he change from de baluk, or child, to de fierce chief, with de bow and arrow a hees hands;" while the old mookhia, whose office it is to perambulate the whole continent of India as one of the couriers of Kaniya, lifted up his eyes as he ejaculated, "Sri Kishna! Sri Kishna!" I gave him a paper addressed to all officers of the British Government who might pass through the lands of the church, recommending the protection of the peacocks and peepul trees, and to forbear polluting the precincts of the god with the blood of animals. To avoid offending against their prejudices in this particular, I crossed the river, and killed our fowls within our own sanctuary, and afterwards concealed the murder by burying the feathers.

OOSURWAS—*October* 16.—There is nothing so painful as sitting down inactive when the mind is bent upon an object. Our escort was yet labouring in the swamps, and as we could not be worse off than we were, we deemed it better to advance, and accordingly decamped in the afternoon, sending on a tent to Oosurwas; but though the distance was only eight miles we were benighted, and had the comfort to find old Futteh, *the victorious*, floundering with his load in a bog, out of which he was picking his way in a desperate rage. It is generally the driver's fault when such an accident occurs: for if there be but a foot's breadth of sound footing, so sensible is the animal, that he is sure to avoid danger if left to his own discretion and the free use of his proboscis, with which he thumps the ground as he cautiously proceeds step by step, giving signals to his keeper of the safety or the reverse of advancing, as clearly as if he spoke. Futteh's signals had been disregarded, and he was accordingly in a great passion at finding himself abused, and kept from his cakes and butter, of which he had always thirty pounds' weight at sunset. The sagacity of the elephant is well known, and was in no instance better displayed than in the predicament above described. I have seen the huge monster in a position which to him must have been appalling; but, with an instinctive reliance on others, he awaited in tolerable patience the arrival of materials for his extrication, in the shape of fascines and logs of wood, which being thrown to him, he placed deliberately in front, and making a stout resistance with head, teeth, and foot, pressing the wood, he brought up one leg after the other in a most methodical and pioneer-like manner, till he delivered himself from his miry prison. Futteh did not require such aid; but, aware that the fault was not his, he soon indignantly shook the load off his back, and left them to get it out in any manner they chose.

Waited to aid in reloading, and it being already dusk, pushed on with my dog Belle, who, observing a couple of animals, darted off into the jungles, and led me after her as fast as the devious paths in such a savage scene would permit. But I soon saw her scampering down the height, the game, in the shape of two huge wolves, close at her heels, and delighted to find rescue at hand. I have no doubt their retreat from my favourite greyhound was a mere *ruse de guerre* to lead her beyond supporting distance, and they had nearly effected their object: they went off in a very sulky and leisurely manner. In my subaltern days, when with the subsidiary force in Gohud, I remember scouring the tremendous ravines near the Antri pass to get a spear at a wolf, my companion (Lieut. now Lieut.-Col. T. D. Smith) and myself were soon surrounded by many scores of these hungry animals, who prowled about our camp all night, having carried off a child the night before. As we charged in one direction, they gave way; but kept upon our quarters without the least fear, and seemingly enjoyed the fun. I do not recollect whether it excited any other feeling than mirth. They showed no symptom of ferocity, or desire to make a meal of us; or a retreat from these ravines, with their superior topographical knowledge, would doubtless have been difficult.

We passed the Bunas river, just escaping from the rock-bound barriers, our path almost in contact with the water to the left. The stream was clear as crystal, and of great depth; the banks low and verdant, and fringed with wood. It was a lovely, lonely spot, and well deserved to be consecrated by legendary tale. In ancient times, ere these valleys were trod by the infidel Tatar, coco-nuts were here presented to the genius of the river, whose arm appeared above the waters to receive them; but ever since some unhallowed hand threw a stone in lieu of a coco-nut, the arm has been withdrawn. Few in fact lived, either to supply or keep alive the traditions which lend a charm to a journey through these wild scenes, though full of bogs and wolves. We reached our journey's end very late, and though no tents were up, we had the consolation to spy the cook in a snug corner with a leg of mutton before some blazing logs, round which he had placed the wall of a tent to check the force of the mountain air. We all congregated round the cook's fire, and were infinitely happier in the prospect before us, and with the heavens for our canopy, than with all our accustomed conveniences and fare. Every one this day had taken his own road, and each had his adventure to relate. Our repast was delicious; nor did any favourable account reach us of tents or other luxuries to mar our enjoyments, till midnight, when the fly of the doctor's tent arrived, of which we availed ourselves as a protection against the heavy dews of the night; and though our bivouac was in a ploughed field, and we were surrounded by wild beasts in a silent waste, they proved no drawbacks to the enjoyment of repose.

Halted the 17th, to collect the dislocated baggage; for although such scenes, seasoned with romance, might do very well for *us*, our followers were ignorant of the name of Ann Radcliffe or other conjurers; and though admirers of tradition, like myself, preferred it after dinner. Oosurwas is a valuable village, but now thinly inhabited. It was recently given by the Rana, with his accustomed want of reflection, to a Charun bard, literally for an old song. But even this folly was surpassed on his bestowing the township of Seesodia, in the valley in advance, the place from which his tribe takes its appellation, on another of the fraternity, named Kishna, his master bard, who has the art to make his royal patron believe that opportunity alone is wanting to render his name as famed as that of the illustrious Sanga, or the immortal Pertáp. I received and returned the visit of an ascetic Sanyasi, whose hermitage was perched upon a cliff not far from our tents. Like most of his brethren, he was intelligent, and had a considerable store of local and foreign legends at command. He was dressed in a loose orange-coloured unga or tunic, with a turban of the same material, in which was twisted a necklace of the lotos-kernel; he had another in his hand, with which he repeated the name of the deity at intervals. He expressed his own surprise and the sentiments of the inhabitants at the tranquillity they enjoyed, without any tumultuary cause being discoverable; and said that we must be something more than human. This superstitious feeling for a while was felt as well by the prince and the turbulent chief, as by the anchorite of Oosurwas.

October 18.—Marched at daybreak to Sumaicha, distance twelve miles. Again found our advanced elephant and breakfast-tent in a swamp: halted to extricate him from his difficulties. The road from Nat'hdwara is but a footpath, over or skirting a succession of low broken ridges, covered with prickly shrubs, as the Khyr, the Khureel, and Babool. At the village of Gong Goorah, midway in the morning's journey, we entered the alpine valley called the Shero Nullah. The village of Goorah is placed in the opening or break in the range through which the river flows, whose serpentine meanderings indicate the only road up this majestic valley. On the banks, or in its bed, which we frequently crossed, lay the remainder of this day's march. The valley varies in breadth, but is seldom less than half a mile, the hills riding boldly from their base; some with a fine and even surface covered with mango trees, others lifting their splintered pinnacles into the clouds. Nature has been lavish of her beauties to this romantic region. The *goolur* or wild fig, the *sitaphal* or custard-apple, the peach or *aroo bódám* (almond-peach), are indigenous and abundant; the banks of the stream are shaded by the withy, while the large trees, the useful mango and picturesque tamarind, the sacred peepul and burr, are abundantly scattered with many others, throughout. Nor has nature in vain appealed to human industry and ingenuity to second her intents. From the margin of the stream on each side to the mountain's base, they have constructed a series of terraces rising over each other, whence by simple and ingenious methods they raise the waters to irrigate the rich crops of sugar-cane, cotton, and rice, which they cultivate upon them. Here we have a proof that ingenuity is the same, when prompted by necessity, in the Jura or the Aravulli. Wherever soil could be found, or time decomposed these primitive rocks, a barrier was raised. When discovered, should it be in a hollow below, or on the summit of a crag, it is alike greedily seized on: even there water is found, and if you leave the path below and ascend a hundred feet above the terraces, you will discover pools or reservoirs dammed in with massive trees, which serve to irrigate such insulated spots, or serve as nurseries to the young rice-plants. Not unfrequently, their labour is entirely destroyed, and the dykes swept away by the periodical inundations; for we observed the high-water mark in the trees considerably up the acclivity. The rice crop was abundant, and the *joar* or maize was thriving, but scanty; the standard autumnal crop which preceded it, the *makhi*, or 'Indian corn,' had been entirely devoured by the locust. The sugar-cane, by far the most valuable product of this curious region, was very fine but sparingly cultivated, from the dread of this insect, which for the last three years had ravaged the valley. There are two species of locusts, which come in clouds, darkening the air, from the desert: the *farka* and the *teeri* are their names; the first is the great enemy of our incipient prosperity. I observed a colony some time ago proceeding eastward with a rustling, rushing sound, like a distant torrent, or the wind in a forest at the fall of the leaf. We have thus to struggle against natural and artificial obstacles to the rising energies of the country; and dread of the *farkas* deters speculators from renting this fertile tract, which almost entirely belongs to the fisc. Its natural fertility cannot be better demonstrated than in recording the success of an experiment, which produced *five crops, from the same piece of ground, within thirteen months.* It must, however, be understood that two of these are species of millet, which are cut in six weeks from the time of sowing. A patch of ground, for which the cultivator pays six rupees rent, will produce sugar-cane six hundred rupees in value: but the labour and expense of cultivation are heavy, and cupidity too often deprives the husbandman of the greater share of the fruits, ninety rupees having been taken in arbitrary taxes, besides his original rent.

The air of this elevated region gave vigour to the limbs, and appetite to the disordered stomach. There was an exhilarating *fraicheur*, which made us quite frantic; the transition being from 96° of Fahrenheit to English summer heat. We breakfasted in a verdant spot under the shade of a noble fig-tree fanned by the cool breezes from the mountains.

SUMAICHA consists of three separate hamlets, each of about one hundred houses. It is situated at the base of a mountain distinctively termed *Rana Paj*, from a well-known path, by which the Ranas secured their retreat to the upland wilds when hard pushed by the Moguls. It also leads direct to the capital of the district, avoiding the circuitous route we were pursuing. Sumaicha is occupied by the Koombhawuts, descendants of Rana Koombho, who came in a body with their elders at their head to visit me, bringing the famed *cukri* of the valley (often three feet in length), curds, and a kid as gifts. I rose to receive these Rajapútras, the Bhomias or yeomen of the valley; and though undistinguishable in dress from the commonest cultivator, I did homage to their descent. Indeed, they did not require the auxiliaries of dress, their appearance being so striking as to draw forth the spontaneous exclamation from my friends, "what noble-looking fellows!" Their tall and robust figures, sharp aquiline features, and flowing beards, with a native dignity of demeanour (though excepting their chiefs, who wore turbans and scarfs, they were in their usual labouring dresses, immense loose breeches and turbans), compelled respect and admiration. Formerly they gave one hundred matchlocks for garrison duty at Komulmér; but the Mahrattas have pillaged and impoverished them. These are the real allodial tenants of the land, performing personal local service, and paying an annual quit-rent. I conciliated their good opinion by talking of the deeds of old days, the recollection of which a Rajpoot never outlives. The assembly under the fig-tree was truly picturesque, and would have furnished a good subject for Gerard Dow. Our baggage joined us at Sumaicha; but many of our camels were already worn out by labouring through swamps, for which they are by nature incapacitated.

October 19.—Marched to Kailwarra, the capital of this mountainous region, and the abode of the Ranas when driven from Cheetore and the plains of the Bunas; on which occasion these valleys received and maintained a great portion of the population of Méwar. There is not a rock or a stream that has not some legend attached to it, connected with these times. The valley presents the same features as already described. Passed a cleft in the mountain on the left, through which a stream rushes, called the "elephant's pool"; a short cut may be made by the foot passenger to Kailwarra, but it is too intricate for any unaccustomed to these wilds to venture. We could not ascertain the origin of the "elephant's pool," but it is most likely connected with ancient warfare. Passed the village of Moorcho, held by a Rahtore chieftain. On the margin of a small lake adjoining the village, a small and very neat sacrificial altar attracted my regard; and not satisfied with the reply that it was *sutti ca macan*, 'the place of faith,' I sent to request the attendance of the village seer. It proved to be that of the ancestor of the occupant: a proof of devotion to her husband, who had fallen in the wars waged by Arungzéb against this country; when, with a relic of her lord, she mounted the pyre. He is sculptured on horseback, with lance at rest, to denote that it is no churl to whom the record is devoted.

Near the "elephant's pool," and at the village of Kheyrlee, two roads diverge: one, by the Birgoola *nal* or pass, conducts direct to Nat'hdwara; the other, leading to Reechair, and the celebrated shrine of the *four-armed god*, famed as a place of pilgrimage. The range on our left terminating abruptly, we turned by Oladur to Kailwarra, and encamped in a mango-grove, on a table-land half a mile north of the town. Here the valley enlarges, presenting a wild, picturesque, and rugged appearance. The barometer indicated about a thousand feet of elevation above the level of Oodipoor, which is about two thousand above the sea: yet we were scarcely above the base of the alpine cliffs which towered around us on all sides. It was the point of divergence for the waters, which, from the numerous fountains in these uplands, descended each declivity, to refresh the arid plains of Marwar to the west, and to swell the lakes of Méwar to the east. Previous to the damming of the stream which forms that little ocean, the Kunkerowli lake, it is asserted that the supply to the west was very scanty, nearly all flowing eastward, or through the valley; but since the formation of the lake, and consequent saturation of the intermediate region, the streams are ever flowing to the west. The spot where I encamped was at least five hundred feet lower than *Arait pol*, the first of the fortified barriers leading to Komulmér, whose citadel rose more than seven hundred feet above the *terre-pleine* of its outworks beneath.

The Mahraja Dowlut Sing, a near relative of the Rana, and governor of Komulmér, attended by a numerous suite, the crimson standard, trumpets, kettledrums, seneschal, and bard, advanced several miles to meet and conduct me to the castle. According to etiquette, we both dismounted and embraced, and afterwards rode together conversing on the affairs of the province, and the generally altered condition of the country. Dowlut Sing, being of the immediate kin of his sovereign, is one of the *babas* or infants of Méwar, enumerated in the tribe called Ranawut, with the title of Mahraja. Setting aside the family of Sheodan Sing, he is the next in succession to the reigning family. He is one of the few over whom the general demoralisation has had no power, and remains a simple-minded straight-forward honest man ; blunt, unassuming, and courteous. His rank and character particularly qualify him for the post he holds on this western frontier, which is the key to Marwar. It was in February 1818 that I obtained possession of this place (Komulmér), by negotiating the arrears of the garrison. Gold is the cheapest, surest and most expeditious of all generals in the East, amongst such mercenaries as we had to deal with, who change masters with the same facility as they would their turban. In twenty-four hours we were put in possession of the fort, and as we had not above one-third of the stipulated sum in ready cash, they without hesitation took a bill of exchange, *written on the drum-head*, on the mercantile town of Palli in Marwar : in such estimation is British faith held, even by the most lawless tribes of India ! Next morning we saw them winding down the western declivity, while we quietly took our breakfast in an old ruined temple. During this agreeable employment, we were joined by Major Macleod, of the artillery, sent by General Donkin to report on the facilities of reducing the place by siege, and his opinion being, that a gun could not be placed in position in less than six weeks, the grilling spared the European force in such a region was well worth the £4000 of arrears. My own escort and party remained in possession for a week, until the Rana sent his garrison. During these eight days our time was amply occupied in sketching and decyphering the monumental records of this singularly diversified spot. It would be vain to attempt describing the intricacies of approach to this far-famed abode. A massive wall, with numerous towers and pierced battlements, having a strong resemblance to the Etruscan, encloses a space of some miles extent below, while the pinnacle or *sikra* rises, like the crown of the Hindu Cybele, tier above tier of battlements, to the summit, which is crowned with the *Badul Mahl*, or 'cloud-palace' of the Ranas. Thence the eye ranges over the sandy deserts and the chaotic mass of mountains, which are on all sides covered with the *cactus*, which luxuriates amidst the rocks of the Aravulli. Besides the *Arait pol*, or barrier thrown across the first narrow ascent, about one mile from Kailwarra, there is a second called the *Hulla pol*, intermediate to the *Hanuman pol*, the exterior gate of the fortress, between which and the summit there are three more, viz. the gate of victory, the sanguinary gate, and that of Rama, besides the last, or *Chougun pol*. The barometer stood, at half-past seven A.M., 26° 65′; thermometer 58° Fahr. at the *Arait pol* : and on the summit at nine, while the thermometer rose to 75°, the barometer had only descended 15′, and stood at 26° 50′,[1] though we had ascended full six hundred feet. Admitting the last range as our guide, the peak of Komulmér will be 3,353 feet above the level of the ocean. Hence I laid down the positions of many towns far in the desert. Here were subjects to occupy the pencil at least for a month ; but we had only time for one of the most interesting views, a Jain temple, and a sketch of the fortress itself, both finished on the spot. The design of this temple is truly classic. It consists only of the sanctuary, which has a vaulted dome and colonnaded portico all round. The architecture is undoubtedly Jain, which is as distinct in character from the Brahminical as their religion. There is a chasteness and simplicity in this specimen of monotheistic worship, affording a wide contrast to

[1] At four o'clock P.M., same position, thermometer 81° ; barometer, 26° 85′.

the elaborately sculptured shrines of the Saivas, and other polytheists of India. The extreme want of decoration best attests its antiquity, entitling us to attribute it to that period when Sumpriti Raja, of the family of Chandragupta, was paramount sovereign over all these regions (two hundred years before Christ); to whom tradition ascribes the most ancient monuments of this faith, yet existing in Rajast'han and Saurashtia. The proportions and forms of the columns are especially distinct from the other temples, being slight and tapering instead of massive, the general characteristic of Hindu architecture; while the projecting cornices, which would absolutely deform shafts less slight, are peculiarly indicative of the *Takshac* architect.[1] Sumpriti was the fourth prince in descent from Chandragupta, of the Jain faith, and the ally of Seleucus, the Grecian sovereign of Bactriana. The fragments of Megasthenes, ambassador from Seleucus, record that this alliance was most intimate; that the daughter of the Rajpoot king was married to Seleucus, who, in return for elephants and other gifts, sent a body of Greek soldiers to serve Chandragupta. It is curious to contemplate the possibility, nay the probability, that the Jain temple now before the reader may have been designed by Grecian artists, or that the taste of the artists among the Rajpoots may have been modelled after the Grecian. This was our temple of Theseus in Méwar. A massive monolithic emblem of black marble of the Hindu Jivápitri, had been improperly introduced into the shrine of the worshippers of the "spirit alone." Being erected on the rock, and chiselled from the syenite on which it stands, it may bid defiance to time. There was another sacred structure in its vicinity, likewise Jain, but of a distinct character; indeed, offering a perfect contrast to that described. It was three stories in height; each tier was decorated with numerous massive low columns, resting on a sculptured panelled parapet, and sustaining the roof of each story, which being very low, admitted but a broken light to break the pervading gloom. I should imagine that the sacred architects of the East had studied effect equally with the preservers of learning and the arts in the dark period of Europe, when those monuments, which must ever be her pride, arose on the ruins of paganism. How far the Saxon or Scandinavian pagan contributed to the general design of such structures may be doubted; but that their decorations, especially the grotesque, have a powerful resemblance to the most ancient Hindu-Scythic, there is no question, as I shall hereafter more particularly point out.

Who, that has a spark of imagination, but has felt the indescribable emotion which the gloom and silence of a Gothic cathedral excites? The very extent provokes a comparison humiliating to the pigmy spectator, and this is immeasurably increased when the site is the mountain pinnacle, where man and his works fade into nothing in contemplating the magnificent expanse of nature. The Hindu priest did not raise the temple for heterogeneous multitudes: he calculated that the mind would be more highly excited when left to its solitary devotions, amidst the silence of these cloistered columns, undisturbed save by the monotony of the passing bell, while the surrounding gloom is broken only by the flare of the censer as the incense mounts above the altar.

It would present no distinct picture to the eye were I to describe each individual edifice within the scope of vision, either upwards towards

[1] See note [3] in p. 26; and also note in p. 276.

the citadel, or below. Looking down from the Jain temple towards the pass, till the contracting gorge is lost in distance, the gradually diminishing space is filled with masses of ruin. I will only notice two of the most interesting. The first is dedicated to *Mama Devi* 'the mother cf the gods,' whose shrine is on the brow of the mountain overlooking the pass. The goddess is placed in the midst of her numerous family, including the greater and lesser divinities. They are all of the purest marble, each about three feet in height, and tolerably executed, though evidently since the decline of the art, of which very few good specimens exist executed within the last seven centuries. The temple is very simple and primitive, consisting but of a long hall, around which the gods are ranged, without either niche or altar.

The most interesting portion of this temple is its court, formed by a substantial wall enclosing a tolerable area. The interior of this wall had been entirely covered with immense tables of black marble, on which was inscribed the history of their gods, and, what was of infinitely greater importance, that of the mortal princes who had erected the tablets in their honour. But what a sight for the antiquary! Not one of the many tables was entire; the fragments were strewed about, or placed in position to receive the flesh-pots of the sons of Ishmael, the mercenary Rohilla Afghan.[1]

On quitting the temple of Mama Devi, my attention was attracted by a simple monumental shrine on the opposite side of the valley, and almost in the gorge of the pass. It was most happily situated, being quite isolated, overlooking the road leading to Marwar, and consisted of a simple dome of very moderate dimensions, supported by columns, without any intervening object to obstruct the view of the little monumental altar arising out of the centre of the platform. It was the Sybilline temple of Tivoli in miniature. To it, over rock and ruin, I descended. Here repose the ashes of the Troubadour of Méwar, the gallant Pirthi-raj, and his heroine wife, Tarra Bhaé, whose lives and exploits fill many a page of the legendary romances of Méwar.

This fair 'star' (*tarra*) was the daughter of Rao Soortan, the chieftain of Bednore. He was of the Solanki tribe, the lineal descendant of the famed Balhara kings of Anhulwarra. Thence expelled by the arms of Alla in the thirteenth century, they migrated to Central India, and obtained possession of Tonk-Thoda and its lands on the Bunas, which from remote times had been occupied (perhaps founded) by the Tâks, and hence bore the name of Taksilla-nuggur, familiarly Takitpoor and Thoda.[2] Soortan

[1] These people assert their Coptic origin: being driven from Egypt by one of the Pharaohs, they wandered eastwards till they arrived under that peak of the mountains west of the Indus called *Suliman-e-koh*, or 'Hill of Solomon,' where they halted. Others draw their descent from the lost tribes. They are a very marked race, and as unsettled as their forefathers, serving everywhere. They are fine gallant men, and, when managed by such officers as Skinner, make excellent and orderly soldiers; but they evince great contempt for the eaters of swine, who are their abomination.

[2] From the ruins of its temples, remnants of Takshac architecture, the amateur might speedily fill a portfolio. This tract abounds with romantic scenery: Rajmahl on the Bunas, Gokurn, and many others. Herbert calls Cheetore the abode of Taxiles, the ally of Alexander. The Tâks were all of the race of *Poorú*, so that *Porus* is a generic, not a proper name. This Taksilla-nuggur has been a large city. We owe thanks to the Emperor Baber, who has given us the position of the city of Taxiles, where Alexander left it, west of the Indus.

had been deprived of Thoda by Lilla the Afghan, and now occupied Bednore at the foot of the Aravulli, within the bounds of Méwar. Stimulated by the reverses of her family, and by the incentives of its ancient glory, Tarra Bhaé, scorning the habiliments and occupations of her sex, learned to guide the war-horse, and throw with unerring aim the arrow from his back, even while at speed. Armed with the bow and quiver, and mounted on a fiery Kattyawar, she joined the cavalcade in their unsuccessful attempts to wrest Thoda from the Afghan. Jeimul, the third son of Rana Raemul, in person made proposals for her hand. "Redeem Thoda," said the star of Bednore, "and my hand is thine." He assented to the terms: but evincing a rude determination to be possessed of the prize ere he had earned it, he was slain by the indignant father. Pirthi-raj, the brother of the deceased, was then in exile in Marwar; he had just signalised his valour, and ensured his father's forgiveness, the redemption of Godwar,[1] and the catastrophe at Bednore determined him to accept the gage thrown down to Jeimul. Fame and the bard had carried the renown of Pirthi-raj far beyond the bounds of Méwar; the name alone was attractive to the fair, and when thereto he who bore it added all the chivalrous ardour of his prototype, the Chohan, Tarra Bhaé, with the sanction of her father, consented to be his, on the simple asseveration that "he would restore to them Thoda, or he was no true Rajpoot." The anniversary of the martyrdom of the sons of Alli was the season chosen for the exploit. Pirthi-raj formed a select band of five hundred cavaliers, and accompanied by his bride, the fair Tarra, who insisted on partaking his glory and his danger, he reached Thoda at the moment the *tazzia* or bier containing the martyr-brothers was placed in the centre of the *chouk* or 'square.' The prince, Tarra Bhaé, and the faithful Sengar chief, the inseparable companion of Pirthi-raj, left their cavalcade and joined the procession as it passed under the balcony of the palace in which the Afghan was putting on his dress preparatory to descending. Just as he had asked, who were the strange horsemen that had joined the throng, the lance of Pirthi-raj and an arrow from the bow of his Amazonian bride stretched him on the floor. Before the crowd recovered from the panic, the three had reached the gate of the town, where their exit was obstructed by an elephant. Tarra Bhaé with her scimitar divided his trunk, and the animal flying, they joined their cavalcade, which was close at hand.

The Afghans were encountered, and could not stand the attack. Those who did not fly were cut to pieces; and the gallant Pirthi-raj inducted the father of his bride into his inheritance. A brother of the Afghans, in his attempt to recover it, lost his life. The Nawab Mulloo Khan then holding Ajmér, determined to oppose the Seesodia prince in person; who, resolved upon being the assailant, advanced to Ajmér, encountered his foe in the camp at daybreak, and after great slaughter entered Gur'h Beetli, the citadel, with the fugitives. "By these acts," says the chronicle, "his fame increased in Rajwarra: one thousand Rajpoots, animated by the same love of glory and devotion, gathered round the *nakarras* of Pirthi-raj. Their swords shone in the heavens, and were dreaded on the earth; but they aided the defenceless."

Another story is recorded and confirmed by Mahomedan writers as to the result, though they are ignorant of the impulse which prompted the

[1] See p. 237.

act. Pirthi-raj on some occasion found the Rana conversing familiarly with an ahdy of the Malwa king, and feeling offended at the condescension, expressed himself with warmth. The Rana ironically replied: "You are a mighty seizer of kings; but for me, I desire to retain my land." Pirthi-raj abruptly retired, collected his band, made for Neemutch, where he soon gathered five thousand horse, and reaching Depalpoor, plundered it, and slew the governor. The king on hearing of the irruption, left Mandoo at the head of what troops he could collect; but the Rajpoot prince, in lieu of retreating, rapidly advanced and attacked the camp while refreshing after the march. Singling out the royal tent, occupied by eunuchs and females, the king was made captive, and placed on an express camel beside the prince, who warned the pursuers to follow peaceably, or he would put his majesty to death; adding that he intended him no harm, but that after having made him "touch his father's feet," he should restore him to liberty. Having carried him direct to Cheetore and to his father's presence, he turned to him saying, "Send for your friend the ahdy, and ask him who this is?" The Malwa king was detained a month within the walls of Cheetore, and having paid his ransom in horses, was set at liberty with every demonstration of honour. Pirthi-raj returned to Komulmér, his residence, and passed his life in exploits like these from the age of fourteen to twenty-three, the admiration of the country and the theme of the bard.

It could not be expected that long life would be the lot of one who thus courted distinction, though it was closed neither by shot nor sabre, but by poison, when on the eve of prosecuting his unnatural feud against his brother Sanga, the place of whose retreat was made known by his marriage with the daughter of the chieftain of Srinuggur, who had dared to give him protection in defiance of his threats.

At the same time he received a letter from his sister, written in great grief, complaining of the barbarous treatment of her lord, the Sirohi prince, from whose tyranny she begged to be delivered and to be restored to the paternal roof; since whenever he had indulged too freely in the 'essence of the flower,' or in opium, he used to place her under the bedstead, and leave her to sleep on the floor. Pirthi-raj instantly departed, reached Sirohi at midnight, scaled the palace, and interrupted the repose of Pabhoo Rao by placing his poniard at his throat. His wife, notwithstanding his cruelty, complied with his humiliating appeal for mercy, and begged his life, which was granted on condition of his standing as a suppliant with his wife's shoes on his head, and touching her feet, the lowest mark of degradation. He obeyed, was forgiven, and embraced by Pirthi-raj, who became his guest during five days. Pabhoo Rao was celebrated for a confection, of which he presented some to his brother at parting. He partook of it as he came in sight of Komulmér; but on reaching the shrine of Mama Devi was unable to proceed. Here he sent a message to the fair Tarra to come and bid him farewell; but so subtle was the poison, that death had overtaken him ere she descended from the citadel. Her resolution was soon formed; the pyre was erected, and with the mortal remains of the chivalrous Pirthi-raj in her embrace, she sought "the regions of the sun." Such the end of the Seesodia prince, and the star of Bednore. From such instances we must form our opinion of the manners of these people. But for the poisoned confection of the chief of Sirohi, Pirthi-raj would have had the glory of opposing himself to Baber, instead of his heroic brother and successor, Sanga.[1] Whether, from his superior ardour of temperament, and the love of military glory which attracted similarly-constituted minds to his fortunes, he would have been more successful than his brother, it is futile to conjecture.

October 20.—Halted till noon, that the men might dress their dinners, and prepare for the descent into "the region of death," or Marwar. The pass by which we had to gain it was represented as terrific; but as both horse and elephant, with the aid of the hatchet, will pick their way wherever man can go, we determined to persevere. Struck the camp at noon, when the baggage filed off, halting ourselves till three; the escort and advanced tents, and part of the *cuisine* being ordered to clear the pass, while we designed to spend the night midway, in a spot forming the natural boundary of Méwar and Marwar, reported to be sufficiently capacious. Rumour had not magnified the difficulties of the descent, which we found strewed with our baggage, arresting all progress for a full hour. For nearly a mile there was but just breadth sufficient to admit the passage of a loaded elephant, the descent being at an angle of 55° with the horizon, and streams on either side rushing with a deafening roar over their rugged beds. As we gained a firmer footing at the base of this first descent, we found that the gallant Manika, the gift of my friend the Boondí prince, had missed his footing and rolled down the steep, breaking the cantle of the saddle; a little farther appeared the cook, hanging in dismay over the scattered implements of his art, his camel remonstrating against the replacing of his *cujavas* or panniers. For another mile it became more gentle, when we passed under a tower of Komulmér, erected on a scarped projection of the rock, full five hundred feet above us. The scenery was magnificent; the mountains rising on each side in every variety of form, and their summits, as they caught a ray of the departing sun, reflecting on our sombre path a momentary gleam from the masses of rose-coloured quartz which crested them. Noble forest trees covered every face of the hills and the bottom of the glen, through which, along the margin of the serpentine torrent which we repeatedly crossed, lay our path. Notwithstanding all our mishaps, partly from the novelty and grandeur of the scene, and partly from the invigorating coolness of the air, our mirth became wild and clamorous: a week before, I was oppressed with a thousand ills; and now I trudged the rugged path, leaping the masses of granite which had rolled into the torrent.

There was one spot where the waters formed a pool or *dé*. Little Cary determined to trust to his pony to carry him across, but deviating to the left, just as I was leaping from a projecting ledge, to my horror, horse and rider disappeared. The shock was momentary, and a good ducking the only result, which in the end was the luckiest thing that could have befallen him. On reaching the Hattidurra, or 'barrier of the elephant' (a very appropriate designation for a mass of rock serving as a rampart to shut up the pass), where we had intended to remain the night, we found no spot capacious enough even for a single tent. Orders accordingly passed to the rear for the baggage to collect there, and wait the return of day to continue the march. The shades of night were fast descending, and we proceeded almost in utter darkness towards the banks of the stream, the roar of whose waters was our guide, and not a little perplexed by the

[1] See Annals, p. 240.

tumultuous rush which issued from every glen, to join that we were seeking. Towards the termination of the descent the path became wider, and the voice of the waters of a deeper and hoarser tone, as they glided to gain the plains of Marwar. The vault of heaven, in which there was not a cloud, appeared as an arch to the perpendicular cliffs surrounding us on all sides, and the stars beamed with peculiar brilliancy from the confined space through which we viewed them. As we advanced in perfect silence, fancy busily at work on what might befall our straggling retinue from the ferocious tiger or plundering mountaineer, a gleam of light suddenly flashed upon us on emerging from the brushwood, and disclosed a party of dismounted cavaliers seated round their night-fires under some magnificent fig-trees.[1]

Halted, and called a council of war to determine our course : we had gained the spot our guides had assigned as the only fitting one for *bivouac* before we reached the plains beyond the mountains ; it afforded shade from the dews, and plenty of water. The *munitions de bouche* having gone on, was a good argument that we should follow ; but darkness and five miles more of intricate forest, through a path from which the slightest deviation, right or left, might lead us into the jaws of a tiger, or the toils of the equally savage Mair, decided us to halt. We now took another look at the group above-mentioned. Though the excitement of the morning was pretty well chilled by cold and hunger (poor sharpeners of the imagination), it was impossible to contemplate the scene before us without a feeling of the highest interest. From twenty-five to thirty tall figures, armed at all points, were sitting or reposing in groups round their watch-fires, conversing and passing the pipe from hand to hand, while their long black locks, and motley-fashioned turbans, told that they belonged to Maroodésa. A rude altar, raised in honour of some " gentle blood " shed by the murky mountaineer, served as a place of rest for the chief of the party, distinguished by the gold band in his turban, and his deer-skin doublet. I gave the usual salutation of " Rama, Rama," to the chief and his party, and inquired after the health of their chieftain of Ganora, to whose courtesy I found I owed this mark of attention. This was the boundary between the two states of Marwar and Méwar, since the district of Godwar was lost by the latter about fifty years ago. The spot has been the scene of many a conflict, and a closer approach disclosed several other altars raised in honour of the slain ; each represented a cavalier mounted on his war-steed, with his lance poised, denoting that in such attitude he fell in defending the pass, or redeeming the cattle from the plundering mountain Mair. A square tablet placed on each contained the date on which he gained " the mansions of the sun." Midnight being past, and bringing no hope of our appetites growing by what they might feed upon, Dr. Duncan and Captain Waugh took the *jhool*, or broadcloth-housing, from the elephant, and rolling themselves in it, followed the example of the chieftain and reposed upon the ashes of the brave, on an altar adjoining the one he occupied. I soon left them in happy forgetfulness of tigers, Méras, hunger, and all the fatigues of the day, and joined the group to listen to the tale with which they enlivened the midnight hour. *This* I can repeat, but it would have required the pencil of a master to paint the scene. It was a subject for Salvator Rosa ; though I should have been perfectly satisfied with one of Captain Waugh's delineations, had he been disposed at that moment to

[1] The burr or banian tree, *ficus Indica*.

exert the pictorial art. Several of my friends had encountered the mountaineer on this very spot; and these humble cenotaphs, covering the ashes of their kin, recalled events not likely to be repeated in these halcyon days, when the names of Bhil and Mair cease to be the synonyms of plunderer. As there may be no place more appropriate for a sketch of the mountaineers, the reader may transport himself to the glen of Komulmér, and listen to the history of one of the aboriginal tribes of Rajast'han.

CHAPTER XXVI

The Mairs or Méras: their history and manners—The 'Barwuttea' of Gocul-gurh—Forms of outlawry—Ajeet Sing, the chief of Ganora—Plains of Marwar—Chief of Roopnagurh—Anecdote respecting Daisoori—Contrast between the Seesodias of Méwar and the Rahtores of Marwar—Traditional history of the Rajpoots—Ganora—Kishendas, the Rana's envoy—Local discrimination between Méwar and Marwar—Ancient feuds—The *aonla* and the *bawul*—Aspect of Marwar—Nadole—Superiority of the Chohan race—Goga of Batinda—Lakha of Ajmér: his ancient fortress at Nadole—Jain relic there—The Hindu ancient arch or vault—Inscriptions—Antiquities at Nadole Eendurira—Its villages—Palli, a commercial mart—Articles of commerce—The bards and genealogists the chief carriers—The "Hill of Virtue"—Khankani—Affray between two caravans—Barbarous self-sacrifices of the Bhats—Jhalamund—March to Jodpoor—Reception *en route* by the Chiefs of Pokurna and Neemaj—Biography of these nobles—Sacrifice of Soortan of Neemaj—Encamp at the capital—Negotiation for the ceremonies of reception at the Court of Jodpoor.

THE *Mair* or *Méra* is the mountaineer of Rajpootana, and the country he inhabits is styled *Mairwarra*, or "the region of hills." The epithet is therefore merely local, for the Mair is but a branch of the *Ména* or *Maina*, one of the aborigines of India. He is also called *Mairote* and *Mairawut*; but these terminations only more correctly define his character of mountaineer.[1] Mairwarra is that portion of the Aravulli chain between Komulmér and Ajmér, a space of about ninety miles in length, and varying in breadth from six to twenty. The general character of this magnificent rampart, in the natural and physical geography of Rajpootana, is now sufficiently familiar. It rises from three to four thousand feet above the level of the sea, and abounds with a variety of natural productions. In short, I know no portion of the globe which would yield to the scientific traveller more abundant materials for observation than the alpine Aravulli. The architectural antiquary might fill his portfolio, and natural history would receive additions to her page in every department, and especially in botany and zoology.[2] I should know no higher gratification than to be

[1] *Méra* is 'a mountain' in Sanscrit; *Mairawat* and *Mairote*, 'of or belonging to the mountain.' I have before remarked, that the name of the Albanian mountaineer, *Mainote*, has the same signification. I know not the etymology of *Maina*, of which the Mair is a branch.

[2] I had hoped to have embodied these subjects with, and thereby greatly to have increased the interest, of my work; but just as Lord Hastings had granted my request, that an individual eminently qualified for those pursuits should join me, a Higher Power deemed it fit to deny what had been long near my heart.

The individual, John Tod, was a cousin of my own, and possessed an intellect

of a scientific party to anatomise completely this important portion of India. I would commence on the Guzzerat, and finish on the Shekhawut frontier. The party should consist of a skilful surveyor, to lay down on a large scale a topographical chart of the mountains; several gentlemen thoroughly versed in natural history; able architectural and landscape draughtsmen, and the antiquary to transcribe ancient inscriptions, as well as to depict the various races. The "Aravulli delineated," by the hand of science, would form a most instructive and delightful work.

A minute account of the Mair, his habits and his history, would be no unimportant feature: but as this must be deferred, I will, in the meanwhile, furnish some details to supply the void.

The Mairs are a branch of the Cheetas, an important division of the Ménas. I shall elsewhere enter at large into the history of this race, which consists of as many branches as their conquerors, the Rajpoots. All these wild races have the vanity to mingle their pedigree with that of their conquerors, though in doing so they stigmatise themselves. The Cheeta-Ménas accordingly claim descent from a grandson of the last Chohan emperor of Dehli. Unail and Anoop were the sons of Lakha, the nephew of the Chohan king. The *coco-nut* was sent from Jessulmér, offering princesses of that house in marriage: but an investigation into their maternal ancestry disclosed that they were the issue of a Ména concubine: and their birth being thus revealed, they became exiles from Ajmér, and associates with their maternal relatives.

Unail espoused the daughter of a Ména chieftain, by whom he had Cheeta, whose descendants enjoy almost a monopoly of power in Mairwarra. The sons of Cheeta, who occupied the northern frontier near Ajmér, became Mahomedans about fifteen generations ago, when Doodoh, the sixteenth from the founder of the race, was created Dawad Khan by the Hakim of Ajmér; and as Athoon was his residence, the "Khan of Athoon" signified the chief of the Mairotes. Chang, Jhak, and Rajosi are the principal towns adjoining Athoon. Anoop also took a Ména wife, by whom he had Burrar, whose descendants have continued true to their original tenets. Their chief places are Burrar, Bairawara, Mundilla, etc. Though the progeny of these Ménas may have been improved by the infusion of Rajpoot blood, they were always notorious for their lawless habits, and for the importance attached to them so far back as the period of Beesildeo, the celebrated prince of Ajmér, whom the bard Chund states to have reduced them to submission, making them "carry water in the streets of Ajmér." Like all mountaineers, they of course broke out whenever the hands of power were feeble. In the battle between the Chohans of Ajmér and the Purihars of Mundore, a body of four thousand Mair bowmen served Nahur Rao, and defended the pass of the Aravulli against Pirthi-raj in this his first essay in arms. Chund thus describes them: [1] "Where

of the highest order. He was only twenty-two years of age when he died, and had only been six months in India. He was an excellent classical scholar, well versed in modern languages and every branch of natural history. His manners, deportment, and appearance were all in unison with these talents. Had it pleased the Almighty to have spared him, this work would have been more worthy of the public notice.

[1] I cannot discover by what part of the range the invasion of Mundore was attempted; it might have been the pass we are now in, for it is evident it was not from the frontier of Ajmér.

hill joins hill, the Mair and Ména thronged. The Mundore chief commanded that the pass should be defended—four thousand heard and obeyed, each in form as the angel of death—men who never move without the omen, whose arrow never flies in vain—with frames like Indra's bolt—faithful to their word, preservers of the land and the honour [1] of Mundore; whose fortresses have to this day remained unconquered—who bring the spoils of the plains to their dwellings. Of these in the dark recesses of the mountains four thousand lay concealed, their crescent-formed arrows beside them. Like the envenomed serpent, they wait in silence the advance of the foe.

"Tidings reached the Chohan that the manly Ména, with bow in hand, stood in the mountain's gorge. Who would be bold enough to force it? his rage was like the hungry lion's when he views his prey. He called the brave Kana, and bade him observe those wretches as he commanded him to clear the pass. Bowing he departed, firm as the rock on which he trod. He advanced, but the mountaineer (Mair) was immovable as Soomair. Their arrows carrying death, fly like Indra's bolts—they obscure the sun. Warriors fall from their steeds, resounding in their armour as a tree torn up by the blast. Kana quits the steed; hand to hand he encounters the foe; the feathery shafts, as they strike fire, appear like birds escaping from the flames. The lance flies through the breast, appearing at the back, like a fish escaping through the meshes of a net. The evil spirits dance in the mire of blood. The hero of the mountain [2] encountered Kana, and his blow made him reel; but like lightning it was returned, and the mountaineer fell: the crash was as the shaking of Soomair. At this moment Nahur arrived, roaring like a tiger for his prey: he called aloud to revenge their chief, his brother,[3] and fresh vigour was infused into their souls. On the fall of the mountain-chief, the Chohan commanded the 'hymn of triumph' [4] to be sounded; it startled the mountaineer, but only to nerve his soul afresh. In person the Chohan sought his foe. The son of Somesa is a bridegroom. His streaming standards flutter like the first falls of rain in Asar, and as he steps on the bounds which separate Mundore from Ajmér, 'Victory! victory!' is proclaimed. Still the battle rages. Elephants roar, horses neigh, terror stalks everywhere. The aids of Girnar and of Sinde now appeared for Mundore, bearing banners of every colour, varied as the flowers of the spring. Both arrays were clad in mail; their eyes and their finger-nails alone were exposed; each invoked his tutelary protector as he wielded the *dodhara*.[5] Pirthi-raj was refulgent as Indra; the Purihar's brightness was as the morning star; each was clad in armour of proof, immovable as gods in mortal form. The sword of the Chohan descended on the steed of the Purihar; but as he fell, Nahur sprung erect, and they again darted on each other, their warriors forming a fortress around the persons of their lords. Then advanced the standards of the Pramar, like a black rolling cloud, while the lightnings flashed from his sword. Mohuna, the brother of Mundore, received him; they first examined each other—then joining

[1] *Lâj* is properly 'shame,' which word is always used in lieu of honour: *lâj rêkho*, 'preserve my shame,' *i.e.* my honour from shame.

[2] Purbut Vira.

[3] The Purihar prince bestowed this epithet merely in compliment.

[4] *Sindoo Râga.*

[5] With two (*do*) edges (*dhara*).

in the strife, the helm of the Pramar was cleft in twain. Now advanced Chaond, the Dahima ; he grasped his iron lance,[1]—it pierced the Purihar, and the head appeared like a serpent looking through the door in his back. The flame (*jote*) united with the fire from which it sprung, while the body fell on its parent earth. By his devotion the sins of his life were forgiven. Nobly did the tiger (Nahur) of Mundore meet the lion of the world. He called aloud, 'Hold your ground as did Bul Raja of old.' Again the battle rages—Doorga gluts herself with blood—the air resounds with the clash of arms and the rattling of banners—the Aswar [2] rains on the foe—Khétrpal sports in the field of blood—Mahadeva fills his necklace—the eagle gluts itself on the slain—the mien of the warriors expands as does the lotos at the sun-beam—the war-song resounds—with a branch of the toolsi on the helm, adorned in the saffron robe, the warriors on either side salute each other." The bard here exclaims, "But why should I enlarge on this encounter ?"—but as this digression is merely for breathing time, we shall not follow him, the object being to introduce the mountain Mair, whom we now see *hors de combat*.

Admitting the exaggeration of the poet, the Mair appears to have been in the twelfth century what he is in the nineteenth, a bold, licentious marauder. He maintained himself throughout the whole of the Mogul domination, alternately succumbing and depredating ; and since the Mahrattas crippled these countries, the Mair had regained all his consequence, and was rapidly encroaching upon his Rajpoot suzerain. But when in 1821 their excesses made it imperative to reduce their holds and fastnesses, they made no stand against the three battalions of sepoys sent against them, and the whole tract was compelled to obedience ; not, however, till many of the descendants of Cheeta and Burrar had suffered both in person and property. The facility with which we reduced to entire subjection this extensive association of plunderers, for centuries the terror of these countries, occasioned no little astonishment to our allies. The resistance was indeed contemptible, and afforded a good argument against the prowess of those who had tolerated the existence of a gang at once so mischievous and weak. But this was leaping to a conclusion without looking beneath the surface, or to the moral and political revolution which enervated the arms of Mair and Mahratta, Pindarri and Pat'han All rose to power from the common occupation of plunderers, aided by the national jealousies of the Rajpoots. If the chieftains of Méwar leagued to assault the mountaineers, they found refuge and support in Marwar ; and as their fortresses at all times presented a sanctuary, their Rawuts or leaders obtained consequence amongst all parties by granting it. Every Mair community, accordingly, had a perfect understanding with the chieftain whose lands were contiguous to their own, and who enjoyed rights granted by the Rana over these nominal subjects. These rights were all of a feudal nature, as *rekwalee* or 'blackmail,' and those petty proofs of subordination, entitled in the feudal law of Europe "*petit serjanterie.*" The token might be a colt, a hawk, or a bullock, and a *nuzzerana*, or pecuniary acknowledgment, perhaps only of half a crown on the chieftain's birthday, or on the Rajpoot Saturnalia, the *Holi*.

[1] *Sang* is the iron lance, either wholly of iron, or having plates for about ten feet ; these weapons are much used in combats from camels in the Desert.

[2] 'Sword '—*Aswar* in the dialect.

But all these petty causes for assimilation between the Rajpoot and the lawless Mair were overlooked, as well as the more powerful one which rendered his arms of no avail. Every door was hermetically sealed against him; wherever he looked he saw a foe—the magical change bewildered him; and when their Khan and his adherents were assailed while in fancied security, and cut off in a midnight attack, his self-confidence was annihilated—he saw a red-coat in every glen, and called aloud for mercy.

A corps of these mountaineers, commanded by English officers, has since been formed, and I have no doubt may become useful. Notwithstanding their lawless habits, they did not neglect agriculture and embanking, as described in the valley of Shero Nullah, and a district has been formed in Mairwarra which in time may yield a lakh of rupees annually to the state.

Some of their customs are so curious, and so different from those of their lowland neighbours, that we may mention a few. Leaving their superstitions as regards omens and auguries, the most singular part of their habits, till we give a detailed sketch of the Ménas hereafter, I will notice the peculiarity of their notions towards females. The Mair, following the customary law handed down from his rude ancestry, and existing long before the written law of Menu, has no objection to a widow as a wife. This contract is termed *nat'ha*, and his civilised master levies a fine or fee of a rupee and a quarter for the licence, termed *kagli*. On such marriage, the bridegroom must omit in the *mor*, or nuptial coronet, the graceful palmyra leaf, and substitute a small branch of the sacred peepul wreathed in his turban. Many of the forms are according to the common Hindu ritual. The *sat-pheera*, or seven perambulations round the jars filled with grain, piled over each other—the *gat-joora*, or uniting the garments—and the *hatléva*, or junction of hands of bride and bridegroom, are followed by the Mairs. Even the northern clans, who are converts to Islâm, return to their ancient habits on this occasion, and have a Brahmin priest to officiate. I discovered, on inquiring into the habits of the Mairs, that they are not the only race which did not refuse to wed a widow, and that both Brahmins and Rajpoots have from ancient times been accustomed not to consider it derogatory. Of the former, the sacerdotal class, the Nagda Brahmins, established at this town long before the Gehlotes obtained power in Méwar. Of the Rajpoots, they are all of the most ancient tribes, now the allodial vassals or bhomias of Rajpootana, as the Chinanoh, Kharwar, Ootain, Dya, names better known in the mystic page of the chronicle than now, though occasionally met with in the valleys of the Aravulli. But this practice, so little known, gives rise to an opinion, that many of the scrupulous habits regarding women are the inventions of the priests of more modern days. The facilities for separation are equally simple. If tempers do not assimilate, or other causes prompt them to part, the husband tears a shred from his turban, which he gives to his wife, and with this simple bill of divorce, placing two jars filled with water on her head, she takes whatever path she pleases, and the first man who chooses to ease her of her load becomes her future lord. This mode of divorce is practised not only amongst all the Ménas, but by Jâts, Goojurs, Aheers, Mallis, and other Soodra tribes. *Jehúr lé or nikela*, 'took the jar and went forth,' is a common saying amongst the mountaineers of Mairwarra.

Their invocations and imprecations are peculiar. The Cheeta or northern Mair, since he became acquainted with the name of the prophet, swears by "*Allah*," or by his first proselyte ancestor, "*Dooda Dawad Khan*," or the still more ancient head of the races, "*Cheeta, Burrar ca án.*" The southern Mairs also use the latter oath: "By my allegiance to Cheeta and Burrar;" and they likewise swear by the sun, "*Sooraj ca Sogun*," and "*Nat'h ca Sogun*"; or their ascetic priest, called the *Nat'h*. The Mahomedan Mair will not now eat hog; the southron refuses nothing, though he respects the cow from the prejudices of those around him, and to please the *Nat'h* or *jogi*, his spiritual guide. The partridge and the *maloli*, or wag-tail, are the chief birds of omen with him, and the former 'clamouring' on the left, when he commences a foray, is a certain presage of success. To conclude; colonies of the Mairs or Méras will be found as far north as the Chumbul, and even in the peninsula of Saurashtra. Mairwarra is now in subjection to the Rana of Méwar, who has erected small forts amidst the most influential communities to overawe them. The whole tract has been assessed; the chiefs of the districts being brought to the Rana's presence presented *nuzzerana*, swore fidelity, and received according to their rank gold bracelets or turbans. It was an era in the annals of Méwar to see the accumulated arms of Mairwarra piled upon the terrace of the palace at the capital; but these measures were subsequent to our sojourn in the glen of Komulmér, from which we have yet to issue to gain Marwar.

October 21.—All hailed the return of daylight with reverence. Captain Waugh and the Doctor uncoiled from the elephant's *jhool*, and I issued from my *palki*, which had proved a welcome retreat against the chills of the night air. By thirst and hunger our appetite for the picturesque was considerably abated, and the contemplation of the spot where we had bivouaced in that philosophical spirit of silence, which all have experienced who have made a long march before breakfast, lost much of its romantic interest. Nevertheless, could I have consulted merely my own wishes, I would have allowed my friends and escort to follow the canteen, and have pursued an intricate path which branched off to the right, to have had the chance of an interview with the outlaw of Goculgurh.

This petty chieftain, who enjoyed the distinctive epithet of outlaw (*barwuttea*), was of the Sonigurra clan (a branch of the Chohans), who for centuries were the lords of Jhalore. He was a vassal of Marwar, now sovereign of Jhalore, and being expelled for his turbulence by his prince, he had taken post in the old ruined castle of Goculgurh, on a cliff of the Aravulli, and had become the terror of the country. By his knowledge of the intricacies of the mountains, he eluded pursuit; and his misdeeds being not only connived at, but his spoils participated by the chief of Deogurh, in whose fief was his haunt, he was under no apprehension of surprise. Inability either to seize the Barwuttea, or drive him from his retreat, formed a legitimate excuse for the resumption of Goculgurh, and the dues of 'blackmail' he derived from its twelve dependent villages. The last act of the Sonigurra was most flagrant; he intercepted in the plains of Godwar a marriage procession, and made captives the bride-groom and bride, whom he conveyed to Goculgurh, where they long languished for want of ransom. A party was formed to lay in wait for him: but he escaped the snare, and his retreat was found empty. Such was the state of society in these districts. The form of outlawry is singular in this country, where the penal laws are satisfied with banishment, even in cases of treason, instead of the sanguinary law of civilization. The criminal against whom the sentence of exile is pronounced being called into his prince's presence, is clad in black vestments, and placed upon a black steed, his arms and shield all of the same sombre hue of mourning and disgrace ; he is then left to gain the frontier by himself. This custom is very ancient : the Pandu brothers were "Barwutteas"[1] from the Jumna three thousand years ago. The Jessulmér annals relate the solemnity as practised towards one of their own princes ; and the author, in the domestic dissensions of Kotah, received a letter from the prince, wherein he demands either that his rights should be conceded, or that the government would bestow the "black garment," and leave him to his fate.

Conversing on these and similar subjects with my Marwarri friends, we threaded our way for five miles through the jungles of the pass, which we had nearly cleared, when we encountered the chieftain of Ganora at the head of his retinue, who of his own accord, and from a feeling of respect to his ancient sovereign the Rana, advanced thus far to do me honour. I felt the compliment infinitely the more, as it displayed that spirit of loyalty peculiar to the Rajpoot, though the step was dangerous with his jealous sovereign, and ultimately was prejudicial to him. After dismounting and embracing, we continued to ride to the tents, conversing on the past history of the province, of his prince, and the Rana, after whom he affectionately inquired. Ajeet Sing is a noble-looking man, about thirty years of age, tall, fair, and sat his horse like a brave Rahtore cavalier. Ganora is the chief town of Godwar, with the exception of the commercial Palli, and the garrison-post Daisoori. From this important district the Rana could command four thousand Rahtores holding lands on the tenure of service, of whom the Ganora chief, then one of the sixteen nobles of Méwar, was the head. Notwithstanding the course of events had transferred the province, and consequently his services, from the Rana of Oodipoor to the Raja of Jodpoor, so difficult is it to eradicate old feelings of loyalty and attachment, that the present Thacoor preferred having the sword of investiture bound on him by his ancient and yet nominal suzerain, rather than by his actual sovereign. For this undisguised mark of feeling, Ganora was denuded of its walls, which were levelled to the ground ; a perpetual memento of disgrace and an incentive to vengeance : and whenever the day arrives that the Rana's herald may salute him with the old motto, "Remember Komulmér," he will not be deaf to the call. To defend this post was the peculiar duty of his house, and often have his ancestors bled in maintaining it against the Mogul. Even now, such is the inveteracy with which the Rajpoot clings to his honours, that whenever the Ganora chief, or any of his near kin, attend the Rana's court, he is saluted at the porte, or at the *champ de Mars*, by a silver mace-bearer from the Rana, with the ancient war-cry, "Remember Komulmér," and he still receives on all occasions of rejoicing a khelat from that prince. He has to boast of being of the Rana's blood, and is by courtesy called "the nephew of Méwar." The Thacoor politely invited me to visit him ; but I was aware that compliance would have involved him in difficulties with

[1] This term is a compound of *bar* and *wuttuna*, literally 'ex patria.'

his jealous prince, and made excuses of fatigue, and the necessity of marching next morning, the motives of which he could not misunderstand.

Our march this morning was but short, and the last two miles were in the plains of Marwar, with merely an occasional rock. Carey joined us, congratulating himself on the ducking which had secured him better fare than we had enjoyed in the pass of Komulmér, and which fastened both on Waugh and myself violent colds. The atmospheric change was most trying: emerging from the cold breezes of the mountains to 96° of Fahrenheit, the effect was most injurious: it was 58° in the morning of our descent into the glen. Alas! for my surviving barometer! Mohés, my amanuensis, who had been entrusted with it, joined us next day, and told me the quicksilver had contrived to escape; so I lost the opportunity of comparing the level of the desert with the plains of Marwar.

October 27.—Halted to collect the scattered baggage, and to give the men rest; the day was nearly over before the whole came up, each party bringing lamentable reports of the disastrous descent. I received a visit from the chief of Roopnagurh, who, like the Thacoor of Ganora, owes a divided allegiance to the courts on each side the mountains. His castle, which gives him rank as one of the most conspicuous of the second grade of the Rana's nobles, was visible from the camp, being placed on the western face of the mountains, and commanding a difficult passage across them. From thence he looks down upon Daisoori and his ancient patrimony, now transferred with Godwar to the Rahtore prince; and often has he measured his lance with the present occupants to retain his ancient *bhóm*, the right derived from the cultivating proprietor of the soil. The chief of Roopnagurh is of the Solanki race, a lineal descendant of the sovereigns of Nehrwalla, and the inheritor of the war-shell of the celebrated monarch Sidraj,[1] one of the most powerful who ever sat on an eastern throne, and who occupied that of Anhulwarra from A.D. 1094, during half a century, celebrated as a patron of literature and the arts. When in the thirteenth century this state was destroyed, the branches found refuge, as already described, in Méwar; for the ancestor of Roopnagurh was brother to the father of "the star of Bednore," and was invested with the estate and lands of Daisoori by the same gallant prince who obtained her hand by the recovery of her father's estates. The anecdote is worthy of relation, as showing that the Rajpoot will stop at nothing "to obtain land." The intestine feuds amongst Rana Raemul's sons, and his constant warfare with the kings of Dehli and Malwa, made his authority very uncertain in Godwar. The Ména and Mair possessed themselves of lands in the plains, and were supported by the Madraicha descendant of the once independent Chohan sovereigns of Nadole, the ancient capital of this region. Sand, the Madraicha, had obtained possession of Daisoori, the garrison-town. To expel him, the prince had recourse to Sadda, the Solanki, whose son was married to the daughter of the Madraicha. The bribe for the reward of this treachery was to be the grant in perpetuity of Daisoori and its lands. Sadda's son readily entered into the scheme; and to afford facilities for its execution he went with his wife to reside at Daisoori. It was long before an opportunity offered; but at length the marriage of the young Madraicha to the daughter of Sugra the Balecho was communicated to the Solanki by his son; who told his father "to

[1] He ruled from A.D. 1094 to 1144.

watch the smoke ascending from the tower of Daisoori," as the signal for the attempt to get possession. Anxiously did Sand watch from his castle of Sodgurh the preconcerted sign, and when the volume of black smoke ascended, he rushed down from the Aravulli at the head of his retainers. The mother-in-law of the young Solanki sent to know why he should make a smoke as if he were burning a corpse, when her son must be returning with his bride. Soon she heard the clash of arms; the Solankis had entered and fired the town, and the bridal party appeared before success was attained. Spears and swords were plied. "'Ware the bull!" (*sandh*), said the Madraicha, as he encountered his foe. "My name is the lion (*singh*) who will devour the bull," replied the Solanki. The contest was fierce, but the Madraichas were slain, and in the morn Pirthi-raj was put in possession of Daisoori. He drew out a grant upon the spot, inserting in it a curse against any of Seesodia blood who might break the bond which had restored the Rahtore authority in Godwar. Although seventeen generations have passed since this event, the feud has continued between the descendants of the lion of Sodgurh and the bull of Daisoori, though the object of dissension is alienated from both.

I could well have dispensed with visits this day, the thermometer being 96°; I was besides devoured with inflammatory cold; but there was no declining another polite visit of the chieftain of Ganora. His retinue afforded a good opportunity of contrasting the Seesodia Rajpoot of fertile Méwar with the Rahtores of Marwar, and which on the whole would have been favourable to the latter, if we confined our view to those of the valley of Oodipoor, or the mountainous region of its southern limit, where climate and situation are decidedly unfavourable. There the Rajpoot may be said not only to deteriorate in muscular form and strength, but in that fairness of complexion which distinguishes him from the lower orders of Hindus. But the danger of generalising on such matters will be apparent, when it is known that there is a cause continually operating to check and diminish the deteriorating principle arising from the climate and situation (or, as the Rajpoot would say, from the *howa pâní*, 'air and water') of these unhealthy tracts; namely, the continual influx of the purest blood from every region in Rajpootana: and the stream which would become corrupt if only flowing from the commingling of the Chondawuts of Saloombra and the Jhalas of Gogoonda (both mountainous districts), is refreshed by that of the Rahtores of Godwar, the Chohans of Haravati, or the Bhatti of the desert. I speak from conviction, the chieftains above mentioned affording proofs of the evil resulting from such repeated intermarriages; for, to use their own adage, "a raven will produce a raven." But though the personal appearance of the chieftain of Gogoonda might exclude him from the table of the sixteen barons of Méwar, his son by a Rahtore mother may be exhibited as a redeeming specimen of the Jhalas, and one in every way favourable of the Rajpoot of Méwar. On such occasion, also, as a formal visit, both chieftain and retainers appear under every advantage of dress and decoration; for even the form of the turban may improve the contour of the face, though the Mairteas of Ganora have nothing so decidedly peculiar in this way as those of other clans.

After some discourse on the history of past days, with which, like every respectable Rajpoot, I found him perfectly conversant, the Ganora chief took his leave with some courteous and friendly expressions. It is after such a conversation that the mind disposed to reflection will do justice to the intelligence of these people : I do not say this with reference to the baron of Ganora, but taking them generally. If by history we mean the relation of events in succession, with an account of the leading incidents connecting them, then are all the Rajpoots versed in this science ; for nothing is more common than to hear them detail their immediate ancestry or that of their prince for many generations, with the events which have marked their societies. It is immaterial whether he derives this knowledge from the chronicle, the chronicler, or both : it not only rescues him from the charge of ignorance, but suggests a comparison between him and those who constitute themselves judges of nationalities by no means unfavourable to the Rajpoot.

October 28.—Marched at daybreak. The Thacoor sent a confidential vassal to accompany me through his domain. We could now look around us, as we receded from the Alpine Aravulli, with nothing to obstruct the vision, over the fertile plains of Godwar. We passed near Ganora, whose isolated portals, without tower or curtain to connect them, have a most humiliating appearance. It is to Raja Bheem, some twenty years ago, that their chieftains owe this degradation, in order to lessen their ability to recover the province for its ancient master the Rana. It was indeed one of the gems of his crown, as it is the only dazzling one in that of Marwar. While we marched over its rich and beautiful plains, well watered, well wooded, and abounding in fine towns, I entered into conversation with the Rana's envoy, who joined me on the march. Kishendas has already been mentioned as one of the few men of integrity and wisdom who had been spared to be useful to his country. He was a mine of ancient lore, and his years, his situation, and his character, gave force to his sentiments of determined independence. He was as quick as touchwood, which propensity occasionally created a wordy war between me and my friend, who knew my respect for him. " Restore us Godwar," was his abrupt salutation as he joined me on the march : to which, being a little vexed, as the point could not be agitated by our government, I said in reply, " Why did you let them take it ?—where has the Seesodia sword slept this half century ? " Adding, " God Almighty never intended that the region on this side the mountains should belong to Méwar ;—nature's own hand has placed the limit between you." The old envoy's blood was roused as he exclaimed, " Even on this principle, Godwar is our's, for nature has marked our limit by stronger features than mountains. Observe, as you advance, and you will find to the further limit of the province every shrub and flower common to Méwar ; pass that limit but a few yards, and they are lost :

" Aonla, aonla Méwar :
Bawul, bawul Marwar.

" Wherever the aonla puts forth its yellow blossoms, the land is of right ours ; we want nothing more. Let them enjoy their stunted babools,[1] their khureel, and the ák ; but give us back our sacred peepul, and the aonla of the border." In truth, the transition is beyond credence marked : cross but a shallow brook, and you leave all that is magnificent in vegeta-

[1] *Mimosa Arabica.*

tion; the peepul, burr, and that species of the *mimosa* resembling the cypress, peculiar to Godwar, are exchanged for the prickly shrubs, as the wild caper, jowas, and many others, more useful than ornamental, on which the camel browses. The argument was, however, more ingenious than just, and the old envoy was here substituting the effect for the cause; but he shall explain in his own words why Flora should be permitted to mark the line of demarcation instead of the rock-enthroned (*Doorga*) Cybele. The legend now repeated is historical, and the leading incidents of it have already been touched upon;[1] I shall therefore condense the Pancholi's description into a summary analysis of the cause why the couplet of the bard should be deemed "confirmation strong" of the bounds of kingdoms. These traditionary couplets, handed down from generation to generation, are the most powerful evidence of the past, and they are accordingly employed to illustrate the *khêâts*, or annals, of Rajpootana. When, towards the conclusion of the fourteenth century, the founder of the Chondawuts repaid the meditated treachery of Rinmull of Mundore by his death, he took possession of that capital and the entire country of the Rahtores (then but of small extent), which he held for several years. The heir of Mundore became a fugitive, concealing himself in the fastnesses of the Aravulli, with little hope that his name (Joda) would become a patronymic, and that he would be honoured as the second founder of his country: that Mundore itself should be lost in Jodpoor. The recollection of the feud was almost extinct; the young Rana of Cheetore had passed the years of Rajpoot minority, and Joda continued a fugitive in the wilds of Bhanduc-perao, with but a few horse in his train, indebted to the resources of some independents of the desert for the means of subsistence. He was discovered in this retreat by a Charun or bard, who, without aspiring to prophetic powers, revealed to him that the intercession of the queen-mother of Cheetore had determined the Rana to restore him to Mundore. Whether the sister of Joda, to give éclat to the restoration, wished it to have the appearance of a conquest, or whether Joda, impatient for possession, took advantage of circumstances to make his entrance one of triumph, and thereby redeem the disgrace of a long and humiliating exile, it is difficult to decide; for while the annals of Méwar make the restoration an act of grace, those of Marwar give it all the colours of a triumph. Were the point worthy of discussion, we should say both accounts were correct. The Rana had transmitted the recall of Chonda from Mundore, but concealed from him the motive, and while Joda even held in his possession the Rana's letter of restoration, a concatenation of circumstances, in which "the omen" was predominant, occurred to make him anticipate his induction by a measure more consonant to the Rajpoot, a brilliant *coup de main*. Joda had left his retreat in the *Roon* [2] to make known to Hurba Sankla, Pabooji, and other *rievers* of the desert, the changes which the bard had communicated. While he was there, intelligence was brought that Chonda, in obedience to his sovereign's command, had proceeded to Cheetore. That same night "the bird of omen perched on Joda's lance, and the star which irradiated his birth shone bright upon it." The bard of Mundore revealed the

[1] See p. 224.

[2] An *alp*, or spot in these mountainous regions, where springs, pasture, and other natural conveniences exist.

secret of heaven to Joda, and the heroes in his train: "Ere that star descends in the west, your pennon will wave on the battlements of Mundore." Unless, however, this "vision of glory" was merely mental, Joda's star must have been visible in daylight; for they could never have marched from the banks of the Looni, where the Sankla resided to Mundore, between its rising and setting. The elder son of Chonda had accompanied his father, and they had proceeded two coss in their journey, when a sudden blaze appeared in Mundore: Chonda pursued his route, while his son Manja returned to Mundore. Joda was already in possession; his *án* had been proclaimed, and the two other sons of Chonda had fallen in its defence. Manja, who fled, was overtaken and slain on the border. These tidings reached Chonda at the pass of the Aravulli; he instantly returned to Mundore, where he was met by Joda, who showed him the letters of surrender for Mundore, and a command that he should fix with him the future boundary of each state. Chonda thought that there was no surer line of demarcation than that chalked out by the hand of nature; and he accordingly fixed that wherever the "yellow blossom" was found, the land should belong to his sovereign, and the bard was not slow in perpetuating the decree. Such is the origin of

"Aonla, aonla Méwar:
Bawul, bawul Marwar."

The brave and loyal founder of the Chondawuts, who thus sacrificed his revenge to his sovereign's commands, had his feelings in some degree propitiated by this arrangement, which secured the entire province of Godwar to his prince: his son Manja fell, as he touched the region of the aonlas, and this cession may have been in '*moondkati*,' the compromise of the price of blood. By such traditional legends, not less true than strange, and to which the rock sculptures taken from Mundore bear evidence, even to the heroes who aided Joda in his enterprise, the *aonla* of the Rajpoots has been immortalised, like the humble *broom* of the French, whose *planta-geneta* has distinguished the loftiest name in chivalry, the proudest race emblazoned on the page of heraldry.

Notwithstanding the crops had been gathered, this tract contrasted favourably with Méwar, although amidst a comparative prosperity we could observe the traces of rapine; and numerous stories were rehearsed of the miseries inflicted on the people by the rapacious followers of Ameer Khan. We crossed numerous small streams flowing from the Aravulli, all proceeding to join the "Salt River," or Looni. The villages were large and more populous; yet was there a dulness, a want of that hilarity which pervaded the peasantry of Méwar, in spite of their misfortunes. The Rajpoots partook of the feeling, the cause of which a little better acquaintance with their headquarters soon revealed. Méwar had passed through the period of reaction, which in Marwar was about to display itself, and was left unfortunately to its own control, or with only the impulse of a long suppressed feeling of revenge in the bosom of its prince, and the wiles of a miscreant minister, who wished to keep him in durance, and the country in degradation.

It creates a refreshing sensation to find the camp pitched in a cool and shaded spot; and at Nadole we had this satisfaction. Here again there was no time for recreation, for there was abundant, nay, overwhelming matter both for the pen and the pencil ; but my readers must be satisfied with the imperfect delineations of the first. Nadole is still a place of some consequence, though, but for its temples, we should not have supposed it to have been the capital of a province. With its neighbour, Nadolaye, five miles to the westward, it was the abode of a branch of the Chohans of Ajmér, established at a very early period. From Nadole sprung the Deoras of Sirohi, and the Sonigurras of Jhalore. The former still maintain their ground, in spite of all attempts of the Rahtores ; but the Sonigurra, who was immortalised by his struggle against the second Alla, is blotted from the list of independent states ; and this valuable domain, consisting of three hundred and sixty towns, is now incorporated with Jodpoor.

There is no spot in Rajpootana that does not contain some record of the illustrious Chohan ; and though every race has had its career of glory, the sublimity of which, the annals of the Seesodias before the reader sufficiently attest, yet with all my partiality for those with whom I long resided, and with whose history I am best acquainted, my sense of justice compels me to assign the palm of martial intrepidity to the Chohan over all the " royal races " of India. Even the bards, to whatever family they belong, appear to articulate the very name as if imbued with some peculiar energy, and dwell on its terminating nasal with peculiar complacency. Although they had always ranked high in the list of chivalry, yet the seal of the order was stamped on all who have the name of Chohan, since the days of Pirthi-raj, the model of every Rajpoot, and who had a long line of fame to maintain. Of the many names familiar to the bard is Goga of Batinda, who with forty-seven sons " drank of the stream of the sword " on the banks of the Sutledge, in opposing Mahmoud. This conqueror proceeded through the desert to the attack of Ajmér, the chief abode of this race, where his arms were disgraced, the invader wounded, and forced to relinquish his enterprise. In his route to Nehrwalla and Somnath he passed Nadole,[1] whose prince hesitated not to measure his sword even with Mahmoud. I was fortunate enough to obtain an inscription regarding this prince, the celebrated Lakha, said to be the founder of this branch from Ajmér, of which it was a fief—its date S. 1039 (A.D. 983). The fortress attributed to Lakha is on the declivity of a low ridge to the westward of the town, with square towers of ancient form, and built of a very curious conglomerate of granite and gneiss, of which the rock on which it stands is composed. There was a second inscription, dated S. 1024 (A.D. 968), which made him the contemporary of the Rana's ancestor, Sacti Khomar of Aetpoor, a city also destroyed, more probably by the father of Mahmoud. The Chohan bards speak in very lofty terms of Rao Lakha, who " collected transit dues from the further gate of Anhulwarra, and levied tribute from the prince of Cheetore."

It is impossible to do full justice to the architectural remains, which are well worthy of the pencil. Here everything shows that the Jain faith was once predominant, and that their arts, like their religion, were of a character quite distinct from those of Síva. The temple of Mahavíra, the last of their twenty-four apostles, is a very fine piece of architecture. Its

[1] Ferishta, or his copyist, by a false arrangement of the points, has lost Nadole in Buzule, using the ب for the ن and the ز for the د.

vaulted roof is a perfect model of the most ancient style of dome in the East; probably invented anterior to the Roman. The principle is no doubt the same as the first substitute of the arch, and is that which marked the genius of Cæsar in his bridge over the Rhone, and which appears over every mountain-torrent of the ancient Helvetii, from whom he may have borrowed it. The principle is that of a horizontal instead of a radiating pressure. At Nadole, the stones are placed by a gradual projection one over the other, the apex being closed by a circular key-stone. The angles of all these projections being rounded off, the spectator looking up, can only describe the vault as a series of gradually diminishing amulets or rings converging to the apex. The effect is very pleasing, though it furnishes a strong argument that the Hindus first became acquainted with the perfect arch through their conquerors. The *torun*, in front of the altar of Mahavíra, is exquisitely sculptured, as well as several statues of marble, discovered about one hundred and fifty years ago in the bed of the river, when it changed its course. It is not unlikely that they were buried during Mahmoud's invasion. But the most singular structure of Nadole is a reservoir, called the *chunna ca bowlee*, from the cost of it being paid by the return of a single grain of pulse (*chunna*). The excavation is immense; the descent is by a flight of grey granite steps, and the sides are built up from the same materials by piling blocks upon blocks of enormous magnitude, without the least cement.

My acquisitions here were considerable. Besides copies of inscriptions made by my Sanscrit scribes, I obtained two originals on brass. Of one of these, dated S. 1218, the memorial of Allandéva, I append a translation,[1] which may be considered curious as a formula of endowment of the Jains. I likewise procured several isolated MS. leaves of very great value, relative to the thirty-six royal races, to the ancient geography of India, and to the founding of ancient cities; also a catalogue of longevity of plants and animals, and an extract from a work concerning the descendants of Srenica and Sumpriti, the potent princes of the Jain faith between Mahavíra and Vicrama. However meagre these fragments may be, I have incorporated their contents into my mosaic. I also made valuable additions to my collection of medals, for I obtained coins of Mahmoud, Bulbun, and Alla, surnamed *Khooni*, or 'the sanguinary'; and another of a conqueror equally meriting that title, Nadir Shah. But these were of little consequence compared with what one of my envoys brought from Nadolaye—a small bag full of curious hieroglyphical (if I may so use the term) medals of the Chohan princes.[2] One side represents a warrior on horseback, compounded out of a character to which I have applied the above term; on some there was a bull; while others, retaining the original reverse, have on the obverse the titles of the first Islamite conquerors, in the same manner as the currency of France bears the effigies of Louis XVI. and the emblems of the Republic. Whoever will pay a visit to Nadole, will find his labour amply rewarded; I had only leisure to glean a few of these relics, which yet formed a rich harvest. Nadolaye, Balli, Daisoori, Sadri, all ancient seats of the Jains, will yield medals, MSS., and rare specimens of the architectural art. From Aboo to Mundore, the antiquary might fill many port-

[1] See Appendix, No. VII.

[2] These will appear more appropriately in a disquisition on Hindu medals found by me in India, in the *Transactions of the Royal Asiatic Society*.

folios, and collect matter for volumes of the ancient history of this people, for this is the cradle of their faith. That I was enabled to obtain so much during a rapid march through the country, arose partly from previous knowledge, partly from the extent of my means, for I had flying detachments to the right and left of my route, consisting of intelligent natives of each city, accompanied by pundits for deciphering, and others for collecting whatever was the object of research ; who, at the close of each day, brought me the fruits of their inquiries. When any remarkable discovery was made, I followed it up in person, or by sending those in whom I could confide. This is not mentioned from a spirit of egotism, but to incite others to the pursuit by showing the rewards which await such research.

October 29.—Camp at Eendurra, eleven miles. This small town, placed on the north bank of one of the nameless feeders of the 'salt river,' is the boundary of Godwar ; here the reign of the yellow aonla terminates, and here commences *Maroost'hali*, or 'the region of death.' The transition is great. We can look back upon fertility, and forward on aridity, which does not, however, imply sterility : for that cunning artist, nature, compensates the want of verdure and foliage to the inhabitants of the desert, by many spontaneous bounties. An entire race of cucurbitaceous plants is the eleemosynary equivalent for the mango and exotics of the central lands of Rajpootana ; while indigenous poverty sends forth her commercial sons from Osi, Palli, and Pokurna, to bring wealth from the Ganges and the Kistna, to the Looni, or to the still more remote oasis, Jessulmér. From Eendurra everything assumed a new character : the sand, of which we had before scarcely a springling, became occasionally heavy ; the shallow beds of the numerous streams were white with saline incrustations ; and the vegetable creation had been gradually diminishing, from the giant race of the sacred fig-tree with leaf "broad as Amazonian targe," to the dwarfish shrubs of the desert. At once the satiric stanza of the bard of a more favoured region was brought to my mind, and as I repeated it to my old friend the Rana's envoy, he enjoyed the confession, and afresh urged his wish that nature should decide the question of their boundaries :

Ak ra jhopra,
Phok ra bâr,
Bajra ra rooti,
Mot'h ra dâl,
Dekho ho Raja, teri Marwar.

'Huts of the âk,
Barriers of thorns,
Bread of maize,
Lentils of the vetch,
Behold Raja, your Marwar!'

The villages are of a construction totally distinct from anything we have seen, and more approaching the wigwam of the western world. Every commune is surrounded with a circumvallation of thorns, *kanta ka kote*, and the stacks of *bhoos*, or 'chaff,' which are placed at intervals, give it the appearance of a respectable fortification. These *bhoos* stacks are erected to provide provender for the cattle in scanty rainy seasons, when the parched earth denies grass, or full crops of maize. They are erected to the height of twenty or thirty feet, coated with a cement of earth and cow-dung, and with a sprinkling of thorns, to prevent the fowls of the air from reposing in them. In this manner, with a little fresh coating, they will exist ten years, being only resorted to on emergencies, when the kine may be said to devour the village walls. Their appearance is a great relief to the monotony of the march through the desert ; which, however, cannot strictly be said to commence till you cross the Looni.

October 30.—A long march of twenty-one miles, in which there was little to record, brought us to Palli, the great commercial mart of western Rajwarra. Like everything else in these regions it bore the marks of rapine ; and as in the civil wars of this state its possession was of great importance to either party, the fortifications were razed at the desire of the inhabitants, who did not admire the noise of war within their gates. From the same feeling, when it was proposed to gird the sister mart, Bhilwara, with walls, the opposition to it was universal. The remnants of the walls lend it an air of desolation. The town is overrated at ten thousand houses. As an emporium its reputation is of ancient date : and, politically, it is connected with the establishment of the reigning family in these regions. A community of Brahmins then held Palli in grant from the princes of Mundore : whence comes a numerous class, termed Palliwal, who follow mercantile pursuits. It was in S. 1212 (A.D. 1156) that Séôji, the founder of the Rahtore dynasty and son to the emperor of Canouj, passed Palli on his return from a pilgrimage from Dwarica to the Ganges. The Brahmins sent a deputation to relieve them from two great enemies to their repose, namely, the Ménas of the Aravulli, and the lions, which had become very numerous. Séôji relieved them from both ; but the opportunity " to acquire land " was too good to be lost, and on the festival of the *Holi* he put the leading Brahmins to death, and took possession of Palli.

Commerce, in these regions, is the basis of liberty : even despotism is compelled to leave it unrestrained. Palli, like Bhilwara, Jhalrapattan, Rinnie, and other marts, enjoys the right of electing its own magistrates, both for its municipal regulations, and the arbitration of all matters connected with commercial pursuits. It was commerce which freed Europe from the bondage of feudality ; and the towns above cited only require the same happy geographical position, to play the part of the Hanse towns of Europe. Like Bhilwara, Palli has its own currency, which, amidst universal deterioration, it has retained undebased. From remote times, Palli has been the connecting link between the sea-coast and northern India. Commercial houses established at Muscat-Mandavi, Surat, and Noanuggur, transmit the products of Persia, Arabia, Africa, and Europe, receiving those of India and Thibet. To enumerate all the articles, it would be necessary to name the various products of each : from the coast, elephants' teeth, rhinoceros' hides, copper, tin, pewter, dates dried and moist,[1] of which there is an immense consumption in these regions ; gum-arabic, borax, coco-nuts, broad-cloths, striped silks, called *putung* ; various dyes, particularly the *kermes* or crimson ; drugs, especially the oxides of arsenic and quicksilver ; spices, sandal-wood, camphor, tea, *mummaye* or mummy,[2] which is much sought after in medicine, and green

[1] The *kharik* and *pind kujoor*.

[2] *Mom* in the language of Egypt signifies ' wax,' says some ancient authority : so it is the usual name of that article in Persian. *Mommy* is probably thence

glass (*kanch*). From Bhawulpoor, soda (*saji*), the dyes called *ál* and *munjeet*, matchlocks, dried fruits, assafœtida, Mooltan chintzes, and wood for household furniture. From Kotah and Malwa, opium and chintzes. From Jeipoor, various cloths and sugars. From Bhooj, swords and horses.

The exports of home production are the two staple articles of salt and woollens; to which we may add coarse cotton cloths, and paper made in the town of Palli. The *looes*, or blankets, are disseminated throughout India, and may be had at from four to sixty rupees per pair; scarfs and turbans are made of the same material, but not for exportation. But salt is the chief article of export, and the duties arising therefrom equal half the land revenue of the country. Of the *aggurs*, or 'salt lakes,' Puchbuddra, Filodi, and Deedwana, are the principal, the first being several miles in circuit.

The commercial duties of Palli yielded 75,000 rupees annually, a large sum in a poor country like Marwar.

The Charuns and Bhats, or *bards* and *genealogists*, are the chief carriers of these regions: their sacred character overawes the lawless Rajpoot chief; and even the savage Koli and Bhil, and the plundering Sahrae of the desert, dread the anathema of these singular races, who conduct the caravans through the wildest and most desolate regions. The traveller avails himself of such convoy who desires to proceed to the coast by Jalore, Beenmahl, Sanchore, and Radhunpoor, whence he may pursue his route to Surat, or Muscat-Mandavi.

To the east of Palli about ten miles, there is an isolated hill, called *Poonagir*, 'the hill of virtue,' which is crowned with a small temple, said to have been conveyed by a Budhist magician from Palit'hana in Saurashtra. Wherever this ancient and numerous sect exists, magical skill is always asserted. Here we found our old friend, Gough, who had been rambling to the south-west amongst Sahraes, Kossas, and all the wild beings of these uncivilised tracts, in search of new breeds of horses. Halted to enjoy his society.

Kharira, 30th.

Rohit, 31st.

November 1.—Khankani, on the north bank of the Looni. There was nothing to arrest attention between Palli and the Looni: all is flat and lonely in the thirty miles which intervene. Our halts were at Kharira, which has two small salt lakes, whence its name; in fact, this superabundant product, *khar*, or salt, gives its name to streams and towns. Both Kharira and Rohit, the intermediate places of halt, are feudal estates, and both chiefs had been involved in the recent civil dissensions: Rohit was under the ban.

Here I had an exemplification of the vulgar adage, "two of a trade," etc. Paimah Naik, the leader of one of the largest *tandas*, or caravans, which frequent the desert for salt, had left his convoy, and with his brethren came to exhibit his wounds and fractures received in a fray with the leaders of another caravan. Both were Bhats; Paimah was the

derived. I remember playing a trick on old Seeloo, our *khuburdar* at Sindia's camp, who had been solicited to obtain a piece of *mummaye* for a chieftain's wife. As we are supposed to possess everything valuable in the healing art, he would take no refusal; so I substituted a piece of indiarubber.

head of the Bhamunia Bhats, so called from the place of their abode, and he counted forty thousand beasts of burthen under his control. Shama had no distinctive epithet : he had no home separate from his *tanda*. His little state when not in motion was on the highways ; hence those who dwell entirely with their cattle are styled *ooboh punti*, 'on the road.' Shama had taken advantage of the greater portion of Paimah's caravan being detached, to revenge an ancient feud ; and had shown himself quite an adept in club-law, as the broken heads of his opponents disclosed. To reconcile them was impossible ; and as the case was to be decided, not by the scales of abstract justice but by calculating which contributed most in duties, Paimah by this summary process, more than from sympathy to his wounded honour, gained a victory by the exclusion of his rival. As before observed, these classes take advantage of their sacred character amongst the Rajpoots, to become the general carriers of the country : but the advantage which might result to the state from the respect paid to them is neutralised by their avarice, and constant evasion of the payment of all established duties. A memorable example of this kind occurred during the reign of Umra the First, with the ancestor of this same Paimah. The Rana would not submit to the insolent demands of the Bhats, when they had recourse to one of the most sanguinary sacrifices ever recorded—the threat alone of which is generally sufficient to extort acquiescence and concession. But the firmness of Umra has been recorded : and he braved them. Collecting the elder portion of their community, men, women, and youths of both sexes, they made a sacrifice to the number of eighty souls with their daggers in the court of the palace. The blood of the victims was on the Rana's head. It was a species of excommunication, which would have unsettled a weaker reason ; for the Rajpoot might repose after the murder of a Brahmin, but that of the prophetic *Vates* would rise against him here and hereafter. For once they encountered a mind too strong to be shaken ; Umra banished the whole fraternity of Bhamunia Bhats from his dominions, and the town of Bhamuni reverted to the fisc. The edict remained uncancelled until these days, when amongst the industrious of all classes whom the proclamations [1] brought once more to Méwar, came Paimah and his brethren. Although tradition had preserved the causes of their exile, it had made no alteration in their sentiments and opinions, and the dagger was always at hand, to be sheathed in their own flesh whenever provocation called it from the girdle. Paimah beset the Rana in all his rides, demanding a reduction, or rather abolition of duties for his *tanda* ; and at length he took up a position on the terrace fronting the 'balcony of the sun,' threatening a '*chandi*,' for such is the term applied to this suicidal revenge. The Rana, who had not the nerve of his ancestor, sent to me to beseech my interference : with his messenger, one from me returned to invite the Bhats to a settlement. They came, as fine, robust, intrepid a set as I ever saw. We soon came to issue : I urged that duties must be paid by all who chose to frequent the passes of Méwar, and that they would get nothing by their present silly mode of endeavouring to obtain remission ; that if they would give a written agreement to abide by the scale of duties laid down, they should receive exemption for five hundred out of the forty thousand bullocks of their *tanda*, and be re-inducted into Bhamuni ; if not, there were daggers (showing them some

[1] See p. 383.

on the table), and they might begin as soon as they pleased. I added, that, in addition to Rana Umra's penalty of banishment, I would recommend confiscation of their entire caravan. Paimah was no fool: he accepted Bhamuni, and the *maufi* for five hundred, and that day received his gold bracelets and clothes of investiture for Bhamuni from the Rana.

November 2.—Jhalamund, ten miles. Although within one march of Jodpoor, we were obliged to make an intermediate halt, in order to arrange the ceremonials of reception; a grave matter with all the magnates of the East, who regulate all such affairs by slavish precedent and ancestral wisdom. On such a novel occasion as the reception of an English envoy at this desert court, they were a good deal puzzled how to act. They could very well comprehend how an ambassador direct from majesty should be received, and were not unfamiliar with the formula to be observed towards a vice-regal legation. But the present case was an anomaly: the governor of all India, of course, could appear only as the first servant of a commercial body, which, with whatever privileges invested, never could be made to rank with royalty or its immediate emanation. Accordingly, this always proved a clog to our diplomatic missions, until the diffusion of our power from the Indus to the ocean set speculation at rest on the formalities of reception of the Company's ambassadors. On the other hand, the eternal rotation of military adventurers enjoying ephemeral power, such as the commanders of the myrmidons of Sindia and Holkar, compelled all the Rajpoot princes to forego much of their dignity; and men like Ameer Khan, Jean Baptiste, or Bapoo Sindia, who but a short time ago would have deemed themselves honoured with a seat in the ante-chamber, claimed equality of reception with princes. Each made it a subject for boasting, how far he had honoured himself by the humiliation of the descendant of the emperor of Canouj, or the scion of Rama. At the same time, as the world is always deceived by externals, it was difficult to concede a reception less distinguished than that granted to the leader of a Mahratta horde; and here their darling precedent was available. To what distance did the Raja send the *istikbal* to meet Ameer Khan? what was the rank of the chieftains so deputed? and to what point did the "offspring of the sun" condescend to advance in person to receive this "lord of the period"? All these, and many similar questions, were propounded through the Vakeel, who had long been with me, to his sovereign, to whose presence he proceeded in order that they might be adjusted, while I halted at Jhalamund, only five miles from the capital. However, individually, we may despise these matters, we have no option, as public servants, but to demand the full measure of honour for those we represent. As the present would also regulate future receptions, I was compelled to urge that the Raja would best consult his own dignity by attending to that of the government I represented, and distinctly signified that it could never be tolerated that he should descend to the very foot of his castle to honour Ameer Khan, and wait the English envoy almost on the threshold of his palace. It ended, as such matters generally do in those countries, by a compromise: it was stipulated that the Raja should receive the mission in his *palkee* or litter, at the central barrier of descent.[1] These

[1] Mr. Wilder, the superintendent of Ajmér, was deputed by General Sir D. Ochterlony, in Dec. 1818, to the court of Jodpoor, and was very courteously received by the Raja.

preliminaries being arranged, we left Jhalamund in the afternoon, that we might not derange the habits of slumber of those who were to conduct us to the capital. About half-way we were met by the great feudatory chieftains of Pokurna and Neemaj, then lords of the ascendant, and the joint advisers of their sovereign. We dismounted, embraced, complimented each other in the customary phraseology; then remounted, and rode together until we reached the tents, where, after I had requested them to be the bearers of my homage to their sovereign, we mutually saluted and parted.

Salim Sing [1] was the name of the lord of Pokurna, the most wealthy and the most powerful of all the baronies of Marwar. His castle and estate (wrested from Jessulmér) are in the very heart of the desert; the former is strong both by position and art. It is a family which has often shaken the foundation of the throne of Marwar. During four generations have its bold and turbulent chiefs made the most resolute of these monarchs tremble. Deo Sing, the great grandfather of the present chief, used to sleep in the hall of the royal palace, with five hundred of his Kompawuts, of which clan he is the chief. "The throne of Marwar is within the sheath of my dagger," was the boast, as elsewhere mentioned, of this haughty noble to his sovereign. His son, Subbul Sing, followed his father's steps, and even dethroned the great Beejy Sing: a cannon-shot relieved the prince from this terror of his reign. Sowaé Sing, his son and successor, acted the same part towards Raja Bheem, and was involved in the civil wars which commenced in 1806, when he set up the pretender, Dhonkul Sing. The catastrophe of Nagore, in which Meer Khan acted the assassin of the Kompawut and all his associates, relieved Raja Maun from the evil genius of his house; and the honours this prince heaped on the son of the Kompawut, in giving him the first office in the state, were but a trap to ensnare him. From this he escaped, or his life and the honours of Pokurna would have been lost together. Such is a rapid sketch of the family of the chief who was deputed to meet me. He was about thirty-five years of age; his appearance, though not prepossessing, was dignified and commanding. In person he was tall, but more powerful than athletic; his features were good, but his complexion was darker than in general amongst the chieftains of Marwar.

His companion, and associate in the councils of his prince, was in every point of personal appearance the reverse of this portrait. Soortan Sing was chief of the Oodawuts, a clan which can muster four thousand swords, all residing on the land skirting the Aravulii; and of which his residence Neemaj, Raepoor, and Chundawul, are the principal fiefs. Soortan was a fine specimen of the Rajpoot; his figure tall and graceful; his complexion fair; his deportment manly and mild; in short, he was a thorough gentleman, in appearance, understanding, and manners.

It would be impossible to relate here all the causes which involved him in the catastrophe from which his coadjutor escaped. It was the misfortune of Soortan to have been associated with Salim Sing; but his past services to his prince amply counterbalanced this party bias. It was he

[1] The sibilant is the *Shibboleth* of the Rajpoot of Western India, and will always detect him. The 'lion' (*sing*) of Pokurna, is degraded into 'asafœtida' (*hing*); as *Halim Hing*.

who prevented his sovereign from sheathing a dagger in his heart on the disgraceful day at Purbutsir; and he was one of the four chieftains of all Marwar who adhered to his fortunes when beset by the united force of Rajpootana. He was also one of the same four who redeemed the spoils of their country from the hands of the multitudinous array which assaulted Jodpoor in 1806, and whose fate carried mourning into every house of Rajast'han.[1] The death of Soortan Sing was a prodigal sacrifice, and caused a sensation of universal sorrow, in which I unfeignedly participated. His gallant bearing was the theme of universal admiration; nor can I give a better or a juster idea of the chivalrous Rajpoot, than by inserting a literal translation of the letter conveying the account of his death, about eight months after my visit to Jodpoor.

"Jodpoor, 2d Asár, or 28th June 1820.

"On the last day of Jait (the 26th June), an hour before daybreak, the Raja sent the *Alligoles*,[2] and all the quotas of the chiefs, to the number of eight thousand men, to attack Soortan Sing. They blockaded his dwelling in the city, upon which for *three watches* they kept up a constant fire of great guns and small arms. Soortan, with his brother Soor Sing, and his kindred and clan, after a gallant defence, at length sallied forth, attacked the foreigners sword in hand, and drove them back. But who can oppose their prince with success? The odds were too great, and both brothers fell nobly. Nagoji and forty of the bravest of the clan fell with the *Thakoor* brothers, and forty were severely wounded. Eighty, who remained, made good their retreat with their arms to Neemaj.[3] Of the Raja's troops, forty were killed on the spot, and one hundred were wounded. Twenty of the town's-folk suffered in the fray.

"The Pokurna chief, hearing of this, saddled; but the Mahraja sent Seonat Sing of Kochamun, the chief of Bhadrajoon, and others, to give him confidence, and induce him to stay; but he is most anxious to get away. My nephew and fifteen of my followers were slain on this occasion. The Neemaj chief fell as became a Rahtore. The world exclaims 'applause,' and both Hindu and Toork say he met his death nobly. Seonat Sing, Buktawar Sing, Roop Sing, and Anar Sing,[4] performed the funeral rites."

Such is the Rajpoot, when the point of honour is at stake! Not a man of his clan would have surrendered, while their chief lived to claim their lives; and those who retreated only preserved them for the support of the young lord of the Oodawuts!

[1] See p. 371, for the murder of the princess of Oodipoor, one of its results.

[2] The mercenary Rohilla battalions, who are like the Walloons and independent companies which formed the first regular armies of Europe.

[3] Which they afterwards nobly defended during many months.

[4] The last, a brave and excellent man, was the writer of this letter. He, who had sacrificed all to save his prince, and, as he told me himself, supported him, when proscribed by his predecessor, by the sale of all his property, even to his wife's jewels, yet became an exile, to save his life from an overwhelming proscription. To the anomalous state of our alliances with these states is to be ascribed many of these mischiefs.

CHAPTER XXVII

Jodpoor: town and castle—Reception by the Raja—Person and character of Raja Maun Sing—Visits to the Raja—Events in his history—Death of Raja Bheem—Deonat'h, the high-priest of Marwar—His assassination—The acts which succeeded it—Intrigues against the Raja—Dhonkul Sing, a pretender to the Gadi—Real or affected derangement of the Raja—Associates his son in the government—Recalled to the direction of affairs—His deep and artful policy—Visit to Mundore, the ancient capital—Cenotaphs of the Rahtores—Cyclopean architecture of Mundore—Nail-headed characters—The walls—Remains of the palace—Torun, or triumphal arch—T'han of Thana Peer—Glen of Pushcoonda—Statues carved from the rock—Gardens at Mundore—An ascetic—Entertainment at the palace—The Raja visits the envoy—Departure from Jodpoor.

THE sand, since we crossed the Looni, had become gradually heavier, and was quite fatiguing as we approached the capital of "the region of death"; but the Marwarries and the camels appeared to move through it as briskly as our men would on the plains of the Ganges. The fort is erected on a mole projecting from a low range of hills, so as to be almost isolated, while, being higher than the surrounding objects, it is not commanded. This table-ridge (mountain we can scarcely term it, since its most elevated portion is not more than three hundred feet in height) is a curious feature in these regions of uninterrupted aridity. It is about twenty-five miles in length, and, as far as I could determine from a bird's-eye view and from report, between two and three in breadth, the capital being placed on the highest part at the southern extremity, and may be said to be detached from it. The northern point, which is the highest, and on which the palace is built, is less than three hundred feet. Everywhere it is scarped, but especially at this point, against which the batteries of the League were directed in 1806, at least a hundred and twenty feet of perpendicular height. Strong walls and numerous round and square towers encircle the crest of the hill, encompassing a space of great extent, as may be judged from the dimensions of the base, said to be four miles in circuit. Seven barriers are thrown across the circuitous ascent, each having immense portals and their separate guards. There are two small lakes under the walls: the *Ranni Talab*, or 'Queen's Lake,' to the east; and the *Golab Sagur*, or 'Rose-water Sea,' to the south, from which the garrison draws up water in buckets. There is also inside a *coond*, or reservoir, about ninety feet in depth, excavated from the rock, which can be filled from these tanks; and there are likewise wells within, but the water is brackish. Within are many splendid edifices, and the Raja's residence is a succession of palaces, each prince since the founder having left memorials of his architectural taste. The city to the eastward of the citadel is encompassed by a strong wall, three coss, or nearly six miles, in extent, on which a hundred and one bastions or towers are distributed; on the rampart are mounted several *raiklas* or swivels. There are seven gates to the capital, each bearing the name of the city to which it leads. The streets are very regular, and adorned with many handsome edifices of freestone, of which the ridge is composed. The number of families some years ago was stated to be 20,000, probably 80,000 souls, an estimate far too great for the present day. The *Golab Sagur* is the favourite lounge of the inhabitants, who recreate amongst its gardens; and, strange to say, the most incomparable pomegranates (*anar*) are produced in it, far superior even to those of Cabul, which they resemble in the peculiarity of being *be-dáná*, 'without grain': rather a misnomer for a fruit, the characteristic of which is its granulations; but this is in contradistinction to those of India, which are all grain and little pulp. The *anars* of the *Kagli-ca-bagh*, or 'Ravens' Garden,' are sent to the most remote parts, as presents. Their beautiful ruby tint affords an abundant resource for metaphor to the Rajpoot bard, who describes it as "sparkling in the ambrosial cup."[1]

On the 4th the Raja received us with due form, advancing beyond the second gate of descent; when, after salutations and greetings, he returned according to etiquette. Giving him time to make his arrangements, we advanced slowly through lines of his clansmen to the upper area, where a display of grandeur met our view for which we were totally unprepared, and far eclipsing the simple and unostentatious state of the Rana. Here everything was imitative of the imperial court of Dehli, where the Rahtore, long pre-eminent, had "the right hand of the king of the world." Lines of gold and silver mace-bearers deafened us with the titles of "*Raj-Raj-Iswara!*" 'the king, the lord of kings!' into whose presence, through mazes of intricate courts filled with his chivalry, all hushed into that mysterious silence which is invariably observed on such occasions, we were at length ushered.

The King of Maroo arose from his throne, and advanced a few paces, when he again courteously received the envoy and suite, who were here introduced. The hall of reception was of great extent: from its numerous square columns, it is styled *shehes stambha*, 'the thousand-columned hall.' They were more massive than elegant; and being placed in parallel rows, at not more than twelve feet from each other, they gave an air of cumbrous, if not clumsy grandeur to an immense apartment, the ceiling of which was very low. About the centre, in a niche or recess, the royal *gadi* or 'cushion' was placed, over which was raised a richly embroidered canopy, supported by silver-gilt columns. On the Rana's right hand were placed those whom the king honoured, the chieftains of Pokurna and Neemaj, who would have been less at their ease had they known that all the distinctions they then enjoyed were meshes to ensnare them. Several other chieftains and civil officers, whose names would but little interest the reader, were placed around. The vakeel, Bishen Ram, was seated near me, almost in front of the Raja. The conversation was desultory and entirely complimentary; affording, however, abundant opportunity to the Raja to display his proficiency in that mixed language, the Hindostannee, which he spoke with great fluency and much greater purity than those who resided about the court at Dehli. In person the Raja is above the common height, possessing considerable dignity of manner, though accompanied by the stiffness of habitual restraint. His demeanour was commanding and altogether princely; but there was an entire absence of that natural majesty and grace which distinguished the prince of Oodipoor, who won without exertion our spontaneous homage. The features of Raja Maun are good: his eye is full of intelligence; and though the *ensemble* of his countenance

[1] *Amrit ra pealu.*

almost denotes benevolence, yet there is ever and anon a doubtful expression, which, with a peculiarly formed forehead, gave a momentary cast of malignity to it. This might have been owing to that deep dissimulation, which had carried him through a trial of several years' captivity, during which he acted the maniac and the religious enthusiast, until the assumed became in some measure his natural character.

The biography of Maun Sing would afford a remarkable picture of human patience, fortitude, and constancy, never surpassed in any age or country. But in this school of adversity he also took lessons of cruelty: he learned therein to master or rather disguise his passions; and though he showed not the ferocity of the tiger, he acquired the still more dangerous attribute of that animal—its cunning. At that very time, not long after he had emerged from his seclusion, while his features were modelled into an expression of complaisant self-content, indicative of a disdain of human greatness, he was weaving his web of destruction for numberless victims who were basking in the sunshine of his favour. The fate of one of them has been already related.[1]

The Rahtore, like many other dynasties not confined to the East, claims celestial descent. Of their Bhat, we may say what Gibbon does of the Belgic genealogist, who traced the illustrious house of Este from Romulus, that "he riots in all the lust of fiction, and spins from his own bowels a lineage of some thousand years." We are certain that there were sovereigns of Canouj in the fifth century, and it is very probable that they ruled there prior to the era of Christianity. But this is accounted nothing by these lovers of antiquity, who never stop short of *Swyambhúva*, and the ark, in which the antediluvian records of the Rahtores may have been preserved with those of the De Coucys. But we will not revert to those "happy times, when a genealogical tree would strike its root into any soil, and the luxuriant plant could flourish and fructify without a seed of truth." Then, the ambition of the Rahtore for a solar pedigree could be gratified without difficulty.

But it requires neither Bhat nor bard to illustrate its nobility: a series of splendid deeds which time cannot obliterate, has emblazoned the Rahtore name on the historical tablet. Where all these races have gained a place in the temple of fame, it is almost invidious to select; but truth compels me to place the Rahtore with the Chohan, on the very pinnacle. The names of Chonda and Joda are sufficient to connect Séôji, the founder, a scion of Canouj, with his descendant, Raja Maun: the rest

> "Were long to tell; how many battles fought;
> How many kings destroyed, and kingdoms won."

Let us, therefore, put forth our palm to receive the *uttur* from his august hand, and the *pân*, acknowledged by a profound *salaám*, and bringing the right hand to my cocked hat, which etiquette requires we should "apply to the proper use:—'tis for the head," even in the presence. At all the native courts the head is covered, and the *en bas* left bare. It would be sadly indecorous to walk in soiled boots over their delicate carpets, covered with white linen, the general seat. The slippers are left at the door, and it is neither inconvenient nor degrading to sit in your socks. The Raja presented me with an elephant and horse caparisoned, an aigrette,

[1] See p. 558.

necklace, brocades, and shawls, with a portion according to rank to the gentlemen who accompanied me.

On the 6th I paid the Raja another visit, to discuss the affairs of his government. From a protracted conversation of several hours, at which only a single confidential personal attendant of the prince was present, I received the most convincing proofs of his intelligence, and minute knowledge of the past history, not of his own country alone, but of India in general. He was remarkably well read ; and at this and other visits he afforded me much instruction. He had copies made for me of the chief histories of his family, which are now deposited in the library of the Royal Asiastic Society. He entered deeply into the events of his personal history, and recounted many of the expedients he was obliged to have recourse to in order to save his life, when, in consequence of the murder of his *Gúrú* (not only his spiritual but his temporal guide, counsellor, and friend), he relinguished the reins of power, and acquiesced in their assumption by his son. The whole transaction is still involved in mystery, which the Raja alone can unravel. We must enter so far into the state secrets of the court, as to disclose the motive for such an act as the destruction of the brave Soortan, and introduce to the reader another high-priest of the Rajpoots as a pendant for the oracle of the Apollo of Nat'hdwara.

The parricidal murder of Raja Ajeet has been the destruction of Marwar, and even "unto the third and fourth generation" Providence would seem to have visited the act with its vengeance. The crown, which in a few years more would have been transmitted by nature's law, was torn from the brow of this brave prince, who has redeemed his lost inheritance from Arungzéb, by the unhallowed arm of his eldest son Abhé Sing ; instigated thereto by an imperial bribe of the vice-royalty of Guzzerat. His brother, Bukhta Sing, was made almost independent in Nagore by the concession of Abhé and the *sunnud* and titles of his sovereign ; and the contests between their issue have moistened the sands of Marwar with the richest blood of her children. Such is the bane of feudal dominion—the parent of the noblest deeds and the deepest crimes.

Raja Maun, accordingly, came to the throne with all the advantages and disadvantages of such a state of things ; and he was actually defending his existence in Jhalore against his cousin and sovereign, when an unexpected event released him from his perils, and placed him on the throne. Bheem Sing had destroyed almost every branch of the blood-royal, which might have served as a nucleus for those intestine wars which desolated the country, and young Maun, the sole intervening obstacle to the full accomplishment of his wishes, was reduced to the last extremity, and on the eve of surrendering himself and Jhalore to this merciless tyrant, when he was relieved from his perilous situation. He attributed his escape to the intercession of the high-priest of Marwar, the spiritual leader of the Rahtores. This hierarch bore the title of divinity, or *Nat'hji* : his prænomen of Deo or Déva, was almost a repetition of his title ; and both together, *Deonat'h*, cannot be better rendered than by 'Lord God.' Whether the intercession of this exalted personage was purely of a moral nature, as asserted, or whether Raja Bheem was removed from this vain world to the heaven of Indra by means less miraculous than prayer, is a question on which various opinions are entertained ; but all agree that nothing could have been better timed for young Maun, the sole victim required to fill up the measure of Bheem's sanguinary policy. When suicide was the sole alternative to avoid surrender to the fangs of this Herod of the Desert, the high-priest, assuming the mantle of prophecy, pronounced that no capitulation was inscribed in the book of fate—whose page revealed brighter days for young Maun. Such prophets are dangerous about the persons of princes, who seldom fail to find the means to prevent their oracles from being demented. A dose of poison, it is said, was deemed a necessary adjunct to render efficacious the prayers of the pontiff; and they conjointly extricated the young prince from a fate which was deemed inevitable, and placed him on the regal cushion of Marwar. The gratitude of Raja Maun had no limits—no honours, no grants, were sufficient to mark his sense of obligation. The royal mantle was hallowed by the tread of this sainted being; and the throne itself was exalted when Deonat'h condescended to share it with his master, who, while this proud priest muttered forth his mysterious benedictions, with folded hands stood before him to receive the consecrated garland. Lands in every district were conferred upon the Nat'h, until his estates, or rather those of the church of which he was the head, far exceeded in extent those of the proudest nobles of the land; his income amounting to a tenth of the revenues of the state. During the few years he held the keys of his master's conscience, which were conveniently employed to unlock the treasury, he erected no less than eighty-four *mindurs*, or places of worship, with monasteries adjoining them, for his well-fed lazy *chélás* or disciples, who lived at free quarters on the labour of the industrious. Deonat'h was a striking example of the identity of human nature, under whatever garb and in whatever clime; whether under the cowl or the coronet, in the cold clime of Europe, or in the deserts of India. This Wolsey of Maroodés exercised his hourly-increasing power to the disgust and alienation of all but his infatuated prince. He leagued with the nominal minister, Induraj, and together they governed the prince and country. Such characters, when exceeding the sphere of their duties, expose religion to contempt. The degradation which the haughty grandees of Marwar experienced, made murder in their eyes a venial offence, provoked as they were by the humiliations they underwent through the influence of this arrogant priest, whose character may be given in the language of Gibbon, merely substituting Deonat'h of Marwar for Paul of Samosata: "His ecclesiastical jurisdiction was venal and rapacious; he extorted frequent contributions from the most opulent of the faithful, and converted to his own use a considerable part of the public revenue. His council chamber and his throne, the splendour with which he appeared in public, the suppliant crowd who solicited his attention, and the perpetual hurry of business in which he was involved, were circumstances much better suited to the state of a civil magistrate, than to the humility of a primitive bishop." But his "full-blown pride" at length burst under him. Sequestrations from the estates of the chief barons of Maroo became frequent in order to swell his rent-roll for the support of his establishments; his retinue on ordinary occasions surpassed that of any chieftain, and not unfrequently he was attended by the whole insignia of the state—the prince attending on such ceremonies. On these occasions, the proud Rajpoot felt that he folded his hands, not to his sovereign, but to his sovereign's sovereign; to a vindictive and vain-glorious priest, who, amidst the mummeries and artifices of religious rites, gratified an inordinate vanity, while he mortified their pride and diminished their revenues. The hatred of such men is soon followed by their vengeance; and though they would not dye their own daggers in his blood, they soon found agents in a race who know not mercy, the myrmidons of that villain Meer Khan, under whose steel, and within the precincts of the palace, Deonat'h fell a victim. It has been surmised that Raja Maun was privy to the murder; that if he did not command, or even sanction it, he used no means to prevent it. There are but two in this life who can reveal this mystery—the Raja, and the *bourreau en chéf* of Rajast'han, the aforesaid Ameer Khan.

The murder of the high-priest was but a prolongation of the drama, in which we have already represented the treacherous destruction of the chieftain of Pokurna and his kindred; and the immolation of Kishna Komari, the Helen of Rajast'han. The attack on the gallant Soortan, who conducted us from Jhalamund to the capital, sprung from the seed which was planted so many years back; nor was he the last sacrifice: victim after victim followed in quick succession until the Caligula of the Desert, who could "smile and stab," had either slain or exiled all the first chieftains of his state. It would be a tedious tale to unravel all these intrigues; yet some of them must be told, in order to account for the ferocity of this man, now a subordinate ally of the British Government in the East.

It was in A.D. 1804 [1] that Raja Maun exchanged the defence of Jhalore for the throne of Jodpoor. His predecessor, Raja Bheem, left a widow pregnant; she concealed the circumstance, and when delivered, contrived to convey the child in a basket to Sowaé Sing of Pokurna. During two years he kept the secret: he at length convened the Marwar chieftains, with whose concurrence he communicated it to Raja Maun, demanding the cession of Nagore and its dependencies as a domain for this infant, named Dhonkul Sing, the heir-apparent of Marwar. The Raja promised compliance if the mother confirmed the truth of the statement. Whether her personal fears overcame her maternal affection, or the whole was an imposture of Pokurna, she disclaimed the child. The chiefs, though not satisfied, were compelled to appear contented with the result of this appeal; and for some years the matter seemed at rest. But this calm was only the presage of a storm, which shook to its base the political edifice of Marwar, and let loose upon her cities a torrent of predatory foes; it dethroned her prince, and, what the planner could not have contemplated, involved his own destruction. The effects of this treachery have for ever destroyed all confidence between the chief and the entire feudal interest. The Pokurna chief, after failing to establish the claims of Dhonkul Sing as pretender to the throne, sent him for safety to the Shekhawut chief of Khetrí, one of the independent nobles of the Jeipoor family. Here he left him till an opportunity again arrived to bring him upon the scene, which was afforded by the contest between the princes of Marwar and Jeipoor for the hand of the Rana's daughter. This rivalry, the effects of which are already related, and which brought into conflict all the northern powers of India, was, in fact, only the under-plot of the deep-laid policy of Sowaé. When once the gauntlet was thrown down for the hand of this fair lady, the Pokurna chief stepped in with the pretended son of Raja Bheem, whose cause, from the unpopularity of Raja Maun, soon brought to his standard almost all the feudality of Marwar. The measures which followed, and

[1] The date of his accession is the 5th of the month Megsir, S. 1860.

the catastrophe, the death of Kishna Komari, have already been related.[1] The assassination of the chief of Pokurna was simultaneous with these events; and it was shortly after that the murder of the pontiff Deonat'h took place.

After being relieved from all external foes by his own strength of mind, and the aid of a few friends whom no reverse could estrange from him, Raja Maun either fell, or affected to fall, into a state of mental despondency bordering on insanity. Suspicious of every one, he would only eat from the hands of his wife, who prepared his food herself; he became sullen and morose; he neglected public business; and finally withdrew entirely from the world. The attempt to rouse him from this real or pretended stupor was fruitless; he did nothing but lament the death of Deonat'h, and pour forth prayers to the deity. In this state, he was easily induced to associate his son in the government, and he bestowed upon him with his own hand the *teeka* of command. Chuttur Sing was the name of the prince, who was still in his minority; thoughtless, and of dissolute habits, he soon gave himself up to the guidance of a junta of the chiefs, who proclaimed Akhi Chund, of the mercantile caste, the chief civil minister of the state.

Such was the condition of Marwar from A.D. 1809 to 1817. At this period, the progress of events made the English arbiters of the destinies of Rajast'han. The regent of Marwar sent an ambassador to treat; but before the treaties were ratified and exchanged the young regent was dead. Various causes were assigned for his death: by some his dissolute habits, occasioning premature decay; by others, with more probability, the dagger of an indignant Rajpoot, the honour of whose daughter he had clandestinely attempted. Upon this event, and the change of political circumstances, the chiefs had no alternative but to turn to the secluded prince. If but one-half is true that I have heard, and from authority of high credit, the occupations of the years which the Raja passed between the murder of the priest and the death of his son, might be deemed an atonement for the deepest crimes. When messengers announced the fate of his son, and that state necessity recalled him to the helm of affairs, he appeared unable to comprehend them. He had so long acted the maniac, that he had nearly become one: his beard was never touched, and his hair, clotted and foul, gave him an expression of idiocy; yet throughout these long years he was resolutely tenacious of life. The party who governed the son and the state had their own menials to wait upon him, and many were the attempts to poison him by their means; in avoiding which, his simulated madness was so perfect, that they deemed he had "a charmed life." But he had one faithful servant, who throughout this dreadful trial never forsook him, and who carried him food in his turban to replace that which was suspected. When by degrees he was led to understand the emergency, and the necessity of leaving his prison, he persevered in his apparent indifference to everything earthly, until he gathered information and the means for a terrible reaction. The treaty with the English put the ball at his foot: he very soon perceived that he might command a force to put down disorder—such was even volunteered; but with admirable penetration he trusted to the impression of this knowledge amongst his chiefs, as a sufficient auxiliary. By disseminating it, he paralyzed that

[1] P. 366.

spirit which maintained rights in the soil of Marwar nearly concurrent with those of the sovereign. No higher compliment could be paid to British ascendancy, than the sentiments of Raja Maun and his nobles; and no better illustration is on record of the opinion of our power, than that its name alone served the Raja's purpose in subjugating men, who, scarcely knowing fear, yet reposing partly on our justice, though mainly on the utter hopelessness of resisting us, were deprived of all moral courage.

In refusing the aid of a mere physical force, the Raja availed himself of another weapon; for by this artifice he threw the chiefs off their guard, who confided in his assumed desire to forget the past. Intrigues for power and patronage seemed to strengthen this confidence; and Salim Sing of Pokurna, the military *maire du palais* or Bhanjgur'h, and Akhi Chund, retained as civil prime minister, were opposed by Jodraj Singwi, who headed the aspirants to supplant them. The Raja complained of their interested squabbles, but neither party dreamed that they were fostered by him to cloak his deep-laid schemes. Akhi Chund had been minister throughout the son's administration; the political and pecuniary transactions of the state were known chiefly to him; to cut him off would have been poor revenge, and Raja Maun was determined not only to extract from him all the knowledge of state-matters transacted during his seclusion, but to make himself master of his coffers, and neither would have been attained by simple murder. Akhi Chund was not blind to the dangers of his position; he dreaded the *appui* his sovereign derived from the English, and laboured to inspire the Raja with distrust of their motives. It suited his master's views to flatter this opinion; and the minister and his adherents were lulled into a fatal security.

Such were the schemes concocting when I visited this court, which were revealed by succeeding events. At this time, the Raja appeared in a state of mental depression, involved in difficulties, cautious, fearful of a false step, and surrounded by the satellites of the miscreant Akhi Chund, who, if he could no longer incarcerate his person, endeavoured to seal up the mind of his prince from all communication with those who might stimulate him to exertion. But all his arts only served to entangle him in the web then weaving for his life. The Raja first made him the means of destroying the most powerful of his chieftains, Soortan being the primary sacrifice to his sanguinary proscription; many others followed, until the best of the feudal chieftains sought refuge from his fury in exile, and found the *sirna* (sanctuary) they sought in the surrounding states, the majority in Méwar. The day of vengeance at length arrived, and the minister and his partisans were transferred from their position at the helm of the state to a dungeon. Deceived with hopes of life, and compelled by the application of some summary methods of torture, Akhi Chund gave in a schedule of forty lakhs of property, of which the Raja realised a large portion, and then dismissed him to the other world. Nagoji, the kelladar,[1] and Mulji Dandul, both fovourites and advisers of the Raja's late son, returned on the strength of a general amnesty, and forgot they had been traitors. The wealth which prodigality had heaped upon them, consisting of many of the crown-jewels, being recovered, their worldly accounts were settled by a cup of poison, and their bodies thrown over the battlements. Success, and the taste of blood, whetted rather than appeased the appetite of Raja Maun.

[1] Commandant of the fortress.

He was well seconded by the new minister, Futteh Raj, the deadly opponent of Akhi Chund, and all the clan of Champawuts, whom he deemed the authors of the murder of his brother Induraj, slain at the same time with Deonat'h. Each day announced a numerous list of victims, either devoted to death, or imprisoned and stripped of their wealth. The enormous sum of a crore of rupees has been stated as the amount of the confiscations.

All these atrocities occurred within six months after my visit to this court, and about eighteen from the time it was received into protective alliance with the British Government. The anomalous condition of all our connections with the Rajpoot states has already been described: and if illustration of those remarks be required, it is here in awful characters. We had tied up our own hands: "internal interference" had been renounced, and the sequestration of every merchant's property, who was connected with the Mehta faction, and the exile of the nobles, had no limit but the will of a bloodthirsty and vindictive tyrant. The objects of his persecution made known everywhere the unparalleled hardships of their case, and asserted that nothing but respect for the British Government prevented their doing themselves justice. In no part of the past history of this state could such proscription of the majority of the kin and clan of the prince have taken place. The dread of our intervention, as an umpire favourable to their chief, deprived them of hope; they knew that if we were exasperated there was no *sirna* to protect them. They had been more than twelve months in this afflicting condition when I left the country; nor have I heard that anything has been done to relieve them, or to adjust these intestine broils. It is abandoning them to that spirit of revenge which is a powerful ingredient in their nature, and held to be justifiable by any means when no other hope is left them. In all human probability, Raja Maun will end his days by the same expedient which secured him from the fury of his predecessor.

Having lifted the mantle which veiled the future, my reader must forget all that has been said to the disadvantage of Raja Maun, and see only the dignified, the courteous, and the well-instructed gentleman and prince. I cannot think that the Raja had coolly formed to himself the plan of the sanguinary measures he subsequently pursued, and which it would require a much more extended narrative to describe. We discoursed freely on past history, in which he was well read, as also in Persian, and his own native dialects. He presented me with no less than six metrical chronicles of his house; of two, each containing seven thousand stanzas, I made a rough translation. In return, I had transcribed and sent to him Ferishta's great *History of the Mahomedan Power in India*; and *Kholasut ul Towarikh*, a valuable epitome of the history of Hindust'han. I little imagined that I should then have to exhibit him otherwise than his demeanour and instructive discourse made him appear to me. In our graver conversation, I was amused with a discourse on the rules of government, and instructions for the guidance of ambassadors, which my better acquaintance with Chund discovered to be derived from that writer. He carried me, accompanied by a single domestic, to various apartments in the palace, whence he directed my view across the vast plains of the desert, whose monarch I envied not. The low hills in the vicinity alone broke the continuity of this arid region, in which a few isolated *neem* trees were thinly scattered, to remind one of the absence of all that is grand in vegetation. After a visit of several hours, I descended to my tent, and found my friends, Captain Waugh and Major Gough, just returned from a successful chase of an antelope, which, with the aid of some Rohilla greyhounds, they had run down. I attributed their success to the heavy sands, on which I have witnessed many pulled down by dogs of little speed; but the secret was revealed on this animal being sent to the *cuisinier*. On depriving him of his hide, between it and the flesh the whole carcase was covered with a large, inert, amorphous white maggot. The flesh was buried in the sands, and no venison appeared again on my table while in India.

November 8.—I set out early this morning to ramble amidst the ruins of the ancient capital, Mundore, an important link in the chain of archæological research, before the *panchranga*, or 'five-coloured banner' of Maroo was prostrated to the crescent. Attended by an escort provided by the Raja, I left the perambulator behind; but as the journey occupied an hour and a quarter, and at a very slow pace, the distance must be under five miles. I proceeded through the Sojut gate, to gain the road leading to Nagore; shortly after which I passed the Maha Mindur, or 'Grand *Minster*'; the funds for the erection of which were provided by Raja Maun, on his escape from ruin at Jhalore. I skirted the range, gradually decreasing in height for three miles, in a N.N.E. direction. We then altered our course to N.N.W., and entered the gorge of the mountains which envelop all that is hallowed of the relics of the princes of this house. The pass is narrow; the cliffs are almost perpendicular, in which are numerous caves, the abodes of ascetics. The remains of fortifications thrown across, to bar the entrance of the foe to the ancient capital of the Puriharas, are still visible: a small stream of pure and sweet water issues from this opening, and had a water-course under an archway. After proceeding a little further, the interval widened, and passing through the village, which does not exceed two hundred houses, our attention was attracted by a line of lofty temples, rising in graduated succession. These proud monuments proved to be the cenotaphs of the Rahtores, erected on the spots where the funeral pyre consumed the crowned heads of Maroo, who seldom burnt alone, but were accompanied by all that made life agreeable or poisoned its enjoyment. The small brook already mentioned flows past the southern extremity of the chief line of monuments, which extend from south to north. At the former point stands that of Rao Maldeo, the gallant opponent of Shere Shah, the brave usurper of the throne of the Moguls. The further point terminates with that of Mahraja Ajeet Sing; while the princes in regular succession, namely, Soor Sing, Oodi Sing, Guj Sing, and Jeswunt Sing, fill up the interval.

These dumb recorders of a nation's history attest the epochs of Marwar's glory, which commenced with Maldeo, and ended with the sons of Ajeet. The temple-monument of Maldeo, which yet throws into shade the still more simple shrines of Chonda, and Joda, contrasted with the magnificent mausoleum of Raja Ajeet, reads us a lesson on the advancement of luxurious pomp in this desert state. The progression is uniform, both in magnitude and elegance, from Maldeo's, who opposed on equal terms the Afghan king (whose memorable words, "I had nearly lost the throne of India for a handful of barley," mark at once the gallantry and the poverty of those whom he encountered), to the last great prince Ajeet.

Even that of Raja Guj is plain, compared to his successor's. These monuments are all erected of a very close-grained freestone, of a dark brown or red tint, with sufficient hardness to allow the sculptor to indulge his fancy. The style of architecture, or rather the composition, is mixed, partaking both of the Sivite and the Budhist ; but the details are decidedly Jain, more especially the columns, which are of the same model as those in Komulmér. I speak more especially of those of Rajas Jeswunt and Ajeet, drawings of which, on a large scale, executed by the Raja's chief architect, I brought to Europe ; but which it would be too expensive to have engraved. They are raised on immense terraces, faced with large blocks of well-polished freestone. That of Jeswunt is somewhat ponderous and massive ; but Ajeet's rises with great elegance and perfect symmetry of proportion.

On ascending the terrace, you enter through a lofty vaulted porch supported by handsome columns to the *sanctum,* which is a pyramidal temple, four stories in height, in the Sivite style, crowned by the *sikra* and *kullus*, elsewhere described. The sculptural ornaments are worthy of admiration, both for their design and effect ; and the numerous columns on the basement, and different stages of ascent, give an air of so much majesty, that one might deem these monuments more fitting sepulture for the Egyptian Cheops, than a shrine—over what ? not even the ashes of the desert king, which were consigned in an urn to the bosom of the Ganges. If the foundations of these necrological monuments have been equally attended to with the superstructure, they bid fair to convey to remote posterity the recollection of as conspicuous a knot of princely characters as ever followed each other in the annals of any age or country. Let us place them in juxtaposition with the worthies of Méwar and the illustrious scions of Timoor, and challenge the thrones of Europe to exhibit such a contemporaneous display of warriors, statesmen, or scholars.

Méwar.	Marwar.	Dehli.
Rana Sanga	Rao Maldeo	Baber and Shere Shah.
	Rao Soor Sing	Hemayoon.
Rana Pertáp	Raja Oodi Sing	Akber.
Rana Umra I. Rana Kurrun	Raja Guj Sing	Jehangír and Shah Jehán.
Rana Raj	Raja Jeswunt Sing	Arungzéb.
Rana Jey Sing Rana Umra II.	Raja Ajeet Sing	All the competitors for the throne after Ferochsér.

From Maldeo to Oodi *le gros* the first *Raja* (hitherto *Raos*) of Marwar, and the friend of Akber, to Jeswunt, the implacable foe of Arungzéb, and Ajeet, who redeemed his country from oppression, all were valiant men and patriotic princes.

"Where were the lions' cubs," I asked of my conductor, "the brave sons of Ajeet, who erected this monument to his manes, and who added provinces to his dominions ?" He pointed to two sheds, where the *kerea-carma* was performed ; there was

> "No funeral urn
> To mark their obsequies" :

but these lowly sheds told, in more forcible, more emphatic language, the cause of this abrupt transition from grandeur to humility, than pen ever wrote; and furnished the moral epilogue to the eventful drama of the lives of these kings of the desert. Abhé Sing's parricidal hand bereft his father of life; yet though his career was one splendid tissue of success and honour, leaving his dominions more than doubled, the contentions of his issue with that of his brother Bukhta Sing, alike accessory, it is said, to the crime, have entailed endless misery upon Marwar, and left them not the power, if they had the inclination, to house his ashes. In the same line with the parricide and his brave brother is the humble monument of the great Beejy Sing, whose life till towards its close was a continued tide of action. I could not avoid an exclamation of surprise: "Shame to the country," I said, "that has neglected to enshrine the ashes of a name equal to the proudest!" His three sons, amongst them Zalim Sing, with the sketch of whom this narrative opened, have their shrines close to his; and but a few yards removed are those of Raja Bheem, and his elder brother Goomân (who died in his minority), the father of the reigning prince, Raja Maun. The last, which closed the line, pertained to Chuttur Sing, who, in all probability, was saved by death from the murder of his parent. I passed it in disgust, asking who had been so foolish as to entomb his ashes better than those of some of the worthies of his race? I found that it was the act of maternal fondness.

The *amavus* (the ides) and the *sancrantis* (when the sun enters a new sign of the Zodiac) of every month are sacred to the *Pitriswara*, on which days it is incumbent on the reigning prince to 'give water' to his ancestors. But the ignorance of my conductor deprived me of much information which I anticipated; and had I not been pretty well read in the chronicles of the Rahtores, I should have little enjoyed this visit to a "nation's dust." They related one fact, which was sufficient to inspire horror. No less than sixty-four females accompanied the shade of Ajeet to the mansion of the sun. But this is twenty short of the number who became *Satis* when Raja Boodh Sing of Boondí was drowned! The monuments of this noble family of the Haras are far more explicit than those of the Rahtores, for every such *Sati* is sculptured on a small altar in the centre of the cenotaph: which speaks in distinct language the all-powerful motive, *vanity*, the principal incentive to these tremendous sacrifices. Boodh Sing was a contemporary of Ajeet, and one of the most intrepid generals of Arungzéb; the period elapsed is about one hundred and twenty years. Mark the difference! When his descendant, my valued friend, the Rao Raja Bishen Sing, died in 1821, his last commands were that none should give such a proof of their affection. He made me guardian of his infant heir;—in a few days I was at Boondí, and his commands were religiously obeyed.

In this account are enumerated the monumental relics below the fort. Upon the mountain, and beyond the walls of the fortress of Mundore, are the *dewuls* of Rao Rinmull, Rao Ganga, and Chonda, who conquered Mundore from the Purihars. Within a hundred yards of this trio of worthies of this house, is a spot set apart for the queens who die natural deaths. But this is anticipating; let me in form conduct my readers step by step from the cemetery of the Rahtores to the Cyclopean city of the Purihars.

Whoever has seen Cortona, Volterra, or others of the ancient Tuscan cities, can form a correct idea of the walls of Mundore, which are precisely of the same ponderous character. It is singular that the ancient races of India, as well as of Europe (and whose name of *Pali* is the synonym of *Galati* or *Keltoe*) should, in equal ignorance of the mechanical arts, have piled up these stupendous monuments, which might well induce their posterity to imagine "there were giants in those days." This western region, in which I include nearly all Rajpootana and Saurashtra, has been the peculiar abode of these "pastor kings," who have left their names, their monuments, their religion and sacred character, as the best records of their supremacy. The *Raj-Pali*, or 'Royal Pastors,' are enumerated as one of the thirty-six royal races of ancient days: the city of Palithana, 'the abode of the Pali,' in Saurashtra (built at the foot of Mount Satrunja, sacred to Budha), and Palli in Godwar, are at once evidences of their political consequence and the religion they brought with them; while the different nail-headed characters are claimed by their descendants, the sectarian Jains of the present day. There is scarcely an ancient city in Rajpootana whence I have not obtained copies of inscriptions from columns and rocks, or medals, gold, silver, and copper, bearing this antique character. All are memorials of these races, likewise termed *Takshac*, the Scythic conquerors of India, ancestors of many of the Rajpoots, whose history the antiquary will one day become better acquainted with. The Purihara, it will be recollected, is one of the four Agnicúlas: races who obtained a footing in India posterior to the Suryas and Indus. I omitted, however, to mention, in the sketch of the Puriharas, that they claim Cashmér as the country whence they migrated into India: the period is not assigned, but it was when the schismatic wars between the Sivites and Budhists were carrying on; and it would appear that the former found proselytes and supporters in many of these Agnicúlas. But of the numerical extent of the followers of this faith we have this powerful evidence, namely, that three-fourths of the mercantile classes of these regions are the descendants of the martial conquerors of India, and that *seven out of the ten and a half* nyâts or tribes, with their innumerable branches, still profess the Jain faith, which, beyond controversy, was for ages paramount in this country.

Let us now ascend the paved causeway to this gigantic ruin, and leave the description of the serpentine *Nagda*, which I threaded to its source in the glen of Pushcoonda, till our return. Half-way up the ascent is a noble *bowli*, or 'reservoir,' excavated from the solid rock, with a facing of cut stone and a noble flight of steps: on which, however, two enormous *goolurs* or wild fig-trees have taken root, and threaten it with premature destruction. This memorial bears the name of Nahur Rao, the last of the Purihars. As I looked up to the stupendous walls,

> "Where time hath leant his hand, but broke his scythe,"

I felt the full force of the sentiment of our heart-stricken Byron:

> "there is a power
> And magic in the ruined battlement,
> For which the palace of the present hour
> Must yield its pomp, and wait till ages are its dower."

Ages have rolled away since these were raised, and ages will yet roll on, and find them immovable, unchanged. The immense blocks are piled upon, and closely fitted to, each other without any cement, the characteristic of all the Etruscan cities termed Cyclopean. We might indeed smuggle a section of Mundore into the pages of Micali,[1] amongst those of Todi or Volterra, without fear of detection. The walls, following the direction of the crest of the ridge, are irregular ; and having been constructed long before artillery was thought of, the Purihar or Pali engineer was satisfied with placing the palace on the most commanding eminence, about the centre of the fortress. The bastions or towers are singularly massive, and like all the most antique, their form is square. Having both fever and ague upon me, I was incapable of tracing the direction of the walls, so as to form any correct judgment of the space they enclose ; but satisfied with gaining the summit, I surveyed the ruin from the site of the palace of the Purihars. The remains, though scanty, are yet visible ; but the materials have been used in the construction of the new capital Jodpoor, and in the cenotaphs described. A small range of the domestic temples of the palace, and some of the apartments, are yet distinctly to be traced ; the sculptured ornaments of their portals prove them to have been the work of a Takshac or Budhist architect. Symbolical figures are frequently seen carved on the large blocks of the walls, though probably intended merely as guides to the mason. These were chiefly Budhist or Jain : as the quatre-feuille, the cross ; though the mystic triangle, and triangle within a triangle ✡ [2] (a sign of the Sivites, only, I believe), was also to be seen. The chief memorials of the Purihara are a gateway and magnificent *Torun*, or triumphal arch, placed towards the south-east angle of the castle. It is one mass of sculpture ; but the pencil was wanting, and I had not leisure even to bring away a rude resemblance of this memento of some victory of the ancient lords of Mundore. A little distance to the northward of my position is the *T'han*, or 'station' of a Mahomedan saint, a disciple of the celebrated Khwaja Kootub, whose shrine at Ajmér is celebrated. This of Thana Peer, as they call him, was a place of great resort to the unsanctified Kafirs, the mercenary Sindies and Afghans, who long prowled about these regions in quest of prey, or plunder, or both. Nearly in the same direction, beyond the walls, are the cenotaphs of the early Rahtores and the Satis already mentioned; but tradition's voice is mute as to the spot which contains the ashes of the Purihars. To the east and north-east, nature has formed at once a barrier to this antique castle, and a place of recreation for its inhabitants ; a lengthened chasm in the whole face, appearing like a dark line, were it not for the superb foliage of goolur, mango, and the sacred burr and peepul, which rise above the cleft, planted about the fountain and perpendicular cliffs of the Nagda, and which must have proved a luxurious retreat to the princes of Mundore from the reverberation of the sun's rays on the rock-built palace ; for there is but a scanty brushwood scattered over the surface, which is otherwise destitute of all vegetation.

[1] *L'Italie avant la Domination des Romains.*

[2] Amongst ancient coins and medals, excavated from the ruins of Oojein and other ancient cities, I possess a perfect series with all the symbolic emblems of the *twenty-four* Jain apostles. The compound equilateral triangle is amongst them : perhaps there were *Masons* in those days amongst the Pali. It is hardly necessary to state, that this Trinitarian symbol (the double triangle) occurs on our (so-called) Gothic edifices, *e.g.*, the beautiful abbey gate of Bury St. Edmunds, Suffolk, erected about A.D. 1377.

Let us now descend by the same causeway to the glen of Pushcoonda, where there is much to gratify both the lover of the picturesque and the architectural antiquary. At the foot of the causeway, terminated by a reservoir of good water, are two gateways, one conducting to the gardens and their palaces erected by the Rahtores; the other, to the statues of the Paladins of the desert. Leaving both for a moment, I pursued the 'serpentine' rivulet to its fountain, where

> " Couched among fallen columns, in the shade
> Of ruined walls that had survived the names
> Of those who reared them,"

I reposed in meditative indolence, overwhelmed with the recollections such scenes inspire. In a recess or cave is a rude altar sanctified by the name of Nahur Rao, the famed king of Mundore, who met in equal combat the chivalrous Chohan in the pass of the Aravulli.[1] A *nye*, or barber, performs worship to the manes of this illustrious Rajpoot, in whose praise Chund is most eloquent. Whence the choice of a barber as a priest I know not; but as he has the universal care of the material portion of the Rajpoot, being always chosen as the cook, so there may be reasons for his having had an interest in the immaterial part in olden days, the tradition of which may have been lost. There is a piece of sculpture containing nine figures, said to represent Ravana, who came from " th'utmost isle Taprobane,"[2] to marry the daughter of the sovereign of Mundore. There was a lengthened legend to account for the name of *nagda*, or, 'serpentine,' being applied to the rivulet, but it is too long to relate. We must therefore quit the fountain, where the gallant Pirthi-raj and his fair bride, the cause of strife between the Chohans and Puriharas, may have reposed, and visit the most remarkable relic within the precincts of this singular place.

A short distance from the foot of the causeway, an archway opens into an enclosed court or area, in the retired part of which, and touching the mountain, is an extensive saloon; the roof is supported by a triple row of columns, of that light form peculiar to the Jains. Here are displayed, in all " the pomp and circumstance of war," the statues of the knights-errant of the desert, armed *cap-à-pie*, bestriding steeds whose names are deathless as their riders', all in the costume of the times in which they lived. They are cut out of the rock, but entirely detached from it, and larger than life. Though more conspicuous for strength than symmetry, the grim visages of these worthies, apparently frowning defiance, each attended by his pundoo or squire, have a singularly pleasing effect. Each chieftain is armed with lance, sword, and buckler, with quiver and arrows, and poniard in his girdle. All are painted; but whether in the colours they were attached to, or according to the fancy of the architect, I know not. Before, however, entering this saloon, we pass a huge statue of Ganésa, placed as the guardian of the portal, having on each side the two Bhiroos, sons of the god of war. Then appears the statue of Chamoonda (the goddess of destruction), and that of the terrific mother, Kankali, treading on the black demon Bhynsasoor, in whose flank her tiger-courser has buried his bloodthirsty tongue: in each of her eight arms she holds a

[1] See p. 540.
[2] *Tapoo Ravana*, 'the isle of Ravana,' wherever that may be.

weapon of destruction. The black Bhiroo (son of time), with a sable flag, bearing *argent* a horse *courant*, marshals the way through the field of blood to his mother. Between her and the heroes whose lives passed "in devotion to the sword," is a statue of the *Nathji*, or 'spiritual guide' of the Rahtores: in one hand he holds his *mala* or 'chaplet'; in the other his *churri*, or 'patriarchal rod,' for the guidance of his flock. Mullinat'h heads the procession, mounted on a white charger, with a lance over his shoulder, to which is attached a flag; his quiver resting on his horse's right flank, and his mistress, Pudmavati, with a platter of food welcoming him from the raid, and who accompanied him when slain to *Suryaloca*, or 'the mansion of the sun.'

Then follows Pabooji, mounted on his famous charger 'Black Cæsar' (*Késar Kali*), whose exploits are the theme of the itinerant bard and showman, who annually goes his round, exhibiting in pictorial delineations, while he recites in rhyme, the deeds of this warrior to the gossiping villagers of the desert.

Next comes Ramdeo Rahtore, a name famed in Maroodésa, and in whose honour altars are raised in every Rajpoot village in the country.

Then we have the brave Hurba Sankla, to whom Joda was indebted for protection in his exile, and for the redemption of Mundore when seized by the Rana of Cheetore.

Goga, the Chohan, who with his forty-seven sons fell defending the passage of the Sutledge on Mahmoud's invasion. Mewoh Mangulia brings up the rear, a famous chieftain of the Gehlote race. It would be tedious to relate any of the exploits of these worthies.

Another saloon, of similar architecture and still greater dimensions, adjoins that just described; it is termed *tyntees cúla* [1] *dévata ra t'hán*, or 'abode of the (tutelary) divinities of the thirty-three races': in short, the Pantheon of the Rajpoots. The statues are of gypsum, or stone covered with that substance; they are of large proportions. First, is the creator, Brimha; then Surya, 'the sun-god,' with his seven-headed steed; then the monkey-faced deity, Hanuman; Rama, and his beloved Síta; Kaniya, in the woods of Vrij, surrounded by the Gopis; and a most grave figure of Mahadeva, with a bull in his hand. These six, with the goddesses of life and death, and of wisdom, constitute the eight chief divinities of the Hindus; whose qualities and attributes, personified, form an assemblage for which St. Peter's and the Vatican to boot would be a confined dwelling.

I now retired to the palace and gardens built by Raja Ajeet; of which, however superb, it is impossible for the pen to give a definite idea. Suites of colonnaded halls, covered with sculpture of easy and even graceful execution, some with screens of lattice-work to secure the ladies from the public gaze, are on the lower range; while staircases lead to smaller apartments intended for repose. The gardens, though not extensive, as may be supposed, being confined within the adamantine walls reared by the hand of Nature, must be delightfully cool even in summer. Fountains, reservoirs, and water-courses, are everywhere interspersed; and though the thermometer in the open air was 86°,[2] the cold within

[1] I imagine the word *cúla*, or 'race,' of which, as often remarked, there are not thirty-three but thirty-six, has given rise to the assertion respecting the thirty-three *crore* or millions of gods of Hindust'han.

[2] Thermometer 55°, 72°, 86°, 80° at daybreak, ten, two, and at sunset; on

doors (if this be not a solecism, considering that there were no doors) was excessive. Some attention was paid to its culture; besides many indigenous shrubs, it boasted of some exotics. There was the golden *chumpa*, whose aroma is overpowering, and if laid upon the pillow will produce headache; the pomegranate, at once "rich in flower and fruit"; the apple of Síta, or *Sitaphala*, which from similitude of taste, we call the custard-apple; a delicious species of the plantain, whose broad, verdant, glossy leaf alone inspires the mind with the sensation of coolness; the *mogra*; the *chamaili*, or jessamine; and the queen of flowers, the *baramasha*, literally the 'twelve-month,' because it flowers throughout the year. It is a delightful spot, and I felt a peculiar interest in it. Let the reader imagine the picture of a solitary Englishman scribbling amidst the ruins of Mundore: in front a group of venerable mango-trees; a little further an enormous isolated tamarind, "planted by the hand of a juggler in the time of Nahur Rao, the last of the Puriharas, before whom he exhibited this proof of legerdemain," and, as the legend goes, from whose branches the juggler met his death:[1] amidst its boughs the long-armed tribe, the allies of Rama, were skipping and chattering unmolested; while beneath, two Rahtore Rajpoots were stretched in sleep, their horses dozing beside them, standing as sedately as the statue of 'Black Cæsar': a grenadier Sepoy of my escort parading by a camp-basket, containing the provender of the morning, completes the calm and quiet scene.

On the summit of the rock, across the narrow valley, several *gophas*, or caves, the abode of the hermit Atteet, were in sight. How the brains of these ascetics can stand the heat and confined air is a wonder, though, if they possessed any portion of that which is supposed to be necessary to the guidance of the machine, they would scarcely occupy such a position, nor consequently, the world's attention. *Mais tout est vanité*, a cause which has produced ten times the number of saints that piety has, and ten times of ten these troglodyte philosophers. Having walked out on the terrace or house-top of the palace, to catch a sunbeam and scare away an ague which tormented me, I discovered one of these animals coiled up on a heap of bat's-dung, in a corner of an apartment of the palace. He was dreadfully emaciated, and but for the rolling of a pair of eyes in a visage covered with hair, there was nothing which betokened animation, much less humanity. There was none but the bat to dispute his reign, or "the spider which weaves its web in this palace of the Cæsars." I had no inclination to disturb the process of ratiocination, or to ask to which sect of philosophers belonged this Diogenes of Mundore, who might, if he had utterance, have desired me to walk downstairs, and not intercept the sunbeam for whose warmth we were competitors. The day was now nearly departed, and it was time for me to return to my friends in camp. I finished the evening by another visit to the knights of the desert; and inscribing my name on the foot of 'Black Cæsar,' bade adieu to the ancient Mundore.

November 13.—The Raja having invited us to a dinner at the palace, we sallied forth, belted and padded, to partake of Rajpoot hospitality. He

the 3rd November, the day of our arrival, the variations were 50°, 72°, 80°, and 75° at those hours.

[1] See the autobiography of Jehangír, translated by that able Oriental scholar, Major Price, for the astonishing feats these jugglers perform in creating not only the tree, but the fruit.

had made a request which will appear somewhat strange—that we would send our *cuisine*, as the fare of the desert might prove unpalatable; but this I had often seen done at Sindia's camp, when joints of mutton, fowls, and fricassees, would diversify the provender of the Mahratta. I intimated that we had no apprehension that we should not do justice to the gastronomy of Jodpoor; however, we sent our tables, and some claret to drink long life to the king of Maroodés. Having paid our respects to our host, he dismissed us with the complimentary wish that appetite might wait upon us, and, preceded by a host of gold and silver sticks, we were ushered into a hall, where we found the table literally covered with curries, pillaus, and ragouts of every kind, in which was not forgotten the *hurea moong Mundore ra*, the 'green pulse of Mundore,' the favourite dish, next to *rabri* or maize-porridge, of the simple Rahtore. Here, however, we saw displayed the dishes of both the Hindu and Musulman, and nearly all were served in silver. The curries were excellent, especially those of the vegetable tribes made of the pulses, the *kakris* or cucumbers, and of a miniature melon not larger than an egg, which grows spontaneously in these regions, and is transported by *kasids*, or runners, as presents, for many hundreds of miles around. The hall was an entire new building, and scarcely finished; it is erected on the northern projection of the rock, where the escarpment is most abrupt, and looks down upon the site of the batteries of the league of 1806. It is called the *Maun mahal*, and, like the hall of audience, its flat roof is supported by numerous massive hewn columns. The view from it to the east is extensive, and we were told that the pinnacle of Komulmér, though eighty miles distant, has been seen, in those clear days of the monsoon when the atmosphere is purified, after heavy showers, from the sand which is held suspended. Great care was taken that our meal should be uninterrupted, and that we should not be the lions to an hour's amusement of the court. There was but one trivial occurrence to interrupt the decorum and attention of all present, and that was so slight that we only knew it after the entertainment was over. One of the menials of the court, either from ignorance or design, was inclined to evince contumely or bad breeding It will be considered perhaps a singular circumstance, that the Hindu should place before a European the vessels from which he himself eats: but a little fire purifies any metallic vessels from all such contamination; and on this point the high-blooded Rajpoot is less scrupulous than the bigotted Mahomedan, whom I have seen throw on the ground with contempt a cup from which his officer had drank water on a march. But of earthenware there can be no purification. Now there was a handsome China bowl, for which some old dowager fancier of such articles would have almost become a supplicant, which having been filled with curds to the *Soodra Fringees* could no longer be used by the prince, and it was brought by this menial, perhaps with those words, to my native butler. Kali Khan, or as we familiarly called him, '*the black lord*,' was of a temper not to be trifled with; and as the domestic held it in his hand, saying, "Take it, it is no longer of any use to us," he gave it a tap with his hand which sent it over the battlements, and coolly resuming his work, observed, "That is the way in which all useless things should be served"; a hint, which, if reported to Raja Maun, he seems to have acted on: for not many months after, the minister, Akhi Chund, who dreaded lest European influence should release his master from his faction and thraldom, was treated by him in the same manner as the china bowl by Kali Khan.

November 16.[1]—This day had been fixed for the Raja's visits to the envoy. In order to display his grandeur, he sent his own suite of tents, which were erected near mine. They were very extensive, modelled in every way after those of the Emperors of Dehli, and lined throughout with the royal colour, crimson : but this is an innovation, as will appear from the formulas yet preserved of his despatches, "from the foot of the throne, Jodpoor." The tent, in fact, was a palace in miniature, the whole surrounded by walls of cloth, to keep at a distance the profane vulgar. The *gadi*, or royal cushion and canopy, were placed in the central apartment. At three, all was noise and bustle in the castle and town ; nakarras were reverberating, trumpets sounding the alarm, that the King of Maroo was about to visit the Fringee Vakeel. As soon as the flags and pennant were observed winding down 'the hill of strife' (*Joda-gir*), I mounted, and with the gentlemen of my suite proceeded through the town to meet the Raja. Having complimented him *en route*, we returned and received him at the tents. The escort drawn up at the entrance of the tent presented arms, the officers saluting ; a mark of attention which gratified him, as did the soldier-like appearance of the men. Hitherto, what he had seen of regulars belonging to the native powers was not calculated to give him a favourable impression of foot-soldiers, who are little esteemed by the equestrian order of Rajpootana. His visit continued about an hour, when the shields were brought in, with jewels, brocades, shawls, and other finery, in all nineteen trays, being two less than I presented to the Rana of Oodipoor. I likewise presented him with some arms of English manufacture, a telescope, and smaller things much valued by the Rajpoots. After the final ceremony of perfumes, and *utr-pân* (which are admirable hints when you wish to got rid of a tiresome guest, though not so in this instance), the exterior wall was removed, and showed the caparisoned elephant and horses, which were part of the khélát. At the door of the tent we made our salaam, when the Raja gave me his hand, which, by the by, was his first salutation on receiving me. It is an ancient Rajpoot custom, and their bards continually allude to extending the right hand—"*dextrâ extentâ*."

November 17.[2]—I went to take leave of the Raja : I had a long and interesting conversation on this our last interview. I left him in the full expectation that his energy of character would surmount the difficulties by which he was surrounded, though not without a struggle, and condign punishment to some of the miscreants, the misleaders of his son, the assassins of his minister and high priest, and consequently the authors of his humiliating and protracted incarceration. Whether the first gratification of vengeance provoked his appetite, or whether the torrent of his rage, once impelled into motion, became too impetuous to be checked, so that his reason was actually disturbed by the sufferings he had undergone, it is certain he grew a demoniac ; nor could any one, who had conversed with the bland, the gentlemanly, I might say gentle, Raja Maun, have imagined that he concealed under this exterior a heart so malignant as his subsequent acts evinced. But the day of retribution must arrive ; the men who

[1] Thermometer 59°, 82°, 85°, 79°.
[2] Thermometer 59°, 73°, 89°, 82° ; at six, ten, two, and sunset.

wrote that dignified remonstrance, which is given in another place,[1] will not tamely bear their wrongs, and as they dare not levy war against their prince, who reposes under British protection, the dagger will doubtless find a way to reach him even in "the thousand-columned hall" of Jodpoor.

Besides the usual gifts at parting, which are matter of etiquette, and remain untouched by the individual, I accepted as a personal token of his favour, a sword, dagger, and buckler, which had belonged to one of his illustrious ancestors. The weight of the sword, which had often been "the angel of death," would convince any one that it must have been a nervous arm which carried it through a day. With mutual good wishes, and a request for a literary correspondence, which was commenced but soon closed, I bade adieu to Raja Maun and the capital of MARWAR.

CHAPTER XXVIII

Nandla—Beesilpoor—Remains of the ancient city—Puchkullia, or Beechkulla—Inscription—Peepar—Inscription confirming the ancient chronicles of Méwar—Geological details—Legend of Lake Sampoo—Lakha Foolani—Madreo—Bhoroonda—Buddun Sing—His chivalrous fate—Altar to Pertáp—Indawur—Jat cultivators—Stratification of Indawur—Mairta—Memory of Arungzéb—Dhonkul Sing—Jeimul, the hero of the Rahtores—Tributes to his bravery—Description of the city and plain of Mairta—Cenotaphs—Raja Ajeet—His assassination by his sons—The consequences of this deed the seeds of the Civil Wars of Marwar—Family of Ajeet—Curious fact in the law of adoption amongst the Rahtores—Ram Sing—His discourtesy towards his chiefs—Civil War—Defection of the Jarejas from Ram Sing—Battle between Ram Sing and Bukhta Sing—Defeat of the former, and the extirpation of the clan of the Mairteas—The Mairtea vassal of Mehtri—The field of battle described—Ram Sing invites the Mahrattas into his territory—Bukhta Sing becomes Raja of Marwar—His murder by the Prince of Jeipoor—His son, Beejy Sing, succeeds—Jey Appa Sindia and Ram Sing invade Marwar—They are opposed by Beejy Sing, who is defeated—He flies to Nagore, where he is invested—He cuts through the enemy's camp—Solicits succour at Bikanér and Jeipoor—Treachery of the Raja of Jeipoor—Defeated by the chieftain of Reah—Assassination of Appa Sindia.

November 19.—We broke ground for Nandla, distant six miles. The first two miles from the capital was through deep sand; for the remainder of the journey the red sandstone protruded, which gives some relief to the footing of the traveller. About half-way we passed a small sheet of water, called after the mother of the pretender, Dhonkul Sing, the Shekhawut Tallao. This lady has constructed a *dhurmsala*, or 'hall for travellers,' on its bank, where she has erected a statue of Hanuman, and a pillar to commemorate her own good works. Not a shrub of any magnitude occurs, for even the stunted *khyr* is rare in this plain of sand; which does not, however, appear unfavourable to the *mot'h*, a vetch on which they feed the cattle. Near the village we crossed the Jogini, the same stream which we passed between Jhalamund and the capital, and which, joined by the Nagda from Mundore, falls into the Looni. The only supply of water for Nandla is procured from two wells dug on the margin of the stream. The water is abundant, and only four feet from the surface, but brackish. There are a hundred and twenty-five houses in Nandla, which is in the fief of the chieftain of Ahore. A few cenotaphs are on the

[1] See p. 159.

banks of a tank, now dry. I went to look at them, but they contained names "unknown to fame."

Beesilpoor, the next place, is distant six estimated coss of the country, and thirteen miles one furlong by the perambulator: heavy sand the whole way. Nevertheless we saw traces of the last autumnal crop of bajra and joar, two species of millet, which form the chief food of the people of the desert; and the vetch was still in heaps. Beesilpoor is situated on a rising ground; the houses are uniform in height and regularly built, and coated with a compost of mud and chaff, so that its appearance is picturesque. It is protected by a circumvallation of thorns, the *kanta-ka-kote* and the stacks of chaff, as described at Eendurra. They are pleasing to the eye, as is everything in such a place which shows the hand of industry. There was an ancient city here in former days, which was engulphed by an earthquake, though part of a gateway, and the fragment of a wall still mark its site. No inscriptions were observed. The water is obtained from a lake.

November 21.—Puchkullia, or Beechkulla, five coss (11 miles 5 furlongs): crossed and encamped on the Jojurri. The soil improving, of a brown sandy texture. Wheat and barley of excellent quality are grown on the banks of the river. It was a relief to meet once more a babool or a neem tree; even our Godwar cypress reared its head on the margin of the Jojurri. Although now only containing a hundred houses, this was once a place of some importance. I found a defaced inscription, in which "the son of Sonung, S. 1224," was still legible; but the mercenary Pat'hans have ruined the harvest of the antiquary. The village is a grant in fee to a Bhatti chieftain. Water is obtained from wells excavated on the margin of the river.

November 22.—Peepar, four coss (8 miles 2 furlongs). Pursued the course of the river, the most extended arm of the Looni, coming from the hills near Purbatsir, on the frontiers of Jeipoor. Its course is marked by the trees already mentioned. The soil, a mixture of black earth and sand, is termed *dhamuni*. Peepar is a town of 1500 houses, one-third of which are inhabited by the Oswals of the Jain faith, the chief merchants of all their country. There are also about two hundred families of Muhaisries, or merchants of the Saiva caste. Peepar carries on a considerable traffic, and has a chintz manufactory, which employs thirty families. It is in the grant of the feudal chief of Neemaj, whose death has been already related. A cenotaph, dedicated to one of his ancestors, has been half destroyed by the Goths of India. Peepar is celebrated in the traditions of the desert as one of the cities founded by Gundrufsén, the Pramara monarch of Awinti, prior to the Christian era. The only inscription I discovered was in a temple of the sea-goddess Lacshmí. It bore the names of Beejy Sing and Dailunji, Rajpoots of the Gehlote race, with the ancient title of Rawul. It was a happy confirmation of the most ancient chronicle of Méwar, which divides the Gehlotes into twenty-four *sachæ* or branches, of which one is called "Peeparia," doubtless from their having conquered this tract from the Takshac Pramara.

There is an abundance of wells, from sixty to eighty feet in depth. Of one recently excavated, I obtained the following details of the strata, which may be gratifying to the geologist. The first twenty feet are composed entirely of that kind of earth called *dhamuni*, chiefly decomposed sandstone with a mixture of black earth, in which occurs a stratum of bluish clay mixed with particles of quartz : this earth is called *morur* in Marwar, and *morund* in Jeipoor. It was then necessary to cut through a rock of red granite [1] for thirty feet ; then several feet of an almost milk-white steatite, succeeded by stalactitic concretions of sandstone and quartz.

Good water is also obtained from a lake called the Sampoo, which is connected with the tradition of the foundation of Peepar. A Brahmin of the Pali tribe, whose name was Peepa, was in the habit of carrying milk to a deity of the Serpent (Takshac) race, whose retreat was on the banks of this lake, and who deposited two pieces of gold in return for the Palliwal's offering. Being compelled to go to Nagore, he gave instructions to his son to perform his charitable office ; but the youth, deeming it a good opportunity to become master of the treasure, took a stick with him, and when the serpent issued forth for his accustomed fare, he struck him violently ; but the snake being "scotched, not killed," retreated to his hole. The young Brahmin related his adventure to his mother ; when the good woman, dreading the vengeance of the serpentine deity, prepared a servant and bullock to convey her son to his father at Nagore. But what was her horror in the morning, when she went to call the youth, to find, instead of him, the huge serpent coiled up in his bed ! Peepa, on his return, was inconsolable ; but stifling his revenge, he propitiated the serpent with copious libations of milk. The scaly monster was conciliated, and revealed the stores he guarded to Peepa, commanding him to raise a monument which would transmit a knowledge of the event to future ages. Hence Peepar arose from Peepa the Pali, and the name of the lake *Sampoo*, from his benefactor the 'serpent' (*sampa*). All these allegorical tales regard the *Takshac* races, the followers of the religion of Budha or Jaina, and their feuds with the Brahminical sects. It is evident that Peepa the Pali worshipped both ; and the very name induces a belief that the whole Palliwal caste are converts from Budhism.

There is a coond or fountain, called after Lakha Foolani, who ruled in ancient times at Phoolra, in the farther corner of the desert, but carried his arms even to the ocean. Wherever I have travelled, tradition is loud in praise of Foolani, from the source of the Looni to its embouchure in the Delta of the Indus.[2]

November 23.—Madreo, five coss (10 miles 2 furlongs). Roads good ; soil as yesterday, but the country very desolate ; only stunted shrubs since we removed from the margin of the river. This is a moderate-sized village, with a tank of good water.

November 24.—Bhoroonda, four coss, or eight miles. The face of the country now changes materially ; our route was over a low undulating

[1] Specimens of all these I brought home.

[2] The traditional stanzas are invaluable for obtaining a knowledge both of ancient history and geography :

"Kuşhup-gurh, Soorajpoora,
Basuck-gurh, Takoh,
Oodhani-gurh, Jugropoora,
Jo Phool-gur'h, i Lakho."

In this stanza we have the names of six ancient cities in the desert, which belonged to Lakha, the Takoh, Tâk, or Takshac, *i.e.* of the race figuratively called the 'serpent.'

ridge of sandstone, in which the stunted shrubs of this region find a bed. At one time the elevation was sufficiently great to allow the chasm through which the road passed to be dignified with the name of 'the Gasooria Pass,' in which a party of the Raja's men is posted for defence, and the levy of transit duties. Bhoroonda is in the fief of Gopal Sing, the chief of Kochamun, one of the most conspicuous of the Mairtea clan. It consists of one hundred and fifty houses; the cultivators are Jats, as are those of all the preceding villages.

I paid a visit to the humble cenotaphs of Bhoroonda; one of them bore the name of Buddun Sing, a sub-vassal of Kochamun, who was slain in the heroic charge against De Boigne's brigades, in the patriot field of Mairta. His name claims the admiration of all who esteem loyalty and patriotism, the inherent virtues of the chivalrous Rajpoot. Raja Beejy Sing had resumed Bhoroonda, when the Thacoor retired to the adjacent court of Jeipoor, where he was well received according to the hospitable customs of the Rajpoot, and had risen to favour at the period when the Mahrattas invaded his *bapótá*, 'the land of his fathers.' Resentment was instantly sacrificed at the altar of patriotism; he put himself at the head of one hundred and fifty horse, and flew to his sovereign's and his country's defence. Unhappily, the whole Mahratta army interposed between him and his countrymen. To cut their way through all impediments was the instant resolve of Buddun and his brave companions. They fell sword in hand upon a multitude; and, with the exception of a few, who forced their way (amongst whom was the chief whose monument is referred to), they were cut to pieces. Buddun Sing lived to reach his ancient estate, which was restored to his family in token of his sovereign's gratitude for the gallant deed. It is valued at seven thousand rupees annual rent, and has attached to it, as a condition, the service of defending this post.

There was another small altar erected to the manes of Pertáp, who was killed in the defence of this pass against the army of Arungzéb.

November 25.—Indawur, five coss (10 miles 2 furlongs). This place consists of two hundred houses; the cultivators are Jats. I have said little of these proprietors of the soil, a sturdy, independent, industrious race, who "venerate the plough," and care little about the votaries of Mars or their concerns, so that they do not impose excessive taxes on them. They are a stout, well-built, though rather murky race. The village is assigned to the ex-prince of Sinde, who derives his sole support from the liberality of the princes of Marwar. He is of the tribe called Kalora, and claims descent from the Abbassides of Persia. His family has been supplanted by the Talpooris, a branch of the Noomries (*the foxes*) of Balochistan, who now style themselves Afghans, but who are in fact one of the most numerous of the Gete or Jit colonies from Central Asia. But let us not wander from our subject.

I will beg the reader to descend seventy or eighty feet with me to view the stratification of Indawur. First, three feet of good soil; five feet of red sandy earth, mixed with particles of quartz; six feet of an unctuous indurated clay; [1]—then follows a sand-rock, through which it was necessary to penetrate about sixty feet; this was succeeded by twenty feet of

[1] Mr. Stokes, of the Royal Asiatic Society, pronounces it to be a steatite.

almost loose sand, with particles of pure quartz embedded ; nodules and stalactitic concretions of sandstone, quartz, and mica, agglutinated together by a calcareous cement. The interior of the well throughout this last stratum is faced with masonry : the whole depth is more than sixty-five cubits, or forty yards. At this depth a spring of excellent water broke in upon the excavators, which supplies Indawur.

November 26.—Mairta, four coss (9 miles 1 furlong). The whole march was one extended plain ; the Aravulli towering about twenty-five miles to our right. To the west a wide waste, consisting of plains gently undulating, and covered with grass and underwood. Natural sterility is not the cause of this desert aspect, for the soil is rich ; but the water is far beneath the surface, and they cannot depend upon the heavens. Joar, mot'h, and sesamum, were cultivated to a considerable extent in the immediate vicinity of the villages, but the product had this season been scanty. The appearance of the town is imposing, its site being on a rising ground. The spires of the mosque which was erected on the ruins of a Hindu temple by the tyrant Arungzéb, overtop the more ponderous and unaspiring *mundurs* which surround it. Notwithstanding this monarch was the object of universal execration to the whole Hindu race, more especially to the Rahtores (whose sovereign, the brave Jeswunt, together with his elder son, he put to death by poison, and kept Ajeet twenty long years from his birthright, besides deluging their fields with the richest blood of his nobles) ; still, such is Hindu toleration, that a marble is placed, inscribed both in Hindi and Persian, to protect the mosque from violence. This mark of liberality proceeded from the pretender Dhonkul Sing, as if with a view of catching golden opinions from the demoralised Pat'hans, by whose aid he hoped to regain his rights. But how was he deceived ! His advances were met by the foul assassination, at one fell swoop, of all his party, by the chief of these mercenaries, Meer Khan.

Mairta was founded by Rao Dooda of Mundore, whose son, the celebrated Maldeo, erected the castle, which he called Malkote.[1] Mairta, with its three hundred and sixty townships, became the appanage of his son Jeimul, and gave its name of Mairtea to the bravest of the brave clans of the Rahtores. Jeimul was destined to immortalise his name beyond the limits of Maroo. Distrusted by his father, and likely to be deserving of suspicion, from the very *ruse* to which Shere Shah acknowledged he owed his safety, he was banished from Marwar. He was hospitably received by the Rana, who assigned to the heir of Mundore the rich district of Bednore, equalling his own in extent, and far richer in soil than the plains he had abandoned. How he testified his gratitude for this reception, nobler pens than mine have related. The great Akber claimed the honour of having with his own hand sealed his fate : he immortalised the matchlock with which he effected it, and which was also the theme of Jehangír's praise, who raised a statue in honour of this defender of Cheetore and the rights of its infant prince. Abulfazil, Herbert, the chaplain to Sir T. Roe, Bernier, all honoured the name of Jeimul ; and the chivalrous Lord Hastings, than whom none was better able to appreciate Rajpoot valour,

[1] Rao Dooda had three sons, besides Maldeo ; namely : First, Raemul ; second, Birsing, who founded Amjerra in Malwa, still held by his descendants ; third, Ruttun Sing, father of Meera Baé, the celebrated wife of Koombho Rana.

manifested his respect by his desire to conciliate his descendant, the present brave baron of Bednore.[1]

The town of Mairta covers a large space of ground, and is enclosed with a strong wall and bastions, composed of earth to the westward, but of freestone to the east. All, however, are in a state of decay, as well as the town itself, which is said to contain twenty thousand houses. Like most Hindu towns, there is a mixture of magnificence and poverty; a straw or mud hut adjoins a superb house of freestone, which "shames the meanness" of its neighbour. The castle is about a gun-shot to the south-west of the town, and encloses an area of a mile and a half. Some small sheets of water are on the eastern and western faces. There are plenty of wells about the town, but the water has an unpleasant taste, from filtering through a stiff clay. There are but two strata before water is found, which is about twenty-five feet from the surface: the first a black mould, succeeded by the clay, incumbent on a loose sand, filled with quartzose pebbles of all hues, and those stalactitic concretions which mark, throughout the entire line from Jodpoor to Ajmér, the stratum in which the springs find a current. There are many small lakes around the town, as the Doodasir, or 'lake (*sir*) of Dooda'; the Baijpa, the Doorani, the Dungolia, etc.

The plain of Mairta is one continuous sepulchre, covered with altars to the manes of the warriors who, either in the civil wars which have distracted this state, or in the more patriotic strife with the southron Goths, have drenched it with their blood. It is impossible to pass over this memorable field without a reference to these acts; but they would be unintelligible without going to the very root of dissension, which not only introduced the Mahratta to decide the intestine broils of the Rajpoot states, but has entailed a perpetuity of discord on that of Marwar. I have already succinctly related the parricidal murder of Raja Ajeet, which arose out of the politics of the imperial court, when the Syeds of Barah—the Warwicks of the East—deposed the Emperor Ferochsér, and set up a puppet of their own. With his daughter (whose marriage with the emperor originated, as already recorded, the first grant of land to the East-India Company), he retired to his dominions, leaving his son Abhé Sing at court, and refusing his sanction to the nefarious schemes of the Syeds. They threatened destruction to Marwar, declaring to the son of Ajeet, that the only mode of averting its ruin was his own elevation, and his subservience to their views, which object could only be obtained by his father's deposal and death. Even the reasoning resorted to, as well as the dire purpose of the miscreants, is preserved, and may serve as an illustration of Rajpoot feeling. When Abhé Sing refused or hesitated, he was asked, "*Máh báp ka saca, ya zumín ka saca?*" which, though difficult to render with accuracy, may be translated: "Are you a branch (*sac'ha*) of the land or of your parents?" As before said, land is all in all to the Rajpoot; it is preferred to everything: Abhé's reply may therefore be inferred. Immediate installation was to be the reward of his revenging the Syeds. That nature could produce from the same stock two such monsters as the brothers who effected the deed, is, perhaps, hardly conceivable, and would, probably, not be credited, were not the fact proved beyond doubt. I should desire, for the honour of the Rajpoot race, whose

[1] See p. 387.

advocate and apologist I candidly avow myself, to suppress the atrocious record: but truth is dearer even than Rajpoot character. Of the twelve sons of Ajeet, Abhé Sing and Bukhta Sing were the two elder; both were by the same mother, a princess of Boondí. To Bukhta Sing, who was with his father, the eldest brother wrote, promising him the independent sovereignty of Nagore (where they then were), with its five hundred and fifty-five townships, as the price of murdering their common sire. Not only was the wretch unstartled by the proposition, but he executed the deed with his own hands, under circumstances of unparalleled atrocity. His mother always dreaded the temperament and disposition of Bukhta, who was bold, haughty, impetuous, with a perpetual thirst for action; and she cautioned her husband never to admit him into his presence after dusk, or when unattended. But the Raja, whose physical strength was equal to his bravery, ridiculed her fears, observing, "Is he not my child? Besides, a slap on the face from me would annihilate the stripling." Upon receiving the note from his brother, Bukhta, after taking leave of his father, concealed himself in a chamber adjoining that where his parents reposed. When all was still the murderer stole to the bed in which lay the authors of his existence, and from a pallet, on which were placed the arms of Ajeet, he seized his sword, and coolly proceeded to exhaust those veins which contained the same blood that flowed in his own. In order that nothing might be wanting to complete the deed of horror, the mother was awakened by the blood of her lord moistening her bosom. Her cries awoke the faithful Rajpoots who lay in the adjacent apartments, and who bursting into the chamber, discovered their prince and father dead: "Treason had done its worst." The assassin fled to the roof of the palace, barring the gates behind him, which resisted all attempts to force them until morning, when he threw into the court below the letter of his brother, exclaiming, "This put the Mahraja to death, not I." Abhé Sing was now their sovereign; and it is the actual occupant of the throne whom the Rajpoot deems entitled to his devotion. Eighty-four Satis took place on this dire occasion, the parent of these unnatural regicidal and parricidal sons leading the funeral procession. So much was Ajeet beloved, that even men devoted themselves on his pyre. Such was the tragical end of the great Ajeet, lamented by his chiefs, and consecrated by the bard, in stanzas in honour of him and in execration of the assassins; which afford proof of the virtuous independence of the poetic chronicler of Rajast'han.

Bukhta, bukhta, baera,
Kyon mara Ajmál[1]
Hindwani ca Sewara
Toorkani ca Sál?

"Oh Bukhta, in évil hour
Why slew you Ajmal,
The pillar of the Hindu,
The lance of the Toork?"

Bukhta Sing obtained Nagore; and Abhé Sing was rewarded with the viceroyalty of Guzzerat, which gift he repaid by aiding in its partition, and annexing the rich districts of Beenmahl, Sanchore, and others, to

[1] The bards give adjuncts to names in order to suit their rhymes: Ajeet is the 'invincible'; Aj-mál, a contraction of *Ajya-mál*, 'wealth invincible.'

Marwar ; on which occasion he added Jhalore to the domain of his brother Bukhta, or as the bard styles him, *bud-bukhta*, 'the unfortunate.' This additional reward of parricide has been the cause of all the civil wars of Marwar.

We may slightly notice the other sons of Ajeet, whose issue affected the political society of Rajpootana. Of these,

Devi Sing was given for adoption to Maha Sing, head of the Champawut clan, he having no heirs. Devi Sing then held Beenmahl, but which he could not retain against the Koli tribes around him, and Pokurna was given in exchange. Subbul Sing, Sowaé Sing, and Salim Sing (whose escape from the fate of the chieftain of Neemaj has been noticed) are the lineal issue of this adoption.

Anund Sing. another son of Ajeet, was in like manner adopted into the independent state of Edur, and his issue are heirs-presumptive to the throne of Marwar.

From these races we derive the knowledge of a curious fact, namely, that the issue of the younger brother maintains a claim, though adopted into a foreign and independent state ; while all such claims are totally extinguished by adoption into a home clan. Under no circumstances could the issue of Devi Sing sit on the *gadí* of Marwar ; when adopted into the Champawut clan, he surrendered all claims derived from his birth, which were merged into his vassal rank. Still the recollection must give weight and influence ; and it is evident from the boast of the haughty Devi Sing, when his head was on the block, that there is danger in these adoptions.

Abhé Sing died, leaving a memorial of his prowess in the splendid additions he made to his territories from the tottering empire of Dehli. He was succeeded by his son Ram Sing, on whose accession his uncle Bukhta sent his aged foster-mother, an important personage in Rajwarra, with the *teeka* and gifts, and other symbols of congratulation. Ram Sing, who had all the impetuosity of his race, received the lady-ambassador with no friendly terms, asking her if his uncle had no better messenger to salute his new sovereign. He refused the gifts, and commanded her to tell his uncle to surrender Jhalore. The offended dame extenuated nothing of the insolence of the message. The reply was, however, courteous, implying that both Jhalore and Nagore were at his disposal. The same sarcastic spirit soon precipitated matters between them in the following manner.

Koosul Sing of Ahwa, the premier noble of Marwar, and of all the clans of Champawut, more brave than courtly, was short in stature, sturdy, boorish, and blunt ; he became the object of his young sovereign's derision, who used to style him the *goorji gunduc*, or 'turnspit dog,' and who had once the audacity to say, "Come, goorji" ; when he received the laconic reproof : "Yes ; the goorji that dare bite the lion."

Brooding over this merited retort, he was guilty of another sarcasm, which closed the breach against all reconciliation. Seated one day in the garden of Mundore, he asked the same chief the name of a tree. "The champa," was the reply, "and the pride of the garden, as I am of your Rajpoots." "Cut it down instantly," said the prince ; "root it out ; nothing which bears the name of champa shall exist in Marwar."

Kunniram of Asope, the chief of the next most powerful clan, the

Kompawut, was alike the object of this prince's ridicule. His countenance, which was not "cast in nature's finest mould," became a butt for his wit, and he would familiarly say to him, '*ao boodha bándur*, "Come along, old monkey." Boiling with rage, the chief observed, "When the monkey begins to dance, you will have some mirth." Leaving the court, with his brother chieftain of Ahwa, they collected their retainers and families, and marched to Nagore. Bukhta Sing was absent, but being advised by his *locum tenens* of his visitors, and of their quarrel with his nephew, he lost no time in joining them. It is said he expostulated with them, and offered himself as mediator; but they swore never again to look in the face of Ram Sing as their sovereign. They offered to place Bukhta Sing on the *gadí of Joda*; and threatened, if he refused, to abandon Marwar. He played the part of our Richard for a short time; but the habitual arrogance of his nephew soon brought matters to a crisis. As soon as he heard that the two leaders of all his vassals were received by his uncle, he addressed him, demanding the instant surrender of Jhalore. Again he had the courtly reply: "He dare not contend against his sovereign; and if he came to visit him, he would meet him with a vessel of water."[1] War, a horrid civil war, was now decided on; the challenge was given and accepted, and the plains of Mairta were fixed upon to determine this mortal strife, in which brother was to meet brother, and all the ties of kin were to be severed by the sword. The Mairtea clans, the bravest, as they are the most loyal and devoted, of all the brave clans of Maroo, united to a man under the sovereign's standard; the chiefs of Reah, Boodsú, Mehtri, Kholur, Bhorawur, Kochamun, Alneawas, Joosuri, Bokri, Bhoroonda, Eerwoh, Chandaroon, collected around them every vassal who could wield a brand. Most of the clans of Joda, attracted by the name of *swámdherma*, 'fidelity to their lord,' united themselves to the Mairteas; though a few, as Ladnú, Neembi, were on the adverse side; but the principal leaders, as Khyrwa, Govindgurh, and Bhadrajoon, were faithful to their salt. Of the services of others, Ram Sing's insolence deprived him. Few remained neuter. But these defections were nothing to the loss of a body of five thousand Jareja auxiliaries, whom his connection with a daughter of the prince of Bhooj brought to his aid. When the tents were moved outside the capital, an incident occurred which, while it illustrates the singular character of the Rajpoot, may be regarded as the real cause of the loss of sovereignty to Ram Sing. An inauspicious raven had perched upon the *kanàt*, or wall of the tent in which was the Jareja queen, who, skilled in the art of the *sookuni*[2] (augur), determined to avert it. Like all Rajpootnis, who can use fire-arms on occasion, she seized a matchlock at hand, and, ere he "thrice croaked," she shot him dead. The impetuous Raja, enraged at this instance of audacity and disrespect, without inquiry, ordered the culprit to be dragged before him; nor was his anger assuaged when the name of the Rani was given. He reviled her in the grossest terms: "Tell the Rani," he said, "to depart my dominions, and to return from whence she came." She entreated and conjured him, by a regard to his own safety, to revoke the decree; but all in vain; and with difficulty could she obtain a short interview, but without effecting

[1] This reply refers to a custom analogous to the Scythic investiture, by offering "water and soil."

[2] *Sookun feerna* means to avert the omen of evil.

any change in her obdurate lord. Her last words were, "With my exile from your presence, you will lose the crown of Marwar." She marched that instant, carrying with her the five thousand auxiliaries whose presence must have ensured his victory.

The Oodawut clans, led by their chiefs of Neemaj, Raepoor, and Raus, with all the Kurrunsotes under the Thacoor of Kewnsir, united their retainers with the Champawuts and Kompawuts under the banners of Bukhta Sing.

Ram Sing's array fell far short of his rival's since the defection of the Jarejas; yet, trusting to the name of sovereign as "a tower of strength," he boldly marched to the encounter, and when he reached the hostile field encamped near the Ajmér gate of Mairta. His rival was not long behind, and marshalled his clans within three miles of the northern portal, called the gate of Nagore. The spot he chose had a sacred character, and was called *mataji ca than*, where there was a shrine of the Hindu Hecate, with a fountain said to have been constructed by the Pandus.

Bukhta Sing commenced the battle. Leaving his camp standing, he advanced against his nephew and sovereign, whom he saluted with a general discharge of his artillery. A vigorous cannonade was continued on both sides throughout the day, without a single man seeking a closer encounter. It is no wonder they paused ere the sword was literally drawn. Here was no foreign foe to attack; brother met brother, friend encountered friend, and the blood which flowed in the veins of all the combatants was derived from one common fountain. The reluctance proceeded from the *ςόργη*, the innate principle of natural affection. Evening advanced amidst peals of cannon, when an incident, which could only occur in an army of Rajpoots, stopped the combat. On the banks of the Baijpa lake, the scene of strife, there is a monastery of Dadoopunti ascetics, built by Raja Soor Sing. It was nearly midway between the rival armies, and the shot fell so thick amidst these recluses that they fled in a body, leaving only the old patriarch. Baba (father) Kishendeo disdained to follow his disciples, and to the repeated remonstrances from either party to withdraw, he replied, that if it was his fate to die by a shot he could not avert it; if not, the balls were innoxious: but although he feared not for himself, yet his gardens and monastery were not "charmed," and he commanded them to fight no longer on that ground. The approach of night, and the sacred character of the old abbot Dadoopunti, conspired to make both parties obey his commands, and they withdrew to their respective encampments.

The dawn found the armies in battle-array, each animated with a deadly determination. It was Raja Ram's turn to open this day's combat, and he led the van against his uncle. Burning with the recollection of the indignities he had suffered, the chief of Ahwa, determined to show that "the cur could bite," led his Champawuts to the charge against his sovereign. Incited by loyalty and devotion "to the gadi of Marwar," reckless who was its occupant, the brave Mairteas met his onset steel in hand. The ties of kin were forgotten, or if remembered, the sense of the unnatural strife added a kind of frenzy to their valour, and confirmed their resolution to conquer or die. Here the Mairtea, fighting under the eye of this valiant though intemperate prince, had to maintain his ancient fame, as "the first sword of Maroo." There his antagonist, the Champawut, jealous of this reputation, had the like incentive, besides the obligation to revenge the insults offered to his chief. The conflict was awful: the chieftains of each valiant clan met hand to hand, singling out each other by name. Shere Sing, chief of all the Mairteas, was the first who sealed his devotion by his death. His place was soon filled by his brother, burning for vengeance. Again he cheered on his Mairteas to avenge the death of their lord, as he propelled his steed against the chief of the Champawuts. They were the sons of two sisters of the Jeipoor house, and had hitherto lived in amity and brotherly love, now exchanged for deadly hate. They encountered, when the "cur" bit the dust, and was borne from the field. The loss of their leaders only inflamed the vassals on both sides, and it was long before either yielded a foot of ground. But numbers, and the repeated charges of Bukhta Sing, who led wherever his nephew could be found, at length prevailed; though not until the extinction of the clan of Mairtea, who, despising all odds, fought unto the death. Besides their head of Reah, there fell the sub-vassals of Eerwah, Sewuroh, Joossurie, and Mehtri, with his three gallant sons, and almost all their retainers.

There is nothing more chivalrous in the days of Edward and Cressy than the death of the heir of Mehtri, who, with his father and brothers, sealed his fealty with his blood on this fatal field. He had long engaged the hand of a daughter of a chief of the Nirookas, and was occupied with the marriage rites, when tidings reached him of the approach of the rebels to Mairta. The knot had just been tied, their hands had been joined—but he was a Mairtea—he unlocked his hand from that of the fair Nirooki, to court the Apsara in the field of battle. In the bridal vestments, with the nuptial coronet (*mor*) encircling his forehead, he took his station with his clan in the second day's fight, and "obtained a bride in Indra's abode." The bards of Maroo dwell with delight on the romantic glory of the youthful heir of Mehtri, as they repeat in their Doric verse,

"Kan a mooti bulbulla
Gulla soni a malla
Asi cos kurro ho aya
Konwur Mehtri-walla."

The paraphernalia here enumerated are very foreign to the cavalier of the west: "with pearls shining in his ears, and a golden chaplet round his neck, a space of eighty coss came the heir of Mehtri."

The virgin bride followed her lord from Jeipoor, but instead of being met with the tabor and lute, and other signs of festivity, wail and lamentation awaited her within the lands of Mehtri, where tidings came of the calamity which at once deprived this branch of the Mairteas of all its supporters. Her part was soon taken; she commanded the pyre to be erected; and with the turban and *toorah* which adorned her lord on this fatal day, she followed his shade to the mansions of the sun. I sought out the cenotaph of this son of honour in the blood-stained field; but the only *couronne immortelle* I could wreathe on the sandy plain was supplied by the Bardai, whose song is full of martial fire as he recounts the gallantry of "*Konwur Mehtri-walla.*"

The Mairteas, and their compeers on the side of the prince, made sad havoc amongst their opponents; and they still maintain that it was owing to the artillery alone that they were defeated. Their brave and loyal leader, Shere Sing of Reah, had fruitlessly endeavoured to recall his brother-in-law from the path of treason, but ineffectually; he spoke with sarcasm of his means to supplant Ram Sing by his uncle. The reply of the old baron of Ahwa is characteristic: "At least I will turn the land upside down;" to which Shere Sing rejoined, angrily, he would do his best to prevent him. Thus they parted; nor did they meet again till in arms at Mairta.

In surveying this field of slaughter, the eye discerns no *point d'appui*, no village or key of position, to be the object of a struggle; nothing to obstruct the doubly-gorged falconet, which has no terrors for the uncontrollable valour of the Rahtore; it perceives but a level plain, extended to the horizon, and now covered with the memorials of this day's strife. Here appears the colonnaded mausoleum, with its airy cupola; there the humble altar, with its simple record of the name, clan, and *sac'ha* of him whose ashes repose beneath, with the date of the event, inscribed in rude characters. Of these monumental records I had copies made of about a score; they furnish fresh evidence of the singular character of the Rajpoot.

Ram Sing retired within the walls of the city, which he barricaded; but it being too extensive to afford the chance of defence against the enemy, he formed the fatal resolution of calling to his aid the Mahrattas, who were then rising into notice. At midnight he fled to the south; and at Oojein found the Mahratta leader, Jey Appa Sindia, with whom he concerted measures for the invasion of his country. Meantime his uncle being master of the field, repaired, without loss of time, to the capital, where he was formally enthroned; and his *án* was proclaimed throughout Marwar. As skilful as he was resolute, he determined to meet on his frontier the threatened invasion, and accordingly advanced to Ajmér, in order to interpose between the Mahrattas and Jeipoor, whose prince, Esuri Sing, was father-in-law to his rival. He wrote him a laconic epistle, requiring him either instantly to unite with him in attacking the Mahrattas, or declare himself his foe. The Jeipoor prince had many powerful reasons for not supporting Raja Bukhta, but he at the same time dreaded his enmity. In this extremity, he had recourse to an expedient too common in cases of difficulty. Concerting with his wife, a princess of Eedur (then ruled by one of the sons of Ajeet), the best mode of extrication from his difficulties, he required her aid to revenge the foul murder of Ajeet, and to recover his son's right. "In either case," said he, "the sword must decide, for he leaves me no alternative: against him I have no hopes of success; and if I march to the aid of an assassin and usurper, I lose the good opinion of mankind." In short, he made it appear that she alone could rescue him from his perils. It was therefore resolved to punish one crime by the commission of another. Esuri Sing signified his assent; and to lull all suspicion, the Rhatorni was to visit her uncle in his camp on the joint frontier of the three states of Méwar, Marwar, and Ambér. A poisoned robe was the medium of revenge. Raja Bukhta, soon after the arrival of his niece, was declared in a fever; the physician was summoned: but the man of secrets, the *védya*, declared he was beyond the reach of medicine, and bade him prepare for other scenes. The intrepid Rahtore, yet undismayed, received the tidings even with a jest: "What, Sooja," said he, "no cure? Why do you take my lands and eat their produce, if you cannot combat my maladies? What is your art good for ?" The *védya* excavated a small trench in the tent, which he filled with water; throwing into it some ingredient, the water became gelid. "This," said he, "can be effected by human skill; but your case is beyond it: haste, perform the offices which religion demands." With perfect composure he ordered the chiefs to assemble in his tent; and having recommended to their protection, and received their promise of defending the rights of his son, he summoned the ministers of religion into his presence. The last gifts to the church, and these her organs, were prepared; but with all his firmness, the anathema of the Satis, as they ascended the funeral pyre on which his hand had stretched his father, came into his mind; and as he repeated the ejaculation, "May your corpse be consumed in foreign land!" he remembered he was then on the border. The images which crossed his mental vision it is vain to surmise: he expired as he uttered these words; and over his remains, which were burnt on the spot, a cenotaph was erected, and is still called *Booro Dewul*, the 'Shrine of Evil.'

But for that foul stain, Raja Bukhta would have been one of the first princes of his race. It never gave birth to a bolder; and his wisdom was equal to his valour. Before the commission of that act, he was adored by his Rajpoots. He was chiefly instrumental in the conquests made from Guzzerat; and afterwards, in conjunction with his brother, in defeating the imperial viceroy, Sirbullund. His elevation could not be called a usurpation, since Ram Sing was totally incapacitated through his ungovernable passions, for sovereign sway; and the brave barons of Marwar, "all sons of the same father with their prince," have always exercised the right of election, when physical incapacity rendered such a measure requisite. It is a right which their own customary laws, as well as the rules of justice, have rendered sacred. According to this principle, nearly all the feudality of Maroo willingly recognised, and swore to maintain, the claims of his successor, Beejy Sing. The Rajas of Bikanér and Kishengurh, both independent branches of this house, gave in their assent. Beejy Sing was accordingly proclaimed and installed at Maroat, and forthwith conducted to Mairta.

The ex-prince, Ram Sing, accompanied Jey Appa to the siege of Kotah, and subsequently through Méwar, levying contributions as they passed to Ajmér. Here a dispute occurred between the brave Rahtore and Sindia, whose rapacious spirit for plunder received a severe reproof: nevertheless they crossed the frontier, and entered Marwar. Beejy Sing, with all the hereditary valour of his race, marched to meet the invaders, at the head of nearly all the chivalry of Maroo, amounting to 200,000 men.

The first day both armies encountered, they limited their hostility to a severe cannonade and partial actions, the inhabitants of Mairta supplying the combatants with food, in which service many were killed; even the recluse Dadoopuntis ran the risk in this patriotic struggle, and several of the old patriarch's disciples suffered. The second day passed in the same manner, with many desperate charges of cavalry, in which the Mahrattas invariably suffered, especially from a select body of 5000 select horse, all cased in armour, which nothing could withstand. The superior numerical strength of Ram Sing and his allies compelled Beejy Sing not to neglect the means of retreat. Throughout the first and second days' combat, the cattle of the train had been kept yoked; on the third, they had carried them to a small rivulet in the rear to water. It was at the precise moment of time when the legion of cuirassiers were returning from a charge which had broken to pieces the Mahratta line, as they approached their friends, the word "*dugga*" spread like wildfire; they were mistaken for Ram Sing's adherents, and a murderous shower of grape opened upon the flower of their own army, who were torn to pieces ere the fatal error was discovered. But such was the impression which this band of heroes had just made on the Mahrattas, that they feared to take advantage of this disaster. A feeling of horror pervaded the army of Beejy Sing, as the choice of their chivalry conveyed the slain and the wounded to the camp. A council of war was summoned, and the aid of superstition came to cool that valour which the Mahrattas, in spite of their numbers, could never subdue. The Raja was young—only twenty years of age; and being prudent as well as brave, he allowed experience to guide him. The Raja of Bikanér, of the same kin and clan, took the lead, and advised a retreat. In the accident related, he saw the hand of Providence, which had sent it to serve as a signal to desist. The Raja had a great stake to lose, and doubtless deemed it wise to preserve his auxiliaries for the defence of his own dominions. It was a case which required the energy of Bukhta: but the wavering opinion of the council soon spread throughout the camp, and was not unobserved by the enemy; nor was it till Bikanér marched off with his aid, towards the close of the day, that any advantage was taken of it. Then Ram Sing at the head of a body of Rajpoots and Mahrattas poured down upon them, and "*sauve qui peut*" became the order of the day. To gain Mairta was the main object of the discomfited and panic-struck Rahtores; but many chiefs with their vassals marched direct for their estates. The guns were abandoned to their fate, and became the first proud trophy the Mahrattas gained over the dreaded Rajpoots. The Raja of Kishengurh, also a Rahtore, followed the example of his brother prince of of Bikanér, and carried off his bands. Thus deserted by his dispirited and now dispersed barons, the young prince had no alternative but flight, and at midnight he took the route of Nagore. In the darkness he mistook the road, or was misled into that of Rayn, whose chieftain was the companion of his flight. Calling him by name, Lall Sing, he desired him to regain the right path; but the orders of a sovereign at the head of a victorious army, and those of a fugitive prince, are occasionally received, even amongst Rajpoots, with some shades of distinction. The chief begged permission, as he was near home, to visit his family and bring them with him. Too dignified to reply, the young prince remained silent, and the Thacoor of Rayn [1] loitered in the rear. The Raja reached Kujwana, with only five of his cuirassiers (*sillahposh*) as an escort. Here he could not halt with safety; but as he left the opposite barrier, his horse dropped down dead. He mounted another belonging to one of his attendants, and gained Deswal, three miles farther. Here the steeds, which had been labouring throughout the day under the weight of heavy armour, in addition to the usual burden of their riders, were too jaded to proceed; and Nagore was still sixteen miles distant. Leaving his worn-out escort, and concealing his rank, he bargained with a Jat to convey him before break of day to the gate of Nagore for the sum of five rupees. The peasant, after stipulating that the coin should be *beeji-sahis*, "the new currency," which still remains

[1] Or *Rahin* in the map, on the road to Jahil from Mairta.

the standard, the common car of husbandry was brought forth, on which the king of Maroo ascended, and was drawn by a pair of Nagori oxen. The royal fugitive was but little satisfied with their exertions, though their pace was good, and kept continually urging them, with the customary cry of "*hank! hank!*" The honest Jat, conscious that his cattle did their best, at length lost all temper. Repeating the sounds "*hank! hank!*" "Who are you," asked he, "that are hurrying on at this rate? It were more becoming that such a sturdy carl should be in the field with Beejy Sing at Mairta, than posting in this manner to Nagore. One would suppose you had the southrons (*dehkhanis*) at your heels. Therefore be quiet, for not a jot faster shall I drive." Morning broke, and Nagore was yet two miles distant: the Jat, turning round to view more attentively his impatient traveller, was overwhelmed with consternation when he recognised his prince. He leaped from the vehicle, horror-struck that he should have been sitting "on the same level" with his sovereign, and absolutely refused to sin any longer against etiquette. "I pardon the occasion," said the prince mildly; "obey." The Jat resumed his seat, nor ceased exclaiming *hank! hank!* until he reached the gate of Nagore. Here the prince alighted, paid his price of conveyance, and dismissed the Jat of Deswal, with a promise of further recompense hereafter. On that day the enemy invested Nagore, but not before Beejy Sing had despatched the chief of Hursolah to defend the capital, and issued his proclamations to summon the ban of Marwar.

During six months he defended himself gallantly in Nagore, against which the desultory Mahrattas, little accustomed to the operations of a siege, made no impression, while they suffered from the sallies of their alert antagonist. Encouraged by their inactivity, the young prince, embued with all the native valour of his race, and impelled by that decisive energy of mind which characterised his father, determined upon a step which has immortalised his memory. He resolved to cut his way through the enemy, and solicit succours in person. He had a dromedary corps five hundred strong. Placing on these a devoted band of one thousand Rajpoots, in the dead of night he passed the Mahratta lines unobserved, and made direct for Bikanér. Twenty-four hours sufficed to seat him on the same *gadi* with its prince, and to reveal to him the melancholy fact, that here he had no hopes of succour. Denied by a branch of his own house, he resorted to a daring experiment upon the supporter of his antagonist. The next morning he was on his way, at the head of his dromedary escort, to the capital of the Cutchwahas, Jeipoor. The "ships of the desert" soon conveyed him to that city. He halted under the walls, and sent a messenger to say that in person he had come to solicit his assistance.

Esuri Sing, the son and successor of the great Sowaé Jey Sing, had neither the talents of his father, nor even the firmness which was the common inheritance of his race. He dreaded the rival Rahtore; and the pusillanimity which made him become the assassin of the father, prompted him to a breach of the sacred laws of hospitality (which, with courage, is a virtue almost inseparable from a Rajpoot soul), and make a captive of the son. But the base design was defeated by an instance of devotion and resolution, which will serve to relieve the Rajpoot character from the dark shades which the faithful historian is sometimes forced to throw into the picture. Civil war is the parent of every crime, and severs all ties, moral and political; nor must it be expected that Rajpootana should furnish the exception to a rule, which applies to all mankind in similar circumstances. The civil wars of England and France, during the conflicts of the White and Red Roses, and those of the League, will disclose scenes which would suffice to dye with the deepest hues an entire dynasty of the Rajpoots. Let such deeds as the following be placed on the virtuous side of the account, and the crimes on the opposite side be ascribed to the peculiarities of their condition.

The devoted sacrifice of Shere Sing, the chief of the Mairtea clan, has already been recorded. When victory declared against the side he espoused, the victorious Bukhta Sing resumed the estates of Reah from his line, and conferred them on a younger branch of the family. Jowan Sing was the name of the individual, and he was now with the chosen band of the son of his benefactor, soliciting succour from the king of the Cutchwahas. He had married the daughter of the chief of Atchrole, one of the great vassals of Jeipoor, who was deep in the confidence of his sovereign, to whom he imparted his design to seize the person of his guest and suppliant at the interview he had granted. Aware that such a scheme could not be effected without bloodshed, the Atchrole chieftain, desirous to save his son-in-law from danger, under an oath of secrecy revealed the plot, in order that he might secure himself. The Jeipoor prince came to the "Travellers' hall" (*dhermsala*), where the Rahtore had alighted; they embraced with cordiality, and seated themselves on the same *gadi* together. While compliments were yet passing, the faithful Mairtea, who, true to his pledge, had not even hinted to his master the danger that threatened him, placed himself immediately behind the Jeipoor prince, sitting, as if accidentally, on the flowing skirt of his robe. The Raja, turning round to the leader of "the first of the swords of Maroo," remarked, "Why, Thacoor, you have taken a seat in the background to-day?" "The day requires it, Maharaja," was the laconic reply: for the post of the Mairteas was the sovereign's right hand. Turning to his prince, he said, "Arise, depart, or your life or liberty is endangered." Beejy Sing arose, and his treacherous host made an attempt to follow, but felt his design impeded by the position the loyal chief had taken on his garment, whose drawn dagger was already pointed to his heart, where he threatened to sheathe it if any hindrance was offered to the safe departure of his sovereign, to whom he coolly said, as the prince left the astonished assembly, "Send me word when you are mounted." The brave Beejy Sing showed himself worthy of his servant, and soon sent to say, "He now only waited for him": a message, the import of which was not understood by the treacherous Cutchwaha. The leader of the Mairteas sheathed his dagger—arose—and coming in front of the Raja, made him a respectful obeisance. The Jeipoor prince could not resist the impulse which such devotion was calculated to produce; he arose, returned the salutation, and giving vent to his feelings, observed aloud to his chiefs, "Behold a picture of fidelity! It is in vain to hope for success against such men as these."

Foiled in all his endeavours, Beejy Sing had no resource but to regain Nagore, which he effected with the same celerity as he quitted it. Six months more passed away in the attempt to reduce Nagore; but though the siege was fruitless, not so were the efforts of his rival Ram Sing in other quarters, to whom almost all the country had submitted: Maroat,

Purbutsir, Palli, Sojut, had received his flag ; and besides the capital and the town he held in person, Jhalore, Sewanoh, and Filodi, were the only places which had not been reduced. In this extremity, Beejy Sing listened to an offer to relieve him from these multiplied difficulties, which, in its consequences, alienated for ever the brightest gem in the crown of Marwar.

A Rajpoot and an Afghan, both foot-soldiers on a small monthly pay, offered, if their families were provided for, to sacrifice themselves for his safety by the assassination of the Mahratta commander. Assuming the garb of camp-settlers, they approached the headquarters, feigning a violent quarrel. The simple Mahratta chief was performing his ablutions at the door of his tent, which as they approached, they became more vociferous, and throwing a bundle of statements of account on the ground, begged he would decide between them. In this manner they came nearer and nearer, and as he listened to their story, one plunged his dagger in his side, exclaiming, "This for Nagore!" and "This for Jodpoor!" said his companion, as he repeated the mortal blow. The alarm was given ; the Afghan was slain ; but the Rajpoot called out "Thief!" and mingling with the throng, escaped by a drain into the town of Nagore. Though the crime was rewarded, the Rahtore refused to see the criminal. The siege continued, but in spite of every precaution, reinforcements both of men and provisions continued to be supplied. It ill suited the restless Mahratta to waste his time in these desert regions, which could be employed so much more profitably on richer lands: a compromise ensued, in which the cause of Ram Sing was abandoned, on stipulating for a fixed triennial tribute, and the surrender of the important fortress and district of Ajmér in full sovereignty to the Mahratta, in *moondkati*, or compensation for the blood of Jey Appa. The monsoon was then approaching ; they broke up, and took possession of this important conquest, which, placed in the very heart of these regions, may be called the key of Rajpootana.

The cross of St. George now waves over the battlements of Ajmér, planted, if there is any truth in political declarations, not for the purpose of conquest, or to swell the revenues of British India, but to guard the liberties and the laws of these ancient principalities from rapine and disorder. It is to be hoped that this banner will never be otherwise employed, and that it may never be execrated by the brave Rajpoot.

The deserted Ram Sing continued to assert his rights with the same obstinacy by which he lost them ; and for which he staked his life in no less than eighteen encounters against his uncle and cousin. At length, on the death of Esuri Sing of Jeipoor, having lost his main support, he accepted the Marwar share of the Salt Lake of Sambur, and Jeipoor relinquishing the other half, he resided there until his death.

CHAPTER XXIX

Madaji Sindia succeeds Jey Appa—Union of the Rahtores and Cutchwahas, joined by Ismael Beg and Hamdani, against the Mahrattas—Battle of Tonga—Sindia defeated—Ajmér retaken, and tributary engagement annulled—Madaji Sindia recruits his army, with the aid of De Boigne—The Rajpoots meet him on the frontier of Jeipoor—Jealousies of the allies—The Cutchwahas alienated by a scurrilous stanza—Battle of Patun—Effects of the Jeipooreans' treachery, in the defeat of the Rahtores—Stanza of the Cutchwaha bard—Suggestion of Beejy Sing: his chiefs reject it, and the prince prepares for war—Treason of the Rahtore chief of Kishengurh—The Mahrattas invade Marwar—Resolution of the chiefs of Ahwa and Asope to conquer or perish—Rahtores encamp on the plains of Mairta—Golden opportunity lost of destroying the Mahratta army—Fatal compliance of the chiefs with the orders of the civil minister—Rout of the camp—Heroism of the Rahtore clans: their destruction—Treachery of the Singwi faction—The chief minister takes poison—Reflections on the Rajpoot character, with reference to the protective alliance of the British Government—Resumption of journey—Jhirrow—Cross the field of battle—*See-kote,* or Mirage, compared with the *Sehrab* of Scripture—Desert of Sogdiana—Hissar—At sea—Description of Jhirrow—Cenotaph of Herakurna Das—Alneawas—Reah—The Mountain Mairs—Their descent upon Reah—Slay its chief—Govindgurh—Chase of a hyæna—Lake of Poshkur: geological details—Description of the lake—Its legend—Aja-pál, the founder of Ajmér—Beesildeva, the Chohan king of Ajmér—Places of devotion on the 'Serpent-rock.'—Ajmér—View of Dhar-ool-Khyr—Geological details—City of Ajmér—Its rising prosperity.

Madaji Sindia succeeded to the command of the horde led by his relation, Jey Appa. He had the genius to discover that his southron horse would never compete with the Rajpoots, and he set about improving that arm to which the Mahrattas finally owed success. This sagacious chief soon perceived that the political position of the great states of Rajast'han was most favourable to his views of establishing his power in this quarter. They were not only at variance with each other, but, as it has already appeared, were individually distracted with civil dissensions. The interference of the Rana of Oodipoor had obtained for his nephew, Madhú Sing, the *gadí* of Jeipoor; but this advantage was gained only through the introduction of the Mahrattas, and the establishment of a tribute, as in Marwar. This brave people felt the irksomeness of their chains, and wished to shake them off. Madhú Sing's reign was short; he was succeeded by Pertáp, who determined to free himself from this badge of dependence. Accordingly, when Madaji Sindia invaded his country, at the head of a powerful army, he called on the Rahtores for aid. The cause was their own; and they jointly determined to redeem what had been lost. As the bard of the Rahtores observes, they forgot all their just grounds of offence [1] against the Jeipoor court, and sent the flower of their chivalry under the chieftain of Reah, whose fidelity has been so recently recorded. At Tonga (the battle is also termed that of Lalsont), the rival armies encountered.

[1] *Put rekho Pertáp ka*
No kote ca Nat'h
Agla goona bukus día
Abki pukero hat'h.

"The lord of the nine castles preserved the honour of Pertáp. He forgave former offences, and again took him by the hand."

The celebrated Mogul chiefs, Ismael Beg and Hamdani added their forces to those of the combined Rajpoots, and gained an entire victory, in which the Rahtores had their full share of glory. The noble chief of Reah formed his Rahtore horse into a dense mass, with which he charged and overwhelmed the flower of Sindia's army, composed of the regulars under the celebrated De Boigne.[1] Sindia was driven from the field, and retired to Muttra; for years he did not recover the severity of this day. The Rahtores sent a force under the Dhabaie, which redeemed Ajmér, and annulled their tributary engagement.

The genius of General Comte de Boigne ably seconded the energetic Sindia. A regular force was equipped, far superior to any hitherto known, and was led into Rajpootana to redeem the disgrace of Tonga. The warlike Rahtores determined not to await the attack within their own limits, but marched their whole force to the northern frontier of Jeipoor, and formed a junction with the Cutchwahas at the town of Patun (*Tuarvati*). The words of the war-song, which the inspiring bards repeated as they advanced, are still current in Marwar; but an unlucky stanza, which a juvenile Charun had composed after the battle of Tonga, had completely alienated the Cutchwahas from their supporters, to whom they could not but acknowledge their inferiority :—

Oodul tyn Ambér ra Rekha Rahtorán.
"The Rahtores guarded the petticoats of Ambér."

This stanza was retained in recollection at the battle of Patun; and if aniversal affirmation may be received as proof, it was the cause of its loss, and with it that of Rajpoot independence. National pride was humbled: a private agreement was entered into between the Mahrattas and Jeipooreans, whereby the latter, on condition of keeping aloof during the fight, were to have their country secured from devastation. As usual, the Rahtores charged up to the muzzles of De Boigne's cannon, sweeping all before them: but receiving no support, they were torn piecemeal by showers of grape and compelled to abandon the field. Then, it is recorded, the brave Rahtore showed the difference between fighting on *purbhom*, or 'foreign land,' and on his own native soil. Even the women, it is averred, plundered them of their horses on this disastrous day; so heart-broken had the traitorous conduct of their allies rendered them. The Jeipooreans paid dearly for their revenge, and for the couplet which recorded it :—

Ghora, joora, pagri,
Mootcha, Kug, Marwar,
Panch rekma mel-lida
Patun myn Rahtore.

[1] "A la gauche la cavalerie Rhatore, au nombre de dix mille hommes, fondit sur les bataillons de M. de Boigne malgré le feu des batteries placées en avant de la ligne. Les pièces bien servies opéraient avec succès; mais les Rhatores, avec le courage opiniâtre qui les caracterise, s'acharnaient à poursuivre l'action, et venaient tuer les artilleurs jusques sur leurs pièces. Alors, les bataillons s'avancèrent, et les Rhatores, qui avaient perdu beaucoup de monde, commencèrent à s'ébranler. M. de Boigne, les voyant se retirer en désordre, réclama l'aide du centre; mais les prières et les menaces furent également inutiles: les vingt-cinq bataillons Mogols, restés inactifs pendant toute la journée, et simples spectateurs du combat, demeurèrent encore immobiles dans ce moment décisif. Les deux armées se retirèrent après cette action sanglante, qui n'eut aucun résultat."

Verbatim :
" Horse, shoes, turban,
Mustachio, sword [of] Marwar,
Five things surrendered were
At Patun by the Rahtore."

Both these "ribald strains" are still the taunt of either race: by such base agencies are thrones overturned, and heroism rendered abortive!

When the fatal result of the battle of Patun was communicated to Raja Beejy Sing, he called a council of all his nobles, at which the independent branches of his family, the Rajas of Bikanér, Kishengurh, and Roopnagurh, assisted, for the cause was a common one. The Raja gave it as his own opinion, that it was better to fulfil the terms of the former treaty, on the murder of Jey Appa, acknowledge the cancelled tribute, and restore Ajmér, which they had recovered by a *coup de main*. His valorous chieftains opposed the degrading suggestion, and unanimously recommended that they should again try the chances of war ere they signed their humiliation. Their resolution swayed the prince, who issued his summons to every Rahtore in his dominions to assemble under their Raja's banner, once more planted on the ensanguined plains of Mairta. A fine army was embodied ; not a Rahtore who could wield a sword but brought it for service in the cause of his country ; and full thirty thousand men assembled on the 10th September 1790, determined to efface the recollections of Patun.

There was one miscreant of Rahtore race, who aided on this occasion to rivet his country's chains, and his name shall be held up to execration—Buhadoor Sing, the chief of Kishengurh. This traitor to his suzerain and race held, jointly with his brother of Roopnagurh, a domain of two hundred and ten townships: not a fief emanating from Marwar, but all by grant from the kings ; still they received the *teeka*, and acknowledged the supremacy of the head of Jodpoor. The brothers had quarrelled ; Buhadoor despoiled his brother of his share, and being deaf to all offers of mediation, Beejy Sing marched and re-inducted the oppressed chief into his capital, Roopnagurh. The fatal day of Patun occurred immediately after ; and Buhadoor, burning with revenge, repaired to De Boigne, and conducted him against his native land. Roopnagurh, it may be supposed, was his first object, and it will afford a good proof of the efficiency of the artillery of De Boigne, that he reduced it in twenty-four hours. Thence he proceeded to Ajmér, which he invested: and here the proposal was made by the Raja for its surrender, and for the fulfilment of the former treaty. Madaji in person remained at Ajmér, while his army, led by Lukwa, Jewa-dada, Sudasheo Bhao, and other Mahratta leaders of horse, with the brigades of De Boigne and eighty pieces of cannon, advanced against the Rahtores. The Mahrattas, preceding by one day's march the regulars under De Boigne, encamped at Nitrea. The Rahtore army was drawn out on the plains of Mairta, one flank resting on the village of Dangiwas. Five miles separated the Rahtores from the Mahrattas ; De Boigne was yet in the rear, his guns being deep sunk in the sandy bed of the Looni. Here a golden opportunity was lost, which could never be regained, of deciding 'horse to horse' the claims of supremacy ; but the evil genius of the Rahtore again intervened: and as he was the victim at

Patun to the jealousy of the Cutchwaha, so here he became the martyr to a meaner cause, the household jealousies of the civil ministers of his prince. It is customary in all the Rajpoot states, when the sovereign does not command in person, to send one of the civil ministers as his representative. Him the feudal chiefs will obey, but not one of their own body, at least without some hazard of dissension. Khoob Chund Singwi, the first minister, was present with the Raja at the capital: Gungaram Bindarri and Bheemraj Singwi were with the army. Eager to efface the disgrace of Patun, the two great Rahtore leaders, Seo Sing of Ahwa, and Maheedas of Asope, who had sworn to free their country or die in the attempt, demanded a general movement against the Mahrattas. This gallant impatience was seconded by all the other nobles, as well as by a successful attack on the foragers of the enemy, in which the Mahrattas lost all their cattle. But it was in vain they urged the raging ardour of their clans, the policy of taking advantage of it, and the absence of De Boigne, owing to whose admirable corps and well-appointed park the day at Patun was lost; Bheemraj silenced their clamour for the combat by producing a paper from the minister Khoob Chund commanding them on their allegiance not to engage until the junction of Ismael Beg, already at Nagore. They fatally yielded obedience. De Boigne extricated his guns from the sands of Alneeawas, and joined the main body. That night the Bikanér contingent, perceiving the state of things, and desirous to husband their resources to defend their own altars, withdrew. About an hour before daybreak, De Boigne led his brigade to the attack, and completely surprised the unguarded Rajpoots. They were awoke by showers of grape-shot, which soon broke their position: all was confusion; the resistance was feeble. It was the camp of the irregular infantry and guns which broke, and endeavoured to gain Mairta; and the civil commanders took to flight. The alarm reached the more distant quarters of the brothers-in-arms, the chiefs of Ahwa and Asope. The latter was famed for the immense quantity of opium he consumed; and with difficulty could his companion awake him, with the appalling tidings, "The camp has fled, and we are left alone!" "Well, brother, let us to horse." Soon the gallant band of both was ready, and twenty-two chiefs of note *drank opium together* for the last time. They were joined by the leaders of other clans; and first and foremost the brave Mairteas of Reah, of Alneeawas, Eerwa, Chanode, Govindgurh; in all four thousand Rahtores. When mounted and formed in one dense mass, the Ahwa chieftain shortly addressed them: "Where can we fly, brothers? But can there be a Rahtore who has ties stronger than shame (*laj*)? If any one exist who prefers his wife and children to honour, let him retire." Deep silence was the only reply to this heroic appeal; and as the hand of each warrior was raised to his forehead, the Ahwa chief gave the word 'forward.' They soon came up with De Boigne's brigade, well posted, and defended by eighty pieces of cannon. "Remember Patun!" was the cry, as, regardless of showers of grape, this heroic band charged up to the cannon's mouth, driving everything before them, cutting down the line which defended the guns, and passing on to assault the Mahrattas, who were flying in all directions to avoid their impetuous valour. Had there been a reserve at this moment, the day of Mairta would have surpassed that of Tonga. But here the skill of De Boigne, and the discipline of his troops, were an overmatch for valour unsustained by discipline and discretion. The Rahtore band had no infantry to secure their victory ; the guns were wheeled round, the line was re-formed, and ready to receive them on their return. Fresh showers of shot and grape met their thinned ranks ; scarcely one of the four thousand left the field. The chiefs of Asope, Eerwah, Chanode, Govindgurh, Alneeawas, Mouriro, and others of lesser note, were among the slain ; and upon the heaps of wounded, surrounded by his gallant clan, lay the chief of Ahwa, pierced with seven-and-twenty wounds. He had lain insensible twenty-four hours, when an old servant, during the night, searched for and found him on the field. A heavy shower had fallen, which increased the miseries of the wounded. Blind and faint, the Thacoor was dragged out from the bodies of the slain. A little opiate revived him ; and they were carrying him off, when they were encountered by Lukwa's *hurkaras* in search of chiefs of note ; the wounded Thacoor was conveyed to the headquarters at Mairta. Lukwa sent a surgeon to sew up his wounds ; but he disdained the courtesy, and refused all aid, until the meanest of his wounded vassals was attended to. This brave man, when sufficiently recovered, refused all solicitation from his sympathising foes that the usual rejoicing might be permitted, and that he would shave and perform the ablutions after sickness, till he could see his sovereign. The Raja advanced from his capital to meet him, and lavished encomiums on his conduct. He now took the bath, preparatory to putting on the honorary dress ; but in bathing his wounds opened afresh, and he expired.

Bheemraj Singwi received at Nagore, whither he had fled, a letter of accusation from his sovereign, on which he swallowed poison ; but although he was indirectly the cause of the defeat, by his supineness, and subsequent disgraceful flight, it was the minister at the capital whose treason prevented the destruction of the Mahrattas : Khoob Chund was jealous of Bheemraj ; he dreaded being supplanted by him if he returned from Mairta crowned with success ; and he therefore penned the despatch which paralysed their energies, enjoining them to await the junction of Ismael Beg.

Thus, owing to a scurrilous couplet of a bard, and to the jealousy of a contemptible court-faction, did the valiant Rahtores lose their independence—if it can be called lost—since each of these brave men still deems himself a host, when " his hour should come " to play the hero. Their spirit is not one jot diminished since the days of Tonga and Mairta.[1]

[1] Three years ago I passed two delightful days with the conqueror of the Rajpoots, in his native vale of Chambéry. It was against the *croix blanche* of Savoy, not the *orange flag* of the Southron, that four thousand Rajpoots fell martyrs to liberty ; and although I wish the Comte long life, I may regret he had lived to bring his talents and his courage to their subjugation. He did them ample justice, and when I talked of the field of Mairta, the remembrance of past days flitted before him, as he said " all appeared as a dream." Distinguished by his prince, beloved by a numerous and amiable family, and honoured by his fellow-citizens, the years of the veteran, now numbering more than fourscore, glide in agreeable tranquillity in his native city, which, with oriental magnificence, he is beautifying by an entire new street and a handsome dwelling for himself. By a singular coincidence, just as I am writing this portion of my narrative I am put in possession of a *Mémoire* of his life, lately published, written under the eye of his son, the Comte Charles de Boigne. From this I extract his account of the battle of Mairta. It is not to be supposed that he could then have been acquainted

By a careful investigation of the circumstances which placed those brave races in their present political position, the paramount protecting power may be enabled to appreciate them, either as allies or as foes; and it will demonstrate more effectually than mere opinions, from whatever source, how admirably qualified they are, if divested of control, to harmonise, in a very important respect, with the British system of government in the East. We have nothing to dread from them, individually or collectively; and we may engage their very hearts' blood in our cause against whatever foes may threaten us, foreign or domestic, if we only exert our interference when mediation will be of advantage to them, without offence to their prejudices. Nor is there any difficulty in the task; all honour the peacemaker, and they would court even arbitration if once assured that we had no ulterior views. But our strides have been rapid from Calcutta to Rajpootana, and it were well if they credit what the old Nestor of India (Zalim Sing of Kotah) would not, who, in reply to all my asseverations that we wished for no more territory, said, "I believe you think so; but the time will come when there will be but one *sicca* throughout India. You stepped in, Mahraj, at a lucky time, the *p'foot*[1] was ripe and ready to be eaten, and you had only to take it bit by bit. It was not your power, so much as our disunion, which made you sovereigns, and will keep you so." His reasoning is not unworthy of attention, though I trust his prophecy may never be fulfilled.

November 28.—Camp at Jhirrow, five coss (11 miles). On leaving Mairta, we passed over the ground sacred to "the four thousand," whose

with the secret intrigues which were arrayed in favour of the "white cross" on this fatal day.

"Les forces des Rajepoutes se composaient de trente-mille cavaliers, de vingt-mille hommes d'infanterie régulière, et de vingt-cinq pièces de canon. Les Marhattes avaient une cavalerie égale en nombre à celle de l'ennemi, mais leur infanterie se bornait aux bataillons de M. de Boigne, soutenus, il est vrai, par quatre-vingt pièces d'artillerie. Le Général examina la position de l'ennemi, il étudia le terrain et arrêta son plan de bataille.

Le dix, avant le jour, la brigade reçut l'ordre de marcher en avant, et elle surprit les Rajepoutes pendant qu'ils faisoient leurs ablutions du matin. Les premiers bataillons, avec cinquante piéces de canon tirant à mitraille, enfoncèrent les lignes de l'ennemi et enlevèrent ses positions. Rohan, qui commandait l'aile droite, à la vue de ce premier avantage, sans avoir reçu aucun ordre, eut l'imprudence de s'avancer hors de la ligne du combat, à la tête de trois bataillons. La cavalerie Rahtore profitant de cette faute, fondit à l'instant sur lui et faillit lui couper sa retraite sur le gros de l'armée, qu'il ne parvint à rejoindre qu'avec les plus grandes difficultés. Toute la cavalerie ennemie se mit alors en mouvement, et se jetant avec impétuosité sur la brigade, l'attaqua sur tous les côtés à la fois. Elle eût été infailliblement exterminée sans la présence d'esprit de son chef. M. de Boigne s'étant aperçu de l'erreur commise par son aile droite et prévoyant les suites qu'elle pouvait entraîner avait disposé sur le champ son infanterie en carré vide (hollow square); et par cette disposition, présentant partout un front à l'ennemi, elle opposa une résistance invincible aux charges furieuses des Rahtores, qui furent enfin forcés de lâcher prise. Aussitôt l'infanterie reprit ses positions, et s'avançant avec son artillerie, elle fit une attaque générale sur toute la ligne des Rajepoutes. Déjà sur les neuf heures, l'ennemi était complètement battu; une heure après, les Marhattes prirent possession de son camp avec tous ses canons et bagages; et pour couronner cette journée, à trois heures après midi la ville de Mirtah fut prise d'assaut.—*Mémoire sur la Carrière Militaire et Politique de M. le Général Comte De Boigne*, *Chambéry*, 1829.

[1] *P'foot* is a species of pumpkin, or melon, which bursts and flies into pieces when ripe. It also means *disunion*; and Zalim Sing, who always spoke in parables, compared the states of India to this fruit.

heroic deeds, demonstrating at once the Rajpoot's love of freedom and his claim to it, we have just related. We this day altered our course from the N.N.E., which would have carried us, had we pursued it, to the Imperial city, for a direction to the southward of east, in order to cross our own Aravulli and gain Ajmér. The road was excellent, the soil very fair; but though there were symptoms of cultivation near the villages, the wastes were frightfully predominant; yet they are not void of vegetation: there is no want of herbage or stunted shrubs. The Aravulli towered majestically in the distant horizon, fading from our view towards the south-east, and intercepted by rising grounds.

We had a magnificent *mirage* this morning: nor do I ever recollect observing this singularly grand phenomenon on a more extensive scale, or with greater variety of form. The morning was desperately cold; the thermometer, as I mounted my horse, a little after sunrise, stood at 32°, the freezing-point, with a sharp biting wind from the north-east. The ground was blanched with frost, and the water-skins, or *behishtis masheks*, were covered with ice at the mouth. The slender shrubs, especially the milky *ak*, were completely burnt up; and as the weather had been hitherto mild, the transition was severely felt, by things animate and inanimate.

It is only in the cold season that the *mirage* is visible; the sojourners of Maroo call it the *see-kote*, or 'castles in the air.'[1] In the deep desert to the westward, the herdsmen and travellers through these regions style it *chittrám*, 'the picture'; while about the plains of the Chumbul and Jumna they term it *dessasúr*, 'the omen of the quarter.' This optical deception has been noticed from the remotest times. The prophet Isaiah alludes to it when he says, "and the parched ground shall become a pool";[2] which the critic has justly rendered, "and the *sehráb*[3] shall become real water." Quintus Curtius, describing the *mirage* in the Sogdian desert, says that "for the space of four hundred furlongs not a drop of water is to be found, and the sun's heat, being very vehement in summer, kindles such a fire in the sands, that everything is burnt up. There also arises such an exhalation, that the plains wear the appearance of a vast and deep sea;" which is an exact description of the *chittrám* of the Indian desert. But the *sehráb* and *chittrám*, the true *mirage* of Isaiah, differ from that illusion called the *see-kote*; and though the traveller will hasten to it, in order to obtain a night's lodging, I do not think he would expect to slake his thirst there.

When we witnessed this phenomenon at first, the eye was attracted by a lofty opaque wall of lurid smoke, which seemed to be bounded by, or to rise from, the very verge of the horizon. By slow degrees the dense mass became more transparent, and assumed a reflecting or refracting power: shrubs were magnified into trees; the dwarf *khyre* appeared ten

[1] Literally, 'the cold-weather castles.' [2] Isaiah, chap. xxxv. 7.

[3] *Sehara* is 'desert'; *Sehráb*, 'the water of the desert,' a term which the inhabitants of the Arabian and Persian deserts apply to this optical phenomenon. The 18th v. chap. xli. of Isaiah is closer to the critic's version: "I will make the wilderness (*Séhra*) a pool of water." Doubtless the translators of Holy Writ, ignorant that this phenomenon was called *Sehráb*, 'water of the waste,' deemed it a tautological error; for translated literally, "and the water of the desert shall become real water," would be nonsense: they therefore lopped off the *àb*, water, and read *Sèhra* instead of *Sehráb*, whereby the whole force and beauty of the prophecy is not merely diminished, but lost.

times larger than the gigantic *amli* of the forest. A ray of light suddenly broke the line of continuity of this yet smoky barrier; and, as if touched by the enchanter's wand, castles, towers, and trees, were seen in an aggregated cluster, partly obscured by magnificent foliage. Every accession of light produced a change in the *chittrám*, which from the dense wall that it first exhibited, had now faded into a thin transparent film, broken into a thousand masses, each mass being a huge lens; until at length the too vivid power of the sun dissolved the vision: castles, towers, and foliage, melted, like the enchantment of Prospero, into "thin air."

I had long imagined that the nature of the soil had some effect in producing this illusory phenomenon; especially as the *chittrám* of the desert is seen chiefly on those extensive plains productive of the *saji*, or alkaline plant, whence by incineration the natives produce soda,[1] and whose base is now known to be metallic. But I have since observed it on every kind of soil. That these lands, covered with saline incrustations, tend to increase the effect of the illusion, may be concluded. But the difference between the *sehráb* or *chittrám*, and the *see-kote* or *dessasúr*, is, that the latter is never visible but in the cold season, when the gross vapours cannot rise; and that the rarefication, which gives existence to the other, destroys this, whenever the sun has attained 20° of elevation. A high wind is alike adverse to the phenomenon, and it will mostly be observed that it covets shelter, and its general appearance is a long line which is sure to be sustained by some height, such as a grove or village, as if it required support. The first time I observed it was in the Jeipoor country; none of the party had ever witnessed it in the British provinces. It appeared like an immense walled town with bastions, nor could we give credit to our guides, when they talked of the *see-kote*, and assured us that the objects were merely "castles in the air." I have since seen, though but once, this panoramic scene in motion, and nothing can be imagined more beautiful.

It was at Kotah, just as the sun rose, whilst walking on the terraced roof of the garden-house, my residence. As I looked towards the low range which bounds the sight to the south-east, the hills appeared in motion, sweeping with an undulating or rotatory movement along the horizon. Trees and buildings were magnified, and all seemed a kind of enchantment. Some minutes elapsed before I could account for this wonder; until I determined that it must be the masses of a floating *mirage*, which had attained its most attenuated form, and being carried by a gentle current of air past the tops and sides of the hills, while it was itself imperceptible, made them appear in motion.

But although this was novel and pleasing, it wanted the splendour of the scene of this morning, which I never saw equalled but once. This occurred at Hissar, where I went to visit a beloved friend—gone, alas! to a better world,—whose ardent and honourable mind urged me to the task I have undertaken. It was on the terrace of James Lumsdaine's house, built amidst the ruins of the castle of Feroz, in the centre of one extended waste, where the lion was the sole inhabitant, that I saw the most perfect specimen of this phenomenon: it was really sublime. Let the reader fancy himself in the midst of a desert plain, with nothing to impede the wide scope of vision, his horizon bounded by a lofty black

[1] Properly a carbonate of soda.

wall encompassing him on all sides. Let him watch the first sunbeam break upon this barrier, and at once, as by a touch of magic, shiver it into a thousand fantastic forms, leaving a splintered pinnacle in one place, a tower in another, an arch in a third ; these in turn undergoing more than kaleidescopic changes, until the "fairy fabric" vanishes. Here it was emphatically called *Hurchund Raja ca poori*, or, 'the city of Raja Hurchund,' a celebrated prince of the brazen age of India. The power of reflection shown by this phenomenon cannot be better described, than by stating, that it brought the very ancient *Aggaroa*,[1] which is thirteen miles distant, with its fort and bastions, close to my view.

The difference then between the *mirage* and the *see-kote* is, that the former exhibits a horizontal, the latter a columnar or vertical stratification ; and in the latter case, likewise, a contrast to the other, its maximum of translucency is the last stage of its existence. In this stage, it is only an eye accustomed to the phenomenon that can perceive it at all. I have passed over the plains of Meerut with a friend who had been thirty years in India, and he did not observe a *see-kote* then before our eyes : in fact, so complete was the illusion, that we only saw the town and fort considerably nearer. Monge gives a philosophical account of this phenomenon in Napoleon's campaign in Egypt ; and Dr. Clarke perfectly describes it in his journey to Rosetta, when "domes, turrets, and groves, were seen reflected on the glowing surface of the plain, which appeared like a vast lake extending itself between the city and travellers." It is on reviewing this account, that a critic has corrected the erroneous translation of the Septuagint ; and further dilated upon it in a review of Lichtenstein's travels in Southern Africa,[2] who exactly describes our *see-kote*, of the magnifying and reflecting powers of which he gives a singular instance. Indeed, whoever notices, while at sea, the atmospheric phenomena of these southern latitudes, will be struck by the deformity of objects as they pass through this medium : what the sailors term a fog-bank, is the first stage of our *see-kote*. I observed it on my voyage home ; but more especially in the passage out. About six o'clock on a dark evening, while we were dancing on the waste, I perceived a ship bearing down with full sail upon us so distinctly, that I gave the alarm, in expectation of a collision ; so far as I recollect, the helm was instantly up, and in a second no ship was to be seen. The laugh was against me—I had seen the "flying Dutchman,"[3] according to the opinion of the experienced officer on deck ; and I believed it was really a vision of the mind : but I now feel convinced it was either the reflection of our own ship in a passing cloud of this vapour, or a more distant object therein refracted. But enough of this subject : I will only add, whoever has a desire to see one of the grandest phenomena in nature, let him repair to the plains of Mairta or Hissar, and watch before the sun rises the fairy palace of Hurchunda,

[1] This is in the ancient province of Heriana, and the cradle of the Aggarwal race, now mercantile, and all followers of Heri or Vishnu. It might have been the capital of Aggrames, whose immense army threatened Alexander ; with Agra it may divide the honour, or both may have been founded by this prince, who was also a *Porus*, being of Pooru's race.

[2] See *Edinburgh Review*, vol. xxi. pp. 66 and 138.

[3] This phenomenon is not uncommon ; and the superstitious sailor believes it to be the spectre of a Dutch pirate, doomed, as a warning and punishment, to migrate about these seas.

infinitely grander and more imposing than a sunrise upon the alpine Helvetia, which alone may compete with the *chittrám* of the desert.

Jhirrow is a thriving village appertaining to a sub-vassal of the Mairtea chief of Reah. There was a small sheet of water within a musket-shot to the left of the village, on whose margin, peeping through a few neems and the evergreen jhal, was erected an elegant, though small *chetri*, or cenotaph, of an ancestor of the possessor. The Thacoor is sculptured on his charger, armed at all points ; and close beside him, with folded hands, upon the same stone, his faithful partner, who accompanied the warrior to Indra's abode. It bore the following epitaph : "On the 2d Megsir, S. 1689 (A.D. 1633), Maharaja Jeswunt Sing attacked the enemy's (Arungzéb's) army, in which battle Thacoor Hernkurna Das, of the Mairtea clan, was slain. To him was erected this shrine, in the month of Megsir, S. 1697."

Water from wells is about thirty-five cubits from the surface ; the strata as follows : four cubits of mixed sand and black earth ; five of kunkur, or calcareous concretions ; twenty of stiff clay and sand ; six of indurated clay, with particles of quartz and mica.

November 29.—Alneeawas, five coss. Half-way, passed the town of Reah, so often mentioned as the abode of the chief of the Mairtea clan. It is large and populous, and surrounded by a well-constructed wall of the calcareous concrete already described, here called *morur*, and which resists the action of the monsoon. The works have a most judicious slope. The Thacoor's name is Buddun Sing, one of the eight great barons of Maroo. The town still bears the name of *Sheer Sing ca Reah*, who so gallantly defended to the death the rights of his young sovereign Ram Sing, against his uncle. A beautiful landscape is seen from the high ground on which the town stands, in the direction of the mountains ; the intermediate space being filled with large villages, relieved by foliage, so unusual in these regions. Here I had a proof of the audacity of the mountaineers of the Aravulli, in an inscription on a cenotaph, which I copied : "On Monday the 3d Magh, S. 1835 (A.D. 1779), Thacoor Bhopal Sing fell at the foot of his walls, defending them against the Mairs, having first, with his own hand, in order to save her honour, put his wife to death." [1] Such were the Mairs half a century ago, and they had been increasing in boldness ever since. There was scarcely a family on either side the range, whose estates lay at its foot, whose cenotaphs do not bear similar inscriptions, recording the desperate raids of these mountaineers ; and it may be asserted, that one of the greatest benefits we conferred on Rajpootana was the conversion of this numerous banditti, occupying some hundred towns, into peaceful, tax-paying subjects. We can say, with the great Chohan king, Beesildeva, whose monument still stands in Feroz's palace at Dehli, that we made them "carry water in the streets of Ajmér" ; and, still more, deposit their arms on the Rana's terrace at Oodipoor. We have, moreover, metamorphosed a corps of them from breakers, into keepers, of the public peace.

Between Reah and Alneeawas we crossed a stream, to which the name of the Looni [2] is also given, as well as to that we passed

[1] A second inscription recorded a similar end of Sewah, the Baôrie, who fell in another inroad of the Mairs, in S. 1831.

[2] I must deprecate criticism in respect to many of my geographical details.

subsequently. It was here that De Boigne's guns are said to have stuck fast.

The soundings of the wells at Reah and Alneeawas presented the same results as at Jhirrow, with the important exception that the substratum was steatite, which was so universal in the first part of my journey from Jodpoor.

Alneeawas is also a fief of a Mairtea vassal. It is a considerable town, populous, and apparently in easy circumstances. Here again I observed a trait of devotion, recorded on an altar "to the memory of Sooni Mull," who fell when his clan was exterminated in the charge against the rival Champawuts, at Mairta, in the civil wars.

November 30.—Govindgurh, distance three coss, or six miles. The roads generally good, though sometimes heavy; the soil of a lighter texture than yesterday. The castle and town of Govinda belong to a feudatory of the Joda clan; its founder, Govind, was grandson to Oodi *le gros*; or, as Akber dubbed him, the "Moota Raja," from his great bulk. Of this clan is the chief of Khyrwa, having sixteen townships in his fief: Bunai, and Musooda, with its "fifty-two townships," both now in Ajmér; having for their present suzerain the "Sirkar Company Behader"; though in lapses they will still go to Jodpoor, to be made "belted knights." These places are beyond the range; but Poosangur, with its twelve villages; Beejathal, and other fiefs west of it, also in Ajmér, might at all events be restored to their ancient princes, which would be considered as a great boon. There would be local prepossessions to contend with, on the part of the British officers in charge of the district; but such objections must give way to views of general good.

This was another desperately cold morning; being unprovided with a great-coat, I turned the *dugla*, or 'quilted brocade tunic,' sent me by the high-priest of Kaniya, to account. We had some capital runs this morning with the foxes of Maroo, which are beautiful little animals, and larger than those of the provinces. I had a desperate chase after a hyæna on the banks of the Looni, and had fully the speed of him; but his topographical knowledge was too much for me, and he at length led me through a little forest of reeds or rushes, with which the banks of the river are covered for a great depth. Just as I was about giving him a spear, in spite of these obstacles, we came upon a blind nullah or 'dry rivulet,' concealed by the reeds; and *Baj Baj* (the royal steed) was thrown out, with a wrench in the shoulder, in the attempt to clear it: the *chirruk* laughed at us.

We crossed a stream half a mile west of Govindgurh, called the Saburmati, which, with another, the Sarasvati, joining it, issues from the Poshkur lake. The Saburmati is also called the Looni; its bed is full of micaceous quartzose rock. The banks are low, and little above the level of the country. Though water is found at a depth of twelve cubits from the surface, the wells are all excavated to the depth of forty, as a precautionary measure against dry seasons. The stratification here was—one cubit

I find I have omitted this branch; but my health totally incapacitated me from re-constructing my map, which has been composed by the engraver from my disjointed materials. It is well known to all practical surveyors and geographers that none can do this properly but their author, who knows the precise value of each portion.

sand ; three of sand and soil mixed ; fifteen to twenty of yellow clayish sand ; four of morur, and fifteen of steatite and calcareous concretions, with loose sand, mixed with particles of quartz.

December 1.—Lake of Poshkur, four coss : the thermometer stood at the freezing-point this morning :—heavy sands the whole way. Crossed the Sarasvati near Naund ; its banks were covered with bulrushes, at least ten feet in height—many vehicles were lading with them for the interior, to be used for the purposes of thatching—elephants make a feast among them. We again crossed the Sarasvati, at the entrance of the valley of Poshkur, which comes from Old (*boora*) Poshkur, four miles east of the present lake, which was excavated by the last of the Puriharas of Mundore. The sand drifted from the plains by the currents of air has formed a complete bar at the mouth of the valley, which is about one mile in breadth ; occasionally the *teebas*, or sand-hills, are of considerable elevation. The summits of the mountains to the left were sparkling with a deep rose-coloured quartz, amidst which, on the peak of Naund, arose a shrine to 'the Mother.' The hills preserve the same character : bold pinnacles, abrupt sides, and surface thinly covered. The stratification inclines to the west ; the dip of the strata is about twenty degrees. There is, however, a considerable difference in the colour of the mountains : those on the left have a rose tint ; those on the right are of greyish granite, with masses of white quartz about their summits.

Poshkur is the most sacred lake in India ; that of Mansurwar in Thibet may alone compete with it in this respect. It is placed in the centre of the valley, which here becomes wider, and affords abundant space for the numerous shrines and cenotaphs with which the hopes and fears of the virtuous and the wicked amongst the magnates of India have studded its margin. It is surrounded by sand-hills of considerable magnitude, excepting on the east, where a swamp extends to the very base of the mountains. The form of the lake may be called an irregular ellipse. Around its margin, except towards the marshy outlet, is a display of varied architecture. Every Hindu family of rank has its niche here, for the purposes of devotional pursuits when they could abstract themselves from mundane affairs. The most conspicuous are those erected by Raja Maun of Jeipoor, Ahelya Baé, the Holkar queen, Jowahir Mull of Bhurtpoor, and Beejy Sing of Marwar. The cenotaphs are also numerous. The ashes of Jey Appa, who was assassinated at Nagore, are superbly covered ; as are those of his brother Suntaji, who was killed during the siege of that place.

By far the most conspicuous edifice is the shrine of the creator Brimha, erected, about four years ago, by a private individual, if we may so designate Gocul Pauk, the minister of Sindia ; it cost the sum of 130,000 rupees (about £15,000), though all the materials were at hand, and labour could be had for almost nothing. This is the sole tabernacle dedicated to the ONE GOD which I ever saw or have heard of in India. The statue is quadrifrons ; and what struck me as not a little curious was that the *sikra*, or pinnacle of the temple, is surmounted by a cross. Tradition was here again at work. Before creation began, Brimha assembled all the celestials on this very spot, and performed the *Yuga* ; around the hallowed spot walls were raised, and sentinels placed to guard it from the intrusion of the evil spirits. In testimony of the fact, the natives point out the four isolated mountains, placed towards the cardinal points, beyond the lake, on which, they assert, rested the *kanats*, or cloth-walls of inclosure. That to the south is called *Rutnagir*, or ‘the hill of gems,’ on the summit of which is the shrine of Sawuntri. That to the north is *Nílagir*, or ‘the blue mountain.’ East, and guarding the valley, is the *Kutchactar Gir*; and to the west, *Sonachooru*, or ‘the golden.’ Nanda, the bull-steed of Mahadeva, was placed at the mouth of the valley, to keep away the spirits of the desert; while Kaniya himself performed this office to the north. The sacred fire was kindled: but Sawuntri, the wife of Brimha, was nowhere to be found, and as without a female the rites could not proceed, a young Goojari took the place of Sawuntri; who, on her return, was so enraged at the indignity, that she retired to the mountain of gems, where she disappeared. On this spot a fountain gushed up, still called by her name; close to which is her shrine, not the least attractive in the precincts of Poshkur. During these rites, Mahadeva, or, as he is called, *Bhola Nath*, represented always in a state of stupefaction from the use of intoxicating herbs, omitted to put out the sacred fire, which spread, and was likely to involve the world in combustion; when Brimha extinguished it with the sand, and hence the *teebas* of the valley. Such is the origin of the sanctity of Poshkur. In after ages, one of the sovereigns of Mundore, in the eagerness of the chase, was led to the spot, and washing his hands in the fountain, was cured of some disorder. That he might know the place again, he tore his turban into shreds, and suspended the fragments to the trees, to serve him as guides to the spot—there he made the excavation. The Brahmins pretend to have a copper-plate grant from the Purihara prince of the lands about Poshkur; but I was able to obtain only a Persian translation of it, which I was heretical enough to disbelieve. I had many grants brought me, written by various princes and chiefs, making provision for the prayers of these recluses at their shrines.

The name of Beesildeva, the famed Chohan king of Ajmér, is the most conspicuous here; and they still point out the residence of his great ancestor, Aja Pal, on the *Nag-pahar*, or ‘serpent-rock’ directly south of the lake, where the remains of the fortress of the Pali or Shepherd-king are yet visible. Aja Pal was, as his name implies, a *goatherd*, whose piety, in supplying one of the saints of Poshkur with daily libations of goats' milk, procured him a territory. Satisfied, however, with the scene of his early days, he commenced his castle on the serpent-mount; but his evil genius knocking down in the night what he erected in the day, he sought out another site on the opposite side of the range: hence arose the far-famed Aja-mér. Manika-Rae is the most conspicuous connecting link of the Chohan Pali kings, from the goatherd founder to the famed Beesildeva.[1] Manika was slain in the first century of the Hijra, when "the arms of Walid conquered to the Ganges"; and Beesildeva headed a confederacy of the Hindu kings, and chased the descendants of Mahmood from Hindust'han, the origin of the recording column at Dehli. Beesildeva, it appears from inscriptions, was the contemporary of Rawul Tejsi, the monarch of Cheetore, and grandfather of the Ulysses of Rajast'han, the brave Samarsi, who fell with 13,000 of his kindred in aid of the last

[1] Classically, Visaladeva.

Chohan Pirthi-raj, who, according to the genealogies of this race, is the fourth in descent from Beesildeva. If this is not sufficient proof of the era of this king, be it known that Udya Dit, the prince of the Pramaras (the period of whose death, or A.D. 1096, has now become a datum),[1] is enumerated amongst the sovereigns who serve under the banners of the Chohan of Ajmér.

The 'serpent-rock' is also famed as being one of the places where the wandering Bhirtrahari, prince of Oojein, lived for years in penitential devotion; and the slab which served as a seat to this royal saint, has become one of the objects of veneration. If all the places assigned to this brother of Vicrama were really visited by him, he must have been one of the greatest tourists of antiquity, and must have lived to an antediluvian old age. Witness his castle at Sehwan, on the Indus; his cave at Alwur; his '*t'hans*' at Aboo, and at Benares. We must, in fact, give credit to the couplet of the bards, "the world is the Pramara's." There are many beautiful spots about the serpent-mount, which, as it abounds in springs, has from the earliest times been the resort of the Hindu sages, whose caves and hermitages are yet pointed out, now embellished with gardens and fountains. One of the latter issuing from a fissure in the rock, is sacred to the Mooni Agust, who performed the very credible exploit of drinking up the ocean.

St. George's banner waved on a sand-hill in front of the cross on Brimha's temple, from which my camp was separated by the lake; but though there was no defect of legendary lore to amuse us, we longed to quit "the region of death," and hie back to our own lakes, our cutter, and our gardens.

December 2.—Ajmér, three coss. Proceeded up the valley, where lofty barriers on either side, covered with the milky toor (*cactus*), and the "yellow aonla of the border," showed they were but the prolongation of our own Aravulli. Granite appeared of every hue, but of a stratification so irregular as to bid defiance to the geologist. The higher we ascended the valley, the loftier became the sand-hills, which appeared to aspire to the altitude of their granitic neighbours. A small rill poured down the valley; there came also a cold blast from the north, which made our fingers tingle. Suddenly we changed our direction from north to east, and ascending the mountain, surveyed through a gap in the range the far-famed Dhar-ool-Khyr. The view which thus suddenly burst upon us was magnificent. A noble plain, *with trees*, and the expansive lake of Beesildeva, lay at our feet, while 'the fortress of the goatherd' crowned the crest of a majestic isolated hill. The point of descent affords a fine field for the mineralogist; on each side, high over the pass, rise peaks of reddish granite, which are discovered half-way down the descent to be reposing on a blue micaceous slate, whose inclination is westward, at an angle of about 25° with the horizon. The formation is the same to the southward, but the slate there is more compact, and freer from mica and quartz. I picked up a fragment of black marble; its crystals were large and brilliant.

Passed through the city of Ajmér, which, though long a regal abode, does not display that magnificence we might have expected, and, like all other towns of India, exhibits poverty and ease in juxtaposition. It was

[1] See *Transactions of the Royal Asiatic Society*, vol. i. p. 223.

gratifying to find that the finest part was rising, under the auspices of the British Government and the superintendent of the province, Mr. Wilder. The main street, when finished, will well answer the purpose intended—a place of traffic for the sons of commerce of Rajast'han, who, in a body, did me the honour of a visit: they were contented and happy at the protection they enjoyed in their commercial pursuits. With the prosperity of Bhilwara, that of Ajmér is materially connected; and having no interests which can clash, each town views the welfare of the other as its own: a sentiment which we do not fail to encourage.

Breakfasted with Mr. Wilder, and consulted how we could best promote our favourite objects—the prosperity of Ajmér and Bhilwara.

CHAPTER XXX

Ajmér—Ancient Jain Temple—Its architecture analysed—Resemblances between it and the Gothic and Saracenic—Fortress of Ajmér—Its lakes—Source of the Looni River—Relics of the Chohan kings—Quit Ajmér—Bunai: its castle—Deorah—Dabla—Bunéra—Raja Bheem—Sketch of his family—His estate—Visit to the castle—Bhilwara—Visit of the merchants—Prosperity of the town—Mandel—Its lake—Arjah, Poor'h—Mines of Dureeba—Canton of the Poorawuts—Antiquity of Poor'h—The Babas, or infants of Méwar—Rasmi—Reception by the peasantry of Méwar—The Suhailea and Kullus—Trout of the Bunas River—Mairta—Visit to the source of the Béris—The Oodi Sagur—Enter the valley—Appearance of the capital—Site of the ancient Ahar—Cenotaphs of the Rana's ancestry—Traditions regarding Ahar—Destroyed by volcanic eruption—Remains of antiquity—Oilman's Caravanserai—Oilman's Bridge—Meeting with the Rana—Return to Oodipoor.

AJMÉR has been too long the haunt of Moguls and Pat'hans, the Goths and Vandals of Rajast'han, to afford much scope to the researches of the antiquary. Whatever time had spared of the hallowed relics of old, bigotry has destroyed, or raised to herself altars of materials, whose sculptured fragments serve now as disjointed memorials of two distinct and distant eras: that of the independent Hindu, and that of the conquering Mahomedan, whose eedgas and mosques, mausoleums and country-seats, constructed from the wrecks of aboriginal art, are fast mouldering to decay. The associations they call forth afford the only motive to wish their preservation; except one "relic of nobler days and noblest arts," which, though impressed with this double character, every spectator must desire to rescue from the sweeping sentence—an ancient Jain temple, a visit to which excited these reflections. Let us rather bless than execrate the hand, though it be that of a Turk, which has spared, from whatever motive, one of the most perfect, as well as the most ancient, monuments of Hindu architecture. It is built on the western declivity of the fortress, and called *Urai din ca jhopra*, or, 'the shed of two and a half days,' from its having occupied (as tradition tells) its magical builders only this short period. The skill of the Pali or Takshac architect, the three sacred mounts of these countries abundantly attest: nor had he occasion for any mysterious arts, besides those of masonry, to accomplish them. In discussing the cosmogony of the Hindus, we have had occasion to convert their years into days; here we must reverse the method, and understand (as in interpreting the sacred prophecies of Scripture) their days as meaning years. Had it, indeed, been of more humble pretensions, we might have supposed the monotheistic Jain had borrowed from the Athenian legislator Cecrops, who ordained that no tomb should consist of more work than ten men could finish in *three days*; to which Demetrius, the Phalerian, sanctioned the addition of a little vessel to contain the ghost's victuals.[1]

The temple is surrounded by a superb screen of Saracenic architecture, having the main front and gateway to the north. From its simplicity, as well as its appearance of antiquity, I am inclined to assign the screen to the first dynasty, the Ghorian sultans, who evidently made use of native architects. The entrance arch is of that wavy kind, characteristic of what is termed the Saracenic, whether the term be applied to the Alhambra of Spain, or the mosques of Dehli; and I am disposed, on close examination, to pronounce it Hindu. The entire façade of this noble entrance, which I regret I cannot have engraved, is covered with Arabic inscriptions. But, unless my eyes much deceived me, the small frieze over the apex of the arch contained an inscription in Sanscrit, with which Arabic has been commingled, both being unintelligible. The remains of a minaret still maintain their position on the right flank of the gate, with a door and steps leading to it for the *muezzim* to call the faithful to prayers. A line of smaller arches of similar form composes the front of the screen. The design is chaste and beautiful, and the material, which is a compact limestone of a yellow colour, admitting almost of as high a polish as the *jaune antique*, gave abundant scope to the sculptor. After confessing and admiring the taste of the Vandal architect, we passed under the arch to examine the more noble production of the Hindu. Its plan is simple, and consonant with all the more ancient temples of the Jains. It is an extensive saloon, the ceiling supported by a quadruple range of columns, those of the centre being surmounted by a range of vaulted coverings; while the lateral portion, which is flat, is divided into compartments of the most elaborate sculpture. But the columns are most worthy of attention; they are unique in design, and with the exception of the cave-temples, probably amongst the oldest now existing in India. On examining them, ideas entirely novel, even in Hindu art, are developed. Like all these portions of Hindu architecture, their ornaments are very complex, and the observer will not fail to be struck with their dissimilarity; it was evidently a rule in the art, to make the ornaments of every part unlike the other, and which I have seen carried to great extent. There may be forty columns but no two are alike. The ornaments of the base are peculiar, both as to form and execution; the lozenges, with the rich tracery surmounting them, might be transferred, not inappropriately, to the Gothic cathedrals of Europe. The projections from various parts of the shaft (which on a small scale may be compared to the corresponding projections of the columns in the *Duomo* at Milan), with the small niches still containing the statues, though occasionally mutilated, of the Pontiffs of the Jains, give them a character which strengthens the comparison, and which would be yet more apparent, if we could afford to engrave the details. The elegant *Cámacúmpa*, the emblem of the Hindu Ceres, with its pendant palmyra-branches, is here lost, as are many emblematical ornaments, curious in design and elegant in their execution. Here and there occurs a richly

[1] See Archbishop Potter's *Archæologia*, vol. i. p. 192.

carved corbeille, which still further sustains the analogy between the two systems of architecture ; and the capitals are at once strong and delicate. The central vault, which is the largest, is constructed after the same fashion as that described at Nadole ; but the concentric annulets, which in that are plain, in this are one blaze of ornaments, which with the whole of the ceiling is too elaborate and complicated for description. Under the most retired of the compartments, and nearly about the centre, is raised the *mumba*, or pulpit, whence the Moollah enunciates the dogma of Mahomed, "there is but one God" : and for which he dispossessed the Jain, whose creed was like his own, the unity of the Godhead. But this is in unison with the feeling which dictated the external metamorphosis. The whole is of the same materials as already described, from the quarries of the Aravulli close at hand, which are rich in every mineral as well as metallic production :—

"I ask'd of *Time* for whom *those* temples rose,
That prostrate by his hand in silence lie;
His lips disdain'd the myst'ry to disclose,
And borne on swifter wing, he hurried by!
The broken columns *whose*? I ask'd of *Fame*:
(Her kindling breath gives life to works sublime;)
With downcast looks of mingled grief and shame,
She heaved the uncertain sigh, and follow'd *Time*.
Wrapt in amazement o'er the mouldering pile,
I saw *Oblivion* pass with giant stride;
And while his visage wore *Pride's* scornful smile,
Haply *thou know'st*, then tell me, *whose* I cried,
Whose these vast domes that ev'n in ruin shine?
I *reck not whose*, he said: they *now are mine*."

Shall we abandon them to cold "oblivion" ; or restore them to a name already mentioned, Sumprithi, or Swámprithi, the *Shah Jéhán*[1] of a period two centuries before the Christian era, and to whom the shrine in Komulmér is ascribed. Of one thing there is no doubt, which is, that both are Jain, and of the most ancient models : and thus advertised, the antiquary will be able to discriminate between the architectural systems of the Saivas and the Jains, which are as distinct as their religions.

Having alluded to the analogy between the details in the columns and those in our Gothic buildings (as they are called), and surmised that the Saracenic arch is of Hindu origin ; I may further, with this temple and screen before us, speculate on the possibility of its having furnished some hints to the architects of Europe. It is well known that the Saracenic arch has crept into many of those structures called Gothic, erected in the twelfth and thirteenth centuries, when a more florid style succeeded to the severity of the Saxon or Romans ; but I believe it has been doubted whence the Saracens obtained their model ; certainly it was neither from Egypt nor Persia. The early caliphs of Bagdad, who were as enlightened as they were powerful, kept alive the light of science when Europe was in darkness ; and the most accomplished noble who accompanied our Cœur de Lion, though "brave as his sword," was a clown compared to the infidel Saladín, in mind as well as manners. The influence of these polished foes on European society it would be superfluous to descant upon. The lieu-

[1] Both epithets imply 'Lord of the Universe,' and of which the name of 'Pirthi-raj,' that of the last Chohan emperor, is another version.

tenants of these caliphs, who penetrated from the Delta of the Indus to the Ganges from four to five centuries prior to this event, when Walid's arms triumphed simultaneously on the Indus and the Ebro, produced no trifling results to the arts. This very spot, Ajmér, according to traditional couplets and the poetic legends of its ancient princes, the Chohans, was visited by the first hostile force which Islam sent across the Indus, and to which Manika Rae fell a sacrifice. What ideas might not this Jain temple have afforded to "*the Light* of Ali!" for Roshun Ali is the name preserved of him who, "in ships landing at Anjar," marched through the very heart of India, and took "Gurh Beetli," the citadel of Ajmér, by assault. The period is one of total darkness in the history of India, save for the scattered and flickering rays which emanate from the chronicles of the Chohans and Gehlotes. But let us leave the temple, and slightly describe the castle of Manika Rae, on whose battlements an infidel's arrow of Roshun's army reached the heir of the Chohan; since which "Lot," for such was his name, has been adopted amongst the lares and penates of this celebrated race. This was the first Rajpoot blood which the arms of conversion shed, and the impression must have been strong to be thus handed down to posterity.

The mind, after all, retires dissatisfied: with me it might be from association. Even the gateway, however elegant, is unsuitable to the genius of the place. Separately considered, they are each magnificent; together, it is as if a modern sculptor were (like our actors of the last age) to adorn the head of Cato with a peruke. I left this precious relic, with a malediction upon all the spoilers of art—whether the Thane who pillaged Minerva's portico at Athens, or the Toork who dilapidated the Jain temple at Ajmér.

I did not see very much of this far-famed fortress: for there was nothing to induce me to climb the steep, where the only temple visible was a modern-looking whitewashed mosque, lifting its dazzling minarets over the dingy antique towers of the Chohan: "he who seven times captured the sultan, and seven times released him." The hill rises majestically from its base to the height of about eight hundred feet; it crest encircled by the ancient wall and towers raised by Ajipál—

> There was a day when they were young and proud,
> Banners on high, and battles passed below;
> But they who fought are in a bloody shroud,
> And those which waved are shredless dust ere now,
> And the bleak battlements shall bear no future blow; [1]

unless the Cossack should follow the track of Roshun Ali or Mahmood, and try to tear the British flag from the *kangras* of Ajmér. On the north side, a party of the superintendent's were unlocking the latent treasures in the bowels of the mountain. The vein is of lead; a sulphuret, or galena.

I have already mentioned the lake, called after the excavator, the *Beesil Táláb*. It is about eight miles in circumference, and besides the beauty it adds to the vale of Ajmér, it has a source of interest in being the

[1] *Childe Harold*, Canto iii.

fountain of the Looni, which pursues its silent course until it unites with the eastern arm of the Delta of the Indus: the point of outlet is at the northern angle of the *Doulut Bag'h*, 'the gardens of wealth,' built by Jehangír for his residence when he undertook to conquer the Rajpoots. The water is not unwholesome, and there are three outlets at this fountain-head for the escape of the water fitting its periodical altitudes. The stream at its parent source is thence called the Sagur-Mati. It takes a sweep northward by Bhowtah and Pisangun, and close to where we crossed it, at Govindgurh, it is joined by the Sarasvati from Poshkur; when the united waters (at whose *sangum*, or confluence, there is a small temple to the *manes*) are called the Looni.

The gardens erected on the embankment of the lake must have been a pleasant abode for "the king of the world," while his lieutenants were carrying on the war against the Rana: but the imperial residence of marble, in which he received the submissions of that prince, through his grandson, and the first ambassador sent by England to the Mogul, are now going fast to decay. The walks on which his majesty last paraded, in the state-coach sent by our James the First, are now overgrown with shrubs.

The stratification of the rock, at the point of outlet, would interest the geologist, especially an extensive vein of mica, adjoining another of almost transparent quartz.

Eastward of this lake about a mile, is another named the *Anah-sagur*, after the grandson of Beesildeo, who has left the reputation of great liberality, and a contrast with Visala. The vestiges of an island are yet seen in the lake, and upon its margin; but the materials have been carried away by the Goths. There are two small buildings on the adjacent heights, called "the annulets of Khwaja Kootub," and some other saint.

Such are the wonders in the environs of Dhar-ool-Khyr, "celebrated in the history of the Moguls, as well as of the Hindus." But my search for inscriptions to corroborate the legends of the Chohans proved fruitless. I was, however, fortunate enough to add to my numismatic treasures some of the currency of these ancient kings, which give interest to a series of the same description, all appertaining to the Budhists or Jains. The inscription occupying one side is in a most antique character, the knowledge of which is still a desideratum: the reverse bears the effigies of a horse, the object of worship to the Indo-Scythic Rajpoot. It is not improbable that the Agnicúla Chohan may have brought these letters with him from higher Asia. Researches in these countries for such monuments may yet discover how far this conjecture is correct. At Poshkur I also found some very ancient coins. Had the antiquary travelled these regions prior to the reign of Arungzéb he would have had a noble field to explore: many coins were destroyed by this bigot, but many were buried under-ground, which time or accident may disclose. He was the great foe of Rajpoot fame; and well might the bard, in the words of the Cambrian minstrel, bid

"Ruin seize the ruthless king."

They did repay his cruelties by the destruction of his race. In one short century from this tyrant, who grasped each shore of the peninsula, the Mogul power was extinct; while the oppressed Rajpoots are again on the ascendant. But the illiterate and mercenary Afghan, "the descendant of the lost tribes of Israel,"[1] if we credit their traditions, may share the iniquity with Arungzéb: for they fulfilled literally a duty which their supposed forefathers pertinaciously refused, and made war against every graven image. Had they even spared us a few of the monsters, the joint conceptions of the poet and the sculptor, I might have presented some specimens of griffins (*grâs*) and demons almost of a classical taste: but the love of mischief was too strong even to let these escape: the shoe was applied to the prominent features of everything which represented animation.

By a medium of several meridian observations, I made the latitude of Ajmér 26° 19′ north; its longitude, by time and measurement from my fixed meridian, Oodipoor, 74° 40′, nearly the position assigned to it by the father of Indian geography, the justly-celebrated Rennell.

December 5.—At daybreak we left the towers of Manika Rae, enveloped in mist, and turned our horses' heads to the southward, on our return to Oodipoor. While at Ajmér, I received accounts of the death of the prince of Kotah, and did intend to proceed direct to that capital, by Shapoora and Boondí; but my presence was desired by the Rana to repair the dilapidations which only two months' absence had occasioned in the political fabric which I had helped to reconstruct. Other interesting objects intervened: one, a visit to the new castle of Bheemgurh, erecting in Mairwarra to overawe the Mairs; the other to compose the feuds which raged between the sectarian merchants of the new mart, Bhilwara, and which threatened to destroy all my labour. We made two marches to Bunai, in which there was nothing to record. Bunai is the residence of a Rahtore chieftain, whose position is rather peculiar. Being placed within the district of Ajmér, and paying an annual quit-rent to the British, he may consider the Company as his sovereign; but although this position precludes all political subordination to the chief of the race, the tie would be felt and acknowledged, on a lapse, in the anxiety for the usual *teeka* of recognition to his successor, from the Raja of Marwar. I argue on knowledge of character and customs; though it is possible this individual case might be against me.

The castle of Bunai is a picturesque object in these level plains; it is covered with the *cactus*, or prickly pear, so abundant on the east side of the Aravulli. This was anciently the residence of a branch of the Purihara princes of Mundore, when held as a fief of the Chohans of Ajmér; and from it originated a numerous mixed class, called the Purihara Ménas, a mixture of Rajpoot and aboriginal blood.

December 6.—Deorah, near the northern bank of the Khari, the present boundary of Ajmér and Méwar. From Ajmér to Deorah, the direction of the road is S.S.E., and the distance forty miles. This important district in the political geography of Rajpootana, which, with the posts of Neemuch and Mhow, is the connecting link between the British dominions on the Jumna and in the Dekhan, was obtained by cession from Sindia in 1818. A glance at the map is sufficient to show its importance in our existing connection with Rajpootana. The greatest breadth of the district is between the Aravulli west, and the Bunas east, and measures about eight miles. The greatest length is between the city of Ajmér and Jhâk, a post in Mairwarra, measuring about forty miles. The narrowest portion is that

[1] They claim Ishmael as their common ancestor.

where we now are, Deorah, whence the Kishengurh frontier can be seen over a neck of land of about twelve miles in extent. Within these bounds, a great portion of the land is held by feudal chieftains paying a quit-rent, which I believe is fixed. I had to settle a frontier dispute at Deorah, regarding the right of cultivating in the bed of the Khari, which produces very good melons. The soil of Ajmér cannot be called rich, and is better adapted for the lighter than the richer grains. Marks of war and rapine were visible throughout.

December 7.—Dabla.—This town was a sub-fee of Bunéra; but the vassal, a Rahtore, had learned habits of insubordination during Mahratta influence, which he could not or would not throw aside. In these he was further encouraged by his connection by marriage with the old ruler of Kotah, who had exemplified his hostility to the Dabla vassal's liege lord by besieging his castle of Bunéra. Having so long disobeyed him, his Rajpoot blood refused to change with the times; and though he condescended, at the head of his twenty retainers, to perform homage on stated days, and take his allotted position in the Bunéra durbar, he refused to pay the quit-rent, to which numerous deeds proved his suzerain had a right. Months passed away in ineffectual remonstrances; it was even proposed that he should hold the inferior dependencies free of quit-rent, but pay those of Dabla. All being in vain, the demand was increased to the complete surrender of Dabla; which elicited a truly Rajpoot reply: "His head and Dabla were together." This obstinacy could not be tolerated; and he was told that though one would suffice, if longer withheld both might be required. Like a brave Rahtore, he had defended it for months against a large Mahratta force, and hence Dabla was vauntingly called "the little Bhurtpoor." Too late he saw his error, but there was no receding; and though he at length offered a nuzzerana, through the mediation of the Kotah vakeel, of 20,000 rupees, to obtain the Rana's investiture, it was refused and a surrender was insisted on. Being an important frontier-post, it was retained by the Rana, and compensation was made to Bunéra. Every interest was made for him through the Nestor of Kotah, but in vain; his obstinacy offered an example too pernicious to admit of the least retrocession, and Dabla was forthwith incorporated with the appanage of the heir-apparent, Jowan Sing.

Almost the whole of this, the Bednore division, of 360 townships, is occupied by Rahtores, the descendants of those who accompanied Jeimul to Méwar: the proportion of feudal to fiscal land therein is as three to one. It is a rich and fertile tract, and it is to be hoped will maintain in ease and independence the brave men who inhabit it, and who have a long time been the sport of rapine.

I received a visit from the chief vassal of the Bednore chief, then at the capital; and as I found it impossible to visit Mairwarra, I subsequently deputed Captain Waugh who was hospitably received and entertained at Bednore. He hunted, and played the *holi* with the old baron, who shows at all times the frankness of his race: but it being the period of the Saturnalia, he was especially unreserved; though he was the greatest stickler for etiquette amongst my many friends, and was always expatiating on the necessity of attending to the gradations of rank.

December 8.—Bunéra.—The castle of Bunéra is one of the most imposing feudal edifices of Méwar, and its lord one of the greatest of its chieftains.

He not only bears the title of *Raja*, but has all the state-insignia attached thereto. His name happens to be the same as that of his sovereign—his being Raja Bheem, the prince's Rana Bheem,—to whom he is nearly related, and but for blind chance might have been lord of all the Seesodias. It may be recollected that the chivalrous antagonist of Arungzéb, the heroic Rana Raj, had two sons, twins, if we may so term sons simultaneously born, though by different mothers. The incident which decided the preference of Jey Sing to Bheem has been related ;[1] the circumstance of the latter's abandoning his country to court fortune under the Imperial standard—his leading his Rajpoot contingent amongst the mountains of Candahar—and his death by dislocation of the spine, through urging his horse at speed amongst the boughs of a tree. The present incumbent of Bunéra is the descendant of that Raja Bheem, who was succeeded in the honours of his family by his son Sooraj, killed whilst heading his contingent at the storm of Beejapoor. The infant son of Sooraj had four districts assigned to him, all taken from his suzerain, the Rana. In such esteem did the emperor hold the family, that the son of Sooraj was baptized Sultan. He was succeeded by Sirdar Sing, who, on the breaking up of the empire, came under the allegiance of his rightful sovereign the Rana. Raé Sing and Hamir Sing complete the chain to my friend Raja Bheem, who did me the honour to advance two miles from Bunéra to welcome and conduct me to his castle. Here I had a good opportunity of observing the feudal state and manners of these chiefs within their own domains, during a visit of three hours at Bunéra. I was, moreover, much attached to Raja Bheem, who was a perfectly well-bred and courteous gentleman, and who was quite unreserved with me. From his propinquity to the reigning family, and from his honours and insignia being the gift of the king's, he had been an object of jealousy to the court, which tended much to retard the restoration of his authority over his sub-vassals of Bunéra ; the chief of Dabla is one instance of this. I found little difficulty in banishing the discord between him and his sovereign, who chiefly complained of the Bunéra kettle-drums beating, not only as he entered the city, but as far as the *Porte*—the sacred *Tripolia* ; and the use of *Chamur* in his presence. It was arranged that these emblems of honour, emanating from the great foes of Méwar, should never be obtruded on the eye or ear of the Rana ; though within his own domain the Bunéra chieftain might do as he pleased. This was just ; and Raja Bheem had too much good sense not to conciliate his " brother and cousin," Rana Bheem, by such a concession, which otherwise might have been insisted upon. The estate of Bunéra is in value 80,000 rupees of annual rent, one-half of which is in sub-infeudations, his vassals being chiefly Rahtores. The only service performed by Raja Bheem is the contributing a quota for the commercial mart of Bhilwara, with the usual marks of subordination, personal duty and homage to the Rana. His estate is much impoverished from its lying in the very track of the freebooters ; but the soil is excellent, and time will bring hands to cultivate it, if we exercise a long and patient indulgence.

The " velvet cushion " was spread in a balcony projecting from the main hall of Bunéra ; here the Raja's vassals were mustered, and he placed me by his side on the *gadí*. There was not a point of his rural or

[1] See p. 312.

domestic economy upon which he did not descant, and ask my advice, as his "adopted brother." I was also made umpire between him and my old friend the baron of Bednore, regarding a marriage-settlement, the granddaughter of the latter being married to the heir of Bunéra. I had, besides, to wade through old grants and deeds to settle the claims between the Raja and several of his sub-vassals; a long course of disorder having separated them so much from each other as to obliterate their respective rights. All these arbitrations were made without reference to my official situation, but were forced upon me merely by the claims of friendship; but it was a matter of exultation to be enabled to make use of my influence for the adjustment of such disputes, and for restoring individual as well as general prosperity. My friend prepared his gifts at parting; I went through the forms of receiving, but waived accepting them: which may be done without any offence to delicacy. I have been highly gratified to read the kind reception he gave to the respected Bishop Heber, in his tour through Méwar. I wonder, however, that this discerning and elegant-minded man did not notice the peculiar circumstance of the Raja's teeth being fixed in with gold wire, which produces rather an unpleasant articulation.

Bunéra adjoins the estates of the Rahtores, and is no great distance from those of the Sangawuts and Jugawuts, which lie at the base of the Aravulli. All require a long period of toleration and unmolested tranquillity to emerge from their impoverished condition. My friend accompanied me to my tents, when I presented to him a pair of pistols, and a telescope with which he might view his neighbours on the mountains: we parted with mutual satisfaction, and I believe, mutual regret.

December 9.—Bhilwara.—I encamped about half a mile from *our* good town of Bhilwara, which was making rapid strides to prosperity, notwithstanding drawbacks from sectarian feuds; with which, however, I was so dissatisfied, that I refused every request to visit the town until such causes of retardation were removed. I received a deputation from both parties at my tents, and read them a lecture for their benefit, in which I lamented the privation of the pleasure of witnessing their unalloyed prosperity. Although I reconciled them to each other, I would not confide in their promises until months of improvement should elapse. They abided by their promise, and I fulfilled mine when the death of the Boondí prince afforded an opportunity, *en route* to that capital, to visit them. My reception was far too flattering to describe, even if this were the proper place. The sentiments they entertained for me had suffered no diminution when Bishop Heber visited the town. But his informant (one of the merchants), when he said it ought to have been called *Tod-gunj*, meant that it was so intended, and actually received this appellation: but it was changed, at my request, and on pain of withdrawing my entire support from it. The Rana, who used to call it himself in conversation "*Tod Sahib ca bustee*," would have been gratified; but it would have been wrong to avail myself of his partiality. In all I was enabled to do, from my friendship, not from my official character, I always feared the dangers to his independence from such precedent for interference.[1]

December 10.—Mandel.—I deviated from the direct course *homewards* (to Oodipoor) to visit this beautiful spot, formerly the head of a flourishing

[1] See p. 383.

district ; but all was dilapidated. The first revenue derived from Mandel was expended on the repairs of the dam of its lake, which irrigates a great extent of rice-land. The Goths had felled most of the fine trees which had ornamented its dam and margin ; and several garden-houses, as well as that on the island in the lake, were in ruins. Not many years ago, a column of victory, said to have been raised by Beesildeva of Ajmér, in consequence of a victory over the Gehlotes, graced this little isle. Mandel is now rising from its ruins, and one of the exiles was so fortunate as to find a vessel containing several pieces of gold and ornaments, in excavating the ruins of his ancient abode, though not buried by him. It involved the question of manorial rights, of which the Rana waived the enforcement, though he asserted them. To-day I passed between Pansil and Arjah, the former still held by a Suktawut, the latter now united to the fisc. I have already related the feud between the Suktawuts and the Poorawuts in the struggle for Arjah, which is one of the most compact castles in Méwar, with a domain of 52,000 bígas, or 12,000 acres, attached to it, rendering it well worth a contest ; but the Suktawut had no right there, say the Poorawuts ; and in fact it is in the very heart of their lands.

December 11.—Poor'h.—This is one of the oldest towns of Méwar, and if we credit tradition, anterior in date to Vicrama. We crossed the Kotaserri to and from Mandel, passing by the tin and copper mines of Dureeba, and the Poorawut estate of Peetawas. *Poor'h* means *par éminence*, 'the city,' and anciently the title was admissible ; even now it is one of the chief fiscal towns. It is in the very heart of the canton, inhabited by the *Babas*, or 'infants' of Méwar, embracing a circle of about twenty-five miles diameter. The broken chain of mountains, having Bunéra on the northern point and Goorla to the south, passes transversely through this domain, leaving the estate of Bagore, the residence of Sheodan Sing, west, and extending to the S.E. to Mungrope, across the Béris. The policy which dictated the establishment of an isolated portion of the blood-royal of Méwar in the very centre of the country was wise ; for the Babas rarely or ever mix with the politics of the feudatory chieftains, home or foreign. They are accordingly entrusted with the command of all garrisons, and head the feudal quotas as the representative of their sovereign. They have a particular seat at court, the *Baba ca Ole* being distinct from the chieftains', and in front. Though they inhabit the lands about Poor'h, it is not from these they derive their name, but as descendants from Pooru, one of the twenty-five sons of Rana Oodi Sing, that blot in the scutcheon of Méwar.

About a mile east of Poor'h there is an isolated hill of blue slate, in which I found garnets imbedded. I have no doubt persevering adventurers would be rewarded ; but though I tried them with the hammer, I obtained none of any value. They are also to be obtained on the southern frontier of Kishengurh and Ajmér, about Serwar. I received the visits of the 'infants' of Goorlah and Gadermala, both most respectable men, and enjoying good estates, with strong castles, which I passed the next day.

December 12.—Rasmi, on the Bunas river.—We had a long march through the most fertile lands of Méwar, all belonging to the Rana's personal domain. The progress towards prosperity is great ; of which Rasmi, the head of a tuppa or subdivision of a district, affords evidence, as well as every village. On our way, we were continually met by peasants with songs of joy, and our entrance into each village was one of triumph. The patéls and other rustic officers, surrounded by the ryots, came out of the villages; while the females collected in groups, with brass vessels filled with water gracefully resting on their heads, stood at the entrance, their scarfs half covering their faces, chaunting the *suhailea*; a very ancient custom of the Hindu cultivator on receiving the superior, and tantamount to an acknowledgment of supremacy. Whether vanity was flattered, or whether a better sentiment was awakened, on receiving such tokens of gratitude, it is not for me to determine: the sight was pleasing, and the custom was general while I travelled in Méwar. The females bearing the *kullus* on their heads, were everywhere met with. These were chiefly the wives and daughters of the cultivators, though not unfrequently those of the Rajpoot sub-vassals. The former were seldom very fair, though they had generally fine eyes and good persons. We met many fragments of antiquity at Rasmi. Captain Waugh and the doctor were gratified with angling in the Bunas for trout; but as the fish would not rise to the fly, I set the net, and obtained several dozens: the largest measured seventeen inches, and weighed seventy rupees, or nearly two pounds.

December 16.—Mairta.—After an absence of two months, we terminated our circuitous journey, and encamped on the ground whence we started, all rejoiced at the prospect of again entering "the happy valley." We made four marches across the *do-áb*, watered by the Béris and Bunas rivers; the land naturally rich, and formerly boasting some large towns, but as yet only disclosing the germs of prosperity. There is not a more fertile tract in India than this, which would alone defray the expenses of the court if its resources were properly husbanded. But years must first roll on, and the peasant must meet with encouragement, and a reduction of taxation to the lowest rate; and the lord-paramount must alike be indulgent in the exaction of his tribute. Our camels were the greatest sufferers in the march through the desert, and one-half were rendered useless. I received a deputation conveying the Rana's congratulation on my return "home," with a letter full of friendship and importunities to see me: but the register of the heavens—an oracle consulted by the Rajpoot as faithfully as Moore's Almanack by the British yeoman—showed an unlucky aspect, and I must needs halt at Mairta, or in the valley, until the signs were more favourable to a re-entry into Oodipoor. Here we amused ourselves in chalking out the site of our projected residence on the heights of Toos, and in fishing at the source of the Béris. If the reader allows his imagination to ascend the dam which confines the waters of the lake, he may view the *Oodi-sagur*, with its islets; and directing his eye across its expanse, he may gain a bird's-eye view of the palace of the Késâr of the Seesodias. The dam thrown across a gorge of the mountains is of enormous magnitude and strength, as is necessary, indeed, to shut in a volume of water twelve miles in circumference. At its base, the point of outlet, is a small hunting-seat of the Rana's, going to decay for want of funds to repair it, like all those on the Tiger Mount and in the valley. Nor is there any hope that the revenues, burthened as they are with the payment of a clear fourth in tribute, can supply the means of preventing further dilapidation.

December 19.—Tired of two days' idleness, we passed through the portals of Dobarri on our way to Ar, to which place the Rana signified his intention of advancing in person, to receive and conduct me " home ": an honour as unlooked-for and unsolicited as it was gratifying. Oodipoor presents a most imposing appearance when approached from the east. The palace of the Rana, and that of the heir-apparent, the great temple, and the houses of the nobles, with their turrets and cupolas rising in airy elegance, afford a pleasing contrast with the heavy wall and pierced battlements of the city beneath. This wall is more extensive than solid. To remedy this want of strength, a chain of fortresses has been constructed, about gunshot from it, commanding every road leading thereto, which adds greatly to the effect of the landscape. These castellated heights contain places of recreation, one of which belongs to Saloombra ; but all wear the same aspect of decay.

Ar, or Ahar, near which we encamped, is sacred to the manes of the princes of Oodipoor, and contains the cenotaphs of all her kings since the valley became their residence ; but as they do not disdain association, either in life or death, with their vassals, Ar presents the appearance of a thickly-crowded cemetery, in which the mausoleums of the Ranas stand pre-eminent in " the place of great faith." The renowned Umra Sing's is the most conspicuous ; but the cenotaphs of all the princes, down to the father of Rana Bheem, are very elegant, and exactly what such structures ought to be ; namely, vaulted roofs, supported by handsome columns raised on lofty terraces, the architraves of enormous single blocks, all of white marble, from the quarries of Kankerowli. There are some smaller tombs of a singularly elaborate character, and of an antiquity which decides the claims of Ar to be considered as the remains of a very ancient city. The ground is strewed with the wrecks of monuments and old temples, which have been used in erecting the sepulchres of the Ranas. The great city was the residence of their ancestors, and is said to have been founded by Asa-ditya upon the site of the still more ancient capital of Tamba-nagari, where dwelt the Tuar ancestors of Vicramaditya, before he obtained Awinti, or Oojein. From Tamba-nagari its name was changed to Anundpoor, ' the happy city,' and at length to Ahar, which gave the patronymic to the Gehlote race, namely, Aharya. The vestiges of immense mounds still remain to the eastward, called the *Dhool-kote*, or ' fort,' destroyed by ' ashes ' (*dhool*) of a volcanic eruption. Whether the lakes of the valley owe their origin to the same cause which is said to have destroyed the ancient Ahar, a more skilful geologist must determine. The chief road from the city is cut through this mound ; and as I had observed fragments of sculpture and pottery on the excavated sides, I commenced a regular opening of the mound in search of medals, and obtained a few with the effigies of an animal, which I fancied to be a lion, but others the *gadha*, or ass, attributed to Gundrufsén, the brother of Vicrama, who placed this impress on his coins, the reason of which is given in a long legend. My impious intentions were soon checked by some designing knaves about the Rana, and I would not offend superstition. But the most superficial observer will pronounce Ar to have been an ancient and extensive city, the walls which enclose this sepulchral abode being evidently built with the sculptured fragments of temples. Some shrines, chiefly Jain, are still standing, though in the last stage of dilapidation, and they have been erected from the ruins of shrines still older, as appears from the motley decorations, where statues and images are inserted with their heads reversed, and Mahavíra and Mahadeva come into actual contact: all are in white marble. Two inscriptions were obtained; one very long and complete, in the nail-headed character of the Jains; but their interpretation is yet a desideratum. A topographical map of this curious valley would prove interesting, and for this I have sufficient materials. The *Taili-ca-Serai* would not be omitted in such a map, as adding another to the many instances I have met with, among this industrious class, to benefit their fellow-citizens. The 'Oilman's Caravanserai' is not conspicuous for magnitude; but it is remarkable, not merely for its utility, but even for its elegance of design. It is equi-distant from each of the lakes. The *Taili-ca-Pool*, or "Oilman's Bridge," at Noorabad, is, however, a magnificent memorial of *the trade*, and deserves preservation; and as I shall not be able now to describe the region (Gwalior) where it stands, across the Asin, I will substitute it for the Serai, of which I have no memorial. These *Tailis* (oilmen) perambulate the country with skins of oil on a bullock, and from hard-earned pence erect the structures which bear their name. India owes much to individual munificence.

The planets were adverse to my happy conjunction with the Sun of the Hindus: and it was determined that I should pass another day amongst the tombs of Ahar; but I invoked upon my own devoted head all the evil consequences, as in this case I was the only person who was threatened. To render this opposition to the decree less noxious, it was agreed that I should make my *entrée* by the southern, not by the eastern porte, that of the sun. The Rana came, attended by his son, his chiefs, his ministers, and, in fact, all the capital in his train. The most hearty welcomes were lavished upon us all. "*Rama! Rama! Tod Sahib!*" (the Hindu greeting) resounded from a thousand throats, while I addressed each chief by name. It was not a meeting of formality, but of well-cemented friendship. My companions, Capt. Waugh and Dr. Duncan, were busy interchanging smiles and cordial greetings, when the Rana, requesting our presence at the palace next day, bade us adieu. He took the direct road to his palace, while we, to avoid evil spirits, made a detour by the southern portal, to gain our residence, the garden of Rampeari.

APPENDIX

Translations of Inscriptions, chiefly in the Nail-headed character of the Takshac Races and Jains, fixing eras in Rajpoot history.

No. I.

Memorial of a Gete or Jit prince of the fifth century, discovered 1820, in a temple at Kunswa, near the Chumbul river, south of Kotah.

May the Jit'ha be thy protector! What does this Jit'h resemble? which is the vessel of conveyance across the waters of life, which is partly white, partly red? Again, what does it resemble, where the hissing-angered serpents dwell? What may this Jit'ha be compared to, from whose root the roaring flood descends? Such is the Jit'h; by it may thou be preserved (1).

The fame of RAJA JIT I now shall tell, by whose valour the lands of SÁLPOORA (2) are preserved. The fortunes of Raja Jit are as flames of fire devouring his foe. The mighty warrior JIT SÁLINDRA (2) is beautiful in person, and from the strength of his arm esteemed the first amongst the tribes of the mighty; make resplendent, as does the moon the earth, the dominions of SALPOORI. The whole world praises the JIT prince, who enlarges the renown of his race, sitting in the midst of haughty warriors, like the lotos in the waters, the moon of the sons of men. The foreheads of the princes of the earth worship the toe of his foot. Beams of light irradiate his countenance, issuing from the gems of his arms of strength. Radiant is his array; his riches abundant; his mind generous and profound as the ocean. Such is he of SÁRYA (3) race, a tribe renowned amongst the tribes of the mighty, whose princes were ever foes to treachery, to whom the earth surrendered her fruits, and who added the lands of their foes to their own. By sacrifice, the mind of this lord of men has been purified; fair are his territories, and fair is the FORTRESS OF TAK'HYA (4). The string of whose bow is dreaded, whose wrath is the reaper of the field of combat; but to his dependents he is as the pearl on the neck; who makes no account of the battle, though streams of blood run through the field. As does the silver lotos bend its head before the fierce rays of the sun, so does his foe stoop to him, while the cowards abandon the field.

From this lord of men (*Narpati*) SALINDRA sprung DEVANGLI, whose deeds are known even at *this remote period.*

From him was born SUMBOOKA, and from him DEGALÍ, who married two wives of YADU race (5), and by one a son named VÍRA NARÍNDRÁ, pure as a flower from the fountain.

Amidst groves of *amba*, on whose clustering blossoms hang myriads of bees, that the wearied traveller might repose, was this edifice erected. May it, and the fame of its founder, continue while ocean rolls, or while the moon, the sun, and hills endure. Samvat 597.—On the extremity of MALWA, this minster (MINDRA) was erected, on the banks of the river TAVÉLÍ, by SÁLÍCHANDRA (6), son of VÍRACHANDRA.

Whoever will commit this writing to memory, his sins will be obliterated. Carved by the sculptor SÉVANARYA, son of DWÁRASÍVA, and composed by BÚTÉNA, chief of the bards.

(*Note* 1).—In the prologue to this valuable relic, which superficially viewed would appear a string of puerilities, we have conveyed in mystic allegory the mythological origin of the Jit or Gete race. From the members of the chief of the gods ISWARA or Mahadeva, *the god of battle*, many races claim birth: the warrior from his arms; the Charun from his spine; the prophetic Bhat (*Vates*) from his tongue; and the Gete or Jit, derive theirs from his tiara, which, formed of his own hair, is called *Jit'ha*. In this tiara, serpents, emblematic of TIME (kal) and DESTRUCTION, are wreathed; also implicative that the *Jits*, who are of *Takshac*, or the serpent race, are thereby protected. The "roaring flood" which descends from this *Jit'ha* is the river goddess, Ganga, daughter of Méra, wife of Iswara. The mixed colour of his hair, which is partly white, partly of reddish (*pandúranga*) hue, arises from his character of ARD'HNÁRÍ, or Hermaphroditus. All these characteristics of the god of war must have been brought by the Scythic Gete from the Jaxartes, where they worshipped him as the Sun (*Bálnat'h*) and as XAMOLSCIS (*Yama*, vulg. *Jama*) the infernal divinity.

The 12th chapter of the Edda, in describing BALDER the second son of Odin, particularly dwells on the beauty of his hair, whence "the *whitest of all vegetables is called the eyebrow of Balder, on the columns of whose temples there are verses engraved, capable of recalling the dead to life.*"

How perfectly in unison is all this of the Jits of Jutland and the Jits of Rajast'han. In each case the hair is the chief object of admiration; of Balnath as Balder, and the magical effect of the Runes is not more powerful than that attached by the chief of the Scalds of our Gete prince at the end of this inscription, fresh evidences in support of my hypothesis, that many of the Rajpoot races and Scandinavians have a common origin—that origin, Central Asia.

(*Note* 2).—Salpoora is the name of the capital of this Jit prince, and his epithet of Sal-índrá is merely titular, as the Indra, or lord of Sál-poori, 'the city of Sál,' which the fortunate discovery of an inscription raised by Komarpal, king of Anhulwarra (*Nehrwalla* of D'Anville), dated S. 1207, has enabled me to place "at the base of the Sewaluk Mountains." In order to elucidate this point, and to give the full value to this record of the Jit princes of the Punjâb, I append (No. V.) a translation of the Nehrwalla conqueror's inscription, which will prove beyond a doubt that these JIT princes of SALPOORI in the *Punjâb*, were the leaders of that very colony of the Yuti from the Jaxartes, who in the fifth century, as recorded by De Guignes, crossed the Indus and possessed themselves of the Punjâb; and strange to say, have again risen to power, for the Síkhs (*disciples*) of Nanuk are almost all of Jit origin.

(*Note* 3).—Here this Jit is called of SÁRYÁ SAC'HA, *branch* or *ramification* of the *Saryas*: a very ancient race which is noticed by the genealogists synonymously with the SARIASPA, one of the thirty-six royal races, and very probably the same as the SARWYA of the Komarpal Charítra, with the distinguished epithet "the flower of the martial races" (*Sarwya c'shatrya tyn Sar*).

(*Note* 4).—"The fortress of Takshac." Whether this TAKSHAC-NAGARI, or castle of the Tâk, is the stronghold of SALPOORI, or the name given to a conquest in the environs of the place, whence this inscription, we can only surmise, and refer the reader to what has been said of Takitpoora. As I have repeatedly said, the Tâks and Jits are one race.

(*Note* 5).—As the Jits intermarried with the Yadus at this early period, it is evident they had forced their way amongst the thirty-six royal races, though they have again lost this rank. No Rajpoot would give a daughter to a Jit, or take one from them to wife.

(*Note* 6).—Sálíchandra is the sixth in descent from the first-named prince, JIT SALINDRA, allowing twenty-two years to each descent=132—S. 597, date of ins.=S. 465—56=A.D. 409; the period of the colonisation of the Punjâb by the Getes, Yuti, or Jits, from the Jaxartes.

No. II.

Translation of an inscription in the Nail-headed character relative to the Jit race, discovered at Ram Chundrapoora, six miles east of Boondee, in digging a well. It was thence conveyed, and deposited by me in the Museum of the Royal Asiatic Society.

To my foe, salutation! This foe of the race of JIT, CATHIDA (1), how shall I describe, who is resplendent by the favour of the round bosom of ROODRANI (2), and whose ancestor, the warrior TUKHYA (3), formed the garland on the neck of Mahadeva. Better than this foe on the earth's surface, there is none; therefore to him I offer salutation. The sparkling gems on the coronets of kings irradiate the nail of his foot.

Of the race of BOTÉNA (4) RAJA T'HOT was born; his fame expanded through the universe.

Pure in mind, strong in arm, and beloved by mankind, such was CHANDRASÉN (5). How shall he be described, who broke the strength of his foe, on whom when his sword swims in fight, he appears like a magician. With his subjects he interchanged the merchandise of liberality, of which he reaped the fruits. From him whose history is fair, was born KRITIKA, the deeds of whose arm were buds of renown, forming a necklace of praise in the eyes of mankind. His queen was dear to him as his own existence —how can she be described ? As the flame is inseparable from the fire, so was she from her lord—she was the light issuing from the sun—her name GOON-NEWÁSA (6), and her actions corresponded with her name. By her he had two sons, like gems set in bracelets, born to please mankind. The eldest was named SOOKUNDA, the younger DERUKA. Their fortunes consumed their foes : but their dependents enjoyed happiness. As the flowers of Calp-vricsha are beloved by the gods, so are these brothers by their subjects, granting their requests, and increasing the glory of the race, whence they sprung.—[A useless descriptive stanza left out (7).]

DERUKA had a son, KUHLA, and his was DHUNIKA, whose deeds ascended high—who could fathom the intentions of mankind—whose mind was deep as the ocean—whose ever-hungry faulchion expelled from their mountains and forests the MEENA tribes, leaving them no refuge in the three wolds, levelling their retreats to the ground. His quiver was filled with crescent-formed arrows—his sword the climber (*véla*) (8), of which pearls are the fruit. With his younger brother Dewaka he reverences gods and Brahmins—and with his own wealth perfumed a sacrifice to the sun.

For the much-beloved's (his wife) pleasure this was undertaken. Now the river of ease, life and death, is crossed over, for this abode will devour the body of the foe, into which the west wind wafts the fragrant perfume from the sandal-covered bosom of Lacshmí (9) ; while from innumerable lotos the gale from the east comes laden with aroma, the hum of the bees as they hang clustering on the flowers of the *padhul* is pleasing to the ear.

So long as Soomeru stands on its base of golden sands, so long may this dwelling endure. So long as the wind blows on the *koonjeris* (10), supporters of the globe, while the firmament endures, or while Lacshmí (11) causes the palm to be extended, so long may his praise and this edifice be stable.

KUHLA (12) formed this abode of virtue, and east thereof a temple to Iswara. By ACHIL, son of the mighty prince YASOOVERMA (13), has its renown been composed in various forms of speech.

(*Note* 1).—*Qu.* if this Jit is from (*da*, the mark of the genitive case) Cathay ? the land of the *Cat'hæ* foes of Alexander, and probably of the Cathi of the Saurashtra peninsula, alike Scythic as the Jit, and probably the same race originally ?

(*Note* 2).—Roodrani, an epithet of the martial spouse of Harar-Siva, the god of war, whom the Jit in the preceding inscription invokes.

(*Note* 3).—Here we have another proof of the Jit being of Takshac race ; this at the same time has a mythological reference to the serpent (*takhya*), which forms the garland of the warlike divinities.

(*Note* 4).—Of this race I have no other notice, unless it should mean the race (*cúla*) was from *Bútán*.

(*Note* 5).—Chandrasén is celebrated in the history of the Pramaras as the founder of several cities, from two of which, *Chandrabhaga*, at the foot of the central plateau of India, in Northern Malwa, and CHANDRAVATI, the ruins of which I discovered at the foot of the Aravulli near Aboo, I possess several valuable memoria, which will, ere long, confirm the opinions I have given of the *Takshac* architect.

(*Note* 6).—The habitation of virtues.

(*Note* 7).—This shows these foresters always had the same character.
(*Note* 8).—Véla is the climber or ivy, sacred to Mahadeva.
(*Note* 9).—Lacshmí, the *apsara* or sea-nymph, is feigned residing amongst the waters of the lotos-covered lake. In the hot weather the Rajpoot ladies dip their corsets into an infusion of sandal-wood, hence the metaphor.

(*Note* 10).—Koonjiris are the elephants who support the eight corners of the globe.

(*Note* 11).—Lacshmí is also dame Fortune, or the goddess of riches, whence this image.

(*Note* 12).—Kuhl is the fifth in descent from the *opponent* of the Jit.

(*Note* 13).—Without this name this inscription would have been but of half its value. Fortunately various inscriptions on stone and copper, procured by me from Oojein, settled the era of the death of this prince in S. 1191, which will alike answer for Achil, his son, who was most likely one of the chieftains of KUHLA, who appears to have been of the elder branch of the Pramaras, the foe of the Jit invaders.

No. III.

Inscription in the Nail-headed character of the Mori Princes of Cheetore, taken from a column on the banks of the lake Mânsurwur, near that city.

By the lord of waters may thou be protected! What is there which resembles the ocean? on whose margin the red buds of honey-yielding trees are eclipsed by swarms of bees, whose beauty expands with the junction of numerous streams. What is like the ocean, inhaling the perfume of the Paryata (1), who was compelled to yield as tribute, wine, wealth, and ambrosia (2)? Such is the ocean!—may he protect thee.

Of a mighty gift, this is the memorial. This lake enslaves the minds of beholders, over whose expanse the varied feathered tribe skim with delight, and whose banks are studded with every kind of tree. Falling from the lofty-peaked mountain, enhancing the beauty of the scene, the torrent rushes to the lake. The mighty sea-serpent (3), o'erspent with toil in the churning of the ocean, repaired to this lake for repose.

On this earth's surface was Maheśwara (4), a mighty prince, during whose sway the name of foe was never heard; whose fortune was known to the eight quarters (5); on whose arm victory reclined for support. He was the light of the land. The praises of the race of TWAST'HA (6) were determined by Brahma's own mouth.

Fair, filled with pride, sporting amidst the shoals of the lotos, is the swan fed by his hand, from whose countenance issue rays of glory: such was RAJA BHEEM (7), a skilful swimmer in the ocean of battle, even to where the Ganges pours in her flood (8) did he go, whose abode is *Avanti* (9). With faces resplendent as the moon, on whose lips yet marked with the wound of their husband's teeth, the captive wives of his foes, even in their hearts does Raja Bheem dwell. By his arm he removed the apprehensions of his enemies; he considered them as errors to be expunged. He appeared as if created of fire. He could instruct even the navigator (10) of the ocean.

From him was descended Raja BHOJ (11). How shall he be described; he, who in the field of battle divided with his sword the elephant's head, the pearl from whose brain (12) now adorns his breast; who devours his foe as does RAHOO (13) the sun or moon, who to the verge of space erected edifices in token of victory?

From him was a son whose name was MAUN, who was surcharged with good qualities, and with whom fortune took up her abode. One day he met an aged man : his appearance made him reflect that his frame was as a shadow, evanescent ; that the spirit which did inhabit it was like the seed of the scented *Kadama* (14) ; that the riches of royalty were brittle as a blade of grass ; and that man was like a lamp exposed in the light of day. Thus ruminating, for the sake of his race who had gone before him, and for the sake of good works, he made this lake, whose waters are expansive and depth unfathomable. When I look on this ocean-like lake, I ask myself, if it may not be this which is destined to cause the final doom (15).

The warriors and chiefs of RAJA MAUN (16) are men of skill and valour —pure in their lives and faithful. RAJA MAUN is a heap of virtues—the chief who enjoys his favour may court all the gifts of fortune. When the head is inclined on his lotos foot, the grain of sand which adheres becomes an ornament thereto. Such is the lake, shaded with trees, frequented by birds, which the man of fortune, SRIMAN RAJA MAUN, with great labour formed. By the name of its lord (*Maun*), that of the lake (*surwur*) is known to the world. By him versed in the *alankara*, PUSHHA, the son of NAGA BHUT, these stanzas have been framed. *Seventy had elapsed beyond seven hundred years* (*Samvatisir*), when the lord of men, the KING OF MALWA (17) formed this lake. By SEVADIT, grandson of KHETRI KARUG, were these lines cut.

(*Note* 1).—The Paryat is also called the Har-síngár, or '*ornament of the neck*,' its flowers being made into collars and bracelets. Its aroma is very delicate, and the blossom dies in a few hours.

(*Note* 2).—*Imrita*, the food of the immortals, obtained at the churning of the ocean. The contest for this amongst the gods and demons is well known. *Vrishpati*, or Sookra, regent of the planet Venus, on this occasion lost an eye ; and hence this Polyphemus has left the nickname of *Sookracharya* to all who have but one eye.

(*Note* 3).—His name *Matolaë*.

(*Note* 4).—A celebrated name in the genealogies of the TAKSHAC *Pramara*, of which the *Mori* is a conspicuous *Sac'ha* or branch. He was the founder of the city of *Maheswar*, on the southern bank of the Nehrbudda, which commands the ford leading from *Awinti* and *Dhar* (the chief cities of the Mori Pramaras) to the Dekhan.

(*Note* 5).—The ancient Hindu divided his planisphere into eight quarters, on which he placed the Koonjerries or elephants, for its support.

(*Note* 6).—TWASTHA, or Takshac, is the celebrated *Nágvansa* of antiquity. All are *Agnicúlas*. Cheetore, if erected by the Takshac artist, has a right to the appellation Herbert has so singularly assigned it, namely, *Tacsila*, built by the Tâk ; it would be the *Tâk-sillā-nagar*, the 'stone fort of the Takshac,' alluded to in No. I.

(*Note* 7).—Raja Bheem, the lord of *Avanti* or Oojein, the king of Malwa, is especially celebrated in the Jain annals. A son of his led a numerous colony into Marwar, and founded many cities between the Looni river and the Aravulli mountains. ***All became proselytes to the Jain faith***, and their descendants, who are amongst the wealthiest and most numerous of these mercantile sectarians, are proud of their Rajpoot descent ; and it tells when they are called to responsible offices, when they handle the sword as well as the pen.

(*Note* 8).—*Ganga-Sagur*, or the Island at the mouth of the Ganges, is specified by name as the limit of Bheem's conquests. His memoria may yet exist even there.

(*Note* 9).—*Avanti-Nat'h*, Lord of Avanti or Oojein.

(*Note* 10).—*Paryataca*, a navigator.

(*Note* 11).—Raja BHOJ. There is no more celebrated name than this in the annals and literature of the Rajpoots ; but there were three princes of the Pramara race who bore it. The period of the last Raja Bhoj, father of Udyadit, is now fixed, by various inscriptions discovered by me, A.D. 1035, and the dates of the two others I had from a leaf of a very ancient Jain MS., obtained at the temple of Nadole, namely, S. 631 and 721, or A.D. 575 and 665. Abulfazil gives the period of the first Bhoj as S. 545; but, as we find that valuable MS. of the period of the last Bhoj confirmed by the date of this inscription of his son Maun, namely, S. 770, we may put perfect confidence in it, and now consider the periods of the three, namely, S. 631, 721, and 1091—A.D. 567, 665, and 1035—as fixed points in Rajpoot chronology.

(*Note* 12).—In the head of that class of elephants called Bhadra, the Hindoo says, there is always a large pearl.

(*Note* 13).—The monster Rahoo of the Rajpoot, who swallows the sun and moon, *causing eclipses*, is *Fenris*, the wolf of the Scandinavians. The *Asi* carried the same ideas West, which they taught within the Indus.

(*Note* 14).—Kadama is a very delicate flower, that decays almost instantaneously.

(*Note* 15).—*Máhá-prálàyá!*

(*Note* 16).—The MS. annals of the Rana's family state that their founder, Bappa, conquered Cheetore from Maun Mori. This inscription is therefore invaluable as establishing the era of the conquest of Cheetore by the Gehlotes, and which was immediately following the first irruption of the arms of Islam, as rendered in the annals of Méwar.

(*Note* 17).—As Raja Maun is called *King of Malwa*, it is evident that Cheetore had superseded both Dhar and Awinti as the seat of power. A palace of *Maun Mori* is still shown as one of the antiquities in Cheetore.

No. IV.

Inscription in the Devanagari character, discovered in January 1822 in Puttun Somnat'h, on the coast of the Saurashtra peninsula, fixing the era of the sovereigns of Balabhi, the '*Balhara kings of Nehrwalla.*'

Adoration to the Lord of all, to *the light of the universe* (1). Adoration to the form indescribable; Him! at whose feet all kneel.

In the year of Mohummud 662, and in that of Vicrama 1320, and that of Srimad Balabhi 945, and the Síva-Singa Samvat 151, Sunday, the 13th (*badi*) of the month Asár.

The chiefs of Anhulpoor Patun obeyed by numerous princes (here a string of titles), Bhataric Srimad Arjúna Déva (3), of Chauluc race his minister Sri Máldéva, with all the officers of government, together with *Hormuz of Belacool*, of the government of *Ameer Rookn-oo-Dín*, and of *Khwaja Ibrahim* of *Hormuz*, son of the Admiral (*Nakhoda*) *Noor-oo-Dín Feeroz*, together with the Chaura chieftains Palookdeva, Ranik Sri Someswadéva, Ramdéva, Bheemsing, and all the Chauras and other tribes of rank being assembled;

Nansi Raja, of the Chaura race, inhabiting *Deo Puttun* (5), assembling all the merchants, established ordinances for the repairs and the support of the temples, in order that flowers, oil, and water, should be regularly supplied to *Rutna-iswara* (6), *Choul-iswára* (7), and the shrine of *Púlinda Devi* (8), and the rest, and for the purpose of erecting a wall round the temple of Somnat'h, with a gateway to the north. Keelndeo, son of Modula, and Loonsi, son of Johan, both of the Chaura race, together with the two merchants, Balji and Kurna, bestowed the weekly profits of the market for this purpose. While sun and moon endure, let it not be resumed. Feeroz is commanded to see this order obeyed, and that the customary offerings on festivals are continued, and that all surplus offerings and gifts be placed in the treasury for the purposes afore-named. The Chaura chiefs present, and the Admiral Noor-oo-Dín, are commanded to see these orders executed on all classes. Heaven will be the lot of the obedient ; hell to the breaker of this ordinance.

(*Note* 1).—The invocation, which was long, has been omitted by me. But this is sufficient to show that BAL-NAT'H, the deity worshipped in PUTTUN SOMNAT'H, 'the city of the lord of the Moon,' was the sun-god *Bál*. Hence the title of the dynasties which ruled this region, BAL-CA-RAÉ, 'the princes of Bál,' and hence the capital BALICAPOOR, 'the city of the sun,' familiarly written *Balabhi*, whose ruins, as well as this inscription, rewarded a long journey. The Rana's ancestors, the *Súryas*, or 'sun-worshippers,' gave their name to the peninsula Saurashtra, or Syria, and the dynasties of CHAURA, and CHAULUC, or SOLANKI, who succeeded them on their expulsion by the Parthians, retained the title of BALICARAÉS, corrupted by Renaudot's Arabian travellers into BALHARA.

(*Note* 2).—The importance of the discovery of these *new eras* has already been descanted on in the annals, S. 1320—945, the date of this inscription =375 of Vicrama for the first of the Balabhi era ; and 1320—151 gives S. 1169 for the establishment of the *Sevasinga* era—established by the Gohils of the island of Deo, of whom I have another memorial, dated 927 Balabhi Samvat. The Gohils, Chauras, and Gehlotes are all of one stock.

(*Note* 3).—Arjuna-Déva, *Chaluc*, was prince of Anhulpoor or Anhulwarra, founded by Vanraj Chaura in S. 802—henceforth the capital of the Balica-raes after the destruction of Balabhi.

(*Note* 4).—This evinces that Anhulwarra was still the emporium of commerce which the travellers of Renaudot and Edrisi describe.

(*Note* 5).—From this it is evident that the Islandic Deo was a dependent fief of Anhulwarra.

(*Note* 6).—The great temple of Somnath.

(*Note* 7).—The tutelary divinity of the Chauluc race.

(*Note* 8).—The goddess of the Bhil tribes.

No. V.

Inscription from the ruins of Aitpoor.

In Samvatsir 1034, the 16th of the month Bysák, was erected this dwelling [1] of Nanukswami.

From Anundpoor came he of Brahmin [2] race (may he flourish), Muhee Deva Srí Goha Dit; from whom became famous on the earth the Gohil, tribe :

2. Bhoj.
3. Mahindra.
4. Naga.
5. Syeela.
6. Aprajit.
7. Mahindra, no equal as a warrior did then exist on the earth's surface.
8. Kalbhoj was resplendent as the sun.[3]
9. Khoman, an unequalled warrior ; from him
10. Bhirtrpad, the Tiluk of the three worlds ; and from whom was
11. Singji ; whose Ranee Maha Lakmee, of the warlike race of Rashtra (Rahtore), and from her was born :
12. Sri Ullut. To him who subdued the earth and became its lord,

[1] Aitun. [2] Vipra cúla. [3] Ark.

was born Haria Devi: her praise was known in Hurspoora; and from her was born a mighty warrior in whose arm victory reposed; the Khetri of the field of battle, who broke the confederacy of his foes, and from the tree of whose fortune riches were the fruit: an altar of learning; from him was

13. Nirvahana. By the daughter of Sri Jaijah, of Chauhana race, was born

14. Salvahana.

Such were their (the princes whose names are given) fortunes which I have related. From him was born

15. Secti Koomar. How can he be described?—He who conquered and made his own the three qualifications (*sacti*);[1] whose fortunes equalled those of Bhirtrpad. In the abode of wealth Sri Aitpoor, which he had made his dwelling, surrounded by a crowd of princes; the ***kulpdroom*** to his people; whose foot-soldiers are many; with vaults of treasure—whose fortunes have ascended to heaven—whose city derives its beauty from the intercourse of merchants; and in which there is but one single evil, the killing darts from the bright eyes of beauty, carrying destruction to the vassals of the prince.

No. VI.

Inscription of Kumar Pal Solanki, in the Mindra of Brimha, in Cheetore, recording his conquest of Salpoori, in the Punjâb.

To him who takes delight in the abode of waters; from whose braided locks ambrosial drops continually descend; even this Mahadeva, may he protect thee!

He of Chaulac tribe, having innumerable gems of ancestry, flowing from a sea of splendour, was Moolraj, sovereign of the earth.

What did he resemble, whose renown was bright as a fair sparkling gem, diffusing happiness and ease to the sons of the earth? Many mighty princes there were of his line; but none before had made the great sacrifice.

Generations after him, in the lapse of many years, was Sid Raj, a name known to the world; whose frame was encased in the riches of victory, and whose deeds were sounded over the curtain of the earth; and who, by the fire of his own frame and fortune, heaped up unconsumable wealth.

After him was Kumar Pal Deo. What was he like, who by the strength of his invincible mind crushed all his foes; whose commands the other sovereigns of the earth placed on their foreheads; who compelled the lord of Sacambhari to bow at his feet: who in person carried his arms to Sewaluk, making the mountain lords to bow before him, even in the city of Salpoori?

On the mountain Chutterkote . . . ar, the lord of men, in sport placed this [writing] amidst the abode of the gods: even on its pinnacle did he place it. Why? That it might be beyond the reach of the hands of fools!

As Nissa-Nath, the lord who rules the night, looking on the faces of the fair Kamunis below, feels envious of their fairness, and ashamed of the dark spots on his own countenance, even so does Chutterkote blush at seeing this (Prasishta) on her pinnacle.

Samvat 1207 (month and day broken off).

[1] 1. Pribhoo.
2. Ootchha.
3. Muntri.
} Three Sactis.

No. VII.

Inscriptions on copper-plates found at Nadole relative to the Chohan princes.

The treasury of knowledge of the Almighty (JINA) cuts the knots and intentions of mankind. Pride, conceit, desire, anger, avarice. It is a partition to the three [1] worlds. Such is MAHAVÍRA: [2] may he grant thee happiness!

In ancient times the exalted race of Chohan had sovereignty to the bounds of ocean; and in NADOLE swayed Lacshman, Raja. He had a son named LOHIA; and his BULRAJ, his VIGRAHA PAL; from him sprung MAHINDRA DÉVA; his son was SRI ANHULA, the chief amongst the princes of his time, whose fortunes were known to all. His son was SRI BAL PRESÁD; but having no issue, his younger brother, JAITR RAJ, succeeded. His son was PRITHWI PAL, endued with strength and fiery qualities; but he having no issue, was succeeded by his younger brother JUL; he by his brother MAUN RAJA, the abode of fortune. His son was ALAN-DÉVA.[3] When he mounted the throne, he reflected this world was a fable: that this frame, composed of unclean elements, of flesh, blood, and dust, was brought to existence in pain. Versed in the books of faith, he reflected on the evanescence of youth, resembling the scintillation of the fire-fly; [4] that riches were as the dew-drop on the lotos-leaf, for a moment resembling the pearl, but soon to disappear. Thus meditating, he commanded his servants, and sent them forth to his chieftains, to desire them to bestow happiness on others, and to walk in the paths of faith.

In Samvat 1218, in the month of Sawun the 29th,[5] performing the sacrifice to fire, and pouring forth libations to the dispeller of darkness, he bathed the image of the omniscient, the lord of things which move and are immovable, Sudasíva, with the *panch-amrit*,[6] and made the gifts of gold, grain, and clothes to his spiritual teacher, preceptor, and the Brahmins to their hearts' desire. Taking *til* in his hand, with rings on his finger of the *cusa* (grass), holding water and rice in the palm of his hand, he made a gift of five *moodras* monthly in perpetuity to the *Sandera Gatcha*[7] for saffron, sandal-wood, and ghee for the service of the temple of MAHAVÍRA in the white market (*mandra*) of the town. Hence this copper-plate. This charity which I have bestowed will continue as long as the SANDERA GATCHA exist to receive, and my issue to grant it.

To whoever may rule hereafter I touch their hands, that it may be perpetual. Whoever bestows charity will live sixty thousand years in heaven; whoever resumes it, the like in hell!

Of Pragvavansa,[8] his name Dhurnidhur, his son Kurmchund being minister, and the *sastri* Munorut Ram, with his sons Visala and Sridhara, by writing this inscription made his name resplendent. By SRI ALAN's own hand was this copper-plate bestowed. Samvat 1218.

[1] Tribhawun-loca; or Pátála, Mirtha, Swerga.

[2] *Mahavira*, to whom the temple was thus endowed by the Chohan prince, follower of Síva, was the last of the twenty-four *Jinas*, or apostles of the Jains.

[3] The prince being the twelfth from Lacshman, allowing twenty-two years to a reign, 264—1218; date of inscription, S. 954, or A.D. 898, the period of Lacshman.

[4] *Kudheata*. [5] *Súdi choudus*.

[6] Milk, curds, clarified butter, honey, butter, and sugar.

[7] One of eighty-four divisions of Jain tribes.

[8] Poorvál, a branch of the Oswal race of Jain laity.

TREATY between the Honourable the English East-India Company and Maharana Bheem Sing, Rana of Oudeepoor, concluded by Mr. Charles Theophilus Metcalfe on the part of the Honourable Company, in virtue of full powers granted by his Excellency the Most Noble the Marquis of Hastings, K.G., Governor-General, and by Thakoor Ajeet Sing on the part of the Maharana, in virtue of full powers conferred by the Maharana aforesaid.

First Article.—There shall be perpetual friendship, alliance, and unity of interests between the two states, from generation to generation, and the friends and enemies of one shall be the friends and enemies of both.

Second Article.—The British Government engages to protect the principality and territory of Oudeepoor.

Third Article.—The Maharana of Oudeepoor will always act in subordinate co-operation with the British Government, and acknowledge its supremacy, and will not have any connection with other chiefs or states.

Fourth Article.—The Maharana of Oudeepoor will not enter into any negotiation with any chief or state without the knowledge and sanction of the British Government; but his usual amicable correspondence with friends and relations shall continue.

Fifth Article.—The Maharana of Oudeepoor will not commit aggressions upon any one; and if by accident a dispute arise with any one, it shall be submitted to the arbitration and award of the British Government.

Sixth Article.—One-fourth of the revenue of the actual territory of Oudeepoor shall be paid annually to the British Government as tribute for five years; and after that term three-eighths in perpetuity. The Maharana will not have connection with any other power on account of tribute, and if any one advance claims of that nature, the British Government engages to reply to them.

Seventh Article.—Whereas the Maharana represents that portions of the dominions of Oudeepoor have fallen, by imprope· means, into the possession of others, and solicits the restitution of those places: the British Government from a want of accurate information is not able to enter into any positive engagement on this subject; but will always keep in view the renovation of the prosperity of the state of Oudeepoor, and after ascertaining the nature of each case, will use its best exertions for the accomplishment of the object, on every occasion on which it may be proper to do so. Whatever places may thus be restored to the state of Oudeepoor by the aid of the British Government, three-eighths of their revenues shall be paid in perpetuity to the British Government.

Eighth Article.—The troops of the state of Oudeepoor shall be furnished according to its means, at the requisition of the British Government.

Ninth Article.—The Maharana of Oudeepoor shall always be absolute ruler of his own country, and the British jurisdiction shall not be introduced into that principality.

Tenth Article.—The present treaty of ten articles having been concluded at Dihlee, and signed and sealed by Mr. Charles Theophilus Metcalfe and Thakoor Ajeet Sing Buhadoor, the ratifications of the same, by his Excellency the Most Noble the Governor-General, and Maharana Bheem Sing, shall be mutually delivered within a month from this date.

Done at Dihlee, this thirteenth day of January, A.D. 1818.

(*Signed*) C. T. METCALFE (L.S.).
THAKOOR AJEET SING (L.S.).

END OF VOL. I.

